CRIMINOLOGY
A GLOBAL PERSPECTIVE

LEE ELLIS

Minot State University

ANTHONY WALSH

Boise State University

ALLYN AND BACON

Boston • London • Toronto • Sydney • Tokyo • Singapore

Editor in Chief, Social Sciences: Karen Hanson
Editorial Assistant: Karen Corday
Executive Marketing Manager: Lisa Kimball
Editorial Production Service: Chestnut Hill Enterprises, Inc.
Manufacturing Buyer: Megan Cochran
Cover Administrator: Linda Knowles
Electronic Composition: Omegatype Typography, Inc.

Internet: www.abacon.com

Between time web site information is gathered and published, some sites may have closed. Also, the transcription of URLs can result in typographical errors. The publisher would appreciate notification where these occur so they they may be corrected in subsequent editions.

Library of Congress Cataloging-in-Publication Data

Ellis, Lee
    Criminology : a global perspective / Lee
  Ellis, Anthony Walsh.
        p.   cm.
    Includes bibliographical references and index.
    ISBN 0-205-18708-0
    1. Criminology. 2. Crime. 3. Criminal behavior.   I. Walsh, Anthony, 1941– II. Title.
  HV6025.E553 2000
  364–dc21   99-053006

Printed in the United States of America

10   9   8   7   6   5   4   3   2   1   04   03   02   01   00   99

CONTENTS

PART III
THEORIES OF CRIMINAL/ANTISOCIAL BEHAVIOR   307

CHAPTER 10   COGNITIVE AND EARLY CHILD DEVELOPMENT ENVIRONMENTAL THEORIES   313

PART IV
SPECIFIC CRIMES   485

PREFACE

The goal of this text is to provide students with an understanding of contemporary criminology. In this regard, five features make this text unique. First, in light of the truly mammoth nature of the research now available to criminologists, other texts have become increasingly selective in citing references. We decided that any attempt to be selective fails to provide students and professionals with an appreciation of just how much is now known in criminology. In addition, selectivity runs the risk of bias. This text is therefore encyclopedic in its attempts to present as much evidence as possible on each issue discussed. To accomplish this goal, the text contains numerous tables that indicate the nature of research findings on a particular topic, the number of studies involved, and the countries in which these studies were conducted. Most of the text's tables do not contain actual citations or references. Instead, the relevant citations and references are provided on the World Wide Web at www.abacon.com/ellis.

Second, since the 1930s, the United States has dominated the field of criminology.[1] This preeminence may have come about in part from a recognition of the United States having an unusually high crime rate for an industrialized nation.[2] One consequence of the concentration of criminologists in the United States is that U.S. textbooks have leaned toward primarily citing domestic criminological research. Breaking with this tradition, we have made a concerted effort to represent scientific efforts to understand and control criminal behavior throughout the world. Not only does this give a fairer picture of the breadth and scope of criminology, but it is also in harmony with a growing academic emphasis on multiculturalism and international awareness. We join others in believing that a multicultural perspective in criminology is long overdue.[3]

Third, throughout this text criminal behavior is conceptualized not as an isolated characteristic of a small minority of people but as an aspect of humanity that exists within us all, although certainly to varying degrees. Along these lines, careful attention is given to research on childhood conduct disorders and the antisocial personality disorder as behavioral tendencies closely related to criminality. Also, the well-established links between criminality and such controversial variables as morality and religiosity are given more coverage than in other texts.

Fourth, this text provides the most thorough coverage of criminological theories currently available. Compared with other texts, ours goes beyond discussing the theories emanating from the classical school, the early positivists, and the twentieth-century environmentalists. Students will learn about several theories that have taken shape largely since the 1980s that other criminology texts have been slow to cover. These theories are primarily of two types: One type involves discoveries in neuroscience (the science of the brain), and the other type comes from applying Darwinian evolutionary concepts to the study of criminality. This coverage is in keeping with the growing interdisciplinary nature of criminology.[4]

The fifth feature of this text that makes it unique is its organization. No other text attempts to thoroughly acquaint students with most of the basic variables associated with crime throughout the world before beginning to describe any specific theories. We believe that this new approach puts students in a stronger position to objectively judge the relative merits of each criminological theory than do other methods of organizing chapters around factual and theoretical information.

SPECIAL COMMENTS TO STUDENTS

As you embark on the study of any new field, it is wise to try to anticipate what you will learn, and how your mastery of this knowledge will be assessed. We recommend that you read the chapters carefully, underlining and perhaps taking notes as you go. In addition to the chapters, be sure to read the introductions to each part, especially Part II and Part III. They provide some important information that is fundamental to the arguments contained in their constituent chapters.

SPECIAL COMMENTS TO INSTRUCTORS

This text should provide your students with the basic information needed to gain a clear overview of the vast field of contemporary criminology. We have made a concerted effort to objectively cover all the topics most criminologists want their students to know.

You will see that the organization of the text is like no other currently available. It is divided into four distinct parts. The first deals with the nature of crime and how criminal behavior is measured and distributed over time and space, and with the history of criminology. In the second part, students are acquainted with numerous correlates of crime. The third part provides information about the theories of crime that have been offered since the beginning of the twentieth century. In the fourth part of the text, students are exposed to information about various specific types of offenses, such as sex crimes, serial murders, and white-collar offenses.

In using this text as a teaching tool, we recommend that you go through the first nine chapters as quickly as possible. They provide valuable information, but purposely avoid examining the theories that are understandably at the heart of criminology. The purpose of these initial chapters is to provide students with the knowledge they can use to make objective judgments about the merit of the theories that begin to be described in Chapter 10.

If there are areas you believe have been inadequately covered or that seem to be misleading in any way, please let us know (ellis@warp6.cs.misu.nodak.edu or twalsh@bsu.idbsu.edu). Also, if you have published any material relevant to criminology that could be incorporated into future editions of the text, please provide us with a reference to the publication, or preferably with an actual copy (send it to Dr. Lee Ellis, Division of Social Science, Minot State University, Minot, ND 58707, USA).

The questions in the test bank have been carefully written and tested on our own students to minimize errors and ambiguities. We have tried to maintain the focus of the test questions on each chapter's (and part's) main points.

ACKNOWLEDGMENTS

Many people helped us to complete this text. These people range from those who read parts of, or even all, the text in its numerous draft forms and provided suggestions for making it clearer and more accurate. We thank them very sincerely.

In particular, we would like to express our appreciation to the following people for commenting on various portions of the text in draft form: Robert Agnew, Ron Akers, Jay Belsky, Thomas Bernard, Robert Burgess, Delbert Elliott, Heather Ellis, Timothy Engh, Marcus Felson, Jeffery A. Gray, David Greenberg, John Hagan, David Hawkins, Travis Hirschi, Eric A. Johnson, Satoshi Kanazawa, David Lykken, Linda Mealey, Robert K. Merton, Terry Moffitt, Myrna Nelson, Gerald Patterson, Herbert C. Quay, Richard Quinney, Vernon Quinsey, Adrian Raine, David Rowe, Pieter Spierenburg, Bryan Vila, Jonathan Wagner, and Lorne Yeudall. In addition, we thank the following reviewers for their helpful comments: Karen Baird-Olsen, Kansas State University; Dennis Hoffman, University of Nebraska; John A. Johnson, Pennsylvania State University; William E. Kelly, Auburn University; Randy L. LaGrange, University of North Carolina at Washington; Thomas Petee, Auburn University; and Bryan Vila, University of Wyoming.

We also want to thank Jacinth Berthold, Tammy Gerszewski, Barbara Reiste, and Debora Reynolds for assisting in organizing the tables and in locating and computerizing the references, and Linda Ebertz for her assistance in designing some of the graphs. Finally, thanks for the editing assistance of Stephanie Ritchie and Myrna Nelson.

ENDNOTES

1. Cohn & Farrington 1994; Downes 1996:360.
2. Kalish 1988.
3. Bennett 1980; Hendricks & Byers 1994; Downes 1996; Littler 1996; Zhang & Messner 1996:300.
4. Osgood 1998.

PART ONE

The Nature of Criminal/Antisocial Behavior and the Discipline That Studies It

Most people who take a course in criminology hope to learn why people commit crime. While this is certainly a question addressed in this text, there are many related questions that need attention before tackling ones about crime causation. For example, what exactly is crime and how can it be accurately measured? Or *can* it be measured accurately? In answering such questions, criminologists must keep in mind that most people who commit crimes (however defined) are never caught, and that unknown numbers of people who are arrested, prosecuted, and even convicted are not actually guilty.

Part 1 is comprised of four chapters. Chapter 1 acquaints you with the nature of criminal law and with the scope of the activities that violate criminal statutes. Chapter 2 focuses on two fairly distinct questions: Why have criminal statutes arisen in nearly all parts of the world? And how can criminal behavior be objectively measured given that there are substantial variations in criminal statutes? In Chapter 3, you will learn about the prevalence of criminal behavior throughout the world according to available statistics. And Chapter 4 provides a brief history of the field of criminology.

CHAPTER 1

Introduction
The Nature of Criminal
and Antisocial Behavior

What sort of person comes to mind when you hear the word "criminal"?
*Would you think of someone lying about his child's age in order to save
a couple of hundred dollars on an airline ticket, or occasionally making
unauthorized copies of a computer program or a movie? Would the
concept include shoplifters, drunk drivers, or people who occasionally
disobey stop signs or exceed speed limits? What about tax evaders, or
corporate executives who knowingly manufacture toys that injure
children? Is someone who smokes marijuana a criminal, even if he or
she doesn't inhale?*

The questions just posed underscore the fact that
the word **criminal** can be applied to many types
of behavior, some of which nearly all of us have
been guilty of at some time in our lives. In this
sense, the present text is not about a minority of
"other people"; it is about our neighbors, our relatives, and even ourselves.

However, there is a more restricted sense in
which the word *criminal* is often used. As we will
see in Chapter 3, very few people ever commit
murder, robbery, or major thefts. Those who do,
especially more than once, are what most people
think of as "real criminals". Even so, it is important to recognize that the dividing line between
"real criminals" and most of the rest of us is fuzzy
and difficult to specify with precision.

One indication of how fuzzy the concept of
crime is comes from noting that nearly all of us
can think of acts that we feel *ought* to be criminal
but are not, or acts that should not be criminal but

are. When people commit these acts, should they
be considered criminals?

For those who still think the concept of criminality is simple, try finding others who will agree
with you on how many crimes someone would have
to commit before he or she would be considered a
real criminal? Four or five? Or would the answer
depend on how serious each crime was? These are
the sort of topics addressed in this chapter.

The main purpose of exploring these topics
is to acquaint you with how criminologists conceptualize their discipline, i.e., what they include
and exclude from study. After discussing the
political–legal underpinnings of crime, a three-
dimensional model of criminal behavior will be
presented. Near the end of this chapter, criminality
will be linked to certain closely related concepts
that are not themselves illegal. These concepts include *childhood conduct disorders* and the *antisocial personality disorder.*

3

CRIMINALITY AS A CONTINUOUS VARIABLE

Oddly enough, it is helpful to begin thinking about criminal behavior as having some similarities to people's heights. As everyone knows, a few people are so extreme in their height that any reasonable person would call them *tall*. Likewise, a minority of individuals have violated so many criminal statutes that no one would question the appropriateness of their being called *criminals*. However, where do you draw the line between tall people and those who are not tall, or between criminals and people who are not criminals. Is a person who stands at 6 feet (9.66 meters) tall, or does the answer depend on whether you are discussing males or females? Is a person who has committed two minor crimes a criminal, or does the answer depend on the culture under study?

The point is that both height and criminality can be thought of as existing along a continuum, even though the words we use often imply that people's heights and criminal tendencies come in more or less discrete categories. In other words, just as height varies in fine gradations, so too does involvement in crime.[1] There is another similarity: Most people appear to be in a broad middle range rather than at either extreme with respect to both characteristics. In the case of criminality, you will learn that just about everyone at some point in their life has violated a criminal (or delinquency) statute. If they were all to be called *criminals*, the term would become virtually synonymous with the word *human*!

Of course, there are differences between the concepts of height and criminality. One of the most noteworthy differences is that criminality is a behavior trait that is much more difficult to measure than is the concept of height. In fact, most of Chapter 2 is devoted to discussing the complexities and subtleties of measuring people's involvement in crime.

THE NATURE OF CRIME AND CRIMINALITY

A fundamental point on which all criminologists agree is that **crime** is a legal concept resting on political processes.[2] These political processes were made possible by the invention of written language, which first occurred about 6,000 years ago in or around the Middle East.[3] The fact that crime is a legal, rather than a strictly scientific, concept has fundamental implications for the scientific study of criminal behavior.

One implication is that hypothetically a society could eradicate crime tomorrow simply by rescinding all of its criminal statutes. Of course, this would not eliminate the behavior specified by the laws; in fact, it would probably cause the behavior to increase, because the behavior could no longer be officially punished. While it is absurd to think that a society will ever try to solve its crime problem by eliminating all of its criminal statutes, the point is that legislative bodies are continually revising their criminal statutes. Rarely does a state or national legislative body convene without making some new additions, deletions, or adjustments in its criminal statutes. Think of how these changes in criminal statutes might affect the subject matter of criminology. To some extent, every time criminal statutes change, so too criminologists must change the definition of the behavior they are trying to understand!

Another implication is that some societies are by definition "crime free." These are the small hunter–gatherer (or foraging) societies that remain in a few remote parts of the world.[4] Because the members of these societies neither read or write, they have no formalized criminal statutes.[5] We will discuss these societies more in Chapter 3. To explore the formulation of criminal statutes and the functioning of the criminal justice system, see Appendix A.

THE MOVING TARGET VERSUS THE STATIONARY CORE CONCEPTS OF CRIME

If what constitutes crime differs from one place (and time period) to another, how can criminologists ever hope to agree on a scientific explanation for criminal behavior? Confronting this dilemma brings us to two perspectives on the subject matter of criminology. We will call one perspective the

moving target perspective, and the other is the **stationary core perspective.**

The Moving Target Perspective

Regarding the moving target view, some criminologists have been so impressed by the wide array of activities that have been deemed *criminal* in various parts of the world that they have declared it impossible to generalize about what is and is not "real" crime.[6] As one criminologist wrote many years ago: "Everything the criminal law of any state prohibits today it will not prohibit at a given future time."[7] Indeed, there are numerous examples of a particular act being criminal in one country while being tolerated and sometimes even rewarded elsewhere.[8] An example is provided in Box 1.1, the widespread Muslim custom of men in their twenties or thirties marrying and then having sex with twelve- and thirteen-year-old girls. This constitutes statutory rape in most Western societies.

Here is another example. In several parts of Africa and the Middle East, one finds a custom that is considered child abuse and malicious wounding in most Western countries.[9] The custom, called *female circumcision* (or *clitorectomy*), involves surgically removing the clitoris and sometimes the skin surrounding the vagina.[10] The operation is normally performed by elderly women on prepubertal girls without anesthetic, is often very painful, and has been known sometimes to cause death due to infection.[11]

The two most common explanations for the practice are that it helps to prevent female promiscuity by reducing pleasurable sensations associated with sexual intercourse[12] and simply "tradition."[13] In countries where the practice is common, female virginity is much more important for "respectable" wedlock than it is in modern Western societies. So, despite the pain and occasional serious infections resulting from the operation, tens of thousands of girls are operated on every year with the full support of their parents. Female circumcision (and perhaps male circumcision, as practiced widely in Western countries) is one example of human beings having different cultural traditions with respect to what is and is not considered criminal behavior. Try thinking of other examples of where something that is criminal in one country (or at some point in time) is perfectly legal somewhere else. You could name laws pertaining to abortion, homosexuality, pornography, gambling, prostitution, and euthanasia.[14] For all of these acts, whether they are criminal or not depends on where one lives.

Let us look at a few of the definitions for criminal behavior that have radically changed over time and space. Many state jurisdictions still outlaw homosexual behavior, even though the laws are rarely enforced.[15] In the past, such behavior was not only illegal, but the laws were often harshly enforced, with punishments sometimes including castration and even death.[16]

Another example of substantial change in definitions of crime has to do with drug use and sale. In this case, the trend has been toward increasing rather than decreasing criminal coverage. Until the Harrison Narcotics Act of 1914, there were few legal restrictions in the United States on the sale, possession, or use of any drugs.[17] In fact, in the late 1800, the Bayer Drug Company (which now primarily produces aspirin) was producing and selling heroin as an over-the-counter cough suppressant, and cocaine was being bottled in Coca-Cola as a pep-me-up.[18] Following the Harrison Act, these drugs became controlled substances, and for the first time drug possession became a crime.

Abortion has been another highly contentious issue from a legal standpoint, with many countries historically regarding it as criminal. Today, most industrial countries permit abortions with various legal stipulations. Ironically, in many of these same countries, laws have been passed to make it a crime for mothers to drink excessively or take various drugs during pregnancy that might harm their unborn infant.[19]

In several cultures, infanticide (the killing of infants by one or both parents) is not defined as a criminal act,[20] while in other societies parents can be held criminally liable for failing to take their

Box 1.1

Marriage or Rape?

Cultures Clash over Arranged Nuptials

BY PETER ANNIN AND KENDALL HAMILTON

The November 9 wedding in Lincoln, Neb., was strictly traditional. A joint ceremony, it was planned by a 39-year-old gulf-war refugee from Iraq, who had arranged to marry his two eldest daughters, aged 13 and 14, to two fellow Iraqi refugees, aged 28 and 34. A Muslim cleric, flown in from Ohio, performed the rites before a small gathering of relatives, and then, as custom dictates, the men and women celebrated the new unions separately, at adjacent houses. The trouble began when the older daughter ran away. Concerned, the girl's father contacted her school, which in turn called police. And that's when Islamic tradition ran up against Nebraska law. Not long after the police were done asking questions, the two girls were placed in foster homes, and five adults stood accused of crimes from child abuse to rape.

The controversy has rattled the people of Lincoln, an easygoing college town of 170,000, and revealed a cultural void as vast as the Middle Eastern desert. The police say that not only were the marriages consumated, violating a state law banning sex between anyone over 18 and anyone under 16 regardless of consent, but also that the girls were forced to have sex with their new husbands against their will—a charge the Iraqi men strongly deny. The case even temporarily usurped the hallowed Cornhuskers football team as the hottest topic in town. If some longtime Lincoln residents were taken aback by the arranged marriages in their midst, the Iraqis were equally puzzled by the legal fallout. Such marriages, even among the very young, are common in much of the Muslim world—and those in the city's close-knit Iraqi community say the girls entered the union willingly. "I spoke to both girls in the days before the wedding," says Aeeda Al-Khafaji, a 30-year-old mother of seven who herself wed at 12 in Iraq. "They were both happy and excited. There was no problem at all." Still, the Iraqis say they're willing to respect the laws of their new land. "We are shocked by these allegations, and we are going to be much more careful [about the age at which girls marry]," says Mohamed Nassir, head of the Lincoln Islamic Foundation. "The problem is, we really didn't know what the law was."

But whose job is it to tell them? As refugees, the Iraqis were relocated by the federal government, which contracts with relief agencies like Catholic Social Services in Lincoln to coordinate housing, financial assistance, medical care and general orientation. The agency would release only a terse statement that "we expect all refugees assisted by our agency to obey all proper civil laws of our country." But Sanford J. Pollack, the attorney for the girls' father, says it's naive to ask refugees—who face cultural and language barriers—to absorb legal rules on their own. "When we bring people to the United States," Pollack says, "we need to educate them about our laws and customs."

Now Lincoln's refugees are getting a crash course courtesy of the city prosecutor's office. The husbands, Majed Al-Timimy, 28, and Latif Al-Hussani, 34, have been charged with rape and could face up to 50 years in prison. For his role in arranging the marriage, the girls' father has been charged with child abuse. Their mother is accused with contributing to the delinquency of a minor. Also caught up in the case is 20-year-old Mario Rojas, with whom the elder daughter was found living after her disappearance. He has been charged with statutory rape. All of the accused have entered pleas of not guilty. Lincoln's district attorney has declined to comment on the case, but one prosecutor, Jodi Nelson, has said that ignorance is no alibi. "You live in our country, you live by our laws," she says. Donations for the defense have been received from as far away as Saudi Arabia, where the case has made front-page news.

To experts in Middle Eastern affairs, the situation is frustrating. "What you have here is cultural incomprehension," says Prof. Rashid Khalidi of the University of Chicago. "And the problem is that the law is not a very subtle instrument in dealing with these kinds of cultural issues." Khalidi calls the uproar in Lincoln "a prime example of a case that begs for a nonlegal resolution." Perhaps. But for the accused, the decision may rest ultimately with another bit of unfamiliar culture, a jury.

children for proper medical treatment, even if doing so violates the parent's religious beliefs.[21]

Of course, killing people who are not members of one's own society, such as in war, has been tolerated, and even encouraged, throughout human history.[22] In some societies, the killing of people as a religious ritual was practiced for centuries, most notably among the Aztecs and Incas in Central and South America.[23]

The main point in presenting these examples is this: If what constitutes crime is highly varied, how can criminologists ever expect to find the causes of crime? This predicament has brought some criminologists to argue that just as crimes vary from one place to another, so too are the causes likely to vary.[24] If it is true that the causes of crime are heavily dependent on how different countries and time periods define crime, then the attention of criminology should be less on the causes of crime, and more on trying to understand why legislative bodies decide to criminalize some behavior rather than others.[25]

The Stationary Core Perspective

The moving target perspective has been criticized for missing an important point.[26] The point is that even though a wide variety of human actions have been deemed criminal by a legislative body somewhere in the world, there are certain acts that are all but universally criminalized.[27] Intentionally killing or injuring fellow members of one's society are primary examples of a universally condemned criminal act.[28] Taking other people's property without permission is the other principal example.[29]

Terms often used to make the distinction between acts that are universally criminalized and acts that sometimes are and other times are not criminalized are: **mala in se** (meaning "inherently bad"), and **mala prohibita** (meaning "bad because they are prohibited").[30] Most criminologists focus the bulk of their research and theorizing on the former rather than the latter, although there are exceptions, particularly for criminologists who

specialize in studying offenses committed by juveniles, rather than by adults.

Some of the strongest evidence in support of this stationary core perspective comes from an organization known as **Interpol** (an acronym for the *International Criminal Police Organization*). Interpol was established after World War II, and is headquartered in Lyon, France, with support from over 125 member nations. Besides assisting member nations with investigations of international terrorism and organized crime, Interpol serves as a repository for crime statistics from member nations.

What is striking about Interpol's statistics is that such acts as murder, assault, rape, and theft are all violations of criminal statutes in every single country. While there are variations in exactly what constitutes each of these offenses, most of these variations are minor.[31] Criminologists who subscribe to a stationary core perspective identify these sorts of offenses as ones that are universally criminalized and the main object of their attempts to understand criminal behavior. While it is still important not to assume exact comparability when looking at international crime statistics, as we will see in various later chapters, research has shown Interpol data to be fairly reliable for this purpose.[32]

The essential difference between the moving target and the stationary core concepts of crime are represented in Figures 1.1 and 1.2. In Figure 1.1 the coverage of criminal laws in five hypothetical societies according to the moving target perspective is represented. Notice that there is little overlap in what each society defines as crime. In Figure 1.2 the coverage of criminal statutes in all five societies is shown as overlapping around a stable core of universally condemned offenses.

Without disputing that criminal statutes vary a great deal from one society to another, the approach of this text will be largely from the stationary core perspective. This means that, unless stated otherwise, the focus will be on attempting to understand the origins, the violations, and enforcement of universally condemned offenses. As the next section will show, these universally

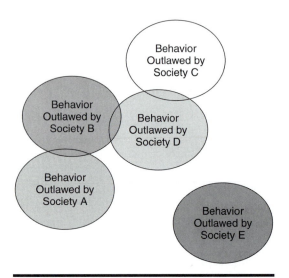

FIGURE 1.1 A diagram illustrating the difference between the moving target perspective.

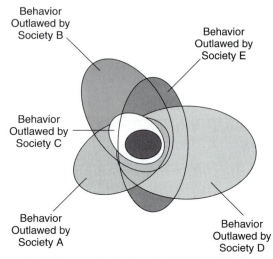

FIGURE 1.2 A diagram illustrating the difference between the stationary core perspective of how criminal statutes come to vary from one society to another.

condemned acts all have certain features in common that distinguish them from nearly all other human activities.*

The Nature of Universally Condemned Crimes

Behavior patterns that are condemned in a criminal sense by most people in all societies may be called **universally condemned crimes.**[33] Collectively, they constitute the **core offenses.**[34] Universally condemned crimes can be separated from all other

*To be thorough, we should mention that the *moving target perspective* in criminology is sometimes also termed the *conflict perspective,* and the *stationary core perspective* is often called the *consensus perspective.*[139] We have chosen not to use these alternative terms here in order to minimize confusion. In Chapter 2, we will discuss the *class conflict perspective* and the *consensus perspective* as ones that offer explanations for the origins of criminal law, which is a different issue than the one focused on here, i.e., what do criminal statutes throughout the world actually prohibit? Another set of terms used to distinguish the moving target perspective and the stationary core perspective is calling the first the *sociological perspective* and the second the *restraint perspective.*[140]

human actions (including other crimes) in terms of the following three concepts: *intentionality, victimization (excluding defensive victimization),* and *extra-group membership exclusion.* Each of these three concepts is described as follows.

1. **Intentionality** Acts are rarely considered criminal if there is no evidence that the person involved in the act could have anticipated, or would have desired, the outcome.[35] In other words, no matter how undesirable an action might be, it is not considered criminal if it was beyond the control of the individual(s) involved. The only important qualification comes in the case of negligence, in which a "reasonable person" should have been able to anticipate a particular outcome, but chose to engage in an act anyway. Such acts are often considered criminal, although to less a degree than acts specifically intended.

2. **Victimization (Excluding Defensive Victimization)** A second criterion that is necessary for an act to be considered criminal is that it must have either injured or deprived

someone of his or her property or privacy.[36] Such acts are called **victimizing acts.**[37] While societies vary somewhat in exactly how they define *injury, property,* and *privacy,* there is sufficient commonality across societies that the details need not concern us here.

The only major exception to criminalizing all victimizing acts comes in the case of an act that is purely defensive in nature. If injury results simply as part of an act of self-defense or defense of a third party, it will rarely be considered criminal.[38]

3. **Exclusion of Nongroup Members** Criminal statutes are normally applied to persons residing within a prescribed geopolitical boundary. By making a distinction between "insiders" and "outsiders," it is possible to harm others and destroy their property in times of war without fear of criminal prosecution.[39]

To test how well you are following these arguments, consider the following six crimes. Three fall under the category of universally condemned offenses, and three do not. Try separating the core offenses from the other three.

- Sale of heroin
- Prostitution
- Illegal gambling
- Manslaughter
- Vandalism
- Burglary

If you guessed that the second column contains the core offenses, you understand the distinction that has just been made. To summarize, if an act intentionally causes injury, property loss, or a loss of privacy to a fellow group member, and this was not the result of self-defense or defense of another, and it occurred within the geopolitical boundaries of where the statutes were enacted, the act will be universally condemned (with very few exceptions).

THREE DIMENSIONS OF CRIMINALITY

The notion of universally condemned crimes or core offenses can be further clarified by conceiving of crime in three dimensional terms: *the victimizing dimension, the political dimension,* and *the serious-*

ness dimension. These dimensions are illustrated in Figure 1.2, and individually discussed below.

The Victimizing Dimension

The **victimizing dimension** pertains to the degree to which there is an identifiable victim. This dimension may be divided into three crime categories: (1) crimes for which there is an obvious intended victim (e.g., most murders and rapes), (2) crimes in which victimization came about as a result of carelessness (e.g., negligent manslaughter), and (3) crimes in which all participation in the crime is voluntary (e.g., prostitution, drug offenses). The first of these three crime categories may be referred to as **victimful offenses,** the second as **marginally victimful offenses,** and the third as **victimless offenses.**[40]

The first specific reference to victimless crimes was made in the 1960s.[41] Basically, the distinction between it and victimful crimes has to do with harm to an unwilling victim.[42] If there is such harm, the crime is victimful; if not, it is victimless.

The distinction between victimful and victimless crimes is fairly close to the much older legal concepts of *mala in se* and *mala prohibita.* Other terms that have been used by criminologists to distinguish victimful and victimless offenses have been *predatory* versus *nonpredatory,*[43] and *nonconsensual* and *consensual.*[44]

Of course, not all crimes fall neatly into one or the other of these two categories. Statutory rape, for example, refers to the act of an "adult" having sexual intercourse with a "child." If the "child" (who often may be fourteen or fifteen years old) has consented to intercourse, statutory rape would not be a victimful offense. However, there is still a sense in which the "child" is still being exploited (or victimized) by an older, more experienced person. Several other sex offenses (to be discussed in detail in Chapter 16) are also only marginally victimful in nature.

As to why so many acts without any obvious victims have been, and continue to be criminalized, most legal scholars would point out that

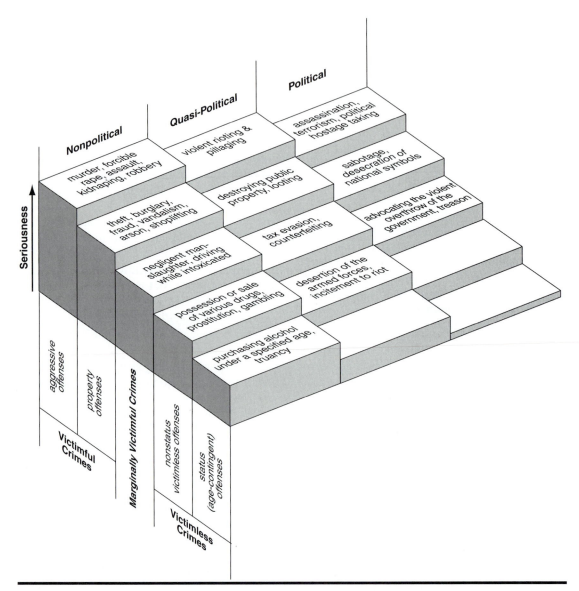

FIGURE 1.3   A diagrammatic representation of the major categories of criminal behavior and of their relative seriousness. (Note that robbery and kidnaping have both aggressive and property crime elements. Also, Quasi-Political and Political offenses can rise in perceived seriousness to levels comparable to their Nonpolitical counterparts if support for the government in power is strong.)

many times the harm done to others and to society in general is not always immediate or obvious. For example, many jurisdictions throughout the world still make gambling illegal.[45] Many of those who continue to support laws against gambling do so because significant numbers of individuals who find gambling "addictive" will lose large sums that would otherwise probably be spent on much more enduring and valuable undertakings, such as caring for the addicted gambler's children. Obviously, wherever gambling is illegal, it is a victimless crime, and yet one can make the argument that the victim is simply not as obvious as in the case of victimful crimes. Many of the laws against alcohol and drug use have been similarly inspired by a desire to prevent harm to remote third-party victims, such as children of those who may use these substances.

As shown in Figure 1.3, victimless crimes are usually subdivided into status and nonstatus offenses. **Status offenses** (also called *age-contingent offenses*) are crimes such as truancy or drinking under a prescribed age, which are illegal for persons under a certain age, but not for those beyond that age.[46] All other victimless crimes (i.e., *nonstatus victimless crimes*) include such things as illegal gambling, prostitution, and drug possession, which are deemed criminal or not criminal regardless of age.

The Political Dimension

Turning to the **political dimension** of criminal behavior, we have already noted that political forces underlie both the creation and enforcement of all criminal statutes. For this reason, special consideration is given to crimes that threaten to destabilize government itself. Thus, offenses such as assassinations and espionage are not just murders and thefts; they are also political offenses. Because political offenses directly threaten the very institutions that make civilized life possible (including the existence of criminal statutes themselves), these offenses are usually dealt with more harshly than the same crime that has no political motivation.

Another category of political crime is one in which governmental actions themselves cause harm to citizens.[47] These are difficult to prosecute in most societies, however, because control over the legal arena in which the crime must be proven is controlled by the government being charged.

There are intermediate types of crime that need to recognized. Certain crimes seriously threaten governmental stability even though this threat may not be what is motivating those who commit the offense. Examples are counterfeiting money (a universal governmental function) and rioting and looting. As shown in Figure 1.3, these are called **quasi-political crimes.**

As you might guess, the vast majority of crimes have no political motivation or significant political ramifications. So, while a few criminologists have come to specialize in studying political (and quasi-political) offenses, the majority of criminologists study nonpolitical crime.

The Seriousness Dimension

The third dimension of crime is **seriousness.** Research has shown that, while almost all crimes are considered serious by some people, the offenses that are most often considered serious are those concentrated in the upper boxes.[48] Over and over again, studies have found substantial agreement both within and across industrial societies regarding the average seriousness ratings given to standard lists of offenses.[49]

Some interesting studies have compared average seriousness ratings given by adults in the United States beginning in the 1920s. These studies concluded that rankings have changed only slightly from then until recent times.[50] Among the slight trends that have been noted, both in the United States and other industrial countries, is an increase in people's seriousness ratings of white-collar crimes, at least compared to their ratings of nonviolent street crimes[51] and a decrease in seriousness ratings given to most offenses associated with "abnormal" sexual behavior.[52]

Overall, U.S. citizens have exhibited a high degree of agreement in their ratings of the seriousness of most offenses.[53] As you might expect, the agreement tends to be stronger in the case of violent crimes than in the case of property and victimless crimes.[54] One of the best predictors of the degree to which people will agree with one another has been education, with highly educated persons exhibiting greater agreement than the less educated.[55] This may be partly artificial in that being well educated better insures that people will be able to read and understand the crime descriptions given on questionnaires.

Besides the United States, studies of crime seriousness have been conducted in countries as diverse as Canada,[56] England and Wales,[57] Puerto Rico,[58] Iran,[59] Kuwait,[60] Papua New Guinea,[61] Germany,[62] and New Zealand.[63] One of the results of these studies is that agreement within a society tends to increase slightly with a country's degree of industrialization.[64] This finding could be simply due to the link between industrialization and the amount of education people have, because most of these studies require that subjects read the crime descriptions.

Some criminologists have asserted that there is little consensus about crime seriousness, especially when comparing offenses that are all fairly similar.[65] However, most studies have shown that, when comparing broad spectrums of offenses, people everywhere in the industrial world appear to have roughly similar views of what are and are not serious crimes.[66] Even in nonindustrial societies, almost no one regards offenses such as gambling and disorderly conduct nearly as serious as committing rape or robbery. Therefore, people everywhere seem to share at least a rough sense of what is "acceptable" behavior under most circumstances.

Interesting studies have been conducted on factors associated with people's assessments of the seriousness of crime. Three of these studies have compared males and females on ratings of crime seriousness. Which sex do you think tends to give higher seriousness ratings to just about all crimes? The answer is females.[67] Part of the reason for this sex difference could be that females are more fearful of being victimized by crime than are men, a point that will be addressed in Chapter 5.

One study asked prisoners to rate the seriousness of crimes and compared their average ratings to those given by the general public. How do you think their ratings compared? Overall, the average ordering was almost exactly the same, although prisoners gave somewhat lower seriousness ratings to all crimes than did the public at large.[68]

What criteria do people use in judging the seriousness of crimes? Researchers have identified

three main factors.[69] The most important is the degree of physical violence or injury to the victim.[70] The second most important is the magnitude of the victim's loss.[71] And the third is the relationship between the offender and the victim. People usually rate an attack on a stranger as more serious than the same attack on someone familiar to the assailant, probably because an attack on a stranger has an element of privacy invasion added to the attack itself.[72]

It should be mentioned that victimless crimes are generally considered less serious than victimful offenses, with the exception of selling certain illegal drugs, which are often seen as comparable to most property offenses in seriousness.[73] Another important qualification to note is that greater agreement can be obtained if details about offenses are given.[74] For instance, the crime of rape includes sexual attacks by strangers using weapons as well as a man refusing to take "later" for an answer from his fiancee.[75] Without disputing that both constitute rape, few would consider the latter as serious as the former offense. Therefore, when people are simply asked to rate the seriousness of rape or any other crime, their ratings will vary more than when the nature of a crime is described in detail.

Table 1.1 provides a list of ten offenses than were among a list given to a sample of adults in Dallas, Texas in 1987. Beside each offense, Table 1.1 presents the average seriousness ratings assigned by the subjects on an 11-point scale, ranging from 0–10 (with 10 being the most serious).[76] Before examining these average ratings, you might want to cover the second column with your hand and assign your own subjective ratings, and then compare them to the averages. More than likely, you will not find major differences.

There is much more to the nature of criminal law than can be delineated by discussing the three dimensions of crime. For a discussion of these topics, you may want to read Appendix A.

Overall, one can generalize by saying that, in all societies, nearly everyone condemns behavior that intentionally victimizes others, especially if

TABLE 1.1. A list of ten offenses, and the average seriousness rating given by subjects in Texas in 1987.[77]

Description of Offense	Average Seriousness Rating
Robbing a store and killing two employees	9.87
Setting fire to an occupied apartment building	9.15
Killing a pedestrian while speeding	8.78
A teenager hitting an old woman in the street	8.14
A teenager forcing his girlfriend into sex	7.67
Stealing an unlocked car	6.69
Evading $500 in federal income taxes	5.07
Painting obscenities on a highway billboard	3.92
Writing a bad check for $10 to a store	3.87
Trespassing in a railroad yard	2.37

the victims are members of the social group to which those making the judgment belong. Victimization comes in three forms: personal injury, deprivation of property, and violations of privacy. To the degree these elements are evident in an act, nearly everyone will condemn the act and support punishment of the offender.[78]

In literate societies (i.e., societies in which a large proportion of citizens can read and write), condemnation of victimizing acts has taken the form of criminal statutes. Even in preliterate societies, victimizing acts are generally disapproved of,[79] although the nature and severity of the sanctions are less predictable.[80]

While a few criminologists specialize in studying political offenses and victimless offenses, the vast majority focus on **victimful nonpolitical offenses.** These offenses are also called the *core offenses* and the *universally condemned offenses.* Where do you find these criminal categories concentrated in Table 1.1?

WHY THE CRIME CONCEPT IS BROADER THAN THE CORE OFFENSES

Even though most people in all societies condemn the core victimful offenses, legal statutes in virtually all societies are not confined to these crimes.

Why? One reason seems to be to discourage people from advocating or even contemplating the commission of core offenses. For example, in many societies, it is not simply illegal to commit a murder or rob a bank, it is illegal to conspire with others to commit these acts.[81] Similarly, truancy has been found to be associated with adolescent crime and drug use.[82] This being the case, it is reasonable to assume that criminality and drug use can be curtailed somewhat by making truancy illegal.[83] In these ways, the web of criminal laws in most societies extends far beyond the core offenses.

Other criminal statutes have come into being to help protect health or improve sanitation. Still other criminal statutes seem merely to support particular religious doctrines. One example is so-called blue laws that make it illegal for taverns and other commercial establishments to be open on Sunday.[84]

There are even instances in which religious traditions sometimes exempt certain acts from coverage by criminal statutes pertaining to core offenses. For example, while it is always a core offense to kill members of one's own society at will, such actions are allowed in some cultures as part of religious ceremonies. Various preliterate African and especially Central American tribal groups, for example, were known to have had special religious ceremonies in which slaves, and sometimes "ordinary citizens" were killed as ritualistic sacrifices to their gods.[85]

Not too dissimilarly, during the sixteenth and seventeenth centuries, officials of the Spanish Inquisition burned thousands of Jews and other heretics for their failure to sincerely convert to Christianity.[86] Instances in which people were identified as witches and burned at the stake or drowned were also known to have taken place in Europe as well as the United States up until the turn of the nineteenth century.[87] These sort of "religious exemptions" from what are obvious violations of core offense statutes, however, have rarely been specifically authorized within the criminal statutes adopted by a state-level government.

In Chapter 3, we will examine international data on crime. As this evidence is examined, caution is in order, because legal statutes vary from one country and time period to another, as do the probabilities of victims notifying police. The variability in legal statutes is especially notable when one goes beyond the core offenses. For example, before 1914, there were no drug offenses. The possession, use, and sale of marijuana, heroin, and cocaine were legal, and other drugs, such as LSD, had not yet been discovered.[88] Some countries appear to be much more prone than others to try to use the criminal justice system to solve what are perceived as social problems, leading to what has been called "over-criminalized societies".[89] Whatever the pros and cons may be regarding criminalizing approaches to the regulation of human behavior, it can have an enormous effect on the number of crimes societies appear to have. We will discuss this issue more in Chapter 3.

THE CONCEPT OF DELINQUENCY AND THE FELONY–MISDEMEANOR DISTINCTION

A term intimately related to criminality is the concept of **delinquency.** As will be discussed more in Chapter 2, a legal distinction between youthful offenders and adult offenders gradually arose in the nineteenth century. The distinction was in part an outgrowth of much older distinctions involving the age at which children could be held legally (and morally) responsible for their actions. Even today, this age varies from one political jurisdiction to another, but is rarely younger than seven years of age, and is often as old as ten or twelve.[90] Beyond that age, full legal responsibility was generally assumed. During the twentieth century, however, most political jurisdictions throughout the world have established a second age cutoff, one between juveniles and adults. This cutoff also varies, largely between fourteen and eighteen years of age.[91] Precedents for the juvenile–adult distinction actually have been traced back centuries under English common law, in which judges usually gave more lenient sentences to younger offenders.[92]

In most political jurisdictions, *delinquency* does not simply refer to criminal offenses committed by persons in their early-to-midteens. Delinquency also includes a number of status offenses. As discussed earlier, status offenses are acts that are only illegal for persons within a specific age category.[93] It is worth noting that delinquency statutes in the United States contain more status offenses than any other country,[94] prompting efforts to curtail them.[95] This provides an instance in which it would be misleading to compare juvenile offending in the United States with juvenile offending in other countries without allowing for the fact that the United States has a greater number of juvenile statutes.

It is important to emphasize that, as with the concept of *crime, delinquency* is ultimately a legal, not a scientific concept.[96] This necessitates that criminologists appreciate the fact that variations exist in what is defined as *delinquency* from one society and time period to another. Nevertheless, at the core of all societal definitions of delinquency are still the victimful offenses that are the stable constituents of what constitute crimes committed by adults throughout the world.

The legal concepts of *felony* and *misdemeanor* are often used in criminological research to help separate the more serious from the less serious offenses. Historically, the term *felony* was used as a synonym for violent and property offenses, while

misdemeanors covered all other crimes, with the exception of political offenses, which were put into a third category.[97] Literally, the word **felony** has the same roots as the word *treachery,* whereas *misdemeanor* comes from a French root meaning "bad motivation" or "bad intention."

Today, the essential distinction between felonies and misdemeanors has to do with the maximum possible punishment that can be legally imposed for an offense. If the maximum possible penalty is greater than one-year imprisonment, then the offense is considered a felony. And, if the maximum possible penalty for an offense is less than one-year imprisonment, the crime is considered a misdemeanor. Obviously, what is a felony in one political jurisdiction may be a misdemeanor in another, and political jurisdictions change their classifications from time to time. Despite this variability, criminologists often use the felony–misdemeanor distinction in their research to separate the study of serious offenses from the study of relatively minor crimes.

THE PRO/ANTISOCIAL CONTINUUM AND THE CONCEPT OF ANTISOCIAL BEHAVIOR

If you were called on to identify behavior that is as close to the complete opposite of *victimful criminality* as you could get, what name would you give to that behavior? Most English speaking people might pick such adjectives as *virtuous, kindly, helpful,* and perhaps even *moral* or *saintly.* In essence, all of these terms refer to the opposite of going out of one's way to hurt others and damage their property.

Social scientists often use the terms **altruism** and **prosocial behavior** to describe the opposite of victimizing criminality.[98] The concept of *altruism* was first used in the nineteenth century by a French sociologist named August Comte to describe self-sacrificing behavior by one human being on behalf of another. He proposed that without altruism human societies would disintegrate.

While it is possible to be altruistic toward some people and antisocial toward others (recall the story of Robin Hood), studies have shown that,

as a rule, people who are most prone to intentionally hurting others are least prone to being helpful and courteous.[99] Thus, pro/antisociality appears to refer to fairly stable behavioral tendencies that are at opposite extremes.[100] Note once again that, as in the case of height and criminality, studies suggest that people can be arrayed along a continuum, with a small proportion being extremely prosocial, a small proportion being extremely antisocial, and the majority being somewhere in between.[101]

Despite the similarities between the concepts of *criminal behavior* and *antisocial behavior,* they should not be equated. The first is a legal concept, while the second is essentially a clinical concept. To better understand their connection, let us look in more depth at the concept of *antisocial behavior.*

Antisocial Behavior over the Life Course

Childhood Conduct Disorders.   Imagine that you were in a clinic that specialized in treating children with behavior difficulties, and a mother came to you for help with her seven-year-old son. She describes him as being chronically defiant toward her and other adults, and as often committing senseless acts of destruction of other people's property, hitting other children with dangerous objects, and stealing and then blatantly lying about doing so.

A variety of names have been given to such behavioral patterns. In recent years, the broad terms of **childhood conduct disorder** or simply **conduct disorders** (CD) has come to be widely used.[102] Other terms that apply to behavior more or less synonymous with *CD* are *externalizing behavior,*[103] *acting out, early delinquency,*[104] *conduct problems,*[105] *disruptive behavior disorder*[106] and *undersocialized aggressive conduct disorder.*[107] In its most severe forms, CD has been referred to as *childhood antisocial behavior.*[108]

The behavioral expression of CD varies considerably in terms of severity and persistence over time.[109] Nonetheless, the main behavioral components include aggression toward peers and adults, destruction and theft of property, chronic defiance, and frequent lying and deception.[110] It is not difficult to surmise that CD children do poorly in school[111] and have relatively few close friends.[112]

According to the most recent version of the **Diagnostic and Statistical Manual of Mental Disorders** (DSM-IV), a widely used clinical reference guide published by the American Psychiatric Association,[113] CD can be defined as "a repetitive and persistent pattern of behavior in which either the basic rights of others or major age-appropriate societal norms or rules are violated." Different subtypes have been identified hinging primarily on the types and amounts of overt aggression involved.[114] When the behavior is evident early in life (i.e., before age 10), it is called *childhood onset type,* and when it occurs later, it is termed *adolescent onset type.*

Two important dimensions (or aspects) have been identified in CD. The first includes fighting and other confrontational acts of disrespect for the rights of others, and the second is more covert, having to do with hyperactivity, an inability to concentrate on long-term tasks, and a tendency to steal and vandalize.[115] As a general rule, both aspects of CD appear together in the same child to a roughly similar degree.

Antisocial Behavior in Adolescence and Adulthood.   Several clinical terms have been used to refer to antisocial behavior that persists beyond childhood, and especially beyond early adolescence. These terms include *psychopathy, sociopathy,* the *antisocial personality syndrome* (APS), and the *antisocial personality disorder* (APD).[116] Prior to the turn of the twentieth century, clinical manifestations of antisocial behavior were referred to as *moral insanity* and *moral imbecility.*[117] Throughout most of the twentieth century, **psychopathy** has been the single most widely used term, but with frequent hopes that a better one would one day be found.[118] In the 1980s, the term **antisocial personality syndrome,** later changed to the **antisocial personality disorder,** was recommended by the committee who devised the Diagnostic and Statistical Manual (DSM) for the American Psychiatric Association. Throughout this text, we will use the two terms *psy-*

chopathy and *antisocial personality disorder* interchangeably.

Why so many different names? Much of the reason has had to do with clinicians not wanting to stigmatize those afflicted by the disorder. However, there has also been a great deal of controversy over just how to define and diagnose persons with the disorder.

Students of criminology should be able to recognize the behavioral characteristics of APD. They are displayed in Table 1.2.[119] As explained more in Chapter 2, several of these characteristics must be present to an appreciable degree to warrant a clinical diagnosis of APD.

While these behavioral tendencies are certainly not criminal in and of themselves, it is not difficult to see that persons who exhibit several of them to extreme degrees will be much more disposed toward a criminal career than persons in general.[120] As discussed in more detail below, studies have shown that there is indeed a strong correspondence between violent and persistent delinquent and criminal histories and an APD diagnosis.[121] Thus, while criminality and APD should not be equated, they should be seen as intimately linked behavioral phenomena.

To further illustrate the concept of APD, consider a study in England in which a group of diagnosed psychopaths and nonpsychopaths read

TABLE 1.2.   Major Behavioral Manifestations of the Antisocial Personality Disorder (APD; psychopathy)

Insensitivity to the feelings of others
Lack of emotional depth or conscience
Extensive history of lying and deception
Impulsiveness and unreliability
Tendencies to blame others, not oneself, whenever
    things go wrong
A grandiose sense of self-worth
Failure to profit from past adverse experiences
A parasitic lifestyle and a lack of long-term life
    goals
Superficial charm
Incapacity for love and impersonal sex life
Untruthfulness and insincerity

stories designed to elicit four categories of emotions: happiness, sadness, embarrassment, and guilt.[122] After hearing each story, the two groups of subjects rated the "dominant" emotional reactions they had to each story. There were no differences between the two groups for the stories about happiness, sadness, or embarrassment. For the story written to elicit feelings of guilt, however, the groups differed significantly. Whereas the comparison group subjects gave high "guilt" ratings to the story, the psychopathic subjects rated their reactions to the story as high on happiness and indifference. What this and similar research has indicated is that while psychopathic subjects are not necessarily criminal, they do have the sort of emotional character that greatly increases their chances of repeatedly becoming involved in crime.

The Link between CD, APD, and Criminality

Is there an association between childhood (or adolescent) CD, APD, and criminality? The answer is yes, although this does not mean that *every*one who is convicted of crime or is diagnosed with APD will have been diagnosed with CD in childhood or adolescence. In the case of mild cases of CD, the chance of serious criminality and APD symptoms appearing later in life is only slightly above the norm, but when CD symptoms are serious and persistent, the chances of serious criminality and APD symptoms are quite high.[123]

When scientists say that complex behavioral tendencies such as CD, APD, and criminality are related, they mean that the tendencies have a substantial likelihood of co-occurring in the same individuals. In more technical terminology, all three variables are said to be positively correlated, meaning that if an individual has one of these three conditions, he or she has an elevated chance of having either or both of the other two conditions. Especially in the case of adult APD, there is almost no chance that, sometime during childhood, a psychopath would not have been diagnosed as being among the 2 to 10 percent of children with CD.[124]

Evidence surrounding connections between CD, APD, and criminality (including juvenile delinquency) will be reviewed in greater detail in Chapter 6. For the time being, suffice it to say that their connections are so close that involvement in criminal conduct is often considered a prerequisite for receiving a diagnosis of APD, although most people who commit crime are never diagnosed as being psychopathic.

Table 1.3 indicates the number of studies that have found a statistically significant relationship between CD, APD, and criminality (including delinquency), and the countries in which the studies were conducted. The number of studies conducted in the United States and Canada are identified in the upper right-hand cells, and the number of studies in all other countries are shown in the lower left-hand cells.

You can see that studies conducted throughout the world have repeatedly documented that there is a substantial statistical link between CD, APD, and criminality. In other words, individuals with childhood CD have a higher than normal probability of being both criminal and diagnosed APD in adolescence and adulthood, and persons with a serious criminal record have a higher probability of being diagnosed psychopathic than those with little or no criminal history.[125] Nevertheless, it is essential to emphasize that these generalizations are all based on statistical probabilities. For example, it would be very misleading to assume that *every*one who is diagnosed with childhood CD, especially the more mild cases, will have a criminal record by age thirty.

Another important qualification to note about the above generalization is that some of the clinical criteria for assessing APD actually include evidence of criminality.[126] This makes the relationship between criminality and APD almost inevitable.[127] Nevertheless, even studies that have focused their diagnostic criteria for antisocial personality strictly on noncriminal symptoms (i.e., those listed in Table 1.2) have still shown a substantial association between antisocial personality and criminality.[128]

In other words, diagnosed conduct disorders in childhood and antisocial personality in adulthood substantially overlap with criminality, but not to the point that these human tendencies should be equated.[129] Part of the reason clinical assessments

TABLE 1.3.   Evidence published pertaining to associations between CD, APD, and delinquency and crime.

	Conduct Disorders in Childhood	Antisocial Personality in Adulthood, or Late Adolescence	Delinquent & Criminal Behavior, especially Serious Victimful Offenses
Conduct Disorders in Childhood		**North America** *Canada*: 2; *United States*: 10	**North America** *Canada*: 4; *United States*: 32
Antisocial Personality in Adulthood or Late Adolescence	**Europe** *England*: 2		**North America** *Canada*: 5; *United States*: 3
Delinquent & Criminal Behavior, especially Serious Victimful Offenses	**Europe** *England*: 4; *Finland*: 2; *Sweden*: 4 **Pacific** *New Zealand*: 3	**Africa** *Nigeria*: 1 **Europe** *England*: 1 **Other** *Several Different Countries*: 1	

Studies listed above and to the right of the shaded squares were based on subjects in the United States; studies listed below and to the left of the shaded squares were based on subjects obtained elsewhere as indicated.)

of either CD or APD and official measures of criminal behavior can not be considered equivalent is the obvious fact that neither CD nor APD are themselves illegal per se. Also, even if CD, APD, and criminality were equivalent, the fact that they all exist along a continuum and are all difficult to measure precisely means that some who are diagnosed with either CD or APD will never be *identified* as criminal.

Nevertheless, nearly all of the studies listed in Table 1.3 have shown that criminality (including delinquency) is much more common among persons who have been clinically diagnosed with CD and/or APD.[130] The more serious and persistent the criminality, the stronger the link to both of these clinical conditions. Also, while the link between CD, on the one hand, and criminality and psychopathy, on the other hand, is substantial for both sexes, it appears to be stronger for males than for females.[131]

Psychopathy can be characterized in terms of two major clusters of behavioral tendencies. The first cluster includes tendencies toward manipulative, callous, and nonempathetic behavior toward others. The second includes tendencies to be impulsive and irresponsible in everyday activities.[132] As with all behavioral criteria used in making clinical diagnoses, those used to identify psychopaths are based on judgments about matters of degree. In other words, nearly everyone is occasionally at least mildly impulsive or callous toward the feelings of others, but persons who are diagnosed as psychopathic or clinically antisocial exhibit these tendencies to extreme degrees.[133]

Finally, a clinical classification category closely related to psychopathy is Briquet's syndrome (or hysteria).[134] This condition refers to flamboyant behavior, usually accompanied by ostentatious grooming and dress, and frequently associated with extreme sexual promiscuity and a chronic failure to form any long-term marital relationships.[135] Briquet's syndrome has been regarded as essentially the female's expression of what is classified as psychopathy in males.[136]

SUMMARY

This chapter has explored the basic concept of criminality. It does so by first noting that criminologists have taken at least two positions regarding the nature of crime. One is the "moving target" view, in which crime is seen as covering a more or less arbitrary and unpredictable set of acts that vary from one society (and time period) to another.[137] The other position, called the "stationary core" perspective, asserts that at the heart of criminal statutes in essentially all societies are certain core offenses that are almost universally condemned.

At the heart of the universally condemned (or core) offenses are three features: (1) the act must have been intentional; (2) the act must have violated another person's physical being, property, or right to privacy, excluding purely defensive actions; (3) the victim must be a fellow group member, rather than an "outsider," so as not to criminalize violent acts during war with another country.

Looking beyond just the core offenses, criminality in the broadest sense can be thought of as consisting of three dimensions: the victimizing dimension, the political dimension, and the seriousness dimension. Regarding the first dimension, some crimes are clearly victimful, others are clearly victimless, and still others are ambiguous with regard to the victimizing dimension, called *marginally victimful.* For the political dimension, it is useful to distinguish political crimes, nonpolitical crimes, and crimes such as rioting and counterfeiting that are quasi-political. In regard to seriousness, offenses vary all the way from trivial to extremely serious, and most people throughout the world are found to agree about the seriousness of various crimes, especially the core offenses. In legal terms, crimes are often divided into those that are considered less serious, called *misdemeanors,* and those that are regarded as more serious, called *felonies.* Criminologists often utilize these two categories in their research.

The concept of delinquency and its relationship to criminality was briefly discussed. Basically, delinquent acts are those committed by juveniles that would be criminal if committed by adults plus a set of *status offenses* that apply only to juveniles.

The formal distinction between delinquent and criminal acts first began to be made in various countries around the beginning of the twentieth century.

The latter portion of this chapter directed attention to the concept of a *pro/antisocial* continuum, and linked it to the concept of *criminality.* Basic to the concept of prosocial is the notion of altruism, or self-sacrificing behavior. The link between criminality and antisocial behavior is that these concepts often refer to the same behavior, although *criminal behavior* is a legal term, whereas *antisocial behavior* is an extra-legal, or clinical, term. While the distinction is important, you will find that many criminologists sometimes use the terms almost interchangeably.

Antisocial behavior encompasses acts that reflect a general disregard for the welfare of others. While being diagnosed antisocial is not itself illegal, studies have shown that persons with such a diagnosis have an increased chance of engaging in illegal behavior. Using clinical terminology, antisocial behavior has come to be called *conduct disorder* when it is exhibited by children (and young adolescents), and *psychopathy* (or *antisocial personality disorder*) when it is exhibited by adults and older adolescents.

Studies have shown that most people are not simply antisocial nor prosocial (or criminal or noncriminal). Rather, people are, for whatever reasons, arrayed along a continuum regarding these behavior patterns, with the majority of us in a broad intermediate position (i.e., neither extremely antisocial nor extremely prosocial in the vast majority of our activities).

Ultimately, criminal and antisocial behavior should be thought of as pertaining to what has been termed *fuzzy sets,* not crisp sets.[138] While it is necessary for the legal system to attempt to draw sharp boundaries around these fuzzy sets in order to hold people responsible for their actions, scientifically speaking it is impossible to make absolute distinctions between what is and is not criminal. Social scientists are used to dealing with fuzzy sets, in that they reflect the reality of human behavioral complexity.

SUGGESTED READINGS_____

U.S. Department of Justice (1977). *Victimless crime: A selected bibliography.* Washington, DC: Law Enforcement Assistance Administration. (Provides a useful set of annotated references to criminological research on victimless crimes up to the mid-1970s.)

Wilson, James Q. (1993). *The moral sense.* New York: Free Press. (A popularly written book on the basic nature of morality and how it underlies human civilization. The link between morality and law abiding behavior is also discussed.)

EXERCISES_____

1. Describe a recent change, or proposed change, in some criminal statute that you have learned about in the mass media. Offer your views on why some people want to make these changes, and why others might resist them. Also offer your opinion on how much impact such changes might make on the level of crime in your area.

2. The following table presents, in no particular order, a list of seven acts that are often considered criminal offenses. Add three more offenses that interest you to this list. Then, rate each of the ten acts on a scale from 1 to 10 in terms of your perception of each one's seriousness (with 10 being the most serious). Put a strip of paper over your ratings, and give the list to a member of the opposite sex, and ask him or her to rate the offenses on the same 10-point scale.

   After he or she is finished, compare the two ratings with the other person present, and discuss each inconsistency of 2 or more ranking points. Write a one- to two-page double-spaced report on what you learned from this exercise about how you and the other person differ and resemble one another in your thoughts about the seriousness of crime. (Recall from studies reviewed in this chapter that on average a sex difference has been found regarding how people rate the seriousness of most crimes. Note whether this was true in your case by adding the total rankings given in both columns.)

Offense	Ranking by Someone Else	Your Ranking
Alcohol consumption by a minor		
Assassinating an unpopular political leader		
Killing a repeatedly abusive spouse		
Raping a stranger with threats from a deadly weapon		
Committing rape on a date by threatening bodily harm		
Driving while extremely drunk		
Molesting a young child		
TOTAL OF ALL RANKS GIVEN		

ENDNOTES

1. Eichelman 1983:391.

2. Conklin 1986:8; Schur 1969:9.

3. Lewin 1988:1129; Pfeiffer 1977:251; Whitehouse & Wilkins 1986:127.

4. Ember & Ember 1985:228.

5. Ellis 1986a.

6. Becker 1963; Chapman 1968:4.

7. Sellin 1938:23.

8. Ginsberg 1965:213; Sheldon et al. 1949:825; Sigvardsson et al.1982:1253; Simmons 1969:33; Wells 1980:66; Wilson 1976:83.

9. Gallard 1995:1593; Toubia 1994:715.

10. Haviland 1990:578; Hicks 1986; Hosken 1979.

11. Gallard 1995.

12. B. J. Ellis 1992:302; Nelson 1987; Toubia 1994:714.

13. Caldwell et al. 1997:1187.

14. Bartol 1980:10.

15. Friedman & Downey 1994:928.

16. Karlen 1980:84.

17. Goode 1984:221.

18. Fishbein & Pease 1996:10.

19. Kantrowitz et al. 1991; Logli 1990.

20. Bonnet 1993:502.

21. Toubia 1994:740.

22. Daly & Wilson 1988:274.

23. Whitehouse & Wilkins 1986:119.

24. Schur 1969:73; Sparks 1980:181.

25. E.g., Greenberg 1977; Quinney 1977; Taylor et al. 1975:44.

26. Eysenck & Gudjonsson 1989:1; Hindelang 1978a:95; Hirschi & Gotfredson 1990:417.

27. Burkett & White 1974:456; Clinard 1959:530; Durkheim 1933:72; Hirschi & Gottfredson 1990:417; Kornhauser 1978:187; Miethe 1982:523; Poznaniak 1980:87.

28. Mukherjee 1981:65.

29. Chase 1963:88.

30. Burkett & Ward 1993:130; Newman 1976:14.

31. Bennett & Lynch 1990.

32. Bennett & Lynch 1990.

33. Segall 1983:18.

34. Ellis 1988.

35. Carroll & Jackson 1983:178; Farrington 1987:34; Glaser 1971:4.

36. Sellin & Wolfgang, 1964.

37. Chilton & DeAmicis 1975:325.

38. Lagerspetz & Westman 1980.

39. Dickstein 1979:40; Glaser 1971:5; Poznaniak 1980:95; Sumner 1940:499; Wolfgang 1975a:477.

40. Ellis 1988.

41. Schur 1965.

42. Stitt 1988:99.

43. Glaser 1978a: 6.

44. Vetter & Silverman 1986:179.

45. Frey & Eadington 1984; Ichniowski 1985.

46. Molotch 1986:175; Streit 1981:411.

47. Johnson & Wasielewski 1982:209.

48. Chilton & DeAmicis 1975; Newman 1976; Rossi et al. 1974:231.

49. Borg 1985; Coombs 1967; Hamilton & Sanders 1983; Warr 1989.

50. Borg 1985; Coombs 1967; Krus et al. 1977.

51. Cullen et al. 1982.

52. Borg 1985; Krus et al. 1977.

53. Carlson & Williams 1993; Durea 1933; Hamilton & Rotkin 1976; Rossi et al. 1974; Sellin & Wolfgang 1964.

54. Abrams & Fave 1976:69; Carlson & Williams 1993; Cullen et al. 1982.

55. Rossi et al. 1974.

56. Akman et al. 1967.

57. Banks et al. 1975:230; Levi & Jones 1985.

58. Valez-Diaz & Megaree 1970.

59. Al-Thakeb & Scott 1981.

60. Evans & Scott 1984.

61. Wuillemin et al. 1986.

62. Borg 1985.

63. Davis & Kemp 1994.

64. Bacon et al. 1963; Brown 1952; Moore et al. 1984; Wuillemin et al. 1986.

65. Cullen et al. 1985; D. F. Hawkins 1980:207; Miethe 1982:469.

66. Davis & Kemp 1994:260; Evans & Scott 1984.

67. Hilton 1989; Kormos et al. 1992; Phillips 1985.

68. Figlio 1975.

69. Gove et al. 1985:489; Hilton 1989.

70. Cohen 1988.

71. Elifson et al. 1983:507.

72. Gove 1985:489.

73. Cullen et al. 1982; Rossi et al. 1974.

74. Messner 1984:437.

75. Ellis 1989a:5.

76. Warr 1989:801.

77. from Warr 1989:801.

78. Newman 1976:44.

79. Wilson & Herrnstein 1985:22.

80. Cormier & Boyer 1963:77 Hoebel 1954.

81. Darley et al. 1996; Feinberg & Gross 1986:593.

82. Fergusson et al. 1995a; Finn & Brown 1971:68; Sellin & Wolfgang 1982:26; Shulman 1961:33.

83. Arnold & Brungardt 1983:29; Ellis 1990a:22.

84. Middleton & Putney 1962.

85. Garfinkel 1967:212; Whitehouse & Wilkins 1986: 33 & 119.

86. Sheldon et al. 1949:846; Willhoite 1977:668.

87. Larner 1984.

88. Fishbein & Pease, 1996:13; Jones et al. 1969:70.

89. Cahalan 1979:9.

90. Eysenck & Gudjonsson 1989:154; Farrington 1987b:35; Loeber 1987:615.

91. Eysenck & Gudjonsson 1989:154; Murrell & Lester 1981:9; Rubin 1949:7; U.S. Department of Justice 1983:61.

92. D. F. Hawkins 1981:207; Rubin 1949:7.

93. U.S. Department of Justice 1983:50.

94. Bortner 1988:101; Farrington 1987a:33; Vanagunas 1979:48.

95. Grygier 1966; National Council on Crime and Delinquency 1975; Rubin 1985:63.

96. Quay 1987b:118.

97. Parmelee 1921:265.

98. Zahn-Waxler et al. 1986:7; E.g., Bonger 1916; Czudner & Mueller 1987; Feshbach & Feshbach 1986; Hinde 1986; Harpending & Draper 1988; McKissack 1975.

99. McKissack 1975:48; Turner 1948.

100. Rushton 1980:82.

101. Eichelman 1983:391; Krebs 1975; Turner 1948.

102. Atkeson & Forehand 1981; Lahey et al. 1994; Offord et al. 1986.

103. Hinshaw 1992a:895; Shaw & Vondra 1995:335.

104. Kazdin 1987:187; Loeber 1987; Quay 1979.

105. Eppright et al. 1993:1233.

106. Costello & Angold 1993; Grizenko & Pawliuk 1994; Zahn-Waxler 1993:79.

107. Quay 1986, 1987b:121.

108. Kazdin & Esveldt-Dawson 1986.

109. Hinshaw 1992a:894; Magnusson 1988:135; Robins 1991:195.

110. Farrington 1991:389; Offord et al. 1986:274; Stewart 1985:324; Stewart & de Blois 1985.

111. Hinshaw 1992; McMichael 1979; Moffitt 1990; Tremblay et al. 1992a.

112. Miller 1994:276; Robins 1991:204; Wheeler & Carlson 1994.

113. American Psychiatric Association 1993:85.

114. Robins 1991:198.

115. Kazdin & Esveldt-Dawson 1986; Magnusson 1988:135.

116. Archer 1995:518; Feldman 1977:174.

117. Brim & Nelson 1981; Hoffman 1986; Lykken 1995:113; Salama 1988:149.

118. Reed 1996:5.

119. Cleckley 1982:204; Farrington 1991:391; Hare 1980; Hare & McPherson 1984a:35; Robins 1966:342.

120. Andrew 1982:366; Blair 1975.

121. Hare & McPherson 1984:35; Haynes & Bensch 1981.

122. Blair et al. 1995.

123. Farrington 1991; Loeber 1982:1413; Robins 1991:203.

124. Miller 1994:274.

125. Vitella 1996:263.

126. Mannuzza et al. 1989:1079; Millon 1981.

127. Hare 1985.

128. Mannuzza et al. 1989:1079.

129. Andrew 1982:366; Eysenck & Gudjonsson 1989:48; Masters & Roberson 1990:314.

130. Ononye & Morakinyo 1994:528.

131. Zahn-Waxler et al. 1995:44.

132. Hare et al. 1988:68.

133. Blackburn & Maybury 1985; Edelmann & Vivian 1988; Hurwitz & Christiansen 1983:117; Wilson & Herrnstein 1985:207.

134. Harpending & Draper 1988.

135. Goodwin & Guze 1984; Guze 1976.

136. Cloninger 1986:188; Cloninger & Guze 1970a, 1970b; Guze 1976; Guze et al. 1986; McMahon 1980:146.

137. Roush 1995:1809.

138. See Clive et al. 1983.

139. Carlson & Williams 1993; Furnham & Alison 1994:41.

140. Hirschi & Gottfredson 1990:417

CHAPTER 2

The Origins of Criminal Law and Options for Measuring Criminal Behavior

Where did criminal laws originate, and why did they come to exist in virtually all societies? Are they for the purpose of protecting the public at large or do they serve the interests of those with enough money and influence to have the laws enacted?

Another question: If law enforcement officials are never notified of most crimes that occur (a fact that this chapter will document), how is it possible for criminologists to objectively measure crime? In this chapter you will learn about the roots of the criminal justice system, and how the statistics generated by the system can be combined with other data to give criminologists a reasonably complete picture of the extent to which criminal laws are violated.

THE ORIGINS OF CRIMINAL LAW

Archaeologists have determined that the practice of writing first appeared about 6,000 years ago in southwestern Asia, often called the *Mideast.*[1] This was a monumental development that probably occurred over several centuries, and coincided with the very earliest beginnings of what is known as **civilization.** Gradually, alphabets and the spelling of words became fairly standardized, and significant minorities of citizens in Middle East societies were able to communicate nonverbally. A major advantage of written language is that, unlike spoken language, it has the potential of existing and continuing to influence others indefinitely. This, we will see, is an important feature for establishing and effectively enforcing rules of human conduct.

As far as is known, the first society to develop a set of written rules of conduct was Babylon, an ancient society covering much of modern-day Iraq. The date was about 4,000 years ago, and the edicts are known as the **Code of Hammurabi,** after the king who reigned over Babylon at the time, and who presumably authorized the formulation of these codes of conduct (see Figure 2.1).[2] The Code of Hammurabi described what sorts of behavior were unacceptable, and prescribed punishment for those caught engaging in such behavior. Let us now focus on the origins of criminal laws at a very fundamental level.

While most agree that, technically speaking, laws can only exist in written form, studies of past and present societies in which there is no writing have shown that there are still basic "understood rules" of acceptable conduct. The origins of these rules have been a major challenge for philosophers and scientists to explain. Some evidence suggests that they are at least partially learned through childhood socialization, or through folklore and songs.[3]

FIGURE 2.1   A black basalt stone engraving with the Code of Hammurabi (the barely visible inscriptions at the base). The two persons depicted in the engraving probably represent the transfer of the codes by the king to his subjects. (R.M.N./Herve Lewandowski)

However, as we will see shortly, there may also be some inherently unlearned aversive feeling that most humans experience when they cause harm to others.

In most early civilizations, criminal laws were not instituted at the outset. Rather, they arose gradually out of laws called **torts.**[4] Torts are laws that permit one citizen to bring charges of wrongdoing against another citizen in order to be compensated or for the state to impose punishment. Eventually, some torts were set aside as offenses that so fundamentally threatened civility and social order that the state, rather than individual victims, brought formal charges against suspected offenders. Today, these offenses form the core of criminal law in nearly all countries.[5]

THE "ULTIMATE SOURCE" OF CRIMINAL STATUTES

With the possible exception of the less than one percent of humans still living in preliterate societies (i.e., societies without reading or writing), all humans are subject to penalties whenever they violate criminal statutes (or they will be when they reach adulthood). What is responsible for the spread of these laws? Five perspectives have been proposed. These are the supernatural/religious perspective, the final arbitrator perspective, the class conflict perspective, the social contract perspective, and the evolutionary perspective. Let us consider each one individually.

The Supernatural/Religious Perspective

Some have proposed that crime statutes, especially those pertaining to core offenses, come from religious teachings and/or directly from God.[6] Supporters of this **supernatural/religious perspective** point out that in many parts of the world religious teachings and legal standards of conduct are similar.[7] The Ten Commandments, for example, contain dictates that are quite similar to criminal statues pertaining to victimful crimes (in particular, "Thou shalt not kill" and "Thou shalt not steal"). Also, for many people, crime, sin, and evil are almost inseparable concepts.[8] The connection between crime and sin provided a rationale for the Catholic Church officiating over many criminal trials throughout Europe during the Middle Ages.[9] Even today, it is a common practice in Islamic countries such as Saudi Arabia and Iran for most criminal trials to be under religious rather than secular control.[10]

The view that God's law has given rise to criminal law could help to explain why certain core offenses are universally condemned. One problem with this perspective is that it implies that only in the societies that are most closely linked to the one "true" religion would one find criminal laws. Instead, societies associated with a wide array of religious beliefs still have somehow come to institute remarkably similar criminal statutes.

The Final Arbitrator Perspective

The very fabric of society can quickly fray, and even unravel, when those who have been criminally victimized take it on themselves to settle grievances against those they suspect of being responsible. Social scientists have documented numerous instances of a phenomenon known as **feuding** (or *blood revenge*), which often starts by one individual being wronged by another (or so believing), and then proceeding to even the score by exacting an eye-for-an-eye. If the suspected perpetrator cannot be punished directly, harm is inflicted on a close relative instead. These vendettas often spin out of control and pit entire kinship groups against one another for generations.[11]

Advocates of the **final arbitrator perspective** contend that one of the most important functions served by political authorities is that of adjudicating disputes between societal members and extracting retribution from perpetrators.[12] In other words, the criminal justice system functions to prevent individuals and families from "taking the law into their own hands." In support of this perspective, research has indicated that societies with well-organized criminal justice systems under centralized governmental control have far less feuding than do societies with poorly organized, or loosely controlled, criminal justice systems.[13] Thus, the risk of a resumption of feuding creates constant pressure on societal leaders to maintain control over a powerful criminal justice system.

The Class Conflict Perspective

According to the **class conflict perspective**, criminal laws have been devised by a society's most powerful interest groups in order to promote and preserve their social and economic advantages.[14]

Proponents of this view see societies being comprised of social classes that compete with one another for power, and contend that among the weapons used are laws and the entire criminal justice system.[15] For example, criminal laws in the United States seem to have been written in such ways as to exempt most profit making from being defined as theft.[16] According to this view, only in "classless societies" is it possible for criminal laws not to end up favoring the rich and powerful. Those who subscribe to this conflict perspective note that laws have proliferated with the accumulation of private property and surplus production.[17]

In support of the conflict perspective, it is worth mentioning that the Code of Hammurabi recognized three classes of citizens: gentlemen, commoners, and slaves.[18] While the gentleman class had certain obligations that slaves and commoners did not have, the gentleman class was exempt from certain laws that slaves and commoners were punished for violating. Supporters of the conflict perspective also point to various ways in which the rich and powerful in most societies avoid being punished for law violations that the less well-to-do fail to escape.

One difficulty with the conflict perspective, at least in its pure form, is that it implies that attitudes toward what is criminal should be linked to one's class position in a society. If so, there should be little agreement about the inherent "wrongfulness" or seriousness of most crimes across social classes.[19] As was noted in Chapter 1, however, there is considerable agreement both within and between societies.

The Consensus (or Social Contract) Perspective

The **consensus perspective** maintains that criminal statutes are fundamental to living in civilized societies.[20] Accordingly, similar sorts of criminal laws should be found in all literate societies.[21] As noted in Chapter 1, this tends to be the case, especially for core offenses.[22]

First advocated by European philosophers in the seventeenth Century, the consensual view often included the assumption that individuals are only bound to society by their own consent, and this consent is based on the assumption that society will do its best to protect them.[23] Probably the most famous proponent of this view was the philosopher Thomas Hobbes,[24] who argued that in order to prevent the outbreak of wars of all against all, social contracts (or "lawful covenants") are instituted in all civilized societies to set reasonable limits on everyone's social interactions.

While it has been difficult to provide a critical test of the consensus hypothesis, it is consistent with the remarkable degree of cross-cultural consistency in laws pertaining to the core offenses.[25] In addition, as mentioned in Chapter 1, researchers have found a fairly high degree of agreement throughout the world on what constitutes serious criminality. Proponents of the consensus perspective maintain that this universal agreement reflects the tendency for most people to inherently appreciate the necessity of setting basic limits on people's overt competition with one another over the necessities and luxuries of life.[26]

The Evolutionary Perspective

According to the **evolutionary perspective** on the origins of law, the origins of law actually go back to our prehuman ancestors.[27] One line of support for this perspective comes from documenting a fascinating type of behavior among nonhuman primates (monkeys and apes). The behavior is known as the **control role** (or *control behavior*). A typical incident in which a primate performs the control role follows the outbreak of a scuffle between two members of a primate society (usually called a troop). If the disturbance does not break up on its own fairly quickly the troop's dominant male deliberately moves toward the combatants. As he approaches, he stares intensely at them and sometimes emits deep grunting sounds. If the fight still persists, the dominant male actually imposes himself between the combatants and threatens one or both of them until they disperse. For an actual example of control behavior, see Figure 2.2. Nearly

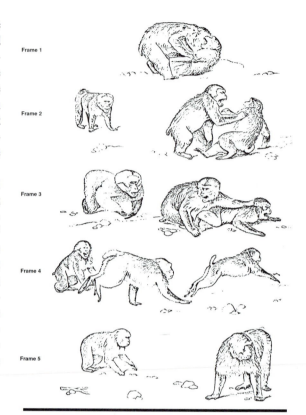

FIGURE 2.2   Five sketches from a series of photographs showing the performance of the control role by a high-ranking adult male Japanese macaque (Japanese macaques are the only species of primate other than humans native to Japan). Frame 1: A fight ensues between two adult females. Frame 2: The adult male approaches in response to screaming from the female being defeated. Frame 3: The male continues to approach slowly until the fight is halted. Frame 4: the male chases one of the two females from the premises. Frame 5: The male remains standing where the fight occurred and stares intently toward the female he had chased. (Episode photographed by K. Modahl and reported by Eaton 1976:100–101).

all instances of control behavior are exhibited by the troop's dominant males or by males closely allied with the dominant male.[28]

Some have suggested that the control role may be fundamental to the evolution of criminal law and law enforcement.[29] In other words, while the criminal justice system cannot exist except where reading and writing have evolved, perhaps there is an underlying desire for social order and peace that we share with many other primate species. Such an evolutionary view would help to explain why a criminal justice system exists in all literate societies, and why, even in nonliterate societies, one finds leaders assuming responsibility for maintaining basic "law and order."[30]

Which of the above five perspectives on the origins of criminal law and the criminal justice system makes the most sense to you? Actually, you do not have to choose just one explanation to the exclusion of all others. More than one, and perhaps all of them, could contain an element of truth. Nevertheless, keeping them distinct is useful, for, as we will see in later chapters, all five perspectives have helped to foster different types of theories of criminal behavior. For additional information on the philosophical and historical underpinnings of criminal law, see Appendix A.

CATEGORIZING AND MEASURING CRIMINAL BEHAVIOR

Scientists commonly distinguish two types of definitions for the variables they study.[31] Criminal behavior, of course, is one of those variables. One type of definition is called a **conceptual definition;** it involves simply using other words to convey the meaning of a variable, such as would be found in a dictionary. For example, *criminal behavior* might be conceptually defined as any behavior that violates a criminal statute within a particular political jurisdiction. This sort of definition is useful but has limitations because it does not give you precise guidelines for actually measuring a large sample of this sort of behavior.

The other type of definition is called an **operational definition.** This one specifies a set of procedures that can be used to measure how intense or widespread a variable is in some identified population. For example, you could opera-

tionally define *criminal behavior* in terms of sorting through last year's conviction records that are on file in a courthouse. Notice how this type of definition of criminal behavior is much more specific and tangible. It is, of course, also more controversial, because some might say that defining criminal behavior in terms of persons convicted will miss many, and possibly even most, offenses that occur.

Another way of roughly distinguishing a conceptual definition of criminal behavior from an operational definition is to say that a conceptual definition essentially reflects whatever criminal statutes specify a crime to be. An operational definition, on the other hand, has to do with how best to measure numerous instances of a criminal act so that it can be objectively studied.

In this section, we will first consider the main crime categories that have come to be most often studied by criminologists. Then we will explore the main ways that criminal behavior has come to be operationalized.

The Major Categories of Crime

As noted in Chapter 1, there are at least three major dimensions to what is known as crime, and most criminological efforts have been aimed toward understanding the most rather than the least serious offenses (p. 11). In this regard, you should also recall the distinction made in Chapter 1 between felonies and misdemeanors (p. 14). Here we will subsume all crimes under six categories: violent crimes, property crimes, drug crimes, sex crimes (except rape), delinquent offenses, and all other crimes. With the exception of the last two categories, these categories reflect those that all member states of Interpol have agreed to use in compiling their annual crime statistics. Let us consider each category individually.

Violent offenses.   These are offenses that cause, or threaten to cause, bodily harm to another human being. In crime statistics maintained in the United

States, the main violent offenses are homicide, assault, forcible rape, robbery, and kidnaping (or abduction). Essentially all violent offenses are felony level offenses. In Canada and all other countries that are part of the British Commonwealth, robbery is usually classified as a property offense rather than a violent crime on the grounds that actual violence is used in only about a third of all robberies.[32]

Property offenses.   These are offenses that deprive another human being of his or her property. If the monetary value of stolen or damaged property is minor, it is often considered a misdemeanor, rather than as a felony. In the United States in recent years, the cutoff for property offenses that are classified as felonies and those that are classified as misdemeanors varies from state to state between $100 and $250.[33] Canada's felony cut off is currently $200,[34] but ultimately the difference is affected by the relative value of the U.S. and the Canadian dollar. The main felony level property crimes are thefts and burglaries (in which homes or businesses are broken into), and of course motor vehicle thefts and arson.

Drug offenses.   Drug offenses cover the possession and sale of numerous mind-altering substances. Political jurisdictions vary in the drugs they declare illegal, but these most often include heroin, cocaine, marijuana, and various hallucinogens such as LSD. Many countries, especially those with large Muslim populations, also have made the possession and sale of alcohol illegal, as did the United States in the early part of the twentieth century.[35]

Sex offenses.   Sex offenses cover a variety of sexually motivated activities, such as pedophilia (child molestation), incest (sexual relationships with close relatives), voyeurism (surreptitiously viewing others when they are disrobed), exhibitionism (exposing one's genitals to an unwilling stranger), statutory rape (having sex with someone under the age of consent), and bestiality (having sexual contacts with animals). Rape (or forcible rape) is usually considered a special type of sex

offense because it usually entails the explicit use or threat of violence. A number of jurisdictions also still regard homosexual behavior as illegal.

Delinquent acts.   The concept of delinquency is important in criminology. The term first began to be used early in the twentieth century following a monumental legislative event in the state of Illinois in 1899. For the first time in history, a legislative body formally separated the "treatment of young offenders" from the "punishment of older offenders." While courts throughout the world have had a long tradition of treating younger (especially first-time) offenders more leniently than they dealt with fully adult offenders, the Illinois legislature was the first to make a formal separation. It designated sixteen as the age separating adults from juveniles, and initially used the term "wayward children" to describe what have since come to be know as delinquents.

The Illinois legislature was encouraged to make the delinquency–criminality distinction by an influential social movement of the late nineteenth Century, known as the **Child Saver Movement.** The reasoning behind this movement was that many young offenders would be less likely to reoffend and would instead develop into productive adults if they were never exposed to the criminal justice system or the hardened criminals it ensnared.

As the juvenile justice system has developed in most states and countries, there have been tradeoffs relative to procedures followed in the criminal justice system. For example, less proof is needed to find a juvenile "involved" than is needed to find an adult "guilty." However, the punishment tends to be much less severe in the juvenile justice system than in the criminal justice system. Another difference was mentioned in Chapter 1: As juveniles, individuals can be tried not only for violating criminal statutes, but also for violating strictly juvenile statutes (i.e., status offenses).

All Other Offenses.   A final category of offenses primarily includes victimless crimes such as illegal gambling, prostitution, vagrancy, and public drunkenness. Various quasi-victimful offenses such as slander, counterfeiting, and perjury also fall into this latter category.

Conduct Disorders and Antisocial Personality Disorders.

As noted in Chapter 1, conduct disorders (CD) and antisocial personality disorders (APD) are not crimes in and of themselves. However, these behavioral disorders are so closely linked to an individual's probability of engaging in criminality that scientists have increasingly considered them and criminality in the same context. Basically, both CD and APD are diagnostic categories into which persons are classified if their behavior habitually interferes with the rights of others not to be injured or have their property confiscated or damaged.

United States and Canadian Nomenclature for Designating Serious Victimful Crimes

In the United States, the Bureau of Justice Statistics (and before it, the Federal Bureau of Investigation) publishes an annual report summarizing the nation's crime statistics. The statistics are collectively known as **Uniform Crime Report** (UCR) data. Canada has a Centre for Justice Statistics that publishes results from what is also called the *Uniform Crime Report* (UCR) data. Whereas the UCRs of the United States go back to the early 1930s, they were not instituted in Canada until 1962.[36] Nevertheless, there were so many state and local jurisdictions in the United States that failed to provide the information requested on the UCRs in the first twenty-five years that the Bureau of Justice Statistics does not normally include data prior to 1960 in any time-series comparisons. As will be noted again in Chapter 3, a time series refers to any attempt to trace the relative occurrence of some category of events (such as crime) over time (usually from year to year).

Canada's UCR data are more uniform than U.S. data because all ten Canadian provinces operate under a single set of criminal statutes, whereas each state in the U.S. has a separate set of statutes.[37] Nonetheless, there is little state-to-state variation in most criminal statutes, especially

in regard to victimful offenses, and each state now used the same reporting format when providing statistical information to the U.S. Bureau of Justice Statistics.

In the United States, the UCR separates crimes into two categories: **Part I offenses** (or **Index Crimes**), and **Part II offenses,** consisting of all crimes other than Part I offenses. Subsumed under the category of Part I offenses are eight victimful crimes. Four of these crimes are aggressive/violent in nature and nearly always involve personal contact between the offender and victim: homicide, assault, rape (excluding statutory rape), and robbery. The other four Part I offenses are property crimes and usually involve no personal contact: larceny (or theft), burglary, motor vehicle theft, and arson. Notice that, as discussed in Chapter 1, these are all universally condemned victimful offenses, although they usually exclude minor thefts. Criminologists who utilize U.S. statistics often confine their statistical analyses to Part I offenses because these offenses correspond with what most people think of as "serious" crime. A description of each of the Index Offenses is provided below.

Homicide or Murder.

Murder is defined as "the willful (non-negligent) killing of one human being by another." Not included in this classification are deaths caused by accident or negligence, justifiable homicides (e.g., self-defense), or attempts to murder not resulting in death.[38] Thus, a murderer is someone who has intentionally caused the death of another person without any legal justification or excuse.

Not all willful killings are considered equally serious. There are various degrees of murder and manslaughter. First-degree (aggravated) murder requires that the act be committed with malice of forethought, deliberation, and premeditation. These three requirements are called the *elements* of the crime, and all three must be proved in order to convict someone of first-degree murder. *Malice of forethought* refers to the intent to cause death or serious harm; *deliberation* refers to the full and conscious knowledge of the purpose to kill, and *premeditation* refers to a design or plan to carry out the act. A contract killing is an example of a murder that fulfills all three elements required to satisfy indictment for first-degree murder.

Second-degree murder is the killing of another with malice of forethought, but without deliberation and premeditation. A bar fight resulting in the knifing death of one of the combatants would satisfy the requirement for this charge. The killer knew that a knife wound could be deadly, but used it anyway. Voluntary manslaughter is the intentional killing of another in the absence of premeditation, such as through carelessness. Involuntary manslaughter is the unintentional killing of another through some act of negligence, such as driving under the influence and committing vehicular homicide.

Forcible Rape. **Forcible rape** is often defined as carnal knowledge of a female forcibly and against her will. The phrase **carnal knowledge** is a roundabout way of referring to intimate knowledge of someone's body, particularly of their genitals. Included are attempts to commit rape by force or threat of force, but **statutory rape** (consensual sexual intercourse with a minor) is not.

Robbery. **Robbery** is defined as "the taking or attempting to take anything of value from the care, custody, or control of a person or persons by force or threat of force or violence and/or by putting the victim in fear."[39] The two primary elements defining robbery are custody and force or threat of force. For instance, Pat leaves her purse on a seat in a restaurant while she goes to the restroom. Seeing this, Jim walks over to her seat, picks up the purse, and leaves the restaurant with it. Jim has not committed robbery (he has committed grand theft, providing the value of the purse and its contents was $250 or more) because he lifted the purse from the restaurant seat, not from Pat's "care or custody." Further, he did not confront Pat or use force or threats to put her in fear.

Aggravated Assault. **Aggravated assault** is defined as "the intentional inflicting, or attempted inflicting of injury upon another person."[40] Aggra-

vated assault is most often charged when some sort of weapon likely to cause death or serious bodily injury, such as a gun, knife, or heavy blunt instrument, is used. It is not necessary for an injury to have actually occurred to charge aggravated assault, and thus attempts are included in this definition. The risk of serious bodily injury, regardless of whether or not it was actually incurred, is the main criterion for charging this crime.

Burglary. **Burglary** is defined as "the unlawful entry or attempted entry of a residence."[41] The method of entry usually involves the use of force ("breaking and entering"), but need only be "unlawful" in the sense that it is obvious to anyone that entry requires the permission of the premises' owners.

Larceny–Theft. **Larceny–theft** is the unlawful taking of the possessions of another.[42] These offenses cover most types of thefts, such as stealing personal items, shoplifting, pickpocketing, and even bicycle thefts. Not included in this category are theft of a motor vehicle, forgery, passing bad checks, or embezzlement, all of which are considered separate offenses.

Motor Vehicle Theft. The U.S. Bureau of Justice Statistics defines **motor vehicle theft** as the theft or attempted theft of a motor vehicle.[43] Motor vehicle theft covers all kinds of motorized land vehicles besides passenger cars, such as motorcycles, buses, automobiles, trucks, and snowmobiles.

Arson. **Arson** is defined as any willful or malicious burning or attempting to burn, with or without intent to defraud, a dwelling, public building, motor vehicle or aircraft, or personal property of another. Some arson offenses involve the burning of one's own property in order to collect insurance; some involve attempts to cover up other crimes such as murder or burglary, and others involve malicious vandalism of random or specifically targeted structures. Arson was added to the U.S. Uniform Crime Reports in 1979, and there still exists a great deal of difficulty in gathering

standardized statistics from reporting agencies. Percentage-wise, however, arson makes a very minuscule contribution to the total number of offenses each year.

Operationally Defining Crime and Delinquency

As mentioned earlier, *operational definitions* are definitions that are in concrete observable terms, not just conceptual terms. For example, saying that criminal behavior is the violation of a criminal statute is helpful in conceptualizing the concept, but it is too vague to be considered an operational definition. On the other hand, if a researcher defined criminal behavior in terms of interviews with persons who appeared in a hospital emergency room with stab and gunshot wounds and asked them how they got their injuries, the researcher would have provided an operational definition of criminal behavior.

Operational definitions of criminal behavior can be grouped into three major categories, with a fourth minor residual category.[44] The three main categories are *official statistics, victimization survey data,* and *self-reported data,* each of which is described below. Most of the scientific studies to be considered throughout the remainder of this text will have utilized one of these three operational measures of criminal behavior.

The Three Main Operational Measures of Criminal Behavior

Official Statistics.   **Official crime statistics** are those derived from the routine functioning of the criminal justice system. The most basic category of official statistics comes from the calls made to police by victims (and sometimes by third-party bystanders). Other major categories of official crime data consist of information about arrests, convictions, and imprisonment and prison release.

In the United States, the federal agency that compiles most official statistics is the Bureau of Justice Statistics (a branch of the U.S. Department of Justice). Before this research agency was established in the 1980s, the Federal Bureau of Investigation (which is also a branch of the U.S. Department of Justice) maintained its own statistics back to the 1930s.[45] The Bureau of Justice Statistics (as well as its counterparts in most other countries) compiles statistics based on information provided by local law enforcement agencies regarding crimes reported to police (including sheriff) departments, arrests that they make, as well as convictions and sentences handed down by courts. We will look at some of these data in Chapter 3.

It is important to interpret official crime statistics with caution for the following three reasons. First, crime statutes vary from one political jurisdiction to another, even within the same country, and they also undergo change over time.[46] However, as noted in Chapter 1, this variability in criminal statutes is largely confined to the noncore offenses rather than the core (universally condemned) offenses.

Second, the likelihood of victims notifying police that a crime has taken place varies. The most important variable affecting reporting probability is crime seriousness. As will be described in more detail when examining victimization data apart from calls made to police, victims are much more likely to notify police of the crimes that involve major property loss or physical injury than for crimes that are not serious in either respect.[47] Another factor affecting the reporting of crimes is technological.[48] For instance, crimes are more likely to be reported in areas of the world with ready access to telephones and modern transportation than in areas in which it is difficult for victims to contact the police.[49] Also, policy-related factors can affect the probability of crimes being reported to police. For example, one study suggested improved police–community relations resulted in a significant increase in the number of calls made to the police department regarding crimes.[50] Furthermore, insurance companies usually require that crimes be reported to police; therefore, as the number of people taking out theft insurance increases, one can expect to find an increase in the proportion of property crimes being made to police.[51] Lastly, there is even evidence that the rate at which police

are able to solve crimes causes a slight increase in the rate at which crimes are reported; the more solved the more reported.[52]

A third reason official crime statistics from one jurisdiction or time period should not be considered completely comparable to statistics from other jurisdictions or times is that between 5 and 20% of all crimes reported to police are not officially recorded.[53] For lack of a better term, these dismissed reports can be called *unsubstantiated crimes*.[54] The reasons that police do not officially record all "crimes" reported to them are numerous, but primarily include decisions that the letter of the law was not actually violated. Another reason is that citizens themselves sometimes retract their allegations, such as when lost objects that they reported stolen are later discovered to have simply been misplaced. Also, in the case of many domestic disturbances, victims often decline to file formal charges or later retract them.[55] Research has shown that some police departments use stricter criteria than do others in screening out unsubstantiated crimes.[56]

Fourth, sometimes factors having nothing to do with either the criminal justice system or the nature of the criminal act itself can affect a region's crime rate. An interesting example has to do with murder. While nearly all murders are detected and accurately recorded in police records,[57] murder rates can be significantly affected by the mere availability of emergency medical services.[58] Specifically, in two otherwise identical areas of a large city, murder rates may vary simply because well-equipped and well-staffed emergency medical facilities are more readily accessible in one area than in the other. As will be discussed in Chapter 3, the availability of emergency medical facilities also means that comparing homicide rates between countries must be done with caution.

Given these sorts of difficulties, should official crime statistics be trusted at all? Over the years, quite a few criminologists have expressed serious reservations about official crime statistics.[59] The most frequent criticism has been that these data are too easily affected by discretionary police policies to be considered reliable.[60] In other words, official statistics are really measuring police behavior as much as they are measuring criminal behavior![61]

Despite these frequently expressed concerns, a recent study of Interpol data (which is based on reports to police in each country) was encouraging with respect to the overall validity of official crime data.[62] This does not mean that all member countries have equally valid data (they do not), but that the data from nearly all countries are sufficiently valid to provide meaningful information about overall variations in crime rates. Keep in mind, however, that saying that it is possible to make meaningful comparisons across (and within) countries is not the same as saying that data should always be taken at face value. More will be said about making international comparisons of crime data in Chapter 3.

Overall, the most common criticism of official statistics is that so many victims fail to report crimes to police that researchers are unsure about what to make of any differences in crime rates that are reported.[63] In other words, are these differences "real," or merely the result of differential citizen reporting or differential police recording practices? The concern is over what criminologists have come to call **dark figures,** meaning all of the crimes committed that never come to official attention.[64] Let us now look at alternatives to official crime statistics in order to better assess the reality of dark figures.

Crime Victimization Survey Data.   **Victimization surveys** involve asking numerous citizens of a city or country whether they have been the victim of crime within some specified time frame regardless of whether they reported the incident to police. Today, these surveys have become a valuable tool used in criminology to better gauge the extent of criminal behavior. However, we will see that victimization surveys have not replaced official statistics for good reason.

The first two victimization surveys were both conducted in Scandinavia, with the very first one dating back to Denmark in 1720.[65] At that time, a concerned citizen of the city of Aarhus went door-to-door asking the city's residents if they had been

the victim of any crime in recent years, and, if they had he asked them for various details. The second survey was carried out over two centuries later in Norway in the late 1940s.[66] Results from these two early surveys are of limited scientific value because of the limited samples and lack of rigor in how subjects were questioned, but they helped lead the way toward numerous nationwide victimization surveys beginning in the 1970s.

The first large-scale pilot victimization survey was completed in the United States in 1967.[67] It was based on interviews of adults from 10,000 households regarding whether they or family members had been the victim of a crime in the past year, regardless of whether the incident had been reported to the police.[68] The reason for the use of such a sizable sample is that it is needed if researchers want to even begin to accurately estimate the frequency of most types of crime. To illustrate, rates of major assaults (those resulting in hospitalization) are typically no more than 3 or 4 per 1,000.[69] Unless samples in the vicinity of 10,000 are surveyed, one can expect to uncover less than thirty or forty such offenses, too few for calculating reliable annual rates, especially for different regions of the country.

Beginning in 1973, the U.S. government began conducting victimization surveys on an annual basis[70] based on samples of 60,000 households comprising over 120,000 citizens each year.[71] Canada followed suit beginning in 1982.[72] We will look at some of the results from these surveys in Chapter 3.

Since the 1970s, victimization surveys have also been conducted in numerous other countries, although usually based on samples of less than 10,000. Countries in which results from these surveys have been published include Australia,[73] Denmark, Norway, and Finland,[74] Israel,[75] Mexico,[76] the Netherlands,[77] Germany,[78] Switzerland,[79] England,[80] and Tanzania.[81]

In nearly all cases, the questionnaires are sufficiently similar to those used in the United States to be compared. Beginning in the late 1980s, victimization surveys using almost identical methodology began to be collected in over a dozen industrialized countries.[82] Some of the results from these surveys will be examined in the next chapter.

How good a job have victimization surveys done in performing their main intended function, i.e., disclosing dark figures? Overall, they have done a good job even though, as we will see, victimization data actually have dark figures of their own, although not nearly as extensive as in the case of official data.

Let us first consider the number of crimes revealed through victimization data compared to the data based on calls made to police. Victimization surveys in both the United States and Canada have indicated that only about a third of all victimful crimes, and little more than half of all serious (felony-level) victimful crimes, are reported to police.[83] Fairly similar findings have come from other countries as well.[84]

Victimization surveys have revealed that some crimes are much more likely to be reported to police than others.[85] Generally, the more serious the crime the more likely people are to have reported it to the police.[86] Thus, as shown in Figure 2.3, over 80 percent of motor vehicle thefts are reported, while less than 10 percent of the thefts involving minor monetary losses are reported.[87] Similar reporting percentages were found in Canada's victimization survey.[88]

The explanations people give to surveyors in victimization interviews for not reporting a crime vary from one type of crime to another. Overall, however, there are two main reasons for not reporting violent crimes: (1) nothing could be done after it had already happened, and (2) it was a personal matter. The two most common reasons given for not reporting property offenses are similar: (1) it was too minor to bother reporting, and (2) nothing could be done after it had already happened.[89]

Now let us consider the fact that even though victimization data were developed primarily to reveal the dark figures inherent in official data, even victimization data themselves do not detect all crimes. One of these failures is rather obvious: Victimization surveys are only helpful for measuring victimful offenses. Thus, crimes such as drug sales, prostitution, and gambling are not

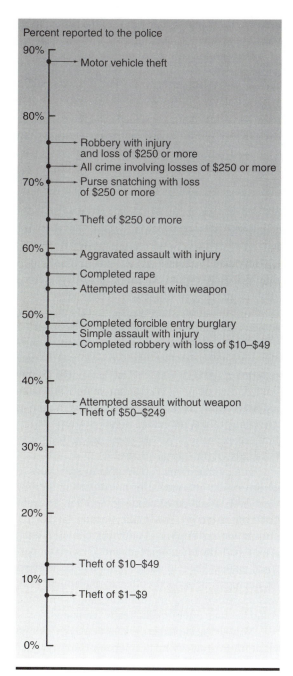

Percent reported to the police

90% — Motor vehicle theft

80%

— Robbery with injury
and loss of $250 or more
— All crime involving losses of $250 or more
70% — Purse snatching with loss
of $250 or more

— Theft of $250 or more

60% — Aggravated assault with injury
— Completed rape
— Attempted assault with weapon

50% — Completed forcible entry burglary
— Simple assault with injury
— Completed robbery with loss of $10–$49

40%
— Attempted assault without weapon
— Theft of $50–$249

30%

20%

— Theft of $10–$49
10%
— Theft of $1–$9

0%

FIGURE 2.3 A chart showing variations in the probability of various types of crimes being reported to police in the United States based on information obtained from victimization surveys (From U.S. Department of Justice 1988:34).

revealed in victimization surveys. In addition, there is one very serious victimful crime that victims never report . . . murder!

Another reason victimization surveys fail to reveal all offenses has to do with lapses in memory.[90] Because people are often being interviewed several months after a crime has taken place, not all of the details, and sometimes not even the event itself, will be recalled. Special studies comparing victimization data with officially reported data have shown that the more time that elapses between when a crime occurred and when the victim was interviewed, the less likely the victim is to report the incident to the surveyor. For this reason, all victimization surveys in the United States ask respondents to recall incidences of victimization only within the past six-months, rather than within the past year. This has been shown to provide more accurate responses, even though annual rates are what researchers are really interested in determining. To get the annual rates, the six-month figures are doubled.[91]

Investigators who have compared official data and victimization data for the same geographical regions and time frames have concluded that they are only modestly comparable, and probably will never be in really close agreement.[92] Of course, this is somewhat ironical, because victimization surveys were initially developed to provide a way of verifying the essential accuracy of calls made to police. Basically, what researchers have concluded is that both types of data provide useful information about criminal behavior, but they have a significantly different focus that only modestly overlaps. Whereas official data focuses on the most serious types of offenses, especially those committed by persons who are strangers to the victim, victimization data focuses on somewhat less serious offenses and includes a greater proportion of domestic assaults.[93]

If the ratio of unreported-to-reported crimes remained constant over time and from one geographical area to another, it would still be possible to compare official statistics directly with victimization data simply by increasing the number of officially reported offenses by some constant per-

centage. Unfortunately, there appear to be too many irregularities in the proportion of crimes reported to police departments from one jurisdiction to another to make this procedure feasible.[94] To illustrate, one study compared official data with victimization data for the same offenses in twenty-six large U.S. cities. The two data sources for motor vehicle theft and armed robbery were in close agreement regarding which cities had the highest and the lowest rates, and in moderately close agreement for burglary. However, for rape and assault, the two data sources were not at all consistent in how they ranked the twenty-six cities.[95]

Research has also shown that at least some crimes are detected better through official data than through victimization survey data. This includes victimless crimes and white-collar crimes such as embezzlement and price-fixing. It also includes a few victimful crimes that people simply forget to report. This failure of recall reduces the number of crimes reported in victimization surveys because the interview often takes place several months after the crime incident, and people simply forget about it, especially if the crime was not particularly serious.[96] A final reason for some of the inconsistencies between official and victimization survey data is that victimization data does not have to meet any stringent legal standards in order to be reported as an offense, whereas official data does (although the standards will vary somewhat from one police department to another).[97]

Self-Reported Crime Measures.   As the name implies, **self-reported measures** of criminal behavior (including delinquency) involve asking subjects how many crimes, if any, they have committed. Most questionnaires used in these studies are completed anonymously, although a sizable proportion are completed via face-to-face interviews.[98] The questionnaires nearly always provide a list of offenses to help subjects remember, and subjects are typically asked to place a check mark (or sometimes a number) beside each offense they recall having committed. Many self-report questionnaires also ask subjects if they have ever been arrested, and, if so, how often.

Of the numerous self-reported crime inventories developed over the years, some focus on special categories of crime—such as aggressive offenses[99] and illegal drug use[100]—while the majority cover a wide spectrum of offenses.[101]

The first two studies of criminal behavior that utilized self-reports were conducted in the United States in the 1940s.[102] With several refinements in methodology, a major study was conducted in the 1950s[103] on which most modern studies have been modeled. Over the years, self-reported crime surveys have continued to rely primarily on college and high school students for subjects.[104] As will be noted shortly, samples drawn from both high school and especially college students substantially underrepresent persons who are most prone toward sustained serious criminal behavior.

In assessing the accuracy of self-reported offenses, the most obvious issue has to do with honesty. Several studies have addressed this question in various ways, and the results have been encouraging, with one important qualification. First, let us consider the encouraging evidence. One study compared crimes reported by subjects on a questionnaire to answers they later gave while being monitored by a polygraph (lie detector). Overall, the answers corresponded well.[105] However, it should be noted that few serious offenders were included in this particular study.

Another study compared self-reported crimes by regular high school students with crimes reported by adjudicated delinquents.[106] Half of the subjects in each group were given one of two slightly different questionnaires at random. One questionnaire "required" subjects to disclose their name (with assurance that they would not be prosecuted for any of their disclosures), while the other questionnaire assured subjects that their answers would be completely anonymous. Regardless of which questionnaire they completed, on average the delinquent group revealed that they had committed almost four times as many offenses as did the regular high school students. Had the researchers not found this sort of difference, the validity of the self-report procedure would have obviously been in doubt. Other studies have also shown that on anonymous questionnaires officially identified delinquents–criminals self-report substantially more offenses than do their peers in the general population.[107] Anonymity itself makes little difference in the number of offenses reported.[108] There appears to be only a slight tendency for those answering on the anonymous version of the questionnaire to self-report more offenses than those answering on the "name required" version.[109]

Additional evidence that self-reports can be relied on to a fair degree for measuring varying degrees of criminality has come from studies of test–retest consistency. Most test–retest studies have involved giving the same group of subjects a self-report questionnaire three or four weeks after they had completed it earlier (without knowing that they would be asked to fill it out a second time). These studies have shown that there is a high level of agreement in overall offenses that were self-reported.[110] A few studies have compared self-reports over time lapses of several years, and again found substantial consistency in self-reported delinquency and crime. For example, subjects who reported a great deal of offending early in their teenage years also tend to report high offending rates a few years later.[111]

One New Zealand study had a group of teenagers complete a self-report questionnaire and then, without being told beforehand, they were given the same questionnaire to complete again one month later. The answers subjects gave on these two occasions correlated very highly.[112] Their responses also coincided fairly well with reports of overall behavior problems given by the teenager's parents and with police and court records.[113] It should be noted that this particular study was not completed anonymously, and that it covered a cross-section of juveniles. Another study compared self-reported delinquency with ratings of delinquent tendencies of the same adolescents by parents and teachers.[114] The study found a substantial (although far from perfect) positive correlation between all three measures. The evidence reviewed so far indicates that self-reported crime measures provide largely accurate information about criminal behavior.[115] But now

for a bit of bad news: For two related reasons, self-reported crime surveys provide a distorted picture of the full extent of serious criminal involvement.

One reason is that, even though most people are forthright in revealing their past criminal involvement on self-report questionnaires, most people also do not have a serious criminal history. For those who do, there is a distinct tendency to underreport their crimes.[116] Basically, as the number of crimes people commit increases (especially if several of the offenses are serious), so too does the proportion of offenses they withhold reporting on self-report surveys.[117] Because they have committed many more offenses than the majority of respondents, however, nearly all of these individuals will still self-report above-average numbers of offenses. The result for research purposes is that self-reports are still useful for roughly identifying people's degree of involvement in criminal behavior, but much less precise than would be the case if the most delinquent and criminal subjects were to respond with the same degree of candor and thoroughness as the least delinquent and criminal subjects.

Among the studies that have brought researchers to conclude that individuals who are most involved in criminal activity are highly prone to underreport their involvement are ones that have asked subjects with known arrest histories whether they have ever been arrested. Twenty-five to 40% of them answered no,[118] and the greatest probability of denial came from individuals who had been arrested for the most serious types of offenses.[119]

Another study re-interviewed subjects who had self-reported having committed at least one serious crime between the ages of ten and twenty-five. In the reinterview, which took place when the subjects were thirty-two years of age, almost half of them denied ever having committed one or more of the offenses they had self-reported earlier in their life.[120]

Yet another indication of substantial underreporting by those who engage in criminal behavior to the greatest extent comes from comparing self-reported recent illegal use of drugs such as marijuana and cocaine by persons arrested or on probation and parole with evidence of use based on analyzing hair and urine samples. Even though the subjects in these studies were assured of not being prosecuted for any drug use they revealed, hair and urine analyses indicated that at least one fourth of those who had recently used one or more illegal drugs self-reported that they had used none.[121]

Why would self-reports be so inaccurate in the case of those who are most heavily involved in crime? A combination of three factors is likely to be involved. First, many persons who are heavily involved in crime may have committed so many similar offenses, and done so almost out of habit, that after a while they simply lose count of the full extent of their criminal involvement.[122] Second, because few people are proud of the crimes they have committed, especially in the case of victimful crimes, they may go out of their way to forget many of them. Third, despite assurances that they will not be prosecuted for any crime they report, those who have committed crimes for which they could be prosecuted may not reveal their involvement to simply "play it safe."[123] Why take a chance that some researcher will honor his or her commitment to keep the information confidential?

The second reason self-report surveys substantially underestimate the full extent of criminal behavior has to do with where most samples are obtained. As noted earlier, most self-report surveys are carried out among subjects who are college students and high school seniors. In Chapter 4, evidence will be reviewed that criminals tend to have much fewer years of education than is the average. For this reason, studies based on student populations, especially college populations, will substantially underestimate involvement in criminal behavior. Even self-reports based on nonstudent populations often underestimate the full extent of criminal activity because such samples almost never include persons who are incarcerated.[124]

For these two reasons—underreporting by the most serious offenders and underrepresentation of the most serious offenders in most self-report surveys—self-report data provide only a minimal estimate of the true extent of serious criminal behavior. However, for measuring minor criminal involvement, especially involvement in victimless crime, self-reported data provide the best estimates that criminologists have yet been able to obtain.[125]

Another point that is important to note about self-reported delinquency and crime measures is that most self-report questionnaires include references to trivial offenses, such as truancy and defying parental authority.[126] Without making light of these infractions, it is legitimate to ask whether they should be included in the same surveys as ones dealing with serious criminality. Because there is no clear line that divides these from other trivial acts of delinquency (such as minor thefts and fights resulting in someone getting a bloody nose), other criminologists assert that as long as what is included is clearly stated, it is appropriate for researchers to include these trivial offenses in self-report measures.

To summarize the evidence on the overall accuracy of self-reports, these data appear to be very accurate for studying offenders who commit relatively minor and/or most victimless offenses. For measuring the full extent of crime by serious offenders, however, self-reports are substantially deficient. Overall, if one's main interest is in studying involvement in serious victimful offending, it is unwise to rely exclusively on self-reports.[127]

The most widely administered self-report questionnaires are those used in a survey that has been conducted annually in the United States among high school seniors since the late 1970s. It is known as the National Youth Survey.[128] Results from this survey will be mentioned several times in later chapters of this book. Countries outside of North America in which individual self-report studies have been conducted are the Philippines,[129] England,[130] New Zealand,[131] and Australia.[132] In the 1980s, an innovative British survey added a set of self-report crime questions to its regular victimization survey questionnaire.[133] In the early 1990s, thirteen European countries cooperated in conducting an international self-report survey.[134] As subsequent chapters will show, self-report studies have been very informative about the nature of criminal behavior, especially among persons whose criminality is fairly minimal.

Other Operational Measures of Criminal Behavior.   Several studies of crime, especially domestic assaults, have utilized data collected from hospital emergency rooms.[135] Other criminological investigations have utilized data from death certificates to study variations in homicide rates,[136] even though not all medical judgments about the causes of death will precisely match legal definitions of homicide.[137] Even insurance claims were utilized in at least one study of property crimes.[138]

Very little research is available pertaining to the reliability of these secondary types of operational definitions for criminal behavior, but there is no reason to believe that they do not provide useful information about criminality.

Comparing the Three Main Operational Measures of Criminal Behavior

Of the three main operational measures, which type is best? In light of the information just reviewed, you should see that the answer must be qualified. Despite numerous criticisms lodged against official data for over a century, various criminologists in recent years have concluded that this is in fact usually the best single source of data for studying serious offenders.[139] On the other hand, for studying less serious (and yet much more common) types of crimes, either victimization or self-report survey data are usually the most complete data sources to use.[140] In other words, if one is interested primarily in drug offenses (a type of victimless crime), self-reports would generally be the preferable data source. However, if a researcher is primarily interested in the full extent to which people are being victimized by crime, the best choice of data will come from victimization surveys.

One notable exception to the use of victimization survey data for measuring the full extent of crime has to do with homicide. For this offense, official data and data from death certificates are the most reliable. Criminologists agree that homicide data tend to be the single most complete category of official data available anywhere in the world.[141] However, as we will see in Chapter 3,

this does not mean that care should not be taken when comparing homicide rates for different countries, or even within a country over time.

Returning to the issue of so-called dark figures, it can now be said that it is not simply official statistics that contain dark figures; there are dark figures in the case of victimization and self-report data also. Figure 2.4 presents three diagrams that show the basic nature of the dark figures for all three of the major operational measures of criminal behavior. (The dark figures are represented by the dark shading in each diagram.)

Without giving any consideration to victimless crimes, each diagram shows the degree to which crimes of varying degrees of seriousness are most likely to be detected by each operational measure. In the top diagram, you can see that very few trivial offenses are detected with official statistics, and many of those that are will be dismissed by police investigators as unsubstantiated crimes. Thus, for official statistics, the dark figures are highly concentrated at the nonserious end of the crime seriousness spectrum. Unfortunately, because of numerous variations in how police departments and even individual police officers operate, the degree to which crimes of varying degrees of seriousness are officially recorded will vary, and criminologists have essentially no control over that variability.

The middle diagram reveals that the dark figures for victimization data are primarily concentrated in the nonserious end of the spectrum, although to much less of a degree than in the case of official data. The failure of victimization data to pick up these minor offenses is largely due to subjects in victimization surveys simply not remembering all incidences of thefts and vandalism after a few months of having been victimized. Because questionnaires and interviewing procedures have become fairly standardized, criminologists can be much more confident in the direct comparability of victimization survey data than is true for official data from the same country or time frame.

Turning to the bottom diagram in Figure 2.4, one can see that most of the dark figures in the case of self-reports are concentrated in the upper

Crimes Reported to Police

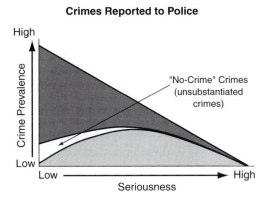

Victimization Survey Data

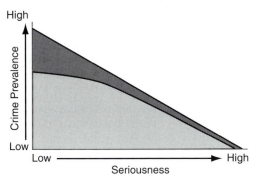

Self-Reported Data

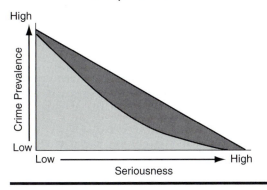

FIGURE 2.4   Representations of how differing proportions of victimful crimes are reported (light shading) and not reported (dark shading) relative to seriousness for the three main operational measures of criminal behavior.

"A cat killer? Is that the face of a cat killer? Cat *chaser* maybe. But hey—who isn't?"

© Gary Larsen. Reprinted with permission of Universal Press Syndicate.

end of the seriousness continuum, rather than the lower end.[142] This is partly due to (1) nearly all self-report surveys exclude most persistent serious offenders from their subject pools, and (2) many of the most serious offenders who remain in self-report subject pools do not reveal the full extent of their criminal histories.[143]

Advantages and Disadvantages of the Three Main Crime Measures

Let us reiterate some of the main features of the three main measures of criminal behavior by specifically discussing each of their strengths and weaknesses as far as providing useful data for criminological research.

Official Data Advantages and Disadvantages. Regarding official statistics, one advantage is that it focuses on serious crime, and reflects some degree of screening to keep "no-crime" crimes from being included in one's data. If you are primarily interested in studying the most serious types of crimes about which there is no doubt of the illegality, it is usually best to utilize official statistics.[144] Another noteworthy advantage of official data compared to the other two types of data is that official statistics has the longest historical continuity.[145] For example, a few early-settled U.S. cities have official crime data that are more than a century old,[146] and in several European countries, official crime statistics (especially on arrests and imprisonments) go back four and five centuries.[147] Beginning in Chapter 3, some of this fascinating data will be examined.

A disadvantage of official data is that it fails to detect a large proportion of the offenses that are committed, and the degree to which this is true will vary from one jurisdiction and time frame to another. Also, official data are limited in the fact that because the vast majority of crimes are never reported to police, let alone solved, criminologists cannot be entirely confident that their studies of persons identified by the criminal justice system are a fair representation of all offenders.

Victimization Data Advantages and Disadvantages.   The main advantage of victimization data is that they provide a more complete picture of the full extent of victimful criminality than do official statistics. As shown in Figure 2.4, the proportion of dark figures is much lower in the case of victimization survey data than in the case of official statistics, except for victimless offenses.

There are four noteworthy disadvantages to crime-victimization survey data. One is that no victimless offenses are detected using this measure. A second disadvantage is that this method is very expensive because of the large sample size that is needed to provide reliable information, especially about the most serious types of offenses.[148] Third, victimization data offers little information about offenders, the only exception being in the case of victims of violence who got at least a glimpse of the perpetrator. Another disadvantage is that little is done in victimization surveys to screen out "no-crime" crimes. In this regard, in victimization interviews, questions are usually phrased in nonlegal terms. For example, instead of asking people if they have been the victim of an assault, surveyors ask "Did anyone beat

you up, attack you, or hit you with anything, say, a rock or a bottle?."[149] It is of course questionable whether all instances of such attacks would meet most jurisdictions' legal definitions of an assault.

Self-Reported Data Advantages and Disadvantages.   The main advantage that self-reported crime measures have over both official statistics and victimization data is that they are the only ones that come close to fully estimating the extent of victimless and the least serious victimful offending.[150] Another advantage is that most self-report studies are relatively easy and inexpensive to conduct. In essence, researchers simply need to locate a few hundred college or high school students willing to complete a questionnaire. One more advantage is that self-report measures allow a researcher to explore in detail how various personality characteristics (which can be self-reported on the same questionnaire as the information about involvement in crime) are related to criminality.[151]

There are two main disadvantages of self-report measures of criminal behavior. One is that most self-report measures focus on relatively minor offenses; and the second is that persons who have committed offenses at the highest levels tend to substantially underreport their offenses.[152] These two shortcomings both have the effect of minimizing people's actual tendencies toward criminality. In later chapters, we will see that this has caused some confusion in criminology over relationships between criminality and a variety of factors.

Overall, while important differences exist between all three main measures of criminal behavior, they are not of the type that makes one measure clearly superior to the other.[153] Rather, all three measures give a more complete picture of the full extent of human criminality than does any one measure.[154]

Operationalizing Conduct Disorders and the Antisocial Personality Disorder

One common set of measures for CD are called *informant measures,* which come from three main sources: parents, teachers, and peers.[155] These measures are also sometimes used to measure delinquency/criminality, although in a "global" sense rather than in terms of involvement in specific offenses. Such assessment scales might ask informants to rate a group of children or adolescents on a ten-point scale in terms of behavior patterns indicative of conduct disorders and/or delinquency.[156]

In addition, interview-based measures of conduct disorders have been developed for use with children over the age of five, usually in conjunction with measures derived from interviewing parents or teachers.[157]

To assess the reliability of these measures, studies have compared ratings given by parents with ones given by teachers (or counselors) for the same children or adolescents. These comparisons have shown that, while far from perfect, parent and teacher ratings of the same children and adolescents exhibit substantial agreement.[158] In addition, ratings given by parents and teachers have also been shown to agree reasonably well with assessments made on the basis of interviewing children[159] as well as with self-reports that teenagers give regarding their delinquency involvement.[160] To make sure that the CD ratings do not simply reflect transient behavioral patterns, counselor ratings for groups of adolescents have been compared for consistency over time and found to be quite consistent.[161]

Currently, the most widely used measure of conduct disorders/childhood antisocial behavior is known as the Child Behavior Checklist (CBCL).[162] The measure involves asking parents and/or teachers to rate children on a list of 113 items, such as engaging in cruelty and bullying, and not seeming to feel guilty after misbehaving. Assessments of the reliability of the CBCL have been favorable.[163]

Several different clinical measures for adult psychopathy have been developed in recent years, among them being criteria developed by a committee of psychiatrists responsible for development of the widely consulted *Diagnostic and Statistical Manual* (DSM-IV).[164] However, at the present time, the single most widely used measure of APD was developed in Canada; it is called the **Psychopathy Checklist.**[165] With this checklist, clinicians rate patients as either having or not hav-

ing each of twenty behavior/personality traits (traits similar to those listed in Table 1.2).[166] The ratings for each trait are made on a three-point scale, with *0* meaning clients lack the particular trait, *1* meaning that they have it to a significant degree, and *2* meaning that they have it to an extreme degree. Persons who receive a total score of *30* or higher are given a diagnosis of psychopathy,[167] with those scoring in the *20*s usually receiving a "borderline" diagnosis.[168]

Careful analysis of this classification scheme has revealed that APD is comprised of two main components (or factors). One component has to do primarily with an insensitivity to the feelings of others, while the second component pertains to a generally unstable and impulsive lifestyle.[169] While these two components of psychopathy sometimes exist independently, usually both are present together in the same individuals in roughly similar degrees.

Psychopathy is also sometimes measured with self-report measures, usually as part of a broader personality assessment questionnaire,[170] or by consulting written clinical records.[171] Self-reports should be used with some caution, however, because of the tendency for psychopaths to be dishonest and generally irresponsible.

Table 2.1 provides a partial list of questions used to measure psychopathy in a general (i.e., noninstitutionalized) population.[172] Like clinical research, self-report studies suggest that there are two major dimensions to psychopathy, one having to do with being deceitful and manipulative of others, and the other primarily associated with not being able to learn from past mistakes and failing to plan ahead.

All you need to know about *factor loadings* is that they provide a mathematical estimate of how well each item epitomizes the two dimensions of psychopathy. The more a particular item comes to epitomize one of the two dimensions of psychopathy, the closer its factor loading approaches 1.00. The negative sign beside a few of the factor loadings means that persons with those particular traits were unusually low, rather than unusually high, in psychopathy.

TABLE 2.1   Items and their factor loadings for a self-report questionnaire for measuring psychopathy (Antisocial Personality Disorder).[173]

Item	Factor Loading
Primary Dimension	
Success is based on survival of the fittest; I am not concerned about the losers.	.67
For me, what's right is whatever I can get away with.	.62
In today's world, I feel justified in doing anything I can get away with to succeed.	.62
My main purpose in life is getting as many goodies as I can.	.62
Making a lot of money is my most important goal.	.61
I let others worry about higher values; my main concern is with the bottom line.	.59
People who are stupid enough to get ripped off usually deserve it.	.57
Looking out for myself is my top priority.	.52
I tell other people what they want to hear so that they will do what I want them to do.	.44
I would be upset if my success came at someone else's expense.	−.50
I often admire a really clever scam.	.50
I make a point of trying not to hurt others in pursuit of my goals.	−.41
I enjoy manipulating other people's feelings.	.39
I feel bad if my words or actions cause someone else to feel emotional pain.	−.33
Even if I were trying very hard to sell something, I wouldn't lie about it.	−.33
Cheating is not justified because it is unfair to others.	−.32
Secondary Dimension	
I find myself in the same kinds of trouble, time after time.	.62
I am often bored.	.51
I find that I am able to pursue one goal for a long time.	−.49
I don't plan anything very far in advance.	.48
I quickly lose interest in tasks I start.	.48
Most of my problems are due to the fact that other people just don't understand me.	.46
Before I do anything, I carefully consider the possible consequences.	−.36
I have been in a lot of shouting matches with other people.	.34
When I get frustrated, I often "let off steam" by blowing my top.	.33
Love is overrated.	.32

As documented in Chapter 1, APD is substantially linked to involvement in serious criminality (see especially Table 1.3), although one should still avoid thinking of psychopathy and criminality as synonymous. Even among persons arrested and convicted of crime, several studies have found a diagnosis of APD predictive of **criminal recidivism** (i.e., the commission of additional offenses after having been convicted).[174] The results of the most recent of these studies was based on following up 300 released Canadian prisoners. Figure 2.5 compares the recidivism rates of three groups of prisoners: those diagnosed with APD while in prison, those diagnosed as not being psychopathic, and those with borderline psychopathic tendencies.[175] As you can see, the psychopathic group had the highest recidivism rate, and the nonpsychopathic group had the lowest. Studies have also found childhood conduct disorders to be predictive of recidivism among juvenile delinquents.[176]

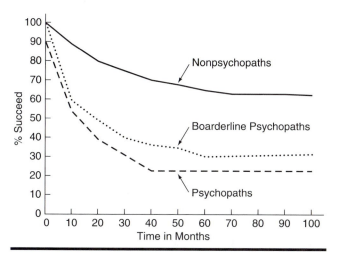

FIGURE 2.5   "Survival curves" for three groups of Canadian prisoners after various months following prison release. One group consisted of diagnosed psychopaths, a second group of nonpsychopaths, and a third group of borderline psychopaths (after Serin & Amos 1995:235). Recidivists would be those who did not "survive," i.e., were returned to prison. Thus, the rate of recidivism would be equal to the percent who succeeded at any given point in time minus 100.

SUMMARY

This chapter has focused on two fundamental issues in criminology. First, what is the basic source for criminal laws, and why do these laws exist in all literate societies? Second, how do criminologists measure variations in criminal behavior? In other words, how can criminologists objectively determine if Person A is more or less criminal than Person B, or if Country A has more crime per capita than Country B?

Regarding the first question, the oldest set of criminal statutes ever found are known as the *Code of Hammurabi,* dating back about 4,000 years to Babylon, a region roughly corresponding to modern Iraq. How fairly similar statutes have come to exist in all other human societies where written communication exists is a question that philosophers and criminologists have struggled

with for many years. Basically, there are five perspectives on why similar criminal statutes, especially regarding the core offenses, exist throughout the world.

The supernatural or religious perspective argues that criminal law basically reflects divine law. The final arbiter perspective asserts that powerful political leaders emerge because some "final arbiter" must be entrusted with the enforcement of criminal laws in order to prevent individuals from enforcing their own set of rules whenever they feel they have been wronged. According to the class-conflict perspective, criminal laws originate from powerful interest groups seeking to institute social customs that help maintain their own power. The consensus (or social contract) perspective holds that most people inherently realize that, without criminal laws, civilized societies would not be possible, and therefore they all agree on certain minimum standards of acceptable conduct. Lastly, the evolutionary perspective contends that the beginnings of the criminal justice system and its supporting legal structure can be traced to life among social animals, pointing in particular to a phenomenon called the *control role* (or *control behavior*) as exhibited in a number of primate societies.

Turning to the categorization and measurement of crime, criminologists often recognize seven fairly distinct broad categories of offenses: violent offenses, property offenses, drug offenses, sex offenses, delinquency, and offenses in general. In the United States, there is an additional frequently used categorization scheme involving distinguishing Part I and Part II offenses. Part I offenses (also called *Index Offenses*) cover four violent offenses (homicide, assault, rape, and robbery), and four property offenses (larceny, burglary, motor vehicle theft, and arson). All other crimes are classified as Part II offenses. In Canada, virtually the same offenses are termed *indictable offenses.*

The idea of operationally defining (or operationalizing) criminal behavior was introduced to acquaint you with the three main ways that criminologists actually measure variations in criminality. The first of these operational definitions involves official statistics, meaning data that is generated by the routine functioning of the criminal justice system. Among the most fundamental of these statistics are data emanating from the calls made to police about crimes that have taken place. The second type of operational definition for criminal behavior discussed was that resulting from victimization surveys. These surveys involve asking thousands of citizens if they have been victimized by crimes within a specified time frame, regardless of whether they reported the incident to police. The third major category of statistical information about criminal behavior comes from self-report surveys, which are usually conducted among high school and college students. Measures of criminality other than these three were also mentioned (such as data from death certificates and hospital emergency room records), as were the main clinical measures for conduct disorders and psychopathy.

It is inappropriate to consider one type of operational measure for criminality better than other measures in all respects. Each measure has advantages and disadvantages, and criminologists have come to understand criminal and antisocial behavior better as a result of using them all. The main advantages and shortcomings of each of the three operational measures of criminal behavior were discussed.

SUGGESTED READINGS

Biderman, A. D., & Lynch, J. P. (1991). *Understanding crime incidence statistics: Why the UCR diverges from the NCS.* New York: Springer-Verlag. (Provides very useful coverage on how and why reports to police (Uniform Crime Reports) differ from survey results [National Crime Survey].)

Block, Richard (Ed.). (1984). *Victimization and fear of crime: World perspectives.* Washington, DC: U.S. Government Printing Office (sponsored by the U.S. Department of Justice). (An excellent resource for information derived from victimization surveys conducted throughout the world.)

Fooner, Michael (1989). *Interpol: Issues in world crime and international criminal justice.* Cincinnati, OH: Anderson. (An informative look at the history of Interpol and how its major restructuring in the 1980s has helped to provide criminologists with even more valuable statistics on international crime than in the past.)

Hindelang, Michael J., Hirschi, Travis, & Weis, Joseph G. (1981). *Measuring delinquency.* Beverly Hills, CA: Sage. (A useful treatment of how self-reported crime measures are developed and utilized.)

Junger-Tas, Josine, Terlouw, Gert-Jan, and Klein, Malcolm W. (Eds.). (1994). *Delinquent behavior among young people in the Western world: First results of the international self-report delinquency study.* Amsterdam: Kugler. (An informative collection of chapters about self-reported delinquency and crime in thirteen countries; also contains a copy of the common survey questionnaire used.)

O'Brien, Robert M. (1985). *Crime and victimization data.* Beverly Hills, CA: Sage. (A valuable book for becoming acquainted with the nature of crime victimization data. Both the strengths and weaknesses of this data source are explored.)

United States Department of Justice (published annually). *Crime victimization in the United States.* Washington, DC: U.S. Government Printing Office. (Provides detailed information from each year's crime victimization survey. Some issues contain analyses of trends and others present copies of the actual survey questionnaires that interviewers complete based on information provided to them by respondents to the survey.)

EXERCISES

1. Consult your college library for either a book or for two or three articles on the origins of criminal law, read this material, and write a one- to two-page summary of what you learned. (Unless your instructor indicates otherwise, the report should be typed and double-spaced.) Indicate at the top of your report what publication(s) you used to prepare your summary. Be sure not to simply copy or paraphrase what you read. Instead, jot down a few notes as you read and then write your summary from those notes and your understanding of what you read.

2. Consult your college library and browse one or more government documents (such as the *Sourcebook of criminal justice statistics,* published annually by the U.S. Department of Justice) for information on some crime-related topic that interests you (your instructor may want to put some limits on the nature of the topic you choose). Examples might be "United States crime trends" or "How age is related to crime rates?" Then write a one- to two-page summary of what the document says about the topic. (Unless your instructor indicates otherwise, the summary should be typed and double-spaced.) Include a photocopy of the one or two pages in the document that contained most of the information you summarized.

3. Examine the sort of self-report items that are used to measure APD (psychopathy) in Table 2.1. Then come up with three items that you think would all get at the same sort of trait. Make two of the items be ones that you think would be positively associated with APD and one that you think would be negatively associated.

4. Examine Figure 2.5. It has to do with recidivism rates among three groups of Canadian prisoners. The graph reveals that psychopaths are more likely to recidivate than the other two groups. What is the probability that each of the three groups will not have recidivated (i.e., "succeeded" outside of prison) after twenty months?

   _____% of nonpsychopaths not being returned to prison

   _____% of borderline psychopaths not being returned to prison

   _____% of psychopaths not being returned to prison

ENDNOTES

1. Lewin 1988:1129; Pfeiffer 1977:251; Whitehouse & Wilkins 1986:127.
2. Chang 1976:11; Haviland 1990:245.
3. Howard & Dunaif-Hattis 1992:519.
4. Barlow 1993:21.
5. Barlow 1993:21.
6. Gruter 1979:47; Howard & Dunaif-Hattis 1992:520; Masters & Roberson 1990:29.
7. Gruter 1979:47.
8. Conrad 1973:209; Hoebel 1954:259 & 264; Masters & Roberson 1990:54.
9. Masters & Roberson 1990:54.
10. Howard & Dunaif-Hattis 1992:520.
11. Boehm 1984:200; Ellis 1990a:90; Masters & Roberson 1990:50.
12. Price 1984:226.
13. Boehm 1984:224.
14. Carlson & Williams 1993:190; Gibbons 1987:57; Jackson & Carroll 1981:291; Michalowski 1977:26; O'Leary 1982:1.
15. Barkow 1991:261; Quinney 1970, 1977:107; Taylor et al. 1973.
16. Krohn 1986:595.
17. Krohn 1986:595.
18. Whitehouse & Wilkins, 1986:139.
19. Newman 1976:15.
20. Carlson & Williams 1993:190; McGarrell & Castellano 1991:175.
21. Bohannan 1973:310.
22. Newman 1976:117.
23. Masters & Roberson 1990:84.
24. Hobbes 1914:72.
25. Raine 1993:28.
26. Gibbons 1987:58.
27. Daly & Wilson 1988:226; Ellis 1990b; Masters 1990:4.
28. Banks et al. 1979:197; Bramblett 1976:98; Eaton 1976; Oi 1990:353; Smith 1973.
29. Ellis 1990b:83; Masters 1990:4.
30. Cormier & Boyer 1963:77; Ellis 1990b.
31. Ellis 1994:20.
32. Williamson et al. 1987:454.
33. Klotter 1994:254.
34. Evans & Himelfarb 1987:56.
35. Jones et al. 1969:67.
36. Evans & Himelfarb 1987:57.
37. Evans & Himelfarb 1987:54.
38. U.S. Department of Justice Statistics 1993:13.

39. U.S. Department of Justice Statistics 1993:14.
40. U.S. Department of Justice 1993:11.
41. U.S. Department of Justice 1993:12.
42. U.S. Department of Justice 1993:13.
43. U.S. Department of Justice 1993:14.
44. Bowling, Graham, & Ross 1994:42.
45. Conklin 1986:39.
46. Chambliss 1969:99; Palermo et al. 1992b.
47. Gove et al. 1985.
48. Brenner 1976:36.
49. Gurr 1976:20.
50. Schneider et al. 1976:110; also see Biderman & Reiss 1967.
51. Gurr 1976:20; Walker 1988:636.
52. Schwind 1984:65.
53. Black 1970; Ellis 1989a:4; Evans & Himelfarb 1987:44; Lonsway & Fitzgerald 1994:135.
54. Bottomley & Coleman 1976:42; Skolnick 1966:164.
55. Coleman & Bottomley 1976:42.
56. Blumstein et al. 1992:121.
57. Landau & Fridman 1993:186; Messner 1984:442.
58. Giacopassi 1992.
59. Bottomley & Coleman 1976:33; deBeaumont & de Tocqueville 1964; Morrison 1897; Sellin 1931.
60. Cook 1980:250; Kitsuse & Cicourel 1963; McCleary et al. 1982.
61. Blakely et al. 1980:370; Schwind 1984:65.
62. Bennett & Lynch 1990.
63. Walker 1971.
64. Blumstein et al. 1991:238; Kirchhoff & Kirchhoff 1984:58; McClintock 1970; Messner 1984; Skogan 1977a; Wolfgang et al. 1972:15.
65. Clinard 1978b:222.
66. See Wolfgang et al. 1972:16.
67. Ennis 1967.
68. Inciardi 1976:184.
69. U.S. Department of Justice 1991.
70. Wells & Rankin 1995:289.
71. Block 1984a:1; Wells & Rankin 1995:289.
72. Evans & Himelfarb 1987:64.
73. Braithwaite & Biles 1984.
74. Aromaa 1984; Clinard 1978b:222; Hauge & Wolf 1974.
75. Fishman 1984.
76. Manzanera 1984.
77. Block 1984b; Fiselier 1979.
78. Kirchhoff & Kirchhoff 1984.
79. Clinard 1978a.

80. Trickett et al. 1995.
81. See Clinard 1978a:223.
82. van Dijk & Mayhew 1993.
83. Griffiths & Verdum-Jones 1989:82; Skogan 1977a; U.S. Department of Justice 1993:31.
84. See Kirchhoff & Kirchhoff 1984:60.
85. U.S. Department of Justice 1988:34.
86. Evans & Himelfarb 1987:65; U.S. Department of Justice 1988:34.
87. Skogan 1977; U.S. Department of Justice, 1988:34.
88. Evans & Himelfarb 1987:65.
89. Evans & Himelfarb 1987:66; Gottfredson & Gottfredson 1980:36; Griffiths & Verdun-Jones 1989:85; Kidd & Chayet 1984; Schwind. 1984:70.
90. Wells & Rankin 1995:290.
91. Block 1984b:23; Ellis 1994:188; Skogan 1976:114.
92. Gove et al. 1985; Menard & Covey 1988; Messner 1984:439.
93. Menard & Covey 1988:381.
94. Walker 1971.
95. Menard & Covey 1988:376; Nelson 1979:26.
96. Walker 1984:97.
97. Pope 1979:354.
98. Braithwaite 1981:43.
99. Olweus et al. 1980.
100. Kandel et al. 1978.
101. Blakely et al. 1980:377; Clark & Tifft 1966:517; Cullen et al.1985:187; Dentler & Monroe 1961; Elliott et al. 1983, 1985; Hindelang et al. 1981:223.
102. Porterfield 1946; Wallerstein & Wyle 1947.
103. Short & Nye 1957.
104. Bowker 1977:178.
105. Clark & Tifft 1966.
106. Kulik et al. 1968.
107. Cernkovich et al. 1985; Emler et al. 1978; Erickson & Empey 1963; Mak 1993:78.
108. Kulik et al. 1968.
109. Elliott & Ageton 1980:97.
110. Moffitt 1996a:404.
111. Dentler & Monroe 1973; Farrington 1973.
112. Williams & McGee 1994:444.
113. Williams & McGee 1994:444.
114. Caspi et al. 1994:184.
115. Also see Hindelang et al. 1979:1009.
116. Hindelang et al. 1981:175; Rojek 1983.
117. Cernkovich et al. 1985; Gould 1969; Hirschi et al. 1980.
118. Hindelang et al. 1981; Petersilia 1980:327.
119. Farrington et al. 1982:194.
120. Farrington 1989.
121. Baer et al. 1991; Cervenka et al. 1996:206; Mieczkowski 1990:295; Mieczkowski et al. 1993; Rosenfeld & Decker 1993:3.
122. Krueger et al. 1994:329; Moffitt 1996:403; Mulvey et al. 1993:135.
123. Petersilia 1980:335.
124. Farrington 1992:532.
125. Eysenck & Gudjonsson 1989:60.
126. Gould 1981:367; Hirschi et al. 1980; Krueger et al. 1994:329.
127. Kirigin et al. 1982:12; Rosen 1985:561; Wilkinson et al. 1982.
128. Elliott & Ageton 1980:98; Elliott et al. 1985.
129. Shoemaker 1994.
130. Farrington 1989.
131. Moffitt & Silva 1988.
132. Carroll et al. 1996; Mak 1993.
133. Mayhew & Elliott 1990.
134. Junger-Tas 1994.
135. Abbott et al. 1995; Cherpitel 1997; Gin et al. 1991; Goldberg & Tomlanovich 1984; McLeer & Anwar 1989; Stark et al. 1981.
136. Brearley 1932:203; Zahn 1989:217.
137. Messner 1984:440.
138. Clinard 1978a.
139. Gove et al. 1985:489; Hippchen 1978:4.
140. Clinard 1978.
141. Gartner 1995:189.
142. Pope 1979:353.
143. Arnold & Brungardt 1983:43; Mulvey et al. 1993:135.
144. Gove et al. 1985:490.
145. Deutsch 1978.
146. E.g., Gurr 1976:63.
147. Beatie 1975; Cockburn 1977; Weiner 1975.
148. Skogan 1977.
149. Clinard 1978b:227.
150. Braithwaite 1981; Meier & Short 1985:390; Van Dusen et al. 1983.
151. Williams & Gold 1972:227.
152. Elliott & Ageton 1980:107; Emler 1984:180; Hindelang et al. 1979, 1981; Pope 1979:353.
153. Arnold & Brungardt 1983:103; Savitz 1978:78.
154. Cohen & Land 1984; Deutsch 1978; Elliott & Ageton 1980; Hindelang et al. 1979.
155. Milavsky et al. 1982:140; Rutter et al. 1974.
156. Reviewed by Barkley 1987.
157. Kazdin & Esveldt-Dawson 1986.
158. Milavsky et al. 1982:140; Olweus 1973.
159. Kazdin & Esveldt-Dawson 1986.

160. Olweus 1978; Williams & McGee 1994:444.
161. Kelley 1981.
162. Moffitt 1996a.
163. Moffitt 1996a:404.
164. American Psychiatric Association 1995:645.
165. Serin & Amos 1995.
166. Forth et al. 1996; Hare 1991; Thornquist & Zuckerman 1995:527.
167. Hare 1991; Harris et al. 1994:387.
168. Harris et al. 1994:395.
169. af Klinteberg et al. 1992; Forth et al. 1996; Hare et al. 1990; Thornquist & Zuckerman 1995:528.

170. Allsopp & Feldman 1974, 1976; Edelmann & Vivian 1988; Levenson et al. 1995; Penner & Spielberger 1988; Smith 1985.
171. Serin 1993; Wong 1988.
172. Levenson et al. 1995:153.
173. From Levenson et al. 1995:153.
174. Harris et al. 1991, 1992, 1993; Hart et al. 1988; Quinsey et al. 1995; Rice et al. 1990; Serin 1996; Serin & Amos 1995:235; Serin et al. 1990; Wong 1984.
175. Serin & Amos 1995:235.
176. Ganzer & Sarason 1973; Haapanen & Jesness 1982; Osborn & West 1978.

CHAPTER 3

Crime over Time and Space

Where is the most crime-ridden country on the face of the earth? Is crime more prevalent today than in the past, or is it perhaps less prevalent? Unfortunately, there are too many types of crime, and too many ways countries maintain their statistics, to allow anyone to give objective unqualified answers to such questions. However, if you can settle for some reasonable generalizations based on data from a wide variety of statistical sources, you will see that many interesting patterns emerge with respect to variations in offending over time and space.

Criminologists are keenly interested in how prevalent crime is in various parts of the world and how it varies over time within a country. Unfortunately, it is often difficult to provide reliable statistics because methods for maintaining those statistics vary tremendously. Therefore, before we begin to examine national and regional crime statistics, some of the pitfalls and partial remedies need to be discussed.

PROBLEMS COMPARING CRIME

Comparing crime from one country or time period to another can lead to gross misinterpretations. There are at least four reasons for this. They have to do with (1) the instability of legal definitions of crime, (2) incompleteness in reporting and recording crime, (3) extralegal influences on crime, and (4) uncertainties associated with adding across crime categories. Each of these reasons need to be highlighted before actual data are presented.

Instability in Legal Definitions of Crime

As noted in Chapter 1, just as people (even within the same society) disagree on what is and is not criminal behavior, so too do legal definitions of crime vary from one society and time period to another. Nevertheless, as long as attention is focused on victimful offenses (i.e., violent and property crimes), the degree of disagreement tends to be minimized. Consequently, this chapter largely focuses on comparing countries and time periods only with respect to victimful offenses.

Another way problems associated with varying legal definitions of crime can be minimized when comparing across nations is to supplement official data with victimization and/or self-report data. Unfortunately, only a few cross-national studies of crime using victimization and self-report surveys have been conducted. However, in one country—the United States—comparisons of crime rates according to both official and victimization data are available going back to the 1970s. Some comparisons will therefore be made between these two data sources for the same types of offenses.

Incompleteness in Recording Crime

There is no reason to doubt that some countries have criminal justice systems that are much better than others at detecting and keeping statistical records on crime. Therefore, all else being equal, countries with the best funded and organized criminal justice systems will report higher crime rates even if their rates may in fact be below average.[1] While there is still no way to make precise adjustments for the quality of official statistics, one can reduce the variations by confining most of one's comparisons to industrialized countries. Also, as you will see, in recent years, it has been possible to compare countries on the basis of victimization data as well as official crime statistics. Otherwise, the fact that some countries have better methods for recording crime than do others is simply one of the things criminologists have always had to keep in mind whenever they compare crime rates across societies.

Also, it is important to note that the "deeper" you go into the criminal justice system for data on crime, the less complete the information will be with respect to all of the offenses that occurred. In other words, of all offenses that occurred, only a fraction will be reported to police, and, of those reported, only a proportion will result in an arrest, and even fewer will result in prosecution, conviction, or imprisonment. Because of this *attrition* in the statistics as one moves from crimes that occur to the point of someone being identified and punished for the crime, it is generally best to assess crime at the earliest stage of entry into the criminal justice system.[2]

One more point to make regarding the completeness of crime data is to note that most countries follow what is called the *seriousness rule* when encountering multiple crime events.[3] This rule states that if someone commits two or more crimes as part of the same basic episode, only the most serious offense is statistically recorded (even if the offender is prosecuted for several crimes).

Of course, this results in an undercounting of the number of crimes committed, but it is a practice that all countries follow.

To give a hypothetical example, say that in the course of committing a robbery, someone pistol-whips a bank clerk, kills another, shoots several holes into the teller's cash drawer, and then wrecks a stolen getaway car. In court, this person would probably face multiple criminal charges, but, for most statistical purposes, the events would simply be recorded as a homicide.

Extralegal Influences on Crime

Say you lived in a country with few modern emergency medical facilities, and you found that your country had many more murders than another country with the same population size, but with excellent emergency medical facilities and well trained personnel. Could it be that your country had more homicides due to the difficulty in providing assault victims with emergency medical care? This is just one example of where factors having nothing directly to do with crime or the criminal justice system sometimes affect crime statistics. It does not mean that comparisons of crime statistics are a waste of time, but that caution is in order when interpreting them.

Adding across Crime Categories

As a way to compare countries in terms of their "overall crime problem," it is a fairly common practice to add across crime categories in a given year. Doing so has the effect of treating serious crimes (bank robbery) and much less serious offenses (shoplifting) as equivalent, which they obviously are not.

In this regard, less serious crimes are always more common than the most serious crimes, although the extent to which this is true will vary. To illustrate, in the case of victimful offenses, studies in the United States and Canada have shown that approximately 85 percent of all "serious" offenses are property offenses, with only 15% being violent in nature.[4] The same ratio was reported for the former Soviet Union shortly before its disintegration into fourteen separate countries in 1990.[5] Nevertheless, this roughly 15 percent of all victimful crimes being violent cannot be considered a constant, with some countries reporting considerably higher percentages,[6] but always less than 50 percent.

Throughout the present chapter, we will help to reduce the potential for misleading comparisons by not ever adding violent crimes with property crimes, or either of these two categories of victimful crimes with any other crime categories. Nonetheless, even by adding all violent crimes or all property crimes together, one is still mixing offenses with considerable variation in seriousness.

CRIME RATE CALCULATIONS

Before making national and international comparisons, it is important to distinguish numbers of crimes from crime rates. Here is an illustration of the distinction: Few would be surprised to learn that every year there are more homicides in the United States than in Canada. To illustrate, in 1990 there were 24,932 murders in the United States compared to 581 for the same year in Canada. In other words, nearly forty-three times as many people were murdered in the United States as in Canada in 1990. However, one needs to take account of the fact that the U.S. population was (and is) nearly ten times greater than Canada's (249.91 million versus 26.22 million in 1990). Obviously, for the purpose of assessing the risk of each U.S. and Canadian citizen being murdered, adjustments need to be made for population size.

Such adjustments produce what is called a *crime rate.* Regarding the example just cited, the murder rate for the United States in 1990 was .0000996 and the rate for Canada was .0000214. Because these rates are both so minuscule, they are commonly reported in terms of 100,000 citizens. This means that the homicide rate for the United States in 1990 was 9.96 (9.96/100,000) and for Canada it was 2.14 (2.14/100,000). Thus, even though 43 times as many people were homicide victims in the United States as in Canada in 1990,

the U.S. homicide *rate* was "only" about four times higher than Canada's.

Specifics on Crime-Rate Calculations

Here is another example of how crime rates are typically calculated. In 1992, California recorded 3,847 murders while the state of Louisiana recorded 590. Without knowing the population of each state, these figures suggest that California has a much worse problem with murder than does Louisiana. However, if you adjust for population size, you come to the opposite conclusion. Below are the actual calculations per 100,000 citizens:

California's 1992 Murder Rate:

$$\frac{\text{Murders} = 3{,}921}{\text{Population} = 30{,}868{,}000} = .000127 \times 100{,}000 = 12.7$$

Louisiana's 1992 Murder Rate:

$$\frac{\text{Murders} = 747}{\text{Population} = 4{,}287{,}000} = .000174 \times 100{,}000 = 17.4$$

Put another way, the average resident of Louisiana had a 37 percent greater chance of being murdered in 1992 than did the average resident of California. This percentage difference can be determined by subtracting Louisiana's murder rate from California's (17.4 − 12.7 = 4.7) and then dividing the result by California's rate (4.7 divided by 12.7 = .37 or 37 percent).

Choosing the Best Denominator in Crime-Rate Calculations

The most common denominator used in most crime rate calculations is the total population. However, there are instances in which the number of people in an area under study may not be the most appropriate denominator to use in calculating crime rates.

To illustrate this point, see Figure 3.1. This graph shows the relationship between automobile theft and the per capita ownership of automobiles in twenty countries. Notice that there is a strong tendency for the automobile theft rate to be highest in countries where nearly all adults own an

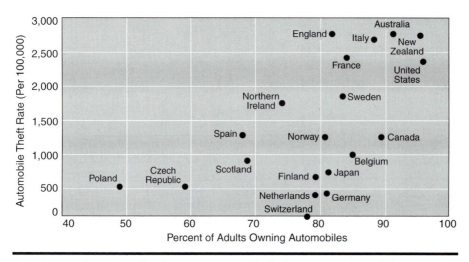

FIGURE 3.1 The relationship between automobile theft rates and automobile ownership rates for twenty countries in 1990 (adapted from van Dijk & Mayhew 1993:11).

automobile. This linkage is so strong that it would be somewhat misleading not to include the per capita automobile ownership in the calculation of the automobile theft rate. The point being made is that while most crime rates are derived by simply dividing by the number of people in the population, sometimes better denominators can be used.[7]

After learning about the potential pitfalls associated with crime rate calculations, you might be tempted to believe that people can "prove anything" they want to with crime statistics. (This attitude has inspired such sayings as "Figures don't lie, but liars figure" and "Lies, damn lies, and statistics"). But cynicism is not warranted as long as you and those providing you with statistics are being careful. You will see that despite all of the potential problems associated with crime statistics, many important conclusions can be gleaned from the mountain of evidence that has accumulated over the years about how countries vary in their crime rates. Some of those conclusions will be surprising, while others may seem so obvious as to be hardly worth mentioning.

CENTURIES OF OFFICIAL CRIME

The first statistics to be examined have been compiled not by criminologists, but primarily by a spe-

cial type of historian, called *social historians*. **Social historians** attempt to reconstruct the past using written records about the lives of more or less ordinary people, rather than the lives of great political figures and events. Thanks to the efforts of social historians over the past few decades, we now have several small windows through which we can see the nature and extent of crime centuries into the past. The oldest records that have so far been located are for various European countries dating back to around 1200 A.D. (in other words, the thirteenth century).

Where would a social historian ever find such ancient information? In the case of homicide, one can imagine that some of the records were found tucked away in the closet of some old coroner's offices. For other types of criminal offenses, the dusty shelves of a centuries-old sheriff's office provided logs on several years of arrests.

Homicide Rates in European and North American Cities, 1200 to Present

Centuries before any country developed the bureaucratic wherewithal for maintaining records on crime rates, a few large cities began doing so. The earliest records on city homicides come from Europe in the thirteenth century, and, fortunately, a few have survived to the present day. Of course, one must be especially guarded in interpreting these ancient statistics because the people who maintained them often did not give detailed accounts of their methodology. Other reasons for caution include:

1. Unknown numbers of persons who were murdered in large cities were actually residents from the surrounding countryside. These "outsiders" would usually be counted as murder victims in the city in which they died, but would not be part of the population based on which the rate was calculated.

2. As will be documented in Chapter 5, crime rates are nearly always higher in urban areas than in rural areas. Therefore, you should not be surprised to find that when we look at countrywide homicide rates, they are usually lower than the rates in large cities of the same country.

3. As noted in Chapter 2, the availability of medical services has a substantial effect on murder rates. Medical services were much less able to save the lives of assault victims centuries ago than are those in more contemporary times.

4. While most early homicide statistics include cases of both manslaughter and infanticide (the killing of infants, usually by mothers), some of the early statistics did not.[8] Social historians are often at a loss to determine exactly what was and was not included in many of the data sets that we will be examining.

With these cautions in mind, let us examine Figure 3.2. It contains the oldest crime data known to exist, the earliest of which goes back to London,

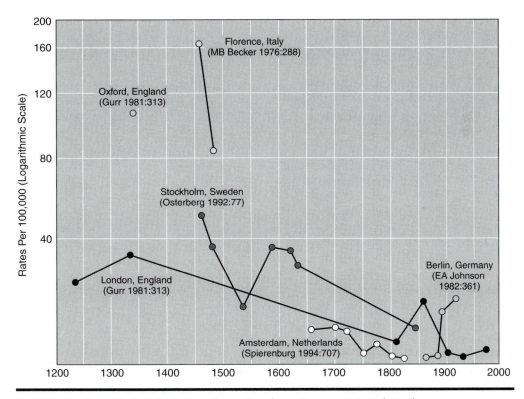

FIGURE 3.2   Trends in homicide rates for various large European cities from the fifteenth through the twentieth centuries.

England in the mid-thirteenth century. At that time, the city's murder rate was estimated to be around 25 (per 100,000 inhabitants), and a century later, the rate had risen to around 35. The next data point provided by the social historians who located these archival statistics was for the early nineteenth century. By that time London's homicide rate had dropped to around ten. All figures for homicide in London throughout the twentieth century have been below five.[9] Clearly, the murder rate in London was higher in the Middle Ages than at any time in recent decades.

A similar dramatic decline in murder rates comes from an analysis of data from Stockholm, Sweden. In 1460, the city's annual murder rate was forty-five, but five centuries later the rate had declined to around five,[10] close to where it remains today.

Other cities shown in Figure 3.2 are Amsterdam and Berlin. Amsterdam experienced a relatively modest drop in its murder rate between the mid-seventeenth century and the beginning of the nineteenth century,[11] while Berlin experienced a rise between the mid nineteenth century to the beginning of the twentieth century.[12]

Overall, what generalization can one make about trends in homicide rates in Europe from the Middle Ages to contemporary times? Basically, there appears to have been a dramatic drop in murder rates.[13] This conclusion has been particularly well documented for England/Wales.[14] When did most of the decline occur? For England/Wales, the decline seems to have taken place mainly between about 1650 through 1800.[15] The same is true for continental Europe.[16]

Why the decline occurred is an unresolved issue, but at least one important factor appears to be the emergence of an increasingly effective criminal justice system in Europe during this period. In other words, following the mid-1600s, the likelihood of a murderer being arrested and brought to justice began to increase substantially. This not only caused murders to drop, but it also helped to curtail revenge killings by victims' families.

One historian suggested that the dramatic decline in Europe's murder rates since the Middle Ages was due to "the 'civilizing' effect of religion, education, and environmental reform."[17] This can be questioned, especially in the case of religion, because the church seems to have had as much, if not more, influence over people's lives in medieval times than it has had since then.

Now take a look at Figure 3.3, which presents the oldest data on homicide rates available for cities in North America—those for Philadelphia, Boston, Chicago, and Miami. Using the same scale as in Figure 3.2, you can see that over the past two centuries, these U.S. cities have had lower murder rates than most European cities did during medieval times. That's the good news. The bad news is that these U.S. cities have had higher murder rates than European cities have had for the past two centuries.

International Trends in Homicide, 1500 to Present

Having looked at social historical data for large cities, let us now give attention to trends in homicide rates for countries as a whole. These statistics first began to be compiled in the late 1500s in Sweden, with England following closely behind. As with the early data on citywide homicide rates, all of the early countrywide data were derived from coroner's reports on cause of death.

Sweden's social historical data on the country's homicide rate are summarized in Figure 3.4, along with a second long series that began being compiled in the county of Kent in England at nearly the same time. Kent county's data is presented instead of data for England as a whole because the Kent county data began being collected earlier, and when data for England as a whole became available (in 1850), it was found to closely resemble the rates for Kent county.[18] Also presented in Figure 3.4 are fairly contemporary homicide rates for a few other countries throughout the world.

Without getting bogged down in details, what does Figure 3.4 allow us to conclude about trends in national rates of homicide? It again supports the general conclusion derived from Figure 3.2: Homicide rates in Europe were relatively high, es-

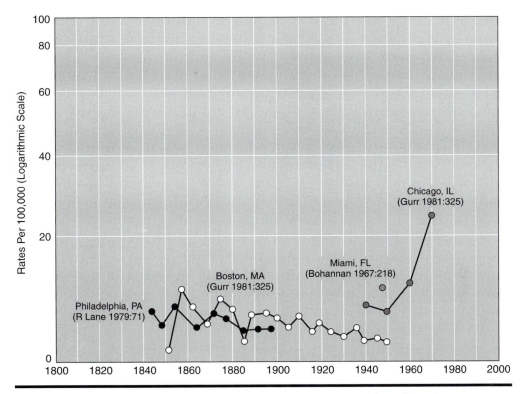

FIGURE 3.3   Trends in homicide rates in large North American cities throughout the nineteenth and twentieth centuries.

pecially prior to the eighteenth century.[19] Figure 3.4 also implies that homicide rates for countries such as the United States and the former Soviet Union around 1990 were only slightly higher than Sweden's about a decade earlier. The rates for all three of these countries were considerably higher than the rates for other industrialized countries with long-term national homicide statistics.

Let us now consider offenses other than homicide. In doing so, keep in mind that comparability becomes considerably more uncertain in the case of nonhomicide offenses.

International Trends for Overall Violent Crime, 1800 to Present

Violent crime other than homicide largely consists of the offenses of assault and armed robbery.

While murder rates are often calculated based on coroner's reports, official statistics on assaults and armed robbery must come from the criminal justice system. The criminal justice system did not begin to take shape in Europe until late in the eighteenth century. Consequently, the oldest data on violent crimes other than homicide go back to the early 1800s. Interestingly, Australia began to compile similar data at about the same time.

Figure 3.5 consists of data for the four countries that have such data going back to at least 1900. Three of these countries are European, and the remaining country is Australia.

As you can see, trends in violent crime rates from these four countries defy any easily recognizable generalization. In terms of comparing countries, rates in France and England/Wales have been consistently lower than the rates in Germany

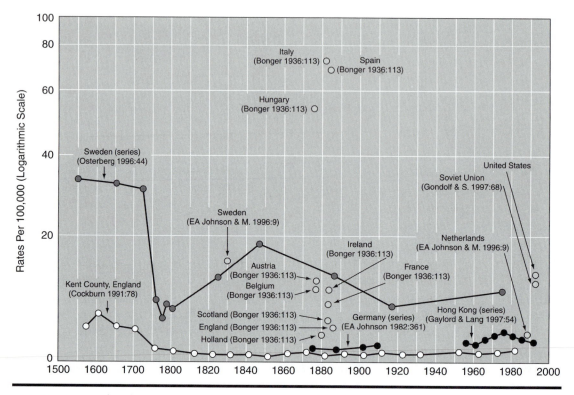

FIGURE 3.4   Trends in homicide rates for various countries from the fifteenth through the twentieth centuries.

and Australia. Of course, one cannot be certain how much of these differences are "real" as opposed to being the result of variations in how crime is defined and measured in each country. Nevertheless, the fact that German and Australian violent crime rates have been at least four times higher than the rates in France and England/Wales in the years where they can be compared suggests that some real differences in violent crime rates may have existed during this period.

International Trends in Property Crime Rates, 1800 to Present

Trends in the prosecutions or convictions for property offenses are shown in Figure 3.6 for the four countries for which data were located that extended back to at least 1900. As you can see, the

longest time series located for property offenses was for Sweden.

Beginning in the early third of the twentieth century, Sweden's property crime rate rose dramatically. For France, on the other hand, property crime rates appear to have dropped, while there was little change in the rates for Germany and England/Wales over the time frames their data were available. Overall, as with official violent crime (other than homicide), it is difficult to generalize about any international trends in property crime rates based on the earliest data sets available.

Contemporary International Comparisons

If one simply wants to compare countries at a recent point in time, the most widely consulted data

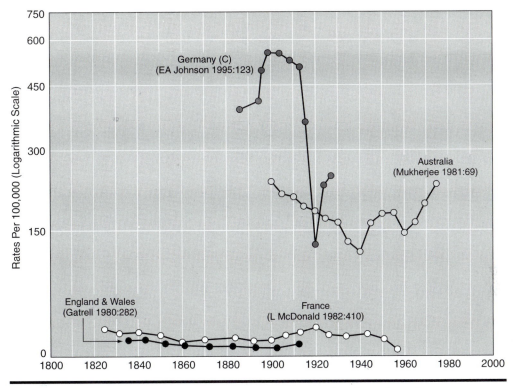

FIGURE 3.5   Trends in rates of violent offenses (except homicides) throughout the nineteenth and twentieth centuries (R = reports to police; P = prosecutions; C = convictions).

source is the one maintained by Interpol based on data provided to it each year by member nations. Table 3.1 provides a list of crime rates for a number of these countries for 1989–1990 for homicide and for total known offenses.

You must be very cautious in comparing the rates shown in Table 3.1, because of country-to-country differences in criminal statutes, in how those statutes are enforced, and in how crime statistics are maintained. Even in the case of homicides, comparisons can be misleading because manslaughter and political killings are counted in some countries but not in others. Basically, while Interpol data have been used in many studies for statistically comparing large groups of countries, they should not be used for comparing a few specific countries with one another (unless, of course,

you have a great deal of familiarity with how the particular countries collect and maintain their data).

What generalization can be made based on Table 3.1? The most striking feature of the table is the tremendous variability one finds in crime rates, even for countries located in the same continental region. Africa, for example, had a homicide rate ranging from less than two to ones in excess of fifteen. Overall, one would be hard-pressed to identify any striking geographical pattern with respect to official crime rates, at least as reported in the early 1990s.

Comparisons among Industrialized Nations.   If one restricts international comparisons to the most highly industrialized countries (mainly in Western Europe, North America, Australia, New Zealand,

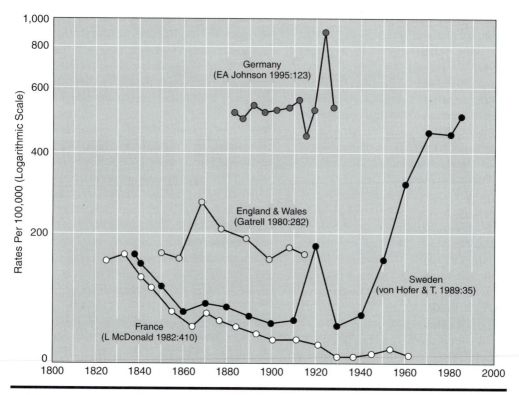

FIGURE 3.6 Trends in rates of property offense prosecutions (or convictions) throughout the nineteenth and twentieth centuries.

and Japan), studies have repeatedly found murder rates to be distinctly higher in the United States.[20] This has been documented repeatedly throughout the twentieth century.[21] Within Europe, Finland appears to have an unusually high violent crime rate, particularly when it is compared to the rates for neighboring Scandinavian countries,[22] but its homicide rate has never matched that of the United States.

When it comes to other types of crime, most researchers still conclude that U.S. rates are unusually high,[23] although we will examine data later in this chapter that call this view into question. In terms of low crime rates, one industrialized country has consistently stood out: Japan.[24] Not only has Japan consistently had low rates of crime of all major types, but it is one of only a few industrialized nations whose crime rates have markedly de-

clined since the end of World War II.[25] Most other industrialized countries had the opposite experience—a substantial rise in crime since the late 1940s[26] and especially since the 1960s.[27] The only industrialized country besides Japan that recorded even modest overall declines in crime rates since the middle of the twentieth century are Switzerland, Belgium,[28] and Denmark.[29]

OFFICIAL CRIME IN NORTH AMERICA

Because many users of this text will be citizens of the United States and Canada, the crime rates of these two countries will be given special attention. In both of these countries, trends will be examined primarily with respect to official data, although some victimization and self-report data will also be considered.

TABLE 3.1.   Officially reported crime rates (per 100,000) for various countries for 1996. (Source: Interpol).

Countries		Crime Rates	
		Homicide	Overall Crime
AFRICA	Botswana	19.50	6,693.00
	Egypt	1.59	3.314.41
	Ghana	1.96	863.81
	Kenya	4.16	364.16
	Syria	1.55	73.40
	Tanzania	6.40	1,249.88
	Zimbabwe	17.88	4,275.50
ASIA	Bangladesh	2.00	16.76
	China	1.90	200.90
	Hong Kong	1.40	1,410.10
	Indonesia	0.85	133.97
	Japan	1.00	1,396.50
	Nepal	2.21	29.05
	Singapore	1.50	1,507.00
	South Korea	1.50	2,637.30
	Thailand	9.50	1,449.00
	USSR	8.67	971.90
EUROPE	Austria	2.30	6,002.70
	Belgium	2.20	3,337.80
	Czechoslovakia	2.03	1,911.49
	Denmark	4.56	10,270.30
	England/Wales	2.26	8,986.13
	Finland	0.70	8,815.90
	France	4.46	6,169.29
	Hungary	3.10	3,287.20
	Ireland	0.82	2,475.76
	Italy	6.40	4,358.33
	Netherlands	14.81	7,613.33
	Northern Ireland	19.49	3,631.62
	Norway	2.61	5,562.74
	Poland	2.80	2,310.70
	Portugal	2.78	804.92
	Scotland	9.45	17,719.19
	Spain	2.43	2635.08
	Sweden	7.02	14,187.76
	Switzerland	1.17	5,275.59
MIDDLE EAST	Greece	2.04	3,306.57
	Israel	2.20	5,233.80
	Saudi Arabia	0.62	119.65
	Thailand	1.66	134.27
NORTH AMERICA	Canada	5.66	11,442.55
	United States	8.70	12,560.67
SOUTH/ CENTRAL AMERICA & CARRIBEAN	Argentina	0.14	177.05
	Barbados	7.05	4,245.30
	Chile	5.81	1,347.18
	Jamaica	20.85	1,926.96
PACIFIC	Australia	3.50	6,476.63
	New Zealand	3.23	14,025.87

As we review the relevant data, bear in mind that crime rates fluctuate in response to numerous still poorly understood factors. In addition, legislators occasionally change their definitions of crime, and police alter the arresting and prosecution guidelines. Therefore, you should not allow your self to jump at one or two of the apparent patterns in crime-rate trends as proof of some current "theory" you may have of why people engage in crime. At the same time, you should not dismiss the data out-of-hand as inherently biased and of no value. Trends in crime data provide criminologists with one piece of a large complex puzzle that is still being slowly assembled.

Overall Crime Rates in Chicago and Toronto

As was the case in Europe, certain large cities in North America began maintaining crime statistics long before either Canada or the United States as a whole did so. The two North American cities for which the longest time series on crime rates are available are Chicago and Toronto, both of which go back to the 1860s. Chicago's longest time series pertains to arrest rates, and Toronto's has to do with reports of offenses made to police. Let us briefly examine both of these two valuable data sets.

As shown in Figure 3.7, Chicago's overall arrest rates were relatively high in the 1860s and 70s, dropped irregularly during the early part of the twentieth century, and then began climbing again around 1950. Its arrest rates reached new highs in the 1990s.

Canada's largest city, Toronto, began to maintain records of crimes reported to police beginning in 1860. Figure 3.8 presents these rates separately for property and violent crimes. As you can see, Toronto, like Chicago, experienced a decrease in both violent and property crimes between 1880 and around 1920. Beyond around 1925, however, reports of both types of crime have gradually risen, although not to the levels reported in the 1880s, particularly in the case of violent crimes.

If you compare Chicago's and Toronto's data, you can see that they roughly parallel one another,

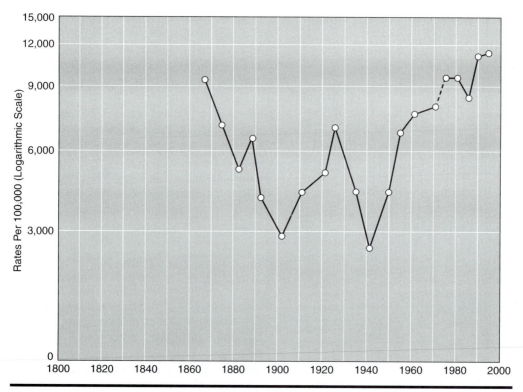

FIGURE 3.7   Trends in arrest rates for the city of Chicago (Gurr 1976:63 for 1868–1970; Division of Research, Chicago Police department for later years.)

except for Chicago's rise in arrest rates between 1910 through 1935, a rise that Toronto did not experience. This was roughly the period of time when Al Capone and other notorious gangsters terrorized Chicago, perhaps explaining the main difference between the two cities.

Homicide Rates in the United States and Canada

Now, let us examine data for the United States and Canada as a whole. The oldest national data for either country has to do with homicide, both of which are derived in very similar ways from coroners' reports.[30] U.S. data goes back to 1900 and Canada's series began in 1921. However, the U.S. data did not include data from all states until 1933,

leading one researcher to question the accuracy of the data prior to that time.[31]

As you can see, since 1921, Canada's homicide rate has been less than one third as high as the U.S. rate.[32] Nevertheless, the trends are very similar in both countries. In particular, both countries experienced two major peaks in their twentieth century homicide rates, one in the early 1930s and the other in the 1970s and 1980s.

An even more striking comparison comes when one compares the murder rates of each country's five largest cities. As shown in Table 3.2, homicide rates are roughly ten times higher in the five largest U.S. cities than in the five largest Canadian cities.

The main reason for this tremendous difference between U.S. and Canadian cities (even though the

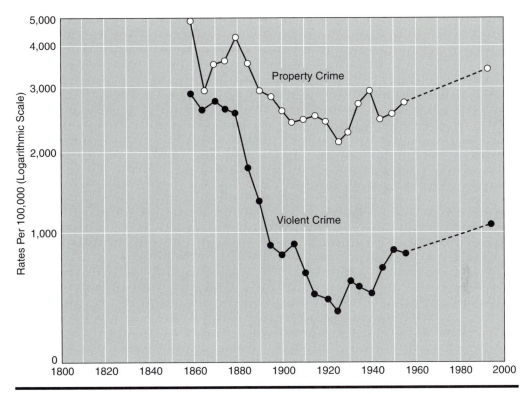

FIGURE 3.8   Trends in rates of crimes reported to the police in Toronto, Ontario from 1860 to 1995 (Sources: Boritch Hagan 1990:575; Toronto Municipal Police Department for data after 1955.)

U.S. murder rate as a whole is only about three times higher than Canada's) is that Canada's highest crime rates are found in the Yukon and the Northwest Territories, two northern provinces in which there are no large cities.[33] For the United States, on the other hand, murder rates tend to be highest in large urban areas. (In Chapter 6, we will discuss the relationship between urbanism and crime in greater detail.)

United States and Canadian Victimful Crime Rates

Since the early 1960s, both the United States and Canada have maintained counts of all offenses reported to police, and, as noted in Chapter 2, both countries call their statistics by the same name—*Uniform Crime Reports*. The UCRs in both the United States and Canada make a distinction between property and violent offenses (as virtually all other countries do).

Despite these similarities, the U.S. and Canadian UCRs should not be equated. The main difference is that Canada does not make the same Part 1/Part II distinction as does the United States. Basically, Canada's crime rates will appear to be higher than they would be if it used the same classifying methodology as is used in the United States.

With this in mind, let us compare Figures 3.10a and 3.10b. As you can see from these graphs, U.S. and Canadian data are similar not only in

FIGURE 3.9   Trends in U.S. and Canadian homicide rates, 1900–1997
(Source: Statistical Abstracts for the United States; Statistics Canada).

TABLE 3.2.   Homicide rates (per 100,000) for the five largest U.S. and Canadian cities, 1990 (U.S. and Canadian government statistics, after Gardner 1995:209).

Five Largest U.S. Cities	Homicide Rate	Five Largest Canadian Cities	Homicide Rate
New York	30.7	Toronto	1.9
Los Angeles	28.2	Montreal	3.4
Chicago	30.5	Vancouver	3.5
Houston	34.8	Ottawa-Hull	1.5
Philadelphia	31.7	Edmonton	3.5

terms of trends, but even in terms of actual rates, both for violent and for property offenses. Again, because of differences in their categorizing procedures, the actual rates in Canada are somewhat higher than they would be if it used the same classifying methods as the United States.

Regarding trends, the fact that they are fairly similar for both property and violent offenses can

be reasonably interpreted as suggesting that similar social forces have been affecting crime rates over the past four decades in both countries. Basically, both countries experienced a rather steady rise in crime throughout the 1960s and 1970s, with irregular leveling off beginning to occur in the mid-1980s, and a slight decline beginning sometime in the 1990s.

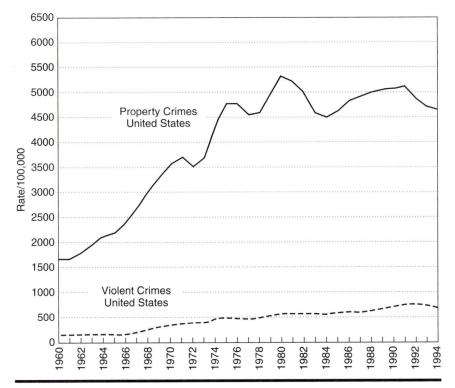

FIGURE 3.10A   Trends in rates of offenses reported to police in the United States for serious violent and property crimes for 1960–1994 (Source: U.S. Bureau of Justice Statistics).

Another noteworthy similarity is that both countries have maintained roughly a 9 to 1 ratio in property offenses relative to violent offenses. The tendency for property offenses to greatly surpass violent crimes is typical of industrialized societies.

VICTIMIZATION DATA

Now that we have gotten a bird's eye view of official crime rates over time and space, let us turn attention to victimization surveys. As discussed in Chapter 2, in 1973, the United States began conducting surveys to determine the rate at which people were being victimized by crime each year regardless of whether victims were notifying the police. Let us examine the results of these surveys. We will do so first for the United States, and then

turn our attention to findings from a couple of recent international victimization surveys.

Trends in U.S. Victimization Rates

U.S. victimization surveys have divided crime (excluding all victimless crime) into three categories: violent crimes, personal thefts, and household thefts. The main difference between the last two types of property crimes is that personal thefts occur outside the home, business, or motor vehicle, while household thefts include thefts that require breaking and entering one of these three sanctuaries.

Figure 3.11 presents the results of victimization surveys since 1973 for these three offense categories. As you can see, violent offenses have

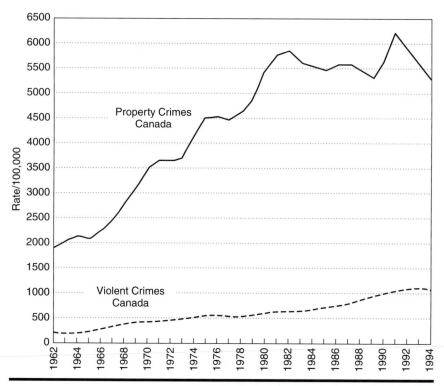

FIGURE 3.10B   Trends in rates of offenses reported to police in Canada for serious violent and property crimes for 1962–1994. (Source: Statistics Canada).

remained relatively stable throughout the period, while both types of property crimes have dropped since the early 1980s.

If you compare the victimization data with the official data since 1973 (refer back to Figure 3.10a), you will notice that the trends are not very consistent. In particular, whereas the official statistics suggest that there was an overall rise in both violent and property crimes at least until 1980 and a general leveling off until the 1990s, the victimization data indicates stability until the early 1980s and a downturn ever since. Several criminologists have sought to explain why these trends are not more consistent.[34] So what's the answer?

It probably comes as no surprise to say that more than one factor appears to be involved. However, the main cause comes from evidence that, at least since the 1970s, crime victims in the United States have gradually increased in their likelihood to call police.[35] As a result, a proportion of the rise in official crime rates since the 1970s is said to be *artifactual,* meaning that it is due to variation in measurement rather than being "real." If you remove the estimated effect of increased reporting from the official data, the curves in Figure 3.10a more closely resemble those in Figure 3.11. In other words, victimization data appear to provide a more reliable estimate of trends in crime victimization rates since 1973 than does official data.[36]

If victimization data are a more accurate reflection of crime rate trends in the United States since 1973, how accurate is the official data prior to 1973? No one knows for sure, but based on the comparisons made since 1973, it is not unreasonable to believe that about a quarter of the rise in crime rates during the 1960s was due to an in-

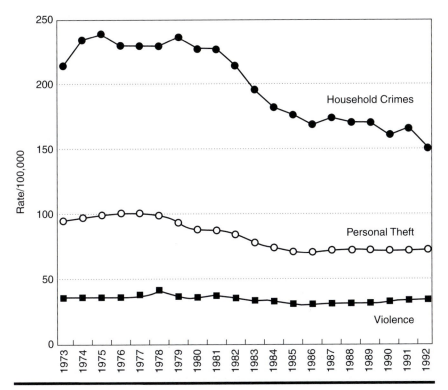

FIGURE 3.11   Victimization Rates for Crimes of Violence, Personal Theft, and Household Crimes from 1973 to 1992.

creased proportion of crimes being reported to police. This implies that the rest of the increase was "real." In later chapters, we will discuss what some of the causes for "real" rises and falls in crime rates might be.

International Victimization Rate Comparisons

Following the lead of the United States, a number of other countries have also begun conducting victimization surveys, if not every year, at least every few years as a way of supplementing their official data. Most notably, England/Wales has been conducting an annual victimization survey since 1981.

In the late 1980s, a consortium of fifteen countries conducted the first ever international victimization survey. What made this effort especially

noteworthy to the field of criminology was that all countries used the same questionnaire and interviewing procedures (except for the languages involved). The only major problem with this international research effort was that the average number of subjects interviewed in each country was around 2,000.[37] You will recall that the survey conducted each year by the United States consists of more than 10,000 interviewees. The main effect of small sample size on the results is that the rates could be off by a substantial amount, especially for the offenses that people experienced least often.

Key findings from this international victimization survey are shown in Figure 3.12. The graph reveals that the highest overall victimization rates were experienced by the United States, although the rates for Canada, Australia, and the Netherlands were not far behind. The lowest victimization rate

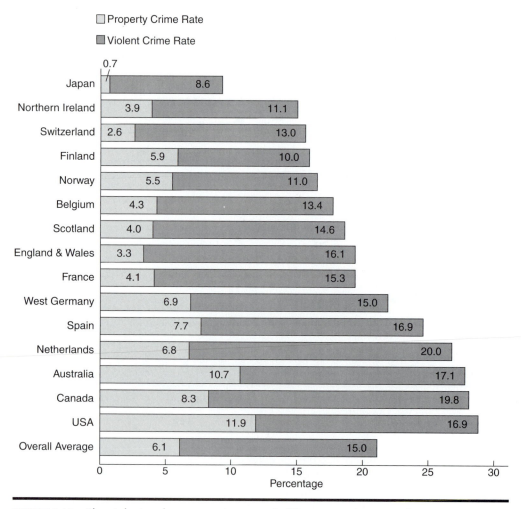

FIGURE 3.12   The violent and property crime rates in fifteen countries, according to simultaneously conducted victimization surveys in 1988–1989. Rates are arranged in descending order, according to the overall crime rates. (Source: Van Dijk et al. 1991:174).

was in Japan, which conforms with evidence from official statistics, indicating that Japan has an unusually low crime rate.

Since England/Wales was the second country to institute an annual victimization survey, it is interesting to compare both its official and victimization data with those of the United States. A recent analysis in this regard concluded that, since 1980, the United States and England/Wales have had similar crime rates, with one country rarely exceeding the other by more than double, and with

rates in England/Wales exceeding those in the United States nearly as often as vice versa, especially since 1990.[38] There was only one glaring exception: homicide. For this offense, the U.S. rate was six times higher.

SELF-REPORTED OFFENDING

The third type of data that can be considered regarding time and space in crime is that based on self-reports. As discussed in Chapter 2, self-reports can provide the most complete measure of criminal involvement, especially in the case of victimless offenses.

The Prevalence of Offending

To get an idea of just how pervasive criminal and delinquent behavior is, consider the results of a study of sixteen-year-old high school students conducted in Omaha, Nebraska in 1990.[39] The results are summarized in Table 3.3. As other self-report surveys have indicated, the Omaha study reveals that self-reported offending is widespread. Notice for example that over 70 percent of the students admitted to having committed a theft. Nonetheless, the results of self-report surveys will vary due to the way questions are phrased, the response options given to subjects, and the degree to which they are assured of anonymity.

The ISR Survey of High School Seniors

The longest running series on self-reported criminal behavior is one begun in 1975 by the University of Michigan's Institute for Social Research. The ISR survey is conducted each year among a representative sample of high school seniors throughout the United States. Some of the key findings from this survey pertaining to victimful offending are presented in Figure 3.13, and those pertaining to illegal drug use are in Figure 3.14.

Self-Reported Victimful Offending.   Taking the four offense categories identified in Figure 3.13 in descending order of occurrence frequency, the first category is theft of something worth less than $50. You can see that this has remained quite stable throughout the reporting period. The next offense category is injuring someone badly enough to require medical attention. Since 1975, the percentage of high school seniors who have reported such behavior has nearly doubled from around 9 percent to around 17 percent.

The third self-reported offending category is theft of items worth more than $50. The percentage of youth reporting such behavior was around 5 percent in the late 1970s, but it had risen to around 10 percent by the 1990s. If one were to scrutinize this trend, it would be qualified somewhat by noting that, due to inflation, the dollar value of most objects has increased. This means that a greater proportion of objects surpass the $50 cutoff today than did so in 1975. Thus, about half of the over-$50 theft category should actually be in the under-$50 theft category, giving each category a 2 to 3 percent rise since 1975.

Finally, students report on whether they have ever taken a weapon, such as a knife or gun, to school. In this case, the percentages have also risen from around 3 percent in the 1970s to about 5 percent in the 1990s.

Self-Reported Drug Use.   The proportion of U.S. high school seniors who report having used drugs in the past year are summarized in Figure 13.14. Six curves are presented, one for the use of all illegal drugs, one for marijuana, the single most widely used illegal drug,[40] and the remaining

TABLE 3.3.   The percentage of Omaha, Nebraska high school students who admitted to having committed particular types of offenses "ever" or during the "past year" (adapted from Marshall & Webb 1993:327).

Type of Offense	Ever	Past Year
Violent (personal) offense	48.2%	34.0%
Property (theft) offense	70.9%	36.9%
Vandalism & illegal carrying of weapons	55.5%	15.0%
Drug offense (possession and sale)	26.0%	17.3%
Status offense (mainly truancy)	56.0%	24.3%

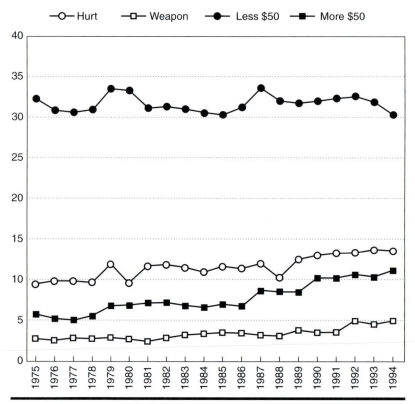

FIGURE 3.13   Trends in Self-Report of Involvement in Victimful Offending by U.S. High School Seniors from 1975–1994.

curves for four other drugs. As you can see, the rates were relatively high in the 1970s, then dropped during most of the 1980s, with a rise again in the 1990s.

International Comparisons Based on Self-Reports

Some international comparisons have been conducted with respect to self-reported offenses, nearly all of which have had to do with drug use. In this regard, drug use in the United States appears to be unusually high, at least in comparison to other industrialized nations.[41] Table 3.4 provides some evidence in this regard by presenting the results of studies on the percentage of college students in var-

ious countries who report having ever used marijuana. As you can see, while all studies conducted on U.S. campuses have found rates in recent years exceeding 59 percent, studies of other industrialized countries are 50 percent or less.

In regard to overall delinquency, one study compared self-reported delinquency among a sample of Filipino youth to youth of comparable age in the United States. The conclusion of this study was that self-reported offending by the U.S. youth appeared to be higher.[42]

"CRIME" IN PRELITERATE SOCIETIES

Today, a small proportion of human beings still live in societies where essentially no one reads or

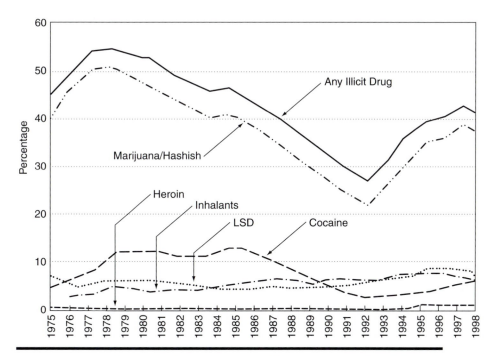

FIGURE 3.14   Trends in Annual Prevalence of an Illicit Drug Use Index for Twelfth Graders.

Note: Use of "any illicit drugs" includes any use of marijuana, LSD, other hallucinogens, crack or other cocaine, or heroin, *or* any use of other opiates, stimulants, barbiturates, methaqualone (excluded since 1990), or tranquilizers that is not under a doctor's orders.

(Source: Mathias 1999:S8)

writes, called *preliterate societies.* Preliterate societies come in several forms, with the simplest form being those known as *foraging* (or *hunter–gatherer*) *societies.* In foraging societies, people live off the land without growing crops or raising livestock. Other preliterate societies have some form of crop cultivation (*horticulture*) or livestock tending (*herding*), or both (*subsistence agriculture*). Today, most of these types of societies are found in the interior of three continents—Africa, South America, and Australia.

So far, this chapter has only examined literate societies with respect to their crime rates. This is reasonable because laws, by definition, must be written. However, if you define crime in terms of the behavior involved rather than in terms of the laws that exist against such behavior, it is reasonable to ask whether preliterate societies exhibit the ***nonlegal equivalent of crime.***

Interesting research has been conducted by anthropologists over the past few decades to determine the level of "crime" in preliterate societies. The focus of all of these studies has been on the willful killing of another person within one's own group (i.e., "homicide"). Most of these estimates of homicide rates were derived either by interviewing large numbers of societal members and asking them to recall the cause of death for each person they knew who had died, or by consulting written records kept by outsiders (such as

TABLE 3.4.   The proportion of college students who self-report ever having used marijuana (studies conducted since 1980).

Country	% of "Ever use"	Citation
Austria	37	Mangweth et al. 1997:466
England	50*	Ashton & Kamali 1995
Spain	25	Hinojal et al. 1983
Spain	17*	Rubio et al. 1984
Spain	25	Queipo et al. 1988
Spain	31	Lopez et al. 1989
Spain	24	Soler et al. 1992
Spain	30	Del Rio et al. 1994
Spain	30	Casanovas et al. 1996
Spain	24	Herreros et al. 1997
United States	61	E. W. Patterson 1988
United States	64	Cuomo et al. 1994
United States	59	Prendergast 1994
United States	59	Mangweth et al. 1997:446

*Students in medical/nursing school.

missionaries). So far, eight studies have reported "homicide" rates in preliterate societies, the results of which are summarized in Table 3.5. As you can see, while there is a great deal of variability, several rates are alarmingly high, reminiscent of European cities during the Middle Ages. It may be noted that the one thing these preliterate societies and medieval Europe had in common was that they essentially lacked a formal criminal justice system.

Studies of societies that lack a formal criminal justice system have shown that ***revenge killings*** are common as a way of "evening the score" when someone's relative or friend has been killed. Revenge killings often set into motion a long series of feuds between families and other social units.[43] Once the criminal justice system has begun to function, revenge killings are often punished as harshly as the original offense being avenged. This forces those who have friends or relatives who have been wronged by another to seek justice from the criminal justice system, rather than through their own actions. As a consequence of the formation of a formal criminal justice system, homicides drop, often dramatically. Other crimes, on the other hand, are only minimally affected by the institution of a criminal justice system.

CLOSING THOUGHTS ON GEOGRAPHIC VARIATIONS AND TRENDS IN CRIME RATES

This chapter has provided a window through which we can get faint glimpses of crime throughout time and space. All of the early crime data are based on official statistics, as provided either by the criminal justice system, or, earlier still, by coroners' offices. The final picture provided by this official data is like a jigsaw puzzle with nearly all of the pieces missing. Even the pieces that have been preserved are almost certainly distortions to varying degrees due to inconsistencies in how crimes are defined and measured.

Other problems are encountered when one turns to self-reports and victimization data. Because these two types of data both bypass the scrutiny of the criminal justice system, the "offenses" being reported may not meet legal definitions of crime or delinquency. Nevertheless, these two alternatives to official data both come closer

TABLE 3.5.   Results from eight studies of homicide rates in preliterate societies.

Population Studied	Geographical Location	Type of Society	Homicides Per 100,000	Citation
Agta	An island in the Philippines	Hunter–gatherer	326.0	Headland 1986:542
Bantu	Southern Africa	Subsistence Farming	4.6	Bohannan 1960b:158
Basoga	Southern Africa	Subsistence Farming	4.0	Fallers & Fallers 1960:71
!Kung	Southern Africa	Hunter–gatherer	29.3	Lee 1979:398
Sebei	Central Africa	Simple herding	11.6	Bolton 1984:2
Ugandan Tribes	South-Central Africa	Subsistence Farming	1.1–11.6	Southall 1960:228
Yanomamo	Northeastern South America	Tribal horticulture	165.9	Melancon 1982:33
Xhosa	Southern Africa	Tribal horticulture	19.3	Thomson 1980:101

to what most people think of as crime and delinquency than is the case for data generated by the criminal justice system.

The bottom line is that criminologists must be cautious with every step they make in attempting to construct a realistic picture of what crime is like over time and throughout the world. Obviously, one would be foolhardy to try to construct an explanation for crime based on what has been acquired so far in the way of generalizations. Nevertheless, one would also be unjustified in completely dismissing all of the information contained in this chapter as worthless. The middle ground is to view this chapter as providing a crude platform from which to examine other aspects of criminology.

Some of the broadest generalizations offered by data summarized in this chapter are the following:

Regarding international trends, it appears safe to say that homicide rates in mediaeval Europe were considerably higher than they are in contemporary industrial societies. This includes the United States, whose homicide rate is significantly higher than for any other fully industrialized nation.

In the case of crimes other than homicide, generalizations become more difficult. Over the past couple of decades, some countries have recorded substantial increases, particularly in the case of property crimes, while other countries have recorded impressive decreases, particularly for violent offenses.

By around the 1960s, most industrialized countries (and many nonindustrialized countries) had established standard crime-recording procedures. While it is still inappropriate to compare one country's crime data with that of another country (except for homicides), standardized recording procedures at least allow one to track a country's crime rate over time with a fair degree of confidence.

Turning to a comparison of the United States and Canada, homicide rates can be traced back to the early part of the twentieth century, but only to the 1960s for all other official data. In all cases, the trends for these two countries are remarkably similar. Nevertheless, the U.S. crime rate, particularly in the case of homicide, has been significantly higher than the corresponding Canadian rates.

Only for the United States is it currently possible to make comparisons between trends in crime rates using all three of the most widely accepted measures of offending: official data, victimization data, and self-reports. What can we say about crime rate trends in the United States based on comparisons of these three measures? Basically, official statistics suggest that crime rates increased throughout the 1960s and 70s,[44] but by the mid- to late-1980s, the rates for most serious crimes began leveling off, and, sometime in the early 1990s, rates began to decline.

Victimization data provides a somewhat different picture, although it only goes back to 1973. According to victimization surveys, U.S. crime rates rose slightly during the 1970s and then began to decrease in the early 1980s, with a slight decrease in rates thereafter.[45] As we mentioned before, there is pretty good evidence that one-fourth to one-third of the apparent increase in the official data during the 1970s was artifactual in the sense that people's tendencies to report increasing proportions of crimes to police rose during this time. If so, the modest increase in crime during the 1970s documented by the victimization data is probably close to accurate.

In regard to self-reported offending by high school students, the first survey was conducted in 1975. Since that time, self-reported victimful offending has been remarkably stable, compared to both official and victimization data. In the case of drug use, rates were relatively high in the last half of the 1970s, then declined during the 1980s, and then begin rising again in the 1990s.[46] As these data sets accumulate over the coming decades, criminologists will be in an increasingly better position to assess how well the various measures of offending parallel one another. So far, the parallels have been only modest.

SUMMARY

This chapter began by sketching some of the problems encountered by those attempting to compare crime statistics over time and space. The problems include changes in exactly how crimes are defined and in the procedures used to identify offenders. Normally, the "deeper" one goes into the criminal justice system to obtain data, the less confidence one can have in the comparability of the data. In other words, for assessing the prevalence of crime in various countries, imprisonment data are usually less comparable than data based on calls made to police by victims. Of all crime statistics, those that are most comparable over the greatest periods of time have been those pertaining to homicide.

We also discussed the misleading conclusion that can come from making comparisons across broad crime categories. The reason is that minor property crimes tend to dominate crime statistics, especially in affluent industrialized societies. Thus, when the rates of property crimes increase even a few percentage points, they can completely overwhelm any changes that might be occurring in the case of more serious types of crimes (such as assaults). The best way to avoid confusion in this regard is to avoid mixing violent and property offenses. Ideally, it is also advisable to make other separations of offenses according to types and/or levels of seriousness.

Next, we discussed the actual procedures used to calculate crime rates. The common practice is to make all calculations in terms of the number of offenses divided by every 100,000 people in the population being studied. However, sometimes it is best to represent the "at risk" population in terms of something other than the number of people in a population. For example, motor vehicle thefts are probably best divided by the number of registered motor vehicles in a country rather than by the number of people in a country.

Of course, all of these rules often have to be compromised with what is actually possible in terms of a particular country's crime-recording practices. Usually, *some* crime data are better than none at all, especially if the data can be considered as *part* of a picture, not as complete picture on its own. In this spirit, this chapter examined much of the oldest and most wide-ranging crime data available in the world.

Centuries of Official Crime

Homicide. The oldest crime data known to exist comes from coroners' reports on the cause-of-death in a few large European cities dating back to the thirteenth century. These data suggest that homicide was alarmingly high during the Middle Ages for most of these cities, but that the rates substantially declined by the beginning of the nineteenth century. The highest homicide rate ever recorded for a large city was for Florence, Italy in the fifteenth century, with a murder rate of 160. This compares to large cities today which have never exceeded forty. Several other mediaeval cities were also quite high until sometime in the eighteenth century.

Homicide data for countries as a whole began to be collected in some European countries in the sixteenth century. According to these statistics, most European countries had high homicide rates when compared to the same countries in the nineteenth or twentieth centuries. Nevertheless, a nation's homicide crime rates are almost always highest in its largest cities. As will be discussed in Chapter 6, this is because urban areas nearly always have higher crime rates than adjacent rural areas.

Crimes Other than Homicides. The earliest period in human history that one finds time series data on violent crime other than homicide is when data first began to be collected by a functioning criminal justice system in the late eighteenth century. Consequently around this time, at least four countries—Australia, England/Wales, France, and Germany—began reporting total violent crime rates. Little is apparent in terms of any common trends for these four countries, but the rates were markedly higher for Australia and Germany than for England/Wales and France.

In the case of property crimes, the longest time series yet located has been for Sweden, whose property crime rate rose dramatically beginning around 1930. The second oldest time series for property crimes was for France, and its rates dropped over roughly the same period of time. Property crime rates for two other countries—England/Wales and Germany—exhibited no overall upward or downward trends.

Contemporary International Comparisons. By the latter half of the twentieth century nearly all countries had begun to routinely tabulate official crime statistics. Only two generalizations seem to be warranted based on these data. First, among industrialized nations, the United States stands out in its official crime rate, particularly with respect to homicides. Second, Japan's offical crime rate is strikingly low in all respects.

Official Crime in North America

Chicago and Toronto. As in Europe, the earliest crime data in the United States and Canada did not cover these countries as a whole, but pertained only to a few of their largest cities. Thus, the oldest North American crime data are for the cities of Chicago and Toronto, both of which began collecting data in the 1860s. Chicago's data were on total arrests, and Toronto's data were on calls made to police, broken down separately for violent and property offenses.

Chicago exhibited a relatively high rate of criminal arrests in the latter part of the 1800s, with a gradual, but irregular, decline in the early decades of the twentieth century, and then a substantial rise to the present time beginning around the 1950s. A fairly similar pattern was revealed in the city of Toronto, although its reports to police were higher in the later decades of the 1800s than they were even in the latter part of the twentieth century, especially for violent offending.

U.S. and Canadian Homicides. By 1900, each state in the United States was providing the federal government with data on the cause of all deaths, and, by 1921, Canada's provinces were doing likewise. This allowed both countries to begin compiling annual statistics on the rate at which people were being murdered. According to these statistics, homicide rates were relatively low in both countries in the early part of the twentieth century, but had risen substantially by the late 1920s and early 1930s. In the 1940s and 1950s, both countries experienced drops in their murder rates, but these rates both rose in the 1960s, eventually reaching new highs in the 1970s and 1980s.

At least since the 1920s, when it became possible to make comparisons, U.S. homicide rates have always been at least three times higher than those in Canada. Even more dramatic differences come from comparing the largest cities of both countries, where U.S. homicide rates are about nine times higher than in Canada.

Overall Crime in the U.S. and Canada   By the 1960s, both countries had devised fairly standard recording procedures for all offenses reported to police. While differences in the types of crimes included do not permit direct comparisons of actual rates, trends in the two countries can be meaningfully compared. In this regard, crime rate trends in the United States and Canada have been similar, with both recording substantial rises in both property and violent offenses during the 1960s and 1970s, and a leveling off in the 1980s. In addition, in both countries police receive nearly nine times more calls pertaining to property offenses than to violent offenses, a ratio that is fairly typical for advanced industrialized societies.

Victimization Data

In 1973, the United States was the first country to begin collecting crime data each year in a way that completely bypasses the criminal justice system. Trends in this data can now be compared to trends in official crime data. The results so far have not been entirely reassuring as to the meaningfulness of both sets of data, because the trends have paralleled one another only modestly. Careful comparative analyses of victimization and official statistics have suggested that victimization data are probably somewhat closer to the real trends in crime rates since the 1970s, due primarily to a gradual increase in the likelihood of people reporting crimes to police over the past few decades.

In the late 1980s, fifteen countries conducted victimization surveys using essentially identical interviewing procedures. This allowed researchers for the first time to compare countries without having to make any allowances for each country's unique criminal justice system. The main shortcoming of this initial fifteen-country survey was that the number of people interviewed in several of the countries was not large enough for highly reliable rate calculations. Nevertheless, overall patterns in crime victimization were fairly consistent with patterns revealed through comparisons of official statistics. In particular, the lowest crime rate among the fifteen countries was Japan, and the highest was the United States, followed closely by Canada and Australia. The close similarity of these three countries is somewhat surprising in light of the much higher homicide rate in the United States than in either of these other two countries. (Of course, homicide victims are not included in victimization surveys!)

Self-Reported Offending

Self-reports reveal that virtually everyone violates the law at least occasionally. Nevertheless, most of the offenses are status and other victimless offenses.

The most ambitious long-term study of offending based on self-reports is the annual survey conducted by the Institute for Social Research. It has determined that, since 1975, the rates of victimful offending has generally remained steady or risen slightly. Regarding drug use, the rates rose until the early 1980s, then declined for a decade, and began to rise again in the 1990s. Studies that have compared the self-reported rates of illegal drug use in the United States with other industrial countries have concluded the U.S. rates are unusually high.

Preliterate Societal "Crime"

Even though preliterate societies have no laws (because they have no writing), nearly all of their members disapprove of intentionally hurting others and confiscating other people's possessions. In this sense, even these societies have crime. Several anthropological studies have sought to determine the rate at which one type of crime—homicide—occurs in various preliterate societies. Their efforts have uncovered a wide range of estimates, all the way from 1 to over 300.

SUGGESTED READINGS

Biderman, Albert D., & Lynch, James P. (1991). *Understanding crime incidence statistics: Why the UCR diverges from the NCS*. New York: Springer-Verlag. (This book will help you understand why there are inconsistencies between various data sources on crime rates in the same country, especially the United States.)

del Frate, Anna Alvazzi, Zvekic, Uglijesa, and van Dijk, Jan J. M. (1993). *Understanding crime experiences of crime and crime control*. Rome: United Nations Publication. (For those who are interested in some of the latest international comparisons on crime victimization, this is a book that is definitely worth consulting.)

Gurr, Ted Robert (1976). *Rogues, rebels, and reformers*. Beverly Hills, CA: Sage. (A widely read book that presents and interprets much of the historical evidence regarding trends in crime rates prior to the twentieth century.)

Junger-Tas, Josine, Terlouw, Gert-Jan, & Klein, Malcolm W. (1994). *Delinquent behavior among young people in the Western world: First results of the International Self-Report Delinquency Study*. Amsterdam: Kugler. (Reports on the first wide-ranging international study of delinquency and crime based on self-report data ever conducted.)

Langan, Patrick, A., and Farrington, David P. (1998). *Crime and justice in the United States and in England and Wales, 1981–1996*. Washington, DC: U.S. Department of Justice (NCJ 169284). (An interesting book that compares both official and victimization crime data in the United States and England/Wales since 1981. Overall, these two countries appear to have fairly similar overall crime rates, with the exception of homicide, which is much higher in the United States.)

Monkkonen, Eric (1996). *The civilization of crime: Violence in town and country since the Middle Ages*. Urbana: University of Illinois Press. (An informative book by a well-known social historian about the history of crime in Europe.)

Neapolitan, Jerome L. (1997). *Cross-national crime: A research review and sourcebook*. Westport, CT: Greenwood. (A valuable book to consult for a wide range of information and references pertaining to how crime rates vary throughout the world and over time.)

Serio, Joseph (Ed.). (1992). *USSR crime statistics and summaries: 1989 and 1990*. Chicago: University of Illinois at Chicago's Office of International Criminal Justice. (Provides some of the first statistical data ever released outside the former Soviet Union about the extent of crime in this country. The publication is in English.)

United States Department of Justice (published annually). *Sourcebook of criminal justice statistics*. Washington, DC: U.S. Government Printing Office. (Presents over 700 pages of detailed statistics each year on every aspect of the criminal justice system in the United States. Much of the information is contained in detailed tables and graphs. Highly recommended reading for serious students of criminology and criminal justice.)

EXERCISES

1. As this chapter has shown, almost everyone has violated a crime or delinquency statute at least once. Also, large proportions of people have been the victim of crime or had a close friend or relative victimized. Write a two- to three-page essay entitled "My brush with crime," in which you describe a real instance of someone close to you having either committed a crime or having been a crime victim. Even if the person is you, describe this person with a fictitious name.

2. Surveys conducted in the United States since 1990 have indicated that most people believe American's crime problem is getting worse. Is this true according to objective statistical evidence presented in this chapter? Write a one- to two-page essay on what might help to explain inconsistencies between public perceptions and reality in regard to increases and decreases in crime.

3. Go to the library and get a copy of Interpol's *International Crime Statistics* for one or more years (you may need to have your instructor procure a copy through interlibrary loan). Prepare a summary table (and/or graph) of some of the data derived from at least two different countries, and prepare a one- to two-page report based on the analysis. For example, you might compare four or five countries with respect to their murder and assault rates. Of course, in making any such comparisons, you will need to be extremely guarded about any statements you make (e.g., "There seems to be a difference . . . ," "The statistics appear to suggest . . . "). The main purpose of this exercise is to acquaint you with some of the official statistics criminologists work with.

ENDNOTES

1. U.N. General Assembly 1977:7.

2. E. A. Johnson 1982:356.

3. Evans & Himelfarb 1987:54.

4. Evans & Himelfarb 1987:60; U.S. Department of Justice 1988:12.

5. Serio 1992b:72.

6. *Australia:* Mukherjee 1981:45; *Malaysia:* Lee 1976:662.

7. Hurwitz & Christiansen 1983:161; Wilkins 1964.

8. Spierenburg 1994:707.

9. Gurr 1981:313.

10. Osterberg 1992:77.

11. Spierenburg 1994:707.

12. E. A. Johnson 1982:361.

13. Beattie 1986:139; Spierenburg 1996:64.

14. Beattie 1977:112; J. D. Rogers 1989:317; Spierenburg 1994:702; Stone 1983:31.

15. Beattie 1977:112; Stone 1983:31; Tobias 1967:37.

16. E. A. Johnson & Monkkonen 1996:8; Osterberg 1996:45; Stone 1983:304.

17. Gatrell 1980:300.

18. Cockburn 1991:78.

19. Daly & Wilson 1988:276; Gillis 1989; Gurr 1976:59, 1981; Lane 1980; Lohdi & Tilly 1973; Osterberg 1996:44.

20. Fingerhut & Kleinman 1990; Kirchhoff & Kirchhoff 1984:60; Richters 1993.

21. Brearley 1932:27; Cortes & Gatti 1972:278; Odom 1927:494; Schur 1969:34.

22. Kaironen 1966; Viemero 1996:88.

23. Grunhut 1951:152; Kalish 1988:1; Scott 1972:4.

24. Dinitz 1987:5; Hechter & Kanazawa 1993:462; Shikita & Tsuchiya 1992.

25. Clifford 1976:2; Martin & Conger 1980:53; D. J. Smith 1995:403; Westermann & Burfeind 1991; Wilson & Herrnstein 1985:453.

26. Balvig 1985; Baur 1964; Mukherjee 1981.

27. Maden 1993:286; Shamsie 1982:633.

28. D. J. Smith 1995:412.

29. Hurwitz & Christiansen 1983:139.

30. Reiss & Roth 1993:52.

31. Eckberg 1995.

32. Russell & Baenninger 1996:177.

33. Gartner 1995:196.

34. Blumstein et al. 1991, 1992; Jensen & Karpos 1993; McDowall & Loftin 1992; S. Menard 1992a; R. M. O'Brien 1996.

35. R. M. O'Brien 1996; U.S. Department of Justice 1988:34.

36. Blumstein et al. 1992; R. M. O'Brien 1996.

37. D. J. Smith 1995:416.

38. Langan & Farrington 1998.

39. Marshall & Webb 1994:322.

40. Mieczkowski 1996:372.

41. S. Black & Casswell 1991; Mangweth et al. 1997.

42. Shoemaker 1994.

43. Boehm 1984.

44. Cronin et al. 1981; Sykes 1980.

45. U.S. Department of Justice 1993:11.

46. L. D. Johnston et al. 1995:84.

CHAPTER 4

Criminological Theorizing:
Popular and Historical Underpinning

Jot down on a piece of paper how you might respond to the following question: In your opinion, what are the one or two main causes of crime in society today? After reading the first few pages of this chapter, you can compare what you wrote down with the results of surveys conducted among representative samples of "the man (and woman) on the street." The second part of this chapter describes some of the colorful history of the earliest ideas about the causes of crime offered in a scholarly context.

If you are completely open-minded, crime could be the result of just about anything. Over the centuries, crime has been blamed on the devil, on witches, and even on astrological forces. In fact the word *lunatic* was originally used to describe someone who became dangerously violent as a result of the appearance of the full moon. Today, few people take these sorts of explanation for crime seriously, but this is not because they have been specifically refuted. In fact, try to imagine how anyone could prove or disprove a theory that most crime is the result of the devil.

SURVEYING PEOPLE'S OPINIONS
ON THE CAUSES OF CRIME

Surveys conducted since the 1950s in the United States and a few other countries (mainly Britain) have revealed that most people explain crime (including delinquency) in terms of causes that can

be subsumed under one or more of the following eight categories:

> Societal and economic factors
> Neighborhood and local institutions
> Family factors
> Interpersonal relationships outside the home
> Mass media influences
> Personality characteristics
> Drugs (including alcohol)
> The criminal justice system

Let us briefly consider the nature of each of these categories.

Societal and economic factors have to do with the way a country functions, including its form of government and economic system. For example, many people believe that criminal behavior will be fostered by societal institutions that encourage competition over wealth or that promote ethnic divisions and rivalries.

Neighborhood and local institutions cover community agencies in charge of educational, religious, business, and recreational activities. (It would also include most criminal justice agencies, but this is considered as a special category below.)

Family factors cover such things as parental discipline and involvement with children as well as the degree of harmony between parents and other family members.

Interpersonal relationships outside the home refer to the people other than family members with whom individuals spend time.

The *mass media* has to do with such factors as television and movies, as well as magazines and, recently, even the Internet.

Personality characteristics pertain to a wide variety of individual traits that people associate with criminality, such as risk-taking tendencies and lack of concern for the rights of others.

Drugs and alcohol pertain to the use of and/or the effects of various recreational drugs on criminal tendencies.

The *criminal justice system* refers to police, court, and correctional policies and practices, particularly the severity of sentences imposed on those convicted of crime.

Variations in Lay Explanations of Crime

In the mid-1940s, the Gallup polling organization asked a representative sample of U.S. citizens what they thought were the main reasons teenagers engage in juvenile delinquency.[1] This marked the first time such an opinion survey on the causes of crime had been conducted. By the 1960s, this sort of question began to be asked more regularly both in the United States and in England. Responses to these surveys are often called **lay theories of crime**.[2]

Table 4.1 summarizes the results of these surveys. To keep the table simple and to make findings comparable, only the three most frequently mentioned causal categories are indicated. In making comparisons, keep in mind that people's answers will vary from one study to the next depending on exactly how questions are phrased

and the sort of response options presented. Therefore, you should look for general patterns, rather than attempting to comprehend all of the minor differences found from one survey to the next.

Using the eight causal categories just presented, Table 4.1 shows that in the United States, most people identify family-based factors as the most important causes of crime, and especially of delinquency. Most often mentioned of these family-based factors are parental discipline and supervision. To illustrate, a poll conducted in the United States in the 1980s revealed that a sizable majority of adult Americans agreed with the statement "We would have less crime in this country if more parents disciplined their children strictly."[3]

Attributing crime and delinquency to inadequate parenting seems to have slipped somewhat in recent years as being perceived as the leading cause of crime in the United States. Notice that in all of the surveys conducted in the 1960s and 1970s, family factors were the single most commonly mentioned cause. However, after 1980, family factors slipped to second and even third place, sometimes behind social and economic factors. Similarly, most of the available surveys conducted in England have shown this country's adults to consider family factors to be the single most important cause of crime (except for one recent study that put family factors behind economic and local institutional variables).

At the bottom of Table 4.1 are the results of two surveys of adolescents, one conducted in Scotland, and the other a cross-cultural study in England and Nigeria. You can see that adolescents in Scotland and England are both less likely to emphasize family factors as the causes of crime and delinquency than is true of adults in England and the United States. This cross-cultural study is particularly interesting because for the first time it offers a window into the perceived causes of crime among non-Westerners. Basically, whereas British children were most inclined to attribute crime to such things as "They do it for fun" and "because they are bored," the Nigerian youngsters chose family and economic factors as the most important causes. In this respect, the Nigerian adolescents were more similar to adults in England and

TABLE 4.1. Summary of the results of public opinion polls about the main causes of crime. Numbers represent the top three ranked factors in people's choices.

Where and When Study was Conducted	Age of Subjects	Explain crime or Delinquency?	Eight Categories of Crime and Delinquency Causation							
			Societal & Economic Factors	Neighborhood/Local Institutions	Family Factors	Relations Outside Home	Mass Media	Personality Factors	Drugs & Alcohol	Criminal Justice System
England, mid-1960s[4]	Adult	Crime		3	1					2
England, early 1970s[5]	Adult	Crime			1		3			2
England, mid-1980s[6]	Mostly adult	Crime		2	1			3	2	
England, early 1990s[7]	Adult	Crime	3		1					
England, early 1990s[8]	Adult	Crime	1	2	3				3	
U.S., 1946[9]	Adult	Delinq.		2	1					
U.S., 1963[10]	Adult	Delinq.		2	1	3				2
U.S., 1964[11]	Adult	Crime			1			3		
U.S., 1966[12]	Adult	Crime			1	2		3		1
U.S., 1972[13]	Adult	Crime			3				2	
U.S., mid-1960s[14]	Adult	Crime	2		1				3	
U.S., late 1960s[15]	Adult	Delinq.		2	1	3				
U.S., mid-1970s[16]	Adult	Delinq.	2		1					
U.S., early 1980s[17]	Adult	Crime	1	2	3					
U.S., 1981[18]	Adult	Crime	1		3					2
U.S., 1989[19]	Adult	Crime	2		3				1	
U.S., late 1980s[20]	Adult	Crime	3	2	1					
U.S., late 1980s[21]	Adult	Crime	1	3	2					
U.S., early 1990s[22]	Adult	Crime	3		2				1	
Scotland, mid-1980s[23]	Adol.	Delinq.		3		1		2		
England, early 1990s[24]	Adol.	Crime				3	2	1		
Nigeria, early 1990s	Adol.	Crime	1		2			3		

adults in the United States until the 1980s in attributing crime primarily to family factors.

Overall, since the 1960s, most adults in the United States and England have considered family variables to be the single most important causes of crime. Nonetheless, surveys have repeatedly found that people view the causes of crime as due to several factors, and accept that the causes may vary, depending on the type of crime being considered.[25]

Demographics and Lay Explanations. Several surveys have been undertaken to determine if demographic variables are related to the answers people give. Regarding gender, women have been found to be more likely than men to attribute crime

and delinquency to family factors; men lean a little more toward economic factors.[26] As far as age is concerned, as was just noted, teenagers are more likely to attribute crime and delinquency to factors outside the home such as economic factors, peer influences, and the lack of recreational opportunities, whereas adults emphasize family variables (particularly the lack of parental supervision).[27]

Regarding socioeconomic factors, only one study was located. It indicated that in the United States, persons of low social status were more prone to blame delinquency on family factors, whereas the upper classes consider various societal and cultural factors (particularly the economy) as a bit more influential.[28]

Political Philosophy and Lay Explanations. Another variable that has been found to bear on what people identify as the causes of crime and delinquency is political philosophy.[29] To discuss this relationship requires noting that political philosophies can be roughly arrayed along a left-wing (liberal) to a right-wing (conservative) continuum. This left–right continuum has been widely documented in all industrialized countries studied so far.[30] As a rule, left-wingers place paramount importance on human equality and forgiveness, especially for those they perceive as "underdogs." Right-wingers, on the other hand, emphasize freedom of action in conjunction with assuming full responsibility for any harm that may result from exercising that freedom.[31] As you might suspect, most people tend to be somewhere in the middle of this left–right continuum, with only small percentages subscribing to the most extreme ends of the continuum.[32]

In the United States, supporters of a left-wing political philosophy usually vote for Democratic candidates, and most supporters of a right-wing political philosophy vote for Republican candidates. In Canada, the largest left-wing party is the Liberal Party, and the main right-wing party is the Progressive Conservative Party. In England, the Labour Party attracts mainly left-wing voters, and the Tory Party attracts mostly right-wing voters.

How do these political views relate to what people identify as the causes of crime? Perhaps you can guess. Studies have indicated that people who have a left-wing political perspective are more inclined to attribute crime and delinquency to social and economic factors such as poverty and racial discrimination.[33] Right-wingers, on the other hand, are most likely to blame crime and delinquency on inadequate education, inadequate parenting,[34] and character flaws.[35]

Comparisons with the Past

Of course, it would be fascinating to know how people's contemporary opinions about the causes of crime compare to the opinions of people who lived centuries ago. But because the earliest survey only goes back to the 1940s, we will never know with a great deal of confidence. The closest that anyone has come to making historical comparisons are those who have studied published writings during various historical periods. In that regard, two historians of eighteenth century America contended that in those days most believed that the causes of crime were to be found primarily in the family and the economy.[36] This, of course, is similar to what surveys have revealed in recent decades.

One study of historical writings from sixteenth-century Europe similarly indicated that most people believed crime was mainly the result of family and local community factors.[37] In weighing this historical evidence, it is important to keep in mind that only a minority of people in past centuries were literate. Therefore, those who wrote the documents that historians have used to make inferences may not reflect the opinions of most people who lived in past centuries.

How Do Criminologists and Criminal Justice Personnel Explain Crime and Delinquency?

A survey was conducted among a representative sample of U.S. criminologists in the late 1980s to determine what they considered the most important causes of crime and delinquency. As you can see from viewing Table 4.2, criminologists are not of one mind on these matters. We will find this point being made again as we explore the history of criminological theories.

Besides the diversity in criminologists' opinions, the most notable conclusion that can be drawn from Table 4.2 is that what most criminologists believe to be the main causes of crime and delinquency is similar to what most adults in the general public believe as well (at least in the United States and England).[38] Notice, for example, that family variables are listed as one of the three leading causes of delinquency by 50 percent of criminologists and as one of the three leading causes of serious criminality by 30 percent. In second place for delinquency was an economic factor, although it was in first place for serious criminality.

TABLE 4.2.   Percentage of each of the following factors that were identified by professional criminologists as one of the three most important causes of "delinquency or minor criminality" and of "serious and persistent criminality" (Ellis & Hoffman 1990:53).

Causes	Percent of Criminologists Identifying This as One of the Three Main Causes	
	Delinquency or Minor Offenses	Serious & Persistent Criminality
Poor supervision in the home or unstable and uncaring family	50%	30%
An economic system that prevents participation by some individuals	38%	56%
Peer influences	34%	13%
Lack of, or inappropriate, moral training by church, family, and school	30%	24%
Bad example by parents or guardians	13%	5%
Lack of education and/or educational opportunities	17%	22%
Bias against the poor in the passage and enforcement of law	15%	18%
Individual differences in succeeding in an industrial society	15%	33%
Availability and use of various mind-altering drugs (including alcohol)	12%	17%
Labeling and perceptions by self and others	12%	17%
Racial discrimination	7%	6%
Failure of the criminal justice system to punish law violators	6%	14%
Bad example by business and community leaders	3%	3%
Brain and hormonal factors	2%	6%
Genetic influences	1%	10%
Mental illness	1%	3%
Inadequate religious training	1%	1%
Other (primarily "Desire for thrill and sensation seeking")	16%	10%

In addition to the general public and criminologists, surveys have also been conducted among people in various criminal justice occupations. Similar to the findings among criminologists, a study of police and corrections officers in Britain revealed that the most popular explanations for serious and persistent crime are economic variables, and the most popular explanations for delinquency and minor criminality are family background variables.[39] Studies carried out among various segments of the criminal justice community have indicated that police personnel are somewhat more likely than other criminal justice officials (such as probation and parole officers) to identify character flaws (e.g., thrill seeking, mental problems) as causing crime, and are less likely to blame the economy and other social factors.[40] As to the source of character flaws among criminals, it should be noted that most criminologists[41] and criminal justice personnel agree[42] that social–environmental factors rather than any inherited factors are the main causes.

An interesting study in Great Britain compared the views of three groups: the general public, police officers, and convicted felons.[43] It found that the explanations given by the ordinary British citizen and those given by the average police officer were almost identical. Both attributed crime primarily to poverty, and secondarily to local institutional factors (such as court leniency) along with poor family conditions. Convicted felons, however, stood out in their emphasis on unjust societal factors and on unfortunate social circumstances as the main causes of crime.

A U.S. study that compared the general public with a sample of probation officers found that, while the most frequently mentioned causes of crime for both groups were social causes, this was significantly more true for probation officers than for the general public. The general public was more prone to also mention individual "predispositional" factors (i.e., character flaws).[44]

Overall, surveys have documented considerable diversity in people's opinions about the causes of crime and delinquency. However, as an overall pattern in the two countries where nearly all of the research has been conducted to date (i.e., the United States and England), most people emphasize family factors and economic factors. As one moves from the young nonserious offender to the older hardened criminal, people tend to shift away from focusing their explanations on family variables.

A BRIEF HISTORY OF CRIMINOLOGICAL THEORY

Having examined the collective opinions of various groups of people about the causes of crime, let us now turn our attention to the views of those responsible for creating the discipline of criminology. We will now trace the field of criminology from its origins about three centuries ago through to the end of the nineteenth century. You will see in subsequent chapters that as we move into the twentieth century so many divergent theories arise that no single chapter can do them justice.

Setting the Stage for the Emergence of Scientific Criminology

An important time in European history began to gradually take shape about 500 years ago with the rise of what has come to be known as the **Renaissance.** The Renaissance was marked by an increase in intellectual and scientific curiosity about topics that people in earlier periods had largely either ignored or simply attributed to supernatural forces. The topics ranged from the movement of

heavenly bodies relative to the earth to the causes of human behavior.

Scientists working during the Renaissance were at risk. In astronomy, for example, Galileo endured humiliation in the early 1600s for publishing evidence that the earth was not the center of the universe. Regarding human behavior, an anatomist named **Franz Joseph Gall** (1758–1828), was fired from his teaching post at the University of Vienna for contending that human emotions and thought were controlled by the brain, rather than by the heart or the soul.[45]

The Renaissance eventually gave rise to a period in the 1700s called the **Enlightenment** (or the **Age of Reason**), which was marked by a strong belief in the abilities of humans to control their own collective destiny through learning and rational discourse rather than through prayer and the mercy of God. For many Enlightenment thinkers, the purest expression of rational thought was scientific observation and logic.

Amidst the turmoil brought on by the Renaissance and the Enlightenment, radically new proposals began surfacing within European universities regarding the causes of human misery, including crime. Instead of maintaining that crime was the result of uncontrollable forces such as the devil,[46] scientific explanations began to receive serious attention.[47] Over the next couple of centuries, three fairly distinct schools of thought would emerge: the Classical School, the Cartographic/Demographic School, and the Positivist School. We will examine each of these schools in turn.

The Classical School

The **classical school of criminology** is so named for two reasons: First, it represents the earliest attempt to deal with crime in a strictly nonsupernatural way. Second, the classical school relied heavily on intellectual "armchair speculation," which is in the tradition of the ancient "classical" Greek philosophers, such as Socrates, Plato, and Aristotle.

The fundamental premise on which the classical school was founded is that human beings are rational agents who will act in their own best interest. Consequently, classical theorists argued that people will choose to obey the law if the sanctions for not doing so are sufficiently severe and have a high probability of being imposed.[48] Fundamental to the classical school's perspective on the causes of crime is a concept known as **hedonistic calculus.** This term refers to people acting in accordance with their desires to maximize pleasure and minimize pain. The two individuals who had the greatest influence on shaping the classical school were Cesare Beccaria and Jeremy Bentham.

Cesare Beccaria.   The founder of classical criminology is the seventeenth-century Italian nobleman and professor of law, **Cesare Beccaria** (*be car' e a*) (1738–1794). Beccaria published the first book to advocate fundamentally reforming Europe's judicial and penal systems. The book, entitled **Dei Delitti e della Pene (On Crimes and Punishment)**, was an impassioned plea to make the criminal justice system rational in the sense that it maximized the probabilities that people would choose not to commit crime.

Beccaria's philosophy contrasted with many common practices in seventeenth-century Europe. For example, the penalties imposed by judges had few restrictions, and appeals were extremely rare. Torture was often used to extract confessions from suspects.

Beccaria accepted the need for punishment, but he believed that criminal statutes should be designed to preserve public safety and order, not simply to avenge the harm caused by an offense.[49] He also took issue with the practice of secret accusations, and of keeping the accused ignorant of the charges brought against them, arguing that such practices led to general deceit and alienation in society. Beccaria argued that accused persons should be able to confront their accusers and know the charges brought against them.

Above all, Beccaria contended that punishment should fit the crime (i.e., be proportionate to the harm done to society), should be the same from one judge to the next, and should be applied without reference to the social status of either the offender or the victim. Beccaria championed the abolition of the death penalty, primarily on grounds that such punishment exceeded the amount of harm any crime (even murder) inflicted on society.

To ensure that prospective offenders would desist in illegal activities, Beccaria said that punishments for specific crimes should be publicly decreed, and judicial discretion in sentencing should be minimized. The judge's task was to determine guilt or innocence, and then to impose the legislatively prescribed punishment if guilt was determined, no more or less.

All of these as well as other reforms advocated by Beccaria had a common theme: to make the criminal justice system fair and standardized. With these qualities, Beccaria argued that crimes could be deterred to the maximum degree. He based this conclusion on the assumption that humans were, by and large, reasoning beings whose actions were guided primarily by weighing the most likely costs and benefits of their actions.

Jeremy Bentham.   At least an equally prominent figure in the classical school of criminology was the British lawyer and philosopher, **Jeremy Bentham** (1748–1832). Bentham supported the basic reforms of criminal law advocated by Beccaria, and wrote extensive critiques of the need for English judicial reform.[50]

Bentham's most widely read book, **Principles of Morals and Legislation** (1789), advocates a philosophy of social control based on what he called the **principle of utility**. This guiding principle was for government to seek to obtain "the greatest happiness for the greatest number." The principle of utility posits that human actions should be judged as moral or immoral according to their effects on the happiness of the majority comprising a civilized society.[51] Thus, the proper function of the legislature was to promulgate laws aimed at maximizing the pleasure and minimizing the pain of the largest number in society.[52]

If legislators are to formulate laws according to the principle of utility, they must understand human motivation, which Bentham summarized as follows: "Nature has placed mankind under the governance of two sovereign masters, pain and pleasure. It is for them alone to point out what we ought to do, as well as to determine what we shall do."[53] Bentham believed that the punishments imposed for crime must be severe and certain enough to insure than no rational being would choose to commit crime.

Cartographic Criminology

Even though the classical school of criminology had a great deal to say about how to reduce crime, it avoided identifying any underlying causes of crime other than to maintain that it occurs whenever the benefits resulting from an offense are perceived as exceeding the ill consequences. While such an assertion would be hard to disprove, it has not been considered a sufficient explanation, especially for crimes that seem to lack rational motivation (e.g., compulsive shoplifting and impulsive assaults). Others writing around the beginning of the 1800s began exploring other ways of understanding criminal behavior.

Adolpe Quetelet. One of these alternative ways was associated with looking for geographical patterns in criminal behavior. Scholars who frequently employ maps and other geographical information in their research are called **cartographers**, thus arose the **cartographic school of criminology.** Cartographic criminology was first championed by an unlikely Belgian named **Adolpe Quetelet** (1796–1874), unlikely because his training was in astronomy rather than in the social sciences. Despite his astronomy background, Quetelet became fascinated by social statistics, including those that had begun to accumulate based on arrest, trial, and imprisonment records throughout Belgium and elsewhere in Renaissance Europe.

Quetelet spent much of his professional career analyzing and interpreting these statistics. As will be mentioned in Chapter 5, he was the first to document gender and age variations in criminal behavior. Gradually, Quetelet offered a theory to explain these and other patterns that he had discovered through his analyses of early crime statis-

tics. What Quetelet proposed was that criminal behavior reflected some yet-to-be-discovered natural laws of collective human behavior, much as the movement of heavenly bodies all seemed to be ruled by natural laws, many of which could be described with mathematic equations. While Quetelet's theoretical ideas are not found in modern criminology, his basic findings, particularly in the area of various demographic correlates of crime, continue to be confirmed.

So influential was Quetelet's research that some writers have credited him with being the founder of criminology.[54] However, we will see that most historians of criminology have bestowed this honor on someone else.

Andre-Michel Guerry. A second prominent contributor to the cartographic school was a French lawyer named **Andre-Michel Guerry** (1802–1866). Writing at the same time as Quetelet, Guerry meticulously shaded maps of various regions of France according to their crime rates. He was the first person known to objectively test the hypotheses that crime was most prevalent among the poor and uneducated. Surprisingly, his analysis suggested that in fact crime (most of which was property crime) was actually most prevalent in the wealthiest regions in France, and that violent crime rates were highest in regions of France where citizens had the highest average levels of education.[55] While his analyses have not been entirely confirmed by subsequent research (discussed in Chapter 6), they are still noteworthy for having paved the way for objectively addressing questions that had earlier received little scientific attention.

Positivist Criminology

In the early-to-mid-nineteenth century, a new approach to the study of human behavior and societies began taking shape. This approach, call **positivism,** was most fully articulated by a French philosopher named **Auguste Comte** (1798–1857).[56]

Comte was what you might call a "grand theorist" in the sense that he had very broad interests and sought to develop an overall understanding of human nature. In his writings, Comte proposed that human intellectual history could be described in terms of three stages. The first stage was a long period of time during which nearly all explanations for human existence were rooted in superstition and religion. The second stage was what Comte called "rational understanding," in which logical reasoning and intuition guided our efforts to comprehend the meaning of life. In the third stage—which Comte called the **positivist stage**—understanding came primarily from applying the scientific method.[57]

Besides playing an instrumental role in formulating the school of thought known as positivism, Comte coined two concepts that are quite relevant to criminology: sociology and altruism. **Sociology** was the name given by Comte to the discipline that would scientifically study human social behavior and human societies. The main importance of sociology in the present context is that it is often considered the "umbrella discipline" under which criminology is subsumed.

You may recall that **altruism** refers to the tendency to be empathetic and self-sacrificing toward others. According to Comte, human societies would not be possible without most of its members being basically altruistic. Notice how different this assertion is from the assumption made by classical theorists that we are all acting in our own self-interest.

The Essence of Positivism.   As it pertains to human behavior, positivism can be thought of as a school of thought resting on three interrelated philosophical assumptions. One assumption is that human behavior is controlled entirely by natural forces.[58] This assumption is in opposition to the view that spiritual forces and free will control our behavior,[59] and is often called the assumption of **determinism.**[60]

The second assumption is that the primary way to achieve an understanding of human behavior is not through contemplation and introspection, but through recording and sharing scientific observations.[61] The process of carefully recording and sharing observations is central to positivist approaches to achieving knowledge.

Third, positivism assumes that as humankind pools its observations and thereby gradually comes to better understand the forces governing human actions, it will be able to collectively direct those actions toward constructive (or "positive") ends.[62] *Positive ends* were usually defined in terms of happiness for as many people as possible. Positivists saw science as playing an increasingly central role in guiding the destiny of humankind.

Positivism's Great Divide: Environmentalism versus Biological Interactionism.   Almost from its inception, a split began to appear within the ranks of positivism. One branch emphasized social environmental causes of human behavior, and the other asserted that biological factors and inherent individual differences also needed to be considered.[63] Nowhere did this positivist schism become more apparent than among the positivists who began specializing in the study of criminal behavior. Let us examine these two positivist factions in more detail.

Environmentalism.   The positivists who felt that only learned social environmental factors needed to be included to fully explained variations in criminal behavior have come to be known as **environmentalists.** In criminology, the most influential early environmentalists were members of the French School,[64] the most prominent of which were Lacassagne, Tarde, and Durkheim.

Antonine Lacassagne (*la cos' ne a*) (1843–1924) was a French physician who took exception to the suggestion that some people were just "born bad." Instead, Lacassagne proclaimed, "Les sociétés ont les criminels qu'elles méritent" (Societies have the criminals they deserve).[65] By this famous proclamation he brought attention to two points. First, societies define what crime is. Second, societies function in ways that provoke criminal behavior in some people more than in others. To Lacassagne, there was no need to assume that individual human beings vary in their propensities to engage in crime except in the sense that each person confronts different circumstances and performs different functions within a society.

Gabriel Tardé (*tar' day*) (1843–1904) was a French lawyer and sociologist. Like Lacassagne, he emphasized that social factors were sufficient to explain why crime varied from one society to another and why crime varied over time within each society. Tardé[66] contended that some people learn to engage in crime much as other people learn legitimate occupations and social customs. According to Tardé, criminal behavior is largely learned from what he called **laws of imitation.**[67] This meant that people imitate others with whom they have frequent contact essentially the same way people copy and come to prefer different styles of clothing.[68] As we will soon see, Tardé's proposals laid a cornerstone for criminological theories that developed decades later in the United States.[69]

Emile Durkheim (*dur' kem*) (1858–1917) was an important positivist who contributed to criminology primarily by speculating about societal variations in attempts to curtail criminal behavior. Durkheim contended that, as societies modernized, they tend to tolerate ever greater variability in behavior, and their forms of punishment become more humane (i.e., less violent).[70] Modernization, especially when linked to rapid social change, was likely to cause an increase in crime, according to Durkheim: Rapid social change brings about a state of what he called **anomie,** by which he meant a feeling of being alienated from any social group and cultural traditions. It was not until after Durkheim's death that anomie and other Durkheimian concepts became incorporated into the field of criminology, as we will see in Chapter 11.

It is also worth noting that Durkheim saw criminal behavior as being a necessary social evil on which societies impose punishments in order to set limits on the behavior of the majority and for the purpose of giving the majority a sense of being united against a common enemy.[72] In other words, without some people being apprehended and publicly punished for violating criminal statutes, the rest of us would not be in a position to know where the normative limits are for our own actions.

Environmental/Biological (E/B) Interactionism: The Italian School.   Around the same time that members of the French School were seeking to find social–environmental causes of crime, another type of positivism was taking shape in Italy.[73] The name given to this version of positivism has included such terms as **hereditarianism** and **biological determinism.**[74] Both of these terms imply that the positivists associated with the Italian School *only* consider biological causes of crime, which was not at all the case. A more apt term to describe the Italian School's version of positivism is **environmental/biological (E/B) interactionism,** because they explicitly envisioned biological and social–environmental factors interacting to affect the probability of criminal behavior.

Interactionists conceive of human behavior not as simply shaped by social learning and environmental circumstances, but as also influenced by individual differences of a biological nature. In other words, even when exposed to the same environment, some people would be more prone to engage in crime than others because their biological constitution was different. The relevant biological influences were of two types: *physical traits* and *cognitive/neurological* (also called *psychological*) traits. As we will see, positivists of the interactionist persuasion almost immediately began to splinter into those who emphasized evolved physical traits that might be linked to crime, and those who focused on cognitive/neurological traits.

Cesare Lombroso (*lam bro' so*) (1835–1909) is most famous for having argued that evolved physical traits are symptomatic of criminal tendencies. Lombroso was an Italian physician (reared in Spain) who spent much of his career tending to the medical needs of men incarcerated in military prisons. During these years, he became interested in Charles Darwin's[75] theory of evolution. (More will be said about Darwin's theory in Chapter 14.) Working from ideas he derived from evolutionary theory, Lombroso came to a novel proposal: Many criminals, he said, might be evolutionary "throwbacks" to more primitive forms of human life.[76] He called this idea **atavism,**[77] and set out to look for evidence among the numerous prisoners that he had been examining over the years. Lombroso concluded that roughly a third of all incarcerated criminals had atavistic physical traits, or what he came to call **stigmata.** These stigmata included such things as protruding brow ridges, twisted and flattish noses, unusually high cheekbones, asymmetrical facial features, long arms relative to the length of the trunk or legs, and an unusually large coccyx (tail bone).[78] He reasoned as follows: The human species is evolving both physically and culturally in ways that allow an ever-increasing mastery over nature. This mastery was being driven primarily by technology and industrialization, which was being fueled by increases in human intelligence and cooperation. However, not all people are evolving at the same rate. Many of those who are the most poorly adapted to the increasingly complex societies end up preying on other societal members. Fortunately, these atavistic individuals often exhibit telltale physical symptoms, called stigmata.

In general, Lombroso[79] believed that for most people who repeatedly committed serious crimes, evolved biological forces are at work, and that rehabilitation efforts for these individuals were not likely to be effective. For the sake of society as a whole, these individuals should be identified and separated from offenders who had a good chance of benefiting from reform efforts.

How has Lombroso's theory fared since it was first proposed in the late 1800s? In fact, not very well, even among his contemporaries.[80] Today, virtually no criminologists support Lombroso's atavism theory, although quite a few still subscribe to Lombroso's basic assumption that biological factors contribute to criminal behavior.

In light of the negative evidence pertaining to his theories, it might surprise you to learn that Lombroso is frequently credited with having been the founder of criminology.[81] How can this seeming contradiction be explained? The answer is that there was a distinctive scientific spirit in Lombroso's writings that set his efforts to understand crime apart from earlier writers.[82] Lombroso devoted little of his time to moralizing about crime, and focused on objectively trying to understand it. While his atavism theory has failed to hold up under the weight of current knowledge, and in fact has very little support among prominent criminologists, Lombroso was still influential in launching criminology as a fledgling scientific discipline. Also, despite the lack of support for his theory, many criminologists then, as now, subscribed to his overarching assumptions that a scientific approach is needed to understand criminal behavior.

Enrico Ferri (1856–1929), a lawyer and socialist legislator, is another famous member of the Italian School of criminology. Like Lombroso, Ferri believed that both biological and social–environmental factors were important for understanding criminal behavior.[83] His main contribution to the promotion of a positivist approach to criminology came from vigorously criticizing the classical doctrine of free will. Ferri argued that it was illogical to hold people responsible for behavior that was actually due to a combination of biological and social factors. Should we therefore not punish offenders? Ferri was opposed to the classical view that narrow limits should be set on the punishment of offenders for specific crimes. Instead, he advocated sentences that could be tailored primarily for the maximum

Cesare Lombruso.
(CORBIS/Beltman)

protection of society, which sometimes meant keeping individuals convicted of the same offenses in prison for different lengths of time.[84]

Rafael Garofalo (1852–1934), also an Italian lawyer and legislator, became a prominent spokesman for the Italian School of Criminology. Garofalo agreed with Lombroso that biological characteristics could help in the identification of serious and persistent criminals. However, Garofalo focused on the brain rather than the external facial and skeletal features, arguing, for example, that criminals had greater development in the rear portions of their brains and slighter development of the frontal regions.[85] In addition, Garofalo suggested that most of the deficiencies exhibited by criminals would ultimately involve "moral abnormalities" rather than physical abnormalities.

To make the study of criminal behavior more scientific, Garofalo emphasized the importance of distinguishing between offenses that were truly im-

moral and those that were merely contrary to accepted customs. Accordingly, he sought to develop what he called a "natural definition of crime."[86] His thoughts on this subject ranged over many complex issues, but much of what he concluded parallels the distinction made in Chapter 1 between crimes that are **mala in se** and **mala prohibita.**

In agreement with Ferri, Garofalo contended that the overriding purpose of criminal sanctions should be to provide protection for the law-abiding majority.[87] To accomplish this, Garofalo stated that the most vicious and persistent criminals should be executed, not because of the need to set an example to insure that others obey the law, but simply because hardened criminals were organically defective and beyond reform. Other criminals could be rehabilitated under proper social conditions, and it was the duty of penal authorities to help provide those conditions.

E/B Interactionism: The Anglo-American School. With his notion of an organic basis for moral reasoning, Garofalo set the stage for other positivists to begin emphasizing the importance of biologically based mental processes in criminal behavior. Among the most important of these was an English prison physician named **Charles Goring** (1870–1919). Goring undertook a study of over 3,000 English male convicts to determine if their physical characteristics matched those identified by Lombroso as atavistic. To help make this determination, Goring compared the offender population to groups of male university students and soldiers in the British army. Overall, Goring[88] found few significant physical differences between these three groups of men, and those that were found largely failed to match Lombroso's theory.

Even though his findings seriously undercut Lombroso's atavism theory, Goring fully accepted Lombroso's belief that biology was an important ingredient in crime causation.[89] Thus, despite his rejection of the idea of criminals being evolutionary throwbacks, two lines of evidence lead Goring to conclude that biology was important in crime causation. First, he found that criminality ran in families, which he interpreted as suggesting genetic influences. Second, criminality seemed to be

Raffaele Garofolo. (Reprinted by special permission of Northwestern University School of Law, *Journal of Criminal Law and Criminology.*)

associated with poor performance in educational settings, what Goring[90] called "defective intelligence." Goring believed that intelligence was substantially inherited,[91] but he had no way of directly testing his assumptions, mainly because IQ tests were just being developed in France at the time he published his ideas.[92]

Working on the heels of Goring was a U.S. psychologist named **Henry Goddard** (1866–1957). Goddard translated Alfred Binet's French test of intelligence into English and administered it to various groups of subjects in the United States. Based on a prison sample, Goddard[93] reached the conclusion that between one fourth and one half of U.S. prisoners were "mentally defective and incapable of managing their affairs with ordinary prudence." His conclusion was given some serious scholarly attention, although by the mid-1920s, it was called into question by a study that suggested that the average IQ score of U.S. prisoners was the same as that for the general U.S. population.[94]

As if his preliminary findings on IQ and criminality were not controversial enough, Goddard went on to propose that most hardened criminals should be sterilized in order to prevent their genes from being transmitted to future generations. Goddard's recommendation was bolstered by the writings of a U.S. anthropologist, named **Earnest Hooton** (1887–1954), who contended that most criminals were both physically and mentally deficient.[95]

Both Goddard and Hooton made their proposals regarding the need to sterilize hardened criminals as part of a social movement known as **eugenics.** This movement emphasized preventing individuals with undesirable genetic traits, such as genes thought to promote antisocial behavior, from having children. The popularity of the eugenics movement peaked in the 1920s and 1930s,[96] waning substantially after it was embraced in Germany under Adolf Hitler's Nazi regime.

Environmentalism: The Chicago School.   Beyond the 1930s, most of the theories to appear in criminology have focused on environmental variables. These will be the theories to be reviewed in the first three chapters of Part III. Many of the early proponents of these environmental theories were associated with the University of Chicago, either as professors or as graduate students. Probably the most distinctive feature of the Chicago School regarding the study of criminal behavior was a strong emphasis on social causes and solutions to the crime problem, and a rejection of any suggested biological predispositions.[97] In this respect the Chicago School built on the tradition of the earlier French School.

The most influential professors at the University of Chicago to specialize in studying criminal behavior from the mid-1920s through the 1940s were **Clifford Shaw** (1896–1957) and **Henry McKay** (1899–1980). Most of the data they collected and carefully analyzed was from the Chicago metropolitan area. In the tradition of Quetelet's cartographic school, Shaw and McKay created maps of how crime varied geographically. Among their most enduring findings was that crime rates tend to be highest in Chicago's central business district, and then gradually diminish as one moves farther and farther out toward the suburbs.[98] Shaw and McKay[99] also found evidence that neighborhood social disorganization, as evidenced by ethnic diversity and high rates of geographical mobility, was associated with high rates of crime and delinquency. We will explore the evidence for these and other "ecological correlates" of crime in Chapter 6.

The most famous graduate of the Chicago Department of Sociology to specialize in criminology was **Edward Sutherland** (1883–1950). Early in his career, Sutherland[100] sharply criticized those who argued that criminals were of low intelligence. He went on to publish a criminology textbook[101] that eventually became the most widely used text in the field for more than two decades. In his text, Sutherland put forth one of the most influential theories of his time, a theory called **differential association theory** (the specifics of his theory will be presented in Chapter 11). Even though Sutherland was as much of a positivist as Lombroso, he adamantly opposed the view that biological factors were responsible for people's varying tendencies to engage in criminal behavior.[102] Instead, Sutherland proposed that environmental factors similar to those first suggested by Tardé (involving learning within a sociocultural context) were the main causes of criminal behavior. Sutherland is undoubtedly one of the most influential figures in U.S. criminology.[103]

Environmentalism: The Socialist School. Because crime is ultimately defined in the political arena of each society, it is not surprising to find that people's varying political philosophies often become intertwined with how they explain crime. In fact, we noted earlier in this chapter that persons with left-wing political views are more apt to identify economic inequality as a major cause of crime than are persons with right-wing political leanings.

One criminologist from the Netherlands became a prominent spokesman for the view that the main causes of crime reside in the unequal distribution of wealth and worldly goods. His name is **Willem Bonger** (1876–1940). Bonger[104] published a book in which he argued that, because of capitalism's emphasis on greed and selfishness, it creates the political and philosophical climate within which crime flourishes. We will explore Bonger's views further in Chapter 12.

On the eve of Nazi Germany's invasion of the Netherlands, Bonger mailed a letter to his son in which he wrote, "I don't see any future for myself and I cannot bow to this scum which will now overmaster us." Later that evening, he committed suicide.

SUMMARY

This chapter on the underpinnings of criminological theorizing began by examining what surveys indicate "the man on the street" believes to be the main causes of crime and delinquency. The second portion of the chapter explored the history of criminology, particularly as it pertains to the earliest attempts to develop theories of criminal behavior.

Results from Opinion Surveys

To date, nearly all of these surveys have been conducted in the United States and Britain. Working in terms of eight causal categories, we noted that the most frequently mentioned cause by most people in both countries has been family factors, particularly parental discipline and supervision. However, there may have been a slight shift away from this view in the United States since the 1980s toward a greater emphasis on economic factors and factors having to do with the severity of criminal sanctions.

Other generalizations drawn from public opinion polls is that females are somewhat more likely to attribute crime and delinquency to family factors than are males, as are adults when compared to teenagers. Political philosophy has been found to have a substantial bearing on how people explain crime, with those on the left wing of the political spectrum being more likely to attribute crime to social and economic factors such as racial discrimination and poverty. Right-wingers, on the other hand, are more likely to attribute crime to local institutional factors (such as lack of education), family factors (such as poor parenting), and character flaws (such as lack of respect for others).

Little can be said about what people believed were the causes of crime prior to the 1940s, although a couple of historians of the eighteenth century have asserted that most writers during that time primarily emphasized family and economic causes. If so, one would have to conclude that, at least in Western societies, people's opinions about the causes of crime have remained fairly stable for at least a century.

A recent survey of criminologists found that they too emphasize family and socioeconomic factors as the primary causes of criminal and delinquent behavior. Basically, as the seriousness and persistence of offenses increase, criminologists shift away from family-based explanations to socioeconomic explanations. For persons affiliated with the criminal justice system, such as police and corrections officers, the most common explanations of crime are again in terms of family and economic factors, with secondary importance given to character flaws. So far, only one study has ever asked criminals themselves what they think causes crime. This British study found that prisoners were considerably more likely than people in general to attribute crime to unjust societal factors and "bad luck."

The History of Criminology

Criminology has had a rich and controversial history. The discipline began to emerge during the European Renaissance, particularly the age of Enlightenment in the late 1700s (eighteenth century). At that time, strictly natural (as opposed to supernatural) explanations began to be offered for everything from the origins of the universe to the behavior of human beings.

The Classical School.   The writings of such theorists as Cesare Beccaria and Jeremy Bentham were primarily aimed toward reforming the criminal justice system rather than being intended as a scientific explanation for criminal behavior. However, implicit in their proposals was the view that humans were essentially rational beings who freely chose to obey or violate criminal statutes after weighing the costs and benefits of their choices. This gave rise to what has come to be called the Classical School of criminology.

The Cartographic School.   In the early 1800s, a more empirically oriented approach to criminology emerged amidst the availability of European crime statistics that allowed scholars to look for geographic and demographic variations. Under the leadership of Adolpe Quetelet emerged the Cartographic School. Quetelet was the first to document that serious criminal behavior was substantially more prevalent among males than among females, and that criminality was heavily concentrated in the second and third decades of life.

A philosophical perspective arose in the early 1800s that eventually had a major impact on the study of criminal behavior. This perspective, called **positivism,** envisioned science being instrumental in helping to create a social climate in which humans would evolve toward increasingly intelligent and civil creatures. Positivism was most forcefully espoused by August Comte, who also coined the important concept of **altruism** and contended that a new science was needed to study human social behavior and to use what was learned to guide humanity in its future evolution. (This discipline was to be called **sociology,** often considered the umbrella discipline under which criminology is subsumed.)

Positivism.   Almost from its inception, the positivist movement began to split along two recognizable branches. On one branch were the environmentalists. They argued that all of the variables that were important for understanding human behavior were social and learning in nature. Those who pursued the alternative branch took the position that genetic/evolutionary/biological factors were also important for understanding human behavior. They are called E/B **interactionists.**

The French School.   By around the middle of the 1800s, some of those working from a positivist perspective began taking an interest in studying criminal behavior. The first to do so are said to be members of the French School of criminology. Most prominent among them were Antonine Lacassagne, Gabriel Tardé, and Emile Durkheim (although Durkheim's interests in criminal behavior were fairly secondary to other sociological interests). Theoretical proposals from these environmentalists included the idea that crime was socially defined and that it was likewise socially determined.

The Italian School.   Paralleling the emergence of the French School was the Italian School, headed by Cesare Lombroso. Lombroso asserted that evolved physical traits could be used to identify individuals who have a biological propensity to commit crime. Joining Lombroso in forming the Italian School were Enrico Ferri and Rafael Garofalo. While they agreed about the importance of biological factors in influencing criminal behavior, their writings emphasized other issues. Ferri spent most of his efforts criticizing the Classical School, and suggesting ways of professionalizing the criminal justice system in ways that recognized the deterministic aspects of human behavior. Garofalo developed a logical/legalist foundation on which to view crime in "naturalistic" terms, rather than in religious or strictly cultural terms.

Criminology in the Early Twentieth Century. By the end of the 1800s, individuals from several countries had begun to study criminal behavior from a positivist perspective. Those who followed the E/B interactionist approach primarily included British and U.S. social scientists with an interest in the evidence linking intelligence and criminality, most notably Charles Goring, Henry Goddard, and Earnest Hooton. Their work led to suggestions that criminals should be prevented from passing their genes on to future generations through sterilization. These ideas became part of a movement whose popularity peaked in the 1920s and 1930s, known as **eugenics.**

Those who subscribed to the environmentalist branch of positivism split into various subfactions, the most prominent of which were members of the Chicago School, particularly Clifford Shaw, Henry McKay, and Edward Sutherland. The other split was lead by Willem Bonger, and came to be known as **socialist criminology.**

SUGGESTED READINGS

Council of Europe (Ed.). (1979). *Public Opinion on Crime and Criminal Justice.* Strasbourg, Sweden: European Committee on Crime Problems (Collected Studies in Criminological Research, Vol. XVII). (This collection of chapters gives valuable coverage to several topics pertaining to how public opinion affects and is affected by the functioning of the criminal justice system.)

Jacoby, Joseph E. (Ed.). (1994). *Classics of criminology (2nd ed).* Prospect Heights, IL: Waveland. (Provides excerpts from the writings of over fifty historical figures in criminology.)

Beirne, Piers (1993). *Inventing criminology.* Albany, NY: SUNY Press. (A clearly written account of criminology's early history.)

Mannheim, Hermann (Ed.). (1973). *Pioneers in criminology.* London: Stevens. (A useful source for detailed information about criminology's vibrant history.)

Vold, George B., Bernard, Thomas J., and Snipes, Jeffery B. (1998). *Theoretical criminology (4th edition).* New York: Oxford University Press. (An informative standard text, useful for exploring the history of criminology and how that history gave rise to contemporary criminological theories.)

EXERCISES

1. Either in the library or through the World Wide Web, do a search for *criminology* and then a subsearch for one of the historical figures mentioned in this chapter. Based on information you find, write a one- to two-page summary of this historical figure's background and views on the causes of and/or cures for crime. Focus on aspects of this person's life and views that were not given attention in the present chapter.

2. Make up a brief (one-page) questionnaire in which you ask people what they believe are the main causes of delinquency and crime. Administer the questionnaire

to at least ten people, either by interview or by having them completeing the questionnaire themselves. Analyze the results to see if your percentages are at all similar to what was reported in Table 4.1. You might also look for any evidence of gender differences in the way your subjects answered your questions. Present a table with your findings, and write a one-page double-spaced narrative about what you found.

ENDNOTES

1. Erskine 1974b:289.
2. Hollin & Howells 1987; Pfeffer et al. 1996.
3. McGarrell & Flanagan 1985:204.
4. Banks et al. 1975:238.
5. Banks et al. 1975:238.
6. Hollin & Howells 1987:206.
7. MORI 1994.
8. Fernham & Alison 1994:41.
9. Erskine 1974b:289.
10. Erskine 1974b:290.
11. Erskine 1974b:290.
12. Erskine 1974b:291.
13. Erskine 1974b:293.
14. Banks et al. 1975:239.
15. Gallup 1973: 1814.
16. Reiderman 1978.
17. Press 1981:47.
18. Shriver 1989:23.
19. Shriver 1989:23.
20. Stalans & Lurigio 1990:340.
21. Campbell & Muncer 1990:415.
22. J. Johnson 1997:10.
23. Abrams et al.1987:406.
24. Pfeffer et al.1996.
25. Hollins & Howells 1987:206.
26. Furnham & Henderson 1983:115; Reuterman 1978.
27. Banks et al. 1975; Reuterman & Durbin 1988.
28. Reuterman 1978.
29. Barlow 1993:26; Furnham & Alison 1994:36; Furnham & Henderson 1983:115.
30. Eysenck 1951; Eysenck & Wilson 1978; Henningham 1996; Sidanius et al. 1983; Wilson & Patterson 1968.
31. Rokeach 1979.
32. Truett 1993.
33. Barlow 1993:26; Furnham & Henderson 1983:115; Ortet-Fabergat & Perez 1992.
34. Furnham & Henderson 1983:115.
35. T. L. Davis et al. 1993.
36. Gulliot 1943; McKelvey 1977:74.
37. Thompson 1968:249.
38. Rock 1979:78.
39. Ortet-Fabregat & Perez 1992.
40. Fielding & Fielding 1991; Goff & Kim 1987; Kennedy & Homant 1986;
41. Ellis & Hoffman 1990:53.
42. Jacobs 1978; Ortet-Fabregat & Perez 1992.
43. Furnham & Alison 1994:41.
44. Stalans & Lurigio 1990:340.
45. Hurwitz & Christensen 1983:22.
46. Gabrielli & Mednick 1983:70.
47. Masters & Roberson 1990:55; Odum 1927:494.
48. Masters & Roberson 1990:84.
49. Beccaria 1963:8.
50. Jones 1986:63.
51. Bentham 1948:127.
52. Bentham 1948:151.
53. Bentham 1948:125.
54. Beirne 1993; Hurwitz & Christensen; 1983:22; Lindesmith & Levin 1937.
55. Beirne 1993:120–127.
56. Lenzer 1997; Masters & Roberson 1990:103.
57. Jeffery 1973:467.
58. Gillespie 1979:8; Masters & Roberson 1990:203.
59. Hirschi & Gottfredson 1994:259.
60. Jeffery 1973:473.
61. Park and Burgess 1921:v
62. Becker & Barnes 1961:501.
63. Lengermann 1974:57.
64. Hurwitz & Christiansen 1983:28.
65. Buikhuisen & Mednick 1988:4.
66. Tarde 1890, 1907.
67. Kinnunen 1996:432; Wilson 1954:5.
68. Tarde 1890:332.

69. Wilson 1954:3.
70. Vold et al. 1998:132.
71. Vold et al. 1998:140.
72. Hurwitz & Christiansen 1983:28.
73. Sutherland & Cressey 1966:56.
74. Adler et al. 1991:57.
75. Darwin 1859.
76. Buikhuisen & Mednick 1988:3.
77. Ferracuti 1996.
78. Ferracuti 1996:136; Lombroso-Ferrero 1972:10–21.
79. Lombroso 1911:376.
80. Adler et al. 1998:56.
81. Flowers 1988:58; Wilson & Herrnstein 1985:74.
82. Wolfgang 1973.
83. Adler et al. 1998:56.
84. Sellin 1968.
85. Allen 1954:379.
86. Allen 1954:379.
87. Ancel 1987.
88. Goring 1913:173.
89. Gilsinan 1990:110; Vold & Bernard 1986:87.
90. Goring 1913:26.
91. Empey 1982:165.
92. Ferentz 1954:300.
93. Goddard 1914:6.
94. Murchison 1926.
95. Hooton 1939:308.
96. Ellis et al. 1988.
97. Knottnerus & Maguire 1995:27.
98. Bullock 1955:567; Shaw 1929:99.
99. Shaw & McKay 1942.
100. Sutherland 1931.
101. Sutherland 1934.
102. Jeffery 1973:491.
103. Masters & Roberson 1990:202.
104. Bonger 1905.

PART TWO

Correlates of Crime

The next five chapters are designed to familiarize you with what have come to be called *correlates of crime*.[1] Knowing the nature of these correlates will give you an objective basis for judging the relative merit of theories of criminal/antisocial behavior that will be presented in Part III of this text.

WHAT IS A CORRELATE OF CRIME?

When researchers say that a variable is a correlate of crime, they mean that studies have repeatedly shown this variable to have a particular type of statistical correlation (or relationship) with criminal/antisocial behavior. The two most common types of relationships are called *positive* and *negative*. The differences between them are illustrated by the four *scattergrams* in Figure II.1. A **scattergram** is simply a graph that shows how two separate variables are related to one another. The points in a scattergram are used to represent subjects (or other sampling units such as cities or states).

Let us briefly describe each of the four graphs in Figure II.1, beginning with Graph A. Notice that this graph has a distinct absence of points in the upper left and the lower right. This means that subjects who score high on Variable Y also tend to score high on Variable X. Such a pattern is said to reflect a positive relationship (or positive correlation). If all of the points were packed together more tightly, ultimately collapsing onto a straight line, it would be considered a strong correlation. Given that the points are quite dispersed, the correlation would be considered weak.

In contrast, Graph B shows a different pattern. Notice that here the absence of points are located in the lower left and the lower right. Such a pattern means that individuals who score high on Variable Y score low on Variable X. This type of pattern is said to reflect a negative (or inverse) relationship.

Now, consider Graph C. In this graph, the points are located more or less evenly throughout the entire scattergram (like a shotgun blast). This sort of pattern is said to reflect the absence of a relationship between the variables involved.

Finally, notice that a still different pattern is represented in Graph D. Unlike in Graphs A and B, the best fitting line would not be straight; instead, it would be curved. The set of points in this graph would be described as **curvilinear** rather than linear. Curvilinear relationships are relatively rare, but as we will see, they do sometimes appear in criminological research.

Using various formulas, researchers are able to represent scattergrams with numbers ranging from 1.00 (an extremely strong positive correlation) to a −1.00 (an extremely

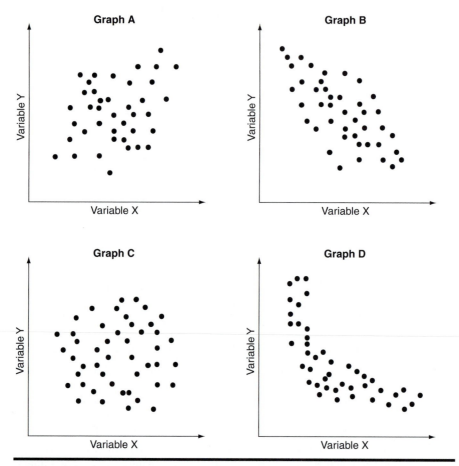

FIGURE II.1   Four hypothetical scattergrams illustrate the concept of correlation.
Graph A represents a modest positive correlation; Graph B, a slightly stronger negative
(inverse) correlation; Graph C, the absence of a correlation; and Graph D, a fairly
strong curvilinear correlation.

strong negative correlation), with 0.00 being the complete absence of a correlation. These
numbers are called *coefficients*. Then, scientists can calculate the probability of a specific
coefficient being the result of chance after taking into account the size of the sample.
When the chances that a coefficient is due to chance are 5 percent or lower, it is said to be
statistically significant.

To find out more on these rules and procedures, you should consult a statistics text or
take a course in statistics. To read the next five chapters, it is not necessary for you to understand these statistical procedures; you only need to be aware of them and that they underlie what scientists mean when they say significant relationships exist between variables.

CRITERIA USED IN ASSESSING CORRELATES OF CRIME

As you will see, not all criminological research is in agreement about whether a particular variable is associated with criminality. Disagreement is especially likely to occur in the case of studies based on small samples (e.g., less than 100 subjects). Other disagreements may arise because of different ways the variables being studied were measured, or differences in where the research was conducted (e.g., some relationships may hold in some countries but not in others).

Throughout the upcoming chapters on correlates of crime, five levels of designation will be used: well-established correlate, established correlate, probable correlate, possible correlate, and unestablished correlate.

In order for a variable to be considered as fitting into any of these five categories, we stipulated that there must have been at least five relevant studies. Based on these five or more studies, we used the findings from each study to calculate a "consistency score." This score was derived simply by dividing the number of studies in the most frequently reported direction by the total number of studies. The only qualification was that if one or more studies suggested the exact opposite of what most of the studies indicated, we added the number of these studies twice to the total number of studies.

Here is a hypothetical example: Say that forty studies have been undertaken to determine if criminals have some trait (Trait X) to a greater degree than do people in general. Let us assume that thirty-four of these forty studies found a significantly higher proportion of criminals with Trait X relative to persons in the general population, and that five of the remaining six studies found no significant difference, and one study actually found criminals with significantly *less* of Trait X than the general population. To calculate a consistency score for this variable, 34 would be divided by 41, yielding an 83 percent consistency score.

The five categorical levels that we designated for the consistency scores appear in the following table:

Categorical Levels	Consistency Criteria
Well-established correlate	95–100% consistency
Established correlate	85–94% consistency
Probable correlate	70–84% consistency
Possible correlate	50–69% consistency
Unestablished correlate	Below 50% consistency

Thus, for the hypothetical example just presented, a consistency score of 83 percent would mean that Trait X would be a *probable correlate of crime.*

ORGANIZATION AND LAYOUT OF THE EVIDENCE

Because the number of studies that will be reviewed in the next five chapters is massive, most of the findings have been condensed into tables, each accompanied by brief narratives.

The tables will give you a bird's eye view of the strength of the scientific evidence and the countries in which the studies were conducted. Nevertheless, you should note that many details and qualifications are omitted in order to maintain a focus on the overall patterns. If details contain a key for properly interpreting how certain variables are correlated with criminality, we discuss these in the narrative about a particular table. Your instructor may mention additional details that he/she will want to bring out with reference to some of the variables to be explored.

Nearly all of the tables follow a similar format. Across the top are identified five different types of official statistics: violent offenses, property offenses, drug offenses, delinquency, and general and undifferentiated offenses (the latter pertains mainly to adults). The next two columns refer to self-report data, which, you will recall from Chapter 2, usually focuses on less serious offenses than is true of official data. One self-report column pertains to offenses in general, and the other is restricted to drug offenses. The last two columns in each table pertain to clinical diagnoses, one for childhood conduct disorders and the other for adult (or older adolescent) antisocial personality disorders. Omitted from the tables are citations specifically to sex offenses, corporate/white-collar crime, serial/mass murder, and organized crime and terrorism, because these special categories of offenses are given focused attention in Part IV of this text.

In each table, research findings are represented according to the countries in which the studies were conducted. The countries are subsumed under the following seven broad geographical regions: Africa, Asia, Europe, the Middle East, North America, South-Central America and Caribbean, and the Pacific. (Note that data specific for Hawaii were listed under *Pacific* rather than *North America*. Also, Mexico is subsumed under *South-Central America and Caribbean* rather than *North America*. Japan and Taiwan are listed under *Asia* rather than *Pacific*.)

As mentioned in the preface, there is a supplement to this text that presents the expanded tables with the actual citations and references. All that is indicated in the text's tables is an indication of the number of studies and the countries within which these studies were conducted.

Finally, note that for aesthetic reasons, information in the tables pertaining to the overall nature of the findings are arranged so that the cells with the largest number of studies appear above those containing the fewest number of studies. This means that in several cases cells pertaining to negative relationships will be listed ahead of those pertaining to positive relationships.

WHAT CHAPTERS 5 THROUGH 9 WILL *NOT* DO

An important point to make about the upcoming five chapters is that they do not address the very important question of *why* correlates of criminality exist. As you read these chapters, feel free to speculate about what those causes might be. However, refrain from settling on firm conclusions in this regard. This is because offering explanations is primarily the function of theories, and these will not be explored until we begin Part III of this text. The logic behind this organization is that knowledge of these correlates of crime will put you in the best position for judging the relative merits of criminological theories.

VARIABLES TO BE COVERED IN EACH OF THE CORRELATES OF CRIME CHAPTERS

Most of the variables to be reviewed in Chapter 5 will pertain to things such as gender, age, race/ethnicity, and social status. Chapter 6 is devoted to research on ecological and macroeconomic variables and involvement in crime. In Chapter 7, the focus will be on the family and peer relationships. Chapter 8 takes up behavioral, intellectual, mental health, and attitudinal variables. Chapter 9 deals with a wide variety of biological factors that have been investigated regarding links to criminality. The purpose of these five chapters is to bring students of criminology up to speed on what close to a century of research has revealed with respect to variables that are (and are not) associated with criminal/antisocial behavior. These chapters set the stage for beginning to explore actual theories of criminality.

ENDNOTE_____

1. Bacon et al. 1963; Bartol 1980:212; Hartnagel 1987; Metfessel & Lovell 1942.

CHAPTER 5

Demographic Correlates of Crime and Crime Victimization

Do you think males or females are more likely to commit crime, or might the answer depend on which country or time period was being studied? Are the poor or the rich more involved in crimes, and where do middle-income people fall? Is criminal behavior more prevalent in some racial or ethnic groups than in others, or should criminologists even ask? What type of people are most likely to become crime victims, and who fears crime the most? Criminologists around the world have been conducting scientific research on questions like these for decades.

The purpose of this chapter is to summarize the accumulated wisdom of their efforts. In Part III of this text, you will be able to use what you learn in the chapters comprising Part II to evaluate specific theories of criminal/antisocial behavior.

Demographic variables are among the most widely studied variables in the social sciences. They include fundamental characteristics of human populations, most notably their gender (sex), age, race/ethnicity, and social status composition. This chapter will acquaint you with what criminologists know about the association between these variables and criminal/antisocial behavior.

As we explore these variables, keep in mind that just because someone possesses traits that happen to be associated with criminal behavior does not mean that he/she is necessarily involved in such behavior. In other words, while it is useful to be aware of the variables criminologists have found associated with crime, it is absolutely essential not to stereotype people on the basis of those findings. Statistical generalizations can only be meaningfully applied to large groups; they

should never be applied to individual members of a group.

Also worth bearing in mind is that some of the demographic variables that are linked to criminal behavior are also substantially linked to one another. For example, people with many years of education tend to have higher incomes than those with few years of education. If both education and income are associated with involvement in crime (which you will see is usually the case), one is left to wonder how much of the relationship between income and crime is simply the result of income being related to education. Researchers have special statistical methods (called *multivariate statistics*) that they use to "pull apart" many of these covariations in order to get a handle on which are the strongest and most fundamental links. The results of these statistical techniques will be given more attention in the chapters dealing with theories of crime.

DEMOGRAPHIC CORRELATES OF CRIME

The first systematic attempt to link demographic variables to variations in criminal behavior was undertaken by the nineteenth-century Belgian astronomer, L. A. J. Quetelet.[1] Quetelet became intrigued by various arrest and imprisonment data that he was able to locate from European governments of his day, and devoted much of his life to statistically analyzing these data. The most common variables contained in the data that Quetelet analyzed pertained to the age and gender (sex) of persons arrested and incarcerated. From the data he examined, Quetelet was struck by how age and sex were associated with crime in consistent ways for all of the countries he examined. As we will see, the regularities he observed persist to the present day.

Gender (Sex)

In keeping with the recent practice of referring to males and females with the term *gender* instead of *sex,* what does the research show regarding gender differences in criminal/antisocial behavior? Overall, the answer is simple: Throughout the world, males have been found to be more involved in criminal activities than females.[2] The more serious and persistent the criminality, the more males tend to dominate in the commission of the offenses.[3] This is not to say that there are no female criminals (there are plenty by whatever measure is used), but simply that their contribution is always less than 50 percent, and, as seriousness of the offenses increases, the proportional contribution being made by females nearly always drops.

Gender is the most thoroughly documented correlate of criminal behavior that has ever been identified.[4] By looking at Table 5.1a, you will see that literally hundreds of studies have reported gender differences in criminal behavior throughout the world, and that they are all but unanimous in indicating that males are more criminal than females. It is fascinating to note that several of these studies extend back five or six centuries into European countries, most notably England.[5]

There are a few studies referenced in Table 5.1a that have failed to find significant gender differences in offending rates, but notice that they are all studies based on self-reports. You should recall that self-reported offending often concentrates on exceedingly trivial offenses (e.g., minor shoplifting and status offenses), where in fact there appear to be few gender differences.

Overall, the consistency score for gender differences in criminal/antisocial behavior was over 96 percent, making it a well-established correlate of crime. If self-report studies are excluded, the consistency score is close to 100 percent.

To be sure, the degree to which males dominate in the commission of crime varies considerably, depending on the types and seriousness of offenses involved and the time and country being studied.[6] Nevertheless, it is fair to generalize that the more serious the offense, the more males tend to dominate in their commission. Thus, males are especially high in their commission of assaults resulting in serious injury or death, with their rates of involvement exceeding female rates by four- or five-to-one.[7] For strictly felony-level offenses, the sex differences often surpass seven-to-one.[8] Similarly, throughout the world roughly three fourths of all murderers are males. If killings and other assaults that have some element of self-defense are excluded, the proportion of offenders who are male is at least five or six times greater than the proportion who are female.

In addition to the evidence summarized by Table 5.1a, victimization survey data have been used to determine the gender of offenders. For certain victimful offenses—assaults, robberies, and purse snatching—victims often see their assailant. Their recollections have confirmed that it is predominantly males that commit these offenses, both in the United States[9] and in Canada.[10] Thus, the overrepresentation of males in arrest and conviction data cannot be attributed to a bias on the part of the criminal justice system.

TABLE 5.1a. Relationship between gender and criminal/antisocial behavior (overall consistency score = 94.4%; established correlate, consistency score with self-reports excluded = 99.2%).

Gender with the Greater Involvment	Type and Seriousness of Offenses								Antisocial Clinical Conditions	
	Official Statistics						Self-Reported Offenses			
	Violent Offenses	Property Offenses	Drug Offenses	Delinquency	General & Unspecified Offenses	Recidivism	Victimful & Overall Offending	Illegal Drug Use	Conduct Disorders	Antisocial Personality
Males more criminal or antisocial	**Africa** *Nigeria:* 2; *Egypt:* 1 **Asia** *India:* 3 **Europe** *Denmark:* 1; *England:* 3; *Finland:* 2; *Germany:* 2; *Iceland:* 1; *Scotland:* 1; *Sweden:* 2 **Middle East** *Israel:* 1 **North America** *Canada:* 4; *United States:* 25 **Pacific** *Australia:* 1; *Japan:* 1; *New Zealand:* 1 **South Central American Caribbean** *Brazil:* 1 **Other** *Various Preliterate Societies:* 6; *Various Preindustrial Countries:* 6	**Europe** *Denmark:* 2; *England:* 1; *Germany:* 1 **North America** *Canada:* 3; *United States:* 10 **Pacific** *New Zealand:*1 **Other** *Several Preindustrial Countries:* 1	**Asia** *China:* 1; *Taiwan:* 2; **North America** *United States:* 3 **Pacific** *New Zealand:* 1	**Asia** *India:* 1 **Europe** *England:* 11; *Finland:* 3; *Norway:* 2; *Poland:* 1; *Spain:* 1; *Sweden:* 3 **North America** *Canada:* 3; *United States:* 37 **Pacific** *Hawaii:* 4	**Africa** *Ghana:* 1; *Several countries:* 4 **Asia** *Japan:* 1; *India:* 4; *Former Soviet Union:* 3; *Taiwan:* 1 **Europe** *England:* 10; *Finland:* 1; *Germany:* 1; *Hungary:* 1; *Italy:* 1; *Scotland:* 1; *Sweden:* 2; *Several European Countries:* 2 **North America** *Canada:* 2; *United States:* 29 **South-Central America & Caribbean** *Argentina:* 2; *Venezuela:* 1 **Pacific** *Australia:* 2 **Other** *Several Industrial Countries:* 4	**Asia** *Japan:* 1 **Europe** *Italy:* 1 **North America** *United States:* 6 **Pacific** *Australia:* 2	**Asia** *India:* 1 **Europe** *Belgium:* 1 *England:* 5; *Ireland:* 1; *Italy:* 1; *Netherlands:* 1; *Spain:* 1; *Sweden:* 1 **Middle East** *Greece:* 1 **North America** *Canada:* 4; *United States:* 28; **Pacific** *Australia:* 4; *Hawaii:* 1; *New Zealand:* 1	**Europe** *Belgium:* 1; *England:* 1; *Germany:* 1; *Italy:* 1; *Spain:* 1; *Switzerland:* 1 **Middle East** *Greece:* 1 **North America** *Canada:* 11; *United States:* 24 **Pacific** *Australia:* 1	**Asia** *China:* 2 **Europe** *England:* 7; *Finland:* 2; *Sweden:* 1; *Netherlands:* 2; *Norway:* 2 **North America** *Canada:* 6; *United States:* 20 **Pacific** *New Zealand:* 1	**Europe** *Denmark:* 3; *Sweden:* 1 **Middle East** *Israel:* 1 **North America** *Canada:* 3; *United States:* 13 **Pacific** *New Zealand:* 1
No significant gender difference						**North America** *United States:* 5		**Europe** *Germany:* 1 **North America** *Canada:* 1; *United States:* 10		
Females more criminal or antisocial								**Europe** *Finland:* 1 **North America** *United States:* 1		

Regarding illegal drug use, all official data indicate that males are more likely to be involved than are females. However, as you can see in Table 5.1a, several self-report studies of illegal drug use found no significant gender differences or actually found females more involved than males. Overall, a safe conclusion seems to be that, throughout the world, males are more likely to use illegal drugs than are females, unless one includes prescription drugs and/or brief experimentation with "light" recreational drugs such as marijuana.

Qualifications

There are five notable qualifications to the generalization that males are more criminal than females. First, in the case of minor thefts, particularly shoplifting, the differences between male and female offending are often minor.

Second, females actually commit more of a few specific types of victimless crimes than do males. These offenses include incorrigibility, prostitution, and running away from home.[11] Also, as shown in Table 5.1a, there are several studies of

drug offenses that have found no significant gender differences, and a few others that have actually found females using drugs more than males; most of these studies have been confined to the use of marijuana.[12] Nevertheless, all studies of a broad spectrum of victimless offenses have concluded that males surpass females in probabilities of offending.

Third, not reflected in Table 5.1a are the results of studies of self-reported violence among dating and married people, at least some of which would be classified as criminal assaults. Instead, studies of gender differences in these two forms of violence are shown in Table 5.1b. The results are divided into all forms of dating and domestic violence and only those forms that are considered "serious," meaning that the assault caused injuries sufficient to require medical treatment.

As you can see, in the case of all instances of dating and domestic violence, there is either no significant gender difference, or males are actually more likely to be the victims of such violence than females. This finding may not ring true to anyone familiar with the fact that nearly all domestic vio-

TABLE 5.1b.   Gender differences in dating violence and domestic violence (spouse abuse) (P = gender of perpetrator; V = gender of victim).

Types of Violence		Type of Violence	
		Dating	**Domestic (Spousal)**
All types regardless of seriousness	Male perpetrators/Female victims more common		
	No significant gender difference	**Europe** *England:* 1 **North America** *United States:* 6	**Europe** *England:* 1 **North America** *United States:* 5
	Female perpetrators/Male victims more common	**North America** *United States:* 6	**North America** *United States:* 1
Serious violence only	Males significantly more involved	**North America** *United States:* 5	**North America** *United States:* 2
	No significant gender difference		
	Females significantly more involved		

lence shelters are for women. In other words, if males are as likely to be victimized by domestic violence as women, why would nearly all spouse abuse shelters be for women?

One can at least partially account for the seeming inconsistency by noting the findings in regard to serious dating and domestic assaults. There, the pattern is the opposite: Males are more likely to be perpetrators and females are more likely to be victims. In other words, while there appears to be little gender difference in the overall tendency to engage in dating and domestic assaults, in the case of assaults causing serious injury, males are more likely to be perpetrators.[13] This, of course, is consistent with the bulk of the studies listed for violent crimes in general.

Fourth, several studies have shown that the degree to which males dominate in criminal behavior is far less extreme in the case of self-reported offenses than in the case of official data.[14] Notice in Table 5.1a that this is especially so for drug offenses, where several recent self-report studies have failed to find a significant sex difference, and some studies have actually found higher self-reported illegal drug use among females than among males. The main qualifier to be made in the case of these studies is that they pertain to "ever use" especially among teenagers. If attention is given to sustained use, especially in adulthood, male use of illegal drugs has always been found to be higher than female use.[15] One indication of this comes from a U.S. study of deaths due to drug overdosing: Three-fourths of victims were males.[16]

This overall pattern of data suggests that sex differences in self-reported criminal behavior are considerably less male dominated than official data. Is it possible, therefore, that the police are biased against males in their arresting, prosecution, conviction, and imprisonment practices? Another possibility is that males are purposely under-reporting and/or females are over-reporting their criminal involvement. In fact, a third possibility appears to be primarily responsible for the over-representation of males in official data relative to self-report data. As mentioned in Chapter 2, those individuals and groups who are least involved in criminal behavior tend to be more diligent in self-reporting each and every instance of their involvement (however trivial) than those who are most heavily involved.

Shifting attention from criminal behavior to clinically diagnosed antisocial behavior, one also finds higher rates among males than among females. This holds true both for childhood conduct disorders and for psychopathy. Most studies have indicated that males are at least three times, and possibly up to five times, more likely to be diagnosed with conduct disorders than females, both in North America[17] and elsewhere.[18] Males also have a much earlier average age of onset for conduct disorders (around age seven) than girls (around age thirteen).[19]

Many clinicians distinguish between predominantly aggressive and nonaggressive forms of conduct disorders, the latter referring mainly to chronic disobedience. When this is done, males dominate primarily in the aggressive form of the disorder.[20]

In the case of psychopathy, males receive such a diagnosis between four and ten times more frequently than do females. Some clinicians have even suggested that psychopathy is virtually unknown among women, giving women a diagnosis of a condition with some similarities to psychopathy, called *Briquet's syndrome* (formerly called *hysteria*), instead.[21] Among the most common symptoms of Briquet's syndrome is flamboyant behavior, accompanied by ostentatious grooming and dress, extreme sexual promiscuity and very unstable marital relationships.[22] Normally absent from the classical symptoms of Briquet's syndrome is the extreme aggression, cruelty, and manipulativeness associated with psychopathy.

Before leaving the issue of gender differences in criminality, it is worth mentioning that a great deal of criminological attention has been directed in recent years toward identifying trends in the extent to which males dominate. In other words, while males are clearly more prone toward criminality than females, might there have been certain times when this was more or less true than it is today? The answer to this question appears to be yes, but the direction of change appears to be complex.

In a review of literature on gender differences in criminality for the United States, one research team found that the proportional involvement of females in crime and delinquency seems to have increased slightly during the decades of the 1960s and 1970s.[23] However, the researchers noted that, when examined in greater detail, all of the increases had to do with relatively trivial property offenses (e.g., shoplifting and other minor thefts), not with serious victimful crimes. As illustrated by trends in Canadian homicide conviction data since 1961, Figure 5.1 similarly suggests that this country has experienced no significant increase in the proportion of murders being perpetrated by females since the beginnings of the modern feminist movement in North America.[24] For serious property and especially for serious violent crimes, the proportional contribution of females seems not to have increased in either the United States or in Canada since the 1960s.

What if one were to go back even farther in time? Doing so with fairly reliable and comparable data is possible for a few Western European countries, particularly England, for several centuries. Figure 5.2 shows changes in the proportion of all criminal indictments and convictions that involved females between the late seventeenth century and the early twentieth century in England. Notice that there is a distinct *down*ward trend in the apparent contribution of females to crime in England throughout this 225-year time span.[25]

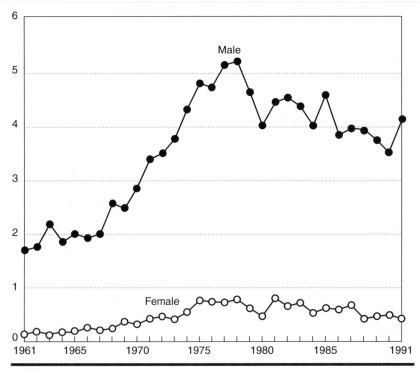

FIGURE 5.1 Trends in Canadian in male and female convictions for homicide, 1961–1991 (Source: Canadian Center for Justice Statistics; adapted from Gartner 1995: 204).

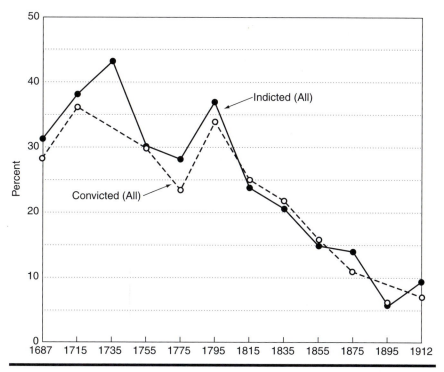

FIGURE 5.2   The percentage of indicted and convicted offenders who were female in England from 1687 to 1912 (adapted from Feeley & Little 1991:722).

These trends could be reflecting all sorts of influences, including tendencies by courts to shift their focus away from trivial to more serious crimes over the past two centuries, or perhaps a relative increase in the cleverness of female criminals! Changes in the gender ratios for crimes will be discussed further in Chapter 12, when feminist theories of crime are considered.

Age (and Age of Onset)

The association between age and criminal behavior has been widely studied, although not to the extent of gender differences. As documented in Table 5.2a, studies have consistently shown that criminal behavior is heavily concentrated in the second and third decades of life, particularly between twelve and thirty years of age.[26] This pattern is illustrated in Figure 5.3 with data from four countries at various points in time. Comparison of these and distribution curves from other countries have shown that differences in the peak probability of crime vary by only three or four years. It is always sometimes in the late teens to early twenties, depending on the exact composition of offenses under scrutiny.

The most notable age-related variations in types of crime involve the two main categories of victimful offenses: Studies have shown that for property crimes, the highest probability is in the mid to late teens, while the maximum probability for violent crimes is in the late teens to early twenties.[27] Also, the relationship between age and crime varies slightly according to gender, with most studies finding males exhibiting peak crime/delinquency probabilities a year or two earlier than females.[28]

Most of the data that has been used to study links between age and criminality have been based

TABLE 5.2a.   Relationship between age and criminal behavior (consistency score: 100%; well-established correlate.)

	Type and Seriousness of Offenses								
	Official Statistics							Self-Reported Offenses	
Peak Age Probability	Violent Offenses	Property Offenses	Drug Offenses	Misdemeanors*	General & Unspecified Offenses	Recidivism	Victimful & Overall Offending	Illegal Drug Use
Between 12 and 30	**Europe** *Former Czechoslovakia:* 1; *Denmark:* 1; *Scotland:* 1; *Germany:* 1; *England:* 1 **North America** *Canada:* 2; *United States:* 26 **Pacific** *Australia:* 1 **Other** *Several Countries:* 2	**Europe** *Denmark:* 1; *England:* 4; *Scotland:* 1; *Germany:* 1 **North America** *Canada:* 1; *United States:* 6 **Other** *Several Countries:* 1	**Asia** *Taiwan:* 1	**Europe** *Denmark:* 1; *England:* 4; *Finland:* 1; *France:* 1; *Germany:* 1; *Sweden:* 1 **Middle East** *Israel:* 1 **North America** *United States:* 4 **Pacific** *Australia:* 1	**Asia** *Former Soviet Union:* 2; *Japan:* 1 **Europe** *England:* 9; *Finland:* 1; *France:* 1; *Germany:* 4; *Norway:* 1; *Sweden:* 3; *Two or More European Countries:* 2 **North America** *Canada:* 2; *Greenland:* 3; *United States:* 27 **South-Central America & Caribbean** *Argentina:* 2	**North America** *United States:* 3 **Pacific** *Australia:* 1	**Europe** *England:* 2 **North America** *United States:* 5 **Pacific** *Australia:* 1 **Other** *Several Countries:* 1	**North America** *United States:* 3
Before 12 or after 30								
No significant Age–Crime Relationship								

*Studies confined to juvenile delinquency were omitted.

on official data. This is because self-report studies are usually restricted in terms of the age range of the subjects. For example, it is most common to give out self-report questionnaires to samples of high school and college students. Nevertheless, within this narrow age range, self-report studies have documented that crime (or delinquency) probabilities generally rise at least through the late teens, just as official data suggest. This is true for crime in general and drug offenses specifically.[29] Only one study so far has used self-reports to follow a representative sample of young adults (the National Youth Survey mentioned on p. 67). This study has confirmed that crime probabilities begin dropping beyond the early twenties,[30] just as offi-

cial data indicate. We will look at some of this data shortly.

Because conduct disorders and antisocial behavior are defined according to the age of those being diagnosed, no evidence is presented in Table 5.2a regarding how these clinical disorders are related to age. Nevertheless, studies of the antisocial personality disorder in several countries have all concluded that, sometime in their thirties, psychopathic symptoms become much less noticeable.[31] This decline in antisocial symptoms has been referred to as **antisocial burnout,** or just **burnout,**[32] and includes a distinct drop in involvement in criminal behavior.[33] In other words, psychopathy almost never appears suddenly in adulthood.[34] As

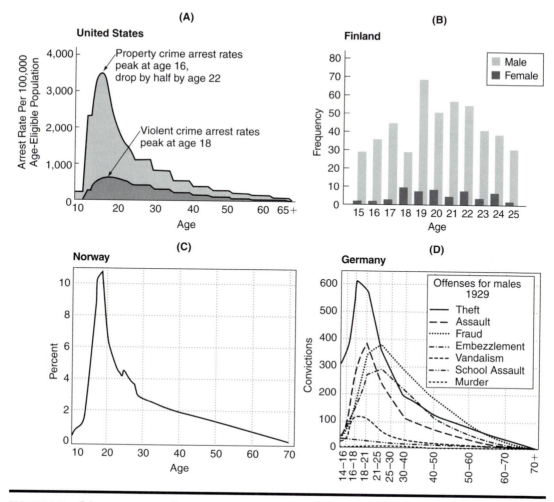

FIGURE 5.3   Crime rates according to age in various countries and time periods:
A. Arrest rates for violent and property felonies in the United States, 1983–1985 (from
U.S. Dept. of Justice 1988:42); B. Convictions in Finland in 1990 of persons 15–25
(Rantakallio 1995: 115); C. Arrests according to age in Norway in 1957 (Hurwitz &
Christiansen 1983:279); D. Convictions of males for various offenses according to age
in Germany in 1929 (Goppinger 1973:354).

with persistent criminality, if someone is going to
exhibit psychopathic symptoms, they will usually
do so long before the age of twenty,[35] usually developing out of childhood conduct disorders.[36]
Overall, throughout early adulthood, psychopathy
is a fairly stable trait within individuals,[37] and its
symptoms only show clear signs of dissipating
with the approach of middle age, not unlike the

pattern documented for criminality itself (see
Figure 5.2).

Closely linked to studies of the relationship
between age and criminality are studies of how the
commission of crime or delinquency at an early
age predicts persistence in offending. Table 5.2b
summarizes the results of this research. As you
can see, nearly all studies have found that the

TABLE 5.2b.   Evidence of a relationship between early age of onset of criminal/delinquent offending and persistence in criminal/antisocial behavior (consistency score = 100%; well-established correlate).

| Nature of the Relationship | Type and Seriousness of Offenses | | | | | | | | Antisocial Clinical Conditions | |
| | Official Statistics | | | | | | Self-Reported Offenses | | | |
	Violent Offenses	Property Offenses	Drug Offenses	Delinquency	General & Unspecified Offenses	Recidivism	Victimful & Overall Offending	Illegal Drug Use	Childhood Conduct Disorders	Antisocial Personality
Positive	**North America** *United States:* 1			**Europe** *England:* 1; *Poland:* 2; *Sweden:* 2 **North America** *Canada:* 1; *United States:* 7	**Europe** *Denmark:* 1; *Sweden:* 1 **North America** *United States:* 1 **Pacific** *Hawaii:* 1	**North America** *Canada:* 1; *United States:* 15	**Europe** *England:* 2 **Pacific** *New Zealand:* 1	**North America** *United States:* 7	**North America** *United States:* 1	
Not significant						**North America** *United States:* 1				
Negative										

earlier individuals begin offending, the longer they tend to persist in doing so. This is true for drug offenses.[38] and for crime/delinquency more generally.[39] In fact, at least one study found early age of offending was the single best predictor of those who will and will not develop a long-term criminal career.[40] As with all generalizations, however, it is inappropriate to conclude from this evidence that everyone who commits a delinquent act early in life will have a long "criminal career."

In summary, age is a strong correlate of criminal and antisocial behavior, with offending probability being the highest during the second and third decades of life. In addition, studies have shown that the earlier an individual begins to exhibit offending tendencies, the longer he/she is likely to persist in such behavior.[41] Even for the most persistent offenders, however, there seems to be a "burn out" that slowly sets in by around age thirty.

Race/Ethnicity

With the possible exception of religion, the most emotionally sensitive topic with which social sci-

entists deal is that of race/ethnicity, and it would be hard to find a discipline for which race/ethnicity is more controversial than criminology. The question of whether one racial/ethnic group is more involved in crime than another is so volatile that most countries do not even maintain statistics on the topic. The main exception has been the United States, perhaps partly because its citizens are much more racially and ethnically diverse than just about any other country, especially among industrialized nations.

Before attempting to review the research linking crime and race/ethnicity, it is important to bear in mind that scientists still disagree about whether race is essentially a biological or a social concept.[42] Also, no matter how race and ethnicity are defined, due to global migration and intermarriage, there are major uncertainties for growing numbers of people as to which race or ethnic category they fit. Evidence of this came from a U.S. governmental health survey in which the race of subjects assigned by an interviewer was compared to the subjects' own self-classification. Nearly 6 percent of the persons who considered themselves black were classified by the interviewer as white, and 70 percent of those who considered themselves to be Native Americans were classified by the interviewer as either white or black.[43] Presumably, most of these inconsistently classified subjects were of varying degrees of mixed racial/ethnic makeup. With so much inconsistency in classification, some have contended that the concept of race/ethnicity is not a legitimate scientific concept. However, you should realize that many of the variables social scientists deal with are similarly difficult to measure precisely. For example, we will soon be discussing social status (or class). What social class do you assign to a janitor who inherited a million dollars and has a college degree? Upper class, middle class, lower class? Social scientists will never agree on how to handle this or other conflicting instances, but still there is meaning in the concept of social status that we will see is helpful in categorizing people. The same principle applies to race/ethnicity: It is a very imprecise concept when applied to many specific individuals, but in aggregate, it is still a useful social science concept.

At least since the seventeenth century, when contact between people of different continents began to be routine, three major racial groups have been recognized among researchers as well as among people at large. Roughly coinciding with the three major continents of the Old World, these racial groups are often termed *black* (African), *white* (European), and *Asian* (or Oriental).[44] Nonetheless, many people of mixed racial ancestry can only be arbitrarily assigned to any one of these three categories,[45] and persons native to India, Australia, and the Americas (before the arrival of Europeans) are often not included in any of the three main racial categories.

Categorizing people into distinct ethnic groups is even more difficult than assigning them to racial categories. All sorts of criteria are used to assess ethnicity, including physical appearances, accents, manors of dress, religion, and even family names. Add to these various criteria high rates of migration and marriage across ethnic lines, and it becomes evident why many people cannot be assigned to just one ethnic category. Given all the difficulties surrounding the concepts of race and ethnicity, let alone difficulties measuring criminality, it is remarkable to find just about everyone (including social scientists) continuing to use the concepts. As we will see, despite the imprecisions of both concepts, many studies have found them related to people's varying probabilities of criminal behavior.

As noted above, the United States has been the main country that has provided data on relationships between race/ethnicity and criminality. This can be understood as the result of two factors. First, the United States is probably the most racially and ethnically diverse country in the world.[46] Second, going back to the 1930s, official crime statistics in the United States have been maintained separately for "white" and "nonwhite," with over 90 percent of the latter being blacks. Beginning in the 1970s, more elaborate racial/ethnic categories came to be used in most U.S. government statistics. To help monitor compliance with laws against discrimination in employment, the following five categories have been officially adopted: white (or Anglo-American), black (or African-American), Asian/Pacific Islander (Asian-American), Native American (Amerindian), and Hispanic (Latino or Spanish-Speaking Americans).[47] About 60 percent of Hispanics are of Mexican ancestry, with most of the remainder from Puerto Rico, Cuba, and various South American countries.[48] To determine which category a person should be assigned to, in most surveys subjects are asked to classify themselves.

In Canada, despite its racial/ethnic diversity, until quite recently no crime data was maintained according to race/ethnicity except in the case of Native Americans (Aboriginals). In 1990, crime data began to be compiled according to racial and ethnic categories on a temporary trial basis amidst considerable controversy. Already, some local Canadian police departments are declining to compile the necessary information.[49]

Those who have criticized collecting crime data according to race and ethnicity have argued that doing so serves to reinforce stereotypes, and is contrary to the fundamental values of a culturally diverse society.[50] Defenders of the practice have asserted that such data is essential for determining if discrimination is taking place, and that such data may eventually be useful in identifying causes and cures for criminal behavior. Aside from the controversy surrounding the collection of crime data according to race and ethnic groupings, many countries simply have such a small minority population as to make such data statistically meaningless.

Six tables summarize the research on race/ethnic differences in criminality. One is devoted exclusively to black–white (Table 5.3a), because this

has received the lion's share of research up to the present time. The remaining five tables (Tables 5.3b through 5.3f) pertain to comparisons between whites and Native Americans, whites and Hispanics, and whites and Asians/Pacific Islanders. Whites (or Anglos) were used as the reference group in all cases, because they are the majority population where most of the research has thus far been conducted. Let us now see what the research indicates.

Black–White Comparisons. Table 5.3a provides a condensed summary of the evidence on how crime rates among blacks compare to the rates among whites. As one can see, the official data is

TABLE 5.3a. Black–white differences in criminality/antisocial behavior (overall consistency score = 68.5%; possible correlate; consistency score with self-reports excluded = 94.3%.)

| Relative to whites | Type and Seriousness of Offenses | | | | | | | | Antisocial Clinical Conditions | |
| | Official Statistics | | | | | | Self-Reported Offenses | | | |
	Violent Offenses	Property Offenses	Drug Offenses	Delinquency	General & Unspecified Offenses	Recidivism	Victimful & Overall Offending	Illegal Drug and Alcohol Use	Childhood Conduct Disorders	Antisocial Personality
Blacks' involvement higher	**Europe** *England:* 1 **Middle East** *Israel:* 2 **North America** *Canada:* 1; *United States:* 75 **Pacific** *Hawaii:* 1	**North America** *United States:* 2	**Europe** *England:* 1 **North America** *United States:* 2	**Europe** *England:* 3 **North America** *United States:* 26	**Asia** *Israel:* 1 **Europe** *England:* 7; *France:* 3 **Middle East** *Israel:* 3 **North America** *Canada:* 1; *United States:* 44 **Pacific** *Hawaii:* 1	**North America** *United States:* 15	**Europe** *England:* 1 **North America** *United States:* 17	**North America** *United States:* 4	**Europe** *England:* 1 **North America** *United States:* 6	**Mideast** *Israel:* 1 **North America** *United States:* 1
No significant difference						**North America** *United States:* 6	**Europe** *England:* 2 **North America** *United States:* 20	**North America** *United States:* 11	**North America** *United States:* 4	**North America** *United States:* 2
Blacks' involvement lower		**North America:** *Canada: 1*					**North America** *United States:* 4	**Europe** *England:* 1 **North America** *United States:* 23		

very consistent in indicating that blacks have higher crime rates than do whites. The extent of black–white differences has been found in regard to both males and females[51] and for all age categories,[52] although the differences appear to be most striking among young males.[53] Overall, there are no geographic regions or periods of time when substantial black–white differences in crime rates have not been documented.

Regarding types of official crimes, studies have found black–white differences to be especially great in the case of violent offenses.[54] Most studies in the United States put the overrepresentation of blacks in violent crimes around three or four times that of whites.[55] Among juvenile offenders, the black–white differences appear to be even greater, especially among males, approaching six or seven to one.[56]

Only one notable exception to the generalization that blacks have higher official crime rates than whites has been documented so far by official data. It has to do with a few white-collar and corporate crimes, such as tax fraud and securities violations, in which blacks are underrepresented.[57] (For more on white-collar and corporate crimes, see Chapter 17.)

Additional evidence that blacks are substantially more involved in serious crime than whites has come from victimization surveys. In these surveys, respondents are asked whether or not they had an opportunity to see the offender. In the case of most assaults and robberies, the answer is yes. Analysis of the answers given by victims indicates that assault and robbery rates are at least three times higher for blacks than they are for whites.[58] More will be said about race differences in crime victimization later in this chapter.

Further evidence of higher crime rates among blacks compared to whites has come from two studies based on reports from mothers of black and white boys, as well as from data collected since the mid-1970s on U.S. college campuses. The two studies based on mothers' reports—one conducted in the United States[59] and the other in England[60]—both indicated that the sons of black mothers were significantly more involved in phys-

ical fighting, thefts, and other antisocial conduct than were the sons of white mothers. Regarding data collected on U.S. college campuses, analysis revealed that the proportion of the student body who were black was substantially correlated with the violent crime rate on campus, although it was not significantly correlated with the property crime rate.[61]

Despite all of this evidence that crime rates are higher among blacks than among whites, many studies based on self-reports have failed to find significant black–white differences. As you can see in Table 5.3a, almost as many self-report studies show no significant black–white differences in criminal involvement as those showing higher crime rates for blacks. Some criminologists have interpreted these findings as suggesting that official statistics are biased against blacks.[62] This interpretation has been criticized by others, in part because of the heavy emphasis that self-reported data place on trivial offenses.[63] In other words, while blacks and whites may in fact differ little in the commission of trivial offenses, the official data could still be correct in indicating substantial black–white differences in the commission of serious crimes.[64] Supporting this interpretation of the data are a few studies of race differences in self-reported crimes that have been able to focus on serious property and especially violent offenses. In all of these studies, blacks have self-reported substantially higher criminal involvement than have whites.[65] Among the most persuasive evidence in this regard comes from a study that asked black and white high school students to self-report their delinquency involvement, which the researchers then grouped into five seriousness categories. As you can see in Figure 5.4, whites were more likely than blacks to report involvement in minor delinquency (e.g., stealing something worth a few dollars), but the reverse pattern emerged with serious forms of delinquency (e.g., dealing in illegal drugs, using force to get money).[66]

Overall, there are at least three reasons to believe that "reality" lies somewhere between the official and the self-reported data, except in the case of the most serious offenses, when the official data

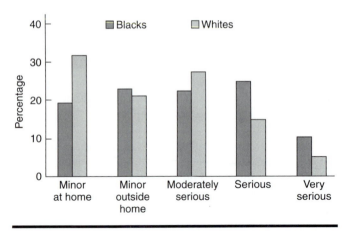

FIGURE 5.4 Percentage of white and black high school youth who self-reported having been involved in delinquent acts that researchers grouped into five levels of seriousness (adapted from Peeples & Loeber 1994:150).

is probably closer to correct than the self-reported data.

First, many self-report surveys, especially in the case of illegal drug use, have been based on samples of high school seniors.[67] In this regard, blacks have considerably higher high school dropout rates than do whites.[68] And, as will be documented in Chapter 7, crime is much more prevalent among high school dropouts than among persons who graduate from high school. This means that studies based on self-reports from high school seniors often fails to find significant black–white differences in crime when real differences exist simply because of the higher proportions of blacks not being included in the sample.

A second reason for the failure of many self-report studies to discover significant black–white differences in crime and delinquency when differences exist involves variations in the completeness of self-reported crime data. As discussed in Chapter 2 (p. 36), several studies have shown that persons who are the least involved in crime tend to be the most diligent in recording even minor infractions of the law. Earlier in this chapter, we noted that this helps to explain why self-reported sex differences in crime are considerably less pronounced

than is indicated by official data (p. 102). In other words, it is not that police are discriminating against males in making arrests, but that females are more conscientious in reporting even minor law violations than are males. Something similar may be occurring in the case of black–white differences in criminal involvement.[69]

Third, several studies have found blacks self-reporting considerably lower drug use than whites, even though arrest rates clearly suggest that use by blacks is higher.[70] Data collected in emergency rooms in the United States on drug overdosing also show the rates for blacks to be much higher than the rates for whites.[71] A study in England found that self-reported illegal drug use was higher among whites than among blacks.[72] However, the researcher noted that, whereas 3 percent of whites failed to complete this part of the questionnaire, 8 percent of the blacks failed to do so. These failures to answer not only could have biased the results toward underestimating black drug use, but they could reflect some fundamental concern about the complete anonymity of the information being provided, especially by minority groups. Collectively, the data suggest that blacks who engage in criminal behavior are more reluctant than whites who do so to disclose the full extent of their involvement. This appears to be true both in terms of victim offenses, as well as victimless crimes, particularly surrounding drug use.

Consequently, despite numerous self-reports to the contrary, crime rates for blacks appear be higher than for whites, with the possible exception of the most trivial forms of delinquency. In the case of serious victimful offenses, black rates are considerably higher, especially for violent offenses among males. Regarding involvement in various acts of delinquency, especially experimental drug use and drinking under the legal age, offending rates appear to be close to black–white equality. Concerning "hard drugs," such as heroin and cocaine, blacks appear to be considerably more heavily involved than are whites,[73] despite some self-reported data to the contrary. Still too little evidence is available on black–white differences in clinically diagnosed antisocial behavior, especially in adulthood, to reach conclusions about their relative prevalence. Therefore, despite a consistency score that puts black–white differences only in the "probable correlate of crime" range, it is safe to say that blacks exhibit significantly higher rates of serious crime than whites, especially regarding violent offenses.

Furthermore, in one recent analysis of self-reported delinquency and crime, all trivial offenses were excluded, leaving only serious offenses. As shown in Figure 5.5, this analysis revealed substantially higher offense rates by blacks than by whites. Notice also that the gender and age variations in self-reported involvement in serious delinquent and criminal behavior are also consistent with official data, as discussed earlier.

Turning to clinical evidence, only a limited number of studies are available, nearly all of which have been confined to the United States. As shown in Table 5.3a, a few studies have found blacks exhibiting symptoms of childhood conduct disorders and adult antisocial personality disorders to a greater degree than whites,[74] although most studies have not found significant average differences.

Before going further, it is important to reiterate that this chapter will offer no *explanations* for racial or any other demographic correlations with criminal behavior. Explanations will begin to be offered in Part III, and you will see that they can become quite complex.

Overall, the evidence indicates that crime rates among blacks are substantially higher than for whites even though Table 5.3a only yielded an 82 percent consistency score. Why inconsistencies exist between official and most self-reports on these differences continues to be the focus of criminological research, but the fact that self-reports concentrate on much less serious types of offenses than do most official data is certainly a factor to keep in mind.

Native American–White Comparisons. The race/ethnic group called Native American are individuals who inhabited North and South America long before Columbus "discovered" America. Anthropological evidence indicates that their ancestors were Asian nomads who arrived in North America at least 10,000 years ago at least in part by way of the Bering Strait.[75]

As you can see in Table 5.3b, nearly all studies of Native Americans (also called Aboriginal Americans, Amerindians) have found them to be overrepresented in official crime statistics when compared to whites. Their overrepresentation is especially high for offenses linked to alcohol consumption, such as public drunkenness and disorderly conduct and more serious forms of violence.[76] This conclusion has been reached based on studies both in the United States[77] and in Canada.[78] It is worth noting that alcohol abuse is considerably higher among Native Americans than for any other commonly designated racial/ethnic group in North America.[79] In Chapter 8, we will discuss the link between alcohol consumption and criminality in greater detail.

Rates of serious crime appear to be significantly higher among Native Americans than among whites. As evidence, studies have found imprisonment rates among Native Americans to be even higher than for blacks, both in the United States[80] and in Canada.[81] Table 5.3b shows that in all but one study of violent offending, Native

Age-Specific Prevalence

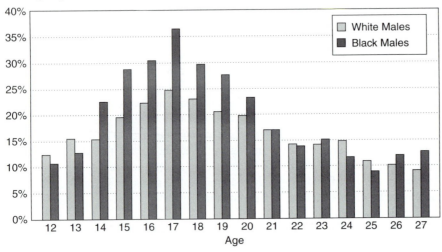

Age-Specific Prevalence

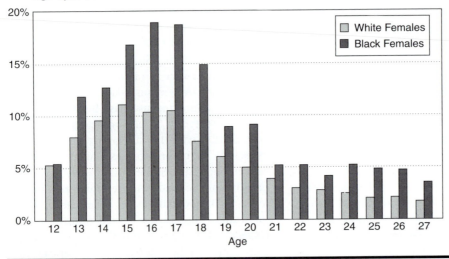

FIGURE 5.5 The proportion of persons between the ages of 12 and 27 who self-reported having committed at least one serious (felony level) crime in the past year. The results are presented according to race and sex (adapted from Elliott 1994:6).

Americans have been shown to have significantly higher rates than the rates for whites.

Regarding self-reports, Native Americans are only modestly higher in overall delinquency than other racial/ethnic groups, at least in the United States. Where their self-reported delinquency rates are several times higher than those for whites is in the use of illegal drugs.[82]

Hispanic–Anglo Comparisons. Hispanic Americans (*Latinos*) are residents of the United States whose ancestors came from Spanish-speaking

TABLE 5.3b.   Native American–white differences in criminal/antisocial behavior (consistency score = 94.6%; established correlate).

| Relative to Whites | Type and Seriousness of Offenses | | | | | | | | Antisocial Clinical Conditions | |
| | Official Statistics | | | | | | Self-Reported Offenses | | | |
	Violent Offenses	Property Offenses	Drug Offenses	Delinquency	General & Unspecified Offenses	Recidivism	Victimful & Overall Offending	Illegal Drug and Alcohol Use	Childhood Conduct Disorders	Antisocial Personality
Native American involvement higher	North America *Canada:* 5; *United States:* 10		North America *United States:* 1	North America *United States:* 2	North America *Canada:* 16; *United States:* 6	North America *Canada:* 3	North America *United States:* 1	North America *Canada:* 2; *United States:* 24 **South and Central America** *Mexico:* 1		
No significant difference	North America *United States:* 1						North America *United States:* 1			
Native American rates lower		North America *United States:* 1								

South and Central American countries. Racially, nearly all Hispanics are considered white, but they are distinguished from European whites, often called *Anglos* (or *non-Hispanic whites*) in many social science research studies. Hispanics are the fastest growing ethnic segment in the United States, with over 10 percent of U.S. citizens classifying themselves as Hispanic since the mid-1970s.[83]

Table 5.3c summarizes the research on how Hispanics and Anglos compare with respect to criminal/antisocial behavior. As you can see, Hispanics have usually been found to have significantly higher crime rates, except for self-reported offending. Differences are especially well documented for homicide, with Hispanic rates being intermediate to the rates for white and black Americans.[84]

In the case of self-reports, you can see that most studies indicate that there are no significant differences between offending rates of Hispanics and Anglos. Regarding self-reported drug offenses, a few studies have even found significantly lower rates of offending among Hispanics than among Anglos, although these studies pertained to marijuana use[85] or engaging in underage alcohol consumption,[86] both relatively minor but widespread drug offense categories. In the case of "harder drugs," such as heroin and cocaine, Hispanics have been found to exceed Anglos in self-reported usage.[87] This latter observation is supported by data collected in hospital emergency rooms, where Hispanic visitation rates for overdosing on heroin and cocaine far exceeded Anglo visitation rates.[88]

While the overall consistency score is in the "possible correlate of crime" range, you can see that nearly all of the exceptional findings have to do with self-reports. If these are excluded, the consistency score rises to 93.9 percent, making an Hispanic–Anglo difference a well-established correlate of crime.

Asian/Pacific Islanders–White Comparisons.
Quite a number of studies have compared crime rates for three groups of identifiable Asian/Pacific

TABLE 5.3c.   Hispanic–Anglo differences in criminal/antisocial behavior (overall consistency score = 65.2%; possible correlate; consistency score with self-reports excluded = 93.9%; established correlate).

Nature of Any Difference Relative to Whites (Anglos)	Type and Seriousness of Offenses								Antisocial Clinical Conditions	
	Official Statistics						Self-Reported Offenses			
	Violent Offenses	Property Offenses	Drug Offenses	Delinquency	General & Unspecified Offenses	Recidivism	Victimful & Overall Offending	Illegal Drug and Alcohol Use	Childhood Conduct Disorders	Antisocial Personality
Hispanic rates higher	North America *United States:* 16		North America *United States:* 1	North America *United States:* 9	North America *United States:* 4		North America *United States:* 4	North America *United States:* 8	North America *United States:* 1	
No significant difference				North America *United States:* 1			North America *United States:* 2	North America *United States:* 9	North America *United States:* 1	
Hispanic rates lower							North America *United States:* 1	North America *United States:* 4		

Islanders with rates for whites. The first group to be discussed are people from East Asian (the Pacific Rim) countries, predominantly those from China (including Taiwan), Japan, and Korea. The second group are those native to the numerous islands in the Pacific, including Australia, New Zealand, and Hawaii, along with the inhabitants of the Philippines. The third group to be compared to whites (or people of European descent) will be persons whose ancestors are from India or Pakistan, most of whom came to settle in England.

Segment One: East (Pacific Rim) Asian–White Comparisons.   Table 5.3d summarizes data comparing crime rates for descendants of Pacific Rim Asian populations and white (European) populations. As you can see, nearly all of the studies have indicated that descendants of Pacific Rim countries have significantly lower crime rates than those for whites. Most of these studies have been conducted in the United States, where the rate of crime among Pacific Rim Asian Americans is typically at least half the rate exhibited by white (European) Americans. As far as official data are

concerned, this is true both for delinquency and crime in general.[89]

Segment Two: Pacific Islander–White Comparisons.   Included in the category of Pacific Islanders here are persons other than whites who reside in one of the numerous Pacific islands. Also included in this category are persons from islands in the Indian Ocean, most notably the Philippines.

Nearly all of the comparisons of crime rates of Pacific Islanders and whites have been conducted in Australia, New Zealand, and Hawaii. Studies from Hawaii have been particularly interesting, because Hawaii is the one land mass that contains sizable proportions of more than one Asian/Pacific Island population along with whites. The results of studies that have compared the crime rate of these groups to those of whites are shown in Table 5.3e. As you can see, most of the evidence indicates that Pacific Islanders exhibit higher crime rates than do whites, the only exceptions appearing in the self-report column.

Let us scrutinize some of the specific studies, beginning with two conducted in Hawaii. The two

TABLE 5.3d.   East Asian–White comparisons regarding criminal/antisocial behavior (overall consistency score = 93.0%; established correlate; consistency score with self-reports excluded = 100%).

| Relative to Whites | Type and Seriousness of Offenses | | | | | | | | Antisocial Clinical Conditions | |
| | Official Statistics | | | | | | Self-Reported Offenses | | | |
	Violent Offenses	Property Offenses	Drug Offenses	Delinquency	General & Unspecified Offenses	Recidivism	Victimful & Overall Offending	Illegal Drug Use	Childhood Conduct Disorders	Antisocial Personality
Asian rates lower	**Pacific** *Hawaii:* 2 **North America** *United States:* 2			**Europe** *England:* 4 **North America** *United States:* 4 **Pacific** *Hawaii:* 1	**Europe** *England:* 1 **North America** *United States:* 8 **Pacific** *Hawaii:* 2		**North America** *United States:* 4	**North America** *United States:* 7	**North America** *United States:* 3 **Pacific** *Hawaii:* 1 **International** *U.S.–China Comparison:* 1	
No significant difference							**North America** *United States:* 2	**North America** *United States:* 1		
Asian rates higher										

TABLE 5.3e.   Pacific Islanders–White comparisons regarding criminal/antisocial behavior (overall consistency score = 86.7%; established correlate; consistency score with self-reports excluded = 100%; well-established correlate).

| Relative to Whites | Type and Seriousness of Offenses | | | | | | | | Antisocial Clinical Conditions | |
| | Official Statistics | | | | | | Self-Reported Offenses | | | |
	Violent Offenses	Property Offenses	Drug Offenses	Delinquency	General & Unspecified Offenses	Recidivism	Victimful & Overall Offending	Illegal Drug Use	Childhood Conduct Disorders	Antisocial Personality
Pacific Islanders higher				**Pacific** *Australia:* 1; *New Zealand:* 3	**Pacific** *Australia:* 2; *New Zealand:* 3	**Pacific** *Australia:* 2	**Pacific** *Hawaii:* 1; *New Zealand:* 1			
No significant difference							**Pacific** *Hawaii:* 1 *New Zealand:* 1			
Pacific Islanders lower										

largest studies of crime and delinquency in Hawaii presented both official and self-reported data. The first of these studies concluded that Chinese and Japanese had the lowest official delinquency rates, followed by whites. The groups with the highest delinquency rates were Filipinos, native Hawaiians, and an "other" category, consisting primarily of Samoans.[90] Regarding self-reports, this study found some ethnic differences, although the differences interacted with gender. The most striking differences were among boys, where Japanese and Filipinos reported the lowest delinquency rates.[91]

The other study of official crime data in Hawaii also found resident Samoans exhibiting an unusually high official crime rate, although Native Hawaiians and Filipinos had crime rates slightly below the rates for whites.[92] Regarding self-reported violence (most of which would have been criminal), college students of various ethnic groups provided the data. Few ethnic differences were found.[93]

In the case of New Zealand, studies have been conducted comparing its aboriginal population (known as *Maori*) with the European immigrants, who began inhabiting New Zealand in the 1800s. Due to intermarriage with the European immigrants, only a few thousand "pure" Maori remain. For statistical purposes, New Zealand's health ministry classifies as Maori anyone with 50 percent or more of exclusive Maori ancestry.[94] According to official data, crime rates are considerably higher among the Maori than among New Zealanders of European decent.[95] However, the one self-report study of delinquency and crime that was conducted found no significant difference between the two groups.[96]

Australian studies based on official data are consistent in indicating that this country's Aboriginal population have much higher crime rates than do its European settler population. This is true both for juvenile offenses[97] and adult offenses.[98]

Segment Three: India/Pakistani–White Comparisons.   The last Asia/Pacific Island group to be compared to whites with respect to crime rates are

persons from India and Pakistan. Because both countries were former British colonies, sizable numbers of Indians and Pakistanis immigrated to England, and now comprise about 3 percent of the entire English population.[99] This has made it possible for several English studies to compare the crime rates for Indians and Pakistanis with those of the white majority. There are also a small proportion of Jews who originated in India now living in Israel,[100] for whom a few comparative crime studies are available.

The results are shown in Table 5.3f. Most of the available studies suggest that Indians and Pakistanis have crime rates that are either slightly lower or not significantly different from those of natives of Britain. The only relevant study conducted outside of England was one pertaining to the prevalence of conduct disorders carried out in the United States. It indicated that children of Indian and Pakistani parents had significantly lower rates of conduct disorders than did white Americans.[101]

Cross-Cultural Studies of Racial Variations in Criminal Behavior.   To this point, we have examined only studies of racial/ethnic variations in criminality conducted within countries. A few studies have also assessed race-crime relationships *between* countries.

A series of international comparative studies have examined how crime rates varied according to the predominant racial composition in each country. These studies have shown that violent crime rates tend to be the highest in countries with predominantly black populations, and lowest in countries with predominantly East Asian populations. Countries with predominantly white populations were typically intermediate in their violent crime rates.[102] Thus, consistent with data comparing racial variations in offending rates within countries, blacks appear to have higher serious crime rates than whites, and whites in turn typically have higher rates than persons of East Asian ancestry. Also, just as there are numerous individuals within each racial category who defy the overall pattern, there are also countries that fail to conform to the overall pattern.[103] Keep in mind that these analyses

TABLE 5.3f. India/Pakistani–White (European) comparisons regarding criminal/
antisocial behavior (overall consistency score = 45.5%; unestablished correlate).

Relative to Whites	Type and Seriousness of Offenses								Antisocial Clinical Conditions	
	Official Statistics						Self-Reported Offenses			
	Violent Offenses	Property Offenses	Drug Offenses	Delinquency	General & Unspecified Offenses	Recidivism	Victimful & Overall Offending	Illegal Drug Use	Childhood Conduct Disorders	Antisocial Personality
Indian/ Pakistani rates lower				**Europe** *England:* 3	**Europe** *England:* 2		**Europe** *England:* 2	**Europe** *England:* 2	**North America** *United States:* 1	
No significant difference				**Middle East** *Israel:* 1	**Europe** *England:* 4				**Europe** *England:* 1	
India/ Pakistani rates higher				**Europe** *England:* 1 **Middle East** *Israel:* 1	**Middle East** *Israel:* 1					

were based solely on comparisons of homicide rates, and that comparisons of other serious offenses may not reveal the same patterns.

One more cross-cultural study compared samples of same-aged children from two countries, China and Sweden, with respect to conduct disorders (as rated by parents and teachers). Consistent with evidence that antisocial behavior tends to be lower among East Asian populations than among European populations, the study found that the proportion of Swedish children with aggressive conduct disorders was significantly higher than was found among the Chinese children.[104]

Overall Assessment of the Race/Ethnic–Criminal Behavior Relationship. Before making some final remarks about the specific nature of race/ethnic variations in criminal behavior, it is important to emphasize the controversial nature of research in this area. Most of the controversy has more to do with the uneasiness that many of us have when studies compare our racial/ethnic group with others. Some of that discomfort can be relieved if everyone keeps in mind that the variability in people's criminal/antisocial behavior is much greater *within* any racial/ethnic group than is the variability in averages *between* groups. Otherwise, scientists are interested in racial/ethnic differences not for the purpose of praising certain groups and embarrassing others, but in order to eventually help to untangle the possible causes of those variations.

The evidence is strong that racial/ethnic group differences do exist with respect to criminal and antisocial behavior. Regarding the three most widely recognized racial groups, there appear to be significant differences in criminal behavior, except possibly for trivial offenses. Overall, blacks have higher crime rates than whites, and whites in turn exceed persons of East Asian ancestry, with the greatest differences involving the most serious violent offenses. All three groups, however, exhibit enormous intragroup variability.

In the case of ethnic groups, Native Americans in the United States and Canada and Hispanic Americans in the United States have higher overall crime rates than do white (Anglo) Americans, with the greatest differences being found for violent offenses (and drug offenses in the case of Native Americans). For Pacific Islanders, the limited evidence usually puts their official crime rates above those of whites, but self-reports have been equivocal. In comparing racial and ethnic groups, it is important to keep in mind that many people are difficult to assign to a single racial or ethnic category, and that there are subgroups within each major category that have higher and lower rates than their particular category's overall average. In sum, while racial and ethnic differences have been demonstrated, the nature of the differences are much more complex than are gender and age differences.[105]

Once again, note that the topic of race/ethnic differences in criminal/antisocial behavior remains extremely controversial. Some of the controversy is scientific in the sense that it is impossible to precisely measure either race/ethnicity or criminal/antisocial behavior. However, the greatest controversy has to do with ethical and emotional repercussions of the research in this area. Some criminologists have questioned the motives of those who would even seek to determine if one racial or ethnic group is more criminal than another, and several countries

have chosen not to compile crime data according to people's race or ethnicity.

Immigrant Status

A variable that is closely related to race/ethnicity is that of being an immigrant or the direct descendant of an immigrant.[106] Over the years, quite a number of studies have examined this variable as a correlate of crime. These studies overlap somewhat with those already reported with reference to race and ethnicity, so those reported here are basically ones in which the researchers chose to focus on the recency of arrival into a host country rather than on the specific race/ethnicity of the immigrant.

As you can see from examining Table 5.4, most of these studies have been conducted in Europe, where substantial immigration has occurred

Table 5.4. Relationships between immigrant status and criminal/antisocial behavior (overall consistency score = 84.5%; established correlate).

| Nature of the Relationship | Type and Seriousness of Offenses | | | | | | | Antisocial Clinical Conditions | |
| | Official Statistics | | | | | Self-Reported Offending | | | |
	Violent Offenses	Property Offenses	Delinquency	General & Unspecified Offenses	Recidivism	Victimful & Overall Offending	Illegal Drug Use	Childhood Conduct Disorders	Antisocial Personality
Positive	**North America** *United States: 3*	**Europe** *England: 1*	**Europe** *Belgium: 1; France: 1; Germany: 4; Netherlands: 8; Sweden: 2; Switzerland: 1; Yugosolovia: 1* **Middle East** *Israel: 4* **North America** *United States: 1* **Pacific** *Australia: 1*	**Europe** *Belgium: 1; England: 2; France: 2; Germany: 9; Netherlands: 2; Sweden: 2* **Middle East** *Israel: 1* **Other** *Europe in general: 1*		**Europe** *Belgium: 1*		**North America** *United States: 1*	
Not significant			**Europe** *Netherlands: 1; Switzerland: 1* **North America** *United States: 1*	**Europe** *Austria: 1*		**Europe** *Netherlands: 1*			
Negative		**Europe** *Germany: 1*				**Europe** *Germany: 1*			

since the 1950s. In particular, Germany, Belgium, the Netherlands, and Sweden have had many immigrant workers from various Middle Eastern countries in recent decades. Also, France experienced substantial immigration from Algeria, a former French colony. Despite speculation about the link between immigration and crime in the United States and Canada during the late nineteenth and early twentieth-century European mass immigration from Europe to North America, little scientific data were compiled to determine if immigrant rates differed from the Europeans who had arrived in earlier decades.

The typical design of the studies summarized in Table 5.4 has involved comparing arrest rates of immigrants or their first-generation descendants to the rates for the host country's indigenous people. Recognizing that young males are more likely to immigrate than most other gender/age groups, many of the studies controlled for gender and age differences between the immigrant and indigenous populations before making comparisons, but others did not.

As you can see, most studies have found crime and delinquency rates to be higher among immigrants and their descendants than among indigenous populations. However, many of the researchers suggested that the country of origin seemed to be more relevant than an individual's immigrant status per se.[107] For example, a French study found that immigrants who came from other European countries had crime rates that were actually lower than the overall French average, but that immigrants from Algeria had higher crime rates than the overall French average.[108] Similarly, three English studies found immigrants from various African countries had higher rates of crime than was true for the indigenous British population, but that immigrants from Asian countries (mainly India and Pakistan) actually had somewhat lower rates.[109] Likewise, a study in Israel found that Jewish immigrants from Africa had higher rates of delinquency, while those from India had essentially the same rates of delinquency as did Jews of European or U.S. decent.[110]

The few comparisons made in the United States have presented a mixed picture. One study in Chicago found that, as the percentage of foreign-born increased in various neighborhoods, the delinquency rates actually decreased.[111] Again, emphasizing the importance of where immigrants originated, rather than their immigrant status per se, one study compared four groups of immigrants to the overall U.S. crime rate. It found no significant difference between the rates for European and Latino immigrants and the U.S. average. For immigrants from India and Pacific Rim countries, the rates were significantly lower than the U.S. average.[112]

The bottom line on research designed to assess any links between criminality and immigration is fuzzy at best. The only safe generalization at this point seems to be that most studies of immigrants to continental Europe suggest that the rates of crime and delinquency among immigrants and their first-generation descendants are significantly higher than for the indigenous populations.

Social Status

Before exploring the evidence regarding the possible relationship between crime and social status, it is important to know what social status is and how it is measured. Overall, **social status** (also called **social class**) refers to people's unequal access to scarce resources.[113] In contemporary societies, social status is usually measured in terms of three indicators: income (or wealth), occupational level, and years of education.[114] Collectively, these three measures are often called **socioeconomic status** (or **SES**).

Given that education, income, and occupational level are all considered indicators of social status, you might expect all three of them to be strongly correlated with one another. However, these three measures of social status are in fact only modestly related to one another.[115] For instance, many people who are highly educated have only modest incomes, and other people with extremely high incomes have only average or below average years of schooling. Nevertheless, when considering large groups of people, there is still a substantial *overall* tendency for income, years of education, and job status to be positively correlated. Therefore, when attempting to measure social status, some social scientists use just one or two of these three indicators, while others will use all three, either separately or in some sort of combination.

How do social scientists measure the social status of people who are still in school, and therefore have no occupation and little if any income? For these individuals, SES is usually defined in terms of the social status of their parents. This type of social status is called **parental** (or **dependent**) **social status.**

The results of research on social status and crime are summarized in two tables, one pertaining to measures of an individual's own social status (Table 5.5a), another with parental social status (Table 5.5b). As you will see, how social status is measured does affect the answer one gives with respect to whether a relationship exists between social status and criminal behavior.

Turning attention first to the individual status indicators, Table 5.5a shows that persons of low social status are more likely to be involved in crime than persons of middle or high status. As you would suspect, most of these studies pertain to adult criminality rather than juvenile delinquency. Few studies have attempted to determine which individual-level SES indicator is most closely linked to criminal behavior. Those that have have generally indicated that educational measures are better predictors of delinquency and criminal involvement than either income or occupational status measures.[116]

In terms of self-reports, only weak (if any) relationships have been documented between education and delinquency/criminality unless attention is focused on serious (especially violent) crimes. Then one does find low education levels associated with high rates of criminality.[117]

Regarding the social status of one's parents, the bulk of the evidence suggests that persons of low status are more involved in crime than persons

of middle and high status. The only notable exception has to do with self-reported offenses. Several of these studies indicate that there is no significant relationship between social status and the probability of offending. A recent Finnish study actually found higher rates of offending reported by upper status youth than by those of lower status,[118] while a Spanish self-report study found the highest overall delinquency rates among middle-class youth.[119] As noted earlier, self-report surveys concentrate on relatively minor offenses, so it may be the case that, for crimes of a less serious nature, there are few if any consistent social status variations, particularly when social status is defined in terms of one's family background rather than in terms of an individual's own achievement.

Also, few if any differences have been found between the middle and upper social strata in overall criminal tendencies either based on official or self-reported data; only when one or both of these groups are compared to the lower social strata do significant differences emerge.[120]

This conclusion could help to explain why many self-report surveys have not found significant social status differences in delinquency and crime. Specifically, because most self-report studies are conducted among high school and college students, persons of low social status and high crime rates are poorly represented in most self-report surveys. This, plus the fact that self-reports concentrate on trivial offenses, reduces the chances of most self-report studies finding significant correlations between status and offending probabilities. The self-report studies that have concentrated on the more serious victimful offenses, and have ensured that the lower social strata were well represented in the sample, have all confirmed the negative relationship found in the official data.[121]

Some criminologists have attempted to determine whether individual or parental status measures are best at predicting criminality. There is obviously no way of knowing in the case of juvenile delinquency, because few if any juveniles have yet established their own social status. But, in the case of adult offenders, studies have indi-

TABLE 5.5a.   Results from studies of the relationship between an individual's social status (except years of education) and criminal/antisocial behavior (overall consistency score =84.3%; probable correlate; consistency score with self-reports excluded = 97.1%; well-established correlate).

| Nature of the Relationship | Type and Seriousness of Offenses | | | | | | | | Antisocial Clinical Conditions | |
| | Official Statistics | | | | | | Self-Reported Offenses | | | |
	Violent Offenses	Property Offenses	Drug Offen.	Delinquency	General & Unspecified Offenses	Recidivism	Victimful & Overall Offending	Illegal Drug Use	Childhood Conduct Disorders	Antisocial Personality
Negative	**Africa** *Nigeria:* 1; *South Africa:* 1 **Asia** *Ceylon:* 2; *Soviet Union:* 1 **Europe**: *Denmark:* 1; *England:* 3; *Italy:* 1; *Scotland:* 1 **North America** *United States:* 4 **South-Central America & Caribbean** *Mexico:* 1	**North America** *Canada:* 1		**Europe** *England:* 2 **North America** *United States:* 1 **Pacific** *Hawaii:* 1 [4]	**Africa** *Uganda:* 1 **Europe** *Denmark:* 1; *England:* 4; *Germany:* 1; *Scotland:* 1 **North America** *United States:* 7 **Pacific** *Australia:* 2		**Europe** *England:* 1 **North America** *United States:* 3		**North America** *United States:* 1	
Not significant				**Europe** *England:* 1			**Europe** *England:* 1 **North America** *United States:* 1	**Europe** *England:* 1 **North America** *United States:* 3		
Positive							**North America** *United States:* 1			

cated that one's own social status, rather than that of one's parents, better predicts degree of involvement in criminal behavior.[122]

It is important to note that the inverse relationship between social status and serious criminal behavior deviates from what statisticians call *linear*. Instead, the relationship has a tendency toward *curvilinearity*.[123] This type of relationship is illustrated in Figure 5.6. Notice that the rate of homicide assailants is distinctly high in neighborhoods where the average income is lowest, but from around the midpoint in incomes toward the highest incomes, there are essentially no differences in assailant rates. In other words, homicide rates do not differ between middle and upper income populations, but dramatic differences exist when either of these groups are compared to the lowest income groups. In statistical terms, the scattering of points for Figure 5.6 is said to conform to a reversed-J curved line rather than to a straight descending line.

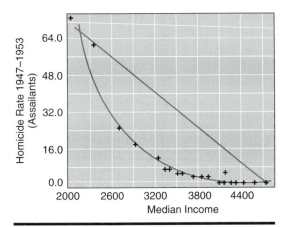

FIGURE 5.6   Results from comparing rates of involvement in homicide and median income between 1947–53 in twenty-one administrative sectors (similar to neighborhoods) in Cleveland, Ohio (Bensing & Schroeder 1960:Table 42).

Before leaving the issue of the relationship between social status and crime, it should be noted that the relationship was the focus of a major controversy among criminologists during the 1970s, when some researchers concluded that there was essentially no relationship between social status and involvement in criminality.[124] Since the 1980s, however, the evidence has mounted in favor of concluding that there is in fact a substantial inverse correlation[125] except in the case of self-reported trivial offenses.[126] It is worth noting that all of the controversy had to do with parental social status, not individual social status, given that the latter is beyond doubt.[127] Also, as illustrated by Figure 5.6, the relationship will only be apparent when a substantial proportion of the persons sampled are of low social status. For this reason, studies conducted among college students will underestimate any social status–criminality relationship.

Overall, what can be concluded about the relationship between social status (or social class) and criminality in light of the evidence summarized by Tables 5.4a and 5.4b? First, the relationship between an individual's social status and his/her involvement in criminality is negative. In other words, persons of lower status are more involved in crime then those of middle or upper status. This generalization has even held true in the case of self-reported offending. Second, the relationship with criminality and an individual's parental social status is much more equivocal, especially in the case of self-reported crime/delinquency. If a statistical link exists between parental social status and criminality, it is almost certainly weaker than the link between individual status and criminality.

DEMOGRAPHICS OF CRIME VICTIMIZATION AND FEAR-OF-CRIME

Besides seeking to determine relationships between demographic variables and criminality, criminologists have also investigated whether demographic variables are linked to either crime victimization or to fear-of-crime. Crime victimization data come in two main forms: The first is derived from homicide data in which demographic characteristics of victims are assessed. The second source of crime victimization data is much more recent, dating back to the 1970s, when the U.S. government began conducting annual victimization surveys.[128]

The main focus of studies designed to assess demographic variations in crime victimizations has been on assaults and threats of assault. This is because the crimes that people are most certain about in terms of victimization, and the crimes they fear the most, are those of a violent nature.

Regarding fear-of-crime, questions have often been incorporated into victimization surveys regarding this variable. The sort of questions used to measure fear-of-crime (or the closely related variable *perceived risk of crime*) are as follows: "How safe do you feel walking along in your neighborhood at night/during the day?."[129]

Gender and Crime Victimization/ Fear-of-Crime

Numerous studies have investigated the relationship between gender and crime victimization. As shown in Table 5.6, these studies have determined

TABLE 5.5b. Results from studies of the relationship between parental social status and criminal/antisocial behavior (overall consistency score = 57.4%; possible correlate; consistency score with self-reports excluded = 85.5%; established correlate).

Nature of the Relationship	Type and Seriousness of Offenses								Antisocial Clinical Conditions	
	Official Statistics						Self-Reported Offenses			
	Violent Offenses	Property Offenses	Drug Offen.	Delinquency	General & Unspecified Offenses	Recidivism	Victimful & Overall Offending	Illegal Drug Use	Childhood Conduct Disorders	Antisocial Personality
Negative	**Asia** *Ceylon: 2* **North America** *United States: 2*			**Africa** *Ghana: 1* **Asia** *China: 1; India: 1; Japan: 2; Korea: 1; Soviet Union: 1* **Europe** *England: 14; Finland: 4; France: 1; Scotland: 2; Spain: 1; Sweden: 4; Yugoslavia: 1* **Middle East** *Israel: 1* **North America** *Canada: 3; United States: 31* **Pacific** *Hawaii: 2* **South-Central America & Caribbean** *Argentina: 2*	**Europe** *Denmark: 4; England: 6; Finland: 1; Sweden: 1* **North America** *United States: 2*	**Europe** *Denmark: 1; England: 1* **North America** *United States: 2*	**Africa** *Uganda: 1* **Asia** *Korea: 1* **Europe** *England: 9; Germany: 2; Sweden: 1* **North America** *Canada: 1; United States: 31* **Pacific** *Philippines: 1* **South-Central America & Caribbean** *Barbados: 1*	**Europe** *Northern Ireland: 1* **North America** *Canada: 1; United States: 9*	**Europe** *England: 3; France: 1* **North America** *Canada: 2; United States: 7* **Pacific** *Australia: 1; New Zealand: 1* **South-Central America & Caribbean** *Puerto Rico: 1*	**North America** *United States: 1*
Not significant				**Europe** *England: 6; Finland: 1; Sweden: 1* **North America** *United States: 6*	**Europe** *Denmark: 1; England: 1*	**Europe** *Sweden: 1* **North America** *United States: 1*	**Europe** *Belgium: 1; England: 3; Germany: 1; Italy: 1; Netherlands: 2; Norway: 1; Portugal: 1; Spain: 1; Switzerland: 2* **North America** *Canada: 1 United States: 9* **Middle East** *Greece: 1* **Pacific** *Australia: 1; New Zealand: 1*			
Positive				**North America** *United States: 2*		**North America** *United States: 1*	**Europe** *Belgium: 1; Finland: 1* **North America** *United States: 9* **Pacific** *Australia: 1; Hawaii: 1*	**Europe** *France: 1* **North America** *Canada: 4; United States: 12* **Pacific** *Australia: 1*		

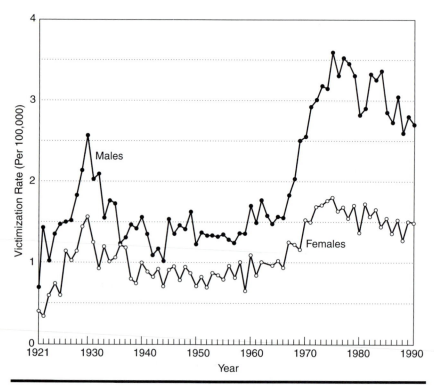

FIGURE 5.7   Trends in Canadian Homicide Vicitimization Rates by Gender, 1921–1990.

Source: Vital Statistics.

that, except for rape, where essentially all victims are female,[130] males have substantially higher victimization rates than do females.[131] Thus, even with rapes included in calculating an overall victimization rate, males run a considerably greater risk of being victimized by violent crime than do females.

The extent to which males are overly victimized has been found to vary from roughly 2- or 3-to-one for assaults and robberies,[132] to 3- or 4-to-one in the case of murder.[133] In some countries, male murder victims have reportedly outnumbered female victims by as much as 8- or 9-to-one, but in a few studies almost no differences have been reported.[134] There is only one study that has ever reported higher murder victimization for females than for males. This was a study of homicides in Italy during the 1800s.[135]

Trendwise, a recent analysis of Canadian data indicated that the degree to which males are victimized more than females has substantially increased since around 1970 (see Figure 5.7).

Regarding crimes other than violent offenses, a few studies have separated gender differences in victimization from property offenses. These have also indicated that males have a higher victimization rate, but not to the degree that is typical of violent offenses.[136]

What about fear-of-crime? Despite their higher risk of being victimized, Table 5.6 shows that numerous studies have found that males report fearing crime less than do females.[137] Various surveys conducted in the United States, for example, have found that over twice as many women as men report being afraid of crime in their neighbor-

TABLE 5.6.   Relationships between gender and crime victimization, and gender and fear-of-crime (consistency score for victimization = 97.1%; well established; consistency score for fear-or-crime = 100%; well established).

Nature of the relationship	Victimization Probability				Fear-of-crime
	Homicide	Violent Crimes Other than Homicide	For Property Offenses	For Crimes in General	
Higher for males than for females	**Africa** *South Africa:* 1; *Uganda:* 1; *Various Tribal Societies:* 2 **Asia** *Ceylon:* 1; *India:* 3 **Europe** *Denmark:* 1; *England:* 4; *France:* 1; *Germany:* 3; *Netherlands:* 1; *Sweden:* 1 **North America** *Canada:* 1; *United States:* 12 **Pacific** *Australia:* 2 **Other** *Various Countries:* 2	**Europe** *England:* 4; *Netherlands:* 1 **North America** *Canada:* 1; *United States:* 14 **Other** *Various Countries:* 1	**North America** *Canada:* 1; *United States:* 1	**Europe** *Scotland:* 1 **North America** *United States:* 9	
No significant gender difference					
Higher for females than for males	**Europe** *Italy:* 1				**Europe** *England:* 5; *Scotland:* 1 **North America** *Canada:* 1; *United States:* 31 **South Central America & Caribbean** *Mexico:* 2 **Pacific** *Australia:* 2; *Japan:* 1 **Other** *Various Countries:* 1

hoods.[138] In fact, just as gender is the single best demographic predictor of who will commit crime, gender is also the strongest demographic predictor of fear-of-crime.[139] Even if sex offenses are excluded from consideration, women express greater fear-of-crime than do men.[140] Overall, males are more often victimized by crime, especially violent crime, than females. Nonetheless, men have less fear of crime than do women.

Age and Crime Victimization/Fear-of-Crime

Results of studies regarding how age correlates with crime victimization and fear-of-crime are shown in Table 5.7. The table documents that, contrary to popular belief, criminals do not prey primarily on the elderly.[141] Instead, research has consistently shown that it is persons in their twenties and thirties who are most likely to be victimized.[142] This holds true for murder, assaults, robberies, and to a lesser degree all property crimes. In the case of murder, for example, the predominant age of victims ranges in the fifteen-year period between twenty-five and forty.[143] Also, based on surveys in fourteen countries, researchers found personal crime victimization rates for sixteen to twenty-four-year-olds to be three times higher than for persons sixty-five years old or older.[144]

Figure 5.8 presents data that show how age and sex interact with homicide victimization up to the age of seventeen. As you can see, males and females have virtually identical victimization rates in the United States until around age twelve, when male rates begin to increase much more dramatically.

Turning to the results on fear-of-crime, one finds that the evidence is somewhat inconsistent. All studies conducted prior to the late 1980s reported that the elderly were more fearful of crime than was true for younger persons (the youngest subjects in nearly all fear-of-crime studies are in their late teens). However, after adjusting for the fact that most elderly persons are women (because their life expectancy in the United States is seven years longer than men's) and using new ways of

TABLE 5.7. Relationships between age and crime victimization, and age and fear-of-crime (consistency score for victimization = 80.1%; probable correlate; consistency score for fear-of-crime = 92.3%; established correlate).

| Nature of the Relationship | Victimization Rate | | | | Fear-of-crime |
	Homicide	Violent Crimes other than Homicide	Property Crimes	Crime in General	
Highest in the mid teens to the mid 30s; Lowest among the elderly	**Africa** *South Africa:* 1 **North America** *United States:* 7	**North America** *Canada:* 1; *United States:* 4 **Other** *Several Countries:* 1	**North America** *Canada:* 2; *United States:* 1	**Europe** *England:* 1; *Germany:* 1; *Netherlands:* 1; *Scotland:* 1 **North America** *Canada:* 1; *United States:* 3	**North America** *United States:* 1
No significant (or complex) relationship with age					**North America** *United States:* 4
Lowest in the mid teens to the mid 30s; Highest among the elderly				**North America** *United States:* 3	**Europe** *England:* 1 **North America** *United States:* 19 **Other** *Various Countries:* 1

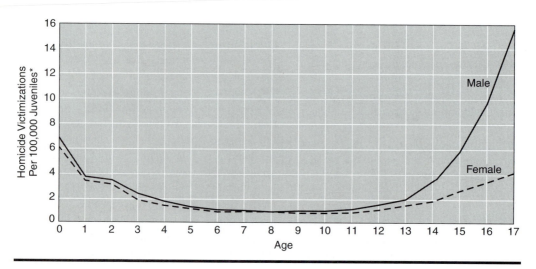

FIGURE 5.8 Until they become teens, boys and girls are equally likely to be murdered.

The rate of homicide victimization is higher for children age five and younger than for those between ages six and eleven. After age eleven the homicide victimization rate increases throughout adolescence, especially for boys.

*Rates are based on the 1976–1991 combined average.

Source: FBI (1993). *Supplementary homicide reports 1976–1991* (machine-readable data files).

phrasing survey questions, recent studies have suggested that little relationship exists between fear-of-crime and age; the aged are among the least fearful.[145]

Another finding that is important to keep in mind with reference to assessing fear-of-crime as it relates to age is that such fear has been shown to be related to health and living arrangements.[146] Specifically, being of poor health and living alone are associated with greater fear, and are both more common among the elderly than for most other segments of the population.[147]

Basically, the more recent studies of age and fear-of-crime have concluded that there is either no relationship, or that the relationship is not due to age per se. One study found a tendency for fear of crime to decrease until around age sixty, and then to increase slightly thereafter.[148] In addition, there may be somewhat different age/fear-of-crime relationships, depending on the type of crimes specified.[149]

Overall, while the evidence is entirely consistent in showing that young adults are the most likely to be crime victims, the evidence is not consistent regarding exactly how age and fear-of-crime are related.

Racial/Ethnic Differences in Crime Victimization/Fear-of-Crime

Nearly all of the studies of racial/ethnic differences in crime victimization and fear-of-crime have been conducted in the United States and have focused on comparing whites and blacks. As shown in Table 5.8a, these studies all indicate that blacks are more likely than whites to be the victim of crime. This is especially true of violent offenses, where blacks have a probability of being murdered that is about six times greater than the probability for whites.[150] In the case of most property crimes, blacks are about one and a half times more likely to be victimized.[151] The magnitude of the race differences for adolescents and young adults since 1940 are shown in Figure 5.9. It indicates that, despite substantial fluctuations in over-

all homicide victimization, blacks have always been at a much greater risk of being killed due to violence than whites. As you can see, this risk is especially high for black males.

Regarding black–white differences in fear, U.S. studies indicate that blacks have greater fear of crime than do whites. However, the only comparable study conducted outside the United States—in England—found the opposite: Whites were more fearful than blacks.[152] This study also found that Asian (mainly East Indians) living in England were the most fearful of all three racial/ethnic groups. One U.S. study considered gender, age, and race all at the same time. It found the least fearful of all groups were young black males, oddly enough the group that was most likely to be victimized by violent crime.[153]

A number of studies conducted in Canada and the United States have contrasted crime victimization rates of Native (Aboriginal) Americans with the remainder of the population. The Canadian studies have all concluded that Aboriginals have homicide victimization rates that are about five times higher than rates for Canadians in general.[154] U.S. studies put the homicide victimization rate of Native Americans at about twice the average for the United States as a whole.[155]

A few victimization studies were found that involved assessing victimization rates of Hispanics (Latin Americans) living in the United States. These concluded that Hispanics had higher victimization rates due to violence than whites, but less than whites due to property crimes.[156] Another compared blacks and Hispanics in fear-of-crime, and concluded that they were considerably more fearful than were blacks, even though their victimization rates tend to be lower.[157]

A final point worth making about the link between race and crime is that most victimful crimes are among members of the same race, rather than between members of different races.[158] This is especially true of nonsexual assaults and homicides.[159] In the United States, for example, over 90 percent of all of the murders committed by blacks involve black victims.[160]

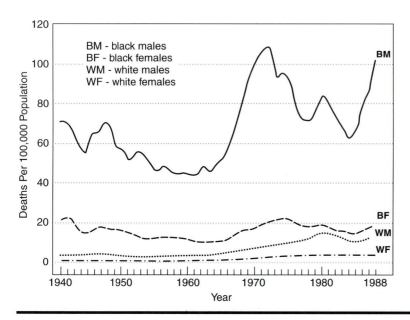

FIGURE 5.9   Homicide victimization rates for persons between 15–24 by race and sex, United States, 1940–1988 (adapted from Reiss & Roth 1993:64).

TABLE 5.8a.   Black–White differences in crime victimization and fear-of-crime (consistency score for victimization = 94.3%; established correlate; consistency score for fear-of-crime = 93.3%).

| Nature of the Relationship | Victimization Rate | | | | Fear-of-crime |
	Homicide	Violent Crimes Other than Homicide	Property Crimes	Crime in General	
Higher among Blacks than among Whites	**North America** *United States:* 17	**Africa** *South Africa:* 1 **Europe** *England:* 1 **North America** *United States:* 11	**North America** *United States:* 1	**North America** *United States:* 2	**North America** *United States:* 1
No significant Black-White differences					
Higher in Whites than Blacks		**North America** *United States:* 14	**North America** *United States:* 1		**Europe** *England:* 1

Social Status and Crime Victimization/ Fear-of-Crime

Studies of the relationship between social status and rates of victimization are summarized in Table 5.9. As you can see, the studies do not provide an entirely clear picture, particularly in the case of self-reported victimization from violent crime. Regarding homicide, however, evidence clearly shows lower status persons are more often victimized, and in the case of self-reported property crime victimization, middle and upper status persons are

TABLE 5.8b.   Native American–White differences in crime victimization and fear-of-crime (consistency score for victimization = 100%; well established).

Nature of the Relationship	Victimization Rate				Fear-of-crime
	Homicide	Violent Crimes Other than Homicide	Property Crimes	Crime in General	
Higher among Blacks than among Whites	**North America** *Canada: 7;* *United States: 2*				
No significant Black-White differences					
Higher in Whites than Blacks					

TABLE 5.9.   Relationships between social status and crime victimization, and social status and fear-of-crime (consistency score for victimization = 46.2%; unestablished; consistency score for fear-or-crime = 100%; well established).

Nature of the Relationship	Victimization Rate				Fear-of-crime
	Homicide	Violent Offenses Other than Homicide	Property Offenses	Crime in General	
Higher in lower classes than in the middle and upper classes	**North America** *United States: 2*	**North America** *United States: 3* **Other** *Various European Countries: 1*			
No significant difference (or complex pattern)		**Europe** *Netherlands: 2*	**North America** *United States: 1*		
Higher in middle and upper classes than in lower classes		**Europe** *Sweden: 1* **North America** *United States: 1*	**Europe** *Netherlands: 1* **North America** *United States: 1*		**North America** *United States: 2*

more frequently victimized. Where is the greatest fear of crime? While the differences are modest, persons of lower social status appear to have more fear than persons of middle and upper status.[161]

Victimization and Fear-of-Crime

Over the years, studies have been conducted to determine if there is a relationship between having been a recent victim of crime and expressing fear-of-crime. As you can see in Table 5.10, most of these studies have found a positive relationship between having been victimized by crime (usually within the past year) and the tendency to express greater fear of crime than those who have not been recently (or ever) victimized.[162] However, all of

the studies that have found a positive relationship have considered it only weak, perhaps because most people who are crime victims are victimized by relatively minor types of offenses.[163]

Being an Offender

In addition to looking for relationships between fear-of-crime and crime victimization, several studies have inquired about the possible link between being an offender and being a crime victim. The evidence is summarized in Table 5.11. As you can see, research strongly supports the conclusion that criminal offenders are considerably more likely to be victimized by crime than are persons in general.[164]

TABLE 5.10. Relationship between having been a recent victim of crime and one's fear of crime (consistency score = 62.5%; possible correlate).

| Nature of the Relationship | Victim Verses Non-Victim | | |
	Of Violent Crime	Of Property Crime	Of Crime In General
Greater Fear Among Victims	**North America** *United States:* 1	**North America** *United States:* 1	**Europe** *England:* 1; *Germany:* 1; *Netherlands:* 1 **North America** *United States:* 5 **Pacific** *Australia:* 1
No significant difference			**Europe** *Netherlands:* 1 **North America** *United States:* 3 **Pacific** *Australia:* 1
Greater Fear Among Non-Victims			

TABLE 5.11. Relationships between being an offender and being a crime victim (consistency score = 100%).

| Nature of the Relationship | How Offending Was Assessed | | | | |
| | In Terms of Official Data | | | | In Terms of Self-Reported Offending |
	Violent Offending	Property Offending	Drug Offending	Offending in General	
Offenders at Greater Risk of Victimization	**North America** *United States:* 2		**North America** *United States:* 1	**Europe** *England:* 1 **North America** *United States:* 4	**Europe** *England:* 1 **North America** *United States:* 9
No significant difference					
Offenders at Lower Risk of Victimization					

SUMMARY

This chapter has provided a highly condensed review of over a thousand studies pertaining to how demographic variables are related to criminal/antisocial behavior and to crime victimization. At the outset, a fundamental distinction was made between *correlates* and *causes* of crime, with correlates referring to variables that are associated with criminal behavior, often without being directly involved in causing such behavior. For example, while evidence is overwhelming in showing that males are more criminal than females, this does not mean that "maleness" is somehow causing criminal behavior. Nor does it mean that all males are criminal and that all females are not. Nonetheless, knowing how gender is correlated with criminal behavior throughout the world can help criminologists to narrow down the possible causes.

Demographic Correlates of Crime.

Beyond doubt, the most thoroughly studied demographic variable with respect to criminal/antisocial behavior is gender. With data extending back several centuries and now covering over fifty countries, researchers have found that males are more involved in crime than females. The only possible exceptions have to do with relatively trivial criminal offenses, where male and female rates of involvement often differ very little. The more serious, violent, and persistent the criminality, the more males have been found to dominate. This tendency for males to offend is also true with respect to childhood conduct disorders and antisocial behavior in adulthood. Nonetheless, the exact degree to which males dominate in the most serious and violent offenses varies quite a bit from one country or time period to another. Official data suggest the gender differences are much greater than do data based on self-reports. To a substantial degree, this probably reflects the fact that official data focus on much more serious victimizing offenses than self-reports do.

Regarding age, crime is heavily concentrated in the teens and twenties. No country has yet been identified in which this basic pattern does not occur, although, as with gender, there are variations from one country to another in terms of exactly what age is most associated with a specific type of crime. All countries, however, have found that the age when violent offenses are most probable are a few years later (usually in the early twenties) than when property offenses are most probable (usually in the mid to late teens). Studies have also consistently shown that the earlier criminal and delinquent behavior begins in youngsters, the longer this behavior is likely to persist.

Turning to the complex and sensitive issue of race/ethnic differences in criminality, studies have found patterns, despite wide variations in how racial and ethnic categories are defined and delineated. In particular, blacks are involved in crime at considerably higher rates than whites, especially in regard to violent offenses. Aboriginal people of the Americas, Australia, Hawaii, and New Zealand also appear to have higher rates of crime than do whites ancestral to Europe. The single major racial group whose crime rates have been shown to be consistently lower than those for whites are East Asians. Crime rates for South Asians (primarily of India and Pakistan) appear to be about the same as for whites. One other ethnic group that has received attention in the United States is Hispanics. Their crime rates have been shown to be intermediate between those of non-Hispanic whites (Anglos) and African Americans, particularly for violent offenses.

Social scientists who study race/ethnic differences in crime rates have been criticized on grounds that their findings are used to stereotype and justify repression of various populations. Those who have defended the collection and publication of such data have countered that it could eventually provide important clues for identifying the causes of criminal behavior, no matter what those causes may be.

A concept that is often closely related to that of race/ethnicity is immigrant status. Most studies of immigrant status in relationship to offending probabilities have been conducted in Europe. Most of these studies have indicated that immigrants and their first-generation descendants engage in crime and delinquency at higher rates than do the people indigenous to the country where the study was conducted.

The next demographic correlate of crime discussed in this chapter was that of social status (also called *social class*). To measure social status, most social scientists consider education, income, and occupational levels, either separately or in some combination. Collectively, these three indicators of social status (or social class) are often referred to as *socioeconomic status* (SES). SES measures are basically of two subtypes: individual and parental. Individual SES measures are derived directly from one's own education, occupational level or income, whereas parental (or family-based) measures are derived from the education, occupation, or income of one's parents.

Research based on individual social status measures is strong in indicating crime is more prevalent among persons of low social status, with little to no difference between persons of middle and upper status. In the case of parental social status, however, a less clear pattern emerges. Regarding official data, the vast majority of the evidence suggests that crime/delinquency and conduct disorders are significantly more prevalent in the lower than in the middle and upper social strata. However, in the case of self-reports, the evidence is almost evenly split between studies indicating higher rates of offending in the lower strata and studies suggesting no significant differences or significantly higher rates in the middle and upper strata.

Many inconsistencies were noted between official data and self-report data as they pertain to demographic correlates of crime. These inconsistencies are most apparent when considering gender, race/ethnicity, and SES. The basic nature of the inconsistencies are that self-reports minimize, and sometimes even completely reverse, patterns that are well established in official statistics. Regarding gender, self-reports indicate that females are much closer to males in criminal/delinquent behavior than official data. For race, black–white differences often disappear, and sometimes are even reversed (in the sense that whites self-report more criminal and delinquent offenses than blacks). Similarly, when using self-reports, the relationship between crime and parental SES often disappears, and several studies even suggest that offending rates are higher among the upper and middle classes than among the lower classes.

The best explanation for these inconsistencies between official and self-reported data has two parts: First, whereas official data focus on much more serious and victimful offenses than is the case for self-reports (the latter focuses on trivial and victimless offenses); second, as noted in Chapter 2 (p. 36), the least crime-prone persons are usually more conscientious and thorough in self-reporting infractions of the law than is the case for those who engage in crime most often. Together, these two facts mean that self-reports provide a somewhat distorted estimate of demographic variations in minor victimless offending and a greatly distorted estimate of demographic variations in serious victimful offending. Therefore, for estimating demographic variations in serious victimful offending—the crimes in which criminologists usually have the greatest interest—official data are generally more reliable.[165]

Demographic Correlates of Crime Victimization and Fear-of-Crime

This chapter also considered demographic variables as they relate to crime victimization and fear-of-crime. Data on crime victimization come from two sources: from government statistics on homicide and from victimization surveys. Overall, these data are consistent in indicating that the most highly victimized persons are young adult males, particularly if they are black and of low SES. These differences tend to be more noticeable in the case of violent offenses than for property offenses. The main exception to the greater victimization of men is in the case of rape and other sex offenses, where young women are victimized at much higher rates than men. Studies have also very consistently found that offenders are more likely to be the victims of crime than is true of nonoffenders, whether offenses are defined officially or in terms of self-reports.

Demographic research on fear-of-crime, however, has revealed some inconsistencies and difficult-to-explain patterns when juxtaposed to the research on crime victimization. Predictably, blacks, particularly those of low social status, are more fearful of crime than whites. Unpredictably, males have been found to be substantially less fearful of crime than are females. Regarding age, there is conflicting evidence, although most stud-

TABLE 5.12.   Capsule summary of demographic correlates of crime.

Correlate	Consistency of the Evidence*					Comments and Qualification
	Well Estab	**Estab**	**Prob**	**Poss**	**Unestablished**	
Gender	(X)	X				Males are more criminal/antisocial than females
Age	X					Criminal/antisocial behavior concentrated in teens & 20s
Age of onset	X					The earlier one begins to exhibit offending behavior, the longer one is likely to persist as such behavior
Black-white comparisons		(X)		X		Except for self-reports, blacks are more crime involved
Native American-white comparisons		X				Native American are more crime involved
Hispanic-Anglo comparisons		(X)		X		Except for self-reports, Hispanics are more crime involved
East Asian-white comparisons	(X)	X				Except for self-reports, whites more crime involved
Pacific Islanders-white comparisons	(X)	X				Pacific Islanders more crime involved
India/Pakistani-white comparisons					X	Most studies indicate that South Asians have lower crime rates, but some suggest opposite
Immigrant status			X			In most countries, persons of immigrant status appear to have higher crime rates than natives
Individual social status	(X)		X			Lower strata are more crime involved
Parental social status		(X)		X		Lower strata appears to be more crime involved, except possibly for minor delinquency

*X – includes self-reports; (X) – excludes self-reports.

ies indicate that fear is greatest among the elderly, despite their relatively low rates of victimization. Thus far, most of the victimization and fear-of-crime data have been collected in the United States, but what has been collected elsewhere is generally confirming the basic pattern just described, especially regarding gender differences.

Finally, in this chapter, we looked at crime victimization in terms of its relationship to having been a former victim and having been an offender. Not surprisingly, most studies have found that former crime victims express greater fear-of-crime than do those who have never been a crime victim. As far as offending is concerned, those who have

TABLE 5.13.   Capsule summary of demographic correlates of crime victimization.

| Correlate | Consistency of the Evidence | | | | | Comments and Qualification |
	Well Established	Established	Probable	Possible	Unestablished	
Gender differences	X					Males more likely victimized, but they are less fearful of crime than females
Age differences			X			Highest victimization in midteens through mid-30s; fear-of-crime is the reverse
Black–white differences		X				Blacks more likely victimized, and are more fearful of crime than whites
Native American–white differences	X					Native Americans more likely victimized than whites, at least for violent crimes in Canada
Social status differences					X	Low status more victimized by violent offenses, middle/upper for property; lower status most fearful
Offenders vs. nonoffenders				X		Offenders more likely victimized than nonoffenders

engaged in crime the most report having been the victims of crimes more other than those who have offended the least.

Overall, it is safe to conclude that numerous demographic correlates of crime and crime victimization exist, and the patterns are similar wherever data have been collected throughout the world. These demographic differences will be among the relationships used later to help judge the merit of various criminological theories.

SUGGESTED READINGS_____

Crime and Justice: A review of Research, 21 (1997). (An entire volume of this annually released journal has been devoted to carefully assessing the complex relationships between race/ethnicity and criminality in various countries, most notably in Canada, England, and the United States. Highly recommended.)

O'Shea, Kathleen A. and Fletcher, Beverly R. (Compilers). (1997). *Female offenders: An annotated bib-*

liography. Westport, CT: Greenwood. (A useful source to consult for information derived from hundreds of studies on gender and crime, and related issues.)

Schwartz, Martin D., & Milovanovic, Dragan (Eds.). (1996). *Race, gender, and class in criminology.* Hamden, CT: Garland. (This edited book provides a useful overview of much of what is currently known about demographic correlates of criminal behavior.)

U.S. Department of Justice (1988). *Report to the nation on crime and justice (2nd ed.).* Washington DC: U.S. Department of Justice (NCJ–105506). (Provides a clear overview of how United States crime rates and crime victimization rates vary according to several demographic traits.)

EXERCISES

1. Write an essay on why the criminal justice system in multicultural societies should or should not maintain crime statistics according to the race/ethnicity of both offenders and victims. You may state which side you favor most, but be sure to fairly present both sides of the issue.

2. Locate an official data source and a self-report data source for the same country (or region of a country). Then compare the information with respect to one or more demographic factors as they relate to differential involvement in the same types of crimes. For example, compare males and females in a particular country with respect to assault rates. Write a brief essay on the differences and similarities. Be sure to cite specific numbers and ratios, and direct the reader to the precise documents and page numbers where you got the information.

3. If you have access to the World Wide Web, do a search for criminal behavior and then a subsearch for one of the demographic, ecological, or victimization variables discussed in this chapter. Based on information you find, write a one- to two-page summary of facts or opinions about how that variable and criminal behavior seem to be related. (Your instructor will probably want you to print out a copy of the source or sources you used. If you do not have access to the world wide web, do your search at the college library.)

ENDNOTES

1. Quetelet 1831.
2. Broom & Selznick 1958:639; Wilson & Herrnstein 1985:144.
3. Elliott et al. 1986:488; Sheldon & Chesney-Lind 1993:73; Warr 1982:196.
4. Metfessel & Lovell 1942:135.
5. Beattie 1975, 1977; Gurr 1981; Weiner 1975; Zehr 1975.
6. Simon & Sharma 1979:394.
7. Cernkovich & Giordano 1979a:132.
8. Hagan et al. 1985.
9. Hindelang 1979; Young 1980:29.
10. Evans & Himelfarb 1992:83.
11. Barker & Adams 1961; Cernkovich & Giordano 1979.
12. Donnermeyer 1992:56.
13. Dobash et al. 1992; Goldberg & Tomlanovich 1984; Nazroo 1995; Stets & Straus 1990.
14. E.g., Gersao & Lisboa 1994:218; Hagan et al. 1985.
15. See Mieczkowski 1996:363.
16. National Institute on Drug Abuse 1994.
17. Campbell et al. 1992:69; Offord et al. 1986:275, 1987:834.
18. Rutter et al. 1970.
19. Robins 1966:154; Robins 1985; Robins & McEvoy 1990.
20. Gabel & Schindeldecker 1991; McGee et al. 1990.
21. Cloninger 1986:188; Harpending & Draper 1988.
22. Goodwin & Guze 1984; Guze 1976.
23. Smith & Visher 1980.

24. Gartner 1995:204; Hartnagel 1987:86.

25. Moffitt 1993.

26. Ellis 1988; U.S. Department of Justice 1988:42; Wilson & Herrnstein 1985:104; Wolfgang 1967:19.

27. Rantakallio et al. 1995:115.

28. Farrington 1987c:44.

29. Kleinman & Lukoff 1978:195.

30. Elliott 1994.

31. *England:* Craft 1969; Gibbens et al. 1955; *United States:* Robins 1966:236, 1991:265; *New Zealand:* Mulder et al. 1994:281; Oakley-Browne et al. 1989.

32. Arboleda-Florez & Holley 1991.

33. Gove 1985:116; Williamson et al. 1987.

34. Loeber 1982:1432; Robins 1978:258; Yahroes 1979:2.

35. Robins 1978:259.

36. Loeber 1982.

37. L. S. Miller 1994:406; Olweus 1979.

38. Kandel 1980a; Potvin & Lee 1980.

39. Loeber 1988:101; Moffitt 1993.

40. Wright & Wright 1995:4.

41. Mason & Frick 1994.

42. Lieberman & Jackson 1995; Sarich 1995:85.

43. Schulman et al. 1995:183.

44. Goldsby 1971; Hurwitz & Christiansen 1983:202; Lester 1973; Marshall 1968; Ogburn & Nimkoff 1958:94; Vogel & Motulsky 1979; Wallace et al. 1985:152.

45. Hurwitz & Christiansen 1983:202.

46. Blue & Griffith 1995:579.

47. Schulman et al. 1995:182; Waters & Eschbach 1995:421.

48. Rouse et al. 1995:345.

49. Johnston 1994:168.

50. Johnston 1994:166.

51. Adler 1975:139; Hendrix 1972; Katzenelson 1975; Sutherland 1939:120.

52. Shin et al. 1977:403.

53. U.S. Department of Justice 1988:47.

54. Blumstein 1982:1280; Pope & McNeely 1981:13; Schuster 1981:109; Wilson & Herrnstein 1985:461; Wolfgang et al. 1972:70; Wolfner & Gelles 1993:203.

55. Wilson & Herrnstein 1985:461.

56. Lykken 1995:213.

57. Roberts & Garbor 1990:297.

58. Blumstein & Cohen 1987; Flowers 1988; Hindelang 1978b:98, 1981:468; Pope 1979:351; Wilbanks 1987; Wolfner & Gelles 1993:202.

59. Tuddenham et al. 1974.

60. Rutter, et al. 1974.

61. Volkwein et al. 1995:663.

62. Quinney 1970:142; Schur 1973:121; Turk 1969; Williams & Gold 1972.

63. Eaton & Polk 1961; Pope 1979:355; Schuster 1981:110.

64. Elliott et al. 1989:31; Pope 1979:353.

65. Elliott 1994:6; Elliott et al. 1986:486; Hill & Crawford 1990:621.

66. Peeples & Loeber 1994.

67. E.g., Kandel et al. 1976; Wallace & Bachman 1991; Welte & Barnes 1987.

68. Jaynes & Williams 1989; Reed 1988.

69. Bowling et al. 1994:56; Junger-Tas 1994:9.

70. Mieczkowski 1996:362.

71. National Institute on Drug Abuse 1994.

72. Leitner et al. 1993:30.

73. Kleinman & Lukoff 1978:190; Mieczkowski 1996:383.

74. also see Eron et al. 1997:144.

75. Scupin & DeCourse 1998:149.

76. Nettler 1984:136.

77. Flowers 1978:106; Graves 1967; Jensen et al. 1977:252; Moyer 1992a:392; Pope & McNeely 1981:13.

78. Roberts & Doob 1997:490.

79. Jensen et al. 1977:253; Mills 1991:12; Schinke et al. 1985; U.S. Indian Health Service 1978.

80. Flowers 1978:106; Jensen et al. 1977:253.

81. Roberts & Doob 1997:479.

82. Jensen et al. 1977; Wallace & Bachman 1991:336.

83. Chapa & Valencia 1993.

84. Martinez 1996:142; Pokorny 1965; Polednak 1989:273; Smith et al. 1986:269; Zahn 1987.

85. Flannery et al. 1996.

86. Robins et al. 1991:265.

87. Johnston et al. 1993:127; Mieczkowski 1996:373.

88. Mieczkowski 1996:382.

89. La Free 1995; E. A. Wells 1992.

90. Voss 1963:323.

91. Voss 1963:326.

92. Blanchard & Blanchard 1983:167.

93. Blanchard & Blanchard 1983:183.

94. Smith et al. 1985:266.

95. Fergusson et al. 1993a, 1993b; Ritchie & Ritchie 1983.

96. Moffitt et al. 1994:361.

97. Gale et al. 1990.

98. Hall et al. 1994; Luke & Cunneen 1995.

99. Smith 1997:108.

100. Roland 1998.

101. Touliatos & Lindholm 1980.

102. Rushton 1990, 1995.

103. Gabor 1994b:153; Rushton 1995:311.

104. Ekblad 1984, 1990.

105. Farrington 1987a:56.

106. Smith 1995:447.

107. Brearley 1932:41; Zimmerman 1966.

108. Desdevises 1980.

109. Batta et al. 1975; Mawby et al. 1979.

110. Amir & Hovav 1976:167.

111. Bursik 1986:52.

112. Touliatos & Lindholm 1980:30.

113. Ellis 1993a:2.

114. Behrman et al. 1980:19; Mayer & Jencks 1989:1441; Thio 1986:198; Townsend 1989:244; Wrong 1958:216.

115. Ellis 1993b:16.

116. Empey 1982.

117. E.g., Terlouw & Bruinsma 1994:119.

118. Aromaa 1994:28.

119. Barberet et al. 1994:250.

120. Garrett & Short 1975.

121. Braithwaite 1981; Hindelang et al. 1979.

122. Braithwaite 1981:50.

123. Loftin & Hill 1974:717.

124. E.g., Tittle et al. 1978.

125. Braithwaite 1981.

126. Bowling et al. 1994:54; Elliott 1994; Evans & Himelfarb 1987:71.

127. Braithwaite 1981; Larzelere & Patterson 1990:316.

128. LaGrange & Ferraro 1989:697.

129. Rountree & Land 1996:1353.

130. Ellis 1998; Gordon et al. 1980:S145.

131. Gartner 1995:201; Gartner et al. 1990:600.

132. Curtiss 1977:165; U.S. Department of Justice 1988:27.

133. Gartner et al. 1990:600.

134. Gartner et al. 1990:593.

135. Pollack 1950:81.

136. Empey 1982:136; U.S. Department of Justice 1988:26.

137. Ferraro 1995:88; Pain 1995.

138. Moore & Trojanowicz, 1988:2; Parker & Ray 1990; Warr 1984.

139. Braungart et al. 1980:56; Ferraro 1995:85; Lira & Andrade-Palos 1993:47.

140. Ferraro 1995:89; Karmen 1991.

141. Evans & Himelfarb 1987:67.

142. M. R. Gottfredson 1986:265; Moore & Trojanowicz 1988:3.

143. Farley 1980:181; Wolfgang 1967:19.

144. van Dijk et al. 1991:64.

145. Ferraro 1995:76.

146. Braungart et al. 1980:56.

147. Braungart et al. 1980:62.

148. Ferraro 1995:81; LaGrange & Ferraro 1989:708.

149. LaGrange & Ferraro 1989:702.

150. Farley 1980:186; also see Kachur et al. 1996.

151. Conklin 1986:125.

152. Walker 1994:377.

153. Ortega & Myles 1987:144.

154. Gartner 1995.

155. Reiss & Roth 1993:70.

156. Empey 1982:139; Reiss & Roth 1993:70.

157. Parker et al. 1993.

158. Blue & Griffith 1995:574; Voss & Hepburn 1968.

159. Curtis 1975:21; Garfinkel 1967:47; Roberts & Doob 1997:490; Wilbanks 1985.

160. Shin et al. 1977:406.

161. Clemente & Kleinman 1977:527.

162. van Dijk 1979:22.

163. van Dijk 1979:22.

164. Sampson & Lauritsen 1994; Singer 1981.

165. Farrington 1987:39.

CHAPTER 6

Ecological and Macroeconomic Correlates of Crime

In what size cities is crime most prevalent: big cities, small cities, ones in-between? Do run-down neighborhoods have higher crime rates than well-kept neighborhoods? What about the state of the economy: Is crime worse during bad times when people are financially destitute or during good times when there's lots to steal? In this chapter, we will examine the evidence pertaining to these types of questions.

This chapter will summarize research on a variety of *ecological variables* that have been considered in relationship to crime. Also to be given attention are variables having to do with the overall state of a national or regional economy, called *macroeconomic variables*. The most distinctive feature of ecological and macroeconomic variables is that they focus not on traits of individuals, but on features of the social and economic environment within which individuals live.

THE NATURE OF ECOLOGICAL VARIABLES

The term *ecology* was first used to refer to the study of plants and animals living in their natural habitats, but gradually the term has also come to be applied to the study of humans living in natural and human-made habitats.[1] Criminological research that is of an ecological nature can be traced back to the cartographic school of the early 1800s. This type of research was later elaborated in the 1930s and 1940s in the United States, primarily by members of the Chicago School.

Ecological research in criminology focuses on comparing crime and delinquency rates of var-ious geopolitical regions, and then looking for features of these regions that might be associated with variations in crime and delinquency rates. The regions studied by ecological researchers are most often neighborhoods, cities, states, and sometimes entire countries. The variables used for comparing regions primarily involve social and economic conditions. For instance, you will find several studies cited in this chapter that have sought to determine if city crime rates are correlated with the proportion of each city's inhabitants who are in their teens and twenties. Notice that this topic is slightly different from the question addressed in Chapter 5 regarding links between age and involvement in criminal behavior. In other words, just because crime is concentrated in the teens and twenties does not mean that you can automatically assume that crime will be higher in cities where a large proportion of inhabitants are in their teens and twenties. In fact, you will see that there are good reasons to doubt that the latter variable has any consistent relationship to offending rates.

It is helpful to be familiar with a term social scientists often use in ecological research. The term is **ecological fallacy.**[2] It refers to a common tendency to assume that because some statistical relationship exists between two variables when studying individuals that the same relationship will be found when studying groups.[3] In other words, even though crime rates are highest among persons in their teens and twenties, one may not necessarily find unusually high crime rates in populations with the largest proportions of persons in that age range. In fact, we will find in this chapter that there is no clear relationship between neighborhood crime rates and the proportion of adolescents and young adults in those neighborhoods.

HOW ECOLOGICAL STUDIES ARE CONDUCTED

Most of the studies to be cited in this chapter come about as the result of combining criminal justice statistics with statistics compiled by other governmental agencies, particularly agencies responsible for maintaining census data (e.g., the U.S. Bureau of the Census). In most of the studies, researchers first decide on what is called the *unit of analysis*. A **unit of analysis** refers to the types of geographical regions or time frames to be used in an ecological study. The most common units of analyses in ecological studies are neighborhoods, cities and counties, states and provinces, and countries (international). In addition, quite a few ecological studies will track a geographical region (such as a country) over a number of years, making time the unit of analysis.

To briefly illustrate how an ecological study might be completed, say that a researcher decides to compare crime rates and divorce rates in one hundred of the largest cities in the United States. In this case, cities would be the unit of analysis. Another researcher might decide to compare fifty countries with respect to their per capita alcohol consumption and their murder rates, which would make countries the unit of analysis.

An element in many ecological studies involves statistically analyzing the data with an eye toward looking for relationships independent of other relationships. For example, a city's divorce rate as well as its crime rate may be influenced by

the age distribution of its citizens. Thus, many ecological studies "statistically control" for some "extraneous" variables in order to better interpret their data. There is no need for you to know how these statistical controls are imposed, but in a few cases they will be mentioned because it seems to bear on some of the findings.

SOCIAL ECOLOGICAL VARIABLES

Two groups of ecological variables will be considered. The first are nine variables having to do with commonly recognized social conditions of a geopolitical region: urban–rural residency and population size, population density, residential mobility, percent divorced/separated, ethnic/racial heterogeneity (percent black [or nonwhite]), average years of education or occupational level, percent owner-occupied residences, and neighborhood/housing conditions in an area. The second group of variables has to do with the availability of such things as gambling, alcohol, and guns in ecological areas.

Urban/Rural Residency and City Population Size

A large number of studies have addressed the question of whether crime rates are higher in cities or in rural areas, and quite a few of those have also compared suburbs to urban/rural differences. Of course, like so many variables studied by social scientists, definitions of what constitutes *urban, rural,* or *suburban* regions are imprecise. Most studies have adopted the practice of classifying rural areas as those consisting of less than 25,000 population, but other criteria have also been used. The concept of *suburban* is even less precisely defined, but basically refers to a residential area that is within a half-hour's drive of a large metropolitan area.[4]

Table 6.1a presents the results of studies of urban/rural (and sometimes suburban) differences in crime rates. Given the imprecision in the definitions of these ecological categories, it is remarkable to note that the evidence is nearly unanimous in indicating that crime rates are higher in urban than in rural areas, with suburban areas being

TABLE 6.1a. Relationship between urban/rural residency and criminality/antisocial behavior (overall consistency score = 87.8%; established correlate).

| Nature of the Relationship | Types and Seriousness of Offenses | | | | | | | | Clinical Conditions | |
| | Official Statistics | | | | | | Self-Reported | | | |
	Violent Offenses	Property Offenses	Drug Offenses	Delinquency	General & Unspecified Offenses	Recidivism	Victimful & Overall Offending	Illegal Drug Use	Conduct Disorders	Antisocial Personality Syndrome
Crime Rate Lower in Rural than in Urban Area	**Europe** *Finland: 1* **North America** *United States: 11*	**North America** *United States: 2*	**North America** *United States: 2*	**Europe** *Denmark: 1* **Middle East** *Israel: 2* **North America** *Canada: 1; United States: 6* **Other** *Several Countries: 1*	**Africa** *Uganda: 1; Zambia: 1; Several Countries: 1* **Asia** *Korea: 1; Taiwan: 1* **Europe** *Denmark: 2; England: 4; Finland: 2; France: 2; Poland: 1; Netherlands: 1* **North America** *Canada: 3; United States: 36* **Other** *Several Countries: 3*		**Europe** *Norway: 1; Spain: 1; Switzerland: 1* **North America** *United States: 6*	**North America** *Canada: 1; United States: 11*	**Europe** *England: 2; Norway: 2* **North America** *Canada: 2*	**Middle East** *Israel: 1*
No significant difference		**North America** *United States: 1*		**North America** *United States: 1*	**Asia** *Former Soviet Union: 1*			**Europe** *Switzerland: 1*		
Crime higher in rural than in urban area							**Europe** *Spain: 1* **North America** *United States: 1*			
Suburban area intermediate to urban/rural areas	**North America** *United States: 2*			**North America** *United States: 2*	**North America** *United States: 5*					
No significant difference										
Suburban area not intermediate										

intermediate. A few studies have come to the same conclusion with respect to conduct disorders and psychopathy: Both conditions appear to occur at higher rates in urban areas than in rural areas.[5]

Most of the exceptional studies shown in Table 6.1a all reported no significant differences, and were usually based on some unusual circumstances. For instance, a study in Switzerland, a country with few large cities, found that persons who grew up in intermediate-sized cities (10–50,000) self-reported higher delinquency and crime rates than persons from larger cities (50,000+), although both surpassed the self-reported offense rates of persons growing up in the smallest communities (<10,000).[6] In one U.S. and one Spanish self-report study, the rates of drug offenses were higher for youth growing up in the rural communities than for those reared in large cities.[7]

Several studies have investigated urban–rural variations in people's fear-of-crime. As you would suspect, these studies have all found that persons living in large urban areas generally have the highest degree of fear, while those living in rural areas have the lowest, and residents of suburban communities have intermediate degrees of fear.[8]

Closely related to the concept of urban/rural residency is that of city population size. This variable is most often used for comparing large cities, all of which would otherwise simply be classified as urban. As Table 6.1b shows, research has generally concluded that as the overall size of an urban population increases, so too does its crime rate.[9] Victimization data has also indicated that the larger and more urban a community is, the higher is its overall crime rate.[10]

Sometimes other factors can distort urban/rural residency or population size as correlates of crime.[11] An example comes from studies in Canada. As shown in Figure 6.1, even though the overall pattern is still consistent with the generalization that large urban centers have higher crime rates than do small rural areas, when communities of less than 5,000 are compared, they have been found to have higher crime rates than communities that are somewhat larger.[12] This higher crime rate for these very small communities reflects the high concentration of Native Americans in villages with less than 5,000 inhabitants.[13] This same pattern was found in a study conducted in Alaska.[14]

A concept frequently mentioned in connection with discussions of urban/rural variations in crime rates is that of the **gradient** (or **concentric zone**) **hypothesis**.[15] This hypothesis states that crime tends to be highest in areas closest to the central business districts of any large city, and then gradually diminishes as one moves out from that the business district (barring some natural barriers such as coastlines or mountain ranges). Various studies have found evidence to support the gradient hypothesis.[16] Note, however, that the gradient hypothesis is merely a descriptive term, not an explanation for why crime rates are nearly always higher in urban areas with high rates of manufacturing and commerce.

One can confidently say that urbanism and community size are positively associated with crime rates.[17] Studies based on victimization surveys (which are not shown in Tables 6.1a or 6.1b, have all come to the same conclusion, both in the U.S.[18] and in Italy.[19] This runs contrary to speculation that

TABLE 6.1b. Evidence of a relationship between city population size and crime/delinquency rates (overall consistency score = 89.3%; established correlate).

Nature of the Relationship	Type and Seriousness of Offenses								Antisocial Clinical Conditions	
	Official Statistics						Self-Reported Offenses			
	Violent Offenses	Property Offenses	Drug Offenses	Delinquency	General & Unspecified Offenses	Recidivism	Victimful & Overall Offending	Illegal Drug Use	Childhood Conduct Disorders	Antisocial Personality
Positive	**North America** *United States:* 9	**Europe** *Slovikia:* 1 **North America** *United States:* 4			**North America** *United States:* 11					
Not significant	**North America** *United States:* 3									
Negative										

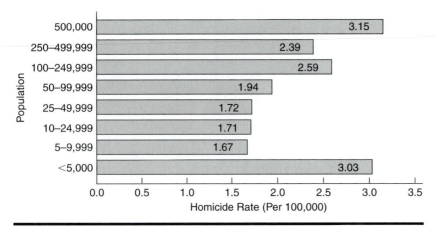

FIGURE 6.1 Average homicide rates according to community size, Canada 1978–90 (adapted from Gartner 1995:198).

differences are due to the greater police presence in urban than in suburban or rural areas.

Technological Development/ Modernization/Industrialization

A concept that quite a number of ecological studies have examined with respect to crime rates is **technological development** (also called *modernization* and *industrialization*). This concept refers to the degree to which the citizens of a society rely on nonagricultural economic activities, such as manufacturing and technological services, to make a living. Most of the studies of the relationship between technological development and crime rates involve making international comparisons.

The results of studies of the link between technological development and crime rates are shown in Table 6.2. As you can see, the findings for crime rates in general are mixed, with nearly half of the studies failing to find significant relationships. However, if you focus just on violent offenses, the evidence generally indicates that technologically developed societies have significantly lower offending rates than do less developed societies.[20] In the case of property offenses, the opposite pattern emerges, with all studies so far reporting significant positive relationships.[21]

Population Density

Population density refers to the number of persons per some unit of space. Two types of space measures are used in these studies: household or room, and square mile or square kilometer.[22] **Household density** is usually measured in terms of the number of persons divided by the square footage or number of rooms in residential households. **Density per square mile** (or **kilometer**) is most often measured by determining the average number of persons per square mile within an urban area (or within an entire country).

As you can see in Table 6.3, the evidence is moderately consistent with the view that population density and criminality are positively correlated, particularly in the case of delinquency and property crimes. In the case of violent crimes, the evidence is mixed, with most studies failing to find a significant relationship.

Residential Mobility and Owner-Occupied Housing

Residential mobility refers to the rate at which people in an area change the homes in which they live. As shown in Table 6.4, many studies have investigated the relationship between residential mobility and offending rates, nearly all of which have found the relationship to be positive. In other words, areas of a neighborhood, city, or state in which people change addresses the most tend to be those in which crime rates are the highest.

TABLE 6.2. Evidence of a relationship between technological development and crime/delinquency rates (overall consistency score = 40.0%; unestablished correlate; consistency score for violent crime = 80%; probable correlate; consistency score for property crime = 100%; well-established correlate).

| Nature of the Relationship | Type and Seriousness of Offenses | | | | | | | | Antisocial Clinical Conditions | |
| | Official Statistics | | | | | | Self-Reported Offenses | | | |
	Violent Offenses	Property Offenses	Drug Offenses	Delinquency	General & Unspecified Offenses	Recidivism	Victimful & Overall Offending	Illegal Drug Use	Childhood Conduct Disorders	Antisocial Personality
Negative	**International** *Several Countries: 8*				**International** *Several Countries: 2*					
Not significant	**South/ Central America & Carribean** *Columbia: 1* **International** *Several Countries: 1*				**Europe** *France: 3*					
Positive		**International** *Several Countries: 5*								

TABLE 6.3. Evidence pertaining to the relationship between population density and criminal/antisocial behavior (overall consistency score = 59.3%; possible correlate).

Nature of the Relationship	Type and Seriousness of Offenses								Antisocial Clinical Conditions	
	Official Statistics						Self-Reported Offenses			
	Violent Offenses	Property Offenses	Drug Offenses	Delinquency	General & Unspecified Offenses	Recidivism	Victimful & Overall Offending	Illegal Drug Use	Childhood Conduct Disorders	Antisocial Personality
Positive	**North America** *United States: 7* **International** *Several Countries: 1*	**Europe** *Germany: 1* **North America** *United States: 3*		**Europe** *Sweden: 1* **North America** *United States: 11*	**North America** *United States: 7*			**North America** *Canada: 1*		
Not significant	**Asia** *India: 1* **Europe** *France: 1; Germany: 1* **North America** *United States: 10* **International** *Several Societies: 9*	**North America** *United States: 1*			**North America** *United States: 1*		**North America** *Canada: 1*			
Negative										

TABLE 6.4. Evidence pertaining to a relationship between residential mobility and criminal/antisocial behavior (overall consistency score = 89.3%; established correlate).

Nature of the Relationship	Type and Seriousness of Offenses								Antisocial Clinical Conditions	
	Official Statistics						Self-Reported Offenses			
	Violent Offenses	Property Offenses	Drug Offenses	Delinquency	General & Unspecified Offenses	Recidivism	Victimful & Overall Offending	Illegal Drug Use	Childhood Conduct Disorders	Antisocial Personality
Positive	**North America** *United States: 5*	**North America** *United States: 2*		**North America** *Canada: 1; United States: 9* **Pacific** *New Zealand: 1*	**Europe** *England: 1* **North America** *United States: 3*	**Europe** Netherlands: 1	**North America** *United States: 2*			
Not significant	**North America** *United States: 1*						**North America** *United States: 1*	**North America** *United States: 1*		
Negative										

Residences are often classified as being either owner-occupied or rental units. Over the years, several studies have examined the possibility that areas in which most of the houses are owner-occupied have lower rates of crime than areas consisting of numerous rental homes.

As you can see in Table 6.5, nearly all of these studies have concluded that as the proportion of homes that are owner-occupied increases crime and delinquency rates decrease. One study conducted in England identified two types of rental homes: privately owned and publicly owned. This study concluded that crime rates were particularly high where most of the rental homes were publicly owned.[23]

Percent Divorced/Separated (Single-Parent Households)

Another social ecological measure that has been frequently investigated with respect to variations in criminal behavior is the proportion of the population that is divorced or separated. This is usually determined on the basis of census information, and therefore has only been studied with reference to official crime data.

As Table 6.6 shows, studies have repeatedly found a positive correlation between regions with high rates of divorced or separated people and high rates of violent crime. However, both studies that focused on property offenses failed to find a significant relationship. Overall, there appears to be a significant link between crime rates and divorce rates at an ecological level of analysis.

Percentage of Teens and Young Adults in the Population

Several studies have attempted to determine whether the proportion of the population in their teens and twenties have unusually high crime rates. Most of these studies have involved comparing neighborhoods in large metropolitan areas or comparing sizable numbers of large cities based on information about age distributions derived from census data. Somewhat varying age ranges have

TABLE 6.5. Evidence of a relationship between the percent of homes occupied by their owners (as opposed to being occupied by renters) and the region's crime/delinquency rate (overall consistency score = 93.3%; established correlate).

| Nature of the Relationship | Type and Seriousness of Offenses | | | | | | | | | Antisocial Clinical Conditions | |
| | Official Statistics | | | | | | Self-Reported Offenses | | | | |
	Violent Offenses	Property Offenses	Drug Offenses	Delinquency	General & Unspecified Offenses	Recidivism	Victimful & Overall Offending	Illegal Drug Use	Childhood Conduct Disorders	Antisocial Personality
Negative	**Europe** England: 1	**Europe** England: 1 **North America** United States: 1		**North America** United States: 7 **Pacific** Australia: 1	**Europe** England: 2 **North America** United States: 1					
Not significant										
Positive					**North America** United States: 1					

TABLE 6.6.   Evidence of a relationship between percentage of adults who are divorced or separated (or single-parent households) in a region and the region's crime/delinquency rate (overall consistency score = 86.7%; established correlate).

| Nature of the Relationship | Type and Seriousness of Offenses | | | | | | | | | Antisocial Clinical Conditions | |
| | Official Statistics | | | | | | Self-Reported Offenses | | | | |
	Violent Offenses	Property Offenses	Drug Offenses	Delinquency	General & Unspecified Offenses	Recidivism	Victimful & Overall Offending	Illegal Drug Use	Childhood Conduct Disorders	Antisocial Personality
Positive	**North America** *United States:* 19			**Europe** *Germany:* 1 **North America** *United States:* 1 **Pacific** *Australia:* 1	**Europe** *Wales:* 1 **North America** *United States:* 3					
Not significant		**North America** *United States:* 2								
Negative	**Europe** *France:* 1									

been used to designate teens and young adults, with the most common being those between 15 and 24 or between 15 and 29, although a few studies have also used 20 to 29.[24]

The results of these studies are shown in Table 6.7, which reveals that most studies have not found significant relationships between the percentage of populations that are teenagers and young adults and the crime rates in those populations. This is noteworthy in light of the clear evidence that crime is highly concentrated in the second and third decades of life. Were one to assume that crime is significantly higher in communities and cities with the highest proportions of citizens who are between 15 and 24 (or 29), one would be committing what social scientists call the *ecological fallacy* (as discussed earlier in this chapter).

Mortality Rates

A number of studies have examined the relationship between average life expectancy in an eco-logical region and its crime rate. Some of these studies have focused on overall mortality rates, whereas others have studied infant mortality.

As Table 6.8 shows, most of these studies have found mortality rates to be higher in regions (usually countries) with the highest crime rates.

Tourism/Gambling

Areas that are major tourist attractions have been compared to regions that are either low or average in their tendencies to attract tourists to see if the former have higher crime rates. Studies have particularly focused on gambling as a tourist attraction.

As shown in Table 6.9, most studies have found a significant correlation between tourism and/or gambling and crime rates. Of course, caution needs to be exercised in attempting to interpret these findings because tourism is probably associated with other ecological correlates of

TABLE 6.7. Evidence of a relationship between percent of a population who are teenagers and young adults and the region's crime/delinquency rate (overall consistency score = 42.9%; unestablished correlate).

| Nature of the Relationship | Type and Seriousness of Offenses | | | | | | | | Antisocial Clinical Conditions | |
| | Official Statistics | | | | | | Self-Reported Offenses | | | |
	Violent Offenses	Property Offenses	Drug Offenses	Delinquency	General & Unspecified Offenses	Recidivism	Victimful & Overall Offending	Illegal Drug Use	Childhood Conduct Disorders	Antisocial Personality
Positive	**North America** *United States:* 5 **International** *Several Countries:* 3	**Europe** *France:* 1 **North America** *United States:* 1			**North America** *United States:* 2					
Not significant	**North America** *United States:* 7 **International** *Several Countries:* 3				**North America** *Canada:* 2					
Negative	**North America** *United States:* 2									

TABLE 6.8. Evidence of a relationship between mortality rates and crime/delinquency rates (overall consistency score = 77.8%; probable correlate).

| Nature of the Relationship | Type and Seriousness of Offenses | | | | | | | | Antisocial Clinical Conditions | |
| | Official Statistics | | | | | | Self-Reported Offenses | | | |
	Violent Offenses	Property Offenses	Drug Offenses	Delinquency	General & Unspecified Offenses	Recidivism	Victimful & Overall Offending	Illegal Drug Use	Childhood Conduct Disorders	Antisocial Personality
Positive	**North America** *United States:* 1 **International** *Several Countries:* 1	**International** *Several Countries:* 2		**Europe** *Germany:* 1 **North America** *United States:* 1	**Europe** *Germany:* 1					
Not significant	**International** *Several Countries:* 2									
Negative										

TABLE 6.9.   Evidence of a relationship between tourism/gambling in a region and its crime/delinquency rate (overall consistency score = 83.3%; probable correlate).

Nature of the Relationship	Type and Seriousness of Offenses								Antisocial Clinical Conditions	
	Official Statistics						Self-Reported Offenses			
	Violent Offenses	Property Offenses	Drug Offenses	Delinquency	General & Unspecified Offenses	Recidivism	Victimful & Overall Offending	Illegal Drug Use	Childhood Conduct Disorders	Antisocial Personality
Positive		North America *United States:* 1			North America *United States:* 5 **Pacific** *Australia:* 1; *Hawaii:* 2 **South/ Central America & Carribean** *Mexico:* 1					
Not significant	North America *United States:* 1				North America *United States:* 1					
Negative										

Per Capita Alcohol Consumption (and Alcohol Availability)

Several studies have looked for evidence of a relationship between the amount of alcohol people consume in a region and that region's crime rate. Because alcohol is taxed almost everywhere it is legally sold, it is possible to calculate per capital alcohol consumption by dividing the revenue derived from alcohol sales by the number of people who live in the area (some studies just count the population that is of legal drinking age).

The results of these studies are summarized in Table 6.10. You can see that most studies have found a significant positive correlation between per capita alcohol consumption and rates of violent crime. However, this positive relationship does not appear to hold for property crimes. Instead, the only two studies bearing on this issue (both conducted by the same researcher), found the opposite pattern: As per capita consumption of alcohol rose, property offenses tended to decrease, both in France[25] and in Germany.[26]

One example of the apparent link between per capita alcohol consumption and rates of violent crime is shown in Figure 6.2. As you can see, homicide rates and rates of alcohol consumption in Sweden tended to closely parallel one another for over a century.

An ecological variable that is closely related to per capita alcohol consumption is one called *alcohol outlet density*. This refers to the number of taverns and/or liquor stores in an area (usually adjusted for the size of the area or the number of people living in it). These studies are nearly always conducted at neighborhood levels within large cities. In Table 6.11, you can see that all of the studies conducted so far have found that neighborhoods with the highest alcohol outlet

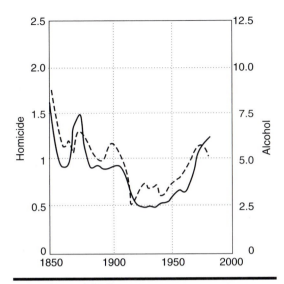

FIGURE 6.2   Trends in homicide rates (solid line) and per capita alcohol consumption (dashed line) from 1850 through 1985 in Sweden (after von Hofer 1990:38).

densities are usually those with the highest crime rates.

It is also worth mentioning that some studies have controlled for the possible confounding influences of such factors as gender and age compositions of the populations under study. These studies have found that at least some of the alcohol outlet density–crime rate relationship is best explained in terms of extraneous factors.[27] Most notably, young males have unusually high crime rates *and* are more likely to visit taverns than females or those who are middle-aged or older. So, if you have a population with an unusually high proportion of young males, there is a good chance that this population will have *both* a high crime rate and high per capita alcohol consumption, making the connection between the latter two variables coincidental. Nevertheless, even after controlling for these sorts of confounding demographics, some of the alcohol consumption/availability–crime relationship seems to remain, especially in the case of violent crime.[28]

TABLE 6.10.   Evidence of a relationship between per capita alcohol consumption and crime/delinquency rates (overall consistency score = 50.0%; possible correlate).

| Nature of the Relationship | Type and Seriousness of Offenses | | | | | | | | Antisocial Clinical Conditions | |
| | Official Statistics | | | | | | Self-Reported Offenses | | | |
	Violent Offenses	Property Offenses	Drug Offenses	Delinquency	General & Unspecified Offenses	Recidivism	Victimful & Overall Offending	Illegal Drug Use	Childhood Conduct Disorders	Antisocial Personality
Positive	**Europe** *Finland:* 1; *France:* 1; *Sweden:* 2 **North America** *United States:* 1									
Not significant	**North America** *United States:* 1									
Negative		**Europe** *France:* 1; *Germany:* 1								

TABLE 6.11. Evidence of a relationship between alcohol outlet density (i.e., the prevalence of taverns and liquor stores in an area) and crime/delinquency rates (overall consistency score = 90.0%; established correlate).

| Nature of the Relationship | Type and Seriousness of Offenses | | | | | | | | Antisocial Clinical Conditions | |
| | Official Statistics | | | | | | Self-Reported Offenses | | Childhood Conduct Disorders | Antisocial Personality |
	Violent Offenses	Property Offenses	Drug Offenses	Delinquency	General & Unspecified Offenses	Recidivism	Victimful & Overall Offending	Illegal Drug Use		
Positive	**North America** *United States: 3*				**North America** *Canada: 1; United States: 5*					
Not significant	**North America** *United States: 1*									
Negative										

Incidentally, we will be revisiting the alcohol consumption–crime relationship in the next two chapters. These chapters will review studies that have examined the relationship based on family and individual levels of analyses (instead of the ecological level, as we are doing here). Ultimately, you will see that it is all but impossible to escape concluding that some sort of important link exists between alcohol consumption and criminality.

Per Capita Gun Ownership

A question that has provoked heated debate over the years has had to do with the relationship between the availability of guns in a region and that region's crime rate. Some have argued the relationship is positive (the more guns, the more crime there will be), while others have argued the opposite (the more guns, the more crime will be prevented).

Since the 1970s, a number of social scientists have sought to shed light on the controversy by comparing regions with high and low rates of gun ownership. Most of these studies have been conducted in the United States, a country with relatively few restrictions on gun ownership, but with substantial state-to-state variations in the laws governing gun ownership. A summary of the findings is presented in Table 6.12. The table indicates that most studies have found a negative relationship between per capita gun ownership and crime, especially in the case of violent crime. In other words, the highest crime rates are in areas where gun ownership is the *lowest*.

One study sought to determine if the type of gun made a difference by comparing ownership of long guns (rifles and shotguns) to handguns. It found that violent crimes were lowest in regions of the country where ownership of long guns was the highest; ownership of handguns had little effect either way.[29] Nevertheless, another study compared states in the United States that recently began allowing people to carry concealed hand guns. It concluded that violent crime rates dropped significantly following the passage of these laws.[30]

You need to be on guard not to "overinterpret" these findings. One confounding problem is that gun ownership (especially of long guns) tends to be higher in rural than in urban areas. As noted earlier in this chapter, nearly all studies have found higher crime rates in urban areas.

TABLE 6.12.   Evidence of a relationship between per capita gun ownership and crime/delinquency rates (overall consistency score=72.7%; probable correlate).

Nature of the Relationship	Type and Seriousness of Offenses								Antisocial Clinical Conditions	
	Official Statistics						Self-Reported Offenses			
	Violent Offenses	Property Offenses	Drug Offenses	Delinquency	General & Unspecified Offenses	Recidivism	Victimful & Overall Offending	Illegal Drug Use	Childhood Conduct Disorders	Antisocial Personality
Negative	**North America** *United States: 5* **International** *Several Countries: 1*				**North America** *United States: 2*					
Not significant	**North America** *United States: 1*				**North America** *United States: 1*					
Positive	**North America** *United States: 1*									

Ethnic/Racial Heterogeneity

The degree to which a geopolitical region is comprised of more than one recognized ethnic or racial group is referred to as its **ethnic/racial heterogeneity.** The opposite of ethnic/racial heterogeneity is ethnic/racial homogeneity.

Various methods have been used to measure ethnic heterogeneity, but the most common is to determine the proportion of a population (usually one comprising a neighborhood) that belongs to each ethnic group, and then calculate the degree to which the groups approach equal proportions. For instance, say that you have two neighborhoods, both of which are comprised of two ethnic groups. One has 5 percent of one ethnic group and 95 percent of the other, while the second neighborhood has 45 percent of one ethnic group and 55 percent of the other. In this example, the second neighborhood would be considered more ethnically heterogeneous than the first neighborhood.

Table 6.13 shows that several studies have been undertaken to determine if heterogeneous areas (most often neighborhoods in large cities) have higher rates of crime than areas that are relatively homogeneous. As you can see, the evidence is fairly consistent in indicating that the more ethnically heterogeneous a population is, the higher its crime and delinquency rates tend to be. Interestingly, the exceptions so far all have to do with violent offenses.

Percent Black (or "Nonwhite")   Numerous studies have been conducted in the United States in which the proportion of a population that is black in a region is correlated with the region's crime rate. In a few of these studies, the term *nonwhite* was used, but the reports all made clear that the vast majority of nonwhites were of African-American heritage.

As shown in Table 6.14, most of these studies have concluded that violent crime rates are significantly higher in cities or neighborhoods with higher proportions of black residents, with tendencies being best established for violent offenses. Regarding property offenses, the studies are nearly evenly split between those that reported a positive

TABLE 6.13. Evidence of a relationship between regional variations in ethnic/racial heterogeneity and regional crime/delinquency rates (overall consistency score = 63.6%; possible correlate).

| Nature of the Relationship | Type and Seriousness of Offenses | | | | | | | | Antisocial Clinical Conditions | |
| | Official Statistics | | | | | | Self-Reported Offenses | | | |
	Violent Offenses	Property Offenses	Drug Offenses	Delinquency	General & Unspecified Offenses	Recidivism	Victimful & Overall Offending	Illegal Drug Use	Childhood Conduct Disorders	Antisocial Personality
Negative	**North America** *United States: 2* **International** *Several Countries: 3*	**Europe** *England: 1* **North America** *United States: 1*			**Europe** *Yugoslovia: 1* **North America** *Canada: 1; United States: 3*	**Europe** *England: 1*		**North America** *United States: 1*		
Not significant	**International** *Several Countries: 6*									
Positive	**North America** *United States: 1*									

TABLE 6.14. Evidence of a relationship between percent black (or nonwhite) in a region and the region's crime/delinquency rate (overall consistency score = 83.9%; probable correlate).

| Nature of the Relationship | Type and Seriousness of Offenses | | | | | | | | Antisocial Clinical Conditions | |
| | Official Statistics | | | | | | Self-Reported Offenses | | | |
	Violent Offenses	Property Offenses	Drug Offenses	Delinquency	General & Unspecified Offenses	Recidivism	Victimful & Overall Offending	Illegal Drug Use	Childhood Conduct Disorders	Antisocial Personality
Positive	**North America** *United States: 35*	**North America** *United States: 7*		**North America** *United States: 5*	**North America** *United States: 9*					
Not significant	**North America** *United States: 3*	**North America** *United States: 4*		**North America** *United States: 1*						
Negative								**North America** *United States: 1*		

correlation and those that reported no significant relationship. The overall conclusion suggested by Table 6.13 is that crime rates are positively correlated with the percent of black people comprising a neighborhood or city, at least as far as violent offenses are concerned.

Percent Foreign Born. One more ecological variable similar to ethnic/racial composition is that of the proportion of a population that was born in another country. Table 6.15 presents the results of studies, primarily conducted in Europe, of the relationship between the percentage of a region's population that was foreign born and the region's crime rate. The results are somewhat mixed but generally consistent with the view that a positive relationship exists.

Average Years of Education and Occupational Levels of Residents

Several studies have sought to determine if crime rates are related to the average years of education and/or the occupational level of persons living in various neighborhoods or large cities. Data per-

taining to income, the other main social status measure, will be considered separately below.

As you can see in Table 6.16, most studies pertaining to average education or occupation levels of people in neighborhoods or cities have concluded that these social status measures have a negative relationship with area crime rates. Nevertheless, there are a few studies that have failed to find significant differences, making years of education and occupation levels of residents only a probable ecological correlate of crime. Note that this again stands in sharp contrast to years of education and occupational levels at the individual level of analysis, both of which are established correlates of crime.

REGIONAL ECONOMIC VARIABLES

Is there a relationship between how wealthy a neighborhood (or city or state) is and its rate of crime? This question has been examined using several different regional economic measures, and, as we will see, these regional measures have not provided entirely consistent answers.

TABLE 6.15. Evidence of a relationship between percent foreign born in a region and the region's crime/delinquency rate (overall consistency score = 66.7%; possible correlate).

Nature of the Relationship	Type and Seriousness of Offenses								Antisocial Clinical Conditions	
	Official Statistics						Self-Reported Offenses			
	Violent Offenses	Property Offenses	Drug Offenses	Delinquency	General & Unspecified Offenses	Recidivism	Victimful & Overall Offending	Illegal Drug Use	Childhood Conduct Disorders	Antisocial Personality
Positive	**Europe** *France:* 1			**Europe** *Germany:* 1	**Europe** *Germany:* 1 **North America** *United States:* 1					
Not significant	**North America** *United States:* 1	**Europe** *France:* 1								
Negative										

TABLE 6.16.   Evidence of a relationship between regional variations in average years of education or occupational level in a region and the region's crime/delinquency rates (overall consistency score = 73.3%; probable correlate).

| Nature of the Relationship | Type and Seriousness of Offenses | | | | | | | | | Antisocial Clinical Conditions | |
| | Official Statistics | | | | | | Self-Reported Offenses | | | | |
	Violent Offenses	Property Offenses	Drug Offenses	Delinquency	General & Unspecified Offenses	Recidivism	Victimful & Overall Offending	Illegal Drug Use	Childhood Conduct Disorders	Antisocial Personality
Negative	**North America** *United States: 4*			**Europe** *England: 1; Germany: 1* **North America** *United States: 2*	**North America** *United States: 2*		**North America** *United States: 1*			
Not significant	**North America** *United States: 1*	**North America** *United States: 2*		**North America** *United States: 1*						
Positive										

Five regional economic measures have been given the most criminological research attention: regional median income, percent living below poverty, neighborhood conditions, unemployment rates, and degree of disparity in income. While it is obvious that there is a substantial overlap between these various regional economic indicators, it is important not to equate them.[31]

Median Income

One measure of a region's economic well-being has involved comparing neighborhoods or cities in terms of the average incomes of their residents. The average income is usually expressed in terms of annual median family earnings (the median is the point about and below which one half of a population is located).

As you can see from Table 6.17, most studies have found that as the average income of a neighborhood or city increased, the rate of crime tends to decrease. Nonetheless, there are several exceptional studies in the sense that they did not find average income to be significantly different in high versus low crime-rate areas. In addition, some stud-

ies of official property crimes and of self-reported offenses have actually found positive correlations between crime rates and area median incomes. Furthermore, studies based on self-reports all either found no significant relationship or a positive relationship. In general, it would be unwise to consider the issue settled at this point regarding any ecological relationship between crime rates and the average income of cities or neighborhoods.

Percent Living below the Poverty Line

Another way to assess the socioeconomic well-being of a neighborhood or city has been to use a *poverty index*. Such an index has been developed mainly in the United States, based on the assumption that a family of a given size needs a certain minimum income in order to "make ends meet." The exact amount of money for this index is adjusted every year for inflation. The proportion of families in a region whose earnings are below this monetary value are said to be living below the poverty line.

Table 6.18 summarizes the findings from studies conducted so far on the relationship between

TABLE 6.17. Evidence of a relationship between regional median income and crime/delinquency rates (overall consistency score = 59.6%; possible correlate; consistency score with self-reports excluded = 66.7%; possible correlate).

| Nature of the Relationship | Type and Seriousness of Offenses | | | | | | | | Antisocial Clinical Conditions | |
| | Official Statistics | | | | | | Self-Reported Offenses | | | |
	Violent Offenses	Property Offenses	Drug Offenses	Delinquency	General & Unspecified Offenses	Recidivism	Victimful & Overall Offending	Illegal Drug Use	Childhood Conduct Disorders	Antisocial Personality
Negative	**North America** *United States:* 10 **International** 4	**North America** *United States:* 2 **International** 1		**North America** *Canada:* 1; *United States:* 3	**Europe** *England:* 1 **North America** *United States:* 6					
Not significant	**North America** *United States:* 2	**North America** *United States:* 2			**North America** *United States:* 2		**North America** *United States:* 1			
Positive		**Asia** *Hong Kong:* 1 **North America** *United States:* 1 **International** 2					**North America** *United States:* 2			

TABLE 6.18. Evidence of a relationship between regional variations in the percent of residents below poverty (or welfare dependent) and regional crime/delinquency rates (overall consistency score = 68.4%; possible correlate).

| Nature of the Relationship | Type and Seriousness of Offenses | | | | | | | | Antisocial Clinical Conditions | |
| | Official Statistics | | | | | | Self-Reported Offenses | | | |
	Violent Offenses	Property Offenses	Drug Offenses	Delinquency	General & Unspecified Offenses	Recidivism	Victimful & Overall Offending	Illegal Drug Use	Childhood Conduct Disorders	Antisocial Personality
Positive	**North America** *United States:* 26	**North America** *United States:* 5		**North America** *United States:* 5	**North America** *United States:* 2		**North America** *United States:* 1			
Not significant	**North America** *United States:* 4	**North America** *United States:* 4			**North America** *United States:* 4					
Negative	**North America** *United States:* 3									

the proportion living below the poverty line and the region's crime rate. You can see that most of the evidence suggests that, as the proportion of a population living in poverty increases in an area, so to does the area's crime rate. Interestingly, the relationship has been better established for violent offending than for property offending.

Neighborhood Conditions

Another measure of regional economic conditions has to do with the overall state of repair of the neighborhood. Over the years, many studies have been conducted to determine if neighborhoods that are well-maintained have lower rates of crime than poorly maintained neighborhoods. Of course, it is to be expected that well-maintained neighborhoods will generally be those with the best tax base, and therefore also have the wealthiest residents.

The results of studies attempting to link neighborhood conditions with crime rates are summarized in Table 6.19. You can see that these studies consistently indicate that poorly maintained neighborhoods have higher crime rates than well-kept neighborhoods.

In general, the evidence supports the conclusion that persons who live in poorly maintained

TABLE 6.19. Results from studies of the relationship between neighborhood and housing conditions and criminal/antisocial behavior (overall consistency score = 92.3%; established correlate; consistency score with self-reports excluded = 100%; well-established correlate).

Nature of the Relationship	Types and Seriousness of Offenses								Clinical Conditions	
	Official Statistics						Self-Reported			
	Violent Offenses	Property Offenses	Drug Offenses	Delin-quencies	General & Unspecified Offenses	Recidivism	Victimful & Overall Offending	Illegal Drug Use	Childhood Conduct Disorders	Antisocial Personality
More offending in poorly maintained Neighborhoods	**North America** *United States: 3*		**North America** *United States: 2*	**Africa** *Egypt:* 1 **Asia** *India:* 1; *Japan:* 1 **Europe** *England:* 9; *Italy:* 1; *Yugoslavia:* 1 **North America** *Canada:* 2; *United States:* 35 **Pacific** *Australia:* 3	**Europe** *England:* 5; *Wales:* 1 **North America** *United States:* 4		**Europe** *England:* 2 **North America** *United States:* 3 **Pacific** *Australia:* 1	**North America** *United States:* 7	**North America** *United States:* 1	
Not significant							**Europe** *Sweden:* 1 **North America** *United States:* 3 **Pacific** *Australia:* 1			
Less offending in poorly maintained neighborhoods							**North America** *United States:* 1			

neighborhoods have higher rates of offending than do those living in well kept neighborhoods. The only possible exception is in the case of self-reported offending, where only about half of the studies have found a link between neighborhood conditions and offending rates.

Unemployment Rate

Yet another economic measure is unemployment. A number of studies have been undertaken to determine if crime rates are higher in areas where rates of unemployment are highest. As you can see in Table 6.20, these studies have reached conflicting conclusions. The overall consistency score reflects the fact that, for violent offenses, property offenses, and crimes in general, there is only a slight tendency for studies to suggest that crime rates are higher in areas with relatively high unemployment rates.

Having considered regional (cross-sectional) variations in unemployment and crime rates, let us consider time variations in unemployment rates and crime. As you can see by inspecting Table 6.21, many studies have investigated the possibility that increases in unemployment in a specific area over time are associated with rises in crime rates. The findings have been mixed, with essentially as many studies reporting no significant relationship as those finding a significant positive relationship.

Income Inequality: General and Racial

Another ecological measure of variation in wealth is a concept known as **income disparity.** This refers to the *differences* that exist between people

TABLE 6.20. Relationship between regional variations in unemployment rates and criminal/antisocial behavior (overall consistency score = 53.1%; possible correlate).

Nature of the Relationship	Type and Seriousness of Offenses								Antisocial Clinical Conditions	
	Official Statistics						Self-Reported Offenses			
	Violent Offenses	Property Offenses	Drug Offenses	Delinquency	General & Unspecified Offenses	Recidivism	Victimful & Overall Offending	Illegal Drug Use	Childhood Conduct Disorders	Antisocial Personality
Positive	**Europe** *England: 2* **North America** *Canada: 1; United States: 8* **International** *Several Countries: 1*	**Europe** *England: 3* **North America** *Canada: 1; United States: 9*	**North America** *United States: 1*	**North America** *United States: 2*	**Europe** *England: 2* **North America** *Canada: 1; United States: 11* **Pacific** *Australia: 1*					
Not significant	**North America** *United States: 10* **International** *Several Countries: 2*	**North America** *United States: 6*			**Europe** *England: 2* **North America** *United States: 9* **International** *Several Countries: 1*					
Negative	**North America** *United States: 3*	**International** *Several Countries: 1*								

TABLE 6.21. Time-series relationships between unemployment rates and rates of crime/delinquency (overall consistency score = 46.8%; unestablished correlate).

| Nature of the Relationship | Type and Seriousness of Offenses | | | | | | | | Antisocial Clinical Conditions | |
| | Official Statistics | | | | | | Self-Reported Offenses | | | |
	Violent Offenses	Property Offenses	Drug Offenses	Delinquency	General & Unspecified Offenses	Recidivism	Victimful & Overall Offending	Illegal Drug Use	Childhood Conduct Disorders	Antisocial Personality
Positive	**Middle East** *Israel: 2* **North America** *Canada: 1; United States: 5*	**Asia** *Taiwan: 1* **Europe** *Sweden: 1* **Middle East** *Israel: 1* **North America** *Canada: 1; United States: 7*		**North America** *United States: 4*	**Europe** *England: 3* **North America** *Canada: 1; United States: 14* **Pacific** *Australia: 1* **International** *Several Countries: 1*					
Not significant	**North America** *United States: 9* **International** *Several Countries: 1*	**Europe** *England: 1* **Middle East** *Israel: 1* **North America** *Canada: 1 United States: 2*		**North America** *United States: 2* **Pacific** *Australia: 1*	**Africa** *Uganda: 1* **Europe** *England: 4; Sweden: 1* **North America** *United States: 8*					
Negative	**North America** *Canada: 4* **International** *Several Countries: 1*	**Europe** *Germany: 1* **North America** *United States: 3*								

or families living in an area, rather than to any measures of poverty per se. To understand this concept, imagine two cities with the same average income. However, in City A, there are no millionaires, whereas in City B, 5 percent of the families are millionaires. For these two cities to have the same average, City B must not only have more millionaires than City A, it must also have many more people who are extremely poor. In other words, in order for the *average* income of both cities to be the same, City A must be made up of nearly all middle income people, whereas City B must have substantial numbers of both very rich and very poor people. One would therefore say

that City B would have a greater degree of income inequality than City A.

To measure income inequality, most studies use what is called the **Gini index,** a measure developed by economists for comparing regions and groups regarding income inequality.[32] It is not necessary for you to know how the Gini index is applied, but it takes into account how much dispersion there is between those in a population who make the highest and the lowest incomes.

Income inequality has been extensively studied as a possible correlate of crime, and the results are presented in three tables. The first of these tables—Table 6.22—summarizes the findings that have compared different regions (such as different cities or states). As you can see, most studies of income disparity have indicated that crime rates are higher in areas where income inequality is the greatest. In other words, neighborhoods, cities, and states in which everyone is more or less equal in their incomes tend to have lower crime rates than areas where the greatest income inequality exists. Nevertheless, there are many studies that have failed to find a statistically significant difference, especially in the case of property offenses, and a few studies that have actually found the opposite pattern.

The second table—Table 6.23—compares income inequality within the same region over time. As you can see, the pattern is similar to the cross-sectional findings: In most studies, increased income inequality is associated with increased offending rates, especially in the case of violent offenses.

Rather than reflecting *overall* income inequality, the third table is concerned with income inequalities between racial groups. Specifically, all of the studies summarized in Table 6.24 were conducted in the United States and had to do with comparing the average incomes of whites and the average incomes of blacks. Some of the studies compared regions, while others made comparisons over time.

These studies have reached conflicting findings regarding violent crimes, with some suggesting that such offenses are highest in cities where average black–white differences in income are the greatest, other studies finding the opposite, and still others finding no significant differences. For

TABLE 6.22. Evidence of a cross-sectional relationship between income inequality within regions and regional crime/delinquency rates (overall consistency score = 60.2%; possible correlate).

Nature of the Relationship	Type and Seriousness of Offenses								Antisocial Clinical Conditions	
	Official Statistics						Self-Reported Offenses			
	Violent Offenses	Property Offenses	Drug Offenses	Delinquency	General & Unspecified Offenses	Recidivism	Victimful & Overall Offending	Illegal Drug Use	Childhood Conduct Disorders	Antisocial Personality
Positive	North America Canada: 2; United States: 19 International Several Countries: 19	North America Canada: 1; United States: 4 International Several Countries: 1			North America United States: 13					
Not significant	North America Canada: 1; United States: 12 International Several Countries: 2	North America United States: 2			North America United States: 2					
Negative	North America United States: 3 International Several Countries: 1	North America United States: 2 International Several Countries: 2			North America United States: 1					

TABLE 6.23.   Evidence of time series relationships between overall income inequality and crime/delinquency rates (overall consistency score = 83.3%; probable correlate).

Nature of the Relationship	Type and Seriousness of Offenses								Antisocial Clinical Conditions	
	Official Statistics						Self-Reported Offenses			
	Violent Offenses	Property Offenses	Drug Offenses	Delinquency	General & Unspecified Offenses	Recidivism	Victimful & Overall Offending	Illegal Drug Use	Childhood Conduct Disorders	Antisocial Personality
Positive	**North America** *United States: 1*	**Asia** *Taiwan: 1* **North America** *United States: 1*			**Asia** *Taiwan: 1* **North America** *United States: 1*					
Not significant		**North America** *United States: 1*								
Negative										

TABLE 6.24.   Evidence of a cross-sectional relationship between racial (black-white) income inequality and crime/delinquency rates (overall consistency score = 33.3%; unestablished correlate).

Nature of the Relationship	Type and Seriousness of Offenses								Antisocial Clinical Conditions	
	Official Statistics						Self-Reported Offenses			
	Violent Offenses	Property Offenses	Drug Offenses	Delinquency	General & Unspecified Offenses	Recidivism	Victimful & Overall Offending	Illegal Drug Use	Childhood Conduct Disorders	Antisocial Personality
Positive	**North America** *United States: 4*	**North America** *United States: 1*								
Not significant	**North America** *United States: 3*									
Negative	**North America** *United States: 2*									

one study of property crimes, a positive link with black–white differences in income was found.

State of the Economy

Another economic variable that has received considerable research attention over the years has been the overall state of the economy. Economists most often measure the state of a region's economy with such indicators as the rate of consumer spending. As the rate of spending increases in a region, its economy is said to be experiencing a surge.

Two tables indicate how the state of the economy relates to offending rates. Table 6.25 presents

TABLE 6.25.   Evidence of a cross-sectional relationship between the state of the economy and crime/delinquency rates (overall consistency score = 45.0%; unestablished correlate).

| Nature of the Relationship | Type and Seriousness of Offenses | | | | | | | | | Antisocial Clinical Conditions | |
| | Official Statistics | | | | | | Self-Reported Offenses | | | | |
	Violent Offenses	Property Offenses	Drug Offenses	Delinquency	General & Unspecified Offenses	Recidivism	Victimful & Overall Offending	Illegal Drug Use	Childhood Conduct Disorders	Antisocial Personality
Positive	**North America** *United States: 7*				**Europe** *Sweden: 1* **North America** *United States: 1*					
Not significant	**North America** *United States: 7*									
Negative		**North America** *United States: 1*		**North America** *United States: 1*						

results based on cross-sectional comparisons, and Table 6.26 presents results based on time-series comparisons. In both cases, the picture is far from being entirely consistent, except that if the state of the economy affects crime rates, it has more to do with violent crime than with property crime.

If one had to generalize based on the studies summarized in these two tables, it would probably be as follows: As the state of the economy improves, violent crime rates as well as delinquency rates tend to increase. However, studies of property crime rates suggest that they move in the opposite direction; they decrease. This is a very odd pattern, and one that will continue to challenge criminologists for an explanation.

PHYSICAL/TEMPORAL ECOLOGICAL FACTORS

The last category of ecological variables to be considered have more to do with the physical environment than with the social environment. One of these variables is seasonality, and the other is distance from the equator.

Seasonality

Over the years, several studies have sought to determine if crime is more common during certain seasons of the year than during others. The results of these studies are summarized in Table 6.27. While crimes are obviously committed throughout the year, you can see that most studies have found violent offending to be most prevalent during the spring and summer months. As far as property crimes are concerned, there appears to be little if any seasonal pattern.

Distance from the Equator ("Southernness")

For over a century, criminologists have reported that crime rates seem to be significantly higher on average the closer one gets to the equator, at least in the northern hemisphere. This has been especially well documented in the case of homicides, although this may be simply because homicides are the only category of official crime that can be confidently compared across countries.

TABLE 6.26.   Evidence of a time-series relationship between the state of the economy and crime/delinquency rates (overall consistency score = 33.3%; unestablished correlate).

Nature of the Relationship	Type and Seriousness of Offenses								Antisocial Clinical Conditions	
	Official Statistics						Self-Reported Offenses			
	Violent Offenses	Property Offenses	Drug Offenses	Delinquency	General & Unspecified Offenses	Recidivism	Victimful & Overall Offending	Illegal Drug Use	Childhood Conduct Disorders	Antisocial Personality
Positive	**Europe** *England: 2* **North America** *United States: 3* **International** *Several Countries: 1*	**Europe** *Sweden: 1* **North America** *United States: 2*		**Asia** *Japan: 2* **North America** *United States: 5* **International** *Several Countries: 1*	**North America** *United States: 1*					
Not significant	**Europe** *Sweden: 1* **North America** *United States: 1*	**Europe** *Germany: 1*			**Asia** *Japan: 2* **Europe** *Germany: 2* **North America** *United States: 1*					
Negative		**Europe** *England: 2; France: 1; Sweden: 1* **North America** *United States: 1*			**Asia** *Japan: 1* **Europe** *England: 3; France: 2* **North America** *United States: 2* **International** *Several Countries: 1*					

As you can see in Table 6.28, the research is very consistent in indicating that the closer one moves toward the equator, the higher crime rates tend to be, at least in the case of violent offenses. Most of the research in recent decades has been conducted in the United States on homicide rates, and nearly all of these studies have indicated that rates in southern states are higher than rates in northern states. A recent study sought to determine if the difference was best considered gradual or dichotomous (with all southern states forming one cluster and all northern states forming a second cluster). The conclusion was that the differences were gradual, such that the farther south in latitude one goes in the United States, the higher the homicide rate tends to be.[33]

In the United States, this phenomenon is usually called the **Southernness Factor.**[34] Several recent U.S. studies have failed to confirm the Southernness Factor, suggesting that if it has been of significance in the past, it is not so any longer.[35] Other U.S. studies have found that the Southernness Factor only seemed to be significant when comparing whites, not when comparing blacks,[36] or that it only applies to homicide, not to any other types of crime.[37]

At least three U.S. studies have also compared crime rates with average temperature in various geographic regions. They all found that regions where the average temperature is high have higher crime rates, particularly for violent crimes.[38] Overall, at least in the northern hemisphere (where

TABLE 6.27.   Evidence of a relationship between seasonality and crime/delinquency rates (overall consistency score = 68.4%; possible correlate).

| Nature of the Relationship | Type and Seriousness of Offenses | | | | | | | | | Antisocial Clinical Conditions | |
| | Official Statistics | | | | | | Self-Reported Offenses | | | | |
	Violent Offenses	Property Offenses	Drug Offenses	Delinquency	General & Unspecified Offenses	Recidivism	Victimful & Overall Offending	Illegal Drug Use	Childhood Conduct Disorders	Antisocial Personality
Highest in Summer and/or Spring	**Asia** *Korea:* 1 **Europe** *England:* 1 **North America** *United States:* 7 **International** *Various Countries:* 2	**North America** *United States:* 1			**North America** *United States:* 1					
Highest in Winter	**North America** *United States:* 1	**Europe** *England:* 2			**Europe** *England:* 1					
Highest in Fall	**Europe** *Germany:* 1									
No significant differences	**North America** *United States:* 1									

TABLE 6.28.   Evidence of a relationship between distance from equator (or "southernness") and regional variations in crime/delinquency rates (overall consistency score = 82.1%; probable correlate).

| Nature of the Relationship | Type and Seriousness of Offenses | | | | | | | | | Antisocial Clinical Conditions | |
| | Official Statistics | | | | | Recidivism | Self-Reported Offenses | | | | |
	Violent Offenses	Property Offenses	Drug Offenses	Delinquency	General & Unspecified Offenses		Victimful & Overall Offending	Illegal Drug Use	Childhood Conduct Disorders	Antisocial Personality
Negative	**Europe** *France:* 1; *Italy:* 2 **North America** *United States:* 24	**Europe** *Slovakia:* 1			**North America** *United States:* 3					
Not significant	**North America** *United States:* 5									
Positive	**North America** *Canada:* 1									

all of the research thus far has been conducted), geographic regions that are relatively close to the equator appear to have higher crime rates, especially for violent crimes.

The clearest exception to the Southernness Factor is Canada. In this country, the highest crime rates, especially for violent offenses, tend to be in the northernmost provinces.[39]

Interpreting the Southernness Factor, as well as other regional variations in crime rates, must be done cautiously. One reason has to do with the fact that crimes are usually officially recorded with respect to where they occurred, not where the offender or the victim resides. This means that regions that are major tourist attractions may appear to have higher crime rates than they would otherwise.[40] Generally, the southern regions of the northern hemisphere are warmer and therefore more attractive tourist attractions.

Another reason for caution in comparing states has to do with the fact that such things as age, race/ethnicity, and degree of urbanization are all related to crime probabilities, and these variables are rarely distributed randomly in geographic terms. As with many other factors related to criminality, the Southernness Factor is interesting, but at best of only modest significance.

CLOSING COMMENTS ON ECOLOGICAL AND MACROECONOMIC CORRELATES

Probably, the most notable feature of studies reviewed in this chapter is the degree of conflicting evidence concerning which ecological and macroeconomic variables are and are not correlates of crime. Even within the various categories of official data, one can find several variables for which the evidence is quite contradictory with respect to any consistent relationship to offending rates.

If one were to try to explain why so many contradictions exist, there are many possibilities, but the two most likely involve difficulty measuring some of the variables of interest and sample size. Regarding sample size, you should know that most nonecological studies utilize samples in the hundreds, and sometimes thousands. For example, the typical study used to assess gender differences in crime rates would have had several hundred members of each gender. In the usual ecological study, on the other hand, the sample size is commonly *less* than one hundred. For example, several of the ecological studies involved comparing the fifty states of the United States, and others involved comparing a few dozen countries or neighborhoods. From a statistical standpoint, small samples of ecological units of analysis make findings less stable. Thus, even when a "real" relationship exists between two variables, researchers are less likely to find it when the number of "sampling units" they are working with is relatively small. Basically, it is fair to assume that many of the "not significant" findings cited in the tables throughout this chapter are likely to have been the result of the relatively small number of units of analyses used in the typical ecological study.

SUMMARY

This chapter has summarized what has been discovered about the relationships between crime rates and ecological and macroeconomic variables. *Ecological variables* have to do with the social or physical environment in which individuals live, and *macroeconomic variables* are concerned with the financial conditions of entire populations, not individuals and families.

In considering ecological and macroeconomic variables, social scientists warn against making the *ecological fallacy:* Just because a particular type of relationship exists at an individual level of analysis does not mean that one will necessarily find the same relationship at various group levels. For example, even though there is a fairly well-established negative relationship between individual income and involvement in criminal behavior, this does not necessarily mean that as average income in a population increases, crime rates will decrease. And, as we have seen in this chapter, any links between average income and crime rates at various ecological levels is still very much up in the air.

Four categories of ecological and macroeconomic variables were considered in this chapter: social ecological variables, regional macroeconomic variables, time-series macroeconomic variables, and physical ecological variables.

Social Ecological Variables

The social ecological variables discussed were urban/rural residency, technological development/modernization, population density, residential mobility and owner-occupied housing, percent divorced or separated, percent teens and young adults, mortality rates; tourism/gambling, per capita alcohol consumption and alcohol availability, per capita gun ownership, ethnic/racial heterogeneity, percent black (nonwhite), percent foreign born, and average years of education and occupational level of residents. Let us review the main conclusions that can be drawn from the available evidence of relationships between these variables and offending rates in various geographical regions.

Regarding urban–rural residency, most studies throughout the world support the generalization that crime rates are more prevalent in urban areas than in surrounding rural areas, with the suburbs exhibiting intermediate rates. Similarly, a substantial majority of studies have shown that crime rates increase with increases in a city's population size.

Technological development/modernization (including industrialization) have been fairly often studied with reference to criminality, usually at the level of comparing different nations or tracking one or a few nations over time. These studies have produced mixed results, with tendencies toward a decrease in violent crime associated with techno-

logical development and an increase in property crime.

In the case of population density, most studies have found rates of crime and delinquency increasing as density increases. This appears to be true using several density measures, e.g., persons per square mile (or kilometer), persons per room in the household. The main exception pertains to violent offenses, where most studies have found no significant relationship.

Research on the relationship between residential mobility and criminality largely supports the conclusion that a positive relationship exists. Studies of the percentage of homes in an area that are owner-occupied (as opposed to being rental homes or public housing) have concluded that crime and delinquency rates are lower in the former. Owner-occupied residency studies indicate that areas with high rates of owner-occupied homes have lower crime rates than do those that are primarily rental homes.

Regarding the percent divorced or separated living in a region, the evidence is consistent in linking this percentage to increased rates of violent offending, but not to increased property offending. Studies of a possible link between the proportion of the population who are in their teens and twenties and crime rates have not found a consistent pattern. Also, studies of mortality patterns generally indicate that areas with the highest mortality rates have the highest rates of crime.

A number of studies have investigated ecological variables such as tourism, gambling, and per capita alcohol consumption. These have generally indicated a positive relationship between these variables and offending rates, although the evidence has not been overwhelming. *Alcohol outlet density,* referring to the number of taverns and bars that are concentrated in a neighborhood, in particular, appears to be positively linked to crime rates.

A very controversial area of ecological research on crime has to do with gun ownership rates. The evidence is somewhat mixed, but, surprisingly to many, most studies have found that crime rates are lowest in areas with the highest rates of gun ownership.

In the case of the racial/ethnic composition of neighborhoods, research has consistently found that crime and delinquency rates are higher in the most ethnically diverse neighborhoods. As far as specific racial/ethnic groups are concerned, nearly all of the research has been confined to the United States. These studies have generally indicated that, especially in the case of violent crimes, rates are higher in predominantly black neighborhoods than in predominantly white neighborhoods. Studies of the percent foreign born in an area (usually a country) have found a tendency for these areas to have somewhat higher-than-average crime rates.

Ecological studies of the average years of education and types of occupations held by people living in the region indicate that as the average years of education and/or levels of occupation of adult residents increase, the rates of crime and delinquency decrease. Nonetheless, several of these studies have failed to find significant differences.

Regional Economic Variables

Variables having to do with the economic conditions of a neighborhood, city, state, or nation have been examined in many studies with reference to ecological variations in crime rates. The variables considered under this category were: average income, percent of households below a designated poverty line, conditions of the neighborhood, unemployment rate, and two relative poverty measures.

Studies of average (median) income have provided a mixed picture with respect to a relationship. While most studies have found a significant inverse relationship, especially in the case of official data, several studies have not.

Numerous studies in the United States have examined crime-rate variations according to the percent of a population living below the officially designated poverty line. Nearly all of these have found that violent crimes are more common in neighborhoods or cities with the highest propor-

tion of persons living in poverty. Surprisingly, however, only about half of the available studies have found any link between rates of property offense and the proportion of persons living in poverty.

Research involving neighborhood conditions has been largely consistent in indicating that crime rates are higher in poorly kept neighborhoods than in those that are well maintained. The only possible exception has to do with self-reported offending, for which studies have often found no significant differences.

When cities or states are compared regarding their unemployment rates, studies have provided quite mixed results. About half of the studies have found a positive relationship, and the other half have found essentially no relationship, regardless of the type of official crimes compared.

Two measures of income disparity have been investigated with reference to criminality: income disparities within a population as a whole (called *relative poverty*), and income disparities between blacks and whites. Results have been mixed in both cases, although most studies have tilted toward the conclusion that as disparities increase, so too do crime rates, especially for violent crimes.

Time-Series Economic Variables

Economic variables that have to do with changes in a region's economic vitality over years, and sometimes decades, are called *time-series macroeconomic variables*. Two such variables have been studied extensively with reference to variations in crime rates: unemployment rates and measures of the state of the economy. Both present an unclear picture with respect to being related to crime rates.

Regarding unemployment, no consistent pattern has yet been identified in the numerous studies that have been conducted. In the case of fluctuations in a region's economy, violent offenses and delinquency appear to rise when the state of the nation's economy improves. However this does not appear to be true for property offenses or for crime in general.

TABLE 7.1b.   Evidence of a relationship between birth order and criminal/antisocial behavior (overall consistency score = 92.9%; established correlate; consistency score excluding self-reports = 100%; well-established correlate).

| Nature of the Relationship | Type and Seriousness of Offenses | | | | | | | | Antisocial Clinical Conditions | |
| | Official Statistics | | | | | | Self-Reported Offenses | | | |
	Violent Offenses	Property Offenses	Drug Offenses	Delinquency	General & Unspecified Offenses	Recidivism	Victimful & Overall Offending	Illegal Drug Use	Childhood Conduct Disorders	Antisocial Personality
Oldest least criminal/ antisocial	**Asia** *India:* 1				**Asia** *India:* 1 **Europe** *England:* 1 **North America** *United States:* 9		**North America** *United States:* 1			
No significant difference							**North America** *United States:* 1			
Oldest most criminal/ antisocial										

Being Married and Age at Marriage

Several studies have investigated how married people compare to single and divorced people of the same age in their criminal/antisocial tendencies. As shown in Table 7.2a, most of these studies have concluded that married people are less involved in criminal behavior than those who are single or divorced. One study included a sample of male widowers, as well as single, married and divorced men, all of about the same average age. It concluded that widowers and married men had comparably low rates of psychopathy; divorced men had the highest rates of psychopathy, and single (never married) men had intermediate levels.[7]

The link between being married and low criminal/antisocial behavior might lead some to conclude that if people would just get married earlier than they do now, we would have less delinquency and crime. This, however, is not supported by available research. Table 7.2b shows that delinquents tend to get married at significantly earlier ages than do nondelinquents. Overall, while *being* married, and *staying* married, appear to be associ-ated with low rates of criminal/antisocial behavior, simply *getting* married, especially at an early age, is not.

Out-of-Wedlock Births or Unwanted Pregnancies

Whether someone is born to unmarried parents or is the result of an unwanted pregnancy are difficult issues to discuss. The stigma attached to out-of-wedlock births is still substantial, even though these births have become increasingly prevalent in most industrialized countries over the past half century. Since 1990, for example, one fourth of all births in the United States have been to unmarried women.[8] Criminologists have examined out-of-wedlock births as a possible correlate of crime since the 1980s.

The degree to which the pregnancy was wanted versus unwanted has also received some research attention.[9] The most common reasons for a pregnancy being unwanted are that the parents were not married or were in the process of

TABLE 7.2a.   Evidence of a relationship between being married and criminal/antisocial behavior (overall consistency score = 73.7%; probable correlate).

| Nature of the Relationship | Type and Seriousness of Offenses | | | | | | | | Antisocial Clinical Conditions | |
| | Official Statistics | | | | | | Self-Reported Offenses | | | |
	Violent Offenses	Property Offenses	Drug Offenses	Delinquency	General & Unspecified Offenses	Recidivism	Victimful & Overall Offending	Illegal Drug Use	Childhood Conduct Disorders	Antisocial Personality
Negative	North America *United States:* 1			Europe *England:* 1 North America *United States:* 2	North America *United States:* 2	Europe *Netherlands:* 1 North America *United States:* 3	North America *United States:* 1	North America *United States:* 2		North America *United States:* 1
Not significant				Europe *England:* 1	North America *United States:* 1	Europe *England:* 1 North America *United States:* 1				
Positive					Middle East *Israel:* 1					

TABLE 7.2b.   Evidence of a relationship between age at marriage and criminal/antisocial behavior (overall consistency score = 100%; well-established correlate).

| Nature of the Relationship | Type and Seriousness of Offenses | | | | | | | | Antisocial Clinical Conditions | |
| | Official Statistics | | | | | | Self-Reported Offenses | | | |
	Violent Offenses	Property Offenses	Drug Offenses	Delinquency	General & Unspecified Offenses	Recidivism	Victimful & Overall Offending	Illegal Drug Use	Childhood Conduct Disorders	Antisocial Personality
Negative				Europe *England:* 2 Middle East *Israel:* 1	Europe *Germany:* 2			North America *United States:* 1		
Not significant										
Positive										

separating, the desire by the women to pursue a career, and the couple already having more children than they wanted.

Table 7.3 presents a capsule summary of the results of research regarding these two closely related variables. As you can see, the findings are largely consistent with the conclusion that children born out-of-wedlock and/or as a result of an un-wanted pregnancy are more likely than children in general to exhibit criminal/antisocial behavior. These studies are further supported by an ecological study in the United States that found that cities with the highest percentages of female-headed households had significantly higher homicide and robbery rates than cities with the lowest female-headed households.[10] Overall, the consistency

TABLE 7.3.   Studies of the relationship between out-of-wedlock births and unwanted pregnancies and criminal/antisocial behavior in the offspring (overall consistency score for out-of-wedlock births = 100%; well-established correlate; overall consistency score for unwanted pregnancy = 88.9%; established correlate).

Nature of Relationship to Criminal/Antisocial Behavior in the Offspring		Type and Seriousness of Offenses							Antisocial Clinical Conditions	
		Official Statistics					Self-Reported Offenses			
		Violent Offenses	Property Offenses	Drug Offenses	Delinquency	General & Unspecified Offenses	Victimful & Overall Offending	Illegal Drug Use	Childhood Conduct Disorders	Antisocial Personality
Out-of-Wedlock Birth	Positively Related	**North America** *United States: 2*				**Europe** *England: 1; Finland: 1; Sweden: 1* **North America** *United States: 1*			**North America** *United States: 2*	
	No significant Relationship									
	Negatively Related									
Unwanted Pregnancy	Positively Related				**Europe** *Sweden: 1*	**Europe** *Czech Republic: 1 Sweden: 1*	**North America** *United States: 1*	**Europe** *Sweden: 1* **North America** *United States: 1*	**Europe** *Czech Republic: 1; Sweden: 1*	
	No significant Relationship					**Europe** *Sweden: 1*				
	Negatively Related									

score suggests that out-of-wedlock births and unwanted pregnancies are established correlates of crime.

Intactness of Parents' Marital Bond ("Broken Homes")

Whether children are reared by a single parent or by both parents living together in the same household is referred to as *intactness of parents' marital bond* or *intact/broken homes*.[11] Homes are "broken" most often because of divorce or separation, although occasionally it is the result of the death of a parent. If parents do not remain together while a child is growing up, the child is said to have come from a nonintact family (or a broken home).

In considering studies of the link between broken homes and criminality, it is important to keep in mind that some children live all their lives with only one parent, while others do so only late in adolescence. Unfortunately, most of the studies on the subject of the link between broken homes and criminal/antisocial behavior have not attempted to examine the timing of the parental separation. Also, researchers have varied in terms of whether they take remarriage and foster parenting factor into account.

Results concerned with broken homes and criminality are summarized in Table 7.4. As you can see, large numbers of these studies have been conducted, with a particularly heavy focus on juvenile delinquency. Also worth noting is that a high proportion of these studies have been conducted in the United States, perhaps because the United States has the highest divorce rate of all industrialized nations.[12]

As Table 7.4 shows, the vast majority of studies have found significantly higher rates of delinquency among persons who come from broken homes than from intact families.[13] The bulk of the exceptional studies were based on self-reported delinquency. This suggests that only for the most trivial types of offenses is one likely not to find a significant relationship between broken homes and criminal/antisocial behavior.[14] For serious delinquency and criminality, the relationship appears to be generally established.[15]

Two studies in the United States analyzed the delinquency-broken home relationship separately for blacks and whites. One found that while a significant relationship existed for both groups, the

TABLE 7.4. Relationship between intactness of parents' marital bond and criminal/antisocial behavior (overall consistency score = 82.2%; probable correlate; consistency score excluding self-reports = 94.3%; established correlate).

Nature of the Relationship	Types and Seriousness of Offenses								Clinical Conditions	
	Official Statistics						Self-Reported			
	Violent Offenses	Property Offenses	Drug Offenses	Delinquency	Unspecified Offenses	Recidivism	Victimful & Overall Offending	Illegal Drug Use	Conduct Disorders	Antisocial Personality Syndrome
Higher in broken homes	**Africa** *Egypt:* 1 **Pacific** *Japan:* 1 **North America** *United States:* 1		**North America** *United States:* 1	**Africa** *Nigeria:* 1; *Ghana:* 1 **Asia** *Former Soviet Union:* 1; *Japan:* 1 **Europe** *Denmark:* 2; *England:* 14; *Norway:* 1; *Sweden:* 2 **North America** *United States:* 80 **Pacific** *Hawaii:* 1; *New Zealand:* 1	**Europe** *Denmark:* 1; *England:* 1; *France:* 2; *Slovakia:* 1; *Sweden:* 1 **North America** *United States:* 9 **Pacific** *Japan:* 1 **South-Central America & Caribbean** *Chile:* 1 **Several Countries:** 1	**Europe** *Finland:* 1; *Netherlands:* 1; *Sweden:* 1 **North America** *United States:* 5 **Pacific** *Hawaii:* 1	**Europe** *England:* 1 **North America** *Canada:* 2; *United States:* 16	**Europe** *England:* 1; *Switzerland:* 1; *Spain:* 1 **North America** *United States:* 22; *Canada:* 4	**Europe** *Sweden:* 1 **North America** *Canada:* 1; *United States:* 11	**Pacific** *New Zealand:* 1
No significant difference		**North America** *United States:* 3		**North America** *United States:* 2 **Europe** *England:* 1		**Europe** *England:* 1	**Europe** *Switzerland:* 1 **North America** *United States:* 22	**North America** *United States:* 9		
Lower in broken homes				**North America** *United States:* 1					**North America** *United States:* 1	

relationship was strongest in the case of blacks.[16] However, another study only found the relationship to be significant in the case of whites.[17]

It is worth noting that some of the studies listed in Table 7.4 as having found positive relationships between broken homes and criminality largely eliminated the statistical relationship by mathematically controlling for other family or demographic variables.[18] Race and social status, for example, are both are associated with being reared in single-parent households, and, as was noted in Chapter 5, they are also related to criminality. Once these demographic variables are statistically eliminated, little or no relationship remains between delinquency and being reared in broken homes.[19]

One study compared three types of families: intact, mother-only, and mother-with-male-partner other than the father. For girls, it found no differences. However, among boys, the highest rates of conduct disorders were found for mother-only families.[20] Similar conclusions were reached by two other studies.[21] They both found conduct disorders for both boys and girls to be lowest for intact marital family structures. Two other studies also concluded that children from divorced homes whose mothers remarried were more delinquent than children from divorced homes in which the mothers remained unmarried.[22]

Another study looked at marital dissolution in terms of whether the parents remarried. It found that divorce was significantly linked to delinquency only when one or both parents remarried within two to three years.[23]

Two other comments are worth making about criminological research pertaining to broken homes. First, a few studies have compared children from homes broken by divorce with homes broken by the death of one of the parents. Children from homes broken by divorce appear to have higher delinquency rates than do children from one-parent families due to the death of a parent.[24] The few studies that have attempted to assess links between the specific timing of parental divorce and offspring delinquency have concluded that the earlier the divorce occurred in a child's life, the higher the risk of serious delinquency,[25] especially in the case of boys.[26] Two other studies, however, have failed to find significant links between the age at which divorce occurred and a child's likelihood of becoming delinquent.[27]

Second, some have argued that broken homes are more closely related to delinquency and crime by females than by males,[28] while other studies have concluded that the relationship holds for both genders.[29] So far, only one study found the relationship more pronounced in males than in females.[30] At this point, the possibility of gender differences in the relationship between broken homes and delinquency has not been settled. However, the overall pattern is clear: A substantial relationship has been documented between broken homes and all forms of delinquency and crime, with the exception of very trivial forms of delinquency.[31]

The bottom line for all of the research so far conducted on the relationship between broken homes and criminal/antisocial behavior is that a modest positive relationship appears to exist. However, numerous factors appear to be interlinked with both of these variables, making any attempt to disentangle them all but impossible. The confounding factors include higher than normal poverty among single parent families,[33] parental discord leading up to and sometimes continuing beyond the divorce,[34] and less time spent by single parents than joint parents with each of their children.[35] Keep in mind that our concern at this point is not with trying to untangle these complex interrelationships, but with becoming familiar with the basic nature of the array of variables associated with criminal/antisocial behavior.

Marital/Family Discord

All married couples have disagreements. However, in some marriages, the parents argue much more often than they do in others, often leading other family members to become embroiled in the disputes as well. Persistent conflicts of this sort are referred to as **marital/family discord.**

Numerous studies have examined the possibility of a relationship between marital/family discord and criminal/antisocial behavior among offspring. As shown in Table 7.5, these studies have consistently shown that children who are reared in families with the greatest degree of discord are significantly more likely to engage in delinquent and criminal behavior than children reared in families generally. At least one study indicated that family discord may be even more closely associated with delinquency than is parental divorce.[35]

While there is no serious doubt that marital/family discord is a correlate of crime, you should avoid jumping to the conclusion that the discord is necessarily causing criminal/antisocial behavior in children. What else might explain such a relationship? Perhaps the antisocial behavior of a child at least partly provokes the parents to argue about how to deal with the misbehavior.

Parent–Child Attachment

Three important aspects of parent–child interaction have been identified: warmth and affection, supervision, and discipline.[36] We will consider each of these as possible correlates of crime.

Parent–child attachment refers to the degree to which parents interact frequently with their children and enjoy doing so. Researchers have measured such attachment with questions directed either toward children or their parents. These questions include ones about how often the family does things together and how well parents and children get along with one another.[37]

Quite a number of studies have examined the relationship between parent–child attachment and variation in criminal/antisocial behavior among the offspring. As you might suspect, most of these studies have concentrated on juvenile delinquency rather than on adult criminality. Table 7.6 shows that the studies have been largely consistent in indicating that loving relationships between parents and children are associated with lower probabilities of delinquency and crime in the child.[38] Nearly all of the exceptional studies had to do with self-reported drug use, particularly the use of marijuana.[39]

As we will see in the upcoming theoretical chapters, criminologists are not of one mind in ex-

TABLE 7.5. Evidence of a relationship between marital/family discord and criminal/antisocial behavior in the offspring (overall consistency score = 100%; well-established correlate).

Nature of the Relationship	Type and Seriousness of Offenses								Antisocial Clinical Conditions	
	Official Statistics						Self-Reported Offenses			
	Violent Offenses	Property Offenses	Drug Offenses	Delinquency	General & Unspecified Offenses	Recidivism	Victimful & Overall Offending	Illegal Drug Use	Childhood Conduct Disorders	Antisocial Personality
Positive	**North America** *United States: 2*			**Asia** *China: 1* **Europe** *England: 1* **North America** *United States: 16; Hawaii: 2*	**Europe** *Denmark: 1* **North America** *United States: 1*	**Europe** *England: 1* **North America** *United States: 2*	**North America** *United States: 13*	**Europe** *England: 1* **North America** *Canada: 2; United States: 9*	**Europe** *England: 2; Sweden: 1* **North America** *United States: 6*	**Pacific** *New Zealand: 1*
Not significant										
Negative										

TABLE 7.6. Relationship between strength of parent–child attachments and criminal/antisocial behavior in the offspring (overall consistency score = 90.6%; established correlate; consistency score excluding self-reports = 95%; well-established correlate).

Nature of the Relationship	Types and Seriousness of Offenses								Clinical Conditions	
	Official Statistics						Self-Reported			
	Violent Offenses	Property Offenses	Drug Offenses	Delinquency	General & Unspecified Offenses	Recidivism	Victimful & Overall Offending	Illegal Drug Use	Conduct Disorders	Antisocial Personality Syndrome
Negative				Asia *China: 1; Russia: 1* North America *Canada: 1; United States: 11*	Europe *Finland: 1; Portugal: 1* North America *United States: 2*		Europe *England: 2* North America *United States: 15*	Europe *Norway: 1* North America *United States: 11*	Europe *England: 1*	
Not significant	Europe *Denmark: 1*							North America *United States: 4*		
Positive										

plaining this relationship. While some see parental actions as the primary causal factor,[40] others have suggested that the behavior of some children elicits less loving responses from parents than does the behavior of other children.[41]

Parental Monitoring and Supervision

Parents vary in the degree to which they monitor and supervise their children. Over the years, many researchers have attempted to determine if these variations have significant links to variations in criminal and antisocial behavior.

As you can see in Table 7.7, the evidence is largely consistent with the view that carefully monitored and supervised children are less involved in delinquent activities than are children who receive little parental attention and guidance. There are only two contrary studies, both of which indicated that parents who were "overly restrictive" in attending to their children's activities had offspring with higher rates of delinquency than did parents in general.[42] Therefore, it may be that

parents can go overboard in supervising and monitoring their children in terms of delinquency prevention, but the overall pattern clearly supports the view that criminal/antisocial behavior are inversely associated with parental supervision and monitoring.

Parenting Competence and Parental Discipline Styles

Even though people do not all agree on *exactly* what constitutes competent parenting, everyone agrees that some parents do a better job than others. Accordingly, several studies have been undertaken to assess the link between competency/ineptness of parenting and criminal/antisocial behavior in offspring. To measure parental competency, researchers have either used ratings based on home observations, or merely the judgments offered by adolescents of their parents' parental competence.

The results of these studies are shown in Table 7.8a. You can see that all studies agree that parents of delinquent and conduct-disordered

TABLE 7.7.   Relationship between degree of parental supervision/monitoring and criminal/antisocial behavior (consistency score = 93.8%; established correlate).

Nature of the Relationship	Types and Seriousness of Offenses								Clinical Conditions	
	Official Statistics						Self-Reported			
	Violent Offenses	Property Offenses	Drug Offenses	Delinquency	General & Unspecified Offenses	Recidivism	Victimful & Overall Offending	Illegal Drug Use	Conduct Disorders	Antisocial Personality Syndrome
Negative	**North America** *United States: 2*		**North America** *United States: 1*	**Europe** *England: 3* **North America** *United States: 10*	**Europe** *England: 2* **North America** *United States: 1*		**Asia** *China: 1* **Europe** *England: 5; Netherlands: 1; Switzerland: 1* **North America** *Canada: 2; United States: 17*	**North America** *United States: 9*	**Europe** *England: 2* **North America** *United States: 3*	
Not significant										
Positive				**Europe** *England: 1* **Pacific** *Australia: 1*						

TABLE 7.8a.   Relationship between parental competence and criminal/antisocial behavior in offspring (consistency score = 100%; well-established correlate).

Nature of the Relationship	Type and Seriousness of Offenses								Childhood Conduct Disorders	
	Official Statistics						Self-Reported Offenses			
	Violent Offenses	Property Offenses	Drug Offenses	Delinquency	General & Unspecified Offenses	Recidivism	Victimful & Overall Offending	Illegal Drug Use	Antisocial Personality	Antisocial Clinical Conditions
Negative				**Europe** *England: 1* **North America** *United States: 1*			**North America** *United States: 1*	**North America** *United States: 1*	**North America** *United States: 3*	
Not significant										
Positive										

youth on average are judged to be significantly more inept (less competent) than is true for parents of children in general.

Because of their greater experience with life and their concern for the welfare of their children, parents lay down rules for their children to follow.

Of course, children do not always see things the way their parents do, and, therefore, at least occasionally disobey the rules. As a result, parents impose various forms of punishment on their children, in various ways, ranging from a few words of warning to physical beatings. Many criminological studies have been directed toward discovering whether some forms of parental discipline are more related to offspring criminality than are others.

One of the problems with this line of research is that researchers have had difficulty specifying and objectively measuring the various types of discipline styles used by parents. Despite these difficulties, fairly clear patterns have emerged about the types of discipline patterns that are most associated with criminal/antisocial behavior.

As shown in Table 7.8a, the type of parental discipline style that has been found most often to be associated with high rates of delinquency and crime in offspring has been described as harsh and inconsistent. Harsh punishment largely includes the use of spanking, and inconsistent punishment is that in which parents sometimes tolerate considerable misbehavior but at other times tolerate little.

Results from one of the relevant studies are shown in Figure 7.1. As you can see, the mothers who never used physical punishment with their children had those with the fewest antisocial behavioral symptoms and those who used physical punishment once or more in the past six months had children with the most symptoms. Caution is in order in interpreting these findings. Not only could the relationship mean that physical punishment somehow encourages children to be antisocial, but it could also mean that children who exhibit antisocial behavior provoke physical punishment by their parents more than is true for children generally.

Some studies have tried to identify the sort of parental discipline styles that are *less* common among delinquent than nondelinquent children. Most of these studies point to loving but firm discipline patterns, meaning patterns that set definite boundaries of acceptable behavior for children, but always do so in the context of caring deeply for them.

In considering the evidence summarized in Table 7.8b, avoid jumping to the conclusion that harsh and inconsistent discipline or totally lax discipline by parents causes children to become delinquent and criminal. That may be true, but

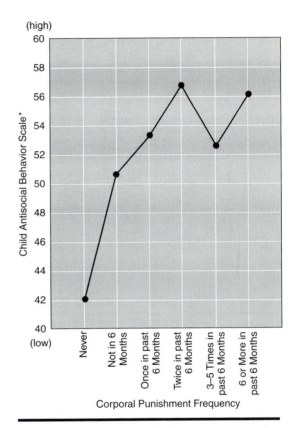

FIGURE 7.1 The relationship between antisocial behavior (conduct disorders) in children and the number of times mothers reported using physical punishments in disciplining the child (after: Straus & Mouradian 1998:364).

there are other ways to explain why such a relationship exists. For example, people appear to "naturally" vary in temperament,[43] and a person who is "naturally" prone to fly off the handle could not only be a troublesome child but might also become a harsh disciplinarian as a parent. And, if temperament is even partially inherited, such a parent would be likely to have children with behavior that often provokes harsh discipline.[44] Such an alternative explanation for why parental discipline patterns tend to correlate with criminal/antisocial behavior remains to be proven, but it serves to illustrate the need for caution in interpreting Table 7.8b.

TABLE 7.8b. Relationship between parental use of physical (harsh) discipline and criminal/antisocial behavior among offspring (consistency score = 90%; established correlate).

Nature of the Relationship	Types and Seriousness of Offenses									Clinical Conditions	
	Official Statistics						Self-Reported				
	Violent Offenses	Property Offenses	Drug Offenses	Delinquency	General & Unspecified Offenses	Recidivism	Victimful & Overall Offending	Illegal Drug Use	Childhood Conduct Disorders	Antisocial Personality
Positive				Asia *China: 1; Russia: 1* Europe *England: 2* North America *United States: 3*	Europe *England: 1*		Pacific *Australia: 2* North America *United States: 1*	North America *United States: 2*	Europe *Sweden: 1* North America *United States: 4*	
Not significant				Europe *Sweden: 1*			North America *United States: 1*			
Negative										

Given that harsh physical punishment is positively associated with offsprings' involvement in criminal/antisocial behavior, it is reasonable to wonder what type of parental discipline patterns are negatively associated. As shown in Table 7.8b, the research on this question is still somewhat limited. Nevertheless, it has been consistent in indicating that children with the lowest probabilities of getting into trouble with the law were reared by parents who set firm limits on their children's behavior, but used "loving" and "warm" discipline when the limits were exceeded. These are obviously somewhat subjective terms, but refer to discipline patterns that are largely devoid of physical punishment or bursts of anger on the part of parents.

Once again, you should be on guard not to read too much into these findings, for it could be that the temperament of children who later get into trouble with the law is such as to elicit anger and physical punishment from parents. If so, the lack of "loving" discipline patterns may be as much of a *reaction* to the behavior of crime-prone children as it is a cause of their behavior.

Child Abuse and Neglect

The concept of child maltreatment encompasses both child abuse and child neglect.[45] Whereas abuse describes active attempts to harm a child, neglect refers to more passive activities that cause harm to a child. Obviously, the dividing line between them is fuzzy, as is the dividing line between child abuse and harsh physical discipline.[46] Most studies of child maltreatment have been concerned with actual physical abuse, and have been based either on reports from social workers or medical per-

TABLE 7.8c.   Relationship between firm but loving (warm) parental discipline and criminal/antisocial behavior among offspring (consistency score = 100%; well-established correlate).

Nature of the Relationship	Types and Seriousness of Offenses									Clinical Conditions	
	Official Statistics						Self-Reported				
	Violent Offenses	Property Offenses	Drug Offenses	Delinquency	General & Unspecified Offenses	Recidivism	Victimful & Overall Offending	Illegal Drug Use	Childhood Conduct Disorders	Antisocial Personality	
Negative							**North America** *United States: 1*	**North America** *United States: 2*	**North America** *United States: 1* **Pacific** *Australia: 1*		
Not significant											
Positive											

sonnel, or on reports by victims themselves, usually years after the abuse had taken place.

The evidence already reviewed, that harsh parental discipline is associated with an increased risk of criminal/antisocial behavior in offspring, provides a hint as to what the evidence has shown when it comes to child abuse. Accordingly, you can see from Table 7.9 that the evidence is very consistent in indicating that persons who are subjected to child abuse as youngsters (and sometimes as teenagers) are more likely to be involved in criminal and delinquent behavior than nonabused children.[47] One research team compared the delinquency rates of abused children not with children in general but with siblings who had not been abused.[48] The conclusion was still that the abused children ended up being more delinquent than their nonabused siblings.

So far, the closest any study has come to questioning the abuse–crime link is a U.S. study that separated its sample by race. While a significant abuse–crime relationship was documented for the sample as a whole (consisting primarily of whites), no significant relationship was found in the case of blacks when considered separately.[49]

It is worth noting that a number of early studies of the relationship between child maltreatment and criminality (i.e., those conducted prior to the 1980s) have been criticized on methodological grounds, such as having been based on inadequate samples and having very loose definitions of abuse.[50] Nonetheless, the studies conducted since the 1980s have come to the same basic conclusion as the earlier studies: Child maltreatment is significantly more prevalent among persons who become most heavily involved in delinquent and criminal behavior than among those who do not.

Several researchers have attempted to determine if child maltreatment is more closely linked to certain types of offending than to others. The results have not been consistent. One study concluded that the strongest correlation between child maltreatment and delinquency appears to involve status offending (particularly the use of illegal drugs) and that it only minimally pertained to violent or property crimes.[51] However, several studies have found that abused children behave more aggressively toward peers than nonabused children do,[52] and that the probability of violent offending seemed to be especially strongly linked to having been an abused or neglected child.[53] Probably the most detailed study of the topic suggested that the linkages are evident across the entire spectrum of offenses.[54] As shown in Figure 7.2, this study found that all aspects of self-reported delinquency were more common among juveniles who had

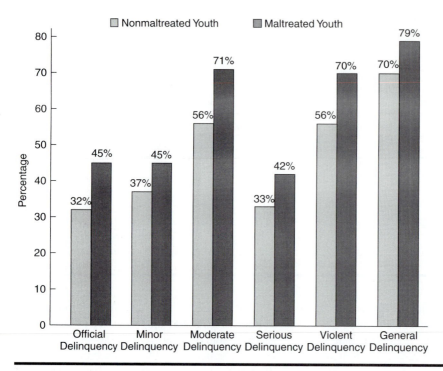

FIGURE 7.2   Relationship between Prevalence of Child Maltreatment and Delinquency.

been physically maltreated as children than among those who had not.

Only one study has given specific consideration to the possibility that child neglect (apart from any active abuse) was a correlate of crime.[55] As you might expect, this study concluded that children who are severely neglected as children are more likely than children in general to have an arrest record.

Finally, it should be mentioned that a few studies have given special attention to one specific type of child abuse, sexual abuse. Sexual abuse may not only involve a parent, a stepparent, but also a sibling or some other family member, as well as an acquaintance or a complete stranger. Also, girls are more likely than boys to be the victims of sexual abuse.[56] The evidence on sexual abuse is still fragmentary but points toward the conclusion that sex-

ual abuse in childhood is associated with an increased risk of delinquency and crime later in life, both in terms of offenses in general[57] and in cases of illegal drug use.[58] Nonetheless, the abuse–crime link does not appear to be as strong in the case of sexual abuse as it is for abuse of a physical nature.[59]

Overall, there is little doubt that physical abuse during childhood is a correlate of crime.[60] The links between offending probabilities and child neglect and sexual abuse are less well established, but point in the same direction.

FAMILY TRAITS

We will now look at traits in the parent that have been investigated with reference to criminal and antisocial behavior in the offspring. The parental traits to be considered are parental criminal/antisocial be-

TABLE 7.9.   Relationship between child abuse (and neglect) by parents and criminal/antisocial behavior in offspring (consistency score = 96.1%; well-established correlate).

Nature of the Relationship	Types and Seriousness of Offenses								Clinical Conditions	
	Official Statistics						Self-Reported			
	Violent Offenses	Property Offenses	Drug Offenses	Delinquency	Unspecified Offenses	Recidivism	Victimful & Overall Offending	Illegal Drug Use	Childhood Conduct Disorders	Antisocial Personality
Positive	Europe *England: 1* North America *United States: 5*		North America *United States: 7*	North America *United States: 25*	North America *United States: 1*		North America *United States: 2*		North America *United States: 7*	North America *United States: 1*
Not significant							North America *United States: 1*		North America *United States: 1*	
Negative										

havior, parental alcoholism and illegal drug use, and parental employment/unemployment.

Familial Criminal/Antisocial Behavior

At least since the 1930s, studies have sought to determine whether crime "runs in families." In other words, do children have a higher probability of becoming involved in crime and delinquency, or of being diagnosed as antisocial, if either of their parents has also been involved? And what about other family members, particularly brothers and sisters? Let us consider these two questions separately.

The results of research on the first question are shown in Table 7.10a. It indicates that numerous studies have assessed the possible link between parental criminality and that of offspring. As you can see, these studies are consistent in indicating that persons who engage in delinquent and criminal behavior are significantly more likely to have one or both parents who have done likewise than is true for persons in general.[61] The same is true for children with conduct disorders.[62] Of course, this does not mean that every antisocial child has an antisocial parent. It simply means that, with large samples of children, criminal/antisocial behavior (or

lack of it) does run in families to a statistically significant degree. Some researchers, in fact, have concluded that criminality in a parent is the strongest family-related variable yet identified for predicting a child's probability of serious delinquency or crime.[63] If both parents happen to have a criminal record, the likelihood of their children also getting into legal trouble appears to be elevated farther than with just one crime-prone parent.[64]

Regarding sibling similarities, the research is much less extensive. Nevertheless, as you can see in Table 7.10b, the available research indicates that, even among brothers and sisters, criminal/antisocial tendencies run in families. In addition, one study looked beyond the nuclear family, and found that even having an aunt or uncle with a criminal record increased the probability of a child being criminal/antisocial.[65] The bottom line is that criminality in the family is linked to an individual's probability of criminal/antisocial behavior. Important qualifiers to this conclusion are that (1) criminologists are still wrangling over the explanation, and (2) there are plenty of exceptions in the sense that many serious delinquents and criminals come from families with little or no criminal history.

TABLE 7.10a.   Evidence of a relationship between an individual's criminal/antisocial behavior and the same behavior by one or both parents (consistency score = 96.3%; well-established correlate).

Nature of the Relationship	Types and Seriousness of Offenses								Clinical Conditions	
	Official Statistics						Self-Reports			
	Violent Offenses	Property Offenses	Drug Offenses	Delinquency	Unspecified Adult Offenses	Recidivism	Victimful or Overall Offending	Illegal Drug Use	Conduct Disorders	Antisocial Personality Syndrome
Positive	**Europe** *England:* 1			**Asia** *Japan:* 1 **Europe** *England:* 9; *Norway:* 1; *Sweden:* 1 **North America** *United States:* 14 **Pacific** *Hawaii:* 1	**Europe** *Denmark:* 4; *England:* 8 **North America** *United States:* 7	**Europe** *England:* 2; *Netherlands:* 1; *Sweden:* 1 **North America** *United States:* 2	**Europe** *England:* 1 **North America** *United States:* 1	**North America** *United States:* 6	**Europe** *England:* 3 **North America** *United States:* 11	**North America** *United States:* 4
Not significant						**Europe** *England:* 1	**North America** United States: 2			
Negative										

TABLE 7.10b.   Evidence pertaining to the relationship between sibling similarity in criminal/antisocial behavior (consistency score = 95.7%; well-established correlate).

Nature of the Relationship	Types and Seriousness of Offenses								Clinical Conditions	
	Official Statistics						Self-Reports			
	Violent Offenses	Property Offenses	Drug Offenses	Delinquency	Unspecified Adult Offenses	Recidivism	Victimful or Overall Offending	Illegal Drug Use	Conduct Disorders	Antisocial Personality Syndrome
Positive			**North America** *United States:* 1	**Europe** *England:* 4 **Pacific** *Hawaii:* 1	**Europe** *England:* 2		**Europe** *Netherlands:* 1 **North America** *United States:* 10		**North America** *United States:* 1	
Not significant							**North America** *Canada:* 1; *United States:* 2			
Negative										

Alcoholism and Drug Use among Parents and Other Family Members

Over the years, quite a number of studies have investigated the link between alcoholism and drug use among parents and criminality among offspring. While defining alcoholism and assessing its prevalence in family members is always problematic, for statistical purposes using fairly large samples, it has been an informative area for criminologists and other social scientists to explore.

Let us consider parental alcoholism and parental illegal drug use separately. In the case of alcoholism, Table 7.11a shows that research findings have been consistent in showing that children of parents who have serious drinking problems are at increased risk of criminal/antisocial behavior.

Turning to parental drug use, studies are summarized in Table 7.11b. These studies have all concluded that parental use of illegal drugs is positively associated with illegal drug use by offspring, as well as with other forms of criminality and with childhood conduct disorders among the offspring.

It is also worth noting that studies have found higher rates of drug and heavy alcohol consumption by parents positively associated with their engaging in child abuse.[66] Furthermore, a couple of studies have indicated that delinquency among children was even positively associated with parental *tolerance* of alcohol use[67] and drug use.[68] Such evidence suggests that a complex web of interrelated variables may exist, rather than just simple one-to-one linkages. Again, theories are needed to help us untangle these possibilities.

Mental Illness and Depression among Family Members

Another type of family trait that has been fairly often investigated in relationship to criminal/antisocial behavior is mental illness, including depression, whether diagnosed as full-blown mental illness or not. The results of these studies are shown in Table 7.12. You can see that most studies have found that mental illness is more prevalent among family members of persons who exhibit the highest rates of offending.

Welfare Dependency and Frequent Unemployment

Families vary in their use of welfare services. Over the years, studies have been undertaken to determine if welfare dependency is associated with involvement in criminal/antisocial behavior. As

TABLE 7.11a.   Relationship between alcoholism by parents and criminal/antisocial behavior in offspring (consistency score = 100%; well-established correlate).

Nature of the Relationship	Types and Seriousness of Offenses								Clinical Conditions	
	Official Statistics						Self-Reported			
	Violent Offenses	Property Offenses	Drug Offenses	Delinquency	General & Unspecified Offenses	Recidivism	Victimful & Overall Offending	Illegal Drug Use	Conduct Disorders	Antisocial Personality Syndrome
Positive			Europe *England: 1* North America *United States: 1*	Asia *Japan: 1* Europe *Sweden: 2* North America *United States: 5*	North America *United States: 3*	Europe *Sweden: 1*		North America *United States: 4*	North America *United States: 10*	North America *United States: 2*
Not significant										
Negative										

TABLE 7.11b.　Relationship between drug use by parents and other family members and criminal/antisocial behavior in offspring (P = parent(s); S = sibling(s) (overall consistency score = 100%; well-established correlate).

Nature of the Relationship	Types and Seriousness of Offenses								Clinical Conditions	
	Official Statistics						Self-Reported			
	Violent Offenses	Property Offenses	Drug Offenses	Delinquency	General & Unspecified Offenses	Recidivism	Victimful & Overall Offending	Illegal Drug Use	Conduct Disorders	Antisocial Personality Syndrome
Positive			North America *United States: 1*	North America *United States: 1*			North America *United States: 1*	North America **Canada:** *2;* *United States: 32*	North America *United States: 4*	North America *United States: 1*
Not significant				North America *United States: 1*				North America *United States: 4*		
Negative										

TABLE 7.12.　Evidence of a relationship between family mental illness and depression and criminal/antisocial behavior among offspring (overall consistency score = 80%; probable correlate).

Nature of the Relationship	Type and Seriousness of Offenses								Antisocial Clinical Conditions	
	Official Statistics						Self-Reported Offenses			
	Violent Offenses	Property Offenses	Drug Offenses	Delinquency	General & Unspecified Offenses	Recidivism	Victimful & Overall Offending	Illegal Drug Use	Childhood Conduct Disorders	Antisocial Personality
Positive				Europe *Sweden: 1* **North America** *United States: 2* **Pacific** *Hawaii: 1*					North America *United States: 6*	North America *United States: 1*
Not significant									North America *United States: 2*	Europe *Denmark: 1* **North America** *United States: 1*
Negative										

you can see from Table 7.13, the evidence is largely consistent with the view that parents who utilize welfare services the most have offspring with greater criminal involvement compared to parents who rarely or never use such services. Welfare dependency is also higher among parents of children who are diagnosed with antisocial behavior disorders.[69]

Regarding frequency of unemployment, a few studies have considered this condition for the male parent, assuming that he is present in the household. These studies have concluded that criminal

TABLE 7.13.   Evidence of a relationship between family welfare dependency and/or parental unemployment and criminal/antisocial behavior among offspring (overall consistency score = 77.8%; probable correlate; consistency score excluding self-reports = 92.3%; established correlate).

Nature of the Relationship	Type and Seriousness of Offenses								Antisocial Clinical Conditions	
	Official Statistics						Self-Reported Offenses			
	Violent Offenses	Property Offenses	Drug Offenses	Delinquency	General & Unspecified Offenses	Recidivism	Victimful & Overall Offending	Illegal Drug Use	Childhood Conduct Disorders	Antisocial Personality
Negative	**Europe** *England: 1*	**Europe** *England: 1*		**Asia** *Japan: 1* **Europe** *England: 3; Finland: 1* **North America** *United States: 3*			**Europe** *England: 1* **North America** *United States: 1*		**North America** *United States: 1* **Pacific New** *Zealand: 1*	**Pacific** *New Zealand: 1*
Not significant				**Europe** *Netherlands: 1*			**North America** *United States: 2*	**North America** *United States: 1*		
Positive										

and delinquent children are more likely to have fathers with a history of unemployment than is true for children in general.

Mother Employed outside the Home

In intact families, it has been most common for the father to work full time outside the home, and for the mother to maintain the home and assume primary responsibility for child care. In recent decades, most industrialized societies have witnessed a gradual shift toward greater involvement of mothers in employment outside the home. Children of parents who both work outside the home have sometimes been dubbed "latchkey kids," because they are often responsible for their own household activities between the time school lets out and their parents arrival home from work.[70]

Over the years, researchers have investigated the possibility that having a mother who works outside the home might be a correlate of crime. The research results are summarized in Table 7.14. As you can see, several studies support the view that a positive relationship exists between having a working mother and being more involved in delinquency, but a number of studies also indicate there is no significant connection. One study in the Netherlands found recidivism to be higher for individuals who were raised in homes with working moms compared to nonrecidivists.

SCHOOL-RELATED VARIABLES

We will now consider variables having to do with education (with the exception of grades, which will be dealt with in Chapter 8). The specific variables to be given attention here are years of education and failure to complete high school, truancy and school discipline problems, and involvement in extracurricular activities.

Years of Education and Failure to Complete High School

As mentioned in Chapter 5, the number of years of education someone has completed is considered one of the key measures of social status. However, we are considering it here as a separate variable. A

TABLE 7.14.   Evidence of a relationship between mother working outside the home and criminal/ antisocial behavior among the offspring (consistency score = 60.0%; possible correlate).

Nature of the Relationship	Type and Seriousness of Offenses								Antisocial Clinical Conditions	
	Official Statistics						Self-Reported Offenses			
	Violent Offenses	Property Offenses	Drug Offenses	Delinquency	General & Unspecified Offenses	Recidivism	Victimful & Overall Offending	Illegal Drug Use	Childhood Conduct Disorders	Antisocial Personality
Negative				**Europe** *Finland:* 1 **North America** *United States: 3*		**Europe** *Netherlands:* 1	**North America** *United States: 2*	**North America** *United States: 4*	**North America** *United States: 1*	
Not significant				**Africa** *Ghana: 1* **Europe** *England: 2; Sweden: 1* **North America** *United States: 2*			**North America** *United States: 1*	**North America** *United States: 1*		
Positive										

closely related variable has to do with whether an adult has graduated from high school. Those who have not are often referred to as *dropouts* (or *high school dropouts*).

The results of studies on the relationship between years of education and completion of high school and involvement in criminal/antisocial behavior are summarized in Tables 7.15a and 7.15b. As you can see, in both cases, the vast majority of studies have found a significant tendency for those who have completed the fewest number of years of education, and those who have dropped out before finishing high school, to be more involved in criminal/antisocial behavior than their more educated counterparts.

The extent to which criminality is associated with low levels of education can be gleaned from noting that whereas three fourths of adults in the United States in recent decades have completed high school,[71] only about one third of persons in U.S. prisons have done so.[72] Despite these substantial differences, bear in mind that they are gen-

eralizations and there are plenty of well-educated crooks.

Recent research has revealed that the crime–education relationship is stronger for persons who come from middle or upper status families, and for those who drop out because they dislike school (as opposed to other reasons for dropping out, such as to get married or because of financial hardship).[73] Researchers have also noted that those who get poor grades tend to drop out of school earlier than those who do well.[74]

The Dropout Dip.   An interesting qualification to the established link between completion of high school and delinquency is a phenomenon called the **dropout dip.** Given that, on average dropouts engage in more delinquency than do those who stay in high school long enough to graduate, you might expect that as soon as dropouts are able to quit school, their delinquency rates would rise. In fact the opposite has been found. As shown in Table 7.16, almost immediately after quitting

TABLE 7.15a.   Results from studies of the relationship between years of education and involvement in criminal/antisocial behavior (overall consistency score = 92.3%; established correlate; consistency score excluding self-reports = 96.6%; well-established correlate).

Nature of the Relationship	Type and Seriousness of Offenses								Antisocial Clinical Conditions	
	Official Statistics						Self-Reported Offenses			
	Violent Offenses	Property Offenses	Drug Offenses	Delinquency	General & Unspecified Offenses	Recidivism	Victimful & Overall Offending	Illegal Drug Use	Childhood Conduct Disorders	Antisocial Personality
Negative	**Europe** *Scotland:* 1 **North America** *United States:* 2			**Africa** *Ghana:* 1 **Asia** *China:* 3 **North America** *United States:* 3 **Pacific** *Hawaii:* 1	**Europe** *Denmark:* 1; *Germany:* 2; *Scotland:* 1 **Middle East** *Israel:* 1 **North America** *United States:* 2	**North America** *United States:* 7	**Europe** *Belgium:* 1 **North America** *United States:* 3	**North America** *United States:* 4	**Europe** *Sweden:* 1 **Pacific** New Zealand: 1	**North America** *United States:* 1
Not significant						**Europe** *England:* 1	**Europe** *Netherlands:* 1; *Sweden:* 1			
Positive										

TABLE 7.15b.   Results from studies of the relationship between dropping out of high school and being involved in criminal/antisocial behavior (consistency score = 100%; well-established correlate).

Nature of the Relationship	Type and Seriousness of Offenses								Antisocial Clinical Conditions	
	Official Statistics						Self-Reported Offenses			
	Violent Offenses	Property Offenses	Drug Offenses	Delinquency	General & Unspecified Offenses	Recidivism	Victimful & Overall Offending	Illegal Drug Use	Childhood Conduct Disorders	Antisocial Personality
Positive				**Europe** *England:* 1 **North America** *United States:* 10	**Europe** *England:* 1 **North America** *United States:* 1		**Europe** *England:* 1 **North America** *Canada:* 1; *United States:* 4	**North America** *Canada:* 1; *United States:* 9	**North America** *United States:* 2	**North America** *United States:* 1
Not significant										
Negative										

school, dropouts appear to reduce their delinquency involvement, although they are still more involved in delinquency than those who graduate from high school.[75]

The dropout dip is illustrated in Figure 7.3. As shown in this figure, dropouts have higher rates of delinquency than their peers who remain in school both before and after the dropouts leave

TABLE 7.16.   Evidence regarding delinquency rates among high school dropouts when compared to their delinquency involvement prior to dropping out (all data based on self-reports) (consistency score = 40.0%; unestablished correlate).

Compared to Delinquency Prior to Dropping Out	Short-Term Effects (within the first year or two)	Long-Term Effects (beyond the second year)
Delinquency decreases after dropout occurs	**North America** *Canada:* 1; *United States:* 5	
No significant difference	**Europe** *England:* 1	
Delinquency/criminality increases		**North America** *United States:* 4

school.[76] Nonetheless, there is a noticeable decline in delinquency for at least the first year after dropping out, especially for dropouts who take up a full-time job immediately after leaving school.

Notice, however, that the dropout dip does not seem to last over the long term.

Truancy and School Discipline Problem Behavior

Truancy refers to unexcused skipping of school by those who have not yet graduated from high school. Technically, truancy is a status offense in most industrialized countries, but it rarely results in any disciplinary action by law enforcement.

School discipline problems encompass a wide variety of activities, ranging from talking and acting up during classes to smoking or engaging in vandalism on school property. Social scientists have collected data about truancy and school discipline problems primarily from school records and from self-reports.

As you can see in Table 7.17, many studies have shown that both truancy and school discipline problems are positively associated with criminal/antisocial behavior. To illustrate the strength of the relationship, one Canadian study found truants self-reporting three times as many delinquent acts as did their peers who attended school regularly.[78]

Extracurricular Activities

Extracurricular activities refer to school-sponsored athletic programs, drama and music programs, along with debate and civic clubs. As Table 7.18 shows, all of the research on connections between involvement in extracurricular activities and offending pertains only to delinquency. The studies thus far have provided a mixed picture with respect to any relationship between involvement in extracurricular activities and offending probabilities. Researchers may eventually find that some types of extracurricular activities may have more of a relationship to offending than others. Currently, most studies that have found a significant relationship have concluded that it is negative.

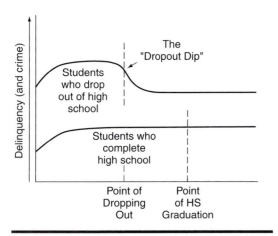

FIGURE 7.3   A diagram illustrating the dip in delinquency that usually accompanies dropping out of high school.

TABLE 7.17. Results from studies of the relationship between truancy and discipline problems in school and being involved in criminal/antisocial behavior (consistency score = 100%; well-established correlate).

| Nature of the Relationship | Type and Seriousness of Offenses | | | | | | | | Antisocial Clinical Conditions | |
| | Official Statistics | | | | | | Self-Reported Offenses | | | |
	Violent Offenses	Property Offenses	Drug Offenses	Delinquency	General & Unspecified Offenses	Recidivism	Victimful & Overall Offending	Illegal Drug Use	Childhood Conduct Disorders	Antisocial Personality
Positive			North America United States: 1	Africa Ghana: 1 Europe England: 2; Netherlands: 1; Sweden: 3 North America United States: 7	Europe Finland: 1; Sweden: 2 North America United States: 1	Europe England: 1; Sweden: 1 North America United States: 6	Europe England: 1 North America Canada: 1; United States: 1	Europe Sweden: 2 North America Canada: 1; United States: 9	North America United States: 4	
Not significant										
Negative										

TABLE 7.18. Results from studies of the relationship between involvement in extracurricular activities and the commission of criminal/antisocial behavior (consistency score = 58.8%; possible correlate).

| Nature of the Relationship | Type and Seriousness of Offenses | | | | | | | | Antisocial Clinical Conditions | |
| | Official Statistics | | | | | | Self-Reported Offenses | | | |
	Violent Offenses	Property Offenses	Drug Offenses	Delinquency	General & Unspecified Offenses	Recidivism	Victimful & Overall Offending	Illegal Drug Use	Childhood Conduct Disorders	Antisocial Personality
Negative				Europe England: 1			North America Canada: 1	North America Canada: 1; United States: 6		
Not significant							North America United States: 2	North America United States: 4		
Positive								North America Canada: 1; United States: 1		

PEER ASSOCIATIONS

We will now review evidence that researchers have collected pertaining to peer associations and involvement in delinquency and crime. We will look at three related issues: overall friendship patterns, associating with others who engage in delinquency and crime, and belonging to a gang.

General Popularity with Peers

Would you guess that delinquents and criminals have more or fewer friends than persons in general? Over the years, quite a few studies have addressed this question, and, as shown in Table 7.19, the findings have consistently shown that delinquents and criminals have fewer friends than do their peers, especially in the case of close friends. In addition, delinquents and criminals are more likely to be avoided and rejected as friends by agemates who know them.[79]

Associating with Delinquents and Criminals

Having shown that persons who engage most often in delinquency and crime generally have fewer friends, especially close friends, than do those who

commit these acts least often, let us ask a related question: Do persons who engage in delinquency and crime most often gravitate toward peer associations with other offenders? In other words, even though delinquents and criminals have fewer friends than most persons overall, do "birds of a feather flock together"?

As you can see by examining Table 7.20, many studies have investigated this question, and the conclusions are thus far unanimous: As the adage goes, "birds of a feather flock together" when it comes to delinquency and criminality. While the vast majority of studies addressing this question so far have been conducted in the United States, what studies there are from other countries all point in the same direction, making preferentially associating with delinquents and criminals a well-established correlate of crime.

Gang Membership

Being a gang member refers to adolescents (and sometimes young adults) who interact fairly regularly with several peers in activities that are rarely supervised by parents or other adults.[80] Beyond that, there is considerable controversy about how gang membership should be assessed.[81] Normally,

TABLE 7.19. Evidence of a relationship between number of friends (or peer popularity) and involvement in criminal/antisocial behavior (consistency score = 97.1%; well-established correlate).

Nature of the Relationship	Type and Seriousness of Offenses									Antisocial Clinical Conditions	
	Official Statistics						Self-Reported Offenses				
	Violent Offenses	Property Offenses	Drug Offenses	Delinquency	General & Unspecified Offenses	Recidivism	Victimful & Overall Offending	Illegal Drug Use	Childhood Conduct Disorders	Antisocial Personality
Negative				Europe *England: 2* North America *United States: 7*	Europe *England:1*		North America *Canada:* 1; *United States:* 10	North America *United States:* 4	Europe *England: 1* North America *United States: 7*	
Not significant							Europe *England: 1*			
Positive										

TABLE 7.20. Relationship between associating with delinquent friends and being involved in criminal/antisocial behavior (consistency score = 100%; well-established correlate).

| Nature of Relationship | Type and Seriousness of Offenses | | | | | | | | | Antisocial Clinical Conditions | |
| | Official Statistics | | | | | | Self-Reported Offenses | | | |
	Violent Offenses	Property Offenses	Drug Offenses	Delinquency	General & Unspecified Offenses	Recidivism	Victimful & Overall Offending	Illegal Drug Use	Childhood Conduct Disorders	Antisocial Personality
Positive				North America United States: 5	North America Canada: 1	North America United States: 2	Asia China: 2 Europe England: 1 North America Canada: 2; United States: 44	Asia China: 1 Middle East Israel: 2 North America United States: 69	North America United States: 1	
Not significant										
Negative										

researchers assess gang membership simply by asking subjects if they consider themselves members of any gang.

Historical accounts of adolescents joining gangs indicate that this phenomenon can be traced back far into antiquity, at least for males,[82] bringing at least one researcher to suggest that many boys seem to have a "gang instinct."[83] Studies of gangs have revealed that membership tends to be constantly changing,[84] with younger new members normally being recruited by those two or three years older.[85] Gangs are almost always comprised of youngsters who reside in the same neighborhood and belong to the same ethnic/racial group.[86]

Turning to the question of a relationship between gang membership and involvement in crime and delinquency, you can see from Table 7.21 that all but a few studies based on self-reported offending have found delinquency to be significantly more common among gang members than their peers who do not belong to a gang. The exceptional studies have indicated that, while the sheer number of self-reported offenses was not significantly different, when offense seriousness was taken into account, even these exceptional studies led to the conclusion that gang members are more criminal than persons in general.

Regarding any sequential order to the gang membership–delinquency relationship, three studies found that the onset of delinquency generally precedes participation in juvenile gangs.[87] Also worth noting is that it does not appear to be the case that gang members specifically organize themselves to engage in delinquency. Instead, it is actually the most "fluid" and poorly organized gangs that appear to be the source of the greatest delinquency rates.[88]

Figure 7.3 presents the results of the largest gang membership study yet undertaken. As you can see, self-reported gang members are more likely to be involved in all major types of delinquency than are their peers who do not belong to gangs.

You might suspect that the links between offending and lack of close friends (see Table 7.20) might not hold up if one were to focus only on delinquents who consider themselves members of a gang. However, even here studies have shown that adolescents who become involved with delinquent gangs are more likely to be rejected by most of their peers as a friend than adolescents in general.[89]

TABLE 7.21.   Evidence of a relationship between gang membership and criminal/antisocial behavior (consistency score = 85.2%; established correlate).

Nature of the Relationship	Type and Seriousness of Offenses								Antisocial Clinical Conditions	
	Official Statistics						Self-Reported Offenses		Childhood Conduct Disorders	Antisocial Personality
	Violent Offenses	Property Offenses	Drug Offenses	Delinquency	General & Unspecified Offenses	Recidivism	Victimful & Overall Offending	Illegal Drug Use		
Positive				North America *United States: 5*	North America *United States: 1*	Europe *England: 1*	Europe *England: 1; Sweden: 1* North America *United States: 11*	North America *United States: 3*		
Not significant							North America *United States: 3*	North America *United States: 1*		
Negative										

RELIGIOSITY

Religiosity refers to the degree to which individuals are actively involved in and/or committed to a particular religious organization and to its belief system. As you might suspect, there are a variety of ways to measure religiosity. In most criminological research, subjects have simply been asked how often they have attended church (or synagogue) services within, say, the past year. However, other religiosity measures have also been explored. These include frequency of prayer, and the strength of such religious beliefs as belief in the existence of God, the devil, or life after death. Yet another religiosity measure is the specific religious denomination to which one belongs.

The research on religiosity and criminality is summarized in five tables, Tables 7.22a through 7.22e. Tables 7.22a pertains to church attendance, by far the most widely used measure of religiosity used by criminologists. All other religiosity measures (except for denominational measures) are summarized in Table 7.22b. Tables 7.22c and 7.22d both pertain to denominational differences in offending rates, the first based on official crime data and the second based on self-reported of-

fending data. In Table 7.22e, the results of ecologically based studies of religiosity are presented.

Church (Synagogue/Mosque) Attendance

Numerous studies have investigated the possible link between involvement in religious services and involvement in criminal/antisocial behavior. To measure church attendance, all of these studies have relied on self-reports (e.g., How often in the past year have you attended religious services?)

You can see from Table 7.22a that the evidence is largely consistent with the view that church attendance is inversely correlated with delinquent and criminal behavior. In other words, persons who engage in delinquency and crime the most are least likely to be regularly involved in church (or synagogue/mosque) services.[90] There are only a few studies that have failed to find significant differences in this regard.

Other Religiosity Measures

In the case of other common measures of religiosity, Table 7.22b shows that the results are much

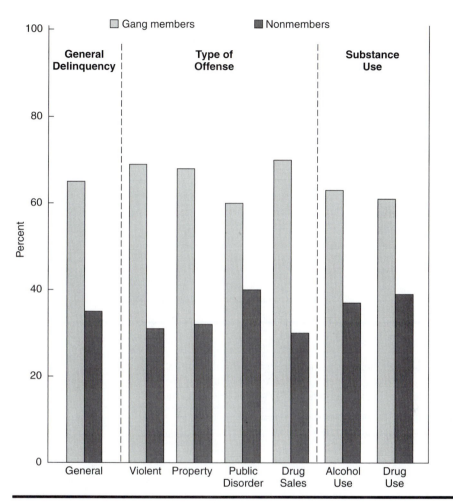

FIGURE 7.4   Based on interviews of 4,000 adolescents in three large United States cities, 30% stated that they were (or had been) gang members. This graph shows the proportion of delinquent offenses that were self-reported by these gang members and by the remaining 70% of the adolescents (adapted from Thornberry & Burch, 1997:3).

more mixed than in the case of church attendance, with a number of studies actually showing positive relationships between religiosity and official delinquency and especially criminality. These patterns have been a genuine challenge for criminologists and other social scientists to explain.[91] Basically, about the only reasonable interpretation is that not only is church attendance the most common measure of religiosity used in criminological

research, but for some reason it appears to be more strongly linked to low involvement in criminal behavior than are any specific religious beliefs or church membership.

Denominations.   As if research on religiosity and criminality were not controversial enough, over the years several studies have sought to determine if members of various denominations might be more

TABLE 7.22a.   Relationship between church (or synagogue/masque) attendance and criminal/antisocial behavior (overall consistency score = 85.7%; established correlate).

| Nature of the Relationship | Types and Seriousness of Offenses | | | | | | | | Clinical Conditions | |
| | Official Statistics | | | | | | Self-Reported | | | |
	Violent Offenses	Property Offenses	Drug Offenses	Delinquency	Unspecified Offenses	Recidivism	Victimful or Overall Offending	Illegal Drug Use	Childhood Conduct Disorders	Antisocial Personality
Negative				North America *United States:* 12	North America *United States:* 2		North America *Canada:* 1; *United States:* 17	Europe *England:* 2; *Ireland:* 1 North America *Canada:* 8; *United States:* 54		
Not significant		North America *United States:* 2		North America *United States:* 2			North America *United States:* 5	Europe *Sweden:* 1 North America *United States:* 6		
Positive										

TABLE 7.22b.   Relationship between religiosity measures other than church attendance and criminal/antisocial behavior (overall consistency score = 68.0%; possible correlate; consistency score excluding self-reports = 50.0%; possible correlate).

| Nature of the Relationship | Types and Seriousness of Offenses | | | | | | | | Clinical Conditions | |
| | Official Statistics | | | | | | Self-Reported | | | |
	Violent Offenses	Property Offenses	Drug Offenses	Delinquency	Unspecified Offenses	Victimful or Overall Offending	Illegal Drug Use	Conduct Disorders	Antisocial Personality
Negative	North America *United States:* 1	North America *United States:* 1		Pacific *Hawaii:* 1	Europe *Slovakia:* 1 North America *United States:* 1	Europe *Netherlands:* 1 Middle East *Israel:* 1 North America *United States:* 13	Europe *England:* 1; *Ireland:* 1 North America *Canada:* 3; *United States:* 34		
Not significant				Pacific *Hawaii:* 1	North America *United States:* 4	North America *United States:* 2	Europe *Sweden:* 1 North America *United States:* 3		
Positive				North America *United States:* 2	Europe *England:* 1 North America *United States:* 5				

or less involved in delinquency and crime than members of other denominations. Throwing caution to the wind, we present the main findings from these studies.

Denominations are impossible to arrange along a continuum (as one can do with other religiosity measures). Therefore, Tables 7.22c and 7.22d summarized the results on denominational studies of criminality in a special format. To orient yourself to the format, notice that there are four main columns in the table. The first indicates the country/state in which the study was conducted, the second notes the type of crime/delinquency data utilized, the third indicates the specific denominations compared, and the last cites the study (according to numbers listed in the endnotes). Whenever significant denominational differences were reported, the subcategories in the third column indicate which denomination had the highest crime/delinquency rate with a 1, the denomination with the next highest rate with a 2, and so forth.

Let us first consider studies based on official data. In Table 7.22c, you can see that in all studies where Christians were compared with Jews, the former had higher crime and delinquency rates. In studies comparing Catholics and Protestants, the former had higher crime and delinquency rates. So far, four studies have compared persons with no religious preference with those who ascribe generally to Christian faiths. Perhaps surprisingly, three of these studies report lower official crime rates among those with no religious preference at all.

In the case of self-reports, the evidence is much less clear-cut. While a study conducted in England and two in the United States both found Jews self-reporting lower offending rates than those reported by Christians, one Canadian study (confined to drug offenses) found Jews and those with no religious preference self-reporting higher rates than Christians. Regarding comparisons between Catholics and Protestants, the evidence from self-reports is not at all consistent.

What can be concluded based on denominational studies? If attention is confined to official data, two generalizations have been well established: Jews are less involved in criminal behav-

ior than are Christians. When comparisons are made within Christian denominations, Protestants (considered as a single group) have been found to have lower offending rates than Catholics.[121]

One recent study classified religions according to their degrees of conservativism (or fundamentalism) and sought to determine if college students reared in religiously conservative families were more or less delinquent than those reared in more religiously liberal families.[122] Based on self-reports, the researchers found no significant differences for either illegal drug use or for other forms of delinquency, except in the case of underage drinking, where students reared in the conservative families drank significantly less. Similarly, a denominational study of drug use (other than alcohol) found no significant differences between Protestants, Catholics, or "others."[123]

Ecological Religiosity.   Apart from the religiosity of individuals, do you think that cities or countries where people are most religious have higher (or lower) crime rates than in cities or countries where people are least religious? Of course, the answer is bound to vary depending on how one defines *religious*.

Table 7.22e is based on ecological studies of religiosity and criminality, where the units of analyses were either cities, states, or nations. These studies were not discussed in Chapter 6 because they seemed more meaningfully understood in the general context of religiosity than in the context of ecology and macroeconomics. A few studies also compare populations in terms of proportional membership in various religious faiths (e.g., percent Catholic).

Overall, the findings from Table 7.22e are mixed, although most suggest that crime rates are lower in areas where the greatest proportions of populations are religious. The greatest inconsistency comes in the area of violent crime, where some studies have actually found religiosity to be positively associated with offending rates.

Considering the research summarized in all five tables together, a couple of generalizations seem warranted. First and foremost, of all aspects

TABLE 7.22c.   Relationships between people's affiliation with various religious denominations and their official involvement in criminal behavior.

Country/State in which Study was Conducted	Type of Offenses	Christian — Protestant: Catholic	Fundamentent	Non-Fund	Baptist	Lutheran	Mormon	None	Muslim	Jew	Other	Reference Number (see endnotes)
Africa												
Nigeria	Delinquency		——— 1 ———							2		92
Europe												
Austria	General & Unspecified		——— 1 ———							2		93
Germany	General & Unspecified	1				2				3		94
Germany	General & Unspecified	1				2				3		95
Germany	General & Unspecified		——— 1 ———							2		96
Hungary	General & Unspecified		——— 1 ———							2		97
Netherlands	General & Unspecified	1	——— 2 ———					3		4		98
Poland	Delinquency		——————— 1 ———————							2		99
Eastern Europe	Delinquency	1	——— 2 ———							3		100
North America												
USA (California)	Delinquency		——————— 1 ———————							2		101
USA (Massachusetts)	General & Unspecified	1	——— 2 ———									102
USA (New Jersey)	General & Unspecified		——— 1 ———							2		103
USA (New Jersey)	Delinquency	1	——— 2 ———							3		104
USA (New York)	Delinquency		——— 1 ———							2		105
USA (New York)	Delinquency		——————— 1 ———————							2		106
USA (New York)	Delinquency		——————— 1 ———————							2		107
USA (Pennsylvania)	General & Unspecified	1	——— 2 ———					4		3		108
USA (Wisconsin)	General & Unspecified	1	——— 2 ———					4		3		109
United States (National)	General & Unspecified		——————— 1 ———————							2		110
United States (National)	General & Unspecified		——————— 1 ———————							2		111
United States	Delinquency	1	——— 2 ———							3		112

TABLE 7.25. Capsule summary of family-based correlates of crime.

	Consistency of the Evidence*					
Correlate	Well Estab	Estab	Prob	Poss	Unestab.	Comments and Qualification
Family size		X				Large family size is associated with increased crime and delinquency
Birth order	(X)	X				First born are less crime involved
Being married			X			Being married, as opposed to single or divorced, may be associated with lower offending rates
Out-of-wedlock births & unwanted pregnancy	X — X					Persons born out-of-wedlock or were unwanted are more crime-involved
Intactness of parent's marital bond	(X)		X			Children reared in broken homes appear to be more crime-involved

*X–with self-reports included; (X)–with self-reports excluded.

TABLE 7.26. Capsule summary of family-based correlates of crime.

	Consistency of the Evidence					
Correlate	Well Estab	Estab	Prob	Poss	Unestab.	Comments and Qualification
Marital/family discord	X					Those from families in which arguing and fighting are common are more crime-involved
Parent-child attachment	(X)	X				Children who are poorly bonded with parents are more crime-involved
Parental monitoring & supervision		X				Children who are minimally monitored or supervised by parents are more crime-involved
Parental discipline patterns	X					Extremely permissive and harsh/sporadic discipline most linked to criminal/antisocial behavior
Child abuse and neglect	X					Children who are abused or neglected are more crime involved
Criminal/antisocial behavior in the family	X					Children from families with criminal/antisocial parents or siblings are more crime-involved

TABLE 7.27.   Capsule summary of family characteristics correlated with criminality.

Correlate	Consistency of the Evidence					Comments and Qualification
	Well Estab	Estab	Prob	Poss	Unestab	
Alcoholism by one or both parents	X					Children with one or both parents who are alcoholic are more crime-involved
Drug use by one or both parents	X					Children with one or both parents who use recreational drugs are more crime-involved
Mental illness in the family			X			Children with mentally ill parents or siblings appear to be more crime-involved
Welfare dependency & paternal unemployment		(X)	X			Children whose parents are dependent on welfare services or whose father is often without employment are more crime-involved
Mother working outside the home				X		Children whose mothers work outside the home may be more crime-involved

that both forms of maltreatment are linked to delinquency and crime among children.

Turning to traits of parents that have been found associated with criminal/antisocial behavior among offspring, evidence was strongly supportive of the view that criminal/antisocial behavior tends to run in families. In other words, if one family member has a serious criminal record or history, there is a substantially increased probability of other family members also exhibiting these traits. In like manner, parental alcoholism and drug use are both unquestionably associated with delinquency and crime among children. Another family-related variable that most studies have shown to be associated with an increased risk of crime and delinquency among children is family welfare dependency or unemployment. In the case of mothers working outside the home, studies are only slightly on the side of suggesting a positive link to criminal and delinquent behavior among offspring.

School-Related Variables

The first school-related variable that was considered was years of education (and failure to complete high school). Studies throughout the world have shown that persons who complete fewer years of schooling and those who drop out of high school before graduating are more involved in delinquency and crime than persons in general. However, a phenomenon called the *dropout dip* has been found in several studies. This refers to a tendency for offending rates to decline during the first year or two following the time that a dropout leaves high school. Nevertheless, rates of delinquency are still higher among high school dropouts than among those who remain in high school to graduation.

Truancy and school discipline problems are associated with relatively high rates of delinquency and crime. Surprisingly for many, however, is that studies have been mixed with respect to finding a relationship between involvement in extracurricular activities and offending probabilities.

Peer Associations

Studies have unequivocally shown that persons who engage in delinquency and crime most have fewer friends than those who do so the least, even early in childhood. The friends that delinquents and criminals do have tend to be other offenders,

TABLE 7.28. Capsule summary of school related correlates of crime.

Correlate	Consistency of the Evidence					Comments and Qualification
	Well Estab	Estab	Prob	Poss	Unestab	
Years of education	(X)	X				As years of education increase, crime involvement decreases
Dropping out of high school	X					Those who drop out of high school before graduating are more crime-involved
Truancy and school discipline problems	X					As truancy and school discipline problems increase, crime involvement increases
Involvement in extracurricular activities				X		Low involvement in extracurricular activities may be associated with high crime involvement

TABLE 7.29. Capsule summary of peer-related correlates of crime.

Correlate	Consistency of the Evidence					Comments and Qualification
	Well Estab	Estab	Prob	Poss	Unestab	
Popularity among peers	X					As popularity with agemates decreases, involvement in crime increases
Associating with delinquents & criminals	X					Those who associate with delinquents and criminals the most are most crime-involved themselves
Gang membership		X				Members of gangs appear to be more crime-involved

including persons who use illegal drugs and gang members.

Religiosity

A controversial area of criminological research has had to do with relationships between religiosity and crime. Numerous types of religiosity variables have been considered in these criminological studies, but the most numerous by far have been studies based on church attendance. These studies have overwhelmingly suggested that persons who attend church most often are less involved in crime and

delinquency than those who attend infrequently or not at all. This relationship is especially well established in the case of self-reported drug offenses.

Other religiosity measures include official church membership, specific religious beliefs, involvement in prayer, and Bible reading. For these types of religiosity measures, the evidence is mixed, particularly in the case of official data.

Another area of religiosity research in connection with crime pertains to denominational differences. The evidence in this regard has consistently shown Jews to have lower crime rates than Christians, with the exception of self-reported drug

TABLE 7.30. Capsule summary of religion-related correlates of crime.

Correlate	Consistency of the Evidence					Comments and Qualification
	Well Estab	Estab	Prob	Poss	Unestab	
Church (synagogue/ masque) attendance	X					Those who attend religious services the least are most crime-involved
Other measures of religiosity				X	(X)	There may be little relationship between most religiosity measures and official criminality; however, self-reported offending appears to be lower for those who are most religious
Religious denominations		(No consistency score calculated)				Among members of major Western religions, crime probabilities are higher for Christians than for Jews
Ecological studies of religiosity				X		There may be little relationship between the religiosity of a state or country and its overall crime rate

use. Among Christians, official data have found Catholics engaging in crime and delinquency at higher rates than Protestants, when the latter is considered as a single group. When major Protestant denominations are investigated separately, complex patterns emerge. In the case of self-reports, no generalizations yet appear to be warranted.

Work-Related Variables

The last category of variables considered in this chapter were work related. In this regard, persons with unstable work histories are more likely to engage in crime and delinquency than persons in general. Similarly, being frequently unemployed is positively linked to criminality. Finally, most studies have found that those who have jobs as teenagers are more likely to be involved in delinquency than those who do not have jobs as youths.

The chapter closed with a cautionary note regarding the importance of not jumping to conclusions based on even well-established correlates of crime. While it is possible that some sort of simple causal relationship exists, very complex causal

TABLE 7.31. Capsule summary of work-related correlates of crime.

Correlate	Consistency of the Evidence					Comments and Qualification
	Well Estab	Estab	Prob	Poss	Unestab	
Stable work history	X					Those with unstable work histories are more crime-involved
Being unemployed		X				Those who are most often unemployed are more crime-involved
Teenage Employment	X					Teenagers who are employed have higher rates of crime than those who are not employed

connections are also possible. As we get into the theoretical chapters, you will see that theories can go a long way toward comprehending the com- plexities of criminality, and of human behavior, generally.

SUGGESTED READINGS

Day, James M., and Laufer, William S. (1987). *Crime, values and religion.* Norwood, NJ: Ablex. (One of only a few books devoted to better understanding how religion may affect criminal behavior.)

Hirschi, Travis and Gottfredson, Michael (Eds.). (1980). *Understanding crime: Current theory and research.* (A collection of chapters primarily having to do with institutional factors related to offending behavior.)

Loeber, Rolf and Stouthamer-Loeber, Magada (1986). Family factors as correlates and predictors of juvenile conduct problems and delinquency. In Michael Tonry and Norval Morris (Eds.), *Crime and justice: An annual review of research,* Volume 7 (pp. 29–149). Chicago: University of Chicago Press. (Provides a valuable synopsis of what researchers have determined about family correlates of crime through the mid-1980s.)

EXERCISES

1. Write an essay about the apparent relationships that exist between family variables and criminal/antisocial behavior. You can use material contained in this chapter, but you should also locate at least two other sources in the library, and cite them in your essay. Unless your instructor states otherwise, the essay should be one to two double-spaced pages in length.

2. Choose three correlates of crime discussed in this chapter, and attempt to construct a logically coherent theory that would explain why these three variables are all correlated with crime as the evidence suggests. While you probably have a lot to learn about theory construction, making an effort at this point should provide you with some good mental exercise, and give you a greater appreciation of the theories that we will begin examining in Chapter 10.

3. Pretend that you are a researcher interested in family, school, peer, or religious correlates of crime. Identify two such variables not specifically discussed in this chapter that you think might be interesting to explore. Then state what you think research would show regarding how these two variables would be related to criminal/antisocial behavior, and explain why you think so. Limit your essay to no more than two double-spaced pages.

4. If you have access to the World Wide Web, do a search for criminal behavior and then a subsearch for one of the family, school, peer, religious, or work-related variables discussed in this chapter. Based on information you find, write a one- to two-page summary of facts or opinions about how that variable and criminal behavior seem to be related. (Your instructor will probably want you to print out a copy of the source or sources you used. If you do not have access to the WWW, do your search at the college library.)

5. Without developing a formal theory, speculate about why teenagers who are employed appear to be more involved in crime and delinquency than is true for teenagers generally. Keep in mind that this appears to be true both for victimful offenses and for drug offenses.

ENDNOTES

1. Ellis 1988; West 1967:73.
2. Friedman et al. 1991.
3. Wilkinson et al. 1982:224.
4. Calhoun et al. 1984; Nield 1976.
5. Wilkinson et al. 1982:224.
6. Sletto 1934; Wilkinson et al. 1982.
7. Robins 1991:283.
8. Gress-Wright 1993.
9. Kubicka 1995:361.
10. Messner & Sampson 1991.
11. Canter 1982:161; Hoffmann 1995.
12. Brearley 1932:45; Ellwood 1919:138; Stack 1992:327.
13. Hurwitz & Christiansen 1983:267; Wadsworth 1979:49.
14. Wilkinson 1980:21.
15. Gold 1970:127; Hurwitz & Christiansen 1983:298.
16. Matsueda & Heimer 1987.
17. Haurin 1992.
18. E.g., Blechman et al. 1977.
19. Hawkins et al. 1988:261; Loeber 1990:17; McCord 1990:132.
20. Vader-Kierman et al. 1995.
21. Achenbach et al. 1991; Pearson et al. 1994.
22. Dornbusch et al. 1985; Johnson 1986.
23. Pagani et al. 1998.
24. Rutter 1971; West & Farrington 1973:70.
25. Behar & Stewart 1984; Wadsworth 1979.
26. Kelly & Baer 1969; Virkkunen 1976:381; Wadsworth 1979.
27. Mednick et al. 1987; West 1982.
28. Bonger 1905:546; Nye 1958; Wilkinson 1980:38.
29. Canter 1982; Dornbusch et al. 1985; Koziey & Davies, 1982; Rosen & Nielson 1982.
30. Johnson 1986:69.
31. van Voorhis et al. 1988:236.
32. Heatherington 1979; Wadsworth, et al.1985.
33. Hawkins et al. 1988:261; Mednick et al. 1990; Quinton et al. 1993; Rutter 1994.
34. McCord 1990:117.
35. Yoshikawa 1994:35.
36. Palmer & Hollin 1996:175.
37. Cernkovich & Giordano 1987:298; Rankin & Kern 1994:501.
38. Rankin & Kern 1994.
39. Donnermeyer 1992:60.
40. Gottfredson & Hirschi 1990; Patterson et al. 1992.
41. Bell 1968; McLeod et al. 1994:595.
42. Mak 1994; Palmer & Hollin 1996:180.
43. Eisenberg et al. 1990:251.
44. Bell 1968; Chess & Thomas 1984; Thomas & Chess 1980.
45. Zingraff et al. 1993:175.
46. Besharov 1981.
47. Garbarino & Plantz 1986; Widom 1994.
48. Bolton et al. 1977.
49. Kruttschnitt & Dornfeld 1991.
50. Widom 1988; Zingraff et al. 1993:176.
51. Zingraff et al. 1993:196.
52. George & Main 1979; Herrenkohl & Herrenkohl 1981; Hoffman-Plotkin & Twentyman 1984.
53. Miller & Knutson 1997.
54. Kelley et al. 1997.
55. Widom 1989.
56. Finkelhor et al. 1990.
57. Benward & Densen-Gerber 1975.
58. Glover et al. 1996.
59. Zingraff et al. 1993:195.
60. Falshaw et al. 1996.
61. Raine 1993:245.
62. Robins 1991.
63. Ferguson 1952:67; Rutter & Giller 1984:182.
64. Robins et al. 1975.
65. Stewart & Leone 1978.
66. Dembo et al. 1987, 1989; Regan et al. 1987; Wright & Moore 1982.
67. V. Johnson & Pandina 1991.
68. McDermott 1984.
69. Bardone et al. 1996:821; Robins & Price 1991.
70. Steinberg 1986.
71. Carpini & Keeter 1991:594; Herrnstein & Murray 1994:144.
72. Beck et al. 1993:3; Winters 1997:453.
73. Beck et al. 1993:3; Jarjoura 1993, 1996; Winters 1997:453.
74. Barro & Kolstrand 1987; Cairns et al. 1989; Coleman & Hoffer 1987; Weng et al. 1988.
75. LeBlanc et al. 1979.
76. Farnworth & Leiber 1989; Jarjoura 1996.
77. Farrington et al. 1986; Pronovost & LeBlanc 1980.
78. Paetsch & Bertrand 1997:29.
79. Kandel 1980.
80. Short 1998:16.
81. Esbensen & Huizinga 1993:569.
82. Puffer 1912.
83. Staub 1965.

84. Esbensen & Huizinga 1993:575.
85. Sarnecki 1986.
86. Moore 1978; Vigil 1988.
87. Glueck & Glueck 1950; Short 1957; Short & Strodtbeck 1965.
88. Cartwright et al. 1970; Gould 1969; Hepburn 1977.
89. Dishion et al. 1991; Patterson & Bank 1989.
90. Cochran et al. 1994; Ellis 1987a; Fernquist 1995:174.
91. Ellis 1985.
92. Asuni 1963:188.
93. Herz 1908.
94. Von Mayr 1917.
95. Aschaffenburg 1933:58.
96. Exner 1939:67.
97. Thon 1904.
98. Bonger 1936:131.
99. Hersch 1937, 1945.
100. Hersch 1936:515.
101. Goldberg 1950.
102. Von Hentig 1948b:337.
103. Kvaraceus 1945:102.
104. Kvaraceus 1944:288.
105. Maller 1932.

106. Peck et al. 1955.
107. Robinson 1958.
108. Lunden 1942:130.
109. Gillin 1946.
110. Levinger 1940.
111. Linfield 1940.
112. Glueck & Glueck 1950:166.
113. Belson et al. 1975:86.
114. Smart et al. 1970.
115. Fejer 1971.
116. Jensen & Erickson 1979:165.
117. Free 1994.
118. Milman & Su 1973.
119. Sarvela & McClendon 1988.
120. Rhodes & Reiss 1970:83.
121. Ellis 1985:509.
122. Free 1994.
123. Sarvela & McClendon 1988.
124. Stark et al. 1982.
125. Bonger 1916:419.
126. Alland 1967:208; Ezekiel 1941:451; Kagan & Freeman 1970:514.
127. DiLalla & Gottesman 1991; Raine 1993:249.

CHAPTER 8

Behavioral and Cognitive Correlates of Crime

What sort of behavior patterns are associated with a person's chances of running afoul of the law? For example, are people who are unusually quiet or accident-prone, or those who are sexually promiscuous, more likely than people in general to be delinquent and criminal? What about those who are stupid or crazy; are they more criminal than other people? While words such as stupid *or* crazy *would not be used in serious scientific discourse, many studies have examined the possibility that intelligence and mental illness are correlates of crime. Despite the sensitive nature of these topics, some interesting, as well as disturbing, discoveries have come out of the pertinent research.*

In Chapter 5, evidence was explored pertaining to how various demographic characteristics are associated with criminal/antisocial behavior. Chapter 6 gave attention to ecological and macroeconomic factors. Then in Chapter 7, we considered how the family and other broad social relationships were linked to involvement in crime. In the present chapter, the findings from studies of several areas of behavior and cognition will be examined, variables that are sometimes collectively known as *psychological variables.*

The present chapter is a particularly long one because of the enormous number of variables involved. However, you will not be overwhelmed by the information if you allow common sense to rule. This is because most of the findings "make sense" in that they provide a fairly consistent picture. As you read, each time a new variable is introduced, see how well you can anticipate what the studies will indicate regarding its relationship to criminality.

GENERAL BEHAVIORAL CORRELATES

Behavioral correlates of crime refer to behavior tendencies that are statistically more common among persons who engage in criminal/antisocial behavior to an usually high or low degree. The behaviors to be considered have been divided into two somewhat overlapping categories: general and specific. General behavior patterns are broader in nature, approaching what are often considered personality traits, while specific behavior patterns refer to a narrower aspect of behavior. Excluded from consideration under the category of behavior are attitudinal variables, because these will be given attention in a separate section near the end of this chapter. The general behavior patterns to be considered as correlates of crime are as follows: impulsivity, sensation seeking, childhood aggression and bullying, extroversion, psychoticism, neuroticism, and trustworthiness/deceptiveness.

Impulsivity

The concept of *impulsivity* (or *impulsiveness*) refers to people's varying tendencies to act on matters quickly, without giving much forethought to the consequences.[1] When researchers study adolescents and adults, impulsivity is usually measured in terms of subjective answers to such questions as "When you have something important to do, how often do you act on the spur of the moment, rather than taking your time to carefully plan every move?" Other ways of measuring impulsivity involve giving subjects various hypothetical scenarios that could elicit impulsive responses, and asking subjects how they would respond.[2] In the case of young children, researchers usually rely on assessments made by parents and teachers using five- to ten-point rating scales.[3]

Whenever social scientists measure a trait such as impulsivity, accuracy is always a legitimate issue. Studies undertaken to determine how well impulsivity can be measured have concluded that subjective self-reports are only modestly reliable.[4] Part of the reason for inaccuracies in measuring impulsiveness is that the tendency to be impulsive will vary for most people depending on the task involved.[5] In addition, studies have revealed that impulsivity is comprised of two fairly distinct dimensions. One dimension involves how quickly people come to decisions (e.g., "I make up my mind quickly"), and the other has to do with how persistent people are in carrying out long-term tasks (e.g., "I don't like work that always demands extreme patience and care").[6]

Despite the difficulties and subtleties in measuring impulsivity, studies of the relationship between impulsivity and criminal/antisocial behavior have yielded consistent findings. The evidence is summarized shown in Table 8.1. As you can see, studies conducted in many countries have concluded that persons who are impulsive have higher probabilities of committing crimes than is true for people in general. Impulsive people also have been shown to have elevated probabilities of being diagnosed with conduct disorders and psychopathy.[7]

Sensation Seeking and Risk Taking

Sensation seeking refers to the desire for varied and complex sensations and experiences, often to the point of taking physical and social risks to have such experiences.[8] As this definition implies, an important element in sensation seeking is the tendency to be reckless.[9] In Chapter 9, we will revisit the topic of health as it relates to risk taking when we consider the relationship between accidental injuries and criminality.

The most widely used measure for sensation seeking is a self-report scale developed in the 1960s.[10] Many studies have been conducted on sensation seeking since that time.[11] Throughout the world, research has indicated that there are at least three other aspects to sensation seeking: boredom susceptibility, adventure seeking, and a tendency to be spontaneous and uninhibited.[12]

Table 8.2 summarizes research findings on the relationship between sensation seeking/risk taking and criminality. The table is segmented into two parts, one concerned with sensation seeking in general, and the other only with risk taking. As you can see, the evidence is quite strong in indicating that a substantial positive relationship exists between sensation seeking and risk taking and probabilities of being criminal and antisocial.[13]

It is worth adding that sensation seeking tendencies seem to precede the appearance of any antisocial behavior. For instance, a Canadian study found "novelty seeking" and impulsivity in five-year-olds to be the two best behavioral predictors of delinquency at age thirteen.[14]

Childhood Aggression and Bullying

Childhood aggression refers to a child's tendency to become involved in physical fights with other

TABLE 8.1.   Evidence of a relationship between impulsivity and criminal/antisocial behavior (overall consistency score = 97.5%; well-established correlate).

Nature of the Relationship	Type and Seriousness of Offenses								Antisocial Clinical Conditions	
	Official Statistics						Self-Reported Offenses			
	Violent Offenses	Property Offenses	Drug Offenses	Delinquency	General & Unspecified Offenses	Recidivism	Victimful & Overall Offending	Illegal Drug Use	Childhood Conduct Disorders	Antisocial Personality
Positive			North America *United States:* 3	Asia *India:* 1 Europe *England:* 5; *Germany:* 2 Middle East *Israel:* 1 North America *Canada:* 2; *United States:* 16 Pacific *New Zealand:* 2	Europe *England:* 1 North America *Canada:* 1; *United States:* 2 Pacific *New Zealand:* 1	North America *United States:* 3	Europe *England:* 1; *Spain:* 2 North America *Canada:* 2; *United States:* 9 Pacific *Australia:* 4; *New Zealand:* 1	Asia *China:* 1 North America *United States:* 3	Europe *England:* 4 North America *Canada:* 1; *United States:* 2	Europe *England:* 1; *Spain:* 1 North America *Canada:* 2; *United States:* 5
Not significant							North America *United States:* 1		Europe *England:* 1	
Negative										

children (and sometimes with adults) to unusually high degrees. Most social science efforts to measure childhood aggression have relied on retrospective self-reports (e.g., "How often did you get into fights as a child?") or on ratings given by parents, teachers, or peers.[15]

Bullying refers to persistent attempts to dominate other children, either through intimidation or through physical aggression. To measuring bullying, researchers have used ratings by teachers, counselors, parents, and peers,[16] as well as self-reports.[17]

The results of research published to date are summarized in Table 8.3. The evidence is supportive of the view that both of these childhood characteristics are associated with increased probabilities of delinquent and criminal behavior later in life.

As we discuss these relationships, keep in mind that research findings only provide generalizations based on examining large numbers of subjects. In the present case, nearly all studies have found that childhood aggression and bullying are on average more prevalent among persons who eventually run afoul of the law (and self-report offending at high rates) than for those who do not exhibit these childhood tendencies.

In recent decades, at least three long-term studies have concluded that persistent childhood aggression is the single best childhood predictor of serious criminality.[18] In any case, there is little room for doubt that childhood aggression is a correlate of crime.[19] Bullying, although studied much less intensely, can also be considered an established correlate of crime.

Trustworthiness/Deceptiveness

After you know people for a while, you develop a general impression of their trustworthiness, meaning the extent to which they will do what they promise or what is expected of them. In a similar vain, some people seem to be highly prone toward

TABLE 8.2.   Relationship between sensation seeking/risk taking and criminal/antisocial behavior (overall consistency score for sensation seeking = 98.4%; well-established; overall consistency score for risk taking = 100%; well-established correlate).

Nature of the Relationship	Type and Seriousness of Offenses								Antisocial Clinical Conditions	
	Official Statistics						Self-Reported Offenses			
	Violent Offenses	Property Offenses	Drug Offenses	Delinquency	General & Unspecified Offenses	Recidivism	Victimful & Overall Offending	Illegal Drug Use	Childhood Conduct Disorders	Antisocial Personality
Sensation Seeking — Positive			North America *United States: 1*	Asia *Russia: 1* Europe *Germany: 2* North America *United States: 8*	Europe *England: 2; Spain: 1; Sweden: 2* North America *United States: 1*	Europe *Spain: 1*	Asia *Russia: 1* Europe *Belgium: 1; England: 2; Spain: 3* North America *United States: 6*	Europe *England: 1; Spain: 1* Middle East *Israel: 1* North America *United States: 16* Pacific *Australia: 1*	Europe *Norway: 1* North America *United States: 4*	Europe *England: 1* North America *United States: 2*
Not significant							North America *United States: 1*			
Negative										
Risk Taking — Positive				North America *United States: 4*			Europe *Sweden: 2* North America *United States: 1*	North America *United States: 2*		
Not significant										
Negative										

deceiving others, either by lying or by bending the truth. To measure such tendencies, social scientists usually rely on reports by parents, teachers, and peers.[20] For obvious reasons, self-reports of such tendencies may not be very reliable, even on anonymous questionnaires. Some self-report questionnaires have been used to measure cheating in school, however.

Studies undertaken to determine if trustworthiness and related tendencies are associated with criminal/antisocial behavior are summarized in Table 8.4. These studies have consistently concluded that significant relationships exist. Specifically, persons who are most prone toward criminal/antisocial behavior are less reliable and trustworthy and more prone toward deception than are persons in general.[21]

The Eysenck Personality Dimensions

In the 1950s, an English psychologist named **Hans Eysenck** (*I' sink*) (1916–1997) proposed that all major variations in personality could be conceptualized within three dimensions. These dimensions were called *extroversion* (or *extroversion/ introversion*), *psychoticism,* and *neuroticism.* Working from theoretical ideas that will be discussed later in this text, Eysenck went on to

TABLE 8.3. Evidence of a relationship between childhood aggression and bullying and criminal/antisocial behavior (overall consistency score for childhood aggression = 95.3%; well-established; overall consistency score for childhood bullying = 100%; well-established correlate).

Nature of the Relationship		Type and Seriousness of Offenses								Antisocial Clinical Conditions	
		Official Statistics						Self-Reported Offenses			
		Violent Offenses	Property Offenses	Drug Offenses	Delinquency	General & Unspecified Offenses	Recidivism	Victimful & Overall Offending	Illegal Drug Use	Childhood Conduct Disorders	Antisocial Personality
A g g r e s s i o n	Positive	Europe *Finland: 2* North America *United States: 1*		North America *Canada: 1; United States: 1*	Europe *England: 2; Finland: 1; Scotland: 1* North America *United States: 6*	Europe *Finland: 1; England: 3; Sweden: 2* North America *United States: 3*	Europe *England: 1; Finland: 1* North America *United States: 1*	Europe *England: 1* North America *Canada: 2; United States: 1*	North America *United States: 11*	North America *United States: 2*	Europe *Finland: 1* North America *United States: 2*
	Not significant										
	Negative								Europe *Sweden: 1*		
B u l l y i n g	Positive	Europe *England: 1*			Europe *Sweden: 1; Norway: 1*	North America *United States: 1*	Europe *England: 1; Scotland: 2* Pacific *Hawaii: 1*	Europe *Switzerland: 1* Pacific *Australia: 1*		North America *United States: 2*	
	Not significant										
	Negative										

hypothesize that criminals will be unusually high in extroversion, and secondarily in psychoticism. His proposal lead to a flurry of research studies in the 1960s and 1970s to determine if his predictions were correct. Let us briefly review the results of these studies.

Extroversion. **Extroversion** refers to people's varying tendencies to be spontaneous and outgoing, especially in social gatherings.[22] Persons who are usually spontaneous and outgoing are said to be *extroverts,* and those who are unusually reserved and prone to avoid chaotic social settings are said to be *introverts.* The majority of people, of course, tend to be in-between, or what are called *ambiverts.* Extroversion is usually measured by asking subjects a series of questions about their preferences for being in lively social gatherings as opposed to being along or in quiet company, and then combining the responses into a single extroversion measure.[23]

Are extroverts unusually prone toward criminal behavior, as Eysenck hypothesized? The answer is uncertain. As Table 8.5 shows, while most studies have found extroverts to be more crime prone, quite a few have failed to find significant relationships. Overall, despite lingering controversy over how Eysenck's scale actually measures people's varying extroversion/introversion tendencies,[24] most studies indicate that offenders are more extroverted than persons in general. Nevertheless, a number of studies have failed to find a significant relationship, suggesting that extroversion is only a probable correlate of crime.

TABLE 8.4.   Relationship between trustworthiness and lying and criminality/antisocial behavior (overall consistency score = 100%; well-established correlate).

Nature of the Relationship		Types and Seriousness of Offenses								Clinical Conditions	
		Official Statistics						Self-Reported			
		Violent Offenses	Property Offenses	Drug Offenses	Delinquency and Misdemeanors	General & Unspecified Offenses	Recidivism	Victimful or Overall Offending	Illegal Drug Use	Conduct Disorders	Antisocial Personality Syndrome
T r u s t w o r t h y	Negative							North America *United States: 1*	North America *United States: 7*		North America *United States: 3*
	Not significant										
	Positive										
L y i n g & C h e a t.	Positive	North America *United States: 1*			Europe *England: 2* North America *United States: 1*	Europe *England: 1; Finland: 1*		North America *United States: 1*	North America *United States: 2*	North America *United States: 1*	North America *Canada: 1* Pacific *New Zealand: 1*
	Not significant										
	Negative										

TABLE 8.5.   Evidence of a relationship between extroversion and criminal/antisocial behavior (overall consistency score = 70.0%; probable correlate).

Nature of the Relationship	Type and Seriousness of Offenses								Antisocial Clinical Conditions	
	Official Statistics						Self-Reported Offenses			
	Violent Offenses	Property Offenses	Drug Offenses	Delinquency	General & Unspecified Offenses	Recidivism	Victimful & Overall Offending	Illegal Drug Use	Childhood Conduct Disorders	Antisocial Personality
Positive				Asia *India: 2* Europe *England: 4* North America *Canada: 1; United States: 2* Pacific *Australia: 1*	Europe *England: 3; Poland: 1* North America *United States: 1*	Europe *England: 1*	Asia *China: 1* Europe *England: 8* North America *Canada: 1; United States: 4* Pacific *Australia: 2*	Europe *Spain: 1* North America *United States: 5*	Europe *England: 1* North America *United States: 1*	North America *United States: 1*
Not significant		Europe *Netherlands: 1*		Europe *England: 6; Portugal: 1* Middle East *Israel: 1*	Europe *England: 1* Pacific *New Zealand: 1*		Europe *England: 2*	North America *United States: 1*	Europe *England: 1*	
Negative				Europe *Scotland: 2*						

Psychoticism. *Psychoticism* should not be confused with either *psychopathy* or *psychosis.* As Eysenck used the term, **psychoticism** refers to a personality pattern typified by aggressiveness and interpersonal hostility.[25] The terms *psychopathy* and *psychosis,* on the other hand, refer to aspects of mental illness. While these are all obviously related terms, the word *psychoticism* has come to be used in describing an aggressive, hostile type of personality.

Studies of the relationship between psychoticism and criminality are summarized in Table 8.6. You can see that most of the studies support Eysenck's assertion that they will be positively correlated. In other words, persons who exhibit a general air of hostility toward others will engage in crime and delinquency at a higher rate than those who score low in psychoticism.

Neuroticism. **Neuroticism** refers to a near-constant state of anxiety and fear. Eysenck made no specific prediction with respect to a possible relationship between neuroticism and criminality, but many studies have used his personality test to examine the possibility that there is a relationship. The results of these studies are summarized in Table 8.7. You can see that most research indicates that criminals and delinquents are more neurotic than is true for people in general, although a fair number of studies failed to find any significant relationship.

Frequent Boredom

Everyone knows what it is like to feel bored, but research has shown that some people experience boredom much more often than do others. So far, the only method of measuring boredom frequency has been to simply ask people, usually using one or more questions about how often they feel bored under various real or hypothetical conditions.[26]

In recent decades, studies have investigated the possibility that there is a relationship between frequent feelings of boredom and involvement in criminal/antisocial behavior. As you can see from Table 8.8, the evidence is supportive of a significant positive relationship, meaning that those who report feeling bored most often are most likely to be high in offending behavior.[27]

TABLE 8.6.   Evidence of a relationship between psychoticism and criminal/antisocial behavior (overall consistency score = 95.5%; well-established correlate).

Nature of the Relationship	Type and Seriousness of Offenses								Antisocial Clinical Conditions	
	Official Statistics						Self-Reported Offenses			
	Violent Offenses	Property Offenses	Drug Offenses	Delinquency	General & Unspecified Offenses	Recidivism	Victimful & Overall Offending	Illegal Drug Use	Childhood Conduct Disorders	Antisocial Personality
Positive				**Europe** *England: 2; Scotland: 1* **Pacific** *Australia: 2*	**Asia** *Bangladesh: 1* **Europe** *England: 3*	**Europe** *England: 1*	**Asia** *China: 1* **Europe** *England: 4* **North America** *Canada: 1* **Pacific** *Australia: 2; New Zealand: 1*		**Europe** *England: 1* **North America** *United States: 1*	
Not significant					**Europe** *England: 1*					
Negative										

TABLE 8.7. Evidence of a relationship between neuroticism and criminal/antisocial behavior (overall consistency score = 61.5%; possible correlate).

Nature of the Relationship	Type and Seriousness of Offenses								Antisocial Clinical Conditions	
	Official Statistics						Self-Reported Offenses			
	Violent Offenses	Property Offenses	Drug Offenses	Delinquency	General & Unspecified Offenses	Recidivism	Victimful & Overall Offending	Illegal Drug Use	Childhood Conduct Disorders	Antisocial Personality
Positive				Asia *India:* 1 Europe *England:* 3 Middle East *Israel:* 1 Pacific *Australia:* 1	Asia Bangladesh: 1 Europe *England:* 3		Asia *China:* 1 Europe *England:* 3	North America *United States:* 1	North America *United States:* 1	
Not significant				Europe *England:* 3; *Scotland:* 1	Europe *Poland:* 1	Europe *England:* 1	Europe *England:* 2 Pacific *New Zealand:* 1		Europe *England:* 1	
Negative										

TABLE 8.8. Evidence of a relationship between frequent boredom and criminal/antisocial behavior (overall consistency score = 100%; well-established correlate).

Nature of the Relationship	Type and Seriousness of Offenses								Antisocial Clinical Conditions	
	Official Statistics						Self-Reported Offenses			
	Violent Offenses	Property Offenses	Drug Offenses	Delinquency	General & Unspecified Offenses	Recidivism	Victimful & Overall Offending	Illegal Drug Use	Childhood Conduct Disorders	Antisocial Personality
Positive							North America *Canada:* 1; *United States:* 3			North America *Canada:* 1
Not significant										
Negative										

SPECIFIC BEHAVIORAL CORRELATES

The somewhat more specific aspects of behavior to be considered now are alcohol and drug use, number of sex partners one has had (and age of onset of sexual intercourse), delayed versus immediate gratification tendencies, and handedness. The nature of the relationships between each of these variables and criminality is described below.

Alcohol and Recreational Drug Use

Even though the use of various drugs has been criminalized in many parts of the world, we will now specifically explore the evidence that drug use—setting aside its legality/illegality—is correlated with criminal/antisocial behavior. In other words, do persons who use drugs (including alcohol and tobacco) exhibit criminal/antisocial tendencies to a greater degree than persons in general? As we examine this question, we will obviously not be considering drug offenses specifically.

The drugs that will be the focus of this inquiry are not over-the-counter medications (such as aspirin or laxatives), nor are they the vast majority of prescription drugs. Rather, this section will concentrate on the use of a relatively small class of drugs that all share one feature in common: they target the brain for their main effects. Such drugs are called **neurologically active drugs.** To distinguish neurologically active drugs that are used for treating specific brain disorders from the drugs that are used "for fun and relaxation," the term **recreational** (or *nontherapeutic*) **drugs** has come to be used.

Most recreational drugs can be subsumed under the following three categories: depressants, stimulants, and hallucinogens.[28] Depressants slow down the functioning of the brain; stimulants help to speed up brain functioning, and hallucinogens cause distortions in the brain's processing of perceptual information. Throughout this section, we will focus on drug use, and not attempt to extend our inquiry into the area of drug abuse or drug dependency. While the dividing line between *drug use* and *drug abuse/dependency* is fuzzy, virtually everyone recognizes the importance of making such a distinction. Our discussion of drug abuse/dependency (including alcoholism) will occur later in this chapter under the category of *mental disorders.* At this juncture, our concern is simply with the occasional (noncompulsive) use of various recreational drugs.

For centuries, in nearly all countries, the most commonly used recreational drug has been alcohol. In terms of scientific research, most methods for measuring the extent to which people use alcohol and other recreational drugs has been through self-reports on anonymous questionnaires. The accuracy of such data is of course not perfect, but appears to be fairly reliable, especially regarding the use of alcohol.[29]

What does the evidence suggest with respect to an association between alcohol and drug use and criminality (setting aside the illegality of possessing many of the drugs in question)? Table 8.9 presents data pertaining to alcohol use. As you can see, the evidence overwhelmingly supports the conclusion that alcohol use and criminality are positively correlated. Alcohol use is more common among persons who engage in serious delinquency, in criminality, as well as those who are diagnosed with conduct disorders and psychopathy.

In the case of property crimes, studies have shown that alcohol use is especially strongly associated with high risk–low payoff offending.[30] Regarding violent offenses, the strongest alcohol–criminality links have involved domestic violence, according to studies conducted both in the United States[31] and in England.[32] Not only is alcohol linked to domestic violence as far as the offender is concerned, but, to a lesser degree, it appears true from the victim's standpoint as well.[33]

One British study sought to determine if adult offenders with a history of serious violent crimes consumed more alcohol per week than did adult offenders who had only been convicted of property and other nonviolent crimes.[34] It found both groups drinking at equally high levels.

Because the use of most recreational drugs other than alcohol is illegal, underreporting is more of a problem for these substances than in the case of alcohol. It would be more reliable to assess involvement in these illegal drugs using urine or hair samples than to rely on self-reports.[35] However, these methods are simply not practical for use in large-scale social science surveys.

Given the consistency of findings regarding an alcohol–criminality link, you may be able to confidently guess the outcome of studies undertaken to determine if recreational drug use other than alcohol is also a correlate of crime. To further bolster your guess, note that the use of alcohol and the use of other recreational drugs are positively correlated.[36] This correlation even holds in the case of tobacco.[37] It will also help you guess the drug use–criminality relationship to know that drug use is positively associated with childhood and adolescent aggression.[38]

Studies that have examined the relationship between recreational drug use and criminality are shown in Table 8.10, and, as you can see, the findings are consistent. Without including drug use it-self as an offense, research has established that recreational drug use is positively associated with involvement in criminal/antisocial behavior.[39] While most studies have not specifically included

TABLE 8.9. Relationships between alcohol use and criminal/antisocial behavior (overall consistency score = 96.2%; well-established correlate).

| Nature of Relationship | Type and Seriousness of Offenses | | | | | | | | Antisocial Clinical Conditions | |
| | Official Statistics | | | | | | Self-Reported Offenses | | | |
	Violent Offenses	Property Offenses	Drug Offenses	Delinquency	General & Unspecified Offenses	Recidivism	Victimful & Overall Offending	Illegal Drug Use	Childhood Conduct Disorders	Antisocial Personality
Positive	**Europe** *Finland:* 1; *Scotland:* 1; *Sweden:* 1 **North America** *United States:* 2 **Pacific** *Australia:* 1	**North America** *United States:* 1		**Europe** *England:* 2; *Finland:* 1; *Sweden:* 2 **North America** *Canada:* 1; *United States:* 3	**Europe** *England:* 1; *Germany:* 1; *Scotland:* 1 **North America** *Canada:* 1; *United States:* 4	**Europe** *Germany:* 1; *Sweden:* 1 **North America** *United States:* 2	**Europe** *England:* 2 **North America** *United States:* 5	**North America** *United States:* 6	**Asia** *Russia:* 1 **North America** *United States:* 8	**North America** *Canada:* 1 **Pacific** *New Zealand:* 1
Not significant						**North America** *United States:* 1				
Negative										

TABLE 8.10. Relationships between recreational drug use and criminal/antisocial behavior (overall consistency score = 97.9%; well-established).

| Nature of Relationship | Type and Seriousness of Offenses | | | | | | | Antisocial Clinical Conditions | |
| | Official Statistics | | | | | | Self-Reported Victimful & Overall Offending | | |
	Violent Offenses	Property Offenses	Drug Offenses	Delinquency	General & Unspecified Offenses	Recidivism		Childhood Conduct Disorders	Antisocial Personality
Positive	**North America** *United States:* 1	**Europe** *England:* 1 **North America** *United States:* 3		**Europe** *England:* 4; *Finland:* 1; *Sweden:* 1 **North America** *Canada:* 1; *United States:* 14	**North America** *United States:* 5	**Europe** *England:* 2 **North America** *United States:* 6	**North America** *Canada:* 1; *United States:* 29	**Europe** *England:* 1; *Sweden:* 1 **North America** *Canada:* 1; *United States:* 17	**North America** *Canada:* 1; *United States:* 4 **Pacific** *New Zealand:* 1
Not significant						**Pacific** *Australia:* 1	**North America** *United States:* 1		
Negative									

the use of nicotine, those that have found it also to be positively associated with involvement in criminal behavior.[40]

Despite the overwhelming evidence that the use of alcohol and various other recreational drugs is positively correlated with involvement in criminal behavior, you should be on guard against assuming that some simple causal connection is involved. One set of findings suggesting that the relationships are complex involves evidence that sensation seeking is positively associated with frequent use of alcohol[41] and with the use of other recreational drugs.[42] It therefore might be that alcohol use, drug use, and criminality (other than drug use) are all correlated with one another because they are all manifestations of sensation seeking. Of course, there may be still other possibilities.

Many have sought to determine which comes first, drug use or criminal/antisocial behavior.[43] The question is difficult to answer partly because both drug use and delinquency often begin intermittently about the same time during adolescence.[44] Also, the answer depends on whether conduct disorders are included in one's conception of criminal/antisocial behavior. If it is, then almost by definition antisocial behavior precedes drug use.[45] One recent study not only found that children with conduct disorders were more likely to eventually use a variety of recreational drugs (including alcohol) than were children generally, but that the severity of conduct disorders was positively associated with the extent of drug use.[46] Such a pattern is referred to as a **dose-dependent relationship.**

Another question that researchers have addressed has to do with trying to identify the one or two drugs that are most strongly related to involvement in serious criminality. While research in this topic is still ongoing, most investigators agree that, at least in the case of violent crime, the drug that is most strongly linked is alcohol.[47]

Another related issue has involved identifying whether any one recreational drug tends to be the first one used. If so, it would be called the **gateway drug.** In this regard, studies have shown that very few drug users start with "hard drugs"

such as heroin or cocaine. Numerous studies conducted in the United States have concluded that nearly all users of hard drugs exhibit a three-stage "progression," starting with alcohol and/or tobacco, then progressing to the use of marijuana, and finally graduating to the harder drugs.[48]

A few studies have identified four stages, starting with beer or wine, moving to cigarettes and/or strong alcohol, then to marijuana, and finally to the hard drugs such as heroin and cocaine.[49] This four-stage model has also been identified in France and Israel.[50] In either case, alcohol appears to be the point of entry for nearly all drug use. Nevertheless, it must be added that the vast majority of persons who consume alcohol do not go on to use hard drugs.

Overall, the conclusions that can be drawn from studies summarized in Tables 8.9 and 8.10 are that the use of alcohol and other recreational drugs are well-established correlates of crime.[51] The mere correlation between these variables, of course, does not speak directly to the question of what exactly is causing what, although the evidence that symptoms of conduct disorders early in childhood are correlated with alcohol and drug use in adolescence suggests that some of the causes precede the onset of criminality per se.

Number of Sex Partners and Age of Onset of Sexual Behavior

Having numerous sex partners can only be scientifically measured using questionnaire responses to questions such as "How many intimate sex partners have you had?"[52] To assess the accuracy of these self-reports, a few studies have surveyed the same people two or more times, presenting them with the same question. These studies have revealed that there is a general tendency to underreport the number of partners one has had, especially by females,[53] and a tendency for at least a small proportion of males to exaggerate.[54] Nonetheless, the answers given by most subjects appear to be accurate.[55]

Age of onset of sexual behavior, as you might suspect, is fairly closely associated with the number of sex partners one has had.[56] Again, self-reports are used to measure age of onset of intimate sexual behavior, with evidence of a fair degree of reporting accuracy.[57]

Table 8.11 presents the findings of research on the relationship between number of sex partners and age of onset of sexual relationships, on the one hand, and involvement in criminal/antisocial behavior, on the other hand. As you can see, the evidence has consistently shown delinquents and criminals reporting more sexual activity, and

to have begun such activities at a younger age, on average than for other persons their age.[58] The same appears to be true of persons diagnosed with conduct disorders and/or psychopathy. Studies have shown this to be true for both premarital as well as extramarital sexual relationships.[59]

Handedness

A curious behavioral variable that has received the attention of several criminological studies over the years has been the variable of handedness. Scientists have yet to find a society in which most people

TABLE 8.11. Relationship between number of sex partners and age of onset of sexual intercourse and criminality/antisocial behavior (overall consistency score for number of sex partners = 98.1%; well-established correlate; overall consistency score for age of onset of sexual intercourse =100%; well-established correlate).

Nature of the Relationship		Type and Seriousness of Offenses								Clinical Conditions	
		Official Statistics						Self-Reported Offenses			
		Violent Offenses	Property Offenses	Drug Offenses	Delinquency and Misde-meanors	Unspecified Offenses	Recidivism	Victimful or Overall Offending	Illegal Drug Use	Conduct Disorders	Antisocial Personality Syndrome
# Sex partners	Positive	**North America** *United States: 1*			**Europe** *England: 2* **North America** *Canada: 1; United States: 8* **Pacific** *Japan: 1*	**Europe** *England: 2*	**Europe** *England: 1*	**Europe** *England: 1* **North America** *United States: 5*	**Europe** *England: 1* **North America** *United States: 21* **Pacific** *Australia: 1*	**Europe** *Sweden: 1* **North America** *United States: 2* **Pacific** *New Zealand: 1*	**North America** *Canada: 2 United States: 1*
	Not significant										**North America** *Canada: 1*
	Negative										
Early Onset	Positive				**North America** *United States: 2*	**North America** *United States: 1*		**North America** *Canada: 1; United States: 8*	**North America** *United States: 13*	**Europe** *Sweden: 1* **North America** *United States: 3* **Pacific** *New Zealand: 1*	**North America** *Canada: 1*
	Not significant										
	Negative										

are not predominantly right-handed.[60] Depending on exactly how handedness is defined, the proportion of humans who are left- or mixed-handed in most societies is only 5 to 10 percent.[61] Why humans are predominantly right-handed remains a mystery. However, as will be discussed in a later chapter, part of the answer lies in the relative contribution of the two halves (hemispheres) of the brain to control over bodily movements.

Handedness is usually measured by asking subjects which hand they most often use in a list of manual tasks, such as brushing their teeth, cutting with a scissors, throwing a ball, and especially writing.[62] The reliability of this information is high.[63]

As shown in Table 8.12, several studies have investigated the possibility that handedness is a correlate of crime. Most of these studies have indicated that delinquents and criminals have a slight but significantly elevated probability of

being left- or mixed-handed when compared to the general population. Nevertheless, a substantial number of studies have failed to find significant differences, and one study actually found the opposite pattern (right-handers were more prone toward delinquency than left-mixed-handers).

ACADEMIC PERFORMANCE AND INTELLIGENCE CORRELATES

That delinquents and criminals have difficulty learning, especially in academic settings, has a long controversial history. Some of the controversy come from the uneasiness most people feel identifying others as "slow" or "dumb," especially if those being identified already have difficulties finding jobs, decent housing, and the like. Nevertheless, as you will see, a great deal of research has examined the possible links between criminality and intelligence (and related variables). The

TABLE 8.12. Evidence of a link between handedness and criminal/antisocial behavior (overall consistency score = 60.0; possible correlate).

| Nature of the Relationship | Type and Seriousness of Offenses | | | | | | | | Antisocial Clinical Conditions | |
| | Official Statistics | | | | | | Self-Reported Offenses | | | |
	Violent Offenses	Property Offenses	Drug Offenses	Delinquency	General & Unspecified Offenses	Recidivism	Victimful & Overall Offending	Illegal Drug Use	Childhood Conduct Disorders	Antisocial Personality
Left/Mixed Handers More Criminal/Antisocial	North America *United States:* 1			North America *Canada:* 1; *United States:* 1	**Europe** *Italy:* 1; *England:* 1 **North America** *United States:* 2	**Europe** *England:* 1	North America *United States:* Ellis & Ames 1989 **Pacific** *New Zealand:* 1		North America *United States:* Grace 1987; **Pacific** *New Zealand:* 1	**Europe** *England:* 1
No significant differences				**Europe** *England:* 1 **North America** *Canada:* 1	**Europe** *England:* 1 **North America** *Canada:* 2; *United States:* 1					
Right Handers more Criminal/Antisocial				**North America** *United States:* 1						

evidence to be reviewed will consider the following topics: academic achievement, intelligence, and learning disabilities. All of these variables can be differentiated from variables reviewed in Chapter 5 dealing with years of education and so forth in that the variables now to be considered have more to do with the qualitative aspects of educational achievement, rather than merely counting the number of years spent attending school.

Academic Achievement (Grade Point Average)

As everyone knows, people vary in the grades they receive in school. While there are certainly exceptions, for most people overall grades earned tend to be fairly consistent from one year to the next.[64] Consequently, educators and other social scientists often summarize grades in terms of averages,

called *GPAs* (or *grade point averages*). Studies have shown that average grades earned each year in high school, and even in elementary school, correlate fairly well with grades earned in college, especially when attention is given primarily to required core curricula (rather than to optional and "activity" courses).[65]

How do the grades of delinquents and criminals compare to those of their relatively law-abiding peers? As shown in Table 8.13, over a hundred studies have investigated this question and very few of them have failed to find a significant inverse correlation. In other words, individuals who receive high grades in school tend to be less criminal and antisocial than persons who get low grades.[66] As will be discussed further, academic performance of delinquents and criminals tends to be especially poor in subject areas that make a

TABLE 8.13. Results from studies of the relationship between academic performance (grade point average—GPA) and criminal/antisocial behavior (overall consistency score = 96.1%; well-established correlate).

Nature of the Relationship	Type and Seriousness of Offenses								Clinical Conditions	
	Official Statistics						Self-Reported			
	Violent Offenses	Property Offenses	Drug Offenses	Delinquency	General & Unspecified Offenses	Recidivism	Victimful & Overall Offending	Illegal Drug Use	Childhood Conduct Disorders	Antisocial Personality
Negative	**Europe** *England:* 1 **North America** *United States:* 1			**Asia** *China:* 1 **Europe** *England:* 8; *Finland:* 1; *Poland:* 1; *Scotland:* 1; *Sweden:* 2 **North America** *Canada:* 4; *United States:* 48 **Pacific** *Hawaii:* 2; *New Zealand:* 1	**Europe** *Denmark:* 1; *England:* 3; *Sweden:* 1 **North America** *United States:* 2	**Europe** *Germany:* 1 **North America** *United States:* 2	**Asia** *China:* 1 **Europe** *Belgium:* 1; *England:* 3; *Norway:* 1; *Switzerland:* 1 **North America** *Canada:* 2; *United States:* 37	**Europe** *England:* 2 **North America** *Canada:* 5; *United States:* 31	**Europe** *England:* 2 **North America** *Canada:* 1; *United States:* 3	**Europe** *England:* 1 **North America** *United States:* 1
Not significant				**North America** *United States:* 1		**North America** *United States:* 1	**North America** *United States:* 5			
Positive										

heavy demand on reading and other linguistic skills, rather than in areas where the primary demands are on mathematical and scientific reasoning skills.[67]

This basic inverse relationship has even been found after statistically holding constant the social status of parents.[68] In other words, even within very specific categories of parental social status, students who received high grades were less involved in delinquency and crime than those who received poor grades.

Intelligence

Over the years, intelligence has been defined in numerous ways, but it basically refers to people's varying abilities to understand and rapidly connect ideas in meaningful ways, especially in an academic setting.[69] The term itself has been criticized as outmoded and misleading. Some critics have suggested that terms such as *mental ability, academic ability, cognitive ability,* or *mental functioning* be used instead of *intelligence.*[70] Others do not challenge the value of the of the concept of intelligence, but question how well tests of intelligence actually measure it.[71] On the other hand, defenders of the concept and its measurement assert that both meet normal scientific standards of importance and reliability.[72] These issues are far too complex to be given attention here, but you may want to keep these controversies in mind as we review research on the relationship between intelligence and criminality.

The first standardized tests of intelligence began to be introduced to the scientific community around the turn of the century in France.[73] The objective of those who developed the tests was to be able to predict academic success.[74] Accordingly, studies have shown that scores on tests of intelligence correlate more strongly with grades, especially in core subject areas, than with any other variable.[75] Scores on intelligence tests are usually standardized according to the age of whoever took the test, yielding what is called an *age-adjusted quotient,* or *IQ* for short.

Most standardized intelligence tests have been designed so that 100 is the average score in whatever population is used in its standardization. Numerous studies have shown that people's IQ scores are roughly distributed in a bell-shaped fashion, with about two thirds of all the scores bunched up within 15 points on either side of 100. This symmetrical distribution is called a *normal* (or *bell-shaped*) *curve.*

Shortly after the first IQ tests were developed, a U.S. researcher, named Henry Goddard,[76] argued that most criminals were "feeble-minded." Over the next few decades, several researchers provided additional evidence that, while criminals on the whole may not be retarded, they do score significantly lower on standardized intelligence tests than the general population.[77] During the same time, however, some other researchers found the IQ scores of criminals not to be significantly lower than average.[78]

What does the evidence suggest with respect to any relationship between intelligence and criminality? The answer is summarized in Table 8.14. As you can see, the bulk of studies indicate that delinquents, criminals, and persons with antisocial tendencies score lower on IQ tests than do their more law-abiding peers. Nonetheless, there are several studies that have failed to find significant differences.

Since the 1950s, evidence has continued to mount in favor of the conclusion that intelligence and criminality are negatively related, meaning that those who engage in criminal behavior the most score lower on IQ tests than those who commit the fewest (and least serious) offenses.[79] All of these reviews have concluded that in virtually all studies based on large representative samples, about an eight-point average difference exists between the IQ scores of criminals and the general population.[80]

Possible "Artificial" Reasons for the IQ–Criminality Relationship. Some have contended that the inverse relationship between IQ and crime that most studies have found may be artificial in the

TABLE 8.14. Relationship between intelligence and criminal/antisocial behavior (overall consistency score = 79.5%; probable correlate; overall consistency score without self-reports = 83.5%; probable correlate).

Nature of the Relationship	Type and Seriousness of Offenses								Antisocial Clinical Conditions	
	Official Statistics						Self-Reported Offenses			
	Violent Offenses	Property Offenses	Drug Offenses	Delinquency	General & Unspecified Offenses	Recidivism	Victimful & Overall Offending	Illegal Drug Use	Childhood Conduct Disorders	Antisocial Personality
Negative	**Europe** *Denmark: 1*			**Asia** *India: 1* **Europe** *Denmark: 1; England: 8; Finland: 3; Spain: 1; Sweden: 4* **North America** *Canada: 1; United States: 43* **Pacific** *Australia:2; Hawaii: 2; New Zealand: 2*	**Europe** *Denmark: 1; England: 4; Finland: 1; Germany: 1* **North America** *United States: 9*	**Europe** *England: 2; Germany: 2; Sweden: 1* **North America** *United States: 2*	**Europe** *England: 3* **North America** *United States: 8* **Pacific** *New Zealand: 3*	**Europe** *England: 3* **North America** *United States: 2*	**Europe** *England: 8; Netherlands: 1; Scotland: 1* **North America** *Canada: 1; United States: 3*	**Europe** *Finland: 1* **North America** *United States: 4*
Not significant				**Europe** *England: 1* **North America** *Canada: 1; United States: 3* **Pacific** *New Zealand: 1*	**Europe** *Germany: 1* **North America** *United States: 3*	**Europe** *England: 2* **North America** *United States: 5* **Pacific** *New Zealand: 1*	**North America** *Canada: 2; United States: 2*	**North America** *United States: 2*		
Positive						**Europe** *England: 2* **North America** *United States: 2*		**North America** *United States: 1*		

sense that it merely reflects the fact that less intelligent offenders are more likely to be arrested and convicted than high IQ offenders.[81] There are two main problems with this argument. First, most studies have not only found IQ scores inversely associated with official crime and delinquency, but also with self-reported offending.[82] Second, the-dumb-ones-get-caught argument does not explain below-average IQ scores among children with conduct disorders, a diagnosis that *precedes* the onset of official delinquency.[83]

Others have suggested that the link between intelligence and criminality simply reflects the link between social status and criminality. In other words, because persons with high IQs on average tend to be of higher social status those with low IQs, the link between intelligence and criminality may be what researchers sometimes call **spurious.**

Basically, a spurious relationship between two variables is one that is entirely explainable in terms of these variables' coincidental relationship with some third variable. This possibility has been investigated by at least three studies. All found that even after controlling for parental SES, a lower but still significant relationship existed between low IQ scores and criminality.[84] In other words, the IQ–criminality link has not been found to be entirely explainable in terms of a coincidental linkage between children's IQ and their parent's social status.

Some Qualifying Remarks about the IQ–Criminality Relationship.

It is interesting to compare Table 8.14 with Table 8.13. Doing so reveals that academic performance (GPA) is more consistently correlated with involvement in criminal/antisocial behavior than is IQ. Thus, while it is difficult to dispute that either academic performance or intelligence are correlates of crime,[85] ability measures appear to be less strongly so than actual performance measures.

Another notable qualification about the IQ–offending relationship comes from a recent Finnish study. While it found an overall negative relationship between IQ and criminality (as most studies have), the researchers sought to determine if there was a point at the lower end of the IQ range when the probability of criminality might no longer increase. Their data indicated that there was. Specifically, persons with IQ scores below 50 had a probability of delinquency that was comparable to those in the normal range; delinquency was most probable for those in the "moderately retarded" range of 50 to 85.[86] Nevertheless, because the proportion of individuals with IQ scores below 50 is very small, they had very little effect on the overall pattern.

Intellectual Imbalance

As you might suspect, intelligence (or mental ability) is complex and cannot be considered a unitary phenomenon. In other words, there appear to be different aspects to our varying mental abilities.[87] Over the years, researchers have identified several different aspects to intelligence,[88] but two major factors (each with several subfactors) stand out in statistical analyses.[89] One of these two factors (or dimensions of IQ) is called *verbal* (or *qualitative*) *intelligence,* and the other is called *performance* (or *quantitative*) *intelligence.*[90]

While these two aspects of mental ability substantially interrelate and seem to facilitate one another,[91] verbal IQ (*VIQ*) primarily has to do with comprehending language, while performance IQ (*PIQ*) is concerned mainly with comprehending physical realities without the use of language. In terms of academic areas of study, persons who get the highest grades in courses such as English, social studies, and the like usually score high in VIQ, whereas those who excel in the physical sciences, and especially in mathematics, are more likely to be high in PIQ. Examples of the kinds of items used on IQ tests to measure these two aspects of intelligence are presented in Figure 8.1.

A number of studies have been undertaken to determine if one of these two dimensions of IQ correlates more closely with criminality than does the other. The results of these studies are presented in Table 8.15. From this table you can see that most studies indicate that criminals and delinquents score significantly lower than average only with respect to VIQ. In other words, nearly all of the deficits in IQ that have been found among persons with criminal and antisocial tendencies have to do with verbal ability rather than with performance ability. This pattern is sometimes called *intellectual* (or *IQ*) *imbalance.*[92] In precise terms, the intellectual imbalance that has been documented in most studies are for crime-prone persons to be deficient only in VIQ.[93]

Most of the studies that have documented this imbalance have found it to be in the range of 3 to 5 IQ points.[94] This is obviously a fairly modest difference, and, as you can see from Table 8.15, it is not one that all studies have confirmed. Because

TESTS OF VERBAL ABILITY

1. **VOCABULARY:** In each row, circle the word that means the same or nearly the same as the underlined word. There is only one correct choice in each line.

       a. <u>arid</u>   coarse   clever   modest   dry

       b. <u>piquant</u>   fruity   pungent   harmful   upright

2. **VERBAL FLUENCY:** For the next three minutes, write as many words as you can that start with F and end with M.

2. **CATEGORIES:** For the next three minutes, list all the things you can think of that are FLAT.

TESTS OF SPATIAL ABILITY

1. **IMAGINARY CUTTING:** Draw a line or lines showing where the figure on the left should be cut to form the pieces on the right. There may be more than one way to draw the lines correctly.

2. **MENTAL ROTATIONS:** Circle the two objects on the right that are the same as the object on the left.

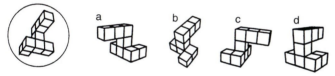

3. **CARD ROTATIONS:** Circle the figures on the right that can be rotated (without being lifted off the page) to exactly match the one on the left.

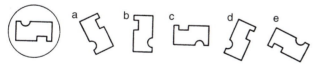

4. **HIDDEN PATTERNS:** Circle each pattern below in which the figure ⌐ appears. The figure must always be in this position, not upside down or on its side.

FIGURE 8.1   Items Used on IQ Tests to Measure Verbal and Performance IQ's.

TABLE 8.15.   The relationship between intellectual imbalance and criminal/antisocial behavior (overall consistency score = 79.4%; probable correlate).

Nature of the Relationship	Types and Seriousness of Offenses									Clinical Conditions	
	Official Statistics						Self-Reported				
	Violent Offenses	Property Offenses	Drug Offenses	Delinquency	Unspecified Offenses	Recidivism	Victimful & Overall Offending	Illegal Drug Use	Conduct Disorders	Antisocial Personality Syndrome	
PIQ significantly higher than VIQ				Europe *Denmark: 1; England: 5; Scotland: 1* North America *United States: 23* Pacific *New Zealand: 1*	Europe *Denmark: 1; England: 1; Germany: 1; Sweden: 1*	Europe *Denmark: 1; England: 1* North America *United States: 3*	North America *United States: 2* Pacific *New Zealand: 1*		North America *United States: 6* Pacific *New Zealand: 2*	North America *United States: 3*
VIQ and PIQ not significantly different				North America *United States: 4*	Europe *England: 1* Pacific *New Zealand: 1*		North America *United States: 2*		Europe *England: 1*	Europe *Finland: 1* North America *United States: 2*
VIQ significantly higher than PIQ							North America *United States: 1*			

there are several studies that have failed to find a significant imbalance, and one study actually found a significantly higher VIQ than PIQ among self-reported offenders, the overall consistency score is in the "probable correlate" range.

Learning Disabilities

What is a **learning disability** (LD)? It is usually defined as a significant discrepancy between an individual's IQ (or some other measure of academic ability) and his/her actual academic performance.[95] Persons who are performing at levels that are substantially below their measured ability are said to be learning disabled.

As you might suspect, there appear to be numerous causes of learning disabilities,[96] including brain abnormalities[97] and physical difficulties hearing or communicating (e.g., stuttering).[98] Sometimes, the causes seem to boil down to a lack

of interest in school or an inability to sit still long enough to pay attention to the teacher.[99]

Research that has explored the possibility that persons prone toward criminal and antisocial behavior have higher rates of learning disabilities than do persons in general are summarized in Table 8.16. As you can see, nearly all of the evidence is in support of the relationship, with the few exceptions found for self-reported offending. (Incidentally, we excluded from this table studies of learning disabilities that have been attributed specifically to difficulties with reading and language comprehension, putting those studies in the table that follows.)

Slow Reading Development and Dyslexia

Studies undertaken to specify the types of learning disabilities that are most associated with criminal/antisocial behavior have often pointed specifically

TABLE 8.16. Results from studies of the relationship between learning disabilities (excluding those specifically attributed to slow reading/language development) and criminal/antisocial behavior (overall consistency score = 95.5%; well-established correlate).

Nature of the Relationship	Type and Seriousness of Offenses								Clinical Conditions	
	Official Statistics						Self-Reported			
	Violent Offenses	Property Offenses	Drug Offenses	Delinquency	Unspecified Offenses	Recidivism	Victimful & Overall Offending	Illegal Drug Use	Childhood Conduct Disorders	Antisocial Personality
Positive				Europe *England: 1; Sweden: 4* North America *Canada: 1; United States: 24*		North America *United States: 1*	North America *United States: 2*	North America *United States: 2*	Europe *England: 3* North America *United States: 2* Pacific *New Zealand: 1*	North America *United States:1*
Not significant							North America *United States: 2*			
Negative										

to reading difficulties.[100] A common form of learning disability having to do with reading is known as **dyslexia,** a condition often associated with difficulty recognizing the differences between letters with the same shapes, but only different in their positioning (e.g., *p, q, b, d*).[101] This condition is also sometimes called *word blindness.*[102]

As you can see from examining Table 8.17, the evidence is very consistent in indicating that several indicators of slow reading development are unusually characteristic of delinquents and criminals. These findings complement evidence that offenders have a special deficit in verbal IQ.

MENTAL DISORDER CORRELATES

Mental disorders refer to a state of cognitive difficulties that generally result in inappropriate social behavior. A "fuzzy" distinction can be made between mental disorder and mental illness. Basically, persons are less likely to voluntarily seek help for mental disorders than for mental illnesses, and are less likely to be treated in an institutional setting. We will discuss links between mental ill-

nesses and offending behavior after considering mental disorders.

The mental disorders that have been frequently examined with respect to criminal/antisocial behavior are as follows: attention-deficit/hyperactivity disorders (ADHD), oppositional defiant disorders (ODD), alcoholism, and drug dependence. Two other widely recognized mental disorders—conduct disorders and antisocial personality disorders—will only be considered indirectly, because these two conditions are considered clinical manifestations of what is legally defined as criminal and delinquent behavior.

Attention Deficit with Hyperactivity Disorder

Have you ever known children who have extreme difficulty paying attention when someone is trying to explain something to them? While every child occasionally has difficulty, those who exhibit attention deficits to the greatest degree are given the diagnosis of *attention deficit disorders* (ADD). If this tendency to be inattentive is accompanied by a high degree of fidgeting and disruptive behavior,

TABLE 8.17.   Evidence of a relationship between slow reading development and criminal/antisocial behavior (overall consistency score = 100%; well-established correlate).

Nature of the Relationship	Type and Seriousness of Offenses									Antisocial Clinical Conditions	
	Official Statistics						Self-Reported Offenses		Childhood Conduct Disorders	Antisocial Personality
	Violent Offenses	Property Offenses	Drug Offenses	Delinquency	General & Unspecified Offenses	Recidivism	Victimful & Overall Offending	Illegal Drug Use		
Positive	North America *United States:* 1			Europe *England:* 3; *Sweden:* 1 North America *United States:* 18 Pacific *Australia:* 1	Europe *Sweden:* 1	North America *United States:* 1			Europe *England:* 1; *Scotland:* 2	North America *United States:* 2
Not significant										
Negative										

the condition is know as **attention deficit with hyperactivity disorder** (**ADHD**).[103] Until the 1980s, the names most commonly given to this condition were *hyperactivity* or *hyperkinesis*.[104] Even though the restless motor movements that constitute a key feature of ADHD usually diminish as affected children become adolescent, their abilities to maintain a focus on long-term tasks assigned by others continue to be abnormally low throughout life.[105]

In the United States, ADHD is estimated to affect about 2 to 9 percent of the childhood population,[106] with estimates in a similar range for other countries as well.[107] A major reason the estimates will vary from one study to the next is that ADHD comes in a substantial range of severity, and not all clinicians will use exactly the same standard in making their diagnoses.

No matter what severity standards are used, however, all studies agree that ADHD is much more common among males than among females, usually by a factor of 4 or 5 to 1, both in the United States[108] and elsewhere.[109] Children who are diagnosed with ADHD tend to do poorly in school,[110] and they are unusually impulsive.[111]

Many studies have examined the possible connection between ADHD and criminal and antisocial behavior, and, as you can see from Table 8.18, the link is well established. ADHD is especially predictive of persistent criminality.[112] The only possible exception has to do with self-reported drug offenses.

Given that ADHD and childhood conduct disorders are closely related clinical conditions (as shown in Table 8.18), it is important to recognize the difference between them. Basically the difference is this: While all hyperactive children have unusual difficulties focusing their attention, many of them are not unusually disruptive and violent toward others.[113] Not only are ADHD and CD separate clinical phenomena, but studies have found that they both predict involvement in serious delinquency and criminality later in life, although CD does so better than ADHD.[114] However, for individuals who receive a combined ADHD–CD diagnosis, the probability of serious delinquency and criminality arising later in life is elevated even more than when either of these conditions appears alone.[115]

"HE'S REALLY FAST. HE CAN GO FROM ZERO TO DRIVING ME BONKERS IN LESS THAN TEN SECONDS."

Oppositional Defiant Disorder

Everyone defies authority figures at times, but some people seem to go out of their way to do so. Persons who are extremely defiant and hostile toward those in authority (such as parents and teachers) are said to have a condition known as **oppositional defiant disorder** (ODD).[116] Diagnosis of ODD is nearly always based on clinical interviews.[117] Obviously, not everyone will draw the line between being ODD and simply being rather stubborn and rude, but clinicians agree that some children and adolescents are so extreme in their tendencies to defy authority and thereby bring misery to themselves and others that a clinical diagnosis is warranted.[118]

In recent years, a number of researchers have sought to determine if ODD is more prevalent among persons who engage in criminal/antisocial behavior. As you can see from the summary presented in Table 8.19, the evidence is consistent with the view that a positive link exists. However, at the present time, most of the evidence of a

TABLE 8.18.   Relationship between attention-deficit/hyperactivity disorders (ADHD) and criminal/ antisocial behavior (overall consistency score = 99%; well-established correlate).

Nature of the Relationship	Type and Seriousness of Offenses								Clinical Conditions	
	Official Statistics						Self-Reported			
	Violent Offenses	Property Offenses	Drug Offenses	Delinquency	Unspecified Offenses	Recidivism	Victimful & Overall Offending	Illegal Drug Use	Childhood Conduct Disorders	Antisocial Personality Syndrome
Positive	**Europe** *Sweden:* 1		**Europe** *Sweden:*1 **North America** *United States:* 5	**Europe** *Norway:* 1 **North America** *Canada:* 1; *United States:* 24 **Pacific** *New Zealand:* 1	**Europe** *England:* 2; *Sweden:* 1 **North America** *United States:* 8	**Europe** *England:* 2 **North America** *United States:* 2	**North America** *United States:* 3 **Pacific** *New Zealand:* 1	**Middle East** *Israel:* 1 **North America** *United States:* 4 **Pacific** *New Zealand:* 1	**Europe** *England:* 6; *Norway:* 1 **North America** *Canada:* 2; *United States:* 22	**North America** *Canada:* 1; *United States:* 8
Not significant							**North America** *United States:* 1			
Negative										

TABLE 8.19.   Evidence of a relationship between Oppositional Defiant Disorders (ODD) and criminal/antisocial behavior (overall consistency score = 100%; well-established correlate).

| Nature of the Relationship | Type and Seriousness of Offenses | | | | | | | | Antisocial Clinical Conditions | |
| | Official Statistics | | | | | | Self-Reported Offenses | | | |
	Violent Offenses	Property Offenses	Drug Offenses	Delinquency	General & Unspecified Offenses	Recidivism	Victimful & Overall Offending	Illegal Drug Use	Childhood Conduct Disorders	Antisocial Personality
Positive				North America *United States: 3*			North America *United States: 2*	North America *Canada: 1*	North America *Canada: 1; United States: 9* South-Central America & Caribbean *Puerto Rico: 1*	North America *United States: 1*
Not significant										
Negative										

positive association has been confined to linking ODD with childhood conduct disorders.[119]

One study of ODD and delinquency concluded that the association is largely confined to early onset delinquency, rather than delinquency that only occurs in the mid to late teens.[120] Studies have shown that early onset delinquency is much more predictive of a long-term criminal career than is true for late-occurring delinquency.[121]

It is worth noting that ODD and ADHD are positively related to one another in the sense that individuals who are diagnosed with either of these conditions have an increased probability of also being diagnosed with the other.[122] In other words, when these two conditions occur in the same individual, the probability of serious violent offending is higher than for those diagnosed with just one or the other of these conditions.

Alcoholism and Other Forms of Drug Dependence

In the preceding chapter, we noted that links have been found between alcoholism and drug abuse in parents and criminality in offspring. Earlier in this chapter, the relationship between alcohol consumption and criminal/antisocial behavior was discussed. Now we give attention to alcoholism and dependency on other drugs as these relate to criminal/antisocial behavior.

While people will never agree on exactly where mere alcohol and drug use leaves off and alcoholism and drug dependency begin,[123] few dispute the need to make a distinction. Basically, individuals who feel compelled to consume several drinks every day are considered alcoholics, especially if their drinking adversely affects family and social relationships.[124] Drug dependence is similarly defined.

Alcoholism.   In recent years, two types of alcoholics have been identified, called Type I and Type II.[125] People with *Type I alcoholism* usually do not begin drinking excessively until at least their mid twenties, and they tend to do so in response to specific frustrating social circumstances. In contrast, *Type II alcoholics* have usually established a pattern of heavy drinking by their early twenties, and do not do so in response to any obvious social provocations.[126] Type II alcoholism has been found to run in families much more often than Type I alcoholism, especially among the males.[127] This strong family transmission pattern for Type II alcoholism has implicated genetic factors as making a substantial contribution to this form of the disease.[128]

Compared to Type I, Type II alcoholism is more heavily concentrated in men than in women,[129] is more closely associated with sensation seeking,[130] childhood ADHD,[131] and with the use of a variety of other mind-altering drugs.[132] From these facts surrounding the distinction between Type I and Type II alcoholism, guess which type is most closely associated with criminal/antisocial behavior.

As you can see from Table 8.20, many studies have found higher rates of alcoholism among persons who are criminal/antisocial. Only a few of these studies distinguished between Type I and Type II alcoholics, but those that did all concluded that it is almost entirely Type II alcoholics who are overrepresented in criminal and antisocial populations.[133]

While both alcohol consumption and alcoholism have been found to be related to criminal/antisocial behavior, the relationship appears to be much stronger in the case of alcoholism.[134] However, some studies have indicated that the tendency to become acutely intoxicated fairly often (such as binge-drinking on weekends) may be more related to criminality than the tendency to merely sustain a stable high alcohol intake day after day.[135]

Table 8.20 shows that numerous countries have contributed to the pool of research on alcoholism and criminality, and that the evidence is unanimous in linking these two phenomena. Overall, there can be no doubt that heavy alcohol consumption/alcoholism is a correlate of crime.[136] There is also evidence that, among alcoholics, persons with the most extreme forms of antisocial behavior tend to begin drinking at an earlier age than is true for alcoholics with few or no antisocial tendencies.[137] Similarly, among convicted offenders, those diagnosed with antisocial personality have been found to have higher rates of alcoholism than those without this diagnosis.[138] All of this evidence reinforces the idea that some sort of nexus exists between criminality, antisocial personality, and susceptibility toward alcoholism, particularly Type II alcoholism.

TABLE 8.20. Relationships between alcoholism and criminal/antisocial behavior (overall consistency score = 100%; well-established correlate).

Nature of the Relationship	Type and Seriousness of Offenses								Antisocial Clinical Conditions	
	Official Statistics						Self-Reported Offenses			
	Violent Offenses	Property Offenses	Drug Offenses	Delinquency	General & Unspecified Offenses	Recidivism	Victimful & Overall Offending	Illegal Drug Use	Childhood Conduct Disorders	Antisocial Personality
Positive	**Europe** *Switzerland:* 1 **North America** *United States:* 1	**Europe** *Switzerland:* 1 **North America** *United States:* 1		**Europe** *England:* 1; *Sweden:* 1	**Europe** *Czech Republic:* 1; *Denmark:* 1; *England:* 1; *Sweden:* 2 **North America** *Canada:* 1; *United States:* 15	**Europe** *Denmark:* 1; *England:* 2; *Finland:* 1 **North America** *Canada:* 2; *United States:* 9	**Europe** *England:* 1 **North America** *United States:* 4	**North America** *United States:* 2	**Europe** *Czech Republic:* 1; *Sweden:* 1 **North America** *United States:* 7	**Europe** *England:* 1; *Sweden:* 1 **North America** *United States:* 13 **Pacific** *New Zealand:* 1
Not significant										
Negative										

Drug Dependency. Without claiming that there is a sharp dividing line, nearly all scientists agree that there is a legitimate distinction to be made between drug use and drug dependency (or drug addiction).[139] The latter term means that drug use must have become fairly habitual and accompanied by distinct feelings of discomfort whenever use is stopped for several weeks (or even days). Social scientists usually assess drug dependency through clinical interviews or via self-reports on anonymous questionnaires.[140]

Many studies have been undertaken to determine if, apart from mere drug use, drug dependency is a correlate of crime. As you can see from the summary of findings presented in Table 8.21, the answer is definitely yes. The overall consistency score for drug dependency makes it a well-established correlate of crime.

Compulsive Gambling

Most people who gamble do so occasionally as a form of recreation. However, some people seem to become addicted to the activity, and, because the odds are always in favor of the gambling establishments, people who gamble most often have the greatest chances of losing substantial amounts of money.

How prevalent is compulsive gambling? According to a survey conducted in the United States,[141] about 2 percent of adults are considered compulsive (or pathological) gamblers.

A number of studies have been undertaken to determine if compulsive gambling is associated with involvement in criminal behavior. The results of these studies, summarized in Table 8.22, have been consistent in indicating that there is a significant positive correlation, both in terms of gambling addiction and even in terms of gambling frequency.[142]

Enuresis

Enuresis, more commonly known as *bed-wetting,* refers to the tendency beyond early childhood to involuntarily urinate while sleeping. Studies conducted in the United States have indicated that most children stop wetting their beds by around age four, with only about a third persisting through age five, and 20 percent continuing to at least occasionally wet their beds beyond the age of seven.[143] Children who are among the last to stop nighttime urination are diagnosed as having enuresis.

TABLE 8.21. Relationships between drug dependence (other than alcoholism) and criminal/antisocial behavior (overall consistency score = 100%; well-established correlate).

Nature of the Relationship	Type and Seriousness of Offenses						Antisocial Clinical Conditions	
	Official Statistics					Self-Reported Victimful & Overall Offending	Childhood Conduct Disorders	Antisocial Personality
	Violent Offenses	Property Offenses	Delinquency	General & Unspecified Offenses	Recidivism			
Positive	North America *United States:* 1	Pacific *Australia:* 1	Europe *England:* 2; *Sweden:* 1 North America *United States:* 1	Europe *England:* 1; *Sweden:* 1 North America *Canada:* 1; *United States:* 11	Europe *Sweden:* 2 North America *United States:* 11	Europe *England:* 2 North America *United States:* 5	Europe *England:* 1; *Sweden:* 2 North America *Canada:* 2; *United States:* 19 Pacific *New Zealand:* 2	Europe *Norway:* 1 North America *United States:* 12 Pacific *New Zealand:* 1
Not significant								
Negative								

TABLE 8.22. Relationships between compulsive gambling and criminal/antisocial behavior (overall consistency score = 100%; well-established correlate).

Nature of the Relationship	Type and Seriousness of Offenses								Antisocial Clinical Conditions	
	Official Statistics						Self-Reported Offenses			
	Violent Offenses	Property Offenses	Drug Offenses	Delinquency	General & Unspecified Offenses	Recidivism	Victimful & Overall Offending	Illegal Drug Use	Childhood Conduct Disorders	Antisocial Personality
Positive			North America *United States: 2*	Europe *England: 1* North America *United States: 1*				North America *United States: 3*		North America *Canada: 1; United States: 1* Pacific *Australia: 2*
Not significant										
Negative										

Over the years, researchers have sought to determine if people with enuresis have an elevated probability of exhibiting criminal and antisocial tendencies. The results are shown in Table 8.23. As you can see, the majority of studies supports the view that enuresis is significantly more common among delinquents and conduct-disordered children than among children in general. Virtually no research has yet been conducted on the possible link between enuresis and adult offending, however.

MENTAL ILLNESS CORRELATES

Many studies have been conducted to determine if mentally ill people have an elevated probability of committing crimes.[144] This research has been almost as controversial as research on the relationship between criminal behavior and intelligence. A major reason for the controversy surrounding mental illness and criminality is that, at least since the 1950s, there has been a trend toward community-based treatment of mental illness, as opposed to institutional treatment.[145]

Few people in the mental health community want to see the trend toward noninstitutional treatment of the mentally ill reversed. However, if mentally ill people have an above-average probability of criminal behavior, some have questioned the wisdom of expanded use of community-based treatment for serious mental illness.[146] One writer went so far as to refer to the movement toward community-based treatment of the mentally ill as the **criminalization of mental illness,** because many patients who would otherwise be receiving care and treatment in a mental hospital end up in jail or prison instead.[147]

By examining Table 8.24, you can see that the vast majority of studies have found a significant positive relationship between mental illness and involvement in criminal behavior.[148] Nevertheless, it is important to add that, despite their increased probabilities of becoming involved in crime, the vast majority of mentally ill persons do not become involved. In fact, one study that separated violent and property crimes found significantly *lower* rates of property crimes among the mentally ill, although they had unusually high violent crime probabilities.[149]

Greater understanding of the crime–mental illness relationship can be achieved by looking at fairly specific categories of mental illness. These relationships are explored below.

TABLE 8.23. Evidence of a relationship between enuresis and criminal/antisocial behavior (overall consistency score = 87.5%; established correlate).

Nature of the Relationship	Type and Seriousness of Offenses								Antisocial Clinical Conditions	
	Official Statistics						Self-Reported Offenses			
	Violent Offenses	Property Offenses	Drug Offenses	Delinquency	General & Unspecified Offenses	Recidivism	Victimful & Overall Offending	Illegal Drug Use	Childhood Conduct Disorders	Antisocial Personality
Positive		**Europe** *France: 1*		**Europe** *England: 2; Sweden: 3* **North America** *United States: 5*		**Europe** *Finland: 1*		**Europe** *Spain: 1*	**Europe** *England: 1; Sweden: 2* **North America** *United States: 3* **Pacific** *New Zealand: 1*	**North America** *United States: 1*
Not significant				**North America** *United States: 1*					**Europe** *Netherlands: 1* **North America** *United States: 1*	
Negative										

TABLE 8.24. Relationship between mental illness in general and criminal/antisocial behavior (overall consistency score = 91.8%; established correlate).

Nature of the Relationship	Type and Seriousness of Offenses								Clinical Conditions	
	Official Statistics						Self-Reported			
	Violent Offenses	Property Offenses	Drug Offenses	Delinquency	Unspecified Offenses	Recidivism	Victimful & Overall Offending	Illegal Drug Use	Childhood Conduct Disorders	Antisocial Personality
Positive	**Europe** *Denmark: 2; Finland: 2; Sweden: 3* **North America** *Canada: 1; United States: 7*	**Europe** *Sweden: 1*	**Europe** *Netherlands: 1; Sweden: 2* **North America** *United States: 12* **Pacific** *Hawaii: 1*	**North America** *Canada: 1; United States: 2*	**Europe** *Denmark: 2; Finland: 3* **North America** *Canada: 4; United States: 26*	**Europe** *Netherlands: 1* **North America** *United States: 1*	**North America** *United States: 3*	**North America** *United States: 1*	**North America** *Canada: 1; United States: 1*	**Pacific** *New Zealand: 1*
Not significant	**Europe** *England: 1*				**North America** *United States: 2*	**North America** *United States: 2*		**North America** *United States: 1*		
Negative		**North America** *United States: 1 1967*								

Schizophrenia

Schizophrenia refers to mental disorders that are most often associated with auditory hallucinations, delusions, and paranoia.[150] Determination of who is afflicted with schizophrenia is nearly always based on clinical interviews with patients and/or their relatives.

The evidence for a significant link between schizophrenia and criminal/antisocial behavior is summarized in Table 8.25. As you can see, it is largely supportive of the view that a positive relationship exists. Studies have also related schizophrenia to general tendencies toward seemingly unprovoked violent outbursts,[151] particularly in the case of delusional forms of schizophrenia.[152] Nevertheless, it is important to add that a couple of recent studies found that the chances of persons who are released from prison with a history of schizophrenia recidivating with a violent crime was actually significantly lower than for prisoners in general.[153]

Also worth adding is that at least four studies have found higher rates of schizophrenia among close relatives of criminals than among relatives of persons in general.[154] In addition, studies have indicated that the schizophrenia–criminality link is strongest when schizophrenia is combined with alcoholism[155] and/or drug abuse.[156]

Unipolar Depression

Depression refers to feelings of sadness and loneliness. Even though everyone has felt depressed over the loss of loved ones or after a major setback in achieving lifetime goals, for some the feelings can be prolonged and overwhelming. To these cases, psychologists and psychiatrists apply the clinical concept of depression.[157] While there is certainly no sharp dividing line, many clinicians find it useful to distinguish between minor and major depression, with the main distinction being the depth of a depressive episode, and the length of time it persists.

TABLE 8.25. Evidence regarding the relationship between schizophrenia and criminal/antisocial behavior (overall consistency score = 85.7%; established correlate).

| Nature of the Relationship | Types and Seriousness of Offenses | | | | | | | | Clinical Conditions | |
| | Official Statistics | | | | | | Self-Reported | | | |
	Violent Offenses	Property Offenses	Drug Offenses	Delinquency	Unspecified Offenses	Recidivism	Victimful & Overall Offending	Illegal Drug Use	Childhood Conduct Disorders	Antisocial Personality Syndrome
Positive	**Europe** *England:* 2; *Finland:* 1; *Germany:* 1; *Sweden:* 1 **North America** *United States:* 5		**Europe** *Sweden:* 1 **North America** *United States:* 4	**Europe** *Germany:* 2	**Europe** *Denmark:* 1; *England:* 1; *Finland:* 1; *Sweden:* 1 **North America** *Canada:* 1; *United States:* 5			**North America** *United States:* 9	**North America** *United States:* 3	**Europe** *Sweden:* 2 **North America** *United States:* 1
Not significant					**North America** *United States:* 3					
Negative						**North America** *Canada:* 1; *United States:* 1				

Table 8.26 provides a summary of the evidence regarding whether a relationship exists between depression and criminal/antisocial behavior. As you can see, most studies indicate that persons who engage in criminal/antisocial behavior to the greatest degree have higher rates of depression than those who rarely, if ever, commit crime. Minor and major depression can therefore be considered correlates of crime, except possibly in the case of self-reported drug use.

Does depression cause crime, does engaging in crime cause depression, or is something else going on? Theory, of course, is needed to help us sort out the most reasonable answers to this sort of causal question.

Manic (Bipolar) Depression

Some types of depression have a special feature, one typified by mood swings between being extremely sad and lethargic at one time, and extremely happy and energetic at another. This type of depression is called **manic depression** (or **bipolar depression**).[158]

While not nearly as many studies have involved manic depression as have considered uni-

TABLE 8.26. Relationships between minor and major depression and criminal/antisocial behavior (overall consistency score minor depression = 86.7%; established correlate; overall consistency score for major depression = 81.3%; probable correlate).

Nature of the Relationship		Type and Seriousness of Offenses								Antisocial Clinical Conditions	
		Official Statistics						Self-Reported Offenses			
		Violent Offenses	Property Offenses	Drug Offenses	Delinquency	General & Unspecified Offenses	Recidivism	Victimful & Overall Offending	Illegal Drug Use	Childhood Conduct Disorders	Antisocial Personality
Minor	Positive	**Europe** *France:* 1			**North America** *Canada:* 3; *United States:* 1	**Europe** *Switzerland:* 1 **North America** *Canada:* 1	**North America** *United States:* 1		**North America** *United States:* 7 **Pacific** *Australia:* 1; *New Zealand:* 1	**North America** *Canada:* 1; *United States:* 7	**Pacific** *New Zealand:* 1
	Not significant								**Europe** *Spain:* 1 **Middle East** *Israel:* 1 **North America** *United States:* 1		**Pacific** *New Zealand:* 1
	Negative										
Major	Positive			**North America** *United States:* 1	**North America** *United States:* 2			**Europe** *Switzerland:* 1	**North America** *United States:* 4	**North America** *United States:* 4	**Pacific** *New Zealand:* 1
	Not significant								**Pacific** *New Zealand:* 1	**North America** *United States:* 2	
	Negative										

TABLE 8.27.   Evidence of a relationship between bipolar depression and criminal/antisocial behavior (overall consistency score = 90.9%; established correlate).

Nature of the Relationship	Type and Seriousness of Offenses								Antisocial Clinical Conditions	
	Official Statistics						Self-Reported Offenses		Childhood Conduct Disorders	Antisocial Personality
	Violent Offenses	Property Offenses	Drug Offenses	Delinquency	General & Unspecified Offenses	Recidivism	Victimful & Overall Offending	Illegal Drug Use		
Positive	North America *United States: 1*				Europe *Switzerland: 1* North America *Canada: 1*				North America *Canada: 1; United States: 3*	North America *United States: 3*
Not significant					North America *United States: 1*					
Negative										

polar depression, the number of studies is sufficient to consider manic depression as a separate correlate of crime. As you can see in Table 8.27, most of these studies have found persons suffering from manic depression to have an increased risk of engaging in crime and of being diagnosed with psychopathy. This increased risk seems to be largely confined to the times when they are in the manic state of their illness rather than when they are in their depressed state.

Suicide

It is not entirely appropriate to think of suicide as a form of mental illness. However, for lack of a better place within which to consider it, and because suicide is often associated with depression,[159] we give suicide attention here.

Suicidal behavior is measured in three main ways: The most obvious is the actual completion of suicide; the second is an attempt to do so, often based on self-reports. The third way is called *suicide ideation.* This refers to self-reports of giving serious thought to committing suicide.

Table 8.28 shows that quite a number of studies have investigated possible links between suicidal behavior and criminal/antisocial tendencies.

As you can see, all studies have found a significant relationship. This does not mean that most criminals have committed or seriously contemplated suicide, but that they have a significantly greater likelihood of having done so than persons in general. The link between suicidal behavior and criminality appears to be especially strong in the case of persons with lengthy histories of alcohol and drug abuse.[160]

In addition to looking for links between suicide and crime at the individual level, some studies have also explored links at the ecological level. Time-series studies have shown that suicide rates and delinquency/crime rates within countries tend to fluctuate together, both in the United States[161] and in Ireland.[162] Similarly, within the United States, a study found that states with the highest crime rates also had higher than average suicide rates.[163] Similarly, across countries, two studies found murder rates and suicide rates to be positively correlated,[164] although one earlier study found the opposite.[165]

Overall, it appears safe to conclude that suicide and criminal/antisocial behavior are positively correlated. This conclusion, of course, can be considered understandable given that criminals and delinquents have above-average rates of depression.

TABLE 8.28.   Evidence of a relationship between suicide and criminal/antisocial behavior (overall consistency score = 100%; well-established correlate).

Nature of the Relationship	Type and Seriousness of Offenses								Antisocial Clinical Conditions	
	Official Statistics						Self-Reported Offenses			
	Violent Offenses	Property Offenses	Drug Offenses	Delinquency	General & Unspecified Offenses	Recidivism	Victimful & Overall Offending	Illegal Drug Use	Childhood Conduct Disorders	Antisocial Personality
Positive			Europe *Sweden: 1* North America *United States: 6*	North America *United States: 1*	Europe *Sweden: 3* North America *Canada: 3* Pacific *Australia: 1*		North America *United States: 2*	Europe *Sweden: 2* North America *United States: 23*	Europe *England: 1* North America *United States: 2*	Europe *Iceland: 1* North America *United States: 2* Pacific *New Zealand: 1*
Not significant										
Negative										

ATTITUDINAL CORRELATES

In addition to religious beliefs (reviewed in Chapter 7), criminologists have investigated differences between delinquents and criminals and persons in general on a number of other attitudinal topics. These include their attitudes toward themselves (self-esteem), their attitudes toward education, and toward conventional authority. Also to be examined under a subsequent heading are empathy and moral attitudes.

Self-Esteem

Self-esteem refers to whether a person by and large views himself/herself favorably or unfavorably. The only way that social scientists have for measuring self-esteem is through self-reports, usually on anonymous questionnaires.[166] Obviously, feelings of self-esteem are bound to fluctuate as people's daily experiences change from positive to negative. Nevertheless, studies have shown that on average some people have much higher average feelings of self-esteem than do others.[167]

Table 8.29 presents the results of studies undertaken to determine if delinquents and criminals have high or low self-esteem relative to persons in general of the same age. You can see that the majority of studies indicate that their self-esteem is below average. Nonetheless, researchers agree that the relationship tends to be fairly weak,[168] meaning that it will sometimes not be statistically significant unless sample sizes of subjects are fairly large.[169]

Some studies have been undertaken to determine which tends to come first: low self-esteem or delinquency. In these studies, researchers interviewed large numbers of early or pre-adolescents. For those who eventually engaged in serious delinquency, the researchers checked to see if and when self-esteem began to drop. Generally, low self-esteem seemed to come first.[170] In fact, engaging in delinquency was followed by a slight rise in self-esteem, although not quite to the level of adolescents in general,[171] and eventually self-esteem seems to continue to drop among persistent delinquents.[172] In interpreting these findings, it may be worth noting that even if low self-esteem precedes delinquency, it may not cause it, because serious and persistent delinquency is itself often preceded by conduct disorders beginning early in childhood.

TABLE 8.29.   Evidence of a relationship between self-esteem and criminal/antisocial behavior (overall consistency score = 73.9%; probable correlate).

Nature of the Relationship	Type and Seriousness of Offenses								Antisocial Clinical Conditions	
	Official Statistics						Self-Reported Offenses			
	Violent Offenses	Property Offenses	Drug Offenses	Delinquency	General & Unspecified Offenses	Recidivism	Victimful & Overall Offending	Illegal Drug Use	Childhood Conduct Disorders	Antisocial Personality
Negative			North America *United States: 2*	**Asia** *Korea: 1* **Europe** *England: 1* **Middle East** *Saudi Arabia: 1* **North America** *United States: 9*	**Asia** *India: 1*	**North America** *Canada: 1*	**Asia** *China: 1* **North America** *Canada: 2; United States: 13* **Pacific** *Australia: 4* **International** *Multiple Countries: 1*	**North America** *United States: 16*	**North America** *United States: 1*	
Not significant				**North America** *United States: 2*		**North America** *United States: 1*	**Europe** *Spain: 1* **North America** *United States: 5*	**North America** *United States: 6*		
Positive						**North America** *United States: 1*		**Europe** *Spain: 1*		

Rebelliousness toward Authority and Defiance of Conventionality

Studies have been undertaken to determine if delinquents and nondelinquents can be distinguished in terms of their general tendencies to be rebellious, particularly toward authority figures. Authority figures not only include government officials and police, but also teachers and even parents.[173] As shown in Table 8.30, these studies have shown that when delinquents are compared to age-mates, they have more hostile attitudes toward widely accepted conventions and they view persons in authority with suspicion and dislike.[174] One study found that delinquents have a tendency to be more hostile and angry toward almost everything than do persons in general.[175] Unfortunately, very little of the research on rebelliousness and these negative attitudes has been extended to samples of adult offenders.

Immediate versus Delayed Gratification and Immediate versus Future Orientation

A famous fairy tale about the ant who worked all day preparing for winter and the grasshopper who spent his time playing the fiddle illustrates the fact that some people seem to live for today, while others carefully plan for the future. Various methods have been used to measure such variation. Among the best known measures has to do with what is called *delayed gratification tendencies* in children. Children are interviewed individually, and, at the end of the interview, they are given a choice of rewards: one piece of candy today or two pieces if they wait until tomorrow.[176] These, along with several similar tests,[177] have shown that some children are much more prone to take the immediate smaller reward, while others consistently opt for delayed larger rewards. Other studies have found

TABLE 8.30.   Evidence of a relationship between rebellious/defiant/negative attitudes toward authority and criminal/antisocial behavior (overall consistency score = 100%; well-established correlate).

| Nature of the Relationship | Type and Seriousness of Offenses | | | | | | | | Antisocial Clinical Conditions | |
| | Official Statistics | | | | | | Self-Reported Offenses | | | |
	Violent Offenses	Property Offenses	Drug Offenses	Delinquency	General & Unspecified Offenses	Recidivism	Victimful & Overall Offending	Illegal Drug Use	Childhood Conduct Disorders	Antisocial Personality
Positive				Europe *England:* 1 North America *Canada:* 1; *United States:* 4		North America *United States:* 1	Asia *Russia:* 1 Europe *England:* 1; *Scotland:* 2 North America *United States:* 9 Pacific *Australia:* 2	Europe *Finland:* 1 North America *United States:* 18	North America *United States:* 3	
Not significant										
Negative										

that when some people are asked about their plans for their lives decades in the future, they have very specific answers, while you can tell that others have hardly even given it a thought. Researchers

© Copley News Service

who study these differences usually refer to their work as *future orientation* research.[178]

Since the 1960s, several studies have been undertaken to determine if either delayed gratification or future orientation is related to criminal/antisocial behavior. You can see from Table 8.31 that nearly all relevant studies indicate that, when they are compared to people in general, delinquents and criminals focus more of their attention on the present than on the future.[179] Perhaps reflecting the same attitudinal tendencies, delinquents also consider themselves less tolerant of frustration than their age-mates according to studies both in India[180] and the United States.[181]

Locus of Control

Back in the 1960s, a U.S. researcher noticed that people vary in the extent to which they perceive forces external to themselves controlling their actions and lives.[182] Since then, a multi-item questionnaire scale has been developed and widely used to measure what is called **internal/external locus of control**.[183] Basically, people who believe they

TABLE 8.31.   Evidence of a relationship between delayed gratification and future orientation and criminal/antisocial behavior (overall consistency score for delayed gratification = 100%; well-established correlate; overall consistency score for future orientation = 83.3%; probable correlate).

| Nature of the Relationship | | Type and Seriousness of Offenses | | | | | | | | Antisocial Clinical Conditions | |
| | | Official Statistics | | | | | | Self-Reported Offenses | | | |
		Violent Offenses	Property Offenses	Drug Offenses	Delinquency	General & Unspecified Offenses	Recidivism	Victimful & Overall Offending	Illegal Drug Use	Childhood Conduct Disorders	Antisocial Personality
G r a t i f i c a t i o n	Negative				North America *Canada: 1; United States: 1*			North America *United States: 3*		North America *United States: 1*	North America *United States: 2*
	Not significant										
	Positive										
O r i e n t a t i o n	Negative				North America *United States: 5*						
	Not significant				North America *United States: 1*						
	Positive										

are very much "masters of their own fate" are said to have internal control, whereas those who believe that much of their behavior is being manipulated by forces outside their own will are said to have external control. The two main sources of external control are chance/fate and "powerful others."[184]

A number of interesting studies have been conducted since the 1970s to determine if persons who are most prone toward criminality might be internals or externals. As shown in Table 8.32, most of the research suggests that perceived external control is significantly more common among those who have engaged in delinquency and crime to the greatest extent. For studies that have probed for which of the two main types of external control seems to be perceived as particularly important for delinquents and criminals, "powerful others" are most often mentioned.[185]

Liberal/Tolerant Attitudes toward Deviance

The word **deviance** is impossible to define precisely, in part because exactly what it refers to varies from culture to culture and over time within cultures. Nevertheless, there are still certain features that nearly all deviant acts share: They tend to be unusual and unpopular within the society under study. No doubt you have noticed that people vary in the degree to which they are comfortable with deviant behavior; some being very tolerant ("anything goes"), while other people are uncomfortable with any behavior that is out of the ordinary.

Table 8.33 summarizes the results of studies undertaken to determine if persons who engage in delinquent and criminal behavior tend to be more or less tolerant of deviance. Results from three categories of deviance are reported. The first involves

TABLE 8.32. Evidence of a relationship between feelings of external locus of control and criminal/antisocial behavior (overall consistency score = 87.5%; established correlate).

Nature of the Relationship	Type and Seriousness of Offenses								Antisocial Clinical Conditions	
	Official Statistics						Self-Reported Offenses			
	Violent Offenses	Property Offenses	Drug Offenses	Delinquency	General & Unspecified Offenses	Recidivism	Victimful & Overall Offending	Illegal Drug Use	Childhood Conduct Disorders	Antisocial Personality
Positive				North America *United States: 4* **Pacific** *Hawaii: 1*		**Europe** *Germany: 1* **North America** *Canada: 1*	**North America** *United States: 3* **Pacific** *Australia: 1*	**North America** *Canada: 1; United States: 2*		
Not significant				**North America** *United States: 1*			**North America** *United States: 1* **Pacific** *Australia: 1*			
Negative										

deviance (or nonconventionality) in general, the second pertains specifically to the use of illegal drugs, and the third has to do with unpopular political views. As you can see, the evidence is largely consistent with the conclusion that tolerance of deviance and/or having deviant attitudes in all three of these realms are associated with increased involvement in criminal/antisocial behavior.

In addition, results from studies of political liberalism are reported. Here, while all of the available evidence is still confined to violation of drug laws, it is consistent in indicating that those who have generally liberal (left-wing) political attitudes engage in criminal/antisocial behavior to a greater degree than those who subscribe to conservative (right-wing) political views.

Negative Temperament (Negative Affect)

You have surely noticed that some people are friendlier than others, while their counterparts almost always seem to be mad at the world for no good reason. A number of research studies have been undertaken to determine if such tendencies are correlated with involvement in criminal/ antisocial behavior. As you can see from Table 8.34, the evidence has rather consistently indicated that delinquents, criminals, and children with conduct disorders are more prone than their peers in general to exhibit a generally "sour" attitude toward life and people around them.

Commitment to Education

Having a commitment to becoming educated or believing in the value of education are measured through self-reports. As shown in Table 8.35, few studies have been conducted among adults, but among adolescents, nearly all studies have found delinquents to have less of a commitment to education than do their relatively nondelinquent peers.[186]

MORALITY AND RELATED ATTITUDINAL CORRELATES

Special attention will now be given to attitudes surrounding morality. This is a sensitive area to probe, but you will see that doing so has uncovered some interesting and possibly important patterns. We begin this section by first exploring empathy and

TABLE 8.33.   Evidence of a relationship between liberal attitudes toward deviance and non-conformity and criminal/antisocial behavior (consistency score for overall deviance = 93.3%; established correlate; overall consistency score for drug-use deviance = 93.8%; established correlate; overall consistency score for political deviance = 100%; well-established correlate).

| Nature of the Relationship | | Type and Seriousness of Offenses | | | | | | | | Antisocial Clinical Conditions | |
| | | Official Statistics | | | | | | Self-Reported Offenses | | | |
		Violent Offenses	Property Offenses	Drug Offenses	Delinquency	General & Unspecified Offenses	Recidivism	Victimful & Overall Offending	Illegal Drug Use	Childhood Conduct Disorders	Antisocial Personality
G e n e r a l	Positive				**North America** *Canada:* 1	**Pacific** *New Zealand:* 1		**Europe** *England:* 1; *Netherlands:* 1 **North America** *United States:* 5	**North America** *United States:* 5		
	Not significant						**North America** *Canada:* 1				
	Negative										
D r u g U s e	Positive							**North America** *United States:* 2	**North America** *United States:* 13		
	Not significant							**Europe** *England:* 1			
	Negative										
P o l i t i c a l	Positive								**North America** *United States:* 5		
	Not significant										
	Negative										

altruism in relationship to criminality; then we turn to the ability to take the role of others, and end with moral reasoning itself.

Empathy and Altruism

You've heard expressions like "I feel your pain." People have been found to vary in the extent to which they are able to empathize. Beginning as

early as two years of age, they readily put themselves in "someone else's shoes" while others find it all but impossible.[187] How would you rate yourself in empathy? High, low, or average? To measure empathy in scientific research, subjects are typically asked to imagine people being tortured or injured in an accident, and then asked to rate the likelihood that they would subjectively "feel" what the victim is feeling.[188]

TABLE 8.34. Evidence of a relationship between negative affect and criminal/antisocial behavior (overall consistency score =86.7%; established correlate).

Nature of the Relationship	Type and Seriousness of Offenses								Antisocial Clinical Conditions	
	Official Statistics						Self-Reported Offenses			
	Violent Offenses	Property Offenses	Drug Offenses	Delinquency	General & Unspecified Offenses	Recidivism	Victimful & Overall Offending	Illegal Drug Use	Childhood Conduct Disorders	Antisocial Personality
Positive				North America *United States: 1*	Pacific *New Zealand: 1*		North America *United States: 1*	North America *United States: 5* Pacific *Australia: 2*	North America *United States: 3*	
Not significant								North America *United States: 1* Pacific *Australia: 1*		
Negative										

TABLE 8.35. Evidence of a relationship between a commitment to education and criminal/antisocial behavior (overall consistency score = 95.7%; well-established correlate).

Nature of the Relationship	Type and Seriousness of Offenses								Antisocial Clinical Conditions	
	Official Statistics						Self-Reported Offenses			
	Violent Offenses	Property Offenses	Drug Offenses	Delinquency	General & Unspecified Offenses	Recidivism	Victimful & Overall Offending	Illegal Drug Use	Childhood Conduct Disorders	Antisocial Personality
Negative				Asia *China: 1* Europe *England: 2; Sweden: 1* North America *United States: 7*			Europe *Switzerland: 1* North America *United States: 22*	North America *United States: 10*	Europe *Sweden: 1*	
Not significant								North America *United States: 2*		
Positive										

Altruism can be thought of as the action component of empathy. In other words, if you feel empathy for someone, then you are motivated to take action in accordance with those feelings, such as trying to help someone who is in trouble.[189] Vari-ous questionnaire scales have been developed for measuring altruistic tendencies.[190] These scales usually involve asking people to imagine various situations in which someone is trouble, and then ask subjects the probability that they would go to the person's aid if at all possible. You might not be surprised to learn that the reliability of these self-assessed altruism scales is rather modest.[191] Other measures of altruism have involved putting subjects in experimental situations that call for them to help someone who appears to be in need and determine if they will actually provide the help.[192] Of course, subjects who readily attempt to provide assistance are said to be more altruistic than those who do not provide assistance, or do so only under the most demanding conditions.

In considering the possible relationship between altruism and criminality, you might recall that in the first chapter of this book we noted that several social scientists have more or less equated altruism with prosocial behavior, and contrasted both with antisocial behavior. Therefore, it would be surprising not to find that highly altruistic people are less involved in crime than persons who are lacking in altruistic tendencies.

Table 8.36 summarizes the evidence on this point. Even though the research thus far has been largely confined to the study of delinquents and childhood conduct disorders, there is little reason for doubt that the same patterns would be found if adult criminals and psychopaths were to be included. Overall, the research indicates that delin-

quents and children with conduct disorders are less empathetic than people in general, especially when attention is given primarily to adolescents and children who are particularly aggressive.[193] The one exceptional study found the same basic negative relationship between empathy and delinquency, but did not consider the strength of the relationship to be statistically significant.[194] These findings are further supported by evidence that prosocial behavior is positively associated with empathy in children.[195]

The studies of altruism, far less numerous than those of empathy, have found that delinquents and criminals tend to be less altruistic than persons in general, particularly in the case of violent offenders.[196] There was an interesting ecological study of altruism and criminality not listed in Table 8.36 that is worth mentioning. This study compared a large number of U.S. cities in terms of the ratio of each citizen's average United Way contributions divided by each citizen's average income (to measure altruism) with each city's violent and property crime rates.[197] Consistent with the view that altruism is associated with low rates of crime, the study found that cities in which the charitable contributions rose as a proportion of overall earnings were also those with the lowest

TABLE 8.36. Relationship between empathy and altruism and criminal/antisocial behavior (overall consistency score = 95.8%; well-established correlate).

Nature of the Relationship		Type and Seriousness of Offenses								Antisocial Clinical Conditions	
		Official Statistics					Self-Reported Offenses				
		Violent Offenses	Property Offenses	Drug Offenses	Delinquency	General & Unspecified Offenses	Recidivism	Victimful & Overall Offending	Illegal Drug Use	Childhood Conduct Disorders	Antisocial Personality
E m p a t h y	Negative				Europe England: 1 North America United States: 8	North America United States: 2		Asia Hong Kong: 1 Europe Spain: 1 North America United States: 2	Europe Spain: 1	Europe England: 1 North America United States: 6	
	Not significant				North America United States: 1						
	Positive										

crime rates. Overall, empathy and altruism can be considered established correlates of crime in the sense that people who are most empathetic and altruistic tend to be the least prone toward criminal/antisocial behavior.

Role Taking/Role Playing

Studies have repeatedly shown that an intimate relationship exists between moral reasoning and the ability to assume the role of someone else.[198] To measure role taking ability, various methods have been used, but the most common has involved asking people to rate their abilities to easily "step into someone else's shoes."[199]

Over the years, studies have compared delinquents and criminals with people generally in terms of their role taking/role playing abilities. The results of these studies are summarized in Table 8.37. As you can see, most of the studies have indicated that people who can assume the role of another person most readily are less likely to become involved in delinquency and crime than those who find role playing most difficult. Some studies have separated emotional aspects of role taking from the purely cognitive or intellectual aspects, and have suggested that it is primarily the emotional aspects that are most strongly inversely correlated with involvement in delinquency.[200]

Moral Reasoning

Morality may seem like a topic that is just too subjective to be studied scientifically. After all, how can one person possibly pass judgment on another person's morality? Social scientists and philosophers have grappled with this question for centuries. The question is of interest to criminologists not only because of the similarity between what is generally considered immoral and what is defined as criminal, but also because many have argued that people with high morals will be less likely to engage in crime than those who are least moral.

Some studies dating back to the 1920s attempted to link delinquency and crime with whether individuals appeared to know right from wrong. Looking for evidence of this obviously required that the researchers make the decision as to what *is* right and wrong, and then assess how closely subjects agreed with their decisions. The results of these studies were disappointing, in that they failed to find noteworthy differences between delinquents and nondelinquents in what was and was not considered wrong.[201]

TABLE 8.37.   Evidence of a relationship between role taking/role playing and criminal/antisocial behavior (overall consistency score = 86.6%; established correlate).

| Nature of the Relationship | Type and Seriousness of Offenses | | | | | | | | Antisocial Clinical Conditions | |
| | Official Statistics | | | | | | Self-Reported Offenses | | | |
	Violent Offenses	Property Offenses	Drug Offenses	Delinquency	General & Unspecified Offenses	Recidivism	Victimful & Overall Offending	Illegal Drug Use	Childhood Conduct Disorders	Antisocial Personality
Negative				North America *United States: 7*	North America *United States: 5*		North America *United States:1*			North America *United States: 1*
Not significant				Europe *England:* 1 North America *United States:* 1	North America *United States:* 1					
Positive										

More recent studies have generally found that those who engage in delinquency and crime consider such behavior less wrong than do those who avoid such activities, although the overlap is considerable.[202] Similarly, a study in China found that adolescents who were officially identified as delinquents generally had weaker commitments to any moral standards than their nondelinquent peers.[203] All of these findings, however, are only a sidelight to what has developed as the main thrust in studies of moral reasoning and criminality.

In the late 1950s, some researchers began to find evidence that delinquents and criminals morally reason at a "lower level" than do persons in general of roughly the same age. More will be said about levels of moral reasoning in Chapter 10, but for now it is only necessary to know that there is considerable evidence that children seem to reason about moral issues differently than do adults. When children are asked to explain why some sort of behavior is wrong, they usually respond in terms of painful or unpleasant consequences that are likely to follow such behavior. Most adults, on the other hand, will explain why something is wrong by referring to the pronouncements of some "moral authority" or by invoking abstract principles of trust and equity as guiding their moral decisions. In this sense, there tends to be a progression from initially equating "wrong" with what results in personal discomfort to eventually using abstract principles in separating "right" from "wrong."

To determine people's levels of moral reasoning, researchers usually present them with a series of hypothetical scenarios that contain moral dilemmas with no easy solution. After subjects state what they would do under these hypothetical situations, they are asked to explain why. In their explanations, researchers seek to determine the level of their moral reasoning. If subjects confine their explanations for why they would take a particular course of action to personal issues of simply avoiding being punished, they are assumed to be reasoning at a lower level than if their explanations are in terms of abstract principles of morality.[204]

What has research indicated with respect to any relationship between moral reasoning and involvement in criminal/antisocial behavior? As you can see from Table 8.38, quite a number of studies have been conducted in this area, and most of the findings support the view that persons who engage in criminal/antisocial behavior tend to exhibit lower levels of moral reasoning than is true of persons in general.[205] In a sense, most studies indicate that delinquents and criminals are closer to toddlers in their moral reasoning than are most of their peers. The only possible exception is in the area of drug offenses, which Table 8.20 showed that studies have not found the same pattern as for other types of offending.[206] This makes sense if you keep in mind that, unlike most victimful offenses, that are *mala in se,* drug and other victimless offenses are largely *mala prohibita.*

Despite the consistency of most of the studies, you can see that there are several studies that have failed to find significant differences. Setting aside those dealing with drug offenses, these exceptional studies may be due to the fact that moral reasoning is a particularly difficult variable to accurately measure (to say nothing about delinquent and criminal behavior being difficult to measure). Furthermore, several of the studies involving official delinquency were based on small numbers of subjects (less than 100),[207] which makes it difficult for findings to reach statistical significance.[208]

To further clarify the relationship between moral reasoning and delinquency and antisocial behavior, some studies have made comparisons within groups of delinquents to see if psychopathic delinquents reasoned at even lower levels than nonpsychopathic delinquents. The results of these studies have been mixed, with some reporting lower moral reasoning among the psychopathic delinquents,[209] and others finding no significant differences.[210]

Before leaving this topic, it should be noted that moral reasoning is fairly strongly linked to other, even better established, correlates of crime. Most notably, empathy,[211] altruism,[212] role taking ability,[213] and intelligence[214] all appear to be positively correlated with moral reasoning. As we have already noted, empathy, altruism, role taking, and intelligence are all established correlates of crime. The fact that these variables are linked to moral

TABLE 8.38.   The relationship between level of moral reasoning and criminal/antisocial behavior (overall consistency score = 78.9%; probable correlate).

Nature of the Relationship	Type and Seriousness of Offenses								Antisocial Clinical Conditions	
	Official Statistics						Self-Reported Offenses			
	Violent Offenses	Property Offenses	Drug Offenses	Delinquency	General & Unspecified Offenses	Recidivism	Victimful & Overall Offending	Illegal Drug Use	Childhood Conduct Disorders	Antisocial Personality
Negative				Europe *England:* 1; *Scotland:* 1 **Middle East** *Israel:* 2 **North America** *Canada:* 1; *United States:* 18	Middle East *Israel:* 1 **North America** *Canada:* 1; *United States:* 7	North America *United States:* 1	Europe *England:* 2 **North America** *United States:* 1		North America *United States:* 3	North America *Canada:* 1; *United States:* 5
Not significant				North America *United States:* 7		North America *United States:* 1	Europe *England:* 1; *Scotland:* 1	North America *United States:* 1	North America *United States:* 1	
Positive								North America *United States:* 1		

reasoning *and* to criminal/antisocial behavior (and probably also to one another) in a web of relationships means that researchers have to be careful in trying to suggest exactly how any one of them might be causing another. Once again, we need theories to guide us in our search for cause and effect, although knowing what relationships exist help us.

UNDERLYING BEHAVIORAL DIMENSIONS OF OFFENDING BEHAVIOR

In bringing this chapter to a close, it is helpful to point to the results of a recent attempt to synthesize much of the research reviewed in this chapter into a two-dimensional model. This model was developed by statistically analyzing the results from a large number of separate studies and was designed to identify the more important underlying factors. The key findings from this analysis are summarized in Figure 8.2. There you will find how a statistical program, known as *factor analy-*

sis, distributes most of the behavioral correlates of crime discussed in this chapter into a two-dimensional space. One dimension, the left–right dimension, is called the *covert–overt dimension,* and the top–bottom dimension is the *destructive–nondestructive dimension.*

This diagram provides a way of spatially conceptualizing how numerous behavioral traits may be interconnected with one another, as well as with criminality. Basically, the closer two characteristics are to one another, the more similar they are in reality, and the more central the characteristics are to any one of the four quadrants of the diagram, the more they epitomize a particular aspect of antisocial behavior. Each quadrant has been given a name that seems to reflect the types of behavior traits that are most commonly found in it.

Figure 8.2 is worth taking a few minutes to examine. Here are a couple of questions to test your comprehension of it: What two traits were found to be most closely associated with "blam-

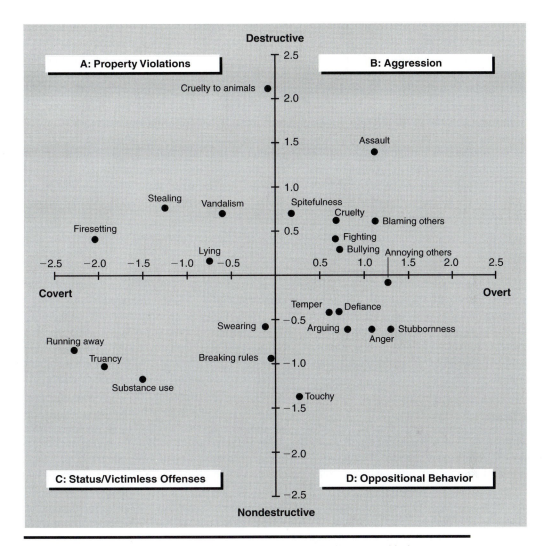

FIGURE 8.2   A diagram representing how various criminal offenses and behaviors correlated with such offenses are inter related according to a factor analysis of results from forty-four published studies (after Frick et.al. 1993).

ing others"? What is the name of the quadrant in which all three of these traits were located?

SOME CLOSING THOUGHTS

As human beings, social scientists have the same emotional feelings other people do when investigating such sensitive topics as variations in intelli-

gence, mental health, and moral reasoning. Certainly, they would feel uncomfortable declaring that those who engage in crime are "stupid," "crazy," and "immoral." If you strip away the scientific language, isn't that what research reviewed in this chapter suggests? The answer depends on how careful you want to be in stating what most of the evidence suggests, and scientists usually want to be extremely careful. In that spirit, the research merely suggests that there are *tendencies* for such traits as intelligence, mental health, moral reasoning—in conjunction with a host of personality/behavior traits—to be statistically associated with varying probabilities of criminality.

It is important to keep in mind that correlational studies mark only a first step in attempting to scientifically understand something as complex as criminal behavior. One can get a hint of just how complex criminality must be by noticing how many variables have now been identified as being correlates of crime. In addition, notice that many

of these correlates of crime are also correlates of one another. For example, studies have shown that ADHD is statistically associated with impulsivity, and that both of these traits are in turn associated with poor academic performance.[215] When these intercorrelations exist, attempts to determine exactly what is causing what can be very frustrating. Fortunately, scientists have strategies that go beyond correlational studies that can help to gradually untangle the causal nature of statistical relationships. Some of these strategies will be revealed when we discuss criminological theories in Part III of this text.

SUMMARY

This chapter has reviewed scientific evidence regarding a wide variety of behavioral traits that have been frequently investigated with reference to criminal/antisocial behavior. In addition, studies linking criminal/antisocial behavior to academic performance, to mental health, and to attitudes were examined.

Behavior Traits

The behavioral traits considered were divided into two categories: general and specific. The general behavior traits of impulsivity are sensation seeking, childhood aggression and bullying, trustworthiness, and the personality traits of extroversion, psychoticism, and neuroticism. The more specific behavior patterns considered were alcohol and drug use, number of sex partners, age of onset of sexual behavior, and handedness.

Studies of impulsivity, sensation seeking, and childhood aggression and bullying were highly consistent in indicating that these were positively associated with criminal/antisocial behavior. Studies of trustworthiness and deception indicate that offenders exhibit high tendencies to lie and low tendencies to meet their commitments. In the case of extroversion, the evidence was fairly consistent in indicating that crime-prone persons are somewhat more extroverted than persons in general. Crime-prone persons also tend to score high on

Eysenck's other two personality dimensions: psychoticism and, to a lesser degree, neuroticism.

With regard to alcohol and recreational drug use—setting aside the legality/illegality of such behavior—the evidence was very strong that such behavior is positively correlated with involvement in criminal/antisocial behavior (discounting offenses directly involving drugs). Studies of sexuality have repeatedly shown that having numerous sex partners and beginning to have sex early in life are positively linked with criminal/antisocial behavior. Most studies of handedness have found significantly higher rates of criminal/antisocial behavior among left- or mixed-handers compared to right-handers, although a fair number of other studies have failed to find significant differences.

Academic Performance and Intelligence

Throughout most of the twentieth century, criminologists and other social scientists have investigated the relationship between intellectual variables and criminal behavior. Accordingly, hundreds of studies have been published on these relationships.

Regarding academic achievement (or grade point average), the evidence is voluminous, and unequivocal in indicating that persons who do poorly in school are more likely to engage in criminal/antisocial behavior than are those who generally receive high grades. In the case of intelligence (or

TABLE 8.39. Capsule summary of general and specific behavioral correlates of crime.

Correlate	Consistency of the Evidence					Comments and Qualification
	Well Estab	Estab	Prob	Poss	Unestab- lished	
Impulsivity	X					Impulsive individuals more crime-involved
Sensation seeking and risk taking	X					Sensation seekers and risk takers more crime-involved
Childhood aggression and bullying	X					Those most prone to aggression and bullying are more crime-involved
Trustworthiness/ deceptiveness	X					Those who are most crime-involved are less trustworthy and more prone to lie
Extroversion/ introversion			X			Extroverts appear to be slightly more crime-involved
Psychoticism	X					Persons who score high on psychoticism are more crime-involved
Neuroticism				X		There is a tendency for those who score high in neuroticism to be more crime-involved
Boredom	X					Those who are most often bored appear to be most crime-involved
Alcohol use	X					Consumers of alcohol are more crime-involved than abstainers
Recreational drug use other than alcohol	X					Those who use recreational drugs other than alcohol are more crime-involved
Number of sex partners	X					Those who have numerous sex partners are more crime-involved
Age of onset of sexual behavior	X					Those who begin having sex at early ages are more crime-involved
Handedness				X		Left- and mixed-handers may be slightly more-crime prone than right-handers

academic ability), the evidence is equally voluminous but somewhat less overwhelming in indicating that those who score high on standardized IQ tests are less involved in criminal/antisocial activities than those who score low.

Another aspect of IQ tests that has received considerable research attention is a phenomenon known as *intellectual imbalance.* This refers to the fact that significant numbers of persons score higher on one of the two main aspects of IQ tests than on the other. Specifically, most studies have shown that those who score significantly higher on the performance (nonverbal) aspects of IQ tests than on the verbal aspects have been found to have an elevated risk of criminal/antisocial behavior.

Another aspect of academic learning is the fact that some persons do poorly in school despite having an average or above-average IQ. These individuals are said to have learning disabilities. Studies have shown that learning disabilities are

TABLE 8.40.   Capsule summary of intellectual correlates of crime.

Correlate	Consistency of the Evidence					Comments and Qualification
	Well Estab	Estab	Prob	Poss	Unestab-lished	
Academic achievement (Grade point aver.)	X					Those with low grades are more crime-involved
Intelligence (IQ) scores			X			Those who score low on IQ tests appear to be more crime-involved
Intellectual imbalance (VIQ>PIQ)			X			Those whose verbal IQs substantially below their performance IQs are more crime-involved
Learning disabilities	X					Learning disabled persons tend to be more crime-involved
Slow reading development	X					Those who develop reading skills at the slowest rates are more crime-involved

positively associated with criminal/antisocial behavior. The type of learning difficulties that have been most often linked to criminality are those surrounding reading skills.

Mental Disorders

Two mental disorders that have been unquestionably found to be more prevalent among persons who engage in criminal/antisocial behavior to the greatest degree are attention-deficit/hyperactive disorders (ADHD) and oppositional defiant disorders (ODD). It is also beyond question that alcoholism and drug dependency are correlates of crime.

Studies of compulsive gambling have consistently linked this behavior to high rates of offending. In the case of a childhood condition known as *enuresis,* research results have been largely consistent with the view that persistent forms are unusually prevalent among persons prone toward delinquency and crime.

Turning to mental illness, evidence was first reviewed for mental illness as a whole. In other words, excluding antisocial personality disorders, are persons who engage in delinquency and crime the most more likely to be diagnosed as being mentally ill compared to those who rarely, if ever, violate the law? The vast majority of scientific studies that have addressed this question have pointed to an affirmative conclusion.

In the case of specific forms of mental illness, the evidence is largely consistent with the view that schizophrenia is more common among persons with serious criminal/antisocial histories compared to persons in general. Both depression and manic depression are even more strongly linked to criminal/antisocial behavior.

For lack of a better place to consider suicide, research on its possible link to criminal/antisocial behavior was considered at the end of the section on mental health. The available research has shown suicidal behavior to be a well-established correlate of crime.

Overall, contrary to assertions that people with mental illness pose no more of a crime threat than do people at large,[216] the evidence suggests that several mental disabilities and illnesses are associated with an elevated risk of criminal behavior.[217] However, this does not mean that most criminals are seriously mentally ill.

TABLE 8.41.   Capsule summary of mental disorders/mental illness correlates of crime.

	Consistency of the Evidence					
Correlate	Well Estab	Estab	Prob	Poss	Unestab-lished	Comments and Qualification
Attention deficits hyperactivity disorder	X					Persons with ADHD are more crime-involved
Oppositional defiant disorder	X					Persons with ODD are more crime-involved
Alcoholism	X					Alcoholics are more crime-involved
Drug dependency	X					Drug addicts are more crime-involved
Compulsive gambling	X					Compulsive gamblers are more crime-involved
Enuresis		X				Enuretics appear to be more crime-involved

TABLE 8.42.   Capsule summary of mental disorders/mental illness correlates of crime.

	Consistency of the Evidence					
Correlate	Well Estab	Estab	Prob	Poss	Unestab-lished	Comments and Qualification
Mental illness in general (aside from psychopathy)		X				Persons with all major forms of mental illness are more crime-involved
Schizophrenia		X				Persons with schizophrenia appear to be more crime-involved
Depression, major Depression, minor		X		X		Persons with major and minor depression appear to be more crime-involved
Manic (bipolar) depression		X				Manic depressives appear to be more crime-involved
Suicide	X					Those who commit or seriously attempt suicide are more crime-involved

General Attitudinal Variables

Two categories of attitudinal variables were considered as correlates of crime. The first was a general category, and the second had to do with fairly specifically with moral reasoning.

Regarding the general category of attitudinal variables, many studies have compared delinquent and criminal populations with people in general regarding self-esteem. Most of these studies have concluded that self-esteem is lower among the former than among the latter.

Attitudinal variables that are well-established correlates of crime have to do with rebelliousness and defiance of authority figures. Similarly, persons who are most prone toward criminal/antisocial behavior have been repeatedly shown to have minimal commitment to educational goals.

A number of studies have compared criminal/antisocial persons to people in general with respect to the immediacy of their goals. By and large, these studies have concluded that criminal/antisocial behavior is negatively associated with people having long-term goals and being willing to delay small immediate rewards for bigger rewards later on.

Some people see themselves almost entirely as the masters of their own fate, while others believe that most of the things in their life course seem to be the result of forces beyond their control. This difference is known as *locus of control*. Research has generally found that persons who are most prone toward criminal/antisocial acts see their lives as determined by outside forces to a greater degree than is true of people in general.

Two more general attitudinal variables that have received sufficient research attention to be considered as correlates of crime are attitudes toward deviant behavior (including criminality), and an overall negative temperament. The available research on both of these two variables has indicated that when crime-prone persons are compared to persons in general, the former are more liberal/tolerant of most forms of deviancy and are more negative or cynical in their overall attitudes toward life, particularly in regard to authority.

TABLE 8.43.   Capsule summary of general attitudinal correlates of crime.

	Consistency of the Evidence					
Correlate	Well Estab	Estab	Prob	Poss	Unestab-lished	Comments and Qualification
Self-esteem			X			Persons with low self-esteem seem to be more crime-involved
Rebelliousness/defiance against authority	X					Persons who are most rebellious and defiant of authority are more crime-involved
Delayed gratification	X					Persons who seek immediate gratification and are most oriented to the present are more crime-involved
Future orientation			X			
Locus of control		X				Those who see their lives being under "internal control" the least appear to be more crime-involved
Liberal/tolerant attitudes toward deviance	X — X					Persons who have the most tolerant attitudes toward deviant behavior are more crime-involved, especially regarding drug use
Negative temperament (negative affect)		X				Individuals who have the most negative attitudes toward things are more crime-involved
Commitment to education	X					Those who are least committed to education are more crime-involved

TABLE 8.44. Capsule summary of variables related to moral reasoning as correlates of crime.

	Consistency of the Evidence					
Correlate	Well Estab	Estab	Prob	Poss	Unestab-lished	Comments and Qualification
Empathy and altruism	X					Persons who are least empathetic and altruistic tend to be more crime-involved
Role taking and role playing		X				Those who are least inclined to assume the role of others are more crime-involved
Moral reasoning			X			Persons who are reasoning at the lowest levels are more crime-involved

Morality and Related Attitudes and Behavior

The last set of correlates considered in this chapter had to do with attitudinal variables closely linked to the concept of *morality*. The first one considered was that of empathy, or the tendency to be able to "feel" the suffering of others. The other variable was altruism, referring to a willingness to be self-sacrificing on behalf of others in need. Research indicates that both of these tendencies are negatively related to involvement in criminal/antisocial activities. A related concept is that of role taking (or role playing). As with empathy and altruism, those who are most able to assume the role of others have been shown in most studies to be unusually low in their involvement in criminal/antisocial behavior.

With respect to moral reasoning itself, studies throughout the world have found such reasoning to gradually develop from a tendency to equate right with what brings pleasure and wrong with what causes pain to oneself. However, as most people mature, they eventually come to reason about moral issues in more abstract terms. Most studies have found that criminals and psychopaths are slower than most people in moving toward more abstract bases of moral reasoning.

The closing section in this chapter reiterated the need to be cautious in offering any quick interpretation of evidence that variables are correlated with criminal behavior. Careless interpretations of these findings sometimes leads to inappropriate stereotyping of people with behavior that strikes us as odd or in violation of some arbitrary cultural norm. In addition, they can be misleading from a strictly scientific standpoint, because there are many ways two variables can be correlated without one of them actually being the cause of the other.

In closing, keep in mind that most scientific understanding is achieved through a long, slow process in which hundreds of people make contributions to a pool of related research. This chapter provides a bird's-eye view of some of that emerging knowledge. Hopefully, it is apparent that criminological understanding is a work in progress.

Also note that criminologists are no strangers to controversy. In Chapter 5, we examined research pertaining to such variables as gender and race. The availability of alcohol and guns in geographic areas were considered in Chapter 6, and Chapter 7 delved into how religion appeared to be linked to criminal/antisocial behavior. In this chapter, intelligence and mental illness were scrutinized. You might wonder if there is any controversy left. In fact, the next chapter gives attention to what many would consider some of the most controversial crime correlates of all: biological correlates.

SUGGESTED READINGS

Collins, James J. (Ed.). (1981). *Drinking and crime.* New York: Guilford. (Provides a useful summary of the evidence available up to the date of publication on the relationship between alcohol use and criminal behavior.)

Hodgins, S. (Ed.). (1993). *Mental disorder and crime.* Newbury Park, CA: Sage. (A valuable book to consult if you are interested in research on mental disorders and criminal behavior.)

Loeber, R., and Dishion, T. (1983). Early predictors of male delinquency: A review. *Psychological Bulletin, 94,* 68–99. (An excellent review of what was known up to the early 1980s of variables that were the most consistently associated with involvement in delinquent behavior by males.)

Peters, Ray DeV., McMahon, Robert J., Quinsey, Vernon, L. (Eds.). (1992). *Aggression and violence throughout the life span.* Newbury Park, CA: Sage. (Provides some up-to-date research findings and theorizing on a variety of behavioral correlates of aggressive and antisocial behavior from childhood through adulthood.)

Quay, Herbert C., (Ed.). (1987). *Handbook of juvenile delinquency.* New York: Wiley. (Consists of a collection of very useful reviews of literature on many of the behavioral/personality correlates of crime and delinquency.)

Walsh, Anthony (1991). *Intellectual imbalance, love deprivation and violent delinquency: A biosocial perspective.* Springfield, IL: Charles C. Thomas. (This book reviews much of the evidence pertaining to the relationship between intelligence and delinquent/criminal behavior, especially evidence bearing on the VIQ–PIQ imbalance.)

EXERCISES

1. This chapter has discussed how nearly all studies have shown that mental illness is significantly more common among serious criminals than among persons in general. What would you say to someone who argued that in light of this evidence we should require that mentally ill persons who are not institutionalized wear ankle bracelets for monitoring their whereabouts? Are there any conditions under which you would favor such a policy, or not favor it? More generally, can you think of any practical applications that might be derived from knowing that mental illness and criminality are statistically related? Write a one- to two-page double-spaced paper on these questions.

2. If you have access to the World Wide Web, do a search for criminal behavior and then a subsearch for one or more of the behavioral or intellectual variables discussed in this chapter. Based on information you find, write a one- to two-page summary of facts or opinions about how that variable and criminal behavior seem to be related. (Your instructor will probably want you to print out a copy of the source or sources you used. You may also do your search at the college library.)

3. Assume that you were writing a letter to someone who had read the present text up to this point, and said that from now on they are going to pick their friends on the basis of their not having any traits that are established correlates of crime. In other words, they will no longer associate with anyone who exhibits a trait that is an established correlate of crime. Write a one- to two-page double-spaced letter in response.

ENDNOTES_____

1. af Klinteberg et al. 1987:238; Jensen & Garfinkel 1988:111.
2. Arbuthnot et al. 1987:148.
3. Vitiello et al. 1990:112.
4. Gerbing et al. 1987; Paulsen & Johnson 1980.
5. Prentky & Knight 1986.
6. Barratt 1994:63.
7. Sher & Trull 1994.
8. Zuckerman 1979:10, 1994:27.
9. Arnett 1996.
10. Zuckerman 1979, 1994:389; also see Arnett 1994.
11. Zuckerman 1994.
12. I. L. Ball et al. 1983:1158; Zuckerman 1971.
13. Arbuthnot et al. 1987:150; Zuckerman 1994:264.
14. Tremblay et al. 1994.
15. Loeber & Stouthamer-Loeber 1987:332.
16. Jonsson 1967:205.
17. Connell & Farrington 1997; Power et al. 1997:210.
18. Farrington 1986a; Stattin & Magnusson 1991; Viemero 1996.
19. Loeber & Dishion 1983.
20. Loeber & Stouthhamer-Loeber 1987:337.
21. Rowe 1986:523.
22. Eysenck & Zuckerman 1978:477.
23. Francis & Pearson 1988:913.
24. Campbell & Reynolds 1984; Francis et al. 1981:103; Rocklin & Revelle 1981.
25. Claridge 1983; Eysenck & Nias 1978:239.
26. Cochran et al. 1994.
27. Wood et al. 1995.
28. Fishbein & Pease 1996.
29. Blumberg et al. 1973; Sobell 1979.
30. Cordilia 1985.
31. Gondolf & Foster 1991; Miller 1990.
32. Gayford 1975; Homer & Gilleard 1990.
33. Murdoch et al. 1990.
34. Myers 1982.
35. Mieczkowski et al. 1991, 1993; Wilcox et al. 1979.
36. Brody 1987; Cockerham 1977; Eisterhold et al. 1979; Fors & Rojeck 1983; McIntosh et al. 1979.
37. McAlister et al. 1979.
38. Kingery et al. 1992; McCormick & Smith 1995.
39. White 1990.
40. Watts & Wright 1990:180.
41. Schwartz et al. 1978; Segal et al. 1980; M. Zuckerman et al. 1972.
42. Andrew & Cronin 1997; Liu & Kaplan 1996; Wood et al. 1995.

43. Loeber 1990:17.
44. Johnston et al. 1978; Kandel et al. 1986.
45. van Kammen et al. 1991.
46. Rutter 1996:496.
47. Mednick & Volavka 1980:136.
48. Brennan et al. 1981; Jessor et al. 1980a; Kandel 1982, 1992; Kandel & Faust 1975; Miller & Volk 1996; Newcomb & Bentler 1986.
49. Kandel & Faust 1975; Single et al. 1974.
50. I. Adler & Kandel 1980.
51. Clayton 1981; Gandossy et al. 1980; Inciardi 1981b.
52. Shrier et al. 1996:378.
53. Gold 1970.
54. Clark & Tifft 1966.
55. Kahn et al. 1988; Rodgers et al. 1982.
56. Durbin et al. 1993.
57. Sheier et al. 1996.
58. West & Farrington 1977.
59. Gebhard et al. 1965:598 & 616.
60. Coren & Porac 1977; Hollis 1875; Spennemann 1984.
61. L. J. Harris 1990:217.
62. Coren et al. 1979; Dean 1982; Steenhuis et al. 1990; Williams 1991.
63. Coren et al. 1979; Steenhuis et al. 1990.
64. Bloom 1964:96.
65. Bloom 1964:95; Bloom & Peters 1961; Ford & Campos 1977.
66. for reviews see Siegel & Senna 1988:302; Silberberg & Silberberg 1971.
67. Hogenson 1974; Sturge 1982.
68. Hawkins & Wall 1980:6; Jensen 1976.
69. Hebb 1978:15; Masters & Roberson 1990:235; Waldrop 1984.
70. Lezak 1988; Shaughnessy 1994:131.
71. Biesheuvel 1972; Cronin et al. 1975; Samuel et al. 1976.
72. Gutterman 1979; Walsh 1991:29.
73. McFarland 1981:311.
74. Ackerman & Heggestad 1997:219; Stelmack et al. 1995:447.
75. Eysenck 1979; Scarr & Carter-Saltzman 1982:831.
76. 1912, 1914, 1921.
77. Healy & Bronner 1939.
78. Reviewed by Ferentz 1954; Weiss & Sampliner 1944; Zelany 1933.
79. Feldman 1977:166; Lynam et al. 1993; Prentice & Kelly 1973; Woodward 1963.

80. Hirschi & Gottfredson 1977; Lynam et al. 1993:187.
81. Doleschal & Klapmuts 1973; also see Quay 1987:107; Rutter & Giller 1984:165.
82. West & Farrington 1973:131.
83. Rutter & Giller 1984:165.
84. McGarvey et al. 1981; Metfessel & Lovell 1942:143; West & Farrington 1977:123.
85. Hirschi & Hindelang 1977; Wilson & Herrnstein 1985:148.
86. Rantakallio et al. 1995.
87. Quay 1987:109.
88. Guilford 1967.
89. Enns & Reddon 1998; Jensen & Faulstinch 1988:926.
90. T. D. Hill et al. 1985; Leckliter et al. 1986; Quay 1987:108.
91. Enns & Reddon 1998.
92. Walsh 1991.
93. Angenent & deMan 1996:52.
94. Law & Faison 1996:699.
95. Broder et al. 1981; Stelmack et al. 1995:447; Winters 1997:452.
96. Pennington & Smith 1983; Pirozzolo et al. 1983.
97. John et al. 1977:1405; Kraus et al. 1996.
98. Cozad & Rousey 1966.
99. Flicek 1992.
100. Buikhuisen 1987:169; Jonsson 1975:184; Williams & McGee 1994.
101. Critchley 1972.
102. Holzman 1979:78.
103. Teicher et al. 1996.
104. Rutter & Gillis 1984:173.
105. Faigel et al. 1995; Gittelman et al. 1985; Klein & Mannuzza 1991; Mannuzza et al.
106. Anderson et al. 1987; Safer & Krager 1988.
107. Bird et al., 1988.
108. Eme 1984; Hinshaw 1992a, 1992b, 1994; Whalen 1989.
109. Norway: Backe-Hansen & Ogden 1996:338.
110. Faigel et al. 1995; Mannuzza et al. 1993.
111. af Klinteberg et al. 1989; Farrington et al. 1990:62.
112. Farrington et al. 1990:73.
113. Werry 1988.
114. Fergusson et al. 1994b; N. Lie 1992; Moffitt 1990a; Taylor et al. 1996; Vitella 1996:263.
115. Forehand et al. 1991; Moffitt 1990a; Vitella 1996:263.
116. American Psychiatric Association 1994:91.
117. Lahey et al. 1994.

118. Angold & Costello 1996.
119. Eme & Kavanaugh 1995:407.
120. Simons et al. 1994.
121. Werner & Smith 1992:107; Crowley et al. 1998:234.
122. Biederman et al. 1996:1198.
123. Barnes 1988:1730; Hurwitz & Christiansen 1983:248.
124. American Psychiatric Association 1994:195; Helzer et al. 1991:81.
125. Cloninger et al. 1981; Sigvardsson et al. 1996; von Knorring et al. 1987:307.
126. Anthenelli & Tabakoff 1995:178.
127. Hallman et al. 1990; Mutzell 1993.
128. Cloninger et al. 1981.
129. Hallman et al. 1990.
130. von Knorring et al. 1985:388.
131. Morrison 1979.
132. von Knorring et al. 1985:51.
133. Sigvardsson et al. 1996; von Knorring et al. 1987:307.
134. Hurwitz & Christiansen 1983:248; Mayfield 1976; McCord 1981a.
135. Collins & Schlenger 1988; Seltzer & Langford 1984.
136. Gibbens & Silberman 1979; Modestin et al. 1996a.
137. Rimmer et al. 1972; Schuckit & Morrissey 1979.
138. C. E. Lewis et al. 1983.
139. Jurich & Polson 1984.
140. Midanik 1988; Stacy et al. 1985.
141. Volberg 1994.
142. Blaszynski et al. 1989.
143. Byrd et al. 1996; Fergusson et al. 1986a.
144. Link et al. 1992; Monahan 1981b, 1992.
145. Fustero 1984:58.
146. Abramson 1972; Solomon et al. 1994.
147. Teplin 1983.
148. Palermo et al. 1992a.
149. Giovannoni & Gurel 1967.
150. American Psychiatric Association 1994:285.
151. Monahan 1992; Swanson et al. 1990.
152. Link et al. 1994.
153. Lidz et al. 1993; Rice & Harris 1995:339.
154. Asnorow 1988; Heston 1970; Kay 1990; Mednick et al. 1987b.
155. Tiihonen et al. 1995.
156. Bartels et al. 1991; Cuffell et al. 1994.
157. American Psychiatric Association 1994:339.
158. MacKinnon et al. 1997:356.
159. Apter et al. 1988; Goldberg 1981; Hoberman & Garfinkel 1988;

160. Woodruff et al. 1972.

161. Loeber 1990:2.

162. McKenna et al. 1997.

163. Boor 1981.

164. Holinger 1979; Palmer 1968.

165. Henry & Short 1954.

166. Bennett et al. 1971; Cobb et al. 1966.

167. Rosenberg 1965.

168. Arbuthnot et al. 1987:152; Bynner et al. 1981:420.

169. McCarthy & Hoge 1984; Moore et al. 1996:541.

170. Bynner et al. 19811; Kaplan 1975a; Rosenberg 1978:271.

171. Bynner et al. 1981:429; Kaplan 1975a.

172. McCarthy & Hoge 1984.

173. Rigby et al. 1987.

174. Gorsuch & Butler 1976; Kazdin 1987:189a.

175. White et al. 1987:729.

176. Mischel et al. 1989:934.

177. Krueger et al. 1996:112; Newman et al. 1992.

178. Arbuthnot et al. 1987:146.

179. Krueger et al. 1996; Tremblay et al. 1994.

180. Misra 1981.

181. Hogan & Jones 1983:17.

182. Rotter 1966.

183. Nowicki & Strickland 1973.

184. Richter et al. 1996.

185. Richter et al. 1996:340.

186. Gibbons & Krohn 1991:101; Kercher 1988:303; Sampson & Laub 1993:101.

187. Zahn-Waxler & Radke-Yarrow 1990:108.

188. Chlopan et al. 1985; Hanson & Mullis 1985:182; Hogan 1969:308.

189. Ellis 1990b:23; Rushton 1980:7.

190. Rushton et al. 1981a; Sawyer 1965.

191. Ma & Leung 1991.

192. Clary & Miller 1986; Smithson & Amato 1982.

193. P. L. Ellis 1982:131.

194. Kendall et al. 1977.

195. Strayer & Roberts 1989.

196. Riley 1986.

197. Chamlin & Cochran 1997.

198. Campbell & Christophier 1996b:39; DeWolfe et al. 1988; Eisenberg & Miller 1990:182; Mullis & Hanson 1983; Selman 1980; Underwood & Moore 1982.

199. Krebs & Gilmore 1982.

200. Arbuthnot et al. 1987:164.

201. Hartshorne & May 1928; Hartshorne et al. 1929, 1930.

202. Gertz & Gould 1995; Smith & Paternoster 1987.

203. Zhang & Messner 1995:377.

204. Rest 1979.

205. Arbuthnot et al. 1987:161; Jurkovic 1980:715; Nelson et al. 1990.

206. Blasi 1980:37.

207. E.g., Hudgins & Prentice 1973; Kohlberg 1958.

208. Jennings et al. 1983:303; Nelson et al. 1990.

209. Campagna & Harter 1975; Jurkovic & Prentice 1974, 1977.

210. Blair et al. 1995:12; Chandler & Moran 1990:243.

211. Dickstein 1979; Hogan 1973; Kozeki & Berghammer 1992:193; Kuhmerker 1975; Lee & Prentice 1988.

212. Blasi 1980:30; Hoffman 1975.

213. DeWolfe et al. 1988; Lee 1983.

214. Gregg et al. 1994.

215. Loeber 1990:14.

216. See Link et al. 1992:275.

217. Link et al. 1992:290

CHAPTER 9

Biological Correlates of Crime

*Are criminals more or less healthy than people in general? Or are there
any unusual ways that their brains work? What about the possibility of
some hormonal or other biochemical factor being related to criminality?
This chapter will review evidence concerning these and other contentious
issues. As we consider the evidence, be on guard against equating biology
with being "born that way." Such thinking is common, but far too
simplistic. The complexity comes in part from the fact that biological
variables themselves are often the result of people's social circumstances.*

Biology is the study of life. Because only living
things—specifically animals—exhibit behavior, it
is reasonable to argue that behavior itself is a biological phenomenon. In this sense, social scientists, including criminologists, are in fact
biologists! Nevertheless, it is common in the social sciences to exclude behavior (especially
complex social behavior) from the scope of *biology*. Keeping with this tradition, the present chapter will review evidence that various biological
variables are associated with criminal/antisocial
behavior.

As with the correlates of crime discussed in
all of the preceding chapters, the only traits to be
reviewed are those for which at least five pertinent studies have been published. The variables to
be discussed are classified under the following
categories: perinatal factors, health, morphology,
physiology, biochemistry, and brain functioning.

PERINATAL CORRELATES

Perinatal literally means "around the time of
birth." It refers to events leading to conception, the

nine or so months of gestation, the birth process
itself, and the few months following birth. Four
perinatal factors have been investigated with respect to criminal/antisocial behavior that they can
statistically be considered correlates of crime.
These factors are birth weight (and gestation
length), perinatal trauma or birth complications,
minor physical anomalies (birth defects), and maternal smoking during pregnancy.

As with other correlates of crime, none of
these variables should be thought of as necessarily
being of a direct causal nature. In many cases, they
may (or may not) simply reflect the effects of social environmental variables, such as the social
status of the mother.

Birth Weight and Gestation Length

When someone we know has a baby, we usually
want to know whether the baby was a boy or a girl,
and how much it weighed. Studies have found that
birth weight is statistically associated with a variety of traits that manifest themselves later in life.
For instance, people who weigh more at birth tend
to be healthier as adults,[1] and to get better grades

in school,[2] and score higher on IQ tests.[3] Because health, grades, and IQ scores all appear to be correlates of crime, is it possible that birth weight is also?

Several studies have investigated the possible link between criminal/antisocial behavior and birth weight. As shown in Table 9.1, this research has so far been confined to measuring criminal/antisocial behavior in terms of delinquency and conduct disorders. The studies have largely concluded that persons who weigh the least at birth have a higher probability of offending and/or exhibiting conduct disorders during childhood than do those who weigh the most.

Perinatal Trauma

Perinatal trauma (including *birth complications* or *birth stress*) refers to any injuries or other difficulties encountered at or around the time of birth. Among the most common types of perinatal trauma are physical blows to the mother's ab-

domen during pregnancy (such as in a fall or a motor vehicle accident), and oxygen deprivation during the birth process (called *hypoxia*).[4] Researchers most often measure perinatal trauma and birth complications using reports by mothers or by an attending physician.

Table 9.2 summarizes the findings from studies undertaken to assess the relationship between birth traumas and birth complications and offspring involvement in criminal/antisocial behavior. As you can see, most of the evidence indicates that these perinatal conditions are significantly more prevalent in criminal/antisocial individuals than in the population at large. One of the studies listed as finding no significant relationship between birth complications and criminality actually did when birth complications were combined with "maternal rejection" throughout childhood.[5]

Overall, more research is called for, but the weight of evidence points toward perinatal trauma and birth complications as being correlated with crime.[6]

TABLE 9.1.   Evidence of a relationship between birth weight and criminal/antisocial behavior (overall consistency score = 83.3%; probable correlate).

| Nature of the Relationship | Type and Seriousness of Offenses | | | | | | | | Antisocial Clinical Conditions | |
| | Official Statistics | | | | | | Self-Reported Offenses | | | |
	Violent Offenses	Property Offenses	Drug Offenses	Delinquency	General & Unspecified Offenses	Recidivism	Victimful & Overall Offending	Illegal Drug Use	Childhood Conduct Disorders	Antisocial Personality
Negative				**Europe** *Denmark:* 1; *England:* 3; *Sweden:* 1 **North America** *Canada:* 1 **Pacific** *Hawaii:* 1					**Europe** *Denmark:* 1; **England:** 1 **North America** *Canada:* 2; *United States:* 3 **Pacific** *New Zealand:* 1;	
Not significant				**Europe** *Finland:* 2 **North America** *United States:* 1						
Positive										

TABLE 9.2.   Evidence of a relationship between perinatal trauma/birth complications and criminal/antisocial behavior (overall consistency score = 58.3%; possible correlate).

Nature of the Relationship	Type and Seriousness of Offenses								Antisocial Clinical Conditions	
	Official Statistics						Self-Reported Offenses			
	Violent Offenses	Property Offenses	Drug Offenses	Delinquency	General & Unspecified Offenses	Recidivism	Victimful & Overall Offending	Illegal Drug Use	Childhood Conduct Disorders	Antisocial Personality
Positive	**Europe** *Denmark: 1* **North America** *United States: 2*			**Europe** *England: 1; Finland: 1* **North America** *Canada: 2; United States: 1* **Pacific** *New Zealand: 1*	**Europe** *Denmark: 1*				**Europe** *Denmark: 1; England: 1* **North America** *United States: 2*	
Not significant	**Europe** *Denmark: 1* **North America** *United States: 1*	**Europe** *Denmark: 1*		**Europe** *England: 2* **North America** *United States: 4*					**North America** *Canada: 1*	
Negative										

Minor Physical Anomalies

Minor physical anomalies (MPAs) refer to quite a number of unusual physical traits, none of which are life-threatening. These include asymmetrical or malformed ears, multiple hair whorls, widely spaced eyes, a high-arched palate, and webbed or widely spaced toes.[7] The causes of MPAs are largely unknown, but are likely to include genetic factors as well as maternal consumption of various drugs and exposure to environmental pollutants during pregnancy.

Research pertaining to MPAs and criminal/antisocial behavior is indicated in Table 9.3. As you can see, quite a few studies have found a significant positive relationship. MPAs appear to be especially strongly linked to criminal aggression among individuals reared in unstable home environments.[8] The links also seem to be more pronounced in the case of males than for females.[9]

Besides being a well-established correlate of crime, MPAs have been found associated with several behavioral correlates of crime. In particular,

studies have found MPAs positively correlated with learning disabilities,[10] with schizophrenia,[11] and especially with ADHD.[12] In addition, MPAs are more common among persons who do poorly in school[13] and who score below average on IQ tests.[14] Persons with one or more MPAs are particularly prone to score low in verbal IQ.[15] You may recall that in Chapter 6, learning disabilities, schizophrenia, low IQ (especially low VIQ), and ADHD all appear to be correlates of crime.

Two studies suggested that MPAs are linked to conduct disorders among offspring who come from homes steeped in dissension and turmoil.[16] This finding reinforces the idea that many biological correlates of crime probably have stronger links to criminality when interacting with social variables than when they are present in isolation.

Maternal Smoking during Pregnancy

Since the 1990s, several studies have found a statistical link between smoking during pregnancy by an expectant mother and conduct disorders among

TABLE 9.3. Evidence of a relationship between minor physical anomalies (MPAs) and criminal/antisocial behavior (overall consistency score = 100%; well-established correlate).

Nature of the Relationship	Type and Seriousness of Offenses								Antisocial Clinical Conditions	
	Official Statistics						Self-Reported Offenses			
	Violent Offenses	Property Offenses	Drug Offenses	Delinquency	General & Unspecified Offenses	Recidivism	Victimful & Overall Offending	Illegal Drug Use	Childhood Conduct Disorders	Antisocial Personality
Positive	**North America** *United States: 2*		**North America** *United States: 1*	**North America** *United States: 1* **Pacific** *Hawaii: 1*			**North America** *United States: 1*	**Europe** *England: 1* **North America** *United States: 3*		
Not significant										
Negative										

offspring. As you can see by examining Table 9.4, these studies have all indicated that women who smoke during pregnancy have a higher proportion of offspring with conduct disorders than do mothers who do not smoke during pregnancy. At least one of the studies statistically adjusted for the fact that smoking is inversely correlated with social status, and still found the relationship to be statistically significant.[17]

Thus far, four studies have followed offspring for a sufficient number of years to determine if delinquency was linked to smoking by the mother during pregnancy. Three of these studies confirmed the existence of a positive statistical relationship.[18] The other study failed to find a significant relationship until it adjusted for the ease of breathing by the infants (called an *Apgar score*). When this adjustment was *combined* with maternal smoking, then a significant positive relationship with offspring delinquency many years later was found.[19]

Worth adding is that studies have linked maternal smoking during pregnancy with the following

TABLE 9.4. Evidence of a relationship between maternal smoking during pregnancy and criminal/antisocial behavior (overall consistency score = 88.9%; established correlate).

Nature of the Relationship	Type and Seriousness of Offenses								Antisocial Clinical Conditions	
	Official Statistics						Self-Reported Offenses			
	Violent Offenses	Property Offenses	Drug Offenses	Delinquency	General & Unspecified Offenses	Recidivism	Victimful & Overall Offending	Illegal Drug Use	Childhood Conduct Disorders	Antisocial Personality
Postive				**Europe** *England: 1;* *Sweden: 1*	**Europe** *Denmark 1*				**North America** *Canada: 3;* *United States: 3*	
Not significant				**North America** *United States: 1*						
Negative										

conditions in offspring: underweight and premature births,[20] ADHD,[21] lower intelligence and academic performance,[22] and increased learning disabilities.[23] All of these variables are themselves correlates of crime.

Overall, several lines of evidence lead to the conclusion that perinatal factors are associated with involvement in criminal/antisocial behavior. Such evidence, in fact, has led one research team to devise a nursing-home visitation program for expectant and early post-term mothers to assist them in delivering and rearing healthy children.[24] Some preliminary efforts to evaluate the effectiveness of this program in preventing childhood conduct disorders and early delinquency have been encouraging, although far from definitive.[25]

HEALTH FACTORS

Links between overall health and/or specific diseases and criminal/antisocial behavior have captured the attention not only of criminologists, but also of public health officials. The studies to be reviewed below are overall health and life expectancy, rates of accidental injuries, and susceptibility to three specific illnesses: hypoglycemia, the perimenstrual syndrome (PMS), and epilepsy.

Overall Health and Life Expectancy

Over the years, numerous studies have compared the health of criminals with that of the general population. Various methods have been used by scientists and health officials to objectively assess health. One obvious way is in terms of age of death; those who die early would be considered less healthy than those who die in old age. This is called a *mortality indicator* of health. Other measures include asking people how many times in the past year they made visits to physicians or spent time in the hospital for specific ailments. This would be an example of what is called a *morbidity indicator*. Additional morbidity indicators are to ask subjects to self-rate their general health, and to report their disability days (days that a person is unable to go to work or engage in routine activities).

Are persons who engage in crime and delinquency more or less healthy than persons in general? The results of research undertaken to answer this question are presented in Tables 9.5a and 9.5b, the first has to do with morbidity indicators of health and the second deals with mortality indicators. Regarding morbidity, as you can see from Table 9.5a, the evidence is largely consistent with the view that criminals are less healthy than the general public.

It is not unreasonable to think that just because crime prone persons tend to be ill more often than people in general, their life expectancy might still be longer. This is in fact the case when you compare men and women: Throughout the world, males on average report feeling healthier,[26] having fewer annual physician visits and disability days per year than do women,[27] even when all pregnancy-related factors are excluded.[28] Yet, men have shorter lives by several years, at least in all modern industrial countries.[29]

So, what does the evidence suggest about criminal behavior and mortality? Is it consistent with the research on morbidity, or does it go in the opposite direction, as in the case of gender? Table 9.5b provides the answer: Persons with criminal/antisocial tendencies have greater morbidity than those with minimal criminal/antisocial tendencies. Thus, offenders are not only less healthy, but they also die at earlier ages than do people in general.

The link between criminality and poor health has even held true in family studies. Specifically, studies have reported that parents of criminals die at an earlier average age than do parents of persons with no serious criminal record.[30]

Accidental Injuries

Accidental injuries refer to significant bodily harm resulting from unintended natural or manmade events. Quite a number of studies have been conducted to determine if persons with serious criminal/antisocial behavior sustain accidental injuries at rates that are higher or lower than for people in general. Table 9.6 presents consistent evidence that ac-

TABLE 9.5a. Evidence of a relationship between morbidity and criminal/antisocial behavior (overall consistency score = 79.2%; probable correlate).

Nature of the Relationship	Type and Seriousness of Offenses								Antisocial Clinical Conditions	
	Official Statistics						Self-Reported Offenses			
	Violent Offenses	Property Offenses	Drug Offenses	Delinquency	General & Unspecified Offenses	Recidivism	Victimful & Overall Offending	Illegal Drug Use	Childhood Conduct Disorders	Antisocial Personality
Positive	**North America** *United States:* 1			**Europe** *England: 4; Sweden: 1* **North America** *Canada: 1; United States: 5*	**Europe** *England: 1* **North America** *United States: 3*		**Europe** *England: 1*			**North America** *United States: 2*
Not significant				**Europe** *Sweden: 3* **North America** *United States: 1*	**North America** *United States: 1*					
Negative										

TABLE 9.5b. Evidence of a relationship between age of death (life expectancy) and criminal/antisocial behavior (overall consistency score = 100%; well-established correlate).

Nature of the Relationship	Type and Seriousness of Offenses								Antisocial Clinical Conditions	
	Official Statistics						Self-Reported Offenses			
	Violent Offenses	Property Offenses	Drug Offenses	Delinquency	General & Unspecified Offenses	Recidivism	Victimful & Overall Offending	Illegal Drug Use	Childhood Conduct Disorders	Antisocial Personality
Positive				**North America** *United States: 3*	**Europe** *Finland: 2* **Pacific** *Australia: 1*				**North America** *United States: 1*	**North America** *United States: 4*
Not significant										
Negative										

cidental injuries are significantly more common among persons with serious criminal/antisocial backgrounds than those without.[31]

Hypoglycemia

The fuel used by the brain to perform its various functions, *including your reading of this very sentence,* is a sugar known as *glucose.*[32] Brain glucose levels are regulated by the blood system, which in turn responds to chemical messages from a small region of the brain called the *hypothalamus* (to be discussed more in Chapter 13).[33] When the hypothalamus detects glucose levels getting either too high or too low, it sends chemical signals to the pancreas to either curtail or increase the

TABLE 9.6.   Evidence of a relationship between accidental injuries and involvement in criminal/antisocial behavior (overall consistency score = 100%; well-established correlate).

Nature of the Relationship	Type and Seriousness of Offenses								Antisocial Clinical Conditions	
	Official Statistics						Self-Reported Offenses			
	Violent Offenses	Property Offenses	Drug Offenses	Delinquency	General & Unspecified Offenses	Recidivism	Victimful & Overall Offending	Illegal Drug Use	Childhood Conduct Disorders	Antisocial Personality
Positive				**Europe** *England:* 3 **North America** *United States:* 7 **Pacific** *Hawaii:* 1	**North America** *United states:* 3 **Pacific** *Australia:* 1	**Europe** *England:* 1	**Europe** *England:* 3 *Netherlands:* 1	**Europe** *Netherlands:* 1	**Europe** *Sweden:* 1 **North America** *United States:* 3	
Not significant										
Negative										

release of insulin into the blood. This regulatory process helps to maintain brain glucose levels at fairly stable levels for most people.

For a variety of reasons, some people have difficulty maintaining glucose levels within a narrow range.[34] These people are said to suffer from **hypoglycemia.** Although the prefix *hypo-* means "low," hypoglycemia can best be thought of as referring to especially unstable glucose levels.

When most people consume sweets, the concentrations of sugar in their blood rises temporarily but in most people it is quickly normalized. For hypoglycemics, however, consumption of sugar can have roller-coaster effects on brain glucose levels, i.e., a dramatic rise followed by a deep plunge.[35] Dramatic fluctuations in brain glucose can cause temporary disturbances in people's thoughts and moods, with the most common symptoms being confusion, difficulty concentrating, and irritability.[36]

Since the 1970s, a number of studies have been conducted to determine if there is any relationship between hypoglycemia and the probability of people engaging in criminal/antisocial behavior. While hypoglycemia is a rare medical condition, Table 9.7 indicates that it is significantly more common among persons with serious criminal histories than for persons in general, particularly in the case of crimes of a violent nature.[37]

In addition, a series of population-wide studies of a Native American tribe in Peru where the homicide rate appears to be extraordinarily high has found that nearly 50 percent of the adults suffered from at least mild forms of hypoglycemia.[38] Along similar lines, mild to severe forms of hypoglycemia have been found significantly correlated with self-reported aggression[39] and hostile fantasies.[40] Also, two studies injected adolescents with high "challenge" dosages of sugar, and found that delinquents responded with higher insulin release than was true for their peers.[41] These findings may be interpreted in other ways, but suggest less stability in glucose regulation among delinquents.

Worth adding to the present discussion is the point that alcohol appears to affect glucose metabolism in ways that make hypoglycemic symptoms worse.[42] Also, experiments with mice indicate that emotional stress can cause the pancreas to release unusually high amounts of insulin, which eventually brings about a depletion of glucose reserves.[43]

Partly because of the evidence linking hypoglycemia to involvement in violent criminal behavior,[44] some have suspected that consumption of sugar even by people without hypoglycemia could

TABLE 9.7.   Evidence of a relationship between hypoglycemia and criminal/antisocial behavior (overall consistency score = 100%; well-established correlate).

Nature of the Relationship	Type and Seriousness of Offenses									Antisocial Clinical Conditions	
	Official Statistics						Self-Reported Offenses		Childhood Conduct Disorders		
	Violent Offenses	Property Offenses	Drug Offenses	Delinquency	General & Unspecified Offenses	Recidivism	Victimful & Overall Offending	Illegal Drug Use		Antisocial Personality
Postive	Europe *Finland: 2* North America *United States: 1*				North America *United States: 1*					Europe *Finland: 2*
Not significant										
Negative										

cause aggression, particularly among children and adolescents.[45] Support for this suspicion, however, has been mixed. A few studies have indicated that high sugar consumption (as well as the consumption of carbohydrates and various artificial food flavorings) increased conduct disorders and/or ADHD symptoms[46] as well as delinquent behavior.[47] However, most studies have failed to find significant causal links between these dietary factors and either conduct disorders or ADHD symptoms.[48]

Overall, current evidence largely supports the view that hypoglycemia is a contributing factor toward criminality, especially of a violent nature. Nevertheless, because the prevalence of this disease is low, especially in its severe forms, it can only be considered a contributor to a tiny proportions of violent offenses.[49]

The Perimenstrual Syndrome

Sex hormone levels in females tend to fluctuate roughly on a twenty-eight- to thirty-day cycle, called the *menstrual cycle.* As a result of these hormonal fluctuations, women often report experiencing changes in mood associated with their menstrual cycle.[50] The most common pattern is for women to report greater depression, irritability, and anxiety in the period shortly before and during menstruation (i.e., perimenstrum).[51] For approximately one third of women, the negative moods associated with perimenstrum are sufficiently severe as to constitute a condition known as the **perimenstrual** (or **premenstrual**) **syndrome** (PMS).[52]

Inspired by an exploratory study in Paris in the 1940s,[53] in the 1960s an English physician, named **Katherine Dalton,** began conducting research into the possibility that women—especially those with severe PMS—might have an increased probability of criminal behavior during perimenstrum. To test her suspicions, Dalton interviewed female convicts, asking them at what point in their menstrual cycle the crime they had been convicted of had taken place. As had been indicated by the Paris study, Dalton discovered that well over half of the women reported that they had committed their offense during the seven days of perimenstrum. Strictly by chance, only about one fourth of all offenses should have occurred during this period.

As shown in Table 9.8, most studies have confirmed Dalton's basic conclusion that female crime is most probable during the perimenstrum period. In addition, at least two studies have found that women who are involved in violent prison disturbances are about twice as likely to do so during the perimenstrum period than at other times.[54]

Despite this consistent finding, several scientists have expressed skepticism, noting that nearly all of the data are based on unreliable retrospective

TABLE 9.8.   Evidence of a relationship between the perimenstrual syndrome and criminal/antisocial behavior (overall consistency score = 85.7%; established correlate).

| Nature of the Relationship | Type and Seriousness of Offenses | | | | | | | | | Antisocial Clinical Conditions | |
| | Official Statistics | | | | | | Self-Reported Offenses | | | | |
	Violent Offenses	Property Offenses	Drug Offenses	Delinquency	General & Unspecified Offenses	Recidivism	Victimful & Overall Offending	Illegal Drug Use	Childhood Conduct Disorders	Antisocial Personality
Higher during perimenstrum	**Europe** *France:* 1 **North America** *United States:* 2	**Europe** *France:* 1 **Europe** *England:* 1			**Europe** *England:* 1	**Europe** *England:* 1					
No significant difference											
Lower during perimenstrum											

accounts.[55] They reason that it is possible that many women who have committed a crime mistakenly recall the timing of the offense as occurring around the time of menstruation. An interesting laboratory experiment found some support for PMS causes crime hypothesis by investigating women with the most severe PMS symptoms. These women were consistently more aggressive on average than women with few or no symptoms, no matter what phases of their menstrual cycle they were in.[56]

Another point to keep in mind is that the exact causal significance of this line of research is still far from settled. For instance, one study found that women who suffer most from PMS report greater use of alcohol,[57] leaving open the possibility that alcohol could account for at least some of the PMS–criminality relationship. Overall, while more research is called for, most of the evidence currently available supports the view that PMS is a correlate of crime.

Epilepsy

Epilepsy is considered an illness of neurological origin. It is typified by **seizures,** which are "electrical storms" in the brain. With varying genetic susceptibility, seizures come about as a result of several environmental factors, among the most

common being physical injuries to the brain, viral infections, low birth weights and birth trauma.[58] Seizures can also be induced by hypoglycemia.[59]

The main behavioral symptoms of epilepsy are known as **convulsions** (or *fits*), although not all people with epilepsy have full-blown convulsive episodes.[60] Mild epileptic episodes may manifest themselves as little more than momentary pauses in ongoing activities accompanied by a glazed stare.

The period of time during which an epileptic seizure is occurring is known as the **ictal phase** of epilepsy, and the remainder is called the **interictal phase.**[61] This terminology is worth knowing, because it may be that increased offending probabilities among people with epilepsy may occur mainly during interictal phases of the disease.

Epilepsy in fact comes in varying degrees, with very mild forms having minimal effect on muscular coordination, either because the area of the brain in which the seizure is occurring is not involved in coordinating bodily movement or because the seizure was of such a short duration that no convulsions had time to occur.[62] Seizures that do not have noticeable debilitating effects on coordination are called **subconvulsive** (or *subclinical*) **seizures.**

Studies of human populations have repeatedly shown epilepsy to be relatively rare, afflicting 1 in every 150 to 200 persons.[63] In prisons, however, the rates of epilepsy are around 1 in 50,[64] or at least three times higher than in the general population. The evidence bearing on this conclusion is summarized in Table 9.9. As you can see, most studies indicate that criminal behavior is more prevalent among persons with epilepsy than among persons in general. Notice, however, that most studies have not found a significant link between epilepsy and delinquency. This could indicate that epilepsy is more common only among persons with the most serious forms of offending.

Further bolstering the possible relationship between epilepsy and criminality are studies in non-human animals with either drug-induced or naturally occurring epilepsy. These studies suggest that epileptic animals have an increased probability of exhibiting violent interictal outbursts than do animals without epilepsy, both in rats[65] and cats.[66]

Some criminologists have strenuously criticized suggestions of a relationship between criminality and epilepsy.[67] Their criticisms have been on two grounds: First, epilepsy is rare among criminals. While true (only about one in fifty serious offenders have epilepsy), the disease is still substantially more common in criminal populations than in general populations.

Second, the crimes that are committed by people with epilepsy only occasionally occur during an actual seizure (the ictal phase of epilepsy).[68] This is true in part because seizures occur intermittently and usually only last a couple of minutes. A few studies have indicated that, during an actual seizure, epileptics exhibit increased rates of defensive forms of aggression.[69] However, these defensive acts usually do not meet most definitions of *criminal intent*. So, on this point, critics also appear to be correct. Nonetheless, it is mainly during the interictal phase that the rate of criminal offending seems to be somewhat higher among people with epilepsy.[70]

It should also be mentioned that epilepsy appears to be associated with other correlates of crime in ways that make any simple deductions about causation difficult to identify. For example, children with epilepsy do poorer in school[71] and score lower on IQ tests than do people who do not have epilepsy.[72] They also appear to suffer from mental illness, particularly schizophrenia, at higher rates than do people in general.[73]

TABLE 9.9.   Evidence of a relationship between epilepsy and criminal/antisocial behavior (overall consistency score = 78.9%; probable correlate).

Nature of the Relationship	Type and Seriousness of Offenses								Antisocial Clinical Conditions	
	Official Statistics						Self-Reported Offenses			
	Violent Offenses	Property Offenses	Drug Offenses	Delinquency	General & Unspecified Offenses	Recidivism	Victimful & Overall Offending	Illegal Drug Use	Childhood Conduct Disorders	Antisocial Personality
Positive	**Europe** *England:* 1 **North America** *United States:* 4			**Asia** *Ceylon:* 1	**Europe** *England:* 2 **North America** *United States:* 6				**Europe** *England:* 1	
Not significant				**Europe** *Finland:* 3 **North America** *United States:* 1						
Negative										

MORPHOLOGICAL FACTORS

The term *morphology* refers to the body's external appearance. Two morphological factors have thus far been investigated with respect to their possible association with criminal behavior: body build and physical attractiveness.

Body Type

Research on the possible relationship between body types and criminality first began to appear in the early decades of the twentieth century. Three extreme body types are recognized: **Endomorphy** refers to persons who are extremely rotund (fat) and nonmuscular. **Mesomorphy** refers to persons who are unusually muscular in their body build. **Ectomorphy** denotes persons who are very skinny and nonmuscular. Finally, in the middle of these three extremes, are persons who are said to have a **balanced body type,** which includes the majority of people.

Since the earliest work on body types, researchers have used a triangular diagram to represent the range of possibilities with regard to body type. Examples of these diagrams are shown in Figure 9.1, which we can discuss before summarizing the evidence for all of the research on body types conducted to the present time.

Each of the dots located within the first diagram comprising Figure 9.1 represents the body type of a male student at Oxford University. As with most college populations, these males appear to be slightly more ectomorphic than a general young adult population (whose dots would be clustered squarely in the center of the diagram). So where are persons of similar age who all have engaged in delinquency or crime located within the same diagrammatic space? As shown in the second diagram, males who had been committed to a training school for delinquency are clustered more in the mesomorphic range (with a slight tendency toward endomorphy).

As indicated in Table 9.10, the diagrams shown in Figure 9.1 illustrate the findings from most of the studies thus far conducted on body

type and criminality. To date, all studies have reported significant tendencies for delinquents and criminals to be more mesomorphic than persons in general. To illustrate the types of findings that have been consistently reported, one of the most famous body type studies found that, whereas 31 percent of nondelinquents were mesomorphic, 60 percent of the delinquents were.[74]

Physical Attractiveness

Physical attractiveness refers to the fact that human beings make judgments about the appearances of other people, particularly with reference to their facial features. Some aspects of the preferences we have appear to be arbitrarily derived from ever-changing cultural standards, while other aspects of our preferences appear to be unlearned.[75] Evidence of unlearned aspects of preferences for facial features have come from studies of neonates (newborn infants who have obviously not had time to learn cultural standards of beauty). These studies have shown that infants stare longer and smile more at what adults generally consider "pretty" faces than at "average" or "unattractive" faces.[76]

As shown in Table 9.11, several studies have investigated the possibility that physical attractiveness is correlated with criminality. These studies have shown that a significant inverse correlation exists, meaning that those who are considered most attractive are less involved in delinquent and criminal behavior than persons who are considered least attractive.[77]

We have listed physical attractiveness as a biological trait for lack of a better category. In trying to make any sense of it, you should keep in mind that physical attractiveness appears to be positively linked with several traits—ranging from general health,[78] to grades,[79] to socioeconomic status[80]—that are themselves correlates of crime. On the other hand, the fact that persons (especially males) with mesomorphic physiques are generally judged more attractive than those with both heavy and slight body builds[81] seems inconsistent with the negative link between physical attractiveness and criminality.

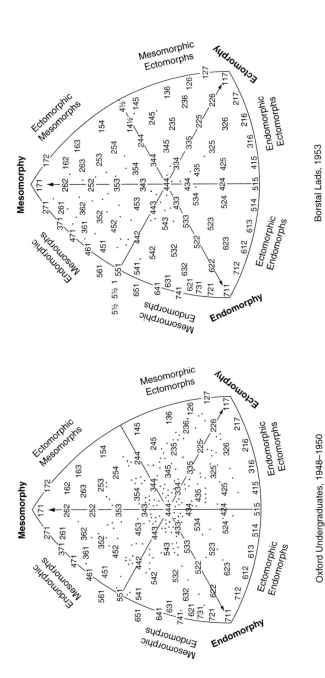

Oxford Undergraduates, 1948–1950
N = 283

Body-build of 283 Oxford undergraduates. Note the fairly even distribution of body types with perhaps a slight preponderance in the lower right-hand corner, signifying lean and slight body-build. From J. M. Tanner, in G. A. Harrison, J. M. Tanner, J. S. Weiner, and N. Barnicut, *An Introduction to Human Biology*, Clarendon Press, New York, 1963.

Borstal Lads, 1953
N = 58

Body-build of fifty-eight juvenile delinquents detained in Borstal institutions. Note the preponderance of endomorphic mesomorphs, i.e., thick-set, brawny lads of an athletic stature, and the almost complete absence of ectomorphs, i.e., the slight, lean, 'beanpole' type. From T. C. N. Gibbens, *Psychiatric Studies of Borstal Lads*, Oxford University Press, New York, 1963.

FIGURE 9.1

279

TABLE 9.10.   Evidence of a relationship between body type and criminal/antisocial behavior (overall consistency score = 100%; well-established correlate).

Nature of Relationship with Criminal/ Antisocial Behavior	Type and Seriousness of Offenses								Antisocial Clinical Conditions	
	Official Statistics						Self-Reported Offenses		Childhood Conduct Disorders	Antisocial Personality
	Violent Offenses	Property Offenses	Drug Offenses	Delinquency	General & Unspecified Offenses	Recidivism	Victimful & Overall Offending	Illegal Drug Use		
Highest among Mesomorphs				Europe *England: 2* North America *United States: 5*	North America *United States: 2*		North America *United States: 1*			North America *United States: 1*
Highest among Endomorphs										
Highest among Ectomorphs										
No significant difference										

TABLE 9.11.   Evidence of a relationship between physical attractiveness (or lack of facial deformities) and criminal/antisocial behavior (overall consistency score = 100%; well-established correlate).

Nature of the Relationship	Type and Seriousness of Offenses								Antisocial Clinical Conditions	
	Official Statistics						Self-Reported Offenses		Childhood Conduct Disorders	Antisocial Personality
	Violent Offenses	Property Offenses	Drug Offenses	Delinquency	General & Unspecified Offenses	Recidivism	Victimful & Overall Offending	Illegal Drug Use		
Negative				North America *United States: 1*	Europe *England: 1* North America *United States: 2*		North America *United States: 1*			
Not significant										
Positive										

PHYSIOLOGICAL CORRELATES

Whereas morphology refers to an animal's external appearance, *physiology* refers to the functioning of body parts that are less externally visible. So far, two physiological variables have been considered as correlates of crime: heart (and pulse) rate and skin conductivity. (The workings of the brain per se will be given separate consideration later in this chapter.)

Resting Heart (and Pulse) Rate

Almost everyone is familiar with having their heart and pulse rates monitored by a physician or nurse. In some cases, patients are tested before and after engaging in strenuous exercise, and other times just their resting heart or pulse rates are monitored.[82] To understand why many studies have been conducted to assess the possible link between heart and pulse rates and offending behavior, think about what an elevated heart or pulse rate is associated with in terms of emotions. We can all recall instances in which we were suddenly startled or told something very upsetting, and felt our heart beginning to pound. This is an extreme example of how fear can help to initiate a rapid heart rate.[83]

What might be the connection between heart or pulse rates and criminality? As shown in Table 9.12, numerous studies have been conducted, and they all indicate the same pattern: When persons who have criminal/antisocial tendencies are compared to those who have few or no such tendencies the heart and pulse rates of the former are significantly slower during normal resting conditions.[84] A couple of studies have even been prospective in the sense that the heart and pulse rates were diagnosed several years prior to the assessment of any criminal/antisocial behavior, and the same pattern emerged.[85] Other studies indicate that the heart and pulse rates of delinquents and criminals tend to rise more slowly in response to mild physical exercise than is true for people in general.[86]

Slow resting heart rates have also been positively associated with several correlates of crime, including impulsivity,[87] bullying,[88] coming from a broken home as well as with being male rather than female.[89] Furthermore, having a slow heart rate under standard testing conditions has been found positively correlated with having one or both parents with a felony conviction.[90]

Skin Conductivity (Galvanic Skin Response)

When we sweat, we exude what is tantamount to diluted urine, containing substantial levels of salt water, and salt water is an excellent electrical conductor. A device, called a **Galvanic Skin Response** (GSR) meter, has been developed to monitor how much we sweat; it does so by measuring electrical impulses passing from one electrode to another through our body (or a portion of our body, such as from one fingertip to an adjacent fingertip). While temperature obviously affects how much we sweat, so too do our emotions. The more emotionally aroused we become (especially in terms of emotions such as anger and fear), the more we sweat, and this increase in sweating can be monitored with a GSR meter.

Studies have examined the possibility that persons who are most prone toward criminal behavior

TABLE 9.12. Evidence of a relationship between slow resting heart (or pulse) rate and criminal/antisocial behavior (overall consistency score = 100%; well-established correlate).

Nature of the Relationship	Type and Seriousness of Offenses								Antisocial Clinical Conditions	
	Official Statistics						Self-Reported Offenses		Childhood Conduct Disorders	Antisocial Personality
	Violent Offenses	Property Offenses	Drug Offenses	Delinquency	General & Unspecified Offenses	Recidivism	Victimful & Overall Offending	Illegal Drug Use		
Positive	Europe *England:* 1			Europe *England:* 2 North America *United States:* 1	Europe *England:* 3 North America *United States:* 2		Europe *England:* 3 North America *Canada:* 1		Europe *England:* 2 North America *Canada:* 1 *United States:* 4	North America *Canada:* 1; *United States:* 1
Not significant										
Negative										

exhibit unusual patterns with respect to their skin conductivity. As shown in Table 9.13, most of the evidence suggests that they do. Specifically, when criminal/antisocial prone persons are compared to persons in general, their GSR responses are lower on average under most testing conditions. This suggests that they tend to experience stress at lower levels than do people in general.

BIOCHEMICAL CORRELATES

A *biochemical* is any chemical naturally produced by a living thing. Even though there are literally thousands of biochemicals that living things, including humans, produce, so far only a handful of these have been sufficiently investigated to be considered here as possible correlates of crime. These biochemicals can be subsumed under three categories: hormones, neurotransmitters, and miscellaneous biochemicals.

Hormones

Hormones are biochemicals produced in one part of the body that travel via the blood system to other parts of the body where they have their primary effects. The two hormonal correlates of criminal behavior thus far associated with criminal behavior are testosterone and cortisol.

Testosterone. **Testosterone** is a sex hormone, meaning that it plays a central role in differentiating males from females. While both genders produce measurable quantities of testosterone throughout most of their lives, males produce much higher levels than do females both perinatally and following the onset of puberty.

The magnitude of the gender differences in testosterone production over the life cycle is illustrated in Figure 9.2. As you can see, male levels are much higher throughout most of gestation (the time we spend in the womb). During the first five months of gestation, testosterone helps to masculinize what will otherwise remain feminine genitals. Then, following the onset of puberty, testosterone in males skyrockets some ten to fifteen times higher than what it was for both sexes from around birth to age ten.[91]

To help illustrate the rather awesome power of testosterone, Figure 9.3 shows how the genitals are modified by the presence of high (male-typical) levels of testosterone between the first through the

TABLE 9.13. Evidence of a relationship between skin conductivity and criminal/antisocial behavior (overall consistency score = 89.5%; established correlate).

Nature of the Relationship	Type and Seriousness of Offenses								Antisocial Clinical Conditions	
	Official Statistics						Self-Reported Offenses			
	Violent Offenses	Property Offenses	Drug Offenses	Delinquency	General & Unspecified Offenses	Recidivism	Victimful & Overall Offending	Illegal Drug Use	Childhood Conduct Disorders	Antisocial Personality
Negative				Europe *Denmark:* 2 North America *United States:* 4	Europe *England:* 1; *Netherlands:* 2 North America *United States:* 2		Europe *England:* 1		Europe *England:* 1 North America *United States:* 1	North America *Canada:* 1; *United States:* 2
Not significant									Europe *England:* 2	
Positive										

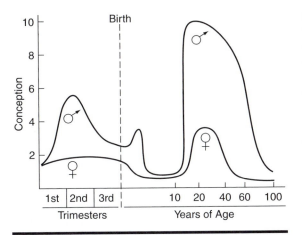

FIGURE 9.2   Testosterone levels of human males and females from conception through old age.

fifth months of gestation. Notice that all of us move from a neutral genital bud one month after conception to recognizable boys and girls by the fifth month. With little or no exposure to testosterone, our genital structures follow the "default" course for mammals, which is female.[92]

Scientists have been interested in testosterone as a possible correlate of crime over the years for various interrelated reasons:

1.   In most species, males are more overtly aggressive than females,[93] and it is difficult to attribute this difference to social training.

2.   Postpubertal testosterone levels have been found associated with aggression in many species of animals see Table 9.15). Castration (removal of the testes, the main organ producing testosterone) usually has "pacifying effects" on aggressive behavior in males.[94]

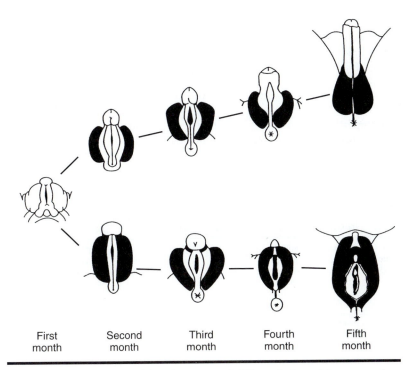

FIGURE 9.3   The two modal paths in sexual differentiation of the external genitals during fetal development. Adapted from Ellis & Ames, 1987:233–258. Copyright 1994 by the authors.

3. Among humans, males engage in crime, especially violent crime, more than do females (Table 5.1a), and their involvement in crime usually rises in the early to midteens (Table 5.2a), which is the same time that male testosterone levels rise.[95]

While no one should equate criminal violence with aggression in general, there are certainly similarities. The above lines of evidence are consistent with the idea that testosterone may be one of the factors responsible for these similarities. Nevertheless, suggestive evidence is far from proof.

To measure testosterone levels in animals, two main sampling sources are used: blood and saliva. Neither of these two methods is ideal from the standpoint of determining what effect testosterone might have on criminal behavior because behavior is controlled not by the blood or saliva, but by the brain. About the only way to determine how much testosterone is in the brain itself is through what is known as a spinal tap, a painful invasion of the body that is not undertaken simply for research purposes.

Another difficulty with blood and saliva samples in measuring testosterone levels involves distinguishing between what is bound and unbound testosterone. In the blood, *bound testosterone* refers to testosterone molecules that are chemically bonded to other biochemical molecules that prevent testosterone from entering the brain (because the newly formed molecules are too large).[96] Also worth mentioning is that, at least outside the brain, testosterone levels fluctuate a great deal throughout the day, usually being highest soon after waking up.[97] For this reason, in most studies of testosterone, subjects are tested at more or less the same time of day, usually early morning. Despite the instability and difficulties in measuring testosterone outside the brain (and then inferring its effects on brain functioning), quite a number of studies have investigated the possible relationship between testosterone and involvement in criminal/antisocial behavior.

As shown in Table 9.14, most studies have found statistically significant relationships between testosterone levels and criminality, both in males[98] and in females.[99] The studies that have

TABLE 9.14.   Evidence of a relationship between circulating testosterone levels and criminal/antisocial behavior (overall consistency score = 72.7%; probable correlate).

| Nature of the Relationship | Type and Seriousness of Offenses | | | | | | | | | Antisocial Clinical Conditions | |
| | Official Statistics | | | | | | Self-Reported Offenses | | | | |
	Violent Offenses	Property Offenses	Drug Offenses	Delinquency	General & Unspecified Offenses	Recidivism	Victimful & Overall Offending	Illegal Drug Use	Childhood Conduct Disorders	Antisocial Personality
Positive	Europe *Finland:* 1 North America *United States:* 3		North America *United States:* 1	North America *United States:* 1	North America *United States:* 5	Europe *Sweden:* 1		North America *United States:* 1	North America *United States:* 1	North America *United States:* 2
Not significant				North America *United States:* 2					North America *United States:* 2	
Negative				North America *Canada:* 1						

failed to find significant relationships mainly have to do with conduct disorders[100] and with juvenile delinquency.[101]

In addition to the studies summarized by Table 9.14 are other studies that have looked at testosterone levels and various forms of noncriminal aggression. The results of these studies are presented in Table 9.15. As you can see, most research has found significant positive relationships between testosterone levels and self-assessed aggressiveness (regardless of its criminality)[102] and self-rated aggressiveness among male delinquents.[103] Peer-rated "toughness" among a sample of young prison inmates,[104] and staff-rated aggression among a group of disruptive children[105] were also found positively correlated with circulating testosterone levels. In addition, most but not all studies of nonhuman species have found a positive relationship between testosterone and aggression.[106] Studies of adolescent and adult males have also found blood levels of testosterone positively correlated with self-reported

measures of aggression, irrespective of this behavior's criminality.[107]

Despite the fairly substantial evidence that a significant correlation exists between testosterone and criminal/antisocial behavior, especially among adults, you should still not jump to any conclusions about causation. Recall that these studies are all based on blood and saliva samples, and that neither the blood nor saliva has any real control over behavior. Another fact about testosterone is that its levels can be greatly affected by environmental events. For example, sleep deprivation and strenuous exercise[108] as well as emotional stress[109] all can cause testosterone levels to temporarily drop. Contrariwise, various sexual experiences, and sometimes their mere anticipation, have been shown to temporarily elevate testosterone levels, both in humans[110] and in other species.[111] Other exhilarating experiences, such as the winning of various athletic contests, also result in rises in testosterone levels.[112] Therefore, comprehension of how testosterone might affect criminal behavior

TABLE 9.15.   Evidence of a relationship between circulating testosterone levels and aggressive/combative tendencies.

		Self-Reported		
	Direct Observation of Aggression and Violence	**Physical Aggression**	**Verbal Aggression**	**Feelings of Hostility and Anger**
Positive	**Europe** *Italy*: 1; *Sweden*: 1 **North America** *United States*: 3 **Nonhuman Primate** *Chimpanzee*: 1; *Rhesus Monkey*: 5; *Talipoin Monkey*: 1; *Vervet Monkey*: 1 **Rodent** *Hamster*: 1; *Mouse*: 1; *Rat*: 3 **Other Mammal** *Deer*: 1; *Dog*: 1 **Nonmammal** *Chicken*: 1	**Europe** *Germany*: 1; *Sweden*: 3 **North America** *United States*: 4	**Europe** *Sweden*: 1	**Europe** *Italy*: 1 **North America** *United States*: 3
Not significant	**Europe** *Netherlands*: 1 **Nonhuman Primate** *Rhesus Monkey*: 2; *Japanese Monkeys*: 1; *Squirrel Monkey*: 1; *Stumptail Monkey*: 1; Nieuwenhuusen et al. 1987; *Talipoin Monkey*: Epple 1978; Eberhart et al. 1980	**Europe** *England*: 1 **North America** *United States*: 2	**Europe** *England*: 1	**Europe** *England*: 1; *Italy*: 1 **North America** *United States*: 3
Negative			**Europe** *France*: 1	

Berry's World

© 1991 by NEA Inc.

"Sorry about getting so aggressive there. I guess my testosterone level is a little elevated."

would have to accommodate the fact that testosterone itself is at least temporarily affected by a variety of social experiences.[113]

Cortisol.   An important group of hormones besides sex hormones are called **stress hormones.**[114] Stress hormones are manufactured mainly by the adrenal glands, and secreted foremost during times of danger and crisis, such as when an animal is being chased by a predator or an infant has been abandoned by its mother. To measure cortisol levels, most researchers use blood or saliva samples.[115] However, a few investigators have used urine and cerebral spinal fluid levels.[116]

Stress hormones primarily include adrenaline, cortisol, and corticosterone, each one tending to be associated with subtle differences in types of stress, with a great deal of individual variation. Because **adrenaline** (also called **epinephrine**) is not only a hormone, but also functions as a neurotransmitter, it will be given attention in the upcoming section rather than here. The stress hormone that has received sufficient research attention to warrant consideration here is cortisol.

Cortisol tends to be released by the adrenal glands most when animals confront frightening or stressful situations that call for a prolonged series of responses,[116] particularly when they lack social support.[118] For instance, studies have found that stress brought on by anticipating having to undergo surgery,[119] speaking in public,[120] and solving arithmetic problems in front of classmates[121] causes cortisol levels to be released by the adrenal glands at rates two to three times higher than normal.

In addition to emotional stress brought on by challenging social circumstances, physical pain often causes a rise in the release of cortisol. For example, cortisol in the blood has been shown to rise more than five times the normal levels for male newborns who have just undergone circumcision.[122] Nonetheless, if stress persists for prolonged periods of time (such as several days or weeks), eventually the release of cortisol subsides to below-normal levels.[123]

When tested over several weeks, even the time of day appears to affect the relationship between chronic stress and cortisol levels.[124] As a general rule, irregular day-to-day stress appears to result in elevated cortisol levels, lasting at least several hours, while stress sustained over several days or weeks often depletes cortisol levels to below normal levels.[125]

As you can see from Table 9.16, most of the relevant studies have found that, when comparisons are made between persons in general and those with a history of criminal/antisocial behavior, the latter exhibit significantly lower average cortisol levels. Nonetheless, Table 9.16 also reveals that more than one study has failed to find significant differences in this respect.

Regarding the possibility of other correlates of crime being linked to cortisol, low cortisol levels appear to be more common among persons who are unusually impulsive[126] and sexually promiscuous.[127] However, one study found no significant relationship between cortisol levels and sensation seeking,[128] and various studies have actually found unusually *high* levels of cortisol associated with both unipolar and bipolar depression[129] and with

TABLE 9.16.   Evidence of a relationship between plasma cortisol and criminal/antisocial behavior (overall consistency score = 75.0%; probable correlate).

Nature of the Relationship	Type and Seriousness of Offenses								Antisocial Clinical Conditions	
	Official Statistics						Self-Reported Offenses		Childhood Conduct Disorders	Antisocial Personality
	Violent Offenses	Property Offenses	Drug Offenses	Delinquency	General & Unspecified Offenses	Recidivism	Victimful & Overall Offending	Illegal Drug Use		
Negative	**Europe** *Finland:* 2; *Sweden:* 1		**North America** *United States:* 1						**North America** *United States:* 6	**Europe** *Finland:* 1 **North America** *United States:* 1
Not significant			**North America** *United States:* 1						**North America** *United States:* 2	**North America** *United States:* 1
Positive										

alcoholism and impulsive aggression.[130]

Overall, most evidence is suggestive of an inverse correlation between cortisol levels and offending probabilities, but the number of studies that have failed to find a significant relationship makes any conclusion somewhat tenuous.

Neurotransmitters

While it is hard to accept that our deepest thoughts are ultimately just electrochemical processes in the brain, the evidence supporting this conclusion is very strong.[131] These electrochemical signals travel at lightning speeds through special nerve cells, called **neurons.** Then, the signals "jump" to adjacent neurons across a very tiny gap, called a *synapse,* and race through the next neuron. The "jumps" between adjacent neurons are made possible by a set of biochemicals, called **neurotransmitters.**

A diagrammatic sketch of how neurons transfer electrochemical signals to one another via various neurotransmitters is shown in Figure 9.4.

In various regions of the brain, specialized *neurotransmitter systems* are found. This means that neurons in certain regions of the brain respond al-

most exclusively to just one type of neurotransmitter. The two neurotransmitter systems that are discussed most with regard to criminal/antisocial behavior are the catecholamine system and the serotonin system. The **catecholamine system** primarily utilizes **dopamine,** along with two chemical derivatives of dopamine, **epinephrine** and **norepinephrine.**[132] The **serotonin system** transmits the neurotransmitter *serotonin.*[133] The general locations of these two neurotransmitter systems (or pathways) in the human brain are shown in Figure 9.5.

As we will see, some neurotransmitters (one in particular) appear to be associated with criminal/antisocial behavior. The first neurotransmitter to be discussed is serotonin. The second to be discussed are the *catecholamines.*

Serotonin.   **Serotonin** (also called *5-hydroxytryptamine* or *5-HT* for short) is an important neurotransmitter. When it is relatively active in our brains, people report feeling calm and contented; and when it is inactive, anxiety and depression increase.[134] Consequently, some drugs designed to treat depression and anxiety disorders have their effects by increasing the presence of serotonin in

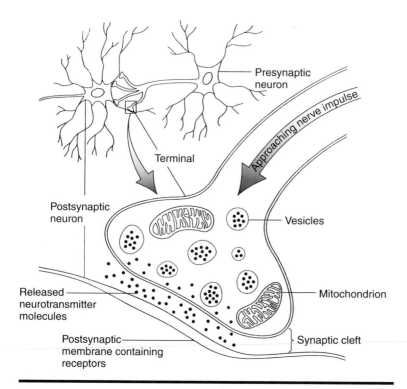

FIGURE 9.4 Sketch of two nerve cells (neurons) at the top, with an enlargement at the bottom showing an axon releasing an unspecified neurotransmitter into a synaptic cleft in order to excite and cause the neighboring nerve cell to excite additional nerve cells. In this way, the billions of nerve cells in our brains communicate with another.

the synaptic cleft. This increased serotonin can elevate mood and aid in impulsive control.[135]

To describe the extent to which serotonin is present in the synaptic gap, neurologists often use the term **serotonergic** (*sĕr ō tō nĕr gĭc*) **functioning.** Basically, when serotonergic functioning is high, the axons in tracks of neurons containing high concentrations of serotonin are releasing relatively large amounts of serotonin into the synaptic gap and/or the serotonin is being retained in the gap rather than being taken back up into the axon.

Unfortunately, it is very difficult to measure serotonergic functioning directly without seriously damaging the brain in the process. However, animal studies have revealed that one can fairly accurately infer serotonergic functioning by measuring a chemical by-product (called a **metabolite**) of

serotonin known as **5-HIAA** (*5-hydroxy indoleacetic acid*) in fluid that circulates through parts of the brain and spinal cord, called **cerebrospinal fluid** (CSF).[136] Studies of CSF 5-HIAA have shown that this serotonin metabolite varies a great deal from one individual to another.[137]

Several studies have investigated the possibility that serotonergic brain functioning might be related to criminal/antisocial behavior, and, as shown in Table 9.17, these studies have consistently found serotonergic activity in the brains of criminal/antisocial persons to be below what is typical of persons in general.[138] This is especially true for individuals whose offenses are impulsive in nature, as opposed to crimes that are carefully planned.[139]

More evidence of a link between low serotonergic activity and criminal/antisocial behavior

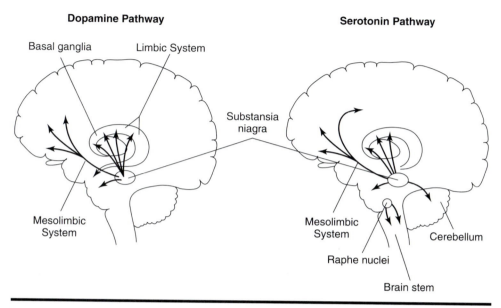

Dopamine Pathway   **Serotonin Pathway**

FIGURE 9.5   The main dopamine and seratonin pathways in the brain (after Kalat 1992:584 and Carlson 1998:105).

TABLE 9.17.   Evidence of a relationship between serotonergic functioning (as inferred from levels of 5-HIAA levels in the cerebrospinal fluid) and criminal/antisocial behavior (overall consistency score = 100%; well-established correlate).

Nature of the Relationship	Type and Seriousness of Offenses								Antisocial Clinical Conditions	
	Official Statistics						Self-Reported Offenses			
	Violent Offenses	Property Offenses	Drug Offenses	Delinquency	General & Unspecified Offenses	Recidivism	Victimful & Overall Offending	Illegal Drug Use	Childhood Conduct Disorders	Antisocial Personality
Negative	**Europe** *Finland: 3* **Middle East** *Israel: 1*	**Europe** *Finland: 1*		**North America** *United States: 2*	**Europe** *Finland: 2; Sweden: 1*	**Europe** *Finland: 3*			**North America** *United States: 3*	**Europe** *Finland: 1* **North America** *United States: 2*
Not significant										
Positive										

comes from studies that have found low serotonergic activity also related to various behavioral and mental health correlates of crime. These relationships are illustrated in Table 9.17 (supplement). As you can see, impulsivity, alcoholism, depression, and suicidal behavior are all linked to low serotonergic activity, ADHD being the only exception documented so far.

In addition, hypoglycemia has been statistically linked to reduced levels of serotonergic functioning.[140] Also, drugs such as *lithium,* which facilitate serotonergic functioning, have been found

TABLE 9.17 (supplement).   Evidence of relationships between serotonergic functioning (mainly as inferred from levels of 5-HIAA levels in the cerebrospinal fluid) and various behavioral correlates of crime.

Nature of the Relationship	Behavioral and Mental Health Correlates of Crime							
	ADHD	Type II Alcoholism/ High Alcohol Consumption	Impulsivity	Depression	Suicide	Pathological Gambling	Perimenstrual Syndrome (PMS)	Impulsive Aggression
Negative		Europe *Finland:* 1 **North America** *United States:* 2 **Mammals** *Nonhuman Primates:* 1	Europe *England:* 2; *Finland:* 1 **North America** *United States:* 3	North America *United States:* 1	North America *United States:* 6	North America *United States:* 1	North America *United States:* 2	Europe *England:* 2; *Finland:* 2 **North America** *United States:* 7 **Mammals** *Nonhuman Primates:* 9; *Rodents:* 9
Not significant	**North America** *United States:* 3							
Positive								**Mammals** *Rodents:* 3

to reduce aggressive tendencies among prison inmates[141] and to reduce impulsive behavior among severe conduct-disordered children.[142]

Furthermore, in the last two columns of Table 9.17 (supplement), you can see that numerous studies have linked low serotonergic activity (or low CSF 5-HIAA) with various forms of aggression, both in humans and in other animals.[143] It is also interesting to note that male monkeys with unusually low CSF 5-HIAA levels died earlier than their male peers, largely due to their incurring more injuries caused by fighting with other males.[144]

Regarding how lowered serotonergic brain functioning could possibly cause an increased probability of impulsive aggression, several studies have indicated that serotonin has a general calming effect on mood. Thus, animals whose brains have low levels of serotonin may generally feel irritable and impatient.[145] These uncomfortable moods may increase the chances of impulsive aggression. These arguments are still somewhat theoretical, and will therefore be pursued in greater depth in a later chapter. Overall, a great deal of research has concluded that low serotonergic functioning is a correlate of crime, especially impulsive violent crime.

Catecholamines.   Three chemically related neurotransmitters are collectively known as the **catecholamines** (*cat e co' la means*). The chemical relationship between these three neurotransmitters has to do with their ability to metabolize (or convert) to one another in a specific order. The most basic neurotransmitter is *dopamine,* which can then convert to *norepinephrine* (also called *noradrenaline*), which in turn can convert to *epinephrine* (also called *adrenaline*). In both cases, the conversions occur in the presence of certain fairly simple chemicals, called **enzymes** (about which more will be said shortly). The catecholamines are also related to one another in the sense that they are involved in transmitting messages in fairly similar regions of the brain.[146]

In addition to being a neurotransmitter, the last of these three biochemicals—epinephrine—is also considered a stress hormone.[147] Because epinephrine is primarily produced outside of the brain in the adrenal glands in response to sudden bursts of fear, it has been nicknamed the *flight-or-fight hormone.* Nevertheless, inside the brain, epinephrine functions as a neurotransmitter.

Various sampling sources and techniques are used to measure catecholamine activity in the brain. Dopamine activity is usually inferred by measuring dopamine's main by-product in the urine, called *homovanillic acid,* although this method is not considered a highly accurate measure because many other factors affect homovanillic acid levels in urine.[148] Regarding epinephrine, urinary output of the biochemical itself is often used,[149] with the assumption that the higher the concentrations of epinephrine in the urine, the more it has been circulating in the body (including the brain). Studies comprising Table 9.18 have suggested that epinephrine and norepinephrine levels are significantly below normal when criminal/psychopathic populations have been compared to populations in general. In the case of dopamine, the evidence is unclear.

A behavioral correlate of crime that has been extensively studied with reference to the catecholamines is ADHD (childhood hyperactivity). As with criminality, studies have found ADHD to be associated with low peripheral levels of epinephrine.[150] Also, the most common medication used to treat ADHD is a stimulant drug know as **Ritalin.** This and similar drugs appear to reduce hyperactive symptoms at least in part by affecting the release of catecholamines.[151]

Beyond these few generalizations, scientists have not yet come to an agreement about the exact nature of any links between the catecholamines and criminal/antisocial behavior, except to note that it appears not to simply involve the amount of these neurotransmitters in the brain.[152] Among the possible complexities surrounding catecholamines and offending behavior are the location and numbers of receptor sites for the neurotransmitters, and even the specific ratio of one catecholamine relative to another.[153] Another possibility is that catecholamines function best within a fairly specific range. Thus, whenever they are excessively low or high, the chances of aggression and other "socially inappropriate" outbursts increase.[154]

Overall, several studies have suggested that a connection exists between one or more of the catecholamines and criminal/antisocial behavior, but the nature of any such relationship is not nearly as

TABLE 9.18.   Evidence of a relationship between the catecholamines and criminal/antisocial behavior (overall consistency score = 76.5%; probable correlate).

Nature of the Relationship	Type and Seriousness of Offenses								Antisocial Clinical Conditions		Non-criminal Impulsive Aggression	
	Official Statistics						Self-Reported Offenses					
	Violent Offenses	Property Offenses	Drug Offenses	Delinquency	General & Unspecified Offenses	Recidivism	Victimful & Overall Offending	Illegal Drug Use	Childhood Conduct Disorders	Antisocial Personality	By Humans	By Nonhuman Animals
Negative			North America *United States:* 1	Europe *Sweden:* 3 North America *United States:* 2	Europe *Sweden:* 1				Europe *Sweden:* 1 North America *United States:* 3		Europe *Sweden:* 2	
Not significant												
Positive											North America *United States:* 2	

well established as in the case of serotonin. What evidence there is has been fairly consistent in suggesting that epinephrine levels outside the brain are lower under stress for persons who are prone toward offending. Regarding norepinephrine and dopamine, evidence of complex relationships have been reported, but are still too poorly understood to be noteworthy in the present context.

Miscellaneous Biochemicals

Cholesterol.   Cholesterol is a fatlike substance found in all animal tissue. Studies have revealed over a four-fold variation in blood cholesterol levels among humans.[155] While most people have come to associate cholesterol with heart disease and other degenerative diseases, in fact, there are different types of cholesterol, not all of which build up fatty deposits in the arteries eventually leading to heart attacks and strokes.[156]

What relationship does cholesterol appear to have with criminal/antisocial behavior? As you can see from Table 9.19, the evidence is thus far consistent in indicating that the relationship is inverse, meaning that persons with low cholesterol levels in their blood are more prone toward criminal/antisocial behavior than is true of persons in general.[157] The more violent the crime, the lower the cholesterol levels of criminals appear to be.[158]

This finding is surprising in light of evidence that low cholesterol levels are associated with lower risk of heart disease,[159] along with evidence that criminals and psychopaths have shorter life expectancies (Table 9.5a). Further puzzling is evidence that heavy use of alcohol (which is unusually common in criminal populations) is associated with elevated cholesterol levels.[160] Nevertheless, studies of monkeys have found that those who were most aggressive exhibited lower cholesterol levels than those who were least aggressive.[161] Also, there is some evidence that low cholesterol helps to depress serotonergic activity in the brain,[162] which was cited earlier as a correlate of crime (Table 9.17).

Monoamine Oxidase.   **Monoamine oxidase** (MAO) is a type of enzyme found throughout the body, including the brain.[163] As noted earlier, an *enzyme* is a relatively small and simple type of biochemical that serves to transform a more complex biochemical into another. Enzymes also help to break down and clear away complex biochemicals after they have performed some function. For example, after a neurotransmitter has helped one neuron to activate an adjacent neuron, an enzyme such as MAO may help to break down the neurotransmitter so that it does not continue to accumulate in the synaptic area, eventually "garbling" subsequent transmissions.

TABLE 9.19.   Evidence of a relationship between cholesterol and criminal/antisocial behavior (overall consistency score = 100%; well-established correlate).

| Nature of the Relationship | Type and Seriousness of Offenses | | | | | | | | Antisocial Clinical Conditions | |
| | Official Statistics | | | | | | Self-Reported Offenses | | | |
	Violent Offenses	Property Offenses	Drug Offenses	Delinquency	General & Unspecified Offenses	Recidivism	Victimful & Overall Offending	Illegal Drug Use	Childhood Conduct Disorders	Antisocial Personality
Negative	Europe *Finland: 3*				North America *United States: 2*				Europe *Sweden: 1*	
Not significant										
Positive										

MAO comes in two slightly different forms, called *MAO-A* and *MAO-B*. Within the brain, both forms of MAO are primarily concentrated near the terminal end of neurons where neurotransmitters are stored and released into the synapses during message transmission. MAO may play an important role in the transmission process by clearing away some of the "chemical debris" that tends to interfere with subsequent transmissions.[164]

Studies have revealed that platelet MAO activity varies a great deal from one human being to another, with some people averaging five to six times as much MAO activity as others.[165] This variability appears to be almost entirely due to genes controlling the production of MAO molecules.[166]

Unfortunately, it is impossible to measure brain levels of MAO activity directly without damaging the brain in the process.[167] Therefore, researchers usually measure MAO in the blood instead, and call the result *platelet MAO*.

The research linking platelet MAO and criminal/antisocial behavior is shown in Table 9.20. As you can see, all but one study has concluded that unusually low levels of MAO activity are found in the blood of criminals and psychopaths. The exceptional study actually found a significant difference, but it was in the opposite direction.[168]

Even though the number of studies linking MAO and criminal/antisocial behavior is still rather modest, studies linking MAO and several correlates of crime are numerous. These studies are summarized in Table 9.20 (supplement). As you can see, platelet MAO activity has been shown to be unusually low among persons who exhibit several established behavioral and mental health correlates of crime, including impulsivity and monotony avoidance, childhood ADHD, learning disabilities, sensation seeking, alcoholism, and recreational drug use.[169] Also, a recent study among male mice found those with low MAO activity exhibiting "enhanced aggression" when compared to mice with normal or above normal MAO activity.[170]

Studies have linked platelet MAO activity to three demographic correlates of crime: gender,

TABLE 9.20. Evidence of a relationship between platelet MAO (mainly MAO-B) and criminal/antisocial behavior (overall consistency score = 86.4%; established correlate).

Nature of the Relationship	Type and Seriousness of Offenses								Antisocial Clinical Conditions	
	Official Statistics						Self-Reported Offenses			
	Violent Offenses	Property Offenses	Drug Offenses	Delinquency	General & Unspecified Offenses	Recidivism	Victimful & Overall Offending	Illegal Drug Use	Childhood Conduct Disorders	Antisocial Personality
Negative	**Europe** *Netherlands:* 1; *Sweden:* 2 **North America** *United States:* 1		**North America** *United States:* 1		**Europe** *Sweden:* 4 **North America** *United States:* 1	**Europe** *Sweden:* 1		**Europe** *Sweden:* 1 **North America** *United States:* 1	**North America** *Canada:* 1	**Europe** *Sweden:* 3 **North America** *United States:* 2
Not significant									**North America** *United States:* 1	
Positive								**North America** *United States:* 1		

TABLE 9.20 (Supplement).   Evidence of relationships between levels of MAO (mainly MAO-B) activity and several behavioral and mental health correlates of crime.

Nature of the Relationship	ADHD	Impulsivity	Academic Performance	Extroversion	Learning Disabilities	Alcoholism of Heavy Alcohol Consumption	PMS	Recreational Drug Use Other than Alcohol	Depression	Sensation Seeking	Schizophrenia
Negative	North America United States: 1	Europe Sweden: 2	Europe Sweden: 1 North America United States: 1	Europe Germany: 1; Sweden: 1 North America United States: 1		Europe Sweden: 4 North America United States: 8 Asia Japan: 1	Europe Sweden: 1	Europe Sweden: 2 North America United States: 3	Europe Sweden: 1 North America United States: 1	Europe Sweden: 1 North America United States: 4 North America United States: 2	North America United States: 1
Not significant				Europe Sweden: 1	North America United States: 1	North America United States: 1					
Positive											

age, and race. Specifically, platelet MAO activity is lower among males than females, particularly during adolescence and early adulthood.[171] In addition, three clinical studies have reported platelet MAO among black males to be significantly lower than among white males.[172]

Recently, MAO-A (rather than MAO-B) was identified in the blood of an extended family in the Netherlands in which several generations of males have been notoriously violent.[173] Exactly how MAO activity in the blood relates to MAO activity in the brain is still being investigated, but platelet MAO seems to reflect the level at which serotonin is active in the brain,[174] as well as the rate of turnover in dopamine.[175]

Overall, the evidence supports the view that low platelet MAO is a correlate of crime, as well as being associated with many of the established correlates of crime, particularly alcoholism and other forms of recreational drug abuse. However, much remains to be learned about why low levels of this enzyme might be linked to criminal/antisocial behavior as most evidence suggests.

NEUROLOGICAL FACTORS

Neurological factors have to do with the brain and how it functions. Three neurological factors have thus far been extensively investigated with reference to criminal/antisocial behavior: "abnormal" brain waves, slow brain waves, and P300 decrements.

"Abnormal" Brain Wave Patterns

Not long after the development of methods for measuring brain waves by attaching electrodes to the scalp, called **electroencephalography** (EEG), researchers in the 1940s began testing samples of criminals and psychopaths to see if any unusual patterns might be found. Unfortunately for research purposes, brain wave patterns are exceedingly complex, making it very difficult for even trained observers of EEG readouts to reliably identify "normal" and "abnormal" patterns.[176] Besides the complexity of brain waves themselves, it is also relevant to note that electrodes located on the skull are unable to detect much of what is happening in the brain except for the activity that is close to the surface.[177] As one writer put it, "There are over 10 billion separate nerve cells in the human brain, woven in a tight latticework of reciprocal interconnections. Even the most precise EEG recordings inevitably detect the chatter of hundreds of thousands of the cells, muted and distorted by the skull."[178] Other writers described the use of EEG recordings for studying the workings of the brain as being "like blind men trying to understand the workings of a factory by listening outside its walls."[179]

Clinicians who interpret EEG readings have come to recognize four basic bands within which to classify most EEG brain waves. These bands are called *alpha, beta, theta,* and *delta,*[180] and are functionally represented in Figure 9.6. **Alpha brain waves** are the most rapid, and tend to be unusually rhythmical and consistent in amplitude. When people emit alpha brain waves (especially in the most rapid range), they are usually alert and relaxed, but focusing their thoughts on some topic of reasonable interest to them.

In the case of **beta waves,** which are somewhat slower than alpha waves, subjects usually have focused their attention on a train of thought, but to a lesser degree than for alpha waves. Brain waves in the **theta** range are slower than alpha or beta, and are commonly emitted when a subject is falling asleep or allowing the mind to wander out of boredom. Finally, **delta brain waves** are slow and usually associated with deep sleep. If you were to inspect an actual EEG readout you would see a confusing mixture of all four brain waves, often running side by side as various regions of the brain are being monitored simultaneously.

Many of the studies of links between EEG patterns and criminality have been published,[181] but are not relevant here because they simply compared different types of offenders, rather than comparing offenders with persons in general. Another problem with many of the early studies of

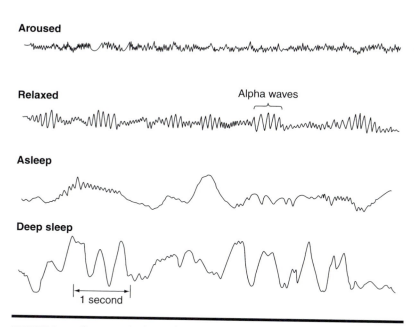

FIGURE 9.6   Some typical EEG brain wave patterns and the cognitive states most associated with them (derived from Pinel 1997:110).

EEG and crime is that the researchers used rather vague terms, such as *abnormal,* to describe EEG readouts, making direct comparisons with other studies virtually impossible. Also, for the studies that did compare offenders with nonoffenders, this was often not done "blind" as to which was which, raising the risk that those who were rating the "normality" of the EEG readings might have unconsciously skewed their results toward what they expected to find.

With the above reservations in mind, let us consider the studies that simply reported on the extent to which offenders exhibited "abnormal" EEG patterns compared to persons in general. As you can see in Table 9.21, most of these early studies concluded that EEG patterns were more "abnormal" for offenders than for persons in general.[182] Nevertheless, for reasons just stated, special caution is in order in considering these findings. Despite the consistent evidence that criminals and psychopaths have higher incidences of "abnormal" EEG patterns compared to persons in general, it is worth mentioning that no significant differences have been documented when comparing psychopathic criminals with criminals not so diagnosed.[183]

Slow Brain Waves

Without suggesting that the conclusion that persons with criminal/antisocial behavior exhibit "abnormal" EEG patterns at higher rates than persons in general is worthless, it would still be desirable to have more specific information about the nature of any abnormalities. Fortunately, some researchers have compared specific features of brain waves in criminal/psychopathic populations with general populations.

As shown in Table 9.22, the main difference that most of these studies have identified is that the brain waves of criminals and psychopaths tend to be slower on average than for persons in general. By *slower* is meant that the brain waves are less often in the alpha, and more often in the beta, delta, or even theta range. Table 9.21 shows that most studies have reported that criminals and psychopaths exhibited a greater proportion of their brain waves in these slower bands than is true for persons in general.[184]

One study repeatedly tested ten individuals who had extensive histories of violence. The purpose of the study was to determine if the times

TABLE 9.21. Evidence of a relationship between "abnormal" brain wave patterns and criminal/antisocial behavior (overall consistency score = 100%; well-established correlate).

| | Type and Seriousness of Offenses | | | | | | | | Antisocial Clinical Conditions | |
| | Official Statistics | | | | | | Self-Reported Offenses | | | |
Nature of the Relationship	Violent Offenses	Property Offenses	Drug Offenses	Delinquency	General & Unspecified Offenses	Recidivism	Victimful & Overall Offending	Illegal Drug Use	Childhood Conduct Disorders	Antisocial Personality
Positive	Europe *England:* 2 North America *United States:* 1			North America *Canada:* 2					Europe *Sweden:* 1	Europe *England:* 1 North America *United States:* 7
Not significant	Europe *England:* 1			North America *United States:* 1						Europe *England:* 1 North America *United States:* 1
Negative										

TABLE 9.22. Evidence of a relationship between overall brain wave speed (proportion of alpha waves) and criminal/antisocial behavior (overall consistency score = 75.0%; probable correlate).

Nature of the Relationship	Type and Seriousness of Offenses — Official Statistics / Self-Reported Offenses								Antisocial Clinical Conditions	
	Violent Offenses	Property Offenses	Drug Offenses	Delinquency	General & Unspecified Offenses	Recidivism	Victimful & Overall Offending	Illegal Drug Use	Childhood Conduct Disorders	Antisocial Personality
Negative	Africa *Egypt: 1*			Europe *Denmark: 2* North America *United States: 1*		Europe *Denmark: 1*			Europe *Sweden: 1* North America *Canada: 1*	Europe *England: 2* North America *United States: 3*
Not significant				North America *United States: 1*			Europe *England: 1*		North America *United States: 1*	
Positive										North America *United States: 1*

these individuals felt most violent and out of control might be associated with any particular brain wave patterns. As predicted, there was a tendency (although not strong) for them to feel most prone toward violence when their brain waves were the slowest (in the delta range).[185]

Overall, Table 9.22 indicates that criminals and psychopaths exhibit a higher frequency of slow brain wave patterns under normal testing conditions than do persons in general.[186] There is also evidence that susceptibility to alcoholism is associated with slow brain wave patterns closely resembling those reported for psychopaths.[187]

P300 Decrements in Evoked Potentials

Another type of brain wave pattern that has shown promise in recent years as being a correlate of crime is called **averaged event-related potentials** (or **evoked potentials**). It refers to changes in electrical activity in the brain in response to external stimuli. To assess variations in evoked potentials, electrodes are hooked up to a subject's scalp, and then he/she is presented with a series of clicks or beeps, whereupon the subject must make some sort of response.[188] After averaging several dozen EEG responses to these simple stimuli, subjects almost invariably exhibit a distinct "dip" in their brain response after 300 milliseconds have lapsed (i.e., just under one-third of a second). However, in some people, the overall brain response is less than for others, and the "dip" is slightly more noticeable.[189] This pattern, illustrated in Figure 9.7, is referred to as a **P300 decrement.**

Several studies have examined the relationship between averaged evoked potentials and criminal/antisocial behavior. As shown in Table 9.23, most of these studies have found P300 decrements to be unusually prevalent in individuals with antisocial tendencies,[190] although one study of aggressive criminality did not find such a pattern.[191]

In addition to the research on criminal and antisocial behavior, it is worth noting that persons with P300 decrements also have been found to be overly impulsive,[192] exhibit attention deficits to most environmental stimuli,[193] and reading

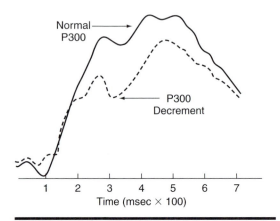

FIGURE 9.7   A normal P300 brain wave pattern versus a P300 decrement brain wave pattern.

difficulties[194] when compared to persons in general. In addition, alcoholism[195] and having a family history of alcoholism[196] are statistically associated with P300 decrements. You may recall that all of these variables are themselves correlates of crime.

MISCELLANEOUS BIOLOGICAL FACTORS

Finally, one biological variable does not fit well into any of the categories already presented: pain tolerance.

Pain Tolerance

Pain tolerance (the opposite of *pain sensitivity*) refers to the ability to withstand painful stimuli at relatively strong intensities. Scientists assess pain tolerance in a number of ways, among them being what is called a *cold water emersion test.* With this test, subjects have their arm strapped to a lever that they can lower into a vat of circulating ice cold water. The subjects are then instructed to lower their arm into the water and hold it there until the pain is too much to bear. Other ways of measuring pain tolerance involve asking subjects to press their bare foot against a fairly sharp object (but not sharp enough to break the skin), and press as hard as they can for as long as they can.[197] Such tests have allowed researchers to objectively measure people's varying tendencies to tolerate pain.

Research on the relationship between pain tolerance and criminal/antisocial behavior is summarized in Table 9.24. As you can see, studies generally indicate that these two variables are negatively (inversely) related, meaning that criminals and psychopaths can usually tolerate more pain than is true for persons in general.[198] One recent study suggested that as far as aggression is concerned, there may be two types of aggressive children, those who are consistently aggressive

TABLE 9.23.   Evidence of a relationship between P300 decrements in evoked potentials and criminal/antisocial behavior (overall consistency score = 87.5%; established correlate).

Nature of the Relationship	Type and Seriousness of Offenses								Antisocial Clinical Conditions	
	Official Statistics						Self-Reported Offenses			
	Violent Offenses	Property Offenses	Drug Offenses	Delinquency	General & Unspecified Offenses	Recidivism	Victimful & Overall Offending	Illegal Drug Use	Childhood Conduct Disorders	Antisocial Personality
Positive									North America *United States:* 1	North America *Canada:* 2; *United States:* 4
Not significant	North America *United States:* 1									
Negative										

TABLE 9.24. Evidence of a relationship between pain tolerance and criminal/antisocial behavior (overall consistency score = 87.7%; established correlate).

Nature of the Relationship	Type and Seriousness of Offenses								Antisocial Clinical Conditions	
	Official Statistics						Self-Reported Offenses			
	Violent Offenses	Property Offenses	Drug Offenses	Delinquency	General & Unspecified Offenses	Recidivism	Victimful & Overall Offending	Illegal Drug Use	Childhood Conduct Disorders	Antisocial Personality
Postive					North America *Canada:* 1				North America *Canada:* 1	Europe *Sweden:* 1 **North America** *Canada:* 2; *United States:* 2
Not significant										North America *United States:* 1
Negative										

and those who are only aggressive when frustrated. The study found that consistently aggressive boys were unusually high in pain tolerance, while those who are aggressive in response to frustration were unusually low in their ability to tolerate pain.[199]

CLOSING THOUGHTS ON BIOLOGICAL CORRELATES

The past four chapters have reviewed the results of literally thousands of studies conducted by scientists throughout the world regarding variables that have been considered as possible correlates of crime. In all cases, these relationships are statistical, meaning that, within the laws of probability, scientists have found various differences and relationships that have less than a 5 percent probability of having occurred by chance. Nevertheless, because of flaws in how variables are sometimes measured and inappropriate sampling procedures, there are several that were in fact just chance observations. The point being made is that scientists never accept any one (or even two) studies as proof for any argument. Instead, answers come slowly after years of painstaking checks and cross-checks by researchers throughout the world comparing their results to those of others. In that sense, science is always a work in progress.

Some of the relationships that we have discussed over the past four chapters may seem so obvious as to scarcely need scientific verification, while other findings might seem to you to completely defy common sense. In any case, correlates of crime can provide objective criteria for assessing theories of criminal/antisocial behavior that have been proposed by criminologists and that will be reviewed in the upcoming chapters of this text.

In the case of the correlates of crime reviewed in this chapter, many are controversial because many people tend to think that if biological factors are related to criminal behavior, there must be little that can be done with criminals except to lock them up and throw away the key. Such simplistic reasoning has caused fear that the discovery of links between biological factors and criminality will lead to "witch hunts" for people with these particular biological markers and efforts to institutionalize them even before they start committing crimes.

While the purpose of this text is not to advocate ethics or policies, we hope that the dangers and flaws in this sort of simplistic reasoning are apparent. The main flaw is that none of the biological or other correlates of crime are anywhere close to providing perfect discrimination between those who do and do not engage in serious criminal/antisocial behavior. Rather, their associations with criminality are all true only in statistical terms. To drive this point home, stop for a moment and think about how many of the correlates of crime named in the past five chapters could be applied to you, and then ask yourself how many of us all would end up in prison if society were to lock up everyone with a fairly good chance of engaging in a delinquent or criminal act sometime in our lives.

If you cannot use the correlates of crime to identify potential offenders and lock them up in advance of their offending, what is the value in learning these correlates? Ultimately, the main value in identifying factors that seem to be statistically related to criminality is that they provide an objective foundation on which to begin assessing the relative merit of various theories of criminal behavior. Once science gets a firm theoretical handle on such behavior, then *perhaps* the human community may decide to use this knowledge to help alleviate the crime problem.

As we bring the present chapter to a close, we wish to reiterate that correlates of crime should not be equated with causes of crime. While a correlate *may* be a cause, many, and perhaps most, of them are not. Consider, for example, the fact that being born prematurely is a correlate of crime. If prematurity is a correlate of crime, wouldn't it also *have* to be a cause of crime? In fact, there are other possibilities, one being that prematurity results from poor nutrition or inadequate prenatal care, and these latter two variables in turn may be mainly due to poverty. If this scenario is correct, prematurity is merely a mediating factor, not really a causal factor. Several other reasonable arguments along these lines are possible.[200]

The point being made is that discovering the causes of such a complex aspect of human behavior as criminality is bound to boggle even the best mind. Fortunately, we have thousands of minds working on the issue and sharing what they find and their best explanations for their findings. Through this collective exchange, many important insights gradually emerge.

SUMMARY

This chapter provides you with an overview of what has been discovered so far regarding possible relationships between biological variables and criminal/antisocial behavior. As with any overview, numerous details have not received attention, and it goes without saying that some of these details could eventually prove to be very important for understanding such behavior.

Perinatal Variables

This chapter considered three perinatal variables, and concluded that one, and possibly two, are correlates of crime: birth weight and minor physical anomalies. In the case of perinatal trauma, the evidence only weakly supported the view that it was a correlate. Smoking by mothers during pregnancy appears to be correlated with offspring offending.

Health Variables

Five health variables were given attention, all of which may be correlates of crime. The two general indicators were, first, various morbidity indicators such as self-assessed health and disability days, and, second, the age of death. In both cases, criminals and psychopaths appear to be less healthy than persons in general. Turning to three fairly specific types of ailments—accidental injuries, hypoglycemia, and, for females, the perimenstrual syndrome—all have been shown to be significantly more prevalent among those who are most prone toward criminal/antisocial behavior when compared to those who are least prone.

Morphologic Variables

The morphologic traits that have been given sufficient research attention to be considered as correlates of crime are body type and physical attractiveness. Body type has been repeatedly linked to criminality such that persons who are most mesomorphic (muscular) seem to have the highest probability of offending, and those who are ectomorphic (skinny and nonmuscular) have the lowest probability. In the case of physical attractiveness (mainly in terms of facial features), those who are generally considered least attractive appear to have higher probabilities of offending than those who are most attractive.

Internal Physiology

Two biological factors having to do with internal physiology have been frequently considered with

TABLE 9.25.   Capsule summary of perinatal, health, morphologic, and internal physiologic biological correlates of crime.

Correlate	Consistency of the Evidence					Comments and Qualification
	Well Estab	Estab	Prob	Poss	Unest	
Birth weight & gestation length			X			Low birth wt/short gestation length infants appear to be more crime-involved
Perinatal trauma				X		Persons who were perinatally traumatized may be more crime-involved
Minor physical anomalies (MPA)	X					Persons with MPAs are more crime-involved
Maternal smoking during pregnancy		X				Offspring whose mothers smoked during pregnancy exhibited higher rates of conduct disorders
Overall health			X			Persons who are less healthy tend to be more crime-involved
Life expectancy	X					Persons who have early ages of death are more crime-involved
Accidental injuries	X					Persons who experience accidental injuries at high rates are more crime-involved
Hypoglycemia	X					People with hypoglycemia exhibit higher rates of crime and psychopathy
Perimenstrual syndrome		X				The perimenstrual syndrome is associated with an increased rate of delinquency and crime
Epilepsy			X			Persons with epilepsy appear to have an increased risk of offending
Body type	X					Persons with mesomorphic body type more crime-involved
Physical attractiveness	X					Persons with unattractive facial features are more crime-involved
Resting heart rate	X					Persons with relatively low resting heart (and pulse) rates are more crime-involved
Skin conductivity (Galvanic skin response)		X				Persons who perspire the least under threatening conditions are more crime-involved

respect to criminal/antisocial behavior. Studies have consistently shown that when they are compared to persons in general, persons with criminal/antisocial tendencies have a lower resting heart rate and are less prone to sweat when facing threatening conditions.

Biochemical Correlates

Three categories of biochemical variables were considered as correlates of crime: hormones, neurotransmitters, and miscellaneous biochemicals. The two hormones considered were testosterone, a major masculinizing sex hormone, and cortisol, an important stress hormone. Testosterone appears to be somewhat higher among criminals and psychopaths than among persons in general, both for males and for females. Delinquency, however, does not appear to be correlated with testosterone levels. Regarding cortisol, its levels tend to be lower among criminals and psychopaths when compared to other people.

The neurotransmitters considered were serotonin and the catecholamines. Research has repeatedly shown serotonin (or serotonergic functioning) in the brain of serious offenders to be lower than for persons in general. Regarding the catecholamines, epinephrine and norepinephrine appear to be lower among offenders also, but the evidence concerning dopamine is mixed.

TABLE 9.26.   Capsule summary of hormonal, neurotransmitter, and miscellaneous biochemical correlates, and of neurological correlates of crime.

| | Consistency of the Evidence | | | | | |
Correlate	Well Estab	Estab	Prob	Poss	Unest	Comments and Qualification
Testosterone			X			Persons with high testosterone levels appear to be more crime-involved
Cortisol			X			Persons with low cortisol levels appear to be more crime-involved
Serotonin	X					Persons with low serotonergic activity in the brain are more crime-involved
Catecholamines			X			Persons with low epinephrine and norepinephrine are more crime-involved; uncertain for dopamine
Cholesterol	X					Cholesterol levels are lower for persons who are more crime-involved
Monoamine oxidase (MAO)		X				Platelet MAO levels are lower for persons who are more crime-involved
"Abnormal" brain wave patterns	X					Persons who are more crime-involved exhibit higher rates of "abnormal" brain waves
Slow brain wave patterns			X			Persons who are more crime-involved exhibit slower brain wave patterns
P300 decrements in evoked potentials		X				Persons who are more crime-involved exhibit more distinct P300 decrements in their evoked potentials
Pain tolerance		X				Persons who are more crime-involved are more tolerant of pain at a given intensity

For the two miscellaneous biochemicals, both cholesterol and monoamine oxidase (MAO) levels appear to be lower among persons with criminal/antisocial tendencies compared to persons in general.

Neurological Correlates

Three neurological variables have been given considerable research attention as correlates of crime: "abnormal" brain waves, slow brain waves, and P300 brain waves. Studies have consistently found "abnormalities" in brain waves to be more prevalent in seriously criminal or psychopathic populations than for populations in general, although the nature of these "abnormalities" has often been poorly specified. In the case of slow brain waves, this appears to be a more specific and measurable aspect of brain functioning that has been fairly often linked to criminal/antisocial behavior. Regarding P300 evoked potentials, most studies have found significant average decrements linked to antisocial behavior.

Pain Tolerance

The final biological correlate of crime that was reviewed was pain tolerance. Most studies have shown that, on average, persons with considerable criminal/antisocial tendencies are more prone toward offending than is true of persons with few or no such tendencies.

The chapter drew to a close with warnings against assuming that any of these biological correlates of crime constitute causes of crime. While some may be causes, most are likely to be linked to criminal behavior in indirect ways. Ultimately, theories are needed to help us gradually piece together a genuine understanding of exactly why biological (and other) correlates of crime exist. It is these theories that we will begin to examine in Part III of this text.

SUGGESTED READINGS

Lewis, Michael and Miller, Suzanne M. (Eds.). (1990). *Handbook of developmental psychology.* New York: Plenum. (A book containing several well-researched chapters about biological underpinnings of criminal and antisocial behavior.)

Lykken, David T. (1995). *The antisocial personalities.* Hillsdale, NJ: Lawrence Erlbaum. (This is a well-written book that presents a valuable overview of how psychopathy may come in two basic forms, one of which may be more highly influenced by biological variables than the other.)

Mednick, Sarnoff, A., Moffitt, Terrie, E., and Stack, Susan A. (Eds.). (1987). *The causes of crime: New biological approaches.* Cambridge, England: Cambridge University Press. (This book contains a useful collection of chapters by a number of the leading researchers on links between biological variables and criminal/antisocial behavior.)

Raine, Adrian (1993). *The psychopathology of crime: Criminal behavior as a clinical disorder.* San Diego, CA: Academic Press. (This book reviews much of what is currently known about how crime and psychopathy are related to biological and other variables. Much of it is written for a professional audience.)

EXERCISES

1. Choose three of the established or well-established biological correlates of crime discussed in this chapter, and construct a logically coherent theory that might explain why they are all linked to criminal and antisocial behavior as the evidence suggests. Confine your theory to one- or two-double-spaced pages.

2. If you were a researcher interested in biological correlates of crime, identify two additional biological correlates of crime you think would be interesting to explore, and state what you think research would show based on things you have learned

about other biological correlates of crime in this chapter. Limit your essay to no more than two double-spaced pages.

3. If you have access to the World Wide Web, do a search for criminal behavior and then a subsearch for one of the biological variables discussed in this chapter. Based on information you find, write a one- to two-page summary of facts or opinions about how that variable and criminal behavior seem to be related. (Your instructor will probably want you to print out a copy of the source or sources you used. If you do not have access to the WWW, do your search at the college library.)

ENDNOTES

1. Hack et al. 1993; Hadders-Algra & Touwen 1990; McCormick 1989.
2. Lagerstrom et al. 1989; McCormick et al. 1990.
3. Marlow et al. 1993; Pharoah et al. 1994; Roussounis et al. 1993; Saigal et al. 1991.
4. Bakan 1990:60.
5. Raine et al. 1994.
6. C. C. Mann 1994.
7. Eysenck & Gudjonsson 1989:20; Pine et al. 1997:395.
8. Mednick & Kandel 1988.
9. Eysenck & Gudjonsson 1989:20.
10. Steg & Rapaport 1975.
11. Campbell et al. 1978.
12. Firestone & Prabhu 1983; Fogel et al. 1985; Gillberg et al. 1983; O'Donnell et al. 1979a; Satterfield 1987; Waldrop & Halverson 1971; Waldrop et al. 1978.
13. Rosenberg & Weller 1973.
14. Firestone & Prabhu 1983; Halverson & Victor 1976; Waldrop & Halverson 1971.
15. Moffitt 1993; Pine et al. 1997:398; Schonfeld et al. 1988.
16. Pine et al. 1997; Sandberg et al. 1980.
17. Wakschlag et al. 1997.
18. Bagley 1992; Rantakallio et al. 1992.
19. Gibson & Tibbetts 1998.
20. R. A. Walsh 1994.
21. Milberger et al. 1996a, 1998; Naeye & Peters 1984.
22. Fogelman & Manor 1988; Milberger et al. 1998; Rantakallio 1983.
23. Butler & Goldstein 1973; Milberger et al. 1996; Naeye & Peters 1984.
24. Olds et al. 1987, 1988.
25. Olds et al. 1997, 1998.
26. Anson et al. 1993.
27. Blaxter 1989:203; Marmot et al. 1991:116; Nathanson 1975; Rahkonen & Lahelma 1992; Rudolf et al. 1992.

28. Klonoff & Landrine 1992:355.
29. Fuller et al. 1993; Hamilton & Hestler 1963; Holden 1987; Nathanson 1978.
30. F. Brown & Epps 1966; Slawson 1926.
31. Junger & Wiegersma 1995.
32. Sokoloff et al. 1977.
33. Bonnet & Pfeiffer 1978:196.
34. Bonnet & Pfeiffer 1978:196.
35. Bonnet & Pfeiffer 1978:197; Chollar 1988:33.
36. Adlersberg & Dolger 1939:1805; Virkkunen 1988:153.
37. Bolton 1984; Virkkunen 1987.
38. Bolton 1973, 1974; Bolton & Bolton 1975.
39. D. Benton et al. 1982.
40. Bolton 1976.
41. Gans et al. 1990; Matykiewicz et al. 1997.
42. Linnoila et al. 1983:2613; Virkkunen 1982:39.
43. Trandaburu et al. 1979.
44. Bolton 1984.
45. Gottlieb 1979; Schauss 1981.
46. B. Weiss 1982.
47. Schoenthaler 1982; Wilder 1947.
48. Conners et al. 1980; Kruesi et al. 1987.
49. Tardiff 1985:636.
50. Moyer 1974:360.
51. Horney 1978:26; Rossi & Rossi 1980.
52. Abraham 1980; Dougherty et al. 1997:381; Frank 1931; Hallman 1986; Woods et al. 1982.
53. Cooke 1945.
54. Dalton 1964; D. P. Ellis & Austin 1971.
55. Binder et al. 1988:492; Dougherty et al. 1997:382; Harry & Balcer 1987:316; Horney 1978; Slade 1984.
56. Dougherty et al. 1997.
57. Tobin et al. 1994.
58. J. L. Cummings 1985:99.
59. Laron 1998:117.
60. Previc 1996:484.
61. J. L. Cummings 1985:99; Griffith et al. 1987.

62. Rose et al. 1987:330.
63. Hauser & Kurland 1975; Kolb & Whishaw 1980:78; Kurland 1959; Merritt 1973:740; Rwiza et al. 1992; Sander & Sharvon 1996:435.
64. Ellis 1987:504; Roth & Erwin 1971.
65. Pine et al. 1977.
66. Griffith et al. 1987.
67. Coleman 1974; MacDonald 1976:223.
68. Delgado-Escueta et al. 1981:715; Turner & Merlis 1962.
69. Albert et al. 1993:416; Harper-Jaques & Reimer 1992:314.
70. Delgado-Escueta et al. 1981; Stevens & Hermann 1981; Treiman 1991.
71. Green & Hartlage 1971; Holdsworth & Whitmore 1974; Pazzaglia & Frank-Pazzaglia 1976.
72. Piness et al. 1937:170.
73. Mendez et al. 1993.
74. Glueck & Glueck 1956:7.
75. Buss 1994:52; L. A. Jackson 1992.
76. Langlois et al. 1987, 1990.
77. Raine 1993:200.
78. Berscheid 1980:14; Dion et al. 1972.
79. Cavior & Dokecki 1973.
80. Buss 1994:63; Dion et al. 1972; Dion & Berscheid 1974; Lerner & Lerner 1977.
81. Cavior & Howard 1973:202; Staffieri 1967.
82. Raine 1996:154.
83. Raine 1996:157.
84. Raine 1993:166.
85. Raine 1988; Raine et al. 1990b.
86. Raine et al. 1990a; Wadsworth 1976.
87. Kagan et al. 1987, 1988; Resznick et al. 1986.
88. Kindlon et al. 1995.
89. Wadsworth 1976:247.
90. Farrington 1997:97.
91. Khan & Cataio 1984:10; Malasanos et al. 1986:702.
92. Ellis 1996:37.
93. Ellis 1986b:525.
94. Bernstein et al. 1983; Potegal et al. 1980.
95. Khan & Cataio 1984:10.
96. Franks et al. 1991; O'Dea et al. 1979.
97. Butler et al. 1989; Dabbs 1990; Foreman & Goodyear 1988.
98. Dabbs et al.1991; Mazur 1995.
99. Rushton 1996.
100. Constantino et al. 1993.
101. Susman et al. 1987.
102. Ehrenkranz et al. 1974; Olweus 1987.
103. Schalling 1987.
104. Dabbs et al. 1987.

105. Scerbo & Kolko 1994.
106. Mehlman et al. 1997.
107. Olweus et al. 1980; Scaramella & Brown 1978.
108. Opstad & Aakvaag 1983; Remes et al. 1985.
109. Aono et al. 1972; Kreuz et al. 1972; F. Singer & Zumoff 1992; Wang et al. 1978.
110. Hellhammer et al. 1985; Knussman et al. 1986; Laye 1981.
111. Bernstein et al. 1978; Nadler et al. 1987.
112. Booth et al. 1993; Mazur 1994:38.
113. Mazur 1995.
114. Selye 1936, 1950.
115. King et al. 1990; Kirschbaum & Hellhammer 1994; Ockenfels et al. 1995.
116. Mason 1986.
117. Wittling & Pfluger 1990:244.
118. Stanton et al. 1987:141.
119. Czeisler et al. 1976; Shannon et al. 1961.
120. Kirschbaum et al. 1992.
121. Bossert et al. 1988; Brantley et al. 1988.
122. Gunnar et al. 1981, 1985; Stang et al. 1988.
123. Bauer et al. 1994; Bourne et al. 1968.
124. Ockenfels et al. 1995.
125. Bourne et al. 1967; Yehuda et al. 1990, 1993.
126. Ballenger et al. 1983; King et al. 1990.
127. Ballenger et al. 1983.
128. Kirschbaum et al. 1992.
129. Rubinow et al. 1984; Traskman et al. 1980.
130. Buydens-Branchey & Branchey 1992.
131. Hoyenga & Hoyenga 1988; Kalat 1992.
132. Zigmond et al. 1980.
133. Soubrie 1986.
134. Kalus et al. 1989; Plaznik et al. 1989.
135. Coccaro & Kavoussi 1997; Salzman et al. 1995.
136. Kruesi et al. 1990:419; Stoff & Vitiello 1996:102; van Praag 1986:104.
137. Higley et al. 1992, 1996a; Kraemer et al. 1989.
138. Raine 1993:82.
139. Bloch & Thompson 1993:53; Linnoila et al. 1983.
140. Roy et al. 1986.
141. Sheard et al. 1976.
142. Siassi 1982.
143. Higley et al. 1996c:1068; Joppa et al. 1997.
144. Higley et al. 1996b.
145. Cloninger 1986; Soubrie 1986.
146. Snyder et al. 1974:1246.
147. Kalat 1992:70.
148. Garreau et al. 1988:93.
149. Olweus 1986.
150. af Klinteberg & Magnusson 1989; Pliszka et al. 1994.

151. af Klinteberg & Magnusson 1989:88; Brown et al. 1979, 1980.

152. Pliszka et al. 1996.

153. Hodgins & Von Grunau 1988:169.

154. Netter & Rammsayer 1991:1016; Stricker & Zigmond 1986; Zigmond et al. 1980.

155. Fox 1961:84.

156. Tierney 1987:83.

157. Hillbrand et al. 1995.

158. Hillbrand & Foster 1993.

159. Langone 1984.

160. Barboriak 1984; Rudel et al. 1981.

161. Kaplan et al. 1991; Muldoon et al. 1992.

162. Hillbrand et al. 1995:42.

163. Westlund et al. 1985; Zuckerman 1980:200.

164. Westlund et al. 1985.

165. Murphy et al. 1976; Robinson et al. 1971.

166. Alexopoulos et al. 1983:1501; Fowler et al. 1982; Oxenstierna et al. 1986; Revely et al. 1983.

167. Redmond et al. 1976:316; Zuckerman 1980:260.

168. Gabel et al. 1994.

169. Ellis 1991:235.

170. Cases et al. 1995.

171. Belmaker et al. 1976; Mann 1979; Robinson et al. 1971; Zeller & Davis 1980:269.

172. Bridge et al. 1985; DeLisi et al. 1981:181; Groshong et al. 1978:1203.

173. Brunner et al. 1993, 1993b; Morell 1993.

174. Anthenelli & Tabakoff 1995:178; Hallman et al. 1990:230; Oreland et al. 1981c.

175. Donnelly & Murphy 1977; Doria 1995:246.

176. Mednick & Volavka 1980:125.

177. Kligman & Goldberg 1975:336.

178. Hassett 1978:102.

179. Margerison et al. 1967.

180. John et al. 1980:1255; Kooi et al. 1978.

181. Raine 1993:175.

182. Syndulko 1978.

183. Murdoch 1972; Small 1966.

184. Bauer & Hesselbrock 1993:577.

185. Milstein 1988.

186. Hare 1970:31.

187. Deckel et al. 1995.

188. Roschke & Fell 1997:108.

189. Kalat 1992:91.

190. Bauer 1997.

191. Branchey et al. 1988.

192. Branchey et al. 1993.

193. Raine 1993:178.

194. Stelmack et al. 1995.

195. Begleiter et al. 1984.

196. O'Connor et al. 1987; Ramsey & Finn 1997.

197. Fowler-Kerry & Lander 1991.

198. Fedora & Reddon 1993; Fowles 1993.

199. Seguin et al. 1996.

200. McLeod & Shanahan 1996:216; Olds et al. 1997.

PART THREE

Theories of Criminal/
Antisocial Behavior

Part II gave you a bird's-eye view of what is currently known (with varying degrees of certainty) about variables related to criminal/antisocial behavior. It is now time to get serious about explaining this behavior. To help accomplish this task, criminologists, like other scientists, rely heavily on theories. The purpose of Part III is to examine theories that have been offered for criminal/antisocial behavior since the early twentieth century.

Most of the theories to be examined go beyond ones discussed in Chapter 4 primarily because more contemporary theories have a more solid footing in scientific research. Nevertheless, don't be surprised to find that theories proposed in the twentieth century have important elements in common with those proposed in earlier periods.

Below are some guidelines to use in judging the merits of the numerous theories that are about to be explored.

THEORIES, "FACTS," AND HOW THEY ARE RELATED

You have probably heard statements such as, "Oh, that's nothing but a theory" when people make a questionable statement. In this sense, theories are often equated with being the opposite of "facts." In science, however, theories and "facts" are often complementary, rather than contrary.

In thinking about the relationship between theories and "facts," you should first realize that, except in casual discourse, scientists avoid using the word *fact* because it implies that there is no longer any reason to doubt something, and scientists are by training and temperament about the most skeptical people on earth. To illustrate this important point, recall that the evidence strongly indicates that throughout the world men are more seriously criminal than women. Even though this gender–criminality relationship has now been confirmed by hundreds of studies conducted throughout the world, is it *possible* that next year one or more studies will report the opposite pattern? There is no way to deny that this is a *possibility,* although it would be pretty stupid to put a wager on it happening. Nevertheless, as long as this possibility exists (and it always will), it is inappropriate to declare the higher criminality of men an unqualified "fact."

Because it is always possible for past observations to be refined and sometimes even completely overturned, scientists avoid words such as *fact* and *proven* to describe their findings. Instead, they use phrases such as "studies have repeatedly shown," "the weight of the evidence," and "well established." While these phrases are more wordy than simply saying this or that is "true," the advantage is that these phrases never close the door on new evidence. This tentativeness is a basic feature of the scientific method.

After finding certain relationships over and over again, scientists often propose theories to explain the relationships. If the theory does nothing more than explain the relationships already established, it is not very impressive; a "good" theory will go on to make additional predictions, the more, the better. Basically, a **theory** is a set of logically related statements about some phenomenon. Theories can be very useful in science because they serve to focus future research and often help to simplify our attempts to understand something.

At the heart of separating "good" and "bad" theories is the process of deriving hypotheses from them. **Hypotheses** are tentative statements about empirical reality which may or may not be confirmed by observation. For example, it is a hypothesis that males are more criminal than females, and, of course, the evidence supporting this hypothesis is very strong. Other hypotheses may not have even been tested yet, let alone confirmed.

A theory of criminal behavior that predicted higher criminality among males than among females would be better than one that was silent about any gender difference. An even better theory would predict that crime is primarily committed by persons in their teens and twenties as well as the observed gender differences. An even better theory would be one that predicts *every*thing that is now established with respect to who is and is not involved in criminal conduct. Finally, the best theory of all would not only predict everything we *currently* know about criminal behavior, but would go on to accurately predict things that have not yet even been investigated.

One more point worth making about scientific theories involves the trouble you probably had learning and remembering all of the correlates of crime covered in Chapters 5 through 9. Presumably, it will someday be possible to know just one theory and from it be able to deduce what all of the correlates of crime are. As we will see, however, no theory has yet been proposed.

CRITERIA FOR JUDGING THE VALUE OF A SCIENTIFIC THEORY

Scientific theories can be thought of as existing at a level of generality that is too broad to fully test. Thus, the best that can be said about a scientific theory is that all of the hypotheses derived from it so far have been confirmed, and that, therefore, the theory has not yet been disproved. Because a scientific theory can*not* be proven once and for all, scientists talk in terms of a theory's "merit" (sometimes called *elegance*). Here are four ways the merit of a scientific theory can be assessed:

Predictive Accuracy and Scope

When a theory leads to hypotheses that are consistent with empirical reality, the theory is said to have **predictive accuracy.** The more hypotheses a theory correctly predicts, the more the theory is said to have **predictive scope.** Predictive accuracy and scope are the two most important criteria used for judging the merit of scientific theories; the greater the accuracy and the broader the scope, the better.[1]

In the context of hypothesis testing, the word *prediction* does not simply mean predicting the future, but also "predicting" what may have already been documented. For example, scientists often discuss how well a theory "predicts" already established facts (sometimes called *postdiction*). In criminology, this would mean that we can ask how well a theory predicts that males are more seriously criminal than females throughout the world, or that crime is heavily concentrated among persons in their teens and twenties.[2]

Simplicity

If two theories are essentially equal in their predictive accuracy and scope, the one that is the least complicated and easiest to understand is considered better. Simplicity basically comes in the form of the number and the difficulty of concepts needed to make the theory comprehensible. Usually, the fewer the concepts, the better.

Aesthetic Appeal

Finally, the sheer aesthetic appeal (beauty) of a theory is used to help assess its scientific merit. Although the beauty of a theory is not the most important criterion nor can it be assessed in totally objective terms, most scientists consider it to be a significant consideration in comparing scientific theories.

You may consider the above criteria as constituting the basic "rules" that scientists use in attempting to sort out "good" and "bad" theories. As the numerous theories of criminal/antisocial behavior are presented in the next six chapters, we will attempt to judge the strengths and weaknesses of each one in terms of these criteria. The primary criteria, of course, will be predictive accuracy and predictive scope.

Attitudinal Appeal

Scientists sometimes judge a theory in part in terms of whether the theory is consistent with the scientists' own overall political or religious perspective. This is especially common for theories having to do with human behavior. Is this an appropriate criterion to use in judging scientific theories? The answer depends on whether one's overall political/religious perspective happens to be correct. If it is correct, any theory that contradicts that perspective is likely to be inaccurate. The problem is that, because so few people agree on all aspects of their basic political/religious philosophy, most people's philosophy must be at least partly incorrect. Overall, even though it is often difficult—some would say impossible[3]—to judge scientific theories with*out* considering their consistency with one's basic political/religious views, trying to do so is advisable.

ORGANIZATION OF THE CHAPTERS COMPRISING PART III

Part III is comprised of six chapters. The first three pertain to theories that use strictly environmental variables to explain criminal behavior. The theories covered in these chapters are also distinguishable by the fact that they give no serious attention to clinical manifestations of antisocial behavior.

The next two chapters pertain to biosocial theories of criminal/antisocial behavior. These are theories that postulate the involvement of both biological and social environmental variables to explain criminal behavior. In addition, these biosocial theories are intended to explain not only criminal behavior but also clinical manifestations of antisocial behavior.

The final theory chapter discusses theories that have been designed to draw together major components of two or more theories covered in the previous five chapters. Nearly all of these *synthesized theories* have been proposed only within the past twenty years.

As you learn about the theories covered in each of the upcoming six chapters, bear in mind that some theories are more easily categorized than others. Accordingly, in a few cases, a particular theory could have been very reasonably placed in a chapter other than the one in which we finally put it.

Tabular Summaries of Research Findings

Throughout Part III, we will be citing specific evidence reviewed in Part II as bearing on many of the theory-driven hypotheses. In other words, if a theory predicts that offenders will be predominantly adolescent and young adult males, we will cite Table 5.2a and Table 5.1a (respectively) as being consistent with this prediction.

Several theories, however, lead to hypotheses that were not specifically discussed in Part II. In these cases, we either cite the few relevant studies (if there are any), or, if there are more than five relevant studies, we again adopt the practice of organizing the evidence into tables. For the tables pertaining specifically to a theory discussed in Part III, we have shaded the cells where evidence consistent with the hypothesis should be located. Then we report a consistency score in terms of the proportion of studies that are in those shaded cells (using the same methodology described in the introduction to Part II). The consistency score formula was as follows: **SS/SS+NSS+(2XCS),** where **SS** refers to the supportive studies, **NSS** refers to the studies that found no significant pattern or difference, and **CS** refers to the studies whose findings were directly contrary to the hypothesis.

Experimental Versus Correlational Research

Nearly all of the research findings reviewed in Part II were nonexperimental in nature. This means that the researchers who conducted the studies made their observations without exercising any control over the degree to which subjects are exposed to the variables being measured. In other words, in nonexperimental (or correlational) research, researchers simply measure the variables they want to study without actually manipulating the exposure to them.

All types of relationships can be of theoretical importance, but most scientific theories stipulate what are called **causal relationships,** rather than mere correlational relationships. In other words, theories usually tell us what variables are causing certain outcomes; they do not *simply* say that two or more variables will be found correlated with each other.

One way that researchers can test theories is by trying to manipulate one of the supposed causal variables, and then determine if this manipulation has the theoretically predicted effect. These types of studies are known as **controlled experiments.** Controlled experiments would be conducted much more often in criminology if they were not usually expensive, time-consuming, and often ethically questionable.

Here is an illustration of how a controlled experiment might be conducted: Say someone puts forth a theory that leads to the hypothesis that we can reduce recidivism (reoffending) among offenders by giving them some new type of counseling. To experimentally test this hypothesis, we might identify 200 offenders that we believe could benefit from such counseling, and divide them into two groups at random. One group (called the *experimental group*) gets the counseling, and the other group (called the *control group*) does not. All 200 subjects are then followed up for, say, two years following their release from prison to determine how many actually recidivated (using the same criteria for judging recidivism, such as being reimprisoned). If our hypothesis is correct, the experimental group should have a significantly lower rate of recidivism than the control group.

Due to difficulties in conducting controlled experiments, researchers also employ various **quasi-experiments** (meaning "sort of" experiments). Here is an example of how a quasi-experiment could be conducted to test the same hypothesis: Say you ask each new inmate coming into a particular prison if he or she would be interested in taking part in a special counseling program, and do this until you get one-hundred who agree to take part in the program. You give them counseling and then compare their recidivism rate to prisoners in general who did not get the counseling. To make the groups more comparable, you make sure that the average age and type of offenses for the two groups are similar.

If the controlled experiment sounds more trustworthy than the quasi-experiment, nearly all scientists would agree. But notice how much better both types of studies would be for identifying whether or not counseling helps to prevent recidivism than would be a study in which you asked people if they have ever had such counseling and how many crimes they've committed, and then make comparisons.

If neither experiments nor quasi-experiments are feasible, researchers often utilize what are called **multivariate correlational studies** to help answer causal questions. These types of studies are very complicated mathematically, but they can be easily understood as follows: Often, a mere correlation between two variables is the result of some third variable operating on both of them. Statisticians have developed various techniques to mathematically "eliminate" extraneous variables from a particular correlation. For reading the following chapters, you do not need to know how these studies are conducted, but simply know that they can be helpful in separating causal relationships from relationships that are actually explainable without being of a causal nature.

In various tables throughout the upcoming chapters, we will summarize the results of studies pertaining to the various theories. In some of these tables, reference will be made to whether the studies were controlled experiments, quasi-experiments, multivariate correlational studies, or mere correlational studies. (These different types are more precisely identified in the supplement to the present text.) All you need to keep in mind is that, for the purpose of identifying causes, controlled experiments are usually considered the most powerful, with quasi-experiments and multivariate studies being roughly of secondary power, and mere correlational studies without multivariate controls are considered the least powerful for identifying causes.

Impartiality and Comprehensiveness

The final comment we wish to make in introducing this third part of the text has to do with our efforts to be fair in characterizing each theory and judging its scientific merit. You will find that we devote more space to describing some theories than others, and you might think that this is because we are more favorably disposed towards them. This is not correct, however. As noted above, an important feature of a good theory is that it is simple. A theory that can be described in a few short paragraphs is in fact a better theory from the standpoint of simplicity than one that takes several pages to describe.

Nevertheless, simplicity is just *one* of the features of a good scientific theory. The most important single feature is the theory's ability to generate the greatest number of testable hypotheses that are ultimately confirmed. This being the case, we made a concerted effort to identify as many of the most obvious hypotheses as we could with respect to each theory. Then we briefly summarize whatever evidence there is bearing on each hypothesis. Our efforts in this regard are bound to be incomplete. To help insure accuracy, we sent drafts of these chapters to most of the still-living proponents of these theories, and asked for their critiques.

ENDNOTES

1. Ellis 1994:203.
2. Braithwaite 1989:44.
3. Collins 1981; Gouldner 1970; Haraway 1989.

CHAPTER 10

Cognitive and Early Child Development Environmental Theories

Are there universally accepted standards of right and wrong? A number of criminologists believe so, and have proposed theories that explain how some people take longer to learn to obey those standards than do other people. Also considered in this chapter are theories that assume that people's social circumstances sometimes may compel them to engage in crime. As we consider these theories, keep in mind that good criminological theories will not only specify what the main causal variables are; they will also indicate how these variables have their criminogenic effects.

Most environmental theories of criminality seek to identify factors that cause people to engage in crime. In fact, most of the theories to be reviewed in this chapter emphasize how certain environmental factors *inhibit* criminal behavior rather than cause it. In other words, these theories assume that people have a "natural" (or given) propensity to engage in crime (as the quickest way to get what they want), but that some of us learn better than others how to avoid acting on these impulses.

Theories reviewed in this chapter make specific proposals about the nature of child development and family relationships that affect the probability of criminal behavior. As we explore these theories, keep in mind that criminologists use various criteria to help them assess the merit of scientific theories. The most important criterion is the theory's ability to predict empirical observations. Chapters 5 through 9 have given you knowledge about the best established empirical correlates of crime. The better a theory is at accu-

rately predicting (and explaining) these correlations, the more the theory is said to have predictive (or explanatory) power.

Five theories will be presented in this chapter: moral maturation theory, two versions of control theory, rational choice theory, and neutralization theory. After presenting a brief sketch of each theory, evidence pertaining to each of them is reviewed.

MORAL MATURATION THEORY:
Developing a Strong Moral Sense Can Inhibit Criminal Behavior

While few equate immorality with criminality, the similarities are striking. First, both moral codes and laws are linguistically expressed, often employing words such as *shall* and *shall not*. Second, at the heart of both concepts is the idea of intentionality, meaning that it is reasonable to hold people both morally and legally responsible for behavior that they intended to happen. Third, most believe that it is appropriate to punish people who violate both moral codes and criminal statutes, unless those people happen to be very young. Finally, there is considerable overlap between the acts that are considered immoral and those that are considered criminal. Let us examine a theory of criminal behavior that has people's development in moral thinking as its focus.

Moral Maturation Theory in Brief

In the 1930s, a Swiss child psychologist named **Jean Piaget** (*pe' a sja*) (1896–1980)[1] proposed that children develop through stages in how they reason about both the physical and the social world around them. Figure 10.1 illustrates experiments used by Piaget to discover that children do not come into the world with an intuitive understanding that matter remains the same regardless of shape. Instead, children gradually develop an understanding of this and many other principles as

their brains mature and their experiences accumulate. Piaget[2] went on to assert that moral reasoning develops gradually in ways that resemble reasoning about the nature of physical objects.[3]

Much more elaborate work on the development of moral reasoning was carried out a few decades later by a U.S. psychologist, named **Lawrence Kohlberg** (1927–1979). Kohlberg[4] reasoned as follows: While everyone begins life without a notion of what is right and wrong, we all acquire a moral sense as we age. From this assumption, Kohlberg[5] developed a theory that asserted that our development of a moral sense progresses through six recognizable stages, which can be subsumed under three levels. For brevity, we will describe only the three levels here (Table 10.1 presents a description of all six stages).[6] The first level is called the **preconventional level,** and is assumed to be where all humans begin at birth. At this level, right is what results in pleasure, and wrong is whatever causes discomfort and unhappiness.

Most people gradually develop to a second level in moral reasoning, called the **conventional**

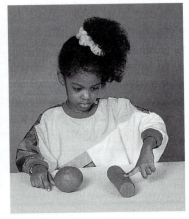

FIGURE 10.1.   In the first frame, a four-year-old girl acknowledges that the two balls of clay are of equal size. In the second frame, she watches as the experimenter rolls one of the two balls into an elongated cylinder shape. The third frame shows her identifying the cylinder piece of clay as being bigger than the ball of clay. This error in judgment is made by nearly all four year olds, but is rarely made by seven year olds. It provides an illustration of what Piaget meant by developing stages in reasoning. Piaget believed that moral reasoning likewise develops through stages. (Marcia Weinstein)

level. Kohlberg said that right and wrong at the conventional level of moral reasoning is primarily defined in terms of authority figures, be they parents, political leaders, or God.

Kohlberg theorized that the highest level of moral reasoning is what he termed the **postconventional level.** Those who reason about moral issues at this level do so primarily in terms of universal principles of equity and justice. In other words, neither pleasure/pain, nor the rules set forth by those in authority guide moral decision making at the postconventional level. Instead, an individual's own internalized sense of right and wrong emerges based on universal principles of the equal worth of human life.

According to **moral maturation** (or *moral development*) **theory,** stages of moral reasoning are universal in the sense that, throughout the world, people progress through these stages in the same sequence.[7] Some have expressed doubts about this assumption,[8] but cross-cultural studies have largely confirmed it.[9] One of these studies compared college students from several Western and Soviet Block countries (before the collapse of the Soviet Union). The study concluded that college students in capitalist and communist countries exhibited virtually identical ordering of their moral reasoning in terms of Kohlberg's six stages.[10]

Despite general support for Kohlberg's assertion that stages in moral reasoning are universal, controversy still surrounds his theory. In particular, some have charged that the theory is biased against non-Western cultures and ethnic groups,[11] mainly because several studies have found subjects from Western industrial nations reasoning at significantly higher stages on average than members of other cultures.[12] Other criticisms that have been lodged against Kohlberg's theory are that it is biased against women,[13] against persons of low social status,[14] and against people with right-wing (as opposed to left-wing) political ideologies.[15]

Considerable research has been devoted to trying to objectively measure the concept of *moral maturation.* In other words, how do you compare people and conclude that one person is reasoning at stage 3 and another is at stage 4? Sometimes self-administered questionnaires have also been used, but most researchers rely on interviews in which subjects are read a series of **moral dilemmas.**[16] Pretend that you are a subject, and are read the following scenario: Say your family was extremely poor, had no medical insurance, and your mother was dying because she lacked an expensive medication that your family could not afford to buy. Would you be morally justified in trying to steal the medicine or not? If yes, why; if no, why not?

TABLE 10.1.   Kohlberg's six stages of moral development.

Levels	Stages	Description
Preconventional	Pure rewards–punishment stage	Pleasure–pain equals good–bad
	Reciprocal stage	Cause pleasure or pain for others, and they will reciprocate in kind
Conventional	Social appearances stage	Behave in ways that assure others that you are a good person
	Law and order stage	Fulfill the expectations of those in authority of one's commitment to the existing social order
Postconventional	Social contract legalistic stage	Behave in accordance with your inherently recognized social obligations to others
	Universal ethical principles stage	Behave in accordance with universal ethical principles

From a Kohlbergian standpoint, there is no absolutely correct answer, but much can be learned from the explanations subjects give for whatever answers they give.[17] In the above example, if you answered that you would be morally justified in stealing the medicine because you thought you could get away with it, you would be reasoning at a preconventional stage. But, if you explained the same answer by saying that you valued human health more than a store's property rights, you would be reasoning at a postconventional level.

If such a method for measuring stages in moral reasoning seems overly subjective to you, don't feel alone.[18] Studies undertaken to assess whether responses to hypothetical scenarios like these compare to moral behavior in the "real world" have come to mixed conclusions.[19] Most researchers in the field seem to agree that, by averaging people's responses to several moral dilemmas, it is possible to get at least a rough fix on how they think about moral issues.

Why would some people develop more rapidly than others through Kohlberg's stages of moral reasoning? Moral maturation theory assumes that the variations are due to different rates of cognitive development, largely in response to environmental experiences.[20] This cognitive development is fostered by what he sometimes called **moral action.**[21] Moral action refers to opportunities to practice behaving in accordance with a moral code in dealing with others.[22] According to Kohlberg and other moral maturation theorists, a particularly important element for advancing moral reasoning is the ability to put yourself in the place of others,[23] especially in the form of role playing with peers.[24]

As applied to the study of criminal behavior, the moral maturation theory contends that persons who move most slowly through the stages of moral development are at the highest risk of offending. It is important to note that moral development theory is only applicable to victimful offenses, because most victimless crimes are not seen as having direct moral implications in the Kohlbergian sense.

Evidence Pertaining to Moral Maturation Theory

Criminal Behavior. As applied to the study of criminal behavior, Kohlberg's theory asserts that persons who engage in criminal and delinquent behavior develop more slowly through the stages of moral development than do persons in general.[25] In other words, if a group of serious offenders is compared to a group of individuals who have rarely, if ever, violated the law, on average the former should be lower in moral reasoning.

Kohlberg himself was the first to test his theory. He did so at the University of Chicago in the 1950s by comparing a sample of convicted juvenile delinquents with a sample of same-aged nondelinquents. While his sample size was small and the differences were only modest, Kohlberg[26] found that, on average, the level of moral reasoning by the delinquents was significantly lower.

Most subsequent studies have confirmed Kohlberg's findings in this regard, although nearly all of the correlations have also found only modest differences, and in several cases the differences were not statistically significant (Table 8.38).[27] Thus, the most direct evidence bearing on moral maturation theory has generally been supportive, although it leaves plenty of room for additional explanations for why people vary in criminal tendencies.

The differences found in most studies may have generally been modest due to the difficulty of measuring both criminality and levels of moral reasoning. It is also worth emphasizing that moral maturation theory applies primarily to victimful offenses, because a number of victimless offenses have no *mala in se* morality implications.[28] The one study that so far specifically examined the relationship between a victimless offense—smoking marijuana—and moral reasoning actually found the relationship to be positive, rather than negative.[29]

Intelligence, Academic Performance, and Years of Education. Piaget and Kohlberg believed that moral maturation is a component of general cognitive maturation.[30] Consequently, moral maturation theory predicts that moral reasoning will be linked to academic ability and intelligence.[31] As shown in Table 10.2, this expectation has been confirmed by most studies. In fact, some researchers have concluded that educational and intelligence variables are the strongest correlates of moral maturation yet identified.[32]

Following the same logic, moral maturation theory predicts that academic performance and intelligence will both be negatively related to frequent involvement in criminal behavior; most studies have supported this deduction, especially in regard to academic performance (Table 8.14). Furthermore, to the extent that doing well in school increases the chances that individuals will stay in school and have favorable attitudes toward education, moral maturity theory is consistent with most of the research linking criminality with truancy (Table 8.35), high school dropouts (Table 8.15b), and attitudes toward school (Table 8.35).

Family Relationships.   Because family and peer relationships are considered important in either promoting or hindering moral development, moral maturation theory predicts that supportive family relationships will be associated with low involvement in crime and delinquency.[33] This prediction would be consistent with evidence of a positive relationship between criminality and poor parent–child relationships (Table 7.6) and abusive family discipline practices (Table 7.8b).

Empathy, Altruism, and Role Taking.   Another prediction that can be made from moral maturation theory is that tendencies toward empathy and altruism will be positively associated not only with criminality (as nearly all evidence suggests) but also with levels of moral reasoning. The findings linking empathy, altruism, and moral reasoning are summarized in Table 10.3, and these findings strongly support theoretical expectations.[34] To clarify the nature of the evidence summarized in Table 10.3, in one study a group of six-year-olds were given a piece of candy as a reward for performing a small task, and then asked in private if they would be willing to donate the candy to a poor child in the neighborhood rather than keep it. The study found that children who had scored high in moral maturation a few weeks earlier were more likely to donate their candy than were those who scored low.[35]

Table 10.3 also presents the results of research linking moral maturation with role-taking behavior. This is in light of Kohlberg's contention that the main way children mature in their moral reasoning is through their ability to assume the perspective of others.[36] While the evidence is limited, it too suggests that moral maturity is positively

TABLE 10.2.   Evidence of a relationship between moral reasoning, on the one hand, and IQ scores and academic performance, on the other hand (consistency score = 95.7%). (The shaded region shows where studies should be located in order to provide support for moral maturation theory.)

Nature of the Relationship	IQ Scores	Grade Point Average	Years of Education
Positive	**Asia** *India:* 2 **Europe** *England:* 1 **North America** *Canada:* 1; *United States* : 12	**North America** *United States:* 1	**Asia** *China:* 2 **North America** *United States:* 3
Not significant	**North America** *United States:* 1		
Negative			

TABLE 10.3.   Evidence of a relationship between moral maturation, on the one hand, and altruism, empathy, and role-taking behavior, on the other hand (overall consistency score = 100%). (The shaded region shows where studies should be located in order to provide support for moral maturation theory.)

Nature of the Relationship	Altruism	Empathy	Role-Taking Behavior
Positive	**North America** *United States: 7* **Europe** *England: 1*	**North America** *United States: 2*	**North America** *United States: 1*
Not significant			
Negative			

associated with the ability to "put yourself in the shoes of another."

Along similar lines, moral maturation theory predicts that empathy, altruism, and role-taking ability will be negatively associated with involvement in criminality, at least in the case of victimful offenses. These predictions have been confirmed (Table 8.36).

Deception and Dishonesty.   According to moral maturation theory, an inverse relationship should exist between moral development and one's involvement in deception and dishonesty. This is consistent with available research on involvement in cheating.[37] Furthermore, the theory predicts that involvement in deception and dishonesty should be associated with criminal behavior, which most studies have also found (Table 8.4).

Religiosity.   Over the years, the relationship between religiosity and morality has been a contentious issue among social scientists. Some have contended that religiosity provides the very foundation on which morality rests.[38] Others, including Kohlberg,[39] have asserted that religiosity and moral reasoning have little in common, except in the case of *mala prohibita* behavior, such as those pertaining to gambling, drug use, and premarital sex.[40] According to this perspective, religion may help to prevent behavior such as drug use and premarital sex, but it is not the basis for *mala in se* behavior (analogous to victimful criminality).

Complicating scientific attempts to understand the nature of any relationship between religiosity and criminality is the fact that human emotions are rarely neutral when it comes to religion. Sometimes emotions can affect how scientists conduct and interpret their findings. Another difficulty has to do with the many ways in which the word *religious* can be used. It can refer to variations in how often people pray, attend religious services, read holy scriptures, or subscribe to various orthodox religious doctrines.

Studies that have thus far addressed the possible connection between religiosity and moral maturation have looked at three distinguishable issues: religious training or knowledge, liberal versus conservative religiosity, and intrinsic versus extrinsic religiosity. To assess liberal versus conservative features of a religious perspective researchers usually rely on the extent to which an individual or a religion, is committed to a literal interpretation of the Bible, Koran, or other religious writings. The concepts of *intrinsic* versus *extrinsic religiosity* refer to the degree to which one is religious even in private (such as praying) or just in public (such as attending religious services).[41]

The results of studies undertaken to assess the relationship between these three measures of religiosity and levels of moral reasoning are shown in Table 10.4. Overall, you can see that the evidence is generally consistent with the view that religiosity, particularly of an orthodox conservative nature, is associated with *lower* moral reasoning, as defined by Kohlberg.[42] This tentative conclusion is contrary to the hypothesis that religiosity promotes moral maturation.

How can this counterintuitive conclusion be explained? Among the ideas that have been offered is that religiosity, particularly that of a conservative nature, emphasizes obedience to authority (e.g., God). Some have proposed that strong beliefs of this nature prevent people from developing beyond the third or, at best, the fourth stages of Kohlberg's six-stage scheme.[43]

Turning to the link between religiosity and criminality, you will recall that the evidence suggests a complex relationship. Regarding illegal drug use, the evidence is overwhelmingly in support of the hypothesis of a negative relationship (Table 8.10). However, for victimful offenses (i.e., those most relevant to Kohlberg's moral maturation theory), studies have been mixed, with most suggesting no significant relationship (Table 8.38). Overall, it would be imprudent at the present time to draw any conclusions about the nature of relationships between religiosity, moral reasoning, and criminality. Nevertheless, most of the scientific evidence does not support the view that religiosity promotes moral maturation, a finding that many will consider surprising.

Gender and Age. One study found males scoring significantly higher on their scale of moral reasoning than was true of females.[44] However, most studies have found no significant gender differences.[45] As others have noted,[46] if the majority of these studies is correct, they would be inconsistent with the voluminous evidence that males are more involved in crime and delinquency than females (Table 5.1a). Some researchers have suggested that there may be subtle differences in *how* males and females think about moral issues,[47] and that these differences could help to explain at least some of the gender differences in offending.[48]

Regarding age, studies of moral maturation have shown that people seem to gradually advance in moral reasoning from the early teens at least through age thirty.[49] This would be fairly consistent with moral reasoning theory.

Parental Discipline. Because moral maturation theory assumes that learning in a social context is at the heart of moral reasoning, one can deduce that parents who encourage children from an early age to consider the moral consequences of their behavior will have less delinquent/criminal children than those who do not encourage such thinking. This deduction is consistent with the findings

TABLE 10.4.   Evidence of a relationship between moral maturation and various measures of religiosity (overall consistency score = 11.1%). (The shaded region shows where studies should be located in order to provide support for moral maturation theory.)

Nature of the Relationship	Type of the Religiosity Measured		
	Extent of Religious Involvement (e.g., Church Membership), Training, or Knowledge	**Conservative (vs. Liberal) or Religious Orthodoxy**	**Type of Religious Commitment: Intrinsic (vs. Extrinsic)**
Positive	**North America** *United States:* 3 **Pacific** *Australia:* 1		
Not significant	**North America** *United States:* 2	**North America** *United States:* 2	**North America** *United States:* 2
Negative	**North America** *United States:* 2 **Pacific** *Australia:* 1; *New Zealand:* 1	**North America** *United States:* 7	**North America** *United States:* 2

from one study that children of parents who used reasoning approaches to discipline had less delinquent youngsters than those who relied mainly on physical punishment.[50] It is also consistent with numerous studies that have found children who were frequently subjected to harsh physical punishment to be more involved with crime and delinquency than children who were minimally disciplined physically (Table 7.8b).

Prevention and Treatment. One of the most important questions you can ask about a theory of criminal behavior is not how well it predicts correlates of crime, but whether it leads to methods for preventing crime or treating offenders. Moral maturation theory has, in fact, inspired a variety of programs for helping to promote moral reasoning,[51] sometimes with the explicit hope of preventing delinquent and criminal behavior.[52]

To illustrate with one particularly innovative example, an Australian researcher recently evaluated a program first developed in Great Britain called the **Victim Awareness Program** (VAP).[53] This program brings offenders together with crime victims, and gives victims an opportunity to describe how having been the victim of a crime affected their lives. Then the offenders are encouraged to verbally reflect and comment on the moral implications of these experiences.[54] Most other programs designed to elevate moral reasoning have consisted of small group sessions in which delinquents are guided through careful discussions of various hypothetical and real moral dilemmas.[55]

What has research indicated with respect to the effects of VAP and other programs designed to raise moral reasoning? A summary of these studies is shown in Table 10.5. As you can see, there is a great deal of evidence that the stage at which delinquents morally reason can be raised.[56]

Of course, the central question here is whether these programs end up reducing crime or delinquency. The available research is supportive of this proposition, although the scientific rigor of some of the evaluations has been somewhat weak. In the most recent of these studies, conduct-disordered boys who were given special training in moral rea-

soning subsequently accumulated fewer court appearances than did a control group of conduct-disordered boys.[57] One study that is not reflected in Table 10.5 found a significant decline in school discipline problems among a group of delinquents following their exposure to a program for moral development training.[58] Another study that may have relevance to moral maturation theory is one suggesting that training in role-taking skills (primarily through training in drama) reduced recidivism among a group of young delinquents.[59]

Closing Comments on Moral Maturation Theory

Moral maturation theory emerged from research and theorizing by Piaget and especially by Kohlberg on how people seem to develop a moral sense. Kohlberg identified six stages, with the earliest equating good and bad with pleasure and pain. In the intermediate stages, moral reasoning relies heavily on authority, and, in the final stages, individuals seem to simply rely on certain abstract principles that value human life and equality.

Very early in Kohlberg's career, he reasoned that the theory he was developing might be relevant to the study of crime and delinquency. Most studies have confirmed his belief that offenders have less developed moral reasoning than their relatively law abiding peers.

Kohlberg's theory makes a number of other predictions, and most of these predictions have been consistent with available research. For example, because Kohlberg and his supporters have envisioned moral reasoning within a more general cognitive framework, it is possible to deduce that criminals and delinquents should be below average in academic performance and intelligence. In addition, the theory correctly predicts that traits such as empathy, altruism, and role-taking ability will be positively associated with moral maturation and negatively linked with criminal involvement.

From a practical standpoint, the theory has lead to programs designed to reduce criminal behavior by teaching offenders and at-risk youth to morally reason at a higher level. While more research is

TABLE 10.5.   Effects of moral reasoning enhancement programs on levels of moral reasoning, on preventing crime or delinquency, or reducing recidivism (consistency score regarding effects on criminal/delinquent behavior = 80%). (The shaded region shows where studies should be located in order to provide support for moral maturation theory.)

Nature of the Effect	Facilitating Levels in Moral Reasoning	Preventive Effects on Criminal and Delinquent Behavior
Positive	**North America** *Canada:* 1; *United States:* 10	**North America** *United States:* 4
Not significant	**North America** *United States:* 3	**North America** *United States:* 1
Negative		

needed, these programs appear to be successful in reducing at least minor forms of offending.

The greatest weakness of moral maturation theory identified so far involves gender and age differences in criminal behavior. Because females are less criminal, the theory implies that they should reason at higher levels than do males, while most evidence suggests that males and females reason about moral issues at essentially identical levels on average. Regarding age, the theory implies that moral reasoning and involvement in crime should co-vary in the sense that ages when crime is most likely is when moral reasoning is at its lowest level. In fact, moral reasoning appears to gradually rise through the teens and early twenties, at the same time that the probability of criminal behavior is also rising.

CONTROL THEORY:
Inhibiting Crime through Social Bonding and Self-Control

Control theory (sometimes also called *social bond theory*) began taking shape in the 1950s with the work of a U.S. sociologist named **Albert Reiss.** Reiss[60] contended that delinquents are often inadequately socialized and thereby fail to develop attachments to conventional others.[61] This theme was elaborated in the 1960s by another U.S. sociologist **Travis Hirschi** (1935–).[62] In 1990, control theory was put into a slightly different form

by Hirschi and yet another U.S. sociologist, **Michael Gottfredson** (1935–).[63]

The central theme in all versions of control theory is that human behavior is largely the result of how children are socialized. This socialization determines the extent to which children come to trust and rely on others, and in turn become emotionally and intellectually committed to them. Control theorists believe that this emotional and cognitive commitment gradually emerges from a long process of being nurtured and socialized by parents or guardians. Children whose socialization experiences contain insufficient degrees of parental love and nurturing will fail to solidify the sense of trust necessary to fully develop a commitment to the well-being of others.

Because control theory was refined in 1990, we will present two separate descriptions of the theory. The original version, as primarily advocated by Reiss and Hirschi, will be called *social control theory*. The more recent version, as put forth by Gottfredson and Hirschi, will be called *self-control theory*. Nevertheless, because both theories make essentially the same predictions, we will be able to discuss hypotheses pertaining to them jointly.

Social Control Theory in Brief

Like moral maturation theory, control theory differs from most other environmental theories of criminal behavior by focusing on determining how most people come to avoid engaging in serious crime, rather than attempting to explain why some people become serious offenders.[64] To answer the question of how most people come to inhibit their criminal impulses, control theorists concentrate on the social environment, particularly the environment in which children grow up. Throughout childhood, if we fail to be sufficiently socialized, we will fail to internalize social norms and rules that normally govern behavior, and this in turn increases the probability of delinquency and crime.[65]

Hirschi[66] described various types of socializing experiences that he felt would serve to inhibit criminal impulses. These experiences can be understood by noting that all societies have institutions (or agencies) that are responsible for most child socialization. The most important of these institutions is the family. Other institutions in most societies are the school and the church.[67] Many control theorists also consider the criminal justice system as a significant control institution,[68] although it tends to function only after all other institutions have failed. According to control theory, failure to socialize to the point of instilling in children a sense of trust, respect, and affection is considered the main cause of delinquent and criminal behavior. Trust and affection are collectively referred to as **bonding.**

According to Hirschi,[69] socialization to the point of forming lasting bonds between a child and society has four elements (or stages). The first element is called **attachment,** which refers to the trust, respect, and intimacy that develops between a child and parents (or other guardians). Attachment comes from the dedicated supervision and guidance that parents give to their children whenever opportunities for antisocial acts first arise.[70] Through this initial aspect of bonding, the beginnings of a sense of moral commitment to others start to form.[71]

Commitment is the second stage in the bonding process. Through commitment, individuals consciously dedicate themselves to maintaining the existing social order and the preservation of their society's norms and values.[72]

The third stage in the bonding process is called **belief.** It refers to the inner feeling that children acquire with regard to the inherent legitimacy and reasonableness of the boundaries being placed on their behavior by those in authority.

The last element in the bonding process is called **involvement.** It refers to the process of devoting time and energy to socially approved activities and avoiding socially disapproved activities, such as crime and delinquency.[73]

At the heart of social control theory is the hypothesis that delinquent and criminal behavior is made more probable by failing to socialize children to a point of their feeling an emotional and intellectual bond to others and to the existing social order.[74]

Self-Control Theory in Brief

The newer version of control theory was called *general theory* by Gottfredson and Hirschi because it was formulated to explain all types of crime and delinquency for all groups of people and times.[75] However, we will not use *general theory* here to refer to their theory, partly because the term was first used to describe an earlier theory.[76] More importantly, the word *general* provides no information about the nature of the variables Gottfredson and Hirschi consider to be the main causes of criminal and delinquent behavior. As most other criminologists have done, we will refer to Gottfredson and Hirschi's theory as **self-control theory.**

Gottfredson and Hirschi note that most crimes seem to be rather spontaneous acts requiring little skill, and usually offer the offender minimal, short-term satisfaction, usually at considerable risk. These characteristics rarely lend themselves to rational explanation. Consequently, Gottfredson and Hirschi reason that people who are most prone toward criminal behavior tend to be low in self-control; i.e., they tend to be impulsive.

People with the greatest self-control are rarely tempted to engage in behavior that harms others, such as thefts and assaults. However, persons with low self-control are often compelled to act on even slight temptations. Gottfredson and Hirschi[77] contend that persons with minimal self-control lack the patience and persistence to work slowly toward long-term goals, and they often find it difficult to relate to other people's feelings. Because they cannot relate to the feelings of others, those who lack self-control do not have a normal sense of guilt when they hurt others.

The bottom line for self-control theory is to envision delinquents and criminals as lacking normal abilities at self-regulation teamed with opportunities to commit delinquency and crime.[78] Due to inadequate socialization, delinquent and crime-prone persons live for the moment, frequently take risks, and think little about how their actions affect others.[79]

What causes this relative lack of self-control? In essence, Gottfredson and Hirschi assert that the same basic deficiencies in socialization by the family and school identified in the original control theory are responsible for failures to learn self-control.[80] In particular, if parent–child bonds fail to form early in life, the child's ability to constrain his or her own behavior later in life is often seriously impaired. Put another way, all of us, by default, are destined to become criminals and delinquents; what diverts most of us from this fate is the socialization we receive during childhood that instills self-control.

In order to test any theory, one needs to measure the key variables. To measure self-control most social scientists have used questions on self-administered questionnaires.[81] Common examples of the statements given to subjects for them to either agree or disagree with are:

I don't deal well with anything that frustrates me.
If someone insults me, I get really angry.
I'm pretty wild.
Rules were made to be broken.

The key difference between social control theory and self-control theory does not have to do with what causes delinquency and crime. Both theories identify the same social environmental factors. The difference is in how these environmental causes are mediated. Social control theory emphasizes the feelings of bonding between children and parents, schooling, and society as mediating the effects, while self-control theory envisions impulsiveness and risk taking as the mediating factors.

Predictions Based on Both Versions of Control Theory

Self-Control.   Except for the variable of self-control (which is explicitly contained only in the newer control theory), identical hypotheses can be derived from both versions of control theory.[82] In the case of self-control, some studies have provided some impressively strong support. Studies both in Switzerland and the United States, for example, found that approximately 25 percent of the variation in self-reported delinquency and crime could be attributed to a lack of self-control.[83]

Variance in these studies can be understood as follows: If both delinquency and self-control could be precisely measured, and lack of self-control were the sole cause of delinquency, then lack of self-control would be said to account for 100 percent of the variance in delinquency. By social science standards, being able to locate a single variable that accounts for a fourth of the variation in another variable is a rare achievement. Nevertheless, other studies of the relationship between measures of self-control and involvement in delinquency have accounted for less than 5 percent of the variance.[84] While considerably more modest, all of these latter findings were still statistically significant.

Family Variables.   Given the emphasis that control theory places on family variables,[85] it is not surprising to find the theory making several predictions about how these variables should be associated with crime and delinquency. Probably the most obvious prediction is that delinquents and criminals should feel less affection toward their parents than is true for their peers.[86] There is overwhelming support for this prediction (Table 7.6).

Control theory also leads one to expect to find factors that diminish opportunities to cultivate close trusting relationships between children and parents to promote delinquent and criminal behavior.[87] Evidence consistent with this prediction would include those suggesting positive links between criminality and broken homes (Table 7.4), large family size (Table 7.1a), and lack of parental supervision (Table 7.7).

School Variables and Intelligence.   School is considered a fundamental socializing institution, second only to the family in its usual importance.[88] Therefore, control theory predicts that individuals who are least involved in, or committed to, education will be most involved in delinquency and crime. From this premise one can deduce that delinquent and criminal involvement would be inversely correlated with academic performance, intelligence, and years of education.[89] The evidence is largely consistent with these predictions (Table 8.14).

Extracurricular and Other Adult-Supervised Activities.   Control theory clearly predicts that crime and delinquency should be lower among persons who are most involved in conventional activities of the community and society in which they live. The evidence weakly supports the hypothesis that involvement in extracurricular school activities is negatively related to delinquency (Table 7.19), except for illegal drug use, for which a negative relationship appears well established.[90]

Attitudes.   According to control theory, because delinquents and criminals are undersocialized, they should hold attitudes that are more contrary to social conventions than is true for their more law-abiding counterparts.[91] In other words, persons who have been socialized to the point of strongly believing in the legitimacy of conventional rules of conduct should have lower rates of delinquency and crime than those who question the legitimacy of these rules.[92] The evidence is largely consistent with control theory on this point. Most studies have shown that delinquents express less conventional (more liberal) attitudes toward drug use and other sociopolitical issues (Table 8.30).

Religiosity.   Control theory also leads to the hypothesis that delinquents and criminals will be less religious than persons in general.[93] This follows from noting that belief and commitment to religious doctrines are acquired through socialization and that these doctrines usually augment the socializing influences of parents and the school.[94] Therefore, one would expect to find virtually all aspects of religiosity inversely correlated with delinquent and criminal behavior. Numerous studies have found church attendance to be inversely associated with delinquency and crime (Table 7.23a). Ironically, this is despite the fact that Hirschi himself headed an early research project that failed to find a significant relationship between church attendance and delinquency.[95]

Nonetheless, not all of the evidence pertaining to the religiosity–criminality relationship appears to be consistent with control theory. For instance, studies suggest that religiosity is more strongly associated with lack of involvement in victimless offenses (particularly drug offenses) than with lack of involvement in victimful offenses.[96] Control theory is hard-pressed to explain why such a difference would exist.

Enuresis.   Most studies have found higher rates of enuresis (postinfancy bed-wetting) and later involvement in delinquency and crime (Table 8.23). If one assumes that enuresis reflects a general delay in self-control, this finding would be consistent with control theory, particularly the self-control version.

Risk Taking.   From the standpoint of control theory, delinquent and criminal behavior are forms of impulsive risk taking.[97] This being the case, it is reasonable to surmise that risk taking and frequency of sustaining accidental injuries should be associated with involvement in criminal and delinquent behavior,[98] as evidence largely suggests (Table 9.6).

Employment.   According to control theory, employment is a type of attachment to conventional social institutions, and it should therefore inhibit criminality.[99] The evidence is somewhat mixed on this point. Regarding adult offending, substantial evidence has shown that crime is diminished by an increase in employment (Table 7.24b). However, several studies have assessed the relationship between self-reported delinquency and employment and found that employment among teenagers is associated with increased offending (Table 7.25). This is directly contrary to control theory.[100]

Ecological Variables.   To the extent that residential mobility disrupts social bonding, one would expect those who frequently move to exhibit unusually high rates of crime and delinquency.[101] This expectation is in accordance with empirical evidence (Table 6.4). Similarly, communities that are poorly maintained may not only have high rates of residential mobility, but may not engender bonding between children and their parents as well as well-kept neighborhoods. This reasoning would allow one to deduce from control theory that undesirable neighborhood conditions would be linked to high crime rates as studies have shown (Table 6.19).

Prevention and Treatment Programs.   As noted in regard to moral maturation theory, one of the most telling features of any criminological theory involves how well programs designed in accordance with the theory actually reduce criminal behavior. Given the success of control theory in generating hypotheses with substantial support, it is somewhat surprising how few programs have been designed around control theory so far. Some of these programs have been aimed toward strengthening the bonding of at-risk youngsters by improving their academic achievement and promoting positive attitudes toward education[102] or by improving their parents' parenting skills.[103] Other programs have been geared more toward enhancing the ability of at-risk youngsters to maintain self-control over their behavior.[104]

As shown in Table 10.6, these programs have been shown to effectively promote bonding and self-control. However, in terms of delinquency

TABLE 10.6.   Effects of programs designed around control theory on: enhanced bonding, enhanced self-control, reductions in crime and delinquency, and reductions in recidivism (O = official data; S = self-reported offending; D = self-reported drug use) (consistency score for effects on offending = 50.0%). (The shaded region shows where studies should be located in order to provide support for moral maturation theory.)

Nature of the Effect	Control Theory Variables		Effects on Offending	
	Bonding	**Self-Control**	**Involvement in Crime and/or Delinquency**	**Recidivism**
Positive (Promoting)	**North America** *Canada:* 1; *United States:* 2	**North America** *Canada:* 1		
Not significant			**North America** *Canada:* 1; *United States:* 3	
Negative (Inhibiting)			**North America** *Canada:* 2; *United States:* 2	

prevention, the evidence has been mixed, with some studies revealing significant beneficial effects and others suggesting no beneficial effects. To date, nearly all of the research aimed toward assessing the effectiveness of intervention programs built around control theory have had to do with the original version rather than with the new self-control version.[105]

Closing Comments On Control Theory

Control theory has been the most popular theory among criminologists in recent decades.[106] In two surveys of members of the American Society of Criminology nearly one quarter of all those respondents identified control theory as the most viable theory of crime and delinquency, and nearly half listed it as one of the top three theories.[107] Control theory has also probably been the most frequently tested theory in criminology in recent decades,[108] and Hirschi is the most widely cited criminologist in modern times.[109]

Despite the popularity of control theory, nearly all tests of it have pertained only to delinquency.[110] The theory's explanatory power has been characterized as modest to moderate, particularly in the case of serious criminality.[111] However, for accounting for delinquency, control theory has repeatedly demonstrated substantial power.[112]

At the heart of control theory is an emphasis on the restraining effects of parental attachment on crime and delinquency.[113] Both versions of control theory make essentially the same predictions, and, as the above brief review shows, the theory has been found to fit well with the findings from numerous empirical studies.[114] Nevertheless, there are many established correlates of crime on which control theory is silent, leading some to assert that control theory seems to be "more incomplete than it is incorrect."[115]

Probably the most glaring shortcoming of control theory is the fact that both versions are silent with respect to gender differences in criminal and antisocial behavior.[116] In other words, neither version of control theory accounts for why parents, schools, and churches throughout the world would socialize children in ways that make males form weaker bonds and have less self-control than females.

Another shortcoming is that both versions of the theory assume that all the influences on behavior are in one direction—from parent to child. No recognition is given to evidence that children come into the world with different personalities and temperaments, and in so doing, affect the behavior of parents from a very early age.[117] The possibility that parents behave affectionately toward some children more than toward others due to personality differences in the child is given no attention in control theory.[118]

Another shortcoming is that nothing in control theory predicts that associating with delinquent friends will enhance the probability of crime or delinquency.[119]

RATIONAL CHOICE THEORY:
A Reinvigorated Classical Criminology

No matter what kind of upbringing we have, when we spot an unattended purse in a vacant room, we all still have the same set of choices: We can leave it alone, we can try to locate its owner, or we can rummage through it for valuables and take them. According to rational choice theorist, the decisions that we make largely depend on the weight we give to the risks and costs involved. If the purse we find contains several hundred dollars, we need the money, and are virtually certain that no one will know who took it, many of us would steal it.

Rational choice theorists would not dispute that there are many factors external to the decision-making process itself that determine whether one violates the law, but they contend that most of these factors play out through a series of rational decision processes. These ideas were not only advocated by the classical theorists, Beccaria and Benthem, but they survived through the twentieth century in what was known as **neo-classical criminology,** an approach that is also central to the field of economics.[120]

Rational Choice Theory in Brief

Rational choice theory rests on the assumption that human beings are reasoning creatures, capable of knowing that their actions have consequences. In other words, except for those who are insane, people's actions come about as a result of considering options and making choices. An inherent part of making choices is sometimes choosing to violate the law. Theoretically, as rational beings contemplate violating a law, they take into consideration such things as the likelihood of being arrested, prosecuted, and imprisoned. As the arrest, prosecution, and imprisonment probabilities increase, the number of persons choosing to violate a particular law should decrease. This has some important qualifications, however. One is that people have to be at least vaguely aware of what the arrest, prosecution, and imprisonment probabilities are, and the other is that the perceived rewards will also be taken into account.

You should note that rational choice theory does not really predict the actions of individuals. Rather it predicts aggregated responses to a set of benefits and costs associated with a particular action, such as committing a crime.[121] To illustrate this point, studies have shown that people who violate a law and don't get caught tend to lower their estimates of being arrested, while those who violate the same law and get caught thereafter raise their estimates of the risk of being arrested.[122] This means that an individual's estimates of being arrested are affected more by personal experience than by an objective assessment of risk. Nevertheless, according to rational choice theory, it is still possible to reduce the rate at which a particular crime occurs by significantly raising the apprehension rate.

The main proponents of rational choice theory are two British criminologists, **Derek Cornish** (1939–) and **Ronald Clarke** (1940–)[123] (Clarke now teaches in the United States). These researchers have emphasized the "reasonableness" of most criminal acts. Their theory differs from the ideas first put forth by the Classical Theorists primarily in that Cornish and Clarke[124] explicitly recognize that every person has a unique **choice structure.** By this they mean that rational thought operates somewhat differently for each human being because everyone has a somewhat unique set of values that affects the decision making process.[125] Basically, choice structure refers to "the constellation of opportunities, costs, and benefits attaching to particular kinds of crime" by an individual at any given point in his or her life.[126] As we age and acquire experiences, our choice structures are bound to change.[127] This means that choices cannot be explained as being simply the result of everyone's common assessment of pleasure and pain; what is highly pleasurable or painful to one person may not be to another.

Rational choice theory can be thought of as combining two criminological subtheories. One is called **deterrence theory.** Its proponents have been mainly interested in identifying the aspects of law enforcement and criminal punishment that is most effective in curtailing criminal behavior.[128] The second sub-theory is called **routine activities theory** (or **opportunity theory**). Its main proponents have been two U.S. sociologists, **Lawrence E. Cohen** (1945–) and **Marcus Felson** (1947–).[129] This version of rational choice theory mainly focuses on identifying environmental conditions (other than the criminal justice system) that are most and least conducive to criminal conduct.

Among the main tenants of routine activities theory is that the time young people spend in unstructured socializing activities has a major impact on their probability of engaging in illegal drug use and other forms of offending behavior.[130] Another tenet is that ecological factors can have a substantial influence on crime rates, both in facilitating and in inhibiting terms. In other words, some environmental settings encourage crime and some discourage it.[131]

Evidence Pertaining to Rational Choice Theory

Deterrence. Rational choice theory is especially relevant to the possible effects of legal sanctions on criminal behavior. Because this theory argues that people usually weigh the probable costs and benefits of their actions, it should be possible to reduce crime rates by increasing apprehension and conviction rates, and by increasing the penalties imposed on those convicted.

Most studies on deterrence are either ecological, in which several states or cities are compared, or a single region is followed over time along with changes in penalties or rates of apprehension. No deterrence researcher expects to find a perfect match between the "costs" of crime and the rate of crime. This is because people are never fully aware of the penalties nor of their likelihood of being caught.[132] In addition, there is evidence that, whenever the penalties for an offense are substantially increased, the probability of defendants being convicted tends to decrease.[133]

Research pertinent to the deterrence effects of sanctions is summarized in Table 10.7. Notice that most studies are supportive of rational choice theory, particularly in the case of violent crimes and the probabilities of conviction and the severity of punishment.[134] While there are quite a number of studies suggesting that no significant effects, many of these simply fell slightly short of reaching statistical significance. This fact is bolstered by noting that there are no studies which have found that raising apprehension rates or making the penalties more severe causes crime to increase.

One area of deterrence research that continues to cause great controversy is the use of the death penalty. As displayed in the last column of Table 10.7, most of the studies on the use of the death penalty do not indicate that it has a significant deterrent effect. In judging these studies, keep in mind that the death penalty is normally compared to life imprisonment (often without parole). If it were to be compared to a $50 fine, there would no doubt be a tremendous deterrent effect. Another point is that research on the deterrent effect of the death penalty is probably not the best test of deterrence theory because many murders are more impulsive and less rationally thought out than the average offense. Also, as just

mentioned, raising the severity of penalties for crimes often has the effect of lowering conviction rates. In other words, jurors who pass judgment on the guilt or innocence of defendants tend to "raise the bar" in terms of the proof of guilt whenever the likely penalties for a crime are made more severe.

In addition to studies summarized in Table 10.7, some researchers have tested the deterrence hypothesis by giving subjects a series of hypothetical scenarios to see if people *think* they would or would not be deterred from various offenses under a variety of circumstances. Findings from these studies are summarized in Table 10.8.

To give a sense of the nature of these studies, one of them found that subjects were sensitive to variations in the potential rewards of crimes, but were almost completely unaffected by the severity of the penalties.[135] This, of course, would not be consistent with the deterrence hypothesis. A study that did support the deterrence hypothesis found that increasing the hypothetical penalties lowered most subjects' self-assessed probability of violating tax laws.[136] However, it is worth noting that even greater compliance with the same laws were achieved by appealing to the subject's sense of fairness and conscience (which seems to make little sense in terms of rational choice).

Consistent with rational choice theory, but not listed in Table 10.8, are a couple of studies indicating that criminals and delinquents underestimate the probability of being arrested when they are compared to peers who have minimally violated the law.[137]

Economic Deprivation. Rational choice theory leads one to expect that crime rates will rise and fall with the state of the economy. In particular, when the economy is depressed, property crime rates in particular should rise, and then decline as the economy improves. A great deal of research has addressed this issue, and it is largely supportive in indicating that whenever a nation's economy worsens, its property crime rate (but not its violent crime rate) goes up (Table 6.26).

TABLE 10.7.   Relationships between crime probabilities and the probabilities of arrest and severe sanctions (overall consistency score = 65.6%). (The shaded regions indicate cells where findings should be to support hypotheses derived from deterrence aspects of rational choice theory.)

Relationship to Crime		Arrest or Conviction Probability		Imprisonment Probability, Sentence Length, or Time Served	
		Arrest or Clearance Rates	Conviction Rates	Imprisonment Rates	Sentence Length or Harshness*
Violent Crime	Negative	**North America** *United States: 2*	**North America** *United States: 4*	**North America** *United States: 3*	**North America** *United States: 6*
	Not significant or Ambiguous	**North America** *United States: 3*			**North America** *United States: 7*
	Positive				
Property Crime	Negative	**North America** *United States: 1*			**Europe** *England: 2* **North America** *United States: 4*
	Not significant or Ambiguous	**North America** *United States: 1*	**Europe** *Sweden: 1* **North America** *United States: 1*		**North America** *United States: 1*
	Positive				
Misdemeanors (Mainly Speeding & Drunk Driving)	Negative	**North America** *United States: 1*		**Europe** *England:1* **North America** *United States: 2*	
	Not significant or Ambiguous			**Europe** *England: 1* **North America** *United States: 2*	
	Positive				
General or Two or More Felony Offenses of Any Type	Negative	**Europe** *England:1* **North America** *United States: 6*		**Asia** *Taiwan: 1* **Europe** *England: 1* **North America** *United States: 4*	**North America** *United States:1*
	Not significant or Ambiguous	**North America** *United States: 2*		**North America** *United States: 1*	**North America** *United States: 2*
	Positive				

Ecological Conditions.   Another prediction by rational choice theory is that crime will vary according to ecological conditions that affect the probability of being identified as an offender. For example, crime should be higher in urban than in rural areas because the chances of being identified are usually lower in large populations. This, of course, is consistent with evidence on urban–rural

TABLE 10.8.   Relationships between self-assessed probability of violating a criminal or delinquency statute and hypothetical increases/decreases in apprehension or penalties (consistency score = 80.0%). (The shaded regions indicate cells where findings should be to support hypotheses derived from deterrence aspects of rational choice theory.)

Probability of Committing the Offense	Type of Criminal Justice Action	
	Increasing Identification/Apprehension	**Increasing Penalties**
Reduced	**North America** *Canada: 1; United States: 5*	**Europe** *Sweden: 2* **North America** *Canada: 1; United States: 3*
Not significant or Ambiguous	**Pacific** *Australia: 1*	**North America** *United States: 2*
Increased		

differences in crime rates (Table 6.1a) and the positive link between crime rates and population density (Table 6.3).

Victimization.   The routine activities version of rational choice theory implies that crime victims will be selected partly on the basis of perceived vulnerability.[138] This prediction has not yet been specifically tested, but seems consistent with research indicating that violent crime, including robbery, is more likely in neighborhoods with the largest number of taverns (Table 6.11). Theoretically, taverns will be frequented by many people who have a relatively low concern for personal safety, and who are sometimes unable to react effectively to an assault.[139]

Gender and Age.   Some have criticized rational choice theory for being largely silent regarding gender differences in offending rates.[140] However, the theory may have some bearing on this point. For example, the greater involvement of males in crime could be at least partly due to their being out-and-about where the opportunities for crime (and crime victimization) are more numerous.

Also, the routine activities version of rational choice theory asserts that males and females should engage in crime at close to the same rates if their opportunities for law violations were the same. Consistent with this reasoning was a study

based on self-reported offenses by a group of teenagers in Iowa.[141] While males self-reported more delinquency, once researchers introduced statistical controls for a variety of opportunity factors (of which males self-reported more), most of the gender differences disappeared.

Regarding age, the routine activities version of rational choice theory predicts that illegal behavior will result from increasing "work and leisure activities outside households."[142] This is consistent with evidence that offending behavior is higher for teenagers who have a job in addition to going to school than do teenagers who simply go to school (Table 7.25).

Prevention and Treatment.   Rational choice theory implies that most rehabilitation programs will be ineffective in preventing recidivism.[143] Because counseling and moral training programs, for example, do not focus their attention on rational (pleasure–pain) aspects of human decision making, they should have minimal effects on offending. This is consistent with research suggesting that counseling programs are ineffective in preventing recidivism,[144] although it is inconsistent with evidence that moral training programs may help to prevent offending in at-risk youth (Table 10.2).

The most promising prevention programs from a rational choice perspective would be those that increase the likelihood of law-abiding behavior yielding desired outcomes, such as financial security. For example, education and job-training programs should help reduce offending to the degree they give people skills that allow them to satisfy their needs without engaging in crime. Because the effectiveness of education and job-training programs are even more relevant to a theory to be discussed in the next chapter, we will review the relevant evidence there. Nevertheless, it can be summarily stated here that the evidence is mixed with respect to the effectiveness of educational and job-training programs in preventing crime and delinquency.[145]

Closing Comments on Rational Choice Theory

Rational choice theorists assert that criminal behavior is largely driven by rational choices. However, unlike the classical theorists, rational choice theorists recognize that not all human beings possess the same choice structures, meaning that they value different things and these differing values affect the choices that are made. As a consequence of differing choice structures, no two individuals will weigh the advantages and disadvantages of violating a criminal statute in exactly the same way. Nonetheless, on average, it should be possible to reduce crime rates either by increasing criminal sanctions or by increasing opportunities to satisfy needs without engaging in crime.

Even the most ardent supporters of rational choice theory acknowledge that there are many more factors affecting criminal behavior than a simple weighing of the probable costs and benefits. Nevertheless, they believe that the extent of the penalties, and the likelihood of being apprehended, have significant effects on offending rates.

Rational choice theory is largely consistent with evidence pertaining to the effects of criminal sanctions on offending rates and with evidence regarding opportunities for legal versus illegal alternatives to satisfying individual desires. Other than that, the theory is limited in its predictions. In particular, rational choice theory is ill-equipped to explain why numerous behavioral/personality traits would be associated with involvement in crime.

In closing, we should note that at least one proponent of the routine activities version of rational choice theory—Lawrence Cohen—has shifted his interest in recent years to a type of evolutionary theory of criminal/antisocial behavior. We will discuss this theory in Chapter 14.

NEUTRALIZATION THEORY: Allowing People to Make Excuses Causes Crime

Have you ever done something you knew was wrong, but found yourself concocting some reasonable-sounding story to make your actions seem acceptable, and maybe even admirable? According to neutralization theory, most criminals are unusually good at this sort of excuse-making, and gullible people often reward them for this behavior.

Neutralization Theory in Brief

The main proponents of neutralization theory are **G. Sykes** and **David Matza.** Beginning in the 1950s, these U.S. criminologists became convinced that criminals, and especially delinquents, often have unusual propensities to rationalize whatever illegal behavior they engage in.[146] This led them to speculate that the rationalizing behavior itself might increase subsequent involvement in crime and delinquency.

Neutralization theory may be characterized in terms of the following three propositions: First, essentially everyone develops a basic moral sense and commitment to a society's standards of conduct. Second, some people learn to use techniques to suspend the applications of these standards to themselves, techniques that are called **neutralization techniques.** Third, persons who use neutralization techniques the most are most likely to engage in crime and delinquency.[147]

Five neutralizing techniques were identified by Sykes and Matza.[148] Two of them pertain to the victim, one asserting that the victim got what he/she deserved (such as when an injury was done in retaliation), and the second denying that the victim was actually harmed (such as a rapist excusing his behavior by saying that the victim actually enjoyed the rape). The remaining three neutralization techniques involve denying responsibility for any harm that was done (e.g., you were drunk or a buddy kept egging you on to break in), condemning the condemner (e.g., those who say you shouldn't have done it have done things just as bad), and appealing to a higher loyalty (e.g., you needed to steal the money to help a friend pay off a debt).

Sykes and Matza contended that most antisocial individuals accept the validity of the prevailing moral order, such as believing that it is wrong to steal or to hurt other people. Furthermore, proponents of neutralization theory assert that most delinquents and criminals do not think of their behavior as bad. In order to make this seemingly contradictory line of reasoning possible, delinquents and criminals invent rational explanations that exempt their particular acts from the "immoral/illegal" category.

Evidence Pertaining to Neutralization Theory

Attitudes.   According to neutralization theory, criminals and delinquents should be unusually tolerant of crime as well as other forms of "deviance." In accordance with this prediction, studies have consistently shown that involvement in criminal and delinquent behavior is associated with liberal or accepting attitudes toward drug use (Table 8.33) as well as deviance in general (Table 8.33).

In the case of victimful offenses, several studies have found criminals and delinquents more prone to offer justifications for stealing and for injuring people than is true for persons in general.[149] Another study found that nondelinquent youth considered the police as being more fair and respectable than did delinquents.[150] In another study, delinquent gang members were found to be less prone to condemn people who were involved in prostitution and in selling stolen goods than were nongang youth.[151] All of these findings are consistent with neutralization theory.

Two studies of attitudes toward offending have not been consistent with neutralization theory. One study found that criminals and delinquents were no more inclined to offer excuses for violent acts directed toward relatives and friends than were persons in general.[152] Only offenses directed toward strangers were more likely to be excused by offenders than for nonoffenders.

The other study was undertaken to test Matza's[153] assertion that people who violate criminal statutes secretly hold more conventional values than they express, especially when they are in the company of delinquent/criminal friends. Contrary to this assertion, the study found that adolescents who reported engaging in extensive illegal behavior rated their own moral standards as generally *stricter* than that of their closest friends.[154]

Locus of Control.   Sykes and Matza[155] contend that one of the main ways to neutralize an illegal act is to assert that something outside of you was really the cause of your actions. This implies that persons who attribute more of their behavior to external forces than to internal forces will be more likely to violate the law. Consistent with this prediction is research on the **locus of control,** which has repeatedly shown that those who lack internal control over their behavior are more likely to commit crime than is true for persons in general (Table 8.32).

Deception.   Neutralization theory leads to the expectation that persons who are generally prone to lie and deceive will be more involved in crime and delinquency than will persons in general. Evidence is largely consistent with this expectation (Table 8.4).

Gender.   Attempts have been made to explain why males are more criminal than females by looking for evidence that males are more likely to try to neutralize their illegal behavior. These studies largely failed to find evidence of gender differences in tendencies to neutralize illegal activities.[156]

Prevention and Treatment Programs.   Neutralization theory implies that crime can be prevented by teaching children to avoid looking for excuses for violating the law. Theoretically, it is through learning to make up excuses that the stage is set for becoming a frequent lawbreaker. Similarly, the theory implies that offenders might be effectively treated by exposing them to individual or group counseling sessions in which they are confronted with the adverse consequences associated with their neutralizing thought processes.

One offender treatment program has been designed to confront hardcore offenders with the inexcusable nature of the antisocial behavior. This program is intended to force psychopathic criminals to own up to the behavior that sent them to prison, and to stop blaming others and "the system" for their current confinement. Until the treatment staff is convinced that an offender in the program has done so, he/she is kept locked up.[157] What are the effects of this program? Unfortunately, no controlled comparisons have yet been published.

Closing Comments on Neutralization Theory

According to neutralization theory, people who engage in crime and delinquency most often have an unusual tendency to conjure up excuses for their offending behavior. To the degree this neutralizing behavior becomes habitual, so too does offending behavior. The theory is vague as to how such tendencies are acquired, but clearly suggests that one can reduce the probability of future offending by making it difficult for people to invoke excuses for criminality.

Neutralization theory is vague as to what causes some people to rationalize their illegal behavior more than other people. In addition, neutralization theory contains little to help explain why demographic and many other established correlates of crime would exist.

Overall, the theory is limited in its predictive scope, but several of its predictions have been well supported by available evidence. Finally, it should be noted that some criminologists simply subsume neutralization theory as a special "plank" under other theories that will be discussed in the next chapter.[158]

GENERAL REMARKS ABOUT THEORIES COVERED IN THIS CHAPTER

This chapter has explored a variety of theories of criminal behavior. The theories all focus on some aspect of how we think and/or how we develop early in life as primarily affecting the likelihood of engaging in criminal and delinquent behavior as we approach maturity. All of these theories have been around in one form or another at least since the 1960s, a time associated with great social turmoil. Most of this turmoil confronted the authority and social responsibility of the criminal justice system.

SUMMARY

This chapter discussed four theories (with one being subdivided into two versions). They all hold in common the view that early childhood experiences and/or intrapersonal thought processes are central to people's probabilities of criminal and delinquent behavior. The theories were moral maturation theory, two versions of control theory, rational choice theory, and neutralization theory.

Moral Maturation Theory

Beginning with Jean Piaget in the 1930s, the idea emerged that humans gradually develop a moral sense through stages. This idea inspired Lawrence Kohlberg in particular to suggest that those who develop most slowly in moral reasoning will be more likely to violate criminal statutes than persons who develop through their stages of moral reasoning most rapidly. In most of his writings, Kohlberg identified six stages, which he subsumed under three levels. Regarding the lowest (or initial) levels, morality is essentially equated with physical pleasure and comfort, while at the highest levels morality is judged on the basis of a hierarchy of certain philosophical principles having little to do with personal feelings. In the intermediate levels, morality is based largely on dictates by authority.

Moral maturation theory makes several predictions besides asserting that criminals and delinquents will score lower than their relatively law-abiding peers on measures of moral reasoning. For example, both Piaget and Kohlberg envisioned moral development as part of an overall process of intellectual maturation. Therefore, such variables as intelligence and grade point averages should be inversely associated with involvement in criminal activities. Evidence of these relationships, in turn, leads one to expect that the average years of schooling one completes will be unusually low for criminals and delinquents.

Another set of predictions that can be derived from moral maturation theory is that such variables as empathy, altruism, and role-taking behavior will be relatively deficient among criminals and delinquents. This is because all of these traits are thought to be components in moral maturation.

As far as crime prevention and treatment programs are concerned, moral maturation theory suggests that programs that help individuals to develop their moral sense will serve to prevent them from engaging in crime. This hypothesis has been tested in two respects. First, quite a number of studies have shown that it is possible to develop discussion group programs in which criminals and delinquents come to think (or at least express themselves) in more advanced levels of moral reasoning, as far as the Kohlberg six-stage scheme is concerned. Second, a couple of studies using these programs with groups of at-risk adolescents have found their subsequent involvement in delinquency was significantly lower than for at-risk adolescents who were not exposed to these programs.

Probably the primary shortcomings in moral maturation theory have to do with being silent regarding the existence of demographic correlates of crime. For example, why would males be more criminal than females, and why would crime rates gradually decline beyond the midtwenties? Such shortcomings do not disprove moral maturation theory, but they suggest that it may at least need some additional theoretical elements.

Control Theory

Building on ideas first articulated by Albert Reiss and Travis Hirschi in the 1950s and 1960s, respectively, the original version of control theory, now called *social control theory,* contends that the process of learning to obey legal statutes comes about slowly through childhood socialization. Those who are exposed to a childhood environment dominated by trust and kindness will gradually develop a strong attachment to others and a commitment to their society's predominant values and norms. On the other hand, individuals who grow up in households and communities dominated by strife and mistrust will often fail to develop these attachments and commitments. According to control theory, criminals and delinquents are primarily drawn from the rank of these latter individuals.

In the more recent version of control theory, commonly called *self-control theory,* Michael Gottfredson and Hirschi elaborate on the internal psychic workings of people with respect to their involvement in crime and delinquency. In a word, those who avoid crime and delinquency to the greatest degree have learned the greatest degree of self-control, and those who become most involved in crime and delinquency have minimally learned self-control. As far as early childhood experiences are concerned, self-control theory and social control theory both agree that early childhood experiences are crucial.

Control theory makes many predictions, and, to its credit, nearly all of those predictions have been confirmed by scientific observation. For example, control theory accurately predicts that many forms of unstable family situations, e.g., divorce, lack of parental affection and guidance, harsh discipline, will be associated with increased probabilities of crime and delinquency. Poor school attendance, and thereby poor school performance, are also fairly easily predicted as correlates of crime based on control theory. The theory also predicts that a variety of negative attitudes toward society, and minimal involvement in religion and work, would be linked to criminality, as most evidence indicates.

Finally, in regard to program intervention, control theory implies that, unless intervention begins early in life for those at-risk, the chances of significantly reducing the prospects of crime and delinquency later in life will be low. If intervention programs are going to be effective, control theory implies that they should be aimed toward giving at-risk youngsters feelings of trust in their social environment and a sense of being an important part of their family, community, and society. A few studies have been geared toward improving parenting skills among the parents of at-risk children and/or improving academic achievement. While the results of these studies have shown that it is possible to increase bonding and self-control among young adolescents, the findings have been mixed so far regarding any significant reductions in subsequent crime and delinquency.

The most glaring weakness of control theory has to do with its silence on a number of variables. For example, it offers little to account for why demographic variables, such as gender and age, would be correlated with offending probabilities. The theory is also silent about any links between criminality and biological variables, and it has had a confusing history with regard to any relationship between offending rates and involvement in religious activities.

Despite these shortcomings, control theory has provided an impressive record in terms of helping to understand variations in criminal and antisocial behavior. Reflecting this fact, it has enjoyed a great deal of popularity among professional criminologists. For instance, in a 1988 survey of U.S. criminologists, about 45 percent indicated that control theory was among their top three choices of theories for explaining criminal and delinquent behavior, nearly 10 percent greater than those choosing the next most popular theory.

Rational Choice Theory

At the heart of rational choice theory is the assumption that people by and large behave rationally, even when they decide to violate criminal laws. The theory's main proponents are Derek Cornish and Ronald Clarke.

According to the theory, rational choices can be socially manipulated to some degree by the sort of penalties placed on violating criminal statutes. In addition, rational choice theorists assert that the opportunities that people have to attain desired goals without violating criminal statutes also affect the extent to which they obey the law.

Rational choice theory encompasses two main subtheories: deterrence theory and routine activities theory. According to deterrence theory, increases in the certainty and/or severity of penalties (all else being equal) will result in fewer offenses being committed. Routine activities (or opportunity) theory maintains that each time a prospective offender encounters an opportunity to engage in crime, he/she roughly assesses the probabilities of being apprehended and weighs this probability against the potential rewards that come from offending.

Quite a number of hypotheses have been derived from rational choice theory, especially as they have to do with deterrence. By and large, scientific observations have been consistent with these hypotheses.

Neutralization Theory

According to Sikes and Matza, criminals have an unusual tendency to blame others or offer excuses for anything they do that they know to be wrong. These excuses range from arguing that they are not really responsible for what happened to downplaying the harm resulting from what they did, to asserting that other people are really worse than they themselves are. To the degree that others accept these excuses, they encourage the commission of future offenses.

The number of hypotheses that can be derived from neutralization theory is fairly limited, confined primarily to attitudinal variables. However, most of the evidence pertaining to these hypotheses have been supportive of the theory.

SUGGESTED READINGS

Beyleveld, D. (1980). *A bibliography on general deterrence.* Farnborough, England: Saxon House. (Provides a very informative summary of research on the effectiveness of deterrent approaches to crime prevention up through the end of the 1970s. It is particularly relevant to rational choice theory.)

Clarke, Ronald V., and Felson, Marcus (Ed.). (1993). *Routine activity and rational choice.* New Brunswick, NJ: Transaction. (This book gives readers a broad sampling of ideas and evidence pertaining to rational decision making in criminal activities.)

Cornish, Derek B., and Clarke, Ronald V. (1986). *The reasoning criminal: Rational choice perspectives on offending.* New York: Springer-Verlag. (Provides substantial and well-organized evidence that most criminal acts make logical sense, at least from the perspective of the offender.)

Felson, Marcus (1998). *Crime and everyday life (2nd ed.).* Thousand Oaks, CA: Pine Forge. (Easy-to-read introduction to rational choice theory.)

Gibbs, John C., Potter, Granville B., & Goldstein, Arnold P. (1995). *The EQUIP Program: Teaching youth to think and act responsibly through a peer-helping approach.* Champaign, IL: Research Press. (This book provides information about one of the most popular programs in moral training that is specifically intended to help reduce antisocial behavior among adolescents.)

Gottfredson, Michael R., and Hirschi, Travis (1990). *A general theory of crime.* Stanford, CA: Stanford University Press. (This book lays out the fundamental arguments in support of self-control theory. It should be near the top of any serious criminology student's list of books to read.)

Kohlberg, Lawrence (1981 & 1984), *Essays on moral development (Vols. 1 & 2.* New York: Harper & Row. (Both of these volumes are classics in moral development theory. Their main focus is on morality, but you will find numerous references to criminal and delinquent behavior as instances of immorality.)

Laufer, William S., and Day, James M. (Eds.). (1983), *Personality theory, moral development, and criminal behavior.* Lexington, MA: Lexington Books. (An edited book containing several very informative chapters on links between moral reasoning and criminality.)

Rest, James R. (Ed.). (1986). *Moral development: Advances in research and theory.* New York: Praeger. (A valuable book for anyone interested in Kohlberg's moral maturation theory.)

EXERCISES

1. Pick your favorite theory in this chapter, and identify two established (or well-established) correlates of crime discussed in Chapters 5 through 9 that are not specifically predicted by this particular theory. Then, either tell how the theory might be modified to explain each of these correlates or why it would be almost impossible to do so. Confine your essay to one to two double-spaced pages. (This exercise is designed to give you some experience attempting to actually think in terms of theories presented in this chapter.)

2. Overall, it appears that people act in more or less rational ways in choosing to avoid or become involved in criminal behavior. Could we therefore dramatically reduce minor and/or victimless offenses, such as shoplifting and possession of drugs, by executing everyone who is caught? Write a one to two double-spaced page report discussing the pros and cons of this idea. Consider the political and moral implications as well as the practical aspects.

3. Read the cover story from the September 7, 1998 issue of *Newsweek* ("Do parents matter?"), and then write a one to two double-spaced page essay on the article in relationship to one or more of the theories covered in this chapter.

ENDNOTES

1. Piaget 1932/1965.
2. Piaget 1978.
3. Lickona 1976.
4. Kohlberg 1979.
5. Kohlberg 1984b.
6. Arbuthnot & Gordon 1987:159.
7. Campbell & Christopher 1996b; Iwasa 1992:3; Vasudev & Hummel 1987.
8. Appell 1980:354; Cortese 1990; E. L. Simpson 1974.
9. Kohlberg 1984; Ma 1988; Snarey 1985.
10. Lind 1986.
11. Cortese 1990; Shweder 1991.
12. Snarey 1985.
13. Gilligan 1982; Hendrixson 1989.
14. Buck-Morss 1975.
15. Emler et al. 1983:1079; J. C. Gibbs & Schnell 1985:1075; Sullivan 1977.
16. Rest 1986.
17. Arbuthnot 1992.
18. Cortese 1984.
19. Blasi 1980:16; Boehnke et al. 1989; Malinowski & Smith 1985.
20. Arbuthnot 1992:307.
21. Kohlberg & Candee 1984.
22. Blasi 1980; Kutnick 1986.
23. Kurdek 1978; Selman 1976.
24. Darley & Shultz 1990:527; Gibbs & Schnell 1985:1074.
25. J. R. Nelson et al. 1990:231.
26. Kohlberg 1958.
27. Kutnick 1986; J. R. Nelson et al. 1990.
28. Lanza-Kaduce et al. 1983:452.
29. Lanza-Kaduce et al. 1983:452.
30. Israely 1985:34; Lickona 1976:230; Piaget & Inhelder 1969.
31. Chiu 1990:195.
32. Chiu 1990:195; Rest 1986.
33. Hayes & Walker 1986:61.
34. Blasi 1980; Rushton 1980:80.
35. Rubin & Schneider 1973.
36. Sharma & Kaur 1992:123.
37. Forsyth & Scott 1984; Malinowski & Smith 1985.
38. Henry & Stansky 1982:24; Johnston & Selby 1978:309.
39. Kohlberg 1981:303.
40. Pargament & Hahn 1986:204; Sharpe 1992:86.
41. Allport & Ross 1967.
42. Rest et al. 1986:131.

43. Lawrence 1979; Rest et al. 1986:126.
44. Kohlberg & Kramer 1969.
45. Reviewed by Brabeck 1983; Bussey & Maughan 1982; Pratt et al. 1988; Thoma 1986; Walker 1984; C. B. White 1988.
46. Reicher & Emler 1985:166.
47. Gilligan 1982.
48. Carlo 1999; Gregg et al. 1994.
49. Colby et al. 1984.
50. Shaw & Scott 1991.
51. Blatt & Kohlberg 1975; Cochrane & Manley-Casimir 1980; Wasserman 1980.
52. Gibbs et al. 1984, 1995; Hickey 1972.
53. Putnins 1997.
54. Launay 1985.
55. Arbuthnot 1992.
56. Arbuthnot 1984; Putnins 1997; Taylor & Walker 1997.
57. Arbuthnot & Gordon 1986.
58. Jennings et al. 1983.
59. Chandler 1973.
60. Reiss 1951.
61. Masters & Roberson 1990:152.
62. Hirschi 1969.
63. Gottfredson & Hirschi 1990.
64. Gottfredson & Hirschi 1990:89; Marcos et al. 1986:137; Masters & Roberson 1990:151.
65. Reiss 1951:196.
66. Hirschi 1969, 1977.
67. Arnold & Brungardt 1983:154; Johnson & Marcos 1988:52.
68. Hagan et al. 1987:567; Sheley 1985:229.
69. Hirschi 1969:27.
70. Rankin & Kern 1994:496.
71. Matsueda 1982:490.
72. Jensen 1976:380; Matsueda 1982:490.
73. Ploeger 1997:662.
74. M. R. Gottfredson 1981:725; Laub & Sampson 1993:303; Lyerly & Skipper 1981:387.
75. Le Blanc 1992:350; Gottfredson & Hirschi 1990:117.
76. Akers et al. 1979.
77. Gottfredson and Hirschi 1990:89.
78. Grasmick et al. 1993:5; Keane et al. 1993:30; Smith & Brame 1994:608; Tittle 1991:1609.
79. Heimer & Matsueda 1994:383.
80. Glaser 1990:428.
81. Evans et al. 1997:502; Gibbs et al. 1998:57; Longshore et al. 1996.

82. Bartusch et al. 1997:18.

83. Evans et al. 1997:490; Vazsonyi 1995, 1997.

84. Longshore et al. 1996; Longshore 1998; Paternoster & Brame 1998:654; Wood et al. 1993.

85. Nagin & Paternoster 1994:583.

86. Wright and Wright 1995:19.

87. Gibbs et al. 1998; Gottfredson & Hirschi 1995:36.

88. Hirschi 1969:110; Thornberry et al. 1985:4.

89. White et al. 1989:723.

90. Downs et al. 1997.

91. Gardner & Shoemaker 1989:484; Menard & Huitzinga 1994.

92. Gibbons & Krohn 1986:128.

93. Marcos et al. 1986; Ross 1996:197.

94. Hawkins et al. 1992.

95. Hirschi & Stark 1969.

96. Burkett & White 1974; Ellis & Thompson 1988.

97. Hagan et al. 1987:793.

98. Junger & Wiegersma 1994:3.

99. Baron & Hartnagel 1997:413; Farrington 1986:336.

100. Ploeger 1997:662.

101. Braithwaite & Biles 1984:6.

102. E.g., D. A. Gottfredson 1986; Hawkins et al. 1992; Schweinhart et al. 1993.

103. Hawkins et al. 1992.

104. Tremblay et al. 1992.

105. Tremblay & Craig 1995:223.

106. Agnew 1985:47; Kelley 1996:332; Simons et al. 1988:294; Kempf 1989:143.

107. Ellis & Hoffman 1990:54; Ellis & Walsh 1999.

108. Bernard 1990:328; Free 1994:152; Stitt & Giacopassi 1992:3.

109. Cohn & Farrington 1998:10.

110. Vold & Bernard 1987:248.

111. Agnew 1985:58; Gardner & Showmaker 1989:481.

112. Polakowski 1994.

113. Gibbs et al. 1998; C. A. Smith & Stern 1997:384.

114. LaGrange & White 1985:19.

115. Rankin & Kern 1994:496.

116. Brannigan 1997:417; S. L. Miller & Burack 1993; Seydlitz 1993:247.

117. Bell 1968; Chess & Thomas 1984; Shaw & Bell 1993; Thomas and Chess 1980.

118. Wright & Wright 1995:20.

119. J. D. Hawkins & Weis 1985:79; Simons et al. 1988:294.

120. Danziger & Wheeler 1975.

121. Hechter & Kanazawa 1997:192.

122. Horney & Marshall 1992.

123. Cornish & Clarke 1986, 1987.

124. Cornish & Clarke 1987:935.

125. Cornish & Clarke 1986:1; Hechter 1994.

126. Cornish & Clark 1987:993.

127. Clarke & Cornish, 1986:8.

128. Decker & Kohfeld 1985; Gibbs 1985; Hechter & Kanazawa 1997:201; Piliavin et al. 1986.

129. Clarke & Felson 1993; Cohen & Felson 1979; Fattah 1993; M. Felson 1987, 1998.

130. Cohen & Felson 1979; Osgood et al. 1996:635.

131. M. Felson 1987, 1998; R. B. Felson & Steadman 1983.

132. Beyleveld 1980:72; von Hofer & Tham 1989:42.

133. Barber & Wilson 1968.

134. Lewis 1986.

135. Piliavin et al. 1986.

136. Schwartz & Orleans 1967.

137. Claster 1967; G. F. Jensen 1969.

138. M. Felson 1987:914.

139. Roncek & Maier 1991:726.

140. Tibbetts & Herz 1996:185.

141. Simons et al. 1980.

142. Land et al. 1990:927.

143. Cornish & Clarke 1987:944.

144. McCord 1978; McCord et al. 1959.

145. Castleman 1984:195; Eysenck & Gudjonsson 1989:192; Jeffery 1977:166.

146. Matza 1964; Matza & Sykes 1961; Sykes & Matza 1957.

147. Landsheer et al. 1994.

148. Sykes & Matsua 1957:666.

149. Agnew & Peters 1986; Austin 1977; Ball 1966, 1968; Ball & Lilly 1971; Buffalo & Rodgers 1971; Hindelang 1970, 1974; Matza 1964:48; Minor 1981; Mitchell et al. 1990; Thurman 1984.

150. Siegel et al. 1973.

151. Gordon et al. 1963.

152. Landsheer et al. 1994.

153. Matza 1964:52.

154. Hindelang 1974.

155. Sykes & Matza 1957.

156. R. A. Ball 1966, 1977.

157. Yochelson & Samenow 1976.

158. Agnew 1994:573; Ball 1983; Cressey 1953.

CHAPTER 11

Social Environmental and Subcultural Theories

Theories explored in Chapter 10 emphasized how cognitive processes and the early family environment may affect the likelihood of people becoming involved in criminal and delinquent behavior. In this chapter, environmental factors of a broader nature are featured (although cognitive and familial factors are not entirely ignored). The theories in this chapter also differ from those presented in the preceding chapter in that they do not assume that standards of right and wrong are universally accepted. Instead, some of the theories now to be explored assume that some subcultures tolerate and even encourage behavior patterns that happen to be considered criminal by other subcultures.

The theories reviewed in Chapter 10 focused primarily on cognition and child development to explain why some people become more criminal (and delinquent) than others. In this chapter, the theories to be reviewed concentrate more on neighborhoods and peers as the causes of offending behavior. Seven theories will be discussed: differential association theory, social learning theory, two versions of strain theory, social disorganization theory, labeling theory, and subculture of violence theory.

DIFFERENTIAL ASSOCIATION THEORY:
Learning Definitions Favorable to Law Violations Causes Crime

Differential association theory was the brainchild of a U.S. criminologist named **Edwin Sutherland** (1883–1950). As noted near the end

of Chapter 4, Sutherland was a very influential figure in criminology.

After teaching at two Baptist colleges in the midwestern United States early in his twenties, Sutherland attended the University of Chicago and earned a Ph.D. in sociology. Thereafter, he accepted a teaching post at the University of Illinois in Urbana, and in 1924 he published the first edition of what eventually became the most widely used criminology text in the United States. By the 1930s, Sutherland[1] had formulated a new theory of criminal behavior that he called **differential association theory,** and around which all subsequent editions of his textbook were organized.[2]

Through his theory and textbook, Sutherland became one of the most influential criminologists of the twentieth century.[3] Following his death, Sutherland's text continued to be periodically updated and republished with joint authorship of another advocate of differential association theory, Donald Cressey (1919–1987).

Differential Association Theory in Brief

As its name implies, differential association theory envisions criminal behavior as being just another kind of behavior that one learns from those with whom one has frequent contact. Sutherland's theory is reminiscent of the theory proposed by Tarde (p. 86) in which crime was explained in terms of cultural transmission and imitation.[4] Differential association theory can be summarized in terms of three propositions, which we have condensed from Sutherland's[5] own nine propositions.

First, criminal behavior is learned as any other complex social behavior is learned, and essentially everyone is equally capable of the requisite learning. This proposition is directly contrary to the assumption that some people are more biologically predisposed toward learning criminal behavior than are other people.[6]

Second, the main process by which criminal and delinquent behavior is learned is through the internalization and acceptance of **definitions favorable to violations of law** relative to definitions unfavorable to law violations.[7] This was a phrase coined by Sutherland to describe attitudes having to do with the appropriateness of illegal as opposed to legal responses to one's environmental experiences. Sutherland believed that people do not simply learn to think of all illegal acts as equally unacceptable; instead, we learn to make many subtle distinctions. For instance, stealing from someone you do not know is often thought of as more acceptable than stealing from a best friend. These variations are part of what Sutherland meant by definitions favorable to law violations.

Third, the primary way definitions favorable to law violations are learned is through associating with persons who themselves have learned varied definitions. Thus, the learning of criminal conduct is more than just a matter of "monkey see, monkey do." Instead, Sutherland argued that it requires a mental process of coming to view certain behavior

as acceptable regardless of how a society at large defines the behavior regarding its illegality.[8] The more an individual has contact with others who view law violating behavior as either trivial or even something to be encouraged, the more one is likely to adopt definitions favorable to law violations himself/herself. Let us now consider the evidence bearing on differential association theory.

Evidence Pertaining to Differential Association Theory

Family and Peer Variables. The most obvious prediction made by differential association theory is that the more individuals interact with criminals and delinquents, the more likely they are to gradually acquire definitions favorable to law violations, and thereby come to commit criminal and delinquent acts. Sutherland asserted that it is not simply the amount of time spent interacting with persons who harbor definitions favorable to law violations, but also the quality of those interactions, and the extent to which the interactions are countered by contacts with people who have definitions unfavorable to law violations.

The main evidence bearing on this hypothesis has come from research on family and peer associations being linked to criminal and delinquent behavior. The evidence in this regard is very supportive of differential association theory.[9] Studies have repeatedly shown that criminal and delinquent behavior tends to run in families (Table 7.10). Similarly, an individual's chances of becoming criminal and delinquent are enhanced if peers and other associates are criminal or delinquent (Table 7.21). Generally, research has shown peer and family variables are among the strongest and best documented relationships with criminal and delinquent behavior.[10] The fact that no other theory places more of an emphasis on these variables than differential association theory speaks well for the theory.

Attitudinal Variables. Differential association theory leads to the expectation that attitudes favorable to law violations will be linked to criminal and delinquent behavior. In other words, delinquents and criminals should believe that their illegal behavior is more acceptable (less wrong) than is true for persons in general.[11] So far, studies bearing on this element of differential association theory have provided mixed support.[12] On the one hand, studies have shown that criminals and delinquents are less likely to condemn illegal drug use when compared to persons in general (Table 8.33), as differential association theory predicts. On the other hand, regarding nondrug offenses, two studies have not found offenders being any more tolerant or accepting of criminal behavior than are persons in general.[13]

A nonsupportive study compared the attitudes of citizens who live in high-crime neighborhoods with those in low-crime neighborhoods. According to differential association theory, citizens in the former should have more tolerant or indifferent attitudes toward crime than people who live in low-crime neighborhoods. One test of this reasoning was not supportive. It found that the average citizens' attitudes in these two types of neighborhoods were not significantly different.[14]

Also, two studies specifically undertaken to determine if attitudes favorable to law violations caused delinquency found little evidence that they did. The researchers interpreted their findings as suggesting that the main reason peers resemble one another in their delinquency is due more to imitation and mutual reinforcement than to similar attitudes.[15] Definitions favorable to law violations, in other words, did not seem to be mediating the similarity in delinquency involvement among peers. However, two other studies found evidence that attitudes were mediating some involvement in adolescent delinquency.[16]

Race/Ethnicity and Social Status.

Differential association theory can explain why crime is more prevalent in some racial/ethnic groups than in others by asserting that groups differ with respect to cultural traditions in attitudes favorable to law violations. Such an explanation, however, does not help to specify *which* racial/ethnic groups will have low- and which will have high-crime rates.[17] Similarly, differential association theory does not predict that crime would be concentrated in the lower social strata.[18] To explain the inverse relationship between social status and crime, Sutherland sometimes suggested that differential association theory could be combined with social disorganization theory.[19]

Gender and Age.

Differential association theory is largely silent about any gender or age differences in crime rates.[20] Regarding age, in fact, the theory implies that the longer a person lives in a particular social setting, his or her offending probability should continue to conform more and more to the norms of that social setting. This is not consistent with the evidence of crime being heavily concentrated in the teens and twenties (Table 5.2a).

In the case of gender, one researcher interpreted differential association theory as asserting that "women are not permitted the same associations as men."[21] Specifically, males are allowed to attach themselves to groups holding antisocial definitions more than is true for females. A problem with this explanation is that it implies that some exceptions should be found, which in turn implies that women should exhibit higher crime rates than men in some societies. At least regarding serious offenses, no societies with higher crime rates among females than among males have yet been found (Table 5.1a).

Prevention and Treatment.

Few prevention and treatment programs have been instituted based on differential association theory. The most ambitious and well-designed of these studies was an experiment conducted in St. Louis, Missouri involving 700 young teenage boys, 500 of which exhibited considerable conduct disorders and early delinquency.[22] The remaining 200 boys were those the researchers used to help provide approximately half of the antisocial youth with guidance and encouragement for exhibiting various forms of law abiding behavior. Results indicated that the boys who had an opportunity to associate with some of the 200 prosocial boys exhibited a significant drop in antisocial behavior compared to the untreated antisocial boys.[23] This study is quite supportive of differential association theory, although other theories to be reviewed in this chapter could also predict the outcome of this experiment.

Closing Remarks regarding Differential Association Theory

The strength of differential association theory is primarily in its implication that family and peer relationships will be substantially related to crime and delinquency, as evidence largely suggests.[24] The theory also suggests that attitudinal variables will mediate the impact of family and friends on criminality, but in this regard the evidence is weak and mixed.

The one well-designed delinquency intervention program based on differential association theory was found to be successful in reducing subsequent delinquency of young offenders. The main shortcoming of differential association theory is that it is largely silent about any possible relationship between offending probabilities and demographic, behavioral and mental health variables. The greatest impact of differential association theory was during the middle half of the twentieth century.[25]

SOCIAL LEARNING THEORY:
Bringing Modeling and Skinnerian Learning Principles into Criminology

In the 1960s, Robert Burgess (1938–) and Ronald Akers (1938–) formulated a theory of criminal and delinquent behavior that was initially called *differential association/reinforcement theory,* but is now more commonly known as **social learning theory.**[26] The theory was specifically designed to improve on differential association theory by being more specific about how definitions favorable to law violations were actually learned.[27] More recent versions of the theory have downplayed the cognitive aspects of social learning, and

concentrated on the environmental reinforcers of illegal behavior.

Social Learning Theory in Brief

To develop a theory that was more specific than differential association theory, Burgess and Akers[28] drew on a branch of psychology that became very influential in the 1950s and 1960s, called **behaviorism.**[29] Led primarily by B. F. Skinner, this approach to psychology concentrated on identifying the fundamental principles of learning from experiments with laboratory animals. These experiments demonstrated that the behavior of rats and pigeons could often be finely controlled by manipulating what are known as **schedules of reinforcement.** These schedules primarily consisted of using different degrees of regularity in rewarding and punishing behavior. In some experiments, animals were rewarded or punished every time they exhibited a behavior, and other times their reward or punishment came irregularly.

Behaviorists such as Skinner found that the rates at which animals continued to exhibit a particular behavior could be greatly affected by these different reinforcement schedules. Among the major conclusions that resulted from the behaviorist experiments were the following: First, reward usually has more predictable effects on behavior than does punishment.[30] Second, the longer one waits to give a reward for a behavior targeted for change, the less effective the reward is in bringing about any persistent changes in behavior.[31] Third, animals are most likely to learn when they are motivated. Motivation in most of the animal experiments was achieved by first making sure the subjects were hungry, and then using food to reward them for their learning various new behavior patterns. In humans, complex social and linguistic rewards can often be used.

Burgess and Akers[32] argued that these and other basic learning principles were central to what Sutherland had simply called "definitions favorable to law violations." They contended that parents and teachers may often inadvertently reward criminal behavior (or its precursors) with what behaviorists called **social reinforcers,** such as simply giving attention to someone who happens to be misbehaving.

A second tradition in the psychology of learning has also become a part of the application of social learning theory to the study of criminal and delinquent behavior. This tradition was developed by **Albert Bandura** (1925–).[33] Unlike Skinner, whose interest was primarily in identifying the most fundamental principles of learning, Bandura mainly sought to understand the most complex forms of learning, such as those found primarily in humans. He argued that most human social behavior was acquired through observation or imitation (or modeling). He seriously doubted that simple rewards and punishments of hungry rats and pigeons had much to do with how humans learned within complex social settings.

Despite its early emphasis on Skinnerian-type learning principles, current versions of social learning theory have been more prone to emphasize observational and imitative forms of learning as well as attitudinal variables. In this regard, Akers and associates[34] identified two classes of "definitions favorable to law violations." They called one class **positive definitions,** and stipulated that these are definitions people use to identify behavior that is socially acceptable. According to social learning theory, people who are most prone toward criminal and delinquent behavior have an unusual proclivity to extend positive definitions beyond normally recognized boundaries. The second type of definition favorable to law violations was called **neutralizing (or rationalizing) definitions.**[35] According to Akers and other social learning theory proponents, law violators are often reinforced for rationalizing their illegal behavior. In this respect, neutralization theory (p. 331) has been incorporated into social learning theory.

Another version of social learning theory has been developed by Oregon psychologist **Gerald Patterson** (1926–) and associates.[36] In this theory, parents, teachers, and peers are seen as sometimes unintentionally reinforcing what starts out to be occasional and rather trivial antisocial behavior in children, but that then escalates into serious of-

fending behavior in adolescence. If parents, teachers, and peers fail to reinforce prosocial behavior and/or inadvertently reinforce antisocial behavior, children can often gradually come to exhibit increasingly serious forms of antisocial behavior.[37]

Unlike other versions of social learning theory, Patterson's version focuses mainly on experiences in the early years of development and little on experiences during adolescence as the causes of delinquency and criminality.[38] The most important difference between Patterson's version of social learning theory and the version mainly espoused by Akers is that Patterson's version does not incorporate Sutherland's concept of *definitions favorable to law violations.* Patterson's version differs from Bandura's version mainly in its emphasis on strictly Skinnerian learning principles, with little attention given to learning through imitation or cultural training.

Patterson's version of social learning theory focuses on deficits in family management skills by parents as the main cause of antisocial behavior by children.[39] He and his colleagues have identified a number of responses that parents make to disruptive and inappropriate behavior of children that may inadvertently increase the reoccurrence of this behavior.[40] For example, when parents of unruly children are compared to parents in general, the former are less likely to praise their children for proper behavior. These parents appear to be less inclined to monitor their children,[41] and less consistent in punishing antisocial acts, even though they are more likely to make threats to do so.[42]

Of course, many acts of delinquency are committed by children with few antisocial behavior symptoms until they reach adolescence.[43] In keeping with its behaviorist roots, Patterson's social learning theory maintains that this late-onset delinquency is mainly due to a loosening of supervisory control by parents.[44]

Evidence Pertaining to Social Learning Theory

Family and Peer Influence. Because social learning theory is an elaboration on differential association theory, it leads to many of the same predictions. Accordingly, the same family and peer influences that differential association theory predicts should be linked to criminal and delinquent behavior are also predicted by social learning theory, and these predictions are quite consistent with available evidence. In particular, criminals and delinquents should come from families and neighborhoods in which such behavior is prevalent, as most studies have shown (for families: Tables 7.10a, 7.10b; for neighborhoods: Table 6.19).

Parental Discipline Patterns.   Social learning theory predicts that children of parents who frequently used harsh discipline will engage in crime and delinquency more than children whose parents did the opposite. Theoretically, such parental behavior provides children with examples for how to behave toward others.[45] Accordingly, nearly all relevant studies have shown that, when compared to persons in general, offenders are more likely to have been harshly disciplined (Table 7.8b) and physically abused (Table 7.9) during childhood. Studies have also linked minimal child–parental affection with offending rates later in life (Table 7.6).

Overall, research supports the hypothesis of a *general* link between children experiencing harsh discipline and abuse and their later engaging in crime.[46] However, this link seems to be no stronger for persons who engage in violent offenses than for those who commit other types of crimes.[47] Also, at least one study failed to find that harsh corporal punishment was a *causal* factor in delinquency; instead, such punishment seemed to be correlated with delinquency simply as another reflection of poor parenting skills.[48]

Broken Homes and Family Discord.   Social learning theory, especially the version developed by Patterson,[49] predicts that all forms of *parental disruption* will increase the probability of childhood antisocial behavior. By this term, Patterson means any failure of parents to cooperate in consistently monitoring and disciplining a child. This concept would lead one to expect that families in which parents either separate and/or are in overt conflict with one another would have children with higher rates of antisocial behavior, predictions that are consistent with most of the available evidence (Table 7.4).

Prevention and Treatment.   Social learning theory goes beyond differential association theory in one more important respect. It has led to the development of related types of treatment strategies for criminal and delinquent conduct. Each of these approaches is discussed below.

The most famous and widely tested of these programs is one begun in the late 1960s for treatment of nonviolent delinquency, called **Achievement Place** (also called *teaching-family group homes*).[50] At Achievement Place and similar types of group homes, juvenile offenders are given a room in a home managed by specially trained "cottage parents." During the first week or two, incoming clients are deprived of essentially all privileges other than a sanitary room and meals. If they wish to watch television, play games, or attend a movie, they must earn points that are being dispensed by the cottage parents or other counselors.[51] The goal of the program is to make rewards contingent on good behavior, such as keeping their room clean and tidy, attending school regularly, completing homework on time, and being considerate of others.

A second type of program inspired by Skinnerian psychology and social learning theory is called **behavioral contracting** (or **contingency management**). In it, parents and other guardians of delinquents are taught skills in behavioral management, including how to draft contracts with their children stating specific types of behavior they must and must not engage in. If the youngsters violate this agreement, they are denied various types of rewards and privileges. The expectations usually include such things as regular school attendance, performing household chores, and being home at prescribed times in the evening. The rewards generally include being able to occasionally

attend movies, or take trips to the mall with acceptable friends on weekends.

Skinnerian psychology and social learning theory also inspired a type of correctional treatment program known as **token economies.**[52] In this program, juvenile and young adult offenders in an institutional setting are given plastic tokens for such things as being polite, attending classes, and keeping their room tidy. In some programs, tokens are taken away for inappropriate behavior. In other programs, the training staff merely maintains logs of appropriate and inappropriate behavior, which are tallied at the end of each week for dispersing rewards.

Studies that have evaluated token economy programs in correctional treatment have generally concluded that they have inhibiting effects on recidivism for at least a few months following custodial release. However, beyond the first few months after discharge, differences between participants in these programs and offenders treated in more conventional ways often disappear.[53]

The fourth treatment program to emerge from social learning theory is called the **therapeutic community** (or TC). This program emphasizes the importance of both group counseling and verbal reinforcement of prosocial values and behavior by correctional personnel and by fellow offenders. TC usually begins in prison and continues in the community after offenders have been released.[54] Nearly all offenders who take part in TC programs have had extensive histories with drug abuse. The TC program is most closely linked to a community-based drug treatment program now found in most large U.S. cities, known as *Phoenix House.*[55]

What effects do these treatment programs have on recidivism? As you can see by viewing Table 11.1, the evidence is mixed. Most of the studies that have evaluated the effects of Achievement Place on recidivism rates have concluded that they have significant preventive effects for the first few months following custodial release, but that the effects seem to disappear over the long term, so that after a year or so participants often

exhibit the same rates of recidivism as do the nonparticipants.[56]

Regarding other programs inspired by Skinnerian psychology, the results again are also mixed. One study involved training parents to use positive reinforcement techniques to reduce childhood conduct disorders. The program failed to have significant lasting effects on the children's behavior.[57] Another study involved a carefully evaluated behavioral contracting with delinquent youth, which concluded that recidivism was significantly reduced, even beyond the first year of implementation.[58]

In the case of TC programs, all of the available studies have indicated that the program significantly reduces rearrest and/or parole violations, particularly for drug abuse offenders.[59]

Overall, several treatment programs inspired by social learning theory have been found to have significant, although modest, depressing effects on recidivism among juvenile delinquents and young adult offenders.[60] Nevertheless, the effects seem to dissipate as the time spent back in the community passes. The programs that may have longer-lasting effects are those following the TC model aimed toward reducing drug abuse.

Closing Remarks about Social Learning Theory

Following the lead of differential association theory, social learning theory asserts that criminal and delinquent behavior is learned behavior. However, social learning theory is not as vague as differential association theory about how such learning occurs. Rather than simply asserting that crime and delinquency results from learning definitions favorable to law violations, social learning theorists have tried to be more specific about how crime and delinquency is learned.[61]

How well has social learning theory held up under empirical scrutiny? Perhaps social learning theory is better equipped to explain some acts of crime and delinquency than others. In particular, the theory seems to be stronger in explaining

TABLE 11.1.   Results from studies assessing the effects of crime and delinquency treatment programs that social learning theory suggests will prevent recidivism. (Shaded regions represent where studies should be clustered in order to support social learning theory.)

Program	Observed Effect on Criminal Recidivism	Main Type of Offending Targeted for Treatment		
		Delinquency in General	Criminality in General	Illegal Drug Use
Achievement Place (Teaching-Family Group Homes)	Preventive Effect	North America *United States:* 2		North America *United States:* 1
	Not significant or Ambiguous Effect	North America *United States:* 3		
	Promotive Effect			
Behavioral Contracting	Preventive Effect	North America *United States:* 2		
	Not significant or Ambiguous Effect	North America *Canada:* 1; *United States* : 3		
	Promotive Effect			
Token Economies	Preventive Effect			
	Not significant or Ambiguous Effect	North America *United States:* 2	North America *United States:* 1	
	Promotive Effect			
Therapeutic Community & Similar Programs)	Preventive Effect		North America *United States:* 2	
	Not significant or Ambiguous Effect			
	Promotive Effect			
Phoenix House (& Similar Programs)	Preventive Effect	North America *United States:* 1		North America *United States:* 1
	Not significant or Ambiguous Effect			
	Promotive Effect			

involvement in victimless offending such as marijuana and illegal alcohol use by adolescents than for involvement in serious property and violent offenses.[62]

Social learning theory is impressive in terms of the number of treatment programs it has helped to inspire. The most unique feature of programs that have developed out of social learning theory

(and Skinnerian psychology, generally) is a heavy emphasis on rewarding prosocial ("good") behavior rather than trying to punish antisocial behavior. The aim is to encourage prosocial behavior to such a degree that antisocial behavior is indirectly eliminated. One of the principal shortcomings of the theory is its silence regarding most demographic correlates of crime. In particular, it offers no explanation for gender or age variations in offending.[63]

Regarding developments in social learning theory, Ronald Akers has remained a supporter, but Robert Burgess has not. Since the 1980s, Burgess has shifted his primary criminological interests to evolutionary theories (to be discussed in Chapter 14). Gerald Patterson and his associates[64] have continued research aimed at identifying the primary reinforcers for antisocial behavior, with an increasing recognition that the reinforcers for childhood-onset offending may be significantly different from the reinforcers for adolescent limited offending.

STRAIN THEORY:
Blocking Economic Opportunities Causes Crime

Strain theory (also called **social structure/ anomie theory** and **blocked opportunity theory**) focuses on the frustration some people feel in attempting to succeed in a competitive socioeconomic environment. The scholar responsible for first formulating strain theory was **Robert K. Merton** (1910–).[65] Merton is a U.S. sociologist with broad theoretical interests, and criminal behavior was certainly one of them. Various names have been given to the theory he proposed, but the one that is most often used is *strain theory.*

In developing his theory, Merton drew on ideas first put forth by Emile Durkheim.[66] Among other things, Durkheim[67] contended that life was not possible unless one's needs are in rough proportion to one's means to satisfy those needs. In addition, you may recall from Chapter 4 that Durkheim introduced the concept of **anomie** to refer to people's lack of a social identity. To Durkheim, the social group provides people with both a reason to live and the space within which to do so. Consequently,

all sorts of behavior problems emanate from people failing to become part of a social group. Now, let us see what Merton and other strain theorists did with these Durkheimian ideas.

Strain Theory in Brief

Merton contended that an interpersonal state of anomie is produced whenever there are discrepancies between the goals that societies create for people and the acceptable means that societies provide for achieving those goals. These goals may be of any sort,[68] but are most often of an economic character, particularly in modern industrial societies.[69]

According to Merton, unrealized desires for status and wealth explain most crime.[70] In modern industrial societies such as the United States, almost everyone learns the importance of being able to make a good living as a fundamental basis on which people's worth is based. Those who are reared in a typical middle- or upper-status home and regularly attend good schools usually acquire the skills necessary to achieve an acceptable standard of living by the time they reach adulthood. However, some do not learn these skills, and, according to strain theory, these are the individuals who are most likely to engage in delinquency and crime.

Another contributor to strain theory was **Albert Cohen**.[71] He drew attention to what he saw as the stress experienced primarily by lower-status youth in their efforts to measure up to middle- and upper-status income standards. Cohen argued that, out of frustration and shame, lower-status youth often develop subcultural values that defy values of the dominant culture that has given them unrealistic goals toward which to strive.[72] Many of these subcultural values lead not only to crime and delinquency, but also to the formation of juvenile gangs, according to Cohen. (More will be said about subcultures later in this chapter.) Other strain theorists contended that it is not just blocked opportunities to legitimate means that affects the probability of crime and delinquency, but also the availability of illegitimate means.[73]

Over the years, other social scientists have elaborated on and extended strain theory,[74] all with essentially the same predictions.[75] The most substantial modification of strain theory was proposed by Robert Agnew.[76] His version of the theory will be discussed separately.

Evidence Bearing on Strain Theory

Socioeconomic Status Variables.   Strain theory is quite explicit in maintaining that crime and delinquency should be concentrated in lower social strata.[77] Evidence is largely consistent with this deduction, with the possible exception of self-reported offending, both in terms of one's own income (Table 5.5a) as well as parental income and occupational status (Table 5.5b).

A related prediction is that crime and delinquency will be lower in societies where competition for wealth is low. This means that socialist countries should have lower crime rates than capitalist countries. And among all types of societies, those where the disparities in wealth are the least should have lower crime rates than societies in which the disparities between the poorest and wealthiest citizens are the greatest.[78] The evidence of income disparities within countries being correlated with crime rates is mixed (Tables 6.22 and 6.23).

Another socioeconomic variable about which strain theory makes a prediction is unemployment. Theoretically, unemployment should primarily affect those who are already experiencing the greatest degree of goals–means incompatibility, and should add further to their frustration. Therefore, crime rates should rise during high rates of unemployment. The evidence regarding this prediction is somewhat mixed, but generally supportive, at least in the case of adult crime (Tables 6.20 and 6.21).

Age and Gender.   The age distribution in crime can be at least partially explained by strain theory if one stipulates that the teens and twenties mark the time when people are under the greatest pressure to become financially independent.

Regarding gender, some have argued that strain theory has difficulty explaining why males are more criminal than females,[79] because there is no evidence that men surpass women in either their desires for material well-being or in their striving to satisfy those desires.[80] However, if one notes that males are under more intense pressure to become financially independent, their greater criminal involvement would be predicted by strain theory. One could reason that, as the pressure on women to become financially self-supporting approaches that of men, their contributions to crime should approach equality as well. As will be discussed in Chapter 12 (in regard to feminist theory), the evidence pertaining to this hypothesis has not provided much support.

Education.   Strain theory predicts that school failure will increase the probability of crime and delinquency, because education is a major vehicle for economic success.[81] As noted in Chapter 7, considerable evidence suggests that a substantial negative correlation exists between criminality and years of education (Table 7.15).

Similarly, strain theory correctly predicts that high school dropouts will have higher crime and delinquency rates than peers who graduate from high school (Table 7.16). However, it would have trouble explaining the "dropout dip" (Table 7.17), i.e., the tendency for offending to decline for at least the first year or so after dropping out of high school. One research team argued that the dropout dip in delinquency was in accordance with strain theory if one assumes that education is largely an unpleasant (strain-inducing) experience for most dropouts.[82] In other words, dropping out of school for those who are doing poorly has at least the temporary effect of removing a significant source of strain, resulting in a temporary reduction in offending. However, because the long-term effect of dropping out is to reduce an individual's chances of making a good living, eventually crime rates by dropouts should once again rise, as evidence suggests (Table 7.17).

Employment and Downturns in the Economy.
According to Durkheim,[83] a state of anomie results from any sudden social change.[84] In strain theory,

this has been interpreted to mean that such events as downturns in the economy will cause increases in crime and delinquency, particularly among lower-status youth who will usually be most likely to be affected by such conditions.[85] Overall, studies of the relationship between unemployment and downturns in the economy in relationship to criminal behavior are largely supportive of this deduction (Table 6.26).

However, the evidence that those who have jobs while they are still in high school engage in more delinquency than youth who do not work while attending high school (Table 6.25) would be difficult to explain in terms of strain theory.

Probability of Achieving Financial Success.

Strain theory implies that youngsters who want to become more financially successful than they can realistically expect should be more prone toward crime and delinquency than persons whose financial goals more closely match what they are likely to achieve.[86] Three studies have tested this hypothesis. One study was supportive,[87] while the other two found no significant difference between serious delinquents and high school students in general regarding the types of jobs they hoped to get and those they actually obtained.[88]

One Canadian study found that corporate crime increased when the economy was performing badly.[89] The researcher who conducted the study suggested that the relationship could be the result of frustration caused by temporarily blocking opportunities to achieve corporate goals.

Social Status and Racial/Ethnic Factors.

Strain theory predicts that persons and groups who are poor will exhibit higher crime and delinquency rates than is the case for those who are financially secure. Thus, it is consistent with evidence of an inverse correlation between social status and offending rates (Tables 5.5a and 5.5b). Nonetheless, strain theory is not consistent with quite a number of self-report studies that have called into question any significant link between being of low social status and involvement in delinquency.[90]

Alienation and Normlessness.

Because Merton based his theory on Durkheim's concept of anomie, some researchers have also looked for relationships between self-reported involvement in delinquency and feelings of alienation. The results have been mixed, with one study finding no relationship,[91] and the other finding weak but significant evidence that people who live in high-crime areas have greater feelings of normlessness and alienation than those who live in low-crime areas.[92]

Goal–Means Incompatibility and Blocked Opportunity.

It is proper to point out that even though strain theory predicts that variables such as social status and school performance will be correlated with criminality, there is more to the theory. In particular, the theory asserts that the key cause of offending is a perception that one's goals are unlikely to ever be realized. Consequently, quite a number of studies have compared offenders to persons in general regarding their perceptions of achieving financial goals.

The results of these studies are summarized in Table 11.2. As you can see, the evidence is mixed, with nearly all of the research so far confined to various types of delinquency, although, if one makes a subtle distinction, there is an aspect of general support for strain theory. While most studies have not supported the hypothesis that delinquents perceive greater incompatibility between their goals and their means to achieve those goals than do people in general, most studies indicate that delinquents are more likely to perceive their opportunities being unfairly blocked by others (fourth column of Table 11.2). In this sense, a fair amount of support has been found for strain theory.[93]

Prevention and Treatment.

Strain theory implies that involvement in crime and delinquency can be achieved in two main ways. One is to increase the opportunities for the poor to achieve the standards of living toward which they strive, and the other is to reduce their expectations.[94] As you might expect, most research efforts have sought the first, rather than the second, alternative.

TABLE 11.2.   Relationship between measures of strain and involvement in crime and delinquency. (The darker shaded regions indicate cells where findings should be to support hypotheses derived from strain theory.)

Nature of the Relationship		Measures of Goals–Means Incompatibility and Blocked Opportunity			
		Self-Assessed Goals–Means Incompatibility	Unrealistic Educational or Occupational Aspirations	Perceptions that One's Opportunities are being Unfairly Blocked	Failure to Meet Parental Expectations
Adult Offenses	Positive			**North America** *United States: 2*	
	Not significant or Ambiguous	**North America** *United States: 2*			
	Negative				
Juvenile Offenses in General	Positive	**North America** *United States: 1*	**North America** *United States: 1*	**North America** *United States: 7*	
	Not significant or Ambiguous	**Europe** *England: 1* **North America** *United States: 5*		**Europe** *England: 1* **North America** *United States: 3*	**North America** *United States: 1*
	Negative				
Drug Offenses	Positive				
	Not significant. or Ambiguous	**North America** *United States: 2*	**North America** *United States: 3*	**North America** *United States: 1*	**Asia** *India: 1* **North America** *United States: 1*
	Negative				
Status Offenses	Positive				
	Not significant or Ambiguous	**Asia** *Hong Kong: 1* **North America** *United States: 1*	**Asia** *China: 1*		
	Negative				

How do you increase opportunities for the poor to achieve a better standard of living than they would otherwise achieve? Most programs have sought to do so by providing them with education and/or skilled job training, such as the 1960s America's War on Poverty under the Kennedy and Johnson Administrations.[95]

Some of these programs had a mandatory evaluation component, allowing for objective assessments of their effectiveness. These evaluations have tended to be disappointing, however, as far as reducing delinquent and criminal activities of their participants.[96] So far, there has been one notable exception. It is a program called the **Perry Project.** The initial evaluation of this basic education program for high-risk preschoolers in the United States indicated that its participants engaged in delinquency at significantly lower rates than comparable youngsters who were not involved in the program.[97] However, this initial report has not yet been successfully replicated.[98]

One study was carried out that attempted to reduce recidivism among delinquents and criminals by lowering their income aspirations.[99] This program involved a series of meetings among young prison inmates and college students in which they discussed career plans and probable salaries. Comparisons of income expectations of the delinquents and criminals before and after the meetings indicated that the program was successful in lowering the inmates' income expectations. In other words, income expectations became more realistic. Unfortunately, the study did not follow the offenders after prison release to assess their recidivism rates.

An interesting Australian experiment was inspired by strain theory in the 1970s. The designers of the experiment reasoned that a less competitive school system might reduce delinquency.[100] Why? The researchers reasoned that competitive school environment subjects poorly performing students to humiliation and encourages all of the students to strive for material possessions that many will never attain.

To test the hypothesis, students attending different high schools in Australia were compared. One type of school placed much more emphasis on grades than did the other. Theoretically, the delinquency rate should be higher for students attending the more competitive schools. In fact, the study found the opposite: Students who attended the least competitive schools reported engaging in more delinquency than did students from the most competitive schools.[101]

Closing Comments on Strain Theory

First proposed in the 1930s, Merton's strain theory asserts that the main cause of crime and delinquency is economic strain, primarily in the sense of financial desires exceeding what one is able to obtain. Support for the theory has been described as "not particularly strong"[102] and "mixed at best."[103] Most criminologists seem to agree that strain theory is only weakly supported by scientific evidence[104] although at least one writer has maintained that support for the theory has been strong.[105]

Probably the main shortcoming of strain theory is that it offers no explanation for why crime and delinquency are associated with numerous family, behavioral, and mental health variables.[106]

No matter what the final assessment of strain theory turns out to be, there is no doubt that it has been one of the most influential and enduring criminological theories of the twentith century.[107]

GENERAL STRAIN THEORY:
Stress and Strain of Many Sorts Causes Crime

The idea that many types of strain (or stress), not just economic stress, may be a cause of crime can be traced back to the 1930s.[108] However, this view was formalized into a theory in the 1980s by a U.S. sociologist named **Robert Agnew** (1953–). He explicitly expanded Merton's original strain theory by arguing that it was not simply economic strain that increased the probability of crime and delinquency, but numerous other forms of social frustration as well. Through this theory, Agnew primarily sought to explain individual variations in offending behavior. A few years later, a version of general strain theory was proposed by another U.S. sociologist, **Thomas Bernard** to help explain racial variations in offending rates.

General Strain Theory in Brief

According to proponents of general strain theory, Merton was correct in underscoring the importance of stress on offending behavior, but focused too narrowly on strain of a financial nature. Agnew[109] reformulated Merton's theory by contending that other types of strain (or stress) can also increase an individual's chances of engaging in crime and delinquency. He arrived at his theory in part by noting that, in laboratory settings, aggression is a common response that subjects make to being repeatedly frustrated or exposed to unpleasant conditions.[110]

According to Agnew, almost any type of social adversity can increase the probability of criminal and delinquent behavior. He stipulated that social adversity falls into three categories: failure to achieve one's goals, removal of positively valued stimuli, and imposition of negative stimuli.[111] Theoretically, whenever any of these unpleasant experiences is confronted, especially if it is chronic and intensely felt, an individual's chances of engaging in criminal and delinquent behavior will increase.[112]

Bernard's[113] version of general strain theory is different only in its tendency to focus on explaining group differences in offending, rather than on individual variations. In particular, Bernard has argued that crime rates, particularly for violent offenses, are unusually high among African Americans due to continual exposure to emotional strain. This strain is not simply economic in nature, but also extends into most other aspects of life,[114] and the reactions are often manifested in the forms of anger and violence.[115]

Evidence Pertaining to General Strain Theory

Because general strain theory builds on Merton's original theory, the hypotheses discussed with reference to the original theory can be considered relevant to the new version. Thus, general strain theory predicts that offending probabilities will be higher among those who fail to achieve financial success, as well as by those who do poorly in school. General strain theory makes predictions about additional variables.

Peer Relationships.   Studies have shown that delinquents are less popular with peers than is true for nondelinquents (Table 7.20). General strain theory predicts that this would be the case.[116]

Family Relationships.   General strain theory predicts that criminal and delinquent behavior will be highest among those who experience poor relationships with parents and spouses.[117] From this prediction one could also reason that families in which harsh and especially abusive discipline is practiced will have higher rates of offending among its members.[118] These predictions all conform with most of the available research (Table 7.8b). Similarly, to the degree that variables such as divorce, child abuse, alcoholism, and drug abuse in one's family or neighborhood can cause stress, general strain theory leads one to expect to find these factors associated with criminality, as

most studies suggest (regarding divorce: Table 7.4; regarding child abuse: Table 7.9; regarding alcoholism and drug abuse: Tables 7.11a & 7.11b).

Physical and Mental Health.   Numerous studies have indicated that prolonged emotional stress adversely affects both physical health[119] and mental health.[120] In the context of general strain theory, this evidence leads to the prediction that offenders will be less healthy and prone toward shorter life expectancies than persons in general. Evidence supports both of these predictions (Table 9.5b). In addition, a general strain theorist would not be surprised to find higher rates of mental illness among offenders, an expectation that is also consistent with most available evidence (Table 8.24).

Sexual Behavior.   Another prediction that can be derived from general strain theory is that being unpopular with members of the opposite sex should lead to delinquency and crime.[121] This prediction is inconsistent with evidence that criminals and delinquents are more sexually experienced (Table 8.11), and begin having sexual experiences earlier in life (Table 8.11), than is true for their more law-abiding peers.

Crime Victimization.   According to general strain theory, as another form of stress, offenders are likely to experience higher rates of crime victimization than is the case for people in general.[122] This expectation is consistent with nearly all of the research concerning the relationship between criminality and crime victimization (Table 5.11). Also consistent with general strain theory in this regard is evidence from a study conducted in Los Angeles. The study found that youth in low-status neighborhoods perceive their environment as more threatening than do youth in general, and that the youth who lived in the low-status neighborhoods exhibited unusually high rates of depression, anxiety, oppositional defiant disorder, and conduct disorder.[123]

Cortisol.   General strain theory implies that one should find physiological evidence of greater feelings of stress among offenders than among people in general. The evidence on this point is somewhat mixed, in that, while short-term stress elevates cortisol, long-term stress seems to lower cortisol levels.[124] Most studies have found that offenders secrete lower levels of cortisol than do persons in general, suggesting that they might be exhibiting an "habituating" response to long-term stress (Table 9.16).

Racial/Ethnic Differences.   General strain theory may help explain why certain racial/ethnic minorities are more heavily involved in crime than others. Theoretically, those that must confront the greatest economic, health, and social hardships should be those that engage in serious offending to the greatest degree. This would coincide with evidence that crime rates are unusually high among generally low social status blacks (Table 5.3a), Native Americans (Table 5.3b), and Hispanics (Table 5.3c) in North America, while generally high social status groups, such as East Asians (Table 5.3d) and Jews (Tables 7.23c and 7.23d), exhibit unusually low rates.

Gender and Age.   To account for gender differences in offending, general strain theory predicts that males experience stress at substantially higher levels than is true for females. However, throughout the world, studies have repeatedly documented the opposite: Females rather than males report experiencing more stress and anxiety in their lives.[125]

In order to accommodate this contrary evidence within general strain theory, proponents of the theory have argued that there seem to be differences in *how* males and females respond to stress that accounts for the higher rates of offending among males.[126] In particular, males appear to be more inclined to respond to stressors with angry combative responses, whereas females respond more with withdrawal self-blaming responses.[127]

In the case of age, general strain theory suggests that the adolescent-early adulthood peek in crime is due to an increase in negative, stressful relationships with others.[128] The relevant research has found only a slight, usually nonsignificant, tendency for teens and young adults to experience higher levels of stress and anxiety than do persons in other age categories.[129]

Closing Remarks about General Strain Theory

According to the original version of strain theory, people become criminal and delinquent out of the frustrations they experience in attempting to achieve financial goals that they are ill-equipped to achieve. Their difficulty in achieving goals is attributed primarily to a lack of academic skills needed to compete in modern societies.

The broader version of strain theory—called *general strain theory*—asserts that many types of stress will produce criminal and delinquent behavior, provided that individuals are repeatedly exposed to it. In general strain theory, the main mediating factors between stressful experiences and offending behavior are emotional feelings of anger and frustration.[130] General strain theory makes several predictions beyond that of the original version, and most of those predictions have been supported by evidence.[131]

In terms of weaknesses, general strain theory has difficulty explaining gender differences in crime rates, although there may be differences in how men and women respond to strain that could support the theory. Also, general strain theory has not yet led to the development of serious attempts to reduce rates of crime or delinquency beyond programs developed under the original version of strain theory.

SOCIAL DISORGANIZATION THEORY:
Disorganization in a Neighborhood Causes Crime

As noted in Chapter 4, the sociology department at the University of Chicago (known as the *Chicago School*) became world famous in academic circles for its studies of societies and social behavior.[132] The period of time during which the Chicago School dominated U.S. sociology was roughly from about 1910 through the 1940s.[133]

Among those who taught and conducted research in the Chicago School was **Robert Park**

(1864–1944). In the 1920s, Park coauthored a book entitled *The City* in which a **concentric-zone theory of urban development** was presented.[134] This theory contended that cities usually develop in a recognizable pattern, with the central business and manufacturing district at the center, surrounded by what Park called a **zone of transition,** then working-class neighborhoods, followed by middle- and upper-class neighborhoods.[135]

Over a decade later, other members of the Chicago School applied Park's concentric-zone theory specifically to the study of crime, most notably **Clifford R. Shaw** (1896–1957) and **Henry D. McKay** (1899–1980). According to Shaw and McKay,[136] the business and manufacturing districts and the zones of transition identified by Park were particularly conducive to crime, and they offered a theory for why this was so.[137]

Shaw and McKay became keenly committed to studying ecological variations in Chicago's crime rates during the turmoil of the 1930s and 1940s, when Al Capone and other notorious gangsters terrorized Chicago neighborhoods. Nonetheless, Shaw and McKay did not direct their research toward studying mobsters. Instead, they concentrated on the most common forms of juvenile offenders.

Social Disorganization Theory In Brief

According to **social disorganization theory,** crime and delinquency are primarily the result of neighborhood social disorganization, particularly as occurs in large urban environments.[138] Three urban conditions are thought to be especially conducive to social disorganization: poverty, cultural heterogeneity, and physical mobility.[139] Under these three conditions, residents of a neighborhood have a diminished probability of perpetuating a common set of social norms, including norms that discourage antisocial conduct.[140]

If one were to identify the type of social ecological conditions that would be *least* conducive to crime and delinquency using Shaw and McKay's theory, it would be a small prosperous community of people who share a common ethnic heritage, and in which there is little in or out migration. Theoretically, crime rates will be unusually low under these conditions because the social norms of the community are well entrenched, and the community's social organization is carefully maintained by individuals who have a clear stake in the community's preservation.[141]

Shaw and McKay were in agreement with other members of the Chicago School that neither genetics nor early childhood experiences were important in affecting crime rates.[142] Instead, they saw the crucial determinants of people's varying tendencies toward crime and delinquency as the socioecological circumstances of the community in which people live.[143]

Historically, it is worth noting that social disorganization theory originated in the 1930s, and that the theory seemed to be instigated by the social upheaval created by several waves of European immigrants to Chicago and other growing U.S. cities throughout the late 1800s and early 1900s. As each new wave of immigrants came into Chicago, they tended to take up residence in the poorest sections of the city (i.e., in the business/manufacturing or zones of transition), just as those in the prior wave could afford to move elsewhere. Shaw and McKay[144] suspected that it was the continual mix of cultures, combined with poverty and the turmoil that comes with moving itself, that was contributing to Chicago's (and the United States') crime problem in the affected neighborhoods.[144]

Evidence Bearing on Social Disorganization Theory

Urban/Rural Factors. Social disorganization theory predicts that crime rates will be highest in urban areas. This prediction is consistent with nearly all of the available evidence (Table 6.1a). In addition, within large cities, intercity areas have higher crime rates than do surrounding suburban areas (Table 6.1a), as social disorganization theory predicts.

Geographical Mobility. Social disorganization theory suggests that crime and delinquency will be higher among persons who frequently change res-

TABLE 11.3. Results from studies that have assessed the effects on recidivism of crime/delinquency treatment programs designed in accordance with labeling theory. (Shaded cells represent where studies should be located in order to be supportive of labeling theory. No relevant controlled experiments were located.)

Program	Observed Effect on Criminal Recidivism	Quasi-Experimental or Comparative Studies
Diversion Program	Preventive Effect	**Europe** *England:* 2 **North America** *United States:* 6
	Not significant or Ambiguous Effect	**North America** *United States:* 6 **Pacific** *Australia:* 1
	Promotive Effect	**North America** *United States:* 1
Self-Concept Enhancement Program	Preventive Effect	**North America** *United States:* 1
	Not significant or Ambiguous Effect	**North America** *United States:* 1
	Promotive Effect	

part of their treatment begins with a bus ride to a maximum security prison. Besides getting a tour of the prison, the youngsters spend two or three hours "rapping" with a half-dozen or so prison inmates specially picked for their no-nonsense depictions of the brutal nature of life behind bars.[189] As each session draws to a close, the youngsters are sternly warned in coarse street language by the inmates that the youngsters themselves are going to end up in "this Hell Hole" unless they change their "#@!*X~!#" ways. It is common for the youngsters to be spirited and jovial in the morning, but sobbing by the time they leave their final session with the inmates.

Supporters of the program believe scared straight is effective, and there are several anecdotal accounts from former participants to bolster this belief.[190] Labeling theorists, on the other hand, would view scared straight as epitomizing how *not* to deal with delinquents, because it is likely to reinforce their deviant self-concept. Along these lines, one critic of scared straight called the program "scared crooked."[191]

What does the evidence suggest? As you can see in Table 11.4, most of the studies of scared straight have indicated that the program has no significant effects on future delinquency. One study

suggested that the program significantly reduced recidivism, and another indicated that it actually increased recidivism to a significant degree. In terms of labeling theory, the bulk of the findings can be considered only slightly supportive because the

Bottom Liners

9/9

"I've learned a lot in the in-prison training program—I don't think I'll get caught again."

TABLE 11.4.   Results from studies that have assessed the effects of scared straight-type programs and shaming programs on recidivism rates. (Shaded cells represent where studies should be clustered if they support labeling theory.)

Program	Observed Effect on Criminal Recidivism	Studies and Countries in Which Studies Were Conducted	
		Controlled Experimental Studies	**Quasi-Experimental or Comparative Studies**
Scared Straight Program	Inhibiting		**North America** *United States:* 1
	Not significant or Ambiguous	**North America** *United States:* 2	**North America** *United States:* 2
	Promoting		**North America** *United States:* 1
Shaming Program	Inhibiting		**North America** *United States:* 1
	Not significant or Ambiguous		
	Promoting		

theory suggests that scared straight should actually increase the probability of future offending or at least have no beneficial effects.

The other type of program that labeling theory suggests will have detrimental effects on offenders is called shaming. **Shaming programs** require offenders to publicly humiliate themselves, such as by wearing placards or displaying bumper stickers proclaiming the nature of the crime they have committed.[192] Shaming has been used extensively in Japan as an integral part of the correctional process.[193] However, it was not until the 1990s that Western societies began to experiment with it on a sizable scale.

An example of a recently tried shaming program has involved shoplifters. As part of their punishment, these offenders are required to stand in front of the store from which they shoplifted wearing a sign reading "I shoplifted at this store, and this is my punishment" for several hours each day for a couple of weeks. Labeling theory predicts that shaming will be counterproductive, because it will serve to reinforce the label of *criminal,* in both the eyes of the offender and those who know him/her.[194]

It should be added that most shaming programs have what proponents term a **reintegrative component.** This refers to a time following the punishment phase when attempts are made to reintegrate the offender into the community.[195] Therefore, shaming programs are not intended to permanently humiliate and reinforce a criminal self-image in offenders. Nonetheless, labeling theory would predict that if shaming programs have any effect, it will be to facilitate criminal labeling, and thereby *increase* future offending.

As you can see in Table 11.4, scientific research on the effects of shaming is in its infancy. The only study published so far on its effects has to do with requiring drunk drivers to put a bumper sticker on their vehicle for a month stating that they had received a drunk driving conviction. Contrary to labeling theory, this study suggested that drunk driving was significantly curtailed subsequent to drunk driving convictions compared to a control group of drunk drivers handled in more conventional ways (warnings and suspended driving).[196]

Closing Comments on Labeling Theory

While its origins go back at least to the 1930s, labeling theory did not catch on in criminology until the 1960s.[197] By the mid-1970s, the theory began receiving heavy criticism for its limited ability to generate supportive hypotheses.[198] Its popularity among criminologists in recent years is low.[199]

One critic charged that labeling theory is "long on theory and short on empirical evidence."[200] Another contended that "the available evidence indicates that deviant labels are primarily a consequence of deviant behavior and [not] a primary cause."[201] If this latter point is valid, it would explain why variables such as self-concept, parental and peer rejection, and social status could all be correlated with criminality without supporting the crux of labeling theory. In other words, what labeling theorists see as causes (the labels) are merely the effects of the criminal and delinquent behavior.[202]

Despite its lackluster performance on strictly scientific grounds, labeling theory has contributed to the diversity of thought in criminology, particularly in terms of inspiring innovative approaches to offender treatment. In addition, as will be seen in Chapter 12, labeling theory helped set the stage for another important theory in criminology—conflict (or critical) theory.

SUBCULTURE OF VIOLENCE THEORY:
Groups and Regions Differ in their Use of Violence to Solve Interpersonal Conflicts

In the 1960s, two U.S. sociologists named **Marvin Wolfgang** (1924–1998) and **Franco Ferracuti** (1927–1992), advanced what has come to be known as the **subculture of violence theory.** With a focus on murders and assaults, the theory maintains that, at least within the United States, some subcultures exist that encourage the use of violence in settling interpersonal disputes.

Subculture of Violence Theory in Brief

Wolfgang and Ferracuti[203] were struck by variations in crime both by region of the United States and according to race/ethnicity. They described the existence of subcultures consisting of young, lower-class, inner-city males in which violence is considered the normal way to settle disputes.[204] You may recall that most studies, especially those conducted prior to the 1980s, found violent crime

rates in the United States to be unusually high in southern states (Table 6.28). Regarding race, U.S. violent crime rates are particularly high for African Americans (Table 5.3a), whose proportions are also particularly high in the southern United States. Wolfgang and Ferracuti theorized that there may be subcultural attitudes and values that are much more prevalent in certain regions, ethnic groups, and even social classes that promote the use of violence, including criminal violence.[205]

Wolfgang, Ferracuti, and other subculture of violence theorists have characterized features of subcultures conducive to violence as those in which settling disputes through the use of force is highly valued.[206] Evidence of high values being placed on the use of physical force would include the use of severe punishment both inside and outside the home.[207]

Regarding factors responsible for the emergence of a subculture of violence in the southern states of the United States, various proposals have been made. These proposals have ranged from blaming the South's defeat in the American Civil War (1861–1865) to suggesting that it still exhibits a lingering "feudal spirit" in which personal disputes are seen as calling for duels and other extralegal "solutions."[208] This latter proposal is in line with the subculture of violence theory in the sense that the relatively high murder rate in the southern United States seems to have preceded the outbreak of the Civil War.[209]

Evidence Pertaining to the Subculture of Violence Theory

Race/Ethnicity. One of the most obvious hypotheses that has been derived from the subculture of violence theory has to do with explaining racial/ethnic variations in crime. In particular, it has been proposed that African Americans have relatively high rates of homicide, robbery, and serious assaults because of their unique experiences in the United States, first as slaves and later as an underclass repeatedly confronted by prejudice and discrimination. Such reasoning is consistent with evidence that African Americans have the highest violent crime rate of all racial/ethnic groups in the United States and South Africa, where slavery has been practiced. However, even in countries with no race-based slave practices, such as England, Israel, and Canada, studies have found violent crime rates to still be unusually high among blacks (Table 5.3a). This led at least one proponent of the subculture of violence theory to propose that the cultural values linked to high rates of interpersonal violence among blacks originated in Africa itself, although prejudice and discrimination by non-Africans may have helped to preserve and exaggerate the behavior in other parts of the world.[210]

The subculture of violence theory would predict that, as the proportion of blacks in a region becomes increasingly concentrated, the rate of violent crime should rise.[211] The reason is that subcultural traditions are assumed to partly depend on the concentration of persons carrying the particular subculture. This deduction is consistent with evidence that the percent black in a population is positively correlated with the population's crime rate (Table 5.3a).

However, you will recall that blacks have unusually high rates of poverty and single-parent families, and both of these latter variables are also correlates of crime (Tables 5.5b and 7.4). Some researchers have proposed that poverty and single-parent households are more important in explaining high rates of violent crime among blacks than any "black subculture." Several studies have been undertaken to test this poverty-causes-violence hypothesis as an alternative to the subculture of violence explanation. The results of these studies have been mixed. At least three studies have concluded that, after controlling for poverty, rates of divorce, and the like (in other words, statistically eliminate their presumed influence), the percent black in a population was no longer significantly correlated with the cities' homicide rates.[212] These findings suggest that such variables as poverty and single-parent households rather than some unique aspect of black subculture are responsible for the link between homicide rates and percent black in a population. However, two other studies were unable to account for most of the higher homicide

rates among blacks by controlling for poverty and other presumably extraneous variables.[213] Unlike the first three studies, these latter two appear supportive of the subculture of violence theory.

Regarding other racial/ethnic groups, one study of counties in the United States found that, as the percent of a county's population that was either Native American or Hispanic increased so too did the county's rates of violent crime, almost as much as did a population's percent black.[214] Such evidence suggests that if blacks really do exhibit a subculture of violence, they are not alone in this regard.

Attitudes.   A hypothesis that can be drawn from the subculture of violence theory is that persons who hold favorable attitudes toward the use of violence will engage in violent crime more than persons who do not hold such attitudes.[215] This hypothesis has received mixed support.

On the one hand, U.S. citizens living in the southern region of the country express more support for (or at least tolerance of) the use of violence to settle problems than do those from other regions of the country.[216] Similarly, a U.S. survey found much greater support for use of the death penalty in the south than in other regions.[217]

As far as social status differences are concerned, several U.S. studies have found that lower status persons express greater approval for use of physical punishment in childhood discipline than is true for middle- and upper-status parents.[218] Similarly, a British study found violence endorsed more by persons of low social status under various types of social conflict than was true for middle- and upper-status persons.[219] These findings would all be consistent with Wolfgang and Ferracuti's theory since violent crime tends to be inversely correlated with social status.

On the other hand, some attitudinal studies have failed to support the subculture of violence theory. For instance, a study of males in the United States found whites more likely to endorse the use of violence in various hypothetical defensive situations than was true for African Americans. In the case of hypothetical offensive situations, there was no significant difference between the two groups.[220] Other studies have found essentially no significant social status differences in attitudes toward the use of violence to settle interpersonal disputes.[221] One study compared prisoners and the general public, and failed to find significant differences in their tendencies to justify the use of violence in most everyday situations.[222]

Self-Esteem.   Another test of the subculture of violence theory involved looking for evidence that self-esteem among violent persons would be higher for those living in violent subcultures than for those living in nonviolent subcultures. This hypothesis was tested by comparing attitudes among subpopulations of relatively poor and well-off Anglo Americans and African Americans in the United States. The conclusion was that there was only a slight nonsignificant tendency for persons who lived in violent subcultures who were themselves violent to have higher self-esteem than their violent counterparts living in nonviolent subcultures.[223]

Child Discipline and Abuse.   To the degree that culture is socially transmitted from parent to child, the subculture of violence theory implies that persons who engage in violence will have been reared by parents who also displayed above average levels of violence. This could explain the well-established relationship between harsh child discipline pattern experienced to an unusual degree by criminals and delinquents (especially those who engage in violent offenses). It could also account for the well-established link between violent crime and child abuse (Table 7.9).

Closing Comments on the Subculture of Violence Theory

According to the subculture of violence theory, certain populations and geographical regions in the United States, have traditions that facilitate and thrive on the use of violence to solve interpersonal disputes. A relatively limited number of hypotheses have been derived from the subculture of violence theory, and only a minority of them have been confirmed.

Probably the greatest shortcoming of the subculture of violence theory is that it has led to only a few testable hypotheses, most notably that violent crime will vary according to subcultural groups such as those linked to race/ethnicity and regionality. The hypotheses have not fit with the evidence very well. Another limitation of the theory is that it was formulated with the United States in mind, and consequently few have attempted to test the theory in any other country.

Also, it should be mentioned that the subculture of violence theory has been criticized for containing circular reasoning.[224] By this, critics mean that high violent crime rates are often used to identify violent subcultures, and then having a violent subculture is used to explain the high violent crime rates.

Despite the shortcomings of the subculture of violence theory, it appears to be the single "most prominent explanation for the disproportionate involvement of blacks in criminal violence."[225] Overall, the subculture of violence theory is a "narrow" theory in three respects. First, it purports only to explain one category of crime: violent offenses.[226] Second, only a few hypotheses have been derived from the theory. Third, the theory was essentially designed only to explain variations in violent crime rates within the United States.

GENERAL REMARKS ABOUT THE THEORIES IN THIS CHAPTER

Theories reviewed in this chapter helped launch criminology into the twentieth century. These theories share the assumption that there are subcultures and ecological conditions that affect how people think about the acceptability of criminal behavior. As we have seen, these theories vary considerably in their predictive power and scope.

One criticism lodged against most of the theories in this chapter is that the concept of *subculture* has never been clearly defined to the satisfaction of most social scientists.[227] This has made it difficult to develop ways to clearly test hypotheses derived from some of these theories.

SUMMARY

Like the theories reviewed in Chapter 10, those in this chapter assume that the causes of crime and delinquency are to be found in the social environment. The theories discussed in Chapter 10 focused on failures to socialize children with regard to universally accepted rules of social interaction. On the other hand, the theories covered by this chapter emphasized how various subcultural elements sometimes instill values that conflict with what the majority culture deems criminal. The six theories reviewed in this chapter were differential association theory, social learning theory, strain theory, social disorganization theory, labeling theory, and subculture of violence theory.

Differential Association Theory

The first theory considered was differential association theory, a theory advocated by Edward Sutherland beginning in the 1930s, and later defended by Donald Cressey. At the heart of differential association theory is the concept of **definitions favorable to law violations.** According to differential association theory, these definitions are gradually acquired through frequent contacts with those who already happen to hold such definitions. Sutherland and Cressey took as a given that definitions favorable to law violations would often vary across classes and subcultures.

Social Learning Theory

Social learning theory was conceived in the 1960s by Robert Burgess and Ronald Akers as one that would improve differential association theory by better accounting for how criminal and delinquent behavior is sometimes viewed as acceptable behavior. According to this theory, reinforced learning may sometimes not even be intended by those who are providing the reinforcement. In addition, imitation and modeling are often elements in intergenerational and peer transmission of definitions favorable to law violations.

A more recent version of social learning theory has been put forth by Gerald Patterson. Without employing the concept of definitions favorable to law violations, Patterson asserts that the responses of parents, teachers, and peers to those who engage in antisocial behavior often serve to reinforce such behavior early in life. From this, Patterson has sought behaviorist approaches to the treatment of various forms of conduct disorders.

Strain Theory

About the same time that Sutherland formulated differential association theory, another U.S. sociologist proposed what has come to be known as strain theory, or goals–means incompatibility theory. This theory asserts that crime and delinquency primarily result from having learned to desire difficult-to-achieve material possessions while having been denied the means to achieve those goals. According to strain theory, those who find their desires continually surpassing their grasp using legitimate means will often resort to the use of illegitimate means. The foremost proponent of strain theory is Robert Merton.

General Strain Theory

Merton's version of strain theory only considered economic strain as leading to crime and delinquency. This prompted Robert Agnew to suggest that any type of strain (stress) can bring about criminal and delinquent behavior. Another proponent of general strain theory is Thomas Bernard, although his focus has been on using the theory to explain racial variations in crime rates.

Social Disorganization Theory

The social disorganization theory of Clifford Shaw and Henry McKay sought the causes of crime among the elements of large city neighborhoods that seemed to be culturally heterogeneous, lacking in social organization, and poverty. Consequently, Shaw and McKay saw in early twentieth century Chicago changing immigrant neighborhoods sowing the seeds for crime and delinquency.

Labeling Theory

Derived from an approach to the study of human behavior called *symbolic interactionism,* labeling theory contends that criminality and other forms of deviance come about because various acts of initial deviance cause people to be stigmatized by others. These stigmatizations have a tendency to become reality, both in the minds of others and, ultimately, in the minds of those who are stigmatized. The main proponents of labeling theory are Lemert and Tannenbaum.

Subculture of Violence Theory

As proposed by Marvin Wolfgang and Franco Ferracuti, the subculture of violence theory was designed to explain why criminal violence seem to be more heavily concentrated in some geographical regions and racial/ethnic groups than in others. In particular, the theory was offered to help account for the unusually high rates of violent crime in the southern United States among African Americans. The theory contends that various historical circumstances have produced certain subcultures that encourage violent "solutions" to interpersonal conflicts.

SUGGESTED READINGS

American Sociological Association (1996). *Social causes of violence: Crafting a science agenda.* Washington, DC: American Sociological Association. (Provides a clearly written summary of proposals regarding social causes of variations in violent crime, with a special emphasis on the importance of most of the variables discussed in this chapter.)

Schur, Edwin M. (1973). *Radical non-intervention: Rethinking the delinquency problem.* Englewood Cliffs, NJ: Prentice-Hall. (This book has as its theme the view that delinquency is often best treated by doing nothing. Such a belief flowed out of the labeling perspective, which asserted that the more attention that is given to an individual's deviant behavior, the more likely he/she is to repeat the behavior.)

Shoham, Giora S., & Rahav, Giora (1982). *The mark of Cain: The stigma theory of crime and social deviance (rev. ed.)* St. Lucia, Queensland, Australia: University of Queensland Press. (For a balanced treatment of the evidence for and against labeling theory that was available up to the early 1980s, this book is highly recommended.)

Sutherland, Edward (1934). *Principles of Criminology.* Philadelphia: Lippincott. (In this classic first edition, Sutherland articulates his original version of differential association theory. By the 1960s, this book had gradually evolved into the most widely used criminology textbook in North America, a position it held until the 1970s.)

Wright, Kevin N., & Wright, Karen E. (1995). *Family life, delinquency, and crime: A policymaker's guide.* Washington, DC: U.S. Department of Justice (Office of Juvenile Justice and Delinquency Prevention). (This short book provides a great deal of useful information on how the family seems to play an important role in crime causation. It is particularly relevant to Patterson's family learning theory, as well as to control theory.)

EXERCISES

1. This chapter reviewed some of the most influential and resilient criminological theories ever proposed. It is noteworthy that four of them are directly traceable to the University of Chicago. What are the names of these four theories? Now write a one- to two-page essay about the University of Chicago's famous sociology department based on information obtained from the library and/or through the Internet.

2. Identify at least two correlates of crime that you think might be relevant to one of the theories discussed in this chapter besides those that are actually discussed. Then write a one- to two-page essay on how you see this theory as being possibly relevant to these two correlates of crime.

3. Locate and read a professional social science article having to do with one of the theories presented in this chapter. Choose an article that seems to objectively test one or more hypotheses derived from the theory that you feel you can understand. Then write a one- to two-page double-spaced paper summarizing the nature of the study and what it found. Unless the expense is prohibitive, you should photocopy the article, making sure the citation is complete, and hand it in with your paper. If you can't photocopy the entire article, at least make a copy of the first page (containing the title, journal name, and abstract). Be sure to write your interpretation of the article using your own words; do not simply paraphrase the abstract or the conclusions.

ENDNOTES

1. Sutherland 1934.
2. Masters & Roberson 1990:204.
3. Gibbons 1987:185; Masters & Roberson 1990:202.
4. Wilson 1954:4.
5. Sutherland & Chressey 1974.
6. Laub & Sampson 1991:1413.
7. Sutherland & Cressey 1974:77.
8. Matsueda 1988; Vold & Bernard 1986:211.
9. Jensen 1972b.
10. Jaquith 1981.
11. Menard & Huizinga 1994:24.
12. Reed & Roundtree 1997:145.
13. Hindelang 1974; Menard & Huizinga 1994:38.
14. Maccoby et al. 1958:48.
15. Jensen 1972b; Warr & Stafford 1991.
16. Heimer 1997; Matsueda 1982.
17. Gibbs 1987:834.
18. Siegel 1998:200.
19. Sutherland & Cressey 1974:77.
20. Gottfredson & Hirschi 1990:124; Masters & Roberson 1990:208.
21. Leonard 1995:61.
22. R. A. Feldman 1992.
23. Tremblay & Craig 1995:195.
24. Rowe & Osgood 1984.
25. Hagan et al. 1998:311.
26. Akers 1977; Akers 1979; Akers et al. 1979; Burgess & Akers 1966.
27. Kandel 1980:253; Winfree et al. 1994:148.
28. Burgess & Akers 1966.
29. Maguin & Loeber 1996:153.
30. B. F. Skinner 1953:188.
31. B. F. Skinner 1953:125.
32. Burgess & Akers 1966.
33. Bandura 1971, 1977, 1985.
34. Akers et al. 1979.
35. Krohn et al. 1987:458.
36. Larzelere & Patterson 1990:305; Patterson 1982, 1996; Patterson & Reid 1970.
37. Patterson & Reid 1984; Snyder & Patterson 1987.
38. D. S. Shaw & Bell 1993.
39. D. S. Shaw & Bell 1993:512.
40. Patterson & Moore 1979.
41. Patterson 1997.
42. Larzelere & Patterson 1990:306.
43. Simons et al. 1994.
44. Patterson & Yoerger 1997:123.
45. Brezina 1998; Hogan & Jones 1983:6.
46. Bandura & Walters 1959.
47. Widom 1989; Zingraff et al. 1993, 1994.
48. Simons et al. 1994.
49. Patterson 1997:91.
50. Binder 1988:275; Braukmann & Wolf 1987; E. L. Phillips et al. 1971.
51. Braukmann & Wolf 1987:136.
52. Ayllon & Azrin 1968; Milan 1987.

53. Jenkins et al. 1974.

54. Hartmann et al 1997:18; Wexler 1994:354.

55. Kratcoski & Kratcoski 1982; Wexler et al. 1990:72.

56. Blakely & Davidson 1984; Braukmann & Wolf 1987:152; Redner et al. 1983.

57. Patterson et al. 1989:333.

58. Stuart 1971.

59. Wexler et al. 1990.

60. Mayer et al. 1986; Wexler et al. 1988.

61. Akers et al. 1979:635.

62. Akers & Cochran 1985.

63. Gove 1985:122.

64. Patterson 1997.

65. Merton 1938, 1968.

66. Nettler 1984:205.

67. Durkheim 1952:246.

68. Merton 1938.

69. Nettler 1984:207.

70. Greenberg 1988:194.

71. A. Cohen 1955, 1965.

72. A. Cohen 1955:121.

73. Cloward & Ohlin 1960.

74. Cloward & Ohlin 1960.

75. Agnew 1984:435; Blau & Blau 1982:117; Myerhoff & Myerhoff 1964:329.

76. 1985, 1992.

77. Brownfield 1986:427; Raine 1993:277; Wilkinson et al. 1982:223.

78. Cohen & Machalek 1988:481.

79. Chesney-Lind & Sheldon 1992; Gove 1985:124.

80. Warren 1979.

81. Agnew 1993:246; Farrington et al. 1986:339; Thornberry et al. 1985:4.

82. Thornberry et al. 1985:16.

83. Durkheim 1952:247.

84. DeGrazia 1948:71.

85. Farnworth & Leiber 1989:264.

86. Cantor & Land 1985:319.

87. Elliott 1962.

88. Polk 1969:210; Quicker 1974:81.

89. Keane 1993.

90. D. H. Kelly & Blach 1971:424.

91. Krohn 1978.

92. Furnham 1984:411.

93. Burton & Cullen 1992.

94. Nettler 1984:206.

95. Jeffery 1977:167; Masters & Robinson 1990:146.

96. Castleman 1984:195; Jeffery 1977:166.

97. Berrueta-Chement et al. 1984.

98. Holden 1990:1402.

99. Greenberg 1988.

100. Braithwaite & Braithwaite 1978:25.

101. Braithwaite & Braithwaite 1978:31.

102. Paternoster & Mazerolle 1994:236.

103. Agnew 1995:371.

104. Agnew 1992:47; Arnold & Brungardt 1983:149; Brownfield 1986:435; Hirschi 1969; Kornhauser 1978.

105. Menard 1995.

106. Raine 1993:272.

107. Agnew & White 1992:475; Farnworth & Leiber 1989:263.

108. Brearley 1932.

109. 1985, 1989, 1992.

110. Berkowitz 1982; Mueller 1983.

111. Agnew 1992.

112. Agnew 1995:365; Paternoster & Mazerolli 1994.

113. Bernard 1990a.

114. Bernard 1990a:81.

115. Agnew 1997:122; Averill 1982:142.

116. Agnew 1989:375.

117. Agnew & White 1992.

118. Brezina 1998.

119. DeLongis et al. 1982; Holms & Masuda 1974; Hui 1993; McEwen & Stellar 1993; Rahe et al. 1967; Zarski 1984.

120. McFarlane et al. 1980; Mueller et al. 1977; Tausig 1982; Vinokor & Kaplan 1986.

121. Agnew & White 1992:483.

122. Agnew 1989:375.

123. Aneshensel & Sucoff 1996.

124. Bauer et al. 1994; Bourne et al. 1968.

125. Barnett & Baruch 1987; Bush et al. 1987; Compas 1987; Compas et al. 1985; Ember 1981:568; Nakazato & Shimonaka 1989.

126. Broidy & Agnew 1997:281.

127. Nolen-Hoeksema 1987.

128. Agnew 1997:123.

129. Costa et al. 1983; Nakazato & Shimonaka 1989.

130. Agnew 1992; Bernard 1990a:81; Paternoster & Mazerolli 1994:253.

131. Paternoster & Mazerolli 1994.

132. Short 1998:5.

133. Blumer 1984.

134. Park & McKenzie 1925.

135. Lachmann 1991:57; Pettiway 1985:191.

136. Shaw & McKay 1942, 1969, 1972.

137. Bursik 1986:37.

138. Empey 1982:190.

139. Siegel 1989:165.

140. Keys 1987:15.

141. Bursik 1986:38.
142. Empey 1982:190; Keys 1987:13.
143. Rose & Clear 1998:443.
144. Shaw & McKay 1969:105.
145. Land et al. 1990:925.
146. Reiss 1986:18; Shaw & McKay 1942; Wirth 1938.
147. Nettler 1984:141.
148. Empey 1982:191.
149. Land et al. 1990:925.
150. Bursik & Grasmick 1993:263.
151. Keys 1987:15.
152. Empey 1982:193; Keys 1987:24.
153. Keys 1987:28.
154. Keys 1987:27; Kobrin 1959.
155. Eysenck & Gudjonsson 1989:193.
156. Gonzales et al. 1996:367.
157. Cooley 1902.
158. Paternoster & Iovanni 1989:362.
159. Weisheit & Culbertson 1985:73.
160. Becker 1963:31.
161. Tannenbaum 1938.
162. Lemert 1951, 1953; also see Becker 1963, 1964.
163. Conklin 1986:249.
164. Evans et al. 1991:60.
165. Lemert 1974.
166. G. A. Fisher & Erickson 1973:178.
167. Lilly et al. 1995:118.
168. Smith & Brame 1994:624.
169. Klein 1986:75; Paternoster & Iovanni 1989:382.
170. Lofland 1969:178; also see Sherman et al. 1992:682.
171. Gove 1975.
172. Paternoster & Iovanni 1989:363.
173. Gold 1970; Gold & Williams 1969; Palamara et al. 1986; Ray & Downs 1986.
174. Farrington 1977.
175. Fisher & Erickson 1973:193; Hayes 1972:84.
176. Farrington et al. 1978; Klein 1974.
177. Evans et al. 1991:61.
178. R. L. Simons et al. 1980:45.
179. J. P. Gibbs 1974; A. R. Harris 1976; Wells & Rankin 1983.
180. Paternoster & Iovanni 1989:384.
181. Klein 1986:75; Sherman et al. 1992.
182. Homant & Kennedy 1982:383.
183. G. A. Fisher & Erickson 1973:179.
184. Downs et al. 1997:1.
185. Gensheimer et al. 1986:52; Whitehead & Lab 1989:282.
186. Stott 1982:71; Wells & Rankin 1983:20.
187. Fitts & Hammer 1969.
188. Wells & Rankin 1983:20.
189. Lundman 1984:136; Waters & Wilson 1979.
190. Finckenauer 1982:211; B. Rice 1980; Waters & Wilson 1979.
191. Finckenauer 1979.
192. Braithwaite 1989; Scheff 1988.
193. Braithwaite & Mugford 1994:140.
194. Braithwaite 1989:16; Farrington 1977.
195. Braithwaite 1988, 1989; Braithwaite & Mugford 1994.
196. Grasmick et al. 1993.
197. Gove 1979:57; Kramer 1980:533; Paternoster & Iovanni 1989:359; Wolff 1987:106.
198. Arnold & Brungardt 1983:174; Grichting 1979:163; Mahoney 1974; Nettler 1984:282; Tittle 1975; Wellford 1975.
199. Ellis & Hoffman 1990:54; Ellis & Walsh 1999.
200. Gibbons 1987:181.
201. Gove 1975:296.
202. Nettler 1984:286.
203. Wolfgang & Ferracuti 1967.
204. McCall et al. 1992:290.
205. Erlanger 1974:83.
206. Staples 1986:139.
207. Gastil 1971:424.
208. Rice & Goldman 1994:371.
209. Gastil 1971:425.
210. Silberman 1978:123.
211. K. R. Williams 1984:284.
212. Blau & Blau 1982; Centerwall 1984; Sampson 1985:61.
213. Messner 1983; K. R. Williams 1984:289.
214. Kposowa et al. 1995:97.
215. D. F. Hawkins 1986:113.
216. Reed 1972.
217. Borg 1998:557.
218. Reviewed by Erlanger 1974:70.
219. Sparks 1976:60.
220. Cao et al. 1997.
221. Ball-Rokeach 1973:747; Gordon et al. 1963; Poland 1978.
222. Ball-Rokeach 1973.
223. Erlanger 1978:168.
224. Bursik & Grasmick 1993b:139; Erlanger 1978:163.
225. R. J. Sampson 1985:47.
226. Fishman 1984:49.
227. Hagan et al. 1998:310

CHAPTER 12

Macroenvironmental Theories

As discussed in Chapter 4, the nineteenth century French criminologist, Lacassagne, was the first to propose that the causes of crime are to be found not in the individual, the family, or even the local community, but in society at large. Even today, his pronouncement, "Societies get the criminals they deserve," strikes many criminologists and laypersons alike as containing more than a mere element of truth. This chapter examines criminological theories that focus on variables that are at the philosophical heart of what makes societies and cultures function.

Macrosociocultural theories (also called **macrotheories** or **structural theories**) focus on variables that pervade a society or culture. These variables include such things as cultural traditions as well as governmental policies and laws. Macrolevel variables can be distinguished from "lower (micro) level" variables such as those pertaining to individuals, families, and neighborhoods. In this chapter, four related theories will be examined. These theories are so wide-ranging that they are sometimes thought of as perspectives instead of theories. The closest we came to considering macrolevel theories before this chapter was in examining the social disorganization theory first developed by members of the famous Chicago School (p. 89). However, this theory really focused on neighborhoods and other social units within a society. Here our focus will be on factors that pervade an entire society or culture.

In addition to being wide-ranging, macrotheories can be distinguished from other criminological theories in at least three ways. First, they are often rhetorical, meaning they are argumentative and emotionally provocative. Second, macrotheories often have political overtones that are more apparent than in other criminological theories. Third, these theories all contend that inequality between social groups is central to understanding variations in crime probabilities. Most macrotheorists do not specifically deny individual variations in propensities toward law-violating behavior, but they choose to focus on explaining variations between classes of people.

The main theories to be examined in this chapter are radical (or neo-Marxian) theory, critical theory, feminist theory, and power–control theory. Each focuses on some aspect of societal inequality as the main driving force behind criminality: Radical theory concentrates on inequality in wealth; critical theory, on inequality in political power; and both feminist theory and power–control theory, on inequality between men and women. Before examining these theories, we will set the stage by discussing the socialist tradition in criminology.

THE SOCIALIST TRADITION IN CRIMINOLOGY:
Capitalism Causes Crime

One of the most influential figures in world history is Karl Marx. He is particularly unique in having simultaneously impacted governmental policies, the course of world history, as well as theorizing in the social sciences. As we will see, this impact has included criminology.

Karl Marx: Returning to Man's Original State

Karl Marx (1818–1883) was a German political philosopher/social scientist. After receiving a Ph.D. in political studies at a German university, Marx became actively involved in writing for various underground socialist newspapers. The basic theme of Marx's articles had to do with exposing the misery of everyday workers in Europe during the mid-1800s, a time when the industrial age was just beginning to envelope continental Europe.

Marx's publications eventually resulted in his expulsion from Germany, whereupon he moved to Paris, and became friends and a writing collaborator with **Frederick Engels** (1820–1895), a well-to-do German businessman. Despite Engels's business background, he became convinced of Marx's arguments about the need for societies to give factory workers fuller access to the profits of their labors, and together they wrote a book proclaiming their belief. It was entitled the **Communist Manifesto.** Soon after this book was published in 1848, Marx and Engels left France, and moved to London. In London, Marx set to writing his most famous book of all, **Das Kapital** (or **Capital**).

A major theme running throughout Marx's writings was that humans are inherently caring and cooperative creatures. To support his argument on this matter, Marx pointed to small foraging societies in which all members share resources and help one another for the common good. Marx believed that once humans began staking out private plots of land and declaring ownership over these plots, a sad perversion of human nature began to occur. Land and other resources became increasingly unevenly distributed. Eventually, surplus goods began to be produced and certain classes of people found themselves barely able to stay alive because of the greed of others. By the time industrial societies had emerged, two fairly distinct classes had emerged. One controlled the means of production and the other did the actual work.

Marx contended that so much wealth would eventually become concentrated in the hands of those who controlled the means of production that the workers would revolt and then establish cooperatives to manage the factories, allowing them to share profits more or less equitably. According to Marx, this revolution would be accomplished by first establishing a governmental bureaucracy that would enforce and oversee a return to human cooperation and sharing. Marx called this phase **socialism.**[1] Eventually, as resistance to the cooperative/sharing mode of production was subdued, the government would "wither away" and **communism** would emerge. In this way, Marx believed that humans would be returning to their original "natural" state, with minimum governmental presence or interference.

The notion of a struggle between social classes is central to Marxian writings.[2] Marx used the term **class** to refer to people's varying degrees of access to the means of generating capital (wealth). In capitalist societies, the owners of the means of production (meaning factory owners) were called the **bourgeoisie** (*bŏr-zhwa ze´*), and those who worked in the factories and stores were the **proletariat** (*prō lĕ tăr´ ē ĕt*).[3]

While Marx wrote little about crime, he (in conjunction with Engels) implied that crime resulted from the suffering brought on by the gross economic inequities inherent in capitalism.[4] Marx believed that capitalism demoralized the proletariat, thereby creating an immoral subclass[5] that he and Engels[6] called **lumpenproletariat,** roughly translated to mean "scum class."[7] The lumpenproletariat was seen as primarily comprised of swindlers, pickpockets, tricksters, and beggars.[8] To Marx, the lack of moral character found in the lumpenproletariat was attributable to their having no stake in preserving the society's existing social order.[9] In effect, they were surplus labor in Europe's emerging capitalist economy.

Marx believed that the bourgeois class was guilty of systematically exploiting the working class,[10] and he felt that this exploitation was a cause of crime.[11] Ultimately, as the temporary socialist state withered away, so too would all formal laws; these laws would be replaced by a less formal and legalistic type of local communal justice.[12]

Willem Bonger: The First Socialist Criminologist

Near the outset of the twentieth century, an Italian socialist[13] argued that property crimes "are the result of economic conditions and proceed directly from the misery . . . in our richest and most civilized countries." The first criminologist to extensively develop this theme was Dutch-born **Willem Bonger** (1876–1940).

As discussed in Chapter 4, Bonger asserted that societies that encourage self-interest to the exclusion of the welfare of the group, and promote competition rather than cooperation, were sowing the seeds for high crime rates. From this reasoning, Bonger concluded that highly capitalistic societies would have higher crime rates than societies that promoted socialist principles.[14]

Originally published in 1905, his book **Criminality and Economic Conditions**[15] is widely recognized as a criminological classic. The theme of the book is that the roots of crime lie in the exploitive and alienating conditions of capitalism. In other words, capitalist philosophy encourages and financially rewards competition and greed. Those who compete most successfully generally do so at the expense of others, and the losers often become understandably embittered and disillusioned with their conditions, and crime is the result.[16]

Bonger distinguished between *egoism,* which he defined as concern for self over others, and *al-truism,* which he defined as concern for others over self. With a focus on victimful offenses, Bonger[17] believed that criminal behavior was rooted in the relative balance between these two perspectives of how people should relate to one another. The more a society encourages egoism over altruism, the more of a crime problem it will have, and Bonger believed that capitalism sets the stage for egoism.[18] Socialism, on the other hand, encourages thinking and behaving altruistically, and altruism was inherently contrary to engaging in crimes that victimize others.

Like Marx, Bonger contended that in primitive societies people were remarkably altruistic and concerned with each other's welfare. However, as societies grew and some people developed the ability to produce more than could be personally consumed, selfishness and hoarding began to spread. This set the stage for thievery and fighting over access to surpluses. According to Bonger, criminal laws were eventually instituted by the rich and powerful to protect the resources they accumulated from the poor and powerless.[19]

It should be noted that Bonger was not inclined to attribute crime entirely to capitalistic ideologies. He[20] accepted that some people were more likely than others to commit crimes largely because of what he called "innate deficiencies in moral qualities." By this, Bonger seemed to have in mind the concept of antisocial personality, although he was not specific. On the idea of innate deficiencies, Bonger parts company with most contemporary neo-Marxian theorists. As we will see, criminologists in the socialist tradition tend to be emphatic about all people having equal propensities to learn criminal behavior; only environmental circumstances determine who does and does not acquire these propensities.[21] However, all neo-Marxian theorists would agree with Bonger[22] that the learning of criminal conduct is most probable in societies that encourage individual competition and selfishness over collectivist cooperation and generosity. Now, let us see how Marx's and Bonger's ideas have developed in the writings of more contemporary theorists.

RADICAL CRIMINOLOGY:
Focusing on Economic Inequality

In the 1970s, several criminologists proposed updated versions of Marxian–socialist criminology. Central to these proposals was the idea that most criminal laws could be traced to people's efforts to protect property, and those who had the most property generally had the greatest legislative influence.[23] These theorists shifted their focus from Who commits crime and why? to Who creates criminal statutes and why? As a result of this new focus, many criminologists concluded that crime reduction could be better achieved by minimizing social inequality than by enforcing laws written mainly by the rich and powerful.[24]

No other criminological theory has gone under more names than the one now to be examined. The names include **Marxian, socialist, neo-Marxian, radical,** and the **new criminology.**[25] The latter name came to be used for a time following the publication of an influential book, entitled **The New Criminology,** in which three British criminologists espoused a version of the theory.[26] Here, we will refer to all versions of this theory as **radical theory.**

Radical Criminological Theory in Brief

At the heart of contemporary radical theory is the same assumption espoused by Marx and Bonger: Capitalism encourages economic inequality, and economic inequality encourages crime.[27] Many radical criminologists argue that the greed fostered by capitalism not only encourages crime, but that excessive profit-making by many corporate owners makes them defacto criminals. This is despite the fact that the laws in capitalist societies have been carefully crafted so as to effectively decriminalize making large profits from the work that others perform.[28]

To explain violent criminal behavior, radical criminologists have pointed to brutalizing and demeaning conditions that capitalism often creates for the working class.[29] In addition, violence is sometimes seen as the only recourse that the poor have for bringing about even modest degrees of change to their benefit.[30]

A topic that is found in the writings of several contemporary radical theorists is that of **surplus labor** (or **underclass**).[31] *Surplus labor* is close to Marx's concept of *lumpenproletariot.* According to many contemporary radical theorists, surplus labor has been created by increased mechanization of industrial production. As this has occurred, growing proportions of the working class—those with the fewest skills that capitalists can exploit—have slid into extremely desperate economic conditions, and prisons have become virtual warehouses for these surplus laborers.[32]

The bottom line is that radical criminologists trace crime primarily to the exploitive actions of wealthy people toward those who must sell their labor to make a living, a type of relationship that they see as an inherent feature of capitalism.[33] Instead of feeling a collective responsibility for one another, as socialism encourages people to do, the fuel for capitalist economies is self-centered greed. Based on this line of reasoning, radical criminologists have concluded that significant reductions in crime in a capitalistic society are unlikely without revolutionary reform of the economic system under which the society operates.[34]

Evidence Bearing on Radical Theory

Crime in Capitalist versus Socialist Societies. The most direct test of radical theory comes from comparing the crime rates found in capitalist societies with those in socialist societies, or from comparing countries that have shifted from one form of economic system to the other. Theoretically, socialist countries should have lower rates of crime, particularly with respect to property offenses.[35]

Two factors have hindered attempts to make such comparisons. One is the fact that property tends to be viewed differently in these two types of societies, and material possessions tend to be much more abundant in capitalist societies.[36] The other problem is that the criminal justice system is usually more formal and bureaucratically organized in capitalist countries than in socialist countries. The less formal and bureaucratized features of the criminal justice system in socialized countries mean that their statistics on crime, especially on property crime, will be difficult to compare to those of capitalist societies. About the only offense that most criminologists feel fairly comfortable comparing is homicide.

No study has yet compared several capitalist and socialist countries with respect to crime rates. However, since the fall of the Soviet Union and its satellite countries in eastern Europe, a few studies have compared crime rates for these countries before and after the transition. Radical theory predicts that these socialist-to-capitalist transitions will be associated with an increase in crime. The evidence collected thus far has been very supportive of this hypothesis.

Russia, for example, experienced a fairly dramatic rise in crime beginning in the early 1990s.[37] Similarly, both the Czech Republic[38] and Slovakia[39] (formerly comprising the country of Czechoslovakia) appear to have experienced substantially increased crime rates after switching from a socialist to capitalist system in 1988. Also consistent with socialist theory was evidence that in Slovakia, the most dramatic rise was in the case of property offenses and delinquency, rather than in violent offenses. Conversely, the rise in crime in the former Soviet Union and Eastern Europe could have had more to do with the general dismantlement of authoritarian governmental control than with the replacement of a socialist with a capitalist philosophy.

Not consistent with radical theory is evidence that Japan's forced transition to a capitalist system (although from a centrally controlled monarchy rather from a socialist economy) following World War II was accompanied by a *decrease* in its crime rate.[40] Also, Japan and Switzerland are two highly capitalistic countries and yet have lower crime rates than appear to exist in more socialistic industrialized nations such as those in Scandinavia.[41]

Nevertheless, the degree of income inequality in Japan is low compared to most other industrialized nations, so it still may not fit the mold of a highly competitive capitalist economy very well.[42]

Two studies tested the hypothesis that socialism helps to reduce crime by correlating crime rates in industrialized democracies with the average proportion of votes cast for socialist party candidates in those countries.[43] One study found that countries with the highest proportions of their citizens voting for socialist candidates had the lowest murder rates.[44] The other study found the opposite pattern for property crimes, i.e., the higher the percentage voting for socialist candidates the higher the property crime rates.[45] After controlling for such factors as the income inequality within the countries sample, this second study was able to reduce the positive correlation to nonsignificance. While radical theory would have predicted the inverse correlation between violent crime and the percentage of a country's citizens who voted for socialist candidates, it would have predicted an even stronger inverse correlation for property crimes, rather than a nonsignificant one.

Overall, the evidence on the main hypothesis derived from radical (neo-Marxian) theory is still fragmentary, and, at best, only modest in providing support.

Poverty and Unemployment Rates.   Radical theory has been tested in quite a number of studies by comparing crime rates to poverty and unemployment rates in various countries or parts of countries. Before considering these studies, it is important to reintroduce a distinction made in Chapter 6 between two types of economic deprivation (or poverty): absolute and relative.[46] **Absolute deprivation** (or **absolute poverty**) refers to conditions in which people lack resources needed to sustain life at a reasonable level of comfort, either for themselves or for their families.[47] While it is impossible to specify exactly where absolute poverty gives way to tolerable economic circumstances, the distinction is still useful for research purposes. **Relative deprivation** (or

relative poverty), on the other hand, has to do with the degree to which individuals or families are poor in comparison to other societal members.[48] Economists and other social scientists have worked out various objective measures for these two concepts.[49]

The distinction between absolute and relative deprivation is illustrated in Figure 12.1. This graph represents the distribution of wealth in three hypothetical societies. The shading at the left end of the graph is intended to represent the state of absolute poverty, or the point at which individuals are lacking sufficient resources to maintain basic health and comfort. Take a moment to study Figure 12.1 and see if you can guess which of these three societies has the greatest and the least degree of absolute poverty. Then guess which of these three hypothetical societies has the greatest and least degree of relative poverty.

Here are the answers: Society A has the greatest absolute poverty, because about half of its population are found in the shaded region of the graph. Society B has the least amount of absolute poverty, because virtually none of its population is in the shaded region.

Regarding relative poverty, one gets a quite different picture. Notice that wealth is most dispersed in Society C. Also note that the sort of dispersion exhibited in Society C is not symmetrical. Instead, the wealth distribution in Society C is said to be *skewed,* with the direction of the skew being toward the upper (or "squished") end of the continuum. Skewed distributions are in fact typical of how wealth is allocated in industrial societies, especially in ones that have the freest market economies.[50] Wealth is least skewed in highly managed socialist economies. If relative poverty is most pronounced in Society C, in which society

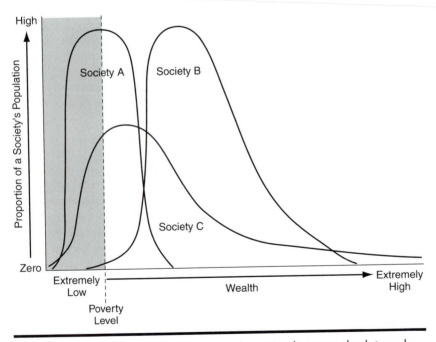

FIGURE 12.1   A diagram for illustrating the distinction between absolute and relative differences in wealth. In this example, absolute poverty would be greatest in Society A, lowest in Society B, and intermediate in Society C. Relative poverty, on the other hand, would be highest in Society C, lowest in Society A, and intermediate in Society B.

is there the least degree of relative poverty? The answer is Society A.

The questions surrounding the distinction between absolute and relative deprivation that are most relevant to radical criminology can be framed as follows: Do societies with a great deal of poverty have higher or lower crime rates than other societies? And, if poverty is associated with crime as radical theorists hypothesize, is it absolute or relative poverty that is the main correlate? Radical theorists have not been of one mind on this point, although they all agree that one or the other type of poverty should be positively linked to crime rates.

According to the absolute poverty version of radical theory, the highest crime rates will be found in societies with the highest proportion of persons who are poor, regardless of their poverty relative to others.[51] The relative poverty version, on the other hand, contends that high crime rates will be mainly associated with degrees of disparity in income, rather than with any measure of the number of persons below a set poverty line.[52]

Much of the evidence relevant to these two versions of radical theory were first reviewed in Chapter 6 in relationship to ecological and macroeconomic correlates of crime. Results from the most relevant of these studies are resummarized in Table 12.1, which shows that the evidence is mixed with respect to providing support for either of the two versions of radical theory.

Let us first consider the absolute poverty version of radical theory. The evidence most relevant to it is located in the column headed the "percent of the population below a standard poverty limit." So far, all of these studies have been conducted in the United States. As you can see, most studies of violent crimes have provided support for radical theory, but beyond the violent crime category, more than half of the studies have failed to find a significant positive relationship between crime and the proportion of a region's population living below poverty.

Regarding the relative poverty version of radical theory, two columns are directly relevant (those listed under relative poverty), and two more are indirectly relevant (those listed under unemployment). You may recall that two relative poverty measures were considered in Chapter 6: general relative poverty and racial relative poverty. General relative poverty refers to the overall degree of scatter in people's wealth within a region, whereas racial relative poverty refers to average differences between two or more racial or ethnic groups within a region. As you can see by examining Table 12.1, numerous studies have been conducted in the United States, and a fair number of international comparative studies are also available. Results from the U.S. studies are mixed, both in the case of violent and property crimes, although they are largely supportive of radical theory in the case of crimes in general. The international studies are entirely consistent with radical theory in the case of violent crimes, but they are not supportive of the theory in the case of property offenses.

Regarding racial relative poverty, all of the relevant research has been conducted in the United States. The results of this research so far has been equally divided between studies supporting radical theory and studies not supporting it.

Turning briefly to unemployment (results of which are summarized in the last two columns of Table 12.1), it is reasonable to argue that, as unemployment goes up, the proportion of persons who are poor will rise and the relative disparities in income should also increase. If so, unemployment rates can be considered indicators of absolute and relative poverty. As you can see, both the regional and the time-series measures of unemployment fail to exhibit consistent relationships with crime rates. Thus, most of the evidence based on unemployment rates also fails to support radical theory.

Historical evidence bearing on the relative version of radical theory comes from making within-country comparisons of wealth over time. Theoretically, to the extent that a country becomes less dispersed in its distribution of wealth, it should experience a reduction in rates of crime. In this regard, most European countries have instituted a series of policies that have significantly

TABLE 12.1.   Relationship between various poverty measures and criminality. (The shaded regions indicate cells where findings should be to support hypotheses derived from one or both versions of radical theory.)

Relationship to Crime		Wealth Disparity Variables			Unemployment Rates	
		Relative Poverty		% Below a Standard Poverty Limit (Table 6.18)	Regional Unemployment Rates (Table 6.20)	Time-Series Unemployment Rates (Table 6.21)
		Overall Relative Poverty (Table 6.22)	Racial Relative Poverty (Table 6.24)			
Violent Crime	Positive	**North America** *United States: 13* **International** *Various Countries: 11*	**North America** *United States: 3*	**North America** *United States: 20*	**Europe** *England: 2* **North America** *Canada: 1, United States: 5* **International** *Various Countries: 1*	**Middle East** *Israel: 2* **North America** *Canada: 1, United States: 4*
	Not significant, or Ambiguous	**North America** *United States: 11*		**North America** *United States: 2*	**North America** *United States: 9*	**North America** *United States: 7*
	Negative	**North America** *United States: 3*	**North America** *United States: 2*	**North America** *United States: 1*	**North America** *United States: 3*	**North America** *Canada: 2* **International** *Various Countries: 1*
Property Crime	Positive	**North America** *Canada 1, United States: 3*		**North America** *United States: 3*	**Europe** *England: 3* **North America** *Canada: 1, United States: 7*	
	Not significant	**North America** *United States: 1* **International** *Various Countries: 1*	**North America** *United States: 1*	**North America** *United States: 4*	**North America** *United States: 4*	
	Negative	**North America** *United States: 2* **International** *Various Countries: 1*			**International** *Various Countries: 1*	
Delinquent Offenses	Positive			**North America** *United States: 1*	**North America** *United States: 2*	
	Not significant					
	Negative					
General or Unspecified Offenses	Positive	**North America** *United States: 10*		**North America** *United States: 1*	**Europe** *England: 1* **North America** *United States: 11* **Pacific** *Australia: 1*	
	Not significant			**North America** *United States: 2*	**Europe** *England: 2* **North America** *United States: 8* **International** *Various Countries: 1*	
	Negative	**North America** *United States: 1*				

diminished disparities in wealth among their inhabitants throughout most of the twentieth century.[53] One of the main ways of helping to more evenly disperse wealth throughout Europe involved enacting various graduated income taxes, meaning taxing the wealthy at higher rates than the poor are taxed. Proceeds from these taxes have primarily gone to the poorer segments of European societies via education, health care, and welfare programs.[54]

England has experienced the most dramatic shift in wealth disparities of any European country. For instance, in the first two decades of the twentieth century, the wealthiest 10 percent of families in England controlled over 90 percent of all the wealth. Over the next five decades, this percentage was substantially eroded so that by 1980 the same 10 percent of families only controlled about 40 percent of England's wealth.[55] Beyond 1980, however, the trend had reversed, with the gap between rich and poor once again widening.[56]

The relative poverty version of radical theory would predict that the dramatic reductions in wealth disparities experienced by England should have been accompanied by a substantial decline in the country's crime rate. Research remains to be conducted on changes in England's crime rates since the 1980s, but the available statistics indicate that England has begun to experience a reduction in crime rates as the gap is again widening. These are not the sort of patterns predicted by the relative poverty version of radical theory.[57]

Similarly, in the United States, a considerably greater proportion of U.S. citizens lived in poverty during the 1930s, when the country was in the grips of the Great Depression, than has been true since the 1950s.[58] If poverty is a significant cause of crime, U.S. crime rates should be much lower in contemporary times than in the 1930s. Crime rates should have been especially low during the 1960s and 70s, when the overall economy was expanding and welfare programs were helping to minimize the number of persons in dire poverty.[59] While nationwide evidence of this sort is always extremely complex, the overall trends in U.S. crime rates do not support the view that reductions in poverty have been accompanied by decreases in crime.[60]

Social Class, Race/Ethnicity, and Gender.   Radical theory implies that groups that lack economic and political power will have higher rates of crime than groups with the greatest power. This prediction is consistent with research suggesting that the higher crime rates are found in the lower strata (Table 5.5b), and in the racial/ethnic groups with the lowest social status (Table 5.3). The hypothesis would also lead one to expect higher crime rates to be found in relatively new immigrant populations than in well-established indigenous populations, which most studies have found (Table 5.4).

However, radical theory would probably incorrectly predict that females will be more criminal than males, at least according to official statistics,[61] which is clearly not the case (Table 5.1a). This latter point will be discussed in greater detail when we get to feminist theory.

Closing Comments on Radical Theory

Radical theory is rooted in Marxian political thought in which humans are believed to be caring and altruistic toward others, but who became selfish as a result of declarations of private property (particularly land). A long history of greed ensued, culminating in an economic system known as capitalism. Radical theorists maintain that capitalism leads to poverty, and poverty leads to crime, especially property crime.

Two forms of poverty are recognized, absolute and relative. Absolute poverty refers to a condition in which a person is essentially incapable of sustaining life. Relative poverty is simply the degree of disparity between rich and poor.

Overall, the scientific evidence pertaining to both the absolute poverty and relative poverty versions of radical theory is mixed. Given the modest nature of the support, one criminologist recently suggested that it may be possible to strengthen radical theory by somehow combining both versions.[62] Another possibility is that some yet-unspecified microlevel variables—such as those considered by theories in the two preceding chapters—need to be integrated with radical theory.

Others have taken radical theory in the direction of what they call **left realism.** This brand of radical theory depicts the poor in society as being doubly victimized, first by capitalism and second by other members of the lower classes who resort to crime.[63] The left realist solution to the crime problem is to work toward social and economic equality.[64]

CRITICAL THEORY:
Focusing on Political Power

Recall that back in Chapter 2, five proposals were explored regarding the origins of criminal laws (p. 25). One proposal—called the **class conflict perspective**—asserted that criminal statutes originated from individuals who seize control over political power. Once they have achieved political control, criminal statutes become a tool for helping them maintain their privileged positions.[65] This perspective has had close kinships with radical theory in criminology, derived in part from noting close links between those who are wealthy and those who leverage political power.[66] In fact, some have even confused radical theory and critical theory.[67] It is worth noting from a historical standpoint that the groundwork for critical theory was actually laid before the writings of Karl Marx. For instance, as early as 1822, a U.S. legislator wrote:

> *Everywhere, with but few exceptions, the interest of the many has, from the earliest ages, been sacrificed to the power of the few. Everywhere penal laws have been framed to support this power.*[68]

Critical Criminological Theory in Brief

Critical theory in criminology is not associated with any specific individual, but began to emerge in the 1970s.[69] Those who work from this perspective have reasoned that their main task should be to study the political process of declaring some acts criminal and others not so. From a critical criminology perspective, the greatest insights into the causes of crime do not come from studying people who violate criminal statutes, but from understanding why criminal laws are passed in the first place.

Whereas other criminologists accept that some criminal statutes are more or less unique to a particular place and time, critical theorists tend to believe that all criminal statutes are arbitrary. Critical theorists minimize the degree to which there may be a set of *universal core offenses.* In the words of one critical theorist:

> *The conflict perspective [sees criminal law as] a set of rules laid down by the state in the interests of the ruling class and resulting from the conflicts inherent in class-structured societies: some criminal behavior is no more than the "rightful" behavior of persons exploited by the extant economic relationships.*[70]

Critical criminology has been characterized as essentially the result of blending radical theory with labeling theory.[71] Critical theorists share with radical theorists a keen interest in inequality. However, whereas radical theorists emphasize inequality in wealth, critical theorists are more concerned with inequality in political power and influence.[72]

Critical theory's kinship with labeling theory has to with both theories assuming that a society's criminal justice system (and the politics that makes it function) determines who will and will not be considered criminal.[73] Because critical theorists believe that the label *criminal* is more or less arbitrary, rather than a term that has a fairly universal meaning, they conclude that those who control the criminal justice system would also control most other aspects of society. All of this boils down to saying that criminologists should mainly attempt to explain rule making and enforcement, rather than trying to explain rule breaking.[74] This idea compliments labeling theorists' emphasis on how societies create criminals through criminal legislation and financial support for law enforcement.

According to critical theory, criminal laws have been designed by the politically powerful (usually with the support of the rich) to help serve their own best interests.[75] For this reason, a society's elite will be able to maintain their positions and resources with fewer risks of being labeled criminal than is true for those with little or no political power.

Critical theorists contend that all theories in the social sciences, including those in criminology, are rooted in political ideology.[76] In other words, critical theorists argue that there are no politically neutral theories of criminal behavior; *every* theory has a political agenda, some are just more explicit than others. Critical theorists, like radical theorists, are openly left-wing, and thus emphasize human equality, even if achieving this equality entails restrictions on individual freedom.[77]

A major difference between critical criminologists and radical theorists is that critical theorists are less inclined to focus on capitalism as the main cause of crime. Instead, political power and influence, no matter what type of economic system a society is operating under, is seen as the main cause of crime. Nevertheless, because capitalism is associated with greater inequality in wealth, many critical theorists are still inclined to consider this form of economic system to be especially susceptible to having its criminal laws fashioned to benefit a small minority of wealthy corporate owners. This reasoning has lead a number of critical theorists since the 1950s to chronicle the way various laws have been designed to discriminate against the poor and powerless in capitalist societies.[78]

Another difference between critical theory and radical theory is that the former is less inclined to advocate overthrowing capitalism, focusing instead on democratizing and deformalizing the criminal justice system in order to reduce the crime problem.[79] Table 12.2 summarizes the main differences between radical theory and critical theory in criminology.

Radical and critical criminologists rarely attempt to explain why various characteristics such as those discussed in Chapters 7 through 9 are associated with involvement in criminal behavior. The only correlates of crime in which they are keenly interested are demographic and ecological correlates, and the demographic and ecological correlates of greatest interest are those having to do with income and social class. Much of the theoretical work by radical and critical criminologists concentrates on understanding crime in terms of class struggle for power and wealth.[80] Table 12.3 provides a summary of how this emphasis differs from most other criminological theories.

Finally, there is a distinct tendency for critical theorists to conceive of most, if not all, offenders as

TABLE 12.2.   Main differences between radical and critical theory in criminology.

Radical Criminological Theory	Critical Criminological Theory
• Less closely tied to labeling theory	• More closely tied to labeling theory
• More inclined to see unequal access to wealth as causing crime	• More likely to see unequal access to political power as causing crime
• More focused on studying economic forces	• More focused on studying the law and the criminal justice system

TABLE 12.3.   Main differences between critical and radical theories and all other criminological theories.

Critical/Radical Theories	Other Criminological Theories
• Mainly focused on explaining why some acts are criminalized and other's are not	• Greater interest in explaining why people vary in their involvement in criminal behavior
• Inclined to confront crime by first creating a society of equals	• Inclined to work within the existing social order to prevent crime

underdogs, and as victims of "the system." In the words of one critic, proponents of critical theory are "too ready to discount sin in low places and unduly prone to exaggerate the incidence of sin in high places."[81]

Richard Quinney's Radical/Critical Criminology

As noted earlier, it is often difficult to clearly distinguish between radical and critical criminology. One of the most widely read criminologists in recent decades who has combined these two theories in criminology is an American sociologist named **Richard Quinney** (1934–).[82] According to Quinney, criminal laws are used by the state and the ruling class to insure survival of capitalist exploitation. He contended that criminologists themselves often unwittingly help to maintain this exploitation by providing the state with information that can be used by those in power to maintain control over the poor and disenfranchised.[83]

Quinney[84] argues that there are essentially three social classes in advanced industrial societies such as the United States. At the top are about 2 percent of the population called the **capitalist** (or **ruling**) **class.** Next are what he (and Marx) called the **petty bourgeoisie,** made up of about 18 percent of the workers. They consist of professionals such as physicians, lawyers, and the like, along with corporate managers and governmental bureaucrats. Last are the remaining 80 percent of the population, consisting of skilled, semiskilled, and unskilled laborers. These people comprise the **working class.**

Quinney's theory of crime can be summarized as follows: Crime is legally defined by the capitalist class in ways that minimize the chances of their members being identified as criminal, and that maximize their chances of maintaining power. The cause of all crime lies in the material conditions of a society.[85] In addition, crime presents a challenge to the existing social order, and for this reason, the ruling class seeks to suppress it, often enlisting the petty bourgeoisie to help. Great sums are spent by the ruling class to maintain functioning of the criminal justice system, because without it challenges to the legitimacy of their control of most of the society's wealth could threaten the entire capitalist system. Those who are most likely to become labeled criminals, therefore, are those who pose the greatest threat to the existing social order and to the perpetuation of unequal distribution of wealth. In the final analysis, crime is an inherent part of the capitalist system.[86]

In recent years, Quinney[87] and others[88] have come to advocate **peacemaking criminology.** This approach to the study of criminal offending emphasizes the need to leave behind the tenets of science in attempting to deal with crime. Instead, everyone needs to become sensitive to the suffering that we all cause one another, both in our interpersonal relationships and as part of a complex and often impersonal social system.[89] Peacemaking criminologists emphasize how groups of people are often pitted against one another and forced to compete by the larger social system within which we live. Not only does this competition often manifest itself in terms of crime, but also in terms of seeking revenge for the crimes committed by others, resulting in a vicious cycle of pain, distrust, and alienation.[90]

Evidence Pertaining to Critical Criminology

Before considering evidence bearing on critical theory, we should note that critical theorists (and radical theorists to a lesser degree) have not emphasized rigorous hypothesis testing to the same degree that most other criminologists have.[91] This is partly because testing macrolevel theories is more difficult than testing microlevel theories. Another reason has been that critical theorists mistrust science as much as they mistrust the criminal justice system. Both are seen as institutionalized tools that are used by those in power to help control those who are not. Rather than conducting scientific research into the causes of crime, critical theorists suggest that criminologists should focus their energies on helping ordinary people to free themselves from oppression by those with power.[92]

The emphasis that critical (and sometimes radical) theorists place on social change rather than research is known as **praxis.**[93] *Praxis* means to undertake intellectual pursuits, including science, for the betterment of humanity, rather than for the sake of "knowledge." This is because "knowledge" is relative and nearly always used by those in power to further their own ends. Therefore, while most other criminologists go about hypothesis testing, critical theorists work to change the course of social history.[94] They believe that one outcome of their efforts will be to dramatically diminish criminal behavior.

Despite the reluctance of many critical (and critical/radical) theorists to engage in hypothesis testing, we will still devote attention to this process. This is because deriving hypotheses from a scientific theory and locating supporting or refuting evidence is still the best way to assess the relative strength of competing theories.

Developments in Criminal Statutes. Critical theory predicts that most changes in legal statutes will be explainable in terms of advantages that these statutes offer to one or more politically powerful interest groups. Among the laws explained in this way are laws against vagrancy (meaning idle loitering), which were first passed in Europe in the sixteenth century. According to one critical theorist, these laws were crafted by the ruling class to "provide powerful landowners with a ready supply of cheap labor."[95] Subsequent changes that were made in the wording of the law over subsequent centuries was interpreted as continuing to provide financial benefits to those in power.

Critical theorists have also cited laws against child labor and mandated school attendance for children under at least their early teens as having criminogenic effects. Rather than enacting these laws primarily to protect children from hazardous industrial injuries and to ensure that they get a good education, one critical theorist hypothesized that the real motivation behind these laws was to keep children and teenagers out of the labor market where they compete with older workers and drive down their wages.[96] The author went on to suggest that a side effect of excluding youth from the world of work was to increase their involvement in crime.[97]

These are two of the better known examples of laws that critical theorists have cited to document that various groups within a society have influenced the criminal justice system to benefit themselves. However, the majority of criminal statutes have not been explained in this way, most notably the statutes pertaining to serious victimful offenses.[98]

Individual Variation in Support for Criminal Statutes. Critical theorists contend that the most powerful members of a society have the greatest influence over a society's criminal statutes.[99] This implies that the upper-class members of a society will hold more favorable attitudes toward most criminal statutes than will lower-class members.[100] Public opinion polls have failed to find support for this hypothesis.[101] Instead, social class appears to have essentially no relationship to people's tendencies to express support for most criminal statutes.[102] In other words, the working class appears to support most criminal statutes as much as do the elite classes.

Race/Ethnicity. Critical theory suggests that racial/ethnic groups that are the most influential in fashioning criminal statutes will do so in ways that insure that they will be less "criminal" than other racial/ethnic groups. In multiracial/ethnic societies such as the United States, this would explain why African Americans and other minority groups, such as Native Americans and Hispanics have higher crime rates than do non-Hispanic whites (Tables 5.3b and 5.3c). However, it would have difficulty explaining why crime rates among most Asian American groups tend to be lower than among whites (Table 5.3d).

Age and Gender. Some critical theorists have sought to explain age and gender variations in crime rates by noting that males during their second and third decades of life are expected to begin exercising their ability to make a living.[103] When young males do so, their actions often threaten those who are currently controlling political and economic power (mainly middle-aged and older males).[104] Therefore, those with the greatest power use criminal statutes to "criminalize" youthful behavior that challenges their authority. This reasoning would predict that it is mainly young males who will be ensnared by the criminal justice system.

Another argument made by at least one conflict theorist has attributed the age distribution in offending to the fact that young people lack power to affect the laws governing the functioning of the criminal justice system.[105] However, this line of reasoning would imply that females should also be convicted of more offenses than men, which evidence clearly refutes (Table 5.1a). Like radical theory, critical theory has considerable difficulty explaining gender differences in offending rates.[106]

Police Presence. The most extensively tested hypotheses derived from critical theory have more to do with the functioning of the criminal justice system than with the causes of crime.[107] Why? This emphasis goes back to the conflict assumption that most of what people define as crime is arbitrarily set by those in control of the criminal justice system.

One such hypothesis that has been derived from conflict (and radical) theory is that the presence of law enforcement should be roughly proportional to the elite's need to maintain their privileged status.[108] This implies that police should be more numerous in populations where the greatest disparities in wealth exist. This hypothesis was tested by correlating the police per capita in large U.S. cities with the degree of disparity in income in those cities. As predicted, a significant positive relationship was found.[109] Another study found that the use of deadly force by police was also correlated positively with the degree of income inequality in a sample of large U.S. cities.[110]

Discrimination in Sentencing. Theoretically, the criminal justice system should deal most harshly with persons who have little or no political power.[111] In other words, if we set aside any differences in criminal involvement, critical theory predicts that persons of low social status, along with racial/ethnic minorities, should receive harsher sentences than other persons.[112] This hypothesis has been tested by numerous studies. A bird's-eye view of the results of these studies is provided in Table 12.4.

The methods used in these studies have varied quite a bit. To measure sentencing severity, most studies have used sentence length or time served, although in the case of serious violent offences, such as murder and rape, a few studies determined whether or not the death penalty was imposed. In all of the studies cited in Table 12.4, the nature of the offense, and the number of prior convictions were statistically controlled because these factors obviously affect sentence severity apart from any biases by the criminal justice system.

In considering Table 12.4, first concentrate on social status. As you can see, while quite a number of studies are consistent with the hypothesis derived from conflict theory regarding sentencing biases, even more studies are not. Most of the studies conducted so far have pertained either to victimless and juvenile offenses or to crimes in general. For both of these crime categories, about twice as many studies have failed to support the discrimination hypothesis as supported it. Only one study of strictly violent offenses was found, and it supported the hypothesis that lower status offenders received harsher sentences than middle- or upper-status offenders for the same offenses.[113] On the other hand, probably the best designed study is one of more than 10,000 prisoners convicted of a wide spectrum of offenses. This study found that the offenders' social status was unrelated to the severity of the sentence they received for specific offenses.[114]

In the case of race/ethnicity, Table 12.4 shows that many studies have been published, mostly in the United States (with a few in England). The studies are of two distinct types. One type has come from analyzing results from actual judicial proceedings. The other type came from what are known as simulated jury studies, which involve presenting subjects (usually college students) with various judicial scenarios, and then asking them how they think they would respond. In the case of

TABLE 12.4.   Relationship between social status or disadvantaged racial/ethnic group membership and disposition/sentence severity (overall consistency score = 41.2%). (The shaded regions indicate cells where findings should support hypotheses derived from conflict theory.)

Relationship between Disposition/Sentence Severity & Lack of Political Power		Regarding Social Class/Status (Actual Judicial or Sentencing Proceedings)	Regarding Race/Ethnicity	
			Actual Judicial or Sentencing Proceedings	Simulated Jury Studies
Violent Crimes	Positive	**North America** *United States:* 1	**North America** *United States:* 10	**North America** *United States:* 6
	Not significant, or Ambiguous*		**North America** *United States:* 4	**North America** *United States:* 3
	Negative		**North America** *United States:* 3	**North America** *United States:* 2
Property Crimes	Positive		**North America** *United States:* 2	
	Not significant, or Ambiguous*		**North America** *United States:* 1	
	Negative		**North America** *United States:* 1	
Victimless & Juvenile Offenses	Positive	**North America** *United States:* 5	**North America** *Canada:* 2, *United States:* 19	
	Not significant, or Ambiguous*	**Europe** *England:* 1 **North America** *United States:* 6	**Europe** *England:* 1 **North America** *United States:* 17	
	Negative	**North America** *United States:* 1		
Two or More Types of Victimful Offenses	Positive	**North America** *United States:* 3	**Europe** *England:* 2 **North America** *United States:* 19	**North America** *United States:* 1
	Not significant, or Ambiguous*	**North America** *United States:* 4	**Europe** *England:* 4 **North America** *United States:* 24	**North America** *United States:* 5
	Negative		**Europe** *England:* 1 **North America** *United States:* 3	

*Studies that are listed as not significant found no statistically significant relationship in either the predicted or the contrary to predicted direction. Studies listed as ambiguous may have found at least one significant difference, but the majority of the findings were either not statistically significant or were mixed with respect to supporting the hypothesis for some types of crime, but not for other types.

race, simulated jury studies usually present groups of whites with information about various "defendants" that are all identical (including the nature of the offense) except for their race. Then, the subjects are asked what they would recommend with respect to disposition of the case (e.g., Would they convict? How long a sentence would they give?). As you can see by examining the last column of Table 12.4, these studies have been close to equally split between those that found support for the discrimination hypothesis and those that did not.[115]

The other type of data comes from statistically analyzing large numbers (often more than a thousand) of outcomes of actual judicial proceedings. Analyses have sought to detect evidence of social status or racial discrimination in case disposition. As Table 12.4 shows, the evidence is mixed with respect to discrimination, with roughly equal numbers of studies supporting and not supporting the hypothesis that the criminal justice system discriminates either in terms of social status or race.[116] Why these inconsistencies would exist is still being actively investigated, but appears to be largely the results of the extraordinary complexity of judicial processes.[117]

At least three qualifying remarks need to be made with reference to the findings summarized in Table 12.4, particularly in the case of race. First, some researchers have suggested that one of the reasons for so much inconsistency in the findings regarding race inequities in sentence severity is that conditions may have changed over time. Particularly in the United States prior to the civil rights movement in the 1960s, there may have been substantial racial discrimination in sentencing. However, since the mid-1970s, most studies have found little or no such evidence.[118] A couple of studies conducted in the 1960s and 1970s found evidence of regional differences in racial discrimination in sentencing, with bias in southern parts of the United States but none in the remainder of the country.[119]

Second, tendencies to discriminate may be largely judge- or jurisdiction-specific, with some judges and some jurisdictions consistently discriminating against African-American defendants

in sentencing, while others may not discriminate against, or may actually do so in favor of, African-American defendants.[120]

Regarding jurisdictional variations, **Darnell Hawkins** (1946–)[121] proposed what he called a **power–threat version of conflict theory.** This version of the theory states that the dominant class or ethnic group responds with harsher sentences toward the subservient class or group to the degree that the latter poses a threat to the power held by the former. From this, one may expect that as the proportion of a dominant group decreases relative to the subservient group, the sentences imposed on the latter will increase. Some attempts to test this prediction have found that, at least in regard to race, African-American defendants receive lighter sentences in predominantly African-American jurisdictions than in predominantly white jurisdictions.[122] These findings support Hawkins' power–threat version of conflict theory, and suggest that one of the confounding factors relevant to some of the inconsistencies in studies cited in Table 12.4 is the result of population compositional factors.

Third, some have argued that most of the studies that have indicated class or racial discrimination may actually have simply failed to control for one or more pertinent variables besides type of offense and number of prior convictions.[123] A related criticism is that some studies used only gross measures of offense type, i.e., they lumped all murders together, rather than considering aggravating circumstances that make some murders much more heinous than others.[124] In this regard, an English researcher found that blacks received longer sentences than whites, but concluded that this was because blacks were more likely to opt for actual trials rather than pleading guilty.[125] A U.S. military study reached a similar conclusion.[126] Studies have shown that regardless of race, defendants pleading innocent but who are found guilty receive longer average sentences than those who plead guilty.[127]

Sentence Severity and Relative Race of Offender and Victim.   Conflict theory would indicate that sentences would be particularly severe for offenders of a disadvantaged group when they had victimized a member of the advantaged group. As shown in Table 12.5, this hypothesis has been tested by several studies and was found to have overwhelming support.[128] In the United States, for all but one study,[129] African Americans who have been convicted of victimizing whites receive harsher sentences on average than do those who victimize one another or whites who victimize either whites or blacks.[130] This tendency seems to have been most prevalent in southern states,[131] and may have declined considerably since the civil rights movement that began in the 1960s.[132] One study of capital punishment in Texas found that the imposition of the death penalty was not only discriminatory when African Americans were convicted of killing whites, but that it was even more so when Hispanics were convicted of killing non-Hispanic whites.[133] Another study found that both African Americans and Hispanics in the United States received harsher sentences for the same types of offenses than did non-Hispanic whites.[134] These patterns are consistent with conflict theory.

Income Inequality and Police/Population Ratio. Another prediction derived from conflict (or conflict/radical) theory is that as income inequality increases, the ratio of police per population should increase.[135] The reasoning behind this expectation is that, as the financial distance between the rich and poor increases in a community, the wealthy will devote increasing financial resources to preserve their social status. This prediction was supported by the results of one study[136] but contradicted by the results of another.[137]

Closing Remarks on Radical and Critical Criminology

Radical theorizing in criminology can be traced back to Karl Marx, who inspired Willem Bonger and others to suggest that the emphasis placed on selfishness in capitalist societies contributed to criminal behavior. Critical theory has similar roots, but also borrows from other theoretical lines of reasoning, particularly labeling theory, and from the simple idea that "power corrupts." By combining these different traditions, critical theory moved away from simply emphasizing that capitalism causes crime to an emphasis on governmental control over the definitions of *criminal* as being at the heart of crime causation.

Throughout the 1970s and early 1980s, radical/critical theory enjoyed considerable popularity among criminologists.[138] In the mid-1970s, for example, 57 percent of criminologists stated that they preferred radical/critical criminology to "mainstream" criminology.[139] By the end of the 1980s, however, in the wake of numerous domestic and international events that called Marxian philosophy into question, radical/critical theory seems to have waned in popularity.[140] A survey conducted in 1988 found that about 20 percent of U.S. criminologists identified either radical or critical theory as one of the three theories they considered most promising for explaining criminal behavior.[141]

TABLE 12.5.   Relationship between race of offender and of the victim and the severity of the sentence (consistency score = 100%). (The shaded regions indicate the cell where findings should be to provide support for the hypothesis derived from conflict theory.)

	Race of the Victim		
Race of Offender	**African Americans more**	**No significant difference**	**Whites more**
African Americans more			**North America** *United States:* 11
No significant difference			
Whites more			

Recent years have seen critical/radical theory give rise to other forms of criminology, one called **peacemaking criminology** and another called **postmodern criminology.**[142] Postmodernists view criminal law as an instrument of oppression by the wealthy and powerful members of society, just as critical and radical theorists do. However, post-modernists also accept these oppressive aspects of society as inevitable. The postmodernist movement in criminology has been described as "withdrawal from political participation on the grounds that the struggle for social change is meaningless and that individual human beings are powerless to influence government and society."[143]

Overall, radical/critical criminologists tend to see themselves as being apart from "mainstream criminology."[144] One reason for their "outsider" status is that critical criminologists shy away from studying individual or family-level traits as causing crime, focusing instead on "the system."[145] Critical theorists sometimes question the motives of mainstream criminologists who are seen as committed to finding things "wrong with criminals," when the real culprits are the business tycoons and politicians who have created societies riddled with inequality, and who commit most of the *real* crimes while rarely being punished.[146]

In terms of prediction, a limited number of hypotheses have been derived from radical or critical theory. Radical theory's greatest strength has been in its hypothesis that crime will be higher in capitalist than in socialist societies. Otherwise, radical theory seems weak from a scientific standpoint.

The predictive ability of critical theory has been largely silent when it comes to explaining why individuals vary in their criminal tendencies. Aside from age, gender, social class, and race/ethnicity, no predictions about people's varying tendencies to engage in crime have been derived from radical or critical theory. Where these theories do make some rather unique hypotheses is in the area of sentencing, although the scientific research has provided mixed support for most of these hypotheses.

Radical and critical theories have had little to say about why various behavioral/personality traits are associated with criminal behavior. For example, neither theory seems to lead to the expectation that alcoholism, ADHD, family size, church attendance, or any biological factors would have substantial relationships to criminality. In fact, some radical and conflict theorists have questioned the ethics of criminologists who spend their time looking for such correlates of crime because they help those currently in power to continue oppressing those who lack power.[147]

FEMINIST THEORY: FOCUSING ON GENDER INEQUALITY

At least in Western countries, the feminist movement has had two waves. The first occurred in the early decades of the twentieth century, and in many North American and European countries it brought about women's right to vote in national elections. The second wave began in the mid-1960s with the main focus on equalizing men's and women's job status and earnings.[148]

During the first wave, a famous lawyer named Clarence Darrow[149] predicted that as women take an equal place in the work force alongside men, they "will commit the crimes that men commit, and furnish their fair quota of the penitentiaries and jails." (You are likely to have heard of Darrow as the defense attorney for a high school biology teacher who was convicted of violating Tennessee's law prohibiting the teaching of evolution in public schools in the 1930s, the famous Scopes Trial.) Darrow suggested that the key to equalizing crime rates for men and women was equal representation in the paid workforce.[150] Several other people not normally linked to feminist theory have similarly predicted that equal earnings and job status for women would cause their crime rates to approach that of men.[151] Nonetheless, from a theoretical standpoint, this prediction is most directly associated with feminist theory.

The sort of information that inspired the second wave of the feminist movement was persistent evidence that women received only a fraction of the wages of men. It is common in industrialized countries for women's earnings to be 60 to 70 percent of the earnings of men.[152] Studies have shown that the differences are partly due to the greater tendency for women to move in and out of the workforce during their reproductive years than is true for men.[153] However, even after statistically adjusting for this sort of factor, a significant differential in average earnings between men and women remains.[154]

In terms of trends, studies in the United States have shown that, since the 1970s, the degree of wage disparity has decreased substantially (see Figure 12.2).[155] This suggests that the second wave of the women's movement has had significant equalizing effects on wage differentials.

As we explore feminist theory itself, it is important to maintain a distinction between the feminist movement and feminist theory in criminology while realizing that people who favor one often (but not always) favor the other. The **feminist movement** refers to efforts to secure equal rights for women (with varying interpretations of the word *equal*). **Feminist theory in criminology** refers to particular types of explanations for criminal behavior and criminal victimization with a focus on gender differences.

Feminist Theory in Brief

In 1975, three feminist writers published books that were of criminological significance. Two of these

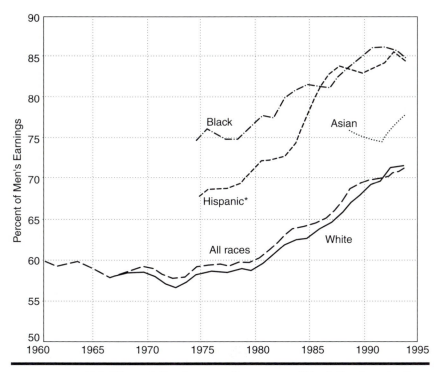

FIGURE 12.2   U.S. Women's Earnings as a Percentage of Men's Earnings, by Race and Ethnicity, 1960–1994

Note: Percentages are based on three-year moving averages of median annual earnings of full-time, year-round workers.

* Hispanics may be of any race.

Source: U.S. Bureau of the Census, unpublished tabulations.

writers were **Freda Adler** (1937–)[156] and **Rita Simon** (1931–).[157] A major theme of both was that as women achieved greater equality with men in social and economic terms, their proportional contribution to crime would increase.[158] Referring to progress in the feminist movement, Adler[159] stated, "Women have lost more than their chains, they have lost many of the restraints which kept them within the law."

The other highly influential early feminist writer in criminology was **Susan Brownmiller** (1935–).[160] In a book entitled **Against Our Will,** she brought attention to women's sexual victimization. Brownmiller maintained that rapists were neither deranged maniacs nor sex-starved Casanovas who won't take no for an answer. Instead, rapist are ordinary men who use rape as a weapon of intimidation to maintain control over women by keeping them in a state of fear.[161] Brownmiller and other feminist writers have seen rape, along with domestic assaults, as means of oppression by men, particularly in capitalist economies.[162]

In the 1970s, feminist writers ushered into criminology a set of ideas that has come to be known as *feminist theory*.[163] The theory assumes that women are oppressed whenever they live in patriarchal societies.[164] **Patriarchy** refers to the tendency for men to be in control of both the family and sociopolitical affairs outside the family.[165] The oppression is thought to come about primarily as a result of men instituting customs and laws that perpetuate their privileged position relative to that of women.[166] This argument is obviously similar to the views of conflict theorists, except that the latter contends that the elite (*regardless* of gender) use the criminal justice system to maintain their privileged position.[167]

Some feminist theorists go on to blame male privilege on capitalism; they are called **radical** (or **socialist**) **feminist theorists.**[168] Other feminist theorists—often called **liberal feminist theorists**—assert that socialist and communist societies are usually just as male-dominated as capitalist societies, and thus patriarchy must be due to factors other than capitalism.[169] Both groups reject any

suggestion that patriarchy has biological origins.[170] Radical and liberal feminist theorists agree that the contribution of women to crime will increase to the degree patriarchy can be eliminated, or at least reduced, by providing men and women equal job status and wages.[171]

Besides offering an explanation for criminal behavior, feminist theorists have been keenly interested in crime victimization, particularly the victimization of women by men in domestic violence and sexual assaults.[172] To account for the disturbing rate at which women are assaulted by men, feminist theorists have contended that males use these forms of violence to maintain their patriarchal authority.[173]

Evidence Pertaining to Feminist Theory

Gender.   The most obvious predictions that can be derived from feminist theory pertain to gender differences in crime rates. Theoretically, to the degree men and women are of equal status, their crime rates should also be equal.[174] This has been called the **emancipation hypothesis.**[175]

The most common ways of testing the emancipation hypothesis have been to either compare countries or follow trends in a single country over time. The results of these studies are shown in Table 12.6. As you can see, the evidence is largely nonsupportive, a conclusion that researchers began reaching by the 1980s.[176] Note that this conclusion directly contradicts assertions by criminologists writing in prior decades. Based mainly on selective comparisons of industrial and nonindustrial societies, these earlier writers contended that as women approach equality with men in wages and occupational status, their crime rates would become more similar.[177]

When comparisons are made within countries or across countries with similar degrees of industrialization, few studies support the emancipation hypothesis. As you can see in Table 12.6, most within-country time-series studies have actually supported the *opposite* of the emancipation hypothesis. That is to say, as countries have moved

TABLE 12.6.   Relationship between women's liberation and the proportion of crimes committed by women (overall consistency score = 24.4%). (The darker shaded regions indicate cells where findings should be in order to provide support for hypotheses derived from feminist theory.)

Nature of the Relationship		Studies	
		Cross-Population	**Time Series**
Violent Crime	Positive		
	Not significant, or Ambiguous*	**North America** *United States: 2*	
	Negative		**North America** *Canada: 1, United States: 5*
Property Crime	Positive		
	Not significant, or Ambiguous*	**International** *Several Countries: 1*	**North America** *United States: 2*
	Negative		**North America** *Canada: 1*
Victimless & Juvenile Offenses	Positive		**North America** *United States: 4*
	Not significant, or Ambiguous*		**North America** *United States: 3*
	Negative		
Overall Offenses	Positive	**International** *Several Countries: 2*	**Europe** *England: 2* **North America** *United States: 3*
	Not significant, or Ambiguous*	**International** *Several Countries: 1*	**Europe** *England: 3* **North America** *Canada: 1, United States: 3*
	Negative		**North America** *United States: 1* **Pacific** *Australia: 1*

*Studies listed as ambiguous may have found a few significant differences, but the majority of the findings were not statistically significant.

toward greater gender equality, the tendency for males to dominate in the commission of crime has actually increased, not decreased. This is especially true for violent offenses: The proportion of offenses committed by males tends to increase as women's involvement in productive labor and wages increases.[178] The only exception that has been fairly well established involves minor property offenses (such as shoplifting and thefts of other small items); women's emancipation appears to be associated with a rise in women's proportional contribution to these types of crime.[179]

Because these findings have surprised almost everyone and are so central to feminist theory, let us briefly examine some of the actual studies. First, consider a study of the proportion of women arrested for crime in Toronto, Canada between 1859 and 1955.[180] This is a particularly interesting set of data because it extends back prior to the first wave of the women's liberation movement.

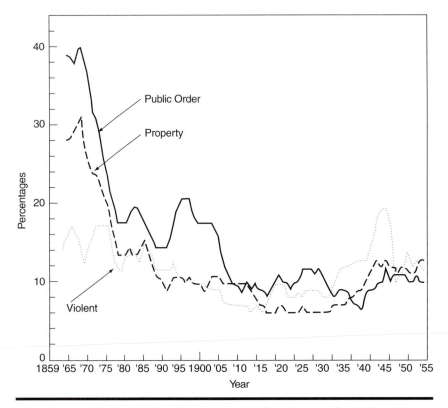

FIGURE 12.3   The proportion of total arrests involving women for violent, property, and public order offenses in Toronto, Canada from 1859 through 1955 (after Boritch & Hagan 1990:588).

As shown in Figure 12.3, women's arrest rates relative to men's dramatically declined over this 96-year period.[181]

A second example comes from a study of trends in U.S. murder rates from 1970 through 1993,[182] a period that would cover most of the second wave of the women's movement. This study found that, despite significantly greater equality in earnings and job opportunities, the proportion of murders committed by women was actually lower in the 1990s than it was in the 1970s. Similar conclusions were reached by another research team when they studied gender ratios in overall index crimes.[183] A third study traced the gender ratios for crime convictions in England from 1892 through 1992, and found virtually no changes.[184]

The fourth study comes from Australia, a country in which the Women's Movement began gaining a foothold in the early 1970s. A study of total arrests in Australia between 1966 and 1986 revealed that the proportion of females being arrested relative to males had actually decreased significantly.[185] The trends are shown in Figure 12.4.

As evidence has mounted against the emancipation hypothesis, attempts have been made to reshape feminist theory in accordance with this evidence. This salvaging effort has come in the form of what is called the **backlash hypothesis.**[186] This hypothesis states that, in the initial stages of women's liberation, males may seek to suppress progress toward gender equality by escalating their violence toward women. This escalation

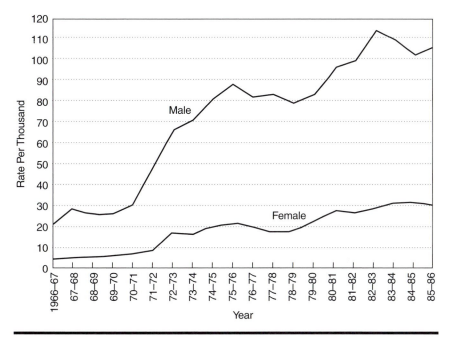

FIGURE 12.4   Male and female total crime rates, Australia, 1966–1986.
Source: Testing the nexis: Crime, gender, and unemployment. *British Journal of Criminology* 29: 144–156.

could result in an overall rise in the proportion of violent crimes committed by males against females. One study has been undertaken to specifically test the backlash hypothesis; its findings were largely contrary to it.[187]

Crime among Feminist and Nonfeminist Women. Studies in the United States have revealed that approximately one third of U.S. women consider themselves feminists.[188] This variation has made it possible to compare the crime rates of supporters and nonsupporters of the feminist movement. Feminist theory would imply that the supporters of women's liberation would be more likely to model their behavior after those of men than would women who are nonsupporters.

So far, two studies have tested this hypothesis. Both studies were conducted in the United States among girls of high school age. One found essentially no relationship between women's liberation attitudes and offending rates, while the

other found that girls who were most sympathetic with feminist issues actually reported significantly less violent offending than did girls who were least sympathetic.[189] In other words, supporters of feminism were *less* like males in their offending behavior than was true of women who were nonsupporters of women's liberation. Thus, neither of these studies provided evidence supportive of feminist theory.

Gender Discrimination by the Criminal Justice System. Feminist theorists have given considerable attention to gender disparities in arresting and sanctioning practices of the criminal justice system.[190] Because the feminist theory sees the criminal justice system as being largely under the control of the male power structure, it leads one to expect that, even if men are more involved in crime than women are, women will still be treated in more discriminatory ways than men by the criminal justice system. The reasoning behind this conclusion is similar to conflict theory's assertion that the class and ethnic groups who lack political and economic power will receive discriminatory treatment by the criminal justice system.

Evidence pertaining to this hypothesis is summarized in Table 12.7. The studies are of three types: arrest and prosecution data, sentencing data, and simulated jury data. Regarding arrests and

TABLE 12.7. Relationship between gender and arrest probabilities or sentence severity (overall consistency score = 33.4%). (Shading shows where evidence should be in order to support feminist theory.)

Type of Offenses and Nature of the Relationship		Aspects of the Criminal Justice System		Simulated Juries
		Arrests/Prosecution	Severity of Sentences	
Violent Crimes	Harsher toward Women			
	Not significant, or Ambiguous*			
	Harsher toward Men		**Europe** *England:* 1	**North America** *United States:* 2
Property Crimes	Harsher toward Women		**North America** *United States:* 2	
	Not significant, or Ambiguous*			
	Harsher toward Men			
Victimless & Juvenile Status Offenses	Harsher toward Women		**North America** *Canada:* 1, *United States:* 15 **Pacific** *Australia:* 1	
	Not significant, or Ambiguous*		**Europe** *England:* 1 **North America** *United States:* 14 **Pacific** *Australia:* 1	
	Harsher toward Men	**North America** *United States:* 1	**North America** *United States:* 2	
Offenses in General	Harsher toward Women			
	Not significant, or Ambiguous*		**North America** *United States:* 1	
	Harsher toward Men	**North America** *United States:* 3	**North America** *United States:* 11	

*Studies listed as not significant found no statistically significant relationship in either the predicted or the contrary to predicted direction. Studies listed as ambiguous may have found at least one significant difference, but the majority of the findings were either not statistically significant or were mixed with respect to supporting the hypothesis for one type of crime, but not for another.

prosecutions, the studies have all documented significant gender discrimination, but the nature of the discrimination is directly contrary to the feminist theory: It is against males rather than females. For example, when self-reported offending has been compared to arrests, males have a higher probability of being arrested than do females.[191]

In the case of gender differences in sentences imposed for specific offenses, numerous studies have been conducted. As you can see in Table 12.7, the findings are mixed with respect to supporting the hypothesis that women are discriminated against by the criminal justice system. However, a pattern is detectable: Males are discriminated against when it comes to sentencing for violent crimes and for offenses in general, whereas females are discriminated against in the case of property crimes. For instance, a U.S. study was conducted in which men and women offenders were matched with respect to the type of offenses they had been convicted of having committed. In terms of sentences handed down, men were significantly more likely than women to be imprisoned (rather than being put on probation) and men received longer sentences for all serious offenses.[192]

However, females are often discriminated against in the case of juvenile offenses, particularly for status offenses.[193] In other words, when it comes to status offenses, females are more likely to receive a formal custodial disposition (such as being sent to foster care) than males are for violating the same ordinance.

To explain this odd pattern of gender discrimination, one criminologist suggested that men are sentenced more harshly than women for most offenses because they have higher risks of recidivating and because their offenses tend to be more serious even within fairly specific crime categories.[194] As to why females would be more likely retained by the juvenile justice system for status offenses, another criminologist proposed that societal and parental concerns over premarital pregnancy is a major factor.[195] In other words, because of the known link between delinquency and early sexual activity (Table 8.11), the juvenile justice system tends to use status offense violations as a pretext for curtailing the sexual behavior of young women at high risk of premarital pregnancy.

Neither of the above explanations, however, is really compatible with feminist theory, because they do not depict men as attempting to maintain a dominant position of power over women. A proposal that is most closely allied with feminist theory is called the **chivalry hypothesis** (or **chivalry factor**).[196] This hypothesis states that the criminal justice system will discriminate against women only when nonlegal social customs become ineffective in maintaining women in their subservient status.[197] In other words, as long as women do not pose a significant threat to the patriarchal system that gives men the upper hand, the criminal justice system will actually discriminate in favor of women.[198] The hypothesis implies that, to the degree women make progress in employment and wage equality, the criminal justice system will eventually come to discriminate against them, or at least treat men and women equally. So far, one study has tested this hypothesis, and found some support for it.[199]

Liberation and Victimization of Women.   A number of feminist theorists have come to focus more on men's victimization of women than on gender differences in crime or sentencing disparities.[200] This may partly reflect the difficulty that feminist theory has had explaining the persistence of gender differences in crime even in countries where women have made substantial strides toward equal employment opportunities and wages.

As you may recall from the discussion of crime victimization in Chapter 5, males tend to be victimized at considerably higher rates than women, especially in the case of violent offenses, with one important exception: rape. For this offense, nearly all of the victims are female, and the perpetrators are overwhelmingly male.[201]

You will recall Brownmiller's assertion that rape is used by men to intimidate women, thereby denying women equal access to political power and status. This hypothesis has been tested by comparing geographical regions of the United States to see if rape rates are higher in areas with the greatest gender disparities in wages, occupational status, and the like. The results have been mixed, with two studies finding geopolitical regions (either states or cities) with the greatest sex disparities in wages or political power having the *highest* rape rates,[202] and one study finding the opposite relationship.[203]

Another prediction derived from feminist theory is that the availability of pornography will be positively associated with rape victimization.[204] The argument surrounding this prediction goes as follows: Pornography treats women as subordinate sex objects rather than as individuals with status and power equal to that of men.[205] Therefore, to the degree men are exposed to pornography, they will come to think of women as sex objects and submissive partners to men's sexual whims. In the views of some feminist writers, pornography is "the central oppressor of women and the chief cause of male violence against us."[206]

Evidence bearing on the prediction that the availability of pornography is associated with rape has been a source of controversy. On the one hand, studies conducted in the United States have shown that states with the highest per capita circulation of "adult magazines" have substantially higher rape rates than do states with the lowest per capita circulation of these publications.[207] The researchers who have conducted these studies rightly emphasize that the relationships they have documented may not necessarily be causal in nature. Nevertheless, self-report studies of male college students have found that students who spent the most time reading or watching pornography had committed the greatest number of sexually coercive acts against women,[208] and comparisons of rapists and other sex offenders with males in general have indicated that the former have availed themselves of pornography more often.[209]

On the other hand, studies conducted in Denmark following repeal of its obscenity laws in the early 1960s found that rape rates remained essentially unchanged.[210] Also, states with the greatest number of adult theaters and adult bookstores per capita in the United States had lower rape rates

than those states with the fewest.[211] International studies, however, have confused the issue further by finding rape rates positively associated with the availability of pornography.[212] (More will be said about sexual assault in Chapter 18.)

Closing Remarks about Feminist Theory

The feminist theory of crime arose out of the second wave of the women's liberation movement in the 1970s. The focus of feminist theory is on gender differences in crime and explains these differences as being due to socialization factors that encourage male dominance and exploitation and female subservice. Consequently, the theory contends that, to the degree women achieve sociopolitical equality with men, their involvement in crime will move toward equality as well. The theory has also drawn attention to male victimization of women in intimate relationships.

So far, most of the hypotheses derived from feminist theory have either been refuted or have called for substantial modifications in the theory. Most importantly from the standpoint of explaining gender differences in crime, the theory has only correctly predicted changes in minor types of property crimes. In the case of serious (especially violent) crimes, progress toward equal pay and job opportunities for women has generally been accompanied by a decrease, rather than an increase, in women's contribution to the crime problem.

Overall, the theory has not held up very well under empirical scrutiny. Of the hypotheses derived from the theory, most have not been supported by the bulk of available research. In particular, nearly all of the evidence has refuted the hypothesis that progress in equalizing job opportunities and wages for men and women will be accompanied by increases in the proportion of serious crime being committed by women.[213] Only fairly minor types of property crime seem to conform to the prediction of feminist theory.

Given this overall assessment, it is not surprising that enthusiasm for feminist theory in criminology has been muted.[214] However, it should be added that this does not mean that criminologists as citizens may not support many of the goals of the feminist movement.

At least one attempt has been made to broaden feminist theory by combining it with radical theory, in the form of what is called **socialist feminist theory.**[215] In this version of the theory, the subservient position of women relative to men is primarily attributed to capitalism.[216] Another respect in which many feminist theorists are allied with radical/conflict theorists is in their opposition to "mainstream" criminology as essentially serving the interests of the state (under the control of wealthy males).[217]

POWER–CONTROL THEORY:
Bringing Marxian Theory into the Family

John Hagan (1946–), an American who now resides and teaches in Canada, is the leading proponent of **power–control theory.**[218] The theory has been described as a "neo-Marxian, class-based" theory that seeks to explain the most common forms of offending.[219] The most common forms of offending that Hagan seeks to explain with his theory are run-of-the-mill forms of juvenile delinquency. Most notably excluded from his theory are serious adult offenses.

In initiating his theory, Hagan noted that neither version of control theory specifically explained gender differences in delinquency. In other words, no element of control theory predicts that males would be socialized in such ways as to have lower self-control, and thereby commit acts of delinquency and crime more often than females.

Hagan and his associates[220] were interested in developing a theory that would predict offending rates at ecological (or aggregate) levels, as well as explain individual variations in offending.[221] To accomplish this, power-control theory borrows concepts from socialist theory, feminist theory,[222] as well as control theory. The concept of **power** refers to authority at the level of the state, and the concept of **control** refers to authority at the level of the family.[223]

Power–Control Theory in Brief

In keeping with its Marxian roots, power–control theory focuses on social class rather than social status. Hagan[224] specifies that there are four basic classes in patriarchal societies. These are the employer class, the professional–managerial class, the working class, and a class of surplus labor.

Power–control theory focuses on how family relationships within a broad societal context affect people's involvement in delinquency and minor criminality. The overarching premise of power–control theory is that the social power structure within the family causes boys and girls to have distinctive relationships with their parents that cause sons to become considerably more delinquent.[225]

Like feminist theory, power–control theory points to patriarchy as fundamental to the understanding of gender differences in offending. The main difference is that, whereas feminist theory depicts patriarchy as typifying how society treats women, power–control theory envisions patriarchy pervading both societal and family relationships. Hagan and Poloni[226] argue that, within the family there are two main types of power structure: **patriarchal** (father-dominated) and **egalitarian** (mother and father share tasks and control equally). The more patriarchal a family, the more boys will be encouraged to be risk takers, and girls will be discouraged from doing so. Furthermore, power–control theory stipulates that, in the upper classes patriarchal families are particularly prone to socialize girls differently than boys, with a premium placed on girls maintaining their "reputations." These differences lead power–control theorists to deduce that gender disparities in offending should be more noticeable in upper-class than in working-class families.

A major cause of movement away from patriarchy toward greater egalitarianism is the ability of women to achieve and maintain financial independence.[227] For this reason, most industrialized societies have witnessed a shift toward egalitarianism in recent decades.

Hagan asserts that, in patriarchal families, parents seek to control daughters more than they control sons, and that parental control is primarily responsible for making children obedient and prone to inhibit risk taking behavior. In accordance with control theory, Hagan believes that risk-taking behavior and a lack of self-restraint are key ingredients in offending behavior.

Theoretically, in patriarchal societies, the upper classes have a greater interest than the lower classes do in controlling the behavior of daughters.[228] As a result, females in the upper classes should be especially prone to avoid engaging in illegal behavior.[229] In relatively egalitarian societies, sons and daughters should end up being more similar in their risk taking and obedience to authority. Consequently, their involvement in delinquency and crime should be more similar, as well.[230]

Overall, power–control theory predicts that societies in which gender equality is promoted will have far fewer disparities between males and females in crime and delinquency rates when compared to male-dominated societies.[231] This should be especially true in the case of gender equality in intrafamily relationships.[232]

Evidence Pertaining to Power–Control Theory

Gender. The prediction that is easiest to derive from power–control theory is that gender disparities in criminal and delinquent behavior will be most pronounced in patriarchal societies. This is because in patriarchal societies girls are socialized to fear and avoid punishment to a greater degree

than boys. Likewise, *within* societies, families that are the most patriarchal should have greater male–female disparities in criminal involvement because of differences in how boys and girls are socialized.

Two studies have specifically tested this prediction, both of which failed to support the hypothesis. One study found fewer disparities in self-reported offending among children reared in patriarchal families than for those reared in egalitarian families.[233] The other study found no significant relationship between patriarchal sex-role attitudes and offending rates.[234]

Power–control theory also implies that females should exhibit greater fear of criminal sanctions than males do especially in patriarchal societies or families.[235] On this hypothesis, the research evidence has been mixed, as shown in Table 12.8.

Parental Supervision. According to power–control theory, parental supervision should be inversely correlated with involvement in delinquency. Numerous studies are consistent with this prediction (Table 7.7). Also, a few studies indicate that gender differences in such supervision may be partially responsible for gender differences in delinquency.[236]

Social Class. Power–control theory led Hagan and others to hypothesize that in patriarchal societies the male–female ratio will be higher in the upper classes than in the worker or surplus labor classes.[237] Evidence consistent with this prediction has been reported.[238] However, a second study found the opposite,[239] while a third study found support for the hypothesis only among

TABLE 12.8. Relationship between gender and fear of criminal sanctions (overall consistency score = 28.5%). (The shaded regions indicate cells where findings should be to support hypotheses derived from power-control theory.)

Nature of the Findings	Fear of Criminal Sanctions
Females More Fearful	**North America** *Canada:* 1; *United States:* 2
No Significant Difference	**North America** *United States:* 4
Males More Fearful	

African Americans; for whites, no social class differences were evident.[240] This hypothesis does not appear to be holding up well.

Economic Conditions.   A social scientist writing in the 1930s argued that delinquency should fall during economic hard times and rise during good times because during hard times unemployed fathers will be spending more time interacting with their sons.[241] Working from power–control theory, McCarthy and Hagan[242] reached almost the opposite conclusion. They contend that, to the extent that, at least in patriarchal societies (where men are the breadwinners and women are the homemakers), males dominate in the commission of delinquency particularly during economic downturns. This is because during hard economic times unemployed males will be able to devote greater time to dominating the family and transmitting patriarchal values, including close supervision of daughters. This close supervision prevents daughters from engaging in delinquency, but does little to prevent males from doing so.

McCarthy and Hagan[243] tested their hypothesis by comparing U.S. gender differences in delinquency over a period of time that included the Great Depression of the 1930s. As predicted, the greatest gender disparity in delinquency was during the Great Depression.

Working Mothers.   Power–control theory asserts that, in patriarchal societies, high rates of mothers in the workforce will be associated with increased rates of delinquency, especially by daughters.[244] According to the theory, this is due to the greater difficulty that working mothers will have exercising control over their children when they are away from the home.[245] Research on a link between working mothers and delinquency is mixed but tilted in a supportive direction (Table 7.14).

Closing Comments on Power–Control Theory

According to power–control theory, most offending by adolescents can be explained in terms of how the exercise of patriarchal power at the societal level impacts the authority structure of the family. (Some feminist theorists have also considered family and societal patriarchy as important in crime causation.)[246] In patriarchal societies, husbands exercise greater authority than in egalitarian societies. Hagan contends that, to the degree husbands wield this authority, it will affect the proportion of males and females who become delinquent. The more husbands control family affairs, the more males will dominate in delinquency.

Power–control theory is limited in terms of the number of hypotheses that have been derived from it. This is partly because it was designed to explain only the most common, and thus *least* serious, forms of offending.[247] Another limitation of power–control theory is that its predictions have been difficult to apply outside of conventional two-parent families. In other words, it is not easy to know how delinquency in single-parent households would be affected by the presence or absence of patriarchy in the society at large. Yet another limitation of power–control theory has been that it makes no predictions regarding individual traits (other than gender and age) that might be linked to offending. Of the hypotheses derived from power–control theory, only about half of them have received clear empirical support.

GENERAL REMARKS ABOUT MACROTHEORIES

Theories that focus on pervasive sociocultural variables as the main causes of criminal behavior have had a long controversial history in criminology (and in social science generally). This controversy can be traced primarily to the fact that these theories have more of a political edge to them than is true for other social science theories. This in no way nullifies their potential value for understanding human behavior. Nonetheless, special caution is called for in attempting to judge the merit of macrotheories. One runs the risk of attributing scientific merit to these theories simply because we happen to agree with the political philosophies that helped to inspire the theories. Likewise, those who do not sympathize with a leftwing political philosophy run the risk of dismissing these theories out of hand.

Another point to make is that macrotheories are not entirely inconsistent with theories covered in previous (or subsequent) chapters. In this regard, one study suggested that poverty seems to cause crime somehow through its effects on such parenting practices as diminished bonding, reduced supervision, and harsher discipline practices.[248] Another study found that lower social-class background leads to violent crime at least in part by lowering a child's educational expectations.[249] These and other studies suggest that more than a

kernel of truth may lie in many of the theories discussed in this and previous chapters.

Just about everyone knows the story of the blind men who feel different parts of an elephant and each comes away with a substantially different impression of what the rest of the beast must be like. Criminologists may be like those blind men. As each one carefully describes what he or she sees and they continually try to put all of their impressions together, a unified picture should one day emerge (even though the phenomenon of criminal behavior is doubtlessly thousands of times more complicated than the anatomical structure of an elephant).

SUMMARY

This chapter described four main criminological theories that share the assumption that the primary causes of criminal behavior are to be found within the philosophical underpinnings of the societies in which we live. The theories subsumed under this category are radical theory, conflict theory, feminist theory, and power–control theory. Central to all of these theories is some type of inequality, be it monetary, political, or interpersonal.

Macrotheories in criminology are usually traced back to Karl Marx and other socialist thinkers of the nineteenth century. Living during the early stages of the industrial revolution, Marx and many of his contemporaries believed that industrialization was giving rise to insidious new forms of economic inequality. Instead of wealthy aristocrats living lavishly off of the labor of peasants, Marx foresaw a bourgeoise class basking in the lap of luxury made possible by the toil of workers in wretched, dangerous factories.

To Marx and his long-time friend, Frederick Engels, a subclass of the proletariat, termed the *lumpenproletariat,* constituted surplus labor, and would become the main source of crime in the emerging capitalist economies. Marx predicted that eventually capitalism would come to a violent end, and out of its ashes would emerge a temporary socialist state. Socialism, in turn, would pave the road for a return to man's original state, which

involved cooperation and equal sharing of resources. Marx called this final state *communism.*

The first criminologist to specifically apply Marxian ideas to the study of criminal behavior was Willem Bonger, writing in the early twentieth century. According to Bonger, societies could encourage their citizens to be either egoistic (self-centered and selfish) or altruistic (concerned for others and willing to share). Societies that encouraged egoism, as capitalism did, were almost certain to have higher crime rates than socialist societies, which were based on principles of a collectivist concern for others.

Radical Theory.   By the 1970s, these philosophical seeds had taken root and began growing into a tree with three branches. One branch is called *radical criminology* (or *radical theory*). Its primary focus is on economic inequality as a cause of criminal behavior. This branch can be thought of as forking into two sub-branches. One—called the *absolute poverty version*—concentrates on the fact that some people simply do not have enough to maintain a decent, let alone comfortable, living. It asserts that this level of deprivation leads to high crime rates. The other sub-branch—called the *relative poverty version*—was more interested in the frustration and envy resulting from relative differences between haves and have-nots as the main cause of crime. Thus, even if no one in a society was in dire poverty, societies in which the gaps between those who were best off and those who were worst off were greatest should have the highest rates of crime.

Critical Theory.   A second theory to emerge out of the socialist tradition in criminology is called *critical criminology* (or *conflict theory*). Rather than seeing economic inequality as the main cause of crime, critical criminologists focus on sociopolitical inequality. They see those with the greatest political power as often tailoring legislation in ways that help to insure retention of their privileged position. In particular, critical criminologists maintain that criminal statutes are biased in the way they are written and enforced to insure that those who lack political influence are most likely to be branded criminals.

A particularly influential spokesman for both the radical and critical perspectives is Richard Quinney. He has tried to combine both of these traditions into a single theory by asserting that all political power is aimed toward controlling scarce resources, and that the ruling class almost invariably tailors societal laws and engineers the criminal justice system so as to perpetuate its own preeminence in resource control. In recent years, Quinney has shifted his focus somewhat to a perspective called *peacemaking criminology,* which attempts to understand crime within a socialist philosophy that is nonetheless resigned to a world in which full equality may never be achieved.

Feminist Theory.   Feminist theory in criminology began to appear in the 1970s with the publication of feminist writings containing both activist and scholarly elements. From the scholarly standpoint, some of these writings sought to explain gender differences in criminal behavior along with women's victimization by men. Most proponents of feminist theory contend that women are being oppressed by men to the extent that the genders do not equally share economic and political power. The tendency for a society (or family) to be male-dominated is called *patriarchy.*

Feminist theory contends that, to the degree patriarchy exists in a society, males will dominate in the commission of crime. In addition, patriarchy will result in women being victimized by men, both sexually and otherwise. Early proponents of feminist theory were Rita Simon and Freda Adler, regarding crime in general, and Susan Brownmiller, with regard to sexual assaults.

Power–Control Theory.   Power–control theory was proposed by John Hagan. It contends that the power exercised within the domain of the family tends to reflect the type of power used in a society's political arena. In particular, authoritarian male-dominated family structures (patriarchy) are thought to suppress females' achievement of personal and financial independence. One consequence of this suppression is thought to be less female involvement in crime and delinquency.

SUGGESTED READINGS

Greenberg, David F. (Ed.). (1993). *Crime and capitalism: Readings in Marxist criminology (expanded and updated edition).* Philadelphia: Temple University Press. (A useful source for many ideas pertaining to Marxian approaches to the study of criminal behavior.)

Inciardi, James A. (1980). *Radical criminology: The coming crises.* Beverly Hills, CA: Sage. (A collection of readings providing a broad interpretation of radical and critical theories in criminology. The

book contains chapters written by authors on both sides of the theoretical controversy.)

Lynch, Michael J., and Groves, W. Bryon (1989). *A primer in radical criminology* (2nd ed.). New York: Harrow & Heston. (This book provides an unusually clear, basic overview of the Marxian/critical tradition in criminology.)

Naffine, Ngaire (1992). *Feminism and criminology.* Philadelphia: Temple University Press. (A book you should consult for feminist theoretical arguments pertaining to gender differences in criminal behavior and criminal victimization.)

Rafter, Nicole Hahn, and Heidensohn, Frances (Eds.). (1995). *International feminist perspectives in criminology*. Bristol, PA: Open University Press. (This book contains a collection of readings bearing on the feminist perspective by proponents from several nationalities.)

Schwartz, Martin D., and Milovanovic, Dragan (Eds.). (1996). *Race, gender, and class in criminology:*

The intersection. New York: Garland. (For those who want to get a broad overview of all of the theories discussed in this chapter, this book is recommended.)

Wilbanks, William (1986). *The myth of a racist criminal justice system*. Monterey, CA: Brooks/Cole. (For those interested in looking critically at critical theory, this book is an informative read.)

EXERCISES

1. Search the Internet and/or the library for information about radical (or socialist) theories of criminal behavior that goes beyond what was presented in this text. Write a one- to two-page double-spaced paper summarizing what you found.

2. Search the Internet and/or the library for information about conflict or feminist theories of criminal behavior that goes beyond what was presented in this text. Write a one- to two-page double-spaced paper summarizing what you found.

3. Locate and read a professional social science article having to do with one of the theories presented in this chapter. Choose an article that seems to objectively test one or more hypotheses derived from the theory that you feel you can understand. Then write a one- to two-page double-spaced paper summarizing the nature of the study and what it found. Unless the expense is prohibitive, you should photocopy the article, making sure the citation is complete, and hand it in with your paper. (If you can't photocopy the entire article, at least photocopy the first page.) Be sure to write your interpretation of the article using your own words; do not simply paraphrase the abstract or the conclusions.

ENDNOTES

1. Rothman 1993:23.
2. Klockars 1980:95.
3. Bohm 1982:567.
4. Krahn et al. 1986:274; Messerschmidt 1988:384; S. S. Simpson & Elis 1994:453.
5. Hirst 1972.
6. Schichor 1980:205.
7. Carter & Clelland 1979:98; Schichor 1980:205.
8. Carter & Clelland 1979:98.
9. Masters & Roberson 1990:168.
10. Friedrichs 1980:38.
11. Schur 1969:123.
12. Friedrichs 1980:38.
13. Loria 1902:107.
14. Hurwitz & Christiansen 1983:157.
15. Bonger 1969.
16. Masters & Roberson 1990:171.
17. Bonger 1905:40.
18. Schur 1969:123.
19. Masters & Roberson 1990:171.
20. Bonger 1969:88.
21. Martindale 1960:193.
22. Bonger 1969:41.
23. Chambliss 1974; Gibbons 1987:62; Sparks 1980:176.
24. Kress 1982:40.
25. Gibbons 1987:125; Henry & Milovanovic 1991:293; Pelfrey 1979:325; Silberman 1994:108.
26. Taylor, Walton, & Young 1973.
27. Buchholz et al. 1974:29.
28. Barlow 1993:26.
29. Klockars 1980:109.

30. T. Alexander 1972:134.
31. Brown 1985:213; Melossi & Pavarini 1981; Schwendinger & Schwendinger 1985:11.
32. Pepinsky 1983:56.
33. Taft & England 1964:130.
34. Gordon 1971; Krisberg 1975.
35. Bailey 1984:544.
36. Hurwitz & Christiansen 1983:158.
37. Krus et al. 1997:751.
38. Krus et al. 1997:75.
39. Lubelcova 1996.
40. Hurwitz & Christiansen 1983:159.
41. Clinard 1978:80; Short 1985:184.
42. Thurow 1987:35.
43. Jackman 1975:216.
44. Braithwaite & Braithwaite 1980.
45. Stack 1984:242.
46. Danziger & Wheeler 1975:113; LaFree & Drass 1996:615; Naffine & Gale 1989:144; Stack 1984:230.
47. Kovandzic et al. 1998:571.
48. LaFree & Drass 1996:629.
49. Amacher & Ulbrich 1995:375; Farley 1984:175.
50. Ellis 1994:35.
51. Hughes & Carter 1981:21; Krahn et al. 1986:274.
52. Patterson 1991:755.
53. Klockars 1980:96.
54. Hill 1988.
55. Eysenck & Gudjonsson 1989:4.
56. Millar 1991:23; Walker & Walker 1987.
57. Hughes & Carter 1981:21.
58. Harrington 1969:178; Lebergott 1976:4.
59. J. Q. Wilson 1975:4.
60. LeFree & Drass 1996:629.
61. A. Morris 1987:10.
62. DeKeseredy 1996:57.
63. Lea & Young 1984; Schwartz & DeKeseredy 1991.
64. Lynch et al. 1994:38.
65. Conklin 1986:9.
66. Friedrich 1980:37.
67. Cardarelli & Hicks 1993:503.
68. Livingston 1822/1968:45.
69. Van Swaaninger & Taylor 1994:183.
70. Chambliss 1976:6.
71. Carter & Clelland 1979:97; Masters & Roberson 1990:174; Wellford 1982:189.
72. Bohm 1982:566.
73. Friday 1977:161; Kaariainen 1997:61; Thornberry & Christenson 1984:399.
74. Friedrichs 1980:44; Jacobs & Brill 1979; Sparks 1980:170.
75. Friday 1977:161; Michalowski 1977:26.
76. Turk 1980:79.
77. Ekehammar et al. 1987; Rokeach 1979.
78. Chambliss 1964; Hall 1952.
79. Friedrichs 1980:39.
80. Quinney 1977:63.
81. Toby 1980:131.
82. Quinney 1974, 1975, 1977.
83. Quinney 1974:267.
84. Quinney 1977:77.
85. Quinney 1977:35.
86. Blau & Blau 1982:117.
87. Quinney 1989, 1991.
88. Caulfield 1996.
89. Caulfield 1996:95.
90. Quinney 1991.
91. Carter & Clelland 1979:106; Lynch et al. 1994:15.
92. Klockars 1980:111; Quinney 1991:7.
93. Habermas 1973:38; Johnson 1980.
94. Klockars 1980:111.
95. Chambliss 1975:15.
96. Greenberg 1977.
97. Sparks 1980:179.
98. Akers 1980:136; Toby 1980:128.
99. O'Leary 1982:1.
100. Masters & Roberson 1990:174.
101. Akers 1980:136.
102. Greenberg 1976; Hopkins 1975.
103. DeKeseredy 1996; Greenberg 1977.
104. DeKeseredy 1996:37.
105. Friday 1977:161.
106. A. Morris 1987:11.
107. Groves & Sampson 1987:182.
108. Silver 1966.
109. Jacobs 1979.
110. Jacobs & Brill 1979.
111. Chiricos & Waldo 1975; Hagan 1975:620; Lizotte 1978; Peterson & Hagan 1984:56.
112. Carter & Clelland 1979:96; Chambliss & Seidman 1971:475; Quinney 1970:141.
113. Swigert 1975.
114. Chiricos & Waldo 1975:766.
115. Sweeney & Haney 1992:186.
116. Kleck 1981, 1985.
117. Conley 1994; Kleck 1981; Pope & Feyerherm 1992.
118. McCarthy & Smith 1986; Peterson & Hagan 1984; Tonry 1995:68; Widmayer & Marquart 1992; Wilbanks 1986:119; Zatz 1987:71.
119. Hindelang 1969:312; Kleck 1981:798.

120. Frazier et al. 1992; Gibson 1978; Unnever & Hembroff 1988:53.
121. Hawkins 1987.
122. Bridges et al. 1987; Bridges & Crutchfield 1988; Dannefer & Schutt 1982; Frazier et al. 1992.
123. Wilbanks 1986:121.
124. Kramer & Steffensmeir 1993.
125. Hood 1992:86, 1993:181.
126. Verdugo 1998.
127. Hood 1992:130; Walsh 1990.
128. Wilbanks 1986:120.
129. E. Green 1964.
130. Keil & Vito 1989.
131. Kleck 1981.
132. McCarthy & Smith 1986.
133. Widmayer & Marquart 1992:187.
134. Petersilia 1985.
135. Jacobs 1979.
136. Jacobs 1979.
137. Greenberg et al. 1983:385.
138. Kress 1982:40.
139. Pelfrey 1980:237.
140. Gibbons 1987:139; Goode 1990:6.
141. Ellis & Hoffman 1990:54.
142. Henry & Milovanovic 1991; James 1996; Milovanovic 1989; Schwartz & Friedrichs 1994.
143. Schwartz & Friedrichs 1994:233.
144. Friedrich 1980:49.
145. Gibbons 1987:24; Herzog & Sudia 1973:148.
146. Taylor et al. 1975:44.
147. Groves & Sampson 1987:182.
148. Austin 1982:20; Binder et al. 1988:499.
149. Darrow 1922.
150. Steffensmeier & Allan 1988:69.
151. Broom & Selznick 1958:639; Hurwitz & Christiansen 1983:274; Nettler 1978a:123.
152. Callan 1991; Marsh 1998:116; Oaxaca 1973.
153. Gilbert & Kahl 1987:194.
154. Oaxaca 1973; Sawhill 1973; Stromberg & Harkess 1978.
155. Bianchi & Spain 1996:24.
156. Adler 1975:24; 1979:94.
157. Simon 1975.
158. Danner 1996:30; Hagan et al. 1987:790.
159. Adler 1975:24.
160. Simon 1975.
161. Brownmiller 1975:15 & 272; Larragoite 1994:160.
162. Ellis 1989a:10; McIntosh 1978:259; Messerschmidt 1986:32.
163. Danner 1996; Dobash & Dobash 1992; Edwards 1989; Gregory 1986.
164. Hartmann 1976.
165. Goldberg 1993.
166. Daly & Chesney-Lind 1988; Yoder & Kahn 1992.
167. Gavigan 1982:40; McIntosh 1977:396.
168. Messerschmidt 1986:32; Rafter & Natalizia 1981:81.
169. Bonta et al. 1995:278; S. S. Simpson 1989:610.
170. Gavigan 1982:44; Goodey 1996:273.
171. Brewer & Smith 1995:177; Caputi 1989.
172. Maguire 1994:282; Schmalleger 1996:487.
173. S. S. Simpson 1989:611.
174. Danner 1996:30; Jurik & Winn 1990:227; Simons et al. 1980:51.
175. Bonta et al. 1995:278.
176. Giordano et al. 1981; Simon & Landis 1991; Steffensmeier et al. 1989.
177. Nettler 1978:123; Sutherland & Cressey 1966:139.
178. Boritch & Hagan 1990:588; Steffensmeier & Steffensmeier 1980.
179. Smith & Visher 1980:697.
180. Boritch & Hagan 1990:588.
181. Boritch & Hagan 1990:293.
182. Stanton et al. 1997.
183. Steffensmeier & Allan 1988:67.
184. Maguire 1994:275.
185. Naffine & Gale 1989:150.
186. Brewer & Smith 1995:177.
187. Brewer & Smith 1995:184.
188. Bellafante 1998:58.
189. James & Thornton 1980.
190. Gavigan 1982:41.
191. Chesney-Lind 1980; Weis 1976.
192. Steffensmeier et al. 1993:435.
193. Feyerherm 1981; Sarri 1983; Steffensmeier et al. 1993:435.
194. Steffensmeier 1980.
195. Ferdinand 1977:13.
196. E. A. Anderson 1976; Chesney-Lind 1978; Krohn et al. 1983; McNeill 1990; Scutt 1979; Visher 1983.
197. Johnson & Scheuble 1991:678; Stang et al. 1978:21; Steffensmeier 1980a:351.
198. Chesney-Lind 1978:43; DeKeseredy 1996:39; Nagel & Weitzman 1971:173.
199. Krohn et al. 1983.
200. C. M. Adler & Polk 1996:396; Maguire 1994:282.
201. Ellis 1998.
202. Baron & Straus 1984; Ellis & Beattie 1983.

203. Baron & Straus 1989:185.

204. Dworkin 1981; MacKinnon 1984; R. Morgan 1980.

205. Dalecki & Price 1994:206.

206. Jacobsen 1995:96.

207. Baron & Straus 1989:123; Scott & Schwalm 1988a.

208. Boeringer 1992, 1994; Boeringer et al. 1991.

209. Marshall 1988; Nutter & Kearns 1993.

210. Ben-Veniste 1971; Kutchinski 1971, 1973.

211. Scott & Schwalm 1988b.

212. Court 1976, 1980, 1984.

213. Klein & Kress 1976:42; Weis 1976.

214. Daly & Chesney-Lind 1988; Danner 1996:43.

215. Triplett & Jarjoura 1997:289.

216. Messerchmidt 1986; Simpson 1989:607.

217. Klein & Kress 1976:34.

218. Hagan & Palloni 1986, 1988; Hagan et al. 1987.

219. Hagan et al. 1985:1151.

220. Hagan 1987:789.

221. Avakame 1997:477.

222. Simpson 1991:122.

223. Hagan et al. 1985:1154.

224. Hagan 1985:1176.

225. Hagan & Palloni 1988:91.

226. Hagan et al. 1987:788.

227. Hagan et al. 1987:789.

228. Brannigan 1997:418.

229. Hagan et al. 1987:791.

230. Hagan et al. 1987:812; Hagan & Palloni 1988:91.

231. Avakame 1997:490; Weisheit 1984:570.

232. Simpson 1991:122.

233. Singer & Levine 1988:640.

234. Avakame 1997:490.

235. Smith & Paternoster 1987:149.

236. Brannigan 1997:419; Hagan et al. 1996:23.

237. Hagan et al. 1985:1156; Triplett & Jarjoura 1997:289.

238. Hagan et al. 1985.

239. Singer & Levine 1988.

240. Jensen & Thompson 1990.

241. Plant 1937:141.

242. McCarthy & Hagan 1987.

243. McCarthy & Hagan 1987:159.

244. Chesney-Lind 1989:181.

245. Brannigan 1997:420.

246. Gavigan 1982:48.

247. Hagan et al. 1985:1174.

248. Sampson & Laub 1994.

249. Jarjoura & Triplett 1993

CHAPTER 13

Neurologically Specific
Biosocial Theories

Have you ever noticed how some people are exceedingly impulsive and seem happy only when they are "living on the edge"? Despite the anguish they sometimes bring to themselves and others, their behavior often persists in one form or another throughout life. Is this sort of behavior learned, or is it at least partly an inherent feature of how their brains work? This chapter will examine various aspects of brain functioning, some of which are linked to traits such as impulsivity, risk taking, and insensitivity to the feelings of others. You will learn how research in a number of these areas has inspired biosocial theories of criminal/antisocial behavior.

Biosocial theorizing in criminology comes in two forms: evolutionary and neurologically specific. Evolutionary theories are aimed toward explaining how criminal/antisocial behavior may have reproductive consequences for both offenders and victims. These theories will be discussed in Chapter 14.

Neurologically specific theories are so named because they identify one or more aspects of brain functioning as influencing criminal/antisocial behavior. Before examining neurologically specific theories, it is important to have an overview of how the brain plays an indispensable role in controlling behavior. Even if you have no background in brain functioning (except as a user!), the next few pages will give you the concepts needed to understand neurologically specific theories of criminal/antisocial behavior.

THE NATURE OF NEUROLOGICALLY SPECIFIC THEORIES

Ground was first broken for neurologically specific theories in the eighteenth century by an anatomist at the University of Vienna, named **Francis Gall** (p. 82). Amidst great controversy, he argued that the brain rather than the heart or soul was responsible for human feelings and actions.[1] He went on to propose that specific areas of the brain controlled specific types of thoughts, behavior, and emotions. This idea of specific regions for specific types of thought led Gall and his supporters to establish a discipline that came to be known as **phrenology,** which explained personality traits in terms of the shape of people's craniums.

So outraged were many religious leaders by Gall's ideas that he was eventually fired from his teaching duties. Today, Gall's main premise—that the brain controls thought, behavior, and emotions—is universally accepted in scientific circles, although Gall's discipline of phrenology fell into disfavor over a century ago. Ironically, the demise of phrenology has been followed by evidence that there *are* regions of the brain that specialize in various types of behavior control.[2] However, this regional brain control over behavior is not to the degree that people's personalities can be analyzed by feeling around on their heads for cranial bumps and indentations.

Today, behavioral scientists agree that it is the functioning of the brain that is responsible for our thoughts, behavior, and emotions. However, this control is not achieved in isolation. Figure 13.1 provides a sketch of how the brain responds to both genetic and environmental factors in exercising its control over how we think, feel and act. To see how neurologically specific theorists use this type of diagram to understand variations in criminal/antisocial behavior requires a rudimentary understanding of how the human brain works.

THE EVOLUTION OF THE HUMAN BRAIN AND HOW IT CONTROLS BEHAVIOR

That the human brain is an evolved organ becomes obvious when you compare it to the brains of other animals.[3] For creatures who are most closely re-lated to humans genetically (i.e., chimpanzees and other apes), there are almost no structural differences between their brains and ours; only the *sizes* of certain brain structures differ.

The Limbic System

If you compare the human brain to the brain of much more distantly related creatures, similarities remain, but obvious differences appear as well, including entire portions of the brain being either present or absent. In reptiles, for example, you will find a more basic brain than is found in mammals, and the more limited behavioral repertoires of reptiles reflects this. For instance, reptiles such as alligators and crocodiles spend nearly all of their time resting, eating, moving in and out of water, periodically having sex, and sometimes fighting with neighbors over hunting territories. Elaborate social activities such as we see in ourselves and other mammals are absent among reptiles.

Another example: Mammals play; reptiles don't. For other differences, consider what female alligators do after laying clutches of eggs. In most reptilian species (but not all), females spend little time feeding and protecting their offspring, and no time teaching them survival skills. Male reptiles do none of these tasks. The main reason for this lack of long-term parental care is that reptiles lack a region of the brain that is responsible for

A Basic Schema for Neurologically Specific Theories

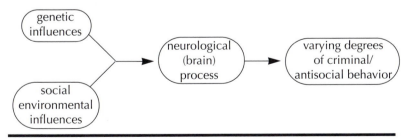

FIGURE 13.1   A comparison of the underlying structure of social environmental and of neurologically specific theories of criminal/antisocial behavior.

learning such behavior. It is called the **limbic system.**[4] In mammals, including all of us primates (monkeys, apes, and humans), the limbic system has evolved to incline adults to provide long-term care to offspring.[5] In most primate species, these parental care tendencies are more pronounced in females than in males, but are present to some extent in both.

The r-Complex

Where is the limbic system located? Because mammals evolved from a type of ancestral reptile, the limbic system was basically just added to the reptilian brain by covering it with a new layer. Thus, the mammalian brain can be said to consist of its reptilian core (called the **r-complex**) plus a covering, known as the limbic system. As we will see later in this chapter, some have argued that the limbic system may have a role to play in causing certain types of criminal acts.

From a behavioral standpoint, the limbic system controls what can be termed "social emotions."[6] These emotions are responsible for mammalian tendencies to be much more "socially responsive" than reptiles. This responsiveness to social factors manifests itself in such forms as play, parenting behavior, pair-bonding between sex partners, and a variety of other social loyalties. Experiments with laboratory animals have shown that when the limbic system (or regions closely linked to it) is damaged, social behavior can be dramatically altered. For example, animals who were once socially considerate and playful often become irritable and vicious when their limbic system is removed or seriously impaired.[7]

The Neocortex

Over the course of mammalian evolution, another major region of the brain emerged, called the **neocortex** (or new layer).[8] As the name implies, the neocortex essentially drapes over the limbic system (which, in turn, overlays the r-complex). The neocortex makes up only a small, thin covering for the brains of many mammals.[9] In humans, however, the neocortex is enormous and is responsible for human brains being larger than those of any other living primate.[10]

What does the neocortex do? It has been described as a "heartless computer," because it appears to be devoid of emotions other than curiosity.[11] The neocortex appears to have evolved primarily to learn and to then weigh options in responding to complex environmental situations, including those of a social nature. Another function of the neocortex in humans is that of acquiring and utilizing language. For a three-dimensional model of the human brain showing the location of its three evolved regions of the human brain, see Figure 13.2.

To briefly elaborate on the significance of this three-part conceptualization of the brain, consider the concept of "brain dead." You may know that persons who are brain dead will often still be breathing, and may even open and close their eyes and make basic facial expressions. However, they can no longer comprehend their surroundings or language in any way. When electrodes are hooked up to their scalps, there will be no activity; this means that their neocortex has ceased to function. The only electrical activity remaining is in lower parts of the brain—where breathing and various reflexive bodily functions are controlled. Sometimes, the functioning of these subcortical regions can be maintained for months or even years, provided that the body is maintained through intravenous feeding.

So, are "brain dead" people alive or not? The answer is one that many families and legislators have had to face as medical technology has made advances in maintaining low brain functioning long after the neocortex has fallen silent due to various types of physical and chemical injuries.

Dividing Up the Neocortex

All three of the basic parts of the brain can be subdivided into numerous components, each making a contribution to various complex behavior patterns. To follow neurologically specific theories of criminal behavior, it is important to focus on subdivid-

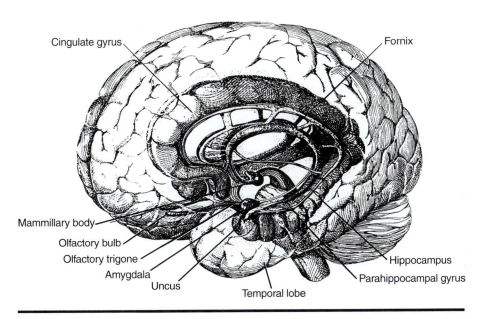

Cingulate gyrus

Fornix

Mammillary body

Olfactory bulb

Olfactory trigone

Amygdala

Uncus

Temporal lobe

Hippocampus

Parahippocampal gyrus

FIGURE 13.2   Sketch of the human brain with the limbic system darkened. Some of the neocortex and the main portion of the R-complex (in the interior of the brain) have been cut away in order to make the limbic structures more visible.

ing the neocortex. This division is of two types. The first has to do with the fact that the neocortex comes in two distinct halves, called the **right hemisphere** and the **left hemisphere.** Studies have shown that these two hemispheres tend to think in distinctive ways. While the left hemisphere usually thinks by stringing a series of logical ideas together to derive a reasonable conclusion, the right hemisphere is more intuitive and holistic in its reasoning pattern.[12] As a result, the left hemisphere tends to be much better at language comprehension, whereas the right tends to be better at mathematics[13] and reasoning in three-dimensional terms.[14] Later in this chapter, you will see that this distinction is central to one of the theories to be explored.

The other way of dividing up the neocortex is in terms of lobes, of which four are recognized. Most important to criminological theory, as we will see, are the **frontal lobes,** which comprise roughly the front third of each hemisphere of the neocortex. The other three lobes are the parietal, the anterior, and the temporal lobes; these have not

been specifically incorporated into any of the theories of criminal behavior to be reviewed.

We are now ready to begin examining neurologically specific theories of criminal/antisocial behavior. The five theories subsumed under this category are suboptimal arousal theory, reward dominance theory, seizuring theory, frontal lobe theory, and hemispheric functioning theory.

**SUBOPTIMAL AROUSAL THEORY:
Crime Reflects a Search
for Environmental Stimulation**

In the 1950s and 1960s, psychologists began documenting that some people are much less sensitive to environmental stimuli than others. This lead two psychologists to speculate about how people's varying sensitivities to environmental stimuli may be responsible for antisocial behavior. They were an American, **David Lykken** (1928–), and a German who moved to England early in his career, **Hans J. Eysenck** (1916–1997). Lykken[15] and

Eysenck[16] independently proposed a similar theory, although Lykken geared his theory mainly toward explaining psychopathy, while Eysenck focused his on criminal/delinquent behavior. The theory they proposed has come to be known as **suboptimal arousal theory** (or sometimes simply **arousal theory**), and has now been elaborated by several other social scientists, most notably Sarnoff Mednick, Frank Farley, and Adrian Raine.[17]

Suboptimal Arousal Theory in Brief

Suboptimal arousal theory is rooted in evidence that people vary in their sensitivities to and preferences for intense environmental stimulation. Some people prefer a great deal of intense environmental stimulation, while others prefer very little (with most preferring something in-between). Lykken and Eysenck both suspected that a region of the brain having to do with our states of sleep–wakefulness and attention was important in this regard. The brain region is called the **reticular formation** (or the *reticular activating system*).

As shown in Figure 13.3, the reticular formation is a diffuse region of the brain originating in the upper portion of the spinal cord and extending up and then flairing outward into the limbic system and neocortex, with especially strong nerve pathways projecting into the frontal lobes.[18] According to suboptimal arousal theorists, this network of neurons plays an important role in causing criminal/antisocial behavior.[19]

The arguments set forth by suboptimal arousal theorists may be summarized as follows: If a person's arousal control center is unusually sensitive to incoming stimuli, he or she will be prone to quickly learn to avoid engaging in behavior that raises the intensity of stimuli to unpleasant levels. On the other hand, if individuals have a reticular formation (and its support networks) that is unusually *in*sensitive to environmental stimuli, they will require a high level of unpleasant stimuli before learning to avoid the behavior that provokes the unpleasant stimuli. According to suboptimal arousal theory, it is these latter individuals who will be unusually prone toward criminal/antisocial behavior.

In addition to predicting that offenders will be difficult to condition with punishment, suboptimal arousal theory also suggests that offenders will go out of their way to have environmental experiences that are unusually provocative. According to

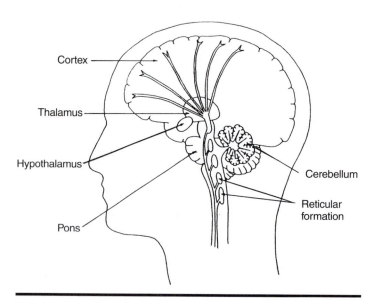

FIGURE 13.3　The reticular formation or activating system.

the theory, this is because the higher brain centers (the limbic system and neocortex) are essentially being starved for stimulation due to the failure of the arousal control regions in the lower parts of the brain to attend to most incoming stimuli.

How is arousal measured? It is usually measured peripherally, meaning that arousal is inferred by measuring things outside the brain itself. The most widely used peripheral measure is the Galvanic Skin Response (or skin conductivity). Theoretically, if physical exertion and temperature are held constant, individuals who are suboptimally aroused will perspire less than those who are unusually high in arousal under the same conditions.[20] So what would suboptimal arousal theory predict with respect to persons who are most prone toward criminal/antisocial behavior? Would they perspire more or less than normal under standard testing conditions? The answer is less.

Other physiological measures of arousal are heart rate and pulse rate under various testing conditions.[21] People whose heart or pulse rates are unusually slow under standard testing conditions when resting or when confronted with a stressful stimuli (such as when they are told to anticipate an electrical shock in thirty seconds) are said to be suboptimally aroused.[22]

Studies have also measured suboptimal arousal using self-reports. This has been done most often by asking subjects how often they find themselves being bored. Those who report becoming bored most often,[23] or those who say they often feel the need for more excitement in their lives,[24] are thought to be most suboptimally aroused.

A simple way to illuminate suboptimal arousal theory is to discuss it with reference to ADHD, an established correlate of crime. Studies have shown that in most cases the hyperactive and inattentive behavior of ADHD children can be temporarily "normalized" by giving them a stimulant drug.[25] The most widely used drug is **methylphenidate** (brand name, **Ritalin**). Ritalin is considered a stimulant drug with potency that falls roughly between two other stimulants: caffeine and amphetamines.

Your first thought might be that the last thing anyone should give to a hyperactive kid is a stimulant. Because stimulants have "calming effects" on most ADHD children, they are sometimes called **paradoxical drugs**.[26] If you think about ADHD neurologically, the seeming paradox disappears. Studies have shown that, like many conduct disordered children, the brains of most ADHD children emit unusually high proportions of slow brain waves.[27] Theoretically, these slow brain waves are experienced as "boredom," which in turn motivates ADHD children to seek and/or create environments with more things going on. Unfortunately, many of their boredom-relieving activities are irritating and disruptive to others. Stimulant drugs "artificially" activate the brain, and thereby temporarily diminish the typical behavior of ADHD children. Suboptimal arousal theory asserts that similar factors often underlie criminal/antisocial behavior.

Lykken has refined his version of suboptimal arousal theory in recent years, arguing that people can be divided into three main categories from the standpoint of genetic susceptibility to antisocial behavior.[28] One category of people are very easily socialized because their brains are disposed toward keen responsiveness to their environments. These individuals have an extremely low probability of engaging in any serious criminal/antisocial behavior. The second category is the one into which he believes most people fall: They are intermediate in terms of being easily socialized, and run a significant risk of becoming serious offenders if they are not properly socialized. The third category, according to Lykken, are individuals whose brains are so extremely resistant to conditioning that even the most diligent parenting will almost always fail to prevent offending. Lykken[29] calls antisocial behavior by the second (most prevalent) category "sociopathy," and termed antisocial behavior "psychopathy."

In summary, suboptimal arousal theory asserts that a substantial amount of human behavior is oriented toward maintaining a preferred (or optimal) level of arousal. Like Goldie Locks, we all seek environmental conditions that are neither too constant nor too varied. However, as with the three bears, what is "just right" for one person may be "too much" or "too little" for someone else. As far as criminal/antisocial behavior is concerned, suboptimal arousal theory stipulates that persons who most often feel "starved" for environmental stimuli will be most likely to offend.

Evidence Bearing on Suboptimal Arousal Theory

Sensation Seeking and Boredom. The most straightforward hypotheses that can be derived from suboptimal arousal theory is that behavioral tendencies such as sensation seeking and risk taking should be correlated with criminal/antisocial behavior. The relationships should be such that persons with the greatest sensation-seeking and risk-taking tendencies will be most involved in crime and delinquency. Research bearing on this hypothesis is very supportive (Table 8.2).

Another line of support for suboptimal arousal is research connecting susceptibility to boredom with offending tendencies. Consistent with the theory, studies have indicated that frequent feelings of boredom are more common among delinquents than among persons in general (Table 8.8).[30]

Impulsivity. Because boredom-prone persons are seeking new experiences more often than most people, it is reasonable to expect that they would be unusually impulsive. Consequently, suboptimal arousal theory would predict a positive correlation between impulsivity and criminality,[31] a prediction supported by considerable research (Table 8.1).

Extroversion. Suboptimal arousal theory asserts that people who are highly extroverted will usually be suboptimally aroused.[32] This would be consistent with evidence that criminal/antisocial behavior is positively associated with extroversion (Table 8.5).

Drug Use and Abuse. Numerous recreational drugs offer a rather obvious way of having new experiences and relieving boredom. Consequently, suboptimal arousal theory predicts that a positive relationship should exist between involvement in criminality (other than drug offenses) and the taking of various recreational drugs. This prediction is consistent with available evidence (Table 8.10).

Sexual Promiscuity. Suboptimal arousal theory predicts that criminals, delinquents, and persons with antisocial tendencies would be more sexually experienced given that most sexual behavior provides an additional source of excitement. The evidence supporting a statistical link between sexual promiscuity and early onset of sexual behavior and offending probabilities is strong (Table 8.11).

Pain Tolerance, Fear, and Stress. Suboptimal arousal theory suggests that persons who are most prone toward criminal/antisocial behavior would respond to pain or threats of pain with relatively little avoidance. This would be consistent with several studies that have found criminals and psychopaths exhibiting greater than normal pain tolerance (Table 9.24).

According to suboptimal arousal theory, criminals and psychopaths should be less fearful and less prone to experience stress than most people.[33] Regarding their fearlessness, one study found psychopaths exhibiting unusually low fear responses when confronted with impending pain.[34] In the case of stress, several studies have found secretion of cortisol (considered a key stress hormone) to be inversely correlated with involvement in criminal behavior (Table 9.16).

Child Abuse and Harsh Discipline. Suboptimal arousal theory suggests a rather novel explanation for the well-established positive relationship between child abuse and criminal/antisocial behavior (Table 7.9). According to the theory, the relationship is not simply due to the experience of child abuse leading to criminality later on. Instead, children who are suboptimally aroused may elicit harsher forms of discipline by parents than most other children. While this hypothesis may be criticized as "blaming the victim," it could at least partly explain why parents of many conduct disordered and delinquent children resort to abusive forms of discipline.

School Performance. Theoretically, youngsters who are suboptimally aroused will find it difficult to focus their attention on routine projects, such as those typically required to do well in school. Therefore, suboptimal arousal theory would predict that school performance and school attendance would be below average among offender populations, and that school discipline problems would be above average. These predictions are all largely consistent with available evidence (Table 8.13).

Religiosity. To the degree that church services and sermons tend to be routine, suboptimal arousal theory predicts that criminals and delinquents would generally avoid religious ceremonies. As a result, their religious beliefs would likely become less orthodox than for persons in general. This reasoning is consistent with evidence that criminals and delinquents are unusually low in religiosity, particularly in the case of church attendance (Table 7.23a).

Mental/Behavioral Disorders. Suboptimal arousal theory predicts that criminal/antisocial behavior will be linked to symptoms of ADHD.[35] This is because, theoretically, the main behavioral symptoms of ADHD result from the brains of some children requiring much more stimulation than the brains of other children.[36] The association between ADHD and criminal/antisocial behavior is well established (Table 8.18).

Heart Rates. Persons whose heart (and pulse) rates are slow under normal conditions and/or slow to speed up under stressful/threatening conditions should be unusually prone toward criminal/antisocial behavior.[37] This is because heart and pulse rates are considered peripheral (i.e., external to the brain) indicators of attention and arousal functioning within the brain.[38] The evidence is consistent with this prediction (Table 9.12).

Skin Conductivity. Recall that under stress, as well as during resting conditions, criminals and psychopaths tend to exhibit below normal elevations in skin conductivity (their Galvanic Skin Response is less than normal). Given that skin conductivity is partly regulated by arousal control centers in the brain, this finding would be predicted by suboptimal arousal theory (Table 9.13).

Brain Waves. Generally slow brain wave patterns in the neocortex are also considered an indicator of suboptimal arousal.[39] Therefore, evidence that criminals and psychopaths have slower brain waves under various testing conditions than do persons in general would be consistent with arousal theory (Table 9.21).

The P300 decrement is also thought to reflect a general failure to fully attend to stimuli as much as most people do.[40] Thus, the evidence of a link between the P300 decrement and criminality/psychopathy is consistent with suboptimal arousal theory (Table 9.23),[41] although, as we will see, it is also consistent with at least one other biosocial theory.

Neurotransmitters. Several neuroscientists have investigated links between key neurotransmitters and symptoms of suboptimal arousal. For example, low serotonin activity in the brain has been linked to ADHD,[42] conduct disorders,[43] and aggressive–impulsive behavior.[44] Studies of laboratory animals have shown that reductions in serotonin activity in the brain cause animals to exhibit impulsive aggression.[45]

Low levels of two other neurotransmitters—norepinephrine and dopamine—have also been linked to two established correlates of crime: ADHD[46] and impulsivity.[47] Other studies suggest that the catecholamine system of ADHD youngsters is underresponsive to normal input from the neocortex.[48] These lines of evidence would be consistent with evidence of relatively low serotonin and possible abnormalities in catecholamine activity in the brains of persistent criminals and psychopaths (Tables 9.17 and 9.18). It is also worth mentioning that stimulants such as Ritalin chemically resemble and seem to mimic the activity of catecholamines in the brain.[49]

Gender and Age. Studies of gender differences in suboptimal arousal have provided mixed support for arousal theory. On the supportive side, studies have consistently shown males to be more prone to boredom than are females.[50] Even as infants, boys habituate to a given stimuli more quickly than do girls.[51]

Confusion has come from studies of arousal based on skin conductivity measures. While some of these studies have reported that males are less responsive to stimuli than females,[52] other studies have reported the opposite.[53] The latter findings appear to be inconsistent with arousal theory. In terms of age, the limited evidence is again inconsistent with arousal theory because middle and older aged persons exhibit lower average skin conductivity than do persons in the highest crime-prone years.[54]

Prevention and Treatment.   Given the established correlation between ADHD and criminal/antisocial behavior, suboptimal arousal theory leads one to believe that drugs that alleviate ADHD symptoms might also help to prevent criminal/antisocial behavior. Recall that stimulants such as Ritalin seem to activate brain functioning of ADHD children so that they are less likely to be hyperactive.

The evidence pertaining to the use of stimulants to treat offending behavior is shown in Table 13.1. In considering the evidence, you should keep in mind that these experiments are all limited in terms of sample size (usually less than one hundred), and nearly always measure only some fairly frequently occurring aspect of the behavior targeted for treatment. A fairly typical study, for example, might identify fifty youth with symptoms of conduct disorders or delinquency, and divide them at random into two groups. One of the groups receives a stimulant drug for the next six months while the other receives a placebo (sugar pill), and various aspects of their behavior are observed by teachers, counselors, or parents.

Table 13.1 shows that studies of Ritalin suggest that it helps to alleviate behavioral symptoms of conduct disorders.[55] Similarly, a couple of studies using other stimulant medications indicated that these drugs significantly reduce externalizing behavior of juvenile delinquents. Mixed results have been obtained so far in using stimulant drugs to treat behavioral symptoms associated with delinquents. Overall, while the evidence is still limited, it supports suboptimal arousal theory in suggesting that the overt behavioral symptoms of conduct disorders can be modestly suppressed with stimulant drugs.

TABLE 13.1.   Results of the use of stimulant drugs in treating conduct disorders and symptoms of juvenile delinquency. (Studies that call stimulant medications into question for treating CD and delinquency are listed after a double slash.) (Note: Except for *methylphenidate,* it is not necessary to know the names of these drugs for examination purposes unless your instructor states otherwise.)

Stimulant Drugs	Type of Subjects	Targeted Behavior	Studies and Findings
methylphenidate (Ritalin)	conduct disordered children	reduction of disruptive, acting out behavior	Klorman 1988a; Barkley et al. 1989 //
	juvenile delinquents	reduction of disruptive, aggressive behavior	// Conners et al. 1971
Benzedrine sulfate & dextroamphetamine sulfate	conduct disordered children	reduction of disruptive, acting out behavior	Conners & Eisenberg 1963; Eisenberg et al. 1965 //
	juvenile delinquents	reduction of disruptive, aggressive behavior	Korey 1944; Eisenberg et al. 1963 //

Closing Comments on Suboptimal Arousal Theory

According to suboptimal arousal theory, people neurologically vary in their preferences for intense environmental stimuli. Some people are most comfortable with very little stimuli, while others quickly feel bored without almost continual exposure to novel and intense stimuli. Suboptimal arousal theory contends that this latter group of individuals will have an elevated risk of becoming involved in crime, especially if alternative avenues for satiating their need for stimulation and excitement are not met.

Considerable evidence supports suboptimal arousal theory.[56] This theory has been found predictive of several established behavioral correlates of crime, as well as certain physiological and neurological variables, such as slow heart rates and slow brain wave patterns. Despite the evidence supporting the theory, it has difficulty accounting for gender and especially age variations in offending probabilities.

It is worth noting that many of the predictions derived from suboptimal arousal theory are similar to those derived from control theory. One interpretation of this similarity is that suboptimal arousal theory may have identified a neurological basis for what Gottfredson and Hirschi define as a lack of self-control.

REWARD DOMINANCE THEORY:
People Whose Brains Focus on Rewards Instead of Punishments Are More Crime-Prone

Herbert C. Quay (1927–),[57] **Jeffrey A. Gray** (1934–),[58] and **Don C. Fowles,**[59] along with other researchers[60] have formulated a neurologically specific theory that is called **reward dominance theory**[61] (and occasionally the **Quay–Gray theory**). The theory is based on the idea that most voluntary behavior is regulated by the relative strength of two opposing behavior control functions in the brain. One is called the **behavioral activation system (BAS)** and the other is called the **behavioral inhibition system (BIS).**

The BAS is thought to motivate or induce behavioral response to cues of probable reward, and the BIS is believed to inhibit behavioral responses to cues of probable punishment.

Reward Dominance Theory in Brief

Reward dominance theory uses the concepts of BAS and BIS to reason as follows: When someone senses that reward is likely to be contingent on a particular course of action, this individual's BAS will engage, and this engagement will motivate him/her to initiate the necessary action sequence. In other words, if steps A, B, and C are perceived as needed to obtain a probable reward, the BAS will begin the action sequence. Contrary-wise, when an individual perceives a high probability of being punished if it takes a particular course of action, the BIS will engage. This means that, if steps X, Y, and Z are seen as likely to result in punishment, an inhibitory region of the brain will prevent the action sequence from being initiated.

According to reward dominance theory, the "strength" of the BAS and the BIS is roughly equal for most people. As a result, most people are sensitive to both the rewarding and the punishing aspects of their actions, and they learn to make decisions accordingly. In the case of criminals and psychopaths, however, reward dominance theory asserts that the BIS is relatively weak and/or the BAS is especially strong (or dominant).[62] Consequently, criminals and psychopaths are hyperresponsive to the prospects of reward and hyporesponsive to the prospects of punishment.[63] This condition is called **reward dominant.** The behavior of criminals and psychopaths, therefore, becomes skewed toward all sorts of reckless and socially inappropriate activities.

Most of the initial research undertaken to test the merit of reward dominance theory involved computerized games. After some initial "easy wins," the computer was programmed to insure greater and greater proportions of losses, so that it behooved players to stop playing beyond the first dozen or so tries.[64] Reward dominance theory predicted that subjects with conduct disorders, psychopathy, and the like will be unusually prone to persist at the game despite the increasing losses. The results of experiments designed to test this prediction with conduct disordered children have been largely supportive,[65] with one failure to replicate.[66]

Theoretically, what is happening is this: Children with conduct disorders become "hooked" on the prospects of reward, and ignore the signs that response contingencies have switched to that of punishment (or nonreward). Thus, unlike children in general, those with conduct disorder (and other strong criminal/antisocial tendencies) seem to be relatively fixated on reward and oblivious to punishment.

Proponents of reward dominance theory have sought to identify specific aspects of brain functioning that might regulate BIS and BAS.[67] There is some evidence that both serotonin and the catecholamines comprising much of the limbic–frontal brain region are important to BIS/BAS functioning.[68] Another possibility is that the brain's natural opiates (called *endorphines*) are involved.[69]

Gray has hypothesized that a network of nerve cells running from the left frontal lobes down through the limbic system could be the main seat of BIS control.[70] This proposal would be consistent with evidence that several factors linked to deficiencies in language skills are related to criminal/antisocial behavior.

Evidence Pertaining to Reward Dominance Theory

Gambling Addiction.   Put yourself in the following circumstances: You are given $20 by an experimenter, who tells you that the purpose of the experiment is for you to use this $20 to make as much additional money as you can. You play against a preprogrammed computer, and can put all or some of your money at risk up to one hundred times. The only thing you are not told is that the computer has been preprogrammed to begin with a very high payoff ratio, and then gradually drop to a zero payoff for all bets after fifty. What do you think you would do? Would you quickly begin to stop betting after an initial run of good luck, or would you keep on risking your money long after the computer makes sure you lose every bet?

Because reward dominance theory sees crime-prone persons as neurologically inclined to focus mainly on the prospects of reward rather than on any risks, they should be more prone than most people to continue risking money long after the computer has stopped making any payoffs. In fact, this is what a number of experiments have shown in children, adolescents, and adults.[71] This pattern of response is called **response preservation,** and it is especially characteristic of criminals and psychopaths,[72] as predicted by reward dominance theory. Theoretically, it is responsible for the positive relationship between offending and gambling addiction (Table 8.22).

Drug Use.   A great deal of research has shown that most addictive drugs have their addictive effects because they act on various reward pathways in the brain.[73] These pathways are primarily located in the limbic system and extend forward into the frontal lobes.[74] If one thinks in terms of reward dominance theory, it would follow that crime-prone persons would be unusually likely to use addictive drugs, as research overwhelmingly suggests (Tables 8.20 and 8.21).

Impulsivity and Delay of Gratification.   The reward dominance theory of criminal/antisocial behavior suggests that offenders will find it unusually difficult to inhibit responses whenever the prospects of reward are even remotely present.[75] Thus, even if responding runs the risk of serious punishment and even if a delayed response would result in an even greater reward later, crime-prone persons should be unusually prone to emit an immediate response to the prospects of reward.[76] This theoretical reasoning is consistent with evidence that offenders are more impulsive (Table 8.1) and are less prone toward delayed gratification (Table 8.31) than are persons in general.

Heart Rate and Skin Conductivity.   The most common peripheral measure of BAS functioning is an elevated heart rate, and to measure BIS functioning, skin conductivity (galvanic skin Response) is often used.[77] Theoretically, criminals and psychopaths (but especially psychopathic criminals) should exhibit a higher heart rate response to the prospects of a reward and a lower GSR in response to the prospects of punishment than would be true of persons in general. Thus far, the results of experiments along these lines have been complicated, and far from clear-cut, although they have provided limited support for reward dominance theory.[78]

Accidental Injuries.   Life always involves risk, but obviously to widely varying degrees. According to reward dominance theory, criminals and psychopaths have an unusually high tendency to take risks. This implies that their rates of accidental injuries will be unusually high as well, which is consistent with most available evidence (Table 9.6).

Conduct Disorders and ADHD.   Reward dominance theory explains ADHD symptoms (mainly inattention and hyperactivity) as due to an underactive BIS relative to their BAS.[79] Consequently, the theory predicts that ADHD and criminal/antisocial behavior should be positively associated with one another, as nearly all relevant evidence has confirmed (Table 8.18).

In addition, the well-established link between conduct disorders in childhood and both criminality and psychopathy later in life (Table 1.3) are predicted by reward dominance theory. The theory suggests that individuals with both conduct disorders and ADHD symptoms should be especially prone toward criminal/antisocial behavior, a prediction not yet tested.

Depression.   According to reward dominance theory, criminal/antisocial behavior should be linked to *low* levels of depression (except for manic depression). This is because an overly active BIS should induce a rather constant state of anxiety (which is thought to lead to depression), and it should inhibit criminal/antisocial behavior.[80] The evidence is largely inconsistent with reward dominance theory in this prediction, because depression tends to be unusually *high* among criminals and psychopaths (Table 8.26).

Closing Comments on Reward Dominance Theory

Reward dominance theory hypothesizes the existence of two types of behavioral control systems: a behavioral activating system (BAS) and a behavioral inhibiting system (BIS). According to the theory, the BAS and the BIS are roughly balanced in relative strength for most people. Persons who are prone toward criminality and psychopathy, however, have a BAS that is considerably stronger than their BIS. As a result, criminals and psychopaths should focus more than most people do on the potential for short-term rewards associated with their behavior, ignoring any potentially punishing aspects of their actions. Theoretically, this "biased" focus has the effect of greatly increasing the frequency of antisocial conduct.

Quite a few hypotheses have been derived from reward dominance theory, most of which fit with current knowledge well. The main difficulty linked with the theory so far has had to do with evidence of a positive relationship between criminality and depression. Theoretically, the relationship should be negative. This is because a relatively strong BAS is not only thought to promote criminal/antisocial behavior, but also to prevent feelings of anxiety and guilt (frequent components of depression).

SEIZURING THEORY:
Limbic Seizures Sometimes Cause Impulsive Offending

In the 1970s, a small group of psychiatrists and neurologists began considering the possible role of the limbic system in certain types of criminal behavior.[81] They were drawn to study this particular region of the brain after noting the bizarre and seemingly senseless nature of some violent crimes, such as attacking a loved one or a drinking buddy over some utterly trivial issue, or gunning down children in a school yard.

Seizuring theory was inspired by research on epilepsy. As you may recall from Chapter 9, epilepsy refers to bursts of electrical discharges in the brain (called *seizures*) that often manifest themselves as uncontrollable motor spasms called **convulsions** (or **fits**). In other words, epileptic seizures occur in the brain, whereas convulsions are among the most obvious outward muscular manifestations of seizures.

Not all seizures cause convulsions. Some seizures are confined to areas of the brain that have little direct control over muscular movements. These seizures are referred to as **subconvulsive** (or **subclinical**) **seizures.** For instance, if a seizure is localized in a small region of the limbic system, it may not affect motor coordination at all, but it could have dramatic effects on emotions because the limbic system has a great deal to do with basic social emotions.

Seizuring Theory in Brief

Seizuring theorists have suggested that subconvulsive seizures in and around the limbic system may sometimes induce behavior of a criminal nature. In other words, persons experiencing seizures in or around the limbic system may engage in actions driven by powerful emotions with little or no input from the higher brain centers (i.e., the neocortex).[82] The term that has often come to be used to describe this phenomenon is **episodic dyscontrol** (or **behavioral disorders**).[83] As a result of limbic seizures, affected individuals might act with no impairment as far as basic coordination is concerned. Nevertheless, the behavior might not only be contrary to "rational thought," but could even surprise the neocortex.

The detection of subconvulsive seizures can be much more difficult than in the case of convulsive (epileptic) seizures. This is not only because subconvulsive seizures, by definition, do not cause convulsive fits, but also because subconvulsive seizures often occur too deep inside the brain to be detectable with electrodes attached to the scalp.[84]

An area of the limbic system that has been most often implicated in the seizuring theory of vi-olent criminality is the **amygdala.**[85] This is partly because the amygdala plays a particularly important role in controlling social emotions (such as jealousy and rage), and also because it has been shown to be the most seizure-prone region of the human brain.[86] Damage to this primitive region of the mammalian brain frequently unleashes a torrent of violent behavior, both in humans[87] and in other mammals.[88] Nevertheless, some types of damage to the amygdala can make aggressive animals more passive and docile.[89] Overall, this small almond-shaped region of the limbic system, located just above each ear, but deep inside the brain, has been a major research focus for seizuring theorists.[90]

Areas in and around the limbic system have also been implicated in the control of basically un-learned urges to possess and control objects.[91] A common expression of these urges in many species of animals may be compulsive hoarding behavior,[92] which sometimes follows extended periods of food deprivation.[93] Based on a case study of a British woman who was anorexic, one writer suggested that humans may also sometimes exhibit compulsive hoarding behavior in the form of kleptomania.[94]

Evidence Pertaining to Seizuring Theory

Epilepsy. Seizuring theory leads one to hypothesize that criminality will be more common among epileptics than among nonepileptics, because seizures in one part of the brain are associated with an increased probability of seizures in other parts of the brain. Except for delinquency, evidence bearing on this hypothesis has been largely supportive, indicating that the prevalence of epilepsy in adult prison populations is four to five times greater than in general populations (Table 9.9).

Types of Offenses. To the degree that seizuring theory has explanatory power, one should find seizures most highly associated with unusually impulsive and "irrational" types of offenses, not with those that are well-calculated and financially lucrative. This hypothesis is difficult to directly test, but would be consistent with studies linking

TABLE 13.2. Results from studies that have sought relationships between the occurrence of subconvulsive (nonepileptic) seizuring and criminal and/or violent behavior. (Shaded regions indicate where studies should be to be consistent with seizuring theory.)

Nature of the Relationship	Criminal Behavior			Impulsive Violence and Acting Out Behavior	
	Violent	**Property**	**Other**	**In Humans**	**In Nonhuman Animals**
Positive	**Asia** *Japan:* 1 **North America** *United States:* 1			**North America** *United States:* 9	**Mammal** *Feline:* 2; *Rodent:* 2
Not significant					
Negative					

seizure disorders with the commission of primarily violent crimes, and with involvement in violent outbursts generally.

Studies that have made such connections are contained in Table 13.2. As you can see, a few studies have linked individuals with a history of seizures with involvement in violent offenses, but none have yet done so for other types of offenses. In addition, several studies have found impulsive violence more common for persons with a history of subconvulsive seizures than for persons with no seizures. Similar findings have been reported by researchers working with various species of laboratory animals: Evidence of brain seizures is associated with an elevated probability of impulsive aggression.[95]

Head Injury. Head injuries have been shown to be one of the main causes of brain seizures.[96] This being the case, seizuring theory would imply that higher rates of injury to the brain would be found in offender populations than in general populations. Several studies have found support for this hypothesis.[97]

Enuresis. Episodic dyscontrol may underlie a general difficulty in voluntarily controlling one's impulses, one symptom of which might be enuresis.[98] This assertion implies that a positive relationship will exist between criminal/antisocial behavior and enuresis, which several studies have indicated (Table 8.23).

Hypoglycemia. Hypoglycemia has been shown to be accompanied by bursts of abnormal, sometimes epilepticlike brain wave patterns.[99] From this observation, seizuring theory would imply that hypoglycemia would be associated with high rates of criminality, especially crimes of a highly impulsive nature. Considerable evidence supports this implication (Table 9.7).

Alcohol. Also supportive of seizuring theory is evidence that alcohol consumption can sometimes trigger seizures for persons with epilepsy, both in humans[100] and rats.[101] This is not to say that alcohol is a direct cause of epilepsy, but that, for susceptible individuals, alcohol may trigger an episode.[102] In the case of criminality, the link to alcohol is fairly strong, especially for violent offenses. Regardless of the criminality involved, several studies of humans[103] and at least one of cats[104] have found alcohol consumption associated with an increased probability of impulsive aggression.

Treatment. One of the strongest lines of support for seizuring theory has come from research on treatment of persons who engage in criminal behavior due to diagnosed episodic dyscontrol. Theoretically, medication that is effective in treating epilepsy should also be effective in treating episodic dyscontrol, and any offending that occurs as a consequence. Most of the drugs used to treat epilepsy are known as **anticonvulsants.**

Table 13.3 provides a brief summary of the outcome of clinical research with anticonvulsants and other epileptic drugs for treating impulsive fits of rage and other unruly acts that are sometimes of a delinquent/criminal nature. As you can see, in the case of three of the four medications listed, studies have concluded that these drugs are helpful in diminishing an array of violent tendencies. This does not mean that the majority of offenders would benefit from such medication, because only persons exhibiting criminal violence as a result of a subconvulsive seizure are ever targeted for treatment with antiepileptic medication.[105] Experiments with laboratory animals also indicate that vicious attacks can be curtailed by anticonvulsants.[106]

Another line of evidence suggesting that a propensity for seizures is a causal factor in some forms of criminal behavior comes from noting that serious criminals and psychopaths, on average, have quicker and more violent tempers than do persons in general.[107] Also, surgery involving the amygdala (or areas adjacent to it) has been found to sometimes help diminish rageful outbursts, often without otherwise affecting overall personality, both in humans[108] and in laboratory animals.[109]

There are even some clinical trials in which anticonvulsive medications have been used to treat addiction to cocaine and marijuana. The evidence from these trials has been mixed, with some suggesting significant beneficial effects,[110] and at least one calling these effects into question.[111]

Closing Remarks about Seizuring Theory

While full-blown epilepsy has such devastating effects on muscular coordination that its victims would rarely be capable of criminal behavior, some seizures are subconvulsive in the sense that they affect areas of the brain that have little direct control over muscular movement. According to seizuring theory, if a seizure occurs in or around the limbic system, it can sometimes trigger fairly primitive emotions that cause acts of violence or property confiscations that violate criminal

TABLE 13.3. Results of the use of anticonvulsant/antiepileptic drugs in the treatment of disruptive behavior, rageful outbursts, and sudden fits of aggression. (Studies following a double slash failed to confirm any treatment effects.) (Note: It is not necessary to know the names of these drugs for examination purposes unless your instructor states otherwise.)

Drugs	Type of Subjects	Targeted Behavior	Studies
Carbamazepine	Conduct disordered children	Reduction of aggressive behavior and episodic dyscontrol	Tunks & Dermer 1977; Cassidy 1990; Kafantaris et al. 1992; Sugarman 1992 //
Diphenylhydantoin	Conduct disordered/ attention deficit children	Reduction of disruptive aggressive behavior	// Lefkowitz 1969; Looker & Conners 1970; Conner et al. 1971
Propranolol (an epileptic medication that is not always classified as an anticonvulsant)	Periodically violent mental patients of various ages	Reduction of rageful and violent behavior	F. A. Elliott 1977; Yudofsky et al. 1981; Williams et al. 1982; Johnson 1984; Sheard 1984; Mattes 1988; Mattes 1990 //
Valproate	Periodically violent adult mental patients & conduct disordered children	Reduction of irritability & aggression	Neepe 1983; Deltito 1993; Wilcox 1994; Wilcox 1995; Donovan et al. 1997 //

statutes. Seizuring theorists call this phenomenon *episodic dyscontrol.*

Putting the theory into an historical context, it is worth noting that, in the early 1800s, Lombroso hypothesized that some criminal acts might be a manifestation of what he termed "latent epilepsy," meaning epilepsy that is usually hidden. Lombroso went on to speculate that latent epileptics might exhibit rage and other "primitive impulses."[112]

Seizuring theory is probably the narrowest theory in criminology, because it purports to explain only a small minority of criminal offenses: those brought on by epilepticlike seizures in and around the limbic system. Nevertheless, it offers explanations for several correlates of crime that no other criminological theory has yet addressed. For example, so far only seizuring theory has offered a coherent explanation for why epilepsy and hypoglycemia are correlates of crime. In addition, only seizuring theory suggests that some of the drugs used in treating epilepsy (called anticonvulsants) are also helpful in treating bursts of aggression that sometimes result in criminal assaults.

FRONTAL LOBE THEORY:
Dysfunctioning of the Frontal
Lobes Causes Crime

As noted in the preceding chapter, the frontal lobes are a particularly prominent feature of the human brain when compared to the brain of other mammals. In modern humans, the frontal lobes comprise approximately a third of the entire neocortex, a proportion that far exceeds any other species.[113] The anterior (or front) half of the frontal lobes are especially well developed in humans, giving rise to what is often referred to as the **prefrontal area** (or **prefrontal cortex**).[114] A sketch of the left hemisphere of the neocortex is presented in Figure 13.4, with its lobes specified.

What do the frontal lobes contribute to human thought and behavior? Considerable progress has been made in answering this question since the 1940s, when researchers first began systematically studying people suffering from serious damage to their frontal lobes. These studies have revealed that most people usually suffer only modest ill effects as far as basic intelligence is concerned, especially if the injuries are confined to the prefrontal area.[115] For example, most people who sustain injuries strictly to the prefrontal area of the frontal lobes are sometimes unaffected in terms of their ability to read and make arithmetic calculations.[116] However, even slight damage to the prefrontal area of the frontal lobes, especially in the left hemisphere (where language is primarily controlled), has been linked to substantial cognitive deficits.[117]

The sort of effects most associated with prefrontal injuries mainly have to do with the ability to plan and reflect on the consequences of various courses of action that must be followed in order to attain long-term goals.[118] These planning skills, collectively known as **executive functions,**[119] are

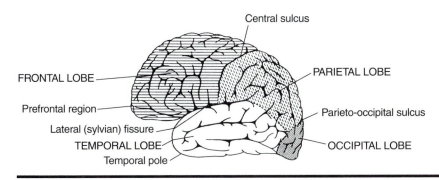

FIGURE 13.4   Lobes of the brain.

often dramatically diminished in patients with pre-frontal injuries.[120]

In addition to having difficulty developing realistic plans for the future, **frontal lobe patients** also tend to be unusually rigid in making responses to new, unfamiliar contingencies.[121] Instead of readily adapting to new contingencies, these patients are usually prone to exhibit what has been termed **response preservation,** meaning stubbornly sticking to the originally established response mode even though doing so is not accomplishing the subject's objective, and may even be counterproductive.[122]

Another evolved function of the frontal lobes, especially of the prefrontal area, appears to be control over empathy and feelings of remorse and shame.[123] This has been accomplished by tightly linking the prefrontal region to the limbic system.[124] Damage to the prefrontal region of the frontal lobes is often associated with emotional "flatness" and an inability to feel genuine sorrow for having caused others to suffer.[125]

Finally, studies have lead researchers to argue that the prefrontal lobes are crucial for moral reasoning.[126] They seem to make their contribution to moral reasoning by monitoring the emotional control centers in and around the limbic system,[127] and then guiding a set of actions that help to comfort one's emotional feeling for any harm done to others.

Dysfunctioning of the prefrontal area should not be thought of strictly in terms of physical injury. Other more subtle causes of frontal lobe dysfunctions may include various genetic factors. In addition, damage sustained during prenatal development by mothers consuming alcohol or other drugs during critical times in fetal brain development may prevent the prefrontal lobes from developing normally.[128]

A challenge to those who have pursued frontal lobe theory of criminal/antisocial behavior has been how to objectively measure dysfunctions in the frontal lobes. Obviously, if someone has sustained massive physical injury to the frontal area of the brain, few would question that the frontal lobes will dysfunction as a result. However, only a small fraction of criminals and psychopaths

have experienced obvious frontal lobe damage. Frontal lobe theorists contend that many people have subtle damage and dysfunctions that can often be measured in one of two ways: behavioral measures and neurological measures.

Behavioral measures of frontal lobe dysfunctions have consisted of presenting subjects with cognitive tasks that primarily challenge their abilities to plan and organize ideas in a hierarchical fashion in terms of importance, and to inhibit responding until sufficient information is presented.[129] The most widely used behavioral measure of frontal lobe dysfunctioning is a test called the **Wisconsin Card Sorting Test (WCST),**[130] although the validity of this measure is still being scrutinized.[131] First developed in the 1940s, the WCST requires subjects to change decision-making strategies in order to get correct answers to various problems.[132] Subjects with frontal lobe dysfunctions tend to answer few questions correctly because they fail to shift their decision-making strategies when it is appropriate for them to do so.[133] Recently, a similar test was designed for use with monkeys, and experimental research demonstrated that the test does indeed make heavy demands on frontal lobe functioning.[134]

Neurological methods of detecting frontal lobe dysfunctions are still being developed, but in recent years they have included EEG brain wave measures, along with computerized axial tomography (CAT) scans, and magnetic resonance imaging (MRI) readings.

Frontal Lobe Theory in Brief

Beginning primarily with **Ethan Gorenstein** (1953–),[135] numerous proposals have been made regarding the possible involvement of the frontal lobes, especially the prefrontal area, in criminal and antisocial behavior.[136] All of these theorists have contended that, in one way or another, the failure of the frontal lobes to function properly may affect higher thought in ways that fail to inhibit criminal and antisocial behavior.

According to frontal lobe theory, the frontal lobes have evolved primarily to help guide behavior that requires long-term planning and foresight, particularly within a complex social environment. The theory also assumes that planning and foresight usually help people satisfy their basic needs and desires without engaging in antisocial behavior. This reasoning leads proponents of frontal lobe theory to attribute much antisocial behavior to **frontal lobe dysfunctions** (or **failures in executive functioning**).

Evidence Pertaining to Frontal Lobe Theory

ADHD.   The frontal lobes are clearly linked to the ability to maintain selective attention.[137] If frontal lobe dysfunctioning is a cause of criminal/antisocial behavior, one would expect offenders to be less able to focus their attention on complex projects than would be true of persons in general. This implies that mental conditions such as ADHD will be associated with criminality. Evidence is strongly supportive of this deduction (Table 8.18). There is also direct evidence linking frontal lobe dysfunctioning with ADHD,[138] which is also consistent with frontal lobe theory.

Delayed versus Immediate Gratification.   Another hypothesis that can be derived from frontal lobe theory is that criminals and psychopaths should be more prone than other people to focus less on long-term outcomes of their actions than on short-term outcomes. This prediction would be consistent with evidence that offenders are not as prone as people in general toward delayed gratification patterns (Table 8.31).

Moral Reasoning.   Given that the frontal lobes appear to play a vital role in moral reasoning, frontal lobe theory would predict that slow development in such reasoning would be associated with involvement in criminal/antisocial behavior. Evidence is largely consistent with this hypothesis (Table 8.38).

Intelligence and Academic Performance.   Frontal lobe theory would lead to the prediction that low IQ and poor academic performance would

be associated with criminality, although not equally so. Regarding intelligence, studies have found that the frontal lobes play a significant role in determining intelligence, although other parts of the brain are also involved.[139] Furthermore, doing well in school has been shown to depend not only on intelligence, but also on planning ability, such as budgeting one's time and sustaining attention on complex tasks.[140] In other words, academic performance appears to depend both on intelligence and on the ability to plan, the latter being almost exclusively a frontal lobe function. From this reasoning, frontal lobe theory implies that academic performance should be more strongly linked to low involvement in criminal/antisocial behavior than is true for intelligence. Research is largely consistent with this reasoning (Tables 8.13 and 8.14).

Massive Frontal Lobe Damage.   Another line of evidence bearing on frontal lobe theory has involved studies of persons who have sustained injury to their frontal lobes. While these case studies are rare, they have been quite consistent in linking serious injury to the frontal lobes with increases in antisocial behavior.[141] Another accompaniment is difficulty planning any complex courses of action.[142]

Figure 13.5 provides an example of one of these case histories. Before sustaining massive prefrontal brain damage from a freak accident, the accident victim was said to have been a very considerate and responsible law-abiding citizen. After the accident, his personality dramatically changed to that of being impulsive, rude, foul-mouthed, and oblivious to the feelings of others.[143] Even though this case occurred over a century ago, scientists were recently able to create a three-dimensional diagram of the neurological damage sustained by the victim based on written accounts.

According to frontal lobe theory, this individual's change in behavior was the result of at least one of his prefrontal lobes having been rendered dysfunctional, and, as a result, he lost much of his control over various aspects of antisocial behavior. Similar case histories have been described for persons diagnosed with ASP[144] and for a child diagnosed with conduct disorders.[145]

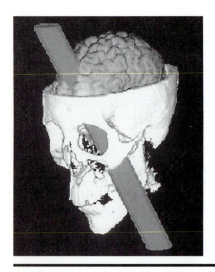

FIGURE 13.5   In 1848 an explosion rocketed an iron rod through the head of a 25-year-old man. The rod was almost immediately removed and despite his injury the man lived to the age of 37. Immediately after the injury, however, the man's personality dramatically shifted from that of a responsive, intelligent, and socially well adapted individual to one who exhibited no respect for social conventions and civility (Damasic et al., 1994, 1402). All that seemed to remain of the original character was intelligence. This was the first well-documented case of massive prefrontal damage.

Next-of-kin allowed the body to be exhumed five years after burial for medical research and in 1990 researchers carefully mapped the skull in order to precisely determine the location of the injury. As these computer simulations from various angles reveal, the injury was largely confined to the prefrontal area. This is among the evidence cited to support the prefrontal theory of criminal and antisocial behavior.

Brain Waves.   Frontal lobe theory would suggest that the brain waves of criminals and psychopaths should be slow relative to the brain waves of persons in general, at least in the frontal lobes. Such slowing would be consistent with evidence of some damage, caused by either physical or chemical insults. Consistent with this prediction is evi-dence from one study suggesting that young delin-quents exhibit a general slowing (or "sluggish-ness") of brain wave patterns primarily in the frontal regions.[146] Very similar abnormalities have been linked to alcoholism, as evidenced by re-duced blood flow to the frontal lobes.[147]

Additional research has suggested that seri-ous criminal offenders have an unusually high rate of dementia (deterioration) of frontal lobe func-tioning (sometimes in conjunction with deteriora-tion in the temporal lobes).[148] These studies must be considered preliminary, because they were based on small clinical samples.

Finally, in regard to brain waves, a recent study aimed at better understanding P300 brain waves concluded that P300 decrements primarily reflected an impairment in the executive functions governing attentional and working-memory con-trol especially in performing multistaged tasks.[149] Thus, high rates of P300 decrements in offenders could not only help to explain their antisocial be-havior (Table 9.23), but could also help to explain why offenders have high rates of ADHD and tend to do poorly on IQ tests and in school.

Blood Flow to the Frontal Lobes.   Recently, a study based on computerized mapping of the brain found that alcoholics, especially those who were also diagnosed with psychopathy, had significantly reduced cerebral blood flow to the frontal lobes.[150] This finding is supportive of frontal lobe theory as far as antisocial behavior is concerned.

Language Deficits.   Various lines of evidence in-dicate that the executive functioning of the frontal lobes plays a vital role in the development of lan-guage skills.[151] The evidence that most of the intellectual and academic deficits seen in per-sons with criminal/antisocial tendencies primarily have to do with deficiencies in language acquisi-tion would be consistent with frontal lobe theory (Tables 8.15 and 8.16).

Parental Alcoholism.   A few studies have found that sons of alcoholic men exhibit executive frontal lobe functioning deficits to an unusually high degree.[152] This would be consistent with frontal lobe functioning theory, given that criminal/antisocial behavior is positively associated with parental alcoholism (Table 7.11a).

Self-Control.   Frontal lobe theory leads to the prediction that persons with frontal lobe dysfunctions will have difficulty exercising self-control. You may recall that, in discussing Gottfredson and Hirschi's self-control theory, that measures of self-control may be capable of accounting for up to 25 percent of the variation people exhibit in offending.[153] This would not be surprising to frontal lobe theorists because they consider the frontal lobes the primary area of the brain that is responsible for long-term self-control.

Closing Comments about Frontal Lobe Theory

There is no doubt that the frontal lobes play a vital role in regulating human behavior. Scientists who study the brain have described this role primarily in terms of **executive functioning,** meaning the master integration of several activities for the achievement of some long-term goals .[154] The prefrontal areas of some people's brains do not appear to be as efficient as those of other people at mastering executive functioning. According to frontal lobe theory, people with the greatest difficulty self-regulating their behavior toward the achievement of long-term goals have frontal lobes that increase their probable involvement in persistent criminal/antisocial behavior.

A major criticism of frontal lobe theory is that it has difficulty measuring frontal lobe dysfunctions other than to infer them from the behavior one is trying to explain.[155] In recent years, however, progress has been made in using sophisticated EEG equipment, CAT scans, and MRI technology to measure the relative activity of the frontal lobes.[156] To the credit of frontal lobe theory, these direct neurological measures have indicated that criminals and psychopaths do seem to have frontal lobes that function less efficiently than is true for persons in general.

A substantial number of hypotheses can be derived from frontal lobe theory. Thus far, all of them appear to be largely consistent with the available evidence.

HEMISPHERIC FUNCTIONING THEORY: Right Hemispheric Dominance or Left Hemispheric Dysfunctioning Causes Crime

Hemispheric functioning theory focuses on the neocortex as contributing to variations in criminal and antisocial behavior. In this respect, it is similar to frontal lobe theory. The primary difference is that hemispheric functioning theory highlights differences in how the two halves of the neocortex function, with a special, although not an exclusive, focus on the frontal lobes.

Many studies have indicated that the two hemispheres tend to function differently, and that these functional differences manifest themselves in terms of different types of thoughts and emotions. Among the best documented differences are three that bear most heavily on hemispheric functioning theory. As summarized in Table 13.4, the right hemisphere is less adept at verbal/linguistic reasoning than is the left hemisphere,[157] and that the right hemisphere is responsible for more negative/unfriendly/rejecting emotions than is true of the left hemisphere.[158] Furthermore, the right hemisphere appears to respond more impulsively to stimuli than is true of the left hemisphere.[159]

What might these differences have to do with criminal/antisocial behavior? Hemispheric functioning theorists speculate that persons whose thought processes are most often focused in the right hemisphere than in the left hemisphere will be unusually nonattentive to verbal stimuli (including laws), and will exhibit more impulsivity and negative (antisocial) feelings toward others.

The Hemispheric Functioning Theory in Brief

Work on hemispheric functioning theory was begun in the 1970s by a Canadian named **Pierre Flor-Henry** (1934–).[160] Without specifically naming the theory, Flor-Henry reasoned roughly

TABLE 13.4.   Evidence of hemispheric differences in thought and emotional processing (overall consistency score = 88.4%).

Nature of the Relationship	Type of Thoughts and Emotions		
	Spatial/Wholistic Reasoning (as Opposed to Linguistic/Serial Reasoning)	**Act Impulsively (as Opposed to Attending to Details)**	**Negative/Unfriendly Emotions (as Opposed to Positive Prosocial Emotions)**
Right hemisphere more involved	**North America** *United States: 7*	**Europe** *England: 2* **North America** *United States: 2*	**Europe** *England: 1* **North America** *United States: 26*
No significant hemispheric differences	**North America** *United States: 1*		**Europe** *Sweden: 1* **North America** *Canada: 1; United States: 2*
Left hemisphere more involved			**North America** *United States: 1*

as follows: The left hemisphere is more involved in attending to linguistic stimuli than is the right hemisphere. Given that laws and other rules of conduct are nearly always expressed linguistically, almost any left hemispheric dysfunctioning could increase the probability of antisocial behavior.

In addition to the diminished focus on language-based reasoning, a shift toward right hemispheric functioning also appears to be associated with greater impulsivity and more negative emotional feelings.[161] As a result, individuals who have the highest proportion of their thinking taking place in the right hemisphere should attend less to linguistic stimuli, should act more often on the spur of the moment, and should have a less positive outlook on life than is true for persons with largely left hemispheric functioning.[162]

How can you determine which hemisphere is having the greatest influence on a person's thought processes? There are a variety of methods for doing so, each one having certain advantages and disadvantages.[163] Some researchers rely on computer-enhanced brain wave measures coming from each hemisphere while subjects perform various intellectual tasks, such as reciting the alphabet backwards or while watching various television programs.[164] However, the most common method is called the **dichotic listening test.**[165] It involves

having subjects put on a set of ear phones, and then feeding separate types of auditory information into each ear. For example, a poem might be recited into one ear, while instructions for getting from Point A to Point B might be recited into the other ear. Then, subjects are asked to repeat what they heard and can remember. Usually, by reversing the messages going into each ear, researchers are able to tell if subjects have a right or left ear advantage for listening to various types of messages.[166]

Studies have documented a phenomenon known as **contralateral control,** meaning that one side of the body, including the ears, tends to be controlled by the opposite side of the neocortex.[167] This phenomenon has allowed the dichotic listening test to estimate the degree to which subjects have a right ear (and thus left hemisphere) advantage for various tasks.

Hypotheses Pertaining to Hemispheric Functioning Theory

Intelligence.   Hemispheric functioning theory leads to the hypothesis that criminals will exhibit deficiencies in language-dependent tasks, but not in other intellectual tasks, such as spatial reasoning.[168] This prediction is consistent with evidence that most of the intellectual deficits found among criminals and psychopaths have more to do with language skills than with nonlinguistic abilities (Tables 8.15 and 8.16).

Attitudes, Peer Friendships, and Depression. Hemispheric functioning theory predicts that criminals and psychopaths should be less friendly and sociable than persons in general. This prediction is supported by evidence that delinquents and criminals express more negative attitudes than do peers, and that they have relatively fewer close friends (Table 7.19). It could also help explain why they have unusually high rates of depression (Table 8.26), suicide (Table 8.28), and lower self-esteem (Table 8.29).

Handedness. Considerable evidence suggests that handedness is linked to hemispheric dominance, with left- (and mixed-) handers being somewhat more prone toward use of the right (contralateral) hemisphere than is true for right handers.[169] This evidence in light of hemispheric functioning theory leads to the expectation that left- (and mixed-) handers will be more involved in criminal/antisocial behavior than right handers. The relevant evidence is weakly supportive of this prediction (Table 8.12).

Gender. A number of studies have indicated that men have higher rates of left- (or mixed-) handedness than do women, although the differences are modest.[170] One study of infants even found higher rates of left-handedness among males than females as young as one-and-a-half years of age.[171] This would suggest that males are "naturally" more prone toward use of their right hemisphere than females, which, according to hemispheric functioning theory, is the hemisphere that is most associated with antisocial thinking and rule breaking.

Direct Brain Measurement. In recent years, a few studies have begun to examine how the two hemispheres function in relationship to criminal and antisocial behavior. These studies provide the most direct test of hemispheric functioning theory.

One U.S. study found that adult psychopaths and conduct disordered children both exhibited unusual activation patterns in their left hemispheres when given mental tasks designed to primarily engage their frontal lobes.[172] In a Canadian study, researchers compared two groups of prisoners, one that had been diagnosed psychopathic and the other that had not received this diagnosis. This study concluded that psychopathic prisoners were more likely than prisoners in general to activate their left frontal lobes in response to various types of test stimuli.[173] Another U.S. study also compared psychopathic and nonpsychopathic offenders; it too found neurological evidence of greater "cognitive deficits" in the left than in the right hemisphere for the psychopathic group.[174] Note that, while all of these studies provide possible support for hemispheric functioning theory, they also can be considered relevant to frontal lobe theory, because the left hemispheric dysfunction in all three cases was primarily located in the frontal lobes.

Working along similar lines, researchers from Canada[175] and the United States[176] investigated psychopathy using the dichotic listening test. Both studies revealed that persons who were diagnosed with the antisocial personality syndrome were more balanced in attending to verbal information than were people in general (the latter having a more distinct right ear–left hemisphere advantage when attending to verbal information). While the differences in both studies were subtle, they are in accordance with hemispheric functioning theory.

Attention. At least three studies have indicated that the right hemisphere is less adept than the left hemisphere at maintaining sustained attention on tasks requiring a focus on detail.[177] This would imply that persons who are most prone toward criminal/antisocial behavior would have difficulty maintaining attention, thereby explaining why their rates of ADHD are unusually high (Table 8.18) and why their school performance is low even after adjusting for any deficits in IQ (Table 8.16).

Sexuality. At least one study has reported that right hemispheric activation was associated with sexual arousal.[178] If so, hemispheric functioning theory would predict that criminals and psychopaths would have an unusually keen interest in sex, a hypothesis that would be consistent with evidence that criminals and psychopaths have more sex partners and an earlier age of onset (Table 8.11) of sexual behavior than for persons in general.

Risk Taking and Accidental Injuries.   One more difference is that at least two studies have found that right hemispheric activation results in a lower estimate of the risk of adverse consequences for various courses of action compared to left hemispheric activation.[179] This difference would lead one to expect criminals and psychopaths to be unusually prone to take risks, and, as a result, to suffer high rates of accidental injuries. Both of these predictions are largely consistent with available evidence (Tables 8.2 and 9.6).

Closing Remarks about Hemispheric Functioning Theory

According to hemispheric functioning theory, the left hemisphere reasons in ways that are more positive and friendly than is true for the right hemisphere. The left hemisphere also reasons more in linguistic terms. Consequently, to the degree persons have a high proportion of their thought occurring in the left hemisphere rather than the right, they will be more prone toward prosocial and "law-abiding" behavior. This theory also suggests that various dysfunctions of either hemisphere could lead to criminal/antisocial behavior by forcing the properly functioning hemisphere to compensate for functions that it is ill equipped to perform.

Hemispheric functioning theory makes a number of unique predictions about how variables should be related to criminal behavior. All of these predictions have been at least modestly supported by the available evidence.

FINAL COMMENTS ON NEUROLOGICALLY SPECIFIC BIOSOCIAL THEORIES

This chapter makes clear that many ideas about the possible biological underpinnings of criminal/antisocial behavior have emerged since the 1950s. So far, however, these theories have had only a modest impact on "mainstream" criminology.[180] In the words of one commentator, "most criminologists do not give biological claims the time of day."[181]

As will be discussed more in the chapter to follow, the tendency for most criminologists to dismiss biological influences on criminal behavior could be due to a lack of training in biology. Another factor seems to be a genuine aversion to biologically oriented theories in light of past political abuses. One need only be reminded of the frightening legacy of Adolf Hitler's attempts to rid Germany of criminals, homosexuals, Jews, and other "inferior misfits" to appreciate this concern. Nevertheless, the misuse of scientific information does not mean that the information is inaccurate, or that it might not also be used in more constructive ways.

We have seen that each neurologically specific theory examined in this chapter focused on somewhat different aspects of brain functioning. As more is learned about how all parts of the brain interrelate, some of these theories are bound to merge with one another. Of course, someday neurologically specific theories may also become integrated with some of the social environmental theories reviewed in earlier chapters.[182]

SUMMARY

Biosocial theorizing in criminology can be divided into two categories: neurologically specific and evolutionary. This chapter has been devoted to exploring the first type. Neurologically specific theories differ from environmental theories in that environmental theories do not identify any aspect of brain functioning as affecting people's probability of engaging in criminal behavior. All neurologically specific theories do. This difference should not obscure the fact that both types of theory recognize that learning is crucial to crime causation.

This chapter began with a brief summary of how the human brain is structured. It was noted that the general structure follows the basic mammalian design. In essence, two cortices cover the innermost core, which mammals inherited millions of years ago from their reptilian ancestors. The inner core is called the *r-complex* and it still has major control over a number of basic survival instincts. The first cortex covering the r-complex is called the *limbic system* and it is responsible for various social emotions, such as those involved in caring for offspring and bonding to sex partners. The outermost cortex, called the *neocortex,* is where mammals carry out their most complex thinking and their most elaborate behavior. In humans, the neocortex is vastly enlarged relative to all other mammals. It includes parts of the brain used to read and interpret this paragraph. Despite the importance of the neocortex, you should never forget that it is not the only part of your brain that has influence over your behavior.

The five neurologically specific theories considered in this chapter were suboptimal arousal theory, reward dominance theory, seizuring theory, frontal lobe theory, and hemispheric functioning theory.

Suboptimal Arousal Theory

Suboptimal arousal theory maintains that all humans prefer levels of environmental stimulation that is neither too low (boring) nor too high (chaotic and even frightening).[183] As far as the brain is concerned, arousal control appears to be a diffuse function, affected in part by the reticular formation, located primarily in the brain stem and projecting up into many other higher brain regions. Primarily for genetic reasons, people vary in terms of how quickly they become accustomed to incoming stimuli at various intensities. Suboptimal arousal theorists contend that persons who need more than the normal amount of environmental stimulation will have an unusually high probability of committing crime.

Suboptimal arousal theory predicts that criminality will be associated with a number of behavioral tendencies, including impulsivity, hyperactivity, risk taking, sensation seeking, the use of mind-altering drugs, and highly varied sexual behavior. Evidence largely supports these predictions. The theory also suggests that offenders will be prone to avoid routine activities such as those associated with school and religion, predictions that are also consistent with most relevant research. There are several proponents of suboptimal arousal theory, but its origins are traced back primarily to David Lykken and Hans J. Eysenck.

Reward Dominance Theory

Reward dominance theory is grounded in two hypothetical concepts: the behavioral activating system (BAS) and the behavioral inhibiting system (BIS). These concepts are thought to have some neurological/neurochemical foundations that remain to be fully specified. Theoretically, crime prone persons have a strong BAS relative to their BIS. This has the effect of causing crime prone persons to concentrate more on the reward aspects of their actions than on the punishing aspects. The main proponents of reward dominance theory have been Herbert C. Quay, Jeffrey A. Gray, and Don C. Fowles.

Seizuring Theory

Seizuring theory contends that some criminal behavior results from seizures in and around the limbic system. This is thought to be most likely in the case of crimes that seem contrary to reason and forethought, such as impulsive assault. Thus, seizuring theory focuses on a relatively narrow category of impulsive, "irrational" criminal acts.

Besides predicting that criminal behavior should be associated with epilepsy (i.e., convulsive seizures), seizuring theory contends that anticonvulsive drugs and sometimes neurosurgery will reduce criminal behavior among persons with limbic seizuring. While the theory is narrow in its predictive scope, the relevant evidence is fairly supportive of the theory. Support for seizuring theory comes from evidence that crime is three or four times more common among epileptics than nonepileptics. There is also considerable evidence that anticonvulsant medications can be used successfully to treat criminal acts that seem to be the result of what seizuring theorists call *episodic dyscontrol*.

Frontal Lobe Theory

The emphasis of frontal lobe theory is on the uniquely enlarged frontal portions of the human neocortex and how its functioning may help to inhibit antisocial behavior. Damage to the prefrontal region of the neocortex has been shown to interfere with the ability to plan and execute flexible courses of action to attain long-term goals. Much of the brain functioning involved in moral reasoning also seems to reside in the frontal lobes.

According to proponents of frontal lobe theory, dysfunctioning of the frontal lobes (due to various causes) may result in individuals who have difficulty engaging in behavior that does not infringe on the rights of others. Among the predictions of the theory are that offending probabilities will be related to ADHD, poor academic performance, and underdeveloped moral reasoning. The main early proponent of frontal lobe theory was Ethan Gorenstein.

Hemispheric Functioning Theory

The main advocate of hemispheric functioning theory is Pierre Flor-Henry. In the case of hemispheric functioning theory, the focus is on the two halves of the neocortex. According to this theory, the right hemisphere is more "criminogenic" in three respects: First, it is less linguistically oriented than the left hemisphere, and therefore less likely to pay attention to and follow linguistic commands. Second, because of its connection with the limbic system, it is less sociable and "friendly" than the left hemisphere. Third, the right hemisphere is more prone to act on impulse than the left hemisphere. Theoretically, these three features of the right hemisphere incline people whose thought processes are more right hemisphere dominant to be more likely to engage in crime than persons whose thought processes are more left hemisphere dominant. Among the predictions of hemispheric functioning theory are that offenders will exhibit higher than average rates of left-handedness, poor linguistic skills, and will be less cheerful and friendly than the average person.

SUGGESTED READINGS

Hare, Robert D. (1993). *Without conscience: The disturbing world of the psychopaths among us.* (An interesting book about psychopaths in which one of the leading researchers in the field discusses the possible underlying neurology.)

Lykken, David T. (1996). Psychopathy, sociopathy, and crime. *Society, 34,* 29–38 (A concise overview of research based on neurologically specific approaches to the study of criminal/antisocial behavior.)

McCord, Joan and Tremblay, Richard E. (Eds.). (1995). *Preventing antisocial behavior.* New York: Guilford. (An informative anthology that explores criminal/antisocial behavior from several biosocial perspectives.)

Millon, Theodore, Simonsen, Erik, Birket-Smith, Morten, and Davis, Roger D. (Eds.). (1998). *Psychopathy: Antisocial, criminal, and violent behavior.* New York: Guilford Press. (A useful book presenting some of the latest findings and theorizing about the neuropsychological underpinnings of criminal/antisocial behavior.)

Rafter, Nicole H. (1997). *Creating born criminals.* Urbana: University of Illinois Press. (The author of this book attacks biosocial theories of criminal behavior as incorrect and dangerous. She states that there is no such thing as a "born criminal" except in the minds of "scientists and social-control specialists" (p. 238).)

Raine, Adrian (1993). *The psychopathology of crime.* San Diego, CA: Academic Press. (This book provides a great deal of information about biosocial influences on criminal and antisocial behavior, particularly as they pertain to arousal theory and reward dominance theory.)

EXERCISES

1. Using the World Wide Web or library sources, look up additional information about one of the three main parts of the mammalian brain (collectively sometimes called the triune brain). Write a one to two-page double-spaced report on how this region could play a role in causing one or more types of criminal behavior.

2. Experiments have shown that criminals and psychopaths exhibit lower levels of emotional stress when they are told to expect a painful electric shock within the next minute (Hare 1978, 1982; Hinton & O'Neill 1978; Woodman 1979). Which one of the theories discussed in this chapter would do the best job of predicting this finding, and why?

3. Using library or Internet resources, search for information about a proponent of one of the theories described in this chapter. The information can include demographic and educational background, as well as broad research interests of the theorist. Write a one to two-page double-spaced report on what you find.

4. Using library or Internet resources, search for more information than is presented here regarding one of the theories presented in this chapter. The information can be about some additional research bearing on the theory or some additional aspect of the theory. Write a one to two-page double-spaced report on what you find.

ENDNOTES

1. Hurwitz & Christiansen 1983:22.
2. Cosmedies & Tooby 1992; Gazzaniga 1985.
3. Aboitiz 1995.
4. MacLean 1985b.
5. MacLean 1985a:412.
6. MacLean 1985a:412.
7. Asher 1982.
8. Aboitiz 1995.
9. Kalat 1992:465.
10. Hofman 1982, 1983.
11. MacLean 1982:309.
12. Gazzaniga 1985; C. A. Nelson et al. 1990; Sperry 1982:1225.
13. Benbow 1988; Troup et al. 1983.
14. Bradshaw 1991; Sobotka & Grodzick, 1989a.
15. Lykken 1957, 1982.
16. Eysenck 1967, 1977; Eysenck & Gudjonsson 1989.
17. L. Ellis 1987c, 1987d; Farley et. al. 1979; Farley & Sewell 1976; Mednick & Hutchings 1978; Raine 1989; Raine & Jones 1987.
18. Graham, 1990:404; Warm & Dember, 1986:49.
19. Raine 1989:1.
20. Raine 1993:159.
21. Margolin et al. 1995:254.
22. Kindlon et al. 1995.
23. Ellis & Thompson 1989b.
24. Wood et al. 1994, 1995.
25. Efron & Barker 1997; Klorman et al. 1988; Sprague et al. 1970; Weiss et al. 1971.
26. Green & Warshauer 1981.
27. Carlton & Advokat 1973; Elmer-DeWitt 1990; Holcomb et al. 1985.
28. Lykken 1998:128.
29. Lykken 1998:125.
30. Cochran et al. 1994; Ellis & Thompson 1989; Wood et al. 1995.
31. Luengo et al. 1994:542.
32. Heaven 1996:52.
33. Lykken 1982; Stattin & Magnusson 1996:626.
34. Patrick 1994.
35. Satterfield 1987.
36. Satterfield et al. 1994.
37. Mezzacappa et al. 1997:458.
38. Raine 1993:167.
39. Ota et al. 1996:26.
40. Garcia-Larrea & Cezanne-Bert 1998.
41. Harmon-Jones et al. 1997; Raine 1989:12.
42. Brase & Loh 1975; Coleman 1971; Greenberg & Coleman 1973; Wender 1969.
43. Pliszka et al. 1988.
44. Brown et al. 1982a; Coccaro et al. 1989; Linnoila et al. 1983; Pucilowski & Kostowski 1983.

45. Garattini et al. 1969; Valzelli 1974.

46. Carter & Pycock 1980; Duterte-Boucher et al. 1988; Robinson & Stitt 1981.

47. Rogeness et al. 1990a.

48. Pliszka et al. 1996.

49. Buchsbaum et al. 1981b; Hernandes et al. 1994; Nurnberger et al. 1981.

50. Sundberg et al. 1991; Vodanovich & Kass 1990; Zuckerman et al. 1978.

51. McCall & Kagan 1970.

52. Coren 1990:551; Eisdorfer et al. 1980; Weller & Bell 1965.

53. Giambra & Quilter 1989; Martinez-Selva et al. 1987; G. D. Wilson 1990:159.

54. G. D. Wilson 1990:160.

55. Barkley et al. 1989.

56. Eysenck & Gudjunsson 1989:123; Raine 1993.

57. Quay 1965, 1988.

58. Gray 1975, 1981, 1987.

59. Fowles 1980.

60. Newman et al. 1987; Shapiro et al. 1988.

61. Scerbo et al. 1990:453.

62. Newman & Kosson 1986.

63. Gray 1987.

64. Matthys et al. 1998:644.

65. Daugherty & Quay 1991; Fonseca & Yule 1995; Matthys et al. 1998; Newman et al. 1987; O'Brien & Frick 1996.

66. O'Brien et al. 1994.

67. Mirkin & Coppen 1980; Raine 1993:93.

68. Fowles 1988; Quay 1993.

69. Gove & Wilmoth 1990.

70. Gray et al. 1983.

71. Reviewed by O'Brien & Frick 1996.

72. Newman et al. 1987; Scerbo et al. 1990.

73. Wise 1996.

74. Olds 1982; Olds & Olds 1965.

75. Lane 1998:742.

76. Gray 1987; Gray et al. 1983; Tremblay et al. 1994:732.

77. Arnett et al. 1997:1415.

78. Arnett et al. 1997; Newman et al. 1990.

79. Braaten & Rosen 1997; Oosterlaan & Sergeant 1996.

80. Gray 1976; Quay 1986; Raine 1993:94.

81. Maletzky 1973; Mark & Ervin 1970; Mark et al. 1975; Monroe 1970, 1977.

82. Mungas 1983.

83. Monroe et al. 1977:241; Suchy et al. 1997.

84. Albert et al. 1993:416; Elliott 1978:152.

85. J. S. Smith 1980; Sweet et al. 1969.

86. Goddard et al. 1969; Stevens 1983:204; Weiger & Bear 1988:90.

87. F. A. Elliott 1976.

88. Albert et al. 1992.

89. Eichelman 1987; Miczek et al. 1974.

90. Albert et al. 1993:416.

91. Barnett 1963; Ellis 1989:59; Maslow 1936, 1940.

92. Dewsbury 1978:53; Etienne et al. 1982.

93. Fantino & Cabanac 1980.

94. Frankenburg 1984.

95. Albert et al. 1992.

96. Ribak et al. 1979:211.

97. Crompton 1971; Lewis et al. 1987, 1988; Yeudall 1977.

98. Michaels 1961:96.

99. Mednick et al. 1982:64.

100. Opitz et al. 1983; Pilke et al. 1984.

101. Mucha & Pinel 1979.

102. Yeudall et al. 1985.

103. Rada 1975; Tinklenbert 1973; Zeichner & Pihl 1980.

104. MacDonnell & Ehmer 1969.

105. Bach-Y-Rita et al. 1971; Maletzky & Klotter 1974.

106. Leavitt et al. 1989; Ray et al. 1987; Sheard 1979.

107. Hare 1980; Millon 1981:182.

108. Heimburger et al. 1966; Suedfeld & Landon 1978:363; Vaernet & Madisen 1970.

109. Ely et al. 1977; Flynn et al. 1970; Kolb & Nonneman 1974.

110. Donovan & Nunes 1998; Donovan et al. 1997.

111. Kosten 1998.

112. Ferracuti 1996:139.

113. Pine 1983:64.

114. Asher 1982:3; Passler et al. 1985.

115. Damasio 1994:1102; Hagberg 1987; Hebb & Penfield 1940; Stuss et al. 1983.

116. Teuber 1964; Weinstein & Teuber 1957.

117. Reiss et al. 1996:1769; Suchy et al. 1997:260.

118. Fuster 1995; Hagberg 1987.

119. Barkley 1997; Giancola et al. 1995; Seguin et al. 1995.

120. Damasio et al. 1994:1102; Luria 1966; Nauta 1971.

121. Damasio et al. 1990:82; Milner 1963, 1964; Milner & Petrides 1984:403.

122. Gorenstein 1982:370; Teuber 1964:410.

123. MacLean 1985a:221, 1985b:415.

124. Kolb & Whishaw 1980:281.

125. Asher 1982:3; Yeudall 1978:221.

126. F. A. Elliott 1978:161; Halstead 1947.

127. Harper-Jaques & Reimer 1992:314.
128. Arnsten 1997.
129. Deckel et al. 1996.
130. Berman et al. 1995; Degl'Innocenti et al. 1998:182; Lueger & Gill 1990:697.
131. Barcelo et al. 1997.
132. Grant & Berg 1948.
133. Drewe 1974; Kolb & Whishaw 1980:284; Shallice 1982.
134. Dias et al. 1996.
135. Gorenstein 1982.
136. Kandel & Freed 1989; Lueger & Gill 1990.
137. Reiss et al. 1996:1771; Rueckert & Grafman 1996.
138. Barkley 1997; Chabot & Serfontein 1996; Mariani & Barkley 1997:123; Rothenberger 1995; Shue & Douglas 1992; Zametkin et al. 1993.
139. Duncan et al. 1996.
140. Cohen et al. 1995:420.
141. Damasio et al. 1990, 1994; Lueger & Gill 1990.
142. Pennington & Ozonoff 1996.
143. Damasio et al. 1994; Kolb & Whishaw 1980:293.
144. Damasio et al. 1990; Saver & Damasio 1991.
145. Lueger & Gill 1990.
146. Deckel et al. 1996.
147. Deckel et al. 1995; Erbas et al. 1992; Kurouglu et al 1996; Nicolas et al. 1993.
148. Blake et al. 1995; B. L. Miller et al. 1997.
149. Garcia-Larrea & Czanne-Bert 1998:260.
150. Kuruoglu et al. 1996.
151. Najam et al. 1997.
152. Giancola et al. 1993; Peterson et al. 1992; Pihl et al. 1990; Pihl & Bruce 1995.
153. Vazsonyi & Flannery 1997:95.
154. Barkley 1997; Fuster 1995.
155. Hoffman et al. 1987; Kandel & Freed 1989.
156. Deckel et al. 1996; Kuruoglu et al. 1996.
157. Mattson & Levin 1990:286; Wapner et al. 1981:17.
158. Alford & Alford 1981; Bear & Fedio 1977:465; Davidson & Fox 1989; Dawson et al. 1992; Fox et al. 1992; Hirskowitz et al. 1984.
159. Gabrielli & Mednick 1983:68; van den Broek et al. 1992.
160. Flor-Henry 1973, 1978, 1989; Krynicki 1978.
161. Davidson & Fox 1989; Dawson et al. 1992; Fox et al. 1992; Schaffer et al. 1983; Silberman & Weingartner 1986.
162. Ellis 1990c.
163. Hugdahl & Franzon 1985; Martinez-Selva et al. 1987; Tancredi & Volkow 1988.
164. Harman & Ray 1977.
165. Kimura 1967; Kimura & Folb 1968; Springer & Deutsch 1981.
166. Zatorre 1989.
167. Heilman & Van Den Abell 1980.
168. Moffitt 1996b:96.
169. Hecaen & Sauguet 1971; Herron 1980; Iaccino & Sowa 1989:1009; Lewis et al. 1988a.
170. Chapman & Chapman 1987; Cosenza & Mingoti 1993; Hugdahl et al. 1990; Perelle & Ehrman 1994:221; Shimizu & Endo 1983.
171. L. A. Archer & Campbell 1988.
172. Deckel et al. 1996.
173. Jutai et al. 1987.
174. Kosson 1998.
175. Hare & McPherson 1984a.
176. Raine et al. 1990b.
177. Friedman 1988; Heilman & Van Den Abell 1980; Wilkins et al. 1987.
178. Tucker & Dawson 1984.
179. Drake 1984, 1985.
180. Wright & Miller 1998.
181. Weitzer 1998:353.
182. Rowe & Osgood 1984:538.
183. Zuckerman, 1979.

CHAPTER 14

Evolutionary Biosocial Theories

As noted in Chapter 3, criminal behavior, or its equivalent, is present in all human societies. Why? This chapter will examine theories that assert that evolutionary forces may be contributing to such behavior. These theories share the assumption that propensities to engage in crime sometimes yield reproductive advantages to offenders and/or reproductive disadvantages to victims. If this assumption is true, criminal/antisocial behavior, as well as efforts to suppress it, may have evolved by natural selection, much as our physical features have evolved. If all of this sounds hard to believe, suspend final judgment until you learn about some little fish called "sneakers."

Evolution is a controversial concept, and yet it provides the bedrock on which modern biology stands.[1] Some oppose the theory for religious reasons, while others feel uncomfortable with its brutal "survival of the fittest" reputation. Especially disquieting has been the application of evolutionary theory to some of the worst aspects of human nature, such as will be considered here.

This chapter will examine a number of recent theoretical proposals having to do with the possible evolutionary foundations of criminal/antisocial behavior. As we delve into these issues, keep in mind that there is a difference between offering a scientific explanation for something and making moral judgments about it. Confusing scientific explanations with moral judgments is referred to as the **naturalistic fallacy**—i.e., the idea that whatever is natural is necessarily "good" (or what *should* be).[2] As we consider the possibility that genetic and evolutionary forces contribute to variations in criminal behavior, be careful not to confuse assertions about "what is" with assertions about "what ought to be." They are separate, although related issues.

The chapter is divided into four sections. The first section introduces you to the dual concepts of *genes* and *evolution,* and describes how these two concepts form the foundation for modern biology. The second section addresses a simple but important question: Do genes contribute to criminal/antisocial behavior? In the third section, a brief sketch of modern evolutionary theory is presented as it has been applied in recent decades to the study of behavior. In the fourth section, evolutionary theories of criminal/antisocial behavior are presented.

EVOLUTION AND GENES: THE MODERN SYNTHESIS

What exactly are genes? Genes are segments of a special type of biochemical called DNA. DNA is usually not thought of as being alive, but it is an essential "transition chemical" between nonliving and living matter. The transition from nonliving to living is made possible by the ability of DNA to self-replicate, meaning that it can draw off "loose" molecules from its immediate environment and use these molecules to construct perfect new copies of itself.

In addition to being able to self-replicate, DNA molecules can also make protein molecules that form the cells within which many DNA molecules reside. DNA can even program cells to join with millions of like cells to make large multicellular organisms, such as ourselves.

In humans, genes are packaged in 46 DNA strands, called **chromosomes.** Half of these strands come from the mother and the other 23 strands come from the father. Along each chromosome are hundreds of tiny segments, called *genes.* It is estimated that there are over 100,000 identifiable genes packaged inside of each cell in our bodies.[3] Genes code for constructing sequences of amino acids that in turn construct proteins that then go on to combine to form all of the features of our bodies, including our brains.

Genetic Mutations and Evolution

No one yet knows where or exactly when the first DNA molecule arose, but once it did, it must have gone wild making billions of copies of itself because the raw material was plentiful, and competition from other DNA did not yet exist. At some point, however, an early DNA molecule made a slight "mistake" in replicating. Although rare, such mistakes still happen thousands of times every day in the billions of living things that now live. Scientists call these mistakes **mutations**.

Many of the mutations that occur are inconsequential for survival. For example, the genes that code for whether we have ear lobes directly attached to the side of our head or ones that droop a little before becoming attached has no bearing on how long we live or how many children we have. While most mutations are either inconsequential or detrimental, on rare occasions a mutation arises that is beneficial to survival and/or reproduction. These beneficial mutations tend to become increasingly prevalent over subsequent generations. The accumulation of these beneficial mutant genes in populations brings about gradual changes in the average appearance of members of existing species. Over hundreds of generations, the accumulation of these mutant genes can eventually lead new species to arise from old ones, especially when the environment is undergoing substantial change. These changes in living things are what scientists call **evolution.** The process by which the environment favors changes in living things is known as **natural selection.**

The first person to propose that natural selection was responsible for the succession of species documented in the fossil record was **Charles Darwin.** The Western world was scandalized by the publication of his theory, with fierce opposition coming from numerous religious spokesmen.[4] Even today, the idea that the human species is an evolved part of the natural world remains a hard pill for most people to swallow. We seem to have nobler origins and purposes (see Box 14.1).

Virtually all modern biologists accept Darwin's theory as the best theory of evolution yet offered, although it has been modified in various ways throughout the twentieth century. The nature of most of the modifications have involved incorporating our growing understanding of **genetics,** a term that was not coined until after Darwin's death.

When biologists were able to combine genetic concepts with Darwin's theory, they were able to go far beyond Darwin in beginning to understand the biochemical basis of evolution. The result of this combination of genetics and evolution is usually called the **Modern Synthesis** or **gene-based evolutionary theory.**

Today scientists know much more than Darwin did, not only about genetics but also about the fossil record, including fossils of several extinct human ancestors.[5] Had Darwin known of these discoveries, his theory could have been considerably more complete than it was, and there may have been no need for the Modern Synthesis.

Comparative and Experimental Approaches to Behavioral Evolution

Normally, natural selection occurs gradually over thousands of years, making it impossible for a

Box 14.1

Religion

Vatican Thinking Evolves, No Longer Interpreting the Bible Literally

The Pope gives his blessing to natural selection—though man's soul remains beyond science's reach

The relationship between faith and science can be vexing, but one way the Roman Catholic Church and mainstream Protestant denominations reconcile the two is to say they each deal with different spheres of knowledge and so are not in conflict. This is a sort of metaphysical version of Christ's admonition to render to Caesar what is Caesar's and to God what is God's, and it is a position that Pope John Paul II reaffirmed last week when he made a statement on evolution. "Consideration of the method used in diverse orders of knowledge allows for the concordance of two points of view which seem irreconcilable," he wrote. "The sciences of observation describe and measure with ever greater precision the multiple manifestations of life . . . while theology extracts . . . the final meaning according to the Creator's designs."

In his message to a meeting of this Pontifical Academy of Sciences, which had taken the origin of life as its theme. John Paul described the shift in the church's view of evolution that has taken place since Pope Pius XII issued his encyclical *Humani Generis* in 1950. "*Humani Generis,*" John Paul wrote, "considered the doctrine of 'evolution' as a serious hypothesis, worthy of a more deeply studied investigation . . . Today . . . new knowledge leads us to recognize that the theory of evolution is more than a hypothesis." Pius was skeptical of evolution but tolerated study and discussion of it; the statement by John Paul reflects the church's acceptance of evolution. He did not, however, diverge at all from Pius on the question of the origin of man's soul: that comes from God, even if "the human body is sought in living material which existed before it."

The statement is unlikely to influence the curriculum of Catholic schools, where evolution has been taught since the 1950s. Indeed, reading the entire Bible literally has not been a dominant practice among Catholics through much of the 20th century. Asked about the Pope's statement, Father Peter Stravinskas, editor of the 1991 *Catholic Encyclopedia,* said, "It's essentially what Augustine was writing. He tells us that we should not interpret *Genesis* literally, and that it is poetic and theological language."

Creationists do not make the distinction between faith and science that John Paul does, and his statement will not discourage them in their battles against the teaching of evolution in states like Tennessee and Alabama. "The Pope is just an influential person; he's not a scientist," says Henry Morris, president emeritus at the Institute for Creation Research in Santee, California. "There is no scientific evidence for evolution. All the real solid evidence supports creation." Bill Hoesch, a spokesman for the institute, says, "[John Paul] would say that man's dignity does not suffer even if God used the process of evolving him from pond scum through the apes to the present so-called dignified position, and we would differ with that."

John Paul stopped short of addressing a point on which Pius was emphatic: that a particular man named Adam must have been our ancestor. Any other theory, Pius maintained, was inconsistent with the doctrine of original sin. But the teaching about Adam has also been superseded, says Father Richard P. McBrien, a liberal theologian at the University of Notre Dame. "No Scripture scholar today would say we are literally descended from two people." To such scholars and John Paul, the evolution of our bodies matters much less than the evolution of our souls.

—By James Collins. Reported by Greg Burke/Rome and Kate Kamlani/New York

Time, November 4, 1996. Reprinted with permission.

---

scientist to directly observe. Therefore, evolutionary scientists often study the fossilized remains of extinct plants and animals as a way of helping to reconstruct the past. However, scientists who are interested in the evolution of behavior are at a distinct disadvantage when all they have to study are fossils.

Behavioral evolutionists have had to rely on carefully comparing the behavior of related living species and on selective breeding experiments to make inferences about how various behavior traits have evolved over time. To see how breeding experiments can help in the understanding of behavior from an evolutionary perspective, Figure 14.1 shows the results of an experiment with laboratory animals in which researchers selected animals who displayed certain behavioral/temperament traits for breeding and denied breeding to the remaining animals. Rats from a standard laboratory population were selected for the degree to which they exhibited weak and strong avoidance behavior when confronted by novel or threatening stimuli. This behavior may be similar to sensation seeking in humans. In each generation, the most extreme male–female pairs were allowed to breed, while the remaining animals were not allowed to do so. As you can see, after twenty generations, two distinct strains of rats had emerged.[6] If scientists can create these sort of differences in twenty generations, imagine what sort of changes natural selection forces could produce over hundreds or even thousands of generations in the wild.

The fact that changes in behavior such as those illustrated in Figure 14.1 were gradual in-

stead of sudden leads to the conclusion that several genes, not just one or two, are responsible for the behavior being selected. Traits that are influenced by several genes are said to be **polygenic** (or *polygenetic*), rather than **monogenic** (or *monogenetic*) As you will see, most of the evidence of genetic influences on criminal/antisocial behavior is consistent with the idea that such behavior is polygenic (influenced by many genes). Because genes code only for amino acids, which in turn convert to proteins, the connection between genes and behavior is always indirect even for monogenic traits.

Other behavior traits that have been artificially selected (as opposed to naturally selected) in various species of laboratory animals include aggression,[9] learning patterns,[10] sexual preferences,[11] alcohol preferences,[12] nest-building behavior,[13] and even color preferences.[14] The diversity of these genetically influenced behavior patterns reinforces the conclusion that genes can have substantial effects on a wide variety of behavior patterns.

Note that natural (or artificial) selection can only affect traits that are at least partially the result

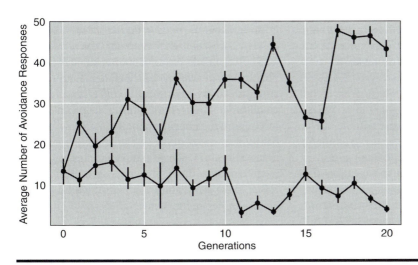

FIGURE 14.1   The results of a selective breeding experiment undertaken to produce two separate strains of rats in terms of learning avoidance responses to certain fear-inducing stimuli. The graph shows the average number of responses exhibited during testing sessions for twenty generations of selectively bred rats (from Brush et al. 1979:312).

of genetic factors. In other words, if genes have no influence on a trait, the prevalence or intensity of the trait will not change as a result of natural (or artificial) selection. This idea is important, because, if it could be proven that genes cannot influence criminal/antisocial behavior, all of the theories that will be reviewed in this chapter would be instantly disproven.

Another point to remember as we look for evidence of genetic influences on criminal/antisocial behavior involves the distinction between **genetic influence** and **genetic determinism.**[15] No evidence has ever been found that genes *determine* whether or not people become criminals. However, as we will see, there is considerable evidence to suggest that genes *influence the probability* of our becoming criminals.

Genes and Criminal/Antisocial Behavior

In recent years, scientists have located genes for specific human diseases, such as cystic fibrosis and Huntington's disease.[16] They have done so through a process known as **genetic mapping**—the identification and functional specification of each segment of DNA. Since the 1970s, there has been an exciting worldwide project underway, known as the **Genome Project,** the goal of which is to eventually map all of the genes on the 23 pairs of human chromosomes with regard to each gene's structure and function.[17]

So far, several hundred genes have been mapped, but this is only a small fraction of the estimated 100,000 genes that exist in each one of our cells.[18] Through the collective efforts linked to the Genome Project, it may be possible sometime in the twenty-first century to know the location and function of all of the genes comprising our species.

Has the Genome Project yet led to the identification of any genes that make some of us more likely than others to engage in crime? No. In this sense, there is still no proof that criminal/antisocial behavior is genetically influenced. However, scientists have not yet located any specific genes for height either.[19] Yet, there is no reason to doubt that height is genetically influenced. How

can scientists be so sure of this? The evidence has come from carefully comparing the height of twins and other types of family relatives.[20] We will explain how these studies are conducted in a moment.

If scientists have found genes for several specific diseases, why have they not yet found any genes for height? The main reason is that height is influenced by multiple genes, and the more genes there are affecting a trait, the harder it is to pinpoint any one of them. If numerous genes influence criminal/antisocial behavior, scientists will also have a great deal of difficulty identifying the location of any of the specific genes.[21]

The Genetic Influence Hypothesis

In recent decades, many researchers have reviewed evidence bearing on the hypothesis that genes influence criminal behavior.[22] The nature of the evidence can be subsumed under seven categories: family studies, twin studies, adoption studies, karyotype studies, biochemical marker studies, studies of genetic influences on correlates of criminality, and studies based on animal models. Each of these lines of evidence is considered separately.

Family Studies.   There is no serious doubt that criminality runs in families (Tables 7.10a and 7.10b). This fact is entirely consistent with the genetic influence hypothesis, but it falls far short of proving it because one could also explain familial similarities environmentally. For example, crime could run in families due to criminal parents either teaching such behavior to their children or by their being inept in supervising and training their children. Therefore, while family studies have provided evidence that is consistent with the genetic influence hypothesis, these studies would be suggestive of genetic influence at best.

Twin Studies.   Twin studies have been employed frequently to look for evidence of genetic influences on criminal/antisocial behavior. Twin studies take advantage of the fact that fraternal twins carry an average of 50 percent of the same genes (just like ordinary siblings), while identical twins carry essentially 100 percent of the same genes. In other words, identical twins are *clones*. Researchers normally assume that identical twin pairs will share experiences to the same degree as do fraternal twin pairs, an assumption that we will see may not be entirely correct. The fact that identical twins share twice as many genes as do fraternal twins makes it possible to study twins with an eye toward separating genetic influences from most environmental experiences.

What do twin studies of criminal/antisocial behavior indicate? As shown in Table 14.1, numerous twin studies of criminal/antisocial behavior have been conducted since the 1930s, nearly all of which have found that identical twins are significantly more **concordant** (similar) in their offending tendencies than are fraternal twins. In other words, if one identical twin has an offending record, the other is more likely to also have such a record than when fraternal twins are compared. Furthermore, as predicted by the fact that identi-

cal twins share twice as many genes (i.e., 100 percent) as do fraternal twins (i.e., 50 percent), most studies have found that identical twins are on average about two times more similar in their probability of offending than are fraternal twins.[23]

Most of these studies involved males because their criminal/antisocial behavior is substantially higher and therefore more easily measured than that of females. Two twin studies have reported some evidence that is not consistent with the genetic influence hypothesis: One U.S. study of conduct disorders[24] and one British study of self-reported delinquency.[25] In both studies, support for the genetic influence hypothesis was found in the case of male twins, but not in the case of female twins, suggesting that female delinquency may not be genetically influenced.[26] However, because the vast majority of delinquents (especially serious and persistent delinquents) are males, both of these twin studies still provided *general* support for the genetic influence hypothesis.

TABLE 14.1.   Evidence from twin studies pertaining to genetic influences on criminal/antisocial behavior (overall consistency score = 87.0%). (Citations in shaded cells refer to studies that are consistent with the genetic influence hypothesis.)

Evidence Pertaining to the Genetic Influence Hypothesis	Type and Seriousness of Offenses								Antisocial Clinical Conditions	
	Official Statistics						Self-Reported Offenses			
	Violent Offenses	Property Offenses	Drug Offenses	Delinquency	General & Unspecified Offenses	Recidivism	Victimful & Overall Offending	Illegal Drug Use	Childhood Conduct Disorders	Antisocial Personality
Evidence favoring the Hypothesis			**North America** *United States:* 1	**Europe** *Denmark:* 1 **North America** *United States:* 1	**Asia** *Japan:* 3 **Europe** *Denmark:* 3; *Germany:* 3; *Netherlands:* 1 **North America** *United States:* 9		**Europe** *England:* 1 **North America** *United States:* 5	**North America** *United States:* 1	**Europe** *England:* 1; *Netherlands:* 1; *Norway:* 1 **North America** *United States:* 12 **Pacific** *New Zealand:* 1	**North America** *United States:* 3
Equivocal evidence	**Europe** *Denmark:* 1			**North America** *United States:* 1	**Europe** *Norway:* Dalgard & 1					
Evidence Contrary to the Hypothesis							**Europe** *England:* 1		**North America** *United States:* 1	

Another noteworthy finding from twin studies is that genetics appears to have important influences on childhood conduct disorders and on adult criminality, but not on most forms of juvenile delinquency.[27] Within the category of adult criminality, one study suggested that genes were more influential in the case of property offending than in the case of violent offending.[28]

Even though findings from twin studies of criminal/antisocial behavior are largely consistent with the genetic influence hypothesis (especially for males), there is at least one reason to remain skeptical. Some have noted that identical twins are not only twice as similar to one another genetically as are fraternal twins, but they are also more similar in the experiences they have had. Therefore, their greater similarity in offending tendencies could be the result not of genetics per se, but of greater similarity in experiences.

A few studies have attempted to test this possibility. Overall, these studies have concluded that shared environments do not explain much, if any, of the greater similarity of identical twins than fraternal twins either for offending behavior[29] or for behavior in general.[30] In other words, the greater similarity in identical twins compared to fraternal twins still appears to be largely due to genetics, not to any greater number of shared experiences they may have had.

Adoption Studies.   In most Western countries these days, about 1 percent of infants are adopted very early in life by persons who are unrelated to them genetically.[31] These children can be said to have two sets of parents: One set gave them their genes, and the other set provided the family environment. Studying adoptees has been a gold mine for social scientists interested in probing nature–nurture questions, including those who study criminal/antisocial behavior. If a sample of adoptees ends up more closely resembling their rearing parents for a trait, this would favor family environmental influences; and if they more closely resemble their genetic parents, genetic influences would be the most reasonable explanation.

Say a group of adopted children are compared to one or both of the parents who reared them. Because criminality is more common in males than in females, assume that all of the adoptees are males and that they are compared to their rearing fathers regarding having been convicted of a felony. Further assume that the same comparisons are made for a group of children from nonadoptive families, where fathers provide both genes *and* the rearing environment to their offspring. If the sons from adoptive families resembled their fathers to the same degree as do sons from genetically intact families, one would be able to attribute the father–son resemblances to rearing influences. However, if adopted sons more closely resembled their genetic fathers than their rearing fathers, and did so essentially to the same degree as sons and fathers in genetically intact families, a genetic interpretation would be warranted.

The above paragraph outlines one way adoption studies are conducted, but there are several other ways as well. For example, some have compared adoptees with both sets of parents, while others have only compared adopted children to one or the other set of parents. Still other adoption studies have involved comparisons of adopted and nonadopted siblings.[32] Therefore, it would be too time-consuming here to describe separately what each adoption study of criminal/antisocial behavior has found. Simply keep in mind that all adoption studies have as their bottom line to determine whether adoptees more closely resemble their genetic relatives (parents or siblings) or their rearing "relatives."

As shown in Table 14.2, all of the evidence from adoption studies so far has been consistent with the genetic influence hypothesis. However, all adoption studies have also found evidence of substantial environmental influence. In adoption studies that have tried to specify the nature of these environmental influences, several aspects of the parental and community rearing environment have emerged. One study of conduct disorders, for example, found that both parental discipline patterns and genetic factors were important contributors to

TABLE 14.2.   Evidence from adoption studies pertaining to genetic influences on criminal/antisocial behavior (overall consistency score = 100%). (Citations in shaded cells show where studies should be consistent with the genetic influence hypothesis.)

Tests of the Genetic Influence Hypothesis	Types and Seriousness of Offenses								Antisocial Clinical Conditions	
	Official Statistics						Self-Reported Offenses			
	Violent Offenses	Property Offenses	Drug Offenses	Delinquency	General & Unspecified Offenses	Recidivism	Victimful & Overall Offending	Illegal Drug Use	Childhood Conduct Disorders	Antisocial Personality
Evidence Favoring the Hypothesis		**Europe** *Denmark:* 1		**Europe** *Sweden: 2* **North America** *United States: 1*	**Europe** *Denmark: 4* **North America** *United States: 4*				**North America** *Canada: 1; United States: 2*	**Europe** *Denmark:* 1 **North America** *United States: 4*
Equivocal Evidence										
Evidence Refuting the Hypothesis										

the condition.[33] Regarding serious offending and antisocial behavior later in life, at least three adoption studies found parental social status interacting with genetics to affect the behavior,[34] while another study found both parental social status and parental alcoholism to be important interactants with genetics.[35]

Overall, the evidence from adoption studies strongly supports the genetic influence hypothesis, although the evidence has also confirmed that environmental factors are important.[36] In a word, adoption studies indicate that genetic and environmental factors *interact* to affect criminal/antisocial behavior.

Karyotype Studies.   Another way scientists have attempted to test the genetic influence hypothesis has been to examine the numbers and configurations of chromosomes. These analyses are called **karyotype studies.**

To conceptualize these studies, recall that humans have 23 pairs of chromosomes, with one of each pair coming from each parent. Twenty-two of these chromosome pairs are known as *autosomes;*

the remaining pair are called the **sex chromosomes** because this pair determines whether someone will be a male or a female. Those who have two **X chromosomes** are females, and those with one X chromosome and one **Y chromosome** are males.

Occasionally, there are exceptions to these rules. For reasons that are not well understood, about one male in every 700 to 1,000 receives an extra Y chromosome, making him **XYY,** and about one in every 500 males receives an extra X chromosome, making him **XXY.**[37] (Note that as long as the Y chromosome is present, an individual is considered a genetic male, regardless of the number of X chromosomes present.)

In terms of appearance, both XYY and XXY males are often indistinguishable from XY males. About the only features that are distinctly more prevalent among XYY and XXY males relative to XY males is that both are above average in height. XYYs, in particular, are almost always in excess of six feet (183 centimeters) tall,[38] and during adolescence they tend to have above average acne problems.[39] XXY males usually have smaller genitals and are somewhat more likely than most males to develop breasts following puberty. However, both XYY and XXY males score significantly below average on standardized tests of intelligence.[40]

What do karyotype studies suggest with respect to criminal/antisocial behavior? The results are summarized in Table 14.3. Note that nearly all of the studies support the genetic influence hypothesis in the sense that persons with either an extra X chromosome or especially an extra Y chromosome have an increased probability of engaging in criminal/antisocial behavior. Most studies have found the proportion of XXY and especially XYY males in prison populations to be more than five times higher than they are in the general male population. Nonetheless, males with an extra Y or X chromosome still comprise no more than 1 or 2 percent of most prison populations.

The most recent karyotype study pertaining to criminal/antisocial behavior was focused on conduct disordered children in Germany. It found significantly higher rates of conduct disorders among XYY males than among XY males (XXY males were not sampled).[41]

Despite some early reports that XYY males are extremely aggressive, studies have failed to find any excess of violent offenses among them.[42] In other words, the types of crimes committed by XYY (and XXY) males seem to be virtually identical to those committed by XY males. The only possible exception is that sex offenses appear to be unusually high among XYY and XXY male offenders than among XY male offenders.[43]

Two karyotype studies in Denmark looked for evidence that the length of the Y chromosome might be related to criminality among normal XY males. One study suggested that there was a relationship[44] and the other concluded that there was not.[45]

One more type of karyotype study that is worth mentioning briefly involves a clinical condition known as the **Fragile X syndrome.**[46] This syndrome affects about one in every 1500 males and one in every 2000 females, and is frequently associated with mild to moderate mental retardation.[47] There are one or more locations on the X chromosome that appear to be unusually prone to

mutate among persons with Fragile X syndrome.[48] The precise location of these mutation-prone areas has been identified using electron microscopes because these areas absorb an unusual amount of staining used in DNA mapping.[49] The reason females are less likely to exhibit symptoms of Fragile X is probably due to the fact that they have two X chromosomes, unlike males, who have only one. Presumably, a second normal X chromosome is often able to compensate for any effects caused by its companion fragile X chromosome.[50]

Several studies have shown that individuals with Fragile X exhibit high rates of conduct disorders,[51] ADHD,[52] learning disabilities,[53] and below average IQ scores.[54] These findings raise the possibility that as adults persons with Fragile X will exhibit higher than normal offending rates, but this possibility has not yet been directly demonstrated.

All and all, karyotype studies have found substantial support for the genetic influence hypothesis. In this case, the studies have focused on the sex chromosomes, a worthwhile avenue to pursue given the substantial gender disparities in criminal/antisocial behavior.

Genetic Influences on Various Correlates of Crime

The next line of evidence pertaining to the genetic influence hypothesis involves looking for evidence that genes influence behavioral or other correlates of crime. The reasoning is that if genes influence numerous correlates of crime, it is likely that some, if not many, of the same genes are influencing criminal/antisocial behavior as well.

Studies relevant to this hypothesis are presented in Table 14.4. This table shows that a substantial number of behavioral and mental health correlates of crime appear to be genetically influenced. The evidence is particularly strong for alcoholism,[55] ADHD,[56] intelligence,[57] and schizophrenia.[58] While none of this evidence proves that criminal/antisocial behavior itself is genetically influenced, finding that a large number of the correlates of crime are genetically influenced is

TABLE 14.3.   Citations to studies regarding criminal and antisocial behavior among XYY males and XXY males relative to XY males (overall consistency score = 93.3%). (Shaded cells are those consistent with the genetic influence hypothesis.)

| Criminal or Antisocial Behavior | Type and Seriousness of Offenses | | | | | | | | Antisocial Clinical Conditions | |
| | Official Statistics | | | | | | Self-Reported Offenses | | | |
	Violent Offenses	Property Offenses	Drug Offenses	Delinquency	General & Unspecified Offenses	Recidivism	Victimful & Overall Offending	Illegal Drug Use	Childhood Conduct Disorders	Antisocial Personality
X Y Y v s X Y — Higher in XYYs				**Asia** *Japan:* 1 **North America** *United States:* 1	**Europe** *England:* 2; *Finland:* 1; *France:* 1; *Scotland:* 1 **North America** *United States:* 2	**Europe** *England:* 1			**Europe** *England:* 1; *Germany:* 1	
No significant difference					**North America** *United States:* 1					
Higher in XYs										
X X Y v s X Y — Higher in XXYs				**Asia** *Japan:* 1	**Europe** *England:* 1; *Finland:* 1 **North America** *United States:* 2					
No significant difference										
Higher in XYs										

definitely consistent with the view that criminal/antisocial behavior is also.

Biological Markers

A **biological marker** is a biochemical that is almost entirely under genetic control. There are many biochemicals naturally produced by the human body that constitute biological markers, but only two so far have been repeatedly linked to criminal/antisocial behavior. One is an enzyme known as **monoamine oxidase (MAO)**, and the other is a brain receptor for dopamine known as the **D$_2$ receptor.**

Monoamine Oxidase.   Twin studies have found 80 to 90 percent of the variations in platelet MAO activity to be the result of genetic factors.[59] MAO activity in the brain appears to help "break down" neurotransmitters. You may recall that low levels of platelet MAO activity have been repeatedly linked to criminal/antisocial behavior.[60]

Given the statistical link between platelet MAO and criminality, and the evidence that this enzyme is almost entirely under genetic control, it is reasonable to suspect that whatever genes are controlling platelet MAO levels must be making a contribution to variation in criminality. This suspicion is bolstered further by evidence that low

TABLE 14.4. Evidence that genes influence several established correlates of crime. (All studies with evidence contrary to the presence of genetic influences are preceded by a double slash. The numbers in brackets represent the ratio of supportive to nonsupportive studies.)

Traits Associated with Criminal and Antisocial Behavior	Evidence that Genetic Factors Influence a Particular Correlate of Criminal/Antisocial Behavior		
	Twin Studies	**Adoption Studies**	**Other Evidence**
Alcoholism (especially Type II Alcoholism)	**Europe** *England:* 1; *Finland:* 3; *Sweden:* 2 **North America** *United States:* 9 **Pacific** *Australia:* 1 //**Europe** *Sweden:* 3; **North America** *United States:* 1 [**13 // 4**]	**Europe** *Denmark:* 3; *Sweden:* 5 **North America** *United States:* 5 //**North America** *United States:* 2 [**13 // 2**]	**North America** *United States:* 13 [**13 // 0**]
Academic achievement		**Europe** *Sweden:* 1 **North America** *United States:* 1 [**1**]	
ADHD	**Europe** *England:* 1; *Norway:* 1 **North America** *United States:* 13 [**15 // 0**]	**North America** *United States:* 2 [**2 // 0**]	**North America** *United States:* 20 **International** Various Countries: 1 [**21 // 0**]
Age of first intercourse	**North America** *United States:* 1 [**1 // 0**]		
Childhood aggression	**North America** *United States:* 2 [**2 // 0**]		
Depression (unipolar)	**Europe** *England:* 1 **North America** *United States:* 5 [**6 // 0**]		**Europe** *England:* 1 [**1 // 0**]
Divorce	**North America** *United States:* 2 [**2 // 0**]		
Drug abuse	**North America** *United States:* 3 [**3 // 0**]	**North America** *United States:* 2 [**2 // 0**]	**North America** *United States:* 4 [**4 // 0**]
Extroversion	**North America** *United States:* 4 [**4 // 0**]	**North America** *United States:* 1 [**1 // 0**]	
Gambling	**North America** *United States:* 1 [**1 // 0**]		
Heart rate/Blood pressure	**Europe** *Italy:* 1 **North America** *United States:* 7 [**8 // 0**]		**Europe** *Sweden:* 1 [**1 // 0**]
Impulsivity	**North America** *United States:* 3 [**3 // 0**]		
Intelligence	**Europe** *Netherlands:* 2 **North America** *United States:* 4 [**6 // 0**]	**North America** *United States:* 3 [**3 // 0**]	**North America** *United States:* 6 [**6 // 0**]
Learning disabilities	**North America** *United States:* 3 [**3 // 0**]	**North America** *United States:* 1 [**1 // 0**]	**North America** *United States:* 1 [**1 // 0**]
Manic depression	**Europe** *Denmark:* 1 [**1 // 0**]		**North America** *United States:* 4 [**4 // 0**]
P300 averaged evoked response	**Europe** *Netherlands:* 1 **North America** *United States:* 4 [**5 // 0**]		**North America** *United States:* 1 [**1 // 0**]
Schizophrenia	**Europe** *England:* 2; *Finland:* 1; *Sweden:* 1 **North America** *United States:* 4 [**8 // 0**]	**Europe** *Denmark:* 1; *Finland:* 1 **North America** *United States:* 2 [**4 // 0**]	**North America** *Canada:* 1; *United States:* 1 [**2 // 0**]
Sensation seeking	**North America** *United States:* 1 [**1 // 0**]		
Serotonin levels/ serotonergic activity			**North America** *United States:* 1 [**// 0**]
Suicidal behavior	**North America** *United States:* 2 [**2 // 0**]		**North America** *United States:* 2 [**2 // 0**]
Testosterone levels			**North America** *United States:* 1 [**1 // 0**]

MAO levels are also associated with a number of correlates of crime. As shown in Table 14.5, these correlates include impulsivity (and monotony avoidance), childhood ADHD, poor academic performance relative to ability, sensation seeking, and recreational drug use, especially excessive use of alcohol.

D₂ Receptors. In the brain, D_2 receptors form along the cell walls of neurons that have a special affinity for dopamine. The number and location of these receptors are determined almost entirely by genes.[61] Since the early 1990s, several studies have found relationships between the prevalence of D_2 receptors in the brain and conduct disorders,[62] official delinquency,[63] and drug abuse.[64] In addition, D_2 receptors have been linked to three correlates of crime: ADHD,[65] gambling addiction,[66] and alcoholism.[67]

In general, while much remains to be learned about how platelet MAO and D_2 receptors in the brain might be related to offending probabilities,

TABLE 14.5.   Evidence that low MAO activity is associated with several behavioral correlates of criminal/antisocial behavior. (Contrary evidence is preceded by a double slash. The numbers in brackets represent the ratio of supportive to nonsupportive studies.)

Behavioral Correlates of Criminal/Antisocial Behavior	Associated with Low MAO Activity
Attention deficit hyperactivity disorder	**Europe** *Sweden:* 1 **North America** *United States:* 1 **[2 // 0]**
Impulsivity	**Europe** *Netherlands:* 1; *Sweden:* 4 **North America** *United States:* 7 **[12 // 0]**
Poor academic performance	**Europe** *Sweden:* 1 **North America** *United States:* 1 **[2 // 0]**
Learning disabilities (including dyslexia)	//**North America** *United States:* 1 **[0 // 1]**
Sensation seeking	**Europe** *Sweden:* 4 **North America** *United States:* 4 **Pacific** *Australia:* 1 //**North America** *United States:* 2 **[9 // 2]**
Recreational drug use (including tobacco but excluding alcohol)	**Europe** *Sweden:* 2 **North America** *United States:* 1 **[3 // 0]**
Excessive alcohol use (Alcoholism)	**Asia** *Japan:* 1 **Europe** *England:* 1; *Sweden:* 5 **Middle East** *Greece:* 1 **North America** *United States:* 6 **[14 // 0]**
Schizophrenia	**Europe** *Germany:* 1 **North America** *United States:* 5 //**Europe** *England:* 1; *Germany:* 1 **North America** *United States:* 4 **[6 // 6]**
Gambling	**Europe** *Spain:* 1 **[// 0]**
Extroversion	**Europe** *Germany:* 2 **North America** *United States:* 1 //**Europe** *Germany:* 2 **[3 // 2]**

they constitute two biological markers that are almost exclusively of genetic origin that have been linked to criminal/antisocial behavior. It would be difficult to explain why these two biological markers would be associated with criminal/antisocial behavior without conceding support for the genetic influence hypothesis.

Animal Models for Aggressive Offending

The last line of evidence bearing on the hypothesis that genes have an influence on criminal/antisocial behavior comes from studying nonhuman animals. This evidence is based on **animal models** of human aggression. As shown in Figure 14.2, several nonhuman species exhibit aggression that is strikingly similar to assaults, murders, and rapes in humans.[68] Animal models of human aggression do not prove that there is a genetic foundation for criminal/antisocial behavior, but it is one more line of evidence that is consistent with such a conclusion.

Overall, we have reviewed seven types of evidence pertaining to the hypothesis that genetic factors substantially influence criminal behavior. These lines of evidence have shown the following:

- Criminal/antisocial behavior has a tendency to run in families
- Genetically identical twins more closely resemble one another in criminality and psychopathy than is true of fraternal twins.
- Adoptees more closely resemble their genetic parents than their rearing parents regarding criminal offending.
- Certain unusual karyotypes involving the sex chromosomes have been found associated with increased risk of criminal behavior.
- Genes have been shown to substantially influence several behavioral and mental health correlates of criminal behavior.
- MAO and dopamine receptors appear to be genetic markers for criminal/antisocial behavior.
- Animal models have been identified for certain forms of violent criminality.

FIGURE 14.2. First photo: A male elephant seal attacks and sexually assaults a female as she attempts to flee to open ocean after a long stay on shore without eating. Such assaults are fairly common among young males who do not control a harem. Photograph provided by Sarah Mesnick. Second photo: A mother langur and her female friend are attempting to prevent a young adult male from snatching and killing the mother's newborn. In human societies, such an act would constitute kidnapping and murder. (Photograph taken by Sarah Blaffer Hedy, and provided by Anthro-Photo). Such murderous behavior is fairly common among langurs, especially by males who have just taken over a troop. By killing the infants, the younger males increase the chances that the troop's females will become sexually receptive earlier than were they to continue to nurse an infant sired by the old "troop owner."

Together, these seven lines of evidence add up to strong support for the genetic influence hypothesis.[69] Nevertheless, a great deal needs to be learned about the location of the genes involved, and exactly how they interact with environmental factors to affect brain chemistry. For instance, numerous studies have indicated that genes affect criminal/antisocial behavior more in the case of upper status boys than boys of lower status,[70] a finding that remains to be theoretically explained.

Overall, the evidence of genetic influences on criminal/antisocial behavior raises many questions. One of the most intriguing of these questions is, why do these genes exist? This is one of the big questions that evolutionary theories of criminality seek to address.

MODERN EVOLUTIONARY THEORIES IN CRIMINOLOGY

Evolutionary theories in criminology can be traced back to Lombroso.[71] However, there has been a resurgence in these theories since the 1980s, the character of which is quite different from Lombroso's belief that criminals are evolutionary throwbacks. Modern evolutionary theorists emphasize that in order for a behavior to evolve, it must be contributing to the reproductive success of organisms exhibiting the behavior. Reproductive success basically refers to the number of offspring that one leaves in future generations. This assumption about reproductive success has led evolutionary criminologists to look for evidence that criminal behavior (especially of a victimizing nature) might actually contribute to reproduction under some environmental conditions.

Along these lines, you will recall that family size is positively correlated with criminality. This suggests that, even though the overall health and life expectancy of offenders is lower than average, the number of children they have is somewhat higher. Such evidence suggests that any genes contributing to criminal/antisocial behavior could be becoming increasingly prevalent, although any tendencies in this regard would not be detectable in just one or two generations. This sort of contro-

versial thinking is one reason many criminologists continue to shy away from evolutionary theory, and why students and professionals alike need to be careful in exploring it.

Evolutionary Theory's "Disposable Vehicle" Concept

Nearly all biologists today accept that Darwin's theory provides a good, although far from complete, explanation for the tremendous diversity of life revealed in the fossil record. Nonetheless, because of advances in genetics, most modern biologists have come to think about evolution somewhat differently than Darwin.

Rather than seeing natural selection as operating on organisms, or groups of organisms, as Darwin did, today's evolutionary thinkers conceive of natural selection as also operating on genes themselves.[72] In other words, genes can be thought of as the units of natural selection at least as much as the traits that organisms possess. Such a view is sometimes referred to as the **disposable vehicle concept,** because organisms themselves are seen as merely temporary carriers of what is potentially immortal in a biological sense: the genes inside each organism. In other words, the genes survive generation after generation, even though the organisms that carry and transport them die.

How do the genes inside of organisms preserve their chances of immortality? By reproducing, and the more times they do so, the better for the genes. Could criminal/antisocial behavior sometimes facilitate reproduction? That is a question of major interest to evolutionary criminologists.

Setting the Stage for Evolutionary Criminology

Let us pursue this unflattering "disposable vehicle" perspective of life a bit further. Consider all the time and effort that female mammals devote to feeding and protecting their young, often with a great deal of personal sacrifice. It is hard to argue that these efforts are in the best interest of the

"The way I see it, we're being exploited by our genes, and by George, I intend to *do* something about it!"

mothers themselves. Instead, modern evolutionists explain maternal investment in offspring in terms of survival of the genes carried by the mothers. In other words, no matter how many offspring a mother has, if she fails to perform her maternal duties, the chances that her genes will be represented in future generations diminish.

Maternal care of offspring is part of what evolutionists call **parental investment** (or **parenting effort**). Other aspects of parental investment include the time females devote to gestating offspring before they are born, and the time spent breast-feeding offspring following birth. Notice that males do not make these initial forms of parental investment. The fact that nearly all of the initial parental investment is made by females becomes an important component in attempts to explain gender differences in criminality from an evolutionary perspective.

Strategies, Counterstrategies, and Deception

In evolutionary terms, a **strategy** is a fairly general option that living things can use to affect their chances of reproducing, and thereby pass their genes to future generations.[73] Evolutionary theorists apply the term *strategy* to both physical and behavioral traits without assuming that the organism has any conscious awareness of the reproductive significance of these traits.

One interesting example of an evolved strategy is this: In numerous species of animals, a female will resist mating attempts by a male at least until he offers her food.[74] This phenomenon is known as **nuptial feeding.** Another example involves a female refusing to mate until after the male has secured a territory and demonstrated his willingness to share it with her.[75]

Why would females have evolved these kinds of strategies? In evolutionary terms, they seem to reflect what is known as **Bateman's rule.**[76] This rule states that whichever gender makes the greatest parental investment will be the most cautious in choosing mates. In nearly all species, the female makes a greater parental investment than does the male. The female parental investment comes in the form of *gestation,* the time between conception and birth when the offspring is being nurtured in the mother's womb.

The principle behind Bateman's rule is fundamental to most of the evolutionary theories of criminal behavior. Here is how that principle can be understood: Picky females often have a reproductive advantage over less choosy females. More precisely, females who choose to mate with males who are most capable of assisting in the care of offspring and are willing to do so will be able to rear more offspring than their less choosy sisters. These choosy females not only do a favor for their own genes by allowing them to combine with genes of males who provide long-term assistance in caring for offspring, but they also help to proliferate the genes of males who are inclined to procure and share resources.

Before you conclude that the evolution of choosy females would have the effect of gradually weeding out all males who were unwilling or unable to procure and share resources, you need to consider what evolutionists call **counterstrategies.** Counterstrategies are physiological or behavioral responses to evolved strategies that circumvent the strategy. Most counterstrategies involve some form of **deception,** i.e., giving false impressions to others.[77] Some deception takes anatomical forms, such as moths that exhibit large fake "eyes" on their wings, fooling prospective predators into thinking the moths are more menacing than is actually true. Other forms of deception are behavioral, such as species of ground-nesting birds that act wounded in order to lure predators away from their nests.[78]

Deceptive counterstrategies have evolved within species as well as between them, and many of these involve male–female relationships.[79] To understand why, again consider Bateman's rule. Given that females should evolve a preference for males who will help care for offspring, the genes of males could either comply with such preferences or they could evolve a counterstrategy.

One counterstrategy to female preferences for males who provide resources would be to behave during courtship as though they will provide resources to offspring, but then renege after insemination has occurred. Another counterstrategy would be to completely bypass the courtship process by simply forcing the female to copulate. It is sad to say that studies have shown that both of these counterstrategies are widespread in the animal kingdom.[80]

With this background, we are ready to explore five recently proposed evolutionary theories of criminal/antisocial behavior: the cheater theory, the r/K theory, the conditional adaptation theory, the alternative adaptation theory, and the evolutionary expropriative theory. While they all are rooted in modern (gene-based) evolutionary theory, each one emphasizes somewhat different aspects of evolution, and thereby leads to somewhat different predictions.

CHEATER (OR CAD VERSUS DAD) THEORY: Criminals/Psychopaths Represent an Alternative Reproductive Strategy

Among bluegill fish, females all look pretty much alike. Males, on the other hand, come in two distinctive forms, called *morphs* (meaning distinct body appearances). One morph is called a *resident male,* so named because he devotes considerable time and energy to procuring and guarding a small territory at the bottom of the pond. Periodically, the resident male will hollow out a small nest in the sand or mud, and when a female approaches overhead, he tries to get her attention and coax her into his territory to inspect his nest.

When a female makes her choice of a mate with a suitable territory and nest, the couple begins courtship. Eventually, the male gently nuzzles her underbelly, which induces her to spawn her eggs in the nest, whereupon the male proceeds to deposit his sperm over the eggs.

While the behavior of courting bluegill sometimes proceeds just as described, there are often complications brought on by the second type of male bluegill. This morph has earned the name **sneaker.** Instead of procuring and guarding a territory like resident males do, a sneaker trespasses onto a resident male's territory while a female and the resident male are in the final stages of courtship. Then, in the blink of an eye, as soon as the female spawns, the sneaker darts over the eggs she has laid and quickly deposits some of his own sperm. He exits as fast as he came to avoid being bitten by the resident male.

In bluegills, sneakers are an example of what biologists call an **alternative reproductive strategy.**[81] It is one of the evolved counterstrategies to female preferences for males who provide reproductively useful resources. In other words, some males have evolved ways to comply with female preferences, whereas others (the sneakers) have evolved ways to circumvent these preferences.

Another example can be found in the mountains of Montana among the bighorn sheep.[82] Among these magnificent animals, one again finds two types of males. One type is called a *tending male* and the other type is called a *coursing male.* Tending males are nearly all fully mature ("middle-aged") sheep who spend most of their time grazing in proximity to fertile females, especially during the rut (the mating season). At the first sign of danger (such as when a predator approaches), tending males usually act to protect the females and any offspring that are nearby.

Coursing males, on the other hand, are predominantly young adults who are shunned by reproductive females, especially during the rut. This rejection occurs despite the fact that coursing males have strong sexual interests in females, and

use a variety of "pushy" tactics to gain access to them whenever possible. For example, coursing males sometimes chase females and literally try to copulate with them as they are running.[83]

In other instances, two or three coursing males will band together to cooperate in cornering a female in order for at least one of them to copulate with her.[84] Why did this rather unpleasant behavior evolve? A recent DNA study found that most lambs born to bighorn sheep were sired by tending males, but about 40 percent were sired by coursing males.[85] In evolutionary terms, a coursing approach to reproduction does not appear to be the most successful reproductive strategy, but it still insures a substantial "reproductive niche" for the males who use it.

What do bluegill and bighorn sheep have to do with crime? Proponents of the cheater theory believe that an alternative reproductive strategy has also evolved in our species. One type of male is more or less law-abiding and loyal to females with whom they usually establish a long-term sexual relationship, while the other males are those we call "hard-core criminals" and "psychopaths."

The Cheater Theory in Brief

Women have a lower reproductive ceiling than do men. What's a **reproductive ceiling**? It is the maximum number of offspring that an individual can possibly produce in a lifetime. Women can partially compensate for their lower reproductive ceiling by being choosy in picking mates. This implies that natural selection favors women who are more cautious in mating than is true for the average male.[86] The result is a constant tension between the sexes: Males seeking to have numerous sex partners, and females seeking to confine their mates to males that will assist in caring for offspring.

When faced with choosy females, males can respond in one of two ways. One way is to comply with their preferences (become a "loyal dad"), and the other is to trick or force them into having sex, and then try to find more mates (become a "royal cad"). Both of these approaches are exhibited by males in various species (i.e., in the bluegill and the mountain sheep). Cheater theorists contend that alternative reproductive strategies have evolved in our species as well.

Building on proposals first articulated in the 1980s,[87] the leading proponent of cheater theory is a U.S. psychologist, **Linda Mealey** (1955–). Mealey[88] believes that alternative reproductive strategies have evolved in humans in two forms, and David Lykken has made a similar proposal.[89] Those who are almost completely genetically programmed to be cheaters and exhibit symptoms early in life are called *psychopaths,* and those who substantially learned this strategy and confine its use to their adolescent years are called *sociopaths.*

Evidence Pertaining to the Cheater Theory

Gender and Age.   If criminal/antisocial behavior is part of a cheater male strategy, the cheater theory predicts that males will dominate in the commission of crime throughout the world. This prediction is consistent with the available evidence, particularly with regard to serious and persistent offending (Table 5.1a).

The cheater theory implies that because criminal/antisocial behavior is part of an overall reproductive strategy, this behavior should be exhibited most intensely during the time that males are initiating their search for mates. Evidence that offending is most prevalent in the two decades following the onset of puberty (Table 5.2a) is consistent with this prediction.

Social Status and Academic Ability.   According to the cheater theory, criminal/antisocial behavior should be exhibited by males who have the greatest difficulty convincing females of their ability and/or willingness to assist in many years of child care. This would imply that criminality would be concentrated in the lower social strata, as most evidence suggests (Tables 5.5a and 5.5b).

Urban–Rural Differences.   Theoretically, alternative reproductive strategies will be more likely to evolve in large impersonal communities than in communities where each member is intimately

known by other members. In other words, the cheater strategy should be more reproductively successful in large urban environments than in rural communities or small towns where nearly everyone knows everyone else. This hypothesis is consistent with evidence that crime and delinquency is more prevalent in urban than in rural areas (Tables 6.1a and 6.1b).

Genetics.   According to the cheater theory, although learning is also involved, there must be genes that promote criminal/antisocial behavior. This prediction is consistent with evidence reviewed earlier in this chapter that significant variations in criminal tendencies, especially among males, are due to genetic factors (Tables 14.1 through 14.5).

Numerous Sex Partners, Unstable Marriages, and Parental Care.   The cheater theory predicts that certain sexual behavior variables will be correlated with criminal/antisocial behavior. Most notably, criminals and psychopaths should be disposed to seek to have numerous sex partners.[90] This prediction is consistent with evidence linking numerous sex partners and early age of onset of sexual behavior with involvement in crime and delinquency (Table 8.11). The cheater theory would also lead one to expect that crime-prone persons would have unstable marriages. The research on these predictions is largely supportive (Table 7.4).

Deception and Lying.   The cheater theory is highly compatible with evidence that criminals and psychopaths are unusually prone toward deception and dishonesty (Table 8.4).

Closing Remarks About Cheater Theory

According to the cheater theory, most women prefer to mate with males who are capable and willing to assist in child care. Theoretically, this preference has evolved because women with such a preference have been able to reproduce at higher rates than women with no such preference.

Men have two general responses they can make to women's desires for assistance in rearing offspring, both of which are reproductively viable. One response is to comply with what women want, and the other is to deceive them into thinking they will comply, and then renege whenever other mating opportunities present themselves. This latter type of response is called the *cheater* or *cad strategy*.

Mealey believes that there are two groups of cheater males. One group consists of males who are all but genetically "hardwired" to be cheaters; these are the true psychopaths. The other group of cheater males essentially learns to use a cheater strategy early in their reproductive careers, but then gradually adopts a more responsible "dad" strategy as they mature. These are termed *sociopaths*.

Cheater theory leads one to expect that the cad strategy will be more favored in the lower than in the upper social strata, because upper strata males will have less need to deceive prospective mates regarding their capabilities to assist in offspring care. Nonetheless, males of all status levels would sometimes be favored for being deceptive regarding their *willingness* to commit to long-term child care.

r/K THEORY:
Criminals Are r-Strategists

The concept of *r/K* was first used in the 1960s to describe how organisms reproduce along a continuum.[91] At one end of the continuum are creatures who reproduce prolifically, often having hundred or even thousands of offspring in a lifetime. Organisms at the other extreme are quite limited in their reproductive capacities, rarely having more than two or three offspring.

Creatures at the rapidly reproducing end of the continuum are said to be **r-strategists** (or **quantitative reproducers**), and those at the other end are called **K-strategists** (or **qualitative reproducers**). Depending on how plentiful the resources needed to reproduce are, sometimes r-strategists have a reproductive edge, and other times K-strategists have the edge.[92] According to r/K theory, as competition for resources becomes increasingly keen, K-strategists will usually, but certainly not always, be favored.

In theoretical terms, an r-strategy is expected to evolve mainly in a "virgin" environment (i.e., one that has all the resources needed to sustain life and few threats). On the other hand, the originators of the r/K concept believe that K-strategists do not tend to evolve until an environment begins to become "saturated" with a particular type of organism, forcing greater competition for dwindling resources. In other words, members of a resource-restricted population will become restrained in the number of offspring they produce as well as in the resources they utilize. Instead of producing large numbers of offspring, these organisms will funnel almost all of their time and energy into caring for a small number of offspring. R-strategists, on the other hand, should seek to use all the resources they can to have as many offspring as possible in a short amount of time. Theirs is a "fast-forward" reproductive strategy, if you will.

To keep these two ends of the r/K continuum straight, remember that *r* refers to rapid rates of reproduction, and *K* refers to reproducing in small numbers, but with great time and care given to insure that all of the offspring survive to reproductive age themselves.

While human beings are an extreme K-strategist species, some evolutionists have argued that the degree to which this is true varies, with some individuals and some ethnic groups being less extreme K-strategists than others.[93] According to the r/K theory, humans who are less extreme in being K-strategists will average more children in a lifetime than those who are the most extreme K-strategists. They should also have children who weigh less at birth, and who become reproductively functional at younger ages, because birth weight and age of onset of reproduction are considered classic indicators of parental investment.[94]

According to the r/K theory, humans who are least extreme in being K-strategists will be most prone toward criminal/antisocial behavior. The main proponents of this theory have been a U.S. sociologist, **Lee Ellis** (1942–) (the first author of this text), and a Canadian psychologist, **Philippe Rushton** (1943–).

The r/K Theory in Brief

Two assumptions are fundamental to the application of r/K theory to the study of criminal/antisocial behavior. The first assumption is that humans vary along the r/K continuum, both as individuals and as numerous breeding populations (even though all humans are still recognized as being near the extreme K-end of the continuum when compared to the rest of the animal kingdom). The second assumption is that criminal/antisocial behavior reflects an r-approach to reproduction. In this regard, property crimes often result in rapidly acquiring resources that can help to attract sex partners.[95] Similarly, many violent crimes such as rape and murder have been shown to be highly motivated by the desire to secure or maintain mating opportunities.[96]

Based on these two assumptions, Ellis[97] and Rushton[98] have contended that criminal/antisocial behavior is a behavioral accompaniment of an r-approach to reproduction. If so, genes that influence criminal/antisocial behavior should also help to promote r-selected traits, such as low weight at birth, large family size, and even multiple birthing (such as twinning).

There is a difference between the Ellis and the Rushton versions of r/K theory. Ellis' version is narrower in its conceptualization of the r/K continuum, limiting the concept primarily to the number of offspring produced in a lifetime, and the time and energy devoted to bringing each offspring to reproductive age. Rushton, on the other hand, has included over sixty variables as comprising the r/K continuum. This difference has no major effects on the hypotheses that will be specified below.

Evidence Bearing on r/K Theory

Reproductive Variables.   The r/K theory predicts that such variables as low birth weights would be correlated with criminal/antisocial behavior. The evidence is largely consistent with this prediction (Table 9.1).

Genetic and Family Variables.   According to the r/K theory, genes should influence criminal/antisocial behavior. Considerable evidence supports this prediction (Tables 14.1 through 14.5). At least in part because of the influence of genes, criminality will run in families. Evidence is supportive of this hypothesis also (Tables 7.10a and 7.10b).

Another family variable that the r/K theory predicts will correlate with offending behavior is family size. Consistent with the theory are studies showing that criminals and psychopaths have more siblings on average than do persons in general of the same age (Table 7.1a).

Gender and Age.   Given the male's higher reproductive ceiling, the r/K theory asserts that males are favored for exhibiting r-traits to a greater degree than for females. This implies that males will exhibit higher rates of criminal/antisocial behavior, as evidence largely suggests (Table 5.1a).

Regarding age, the r/K theory maintains that most victimful offenses have to do with acquiring reproductively significant resources, including sex partners. Thus, offending should be most prevalent during the most active reproductive years. This reasoning is consistent with evidence that criminal behavior is highly concentrated in the second and third decades of life.

Marital Status and Child Abuse.   According to r/K theory, rates of crime and psychopathy should be relatively high in individuals and groups in which parental investment in offspring is low. This implies that criminality will be linked to high rates of divorce and desertion, as most research suggests (Table 7.4), and with child maltreatment, also as evidence indicates (Table 7.9).

Social Status.   It is not possible to state which social status will have high or low rates of criminal behavior using r/K theory. However, the theory asserts that if there are differences in offending, the highest offending rates will be found among the strata with the highest fertility and twinning rates, and those with the lowest birth weights and rates of stable marital bonding.

Table 14.6 presents the evidence relevant to this hypothesis as it relates to social status. As you can see, the table shows that the lower social strata (in which most studies have found the highest rates of offending), exhibit the highest rates of fertility and twinning. Likewise, they have lower birth weights and less pair-bonding stability than do persons in the middle or upper levels. All of these findings are consistent with r/K theory.

Race/Ethnicity.   As with social status, the r/K theory does not predict that any specific racial/ethnic group will be more involved in crime than another. However, the theory does predict that, if there are racial/ethnic differences in offending rates, these differences will be associated with such physiological/reproductive traits as birth weights, family size, twinning rates, and bonding stability of parents. Specifically, whichever racial/

ethnic groups exhibit the highest crime rates should have unusually low birth weights, large family size, high twinning rates, and unstable pair-bonding.[99]

Research pertaining to these controversial hypotheses is summarized in Table 14.7. As you can see, most of the evidence is consistent with r/K theory in that it indicates that the racial/ethnic groups with the highest rates of offending according to most studies (Tables 5.3a through 5.3e) have the lowest birth weights (or gestation lengths), the largest families, the highest rates of twinning, and the most unstable bonding between parents. Nonetheless, there are exceptions, and numerous racial/ethnic groups have not yet been investigated with respect to the relevant physiological/reproductive traits predicted by r/K theory. Among the exceptions, there is little evidence that Asians or Hispanics in the United States differ significantly from whites in average birth weight, despite the

TABLE 14.6.   Evidence of links between social status and birth weight, family size, twinning, and bonding stability (overall consistency score = 95.8%). (Studies in shaded boxes are consistent with r/K theory.)

Nature of the Relationship	Indicators of an r-Approach to Reproduction			
	Birth Weight or Gestation Length	**Twinning Rate**	**Family Size (Number of Siblings, Birth Rates, Fertility)**	**Bonding Stability between Parents**
Negative		**Africa** *Nigeria:* 2 **Europe** *Germany:* 1 **North America** *United States:* 1	**Europe** *England:* 1; *France:* 4; *Sweden:* 1 **North America** *United States:* 7	
Not significant	**Europe** *Sweden:* 1 **North America** *United States:* 2			
Positive	**Asia** *Burma:* 1; *India:* 8; *Java:* 1 **Europe** *Denmark:* 1; *England:* 2 **Middle East** *Iran:* 2 **North America** *United States:* 16 **South/Central America & Caribbean** *Columbia:* 1 **Pacific** *Australia:* 2			**Europe** *England:* 4 **North America** *Canada:* 1; *United States:* 11

TABLE 14.7.   Evidence of links between race/ethnicity, on the one hand, and birth weight, twinning, family size, and bonding stability on the other. (Studies in shaded boxes are consistent with r/K theory.)

Nature of the Relationship Compared to Whites (Europeans)		Indicators of an r-Approach to Reproduction			
		Birth Weight or Gestation Length (G)	Twinning Rate	Family Size (Number of Siblings, Birth Rates; Fertility)	Bonding Stability between Parents
Blacks	Higher		**North America** *United States:* 7 **International** *Two Countries:* 2	**Africa** *South Africa:* 1 **North America** *United States:* 11 **South/Central America & Caribbean** *Brazil:* 1	
	No significant difference				**North America** *United States:* 1
	Lower	**North America** *United States:* 22 **Pacific** *Hawaii:* 1 **International** *Several Countries:* 1			**North America** *United States:* 11
Asians (Pacific Rim)	Higher	**North America** *United States:* 1	**North America** *United States:* 1	**North America** *United States:* 1	
	No significant difference	**North America** *United States:* 2 **International** *Several Countries:* 1		**Pacific** *Hawaii:* 1	
	Lower	**North America** *United States:* 2	**North America** *Canada:* 1; *United States:* 3 **Pacific** *Hawaii:* 1	**North America** *United States:* 6 **South/Central America & Caribbean** *Brazil:* 1	
Native (Aboriginal) Americans	Higher			**North America** *United States:* 3	
	No significant difference	**North America** *United States:* 1			
	Lower	**North America** *United States:* 2			
Hispanics	Higher			**North America** *United States:* 11	
	No significant difference	**North America** *United States:* 7*			
	Lower				**North America** *United States:* 1

*Except for immigrants from Puerto Rico (whose birth weights are lower than those for non-Hispanic whites), U.S. Hispanics have birth weights that are comparable to those of non-Hispanic whites.

fact that Asians have lower crime rates and Hispanics have higher crime rates than whites according to most studies.

Sexual Behavior. The r/K theory predicts that both early onset of sexual activity and having numerous sex partners will be associated with involvement in criminal/antisocial behavior. The evidence is largely consistent with both predictions (Table 8.11).

Closing Comments on the r/K Theory

The r/K theory of criminal/antisocial behavior maintains that genes influence people's approaches to reproduction within a fairly narrow range of the r/K continuum, and those who are most prone toward criminality are toward the r-end of the range relative to persons in general. If this assertion is correct, criminality should be associated with r-strategy traits such as low birth weights and multiple birthing. In addition, criminals should begin reproducing at a relatively early age, and have more offspring and low parental care than noncriminals.

To account for gender differences in offending rates, the theory asserts that men have been favored for exhibiting more r-strategy traits than women. Males have evolved an emphasis on an r-strategy not only because they have a higher reproductive ceiling than females do, but also because they have greater difficulty identifying their genetic offspring. According to the r/K theory, crime is most common in the teens and twenties because this is when males are most likely to be seeking to attract mates, and often have the fewest resources to do so.

Overall, additional research is needed to determine how useful r/K theory is for helping to understand variations in criminal and antisocial behavior. It is not unusual for science to take decades of intense research and debate to gradually come to a rough consensus about a theory. The fact that race is one of the variables that is at the heart of r/K theory adds an additional element of controversy to it.

CONDITIONAL ADAPTATION THEORY: Sensing That Life Will Be Short and Difficult Leads to Antisocial Behavior

Conditional adaptation theory was first formulated in the 1980s by **Jay Belsky** (1952–)[100] in conjunction with two other anthropologists at Pennsylvania State University.[101] This theory has been applied to a diversity of human behavior, including antisocial behavior.[102]

In broad terms, conditional adaptation theory asserts that humans have evolved the ability to unconsciously monitor and make adaptations to their environment early in life that then persist throughout the remainder of life. More specifically, Belsky and colleagues have hypothesized that the first five to seven years of life are crucial in making lifelong adaptations.[103] During this time, youngsters monitor their environments for clues relevant to the stability of interpersonal relationships and availability of resources.[104] Depending on what children unconsciously sense, they will become biologically and behaviorally "wired" to live the rest of their lives either as opportunists or as contributors to the common good. Those whose environments activate the brain for the opportunist mode will be at an increased risk for antisocial behavior.

What evidence led Belsky and his colleagues to their theory? Studies in various species of animals indicate that, when mothers stop nursing offspring relatively early, the offspring reach puberty sooner than when nursing continues to the normal age or beyond.[105] In humans, girls who report having the most strained relationships with their parents (especially their mothers) reached puberty at an earlier average age than did other girls.[106] Also, boys and girls of divorced parents have been found to reach puberty at an earlier average age than children of parents who remain married.[107] Not only do children of divorced parents reach puberty early, they also begin having sexual intercourse at a significantly earlier age than children from parents who remain married.[108] Proponents of conditional adaptation theory recognize that some genetic *variability* may exist in the human species regarding rates of sexual maturation that may affect antisocial behavior.[109] However, their theory focuses on how a common set of genes has evolved in all of us to make our bodies keenly sensitive to childhood environmental conditions.

Overall, if a child's experiences suggest that his/her life will be plagued by scarce resources and unreliable social relationships, Belsky and his associates contend that the child's entire reproductive physiology will be sped up. Theoretically, this "fast forward" life history will incline the child to either consciously or subconsciously emphasize early and frequent reproduction.

Conditional Adaptation Theory in Brief

According to conditional adaptation theory, genes influence antisocial behavior, but most of the influence is indirect. In other words, at least at birth, essentially everyone has the same genetic potential for exhibiting such behavior. Then, depending on one's early life experiences, the offending potentials are changed.

Belsky and his colleagues[110] argue that genes have nearly all of their effects on criminality by programming young children to unconsciously sense the stability of the overall environment in which they grow up. Children who come to sense that close relationships in their environment are unstable and/or resources are scarce are programmed by their genes to shift toward an "opportunistic" mode of reproduction.[111] In recent formulations of the theory, Belsky[112] also stipulates that a minority of people who adopt an opportunistic mode of reproduction may have genes instead of environmental circumstances directing them to do so. (However, most of the impetus for early and frequent reproduction results from sensing that one's early environment that life will be unstable and short.)

Among the strongest indicators of an opportunistic mode of reproduction, according to conditional adaptation theory, are an early age at puberty and engaging in sex and child-bearing early. Because their resources for doing so will

likely be scarce (as they were when they grew up), such individuals often seek to procure resources by any means available, including deception and stealth.[113] At the other extreme, if resources appear to be sufficient and social relationships with parents and peers are stable during the early years, a child will adapt physiologically and behaviorally in ways that are conducive to an orderly acquisition of resources.

Evidence Bearing on Conditional Adaptation Theory

Family Relationships and Child Abuse.   The conditional adaptation theory predicts that strained and unstable family relationships will be associated with criminal/antisocial behavior.[114] Studies linking criminality to divorce (Table 7.4), poor parent–child interactions (Table 7.6), and child abuse (Table 7.9) would be consistent with conditional adaptation theory, especially if these events occur fairly early in a child's life.[115]

Social Status.   According to the conditional adaptation theory, persons who spent their first few years of life in poverty will become involved in crime and delinquency to a greater degree than those who did not. Early life poverty should be considerably more important than poverty in later childhood, adolescence, or adulthood. Such a deduction follows from the assumption that low social status will be frequently linked to unstable supplies of resources. Although evidence does link poverty to elevated crime rates (Table 5.5b), to our knowledge, no study has yet attempted to test conditional adaptation theory's prediction that early life poverty is most likely to have effects on criminal behavior.

Peer Relationships.   In the case of peer relationships, the conditional adaptation theory makes the same prediction as in the case of family relationships: Relationships should be strained and unstable, especially early in childhood. The evidence is supportive of this prediction (Table 7.6).

Age of Puberty.   Central to the conditional adaptation theory is the hypothesis that offenders will reach puberty at an unusually early age. Delinquency research currently bearing on this hypothesis is supportive, both for males[116] and for females.[117]

Number of Sex Partners and Early Onset of Sexual Behavior.   Theoretically, criminals as well as their children should become sexually active at an earlier than average age, and have relatively fewer stable sexual relationships (thus, more sex partners) than persons in general. Evidence strongly supports these predictions (Table 8.11).

Economic Conditions.   According to the conditional adaptation theory, antisocial behavior should rise ten to fifteen years after hard economic times. In other words, persons who were infants and young children during depressions or deep recessions should engage in crime to a greater degree than those who were reared during favorable economic periods. This prediction follows from noting that, according to Belsky's theory, economic conditions largely have their effects on young children, not on people at the time the conditions are being experienced.

You may recall that the current evidence is quite mixed with respect to any links between economic conditions and crime rates (Tables 6.21 and 6.22). None of these studies, however, used a ten- to fifteen-year lag time between the economic conditions and increases in delinquency and crime rates predicted by conditional adaptation theory.

Genetics.   The conditional adaptation theory asserts that essentially everyone has an equal genetic capacity to become criminal and antisocial under conditions of deprivation and uncertainty. This deduction runs counter to evidence that genes *differentially* influence people's criminal/antisocial behavior (Tables 14.1 through 14.5).[118] However, in the most recent versions of the theory, this shortcoming is circumvented by stipulating that a minority of offenders may carry genes that

have more or less direct effects on antisocial behavior.[119]

Closing Comments on Conditional Adaptation Theory

Like other modern evolutionary theories of criminal behavior, the conditional adaptation theory focuses on the reproductive consequences of criminal/antisocial behavior. Its most distinguishing characteristic is its assumption that genetic influences on criminal tendencies are primarily indirect rather than direct. In other words, rather than assuming that genes program the brain to exhibit specific behavior, the conditional adaptation theory maintains that genes program us to monitor our environment early in life and adjust our lifelong approaches to reproduction accordingly. If an individual is reared in harsh and unpredictable social conditions, his/her overall sexual development will be accelerated, both physically and behaviorally.[120] The conditional adaptation theory makes a number of predictions, nearly all of which have been borne out by scientific evidence. On the negative side, the theory is largely silent about mental health and biological correlates of crime. Furthermore, it fails to predict that people would differ in their genetic propensities toward criminal/antisocial behavior, as considerable evidence suggests.

Parenthetically, in Belsky's most recently published article,[121] he has modified his assertion that all people have a more or less equal genetic propensity toward antisocial behavior. Instead, Belsky has now conceded that there may be two types of people in this regard: those with a strong genetic propensity and those whose adverse environments compel them toward such behavior.

ALTERNATIVE ADAPTION THEORY:
Genes Make Criminals Emphasize Mating Effort over Parenting Effort

In the 1990s, a U.S. psychologist named **David Rowe** (1949–),[122] proposed an evolutionary theory of criminal/antisocial behavior that emphasizes the role of gender in combination with certain behavioral/personality traits as the main causal factors. The theory is called **alternative adaptation theory.**[123] This name reflects the fact that Rowe's theory takes a key element of conditional adaptation theory and turns it on its head: the one having to do with the importance of the family environment.

Central to Rowe's theory are the opposing concepts of *mating effort* and *parental effort.*[124] Using evolutionary terminology, **mating effort** refers to the tendency to focus one's reproductive time and energy on seeking copulatory partners. **Parenting effort,** on the other hand, refers to the tendency to direct reproductive time and energy toward caring for offspring. These concepts are similar to the quantitative/qualitative, *r/K* continuum discussed earlier, but Rowe's theory adds some additional conceptual elements and does not consider such features as birth weights and twinning rates.

Rowe asserts that, for genetic reasons, people either emphasize mating effort or parenting effort. He believes that the two strongest predictors of which of these they will emphasize are gender and a suite of behavior traits such as sensation seeking, aggressiveness, and sex drive. Persons who are low in these personality tendencies, especially if they are females, will emphasize parenting effort, whereas persons who are high in sensation seeking, aggressiveness, and sex drive, especially if they are males, will emphasize mating effort.

A third less important predictor of whether a person will emphasize mating effort or parenting effort is intelligence. Theoretically, persons with high intelligence will be able to carry out more long-term and socially complex resource procurement strategies than those with low intelligence. Therefore, those with high intelligence will gravitate toward parenting effort, and those with low intelligence will tend to emphasize mating effort.

Alternative Adaptation Theory in Brief

According to Rowe, the reproductive effort of delinquents and criminals is biased toward mating effort rather than toward parenting effort.[125] For this reason, persons who engage in crime the most are predominantly male and have a relatively strong sex drive.

Rowe[126] explains these and other interconnections roughly as follows: Criminal behavior essentially represents the most direct and immediate ways of getting valued resources, and to be successful at it requires a willingness to risk retaliation from victims. More sophisticated and longer term resource procurement methods, on the other hand, require patience and intelligence.

Like other modern evolutionary theories of criminal behavior, alterative adaptation theory assumes that the bottom line for the prevalence of criminal/antisocial behavior is the number of offspring those who engage in such behavior leave relative to those who avoid such behavior. In this regard, Rowe[127] has asserted that criminality is **frequency dependent,** meaning that it is most likely to contribute to the reproductive success of criminals when there are only a few other criminals in a population. Thus, as the number of persons with genetic propensities toward crime increases, their likelihood of outreproducing noncriminal males diminishes, implying that persons with strong genetic dispositions toward criminality could never become the majority in a human population.

Unlike conditional adaptation theory, Rowe's theory places minimum emphasis on childrearing styles as affecting involvement in criminal behavior. He does so based on studies suggesting that virtually all of the similarities in personality and intelligence between parents and their offspring can be explained in terms of genetic factors rather than in terms of training and modeling influences.[128] In other words, alternative adaptation theory assumes that childhood experiences in the family have essentially *no* effects on the personality and intellectual traits relevant to criminal/antisocial behavior. Instead, Rowe's theory assumes that people vary greatly in their genetic propensities to pursue mating-effort/parenting-effort reproductive strategies, and that this genetic variability is largely responsible for why family members resemble one another in criminal/antisocial tendencies.[129]

Evidence Bearing on Alternative Adaptation Theory

Parental Care.   According to the alternative adaptation theory, parents of offenders, as well as offenders themselves, should devote less time to child care than is true for persons in general. Presumably, this means that they will spend less time with children, and use discipline patterns that reflect little patience and commitment. Nearly all relevant studies support these predictions (Tables 7.7 and 7.8b). In addition, the theory would predict that offenders would be more likely than persons in general to give up their children for adoption, a prediction that remains to be investigated.

Parental Training and Discipline.   According to alternative adaptation theory, parental training and discipline patterns have been found related to criminal/antisocial behavior not because this parental behavior has major effects on offspring behavior, but because it is reflecting the operation of many of the same genes. In other words, genes that incline an individual to be criminal and antisocial inclined his or her parents to shirk their caregiving roles, and to use harsh and even abusive discipline. Separating genetic explanations of the link between parental training and offspring offending probabilities from explanations that assume a direct causal role of the parental training remains to be accomplished.

Gender and Age.   The predominance of adolescent and young adult males among serious persistent offenders is explained by the alternative adaptation theory as a result of evolutionary forces that have favored males who emphasize mating effort over parenting effort. However, with the birth of each new offspring, as a male's remaining years become fewer, natural selection should favor males who gradually shift toward an emphasis on parenting effort. This prediction is consistent with

what has been found regarding the diminished probability of offending following the third decade of life (Table 5.2a).

Immediate versus Delayed Gratification.   Alternative adaptation theory leads one to hypothesize that criminals and psychopaths will be unusually prone toward immediate gratification behavior patterns, an hypothesis that is consistent with available research (Table 8.31).

Numerous Sex Partners.   The alternative adaptation theory clearly leads to the expectation that criminals and psychopaths will seek to be more involved in sexual behavior and begin doing so at an earlier age with a wider variety of sex partners than would be true for persons in general. The evidence is supportive of this prediction (Table 8.11).

Social Status.   According to the alternative adaptation theory, criminal/antisocial behavior should be more common in low than in high status populations because females should be more willing to mate with a high status male than with a low status male. This means that the need to quickly acquire resources using either violent or stealthy tactics should be less prevalent in the upper than in the lower social strata.[130] In addition, some of the behavior associated with high mating effort in males may distract them from pursuing the sort of long-term "legitimate" career opportunities that help them to attain high social status.

Most studies indicate that, with the possible exception of drug offenses, crimes are more prevalent in the lower than the middle and upper strata (Table 5.5a). This is consistent with Rowe's alternative adaptation theory.

Intelligence and Academic Performance.   Alternative adaptation theory leads one to expect that intelligence will be inversely correlated with criminal/antisocial behavior. This expectation is consistent with most of the available evidence (Tables 8.13 and 8.14). The evidence that academic performance is even more consistently correlated with criminal/antisocial behavior than is intelli-

gence is not predicted by Rowe's theory, but does not pose a major challenge to it.

Genetics. Alternative adaptation theory is especially emphatic about the direct role played by genes in affecting criminal/antisocial behavior. The evidence is strongly supportive of this hypothesis (Tables 14.1 through 14.5), and studies suggest that social environmental factors *out*side the family also play a substantial role.[131] The role of nonfamilial environmental influences is recognized by Rowe's theory, but is not clearly spelled out at the present time.

Closing Comments on Alternative Adaptation Theory

The alternative adaptation theory as developed by David Rowe asserts that criminal behavior is a manifestation of an emphasis on mating effort over parenting effort. Mating effort is emphasized primarily by males rather than females because males have a higher reproductive ceiling, and can therefore benefit more than females from having multiple sex partners.

Criminality is thought to be more closely linked to low rather than high intelligence because criminal behavior reflects less long-term planning strategies for resource procurement. The alternative adaptation theory emphasizes the genetic nature of personality and intellectual traits that are thought to underlie an emphasis on mating over parental effort.

The theory makes a substantial number of predictions, nearly all of which have been supported so far by available evidence. A particularly controversial feature of the alternative adaptation theory involves its minimal emphasis on the importance of family background in determining offspring behavior, including criminal/antisocial behavior. The theory is unique in asserting that essentially all of the links between sensation seeking, widely varied sexual behavior with numerous partners, aggressiveness, and criminal/antisocial behavior are actually due to genetics rather than the impact of childrearing.

THE EVOLUTIONARY EXPROPRIATIVE THEORY: Victimful Crime Is an Evolved Tactic for Resource Procurement

The evolutionary expropriative theory was first formulated in the 1980s through the collaborative efforts of three U.S. sociologists: Lawrence Cohen, Richard Machalek (*Ma ka' lek*), and Bryan Vila.[132] The theory maintains that victimful criminality represents one of the many ways of "making a living." The only difference is that criminal behavior causes victims to band together and initiate efforts to repress it; most other ways of making a living do not have these effects.

The Evolutionary Expropriative Theory in Brief

According to the evolutionary expropriative theory, humans, along with other animals, have evolved tendencies to act in ways that help ensure their own survival at least long enough to reproduce. An important component in accomplishing this goal is having access to various resources, particularly food and shelter.

Expropriative theorists argue that there are two ways to acquire resources: generative and expropriative. **Generative resource acquisition** involves such things as growing crops, tending livestock, building homes, and teaching others to do likewise. **Expropriative methods of acquiring resources** involve essentially taking advantage of the work of others, such as stealing and trickery. Theoretically, most victimful criminal behavior constitutes expropriative methods of resource acquisition.[133]

The evolutionary expropriative theory assumes that people have the ability to calculate the likelihood that they can secure needed resources in whatever ecological conditions they happen to live. This makes this theory similar to conditional adaptation theory. However, unlike conditional adaptation theory, the ecological expropriative theory does not assume that there is a critical time during childhood when these calculations are made. Instead, people make their assessments throughout life.

The evolutionary expropriative theory is also distinctive in terms of thinking about resource procurement as if it were an elaborate game (the game of life, if you will).[134] The rules of the game are that players can either procure resources using productive methods (taking resources from nature), or they can procure resources by expropriating them from other human beings. Theoretically, as the number of humans comprising a society grows, so too do opportunities for expropriative tactics. Thus, as societal size increases, the need for an organization that will discourage the use of expropriative tactics grows. This need brings about the criminal justice system.[135]

Hypotheses Derived from Evolutionary Expropriative Theory

Academic Ability.   According to the evolutionary expropriative theory, persons who have poor academic ability will be more likely to adopt expropriative methods of resource procurement than persons with high academic ability. More precisely, persons of all academic abilities may experiment with a variety of methods of procuring resources, but those with high academic abilities and skills will be more likely to abandon those with the greatest risks and short-term payoffs for those with fewer risks and long-term payoffs. The evidence pertaining to intelligence and especially to school grades is supportive of this hypothesis (Tables 8.13 and 8.14).

The Criminal Justice System.   No other criminological theory is more explicit in offering an explanation for the emergence of the criminal justice system than is the evolutionary expropriative theory. According to this theory, the probability that a criminal justice system will evolve is largely dependent on the size of the society, because the effectiveness of informal methods of social control diminishes as the size of the social group (and the anonymity of its members) increases. Overall, the evidence is consistent with this hypothesis (Tables 6.1b and 6.3). This hypothesis could also help to explain why per capita crime rates are lower in rural areas than in suburban, and especially urban areas (Table 6.1a).

Genetics.   Like the conditional adaptation theory, the evolutionary expropriative theory assumes that essentially everyone has the capacity to exhibit criminal and antisocial behavior when conditions of resource deprivation are severe. If so, whatever genetic propensities there are to engage in criminal/antisocial behavior are present in virtually all of us. This means that humans should all have a more or less equal genetic propensity to engage in criminal/antisocial behavior, a deduction that is contrary to the evidence of substantial variability toward such behavior (Tables 14.1 through 14.5). Such evidence does not completely invalidate the evolutionary expropriative theory, but it does suggest that the theory may need to be amended.

Unemployment and Economic Downturns.   The evolutionary expropriative theory leads one to expect that crime rates would be highest when economic conditions are bad. Somewhat contrary to this prediction, studies have not found clear links between offending rates and such factors as high unemployment (Tables 6.20 and 6.21) or other measures of poor economic conditions (Tables 6.25 and 6.26).

Closing Comments on Evolutionary Expropriative Theory

The evolutionary expropriative theory contends that criminal behavior is primarily undertaken as one of two fundamental ways of procuring reproductively useful resources, the other method mainly involving the creation of new resources, often in cooperation with others. Theoretically, everyone has the potential of resorting to criminal and other expropriative methods of resource procurement, but those who have the greatest difficulty obtaining resources creatively have the highest offending probabilities.

The theory is distinctive in its conceptualization of criminality as part of a serious game, a game that eventually gives rise to the criminal jus-

tice system. According to the theory, as societies become larger and more impersonal, the criminal justice system inevitably arises as a way of countering the advantages of using expropriative methods of resource procurement.

Overall, the theory is not as broad as other evolutionary theories in criminology, and the evidence pertaining to it has provided only mixed support. A particularly unique feature of the evolutionary expropriative theory is that it predicts that the criminal justice system will arise in societies as they develop in size and complexity, as evidence suggests.

GENERAL REMARKS ABOUT EVOLUTIONARY THEORIES

All but one of the theories reviewed in this chapter (the evolutionary expropriative theory) assume that (1) genes help to account for variations in criminal/antisocial behavior, and (2) these genes are the result of natural selection forces that have operated over countless generations. Despite the substantial evidence now supporting the genetic influence hypothesis, most criminologists remain skeptical of genetic and evolutionary influences on criminal behavior.[136] Why? At least four interrelated factors may be involved.

One reason for skepticism involves a long tradition in the social sciences of emphasizing the role of sociocultural learning in determining human behavior. In this regard, it is important to remember that genetic influences and learning are not mutually exclusive. Even if a type of behavior is entirely learned, individuals could still be differentially genetically disposed to learn some behavior more readily than other behavior.

A second reason criminologists have found it difficult to believe that genes contribute to criminal behavior is the fact that crime is socially defined and the definitions vary from one culture to another (and over time within the same culture). Nevertheless, there appears to be a set of core offenses that are recognized in all cultures and have been remarkably stable over time.

A third factor that may contribute to the dismissal of the genetic influence hypothesis is that most criminologists have had little training in biology, and even less in genetics. This makes it difficult to follow the research linking genetics and other biological influences with criminal/antisocial behavior.

Fourth, many criminologists have been hostile toward the genetic influence hypothesis (and biological theories in general) because they fear the political implications. As one writer stated, "biological theories often are used for the political purpose of blaming the powerless for crime . . . by the wealthy and powerful."[137] Others noted how biological theories helped to foster Nazi Germany's "final solution" to its "Jewish problem."[138] After all, if genes are responsible for criminal behavior, why not deal with the crime problem by making sure that criminals don't contaminate the human gene pool? These are obviously frightening ideas were they to get into the minds of the wrong political leaders.

A Canadian sociologist recently offered an evolutionary theory of genocide.[139] He argued that humans, like other animals, may have evolved a fear of strangers. This fear, especially when encouraged by governmental policies, could lead many people to engage in genocide. If such a vicious side has evolved as a part of human nature, the best way to control it may be through understanding its biological and evolutionary underpinnings.

All five theories reviewed in this chapter assume that genetic factors contribute to criminal behavior, and that this influence has been subject to natural selection. These assumptions continue to be very controversial from the standpoint of "political correctness." This is especially true of the three theories that imply that genes *differentially* incline people's brains to increased involvement in criminal/antisocial behavior (i.e., cheater theory, r/K theory, and alternative adaptation theory).

It is worth mentioning that there is considerable overlap between evolutionary explanations of criminality and neurologically specific explanations.[140] This can be understood by making a distinction between proximate and distal causes.

FIGURE 14.3   Following a recent American conference at which scientists exchanged the latest evidence concerning genetic influences on criminal behavior, this cover story appeared in *U.S. News and World Report.* (Theo Westenberger/Liaison Agency)

Proximate causes of behavior have to do with how the brain learns and responds to environmental conditions. **Distal (or ultimate) causes,** on the other hand, are causes of an evolutionary nature because they have to do with how individuals and groups have reproduced at varying rates over past generations. Thus, to the extent that criminality affects the reproductive rates of either offenders or victims, genes conducive to various behavior patterns may have accumulated at different rates in various populations. Most biosocial theorists see efforts to identify the proximate and distal causes of criminality as complementing one another.

Finally, it is important to keep in mind that you should never equate *genetic influence* and *genetic determination.*[141] Because genes never completely determine a complex behavior such as criminality, advances in understanding how genes make their contributions to offending probabilities may make it possible to develop new approaches

to crime prevention and treatment that will be more humane than those used in the past. Thus, the work being done on the genetic and evolutionary factors underlying criminality should not be seen as just another way for society to escape the blame for crime.

Currently, people who are genetically disposed to heart disease can often have their lives extended by learning how to regulate their diet, take various medications, and exercising. Similar preventive measures *may* eventually arise from the evidence and theories reviewed in this chapter.

SUMMARY

The fossil record provides irrefutable evidence that the types of organisms that have existed on earth have dramatically changed over millions of years. Biologists call this record of change *evolution.* Over the past couple of centuries, various theories have been proposed to explain why evolution has occurred. So far, one theory—that of Charles Darwin—has done the best job of explaining what has been learned about the gradual changes in life forms on earth. His theory has been further empowered by incorporating modern knowledge of genetics, leading to a revised theory, variously named *Neo-Darwinian theory,* the *Modern Synthesis,* or *gene-based evolutionary theory.*

What makes evolution possible are thousands of genes that exist as segments of DNA. Naturally separated strands of DNA are called *chromosomes,* of which most humans have 46. Occasionally, the genes on these chromosomes undergo slight changes in their chemical structure; these changes are called *mutations.* Sometimes mutations spread throughout a population because they provide their carriers with a trait that helps them to adapt to a particular environment better than species members lacking the particular trait.

At the heart of all versions of Darwin's theory is the idea that species arise and eventually become extinct as a result of individual species members reproducing at varying rates, depending on environmental conditions. Darwin called this phenomenon *natural selection.*

Neo-Darwinian Theory in Criminology

Most evolutionists assume that natural selection operates as much on behavior as it does on anatomical and physiological traits. Following this assumption, some criminologists have applied Darwinian ideas to the study of criminal behavior. Thinking about criminality in evolutionary terms has led to questions about the reproductive consequences not only of offending, but also of crime prevention efforts. Perhaps both have at least partly evolved by natural selection.

Evidence That Genes Contribute to Offending Probabilities

Evidence that genes contribute to variation in criminal behavior does not prove that evolutionary theory can help in understanding such behavior. However, if genes are not responsible for significant variation in such behavior, the argument that evolutionary theory could help in understanding criminal behavior would be seriously undercut. Consequently, researchers working from an evolutionary perspective have been keenly interested in the *genetic influence hypothesis.*

Seven lines of evidence have pointed toward genetic influences on criminal/antisocial behavior. These lines are as follows:

- Criminal behavior tends to run in families
- Twins who share 100 percent of their genes (identical twins) more closely resemble one another in criminality and psychopathy than do twins who only share 50 percent of their genes (fraternal twins).
- Regarding persistent involvement in criminality, adoptees have been found to more closely resemble their genetic parents than the parents who reared them.

- Extra X and Y chromosomes have been found associated with increased involvement in criminal behavior.
- Studies have disclosed that genes influence several behavioral and mental health correlates of crime.
- At least one genetic marker—that for low MAO activity—has been linked to criminal/antisocial behavior.
- Behavior that is similar to criminality in humans has been identified in nonhuman animals and may have evolved by natural selection.

In the present chapter, five recently proposed evolutionary theories were reviewed: the cheater theory, the r/K theory, conditional adaptation theory, alternative adaptation theory, and the evolutionary expropriative theory. While all five theories are rooted in the Neo-Darwinian theory of evolution, each one emphasizes somewhat different features of this theory.

Cheater Theory

The cheater theory was inspired by evidence that, in several species, males have evolved what are termed *alternative reproductive strategies.* These strategies are made possible by the fact that males do not need to gestate offspring in order to reproduce. This gives males a much higher reproductive ceiling than females, which in turn offers them greater latitude than females have in their approaches to reproduction.

In species that have evolved distinct alternative reproductive strategies at least two subpopulations of males are found. Among the names given to these subpopulations are *dads* and *cads.* Dads reproduce mainly by complying with female preferences for males who are able and prone to provide substantial parental care for offspring. Cads, on the other hand, have evolved various methods of using either force or deception in order to copulate while providing little or no offspring care.

According to proponents of the cheater theory, persistent criminals and psychopaths are human cads. Proponents of the cheater theory, such as Linda Mealey, have contended that some males may simply learn to become cads, while others are genetically inclined to approach reproduction in this way.

To put the cheater theory more formally, females have evolved preferences for males who will provide resources and assistance in rearing offspring. In a number of species, the genes programming males have responded to this female preference with an alternative reproductive strategy: that of a cheater or cad. Theoretically, cheater males have evolved in human populations just as in several other species, especially in large impersonal societies in which their strategy is hardest to detect.

r/K Theory

According to r/K theory, animals can be arrayed along a continuum of successful approaches to reproduction, and a number of traits vary in predictable ways in conjunction with this continuum. Individuals or groups that evolve tendencies to reproduce slowly not only must have fewer offspring but must spend more time gestating each one and then caring for them more carefully after birth. Rapidly reproducing organisms, on the other hand, tend to emphasize producing larger numbers of offspring, but without spending as much time gestating and caring for each one.

Those who have applied the r/K concept to the study of criminal behavior have made two assumptions: First, even though humans as a whole are extremely K in their approach to reproduction, there is still some intrahuman variability. Second, victimizing behavior within a species is an expression of a relatively r-approach to reproduction. If so, criminals and psychopaths can be thought of as being more prone toward an r-strategy than people in general.

According to the r/K theory, criminals and psychopaths will have shorter gestation lengths, lower birth weights, larger numbers of siblings and

offspring, and they will begin engaging in sexual behavior earlier and with more partners than is true for people in general. To account for why males are more criminal than females, the theory asserts that males are more prone toward an r-approach toward reproduction than females. The main proponents of this theory are Philippe Rushton and Lee Ellis.

Conditional Adaptation Theory

The conditional adaptation theory asserts that antisocial behavior is part of a broad adaptive response to an unstable and hostile environment. The theory's proponents believe that essentially people are genetically inclined to begin early in life weighing their environmental options as far as reproduction is concerned. During the first few years of life, children who sense that their environments are chaotic and hostile will begin puberty early, and will complement this early physical development with an early onset of sexual activity. In adulthood, these same individuals will have unstable pair bonds and minimal inclinations to engage in childrearing.

Conditional adaptation theory asserts that, if the same individuals were to be reared in predictable, caring environments, their reproductive development would be delayed, as would the onset of sexual activity. In addition, a stable caring environment would prevent most children from developing the sort of opportunistic approaches to reproduction that incline them to violate criminal statutes. The main proponent of conditional adaptation theory is Jay Belsky.

Alternative Adaptation Theory

According to David Rowe, the main proponent of alternative adaptation theory, humans are genetically programmed to vary in tendencies to engage in criminal/antisocial behavior. In other words, some people have strong antisocial tendencies, some have virtually none, and most are intermediate. This assumption is the opposite of the one made by proponents of the conditional adaptation theory, who assume that all humans have nearly an equal genetic potential for criminal/antisocial behavior.

Rowe distinguishes between mating effort and parenting effort, and asserts that those who are most prone to engage in criminal/antisocial behavior have evolved tendencies to emphasize mating effort. From these premises, alternative adaptation theory leads to the hypothesis that offenders will be males, prone toward sensation seeking and aggression, and have a strong sex drive.

Evolutionary Expropriative Theory

Lawrence Cohen, Richard Machalek, and Bryan Vila have proposed an evolutionary theory that shares with conditional adaptation theory the assumption that, from a genetic standpoint, all humans have an equal potential for criminal/antisocial behavior. According to the evolutionary expropriative theory, genes incline all of us to organize our lives around the acquisition of resources that will help us to reproduce. Two extreme approaches to resource acquisition are identified: productive and expropriative. Whereas productive means of resource acquisition involves creating resources from more fundamental elements, often in cooperation with others, expropriative resource acquisition entails manipulation and victimization as resource acquisition strategies. Criminal/antisocial behavior represents the main forms of expropriative strategies.

The theory asserts that people engage in crime in response to resource deprivation or in anticipation of such deprivation in the future. Furthermore, the theory contends that victims of expropriative tactics often attempt to retaliate, either individually or collectively, giving rise to the criminal justice system.

Overall, evolutionary theories of criminal/antisocial behavior attempt to explain such behavior in terms of its long-term reproductive consequences. Two of the theories—the r/K theory and alternative adaptation theory—assume that genes operate differentially on people's tendencies to engage in criminal/antisocial behavior. Two other theories—conditional adaptation theory and evolutionary expropriative theory—assume that genes incline everyone to adjust their behavior to environmental circumstances in ways that make some people more likely than others to exhibit criminal/antisocial tendencies. The other theory— the cheater theory—assumes that two types of criminals/psychopaths have evolved, ones who are genetically hardwired and ones who largely learn their offending behavior. The latter are thought to be more likely to abandon their offending behavior by the time they reach adulthood than are the former.

SUGGESTED READINGS

Buss, David (1998). *Evolutionary psychology.* Needham Heights, MA: Allyn & Bacon. (A clearly written text that provides many illustrations in the use of modern evolutionary theory to help understand human [and nonhuman] behavior.)

Barash, David (1979). *The whisperings within.* New York: Harper and Row. (An easy-to-read book that explains how behavior can be interpreted from an evolutionary perspective.)

Daly, Martin and Wilson, Margo (1988). *Homicide.* New York: Adline de Gruyter. (This book presents arguments and detailed evidence to suggest that much of the variation in violent crimes can be understood from the standpoint of modern evolutionary theory. It is one of the few books on criminal behavior specifically written from an evolutionary perspective.)

Wright, Robert (1994). *The moral animal.* New York: Pantheon. (A widely read book on the application of evolutionary theory to the study of human morality and altruism. Several parts of this book are relevant to criminology.)

EXERCISES

1. Chapter 5 presented evidence that males are more likely to be victimized by violent offenses than females, except when sexual offenses are involved. Offer an evolutionary account for why males, especially young males, would be more involved in violent crimes (both as offenders and victims), while females would be mainly victimized by sexual offenses. (In answering, keep in mind that evolutionary explanations focus on the reproductive consequences of what one is trying to explain.) Write one to two double-spaced pages.

2. Read the cover story from the April 21, 1997 issue of *U.S. News and World Report,* and/or articles from one or more Internet sites (or from the library) on genetics and criminality. Then, write a one to two-page double-spaced report on the nature of the controversy concerning this topic. (While you can offer your own opinion, be sure to also mention what others have argued.)

3. Using library or Internet resources, search for information about a proponent of one of the theories described in this chapter. The information can include personal background information as well as research interests of the theorist. Write a one- to two-page double-spaced report on what you find.

4. Many of the theories in this chapter make similar predictions, especially regarding gender and criminal behavior, and aggression in general. In one to two double-spaced pages, explain why. Hint: What is it about gender that is indispensable from the standpoint of evolution?

ENDNOTES

1. Dennett 1995; Scott 1997:264.
2. Beckstrum 1993:2; Buss 1994:16.
3. Herman 1984:266; Noble 1996a:337.
4. Ruse 1982:26.
5. Haviland 2000; Jarmain et al. 1998.
6. Brush 1979:312.
7. Broadhurst 1967:126.
8. Wimer & Wimer 1985.
9. Hyde & Sawyer 1979, 1980; Lagerspetz 1964; Shrenker & Maxson 1982.
10. Brush et al. 1979, 1988; Satinder 1980.
11. Yamazaki et al. 1978.
12. Wilson et al. 1984.
13. Broida & Svare 1982; Lynch 1981.
14. Kovach & Wilson 1981.
15. Alper 1998.
16. Horgan 1993.
17. Lander 1996.
18. Collins et al. 1996:14771; Noble 1996a:337.
19. Hay 1990:638; Lasker & Tyzzer 1982:71.
20. Cavalli-Sforza & Bodmer 1971; de Castro 1993; Horgan 1993; Wilson 1986.
21. Devor 1993.
22. Carey 1992, 1994; DiLalla & Gottesman 1989; Eysenck & Gudjonsson 1989:108; Goldsmith & Gottesman 1995; Raine 1993; Walters 1992:604.
23. Ellis 1982:48.
24. Stevenson & Graham 1988.
25. Rushton 1996.
26. Rushton 1996:88; Rutter 1996:9.
27. DiLalla & Gottesman 1989; Edelbrock et al. 1995; Lyons et al. 1995:906; McGuffin et al. 1994; O'Connor et al. 1998b; Thapar & McGuffin 1996:1116.
28. Mednick & Kandel 1988.
29. Rowe 1983.
30. Kendler & Gardner 1998; Plomin et al. 1976.
31. Cadoret 1986:45.
32. Grove et al. 1990.
33. Ge et al. 1996.
34. Cadoret et al. 1987; Duyme 1990; Van Dusen et al. 1983.
35. Cadoret et al. 1990.
36. Rutter 1996:9.
37. Hoffman 1977:447.
38. Horgan 1993.
39. Witkin et al. 1976.
40. Clark et al. 1970; Hoffman 1977:447; Horgan 1993; Hunter 1977; Nielsen & Tsuboi 1970.
41. Ratcliffe 1994.
42. Price & Whatmore 1967; Wilkin et al. 1976.
43. Reiss & Roth 1993:118.
44. Soudek & Laraya 1974.
45. Akessen & Wahlstrom 1977.
46. Franke et al. 1996.
47. Kluger et al. 1996:358; Nussbaum & Ledbetter 1986.
48. Heitz et al. 1991:1236; Oostra & Halley 1995.
49. Nussbaum & Ledbetter 1986:111.
50. Nussbaum & Ledbetter 1986:125.
51. Hagerman et al. 1992; Lachiewicz & Dawson 1994; Lachiewicz et al. 1994.
52. Einfeld et al. 1991; Fisch 1993; Hagerman et al. 1992, 1994.
53. Hagerman et al. 1994.
54. Fisch 1993; Kluger et al. 1996.
55. Johnson et al. 1996:67.
56. Levy et al. 1997; Sherman et al. 1997a, 1997b; Thapar et al. 1995.
57. Bouchard et al. 1990; Plomin & Neiderhiser 1992; Teasdale & Owen 1984; L. A. Thompson et al. 1993.
58. Onstad et al. 1991; Stabenau & Pollin 1993.
59. Pedersen et al. 1993.
60. Davis et al. 1983:534; Haier et al. 1980:341; Von Knorring et al. 1984; Yu et al. 1984.
61. Perry et al. 1991; S. S. Smith et al. 1992.
62. Comings 1995; Comings et al. 1996b.
63. Comings et al. 1994a.
64. Comings et al. 1991; Noble et al. 1993; S. S. Smith 1992.
65. Comings 1995.
66. Comings et al. 1996a.
67. Noble 1993.
68. Ellis 1998.
69. Dinwiddie 1996.
70. Cadoret et al. 1987; Duyme 1990; Van Dusen et al. 1983; Venables 1987; Walsh 1992b.
71. Lombroso 1911.
72. Dawkins 1976:v; Grene 1982:1.
73. Rowe 1996:269.
74. Buss 1989:2; Ellis 1989a:51; Trivers 1985:252; Yosef & Pinshow 1989.
75. Bateson 1983; Searcy 1982.
76. Bateman 1948.
77. Jolly 1985a:414, 1985b; Trivers 1985:395.
78. Gramza 1967.
79. Cheney et al. 1986:1364; de Waal 1982:74; Mitchell & Thompson 1986; Tooke & Camire 1991.
80. Alcock 1993; Ellis 1998; Trivers 1985.

81. Bass 1996; West-Eberhard 1986.
82. Hogg 1984.
83. Hogg 1984:257.
84. Ellis, 1998:95.
85. Hogg & Forbes 1998.
86. Bereczkei et al. 1997; Buss 1994.
87. Draper & Harpending 1982; Kofoed 1988; MacMillan & Kofoed 1984.
88. Mealey 1995.
89. Lykken 1995.
90. Seto et al. 1997.
91. MacArthur & Wilson 1967; Pianka 1970.
92. B. H. Smith & Tompkins 1995:263.
93. Cunningham 1981:85.
94. Chisholm 1988:81; Relethford 1990:498.
95. Burgess & Draper 1989.
96. Daly & Wilson 1988.
97. Ellis 1987, 1989 a or b?.
98. Rushton 1990, 1995.
99. Cunningham & Barbee 1991; Ellis & Walsh 1997:253.
100. Belsky 1980, 1993; Belsky et al. 1991.
101. Draper & Harpending 1982; Harpending & Draper 1988.
102. Barber 1998; Belsky 1997; Draper & Belsky 1990; Kim et al. 1997.
103. Belsky et al. 1991.
104. Belsky et al. 1991; Kim et al. 1997:110.
105. Evans & Hodges 1984; Tardiff 1984.
106. Graber et al. 1995; Moffitt et al. 1992; Steinberg 1988; Surbey 1990.
107. Reviewed by Kim et al. 1997:112.
108. Aro & Taipale 1987; Magnusson et al. 1986; E. Smith et al. 1985.
109. Belsky et al. 1991:662; Kim et al. 1997:137.
110. Belsky et al. 1991.
111. Hill et al. 1997.
112. Belsky 1999.
113. Harpending & Draper 1988; Harpending & Sobus 1987.
114. Belsky et al. 1991:655.
115. Belsky 1997:369.
116. Duncan et al. 1985; Susman et al. 1987.
117. Magnusson 1988; Magnusson et al. 1985, 1986; Sonis et al. 1985.
118. MacDonald 1997.
119. Belsky 1999.
120. Belsky et al. 1991:659.
121. Belsky 1997.
122. Rowe 1996.
123. Rowe et al. 1997.
124. Rowe 1996:270.
125. Rowe et al. 1997.
126. Rowe 1996:285.
127. Rowe 1996:302.
128. J. R. Harris 1998; Rowe 1994; Scarr et al. 1981:888.
129. Rowe et al. 1997.
130. Rowe et al. 1997:113.
131. Rowe 1994.
132. Cohen & Machalek 1988; Vila 1994, 1997; Vila & Cohen 1993.
133. Cohen & Machalek 1988.
134. Colman & Wilson 1997.
135. Vila & Cohen 1993:878.
136. Ellis & Hoffman 1990; Ellis & Walsh 1999.
137. Farley 1998:179.
138. O. D. Jones 1994:275; Wright & Miller 1998:9.
139. Brannigan 1998.
140. Lykken 1995; Raine 1993.
141. van den Oord et al. 1996:355

CHAPTER 15

Synthesized Theories

Criminology is a vibrant discipline with hundreds of researchers throughout the world contributing new information to our store of knowledge and cross-checking old information every year. As this knowledge continues to grow, criminologists are challenged to devise new theories that better fit the increasing evidence. Theories proposed in recent decades have tended to borrow from two or more older theories, often adding some new concept in the process and then blending them into what are called synthesized theories. *In this chapter, we will examine these theories.*

Beginning in the late 1970s, criminologists began proposing what are called **synthesized theories** of criminal behavior.[1] Such theories arise by combining two or more recognized "parent" theories, usually with the addition of at least one new conceptual component. As you would suspect, synthesized theories tend to be more complex than the theories examined in the preceding chapters. Of course, complexity is not a virtue when it comes to scientific theories. The only justification for complexity is that such theories have greater explanatory power than simpler theories.[2]

As with the theories reviewed in previous chapters, synthesized criminological theories can be either environmental or biosocial. Those that stipulate the involvement of no biological variables are environmental theories, and those that assert that at least one biological variable is involved (in conjunction with one or more environmental variables) are biosocial theories.

Four synthesized theories will be reviewed in this chapter, two are of an environmental nature and the other two are biosocial. The synthesized

environmental theories are the integrated theory and the social development model. The biosocial theories are the two-path developmental theory and the evolutionary neuroandrogenic theory.

INTEGRATED THEORY:
Linking Strain, Control, and Social Learning Theories

Delbert Elliott (1933–)[3] and associates[4] proposed a theory that primarily combines the elements of three theories discussed in earlier chapters. These theories are strain theory (p. 347), control theory (p. 321), and social learning theory (p. 342).

Integrated Theory in Brief

In a nutshell, here is how Elliott constructed his integrated theory: From strain theory, he borrowed the idea that offending behavior is encouraged when people are frustrated with efforts to attain economic goals they have set for themselves. This

frustration is seen as particularly difficult to accept by those in their teen and early twenties.

Elliott abstracted from control theory the idea that inadequate socialization, particularly in the home, is a major contributor to crime. He also noted that poorly organized local communities can also foster criminality by failing to provide clear boundaries between acceptable/unacceptable behavior, and by not imposing sanctions on lawbreakers. It can be noted that this latter point contains some elements of social disorganization theory.

In the case of social learning theory, the main assumption incorporated into Elliott's integrated theory was that young people are prone to imitate the behavior of peers with whom they associate. In this way, youth who are most prone to violate the law associate with one another and reinforce one another's behavior.

Overall, once you are familiar with strain theory, control theory, and social learning theory, Elliott's integrated theory is easily understood. It basically states that offending is the result of (1) inadequate socialization in the home, (2) strain resulting from not being able to attain ones economic goals, and (3) frequent associations with peers who engage in and reward others for engaging in antisocial behavior.[5]

Evidence Relevant to Integrated Theory

Because the integrated theory merely combines three earlier theories without adding any new conceptual elements, hypotheses derived from it are basically the sum of all those derived from its three parent theories. Nevertheless, integrated theory implies that the variables identified in its three parent theories may often interact to affect offending behavior in ways that any one of the parent theories would not anticipate. However, if there are such interactive effects, they remain to be specified.

You may recall that strain theory and social learning theory are both fairly strong in the sense of correctly predicting quite a few hypotheses. Even stronger still is control theory. By combin-

ing these three theories, Elliott's integrated theory holds substantial promise in terms of predictive power.

Closing Comments on Integrated Theory

By combining three relatively strong environmental theories into one, the integrated theory is immediately catapulted into a leading position in contemporary criminology as far as its predictive power is concerned. Nevertheless, the integrated theory is more complicated than any of the three parent theories out of which it was constructed. Some defenders of the parent theories might argue that it is difficult to justify the additional complexity of Elliott's integrated theory in light of its inability to make any predictions beyond those derived from its parent theories.

THE SOCIAL DEVELOPMENT MODEL:
Linking Control Theory and
Social Learning Theory

In the 1980s, **David Hawkins** (1945–), in conjunction with **Joseph Weis,** formulated what has come to be called the **social development** model for antisocial behavior.[6] The word *model* was used instead of *theory* as a way of emphasizing that their theory was primarily intended for use in designing effective approaches to the *prevention* of delinquency and crime. Only secondarily was the social development model designed to help *explain* such behavior.

Hawkins and Weis[7] created the social development model by combining control theory and social learning theory.[8] Recall that social learning theory is an extension of differential association theory; therefore, the social development model can be said to also incorporate differential association theory.[9]

You may recall that control theory contends that delinquent and criminal behavior results from a failure by families or other social institutions to help individuals form strong emotional bonds and a sense of commitment to the society and to its values (p. 321). Social learning theory, you may

recall, asserts that most delinquent and criminal behavior results from individuals not being reinforced for engaging in prosocial interactions and activities, and thus learning definitions favorable to law violations (p. 342).

The Social Development Model In Brief

Hawkins and Weis, as well as others,[10] have asserted that despite the strengths of both theories, control theory and social learning theory have serious deficiencies that can be overcome simply by combining them into a single theory. The most notable deficiency they saw in control theory was its inability to explain why delinquents form relationships with one another, and, by so doing, usually become even more delinquent. As noted in Chapter 10, both versions of control theory imply that the formation of any social bonds and commitments should reduce, rather than increase, delinquent and criminal behavior.

Social learning theory explained why associating with delinquent peers led to delinquency. However, it failed to give recognition to the importance of strong emotional ties between child and parent as well as other primary socializing forces in preventing delinquency and crime.[11]

The social development model assumes that the prevention of delinquency and crime requires both a formation of a genuine commitment to social order and reinforcement for prosocial behavior. Theoretically, three factors help to insure that this emotional bonding occurs: First, there must be numerous opportunities for involvement in social activities between children and their parents and their community. Second, the child must acquire the intellectual and physical skills needed to maintain meaningful relationships with parents and local communities. Third, the child must receive frequent reinforcement from parents and the community at large for maintaining these relationships. If any three of these factors are inadequate, the child will become a loner or will come to associate with other children who have also failed to become an integral part of their families

and communities. As a consequence, the child will become delinquent and/or criminal.[12]

In the most recent version of the social development model, suboptimal arousal is hypothesized to be operating in addition to strictly social environmental factors.[13] However, the earlier versions of this theory did not mention suboptimal arousal or any other biological component. Therefore, we are currently treating the social development model as being strictly an environmental theory.

As already noted, Hawkins and Weis[14] set as their goal to devise a theory that would be of maximum utility in formulating delinquency prevention programs. So far, their efforts to evaluate the effectiveness of the social development model has focused on curtailing adolescent use of illegal drugs.[15] However, a few other researchers have utilized the model to develop strategies for generally improving parenting skills by parents of youngsters at risk for drug use.[16]

Evidence Relevant to the Social Development Model

Because the social development model simply combines control theory and social learning theory, all of its basic hypotheses are those already reviewed in connection with these two parent theories. This makes the social development model a formidable theory, because control theory and social learning theory each make a substantial number of accurate predictions on their own. However, there is little to be said about evidence pertaining to the social development model except as it has to do with delinquency prevention.

Delinquency Prevention. Because the social development model was primarily formulated for use in delinquency prevention, it is appropriate to pay special attention to the theory's performance in this regard. So far, only a few studies have been conducted on the effectiveness of programs based on the social development model in terms of preventing delinquency, and most of these have focused on the use of illegal drugs.[17] Programs designed in

accordance with the social development model emphasize encouraging close bonding between offspring, parents, and teachers, and give parents and teachers skills to use in managing children's behavior primarily through reinforcement rather than punishment. So far, three published studies have reported findings relevant to the effects of these programs on delinquency and/or conduct disorder behavior.

One program based on the social development model was developed for children with conduct disorders. In this program, parents of aggressive conduct disordered children were given special training in behavioral management using Skinnerian learning principles of reward. The results were that the conduct disordered behavior was significantly reduced for white male children. However, for African-American males and for females of both racial groups, no significant effects were found.[18]

Another program inspired by the social development model involved giving young at-risk adolescents ten weeks of **resistance skills training** to help prevent drug abuse. In these programs, trained counselors encourage youngsters to imagine being confronted with opportunities to begin using drugs, and then to practice in role-playing ways of resisting these opportunities.[19] In addition, the youngsters are made aware in unambiguous ways of the social, health, and legal costs of drug use.[20] These programs have been found to significantly curtail drug use at least until high school, particularly for marijuana.[21]

In yet another program designed in accordance with the social development model, middle-school youngsters at risk of dropping out were put into special classes that maintained them in a small homeroom setting where a single teacher could more carefully monitor their behavior and work with parents in managing any problems that arose. The results suggested that not only did their grades improve more than those of a control group of youngsters, but that they ended up staying in school longer and engaging in delinquency less.[22]

Closing Comments on the Social Development Model

The social development model combines two popular environmental theories: control theory and social learning theory. David Hawkins and other proponents of the social development model believe that criminal and delinquent behavior will be lowest under the following conditions: First, strong bonds need to form between a child and his/her social surroundings early in life. Second, the child should be given numerous opportunities to engage in desired behavior so as to avoid undesirable (antisocial) behavior.

Because the social development model was primarily developed as a practical guide for actually preventing delinquency and crime, rather than simply explaining such behavior, it is important to ask how well it has done in this regard. Currently, there is some evidence that preventive strategies designed around the model can serve to reduce illegal drug use and possibly other forms of delinquency.

In terms of weaknesses, the social development model has the same shortcomings as are common to its two parent theories. In particular, it is hardpressed to explain the universal tendency for males to engage in crime at higher rates than is true for females. At least one attempt has been made to explain this pattern within the social development model by asserting that girls are usually monitored more closely by their parents than is true for boys.[23] However, nothing in the social development model would explain why parents would monitor girls more than males in all societies.

THE TWO-PATH DEVELOPMENTAL THEORY: Failure in Neurological Development of Language Skills Leads to Criminality

Most people who become offenders start doing so in their teens (Table 5.2a). Nevertheless, a sizable proportion of offenders begins exhibiting severe antisocial symptoms much earlier in life, and studies have shown that these individuals are the most

likely to continue offending well into adulthood.[24] This evidence inspired a U.S. psychologist, **Terry Moffitt** (1955–), to propose a biosocial theory of criminal/antisocial behavior. Her theory asserts that two distinct types of offenders exist, and the causes for each of them are also distinct.

The Two-Path Developmental Theory in Brief

Following her involvement in a long-term study of young males in New Zealand,[25] Moffitt[26] came to the conclusion that there are actually two distinct types of offenders. She calls one type *adolescent-limited* and the other type *life-course-persistent.* As these names imply, one group confines nearly all of its antisocial behavior to the adolescent years, whereas the other group begins in childhood and persists at offending often through middle age. She estimates that adolescent-limited offenders are three to four times more common than life-course-persistent offenders.[27]

When it comes to causation, Moffitt believes that it is particularly important to consider these two types of offenders separately. Let us begin with the more serious and long-term type.

Causes of Life-Course-Persistent Offending

Regarding life-course-persistent offending, Moffitt attributes this behavior to two specific neuropsychological impairments, one having to do with executive functions and the other with language skills. Combined difficulties in these two areas is what Moffitt postulates to cause offending that begins in childhood and nearly always persists well into adulthood.

You may recall from the preceding chapter that the term *executive functions* pertains to the ability of the neocortex, particularly the frontal lobes, to coordinate a series of actions toward achieving some long-term goal (p. 419). Moffitt asserts that poor executive functions in conjunction with slow development in language skills impede the process of socialization.[28] In her words, "Children with neuropsychological prob-

lems evoke a challenge to even the most resourceful, loving and patient families."[29]

Causes of Adolescent-Limited Offending

Regarding adolescent-limited offenders, the two-path developmental theory asserts that criminal/antisocial behavior is initiated by maturational changes accompanying puberty. These changes signal young people that they should be entitled to adult social status.[30] However, adolescents rarely have either the financial security or the social influences of adults, so their attempts to break free of childhood restrictions are often frustrated.

At this point, many adolescents turn to what Moffitt calls *social mimicry* of peers whom they see getting what they want by engaging in antisocial behavior.[31] In other words, many "normal" adolescents experiment with imitating life-course-persistent offenders. As a bottom line, "Delinquent acts hold symbolic value as evidence that teens have the ability to resist adult demands and the capacity to act without adult permission."[32] Once the delinquent act of an adolescent becomes known to another, it is often admired as an act of independence by other adolescents and is thereby often further reinforced and imitated.[33]

Finally, given all of this adolescent learning of antisocial behavior, why would adolescents stop the behavior by the time they become adults? According to Moffitt,[34] within a few years, most adolescents learn that there are more effective and less risky ways to attain the privileges of adulthood. Basically, this means they join the productive work force and begin earning wages and taking on family responsibilities.

Evidence Bearing on the Two-Path Developmental Theory

Existence of Two Distinct Paths.
Are there really two distinct types of offenders? The evidence so far is mixed. On the supportive side, one study indicated that conduct disordered children who become delinquent can be distinguished from the

"typical" delinquent in terms of having significantly lower VIQ scores, lower impulse control, and higher rates of violent crimes.[35] Studies have also reported two fairly distinct "pathways to delinquency," one exhibited by early starters, and the other exhibited by late (adolescent) starters.[36] Probably the most supportive evidence for Moffitt's dichotomy is that which has shown that nearly all persons who commit serious offenses beyond their midtwenties were diagnosed with conduct disorders as children.[37] In other words, while delinquency is widespread among teens, only a few go on to commit serious crimes in adulthood, and nearly all of these exhibited serious conduct disorders in childhood.

On the nonsupportive side are studies that have either suggested that there are three or more distinct types of offenders in terms of their age of onset and termination,[38] or indicated that onset and termination of offending actually exist along a wide indistinguishable continuum.[39] All of these counterproposals have been based on analyses of large data sets using rather complicated mathematical models, and are far from settling the controversy.

Social Mimicry. Is there evidence that adolescent-limited offenders commit their offenses because they are mimicking what seem to be successful tactics by life-course-persistent offenders? As support for this hypothesis, Moffitt has pointed to evidence that associating with delinquents appears to be much more important in affecting an adolescent's own delinquent behavior than are any attitudes that adolescents have about delinquency.[40] Other supportive evidence would include studies showing that delinquents tend to associate with one another (Table 7.21).

Age. There is some evidence that the age of the average offender has gradually dropped in many Western countries, at least since the beginning of the twentieth century.[41] Moffitt's theory explains this decline in terms of a decline in the average age of puberty, brought on by improvements in nutrition and health in combination with less of a need

for relatively unskilled workers in industrial societies.[42] The end result of these two forces is that adolescents are forced to retain their "subadult status" longer than was the case in earlier times.

The two-path developmental theory also predicts that those who reach puberty earliest should be more delinquent than those who are late in reaching puberty. Why? Because those who mature the earliest will be most likely to retain their "subadult status" the longest. Most of the evidence bearing on this hypothesis has been obtained from females, because they have more obvious symptoms of puberty onset than is true for males. These studies support the hypothesis that early puberty is associated with higher rates of delinquency.[43]

Intelligence and Academic Performance. According to the two-path developmental theory, life-course-persistent offenders should exhibit substantial intellectual deficits, particularly in the area of language. This hypothesis is consistent with numerous studies indicating that relatively low IQ scores (Table 8.14) and poor academic performance (Table 8.13) are associated with delinquent and criminal behavior. According to Moffitt's theory, these intellectual deficits should not be a significant cause of delinquency in adolescent-limited offenders, only in the life-course-persistent group.[44] Research undertaken to specifically test this hypothesis has so far been supportive.[45]

Child Abuse. Research has repeatedly shown a statistical relationship between criminal/antisocial behavior and being subject to child abuse (Table 7.9), and even harsh discipline (Table 7.8b). Most explanations of these relationships have been in terms of the abuse being the cause of the antisocial behavior by the child later on. The two-path development theory suggests that the causal order may not be that simple. Moffitt[46] argues that children with neuropsychological problems associated with life-course-persistent offending will often pose special challenges for parents. One result of the frustration parents experience in rearing children with neurological symptoms of life-course-

persistent offending is that these children will be at an increased risk of being abused by their parents.

Becoming a High School Dropout.

Recall the puzzling tendency for high school dropouts to engage in less crime after dropping out than they did before dropping out (Table 7.16). Moffitt's theory offers a unique explanation for this "dropout dip" by asserting that the process of leaving high school is a tangible symbol of adult status.[47] Such an explanation, however, would lead one to expect that those who stay in school the longest would be more involved in delinquency than those who leave early, which studies have *not* found (Table 7.16).

Employment.

Moffitt's theory predicts that there will be positive relationships between offending probabilities and such interpersonal variables as maintaining stable employment. This is consistent with evidence that those who are most often involved in long-term employment have lower involvement in crime and delinquency than those who have extensive histories of unemployment (Table 7.24a). However, the theory does not explain why unemployment rates over time show no consistent relationship to offending rates (Table 6.21).

Race/Ethnicity.

To account for why life-course-persistent offending is more prevalent in some racial/ethnic groups than in others, the two-path developmental theory attributes differences to perinatal factors, particularly those involving nutrition, environmental toxins, and infectious agents. These perinatal factors, in turn, may be the result of poverty and racial discrimination.[48] Regarding adolescent-limited offending, the two-path developmental theory implies that racial/ethnic groups who spend the most time between the onset of puberty and the time they become involved in productive work will be the most involved in offending.

Gender.

Moffitt's explanation for why males are more criminal/antisocial than females remains true to the two-path concept in her theory. Regarding life-course-persistent offenders, she attributes the difference to higher rates of neurological damage during or shortly before birth among males.[49] Supportive of her deduction, there is some evidence that males have higher rates of neurological abnormalities due to birth complications than do females,[50] and birth complications do appear to be a correlate of crime (Table 9.2).

In the case of adolescent-limited offending, Moffitt's theory implies that there should be considerable variability. Theoretically, as females have increased contact with life-course-persistent offenders relative to the contact that "normal" males have with life-course-persistent offenders, the proportional contribution of females to delinquency should rise.[51] To our knowledge, there is no research yet available to test this particular deduction from the two-path development theory.

Concluding Remarks on the Two-Path Developmental Theory

Moffitt has proposed a synthesized theory that draws on both biological and social learning variables. The theory identifies two distinct paths to becoming involved in criminal/antisocial behavior: the life-course-persistent path and the adolescent-limited path.

To explain life-course-persistent offending, the theory contends that it results from two neuropsychological deficits. One deficit has to do with *executive functioning*, a concept also employed by Gray and Quay and other frontal lobe theorists (p. 413). The other type of neuropsychological deficit involves the slow acquisition of language skills.

According to the two-path developmental theory, causes of adolescent-limited offenders are entirely of a social nature. Moffitt maintains that when children reach puberty, they begin to feel entitled to the status and privileges of adults. These feelings often prompt them to imitate the behavior of life-course-persistent offenders and thereby exhibit behavior that "real" adults consider offensive and inappropriate, often to the point of being criminal. Theoretically, the longer adolescents linger between childhood and adulthood, the greater their risk of offending becomes.

Among the weaknesses of the two-path developmental theory is that the term *neuropsychological* is vague. Moffitt has not specified the brain regions she believes to be involved in affecting life-course-persistent offending, and the term *psychological* is used to refer both to cognitive processes and to behavior itself.

The two-path developmental theory can also be criticized for offering no explanation for why the desire for adult status and privileges would begin in adolescence. Is there some sort of biological trigger, or perhaps a cultural one?

A final comment worth making in regard to Moffitt's theory involves noting parallels between it and a theory reviewed in Chapter 14, Linda Mealey's cheater theory (p. 449). One parallel is that both theorists postulate that there are two types of offenders, and contend that one type is confined to adolescence, while the other begins early in childhood and persists well into adulthood. Second, both theorists attribute the adolescent-limited type of offending almost exclusively to social factors and the longer-term form of offending to biological factors. Beyond that the two theories diverge, however, because Moffitt's biological focus is on neuropsychological factors, while Mealey's focus is on the reproductive consequences of offending.

EVOLUTIONARY NEUROANDROGENIC THEORY: Exposing the Brain to Male Hormones Causes Crime Due to Sexual Selection of Overtly Competitive Males

Theories, especially synthesized theories, can get complicated. The theory now to be described has several conceptual elements, but, if you take one element at a time, the theory is fairly easy to understand.

As noted in Chapter 14, evolution refers to the process of gradual changes in life forms due to genes and differential rates of reproduction by organisms carrying those genes. In elaborating on his theory of evolution, Charles Darwin extended his concept of *natural selection* to include a special subtype that he called **sexual selection**. Darwin

meant by this term natural selection that occurred among and between the sexes of a given species. To illustrate the concept of sexual selection, say that in some species there was a male who had inherited a trait that made him sexually attractive to females. Assume that the trait was of no other benefit; it just attracted females. Even if this male might run a higher risk of dying at a younger age than most males, he might mate with so many females in his brief lifetime that his special trait would become increasingly prevalent in the population. This would be one example of sexual selection. The theory now to be reviewed asserts that sexual selection could help to account for why large proportions of males engage in criminal/antisocial behavior.

Other key concepts in the theory to be reviewed are neurology and androgens. *Neurology* refers to anything pertaining to the brain, and *androgens* are sex hormones that are more prevalent in males than in females. Androgens are sometimes called "male sex hormones," although females have them also, only in smaller average amounts. The most widely studied, and probably the most important androgen is testosterone, a hormone that a number of studies have found associated with criminality, especially of a violent nature (Table 9.15).

The Evolutionary Neuroandrogenic Theory in Brief

The **evolutionary neuroandrogenic (ENA) theory** focuses on how male sex hormones influence brain functioning to affect the probability of criminal/antisocial behavior, and how this and related behavior might be sexually selected. According to the theory, testosterone and other androgens act on the brain in ways that increase overtly competitive behavior, and overtly competitive behavior has been sexually selected. In other words, males who are overtly competitive over the centuries have passed on their genes to future generations at above average rates, mainly because females have been naturally selected for choosing males who compete for resources that females can then use to rear children.

According to the ENA theory, most criminal/antisocial behavior is an expression of overtly competitive behavior. Other expressions of competitiveness are various deceptive business practices, including ones that border on illegality.[52]

Lee Ellis (1942–), the first author of this text, has been the main proponent of the ENA theory.[53] At the heart of the ENA theory is the idea that male sex hormones have evolved ways of affecting the human brain so as to incline males to be more overtly competitive than females. This male pattern has evolved primarily because females have evolved mating preferences for males who are driven to acquire the resources needed to assist females in childrearing. In other words, females who in the past have chosen competitive males have successfully reared more offspring than females who have chosen to mate with less competitive males.

How are male brains affected by androgens to be more overtly competitive? According to the theory, the effects are achieved in a two stage process: the perinatal stage and the postpubertal stage (p. 283). During the perinatal stage, the neurological foundations for overtly competitive behavior involve two main processes. One is a reduction in sensitivity to stimuli, called the *suboptimal arousal effect*. The other process involves shifting hemispheric functioning away from the left hemisphere and toward the right hemisphere, thereby facilitating spatial reasoning while impeding language acquisition. This is called the *rightward shift effect*.

According to the ENA theory, these two neurological effects are laid down prior to birth, although they are usually not fully activated until the onset of puberty. Basically, the more a brain is exposed to testosterone during fetal development, the more his/her brain will be suboptimally aroused and rightward shifted, with the full impact not occurring until the brain is exposed to high levels of testosterone beginning in the teenage years.

The exact form that the overtly competitive behavior takes will vary, depending not only on the degree of androgen exposure perinatally, but also on learning. Some males rather quickly learn how to express their overtly competitive behavior in ways that do not elicit retaliation from others. Other males are so blatant in expressing the behavior that they repeatedly provoke retaliation. Theoretically, males who have the greatest difficulty learning will be those who will take the longest to express their overtly competitive behavior in relatively nonoffensive ways. Because rules and laws are expressed linguistically, difficulty learning language will be particularly conducive to slow learning of how to be overtly competitive without eliciting retaliation. In addition, persons who are suboptimally aroused and/or rightward shifted in neocortical functioning to the greatest degree should be slow in learning to express their overtly competitive behavior in nonoffensive ways.

The ENA theory contends that females have had to take care not to choose males who are so competitive that they fail to share whatever resources they acquire. This has sexually selected some males both toward a wide range of honest and deceptive behaviors. Males who are least capable of nonoffensive competitive behavior should gravitate toward the deceptive end of the continuum. Because deception only tends to be effective in the short run, these males will need to opt for short-term (r) approaches to reproduction.

Hypotheses Derived from the Evolutionary Neuroandrogenic Theory

The ENA theory resulted in part from synthesizing three theories discussed in earlier chapters: suboptimal arousal theory (p. 407), hemispheric functioning theory (p. 423), and r/K theory (p. 450). The other main component of the theory involves the effects of androgens (primarily testosterone) on brain functioning. When all of these theoretical elements are linked together, the ENA theory leads to many hypotheses. Many of these hypotheses will not be discussed here because they were dealt with earlier in connection with the parent theories. Nevertheless, several additional hypotheses remain that can either be derived from or extended based on ENA theory.

Gender and Age. Fundamental to the ENA theory is that offenders will be predominantly male. However, because some females are exposed to high levels of androgens when their brains are developing, some females may become as overtly competitive as the average male. If these females have difficulty learning, their offending behavior may resemble that of many males. There is currently no evidence to either support or refute the hypothesis that female offenders were exposed to high perinatal levels of testosterone.

In terms of age, the ENA theory contends that offending will be most frequent shortly after the onset of puberty, and will decline after a few years, particularly for individuals who are able to quickly learn alternative ways of expressing their overtly competitive impulses. Consistent with ENA theory, studies have shown that offending probabilities peak in the teens and subside by the midtwenties (Table 5.2a).

Testosterone. According to the ENA theory, positive associations should exist between androgens and involvement in criminal/antisocial behavior. More precisely, brain exposure to androgens should account for both inter- and intragender variations in offending rates. So far, nearly all of the pertinent research has involved comparing postpubertal levels of testosterone. Consistent with the hypothesis, studies have shown that males exhibit higher levels of testosterone than do females, especially following the onset of puberty.[54] Regarding intragender comparisons, the evidence is less clear, but generally consistent with the view that a modest positive correlation exists between circulating testosterone levels and offending behavior (Table 9.2).

If the ENA theory is correct, one should find other factors linked to offending that are at least partly linked because of increased testosterone levels. In this regard, one study has suggested that the link between offending and unstable marriage patterns may be partly due to testosterone levels, at least among males. The study sampled testosterone levels of more than 1800 U.S. Air Force veterans on four different occasions over a ten-year period. Among its findings were that divorce probabilities rose when testosterone levels were high.[55] The researchers speculated that testosterone may therefore at least partly account for why marriage is often found associated with low involvement in crime.[56]

Brain Functioning. The ENA theory assumes that androgens influence offending primarily by altering brain functioning. This assumption leads one to expect that average differences in brain functioning will be found when comparing those who have high versus low involvement in criminal/antisocial behavior. As noted in Chapter 9, several studies have found brain wave patterns associated with involvement in such behavior (Tables 9.21 through 9.23).

Neurotransmitters. Some animal studies indicate that high perinatal exposure to testosterone causes a reduction in serotonergic activity in the brain.[57] This would be consistent with the evidence that serotonin levels are lower among offenders than among persons in general (Table 9.17). In a related vein, studies have shown that testosterone serves to lower MAO levels in the blood,[58] and most studies have indicated that platelet MAO is a negative correlate of offending (Table 9.20).

Another neurotransmitter that appears to be influenced by testosterone is dopamine.[59] Research has suggested that dopamine concentrations (especially in the frontal–limbic area) decline substantially in males between ages twenty-five through thirty-five (and much more gradually for females).[60] Dopamine plays a central role in reinforcing behavior.[61] It has been proposed that a decline in dopamine concentrations in the frontal–limbic area may temper youthful desires for intense and varied experiences, and make it possible for more everyday experiences to be reinforcing.[62] If so, testosterone may affect dopamine functioning in the brain in ways that cause offending behavior to subside in most males beyond their

midtwenties. Current evidence is not particularly supportive of this hypothesis (Table 9.18).

Pain Tolerance.   Because the ENA theory asserts that brain exposure to testosterone decreases sensitivity to environmental stimuli, one would expect to find offenders exhibiting greater pain tolerance than nonoffenders.[63] Evidence is largely consistent with this prediction (Table 9.24).

The theory also predicts that because male brains are exposed to higher levels of testosterone than female brains, males in general should be less sensitive to pain than females. Many are surprised by the outcome of tests of gender differences in pain sensitivity, but males appear to tolerate pain at more intense levels than do females. This is not only true in humans,[64] but also in other species.[65] Greater tolerance of pain has even been found for boys than in girls who are under two weeks of age.[66]

Experiments with laboratory animals suggest that brain exposure to testosterone (especially perinatally) is the main cause of these average gender differences.[67] Such evidence would be consistent with the ENA hypothesis that androgens help to make males less sensitive to environmental stimuli and so contribute to their overtly competitive behavior.

Intelligence and Learning.   According to the ENA theory, individuals who have difficulty learning, especially in regard to linguistic rules, will be more likely to violate criminal laws than those who learn quickly. This prediction follows from noting that while testosterone appears to promote overt competitiveness, knowing how to compete in ways that do not elicit retaliation is learned. Thus, any neurological damage and/or a lack of careful supervision and training by parents should increase the chances of offending behavior.

This reasoning predicts that both poor school performance and low intelligence will be associated with involvement in criminal/antisocial behavior. Learning disabilities should also increase the risk of offending. The evidence is largely consistent with all three predictions (Tables 8.13, 8.14, and 8.16).

Intellectual Imbalance, Handedness, and Depression.   The ENA theory implies that the main intellectual deficits associated with offending probabilities will be linguistic in nature. This is because the theory asserts that testosterone mainly causes thought to shift from the left to the right hemisphere.[68]

If this assertion is true, one would expect to find a link between "intellectual imbalance" (i.e., PIQ > VIQ) and offending behavior, a prediction that is supported by most studies (Table 8.15). A rightward shift in higher thought should also lead to a positive link between offending and left-mixed-handedness, a prediction for which there is only weak support (Table 8.12).

Given that the right hemisphere has been shown to have a more negative emotional tone than the left hemisphere,[69] the ENA theory predicts that offenders will exhibit less positive emotions than persons in general. This would be consistent with studies showing unusually high rates of depression among the offending (Table 8.26), and with studies that have found them to be less friendly than persons in general (Table 8.34).

Evolution.   The ENA theory has been conceptually linked to r/K theory (p. 450) by making a single critical assumption: That testosterone promotes r-approaches to reproduction.[70] Recall that an r-approach to reproduction emphasizes reproducing in relatively large numbers at the expense of providing intense parental care for each offspring. In other words, the ENA theory assumes that testosterone (and possibly other male sex hormones) has evolved to help promote an approach to reproduction that emphasizes having large numbers of offspring with diminished parental care. If testosterone is one of nature's main biochemicals for promoting r-approaches to reproduction, and criminality is linked to r-approaches to reproduction, one should expect high testosterone to not only be associated with offending probabilities, but also with diminished parental care and large family size. These predictions have not yet been tested.

Closing Comments on the Evolutionary Neuroandrogenic Theory

The ENA theory boils down to asserting that male brains have been sexually selected to exhibit overtly competitive behavior to a greater degree than female brains. From a biochemical standpoint, the ENA theory contends that male brains are made more overtly competitive due to exposure to androgens. Among the behavioral expressions of this overt competition are increased aggression and a tendency to resort to relatively ruthless/desperate means of acquiring scarce resources. Theoretically, overtly competitive behavior does not begin to be fully expressed until the onset of puberty. At that time, its expression is usually rather "crude" and offensive to others, often taking criminal forms.

The ENA theory is a unique criminological theory in two respects: First, while proposals have been made over the years that male sex hormones may be a cause of criminal/antisocial behavior, especially for violent offenses,[71] this proposal has never before been incorporated into a formal theory.

The second unique feature of the ENA theory is that it is the only one so far to combine both evolutionary and neurological concepts as causal factors. In this regard, the theory asserts that exposing the brain to testosterone has two main neurological effects. One effect is to make the brain less sensitive to incoming stimuli, and the other effect is to shift higher thought away from the left (language) hemisphere toward the right (spatial) hemisphere.[72] Ellis contends that all of these effects have evolved to help make males more overtly competitive, which has evolved in turn because females have been favored for choosing males who are capable providers.

Why does offending probabilities for males drop substantially beyond the midtwenties even though testosterone levels remain high? According to the ENA theory, the decline in offending is due to most males learning within a few years the basic limits within which they can express their competitive urges without provoking retaliations.

This explanation leads one to expect that persons with low intelligence and/or learning disability will persist in offending longer than is true for persons in general.

The ENA theory makes numerous predictions, most of which appear to have at least moderate support. Nevertheless, it is also a relatively complicated theory, and many of its assumptions remain largely untested. In particular, there is currently little evidence to either support or refute the assumption that perinatal-plus-postpubertal exposure to androgens causes the brain to function in ways that facilitate overtly competitive behavior.

In terms of weaknesses, the ENA theory has difficulty explaining why there would be considerable variation from one population (or time period) to another in the proportional contribution of males and females to criminal/antisocial behavior. While the levels of androgens are likely to vary from one population and time period to another during both the perinatal and postpubertal stages, it remains to be established that these variations can account for male–female variations in offending ratios.

FINAL COMMENTS ON SYNTHESIZED THEORIES IN CRIMINOLOGY

In recent decades, there seems to have been a growing trend in criminology toward combining the essential elements of two or more already proposed theories into a new synthesized theory. These theories are almost inevitably more complicated than the parent theories from which they were created. In assessing these more complicated theories, keep in mind that the purpose of scientific theories is not only to predict and explain, but to do so in as simple a way as possible. This means that synthesized theories are not without disadvantages, even if they lead to more testable hypotheses than some of the earlier theories. If the trend really is toward synthesized theories in criminology, future versions of the present chapter are likely to grow in coverage more than any of the other theory chapters.

SUMMARY

Four synthesized theories were reviewed in this chapter. Two fit into the category of environmental theories. They were the integrated theory and the social development model. The other two—the two-path development theory and the evolutionary neuroandrogenic theory—were both biosocial theories. Let us briefly summarize each one.

Integrated Theory

Delbert Elliott's integrated theory is an amalgamation of three earlier theories: strain theory, control theory, and social learning theory. By and large, integrated theory asserts that criminality is caused by a combination of strain brought on by frustrated attempts to attain one's economic/lifestyle goals, by inadequate socialization in the family, and by associating with antisocial peers and the mutual reinforcement of one another's behavior and attitudes.

The Social Development Model

The theory put forth by David Hawkins in conjunction with Joseph Weis is known as the social development model. It was called a model, rather than a theory, in order to emphasize that it was proposed primarily to guide the development of crime and delinquency prevention measures, and only secondarily to theoretically explain offending.

According to the social development model, offending behavior is partly learned through associating with, and then imitating, peers and others who are already exhibiting antisocial behavior. This idea was largely borrowed from social learning theory. In addition, offending behavior is learned as a result of a failure to bond with individuals who are committed to conventional values supportive of societal order and respect for others. This line of reasoning was first championed by proponents of control theory. From these two theoretical foundations, the social development model suggests that essentially all children can be diverted from extensive involvement in antisocial be-

havior. The diversion is achieved by parents or other caring adults taking time to reinforce belief in, and a commitment to, conventional values, as well as associations with other like-minded peers.

The Two-Path Development Theory

In the two-path development theory, Terry Moffitt argues that offenders can be divided into two distinct types: life-course-persistent and adolescent-limited. Theoretically, the causes of the first of these two types are neuropsychological mechanisms responsible for executive control over behavior and the acquisition of language skills. In the case of adolescent-limited offending, the causes are social, rather than neuropsychological. Motivated by a desire for adult status, the social causes of adolescent-limited offending primarily include the imitation of life-course-persistent offenders and incomplete socialization into the assumption of adult life.

The Evolutionary Neuroandrogenic Theory

Lee Ellis's evolutionary neuroandrogenic theory uses the concept of sexual selection to argue that males who are overtly competitive tend to have a reproductive edge over males who are not. In other words, when given a choice, most females choose to mate with males with resources or at least the ability to obtain resources. This preference has resulted in the evolution of males who are, on average, more overtly competitive than females.

From a neurohormonal standpoint, androgens (particularly testosterone) have evolved in part to affect brain functioning in two ways that promote overtly competitive behavior. One way is by making the brain less sensitive to environmental stimuli, such as pain, and the other is to shift neocortical functioning away from the left (language) hemisphere more toward the right (spatial/holistic reasoning) hemisphere. Theoretically, these neurological effects are produced during two developmental stages, one occurring before (and very shortly after) birth, and the other occurring following the onset of puberty.

According to the ENA theory, most male brains are not activated to begin fully expressing overtly competitive behavior until puberty. At the onset of puberty, therefore, the expression of overtly competitive behavior is often rather crude, which includes fighting and stealing. Within a few years, however, most adolescent males learn how to express their overtly competitive tendencies without provoking retaliation. Those who take the longest to do so are those who have the greatest difficulties learning and/or the fewest opportunities to learn. They are also those who have the highest probability of running afoul of the law.

SUGGESTED READINGS

Adler, Freda and Laufer, William S. (Eds.). (1993). *New directions in criminological theory,* volume 4. New Brunswick, NJ: Transaction. (A collection of chapters which both reflect and have inspired efforts to develop new and more powerful criminological theories.)

Cordella, Peter and Siegel, Larry (Eds.). (1996). *Readings in contemporary criminological theory.* Boston: Northeastern University Press. (Gives readers a wide range of theoretical perspectives and the research findings bearing on those perspective.)

Gregg, Barak (1998). *Integrating criminologies.* Boston: Allyn & Bacon. (This book explores and attempts to draw together a number of theoretical traditions in criminology.)

Thornberry, Terence P. (Ed.). (1997). *Developmental theories of crime and delinquency.* New Brunswick, NJ: Transaction. (Provides a collection of chapters in which several arguments appear on how various theoretical traditions in criminology can be drawn together to provide a more complete picture of criminal/antisocial behavior.)

EXERCISES

1. Locate and read a social science article bearing on one of the theories presented in this chapter. Choose an article that you can understand, and that seems to objectively test one or more hypotheses derived from one of this chapter's theories; then write a one- to two-page double-spaced paper summarizing the nature of the study and what it found. Unless your instructor tells you otherwise, you should hand in a photocopy of the article you summarized. Be sure to write your interpretation in your own words; do not simply paraphrase the abstract or the conclusions of the article itself.

2. Using library or Internet resources, search for information about a proponent of one of the theories described in this chapter. The information can include demographic and educational background, as well as research interests of the theorist. Write a one- to two-page double-spaced report on what you find.

ENDNOTES

1. Bernard & Snipes 1996.
2. Bartusch et al. 1997:17.
3. D. Elliott 1985.
4. D. Elliott et al. 1979.
5. Bernard & Snipes 1996:311.
6. Catalano & Hawkins 1996.
7. Hawkins & Weis 1985; Weiss & Hawkins 1981.
8. Catalano et al. 1996:430; Spoth et al. 1995:450.
9. Catalano & Hawkins 1996:155; O'Donnell et al. 1995.
10. Winfree & Bernat 1998.
11. Hawkins & Weis 1985:79.
12. Hawkins & Weis 1985:79.

13. Catalano & Hawkins 1996:161.
14. Hawkins & Weis 1985.
15. Catalano et al. 1996; Hawkins et al. 1986, 1988, 1992, 1995.
16. Spoth et al. 1995.
17. Catalano et al. 1996; Hawkins et al. 1992, 1995.
18. Hawkins et al. 1991a.
19. Botvin 1986.
20. Hawkins et al. 1991b.
21. Hawkins et al. 1989; Pentz et al. 1989.
22. Felner & Adan 1988.
23. Catalano & Hawkins 1996:160.
24. Farrington & Hawkins 1991; Patterson et al. 1989; Simons et al. 1994.
25. Silva & Stanton 1996.
26. Moffitt 1990, 1993, 1994, 1997.
27. Moffitt 1997:44.
28. Bartusch et al. 1997:16.
29. Moffitt 1997:18.
30. Bartusch et al. 1997:16; Moffitt 1997:25.
31. Moffitt 1997:25.
32. Moffitt 1997:31.
33. Moffitt 1993:685.
34. Moffitt 1997:35.
35. Bartusch et al. 1997:38.
36. Moffitt 1990; Patterson & Yoerger 1993; Simons et al. 1994.
37. Robins 1966, 1978a.
38. D'Unger et al. 1998; Nagin & Land 1993:352; Tracy et al. 1990.
39. Patterson et al. 1998.
40. Nagin & Paternoster 1991; Warr & Stafford 1991.
41. Farrington 1986b; Greenberg 1977.
42. Moffitt 1997:38.
43. Caspi et al. 1993; Sonis et al. 1985.
44. Moffitt et al. 1996:402.
45. Moffitt 1990a; Moffitt et al. 1994.
46. Moffitt 1997:18.
47. Moffitt 1997:36.
48. Moffitt 1994:38.
49. Moffitt 1994:3.
50. Geshwind & Galaburda 1985b:547; Kawi & Pasamanick 1959:19.
51. Moffitt 1994:39.
52. Ellis 1987a:153.
53. Ellis 1986a, 1987b, 1989b, 1990c; also see Ellis & Coontz 1990; Eysenck & Gudjonsson 1989:125.
54. Malasanos et al. 1986:702; Sherwin et al. 1985:342; Susman et al. 1987; Udry & Talbert 1988.
55. Mazur & Michalek 1998.
56. Mazur & Michalek 1998:328.
57. Giulian et al. 1973; Ladosky & Gaziri 1970.
58. Briggs & Briggs 1972; Broverman et al. 1968:40; Itil 1976:106; Klaiber et al. 1976.
59. Everitt 1984.
60. Pine 1983:67; Wong et al. 1984:1394.
61. Phillips & Fibiger 1973.
62. Ellis & Coontz 1990:177.
63. Ellis 1991.
64. Berkley 1997; Buchsbaum et al. 1981a, 1981b; Feine et al. 1991; Fowler-Kerry & Lander 1991; McGrew 1979:443; Mechanic 1975:357; Mogil et al. 1993; Riley et al. 1998.
65. Beatty 1978; Ellis 1986:530; Gandelman 1983; Kavaliers & Innes 1990.
66. Barfield 1976:70; Bell & Costello 1964.
67. Beatty & Beatty 1970; Beatty & Fessler 1977a; Redmond et al. 1976:322.
68. Ellis & Coontz 1990:176.
69. Davidson & Fox 1989; Dawson et al. 1992; Fox et al. 1992; Schaffer et al. 1983; Silberman & Weingartner 1986.
70. Ellis 1989b, 1989/90.
71. Dabbs & Morris 1990; Konner 1982:200; Rutter & Gilles 1984:125; Venables 1988;.
72. Ellis 1990a

PART IV

Specific Crimes

In Part III we discussed at length what scientists from a variety of disciplines have considered causal explanations for why people become criminals. These theories had to do with criminal behavior in general, and tried to answer question such as "Why are people from broken homes more prone to crime?" and "What influence does having delinquent friends have on the individual's own delinquency?" Rather than looking at generic criminal behavior, this final part of the book looks at specific kinds of criminal behavior. In choosing what kinds of specific criminal behaviors to look at, we decided to include those behaviors that probably generate the greatest degree of shock, horror, fear and disgust—as well as controversy—among the greatest number of people. These crimes are mass, spree, and serial murder, terrorism, white-collar crime, organized crime, and sex crimes.

In Chapter 16 you will learn about multiple murder and about terrorism. We will acquaint you with types of multiple murderers and terrorists, the prevalence of this kind of behavior, and with the efforts that have been made to explain it. Mass, spree, and serial murder are often thought of as the epitome of mindless evil, thus defying any sort of scientific explanation. Nevertheless, scientific explanations are sorely needed. Terrorism is also often seen as "senseless," although we will see that there is a sort of immoral rationality behind many acts of terrorism. We will explore this rationality and see what, if anything, traditional crininological theories can tell us about the kind of person who joins terrorist organizations.

Chapter 17 looks at white-collar crime and organized crime. White-collar crime is more costly to the economy, and results in greater loss of life, than street crime. Yet very little is done to thwart it compared to the much vaunted "war on (street) crime." We will explore a number of issues in this section, including the issue of whether white-collar criminals are all that different from street criminals. Organized crime takes you into the world of people who make a business out of crime where you will meet la Cosa Nostra, outlaw motorcycle gangs, the Yakuza, and various other organized crime groups. We will explore the kinds of social conditions that provide the impetus for organized crime, and ask what sort of individuals become organized criminals. We look at white-collar and organized crime and ask whether or not theories designed to explain street crime are applicable to them.

Finally, in Chapter 18 we look at sex crimes, primarily rape and child molesting, considering such questions as "How prevalent is it?" "Who commits it?" and "Who is at greatest risk for being victimized by it?" As with the other topics in this part of the book, we look at the ways in which a variety of scholars have approached and attempted to explain these kinds of behavior.

CHAPTER 16

Multiple Murder and Terrorism

In April of 1973, Edmund Kemper, a six-foot-nine-inch, 300-pound, twenty-five-year-old hate machine crept into his mother's bedroom and bludgeoned her to death. This hulk of a man, who had already killed his grandparents and at least six young women since he was fifteen years old, then decapitated her, had sex with her headless body, and played darts with the head. He had also decapitated and sexually assaulted the corpses of his previous female victims, and on at least two occasions he preserved their heads so that he could use them later for perverse sexual activity. He even ate the flesh of some of his victims, cooking it into a macaroni casserole. Kemper's biggest thrill, however, was not sex, murder, or cannibalism, it was the act of decapitation. In Kemper's own words: "You hear that little pop and pull their heads off and hold their heads up by the hair. Whipping their heads off, their body sitting there. That'd get me off."[1]

This chapter deals with the most bizarre and horrific of all criminal activities, the slaughter of the innocent by the seemingly insane. The first part of this chapter examines the phenomenon of multiple murder, specifically, the kinds of multiple murder that seem to lack rational motivation. Criminologists have identified three such types of murder: *spree, mass,* and *serial* murder. This section of the chapter emphasizes the nature, prevalence, and causes of serial murder. The second part of the chapter deals with terrorism, which, while seemingly mindless to many observers, has its own brand of rationality. We will explore many aspects of terrorism, including its history, prevalence, and possible causes. This chapter differs from previous ones in that the nature of its subject matter requires the mentioning of several specific

names and cases that are important only for illustrative purposes.

WHAT IS MULTIPLE MURDER?

As indicated above, *multiple murder* is a term encompassing what criminologists have called *spree, mass,* and *serial* murder. Because most such crimes are considered to lack rational motivation,[2] we exclude from consideration multiple murders committed for political or financial reasons. The kinds of mass murderers we focus on are individuals for whom the act of murder is its own reward, and from which no other gain is expected. Thus, we exclude people such as professional "hit men" and crimes committed for ostensibly political reasons, such as the biggest mass murder in U.S. history, the

Oklahoma City Federal Building bombing of April, 1995, which took the lives of 169 people and injured over 500 others. We know very little about the recently convicted bomber, Timothy McVeigh, or his motives, but they seem to have been political, and thus the bombing is classified here as an act of terrorism rather than an act of mass murder.

When we exclude murders committed for some instrumental purpose we are left with murders seemingly committed for their own sake; that is, committed because the offender enjoys it and seeks no other reward from it beyond the pleasure it affords him. Although murder is usually considered the most serious crime a person can commit, murder for revenge or for personal gain is understandable because the motives have rational elements. While we still condemn such murders, we can all think of circumstances under which we might commit them. The gruesome bloodlust of killers like Edmund Kemper, however, baffle and terrify us because they lack any objectively rational motivation, unless we are willing to call seeking bloodlust thrills a rational motivation. But they also hold a morbid fascination for us, as the number of books and movies devoted to them attest. In 1988, the media marked the centennial of the infamous Jack the Ripper case with a slew of heavily watched movies and television docudramas. The legend that grew around the Ripper case probably had a lot to do with its "novelty" (Jack is often falsely considered to be the first serial killer). Or it may have had a lot to do with the fact that Jack's six or so murders constituted a little over 3 percent of England's murders in 1888.[3] Many serial killers both before and after Jack have far surpassed him in the number of their victims and the sadistic brutality of their actions, thus making the study of the phenomenon an important item on the criminological agenda.

Mass and Spree Murder

The primary characteristic differentiating mass, spree, and serial murder is the time frame in which the murders take place. **Mass murder** is the killing of several people at one location. Such incidents typically begin and end within a few minutes or hours. **Spree murder** is the killing of several people at different locations over a period of several days. Research suggests that the time frame involved is the only factor that differentiates mass and spree killers, and that both mass and spree killers are quite different from the serial killer.[4] We will thus consider mass and spree killers together.

There are relatively few generalities we can make about mass and spree killers. Most research on these individuals is necessarily retrospective (interviews with families and friends, and sometimes notes left by the offender) because they typically commit suicide or are killed by police at or near the scene of their crime. The exceptions to this rule are felony-related and gang-related mass murder.[5] However, reviews of the literature on mass murder from the 1960s to the mid-1990s[6] note several commonalities shared by mass and spree murderers:

- They are typically white males with an age range broader than that of serial killers.
- They have previously displayed impulsive, violent, frustrated, depressed, alienated, and anti-authoritarian behavior, probably arising from a deep sense of having been wronged.
- They tend to have a morbid fascination with guns and to own many of them.
- Their behavior at the time of the crime, as well as the fact that it is typically committed in public places, make it obvious that they are unconcerned about their own death, leading some researchers to view this type of murder as an elaborate suicide attempt. This is not true of felony- and gang-related mass murderers.
- They seem to contemplate committing murder and prepare for the act, although the time and place where it takes place is not generally preestablished.
- Spree and mass murders increased considerably in the United States during the 1960s through the 1990s.
- Young, nonwhite male predominate in felony-related (58.3%) and gang-related (100%) mass murder incidents.

- The average age of all mass murderers over the past thirty years is twenty-nine, and the average number of victims per incident is 4.89.

As we have said, mass murder involves the murder of several victims at the same location over a relatively short period of time. Mass murderers typically remain at the murder site until they are killed by police, take their own lives, or (rarely) surrender. Noninstrumental mass murderers can be roughly divided into two types: (1) Those who chose specific targets that the killers believe to have caused them stress (e.g., disgruntled workers attacking supervisors and other company representatives), and (2) those who attack random targets having no connection with the killer but who belong to groups the killer dislikes. For instance, James Huberty disliked Hispanics and children and selected them as his targets in a McDonald's restaurant in San Ysidro, California. He killed twenty-one people, mostly Hispanic children, and wounded nineteen before being gunned down by police. In a similar scenario, woman-hater George Hennard drove his pickup truck through a cafeteria window in Killeen, Texas, in 1991 and killed twenty-two people, fourteen of whom were women, before committing suicide. Another woman-hater, Canadian Marc Lepine, entered a classroom in the engineering building at the University of Montreal, in 1989, ordered all the men out, and began shooting women, killing fourteen and wounding thirteen others.[7] The personal histories of all three men illustrate the attitudinal and behavioral patterns outlined in the reviews of Palermo and Petee, Padgett, and York.

Spree murder involves the killing of a number of victims at different locations over a period of several days or even weeks. Spree killers move from victim to victim in fairly rapid succession, and, like mass murderers, make little effort to hide their activities or avoid detection, moving from victim to victim as if driven by some frenzied compulsion.

Two particularly notorious spree murder cases that illustrate a common pattern are the cases of American Mark Essex and Australian Christopher Wilder. Mark Essex was a frustrated African American who frequently voiced his hated of whites, especially white cops. His spree began on New Year's Eve of 1974, when he ambushed and shot two police officers right outside the New Orleans Police Department building, after which he ambushed and killed another officer responding to a burglary alarm. The next day he killed a grocery store manager and three other people in a hotel. Essex held responding officers at bay for most of the night before he was finally gunned down. When it was all over, Essex had killed nine people and seriously wounded ten others.[8]

Australian-born Christopher Wilder, owner of a prosperous construction company and race-car driver, was a spree killer who showed that a person does not have to be a failure in life to engage in spree killing. On a wild cross-country ride from California to the east coast, Wilder killed at least eight women before being gunned down near the Canadian border by a state trooper in 1984. Wilder was also suspected in a number of states and in Australia of the murders of several women prior to his final cross-country spree.[9]

Spree and mass murders have increased steadily in the United States since the middle of the century. In the 1950s, there were just four cases of spree or mass murder, and in the 1960s there were only seven.[10] During the period from 1977 to 1991 such incidents increased tenfold. The Justice Department lists 157 incidents of mass murder in which 964 people were killed, and 112 incidents of spree murder in which 483 people were killed during that period.[11] This amounts to about one incident of spree or mass murder every twenty days in the United States over the fifteen-year period compared to one every 912 days in the 1950s.

Serial Murder

The consensus among criminologists is that **serial murder** is the killing of three or more victims over an extended period of time.[12] We usually hear about spree or mass murders after they are over and the perpetrator is dead or in police custody, but a serial killer can haunt a community for months or years. In addition to this time-frame distinction, there are several generalities that differentiate the serial killer from spree and mass killers, as well as from the "typical" (nonmultiple) murderer:

- Whereas spree and mass killers almost invariably use firearms and kill their victims quickly, serial killers generally prefer to stalk and often torture their victims.
- The "typical" serial killer is a white male who is older than the "typical" homicide perpetrator.
- African Americans are slightly overrepresented among known serial killers, and Asian Americans and women are greatly underrepresented.
- A number of researchers have reported that the United States has produced more serial killers than the rest of the world combined.
- Researchers have identified four general types of serial killers: visionary, mission-oriented, hedonistic, and power/control.
- Since 1977, the prevalence of serial murderer has been more than twice that of spree or mass murders and has accounted for more than twice the number of victims.[13]

These generalities will be discussed in more detail.

The Extent of the Problem

The true extent of the serial killer problem is difficult to gauge, and the sensational nature of the phenomenon has led to many exaggerated claims. A figure often quoted is that about 20 percent of murders in this country (about 4,000–5,000) every year are committed by serial killers.[14] Their justification for this figure has been the steady rise in "uncleared" murder cases since the 1960s. Despite the increase in size, training, and technical ability of police departments, the clearance rate for murder in the United States dropped from 86 percent in 1968 to 67.2 percent in 1990.[15] Murder is considered the most easily solved of all crimes because it is usually committed by someone known to the victim for defined reasons, but a randomly chosen murder victim with no previous connection to the killer often leaves the police literally "clueless."

With the continual drop in clearance rates noted in successive Uniform Crime Reports since 1968, it became common to equate "motiveless" and "uncleared" murder with "serial murder." However, many victims of uncleared murders are sexually unmolested adult males (not the typical targets of serial killers), and the increase in "gang-banging" and territorial wars among drug dealers may have more to do with the increase in uncleared murders than serial killers.[16] From a variety of data sources, it was estimated that serial killers account for no more than 300 to 400 murders each year, which, while a horrible toll on innocent human lives, falls far short of sensationalized claims.[17]

Serial killing is not just a modern phenomenon, as the data presented in Figure 16.1 show. Although the numbers of *known* serial killers in the earlier years of this country's history are modest by modern standards, the rates (number of killers divided by the average population of the United States during the period examined) show a fairly consistent pattern across time. The almost fourfold increase in the rate of killers from the 1960–1974 period to the 1975–1992 period is probably only partly a real increase in the number of serial killers. An unknown portion of that increase may be attributed to much improved law enforcement methods (discussed later) initiated during that period. The increase in other forms of homicide, including spree and mass murder, which are not subject to the same classification difficulties, however, leads us to conclude that part of the reported increase represents a real increase.

A Typology of Serial Killers

Although all serial killers have the same killing goal, they have different psychological motives. Among a number of typologies of serial killers, that of Holmes and DeBurger[18] has perhaps gained the widest acceptance. Their typology divides serial killers into four broad types: *visionary, mission-oriented, hedonistic,* and *power/control.* These are ideal types, not definitive categories; many serial killers may evidence aspects of all types at various times, and there is considerable overlap of cate-

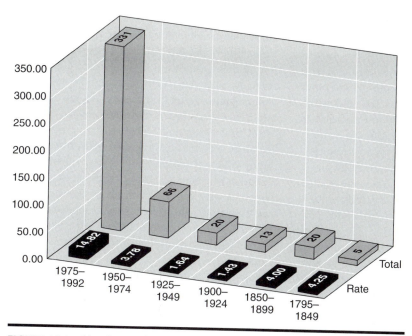

FIGURE 16.1   Number and Rate per 10 Million of Serial Killers in the United States, 1795–1992

Source: Adapted from U.S. Justice Department figures as reported by Jenkins (1994). Rates per 10 million population computed by authors.

gories from killer to killer. Some specific cases will be used to illustrate each type.

The **visionary serial killer** feels impelled to commit murder by visions or "voices in my head." These visions or voices may be thought of as coming from God, from demons, from a dead parent, or even from a howling dog, as in the case of David Berkowitz (the "Son of Sam"), but all command the person to kill. Visionary killers are typically out of touch with reality, and may be diagnosed as psychotic or schizophrenic. The sexual assault of victims is not usually a component of the visionary killer's pattern. Berkowitz, for instance, shot most of his victims (young women and their male companions parked in "lover's lanes") and then fled.

Mission-oriented killers feel it to be their mission in life to kill certain kinds of people. Unlike visionary killers, they do not have visions or hear voices, and they define their own "undesirables" and set out to eliminate as many as they can. Prostitutes and homosexuals are frequent targets of mission-oriented serial killers, but targets may also be people of particular races, religions, or ethnic groups. Although most serial killers operate alone, groups of individuals sometimes act together. An example of a mission-oriented serial killing group is a Black Muslim group that operated in southern California during the early 1970s called the *Angels of Death* (the "Zebra killers"). Each member, the most notable of whom included Larry Green and Jesse Cooks, was to kill at least four "evil blue-eyed devils" (whites), for which they received a free trip to Mecca and the respect of other members. Many of these killings involved long torture sessions in which various body parts were cut off one by one.[19] Sexual activity is also typically not involved in mission-oriented killings.

Hedonistic serial killers kill for the pure thrill and joy of it. The hedonistic killer is such a self-centered psychopath that he considers someone's life less important than the achievement of an orgasm for himself. The majority of serial killers are of the hedonistic type.[20] Killing, and the cruel and perverted sexual activity that is part of it, become the greatest of pleasures for these people. Torture, cannibalism, necrophilia, and other bizarre activities are central to the hedonistic killer's pattern of sexuality. Edmund Kemper is an example of this kind of killer (although Kemper had been institutionalized and found to be psychotic after killing his grandparents, he never claimed that "voices" made him do what he did). Many hedonistic killers are sexually dysfunctional and only achieve satisfactory orgasm while "penetrating" their victims with a knife (*picquerism*). Killing becomes an addiction among hedonistic killers, and it becomes amalgamated into their lifestyles in much the same way that drugs dominate the lifestyles of drug addicts.[21]

The **power/control** serial killer gains more satisfaction from exercising complete power over his victims than rather than from "bloodlust," although sexual activity is almost always involved. Like the hedonist killer, the power/control killer frequently suffers from some form of sexual inadequacy. Ted Bundy was of this type. Bundy would keep the bodies of some of his victims for several days before disposing of them, during which time he would frequently wash and groom them like dolls. The prime example of this type is Jeffrey Dahmer. Dahmer tried to create sex slaves of some of his victims (all males) by performing "lobotomies" on them by drilling holes in their heads and pouring acid into them. Dahmer's goal was to exert complete control over mindless human beings; even his acts of cannibalism may be viewed as attempts to fully possess at least parts of his victims.

Race and Multiple Murder

Although we have said that the typical serial killer is a white male, between 13 and 16 percent of the known U.S. serial killers operating in the present century (a period in which African Americans constituted between 10 and 12 percent of the population) have been African American.[22] A study of 337 serial killers operating since 1825 found

that 22 percent were African-American,[23] and a study that included mass and spree murderers with serial killers put the figure at 20 percent.[24] Relative to their proportion in the general population, then, African Americans are slightly overrepresented among serial killers, although few African-American serial killers are well known.

Coral Watts and Milton Johnson are two of the most notorious examples of African American serial killers of recent years. Watts, known as the "Sunday Morning Slasher," confessed to ten murders and was linked to ten others between 1978 and 1983, and Milton Johnson was responsible for at least seventeen murders in 1983. The latest known African-American serial killer is Henry Louis Wallace, who raped and strangled at least nine women from 1993 until his capture in 1996. His short (by usual serial killer standards) killing career is attributed to the fact that his victims were all acquaintances, which according to FBI experts makes him unique among serial killers.[25] While Watts's, Johnson's, and Wallace's figures fall short of figures attributed to Caucasian killers such as Ted Bundy or John Wayne Gacy, they exceed the figures attributed to more publicized killers such as David Berkowitz and Jeffrey Dahmer.[26] The extensive media coverage of the Bundy, Gacy, and Berkowitz cases has made these killers almost household names, but Watts and Johnson are practically unknown, despite having operated within the same general time frame. Wayne Williams (the Atlanta Child Murders) is the only African American to gain a modicum of the notoriety attached to his white counterparts.

Philip Jenkins[27] suggests three reasons why African-American serial killers do not attain the notoriety of their Caucasian counterparts. First is the media's perception that books and movies featuring African-American characters are not likely to appeal to mass audiences. For instance, two very similar cases occurred in Philadelphia in the mid-1980s, one in which the killer was Caucasian, and the other in which he was African-American. Both men kidnaped and imprisoned a number of women and held them in their basements where they tortured and killed them. The Caucasian killer, Gary

Heidrick, received widespread national attention, and became the subject of books and television shows; the African-American killer, Harrison Graham, received virtually no media attention, despite having been convicted of seven murders, four more than Heidrick.[28] Second, the language often used to describe serial killers (e.g., *primitive, monsters, animals*) would be considered racist if applied to African Americans. Third, law enforcement agencies are less likely to take black crimes seriously unless the victims are Caucasian. For instance, Albert Fish, a notorious sadomasochistic Caucasian serial killer who preyed on African-American children from 1910 to 1935, was only caught after he murdered the daughter of a Caucasian middle-class neighbor. Given this relative lack of interest, Jenkins is of the opinion that African-American serial killers may be more "hidden," and thus more prevalent, than the record indicates, especially during earlier periods of the century.[29]

According to Jenkins,[30] Asians are as underrepresented in serial killing as they are in other kinds of violent crime. The only *known* Asian-American serial killer operating in the United States this century was Charles Ng. Ng and his Caucasian partner, Leonard Lake, tortured and killed at least nineteen people in the early 1980s. If there have been other Asian-American serial killers, and if, like African Americans they largely killed within their own communities, they also may have been shielded from exposure by lower levels of public and police concern for nonwhite victims characteristic of earlier times.

Female Serial Killers

In 1991, Aileen Wuornos was arrested and charged with the shooting deaths of seven males whom had she had picked up while working as a prostitute. She became an instant hero in some radical feminist and lesbian circles, where she is viewed as a sacrificial lamb, condemned to die by a patriarchal society for defending herself against brutal male johns.[31] Wuornos was dubbed by the FBI and the media as "America's first woman serial killer" because she fit the definition of a "true"

serial killer as a person who kills for no rational motive.[32] Wuornos is not the first female to commit multiple murders, however. Indeed, nursing home proprietor Amy Archer-Gilligan may have murdered up to one hundred patients in her charge (including five whom she married) between 1907 and 1914, and may be among the most prolific serial killers in U.S. history.[33] However, the key distinction between male and female serial killers may be that, "There are no female counterparts to a Bundy or a Gacy, to whom sex or sexual violence is a part of the murder pattern."[34]

It is generally accepted among scholars of serial murder that female serial killers typically kill for instrumental reasons or from twisted notions of mercy (as is often the case in "medical" murders), and thus do not fit the definition of predatory killers who seek out strangers and kill for the sake of killing.[35] This is what made the Wuornos case so interesting: she did seek strangers (or at least, she allowed herself to be sought) and killed them without apparent motive, unless we accept her claim that each murder was an act of self-defense. Sex was certainly not her motive, for she was a lesbian who hated men.[36] Wournos also reversed the male killer/prostitute victim relationship, and her victims were heterosexual males as opposed to the more vulnerable female, child, or gay victims of male serial killers.

There had been cases prior to Wuornos in which females had killed random strangers without any apparent motive, but did so at the instigation of male companions. Female "disciples" of Charles Manson's "family," such as Susan Atkins and Patricia Krenwinkle, boasted to authorities about their part in the Tate (five victims) and LaBianca (two victims) murders in 1969. Then there was Carol Bundy (no relation to Ted) who helped her lover, Douglas Clark, decapitate and sexually assault at least six females and one male in the early 1980s. Carol was totally under the spell of the handsome Clark and became his disciple in the same sense that Atkins and Krenwinkle became disciples of Manson. Initially she only wanted to please Clark, but apparently she came to enjoy the killing.[37]

An in-depth study of fourteen female serial killers (including Aileen Wuornos) revealed some interesting gender differences between male and female serial killers.[38] None of the sixty-two victims of these women had been tortured, sexually assaulted, or mutilated, and none had been victims of stalking. Poisoning accounted for the majority (57%) of the killings, followed by smothering (29%), firearms (11% [all Wuornos's]) and "other" (3%). About half of the women were described as having instrumental and half affective (emotional) goals. One nurse's affective desire to be "super-nurse" led her to induce seizures in children and then rush to the rescue with the appropriate antidote. Her presence in the sample shows she was unsuccessful on a fair number of occasions.

Multiple Murder Overseas

Excluding acts of terrorism, mass or spree murder is relatively rare in developed countries outside the United States. Other countries have their "crazies" and their disgruntled, but strict gun-control laws often deny them the tools that are practically essential to the commission of such acts.[39] But mass and spree murder does occur overseas. Michael Ryan killed fourteen people and wounded sixteen before committing suicide in Hungerford, England, in 1987, and sixteen were gunned down by Eric Borel in Toulon, France, in 1995. In March of 1996, Thomas Hamilton gunned down sixteen elementary school children and their teacher in Dunblane, Scotland, before killing himself, and, in May of the same year, Martin Bryant killed thirty-five and wounded fifteen in Tasmania, Australia, before being captured by police.[40]

Strict gun controls may help to prevent some would-be mass or spree killers overseas, but they do not prevent serial killers, who prefer to use more "hands-on" weapons. The United States has more than its fair share of serial killers: Norris[41] claims that the United States has produced 75 percent of the world's known serial killers over the last twenty to thirty years, and Michael Newton indicates that the United States has accounted for 74 percent of the world's known serial killers in the twentieth century.[42] Note that we say *known* serial killers. Because the writers making this claim are Americans, it is reasonable to assume that they are in a better position to document U.S. serial killers than foreign serial killers. It has been noted that foreign writers document larger numbers of serial killers in their own countries than do U.S. writers.[43] Some of these foreign killers are profiled in Table 16.1.

A number of the serial killers profiled in Table 16.1 shows that other countries have had their share. The first two columns list the case and the apparent motive as we believe it to have been. The column labeled *modus operandi* briefly describes the killer and his typical "operating style," based on our assessments. The hedonistic type appears to predominate. Note that the killers come from all walks of life and vary greatly in status. They include a Marshal of France, a physician, an engineer, an ex-police officer, a law student, several "ordinary" working men, and a number of drifters. The next column indicates the country and time period in which the cases occurred, which dispels the notion that serial killing is largely a modern U.S. phenomenon.

Explaining Serial Murder

Looking for the causes of serial murder might be described as trying to make sense of the senseless. No one has tried, except in the most cursory manner, to apply any of the more traditional criminological theories to the phenomenon, although certain aspects of family and developmental theory are frequently invoked. Because of the relative rarity of serial murder, it is especially important to differentiate between efforts to explain the prevalence (the increase or decrease in the proportion of the population engaging in the behavior) of serial murder and efforts to explain why those who commit it do so. This section examines some social, psychological, and biological explanations that have been offered by various theorists.

Social Change and Serial Killers.
Significant changes in the prevalence of any behavior always

TABLE 16.1 Some Notorious Serial Killers in History

Case	Apparent Motive	Modus Operandi	Country and Time	Number Victims	Citation
Gilles de Rais	Hedonistic bloodlust; practice of black magic	Gilles de Rais was Marshal of France and hero of the 100-year war with England. Mostly enjoyed killing young boys in his castle where he would sodomize them before and after death. He was hanged and burned in 1440.	France, 15th century	140–300	Wolf, L. (1980). *The life and crimes of Gilles de Rais.* New York: Potter.
"Jack the Ripper"	Hedonistic bloodlust, probable cannibalism, self-aggrandizement	Preyed only on prostitutes. He enjoyed dismembering his victims and neatly laying the parts around the corpse. Made no attempts to hide his victims and enjoyed taunting the police. "Jack" may have felt himself to be on a mission to rid society of prostitutes. He was never found or identified.	England, late 19th century	5–6	Wilson, C. (1984). *A criminal history of mankind.* London: Pantheon.
H. H. Holmes	Hedonism and sadism. Also killed for profit	A physician who made a fortune in the drugstore business. He owned a "torture castle" in which he rented rooms to unwary visitors. He often skinned his victims and experimented with their bodies. Killed many men, women, and children in various insurance scams. Police found the remains of over 200 people in the burned ruins of Holmes's castle. He was hanged in 1896.	United States, late 19th century	200+	Hickey, E. (1997). *Serial murderers and their victims.* Belmont, CA: Wadsworth.
Pedro Alonzo Lopez	Hedonistic bloodlust	The "monster of the Andes" killed many young girls in Columbia, Ecuador, and Peru. Kicked out of his home at age 8 and repeatedly sodomized on the streets and in prison, Pedro took his hatred out on girls he considered "gentle, trusting, and innocent." Pedro, who was executed in 1983, was probably the deadliest serial killer in history.	Ecuador, Peru & Columbia, late 20th century	300+	Hickey, E. (1997). *Serial murderers and their victims.* Belmont, CA: Wadsworth
Henry Lee Lucas and Ottis Toole	Hedonistic bloodlust, sadism	A serial-killing tag team. Lucas killed his prostitute mother and raped her corpse. After release from prison in 1976 he teamed up with Toole (a transvestite who was psychotic and retarded) to begin a spree of killing across the country. Lucas was a sadist and necrophile, while Toole was more interested in cannibalism. Toole died in prison of cirrhosis of the liver in 1996; Lucas awaits execution in a Texas prison. Both men were unemployed drifters.	United States, late 20th century	200+ (many doubt this claim)	Lester, D. (1995). *Serial killers: The insatiable passion.* Philadelphia: Charles Press.

continued

TABLE 16.1 Continued

Case	Apparent Motive	Modus Operandi	Country and Time	Number Victims	Citation
Bruno Ludke	Hedonistic bloodlust	Ludke, a laundry delivery man, began killing in 1927 at the age of 18. Arrested in 1936 for rape and castrated, he continued his deadly business until rearrested in 1944. He was used as a guinea pig in Nazi experiments before execution in the same year.	Germany, early 20th century	85	Wilson, C. (1984). *A criminal history of mankind*. London: Pantheon.
Andrei Chikatilo	Hedonistic bloodlust, cannibalism	Chikatilo, a part-time school teacher and engineer, murdered women, boys, and girls between 1978 and 1990. A cannibal and sexual sadist, he found most of his victims in train and bus stations. He was executed in 1994.	Russia, late 20th century	50+	Hickey, E. (1997). *Serial murderers and their victims*. Belmont, CA: Wadsworth
Anatoly Onoprienko	Visionary killer, also bloodlust and profit	Onoprienko, a forestry student and drifter, enjoyed wiping out entire families living in isolated areas during his murderous sprees, which lasted from 1989 to 1996. He claimed that "voices" made him kill, but he also often looted homes after killing the occupants. He was arrested in 1996.	Ukraine, late 20th century	50+	*The European* (1996). April 25–May 1.
John Wayne Gacy	Power/control, sadism	Gacy was a building contractor, convicted child molester, and prominent member of Chicago's "do-gooder" crowd. When not volunteering to entertain kids in hospitals with his clown act, Gacy was searching for young males to rape, beat, and torture to death. When police finally searched his home they found 30 bodies decomposing in his crawlspace. Gacy was executed in 1994.	United States, late 20th century	30+	Lester, D. (1995). *Serial killers: The insatiable passion*. Philadelphia: Charles Press.
Dean Corll	Hedonistic bloodlust	Corll, a.k.a. "The Candyman," would invite young males into his home to take drugs and have sex. Boys who became incapacitated found themselves chained to the wall where they remained until death. Corll would abuse them for days, and would end it all by biting off the boys' penises. Corll was shot dead by Elmer Henly, a teenager who worked to procure new victims for him.	United States, late 20th century	27	Hickey, E. (1997). *Serial murderers and their victims*. Belmont, CA: Wadsworth
Jeffrey Dahmer	Power/control, cannibalism	Dahmer searched gay bars for his victims. He would lure them to his apartment where he would often drug and kill them. He enjoyed having sex with their corpses (using condoms) more than with their live bodies. He would keep bodies for days before cutting them up, preserving some of the parts for food.	United States, late 20th century.	17	Lester, D. (1995). *Serial killers: The insatiable passion*. Philadelphia: Charles Press.

TABLE 16.1   Continued

Case	Apparent Motive	Modus Operandi	Country and Time	Number Victims	Citation
Albert Fish	Sadomasochism, cannibalism	Fish, a house painter, enjoyed torturing children of both sexes and hearing them scream. He would sometimes make and eat a stew of their remains, and at least once sent the recipe to a victim's parents. He also enjoyed pain himself; driving needles into his scrotum and stuffing alcohol-soaked cottonballs up his rectum and lighting them. He supposedly looked forward to his electrocution in 1936 with great excitement.	United States, early 20th century	15+	Wilson, C. (1984). *A criminal history of mankind*. London: Pantheon.
Ted Bundy	Power/control	Bundy was a handsome, intelligent, and charming ex-law student and hot-line counselor who liked to abduct and kill pretty young college girls. Bundy liked to have sex with their corpses because he could exert complete control over them. He was executed in 1989.	United States. late 20th century	22+	Hickey, E. (1997). *Serial murderers and their victims*. Belmont, CA: Wadsworth
Alexander Specsivtsev	Hedonistic cannibalism	When police raided Specsivtsev's apartment in 1997 in response to neighbor's complaints of odors, they found an inventory of cooked and uncooked human body parts. His 57-year-old mother lived in the same apartment and helped him to dress and cook the parts. He was arrested, but his fate was unknown at the time of writing.	Russia, late 20th century	26	Saffron, I. (1997). Chance leads to capture in serial killer–cannibal case. *Idaho Statesman* news story, Feb. 2
Dennis Nilsen	Power/control	Britain's Jeffrey Dahmer. Nilsen, an ex-London police officer, murdered homosexuals and drifters after having sex with them. Like Dahmer, Nilsen enjoyed having sex with their corpses and washing and grooming them. He disposed of his victims by cutting them up and shoving them into the plumbing system, which was his undoing. He received 25 years to life on six counts of murder.	England, late 20th century.	15 bodies found in his flat. May have been others.	Eggers, Steven. (1998). *The killers among us*. Saddle River, NJ: Prentice-Hall.
Fritz Haarmann	Hedonistic, Power/control	A lover and killer of young boys who stalked railway stations for victims. After he had killed and sodomized his victims he would sell their clothes and their flesh (suitably disguised as beef) for profit. He was caught when the police traced a coat belonging to a missing boy to him. Haarmann boasted of killing 40 young men. He was beheaded in 1925.	Germany, early 20th century.	27+ bodies dredged out of river.	Wilson, C. (1984). *A criminal history of mankind*. London: Pantheon.

require explanations be couched in terms of sociocultural factors. The fairly dramatic increase in the number of serial killers since the early 1960s points to some very important social changes occurring since then. The change in the age distribution during the period (a greater percentage of young people), which is frequently invoked to account for the general increase in violent crime during the period, cannot account for the increase in the rate of serial killing for two important reasons. First, conventional homicides during the period only doubled, but serial killing rose about five times faster.[44] Second, while the age of those arrested for conventional murder peaks in the early twenties, most serial killers begin killing in the mid- to late-twenties.[45]

It has been suggested that the disinhibited counterculture that arose during the period had something to do with the increased prevalence.[46] As we have seen, the 1960s and 1970s were tumultuous years in which many traditional values were questioned and rejected. The countercultural ethos of the late 1960s and early 1970s, despite its rhetoric of flower power and peace, was essentially an ethos of personal satisfaction ("Do your own thing") and not feeling bad about it ("Don't get hung up on guilt"). Following that period many more people crossed the line to engage in a variety of aberrant behaviors because of what has been called "society's recent war against guilt."[47] The personal satisfaction ethos can be liberating, but taken to extremes it can produce the worst kind of monsters. The late 1960s also saw an explosion of pornography, some of which depicted scenes of bondage, torture, and violent rape, which may have fed and shaped the sexual fantasies of some people, a proportion of whom subsequently acted them out in the name of personal satisfaction.[48]

The 1960s also marked the beginning of the decarceration movement in the mental health system. If psychiatric hospitals housed the same proportion of the population in 1997 that they did in 1955 they would have had over 900,000 patients rather than the 70,000 they actually had.[49] A number of men who became "celebrated" serial killers incarcerated under the old sexual psychopath laws were released from custody, some despite the warnings of the killers themselves that they would kill if released.[50] Henry Lee Lucas, for instance, after serving nine years for knifing his mother to death, warned prison officials that if they let him out he would leave them "a present on the doorstep." He did just that, leaving a young female victim dead within walking distance of the prison gates on the day of his release.[51] Many other individuals arrested early in their criminal careers—including John Wayne Gacy (see Table 16.1)—who would have been firmly locked away on compulsory commitment orders prior to the 1960s, were released to prey on the public.

Family and Developmental Factors. Whatever the social factors accounting for the increased prevalence of serial killing may be, only an infinitesimally small number of people experiencing them ever kill once, never mind become serial killers. Thus, the developmental histories of those who become serial killers should be explored and their common experiences noted. One factor linked to serial killers that researchers appear to be unanimous about is that their childhood experiences were almost uniformly characterized by an extreme level of maternal deprivation. Most serial killers are children born illegitimately and/or adopted, institutionalized, or reared by mothers married three or more times,[52] and may experience these things "as the ultimate form of rejection."[53] Others contend that the great majority of serial killers experienced early separation from their mothers or were "otherwise deprived of the mother's direct emotional involvement,"[54] and that "the serial killer's childhood is marked by a lack of nurturing and love."[55] A Russian psychiatrist pointed out that the breakdown of the family also provides would-be serial killers with large numbers of rootless potential victims.[56] The neglect, abuse, and social isolation experienced by many serial killers in their early years leaves them angry and unable to relate to others in conventional ways. After reviewing the case histories of a number of such killers, one researcher concluded: "And so insecure social bonds prevent a capacity for love and affection from being channeled into stable relationships, and the resentment lies dormant, like a volcano, waiting to be detonated into violence."[57]

Cognitive Factors. Demographic profiles, while useful, are certainly not the whole story. About one-fourth of U.S. children were born out of wedlock in 1990,[58] and while many of them may suffer greater deprivation than children born in wedlock, only a handful of this multitude will become serial killers. Likewise, many other abused and deprived children grow up relatively healthy, which means we must explore the peculiar psychology of serial killers. Two cognitive factors commonly imputed to serial killers, especially hedonistic killers, are strong feelings of sexual inadequacy and a rich fantasy life.

Edmund Kemper's necrophilia was supposedly tied to his concerns about his small penis;[59] Henry Lucas stated that he had to kill to gain sexual release because he was impotent with a live person;[60] Andrei Chikatilo suffered from extreme premature ejaculation, frequently ejaculating without even attaining an erection when sexually excited.[61] With sexuality being such a central part of human life, extreme sexual dysfunction may result in deeply embedded feelings of worthlessness and powerlessness, the seeds of which may have already been implanted by childhood abuse and neglect. Serial killers may be trying to counteract these feelings by controlling, manipulating, punishing, and destroying vulnerable members of the sex (i.e., women) whom they may see as the cause of their feelings.

A study of thirty-six serial murders revealed a pattern of long-standing preoccupation with fantasies devoted to sexualized violence.[62] It has often been noted that children raised in abusive and neglectful homes retreat into a private fantasy world where they can escape their fears and exert control, thus gaining in their minds that which is unavailable in reality.[63] Fantasies often reflect the violence children experience in their lives, and, if combined with the compulsive masturbatory behavior also characteristic of serial killers,[64] may become firmly ingrained in the neural pathways to the brain's pleasure centers, thus fusing sexual pleasure and violence. It has been reported that some serial killers enter a semihypnotic state while fantasizing that eventually leads to a "divided self," one part being relatively normal and the other totally preoccupied with acting out the fantasy.[65] Partly because of their isolated fantasy lives, serial killers rarely develop caring relationships with others, making it easier to view their victims simply as "things" to be used for self-gratification.[66]

Biological Factors. Needless to say, millions of men feel sexually inadequate and millions more enjoy rich fantasy lives (including fantasies of violent sexuality) without becoming serial killers. Perhaps the sexually inadequate fantasizers who become serial killers differ in some biological ways from those who do not. Because it is not standard procedure for serial killers to be neurophysiologically assessed as part of the usual assessment process, we know relatively little about them in this area. Among those who have received psychoneurological testing via CAT or PET scans, a large percentage have been found to have significant damage to the frontal lobes of the brain.[67] This damage may be either the result of congenital defects or head injuries. Damage to this part of the brain can seriously undermine the person's ability to control primitive violent impulses, as well as disrupt appropriate emotional responses to all sorts of environmental stimuli.[68]

Some studies reviewed by Norris[69] point to a particular kind of biochemical profile characterizing a number of serial killers. In one study of ten serial killers (which included Charles Manson and Henry Lee Lucas) it was found that nine of them had what has been called *Type B chemical imbalance,* so named because it is a profile first detected in Type B (consistently violent) psychopaths. This profile includes elevated levels of lead and cadmium in the blood and urine and depressed blood zinc. The single exception in the sample suffered from brain damage from a motorcycle accident. Norris further theorizes that this profile is due to a combination of genetic factors and abnormal fetal development of the brain and autonomic nervous system (ANS). This abnormal development may be due to maternal alcohol and/or drug abuse and to the secretion of stress and anxiety hormones resulting from protracted abuse and neglect.[70] The abnormal development of the brain and ANS may result in individuals who require higher levels of stimulation for sexual satisfaction. A subset of these individuals may be so suboptimally aroused that only the dangers and sexual depravity of sadistic serial murder provide sufficient stimulation to "turn them on."[71] Much more study is needed before we can make more definitive statements about the neurohormonal profiles of serial killers.

An Integrated Theory. One theory that has attempted to integrate all levels of analysis to explain serial murder is the *diathesis–stress* model of Stephen Giannangelo,[72] who formulated it from in-depth case studies of serial killers on whom we have the most information. He acknowledges that a more comprehensive sample of lesser known killers might lead to different conclusions. Giannangelo believes that all serial killers have a congenital susceptibility to behave and think in ways that lead to serial killing if combined with the kinds of environmental stressors/traumas we have been discussing. This combination may lead to the development of self-esteem and self-control problems and sexual dysfunction, all of which feed on one another. These problems lead to the development of maladaptive social skills, which may move the person to retreat into his private pornographic fantasy world. As he dwells longer and longer in this world he enters a dissociative process (the "divided self") in which he takes his fantasies to their moral limits. At this point the killer seeks out victims to act out his fantasies, but the actual kill never lives up to his expectations or to the thrill of the hunt, so the whole process is repeated and becomes obsessive–compulsive and ritualistic.

LAW ENFORCEMENT'S RESPONSE

Offender Profiling

Law enforcement agencies have responded to the challenge presented by serial killers in a variety of ways. The most publicized response (particularly by the movie *Silence of the Lambs*) was the establishment of the FBI's *Behavioral Science Unit* (BSU) in the early 1970s at Quantico, Virginia. The BSU, now part of the National Center for the Analysis of Violent Crime (NCAVC), has developed methods of *profiling* serial killers and other violent offenders. Profiling is done by extensive interviewing and formal psychological testing of incarcerated killers in order to develop a typology (the classification of offenders into different types) based on personality and other offender characteristics.[73]

Crime Scene Analysis

Offender profiling is augmented by crime scene analysis, which often tells experienced investigators a lot about the perpetrator. Crime scene analysis involves reconstructing the sequence of events preceding, during, and after the murder. Reconstructing the events preceding the murder based on the evidence available helps investigators answer many questions, including the following:

- Was the victim carefully targeted (a specific type of victim taken in a specific manner)?
- What was the element of risk involved for the offender in selecting this victim (was she/he abducted from a public place or some more secluded place; did she/he struggle)?
- Was the crime planned (as evidenced by the presence of ropes, tape, or other equipment, or was it apparently the result of an unexpected opportunity)?
- Does the state of the corpse (tortured, mutilated) indicate that the offender is playing out violent sexual fantasies? Is the body crudely sexually displayed for "shock" effect?
- Has the crime scene been staged to confuse the police, or is the offender an "amateur"?
- If it is reliably established that the crime was committed by a serial killer, are there indica-

tions that he is escalating (shorter time between crimes, more mutilation of the body, crime better planned), or is he getting sloppier as he seeks more frequent victims for his escalating need for gratification?

There are many other clues that investigators take from a crime scene that, when combined with BSU profiles, can provide investigators with a fairly accurate (sometimes uncannily accurate) picture of the kind of person they are looking for.[74]

The Linkage Blindness Problem

Consisting of over 20,000 different federal, state, county, and municipal agencies, U.S. policing is extremely decentralized and fragmented.[75] This level of decentralization often causes problems in the investigation of crimes committed in several different jurisdictions, which is sometimes the case with serial killers. Many serial murders may occur in diverse police jurisdictions without law enforcement being able to note the connections between them. This problem has been termed *linkage blindness*. In response to this problem, in 1985 the FBI created the Violent Criminal Apprehension Program (VICAP), which is a national clearinghouse that collates information on unsolved violent crimes from different jurisdictions. VICAP is a computerized system that analyzes modus operandi (M.O.s), physical evidence, victim characteristics, crime scene analyses, suspect descriptions, and so on, from crime reports submitted by police agencies from all over the United States, to see if similarities exist.[76] When the computer "hits" on similarities, the agencies involved are informed and they can then coordinate their investigations and, hopefully, end the careers of serial killers earlier than would otherwise have been the case.

The implementation of VICAP probably accounts for a fair portion of the large increase in known serial killers noted during the 1975–1992 period over the previous period (see Figure 16.1). Law enforcement authorities now have the ability to link a number of homicides committed in different jurisdictions to a single individual or indi-

viduals. Before VICAP, these homicides may have been considered separate homicides committed by several different killers because of the linkage blindness problem.

TERRORISM

PanAm Flight 103 from Frankfurt to New York via London was right on schedule. It had been about an hour since takeoff from London and passengers were settling in for the long flight. There were all kinds of people on board: babies, grandmothers, teenagers, British businessmen, German entertainers, catholic nuns, Arab merchants, but they were mostly U.S. students, military personnel, and miscellaneous expatriates flying home for Christmas on December 21, 1988. Just as a young girl in a Notre Dame sweatshirt was ordering a 7UP, all 259 human beings aboard the aircraft were torn apart by a monstrous explosion. Engines and other parts of the disintegrating aircraft plunged into the little village of Lockerbie, Scotland, claiming another eleven victims. These 270 souls were victims of a bomb placed aboard the aircraft in Frankfurt by fanatics (probably terrorists working for Libya) who doubtless believed that what they were doing was justifiable.

Actions such as the bombing of Flight 103 lead many people to think of terrorists as subhuman creatures, and terrorism as something peculiar to the alienated twentieth century. In this part of the chapter we will attempt to come to grips with what terrorism is, why it is practiced, and who the "typical" terrorist is. Terrorism has a long history, although we will see that there was a dramatic upturn in such activities in the 1960s. Terrorism is "as old as the human discovery that people can be influenced by intimidation."[77] In this section you will learn that terrorists have rational motives and that these motives and the terrorist groups that give them voice are rooted in history and politics.

The earliest known terrorist group was a Jewish nationalist/religious group called the *Sicarii.* They operated against occupying Roman forces around 70 A.D. using deadly savage methods against Romans and Jews alike.[78] Another early group, the *Ismailis* or *Assassins,* responding to what they considered religious oppression, carried out a reign of intimidation throughout the Islamic world from about the eleventh to the mid-thirteenth centuries, and have been called the most effective terrorists in history.[79] The term *terrorism* itself is believed to have originated with the French Revolutionary Jacobins who instituted France's domestic Reign of Terror.[80] Many other examples of pretwentieth-century terrorism could be given to show that the phenomenon is neither new nor alien to human nature.

Terrorism Defined

Terrorism is like spree, mass, and serial murder rolled into one. Although revenge and hatred are usually integral to terrorist activity, the difference between it and other forms of multiple murder is that terrorism is highly organized and conducted primarily for sociopolitical reasons. If we define *terrorism* as the mass murder of innocent civilians by highly organized killers for political or social purposes, then the former Soviet Union (62 million victims), The People's Republic of China (35 million victims), and Nazi Germany (21 million victims) stand as the bloodiest terrorists in human history, with most of the victims being their own nationals.[81] Such state-sanctioned terrorism, insidious as it may be, is not considered here. Terrorism as we discuss it here is the *criminal* (unsanctioned by the state) murder of innocent victims for political or social purposes. The definition of *terrorism* adopted by the FBI stresses its unlawfulness and antigovernmental nature: "the unlawful use of force or violence against persons or property to intimidate or coerce a government, the civilian population, or any segment thereof, in furtherance of political or social goals."[82] Radical

criminologists view definitions such as this as another example of the state's monopoly over criminal definitions, and would like to substitute their own "value neutral" definition of terrorism as "behaviors which menace the social, economic and political order."[83]

Why Terrorism?

Terrorism is a tactic used by antigovernmental groups to influence the behavior of others through intimidation. For instance, the bombing of abortion clinics and the murder of physicians who work there are attempts by radical fringes of the pro-life movement to intimidate people who seek abortions or people who perform them. You may be horrified that some people feel it necessary to use bombs and the bullets to change the minds and/or behavior of others who believe differently, but often those who resort to such tactics sincerely believe that they have no other choice and that their behavior is morally justifiable. They typically appeal to a higher moral "good," such as ethnic autonomy or some religious or political dogma to justify the killing of innocents. Most terrorist groups (e.g., the IRA and the Basque ETA) appear to embrace an ideological mixture of nationalism and Marxism, while others may primarily invoke religious fundamentalism (e.g., Iraq's *al-Da'wa* or Lebanon's *Hizballah*). A set of moral and ideological justifications akin to the techniques of neutralization discussed in Chapter 10 are provided to the individual terrorist by the terrorist group, which, because of its isolation from mainstream society, often becomes the sole source of self-identity and social support, as well as the sole definer of reality, for its members.

All terrorist groups see themselves and the people for whom they claim they are fighting as oppressed victims of an unjust regime, which may be a view with at least some truth to it. But why strike at innocents, some of whom may be fellow "victims"? They strike at innocents because the very essence of terrorism is public intimidation, and the randomness of terrorist action accomplishes this better than targeting specific individuals would. Victims are incidental to the aims of terrorists; they are simply instruments in the objectives of (1) publicizing the terrorists' cause, (2) instilling in the general public a sense of personal vulnerability, and (3) provoking a government into unleashing repressive social control measures that may cost it public support.[84] Terroristic violence, while it may be cruel and immoral, is thus not "senseless" violence because it has an ultimate purpose. There is a logic to terrorism by which evil means are justified by the ends they seek. Every time terrorists gain an objective they have sought, the rationality of terrorism is demonstrated along with its immorality.

Is There a Difference between Terrorists and Freedom Fighters?

Do you accept the cliché that one person's terrorist is another's freedom fighter? Although many people do, this attitude has been called "sophomoric moral relativism."[85] Although all terrorists probably claim to be freedom fighters, there are two important distinctions between terrorists and freedom fighters (or guerrillas) that go beyond semantics implying their moral equivalence. First, freedom fighters are fighters in wars of national liberation against foreign occupiers or against oppressive domestic regimes they seek to overthrow. Terrorists are typically fighting to gain some sort of ethnic autonomy or to right some perceived inequity, and rarely have illusions of overthrowing the government they are fighting against. While guerrillas may occasionally use terrorist tactics against noncombatants, widespread use of such tactics will deprive them of the popular support they need, and thus they tend to confine their activities to fighting enemy combatants.[86]

The second important distinction is that guerrilla activity is overwhelmingly confined to third-world dictatorships or one-party states, while terrorists overwhelmingly operate against liberal Western democracies, which are less well-equipped to deal with the problem because of legal and moral restraints than are ruthless dictatorships or one-party states. Because of the political con-

texts in which they operate, it may be said that guerrillas literally have no choice other than armed insurgence to accomplish change because they are outside of the system that oppresses them. Terrorists, on the other hand, often have access to the system, but they have spurned the ballot box and embraced the bomb. For instance, although the people of Puerto Rico have consistently voted to maintain ties with the United States, various Puerto Rican terrorist groups continue their bombing campaign to "free" Puerto Rico. Likewise, the British government has consistently said that Northern Ireland will be reunited with the Republic of Ireland any time the majority of the people of Northern Ireland express their wish for it at the polls, but the IRA has not accepted this. Of course, not all claims of injustice can be righted at the polling stations, and thus the distinctions we have made here may be overdrawn to some extent. They are real enough, however, to conclude that the moral conflation of *terrorist* and *freedom fighter* is probably not warranted.

The Extent of Terrorism

Although we have said that terrorism has ancient roots, it became far more prevalent after the 1960s. The increased prevalence can be attributed to a number of factors. The instability experienced by many countries following World War II provided fertile soil for conflict, much like the instability and conflict that followed the recent breakup of the Soviet Union and Yugoslavia. There was also a general air of discontent, protest, and alienation surrounding the 1960s as people demonstrated against the Vietnam war and for civil rights for African Americans, women, and gays. Although these protests originated in the United States, they soon spilled into other democratic countries. The resurgence of the IRA, for instance, occurred after Catholic civil rights marchers were attacked by Protestant loyalists. The 1960s was also the high point of conflict between the superpowers, with each having their zones of influence and with each supporting armed opposition within the other's zone. Terrorism is also much easier to accomplish than ever before. Modern transportation systems allow terrorists to slip in and out of areas of operation with speed and efficiency, and the same systems provide terrorists with convenient targets because they bring large numbers of people together in places such as airports and railroad stations. Modern technology also makes the terrorist's life easier in that it provides easily concealed and relatively cheap weapons and explosives of great destructive power.[87]

To give you some idea of the recency of most terrorist groups, of the seventy-six groups that were active in 1990, only three originated before 1960.[88] Terrorist incidents also rose dramatically after 1960, but have fallen off in recent years. U.S. State Department statistics presented in Figure 16.2 show that the number of international terrorist incidents rose from a low of 345 in 1975 to a high of 665 in 1987, and then dropped to a new low of 296 incidents in 1996. These 296 incidents resulted in 311 deaths and 2,652 injuries.[89] Although these deaths and injuries are matters of concern, the damage to society as a whole is more psychological than physical. The death, damage,

and loss attributable to international terrorism is minuscule when compared to that attributable to traditional crime.[90] To put the problem in perspective, compare the 296 deaths *worldwide* in 1996 attributable to international terrorism to the 19,645 homicides committed in the United States alone in the same year.

Terrorism and Common Crime

Like any organization, terrorist organizations must be financed. Some funding for terrorist groups comes from governments sympathetic to their cause, or hostile to the governments against which the terrorists operate. The United States government has designated Cuba, Iran, Iraq, Libya, Sudan, Syria, and North Korea as terrorist-sponsoring nations, with Iran the most active of them.[91] Some funding comes from private sympathizers, but most of it comes from common criminal activities like drug trafficking, extortion, and bank robbery. The IRA, for instance, has raised vast sums of money by extorting "protection" money from the very shopkeepers and businesspeople they claim to be

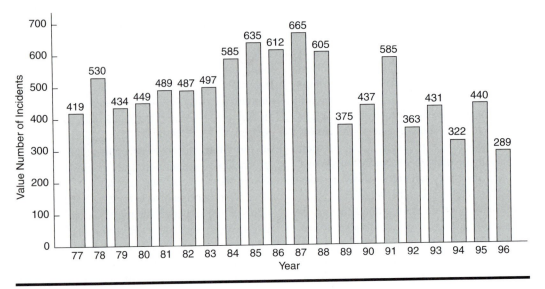

FIGURE 16.2 International Terrorist Incidents, 1977–1996

Adapted from (1997) *Patterns of Global Terrorism, 1996*. United States Department of State, Washington, DC: p. 70.

fighting for. They have made so much money from this and other criminal activities that they have had to branch out into legitimate businesses and have launched money-laundering schemes.[92] Although political ideology remains an important binding link in the IRA, evidence suggests that many IRA groups now exist with the primary purpose of developing wealth for their members.[93]

Terrorist groups in South America, such as the Marxist/Maoist *Shining Path* of Peru, make enormous profits from drug trafficking, and European groups, such as Germany's Red Army Faction and Italy's Red Brigades (both Marxist oriented), finance their activities through bank robberies and kidnaping. The widespread involvement of terrorist groups in such pecuniary practices casts serious doubt on the ideological idealism that they claim motivates their activities. The large amounts of money involved can corrupt the most dedicated ideologue in time, especially if fellow terrorists are lining their pockets. It has been said that, "Gradually, the [criminal] activities become ends in themselves and terrorist groups begin to resemble ordinary criminal organizations hidden behind a thin political veneer."[94]

Some Important Terrorist Groups

The Irish Republican Army (IRA).   The IRA is perhaps the terrorist organization best known to people in the United States. The IRA traces its origin to the ill-fated Easter Rebellion against British rule in 1916. It began as an organization devoted to reuniting the predominantly Catholic Republic of Ireland with the predominantly Protestant Northern Ireland (which is now a part of the United Kingdom) under a Marxist government. The IRA was almost destroyed by Irish government forces during the Irish civil war in the 1930s, but reemerged strongly in the late 1960s. The IRA has carried out terrorist activities in the Republic of Ireland, Northern Ireland, the British mainland, and against British military bases in Germany. After some bloody internal struggles in the early 1960s, some IRA members, disenchanted with the Official IRA's (OIRA) Marxist orientation and willingness to seek peace with the British, broke off to form the Provisional IRA (PIRA). When we hear of IRA terrorist activity today, it refers to PIRA activity. The PIRA has been responsible for many hundreds of murders since the late 1960s and has done everything that it could to sabotage Anglo–Irish agreement.[95] In September, 1994, the PIRA agreed to join the OIRA in a cease-fire, although some PIRA units have carried out conventional robberies.[96] The 1994 cease-fire was unfortunately shattered by two IRA bombings in London in early 1996, but prospects have improved once again with the victory of the more conciliatory Labour Party in Britain in the 1997 election.

The activities of the PIRA spawned the terrorist activities of fiercely pro-British and anti-unionist Protestant groups such as the *Ulster Volunteer Force, Ulster Freedom Fighters,* and the *Red Hand Commandos.* Despite their pro-British stance, these groups have sometimes fought British security forces attempting to thwart terrorist activities aimed at Catholic IRA supporters. The Ulster Volunteer Force officially renounced terrorism in 1976, but it continued to engage in criminal violence.[97] The emergence of these groups points to the intractable nature of terrorism. If the reunification of Ireland were to occur, the Irish government would probably be faced with the same problem from Unionist terrorists that the British have faced from the IRA.

Palestine Liberation Organization (PLO).   The PLO is not a terrorist organization per se. It serves as an umbrella organization for several such groups serving a variety of ideologies and agendas united by Palestinian nationalism. Although groups under the PLO umbrella, such as the Arab Liberation Front, *al Fatah* and the Palestine Liberation Front, engage in numerous terrorist acts against noncombatants, even noncombatants from neutral nations. They also conduct guerilla warfare against the Israeli military.

The PLO was created at the first Arab Summit meeting in Egypt in 1964 with the aim of liberating Palestine from the Israelis. The irony of this aim is that Palestine did not exist until the end of

World War I. Up until then, the area now called Palestine or Israel was part of the Turkish (Ottoman) Empire organized into Jewish, Christian, and Muslim religious communities without any kind of national identity.[98] During World War I, the British promised to support Arab nationalism in the area in exchange for Arab support against the Ottoman Empire, which was allied with Germany and Austria/Hungary, but they also supported a national homeland for the Jews in the same area. After World War II, the United Nations voted to partition the area into Arab and Jewish areas under British supervision. The Arabs did not accept this, and the day after the British (who were harassed during their mandate by Israeli terrorist organizations such as the *Irgun* and the *Stern Gang*) left the newly proclaimed state of Israel, a number of Arab armies invaded the new country and were soundly defeated. Israel's victory and expansion of its territory became the impetus for the formation of the various Palestinian liberation groups.

After thirty years of bloody violence, the Arab–Israeli conflict may be on the brink of peaceful resolution with the 1994 agreement between Israel and the PLO providing for Palestinian self-rule in the West Bank and Gaza Strip. Relations between Israel and other Arab governments also improved with the demise of the Soviet Union and the support it used to provided those governments and for terrorism in general. Unfortunately, fanatical groups opposing the peace process, especially Iranian-backed groups, who continue to demand the destruction of Israel, have increased their terroristic activities since the 1994 agreement.[99]

Hizballah. *Hizballah* ("Party of God") is the best contemporary example of a state-sponsored terrorist organization. Hizballah ultimately owes its existence to the religious split between *Sunni* Muslims, who believe in the legitimacy of the secular state, and *Shi'ite* Muslims, who do not. It was organized by the *Shi'ite* religious leader Ayatollah Khomeini to fight the secular rule of the Shah of Iran. It emerged on the international stage after the Israeli invasion of Lebanon in 1982, which drove the PLO out of that country. Ironically, the PLO had been the chief opponent of the Lebanese *Shi'ites* prior to the invasion. *Hizballah* fighters were sent to Lebanon by Khomeini, ostensibly to aid in the fight against Israel, but with the long-range goal of establishing an Iranian-style Islamic regime in Lebanon. *Hizballah* has claimed responsibility for a number of spectacular terrorist operations that helped hasten the withdrawal of U.S. and Israeli forces from Lebanon. Among these actions where the bombing of the U.S. Marine barracks in 1983, killing 251 U.S. and 56 French soldiers, and the kidnaping and/or murder of several U.S. and European citizens.

Hizballah has a sense of engaging in a sacred mission that transcends the confines of Lebanon. Much as Christian crusaders several centuries before them saw the Muslim presence in the Holy Land as an affront to Christianity, the more radical among modern *Shi'ites* view the existence of a Jewish state in an area they also consider holy to be an affront to Islam.[100] They are fiercely anti-Israeli and anti-American, viewing the United States as the decadent, drug-infested, crime-ridden, sex-perverted "Great Satan" of the world. *Hizballah*'s leadership is composed of Islamic clerics, which poses a problem because terrorism is against Islamic law. For this reason the organization has several *noms de guerre* ("war names") such as Islamic Jihad, Revolutionary Justice Organization, and Islamic Jihad for the Liberation of Palestine.[101] Directed and financed by Iran, *Hizballah* is headquartered in Lebanon and has established cells in Europe, North and South America, and Africa.[102]

Table 16.2 provides brief descriptions of some other terrorist organizations identified by the United States Department of State.

Terrorism in the United States

Americans have been targeted by terrorists while traveling abroad, but the terrorist organizations responsible for those attacks have found it difficult to do so within the borders of the United States, thanks largely to the great distances between this

TABLE 16.2   Examples of Other Terrorist Organizations

Group	Description & Activities	Ideology	Approximate Strength	Funding Sources
Abu Nidal Organization: a.k.a. Black September	Split from the PLO in 1974, this group has carried out attacks in 20 countries, killing or injuring almost 900 persons. Responsible for attacks on Rome and Vienna airports in 1985 and hijacking of Pan Am Flight 73 in 1986. Currently headquartered in Libya, Lebanon, and Sudan.	Nationalist and weakly socialist	Several hundred	Iraq, Syria, Libya
ETA (Basque Fatherland and Liberty)	Founded in 1959 with the aim of creating an independent Basque homeland in northwest Spain and southwest France. Its activities have been aimed primarily at Spanish government officials and security forces, but French interests have also been attacked.	Nationalist & weakly Marxist	Unknown, but has may supporters in Basque regions	Primarily via criminal activity; has received training in Libya and Lebanon
Japanese Red Army	A radical breakaway group of the Japanese Communist League with the goal of fermenting world revolution. The group was responsible for a number of aircraft hijackings in the 1970s, and for the Lod Airport massacre in 1972.	Radical Marxist	A few hardcore members with unknown number of sympathizers	Unknown
Kurdistan Worker's Party	Composed of Turkish Kurds seeking an independent Kurdish state in Turkey. Have attacked Turkish diplomats in many countries and attempted to disrupt tourism in Turkey by bombing hotels, historical sites, and kidnaping tourists.	Marxist	10,000–15,000	Syria, Iraq, Iran
Liberation tigers of Tamil Eelam (LTTE)	Composed of ethnic Tamils seeking an independent Tamil state in Sri Lanka, primarily through the use of bombings and assassinations. The LTTE have refrained from targeting Western tourists for fear of drying up funds from overseas Tamils.	Nationalism	10,000	Funds from Tamil communities overseas and some drug smuggling
Mujahedin-e Khalq	Formed in the 1960s to counter the westernization of Iran under the Shah. It supported the overthrow of the Shah but is presently fighting against Iran's Islamic fundamentalist regime. Carries out attacks on Iranian diplomats and Iranian property.	A mixture of Marxism and Islam	Several thousand	Contributions from Iranian expatriates
Red Brigades	Formed in 1969 with the intention of creating a revolutionary state in Italy and taking the country out of the Western alliance. Carried out many high-profile murders and kidnapings of prominent Italians, as well as small-scale attacks on NATO targets.	Marxist–Leninist	50?	Criminal activity, some from PLO and other terrorist groups
Sendero Luminoso (Shining Path)	Perhaps the world's most ruthless terrorist group. Formed in late 1960s to destroy existing Peruvian institutions and replace them with a peasant revolutionary regime. Almost all Peruvian institutions have been brutally targeted in Peru and abroad.	Marxist/Maoist	2,000+	Mostly drug trafficking and other forms of crime.

Source: Department of State (1996). *Patterns of global terrorism.*

country and the countries in which the terrorist groups are based. But as the bombings of the World Trade Center in 1993 and of the Oklahoma City Federal Building in 1995 attest, the United States is not immune to such attacks. Although the World Trade Center bombing was the work of foreign Islamic fundamentalists, the United States has its share of domestic terrorists. For instance, there have been at least nine Puerto Rican groups operating since the 1970s that have used terrorist tactics in their struggle to gain independence from the United States.[103] Terrorist groups in the United States are decidedly amateur compared with their foreign counterparts, but the bombing in Oklahoma City demonstrates that even the acts of amateurs can have devastating results. We may divide domestic American terrorists into three general types: *ideological, nationalist,* and *special-issue,* with the ideological type being further divided into left- and right-wing groups.

Ideological: Left-Wing. Left-wing terrorism in the United States became prevalent in the turmoil of the 1960s, although there had previously been left-wing groups here that occasionally used terrorist-type tactics. The most prominent groups in the 1960s were the *Students for a Democratic Society* (SDS) and its more radical offshoot, the *Weather Underground* (WU). Solidly middle-class, mostly white, and fiercely Marxist, the WU focused its attacks on symbols of "capitalist oppression" such as banks, corporate headquarters, and military facilities. It was thought to be defunct after the arrest of many of its leaders in the 1970s, but it renewed its robbery and bombing campaign in the 1980s.[104] An even more radical group, *The May 19 Communist Organization* (M19CO) have joined in bombing operations of U.S. military facilities with Puerto Rican groups and developed ties with European and Middle Eastern terrorist groups.[105]

Perhaps the most dangerous of contemporary left-wing groups is the *Revolutionary Armed Task Force* (RATF), a group forged from the alliance of the May 19th Coalition and the *Black Liberation Army.* Although this group has earned its terrorist credentials by bombing a number of capitalist

symbols, including the FBI's headquarters in New York, much of its activity seems to be concentrated on conventional crimes such as robbery and drug trafficking. The RATF recruits from minority prisoners and parolees, especially those who see themselves as victims of a capitalist and racist United States.[106]

Ideological: Right-Wing. Most right-wing U.S. groups characterized as terrorist are *extremist* rather than terrorist groups in that they hold views that are to the extreme right of mainstream views, but they do not necessarily translate their views into terrorist action. However, if the Oklahoma City bombing turns out to be more than the work of a deranged individual, this assessment will have to be changed. An example of such a group is the *Aryan Nations,* a right-wing group headquartered in Idaho that espouses white supremacy, anti-Semitism, tax resistance, and radical libertarianism. Although this group has never been linked to terrorist activities, and although they specifically disavow violence, the danger of escalation is always present among people who are motivated by hate. In 1983, ultraradical members of the Aryan Nations, who felt that more violent tactics were called for, broke away and founded *The Order.* Espousing the same views as their parent organization, this group has been responsible for several bank robberies and politically motivated murders. Law enforcement officials have identified about 150 members of this group, although many of its leaders have been arrested.[107] Much of the money stolen by The Order has been used to fund other white hate groups such as the Ku Klux Klan (KKK) and various neo-Nazi groups.[108]

The KKK is one of the oldest terrorist groups in the world, although today it is a generic name for a number of autonomous groups, which range from those that never go beyond rhetoric and cross burning to those who actively practice terrorism.[109] At its peak, the KKK boasted a membership of four million, and many members engaged in murders, bombings, beatings, and cross burnings to intimidate African Americans and white civil rights workers. The KKK shares with most

other U.S. right-wing extremist/terrorist organizations an extreme Christian fundamentalism, the
advocacy of paramilitary survivalist training, and a
conspiratorial view of politics. They refer to the
U.S. government as ZOG (Zionist Occupational
Government), which they say is run by Jews, lib-
erals, and African Americans.[110]

Just as there are substantial differences in the
ideologies of right- and left-wing groups, there are
substantial differences between their individual
members. Left-wing groups are younger (average
age at arrest = 35), and have more female (27%)
and minority (71%) members than right-wing
groups. The average age at arrest of right-wing
group members is thirty-nine, and their numbers
include only a small number of females (7%) and
minorities (3%, all Native American). Left-wing
groups tend to be concentrated in urban areas,
have a middle-class membership, most of whom
hold a college degree (54%); right-wing groups
tend to be rural and working class, with only 12
percent holding college degrees.[111]

Nationalist and Special-Issue Domestic Terrorists

Nationalist terrorists in the United States consist of
a variety of groups with a mostly émigré membership and with aims generally having little to do
with the United States. The exception are the already mentioned Puerto Rican groups whose aim
is an independent Puerto Rico. Emigré groups in
the United States bring with them old hatreds and
causes from their homelands. These groups include
the Armenian Secret Army of the Liberation of Ar-
menia (ASALA) and a variety of anti-Castro
Cuban groups. The ASLA is now defunct, but
when it was operating it primarily operated against
Turkish targets, including the assassination of the
Turkish Consul-General in Los Angeles in 1982.[112]
The activities of the various expatriate Cuban
groups target supporters of the Castro regime.

Special-interest terrorists are usually people
on the outer fringes of otherwise legitimate special-
interest groups such as pro-life and animal rights
activists. The vast majority of people concerned

with these issues pursue their causes peacefully by
demonstrating and lobbying, but radical activists
plant bombs, start fires, ransack buildings, and
commit murder in their attempts to influence public policy. Most members of special-issue groups
soundly condemn such actions as damaging to
their cause.

THE CAUSES OF TERRORISM

You may have guessed from our brief discussion
of domestic and foreign terrorists that, from a political and historical point of view, there are as
many causes of terrorism as there are terrorist
groups. As our brief histories of the IRA, PLO,
and Hizballah implied, terrorism cannot be understood without understanding the *specific* historical, social, political, and economic conditions
behind the emergence of each terrorist group. Although certain kinds of people may be drawn to
terrorism, to view terrorists as a bunch of "sicko-
weirdos" wreaking havoc around the world like so
many mission-oriented serial killers is to ignore
the diversity of histories, purposes, causes, and
people associated with terrorism. The one generality we can make is that all groups originated in
response to some perceived injustice. However,
beyond the sociopolitical conditions and the perceived injustices we need to seek more specific
causes located within the individuals, because the
vast majority of people exposed to the same situations do not resort to terrorism.

Is There a Terrorist Personality? Despite self-
selection for membership in terrorist groups, no
study of terrorist psychology has ever produced a
psychological profile, leading us to suspect that
there is not any such thing as a "terrorist personality." On the other hand, the absence of a uniform
terrorist personality does not mean that certain
traits are not disproportionately present among
those who join terrorist groups. Terrorist groups
live on the fringes of society and espouse a vio-
lently radical vision of reality, factors that make it
unlikely that terrorist organizations attract members from across the spectrum of personality types.

Some theorists are of the opinion that we should look at what terrorist groups have to offer if we want to understand why individuals join them: "Terrorism can provide a route for advancement, an opportunity for glamour and excitement, a chance of world renown, a way of demonstrating one's courage, and even a way of accumulating wealth."[113] In other words, terrorism is much like organized crime in that it provides illegitimate ways to get what most of us would like to have— fame and fortune. Terrorists also have a bonus in that they, and their comrades and supporters, see themselves as romanticized warriors fighting for a just and noble cause.

An exhaustive study of 250 incarcerated West German terrorists found them to have traits very much like those found among common criminals. Many of them had suffered the early loss of one or both parents, they were involved in frequent conflicts with authorities prior to joining their groups, and they had frequently failed in school and work endeavors. Psychologically, they were found to be stimulus-seekers, to be hostile, suspicious, aggressive, defensive, to be extremely dependent on the terrorist group, and to have a preference for a parasitic lifestyle.[114] This dovetails with claims that the two most commonly found traits among terrorists are low self-esteem and a predilection for risk taking.[115]

Some scholars view terrorists as people with marginal personalities drawn to terrorist groups because their deficiencies are both accepted and welcomed by the group.[116] These scholars also see the terrorist group as made up of three types of individuals: (1) The *charismatic leader,* (2) the *antisocial personality,* and (3) the *follower.* The charismatic leader is socially alienated, narcissistic, arrogant, and intelligent, with a deeply idealistic sense of right and wrong. The terrorist group provides a forum for his narcissistic rage and intellectual ramblings, and the subservience of group members feeds his egoism. Antisocial (or psychopathic) individuals have opportunities in terrorist groups to use force and violence to further their own personal goals, as well as the goals of the group. For the psychopath, the group functions like an organized crime family, providing greater opportunity, action, and prestige than could be found outside the group. The majority of terrorists, however, are simple followers with deep needs for acceptance, which makes them susceptible to all sorts of religious, ideological, and political propaganda.

Becoming a Terrorist. Some terrorism theorists, while agreeing that terrorist groups may attract a disproportionate number of criminals and "crazies," believe that the bulk of terrorists are probably better characterized as crusaders convinced of the moral rightness of their cause.[117] If these theorists are right, we have to explain how it is that "normal" people are persuaded to commit brutal acts against innocent people. When moral people are required to commit immoral acts there must be some sort of personal transformation that makes it possible. In other words, the willingness to perform terrorist acts may reflect a *process* of moral disengagement more than a manifestation of pathological and/or criminal traits the individual brings to the terrorist group.[118] If the essence of terrorism, is "the complete transformation of sane human beings into brutal and indiscriminate killers,"[119] terrorist acts doubtless generate significant levels of cognitive dissonance in the new recruit which must be resolved. As we saw in Chapter 10, inconsistencies between attitudes and behavior (the stuff of cognitive dissonance) are usually resolved by changing attitudes rather than behaviors. For the terrorist this typically means a deepening of the belief that the cause is just, the further dehumanizing of their targets, and any of a number of other ways that humans have for exorcizing behavior-inhibiting guilt.[120]

LAW ENFORCEMENT RESPONSE AND GOVERNMENT POLICY

There are any number of ways a democracy can respond to terrorism, ranging from making concessions to military intervention. Concessions are only likely only when there is moral substance to the terrorist cause, and when such concessions are reasonable. For instance, Spain has granted considerable autonomy to its Basque region in response to Basque terrorism, but Israel can hardly make concessions to Islamic terrorists whose "only" demand is the complete destruction of the state of Israel. Military intervention may be used when the terrorist threat is too big for civilian authorities to handle. But besides being distasteful to the democratic spirit, military intervention, even though successful in the short term, may be detrimental in the long term, as Israel discovered after it invaded Lebanon in 1982. On the other hand, the use of certain military units, such as Germany's *Grenzschutzgruppe* 9 (GSG9) and Britain's almost legendary SAS (Special Air Service), have proved spectacularly successful.[121]

International law has been applied against terrorists, sometimes successfully, sometimes not. The principle of international law known as *aut dedire aut punire* (Latin for 'either extradite or punish') obligates countries to either extradite terrorists to the country where their crimes were committed or to punish them themselves. Some countries neither extradite nor punish for one reason or another (they may support the terrorist's cause, or they may fear reprisals). The courts in some countries sometimes have difficulties with the terrorist/freedom fighter distinction, and sometimes even closely allied countries (e.g., Canada, Germany) refuse to extradite anyone to the United States if that person may face the death penalty.[122]

The United States has a clear-cut policy to combat terrorism. According to the U.S. State Department, the government's counterterrorist policy follows three general rules:

(1) Do not make deals with terrorists or submit to blackmail. We have found over the years that this policy works.
(2) Treat terrorists as criminals and apply the rule of law.
(3) Bring maximum pressure on states that sponsor and support terrorists by imposing economic, diplomatic, and political sanctions and urging other states to do likewise.[123]

Of course, these policies cannot always be strictly adhered to. The Iran/Contra affair of 1986 was a classic example of the government breaking its own rules (by violating its own arms embargo against Iran, the United States hoped to gain the release of U.S. citizens held hostage in Lebanon). Nevertheless, declining terrorist activity in democratic countries indicates that counterterrorist policies have fared somewhat better than have policies aimed at the reduction of common crime. But we cannot be complacent about recent democratic successes. Some authorities feel that the threat to the United States and other democracies from terrorism is a greater threat than conventional war, particularly given the apparent availability of nuclear weapons and components on the black market following the collapse of the Soviet Union.[124] When all is said and done, perhaps the only real defense against terrorism is a proactive one in which we attempt to address the social and political grievances on which terrorism feeds.

SUMMARY

Spree, mass, and serial murder are "motiveless" or irrational murders. All types have increased dramatically since the 1960s, especially serial murders, but not so dramatically as popular accounts sometimes claim. Nevertheless, serial murder was eight to sixteen times more common between 1970 and 1990 than it was between 1940 and 1969. Serial murder is the murder of four or more victims over an extended period of time. Researchers have developed a number of typologies of serial killers, with the most popular being Holmes and DeBurger's visionary, mission-oriented, hedonistic, and power/control types. Visionary killers are usually psychotic, and mission-oriented killers feel that it is their duty to rid the world of people they consider undesirable. Hedonistic killers (the most common) kill for the pure joy of it, while power/control killers get more satisfaction from exerting complete control over their victims.

Although African Americans are slightly overrepresented in the ranks of serial killers relative to their numbers in the population, Wayne Williams is the only African American to achieve anywhere near the same degree of notoriety that his white counterparts have. It is thought that African-American serial killers are not subjected to the same scrutiny as their white counterparts because stories featuring African-American characters are not likely to have wide media appeal, because the language often used to describe serial killers would be considered racist if applied to them, and because there has been traditionally less police concern for African-American victims.

Females are even more underrepresented among serial killers than they are among other kinds of criminals. There have been a number of women who have killed multiple times, but they have not been considered serial killers because at the core of the definition of *serial killer* is the idea of the motiveless bloodlust for killing strangers. Female multiple murderers typically have an instrumental reason for killing, and they usually kill someone known to them. If we define serial killing as motiveless (noninstrumental), then only Aileen Wournos fits the definition.

Other female serial killers have been female disciples of male killers. These are women who are totally under the control of the men in their lives, and whose only desire is to please their men. However, some women evidently do come to enjoy killing after a while.

The United States has more than its fair share of serial killers, and some authors make the claim that this country accounts for about 75 percent of the world's known serial killers over the past twenty to thirty years. However, many other countries have their own serial killers, who are often unknown to U.S. writers.

In trying to explain the phenomenon of serial killing, we have to explain both why the rate has increased and who those who commit it do so. Numerous social changes since the 1960s, such as the rejection of traditional morality, the mass marketing of pornography, and the decarceration movement have been used to explain the increased

prevalence of serial killing. In terms of explaining why individuals become serial killers, the one area of agreement among researchers is that such people have suffered a high degree of emotional deprivation and abuse.

It was pointed out that millions of children are deprived of their mother's emotional involvement without becoming serial killers, so we have to go beyond mere demographics to explore cognitive factors. Two factors commonly imputed to serial killers are strong feelings of sexual inadequacy and a rich fantasy life. They tend to be loners who project the blame for their sexual inadequacies onto women and fantasize about "getting even." Their fantasies are often combined with compulsive masturbation, a combination that may lead to the cognitive fusion of sex and violence, the epitome of which is the sadistic bloodlust of the serial killer.

Among the posited biological causes of such behavior is damage to certain areas of the brain, which results in difficulties controlling impulses. Some studies have also pointed to a particular chemical profile related to serial killing (and psychopathy in general), and other studies have shown that serial killers have severely unreactive ANSs, suggesting that only the most depraved and sadistic acts provide sufficient emotional stimulation to turn them on.

An integrated theory of serial killing (the diathesis–stress model) posits that serial killers have a biological disposition to kill that is exacerbated by severe environmental stress during childhood. These people develop self-esteem and self-control problems as well as sexual dysfunctions, which result in maladaptive coping skills and a retreat into a fantasy world.

Offender profiling, crime scene analysis, and the VICAP program have provided law enforcement with powerful tools in combating all sorts of violent crime, but particularly in combating serial murder. The ability to address the linkage-blindness problem probably accounts for a good part of the increase in known serial killers after VICAP was implemented.

Terrorism is an ancient method of intimidating the public by the indiscriminate use of violence for social or political reasons. Terrorists are different from freedom fighters or guerrillas in that terrorists usually operate against democracies and freedom fighters against foreign colonialists or oppressive domestic regimes. Terrorism increased rather dramatically from the 1960s to the mid-1980s and has steadily dropped off since then. In 1996 there were 296 international terrorist incidents resulting in 311 deaths worldwide. Many terrorist groups tend to evolve into organized crime groups hidden behind an ideological veneer.

The IRA and the PLO are probably the best-known terrorist groups. Both groups reached accords with their target countries (Britain and Israel, respectively) in the late 1990s and suspended operations, although there have been subsequent incidents. Hizballah, a radical pro-Iranian Islamic fundamentalist group, appears to be the most active and most deadly terrorist group presently operating. Its goal is the destruction of Israel and the establishment of an Islamic republic in Lebanon.

Although U.S. terrorists are decidedly amateur in comparison with their foreign counterparts, there are a fair number of terrorist groups operating in this country. These groups may be divided into ideological (left- and right-wing), nationalist, and special-issue groups.

From a historical and political point of view, there are as many causes of terrorism as there are terrorist groups. Each group has its origins in some perceived social, economic, or political injustice, but only a minuscule number of people react to such conditions by joining terrorist organizations. This observation leads many researchers to look for a "terrorist personality." There is no uniform terrorist personality, although there are certain traits found more frequently among terrorists than among the general population. The most common traits found are low self-esteem and a predilection for risk taking. Because most terrorists are not mentally ill, a process of moral disengagement is posited to explain their transition from sane human beings to killers.

Democracies have considerable difficulty responding to the terrorist threat because of legal restraints. The use of military units is distasteful to the democratic spirit, although the short-term use of special units has proven very useful. The international community has evolved certain processes for dealing with terrorists. One has been the passage of laws that obligate a country to either extradite terrorists in their custody to the country where the terrorism took place, or to punish the offenders themselves. As for the United States, it has a clear-cut policy of treating terrorists like common criminals, not making deals with them, and imposing sanctions against nations that sponsor terrorism. The threat to democracies from terrorism may be greater than the threat from conventional warfare, particularly if fanatical groups are able to get their hands on nuclear weapons.

EXERCISES

1. Examine the traits and characteristics associated with psychopathy found in Chapter 16 and write a paragraph or two indicating how these same factors might be useful to serial killers.

2. Look up a story in one of the major news magazines, such as *Time* or *Newsweek* on any of a number of recent school shooting sprees committed by schoolchildren. Can you find any commonalities among all the cases in terms of the kind of children that commit these crimes?

3. What is your explanation for why females are not represented among serial killers who kill for the joy of killing and who enjoy sexual bloodlust?

4. Do you agree or disagree that there is a moral difference between terrorists and guerillas?

5. Mass and spree murderers almost by necessity need guns to carry out their activities. Would a ban on private ownership of weapons be an acceptable price to pay to save the lives of victims of these acts (as well as other victims of guns)?

ENDNOTES

1. Leyton 1986:42.
2. Keeney & Heide 1995.
3. Jenkins 1988b:7.
4. Palermo 1997.
5. Petee et al. 1997.
6. Palermo 1997; Petee et al. 1997.
7. Lester 1995:85.
8. Leyton 1986.
9. Egger 1998.
10. Holmes & Holmes 1992:54.
11. Jenkins 1994:28.
12. Keeney & Heide 1995.
13. Jenkins 1994:28.
14. Holmes & DeBurger 1985:29.
15. Federal Bureau of Investigation 1969; 1991.
16. Jenkins 1988a:4.
17. Jenkins 1988a:3.
18. Holmes and DeBurger 1985.
19. Levin & Fox 1985: 86.
20. Ressler et al. 1988:3.
21. Norris 1988:19.
22. Hickey 1991:133; Jenkins 1994:169; Newton 1992:49.
23. Hickey 1997:136.
24. Levin & Fox 1985:51.
25. Powell 1996.
26. Jenkins 1994:170.
27. Jenkins 1994:173.
28. Jenkins 1994:172.
29. Jenkins 1994:175.
30. Jenkins, personal communication, 1996.
31. Jenkins 1994:155.
32. Keeney & Heide 1995.
33. Jenkins 1994:151.
34. Segrave 1992:5.
35. Holmes et al. 1991; Keeney & Heide 1994.
36. Jenkins 1994:154.
37. Levin & Fox 1985:74.
38. Keeney & Heide 1994.
39. Jenkins 1988b:12.
40. Rufford 1996.
41. Norris 1988:19.
42. Cited in Jenkins 1994:41.
43. Lester 1995:26.
44. Jenkins 1992:14.
45. Levin & Fox 1985:59.
46. Levin & Fox 1985.
47. Levin & Fox 1985:72.
48. Sears 1991:98.
49. Torrey 1997.
50. Jenkins 1992.
51. Norris 1988:115.
52. Leyton 1986:315.
53. Levin & Fox 1985:37.
54. Norris 1988:187.
55. Sears 1991:79.
56. Saffron 1997:19a.
57. Wilson 1984:623.
58. Popenoe 1993:532.
59. Levin & Fox 1985:35.
60. Norris 1988:124.
61. Cullen 1993:218.
62. Burgess et al. 1986.
63. Carlisle 1993; Ressler et al. 1988:28.
64. Ressler et al. 1988:29.
65. Carlisle 1993.
66. Drukteinis 1992:535.
67. Norris 1988:42.
68. DeHart & Mahoney 1994:33.
69. Norris 1988.
70. Norris 1988:193–194.
71. Drukteinis 1992:534.
72. Giannangelo 1996.
73. Jenkins 1994:56.
74. Douglas et al. 1986.
75. LaGrange 1993:40.
76. Brooks et al. 1987.
77. Hacker 1977:ix.
78. Vetter & Perlstein 1991:30.
79. Wheeler 1991:25.
80. Wheeler 1991:8.
81. Rummel 1992.
82. Smith 1994:9.
83. Lynch & Groves 1989:39.
84. Bandura 1990:162–163; Sederberg 1989:86–87.
85. Sederberg 1989:28.

86. Ezeldin 1987:47.
87. Ezeldin 1989; Kerstetter 1983.
88. Crenshaw 1991:76–77.
89. U.S. Department of State 1997:69.
90. Albanese & Pursley 1993:98.
91. U.S. Department of State 1995:20.
92. White 1991:128.
93. Carter 1994:254.
94. Albanese & Pursley 1993:100.
95. White 1991:36.
96. U.S. Department of State 1995:9.
97. Long 1990:46.
98. Long 1990:32.
99. U.S. Department of State 1995:iv.
100. Kramer 1990:135.
101. U.S. Department of State 1995:43.
102. U.S. Department of State 1995:43.
103. Albanese & Pursley 1993:104.
104. White 1990:30.
105. Stinson 1987:62.
106. Albanese & Pursley 1993:107.
107. Stinson 1987:63.
108. Albanese & Pursley 1993:111.
109. White 1990:25.
110. Vetter & Perlstein 1991:58.
111. Smith 1994:46–47.
112. Vetter & Perlstein 1991:61.
113. Reich 1990:271.
114. Reich 1990:270.
115. Long 1990:18.
116. Johnson & Feldmann 1992.
117. White 1991:112.
118. Bandura 1990.
119. Sprinzak 1991:58.
120. Bandura 1990.
121. White 1991:250.
122. Vetter & Perlstein 1991:203.
123. U.S. Department of State 1995:iv.
124. Albanese & Pursley 1993:126; Vetter & Perlstein 1991: 241.

CHAPTER 17

White-Collar and Organized Crime

In Chapter 1 we asked you what images pop into your head when you hear the word crime. *Whatever images you conjured up, we wager that the image of a well-dressed, middle-aged person, sitting in a leather recliner dictating a memo authorizing the marketing of defective automobiles or the dumping of toxic waste was not among them. We seldom think that the chain of events set into motion by a business memo may do more harm than the activities of any "street punk." It's true: People who wear white collars to work rob and kill too, only they use guile and deceit rather than a gun or knife and force and threats of force. When people are polled regarding their fears about crime they consistently report fear of being victimized by "street crimes," and rarely, if ever, report any concern about "suite crime."[1] Is this fear misplaced? Far more money is stolen and far more people killed every year as the result of scams and willful illegal corporate activity than as the result of street criminals: "By virtually any criterion, white collar crime is our most serious crime problem."[2] But you be the judge.*

THE CONCEPT OF WHITE-COLLAR CRIME

Our discussion of white-collar crime focuses on three broad areas. First, we introduce and define the concept and differentiate between occupational and corporate white-collar crime. Second we address the issue of the applicability of traditional criminological theories to occupational crime, particularly to embezzlement, forgery, and fraud. Third, we explore the world of corporate crime and criminologists' attempts to explain it, as well as their attempts to explain why corporate crime is rarely punished with the severity that street crime is.

The term *white-collar crime* was coined in the 1930s by Edwin Sutherland of differential association fame. Although sociologists previously stud-

ied crime among the upper classes, it tended to be a neglected area in criminology because factors such as poverty, subcultural norms, and social disorganization were considered the major causes of crime, and still are among many criminologists today. The fact that the bright and successful committed crimes posed a challenge to such theories, although conflict and Marxist theorists had always considered crimes of the "upperworld" to be very serious. Sutherland's focus on the white-collar criminal allegedly proved useful in that, "it falsified poverty pathology theory and it revealed the criminality of the privileged classes and their impunity to the law."[3]

Sutherland defined white-collar crime as crime "committed by a person of respectability and

516

high social status in the course of his occupation."[4] Although this definition became enshrined for a long time as *the* definition of white collar crime, and it governed research for a long time, it was wrong in three important ways: (1) most white-collar criminals are not of "high social status," (2) many are not otherwise respectable people, and (3) it fails to distinguish between crimes committed by individuals acting for personal gain, and crimes committed on behalf of the employer with the employer's blessing and support. Another problem related to Sutherland's definition was that many criminologists began viewing crime as something committed either by low or high status persons, thereby ignoring middle-class crime.[5] Crimes are committed on Main Street as well as on Mean Street and Wall Street, and any analyses of white-collar crime must include "Main Street" crimes.

A contemporary definition of *white-collar crime* that focuses on the characteristics of the offense rather than of the offender defines **white-collar crime** as "an illegal act or series of illegal acts committed by nonphysical means and by concealment or guile, to obtain money or property, or to obtain business or personal advantage."[6] This definition was adopted as the "official" one by Congress in 1979 in its *Administration Improvement Act.* Although avoiding the problem of social status, this definition still fails to differentiate between persons who commit crimes for personal gain and those who do so primarily on behalf of an employer. Our analysis of white-collar crime will differentiate between individuals who steal, defraud, cheat, and embezzle, both in and out of an occupational context, and those who commit a wide variety of offenses attributed to a business corporation. We reserve the term *occupational* crime for the former, and *corporate* crime for the latter, although many crimes that have been called *white-collar* defy neat placement into either category.

Occupational Crime

Occupational crime is crime committed by individuals in the course of their employment. The most obvious and common form of occupational crime is employee theft and vandalism. This might range from the draining of company funds by creative bookkeeping or sophisticated computer techniques to stealing small items of little value from the office or factory floor. Likewise, vandalism by disgruntled employees may run the gamut from scrambling important computer data to scratching graffiti on newly painted walls. Although such activities may seem relatively mundane to most of us, computer fraud alone is estimated to cost as much as $5 billion each year,[7] and the annual losses from all kinds of employment-related crime have been estimated to amount to more than the annual losses from all street crimes combined.[8] Although these figures are derived more from educated guesses than from hard data, they do provide us with a rough idea of just how serious employee crime is. Just as we all pay for street crime through the portion of our taxes that goes to support the criminal justice system, we all pay for employee crime because victimized companies merely pass on their losses to its customers via higher prices. Additionally, about one thousand businesses go bankrupt every year because of employee theft, which also means the loss of the jobs these businesses provided.[9]

The FBI's "Big Three" White-Collar Crimes. The only white-collar crimes appearing in the Uniform Crime Reports annual report are embezzlement, fraud, and forgery/counterfeiting. These crimes may or may not be committed in an occupational setting. As previously noted, contemporary researchers define *white-collar crime* by the nature of the offense rather than by the social status of the offender, so blue- and pink-collar workers, the unemployed, and welfare recipients can commit the kinds of white-collar crimes described below.

Embezzlement is the misappropriation or misapplication of money or property entrusted to the embezzler's care, custody, or control. Being in positions of trust, embezzlers are usually able to cover up the theft for a long period of time. Most embezzlers do what they do because they have some form of pressing financial problem, or simply because they have access to large amounts of money and the ability to hide any discrepancies for some time. After being exposed, many embezzlers insist that they were only "borrowing the money," and that they fully intended to pay it back.[10] Embezzlement is is at once the most costly and the rarest of occupational crimes, with only 11,499 cases being reported in the UCR in 1996. It is also the crime in which the percentage of female offenders (44.7%) most closely matched the percentage of male offenders (55.3%) in 1996.[11]

Fraud is theft by trick, i.e., obtaining the money or property of another through deceptive practices such as false advertising, impersonation, and other misrepresentations. Examples of fraud include door-to-door roofers who are never heard from again after taking your deposit, telemarketing fraud, offers of quack medical cures, phony faith healers, price gouging, and diploma mills promising "accredited" college degrees for a lot of money and little study. We could go on and on with examples, and we bet that you have one or two of your own. The FBI reported that 58.3 percent of those arrested for fraud in 1993 were males and 41.7 percent were females, indicating a very small sex difference in the commission of this crime.[12]

Forgery is the creation or alteration of documents to give them the appearance of legality and validity with the intention of gaining some fraudulent benefit from doing so. A person finding a paycheck belonging to someone else, signing that check with the name appearing on it, and then cashing it, has committed theft by forgery. **Counterfeiting,** the creation or altering of currency, is a special case of forgery. The FBI reported that 64.6 percent of those arrested for forgery/counterfeiting in 1996 were males and 35.4 percent were females.[13]

There are a number of other subcategories of noncorporate white-collar crimes. Crimes committed by professionals, such as physicians and lawyers, in the course of their practices are difficult to categorize because they commit them for personal gain, but in many cases the professional and the "corporation" are one and the same. Frauds committed by physicians include such practices as filing insurance claims for tests or pro-

cedures not performed, performing expensive and unnecessary operations, steering persons to laboratories, pharmacies, or any facility in which the doctor has a financial stake, referrals to other doctors in return for kickbacks, and prescribing and charging for brand-name drugs and substituting generic drugs.

Medicare and Medicaid programs are viewed by many as welfare programs for physicians. Fraud within these programs has been estimated to cost between $50 and $80 billion per year,[14] and overall medical fraud is estimated to be about $100 billion, or about 10 percent of the total U.S. health-care bill.[15] Fee-for-service medicine essentially means that physicians earn more money the more they perform expensive procedures (even fraudulent ones, such as pregnancy tests on seventy-five-year-old women). A Congressional subcommittee on medical fraud estimated that about 2.4 million unnecessary surgeries are performed each year, a number that allegedly costs the public approximately $4 billion dollars and the loss of about 11,900 lives.[16]

Most lawyers also work on a fee-for-service basis, thus generating the same temptations to increase their incomes by fraudulent means, although they usually do not have the same deadly consequences as medical fraud. Frauds perpetrated by lawyers include persuading clients to pursue fraudulent or frivolous lawsuits, billing clients for hours not worked, filing unnecessary motions, and complicating a simple legal matter to keep clients on the hook, "I will defend you, all the way to your last dollar." Thus, it seems that every occupational category generates a considerable number of occupational criminals, and the higher the prestige of the occupation the more their criminal activities cost the general public.

Causes of Occupational White-Collar Crime

Does white-collar crime require specific explanatory theories that are different from theories attempting to explain street crime? Some criminologists believe that crime is a unitary phenomenon and thus all crimes can be explained by the same set of causes; others believe that each kind of crime is so different that each requires its own explanation. The former is exemplified by self-control theory (low self-control is the basic cause of all crime), and the latter by rational choice theory (the causes of crime are found in the interaction of offenders and criminal opportunities, and the more specific the explanation the more useful it is).

Much of Edwin Sutherland's interest in white-collar crime had to do with his desire to show that all crime could be explained by his theory of differential association. However, it is difficult to posit that embezzlers gain normative support at the bank for their crimes, or that physicians are socialized into excepting an excess of definitions favorable to Medicare fraud. Few criminologists today argue that differential association theory can be a general theory of crime, and whatever side of the general/specific argument they may be on, most seem to agree that white-collar crime places a limit on a general theory of crime.[17] If we think of crime in terms of Mean Street or Wall Street, it is almost self-evident that crimes committed by individuals whose personal characteristics and demographic profiles are poles apart require different explanations. But if the typical white-collar criminal is not too very different from the typical street criminal, then the possibility of a general theory exists.

Are Occupational White-Collar Criminals and Street Criminals All That Different?

According to Hirschi and Gottfredson,[18] occupational crime differs from common street crime only in that it is committed by people in a position to do so: Medicaid fraud can typically only be committed by physicians, and bank embezzlement by bank employees in a position of trust. The motives of occupational criminals are the same those of street criminals, that is, to obtain benefits relatively quickly with minimal effort. Furthermore the age, sex, and race profiles of occupational criminals are not that much different from those of street criminals. Using UCR data, Hirschi and Gottfredson determined that rates for fraud, forgery, and em-

bezzlement peak in the early twenties and decline with increasing age to approximately one half by age forty-one.[19] Similarly, they found that male rates were higher than female rates, and that African-American rates were higher than white rates. From these data they concluded: "When opportunity is taken into account, demographic differences in white collar crime are the same as demographic differences in ordinary crime."[20]

Others argue that the UCR categories of embezzlement, forgery, and fraud are not appropriate indicators of occupational crime because most are committed in a nonoccupational context, and that the demographic profiles of UCR white-collar and street criminals are not the same.[21] We won't debate what are or are not appropriate indicators of occupational crime, but the claim that the demographic correlates of the two groups are or are not the same is very important for criminological theory. No study of the issue finds that the demographics of the two groups are different in *kind* (i.e., old, female, and white rather than young, male, and African-American), but only in *degree.* Individuals arrested for embezzlement, fraud, and forgery *do* tend to be disproportionately young, male, and African-American, but older persons, females, and whites are proportionately more represented in occupational crime than they are in street crime.

When we look at white-collar crimes that require high status occupations for their commission we find a different story. An analysis of 1,094 white-collar criminals processed through the federal courts (all non-UCR white-collar crimes are federal crimes) in the 1980s found that the sociodemographic characteristics of the typical high-status white-collar offender differed radically from those of street criminals.[22] Antitrust offenders were 99.1 percent white, 99.1 percent male, and averaged fifty-three years of age. Securities fraud offenders were 99.6 percent white, 97.8 percent male, and had an average age of forty-four. Offenders in other federal crime categories (tax, credit, mail fraud, bribery, and false claims) were also older by about ten years than the average street criminal. Males were even more heavily overrepresented than they are in street crime, and nonwhites were also overrepresented (ranging from 17% of the bribery offenders to 38% of the false claim offenders), although not to the extent that they are among street criminals.[23] It was also found that 43.4 percent of the sample had a prior adult arrest, compared with 89.5 percent of a sample of street criminals and about 17 percent of the general public.[24]

Explaining Crimes of the Middle Classes

These data seem to indicate that white-collar criminals occupy a middle position between the general public and street criminals. The authors of the study dismiss the notion that the kinds of crimes they examined could have been caused by low self-control, stating that if this was the case they would have to say that "The securities fraud offender should have been a youthful mugger but missed the boat."[25] Their explanation for white-collar crime is in the anomie/strain tradition, believing that it is "normal" in a business environment that encourages competition and innovation: "We have about the rate of white-collar crime that we 'need' in order to encourage the amount of freedom, aspiration, and upward mobility that we seem, as a society, to want."[26] The authors also note that many white-collar criminals were trying to hold on to the positions and wealth they had worked so hard to gain and were in danger of losing.[27] This explanation is consistent with a proposition from general strain theory that defines strain not only in terms of wanting what we do not have, but also in terms of not wanting to lose what we do have.[28]

CORPORATE CRIME

Corporate crime is criminal activity on *behalf* of a legitimate business organization, the kind of crime that Sutherland most had in mind when he defined *white-collar* crime. Corporate crime is certainly not a new phenomenon, but concern about it is relatively new. During much of U.S. history, the primary legal stance relating to the activities of business was decidedly *laissez-faire* ('leave it

alone to do as it will'). Under the influence of capitalist philosophy and social Darwinism, U.S. courts traditionally adopted the view that government should not interfere with business by attempting to regulate it. For a very long period in our history, victims of defective and dangerous products could not sue corporations for damages because the guiding principle was *caveat emptor* ('let the buyer beware'), and unhealthy and dangerous working conditions in mines, mills, and factories were excused under the freedom-of-contract clause of the Constitution.[29] Thus, the defrauding, maiming, and killing of innocent consumers and workers by business enterprises was not only tolerated for much of our history, it was legally protected.

This attitude shifted somewhat with the passage of the Sherman Antitrust Act in 1890. This act was designed to encourage competition by forbidding the formation of trade monopolies. Antitrust offenses include conspiracies to fix prices, bid-rigging, bribery, and any other efforts to be anti-competitive and monopolistic. Other corporate crimes and illegalities include toxic waste dumping, securities fraud, violations of safety and health regulations, kickbacks, unfair labor and business practices, and manufacturing defective or dangerous products, either knowingly or unknowingly. These crimes of concealment, fraud, and misrepresentation victimize all sorts of groups and individuals in our entire society. Crimes such as these are actions committed during the course of fulfilling the legitimate role of the corporation, and in the name of corporate profit and growth. Three famous examples of corporate crime are described below.

The Dark Side of Corporate America: Conspiracy, Looting, and Homicide

The Electrical Equipment Conspiracy: "Everybody's Doing It." In *The Wealth of Nations*, English economist Adam Smith wrote that "Seldom do members of a profession meet . . . that is does not end up in some conspiracy against the public or some contrivance to raise prices."[30] The heavy electrical antitrust conspiracy cases of 1961, which involved such corporate giants as General Electric and Westinghouse, provide us with a fairly modern example of Smith's observation. This conspiracy constituted the most serious violation of the Sherman Antitrust Act since its passage.[31] Executives of the twenty-nine companies involved in the conspiracy met on a regular basis to discuss price-fixing and bid-rigging with the express purpose of dividing their industry's business "fairly" among themselves. They knew that they were engaging in an illegal conspiracy, as evidenced by the lengths they went to to keep their meetings secret. They called their meetings "choir practice," and the roster of those attending (under false names) was known as the "Christmas card list."[32] Sometimes these meetings could degenerate into verbal brawls if one company or the other felt that it was not getting its fair share of the spoils, or if some company was accused of failing to live up to previously agreed arrangements. These "choir practices" were not much different from organized crime's "family" meetings wherein similar disputes are discussed. Companies participating in the conspiracy benefited from their illegal activities to the tune of about $2 billion (equivalent to about $12 billion in 1998 dollars). It is interesting to note the participants' explanations of why they engaged in these activities. They claimed that what they were doing was illegal, "but not criminal," that they were simply "following orders," that "Everyone was doing it," that "If I didn't do it, someone else would," that "No one got hurt," and that what they were really doing was "stabilizing prices."[33] These "techniques of neutralization" enabled all forty-five defendants to cast themselves as respectable businessmen who had been unfairly singled out for punishment by overzealous government regulators. None of the indicted conspirators seemed to have suffered at all from the experience; they all either remained employed with their companies or obtained employment elsewhere, mostly at higher salary levels.[34]

The S & L Scandal: The Best Way to Rob a Bank Is to Own One.

The savings and loan (S & L) scandal of the 1980s amounted to the most costly crime spree in U.S. history and is likely to cost the U.S. taxpayer up to $473 billion.[35] This staggering amount is far greater than losses from all the "regular" bank robberies in U.S. history put together.[36] The S & L scandal occurred in a decade noted for its greed and corruption.[37] The atmosphere during the Reagan–Bush era was decidedly one of "rugged capitalism" and greed, as exemplified by the words of the corporate raider played by Michael Douglas in the 1987 movie *Wall Street*: "Greed—for the lack of a better word—is good. Greed is right. Greed works." Deregulation was in vogue, and industries that remained regulated found that their regulatory bodies had been rendered impotent to investigate wrongdoing or to enforce compliance. This climate of greed and corruption, deregulation, impotent regulatory bodies, and "trickle-down" economics, combined with certain other structural factors to produce the S & L scandal.

The hyperinflation of the 1970s left many S & L's holding low-interest mortgages, which combined with low growth in the economy squeezed them at both ends, and many began to fail. The S & L industry was deregulated in 1980 under the assumption that the free market cures all economic problems, but it became "the cure that killed."[38] Deregulation allowed for massive embezzlement of funds by S & L owners and executives, thus making these crimes hybrids of occupational and corporate crime in that they constituted crime *by* the corporation *against* the corporation. Most of the looting took the form of extravagant salaries, bonuses, and perquisites (luxury cars, private jets, first-class European vacations, and so forth) that executives awarded themselves as their banks sank ever further into debt. Other methods involved selling land back and forth ("land flipping") within a few days until its paper value far exceeded its real value, and then finding "sucker" institutions to buy it at the inflated price, and loans made back and forth between employees of different banks with the knowledge that the loans would never be called in. A variety of scams with their own playful names such as "cash for trash," "kissing the paper," "daisy chains," and "dead cows for dead horses," convey the contempt these upper-middle-class executives had for their victims, and the gamelike way in which they viewed their activities.[39]

The Ford Pinto Case: Our Money or Their Lives? Corporate crime is generally committed by highly educated, highly intelligent and rational white males with the ability to weigh the costs and benefits of violating a law, ignoring a regulation, or marketing a defective product. The cold calculations of the corporate offender somehow seem more "evil" than the ill-considered calculations of the uneducated street crook, especially when those calculations pit lives against profits, as they did in the famous Ford Pinto case. This case involved the 1971 through 1977 Ford Pinto models, which were fitted with gas tanks that ruptured and burst into flames in rear-end collisions of over 25 miles per hour.

The Pinto was manufactured under strict cost and weight constraints set by Ford's then-president, Lee Iacocca. According to Ford engineers, safety was not a popular word around Iacocca, who would dismiss safety issues with a curt: "Read the project objectives and get back to work."[40] The fuel rupture problem could have been fixed at a cost of $11 per vehicle, but with 11 million Pintos and 1.5 million light trucks with the problem, Ford accountants calculated that it would cost the company $137 million to fix. It was calculated that *not* fixing it would result in 180 burn deaths, 180 serious burn injuries, and 2,100 burned vehicles, which they estimated would cost about $49.5 million dollars in lawsuits and other claims. Comparing those two figures, it was determined that in light of the $87.5 million it would save by not fixing the gas tank problem, to fix it would be unprofitable, and therefore irrational.[41]

Such disregard for human life did not seem to bother the consciences of this gang of suite criminals. Ford executives openly used these figures in a cost/benefit chart to lobby against federal fuel leakage standards to show just how unprofitable such standards would be! According to Harley Copp (a former Ford chief engineer who resigned because of his concern with safety), 95 percent of the 700 to 2500 people who died in Pinto crashes would have survived had the problem been fixed.[42] If this is anywhere near an accurate estimate of deaths caused by the Pinto defect, the executives who conspired to ignore the defect may be the worst multiple murderers in U.S. history. Yet no Ford executive was ever imprisoned, and many went on to bigger things.

Punishing Corporate Crime

Corporate crime is monitored and responded to by a variety of criminal, administrative, and regulatory bodies, but very few corporate crooks are ever the recipients of truly meaningful sanctions. In the electrical conspiracy, only seven of the executives involved served any prison time (all thirty days or less in a federal "prison without walls," complete with tennis courts and golf courses), and fines assessed against individuals and corporations totaled less than 10 percent of the amount gained from their illegal activity.[43] Two of the biggest "players" in the S & L scandal were sentenced to less than two years imprisonment for stealing $20 million dollars in one case, and $30 million in another.[44] In a bad-check scheme headed by E. F. Hutton stockbrokers that resulted in a multibillion dollar loss to 400 banks, the conspirators were only fined $2.75 million and ordered to pay restitution. Commenting on this case, Senator Paul Simon said that it gives people the impression that "If you rob a service station of $25 you're going to prison. But if you're with a big brokerage firm and you rob millions of dollars, nothing's going to happen to you."[45]

The Ford Motor Company was financially punished for its wanton disregard for human life in the civil courts, but such punishment was factored into their decision making anyway. However, they never counted on criminal prosecution, a rare threat for the corporate criminal. Despite all the deaths caused in fiery Pinto collisions, Ford was only criminally indicted for reckless homicide in Indiana, where three teenage girls had been burned alive in a Pinto. Although Ford was found not guilty (on a technicality), it did send a message to corporate America that there are those in the criminal justice system who feel that corporate murderers are as culpable as street murderers.[46]

An almost endless number of cases could be cited in which rich corporations received lenient penalties—usually in the form of fines that amount to little more than pocket change for them—on conviction for outrageous criminal acts. More interesting is why corporate crime, our largest and most costly form of crime, is treated so leniently. Radical theorists may invoke the Golden Rule ("Those with the gold make the rules") to explain the substantial differences in severity of punishment between street and corporate criminals. We do not have to be Marxists to acknowledge that great wealth confers a certain degree of immunity from prosecution and/or conviction, and even from the criminalization of acts typically committed by the wealthy. The degree to which this is true fluctuates with the ideological times. The liberal Carter administration made the prosecution of corporate crime an important item on its agenda, but the conservative Reagan administration wasted little time in reversing this trend when it took office. The power of corporate America can be gauged by the 1990 U.S. Justice Department's withdrawal of its support for proposed tougher sentences for corporate offenders in response to heavy lobbying by many prominent industries, the targets of the proposal.[47] This action adds credence to radical theorists' assertions that wealth and power go a long way to determine which behaviors are criminalized and which are not, for we seriously doubt that street criminals would get very far lobbying against proposals for stricter penalties for them.

Corporate Recidivism

Lenient penalties for corporate criminals cannot be explained by the argument that many corporate crimes are merely mistakes of judgment that are unlikely to reoccur once uncovered. Many corporations are serious recidivists, with General Electric being perhaps the worst offender. This company has been accused of well over 100 acts of "wrongdoing" since 1911, and in 1990 alone paid fines in sixteen cases of abuse and fraud in government contracting.[48] One study of 477 major U.S. corporations found that 60 percent of them were known to have violated the law, and that 13 percent of the violator companies accounted for 52 percent of all violations, with an average of 23.5 violations per company.[49] A study of brokerage firms found that many of the biggest names in the securities business, such as Prudential, Paine Webber, and Merrill Lynch, have had an average of two or more serious violations *per year* since 1981.[50] "Three-strikes-and-you're-out" laws evidently do not apply in the world of pinstripe suits.

The *Mens Rea* Dilemma

An ironic aspect of lenient punishment for corporate offenders is that a stigmatizing criminal label and the threat of imprisonment would probably have a significant deterrent effect on upper-middle-class corporate executives who have so much to lose. The biggest obstacle to criminalizing many acts of corporate wrongdoing is the difficulty in establishing **mens rea** (criminal intent). Our legal system requires that, for an act to be considered criminal, the law must establish intent—a person or a group of persons *specifically intending* to hurt another person or group of persons. This requirement prevents criminal prosecution in many cases of corporate wrongdoing. The common murderer usually *wants* to harm his or her victim, but the Ford executives who decided not to recall the Pinto did not *want* to harm anyone, and would have preferred that no one was. Further, the gas tank problem was not the *proximate* cause of anyone's death, the rear-end collisions were. This may all seem like hairsplitting; Pinto victims are just as dead regardless of whether their deaths were intended or simply a side effect of corporate greed and callousness, and Ford executives *were* fully aware that a certain number of people would die. Nevertheless, establishing *mens rea* is problematic, as is applying the concept of crime and responsibility to bloodless corporate bodies as opposed to specific persons.

Most corporate wrongdoing is considered violation of administrative law, and is thus resolved by sanctions such as fines, injunctions, and consent degrees, rather than violations of the criminal law, which alone can result in sanctions of imprisonment. If an administrative agency determines that a wrongdoing warrants criminal prosecution, it must relinquish the case to the criminal justice system, which requires a higher standard of proof than administrative law, achieves fewer convictions, and often imposes lower financial sanctions.[51] If a criminal prosecution is initiated, prosecutors with limited budgets must contend with the enormous legal resources enjoyed by corporations. In light of these practical problems, it is understandable why administrative agencies rely heavily on noncriminal procedures to combat corporate wrongdoing unless the circumstances strongly suggest that criminal prosecution is warranted.

Although administrative sanctions are more certain and financially more severe than criminal sanctions, they obviously have little deterrent effect. Many penalties are never paid, and many businesses openly admit that such penalties have little or no effect on their behavior.[52] The only way to deter corporate crime appears to be to change the criminal law to make prosecution easier (without violating the principle of *mens rea*). Some states dispense with strict interpretation of *mens rea* for murder charges other than first-degree murder, requiring that only "reckless indifference" or "reckless disregard" for human life be proven. Ford executives certainly could have been convicted on those grounds. We could also enact statutes requiring corporate executives at all levels to report products or actions that may cause death or injury to consumers or workers. Failure to do so would result in criminal prosecution of *individual executives*, not a bloodless corporation. The spectacle of company executives serving lengthy prison sentences alongside murderers and rapists in state prisons (not federal "country clubs") may shock corporate America into behaving more responsibly.[53]

The Causes of Corporate Crime

Contrary to those who believe that traditional criminological theories are silent on the subject of corporate crime, many of them have something to tell us. For obvious reasons, theories focusing on such factors as poverty and social disorganization have

nothing to offer us. Other theories, while developed in contexts of lower-class crime, are not limited to it, and some propositions from them may be better suited to explaining corporate crime than they are to explaining lower-class crime. After all, the only difference between the S & L crooks and Los Angeles rioters is the way they looted.

Given classical assumptions about human nature, the motivation for individuals to engage in corporate crime is easily appreciated. Opportunities abound in corporate America to gain wealth far beyond what individuals could earn legitimately, and they can do so with relatively little effort. The prevalence of corporate crime can also be appreciated given the weakness of formal and informal controls over business activities and the lenient penalties imposed. Combine the absence of meaningful controls with the seductive lure of big money, and corporate crime is more easily understood by the neoclassical criminologist than is street crime, with its more meager rewards and more certain and more severe penalties. We may expect business executives to have assimilated the egoism, acquisitiveness, and competitiveness fostered by capitalism more completely than most. This, combined with the power to avoid criminal labeling, renders corporate crime fully understandable to criminologists.

But general explanations such as these, which invoke assumptions about human nature or about the economic system, do not explain differences between companies and individuals who do and do not participate in illegal activities. All companies and their executives are exposed to the capitalist ethos and opportunities for illegal gains, but they respond to these pressures differently. We might say that corporate criminals are "high-class innovators," to borrow a phrase from strain theory. But what differentiates "innovators" from others?

Corporate Characteristics

Just as there are criminogenic neighborhoods, the literature on corporate recidivism suggests that there are criminogenic corporations with a "tradition" of wrongdoing. Newcomers entering such corporate environments are socialized into the prevailing "way of doing things." Just as slum children are alleged to adopt the criminal "definitions" of their peer groups, professional socialization into an organization rife with unethical and illegal practices will influence the newcomer's behavior in the same direction. This process can produce a sort of moral apathy in well-socialized executives striving to do their jobs in their own and their company's best interests.[54] If their consciences are pricked by what is happening, they have ready access to techniques of neutralization to quieten them and to make further wrongdoing that much easier.

Certain kinds of corporations are more prone to wrongdoing than others. A number of studies indicate that we can best understand corporate wrongdoing by exploring the variables of pressure, opportunity, and predisposition.[55] The *pressure* of a highly competitive and heterogeneous market environment, intense competition, and having to deal with a large number of suppliers, regulatory agencies, creditors, and consumer groups creates strong motives to cut many corners.[56] The *opportunity* for wrongdoing is created in large, rich companies expecting innovation and excellence from its executives, and which are faced with ambiguous and frequently changing regulatory laws.[57] *Predisposition* is created in companies operating in mature industries in which the prevalence of illegality is high, which have established relationships with regulatory agencies, and which have highly committed employees.[58]

Pressure, opportunity, and predisposition are independent but often interacting causal factors. Pressure leads to both intentional and unintentional illegality out of the need for corporate survival, and is a function of intense competition and scarce resources. These factors, particularly scarce resources, are more likely to result in violations of administrative law rather than violations of criminal law. Opportunity leads to intentional wrongdoing when individuals take advantage of situations that the business environment creates and facilitates. Such an "enabling" environment tends to exist when a corporation enjoys relatively light competition and plentiful resources. Finally, predisposition functions as both a facilitator and perpetuator of corporate wrongdoing. Mature corporations in certain industries, most notably the oil, automobile, pharmaceutical, and heavy equipment industries, tend to create an ethos in which the established routine is to reward innovations that stimulate business regardless of the methods involved.[59]

Individual Characteristics

Because most people exposed to the highly competitive and pressurized environment of U.S. business do not engage in criminal activity, it is necessary to look at individual characteristics also. Individual traits, such as low IQ, low self-control, and poor conditionability, obviously do not apply to people who have spent many years of disciplined effort to achieve high status positions. However, it appears that people who choose business careers tend (on average) to have lower ethical and moral standards than people who choose other legitimate careers. A number of studies have concluded that business students are, on average, less ethical than students in other majors,[60] and that entering MBA students make fewer decisions judged as ethical and moral than entering law students.[61] Yet there are many who elect not to engage in illegal activities, even when pressured by superiors to do so, and there are even whistleblowers who risk their careers by reporting such behavior to the appropriate authorities.

Efforts to differentiate between offenders and nonoffenders have focused largely on the variables of *locus of control, moral reasoning,* and *Machiavellianism.* Psychologists view people as either having an internal or external *locus of control.* People with an internal locus of control tend to believe that they can influence outcomes, and are relatively resistant to coercion and influence from others. People with an external locus of control put more emphasis on the environment, feeling that circumstances have more influence over situations than they themselves do. The literature indicates that those who engage in corporate crime tend to have an external locus of control, and that whistle blowers tend to have and internal locus of control.[62] An external locus of control renders a person susceptible to definitions favorable to corporate crime if those definitions are held by superiors.

Closely related to locus of control is moral reasoning. People operating at higher stages of cognitive moral development are more self-reliant and tend to behave according to their own beliefs about right and wrong. People at lower stages tend to emphasize conformity to group norms. Thus, the lower the stage of moral development, the more likely the person will engage in corporate wrongdoing.[63]

The final individual characteristic frequently looked at by corporate crime researchers is *Machiavellianism,* the manipulation of others for personal gain. People high on this trait are shallow individuals who exploit superiors and equals by de-

ceit and ingratiation, and subordinates by bullying. In the business world, as elsewhere, these people may be willing to use any means necessary to accomplish their goals, including criminal activity.[64]

Figure 17.1 presents a model summarizing corporate and individual traits that are assumed to lead to corporate crime and illegality. Although some criminologists may balk at separating corporate illegality from corporate crime, correctly arguing that these definitions are simply a function of differential ability to avoid criminal labeling, it does reflect the legal situation as it now exists. Illegality and crime may be separate phenomena in the sense that corporations that routinely engage in violations of administrative law may be reluctant to expose themselves to criminal sanctions by engaging in violations of criminal

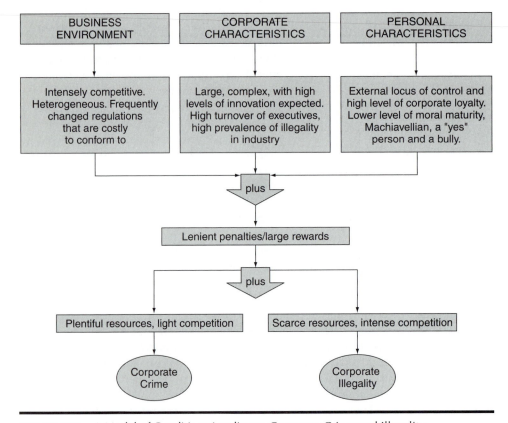

FIGURE 17.1 A Model of Conditions Leading to Corporate Crime and Illegality

law. Given the damage caused to society by corporate illegality, this may be a good argument for extending the reach of the criminal law into America's corporate boardrooms.

ORGANIZED CRIME

Corporate crime is "organized crime" in some senses, but its practitioners don't pack pistols, fit whistle-blowers with concrete footwear, or drive their competitors out of business by blowing up their offices. Human nature being what it is, these differences make "real" organized crime more interesting than corporate crime to students. Organized crime has existed in one form or another since our ancestors lived in caves. The Greek pirates who harried the Roman Empire and the English buccaneers who plundered the Spanish Main could be considered organized criminals who used violence for personal gain. Today's organized criminals are not so swashbuckling, but they still seem to fascinate us. The "Mafia mystique" has been capitalized on by numerous novels and movies, and many key figures in organized crime such as "Lucky" Luciano, Meyer Lansky, Al Capone, and Bugsy Siegel have practically become household names.

Organized Crime Defined

Despite the general public's fascination with organized crime, criminologists have had a difficult time deciding just what it is, where it came from, where it is going, what groups should be included as "organized," and just how organized it is. These are among the issues we will discuss in this section. One thing academics no longer debate, however, is the existence of organized crime; it exists and it is very big business. The President's Commission on Organized Crime (PCOC) estimated that its gross income was about $66 billion in 1986,

and that in the 1980s it employed at least 280,000 members and associates in the United States.[65]

As is the case with white-collar crime, criminologists have wrestled to arrive at a useful definition of organized crime. Organized crime is different from other forms of criminal enterprise, and we need to understand what these differences are. Some definitions are so broad as to encompass almost any kind of planned crime committed by more than one individual, while others are so narrow that they miss key characteristics of organized crime that should be included. An excellent succinct definition based on a fairly wide consensus of organized crime specialists, is that **organized crime** is "a continuing criminal enterprise that works rationally to profit from illicit activities that are often in great public demand. Its continuing existence is maintained through the use of force, threats, and/or corruption of public officials."[66] This section expands on this definition, drawing from findings of the PCOC and concentrating on *La Cosa Nostra* (literally, 'our thing') because more is known about this group than others and because it is the most famous of crime groups. It should not be inferred from this that *La Cosa Nostra* (LCN), also known as the Mafia, the Syndicate, or the Mob, and organized crime are synonymous. There are many other organized crime groups in the United States and around the world, some predating LCN.

Structure.   The first characteristic that differentiates organized crime from other kinds of crime is its formal structure. LCN groups are structured in hierarchical fashion reflecting various levels of power and specialization. There are alleged to be twenty-four families with a national ruling body known as the *Commission,* which was established by Salvatore "Lucky" Luciano in 1931.[67] The Commission, which serves primarily as a judicial body, consists of the bosses of the five New York families (the Genovese, Gambino, Lucchese, Bonanno, and Columbo/Profaci, families) and four bosses from other important families. Members know and respect the hierarchy of authority in their organization just as corporate executives know and respect ordered ranks of authority in their corporation. Although there are occasional family squabbles and coups that may remove individuals from the hierarchy, the structure remains intact. Figure 17.2 is a diagram of the formal structure of an LCN family.

At the top of the family structure is the boss (the *don* or *capo*) whose rule within it is absolute, although he may be overruled by the national commission. Beneath the boss is a counselor (*consigliere*) or advisor, and an underboss. The counselor is usually an old family member who is wise in the ways of crime, and the underboss is a sort of vice president being groomed for succession to the top position. The lieutenants or captains (*caporegimas*) supervise the day-to-day operation of the family and enjoy considerable power. The number of lieutenants depends on the size of the family. Below the lieutenants are the soldiers, who, although the lowest rank in the family, may each run their own crew of nonmember associates.

LCN members are not employees of the family in the traditional sense of the term. Membership entitles the member to run his own rackets using the family's connections and status. A certain percentage of a soldier's earnings is paid to his lieutenant, who also has his own enterprises from which he pays a percentage to the underboss, and so on up the line. This kind of pyramidal payment scheme works like a franchise operation, and has been referred to as "the McDonald's-ization of the Mafia."[68]

The LCN model just presented is known as the *corporate model* because of its similarity to corporate structure, i.e., a formal hierarchy in which the day-to-day activities of the organization are planned and coordinated at the top and carried out by subordinates. Although it is the model favored by law enforcement and the PCOC, some academics favor what is known as the *feudal model.* This model views the LCN as a loose collection of criminal groups held together by kinship and patronage. The semiautonomous operations of Mafia soldiers and lieutenants, and the provision of status and protection from the family in exchange for a cut of their earnings, provides evidence that LCN bosses are more like feudal lords than corporate CEOs. Perhaps it is best to view LCN as a highly structured feudal system.

Continuity. Organized crime is like a mature corporation (or a feudal system for that matter) in

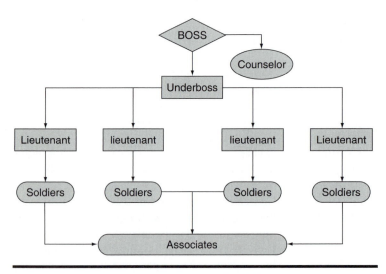

FIGURE 17.2   Hierarchical Structure of a Typical Organized Crime Family
Adapted from *President's Commission on Organized Crime,* 1986, p. 469.

that it continues to operate beyond the lifetime of its individual members. It does not disintegrate when key leaders are arrested, die, or are otherwise absent. The criminal group takes on a life of its own, and members subordinate their personal interests to those of the family. This makes organized crime quite different from gangs that spring up and die with their leaders.

Membership.   LCN is not an equal opportunity employer. Membership is restricted to males of Italian descent who have already proven their criminal expertise. New members must be sponsored by "made guys" (established members), who are held responsible for the behavior of the initiate during his probationary period. Applicants are usually known for their criminal activity and loyalty before applying, and only the most "promising" applicants are accepted. A lifetime commitment to the group is required from the newcomer, and in return he receives a guaranteed and rather lucrative criminal career as part of a "prestigious" organization. A criminal who is not of Italian descent, but who has qualities useful to the organization, may become an "associate" of LCN. The FBI estimates that for every formal member of LCN there are ten associates.[69]

Criminality.   Like any other kind of business, organized crime seeks to make a profit. Most of organized crime's income is derived from supplying the public with goods and services not generally available in the legitimate market, such as drugs, gambling, and prostitution. Much of organized crime's income is funneled into legitimate businesses after its "dirty" (illicit) money is "laundered." Thus, although organized crime is roughly structured and motivated similarly to mainstream business enterprises, it differs from them in the illicit nature of its product and its reason for being. Corporate criminals may cost the nation dearly (more than organized crime), but criminal activity is peripheral to their primary concern. We might say that corporate criminals make a crime out of business, and that organized criminals make a business out of crime.

A Brief History of Organized Crime in the United States

One of the unfortunate consequences of the media attention and sensationalizing of organized crime is that many Americans have come to view it as an alien conspiracy, primarily of Italian origin. The truth, however, is that organized crime groups existed long before there was any major Italian presence in the United States, and that most organized crime scholars believe that the phenomenon is a "normal" product of the competitive and freewheeling nature of U.S. society.[70] Scholars place a variety of dates on the beginnings of organized crime in the United States as we have defined it, but the two major candidates are the founding of the *Society of Saint Tammany* in the late eighteenth century, and *Prohibition* in the early twentieth century.[71]

Tammany Hall.   The Tammany Society began as a fraternal and patriotic society, but soon evolved into a corrupt political machine consisting mostly of ethnic Irishmen. Tammany, which became synonymous with the Democratic Party in New York City, ran the city well into the twentieth century from the "Hall" (Tammany Hall), making use of Irish street gangs to threaten and intimidate political rivals.[72] Prominent among these gangs were the *Whyos* and the *Five Points* gangs, which by all accounts were every bit as vicious as the modern *Bloods* and *Crips* gangs. In order for a new member to be accepted by the Whyos, which at its peak had over 500 members, he had to have killed at least once. The Whyos plied their trade among New York's citizenry by passing out price lists for the services they provided (ranging from $2 for punching to $100 for murder) as casually as pizza vendors.[73] The Five Points gang, headed by Paul Kelly, was a confederation of neighborhood gangs, and was said to have over 1,500 members at one time. Among the future luminaries of organized crime associated with Kelly's confederation were John Torrio, Al Capone, and Lucky Luciano.[74]

The Prohibition Period.   Organized crime existed on its earnings from gambling, prostitution, protection, extortion, and labor racketeering during the early part of the twentieth century. During this period, members of these criminal organizations were often employed by politicians, who used them as errand boys and enforcers, a relationship that was to reverse itself after 1920. In 1920, the United States Congress handed every petty gang in the United States an initiation to unlimited expansion with the ratification of the Eighteenth Amendment (the Volstead Act, or Prohibition), which prohibited the sale, manufacture, or importation of intoxicating liquors within the United States. Prohibition ushered in a vicious ten-year period of crime, violence, and political corruption as gangsters fought over the right to provide the drinking public with illicit alcohol. More than 1,000 gangsters were killed in the New York wars alone during the 1920s.[75]

Johnny Torrio, a product of New York's Five Points gang, became the leading figure in Chicago's gangland. A master strategist, he realized that violence was counterproductive, and was able to broker a truce among warring factions and organize them into a sort of loose confederation. These cooperative agreements did not always hold up, and Torrio himself was critically wounded by members of a rival Irish gang. After recovering from his wound, Torrio returned to New York in 1924, leaving his protégé, Al "Scarface" Capone, in charge of the Chicago operation.

The Capone era provided America with its stereotypical image of organized gangsters and gangsterism. Capone was a ruthless criminal and a flamboyant man whose generosity endeared him to many members of the media and to many of Chicago's poor people for whom he provided soup kitchens and shelter.[76] Only twenty-five years of age when he succeeded Torrio, he soon established a criminal empire that, at the height of Prohibition, consisted of over 700 gunmen.[77] The wealth Capone accumulated from his bootlegging and prostitution enterprises got him into the *Guiness Book of Records* as having the highest gross income ($105 million) of any private citizen in the United States in 1927.[78] But all good things come

to an end. The Depression cut into Capone's income, and the Supreme Court ruled that unlawful income, as well as lawful income, was subject to taxation. It was this law that spelled his doom. He was sentenced to eleven years imprisonment for tax evasion in 1931, and was released in 1939. Suffering from terminal syphilis, he retired to his estate in Florida, where he died in 1947 of pneumonia following a stroke at age forty-eight.

Post-Prohibition.   With the repeal of the Eighteenth Amendment in 1933, organized crime entered a new and quieter phase. The Castellammarese war between the Masseria and Maranzano gangs in New York ended with the deaths of both leaders in 1931, and with the subsequent emergence of the five New York LCN families active today. It also saw Luciano become the most important figure in LCN, enabling him to set up the organization's national commission and to claim the title of founding father of Italian-American organized crime.[79]

In 1936, Luciano was sentenced to prison on compulsory prostitution charges but was granted clemency in 1945 for assistance rendered to the United States government during the war. Luciano's control over the waterfront unions enabled him to prevent wartime shipping disruptions due to union unrest, and to place intelligence operatives on the waterfront to combat German infiltration. On his release from prison he was deported to Italy, where he died in 1962.

Reaffirming the Existence of Organized Crime

Interest in organized crime activities waned considerably after the war, and many law enforcement officials, including FBI director J. Edgar Hoover, refused to acknowledge its existence. (Tapping into veins of Italian resentment and civil rights reformism, Joe Columbo, former capo of the Columbo/Profaci Family, organized the Italian-American Civil Rights League around the issue of the nonexistence of the Mafia). Three events—the Kefauver Committee, the Appalachian "summit," and the McClellan Commission—reaffirmed the reality of its existence. In 1950, the (Senator Estes) *Kefauver Committee* on organized crime was formed to investigate the extent to which organized crime was involved in interstate commerce. The Kefauver Committee did little except perpetuate and publicize the notion of the Mafia as an alien conspiracy (committee hearings were extensively televised), and to embarrass President Harry Truman, who was a product of Kansas City's corrupt Pendergast machine, which had strong ties to the Kansas City LCN.[80]

The *Appalachian meeting,* held in Appalachia, New York, in 1957, provided strong evidence for the existence of a national and coordinated crime syndicate, and once again riveted national attention on it. Major LCN figures met on this occasion to confirm Vito Genovese as the *capo di tutti capi* ('boss of bosses') and to discuss other matters. The meeting was raided by police, and sixty-three people were arrested. No convictions came out of this raid, but it destroyed LCN's hope that it could stay out of the public spotlight. It finally confirmed the existence of organized crime, and law enforcement began to focus more seriously on combating it.[81]

The (Senator John L.) *McClellan Commission* was formed in 1956 to look into financial irregularities in the Teamster's Union, but the star witness was a drug trafficker and "made man" in the Genovese Family named Joe Valachi. While in prison on drug charges, another "made man" accused Valachi of being an informer, which probably meant to Valachi that he was marked for death. Rather than face this prospect, Valachi decided to testify as to what he knew about the Mafia before the McClellan Commission. Valachi revealed much about the operation of the "Mafia," including the fact that members of Italian organized crime no longer used that name, if they ever did. According to Valachi, the organization called itself "Cosa Nostra," a term unfamiliar to law enforcement officials up to then. Commission member Senator Robert Kennedy called Valachi's

testimony the "biggest intelligence breakthrough yet in combating organized crime."[82]

Law Enforcement's Response to Organized Crime

Valachi's testimony, along with a number of other events, led to the passage of federal legislation that enabled law enforcement to launch massive attacks on organized crime. Among the most important new tools forged for law enforcement were the *Organized Crime Control Act* (OCCA) and the *Bank Secrecy Act* (BSA), both passed in 1970. Included in the provisions of OCCA are witness immunity from prosecution, the witness protection program, and the Racketeer Influenced and Corrupt Organizations (RICO) statutes.

The *witness immunity* provision allows federal prosecutors to grant lower-level members of organized crime groups immunity from prosecution for their own crimes in exchange for testimony incriminating higher-level members. Witnesses who do not want to testify or be granted immunity are immunized anyway and then forced to testify under pain of contempt of court charges, which could result in indefinite imprisonment.[83]

Witnesses are still often reluctant to testify despite the grant of immunity because they realize that doing so places their lives in jeopardy. To counter this problem, federal authorities instituted the *witness protection program,* administered by the U.S. Marshals Service. The program provides for around-the-clock protection while witnesses are in "hostile territory" (such as in "safe houses" awaiting court appearances). After testifying, witnesses in the program are provided with new identification documents, employment, housing, and other assistance until they become reestablished. There were 12,500 persons (witnesses and their families) in the program in 1988 at an annual per-family cost ranging from $47,000 to $84,000.[84] An interesting sideline underscoring the difficulties in rehabilitating confirmed criminals is that, despite being given a new start in life, 21 percent of criminals entering the witness protection program are arrested under their new identities within two years of entry.[85]

The RICO statutes address ordinary crimes such as murder, robbery, extortion, fraud, and kidnaping, but they differ from traditional statutes relevant to these same crimes in that they specifically target the continuing racketeering activities of organized criminals. RICO statutes provide for more severe penalties for the same crimes committed under traditional criminal statutes, and also for the seizure of property and assets obtained from or involved in illegal activities. RICO even provides for the seizure of the assets of a legitimate business if the business was used for money-laundering.

The primary function of the BSA (supplemented by the *Money-Laundering Control Act* of 1986) is the prevention and detection of money-laundering. Money-laundering—making illegitimate money appear legitimate—is a vital component of organized crime's ability to carry on its activities. The vast amount of illicit money that flows through the hands of organized crime must be "laundered" into legitimate money so that income taxes can be paid on it (the lesson of Al Capone's conviction for income tax evasion was not lost on organized crime) and so that it can be openly used. Under this act, banks must file a report if funds over $10,000 in cash are either deposited or withdrawn, and a report must be filed with the U.S. Customs Service if more than $10,000 in cash enters or leaves the United States.

Armed with these new weapons, through the 1980s and into the 1990s the government successfully prosecuted hundreds of organized crime figures. Particularly important were the *Commission trials* (a reference to the LCN commission), which took place from 1983 through 1987. Over 5,000 indictments were handed down in 1985, and leaders of sixteen of the twenty-four LCN Families were indicted. Anthony Salerno, Anthony Corallo, and Carmine Persico, leaders of the Genovese, Lucchesi, and Columbo Families, respectively, were sentenced to one hundred years each on racketeering charges, and Philip Rastelli, leader of the Bananno Family, received twelve years.[86] The leader of the Gambino Family, Paul Castellano,

avoided prosecution by getting himself murdered. Castellano's successor (and murderer), John Gotti, was sentenced to life in prison in 1992 after being convicted of thirteen federal charges. Formerly known as "the Teflon don" because of his ability to avoid prosecution, Gotti was betrayed by his former underboss, Salvatore "The Bull" Gravano, who testified against him.

No one knows how much damage these convictions have done to the LCN. It may continue to operate for many years to come, but probably as a pale reflection of its former self. Skillful use of the provisions of the OCCA has seriously undermined the old code of *omerta* (silence), and many "made men" have turned informant since Joe Valachi. The generational gap pitting the discipline, loyalty, and honor of the old Mafiosi against the more Americanized attitudes of younger mobsters, who disdain such "old fashioned" values, has also contributed to the rot of the LCN from within.[87] Even if Italian organized crime erodes along with the values that helped to create and maintain it, there are many other organized groups to keep law enforcement very busy.

Outlaw Motorcycle Gangs

It has been estimated that some 900 motorcycle gangs exist in the United States, with four—the Hells Angels, the Outlaws, the Bandidos, and the Pagans—having evolved into a serious organized crime problem.[88] All clubs got their start after World War II, with the Hells Angels (who began as the "Pissed Off Bastards of Bloomington"), consisting mainly of war veterans, being the first. The organizational structure of these groups is similar to that of LCN, and typically consists of a president, vice president, secretary–treasurer, sergeant-at-arms, road captain, and enforcer. Each chapter or club belongs to a regional entity, and to a national organization headed by a "mother club," which is usually the founder club. Membership is open to all ethnic groups except African Americans. Prospective members must be sponsored, and be willing to demonstrate their criminality in front of "made" members. Women can join the gangs as associates, but their status is little more than sexual playthings. Wives or steady girlfriends of gang members are referred to as *Old Ladies,* and are the exclusive "property" of their men. Other women are referred to as *Mammas* or *sheep,* and are the sexual "property" of any gang member desiring to use them or to prostitute them to nonmembers.

All outlaw motorcycle gangs are involved in a variety of crimes, the manufacturing and distribution of drugs being their main source of income, with prostitution, pornography, and massage parlors being other sources. The Hells Angels and the Outlaws, who are often in bitter conflict with each other, are known to have ties to LCN and have performed contract killings for it.[89] Outlaw gangs are also investing heavily in legitimate businesses, mostly of a cash-intensive nature such as the vending, catering, and service industries, which facilitate money-laundering. Some Hells Angels have abandoned their outlaw image (bearded and long-haired men sporting tattoos, earrings, and gang "colors" are easily identified) and have taken to wearing suits and driving cars when conducting "business." The image polishing by the ex-"pissed off bastards" is reminiscent of the evolution of Italian organized crime from a bunch of rowdy rebels into a sophisticated criminal organization.[90]

The Japanese *Yakuza*

Japanese organized crime (JOC) groups are probably the oldest and largest in the world, with total membership about twenty times larger than LCN and estimated at 103,955 in 1980.[91] Although the term *Yakuza* (literally, 'a useless person') properly refers to the individual members of the criminal groups, it is commonly used as a synonym for JOC.[92] JOC evolved from masterless samurai warriors who contracted their services out for assassinations and other illegal purposes.[93] The defeat of Japan in WW II and the ensuing chaos provided the catalyst for the growth of JOC. This period saw many gang wars erupt over control of lucrative illicit markets. As in the United States, these gang wars led to the elimination of some gangs

and to the consolidation and strengthening of others. The *Yamaguchi-gumi* group, with an estimated membership of over 10,000, is the largest of these groups, followed by the *Sumiyoshi-rengo,* with about 6,000 members.[94]

There are a number of interesting similarities and differences between the Yakuza and LCN. The basic unit of the Yakuza is the *ikka* ('family'), which is headed by an *oyabun* ('leader') under whom are his *kobun* ('subordinates'). The *Sumiyoshi-rengo* group is structured along the lines of a confederation of gang bosses with an elected president, while the *Yamaguchi-gumi* has more of a pyramidal power structure, with the *oyabun* exercising absolute power. Membership in these groups is recruited heavily from the two outcast groups in Japanese society—the *burakumin* (outcasts because their ancestors were butchers, a trade that violated Buddhist religious proscriptions) and Japanese-born Koreans. Once admitted, a kobun must pledge absolute loyalty to his superiors, and, like his LCN counterpart, must generate his own income and contribute part of it to the *ikka.* Discipline is strict; any member who fails to complete some required task is expected to demonstrate his repentance by committing *yubitsume* (cutting off his little finger).[95]

Organized crime constitutes a much greater proportion of Japan's total crime than it does in the United States. In 1988, gang members accounted for 64 percent of all arrests for threat, 41 percent for blackmail, 25 percent for murder, 21 percent for assault, and 19 percent for robbery.[96] It is estimated that 30 percent of all inmates in Japanese prisons are Yakuza.[97]

Why is it, in a low-crime country like Japan, that the Yakuza are not subject to concentrated efforts to eliminate them? A major reason is the unique position of JOC groups in Japanese society. Their historical connection with the samurai, their espousal of traditional norms of duty, loyalty, and manliness, their support for nationalistic programs, and their "law enforcement" functions (neighborhoods in which the Yakuza do business are safe from common criminals) endow them with a certain level of respect and admiration among the Japanese. Furthermore, the Yakuza are not shadowy underworld figures; their affiliations are proudly displayed on insignia worn on their clothes and on their offices and buildings, and they publish their own newsletter. The headquarters of one crime group, complete with the gang emblem hanging proudly outside, is only three doors away from the local police station.[98]

The police tend to tolerate Yakuza activity in certain areas as long as it involves only the provision of some illicit goods and services demanded by the public, but they crack down hard when firearms and drugs are trafficked, or when innocent civilians are harmed. The United States is a major source of guns, drugs, and pornography for the Yakuza, and some Yakuza groups are involved with LCN. The Yakuza have also invested heavily in U.S. businesses in an attempt to hide their money from the Japanese tax collector.[99]

The Russian *Mafiya*

No discussion of organized crime is complete without mentioning the Russian *Mafiya,* a group of organized gangs that many experts consider to be the most serious organized crime threat in the world today.[100] There has been an explosion of crime in Russia since the breakup of the Soviet Union. Two factors—the loosening of rigid social controls and efforts to build a market economy on the ruins of the old system—are the main culprits. Even in the old Soviet Union there had been significant organized crime activity as the "shadow economy" exploited the shortage of all kinds of consumer goods created by the centrally planned economy.[101] The crime, bribery, political and police corruption in modern Russia make the Prohibition period in the United States look positively benign. A 1995 *CNN Presents* investigative report (*Wild, Wild East*) reported that over 5,000 organized crime groups exist in Russia, that 98 percent of street vendors pay protection money, that 50 percent of the capital raised by the new economy is controlled by Russian organized crime (ROC), and that 50 percent of Russians had either paid a bribe or knew someone who had.

Unfortunately, very little is known about ROC because its existence (like the existence of LCN in the United States) was denied by the Communists, and because only recently has it experienced prolific growth.[102] However, we know that ROC has existed since at least the seventeenth century, and that it became firmly entrenched in Russian society in the 1920s. The major group in ROC is known as the *vory v zakone* ('thieves-in-law'), which began as a large group of political prisoners imprisoned following the Bolshevik Revolution in 1917. The Soviet prison system used this group to maintain order over the general prison population in exchange for many favors. These "elite" prisoners developed their own structural hierarchy and strict code of conduct or "laws" (hence thieves-"in-law"). One of their strictest rules was that there is to be absolutely no cooperation with legitimate authority for any reason. This rule generated a major split in their ranks when a large number of them were recruited to fight the German invasion of the Soviet Union in 1941. Because they had violated the code of noncooperation, thieves who fought in the war were declared "scabs," and were met by animosity when they returned. This animosity soon escalated to the "scab wars" of the 1940s and 1950s, with the scabs getting secret assistance from the Soviet secret police.[103] Russian organized crime wars are still taking place among a wide variety of Russian and other ethnic group gangs.

Because of the ethnic diversity of ROC, it is loosely organized at present and may be undergoing the weeding-out and consolidation phases that the LCN underwent in the 1930s and the Yakuza underwent after WW II.[104] The threat is a dire one. A high-ranking official in the Russian Ministry of Interior stated that crime is the biggest factor threatening Russia's democratization, economic development, and public security.[105] It threatens democratization because if a democratic government cannot control it an authoritarian one will. It threatens economic development because foreign companies are reluctant to make the much needed investments in an economy rife with the murder and extortion of business leaders. It threatens public security because many police officers and KGB

personnel have left public service for the more lucrative opportunities available with organized
crime.[106]

Among the most structured crime groups in
Russia are the ethnic crime groups, particularly the
Chechens. One of the stated reasons for Russia's
1994 invasion of the semiautonomous region of
Chechnya was the perceived impact of Chechen
crime in Moscow, where there were an estimated
1,500 Chechen gangsters operating in 1991.[107] The
Chechens (consisting of only 700,000 people) have
proven their courage, organization, and ability to
acquire weapons in their fight against Russia.
Many of these weapons, including tanks and ar-
tillery, were acquired from Russian troops, from
generals selling whole arsenals to privates selling their rifles.[108] This easy access to powerful
weapons (including nuclear weapons) is the biggest
threat posed by ROC. In 1994 German police
recorded 267 ROC offers to supply nuclear materials to various terrorist organizations and "outlaw"
nations in 1994.[109] The specter of nuclear blackmail by fanatical groups or nations some time in
the future demonstrates that the nuclear threat from
Russia did not end with the end of the cold war.

Other Organized Crime Groups

There are numerous other domestic and foreign
organized crime groups in the world. Domestic
groups include the Mexican Mafia, the Aryan
Brotherhood, the Texas Syndicate, and the Black
Guerrilla Family, all of which began as prison
gangs, and all of which have extended their activities beyond prison walls. The Marielito gangs in
Florida formed in the 1980s when Castro emptied
many of his prisons and shipped the inmates to the
United States. The Russian "humanitarian" emi-
gration policy for "dissidents" during the 1970s
also provided a way for the Russians to rid themselves of many criminals who later formed the nucleus of Russian organized crime groups in the
United States.[110] The United States has been and
perhaps always will be a prime target for organized crime because of its lucrative markets for illicit goods. The Chinese Triads, the Columbian

Medellin and Cali cartels, and the Jamaican Possess groups have had a devastating impact on U.S.
society through their drug trafficking, and the next
substantial organized crime threat to the United
States is widely assumed to be coming from Eastern Europe, particularly from Russia.[111]

Explaining Organized Crime

An early attempt to explain organized crime emphasized that the United States is cursed by it because it has a tradition of criminal activity in high
places, and because it tends to criminalize goods
and services—gambling, illicit sex, alcohol, and
drugs—that a significant proportion of Americans
demand.[112] When such demands are not be met
legally, there are always those who are willing to
supply them illegally if the price is right. Recall
that Prohibition provided the catalyst for organized
crime in the 1920s, just as drug trafficking keeps it
going today, and that the Yakuza traces its modern existence to the prohibition against gambling
in Japan.[113]

Organized crime exists because of huge economic incentives to supply people with goods and
services legally denied them. This early theory of
organized crime relied on anomie/strain theory,
describing the gangster as "a man with a gun, acquiring by personal merit what was denied him by
complex orderings of stratified society," and saw
each successive wave of immigrants ascending a
"queer ladder of social mobility" in U.S. society.[114] Each ethnic group denied legitimate means
to success in mainstream America climbed its own
"queer ladder" until it gained acceptance and legitimate success.

The memoirs of a number of LCN figures,
however, do not support the notion that they turned
to crime because they were denied legitimate opportunities. Many of them had received good edu-
cations, came from involved and intact families,
and had many opportunities to enter legitimate careers.[115] Rather, these men saw organized crime as
a more lucrative and desirable career than any alternative, with many of them expressing the opinion that "working stiffs" are "suckers." However,

these memoirs were mostly written by high-ranking figures born into the mob or by "made men," so the lack of legitimate opportunities remains a possible factor explaining the participation of the more numerous mob associates. It is also true that the major source of recruitment for the Yakuza are social outcasts denied economic and social opportunities in the "straight" world.[116]

Differential association theory may provide an alternative explanation. Almost all mob members lived in neighborhoods where they were constantly surrounded by criminals and criminal values. They grew up hero-worshiping the neighborhood "made men," emulated their dress and mannerisms, and dreamed of becoming one of them. It was the mobster who had the beautiful women, the sleek cars, the fancy clothes, and the respect, not the "working stiff" who was always worrying about paying bills and getting laid off. Such neighborhoods proved to be fertile ground for the constant cultivation of new batches of criminals.

Yet most people in these neighborhoods saw the same things and did not become criminals, nor are there any outcast groups analogous to the *burakumin* in the United States today. Although there are criminogenic neighborhoods that will produce proportionately more criminals than other neighborhoods, there is no reason to assume that the rank-and-file LCN associate (or any other organized gang member) is any different in background and personal characteristics than the ordinary unaffiliated street criminal. The leadership of these groups may be intelligent and shrewd men who hatch complicated criminal plots, but their subordinates engage in mundane crimes like burglary and robbery to support themselves and their masters. Their strong desire to belong and to gain instant respect by displays of "manliness" and aggression, their fatalism, their sensation seeking, their lack of empathy, and their involvement in many high-risk/low-profit crimes mark them as very ordinary street criminals.[117]

SUMMARY

Although rarely thought of as such, white-collar crime is our costliest and most deadly form of crime. Criminological theories focusing on poverty and social disorganization led to the neglect of this kind of crime until Edwin Sutherland spotlighted it. We have divided white-collar crime into occupational and corporate crime. Occupational crime is crime committed against an employer or the general public in the course of an individual's employment. The annual loss from all employment-related crime is probably greater than for all street crimes combined.

Embezzlement, fraud, and forgery/counterfeiting are the only white-collar crimes reported in the UCR. Although comparatively rare, embezzlement is the most costly of occupational crimes. Examples of other occupational crime are frauds committed against individuals, insurance companies, and government agencies, and professional fraud committed by physicians and lawyers. Illegal medical activities are particularly costly and deadly.

Criminologists argue about whether or not they can explain occupational crime with the same set of theories used to explain street crime. Hirschi and Gottfredson provide data purporting to show that people who commit the UCR white-collar crimes are similar to those who commit street crimes. Others disputed these findings, but only showed that white-collar criminals were different in degree, not in kind. The study by Weisburd and his colleagues offered support for both positions for all white-collar crimes except those requiring high-status occupation for their performance. It was determined that white-collar criminals occupy a middle position between street criminals and "respectable" people in terms of criminal convictions, and that the age, sex, and race demographics are the same as those for street criminals, but not to the same degree. It may be possible, therefore, to explain white-collar crime with the same theories (e.g., anomie or differential association) used to explain street crime.

Corporate crime—criminal activity on behalf of the organization—is more costly and deadly than occupational crime, although it was not considered problematic in the early days of U.S. industrialization. Three examples of corporate crime were given: the electric equipment conspiracy, the Ford Pinto case, and the S & L scandal. These crimes involved the loss of billions of dollars, and, in the Pinto case, of hundreds of lives. Despite the great harm caused by corporate crime, very few corporate crooks are ever meaningfully punished. Corporate crime is typically punished by monetary fines, which amount to little more than pocket change for corporate entities.

The lenient penalties for corporate crime does not deter corporate criminals, as the literature on corporate recidivism attests. Corporate wrongdoing is typically investigated and punished by administrative agencies rather than by the criminal justice system, which alone can impose sentences of imprisonment. The primary reasons that the criminal justice system rarely gets involved with corporate crime is the difficulty of proving *mens rea* (intent), and the limited resources of the prosecutor's office relative to those enjoyed by corporate entities.

Corporate crime and illegality were explained by a variety of factors, including the juxtaposition of lucrative opportunities and lenient penalties. The variables of pressure, opportunity, and predisposition were invoked to explain corporate crime and illegality, with companies enjoying plentiful resources and light competition being more prone to crime, and companies with scarce resources and intense competition being more prone to corporate illegality. Personal characteristics associated with corporate criminality include an external locus of control, a low level of cognitive moral development, and a high level of Machiavellianism.

Our discussion of organized crime (OC) focused on La Cosa Nostra (LCN), which is a confederation of families that restrict membership to ethnic Italians. Modern U.S. OC grew out of the corrupt political machine and its supporting street gangs known as Tammany Hall, and received its biggest boost from Prohibition. Many of the gangsters who rose to national prominence during this period got their start in the variety of gangs that supported Tammany Hall. The repeal of Prohibition ushered in a quiet period in OC's history, particularly after the founding of the "commission"

by Lucky Luciano as a judicial body to settle interfamily disputes without resorting to war.

Things became so quiet that people denied that LCN existed. Three events—the Kefauver Committee, the Appalachian meeting, and the McClellan Commission—put an end to denials and helped to launch major assaults on LCN. These assaults were made possible by the passage of the Organized Crime Control Act (OCCA) and the Bank Secrecy Act. Included in the OCCA were the RICO statutes and provisions for witness immunity and protection programs. Although the prosecution of major LCN figures has met with considerable success, LCN continues to exist.

Among our nation's many outlaw motorcycle gangs, four—Hells Angels, Outlaws, Banditos, and Pagans—have evolved into organized crime groups. All gangs began after WW II, have many characteristics (structure, membership criteria, etc.) in common with LCN, and appear to be evolving similarly in that they are shedding some their rowdy ways and becoming "respectable" by investing heavily in legitimate businesses.

The Japanese Yakuza are probably the oldest and biggest organized crime group in the world. Having evolved from masterless samurai warriors, it received a major boost by the chaos existing in Japan after its defeat in WW II. The Yakuza has many characteristics in common with LCN, but its differences are more interesting. It is responsible for a much larger proportion of Japanese crime than LCN is responsible for in the United States, yet it operates openly and proudly, even publishing its own newsletter. The police do not crack down on the Yakuza unless innocent people are harmed, or if drugs and guns are being trafficked.

The Russian "Mafia" is considered by many to be the biggest OC threat to the world today. The widespread chaos and corruption following the breakup of the U.S.S.R. allowed Russian OC to come out of the closet and proliferate. Not only is Russian OC preventing the democratization and economic stability of Russia, it is spreading its influence to many Western nations and is involved in the acquisition and sale of nuclear materials.

Organized crime flourishes wherever and whenever goods and services demanded by a significant percentage of the population are unavailable through legitimate channels. The U.S., Japanese, and Russian examples indicate that OC proliferates in times of social chaos, in a process in which some gangs are weeded out and others consolidate their power. Of special interest is the overrepresentation of minorities in OC (the Italians in the United States, the Koreans in Japan, and the Chechens in Russia), providing support for Daniel Bell's "Queer ladder of social mobility" thesis.

There is also some support for differential association theory provided by Mafia figures in their memoirs relating how their early environments were permeated with criminal attitudes and values. However, most people in those same environments did not become criminals, organized or otherwise. As suggested by their attitudes and behavior, most of the rank-and-file members of OC are no different from ordinary "unaffiliated" street criminals.

EXERCISES

1. We have learned that when people are asked questions about their fears of crime they almost always report a fear of being victimized by common street crimes. We have also learned that people are more likely to be victimized by white-collar crime than by street crimes. Why do you think most people fear street crime more than white-collar crime? Do they view corporate crime as being less serious than street crime? Ask a number of your friends the same questions.

2. Do you think there is really any moral difference between (1) setting off a bomb outside a building for some political reason knowing that a certain number of people would be killed, and (2) marketing 11 million defective automobiles knowing that a certain proportion of them will explode into flames when rear-ended and burn the occupants alive?

3. Do you think that white-collar crime (occupational and corporate) can be explained by the same principles as street crime? Read one or two of the relevant cited articles for guidance.

4. What do you think the relationship is (if any) between social morality and the *prevalence* of organized crime?

5. Some observers believe that law enforcement's response to organized crime in the United States (e.g., the RICO statute) goes too far, and threatens everyone's civil liberties. Do you agree?

ENDNOTES

1. Schmalleger 1996:16–18.
2. Coleman 1985:7.
3. Hirschi & Gottfredson 1987:950.
4. Sutherland 1940:9.
5. Weisburd et al. 1991:178.
6. Edelhertz, as cited in Weisburd et al. 1991:7.
7. Albanese & Pursley 1993:42.
8. Coleman 1985:78; McCaghy & Capron 1994:263.
9. McCaghy & Capron 1994:269.
10. McCaghy & Capron 1994:268.
11. Federal Bureau of Investigation 1997:231.
12. Federal Bureau of Investigation 1997:231.
13. Federal Bureau of Investigation 1997:231.
14. Witkin et al. 1992.
15. Rosoff et al. 1998:410.
16. Coleman 1985:113.
17. Braithwaite 1993.
18. Hirschi and Gottfredson 1987.
19. Hirschi and Gottfredson 1987:961.
20. Hirschi & Gottfredson 1987:967.
21. Steffensmeier 1989.
22. Weisburd et al. 1991.

23. Weisburd et al. 1991:50.
24. Weisburd et al. 1991:67.
25. Weisburd et al. 1991:187.
26. Weisburd et al. 1991:192.
27. Weisburd et al. 1991:189.
28. Agnew 1992:50.
29. Abadinsky 1991:52–68.
30. Smith 1953:137.
31. Rosoff et al. 1998.
32. Geis 1967:143.
33. Rosoff et al. 1998:50.
34. Geis & Meier 1986:439.
35. Calavita & Pontell 1994:460.
36. Schmalleger 1996:327.
37. Ross 1988:1.
38. Calavita & Pontell 1994:462.
39. Calavita & Pontell 1994:1969.
40. Cullen et al. 1987:161.
41. Cullen et al. 1987:162.
42. Mokiber 1988:377.
43. Browning & Gerassi 1980:410.
44. Rieman 1995:131.
45. Cited in Cullen et al. 1987:341.
46. Cullen et al. 1987:294.
47. Hagan 1994:397.
48. Byrnes 1994:32.
49. Clinard & Yeager 1980:116.
50. Wells 1995:1E.
51. Baucus & Dworkin 1991; Snider 1990.
52. Mokhiber 1988:29.
53. Mokhiber 1988:39.
54. Coleman 1985:215; Rosoff et al. 1998:400.
55. Baucus 1994; Baucus & Dworkin 1991; Baucus & Near 1991.
56. Baucus 1994:704.
57. Baucus 1994:707.
58. Baucus 1994:711.
59. Daboub et al. 1995:152.
60. Useem 1989; Zinkham et al. 1989.
61. McCabe et al. 1991.
62. Dozier & Miceli 1985; Trevino & Youngblood 1990.
63. Trevino & Youngblood 1990; Weber 1990.
64. Baucus 1994.
65. President's Commission on Organized Crime 1986:423.
66. Albanese & Pursley 1993:58.
67. President's Commission on Organized Crime 1986:37.
68. Abadinsky 1987:43.
69. President's Commission on Organized Crime 1986:41.
70. Bynum 1987:3.
71. Lupsha 1986:32.
72. Abadinsky 1988:95.
73. Browning & Gerassi 1980:289.
74. Lupsha 1986:43.
75. Peterson 1983.
76. Browning & Gerassi 1980:331.
77. Abadinsky 1987:44.
78. Abadinsky 1988:144.
79. Lupsha 1987:32.
80. Abadinsky 1988:312–313.
81. President's Commission on Organized Crime 1986:22.
82. In Wilson 1984:566.
83. Albanese & Pursley 1993:75.
84. Rush 1991:323.
85. Albanese & Pursley 1993:75.
86. Albanes & Pursley 1993:63.
87. Firestone 1993:213.
88. PCOC 1986:59–62.
89. PCOC 1986:64.
90. PCOC 1986:65.
91. Iwai 1986:208.
92. Huang & Vaughn 1992:19.
93. Hoshino 1988.
94. Iwai 1986:211.
95. Huang & Vaughn 1992:34.
96. Huang & Vaughn 1992:28.
97. Johnson 1990.
98. Bornoff 1991:334.
99. PCOC 1986:102.
100. Carter 1994; Serio 1993a.
101. Serio 1993a:11.
102. Volobueve 1990:75.
103. Mogek 1996.
104. Carter 1994:249.
105. Carter 1994:255.
106. Carter 1994:255.
107. Serio 1992:6.
108. Serio 1993b.
109. CNN Presents 1995.
110. PCOC 1986:112–122.
111. Carter 1994.
112. Bell 1962:128.
113. Iwai 1986:208.
114. Bell 1962:129.
115. Firestone 1993.
116. Huang & Vaughn 1992:23.
117. Gottfredson & Hirschi 1990:213; Huang & Vaughn 1992:33; Iwai 1986:224.

CHAPTER 18

Sex Offenses and Offenders

Someone once wrote that sex is the most fun you can have without laughing, but from the large number of criminal offenses associated with sexual behavior it seems that it is anything but a laughing matter. Our culture is more than a bit schizoid about sex and sexuality. On the one hand we sexualize and eroticize almost everything, and on the other we suspend six-year-old boys from school for kissing female classmates on the cheek. What do you consider appropriate sexual behavior? Have you ever had premarital or extramarital sex, or engaged in anal or oral sex with a member of either sex? If so, you have committed a crime in many states. At what age do you think it appropriate for children to give their consent to an adult for sexual activity with them? Colonial Americans used to consider ten appropriate; adults having sex with children that young today would find themselves in big trouble. In this chapter you will learn about what scientists, laypersons, and the legal system know (or think they know) about sex offenders and their offenses.

This chapter deals with a variety of sex offenses ranging from forcible rape to exhibitionism. No other category of offenses covers such a wide range of behavior, and few others generate as much discussion. You should realize that all sexual crimes are considered deviant acts, but not all sexually deviant acts are considered crimes. The American Psychiatric Association's (APA) *Diagnostic and Statistical Manual* lists a number of sexual behaviors considered deviant that are called *paraphilias* (literally, 'other loves'), only some of which are illegal. A paraphilia is defined by the APA as "recurrent, intense sexually arousing fantasies, sexual urges involving (1) nonhuman objects, (2) the suffering or humiliation of oneself or one's partner, or (3) children or other nonconsenting partners.[1] Paraphilias such as urophila (urinating on someone or being urinated on) or klismophilia (giving or receiving enemas) are not crimes if participated in with a willing partner, but acts such as voyeurism (peeping) and exhibitionism (exposing one's genitals) are. We will concentrate only on sexually deviant acts that have been criminalized, particularly rape. We examine the characteristics of both perpetrators and victims of rape, and the major theoretical explanations for its occurrence. Our discussion of rape is followed by a discussion of child molesting in which the same theoretical issues will be explored. We conclude the chapter with a short discussion of the clinical treatment of sex offenders.

SEX AND U.S. SOCIETY

It has been claimed that U.S. laws pertaining to sex have few parallels in the modern world, and that "Western European nations have generally abandoned similar legislation, in some cases as long as a century ago."[2] For example, if you live in one of the states that has antisodomy laws you could be imprisoned for engaging in consensual oral and/or anal sex with a member of either sex. Most cases in which sodomy is charged involve male homosexuals caught engaging in sex in public places, but oral and anal intercourse engaged in by consenting spouses in the privacy of their own homes have been prosecuted in the contemporary United States.[3]

Sexual offenses encompass such a wide range of behaviors that the wisdom of placing them all in a single category is questionable. The exhibitionist is as different from the rapist as the check forger is from the armed robber. No common denominator distinguishes all sex offenders from one another, or indeed from the "normal" person. A sex offender can be everything from a sexual sadist who uses his penis to defile and degrade his victim, to the gentle and unassuming minister who "playfully" touches a child where he shouldn't. A sex offender may also be someone who succumbs to temptation once in his life, or he can be someone whose whole life has been consumed by compulsively looking for opportunities to sexually offend (we use the masculine pronoun because, although we occasionally find female sex offenders, they are extremely rare). Sex offending is thus a much wider category than any other category of offending. It encompasses behaviors defined as criminal or noncriminal according to such factors as the nature of the relationship between the parties involved (kin versus nonkin), age differentials, gender (same versus opposite), the degree of consent of the partner, the setting in which the act takes place (public versus private), and the type of act performed.

The Public Image of the Sex Offender

Americans generally have extremely negative and punitive attitudes toward sex offenders. We are convinced that sex offenders are either insane, mentally retarded, brutal, depraved, immoral, or all the above.[4] Public animus is reflected in a number of criminal statutes aimed specifically at sex offenders, such as sexual psychopath laws, Washington State's Violent Predator Act (VPA), and public notification/registration laws enacted by a number of states. Although sexual psychopath laws are no longer operative, laws such as the VPA, which allows for the indefinite civil commitment of sex offenders *after* they have completed criminal sentences, perform much the same function.[5] In 1997 the United States Supreme Court (*Kansas versus Henrick,* 1997) upheld an "indefinite commitment" case from the state of Kansas, which will probably serve as a green light for more states to pass such laws. Public notification and/or registration laws exist in at least thirty-eight states. These laws require police, prosecution, media, victim, and neighborhood notification that a sex offender is to reside in the area, and registration means that the offender must register as a sex offender with local law enforcement agencies.[6] No other class of offenders are so deprived of their rights after having completed their prison sentences.

RAPE AND RAPISTS

Definition and Incidence

Forcible rape is defined in the Uniform Crime Reports (UCR) as, "the carnal knowledge of a female forcibly and against her will."[7] This definition excludes statutory rape (consensual sex with an underage female) and the rape of males, although almost all states include male rape in their rape figures. A sexual assault may also be defined as rape in some jurisdictions if nonvaginal (oral or anal) penetration was accomplished or if vaginal penetration was accomplished with objects other than the penis, such as with fingers, tongue, or inanimate object. According to the 1997 UCR, there were 94,769 reported rapes in 1996 (a rate of 71 per 100,000 females), which is 1 percent lower than the 1995 rate. The clearance rate for forcible rape in 1996 was 52 percent.

As we saw in Chapter 2, precise crime rates are impossible to obtain, and precise rape figures have been considered the most difficult to obtain. We also saw that victim survey data are often used to help researchers uncover hidden crimes. In 1993, the Bureau of Justice Statistics (BJS) published a twentieth anniversary issue of the National Crime Victimization Study (NCVS).[8] The most surprising finding in comparing UCR and NCVS data was that the discrepancy between the figures for rape contained in the two sources was less than for any other crime, with a NCVS/UCR ratio of 1.75:1.

Some Facts about Rape

Major findings from twenty years of NCVS surveys on rape include the following facts:

- About half of all rapes are committed by someone known to the victim.
- The offender was armed in about 20 percent of the cases. Stranger rapists were more likely to be armed with a weapon (29%) than were rapists known to the victim.
- Among the victims who fought their attackers or yelled and screamed, more reported that it helped the situation rather than made it worse.
- Slightly more than half of the victims report the assault to the police. Victims are more likely to report the incident if the perpetrator was armed or if they sustained physical injuries. The relationship the victim had with the offender (stranger versus nonstranger) did not influence the decision to report the crime to the police.

Rape Internationally

Although rape occurs everywhere, rape rates vary considerably from country to country. For instance, the *reported* rape rate in the United States is typically four times higher than that of Germany, thirteen times higher than Britain, and twenty times higher than Japan.[9] We emphasize *reported* because determining "true" rape rates is extremely difficult, and comparing international rape rates is more difficult yet. Some countries include statutory rape in their rape reports, others do not, and some do not differentiate between rape and other sexual offenses.[10] We also have to be sensitive to the degree of stigma attached to rape victims in different cultures. To the extent that rape victims are considered "spoiled goods," or to have in some way contributed to their victimization, they are not likely to report the incident to the police. To gain some inkling of the role of culture in the propensity to report rape, consider that Egypt, a nation of about 54 million people, reported just three rapes to INTERPOL in 1992, while France, with approximately the same population, reported 4,582.[11]

Characteristics of Rapists

What kind of men rape, and why do they do it? Answering this question is difficult because studies designed to do so have typically been limited to the small proportion of rapists who have been caught and convicted. Given this, it should be kept in mind as we describe the characteristics of rapists that we are actually describing the characteristics of rapists who have been reported, arrested, tried, and convicted.

From a variety of studies it has been found that about 75 percent of rapists are under thirty, about 80 percent are either from the ranks of the unemployed or the blue-collar working class, and only about 20 percent have a high school education or better.[12] The UCR[13] reports that about 56.2 percent of arrested rapists were white and 41.4 percent African American, with the remainder classified as "other." Most males arrested and convicted of forcible rape (about 80 percent) have previous criminal convictions, a small number have prior rape convictions, and about one third have prior convictions for other violent crimes.[14]

Highlights from a variety of studies include the following facts about rapists: Compared with other men, they are more likely to condone all kinds of violence against women, to be hostile against women, to hold traditional sex-role attitudes, to be more sexually experienced, to be aroused by visual and audio depictions of rape, to be more irresponsible, to lack social conscience, and to have a history of substance abuse.[15]

There are significant demographic differences between stranger and date rapists. One study found that stranger rapists had significantly more serious criminal histories, were significantly younger, of lower class, more likely to be drug and/or alcohol addicted, and to cause physical harm to their victims.[16] As has been found in many other studies, in most instances of date rape force is used only after a variety of nonviolent tactics (getting the victim drunk or high, verbal pressures, false pledges of love, threatening to terminate the relationship, and so on) have been tried.[17]

Groth's Typology of Rapists

Several typologies of rapists have been developed, with the typology developed by Nicholas Groth[18] being the most familiar. Groth assumes that rape is a "pseudosexual" act in which the primary motivation is the assertion of the rapist's power. Because he views rape as an aggressive act symptomatic of psychological dysfunction, Groth labels his three major categories of rape—*anger, power,* and *sadistic rape*—depending on the rapist's primary motivation. It is important to note that the typology was formulated and the motivations inferred by noting the characteristics of the assault rather than the *known* motives of the assailant.

The *anger rapist* is thought to be mad at the world in general and at women in particular. He uses a great deal more force than is necessary to make his victim comply, and then forces her into a variety of acts designed as much to degrade and humiliate his victim as to satisfy himself. The anger rapist is satisfied to the degree that he can degrade and humiliate his victim, and is viewed as a man who is frustrated with his lot in life and trying to get back at it through the brutalization of women. Groth estimates that 40 percent of the rapists treated by his agency—the Connecticut Sex Offender Program (CSOP)—are anger rapists.[19]

Power rapists are interested more in establishing complete dominance and control over their victims rather than humiliating and degrading them, although they will use considerable force if their victim fails to comply with their demands. Power rapists may kidnap and hold their victims captive so as to further assert their authority, mastery, and dominance. The power rapist is satisfied to the degree to which he can establish the complete submission of his victim. He is seen as a man who has a poor self-image and feels a need to prove his masculinity. Groth indicates that the power rapist is the most common type (55%) treated at CSOP.[20]

The *sadistic rapist* achieves sexual arousal by torturing and otherwise mistreating his victims. He is a combination of the anger and power rapist except that his goal is to physically hurt and injure his victim rather than just humiliate her. Many sadistic rapists choose women who symbolize something they consider to be "bad," such as prostitutes, and use rape to punish them. The sadistic rapist is about one step away from becoming a serial killer, and is the most dangerous of the three types of rapists. Thankfully, only about 5 percent of convicted rapists are of this type.[21]

Characteristics of Victims

Are there any identifiable characteristics of women that put them at greater risk of becoming victims of rape? A number of large surveys of high school and college students have shown that a majority of males and a significant minority of females believe that it is justifiable for a man to use some degree of force to obtain sex if the victim had somehow "led him on."[22] This would appear to indicate that some people may believe that there could be an act labeled "justifiable rape" in the same sense that there is justifiable homicide. These same surveys also indicate that many people continue to believe that rape victims are often at least partially responsible for their rape because of such factors as dress and lifestyle, and because of the belief that "nice girls don't get raped."[23] By including this section on victim characteristics by no means indicates that we endorse these beliefs. What these data show is that as a nation we are still desperately in need of education about the nature of rape.

Age and SES.   Although infants and old women have been victimized by rape, rape victims are most likely to be young women. The Bureau of Justice Statistics (BJS) indicates that females aged between 16 and 19 are at the highest risk for rape (a rate of 5.1 per 100,000), with women over 65 having the lowest risk (a rate of 0.1). The poorest of women (annual income less than $7,500) are almost eight times as likely to be raped than women from households with an annual income greater than $75,000, with rates of 6.7 and 0.9, respectively.[24] Most victims of sexual assault (64.2%) knew their assailants, but a "completed rape" is most likely to have been committed by a stranger (77.2%).[25] This does not necessarily mean that 77 percent of all completed rapes are committed by strangers. Women raped by husbands, other relatives, and boyfriends are probably less likely to report their victimization either to the police or to survey-takers.

Race.   Although white women constitute most of the rape victims, the white rate of 1.9 is less than the Hispanic (2.5) or African American (2.7) rates. Most rapes are *intra*racial, but some researchers have suggested that, because of the frequency with which African Americans select white victims (about 55 percent of the time), it could be considered an *inter*racial crime.[26] Some theorists attempt to explain this by indicating that African Americans who rape whites gain status and power among their friends, and that they get more of a thrill out of raping a white woman because it violates a powerful taboo.[27] Others dispute this, saying that, once the relative size of the African-American and white populations is considered, there are no grounds for considering the rape of whites by African Americans anything other than a random process. Potential white victims far outnumber potential African American victims, and we should therefore mathematically "expect" more white victims to be sexually assaulted by perpetrators of any race.[28]

Lifestyle.   There are behavior patterns or lifestyle choices that put women more at risk for being sexually victimized. It has long been known that many cases of reported rape occur at times when both the offender and the victim had been drinking.[29] A recent theory of rape victimization asserts that rape victims are women who lack "suitable guardians" (college students away from home or single women living alone) who go out drinking more frequently and drink more heavily than other women. The authors of this study emphasize that it should not be taken as an attempt to blame women for their victimization or to remove it from the assailants. They indicate that their study supports the feminist notion that women are less free in their movements in society, and that the solution to rape is not to keep women away from bars but rather to change U.S. society.[30]

Theories of Rape

Rape is a violent crime that has devastating consequences for many of its victims. In addition to any physical injuries and financial costs victims may suffer, they often also suffer from a loss of self-esteem, and from depression, anger, and guilt ("Did I contribute to it?" "Could I have done more to prevent it?"). Because of rape's terrifying nature, it is imperative that scientists come to understand it more thoroughly so that we can deal more effectively with it. Unfortunately, theories of rape have been colored by ideological issues to a greater extent than theories about crime in general. The three primary theories of rape are the *feminist, social learning,* and *evolutionary* theories. Each theory provides some answers to the puzzle of rape causation, and none should be uncritically embraced or summarily dismissed. As always, you should realize that there is no single feminist, social learning, or evolutionary theory, and that our presentation represents what we believe to be the most accepted versions of these theories. A fourth theory has recently been proposed that integrates the existing theories into a *biosocial* theory.[31] We begin with a discussion of feminist theory.

The Feminist Theory of Rape.   The fundamental assumption of the feminist theory of rape is that it is motivated by power, not sexual desire. It is viewed as a crime of violence and degradation designed to intimidate and keep women "in their place."[32] According to most feminist theorists, to understand their view of rape we have to understand three things about gender relations in the United States:

1. There are large social, legal, and economic power differentials between men and women.
2. These power differentials affect all social interactions between men and women, as well as the actions of individual men and women.
3. Those who enjoy the advantages of these power differentials (men) use any and all means to control those who do not (women). Men use a variety of control tactics, such as coercion, overt force, and ideology supportive of male dominance touted by the media and the church, without necessarily being consciously aware of the "true" intent of these tactics.

Feminist theories of rape were developed, in part, in reaction to the *victim-precipitated* perspective. This perspective views rape as the culmination of a series of events in which the behavior of the victim is interpreted by the offender as inviting sexual activity, or at least as indicating that she will eventually agree to it if he continues to pressure her.[33] Although this perspective was interpreted by many as blaming the victim for her own victimization, in actuality it saw the victim as inadvertently *contributing* to, not *causing,* the outcome by her passive behavior or by her initial assent to kissing and/or necking, interpreted by her assailant as the victim "wanting it." Nevertheless, feminists were outraged by this deemphasis on the assailant's culpability, and by dressing prevailing cultural stereotypes of rape and rape victims ("She asked for it," "Good girls don't get raped") in scientific clothing.[34]

According to one of the earliest and most famous versions of feminist rape theory, males in our society are socialized to rape via the many gender-role messages society sends them asserting their authority and dominance over women.[35] Rape is the major weapon males have used to establish and maintain both the general social patriarchy and the dominance of individual men over individual women. Rape and the threat of rape force a woman to seek the protection of a man from the predations of other men, thus forcing her into permanent subjugation. The most extreme statement of this position is that rape "is nothing more or less than a conscious process of intimidation by which *all* men keep *all* women in a state of fear."[36] Although Brownmiller was aware that most men do not rape and that most women are not raped, to her the act is central to understanding the social, economic, and political relationships between the sexes. It is for this reason that many feminists view rape as a violent *political* act, not a sexual act.

Given this politicized view of rape, many feminist theorists are of the opinion that rape is not an act committed by a few psychologically unhealthy men. Rather, as the master symbol of women's oppression; it is an act that practically all men may commit and is indicative of a general hatred of women that characterizes the behavior of "normal" adult men.[37] To support this notion feminists point to the widespread use of rape by victorious armies during wartime, and to various "rape proclivity" studies that indicate that between 35 and 69 percent of surveyed males admit that they would commit rape given assurances of never being exposed and punished.[38] Additionally, no edition of the APA's *Diagnostic and Statistical Manual* has ever listed rape as a sexual deviation. In other words, the APA does not recognize any clear syndrome associated with rape that could be called "rapism," which essentially means that the APA does not consider rape to be clinically abnormal behavior.

Social Learning Theory of Rape.   The social learning theory of rape is similar to the feminist theory in many ways. According to both theories, rape is caused by differences in the way women and men are socialized about sexual matters. Men are socialized to aggressively pursue sexual opportunities while women are socialized to be passive and to delay sex until a male has committed to them. The implication is that if women were socialized like men they would be equally as likely to use sexually coercive tactics, and that if men were socialized like women they would be equally unlikely to use such tactics. The major difference between the two theories is that social learning theory places less emphasis on sexual politics and is generally agnostic about what the "ultimate" purpose of rape is (i.e., to "keep women in their place"). Social learning theorists are also unlikely to view rapists as "normal" men, as Groth's (a social learning theorist) typology discussed earlier indicates.

Social learning theorists agree with feminists that the negative images of women as the sexual playthings of men promulgated in advertising, pornography, and in some modern teenage music, play a critical role in increasing the probability of rape. Studies have shown that sex offenders are about three times more likely to own pornography than "normal" male controls,[39] and that frequent consumers of it are less satisfied with "normal" sex and with their wives or lovers.[40] The cumulative effect of pairing women with eroticized violence and impersonal sex is that people become immune to the suffering inherent in the content of these images.[41] Men come to "objectify" women, to view women as "things," who are useful only insofar as they can be used to satisfy sexual needs.[42]

As you might expect, many convicted rapists hold traditional masculine values that glorify sexual prowess and divide women into "whores" and "Madonnas." Many also have difficulty understanding how their victims could accuse them of rape, feeling that once a woman's initial protests are overcome in the forceful "masculine" way of the movie tough guy, she should just melt into their arms. Another major difference between the feminist and social learning theories is that the feminist theory is primarily a structural theory while the social learning theory attempts to explain rape at the individual level. Feminists concentrate on the social structural factors that put *all* men at risk for committing rape; social learning theorists identify characteristics of *specific indi-*

viduals who have actually committed rape and explore their specific learning histories to identify social structural factors that may have contributed to their behavior.

Evolutionary Theory of Rape.   The evolutionary theory of rape holds the view that coercive sexuality is a male adaptation designed by natural selection. Evolutionary theorists point out that forced copulation is observed throughout much of the animal kingdom, especially among primate species.[43] According to evolutionary theory, the key to understanding rape is the wide disparity in parental investment between the sexes. Having no *necessary* parental investment other than insemination, males have evolved a propensity to seek copulations with multiple partners. The more successful a male is in this endeavor the greater his reproductive success, and the greater the representation in subsequent generations of genes for the traits that gave him an edge in the mating game. On the other hand, a female's parental investment is enormous. Her best reproductive strategy is to secure parental investment from a male to assist her in this task. Females cannot increase their reproductive success by promiscuous mating; indeed, such a strategy would be more likely to minimize reproductive success because few men would be expected to assist a female in rearing offspring whose paternity is in doubt. Because our ancient female ancestors faced this problem, women today are more inclined to resist casual copulations than are men. Thus, evolutionary theory posits two conflicting reproductive strategies arising from different levels of parental investment between males and females: the female strategy, which is careful and discriminating, and the male strategy, which is reckless and indiscriminate. Rape is sometimes the result of this discrepancy: "human rape is a maladaptive consequence of an adaptive general mating strategy of men."[44]

There are arguments among evolutionary theorists as to whether rape is an evolutionary adaptation per se, or a "side effect" of other psychophysiological adaptations that themselves aid reproductive success in males, such as aggressiveness and strength of sex drive. If rape is an adaptation rather than a side effect, it means that rape behavior was *specifically* designed by natural selection because of its effectiveness in promoting male reproductive success. As is the case with any other trait, the more coercive sexuality aided reproductive success in evolutionary environments the more strongly it was selected for. Many evolutionary theorists believe that the genes underlying rape behavior are virtually invariant in the male gene pool (every male has them). The conclusion that follows from this rape-as-an-adaptation hypothesis is that the male use of coercive tactics will not vary with genetic differences but with environmental differences.[45] Evolutionists thus agree with feminists on at least two points: (1) all men are potential rapists, and (2) men who employ coercive tactics do so because of environmental factors (if all men have genes conducive to rape, rape behavior must be accounted for by environmental factors because differences in any behavior can only be accounted for by factors that vary). The environmental factors stressed by evolutionary theorists are differences in male status and resources.

Because older males monopolize females by virtue of their control over resources valued by females, forced copulation throughout much of the animal kingdom is a strategy employed primarily by young, resource-poor males.[46] Human females have also been found crossculturally to prefer to mate with males of high status, or who at least have the potential of achieving it.[47] Because of this preference, many younger and low-status males may be denied the opportunity to mate legitimately with the most attractive females. Evolutionary theory therefore predicts that most rapists will be young males of low socioeconomic status, a prediction that is confirmed with data from around the world.[48] Although this fact is consistent with evolutionary theory, we have to remember that almost all studies of rapists are studies of *convicted* rapists.

Evaluation of the Theories

The main contribution of feminist theory is political and legal rather than scientific in that it has managed to make us more aware of the horrible nature of rape and to challenge stereotypes associated with rape and rape victims. Scientifically, feminist theory's major contribution has been to demonstrate the link between social structure and cultural values and the propensity to rape. They have demonstrated that cultures with high rape rates evidence a stronger acceptance of violence as a way of dealing with problems than do cultures with low rape rates.[49]

The major problematic area in both the feminist and social learning theories is the insistence that rape is a pseudosexual act. While it is obvious that rape is a violent act, it is just as obvious to critics of these theories that it is a sexual act also. Most clinicians engaged in the treatment of rapists insist that rape is primarily sexually motivated.[50] Very few laypersons (about 9% of males and 18% of females) believe that power and anger are the primary motives for rape,[51] as feminist and social learning theories argue. Some recent feminist writings recognize the sexual, as well as the violent, nature of rape, but insist that the "not-sex" argument was necessary initially to emphasize that women received no sexual pleasure from being raped.[52] Some theorists even consider the "not-sex" belief to be dangerous because it prevents us from learning more about the causes of rape, "at the expense of an increased number of rape victims."[53]

Evolutionary theory draws the most severe criticism, both because of its novelty (few social scientists are familiar with evolutionary biology), and because its claims give many the impression that it dehumanizes both women and men. Perhaps the major criticism of the theory is that, by claiming that rape is a natural or normal phenomenon (i.e., a product of natural selection), we dignify and justify it,[54] or imply that it is inevitable and even morally acceptable.[55] Such criticisms are further examples of the naturalistic fallacy, which you will recall is the confusion of "is" with "ought."[56] Nature simply *is,* what *ought* to be is a moral judgment. To say that forced copulation is normal mammalian behavior from a scientific viewpoint is no more a moral statement than it is to say that disease and death are natural and normal processes, however unwelcome they may be. Evolution is morally blind in that it "allows" for the selection of traits to the extent that they aid in reproductive success regardless of how morally reprehensible they may be. Evolutionary theorists are among the first to denounce rape as a crime in need of severe punishment precisely *because* they view it as a potential behavior of all men requiring strong environmental deterrents.

This perspective's emphasis on reproductive success has led to the criticism that it cannot explain instances in which there is no possibility of reproduction, such as rapes involving males, children, and postmenopausal women, as well as rapes that do not include vaginal intercourse.[57] This criticism is another misunderstanding of evolutionary logic. Organisms are not adapted by natural selection to directly seek ultimate goals (reproductive success), rather they are selected to seek proximate goals (in this case, sexual pleasure) that themselves serve ultimate goals without awareness.[58] Even the vast majority of voluntary copulations are not engaged in to increase "reproductive success"; instead, we often take pains to subvert this "goal" via the use of contraception. Nonreproductive sex can be likened to the diffusion of human nurturance to animals, which has no fitness-promoting advantage at all for the nurturer. Human nurturance is certainly an adaptation, but only insofar as that nurturance was directed at genetic kin. Both nonreproductive sex and animal nurturance provide us with pleasurable effects that are themselves wholly extraneous to the effects responsible for their evolutionary selection.[59]

The Synthesized (Biosocial) Theory of Rape

If rape behavior is an adaptation in its own right rather than a side effect of more general psychological adaptations, how useful can such knowledge be? To say that men rape because such behavior is part is part of our primate heritage may well be true, but it also begs an awful lot of questions. Most men never exercise this "rape potential," so we would like to know what the differences are between those who do and those who do not.

In other words, we need a theory of rape that goes beyond examining phenomena common to all men, whether it be a common phylogenetic heritage or a common patriarchal society. Such a theory is the synthesized *biosocial theory* of rape. This theory incorporates the most empirically supportable claims of feminist, social learning, and evolutionary theories, and adds neurohormonal variables.[60] The theory contains four propositions:

1. *The sex drive and the drive to possess and control motivates rape.*

The basis of the biosocial theory is that rape (as well as all other sexual behavior) is motivated by two drives that have evolved via natural selection: the sex drive and the drive to possess and control. All sexually producing organisms possess an unlearned sex drive, although the manner in which it is expressed is mostly learned. The contention that rape is sexually motivated rests on many kinds of evidence. The two most compelling are: (1) nonstranger rapists are overwhelmingly likely to use force only when other tactics (use of alcohol, pleading, false claims of love, etc.) have failed, making it very difficult to claim that rape is "nonsexual"; (2) forced copulation exists in many animal species, making it difficult to maintain claims that similar behavior among human males is motivated by hatred of females, that rape occurs because males and females are differentially socialized, or that males are attempting to protect their privileged political and economic positions when they rape.

Animals also possess a strong drive to possess and control, as evidenced by the catching, hoarding, burying, and protection of resources. The drive to possess and control is especially strong where sex partners are concerned. Among humans there is plentiful evidence that men and women are extremely possessive of one another. Jealousy and male sexual proprietariness is responsible for an overwhelming percentage of spousal and lover homicides in the United States, and probably elsewhere also.[61]

2. *The average sex drive of men is stronger than the average sex drive of women.*

Among the many facts called on to support this proposition are that males commit the vast majority of sexual crimes, consume the vast majority of pornography, constitute practically all the customers of both male and female prostitutes, masturbate more frequently, and have a much greater interest in casual sex with multiple partners. Not only are these and many other indices of strength of sex drive found across cultures but also among all other primate species. Opposing the male tendency to readily learn forceful copulatory tactics is the evolved female tendency to resist them. As pointed out earlier, the disparity in parental investment between the sexes has produced these opposing tendencies, and the tension generated by them sometimes results in rape.

3. *Although the motivation for rape is unlearned, the specific behavior surrounding it is learned.*

Biosocial theory contends that the behavior surrounding rape is learned via experiential (operant) learning, and contends that individuals with the strongest sex drives will learn rape behavior more readily. We know that behavior tends to be repeated when it is reinforced. Thus, men who have successfully used "pushy" (but not necessarily forceful) tactics to gain sexual favors in the past have learned that those tactics pay off. A male's initial "payoff" may be little more than a necking or petting session, but if he finds that each time he escalates his pushiness he succeeds in gaining greater sexual access, his behavior will be gradually shaped by reinforcement in ways that could lead to rape. While biosocial theory does not deny that other kinds of learning (e.g., attitudinal, modeling) can affect the probability of rape, the kind of learning it emphasizes is the most powerful method of learning known to psychology.[62]

4. *Because of neurohormonal factors, people differ in the strength of their sex drives and in their sensitivity to threats of punishment.*

The brains of all mammals are destined to remain female unless masculinized/defeminized by androgen hormones *in utero*. This "sexing" of the brain results not only in a stronger male sex drive, but also in variations in the strength of the sex drive among both males and females. The exposure of the brain to varying levels of androgens during fetal development leads to varying intensities of the sexual drive, and, because males receive more of these androgens, they are more likely than females to forcefully seek sexual copulation. Exposure to fetal androgens also results in lessened male sensitivity to environmental stimuli later in life. Compared to females, males in many species are less sensitive to noxious stimuli, leading them to somewhat discount the consequences of their behavior, both for themselves and for their victims. Unfortunately, individuals with the strongest sex drives are usually the same individuals who are the most insensitive to environmental stimuli because the same neurohormonal factors are responsible for both. These are the individuals who are most likely to rape and to be engaged in criminal activity in general.

Figure 18.1 presents a diagrammatic model of the synthesized biosocial model of rape. Note that the probability of learning deceptive/coercive tactics depends on the strength of a person's sex drive and his/her insensitivity to the suffering of others, which vary with neurohormonal differences. Unlike other theories of rape, the biosocial theory predicts that some females will also employ coercive and/or deceptive tactics to obtain copulations. According to Figure 18.1, about one third of all women and about three fourths of all men have at least a minimal probability of learning deceptive copulatory tactics, and that about 5 percent of females and about 45 percent of males have at least a minimal probability of learning forced copulatory tactics.

CHILD MOLESTERS

Child molesters are sexually mature persons who abuse children by enticing them to engage in behavior designed to sexually gratify the molester. Child molesting (also sometimes referred to as *pedophilia, child rape, child sexual abuse,* or legally as *lewd and lascivious conduct* or *gross sexual imposition*) may constitute the most common form of illegal activity against the person in the United

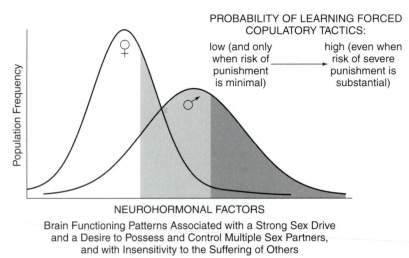

FIGURE 18.1   A diagrammatic model of the biosocial theory of sexual assault
(From Ellis, 1991, *Journal of Clinical and Consulting Psychology*)

States.[63] Several clarifying points should be made regarding this broad definition:

1. A child molester need not necessarily be an adult. Minors may also be accused of child molestation if they are five or more years older than their victims.

2. We said "persons" rather than "males" because, although rare, females can be child molesters, too. We discuss the issue of female perpetrators later in this chapter.

3. The definition of *child* is problematic because to some extent it is arbitrary. The "age of consent" (the age at which a person is considered mature enough to give informed consent to sexual activity) varies from state to state, from country to country, and from time to time. During much of the nineteenth century it was ten in the United States. It has risen steadily until today it ranges from fourteen (in Hawaii)

to eighteen in about twelve states, with sixteen being the most common threshold in the United States and Europe.[64]

4. It is not always the adult who initiates sexual contact with children. Although extremely rare, children sometimes entice adults to engage in sex with them in exchange for money and/or other favors. There has been documented evidence of child prostitution rings formed and operated by the children themselves.[65] It should be emphasized that whatever role children may play in such instances the adults involved are morally and legally responsible for what transpires.

Who Gets Victimized and How?

Any child is potentially at risk for child sexual abuse, although some children are more at-risk than others. It is more difficult to accurately gauge the prevalence of child molesting than it is to gauge the prevalence of rape, with rates depending on how broad or how narrowly molesting is defined. A "best guess" arrived at from a variety of sources is that the percentage of children in the United States experiencing sexual abuse sometime during their childhood is 25 percent for girls and 10 percent for boys.[66] Girls are more likely to be abused within the family by fathers, stepfathers, brothers, and other relatives, and boys are more likely to be victimized by acquaintances outside of the family and by strangers.[67] A Child Protection Services analysis of official reports covering the period from 1976 to 1982, inclusive, indicated that the average age of victims is 10.5 years, that about two thirds of sexually abused children are victimized "only" once, and that the molesting tends to be in the form of fondling and/or oral sex rather than vaginal or anal penetration.[67] The strongest single predictor of victimization for girls is having a stepfather. Stepfathers are about five times more likely to sexually abuse their daughters than are biological fathers.[69] The strongest predictor for boys is growing up in a father-absent home.[70]

There are many other factors predictive of child sexual abuse, and the more that are present the more likely abuse is to occur. Finkelhor[71] developed a *risk factor checklist* for the likelihood of girls' victimization that contains the following predictors: stepfather; ever lived without mother; not close to mother; mother never finished high school; sex punitive mother; no physical affection from [biological] father; family income under $10,000 [in 1980 dollars]; two friends or fewer in childhood. Finkelhor found that the probability of victimization was virtually zero among girls with none of the predictors in their background and rose steadily to 66 percent among girls with five.

Causes of Child Sexual Abuse

Many of the same factors alleged to cause rape are invoked as causes of child sexual abuse also. Cultural norms and stereotypes defining children as possessions, child pornography, and the toleration of child sex advocacy groups such as the Rene Guyon Society and the North American Man–Boy

Love Association (whose slogan is, "Sex by year eight or else it's too late") are blamed for child sexual abuse.[72] As we indicated when discussing rape causality, sociocultural factors by themselves are not sufficient to explain a phenomenon like child molesting. Such factors "set the stage," but they do not constitute the play. We would like to know why some people on the stage emerge as sexual predators and others do not. Rather than repeat many of the ideas contained in the various theories of rape, we will concentrate on distinguishing between child molesters and rapists and discussing the pedophile.

Characteristics of Offenders

Convicted child molesters are a more heterogeneous group of offenders than are rapists. About two thirds of convicted child molesters are from unskilled and semiskilled occupations, but members of the more prestigious occupations such as law, medicine, and the clergy are far more likely to be found among convicted child molesters than among convicted rapists.[73] They are also older on average: About 75 percent of convicted rapists are under thirty, while about 75 percent of child molesters are over thirty.[74] Of course, child molesters exist among people of all ages, races, and socioeconomic classes.

The overwhelming number of individuals charged with child sexual abuse do not manifest any pronounced clinical symptoms. However, a small proportion are classified as pedophiles. *Pedophilia* (literally, 'love of children') is a psychiatric diagnosis for individuals who are preferentially sexually attracted to children. Most child molesters are individuals who normally prefer adult relationships, but pedophiles *prefer* to interact sexually with children, sometimes exclusively.[75] Most pedophiles are found to be timid, shy, and haunted by feelings of inadequacy, which is probably why they select targets who are easy to control and who won't ridicule them.[76]

Finkelhor's Four-Factor Causal Model

Perhaps the best known theory of child molestation is Finkehor's four-factor model, which tries to integrate insights from a variety of child sexual abuse theories. The four factors—emotional congruence, sexual arousal to children, blockage, and disinhibition—are described below.

Emotional Congruence (ECon) refers to a "fit" between the offender's emotional needs and the child's characteristics that the offender finds satisfying. The idea behind ECon is that, because of low self-esteem and arrested psychological development, the molester is better able to relate to children as equals than he is to adults. Relating to children gives offenders the feelings of dominance, control, and efficacy they are unable to attain with adults.

Sexual Arousal to Children (SexA) refers to attempts to explain why molesters find children sexually arousing. A person who attains emotional satisfaction in nonsexual ways in the company of children is also more likely than others to find children sexually arousing. This may also be a result of the offender's own childhood victimization or of a preoccupation with child pornography. Finkelhor[77] acknowledges that many men may find underage children sexually arousing, but he indicates that the question is why some men are more aroused than others, and why only a proportion of men who are sexually aroused to children act on their arousal.

Blockage (Blk) refers to the offender's lack of a legitimate sex partner. Many theories of incestuous offending rely on this factor to explain it. If a man is denied sexual access to his wife because of alienation, inhibition, or his wife's illness, he may turn to his daughter as a substitute wife. Alternatively, the blockage may be the result of the offender's history of awkwardness, timidity, and perhaps impotence with age-appropriate sex partners, which may have lead him to abandon efforts to achieve sexual gratification with adults and to focus on children.

Disinhibition refers to how molesters overcome social inhibitions against adults having sex with children. Finkelhor divides this factor into three subfactors: *Internal Inhibition* (InIn), *External Inhibition* (ExIn), and *Child Resistance* (CRes). An offender must not only be motivated to commit sexual abuse, he must also overcome internal and external constraints acting against his desire to abuse. A poorly socialized person, an impulsive person, a person without strong feelings of guilt and empathy, will find it easy to discount social inhibitions against child sex, even if his motivation is weak (low emotional congruence, weak arousal to children, and no blockage). Factors such as senility, drunkenness, and mental retardation may also disinhibit child molestation.

External inhibition refers to factors outside the offender that restrain child sexual abuse. The most important of these restraints is the protection and supervision a child receives from others, such as parents, other relatives and responsible adults, siblings, and peers. The rigorous pursuit and prosecution of child molesters is also a strong external inhibitor.

Child resistance (CRes) refers to the ability of the child to fend off sexual advances by running away, screaming, threatening to tell, refusing to cooperate, or by any other tactic let the potential molester know that this particular child is no easy mark. A child who feels needy, powerless, and lacking in feelings of self-worth is less likely to offer effective resistance to a molester (or to any other potential victimizer, such as the school bully) than is a confident and assertive child.

Finkelhor expresses the probability of child molesting ($P_{child\ molesting}$) as a ratio of motivating to inhibiting factors of the following form:

$$P_{child\ molesting} = \frac{ECon + SexA + Blk}{InIn + ExIn + CRes}$$

Finkelhor notes that none of the motivating factors alone is sufficient to result in actual child molesting, and that we have to look at the pushes, pulls, and varying strengths of each of them in interaction with the others. However, disinhibition, without which abuse will not occur despite the strength of a person's motivation, *is* a requirement.[78] The disinhibiting factors themselves vary in strength and interact with one another in many predictable and idiosyncratic ways.

Female Sex Offenders

Biosocial theory predicts that we should expect at least some female sex offenders. Cultural stereotypes make it difficult for most people to imagine a woman as a sexual victimizer. Women are thought of as mothers and wives who provide care and comfort for others, not as people who cause harm or abuse, and few behaviors depart so far from cultural norms and beliefs as female sexual offending.[79]

It is difficult to determine what percentage of sex offenders is female. Over the past decade the UCR has consistently reported that between 0.9 and 1.3 percent of rape arrestees have been women. Despite the curiosity that female perpetrators of this most "male" of crimes should generate, studies of female rapists are almost nonexistent. One study documented eleven "forcible rapes" of males by females, but the majority of these incidents were either women charged with aiding and abetting males to commit rape or "baby sitter" abuse rather than the kinds of forced sexual activity we associate with the term *rape*.[80] Doubtless there have been cases in which women have used force to compel males to copulate with them, but there are so few of them that systematic research has not been feasible.[81]

Because females are physically weaker than males, and because they do the majority of child care, females are more likely to be child molesters than rapists. However, despite the much greater opportunity women have to commit it, male molesters greatly outnumber female molesters. The exact percentage of female molesters is impossible to determine, but based on official statistics they constitute no more than 2 percent of all child molesters. Perhaps the earliest study of crime statistics ever done found that females constituted just 0.85 percent of convicted child molesters in France during the years 1826 through 1831.[82] Statistics on all sex offenses committed over a ten-year period in the United Kingdom found that less than 1 percent were committed by females.[83] Studies based on official statistics from the United States find a female offending rate of about 1.5 percent.[84] A study of over 600 molestation cases in New Hampshire and Vermont found only nine cases in which the perpetrator was a woman.[85] In all cases the women's IQs were in the retarded to dull normal range, most had a variety of character disorders, and four of the nine committed the offense in the company of a dominant male partner.

These statistics were all based on official records of convicted women; unofficial records paint a different picture. A nationwide study found that 13 percent of female victims and 24 percent of male victims were victimized by a female. However, these figures are inflated by definitional problems. Females were considered to be active perpetrators *without engaging in actual sexual contact* if, as mothers or legal guardians, (1) they neglected to provide protection for the child while the father/stepfather abused him/her, or if (2) they provided inappropriate or inadequate supervision of a child's "voluntary sexual activities."[86] If figures are cited without providing the definitions on which they are based we get a distorted picture of female *sexual* offending.

Why Are Women Low-Level Perpetrators of Sex Crimes?

Although cultural stereotypes used to tell us that "women just don't do such things," now that we know that they sometimes do, it becomes important to understand why it is such a rarity. Perhaps by understanding why females are so unlikely to sexually offend we may gain further understanding of why males are. Finkelhor's [87] review of the literature found a variety of alleged reasons why women are unlikely to engage in child sexual abuse, which we paraphrase below.

1. Females generally prefer partners who are older, larger, and more powerful than themselves while the male preference is exactly the opposite. Thus, being in a position of dominance and authority over children is a relationship that is not what most women find sexually arousing, but congruent with what most men find sexually arousing.

2. Women do not generally initiate sexual activity, and, because children are not likely to invite them to engage in sex, such activity is less likely to arise. Males are typically the sexual initiators, thus initiating sexual activity with a child is more likely to arise.

3. Males are more promiscuous than females, and much more likely to seek novel sexual

stimuli, thus they are more likely than women to sexualize their relationships with children.

4. Males are aroused easily by sexual stimuli divorced from a relationship context while females rely more on the totality of the relationship with their sexual partner to be aroused. The relationship a woman has with children is likely to preclude her viewing them as sex partners; a male can more easily separate the relationship and sexual arousal components.

5. Having sexual opportunities is more important to the maintenance of self-esteem for males than for females, who are more concerned about love relationships for self-esteem maintenance. Thus, when adult sexual outlets are blocked males are more likely to turn to children than are females.

6. Women are better able to empathize with the potential harm that may result from child molestation because they are the targets of sexual exploitation themselves more often than men.

OTHER PARAPHILIAS

Other than pedophilia, the most common paraphilias that have been criminalized are exhibitionism and voyeurism. Paraphilias typically begin in early adolescence and become better defined and elaborated during early adulthood. For some individuals, paraphiliac stimuli are necessary for sexual arousal and are always a component of their sexual activities; for others such stimuli simply add novelty or spice to their sexual lives and are only occasionally engaged in. According to the APA, paraphilia is virtually unique to males: "Except for sexual masochism, where the sex ratio is estimated to be 20 males for each female, the other paraphilias are almost never diagnosed in females."[88]

Exhibitionism involves the exposure of one's genitals (sometimes while masturbating) to a stranger of either gender for sexual pleasure. There is usually no attempt at further sexual activity with the victim, although such attempts do sometimes occur. Contrary to the "dirty-old-man-in-a-greasy-raincoat" stereotype, the APA reports that exhibitionism becomes less severe after age 40.[89]

Voyeurism is the act of secretly observing ("peeping") unsuspecting persons who are naked, in the process of disrobing, or engaging in sexual activity. Such behavior is highly arousing for the voyeur, who may masturbate while he is watching or while fantasizing about it afterward. No other sexual activity with the observed person is typically sought, although voyeuristic activity can sometimes result in rape.[90] Research has shown that many rapists have histories of voyeurism before the emergence of rape behavior.[91]

Toucheurism and **frotteurism** are two closely related paraphilias. Toucheurism involves the desire to intimately touch a woman, and frotteurism involves the desire to press the penis against a woman. In each case it is necessary for sexual arousal that the women touched or rubbed against be strangers to the offender. Both of these behaviors typically take place in crowded areas such as shopping areas and elevators.

PARAPHILIAS AS COURTSHIP DISORDERS?

It has been proposed that the most common paraphilias represent a pathological distortion of normal courtship phases.[92] These paraphilias differ from the normal courtship pattern in that the target must always be a stranger, and in that the person displaying the paraphilia develops an intensified preference for a single phase and may show little interest in other phases. Normal courtship behavior typically consists of the four phases listed on the left side of the following table, and their paraphilic distortions are listed on the right side:

Normal	Distortion
1. Searching for and locating a potential sex partner	Voyeurism
2. Engaging in pretactile (verbal and nonverbal indicators of interest) interaction with him or her	Exhibitionism
3. Tactile interaction (kissing, necking) with him/her	Toucheurism/frotteurism
4. Sexual intercourse	Preferential rape pattern

CAUSES OF PARAPHILIAC BEHAVIOR

Paraphiliac behavior is sexual behavior, and as such we need not repeat what we have already said in discussing rape and child molesting regarding the role of biological drives, modeling, imitation, the media, and so forth. Because many paraphilias involve stimuli that the great majority of individuals find sexually neutral (shoes, enema hoses, whips, etc.), a theory of how sexually neutral stimuli take on sexual properties for some individuals is required. Part of the answer to this question lies in the principles of *classical conditioning*.[93] Classical conditioning involves learning to transfer a natural (unlearned) response from one stimulus to a neutral stimulus. The Russian psychologist Ivan Pavlov first experimented with classical conditioning by conditioning a dog to salivate at the sound of a bell (the neutral stimulus). He did this by pairing the sound of a bell with the presentation of food to the dog. The food is an *unconditioned* (natural) stimulus with intrinsic properties that lead the animal to salivate, which is an *unconditioned* (natural) response. The sound of the bell accompanying the food is known as a *conditioned* stimulus, and the reaction of the dog to the conditioned stimulus is known as the *conditioned* response. The point is that dogs do not normally salivate at the sound of a bell, but will learn (be conditioned) to do so if it is paired with an unconditioned stimulus often enough.

We can apply this to the process of learning aberrant sexual behavior: sexual stimuli (sights, sounds, touches, and smells) are unconditioned stimuli because they have the intrinsic property of eliciting unconditioned natural responses (sexual arousal) that are intrinsically rewarding. If sexual stimuli somehow become paired with an unconditioned stimulus, that stimulus may become a conditioned stimulus capable of eliciting the unconditioned responses by itself. This unconditioned stimulus can be anything associated with the various paraphilias. Such unconventional patterns of conditional stimuli may create a preference for deviant rather than conventional sexual behavior.

ASSESSMENT AND TREATMENT OF SEX OFFENDERS

Although public outrage has made the idea of treating sex offenders rather than punishing them an unpopular idea, the realization that most incarcerated sex offenders will eventually be released makes it imperative that we do what we can to insure that they do not continue to offend after they are released.[94] There is a great deal of pessimism surrounding sex offender treatment. While it is true that nothing works for some offenders, the professional literature is cautiously optimistic. Most studies report at least some success comparing treated and untreated offenders. A recent review of twelve meta-analyses covering a total of 356 different studies found that nine of the meta-analyses were positive (treatment "works"), three were inconclusive, and none were negative.[95] Treatment efforts with incestuous offenders tend to be most successful and efforts aimed at homosexual pedophiles the least.[96] What is counted as "success," however, varies wildly from study to study, and recidivism rates continue to be unacceptably high.

A variety of treatment modalities have been implemented by public and private agencies, with the most frequently relying almost exclusively on behavioral and cognitive treatment, such as group therapy, interpersonal communication skills, and psychoeducational programs (i.e., social and self-control skills). The efficacy of such modalities has been questioned by a number of researchers who feel that psychometric assessment by itself is of limited utility for the assessment and treatment of sex offenders.[97]

The assessment of a sex offender typically begins with the administration of a series of interviews and psychological tests. Many modern treatment programs go beyond psychosocial assessment and use physiological assessment using the polygraph and penile plethysmograph (PPG) along with psychosocial assessment.[98] The PPG is a rubber band-like device hooked to an electronic recording monitor. The band is placed around the penis and expands and contracts as the penis erects and deflates in response to visual and audio depictions of sexual activity. The aim of PPG assessment is to measure level of arousal to deviant sexual activity. Most men will have some level of arousal to deviant sexual activity, but unlike "normal males," offenders who are preferentially attracted to such activity will have higher PPG readings than they will to nondeviant sexual activity. If a rapist achieves a 30 percent erection when viewing stimuli depicting consensual sex and one of 80 percent when viewing violent sex, we can conclude that he is preferentially interested in violent sex and that he is probably a dangerous individual.[99]

Psychosocial treatment of sex offenders tends to center around group counseling sessions to correct "thinking errors" in which stereotypical images of women and false perceptions are brought out into the open and discussed. Educating males to accept women as equals who have the right to say no can go a long way toward preventing a reoccurrence of rape, and showing child molesters the damage that can occur as a result of their actions may help to prevent future offenses. It is a sad fact that many men do believe that women "ask for it" if they accept a date and engage in a little mild petting, and there are child molesters who believe that "no harm is done," although that is probably more of a rationalization than a genuine belief. Egocentric thinking—believing that everyone thinks as we do—leads some men to the conclusion that, "Hey, I'm aroused and ready to go, she must be too." The kind of men who believe these things are "masculine" males in the traditional "Real-men-don't-take-no-for-an-answer" sense of the word.[100]

The results of treatment efforts for the preferential rapist have been discouraging. Treatments using aversive conditioning (pairing sexually arousing deviant stimuli with some sort of punishment, such as an electric shock) and therapeutic castration have been drastically curtailed in the United States because of civil rights considerations.[101] Yet the most effective form of treatment for sex offenders is probably therapeutic castration. A review of the literature involving 2055 European sex offending castrates followed over periods for up to twenty years found recidivism rates ranging from zero to 7.4 percent.[102] Rapists in the United States have known recidivism rates as high as 50 percent, regardless of whether treated with psychosocial counseling or not.[103]

Although surgical castration has been curtailed in the United States, it remains to be seen how the courts will view chemical "castration" with drugs such as medroxyprogesterone (Depo-Provera) or cyproterone acetate (Andocur). Offenders with excessive sex drives that place them at risk for reoffending are particularly good targets for this kind of therapeutic intervention. Depo-Provera reduces libido by drastically reducing testicular production of testosterone, and Andocur does the same thing by blocking testosterone receptors.[104] Such drugs have been called "limbic–hypothalamic tranquilizers" because they "allow the offender to concentrate on his psychosocial problems without the distracting fantasies and urges accompanying androgen-driven limbic–hypothalamic activity."[105] These drugs reduce the level of activating testosterone, which diminishes arousal or responsiveness to sexuality and violence. With the seething activity of the more primitive brain area dampened, offenders can concentrate on combating their psychosocial weaknesses with their counselors.

SUMMARY

This chapter has dealt with a variety of sex offenses. We have emphasized rape and child molesting, but the term *sex offenses* covers so many diverse behaviors and involves so many nonsexual considerations that it may not be entirely advisable to treat them alike for analytical purposes. The United States has criminalized many different sexual acts that other Western countries have long ago legitimized, and Americans tend to have particularly negative attitudes about sex offenders. Sex offenders are the targets of special control methods, such as indefinite civil commitment laws and mandatory registration, that are not applied to other kinds of criminals.

Rape is a violent sexual offense committed overwhelmingly by males against females, but also against other males. It is extremely difficult to obtain precise data on rape, but according to victimization data, about 75 percent more rapes are committed than are reported to the police. The United States has particularly high rates of *reported* rape, although differences in definitions and what acts are included (statutory rape, attempted rape, etc.) under the heading of rape make it very difficult to compare rape figures internationally. Also, the way rape cases are handled and the degree of stigma attached to rape victimization in different countries presents further problems of comparison.

With the reminder that when we speak of characteristics of rapists we are talking about convicted rapists, we explored these characteristics. Most rapists tend to be young, lacking in education, mostly unemployed or working in low-status occupations, have previous criminal convictions, and generally hostile toward women. Stranger rapists are particularly more likely to physically injure their victims. We also saw that rapists may be categorized as anger, power, and sadistic types, with the power rapist being the most common, and the sadistic rapist the least common.

Just as there are characteristics associated with men who are convicted of rape, there are certain characteristics associated with the probability of being victimized by rape. Women most at risk for rape are between the ages of sixteen and nineteen, white, poor, who are living alone, and who drink more frequently and in greater amounts than other women. Women least likely to be victimized are married women over sixty-five from homes with incomes of $75,000 a year or more.

There are several theories of rape causation that can be placed into three general categories: the feminist, social learning, and evolutionary theories. The earlier feminist theories were devised in reaction to the notion that women could be somehow responsible for their own victimization. Characterizing rape as a crime of violence rather than a sex crime, feminists viewed it as a political act designed to intimidate and degrade women in order to "keep them in their place." Rape cannot be understood without understanding the disparity of power that exists between men and women and the efforts of men to maintain that disparity. Feminists view rapists as "normal" men who may commit rape under certain circumstances, and point to its frequent use in war, the fact that it is not listed as a paraphilia by the APA, and studies that consistently show that between 35 and 69 percent of surveyed males admit that they would commit rape if they were sure they would not be punished.

The social learning theory agrees with feminist theories that rape is learned by men assimilating the sexist values and attitudes of their cultures. They also agree that the print and electronic media promote rape by depicting women as sex objects. Social learning theorists are more concerned with explaining rape at the individual level, however, and reject the idea that all men are equally likely to rape under similar environmental conditions. They believe that to understand why men rape they must understand the specific learning histories of men who commit it.

According to the evolutionary perspective, rape is a male adaptation forged by natural selection because it increased reproductive success in our distant male ancestors who practiced it. Thus, this perspective agrees with feminist theorists that all men are potential rapists, but not because they are exposed to sexist attitudes and a patriarchal society, rather because they are heirs to an evolved biological strategy. Noting that coerced copulation occurs in most species of animals, they attribute it to the wide disparity in parental investment. Whereas males need invest very little in parenting and may therefore readily engage in casual sex, the female investment is enormous. Females have evolved to be more careful and "choosy" about the men they will mate with, and this reticence often collides with male desire and may result in rape. Other evolutionary theorists deny that rape per se is an evolutionary adaptation and that it is more likely to be a "side effect" of other adaptations, such as aggression and a strong sex drive, which themselves contribute to the probability of rape.

The main contribution of feminist theory was to alert us all to the horrible nature of rape. Many feminist theorists have gone beyond the "not-sex" argument of earlier times, indicating that such a position was needed initially to rid people of the many myths and stereotypes surrounding rape. Most scientists and clinicians today understand that rape is both a violent and a sexual crime, and that sex and aggression are linked together, even in acts of consensual sex.

Evolutionary theories have been severely criticized as condoning and justifying rape, although evolutionary theorists strongly reject such criticisms as examples of the naturalist fallacy. Evolutionary theories have also been criticized for not being able to account for nonreproductive coercive sex crimes, such as the rape of the extremely young or extremely old, and for male rape and nongenital sexual activity. The response to this is that no organism is designed by natural selection to seek ultimate goals. Rather organisms are designed to seek proximate goals, and these goals can be realized in many diverse ways.

Biosocial theory synthesizes these three theories, and it contains four general propositions:

1. The sex drive and the drive to possess and control motivates rape;
2. The average sex drive of men is stronger than the average sex drive of women;
3. Although the motivation for rape is unlearned, the specific behavior surrounding it is learned; and
4. Because of neurohormonal factors, people differ in the strength of their sex drives and in their sensitivity to threats of punishment.

Although this theory integrates a great deal of diverse data, it has been criticized for its failure to recognize the patriarchal nature of society and how patriarchy contributes to rape.

Child molesting may be the most common crime committed against the person in the United States. The age at which child molestation may become consensual sex varies from state to state, with sixteen being the most common age.

Both boys and girls can be victims of this crime, and females as well as males can be perpetrators. Girls are most likely to be victimized by relatives (especially stepfathers) and boys are most likely to be victimized outside of the family. Finkelor's checklist of factors for the likelihood of victimization of girls indicates a risk of about 66 percent for girls having five of the factors to near zero for girls having none of them in their backgrounds.

There are some striking differences between rapists and child molesters. Convicted rapists tend to be overwhelmingly from unskilled and semi-skilled occupations whereas child molesters include many individuals from high-status occupations. Child molesters also tend to be older, with 75 percent being over thirty, while 75 percent of rapists are under thirty. Although many child molesters are preferentially sexually attracted to adults, there is a category of child molesters known as *pedophiles* whose primary sexual attraction is to children. These individuals tend to be shy, introverted, timid, and are haunted by feelings of inadequacy. Finkelor's Four-Factor Causal Model attempts to explain why some individuals are preferentially attracted to children. The model views an incident of child molesting as a ratio of motivating factors to disinhibiting factors.

Although many people find it difficult to believe, females have also been known to commit sex crimes. Females constitute about 1 percent of arrests for rape every year in the United States, although most cases turn out to be cases of women aiding and abetting males to commit rape or cases of child molesting. Even in cases of child molesting (where women have considerable more opportunities than men) women are vastly underrepresented. Female child molesters are also typically found to be of low intelligence and suffer from a variety of character disorders. A number of reasons for low female sex offending were given.

The paraphilias of exhibitionism, voyeurism, toucheurism, and frotteurism were then addressed as distortions of normal courtship behavior. We also discussed ways in which sexually neutral behaviors may take on sexual properties according to the principles of operant conditioning.

The treatment of sex offenders, while not particularly popular with the public, has achieved a certain level of success. Many modern sex offender treatment programs include physiological assessment using the polygraph and penile plethysmograph before commencing treatment. The most common form of treatment for sex offenders today is still psychosocial counseling. However, given the very high success rates of of-fenders treated with antiandrogen compounds such as Depo-Provera and Andocur, it would seem that such treatment prior to counseling would have a welcome effect on the sex offending recidivism rate. Of course, other treatment methods of a psychosocial nature should also continue to be a part of any sex offender treatment program.

EXERCISES

1. What are your thoughts on the continued confinement of sex offenders after they have completed their prison sentences? Are we violating basic principles of law in order to protect society from what might happen?

2. Which theory of rape makes the most and least sense to you? Give your reasons.

3. Why do you think that the American Psychiatric Association has never defined rape as paraphillic behavior requiring treatment?

4. Recalling what has been said about female offending in general throughout this book, why do you think females are such low-level sex offenders?

5. Should all repeat sex offenders be required to undergo therapeutic castration (either surgical or chemical)? Give your reasons why or why not.

ENDNOTES

1. American Psychiatric Association 1994:523.
2. Robertson 1987:251.
3. Inciardi 1994:82.
4. Walsh 1997:262.
5. Cohen 1995.
6. Schwartz 1995.
7. United States Department of Justice 1997: 23.
8. Zawitz et al. 1993.
9. Schwartz 1995:3–2.
10. Kadish 1988:6–7.
11. INTERPOL 1992:54.
12. Bartol 1995:286.
13. Federal Bureau of Investigation 1997.
14. Bartol 1995:286.
15. Bartol 1995; Harney & Muehlenhard 1991.
16. Walsh 1997:265.
17. Ellis 1989; Koss & Leonard 1984.
18. Groth 1979.
19. Ibid:58.
20. Ibid.
21. Ibid.
22. Goodchilds & Zellman 1984; Herman 1990.
23. Bartol 1995:289.
24. BJS 1996:231.
25. BJS 1996:236.
26. LaFree 1982; O'Brien 1987; Wilbanks 1985.
27. Scully & Marolla 1985:259.
28. Koch 1985.
29. Bohmer & Parrot 1993.
30. Schwartz & Pitts 1995:28.
31. Ellis 1989; 1991.
32. Gilmartin 1994:60.
33. Amir 1967:493.
34. Gilmartin 1994:57.
35. Brownmiller 1975.
36. Brownmiller 1975:5; emphasis original.
37. Clark & Lewis 1977:140; Herman 1991:178.
38. Reviewed in Skinner et al. 1995.
39. Murrin & Laws 1990:85.
40. Kenrick et al. 1989.
41. Gilmartin 1994:63.
42. Robertson 1987:259.
43. Ellis 1989; Smuts 1992; Thornhill & Thornhill 1992.
44. Thornhill & Thornhill 1987:5.
45. Thornhill & Thornhill 1992:365.
46. Smuts 1992.
47. Buss 1989; Wiederman & Allgeier 1994.

48. Bartol 1995:287; Ellis & Walsh 1997; Koch 1995.
49. Marshall & Barbaree 1990:265.
50. Barbaree & Marshall 1991:621.
51. Hall 1987:38.
52. Gilmartin 1994:65; Herman 1990:182.
53. Palmer 1994:59.
54. Brownmiller & Mehrhof 1992:382.
55. Dupre 1992:383.
56. Beckstrum 1993:2.
57. Grauerholz & Koralewski 1991:192.
58. Thornhill & Thornhill 1992:414.
59. Lykken 1995:50.
60. Ellis 1989; 1991.
61. Daly & Wilson 1988.
62. Lykken 1995:70.
63. American Psychiatric Association 1994:523.
64. Knudson 1991:17.
65. Glaser & Frosh 1993:16.
66. Bartol 1995:301.
67. Knudsen 1991:21; Walsh 1994.
68. Knudsen 1991:21–22.
69. Glaser & Frosh 1993:19.
70. Walsh 1988.
71. Finkelhor 1984.
72. Stermac et al. 1990.
73. Walsh 1997:269.
74. Bartol 1995:304–305.
75. Langevin 1990:108.
76. Bartol 1995:309.

77. Finkelor 1984:40.
78. Ibid. 58.
79. Allen 1991:11.
80. Sarrel & Masters 1982.
81. Schwartz & Cellini 1995:5–11.
82. Quetelet, 1842/1972.
83. O'Connor 1987.
84. Rowan et al. 1988.
85. Ibid.
86. Finkelhor 1984:173.
87. Ibid., 182–183.
88. American Psychiatric Association 1994:524.
89. Ibid., 525.
90. Ibid., 532.
91. Freund 1990, 106.
92. Freund 1990; 1991.
93. Laws & Marshall 1990.
94. Gendreau & Ross 1987, 381.
95. Lotke 1996, 2.
96. Gendreau & Ross 1987, 383.
97. Hall & Proctor 1987; Marsh & Walsh 1995.
98. Marsh & Walsh 1995.
99. Earls & Proulx 1987.
100. Bernard et al. 1985.
101. Pallone 1990.
102. Bradford 1990.
103. Maletzky 1987.
104. Emory et al. 1992.
105. Marsh & Walsh 1995, 87.

Crime, the Law, and the Criminal Justice System

THE LEGAL MAKING OF A CRIMINAL

What is a criminal? The simple answer to this question is someone who has committed a crime. The formal process of becoming a legally defined criminal is much more complicated than that, however. Whatever factors criminologists decide might lead to criminal behavior, a person is not "officially" a criminal until he or she has been defined as such by the law. This process of defining what constitutes a crime and who will be defined as a criminal is an important part of criminology. Before the law can properly call a person a criminal, it must go through a series of actions governed at all junctures by well-defined legal rules collectively called *criminal procedure*. These procedural rules vary greatly from culture to culture, but almost all modern cultures have a set of rational (i.e., predictable) rules guiding the serious business of officially labeling a person a criminal.

In this appendix we discuss these procedures in U.S. and Canadian law as we take you from arrest to conviction and beyond. We will also briefly discuss other traditions of law outside the English-speaking tradition. Any comparative study is always biased to some degree by the point of view of what we know most intimately, but we make no attempt to define a "best" system. What is best for a given society must be gauged with reference to its own unique history, culture, philosophy, and needs, and these are issues we cannot concern ourselves with here. The primary value of a comparative study of criminal law (or of anything else for that matter) is that it lifts some of the veils of uncritical ethnocentrism favoring "ours" over "theirs," and the bonus is that some understanding of other systems helps us to better understand our own.

We will first introduce you to the U.S. criminal justice system by following the processing of felony cases from arrest to trial and beyond, and then repeat the process with respect to the Canadian criminal justice system. We then acquaint you with the four great traditions of law existing in the world today.

BASIC PRINCIPLES OF U.S. AND CANADIAN CRIMINAL LAW

Although Canadian and U.S. criminal law differs in many ways, both systems have their origins in English common law and both systems remain faithful to its general principles. Any differences between the two systems are mainly differences in specifics rather than basic underlying legal philosophy. This section is thus applicable to both legal systems and to all other systems sharing the common law tradition, although there may be slight differences of interpretation from country to country.

Corpus Delicti: What Constitutes a Crime?

Corpus delicti is a Latin term meaning 'body of the crime,' and refers to the elements of a given act that must be present in order to legally define it as a crime. As we saw when discussing the eight index crimes in Chapter 2, all crimes have their own specific elements, the essential constituent parts that define the act as criminal. In addition to their specific elements, all crimes share a set of general elements or principles underlying and supporting the specific elements. There are seven of these principles, and a person cannot be "officially" labeled a criminal unless all of them are present. In actuality, it is only necessary for the state to prove two to satisfy *corpus delicti: actus reus* and *mens rea*. The other principles, while just as important to the legal definition of a criminal, are either abstract principles of no concern to the particular case at hand, or are proven in the course of proving *actus reus* and *mens rea*.

Actus reus means *guilty act,* and refers to the principle that a person must commit some forbidden act or neglect some mandatory act before he or she can be subjected to criminal sanctions. In effect, this principle of law means that people cannot be criminally prosecuted for thinking something or being something, only for *doing* something. This prevents governments from passing laws criminalizing statuses and systems of thought they don't like. For instance, although homosexual *behavior* may be a punishable crime in some states, *being* homosexual cannot be punished because "being" something is a status, not an act. Attempted criminal acts, although not accomplished for one reason or another, are crimes, as is conspiracy to commit a crime the moment the conspirators take some action to put their plan into motion.

Mens Rea means *guilty mind,* and refers to whether or not the act was intentional, that is, whether the suspect had a wrongful purpose in mind when carrying out the *actus reus*. For instance, although receiving stolen property is a criminal offense, if you were to buy a stolen television set from an acquaintance without knowing it had been stolen, you would have lacked *mens rea*, and would not be subject to prosecution. If you were to be prosecuted, the prosecutor would have to prove that you knew the television was stolen. Negligence, recklessness, and carelessness that result in some harmful consequences, even though not intended, *does not* excuse such behavior from criminal prosecution under *mens rea*. Conditions that may preclude prosecution under this principle are self-defense, defense of others, youthfulness (a person under seven years of age cannot be held responsible), insanity (although being found insane does not preclude long-term confinement), and extreme duress or coercion.

Nullem crimen, nulla poena sine lege is a Latin phrase which literally means that there can

be no crime or punishment except as the law prescribes, sums up two of the remaining five principles: the principles of *legality* and *punishment.* **The principle of legality** specifies that no crime can be committed unless there is a law that defines it as such. Although this may seem obvious and redundant, actually it is an extremely important principle of common law. The principle functions to prevent the passage of *ex post facto* laws, which means that if a law is passed next week forbidding some act, you cannot be held criminally responsible if you engage in that act today (but watch out after next week). A person must have "fair warning" that an act is illegal before he or she can be prosecuted for engaging in it. The making of "after the fact" laws is a common practice of authoritarian and totalitarian regimes to stifle any potential opposition. Any organized opposition to such regimes would be constantly off-balance because it would not know whether its actions would be retroactively defined as illegal.

The **principle of punishment** asserts that no act can be considered criminal unless the punishment for its commission is specified by law. An act cannot be simply "forbidden" or "against the law," it must have a specified penalty attached to it, which must be specified. This principle protects criminal defendants from arbitrary and capricious punishment.

Concurrence means that the act (*actus reus*) and the mental state (*mens rea*) concur in the sense that the criminal intention actuates the criminal act. For instance, if John sets out with his tools to burglarize Mary's apartment, does so, and takes her VCR, he has fused the guilty mind with the wrongful act and has therefore committed burglary. However, assume that John and Mary are friends in the habit of visiting each other's apartment unannounced and making themselves comfortable. One day John decides to visit Mary, finds her not at home, but walks in and sits down as he has done with her blessing many times before. While sitting there, John suddenly decides that he could sell Mary's VCR for drug money, and leaves her apartment with her VCR. Has John committed burglary in this scenario? Although the loss to Mary is the same in both scenarios, in the latter instance John cannot be charged with burglary because he did not enter her apartment "by force or fraud," the crucial element needed to satisfy such a charge. In this case, the concurrence of guilty mind and wrongful act occurred after lawful entry, so he is only charged with grand theft, a less serious crime.

Harm refers to the negative impact a crime has either to the victim or to the general values of the community. Although the harm caused by the criminal act is often obvious, the harm caused by many "victimless crimes" (drug abuse, gambling, prostitution, pornography) is often less obvious. Yet some such crimes can cause more social harm in the long run than many crimes with specific victims.

Causation refers to the necessity to establish a causal link between the criminal act and the harm suffered. This causal link must be proximate, not ultimate. For instance, suppose Tony wounds Frank in a knife fight. Because Frank has no medical insurance, rather than seeking professional medical treatment, he pours alcohol on his wound and bandages it himself. Three weeks later, Frank's self-treated wound becomes severely infected and results in his death. What crime could the prosecutor charge Tony with? Certainly the wounding led to Frank's death, but Frank's own disregard for the seriousness of his injury, not the fight, was the most proximate cause of his death. The question the law asks in cases like this is, "What would any reasonable person do?" We think most people would agree that the reasonable person would have sought medical treatment. This being the case, Tony cannot be charged with any form of homicide; the most he could be charged with is aggravated assault.

AN EXCURSION THROUGH THE U.S. CRIMINAL JUSTICE SYSTEM

Now that you are aware of the principles behind the process of "officially" labeling someone a criminal, we will discuss the process itself. The best way to explain the process within the space available is to follow the processing of felony cases from arrest to trial and beyond. There are many points at which the arrested person may be shunted off the criminal justice conveyor belt via the discretionary decisions of a variety of criminal justice officials. This process will vary in some specifics from state to state, but the principles underlying the specifics are uniform. Presented here are the stages and procedures that are most common among our fifty state court systems for the processing of felony offenses.

Arrest

A felony suspect first enters the criminal justice system by arrest. When a person has been legally detained to answer criminal charges, he/she has been arrested. Some arrests are made on the basis of an *arrest warrant,* which is an official document signed by a judge (usually) on the basis of evidence presented by law enforcement officials indicating that the person named in the warrant has probably committed a crime. The warrant formally authorizes the police to execute the arrest, although the great majority of arrests are initiated by the police without a warrant. A police officer making a warrantless arrest is held to the same legal constraints involved in making application for a warrant. To make a legal felony arrest the officer must have *probable cause. Probable cause* means that the officer must possess a set of facts that would lead a reasonable person to conclude that the arrested person had committed a specific crime. Although a person can be stopped on the basis of an officer's suspicion and frisked for a weapon, he or she cannot be arrested on the basis of suspicion alone, even if illegal items such as drug paraphernalia are discovered (the discovery of a weapon, however, would constitute probable cause for arrest). It is only after a formal arrest that the Fifth Amendment rights (Miranda Rule) against self-incrimination come into play.

Preliminary Arraignment

After arrest and booking into the county jail, the felony suspect must be presented in court for the preliminary arraignment before a magistrate or municipal judge. The preliminary arraignment must take place at the earliest opportunity. The preliminary arraignment has two purposes: (1) To advise suspects of their constitutional rights (right to counsel and right to remain silent) and of the tentative charges against them, and (2) to set bail. Bail can be either granted or denied at this point. The suspect may be released on monetary bail or on his or her own recognizance. If bail is denied it is usually because of the gravity of the crime, the risk the suspect poses to the community, or the risk that the suspect might flee the court's jurisdiction. There is no constitutional right to bail. The Eighth Amendment only states that "excessive bail shall not be required." The traditional assumption has been that bail is only designed to assure the suspect's appearance at the next court hearing, and that "excessive" means that the amount set should be within the suspect's means. Under these assumptions, many dangerous offenders were released on bail in the past. Although this still happens, it does so less than in the past. The 1984 Bail Reform Act, which has passed constitutional muster, established the principle that individuals deemed dangerous to the community could be detained pending disposition of the case.[1]

Preliminary Hearing

The preliminary hearing usually takes place about ten days after the preliminary arraignment, and is a proceeding before a magistrate or municipal judge in which three major matters must be decided: (1) Whether or not a crime has actually been committed, (2) whether or not there are reasonable grounds to believe that the person before the bench committed it, and (3) whether or not the crime was committed in the jurisdiction of the court. These matters determine whether the suspect's arrest and detention is legal. The onus of proving the legality of the suspect's arrest and detention is on the prosecutor, who must establish probable cause, and present the court with evidence pertinent to the suspect's probable guilt. This is usually a relatively easy matter for the prosecutor because defense attorneys rarely cross-examine witnesses or introduce their own evidence at this point.[2] Defense attorneys' primary use of the preliminary hearing is to discover the strength of the prosecutor's case.

The Grand Jury

If the prosecutor is successful, the suspect is *bound over* to a higher court for further processing. Prior to the suspect's next court appearance, prosecutors in some states must seek an indictment (a document formally charging the suspect with a specific crime or crimes) from a *grand jury*. The grand jury, so called to distinguish it from the "petit" or trial jury, is nominally an investigatory body and a buffer between the awesome power of the state and its citizens, but some see it as an historical anachronism that serves only prosecutorial purposes.[3] The grand jury is composed of citizens chosen from voter or automobile registration lists and number anywhere from seven to twenty-three members.[4]

Arraignment

Armed with an indictment (or an *information* filed on the basis of the preliminary hearing outcome in states not requiring grand jury proceedings), the prosecutor files the case against the accused in felony court (variably called a *district, superior,* or *common pleas court*), which sets a date for arraignment. The arraignment proceeding is the first time defendants (the accused's status has changed from suspect to defendant on the basis of the indictment or information) have had the opportunity to respond to the charges against them. After the charges are read to the defendant, he or she must then enter a formal response to them, known as a plea.

The plea alternatives are guilty, not guilty, or no contest (*nolo contendere*). A guilty plea is usually the result of a plea bargain agreement concluded before the arraignment. About 90 percent of all felony cases in the United States are settled by plea bargains in which the state extends some benefit to the defendant (e.g., reduced charges, a lighter sentence) in exchange for his or her cooperation.[5]

By pleading guilty, defendants give up their right to be proven guilty "beyond a reasonable doubt," their right against self-incrimination, and their right to appeal. A number of studies have demonstrated that defendants who insist on their constitutional right to a trial are subjected to harsher penalties than those who plead guilty by a system that relies on plea bargains to keep functioning.[6]

A "no contest" plea is the equivalent of a "guilty" plea in terms of criminal processing, and is treated as such. Defendants usually plead no contest rather than guilty to protect themselves from civil litigation arising from the same set of circumstances involved in the criminal case. A guilty plea is a direct admission of guilt, and can thus be used in civil proceedings, but a no contest plea admits nothing, thus the conviction based on it cannot be used in civil court. A "not guilty" plea results in a date being set for trial; a "guilty" or "no contest" plea results in a date being set for sentencing.

The Trial

A trial by a jury of one's peers is a right going back as far as the Magna Charta in 1215, and is enshrined in the Sixth Amendment to the Constitution. A trial is an examination of the law and the facts of a case by a judge or a jury for the purpose of reaching a judgment. If a defendant wishes, and state statutes allow for it, he or she can forgo the constitutional right to a jury trial and submit to a bench trial (trial by judge, or sometimes, judges). The trial is an adversarial process pitting the prosecutor against the defense attorney, with each side trying to "vanquish" the other. There is no pretense that each side is interested in seeking truth or justice in this totally partisan process. It is the task of the judge to ensure that both sides play by the rules. The prosecution's job is a little more difficult than the defense's because it must "prove beyond a reasonable doubt" that the accused is indeed guilty. Except in states that allow for nonunanimous jury decisions, the defense need only plant the seed of reasonable doubt in the mind of one stubborn juror to upset the prosecution's case.

Having heard the facts of the case, and having been instructed by the judge on the principles of law pertaining to it, the jury is charged with reaching a verdict. The jury's verdict may be guilty or not guilty, or if it cannot reach a verdict (a "hung" jury), the judge may declare a mistrial. A hung jury results in either dismissal of the charges by the prosecutor or in a retrial. If the verdict is guilty, in most cases the judge will delay sentencing (usually for a period of about thirty days) to allow time for a presentence investigation report to be prepared. It is at the point of conviction that the person officially becomes a criminal.

Probation

The presentence investigation report (PSI) is prepared by a probation officer. It contains a variety of information about the crime and offender's background, such as criminal record, education and work history, marital status, use of alcohol/drugs, and offender's attitude. On the basis of his or her investigation, the probation officer completes the PSI by offering a sentencing recommendation. The most important factors influencing these recommendations are seriousness of the crime and the criminal history of the defendant. Other factors, such as the officer's assessment of the rehabilitative potential of the defendant, are important, but much less so. A variety of studies have found that these recommendations are followed by judges around 90 percent of the time.[7]

One of the sentencing options open to the judge is to place the offender on probation, the most common sentence for felonies in the United States today.[8] A probation sentence is actually a suspended commitment to prison that is conditional on the offender's good behavior. If at any time during their probationary period offenders do not abide by the imposed probation conditions (consisting of a variety of general and offender-specific conditions), they may face revocation of probation and the imposition of the original prison sentence. Probation officers supervise and monitor offenders' behavior and assure that all conditions of probation (e.g., substance abuse counseling, fines and restitution paid, restraining orders followed) are adhered to. Probation officers thus function as both social workers and law enforcement officers, sometimes conflicting roles that officers may find difficult to reconcile.

Incarceration

If the sentence imposed for a felony conviction is some form of incarceration, the judge has the option of sentencing the offender to a state penitentiary, a county jail, or a county work-release program. The latter two options are almost invariably imposed as supplements to probation orders. U.S. prisons are terribly overcrowded despite the boom in building new prisons that occurred in the 1980s. Such overcrowding has led to serious problems such as prison riots, the early release of dangerous offenders, and the frequent inability of the courts to impose custodial sentences on serious criminals.[9]

We often hear that the U.S. criminal justice system is "soft on crime," but a comparison of our incarceration rates with those of other countries shows that the United States has by far the highest incarceration rate of any country with values and a political system closely matching its own.[10] As of June 30, 1994, the United States's Federal and state prisons held a staggering 1,012,851 inmates, which represents a rate of about 402 inmates per 100,000 population.[11]

As large as differences in incarceration rates between the United States and other nations might seem (ranging from about 1.5 times the South African rate to over 13 times the rate in India), caution should be exercised when interpreting them because such figures only indicate what proportion of the *general population* is behind bars, not what proportion of the *criminal population* is behind bars, and thus really doesn't say anything about how "soft" or how "hard" the United States is relative to other countries. The incarceration data would only bear on such a question if every country had an equal proportion of its citizens engaged in criminal activity. From the international crime rate comparisons given in Chapter 3, we

have a fairly good idea that this is not so. In fact, when level of crime is taken into consideration, the United States may indeed be somewhat "softer" on crime than many other countries.[12]

If incarceration rates are fairly similar across comparison countries once we take into consideration the differences in crime rates, what about time actually spent in prison for those who are incarcerated? In comparing length of sentences imposed for homicide, robbery, burglary, and theft in the United States with those of Canada, England and Wales, and West Germany, it was found that U.S. courts imposed significantly longer sentences than these other countries for all crimes.[13] When comparing time actually served, however, U.S. prisoners served about the same amount of time as did inmates in those countries.[14]

Parole

Parole, a conditional release from prison, is granted to inmates some time prior to the completion of their sentences. An inmate is granted parole by an administrative body called a *parole board,* which decides for or against parole based on such factors as inmate behavior while incarcerated and the urgency of the need for cell space. Once released on parole, parolees are supervised by parole officers, whose job is almost identical to that of a probation officer. In many states, probation and parole officers are one and the same. The primary difference between probation and parole is that probationers are under the supervision of the courts and parolees are under the supervision of the state Department of Corrections. Revocation of probation is a judicial function, revocation of parole is an executive administrative function.

AN EXCURSION THROUGH THE CANADIAN CRIMINAL JUSTICE SYSTEM

An excursion through the Canadian criminal justice system from arrest to parole is not that much different from the U.S. trip we have just completed. There are probably no other two independent countries in the world that so parallel to one another in this regard, and have been so more and more since the adoption of the *Charter of Rights and Freedoms* by the Canadian Parliament in 1982. There are some interesting differences between the two systems that remain, however. These differences are specific differences in procedure rather than major differences of principle.

We should first point out that the U.S. model of justice has been characterized as a *due process* model. This model places primary emphasis on the rights of the accused (as outlined in the *Bill of Rights*) and correct legal procedure, even at the expense of truth, efficiency, and community safety.[15] Canada, on the other hand, has leaned more towards the *crime control* model, which puts emphasis on the protection of the community and the efficient maintenance of social order. Although these comparisons are somewhat overdrawn, they are exemplified in the objectives of "life, liberty, and the pursuit of happiness" in the United States's *Declaration of Independence,* and "peace, order, and good government" in Canada's *British North America Act.* Both countries have respected civil liberties better than most others throughout their histories, but it is fair to say that Canada has been more conservative in its insistence that civil liberties can have meaning only in an orderly society.[16] With this background in mind, we commence our journey.

Arrest

The primary reason for arrest in Canada is to compel the accused's attendance at trial. As in the United States, a police officer may arrest a suspect without a warrant if the officer has reasonable and probable grounds to believe that the arrested party has committed, or is about to commit, an indictable offense. An officer may also arrest for a summary offense if the officer believes that not doing so may result in further criminal activity (indictable and summary offenses are analogous to U.S. felony misdemeanor offenses). Officers are typically discouraged from making arrests for summary offenses "unless they have reasonable grounds to believe that the 'public interest' can be satisfied

only by adopting such a course."[17] A person accused of a summary offense is issued a summons, a formal document setting forth the charges against the accused and informing him or her of the time and place to appear in court. Under the *Charter of Rights and Freedoms,* an arrested or detained person has the right to "be informed promptly of the reasons therefore," and to retain and instruct counsel without delay and to be informed of that right."[18] Failure to allow the accused to exercise this right may result in any statements made by the accused being declared inadmissible.

Preliminary Inquiry

After arrest and booking, the individual accused of an indictable offense may appear before a provincial court judge who conducts the preliminary inquiry to determine if there is sufficient evidence to commit the accused to trial. Sometimes the preliminary inquiry is waived and the case proceeds directly to trial unless the accused has entered a guilty plea, in which case the next step is sentencing. The preliminary inquiry performs roughly the same functions that the preliminary arraignment, the preliminary hearing, and arraignment combined do in the United States. There are three major differences between the processes in the two countries that are outlined below.

1. Although not a trial, the crown prosecutor may present witnesses he or she will call in the event of a trial and the defense counsel may cross-examine them. The cross-examination of witnesses does not occur in the United States until the trial.

2. A provincial court is not a "lower" court in the same sense that a municipal court is in the United States. We have seen that if a U.S. municipal judge finds sufficient evidence to warrant committing the accused to trial, he/she declares the case "bound over" to the felony courts, which have original and exclusive jurisdiction over felonies. Some indictable offenses, however, fall under the jurisdiction of the Canadian provincial courts, and the judge can elect to try the case immediately or set a later date for the trial if the case before the court is within its jurisdiction. Other indictable offenses are moved to higher courts known as *Superior, Supreme, District, County,* or *Queen's Bench* courts, depending on the province.[19]

3. If a judge finds sufficient evidence to warrant committing the accused to trial, he/she has the power to impose a news blackout regarding the evidence heard in court, and even with regard to the suspect's identity. This is done to avoid the kind of pretrial publicity and damaged reputations that often accompany legal accusation in the United States, where judges do not enjoy such power. This rule implies a stricter interpretation of the "innocent until proven guilty" assumption than that which exists in the United States. This is an interesting switch in which Canadian law is more protective of the individual whereas U.S. law has opted to support the community's right to know (derived from the freedom of speech clause of the First Amendment) over the individual's right to privacy.

As in the United States, the Canadian suspect has the right to have bail granted at any time after arrest under the presumption of innocence. Prior to 1972 it was fairly difficult for poor suspects to post bail (about 40 percent of suspects were retained in custody pending their trials), and many suspects denied bail subsequently found themselves legally disadvantaged in terms of trial outcome.[20] Under the 1971 *Bail Reform Act,* there is a strong presumptive right to bail, and the onus is now on the Crown to show why bail should be denied. This presumptive right was further strengthened by the *Charter of Rights and Freedoms,* which stipulates that a suspect is "not to be denied reasonable bail without just cause." An arrested party can be released on bail by the police, a justice of the peace, or by a judge at a formal bail hearing.[21]

Indictment

At the conclusion of the preliminary hearing, but only if the accused is to be tried outside of the provincial court system, the next step the prosecutor must take is to prefer an indictment. This serves the same purpose as an indictment in the Unites States, although the process of obtaining an indictment does not require grand jury proceedings (grand juries no longer exist in Canada). The indictment, or formal accusation, is made by the Attorney General or by a Crown counsel (prosecutor) that the defendant has committed the offense in the indictment.

The accused may at any time enter a plea of guilty. It is a fairly common tactic in Canada for the defense to exercise its right to have a case heard in a higher court in order to obtain discovery (learn the strength of the Crown's case) and then to elect to return to the lower court with the intention of pleading guilty.[22] Although plea bargaining is looked down on with a certain amount of ethical disdain by the Canadian legal system, it is nevertheless firmly entrenched, with about 80 percent of criminal cases being disposed of by this method.[23] The inducements to plead guilty are not quite as attractive in Canada as in the United States, but a fair number of Canadian defendants obviously find sufficient motivation to relinquish their right to a trial and formally admit their guilt.

Trial

A trial may be conducted by a judge or by a judge and a jury. Canadian defendants have the right to a trial, but they only have the right to a *trial by jury* if the offense listed in the indictment carries a maximum penalty of imprisonment for five years or more years. Only the most serious indictable offenses that must be heard by a superior court judge (such as murder) fall into this category. Other indictable offenses (such as theft) may be heard by a provincial judge sitting alone or sometimes with two or more judges. A third class of indictable offenses, including robbery and sexual assault, may be tried in any manner previously discussed (trial by provincial judge, by superior court judge alone, or by superior court judge and jury) according to the wishes of the defendant. Significantly, it has been found that defendants who may choose their method of trial elect to be tried by a judge alone in 90 percent of the cases.[24] Summary offenses are tried by a provincial court judge sitting alone, although under certain circumstances a case may be heard by two judges sitting together. Summary offence trials can proceed without the accused if the accused does not wish to be present in court. However, if the Court requires the accused's presence, the accused can be compelled to appear.

Sentencing

If a defendant has been found guilty, he or she then becomes the subject of a presentence investigation conducted by a probation officer. The Canadian presentence report contains much the same information as its U.S. counterpart. Given the discretionary latitude allowed Canadian judges, the sentencing/treatment recommendations contained in the presentence report strongly influence the actual sentence received by the convicted defendant.

The Canadian system makes a distinction between sentencing and punishment, with sentencing being a statement ordering the imposition of a sanction (which may not be punitive), and punishment being the actual imposition of some form of deprivation, such as imprisonment.[25] One of the sentencing options for minor first offenders may be an absolute discharge, meaning that he or she is removed entirely and without condition from correctional authority as if the offense had never occurred.

Probation

Probation is the most common outcome for a convicted Canadian defendant except for the most minor offenses (where a fine is most common) or the most serious offenses. A Canadian probation order can continue in force for a maximum of only three years.[26] Probation in Canada may be successfully terminated without serving a minimum amount of time if the probationer fulfills a key provision of his or her probation order, such as paying full restitution to the victim.

Incarceration

Although there are federal and provincial prisons in Canada, there are no separate federal or provin-

cial criminal codes. Therefore, whether a convicted person goes to a federal or provincial penitentiary in Canada depends not on having violated a different code, but rather on the length of the sentence received. In general, commitments of two years or more are served in federal penitentiaries and sentences less than two years are served in provincial penitentiaries.

Although Canada has an incarceration rate only one fourth that of the United States, it has a rate higher than any European country other than Hungary.[27] As indicated in our earlier discussion of the U.S. system, Canadian defendants usually receive lighter sentences than their U.S. counterparts, but in terms of actual time served there is no significant difference between the two countries.[28]

Although the average Canadian prison is far smaller than the average U.S. prison, Canadian prisons experienced a higher rate of prison riots during the period encompassing 1971 through 1983.[29] However, Canadian prison riots tended to result in fewer injuries, despite the fact that Canadian prison officials relied less on alternatives to force than Americans to resolve the situation.[30] Interestingly, the major cause of prison riots in the United States (race) did not even appear as a cause in Canadian riots. The major cause of Canadian prison riots was escape attempts, which was not listed as a cause in U.S. prison riots. The U.S. riots also seemed to be sparked often by inmate complaints against both treatment and security staff, which was not listed as a cause of Canadian riots.

Parole

Parole in Canada is under the Jurisdiction of the National Parole Board (NPB). There are three primary forms of prison release in operation in the Canadian correctional system: *temporary absence, day parole,* and *full parole.* Temporary absence and day parole are designed to allow brief periods away from an institution for a number of reasons, such as participation in a rehabilitative program, work, education, or family-related matters. Temporary absences can last longer than one day, and are generally awarded near the completion of an inmate's sentence as a way of "easing" or reintegrating the inmate back into the community.

As in the United States, full parole is the release of an offender into the community under the supervision of a parole officer for the remainder of his or her sentence. Canadian inmates are typically eligible for parole after serving one third of their sentence or after serving seven years, whichever is the shorter period.[31] Most periods of parole last between one and two years.[32]

THE FOUR TRADITIONS OF LAW

The four main traditions or "families" of law in the world today are *civil law, common law, Islamic law,* and *socialist law.*[33] Of course, there are many systems of law in the world, each unique in many respects, but just about all of them are related to some degree to one of these four traditions. Some legal systems, due to the legacy of conquest and/or colonization, and sometime voluntary borrowing, are mixtures of one or more of these traditions, with native elements also thrown into the mix. Even among members of the same legal tradition there are often numerous specific differences, such as between England and the United States within the common law tradition, or between France and Germany within the civil law tradition.

All modern legal traditions have four basic elements in common:

- A set of written statutes defining behaviors that are forbidden or required, along with a set of written procedures outlining how people accused of violating those statutes will be dealt with.
- A body of people trained and empowered to enforce these statutes, called *police officers.*
- A formal system of determining the guilt or innocence of persons arrested by the police for violating the law.
- A system for punishing those found guilty.

As with many other areas of inquiry, differences between and among things are more interesting than commonalities. Thus we compare and contrast the common law tradition with other legal traditions with respect to the most basic of principles that define it.

Common Law

The **common law** tradition originated in England and has spread its influence around the world. India is the world's most populous common-law country, although Indian law is liberally sprinkled with indigenous Hindu law.[34] In addition to the widespread British influence, various aspects of common law have spread to countries formerly occupied by the United States such as the Philippines, Japan, and Italy, where common-law procedural principles were superimposed on a civil law structure.[35] However, no system of law is imported whole. Even Britain's daughter countries—the United States, Canada, Australia, and New Zealand—and sometimes England itself, have often found it necessary to depart from some specific practices to varying degrees without violating its general principles. Nevertheless, it remains the major source of modern criminal law in all English-speaking countries except Scotland and South Africa.[36]

Historical Aspects of Common Law.   The origin of the English common law is traditionally traced to the Norman conquest of England in 1066.[37] Prior to the Norman invasion, English law was a mixture of ancient custom, church law, and remnants of Roman and Germanic law. The principles and applications of these laws varied greatly from area to area within England. The "law" of the land was determined by powerful feudal lords, who often settled their disputes by combat. Because the lords relied on combat, and because their subjects had few rights, law as we know it was not really needed.[38] After the Norman invasion, William the Conqueror and his royal successors set out to provide the English with a law common to all (hence the term *common law*), both as a means of unifying England and to increase royal power at the expense of the feudal lords.

These Norman kings did not seek to impose alien laws on the English. The common law is fashioned from local customs and practices, shaped and formalized by judicial decisions based on the facts judges had before them. These decisions ultimately became the basis for future judicial decisions for judges confronted with similar cases in what became known as the *doctrine of precedent,* or **stare decisis.** Eventually these decisions, as well as the arguments made by lawyers involved in the cases, were written down and circulated for review by other judges and lawyers.[39] Thus much of English law is "judge-made," or case law, which has evolved over the centuries in response to the problems of the common person. In a very real sense, the common law represents the crystallization of custom as it existed at the time of its inception.

Of particular interest to U.S. students is the fact that many of the principles of common law found in U.S. criminal law procedure arose from the struggles between Parliament and the monarchy in the seventeenth century. The legal principles and procedures that resulted from the Parliamentary victory in that struggle were imported into the New World by English colonists. Most of the criminal procedural rules contained in the Fourth, Fifth, Sixth, and Eighth amendments of the Bill of Rights are based on the English Bill of Rights, many of them taken verbatim from it.[40]

Basic Features of Common Law.   The common law is distinguished from other systems of law in five important ways briefly described below.

1. *Common law is unwritten:* When we say that the common law is unwritten, we do not mean that it is literally not written down or that it lacks precision of meaning. The term is used to distinguish its origin in the customs of the people as formalized by judges from the "written" or statutory laws of the civil tradition, which were imposed on citizens from above.[41] Common law, however, has long surrendered its lawmaking role to legislative statutes and codified criminal law, while maintaining its role in procedural law. It is in the United States rather than England where judges retain a modicum of the old common law law-making role. In England, the laws of Parliament (the British legislative body analogous to the United States Congress) are not subject to judicial review. If a judicial body in the United States rules a legally enacted statute to be "unconstitutional," it is, almost by definition, engaging in judicial lawmaking.[42]

2. *Common law respects precedent:* The common law's respect for precedent flows from its origin as case law, which reflects the accumulated wisdom of generations of judicial decisions. Precedent operates in vertical and horizontal dimensions. The vertical dimension means that decisions made by higher courts should always be considered by lower courts in their deliberations, and the horizontal dimension means that courts at the same level maintain consistency in their interpretations of the law.[43] The doctrine of precedent allows for predictability, consistency, and rationality in the legal system.

3. *Common law is adversarial:* The adversarial nature of common law stems from the "trial by combat" method of settling disputes in medieval times. In an adversarial system both the prosecution and defense are expected to vigorously pursue their self-interest; some legal experts even argue that this should be extended to the point where it may be considered ethical to present a "false defense."[44] Judges in common law countries are supposed to function as disinterested referees, making sure that the opposing sides follow the rules. Judges do not control the flow of information to the court, do not question suspects or witnesses, and do not pass judgments of guilt or innocence (a bench trial is an exception to this).

4. *Common law uses grand and petit juries:* Indictment by grand jury and trial by petit jury have been cherished procedures in common-law countries. They were traditionally viewed as bodies of citizens interposing themselves between the power of the state and the accused. The expense of grand juries, as well as the various criticisms laid against them, led to their abolition in England and Canada, and to the ever-decreasing use of them in the United States (only four states require grand jury indictment for all crimes). Likewise, many practical considerations have led to less use of trial juries than was previously the case, and to the use of nonunanimous jury decisions and juries of less than twelve members in some states.[45]

5. *Common law uses judicial review:* Judicial review refers to the judiciary's examination of the legality of the actions and decisions of executive and administrative officers of the government, as well as appellate review of lower court decisions. The scope of judicial review is limited to various degrees in different common law countries. For instance, the U.S. Supreme Court can rule any legislation or executive order to be unconstitutional, but no judicial power in Britain has the power to overrule a Parliamentary act. The Supreme Court of Canada is beginning to evolve along the lines of its U.S. counterpart, although Canada's fear of judicial lawmaking applies the brakes to excessive judicially interference in legislative business.[46] Judicial review of criminal cases from the lower courts follows similar lines in all common-law countries.

Civil Law

The most pervasive legal system in the world is the civil law tradition. It is found in all countries of western Europe except England and Wales, in all Central and South American countries, in many African countries, and a number of Asian countries.[47] The civil law tradition is sometimes called *continental law,* or *code law* to avoid confusion with the civil branch of law in common-law countries, which deals with noncriminal matters. As within the common-law tradition, the civil law tradition encompasses a variety of systems that differ on many specifics.

Historical Origins of Civil Law. The civil law has a long history of development. Although its development is not so centered on one country as the development of common law is centered on England, it probably owes most to ancient Rome and nineteenth century France and Germany. As indicated in Chapter 1, the first historical example of a written code of laws can be traced back to the edicts of King Hammurabi (the Code of Hammurabi), who reigned in Babylon about 4,000 years ago. More relevant to the development of

modern civil law is early Roman law, beginning with the Twelve Tables, a compilation of rules regulating family, economic, and religious conduct, written around B.C. 450. A further advance in Roman law did not occur for almost another 1,000 years, when the Emperor Justinian published the *corpus juris civilis,* or *Code of Justinian,* in 533 A.D.[48] Modern civil law owes most to France's Napoleonic Code, or *Code Civil des France,* published in 1804, for it became the blueprint for almost all subsequent civil law codes.

Basic Features of Civil Law. The basic features of civil law are almost mirror opposites of the features of common law, although the two systems are not so far apart in theory and practice as this statement might imply. We will discuss civil law features with reference to their common law counterparts.

1. *Civil law is written rather than unwritten:* As opposed to the common law's slow accumulation of case law derived from decisions based on local customs, the Twelve Tables, the Code of Justinian, the Napoleonic Code and its successors, are all codes of conduct (statutes) written from above and imposed on citizens and subjects below. This comparison of principles may be overdrawn, however. Most law in common-law countries today is code (statutory) law based on legislative fiat rather than case law, and the legal prescriptions and proscriptions outlined in the various civil law codes were mostly consistent with the norms and customs that prevailed at the time of their publication.

2. *Precedent is not officially recognized:* Theoretically, the codes laid down in civil law are complete the day they are enacted and are not subject to judicial review. As such there is no need to refer to past cases for guidance; the code itself is all the guidance needed. In practice, however, no code is so complete as to provide unambiguous guidance in all matters coming before the courts, and civil law judges in practice often refer to and rely on case law, and thus to precedent.[49]

3. *It is inquisitorial rather than adversarial:* This is the primary distinguishing feature of civil law vis-à-vis common law. The term *inquisitorial* conjures up images of the Spanish Inquisition, torture, and the notion that the accused is assumed guilty unless he/she can prove innocence, all of which is untrue. *Inquisition* refers to the extensive investigation, interviews, and interrogations that are carried out in civil law countries to ensure that an innocent person is not subjected to trial.[50] The focus is on truth, and not so much on procedure, so many of the protections afforded suspects in common-law countries (such as the right to remain silent) do not exist. This does not mean that these systems run roughshod over individuals. More than one comparative legal scholar has voiced the opinion that the civil law is more protective of the innocent, and that the common law is more protective of the guilty.[51] This strongly suggests that civil law procedure is more likely to arrive at the truth and serve the purpose of justice than is common-law procedure. The intensive pretrial investigations minimize the likelihood that an innocent person will be brought to trial, but it also implies a strong presumption of guilt if the investigation does lead to a trial.

4. *It has traditionally made little use of juries:* There is some use of juries in some civil law countries, but they don't have exactly the same role that they have in common-law countries. Civil law juries do not have access to the totality of the evidence contained in the written inquiry of the case, and they do not receive defense and prosecution summations. They are thus much more reliant on the judge's direction than are common law juries.[52] Very serious criminal cases are decided by a "jury" of twelve members in France, but this tribunal consists of three professional judges and nine laypersons.[53] A very similar situation exists in Germany.[54] Civil law legal scholars see no problem with this. After all, judges in civil law countries are highly trained civil servants who owe their positions to education and experience, not political patronage. They are active participants in trials and see their job as seeking the truth by directly questioning suspects, witnesses, and other trial participants. In essence, civil law judges play to various degrees all parts played in common law

systems by judges, prosecutors, defense attorneys, and jury members.

5. *Judicial review is used sparingly:* There is no judicial review of legislatively determined statutes in most instances, although it is more common in some civil law countries than in others, it is not nearly so widespread as it is in the United States. On the whole, civil law countries tend to view the practice of judicial review as antidemocratic, as do many common law countries, including England itself. Appeals to higher courts are permissible on criminal matters, however. Unlike common-law appellate courts, whose function is to rule on points of law only, civil law appellate courts in some countries can rule on law and on facts. In some instances an appeals court may hold a new trial if new evidence is brought before it, and it can increase or decrease a criminal sentence on appeal.[55] Neither of these options is available to appeals courts in common law countries.

Socialist Law

Socialist law originated in 1917 when after the Russian Revolution, the Union of Soviet Socialist Republics (USSR) was established. Although the collapse of the USSR has led to the demise of socialist law in Russia and its former Eastern European satellites, variants of socialist law continue to exist in China, North Korea, Vietnam, and Cuba.[56] Because socialist law is based on Marxist/Leninist ideology, it is the only system of law considering itself to be a temporary anachronism.[57] Marxist/Leninist ideology envisions the eventual "withering away" of the state and an ensuing "dictatorship of the proletariat" in which law will no longer be needed (it was believed that Communism would release the "natural goodness" in all people).

Despite the alleged natural goodness of people, the state tried to control every aspect of Soviet life under the slogan of "socialist legalism," and saw itself as a parent and teacher of the masses. The law was viewed as a means of training the people to fulfill the responsibilities the state imposed on them.[58] While all systems of law have a "social engineering" function to some extent, this is a major function of Socialist law. "Legal" decisions, especially during the Stalin years, were often made by the secret police and revolutionary tribunals on a more or less ad hoc basis. The use of vague concepts like "counterrevolutionary" allowed for the creation of "instant" offenses not designated as crimes in any penal code. As we have seen, such practices are expressly forbidden in common law under the principle of legality ("no crime without law"), but they were justified by the Soviets and the Chinese as necessary to preserve the revolution, which was considered the only legitimate role of law anyway.[59]

Since the breakup of the Soviet Union, China is the most important country that has retained socialist law. We thus restrict our comparison to socialist law as it is practiced in China.

1. *Socialist law is written rather than unwritten.* Although Chinese law shares this characteristic with French civil law, it lacks the strict formalism of the latter and allows for a high degree of the ad hoc nature of statutory and procedural definitions noted earlier. Indeed, it wasn't until 1979 that China got its first legal and procedural code.[60] There have been recent attempts to liberalize the law and to bring it in line with other modern nations,[61] but it remains to be seen what effects this will have on actual practice.

2. *Precedent has no place in socialist law.* The concept of precedent is a totally alien to socialist law for a number of reasons. First, because the law is often changed to suit the changing political needs of the state, it would be useless as a guide for judicial decision making. Second, law is imposed from above by the Communist Party, and is thus complete as soon as it is enacted and cannot be amended by case law. Third, because judges are subservient to the party, they cannot be allowed either to make or interpret party law. Finally, in the Chinese case, the recency of its criminal code hardly affords time for the accumulation of case law.

3. *Socialist law is primarily inquisitorial.* Although Chinese law is primarily inquisitorial, it has adversarial aspects. Defendants have the right to defend themselves (literally) in court, to hire a lawyer (lawyers are extremely rare in China), or to appoint a relative or friend to advocate for them, mostly in the form of arguing for leniency in sentencing.[62] There is no presumption of innocence at any stage of Chinese criminal justice processing, and the Chinese do not look kindly on defendants who insist on denying their guilt. Confession and remorse are viewed most positively, however. There is such an emphasis on contrition and reintegration that the authorities do not let defendants know what evidence there is against them on the assumption that it would taint the voluntariness of confession to do so.[63]

4. *Socialist law does not make use of juries.* A Chinese trial is much like a trial in the civil law tradition, i.e., a review of the facts and a consideration of sentence. It is presided over by either a panel of one judge and two lay assessors, or by a panel of three judges. The judge, prosecutor, lay assessors, victim, or victim's representative may all interrogate the defendant, who does not have the right to remain silent. Following this phase, the defendant has the right to debate any of those who had questioned him or her. The panel then decides both the verdict and the punishment by majority vote.

Although the emphasis in the Chinese criminal justice system is, in principle, on rehabilitation and reintegration, punishment for those considered to be beyond rehabilitation is severe. The death penalty is applied to nearly seventy different offenses in China; there were 4,367 confirmed executions in 1996.[64] After adjusting for population size, this amounts to about fifteen times as many executions as there were in the United States (74) in the same year.

5. *Socialist law does not permit judicial review.* Whereas the French oppose judicial review of legislation on the grounds that it thwarts the democratic will of the people, for the Chinese it cannot even be imagined given the subservient nature of both the judiciary and the law itself to the state. However, criminal court decisions can be appealed to a higher court or adjudication committee, whose decision is forever binding (the decision cannot be further appealed to an even higher court). Both the defendant and the prosecutor can appeal a verdict, which indicates that the concept of double jeopardy is also an alien concept in socialist law.

Islamic Law

Islamic law has its origins in the collected revelations and thoughts of the Prophet Muhammad (who lived from 570 to 632 A.D.) contained in Islam's holy book, the *Qu'ran* (Koran). Islamic law spread with Arab conquests that stretched from Muhammad's time to the late eleventh century.[65] Islamic law is practiced primarily in Arabic countries, most of North Africa, and in Pakistan and Bangladesh, regions of the Indian subcontinent. The major difference between Islamic law and the other three traditions is that it is a theocratic (religious) system that claims to be based on direct revelation from God (*Allah*). As with other legal traditions, however, there are differences from country to country in the way the law is interpreted and applied. The *Qu'ran* is strictly followed in fundamentalist Iran, and has been formally adopted as the constitution of Saudi Arabia, but countries such as Turkey and Egypt have a much more secularized approach to law.[66] Because Saudi Arabia is the country that most closely follows Islamic law, we confine our discussion to that country.

1. *Islamic law is written but augmented by case law.* The *Qu'ran* is considered the ultimate source of Islamic law. It contains numerous moral precepts relating in a general way to all aspects of life, but it is not a legal code in the Western sense of the word. The generality of the *Qu'ran's* moral precepts necessitates their augmentation by the commentary of legal scholars and case law. The *Qu'ran* functions as a sort of constitution, laying out general principles, that must be interpreted and applied to a variety of specific cases.[67] What emerges from the *Qu'ran,* case law, and scholarly commentaries is called *Shari'a,* "the path to follow."

2. *Islamic law recognizes precedent but is not bound by it.* As mentioned above, the generality of the *Qu'ran* (imagine trying to run a legal system based solely on the Bible) necessitates the accumulation of case law that judges may refer to when making decisions. However, case law functions more as a guide than as principles binding on lower courts until overturned at a higher level. Many Western scholars view Islamic law as lacking a set of generalized legal (as opposed to religious) principles. As such, they view it as a system of ad hoc justice more akin to informal dispute resolution than to the predictable systems of the West.[68]

3. *Islamic law is accusatory.* Under Islamic law the victim of a crime (the accuser) is responsible for initiating a court action by bringing a complaint against the wrongdoer. Except in highly involved crimes, crimes against the state, or in instances where foreigners are involved, there is little if any formal investigation of the complaint or of the accused (Islamic law is therefore not inquisitorial). The case is settled in court by the practice of oath-taking in which both parties in the dispute make a series of statements under oath regarding various aspects of evidence and of personal character (augmented by witnesses) for the *qadi* (judge) to evaluate. The parties represent themselves in these instances, so in a sense Islamic law is adversarial, but certainly not in the common-law sense. The climax of a trial comes when the qadi, at his discretion, challenges one of the parties to swear an oath that he is telling the truth. If the person challenged declines to swear the oath (and this happens fairly often) he automatically loses the case. If he does swear the oath, he automatically wins.[69]

4. *Islamic law does not make use of juries.* The qadi is the sole finder of fact and law in an Islamic law trial. Because of the practice of oath-taking, however, his main concern is often deciding which party should be challenged to swear it. Procedure in Saudi Arabian courts is therefore extremely informal compared with procedure in other systems. There is no skillful cross-examination by prosecutors or defense attorneys, no juries to be swayed by emotional appeals, and no fine points of law to be ruled on by the judge. Given the great power of the qadi, it is interesting to note that the primary training for such work in Saudi Arabia is religious, and that formal legal training in that country is

deemed more important for practicing civil (non-criminal) than criminal law.[70]

5. *Islamic law allows limited judicial review.* The accusatory process we described under point 3 applies only to the most serious crimes, the *Huddud* crimes. *Huddud* crimes and their penalties are adultery (death), sodomy (death), fornication (eighty lashes), false accusation of any of the foregoing crimes (one hundred lashes), alcohol consumption (whipping—varies, death is possible after third offense), apostasy—religious conversion from Islam to some other faith (death), theft (amputation of hand), and robbery (amputation of alternate-side hand and foot). *Huddud* crimes and the penalties attached to them are considered God-prescribed, and no judge or legislative body can alter the penalty for them.[71] Because the law is based on the will of Allah as written in the *Qu'ran,* the only form of judicial review can be to determine if a case was conducted in conformity with it. However, because the oath deciding the case is considered binding, the appeal applies only to the sentence imposed. Appeals are heard by a panel of three to five judges. Because the *Qu'ran* does not envision conflict between the interests of the rulers and the ruled, and because the law is of divine origin and valid for all time, there can be no provision for judicial review of governmental actions.[72]

SUMMARY

No matter what offensive behavior a person may commit, he or she is not "officially " a criminal until legally defined as such. In order to be so defined, the person must be processed through a series of steps or procedures designed for that purpose. These procedures are part of a set of rules each society has for governing itself called *the law.*

In order to apply the label of "criminal" to someone in the United States, the state must prove *corpus delicti,* or "body of the crime." To prove corpus delecti, the state must prove that the person who is to be labeled actually committed a criminal act (*actus reus*), and did so with the full and conscious knowledge that the act was wrong (*mens rea*). *Actus reus* and *mens rea* are two of a set of seven important legal principles of U.S. law. The other five principles are (1) legality, (2) punishment, (3) concurrence (4) causation, and (5) harm.

A suspect's journey through the U.S. criminal justice system begins with arrest, for which a warrant must be issued, or for which a police officer must have probable cause to believe that a felony crime has been committed. On arrest the suspect is booked into the county jail to await a preliminary arraignment, which should take place at the earliest possible time after arrest. The purpose of the preliminary arraignment is (1) to advise suspects of their constitutional rights, and, (2) set bail. There is no constitutional right to bail.

The next step in the process is the preliminary hearing held before a lower-court judge to determine if the suspect's arrest and detention were legal, and to determine if the prosecution has enough evidence to warrant the case being bound over to a higher court. If the prosecutor is successful, he or she must seek an indictment from the grand jury, formally charging the suspect with the crime he or she is accused of. A grand jury indictment is not necessary in all states or in all crimes.

The next step is arraignment before a felony trial judge in which the defendant enters a formal plea of "guilty," "not guilty," or "no contest" to the charges specified in the indictment. A "guilty" or "no contest" plea results in a date being set for sentencing; a "not guilty" plea results in a date being set for trial. The criminal trial is a process by which the state must prove "beyond a reasonable doubt" (usually to a jury) that the defendant committed the crime he or she has been accused of.

If the state fails to do this, the defendant is set free; if the state succeeds, he or she is usually referred to the probation department for a presentence investigation report (PSI). The PSI contains pertinent facts about the offense committed and about the defendant's background, which is used to make a sentencing recommendation. The defendant can be sentenced to a variety of punishments, including probation or prison. The United States is often considered to be the most punitive of Western nations in its sentencing, but, looking beyond the surface, figures reveal that although sentences are longer, time actually served is similar to other Western nations.

We then took an excursion through the Canadian criminal justice system, noting that it is quite similar to the U.S. system. Although both countries share the common-law tradition, and although an exemplary champion of civil liberties, Canada was characterized as more of a crime-control system than a due-process system because of its emphasis on community protection. There are only minor differences between the Canadian and U.S. criminal justice systems at each stage of criminal processing.

We next discussed the four traditions of law in existence today. The first legal tradition examined was the common law, which is the legal system of England and most of her former colonies. The common law is adversarial in nature, relies extensively on the principle of precedent, is "unwritten," makes great use of laypersons (in grand and petit juries), and uses judicial review. By way of contrast, the civil law system (the most common tradition in the world) is characterized by factors that are essentially the opposite of the common-law tradition. It is not so concerned with the procedural rights enjoyed by suspects in common-law traditions, but many scholars feel that it serves the purposes of truth and justice better.

The socialist tradition is a tradition seemingly destined to the dustbin of history. It was developed in the former Soviet Union to serve the purpose of the Communist revolution. In doing so, it violated many of the legal principles of both the common and civil law traditions. China is the most important country still operating under the socialist system today. We characterized Chinese law as written and primarily inquisitorial, noted that it makes no use of precedent, juries, or judicial review. Many former Communist countries appear to be returning to a more traditional civil law system.

The final tradition examined was the Islamic tradition, using Saudi Arabia as our exemplar nation. Unlike the other traditions, the Islamic tradition is a religious one, based as it is on the holy book of Islam, the *Qu'ran*. We noted that Islamic law is written (the *Qu'ran*) and augmented by case law, which means that there is a certain amount of respect for precedent, although it is not binding, and that it is an accusatory system. We also noted that it does not make use of juries or judicial review.

EXERCISES

1. Why is law essential to any modern society regardless of its political ideology?
2. Do you think that the presentence report is necessary for "proper" sentencing, or do you believe that everyone convicted of the same crime should receive the same punishment, period?
3. Do you see the U.S. criminal justice system as "softer" or "harder" on criminals than systems in other democratic nations?
4. What are the advantages or disadvantage of the principle of *stare decisis*?
5. What are the advantages and disadvantages of common and civil law systems for (a) society, (b) an innocent defendant, (c) a guilty defendant?
6. Do you think that the severe punishments of the Islamic system would reduce crime in this country? Would you like to see such a system here?

ENDNOTES

1. Robin & Anson 1990:248.
2. Robin & Anson 1990:35.
3. Schmalleger 1993:23.
4. Rush 1991:141.
5. Robin & Anson 1990:282.
6. Uhlman & Walker 1980; Walsh 1990.
7. Myers 1979; Walsh 1985.
8. Schmalleger 1993:375.
9. Schmalleger 1993:434–435.
10. Kappeler et al. 1993.
11. *Law Enforcement News* 1994:7.
12. Lynch 1987.
13. Lynch 1993.
14. Lynch 1993:650.
15. Schmalleger 1995:19.
16. Hagan & Leon 1978:182.
17. Griffiths & Verdun-Jones 1989:97.
18. Griffiths & Verdun-Jones 1989:99.
19. Cunningham & Griffiths 1997.
20. Brannigan 1984:191.
21. Cunningham & Griffiths 1997:173.
22. Brannigan 1984:135.
23. Griffiths & Verdun-Jones 1989:266–70.
24. Griffiths & Verdun-Jones 1989:205.
25. Griffiths & Verdun-Jones 1989:285.
26. Brannigan 1984:220.
27. Kappeler et al. 1993.
28. Lynch 1993.
29. Montgomery 1987.
30. Montgomery 1987:63.
31. Griffiths & Verdun-Jones 1989:449.
32. Brannigan 1984:220.
33. Derrett 1968; Fairchild 1993; Opolot 1981.
34. Derrett 1968:80.
35. Weigend 1983:542.
36. Schmalleger 1993:99.
37. Rush 1991:59.
38. Opolot 1981:570.
39. Abadinsky 1991:9.
40. Fairchild 1993:35.
41. Opolot 1981:67.
42. Fairchild 1993:35.
43. Carter 1984.
44. Mitchell 1987.
45. Robin & Anson 1990:327–329.
46. Thompson 1985:70.
47. Fairchild 1993:29.
48. Abadinsky 1991; Merryman 1985.
49. Abadinsky 1991:18; Shapiro 1981:135.
50. Fairchild 1993:125; Opolot 1981:27.
51. Fairchild 1993:125; Maechling 1993:42; Merryman 1985:139.
52. Terrill 1984:135.
53. Fairchild 1993:169.
54. Jescheck 1970.
55. Abadinsky 1991:20.
56. Vago 1991:12.
57. Opolot 1981:109.
58. Allen 1993.
59. Opolot 1981:111.
60. Davidson & Wang 1996.
61. *Economist* 1997.
62. McCabe 1989.
63. Reichel 1994:219.
64. *Economist* 1997.
65. Durant 1949:187.
66. Jones 1992.
67. Jones 1992.
68. Abadinsky 1991; Reichel 1994.
69. Reichel 1994:115.
70. Fairchild 1993:157.
71. Souryal Potts & Alobied 1994.
72. Reichel 1994:165

Abadinsky, H. (1987). The McDonaldization of the Mafia. In T. Bynum (Ed.), *Organized crime in America: Concepts and controversies* (pp. 43–54). Monsey, NY: Willow Tree Press.

Abadinsky, H. (1988). *Organized crime* (2nd ed.). Chicago: Nelson-Hall.

Abadinsky, H. (1991). *Law and justice: An introduction to the American legal system.* Chicago: Nelson-Hall.

Abbott, J. C., Dunbrack, R. L., & Orr, C. D. (1985). The interaction of size and experience in dominance relationships of juvenile steelhead trout (*Salmo gairdneri*). *Behaviour, 92,* 241–253.

Abel, G., & Rouleau, J. (1990). The nature and extent of sexual assault. In W. Marshall, D. Laws, and H. Barbaree (Eds.), *Handbook of sexual assault: Issues, theories, and treatment of the offender* (pp. 9–21). New York: Plenum.

Aboitiz, F. (1995). Homology in the evolution of the cerebral hemispheres: The case of reptilian dorsal ventricular ridge and its possible correspondence with mammalian neocortex. *Journal of Brain Research, 36,* 461–472.

Abraham, G. (1980). Premenstrual tension. *Current Problems in Obstetrics and Gynecology, 3,* 1–39.

Abrams, D., Simpson, A., & Hogg, M. A. (1987). Different views: The impact of sex, area of residence, and victimization on teenagers' explanations for delinquency. *Journal of Youth and Adolescence, 16,* 401–413.

Abrams, J. K., & Fave, L. R. D. (1976). Authoritarianism, religiosity, and the legalization of victimless crimes. *Sociology and Social Research, 61,* 68–82.

Abramson, M. (1972). The criminalization of mentally disordered behavior: Possible side effect of a new mental health law. *Hospital and Community Psychiatry, 23,* 101–105.

Achenbach, T. M., Howell, C. T., Quay, H. C., & Conners, C. K. (1991). Methodological and substantive lessons: Reply monographs-of-the society for research in child development. *Child Development, 56,* 128–130.

Ackerman, P. L., & Heggestad, E. D. (1997). Intelligence, personality, and interests: Evidence of overlapping traits. *Psychological Bulletin, 121,* 219–245.

Adler, C., & Polk, K. (1996). Masculinity and child homicide. *British Journal of Criminology, 36,* 396–411.

Adler, F. (1975). *Sisters in crime: The rise of the new female criminal.* New York: McGraw-Hill.

Adler, F. (1979). Changing patterns. In F. Adler & R. Simon (Eds.), *The criminology of deviant women* (pp. 91–94). Boston: Houghton Mifflin.

Adler, F., Mueller, G. O. W., & Laufer, W. S. (1991). *Criminology.* Boston: McGraw-Hill.

Adler, F., Mueller, G. O. W., & Laufer, W. S. (1998). *Criminology* (3rd ed.). Boston: McGraw-Hill.

Adler, I., & Kandel, D. B. (1980). *Cross-cultural perspectives on developmental stages in adolescent drug use.* New York: Columbia University Press.

Adlersberg, J., & Dolger, J. (1939). Medico-legal problems of hypoglycemic reactions in diabetes. *Annals of Internal Medicine, 12,* 1804–1807.

af Klinteberg, B., Humble, K., & Schalling, D. (1992). Personality and psychopathy of males with a history of early criminal behaviour. *European Journal of Personality, 6,* 245–266.

af Klinteberg, B., Levander, S. E., Oreland, L., Asberg, M., & Schalling, D. (1987). Neuropsychological correlates of platelet monoamine oxidase (MAO) activity in female and male subjects. *Biological Psychology, 24,* 237–251.

af Klinteberg, B., Magnusson, D., & Schalling, D. (1989). Hyperactive behavior in childhood and adult impulsivity: A longitudinal study of male subjects. *Personality and Individual Differences, 10,* 43–50.

Agnew, R. (1984). Goal achievement and delinquency. *Sociology and Social Research, 68,* 435–451.

Agnew, R. (1985a). Social control theory and delinquency: A longitudinal test. *Criminology, 23,* 47–61.

Agnew, R. (1985b). A revised strain theory of delinquency. *Social Forces, 64,* 151–167.

Agnew, R. (1989). A longitudinal test of the revised strain theory. *Journal of Quantitative Criminology, 5,* 373–387.

Agnew, R. (1992). Foundation for a general strain theory of crime and delinquency. *Criminology, 30,* 47–87.

Agnew, R. (1993). Why do they do it? An examination of the intervening mechanisms between social control variables and delinquency. *Journal of Research in Crime and Delinquency, 30,* 245–266.

Agnew, R. (1994). The techniques of neutralization and violence. *Criminology, 32,* 555–580.

Agnew, R. (1995). Testing the leading crime theories: An alternative strategy focusing on motivational processes. *Journal of Research in Crime and Delinquency, 32,* 363–398.

Agnew, R. (1997). Stability and change in crime over the life course: A strain theory explanation. In T. P. Thornberry (Ed.), *Developmental theories of crime and delinquency: Advances in criminological theory* (Vol. 7, pp. 101–131). New Brunswick, NJ: Transaction.

Agnew, R., & Peters, A. A. R. (1986). The techniques of neutralization: An analysis of predisposing and situational factors. *Criminal Justice and Behavior, 13,* 81–97.

Agnew, R., & White, H. R. (1992). An empirical test of general strain theory. *Criminology, 30,* 475–499.

Akers, R. L. (1977). Deviant behavior: A social learning approach (2nd ed.). Belmont, MA: Wadsworth.

Akers, R., L. (1980). Further critical thoughts on Marxist criminology: Comments on Turk, Toby, and Klockars. In J. Inciardi, A. (Ed.), *Radical criminology, the coming crises* (pp. 133–138). Beverly Hills, CA: Sage.

Akers, R. L., & Cochran, J. K. (1985). Adolescent marijuana use: A test of three theories of deviant behavior. *Deviant Behavior, 6,* 323–346.

Akers, R. L., Krohn, M. D., Lanza-Kaduce, L., & Radosevich, M. (1979). Social learning and deviant behavior: A specific test of a general theory. *American Sociological Review, 44,* 636–655.

Akesson, H. O., & Wahlstrom, J. (1977). Length of the Y-chromosomes in men examined by forensic psychiatrists. *Human Genetics, 39,* 1–5.

Akman, D., Normandeau, A., & Turner, S. (1967). The measurement of delinquency in Canada. *Journal of Criminal Law, Criminology, and Police Science, 58,* 330–337.

Albanese, Jay, & Pursley, Robert (1993). *Crime in America: Some existing and emerging issues.* Englewood Cliffs, NJ: Regents/Prentice-Hall.

Albert, D. J., Jonik, R. H., & Walsh, M. L. (1992). Hormone-dependent aggression in male and female rats: Experiential, hormonal, and neural foundations. *Neuroscience and Biobehavioral Reviews, 17,* 405–425.

Albert, D. J., Walsh, M. L., & Jonik, R. H. (1993). Aggression in humans: What is its biological foundation? *Neuroscience and Biobehavioral Reviews, 17,* 405–425.

Alcock, J. (1993). Animal behavior: An evolutionary approach (5th ed.). Sunderland, MA: Sinauer.

Alexander, T. (1972). The social engineers retreat under fire. *Fortune,* 86 (October), 132–148.

Alexopoloulos, G. S., Lieberman, K. W., & Frances, R. J. (1983). Platelet MAO activity in alcoholic patients and their first-degree relatives. *American Journal of Psychiatry, 140,* 1501–1504.

Alford, R., & Alford, F. (1981). Sex differences in asymmetry in the facial expression of emotion. *Neuropsychologia, 19,* 605–608.

Alland, A. (1967). *Evolution and human behavior.* London, England: Tavistock.

Allen, C. (1991). *Women and men who sexually abuse children.* Orwell, VT: Safer Society Press.

Allen, F. A. (1945). Pioneers in criminology—Raffaele Garofolo (1852–1934). *Journal of Criminal Law, Criminology, and Police Science, 45,* 373–389.

Allen, Fredrick (1993). Restructuring justice in Russia: A new era of challenges. *Federal Probation, 57,* 54–58.

Allport, G. W., & Ross, J. M. (1967). Personal religious orientation and prejudice. *Journal of Personality and Social Psychology, 5,* 432–443.

Allsopp, J. F., & Feldman, M. P. (1974). Extroversion, neuroticism, psychoticism, and antisocial behaviour in school girls. *Social Behaviour and Personality, 2,* 184–189.

Allsopp, J. F., & Feldman, M. P. (1976). Item analyses of questionnaire measures of personality and anti-social behaviour in school. *British Journal of Criminology, 16,* 337–351.

Alper, J. S. (1998). Genes, free will, and criminal responsibility. *Social Science and Medicine, 46,* 1599–1611.

Alschuler, A. (1976). The trial judge's role in plea bargaining. *Columbia Law Review, 76,* 1059–1154.

Al-Thakeb, F., & Scott, J. E. (1981). The perceived seriousness of crime in the Middle East. *International Journal of Comparative and Applied Criminal Justice, 5,* 129–143.

Amacher, R. C., & Ulbrich, H. H. (1995). *Microeconomic principles and policies.* Cincinnati: South-Western.

American Psychiatric Association, D.-I. (1993). *Diagnostic and statistical manual of mental disorders.* (4th ed.). Washington, DC: American Psychiatric Association.

American Psychiatric Association. (1994). *Diagnostic and statistical manual of mental disorders,* (4th ed.). Washington, DC: American Psychiatric Association.

Amir, M., & Hovav, M. (1976). Juvenile delinquency in Israel: Major trends in statistical data. *Israel Annals of Psychiatry, 11,* 161–172.

Amir, M. (1967). Victim precipitated forcible rape. *Journal of Criminal Law, Criminology, and Police Science, 58,* 493–502.

Ancel, M. (1987). *Social defense: The future of penal reform.* Littleton, CO: Fred B. Rothman.

Anderson, E. A. (1976). The "chivalrous" treatment of the female offender in arms of the criminal justice system: A review of the literature. *Social Problems, 23,* 350–357.

Anderson, J. C., Williams, S., McGee, R., & Silva, P. (1987). DSM-III disorders in preadolescent children: Prevalence in a large sample from the general population. *Archives of General Psychiatry, 44,* 69–76.

Andon, H. B. (1997). Patterns on injury mortality among Athabascan Indians in interior Alaska 1977–1987. *American Indian and Alaska Native Mental Health Research, 7,* 11–32.

Andrew, J. M. (1982). Memory and violent crime among delinquents. *Criminal Justice and Behavior, 9,* 364–471.

Andrew, M., & Cronin, C. (1997). Two measures of sensation seeking as predictors of alcohol use among high school males. *Personality & Individual Differences, 22,* 393–401.

Aneshensel, C. S., & Sucoff, C. A. (1996). The neighborhood context of adolescent mental health. *Journal of Health and Social Behavior, 37,* 293–310.

Angenent, H., & De Man, A. (1996). *Background factors of juvenile delinquency.* New York: Peter Lang.

Angold, A., & Costello, E. J. (1996). Toward establishing an empirical basis for the diagnosis of oppositional defiant disorder. *Journal of the American Academy of Child and Adolescent Psychiatry, 35,* 1205–1212.

Anson, O., Paran, E., Neumann, L., & Chernichovsky, D. (1993). Gender differences in health perceptions and their predictors. *Social Science and Medicine, 36,* 419–427.

Anthenelli, M. D., & Tabakoff, B. (1995). The search for biochemical markers. *Alcohol Health and Research World, 19,* 176–181.

Aono, T., Kurachi, K., & Mizutanai, S. (1972). Influence of major surgical stress on plasma levels of testosterone, luteinizing hormone and follicle-stimulating hormone in male patients. *Journal of Clinical Endocrinology & Metabolism, 35,* 535–542.

Appell, G. N. (1980). Talking ethics: The uses of moral rhetoric and the function of ethical principles. *Social Problems, 27,* 350–357.

Apter, A., Bleich, A., Plutchik, R., Mendelsohn, S., & Tyano, S. (1988). Suicidal behavior, depression, and conduct disorder in hospitalized adolescents. *Journal of the American Academy of Child and Adolescent Psychiatry, 27,* 696–699.

Arboleda-Florez, J., & Holley, H. L. (1991). Antisocial Burnout: An exploratory study. *Bulletin of the American Academy of Psychiatry and Law, 19,* 173–183.

Arbuthnot, J. (1984). Moral reasoning development programs in prison: Cognitive-developmental and critical reasoning approaches. *Journal of Moral Education, 13,* 112–123.

Arbuthnot, J., Gordon, D. A., & Jurkovic, G. J. (1987). *Handbook of juvenile delinquency.* New York: John Wiley & Sons.

Arbuthnot, J. (1992). Sociomoral reasoning in behavior-disordered adolescents: Cognitive and behavioral change. In J. McCord & R. E. Tremblay (Eds.), *Preventing antisocial behavior: Interventions from birth through adolescence* (pp. 283–309). New York: Guilford.

Arbuthnot, J., & Gordon, D. A. (1986). Behavioral and cognitive effects of a moral reasoning development intervention for high-risk behavior-disordered adolescents. *Journal of Consulting and Clinical Psychology, 54,* 208–216.

Archer, L. A., & Campbell, D. (1988). A prospective study of hand preference and language development in 18- to 30-month olds: I. Hand preference. *Developmental Neuropsychology, 4,* 85–92.

Archer, R. P. (1995). The many faces of psychopathy. *Contemporary Psychology, 40,* 518–520.

Arnett, J. (1994). Sensation seeking: A new conceptualization and a new scale. *Personality and Individual Differences, 16,* 289–296.

Arnett, J. (1996). Sensation seeking, aggressiveness, and adolescent reckless behavior. *Personality and Individual Differences, 20,* 693–702.

Arnett, P. A., Smith, S. S., & Newman, J. P. (1997). Approach and avoidance motivation in psychopathic criminal offenders during passive avoidance. *Journal of Personality and Social Psychology, 72,* 1413–1428.

Arnold, W. R., & Brungardt, T. M. (1983). *Juvenile misconduct and delinquency.* Boston: Houghton Mifflin.

Arnsten, A. F. T. (1997). Catecholamine regulation of the prefrontal cortex. *Journal of Psychopharmacology, 11,* 151–162.

Aro, H., & Taipale, V. (1987). The impact of timing of puberty on psychosomatic symptoms among fourteen- to sixteen-year-old Finnish girls. *Child Development, 58,* 261–268.

Aromaa, K. (1984). Three surveys of violence in Finland. In R. Block (Ed.), *Victimization and fear of crime: World perspectives* (pp. 11–21). Washington, DC: U.S. Government Printing Office.

Aromaa, K. (1994). Self-reported delinquency in Helsinki, Finland, 1992. In J. Junger-Tas, G.-J. Terlouw, & M. W. Klein (Eds.), *Delinquent behavior among young people in the Western world: First results of the international self-report delinquency study* (pp. 16–41). Amsterdam: Kugler.

Aschaffenburg, G. (1933). *Das Verbrechen und seine Bekampfung.* Heidelberg: Carl Wingers Universitatstiuchhandlung.

Asher, J. (1982). The concept of the family as seen as deeply rooted in human brain. *Alcohol, Drug Abuse, and Mental Health Administration News,* June 18, 1–3.

Ashton, C. H., & Kamali, F. (1995). Personality, lifestyles, alcohol and drug consumption in a sample of British medical students. *Medical Education, 29,* 187–192.

Asnorow, J. R. (1988). Children at risk for schizophrenia: Converging lines of evidence. *Schizophrenia Bulletin, 14,* 333–342.

Associated Press (1996). U.S. fugitive convicted in Cuba. *The Idaho Statesman,* Tuesday, August 27, p. 6a.

Asuni, T. (1963). Preliminary study of juvenile delinquency in western Nigeria. *Proceedings of the 12th International Course in Criminology, 1,* 186–194.

Atiyah, P., & Summers, R. (1987). *Form and substance in Anglo-American law: A comparative study in legal reasoning, legal theory and legal institutions.* Oxford: Oxford University Press.

Atkeson, B. M., & Forehand, R. (1981). Conduct disorders. In E. J. Mash & L. G. Terdal (Eds.), *Behavioral assessment of childhood disorders* (pp. 185–219). New York: Guilford.

Austin, R. L. (1977). Commitment, neutralization, and delinquency. In T. N. Ferdinand (Ed.), *Juvenile delinquency: Little brother grows up* (pp. 121–137). Beverly Hills, CA: Sage.

Austin, R. L. (1978). Race, father-absence, and female delinquency. *Criminology, 15,* 487–504.

Austin, R. L. (1982). Women's liberation and increases in minor, major, and occupational offenses. *Criminology, 20,* 407–430.

Avakame, E. F. (1997). Modeling the patriarchal factor in juvenile delinquency: Is there room for peers, church, and television? *Criminal Justice and Behavior, 24,* 477–494.

Averill, J. R. (1982). *Anger and aggression.* New York: Springer-Verlag.

Ayllon, T., & Azrin, N. (1968). *The token economy: A motivational system for therapy and rehabilitation.* New York: Appleton-Century-Crofts.

Bach-y-Rita, G., Lion, J. R., Climent, C. E., & Ervin, F. R. (1971). Episodic dyscontrol: A study of 130 violent patients. *American Journal of Psychiatry, 127,* 1473–1478.

Backe-Hansen, E., & Ogden, T. (1996). Competent girls and problematic boys? Sex differences in two cohorts of Norwegian 10- and 13-year-olds. *Childhood, 3,* 331–350.

Bacon, M. K., Child, I. L., & Barry, H. (1963). A cross-cultural study of correlates of crime. *Journal of Abnormal and Social Psychology, 66,* 291–300.

Baer, D. J., Baumgartner, W. A., Hill, V. A., & Blahd, W. H. (1991). Hair analysis for the detection of drug use in pretrial, probation, and parole populations. *Federal Probation, 55,* 3–10.

Bagley, C. (1992). Maternal smoking and deviant behavior in 16 year olds: A personality hypothesis. *Personality and Individual Differences, 13,* 377–378.

Bailey, W. C. (1984). Poverty, inequality, and city homicide rates: Some not so unexpected findings. *Criminology, 22,* 531–550.

Bakan, P. (1990). Nonright-handedness and the continuum of reproductive casuality. In S. Coren (Ed.), *Left-handedness* (pp. 33–74). North-Holland: Elsevier.

Balkwell, J. W. (1990). Ethnic inequality and the rate of homicide. *Social Forces, 69,* 53–70.

Ball, I. L., Farnill, D., & Wangeman, J. (1983). Factorial invariance across sex of the form V of the sensation-seeking-scale. *Journal of Personality and Social Psychology, 45,* 1156–1159.

Ball, R. A. (1966). An empirical exploration of neutralization theory. *Criminologica, 4,* 22–32.

Ball, R. A. (1968). An empirical exploration of neutralization theory. In M. Lefton, J. Skipper, & C. McCaghy (Eds.), *Approaches to deviance* (pp. 255–265). New York: Appleton-Century-Crofts.

Ball, R. A. (1977). Emergent delinquency in an urban area. In T. N. Ferdinand (Ed.), *Juvenile delinquency: Little brother grows up* (pp. 101–120). Beverly Hills, CA: Sage.

Ball, R. A. (1983). Development of basic norm violation: Neutralization and self-concept within a male cohort. *Criminology, 21,* 75–94.

Ball, R. A., & Lilly, J. R. (1971). Juvenile delinquency in an urban county. *Criminology, 9,* 69–85.

Ball-Rokeach, S. J. (1973). Values and violence: A test of the subculture of violence thesis. *American Sociological Review, 38,* 736–749.

Ballenger, J. C., Post, R. M., Jimerson, D. C., Lake, C. R., Murphy, D. L., Zuckerman, M., & Cronin, C. (1983). Biochemical correlates of personality traits in normals: An exploratory study. *Personality and Individual Differences, 4,* 615–625.

Balvig, F. (1985). Crime in Scandinavia: Trends, explanations and consequences. In N. Bishop (Ed.), *Scandinavian criminal policy and criminology 1980–1985* (pp. 7–17). Copenhagen, Denmark: Scandinavian Research Council for Criminology.

Bandura, A. (1971). *Social learning theory.* Morristown, NJ: Ronald Press.

Bandura, A. (1977). *Social learning theory.* Englewood Cliffs, NJ: Prentice-Hall.

Bandura, A. (1985). *Models of causality and social learning theory.* New York: Plenum.

Bandura, A. (1990). Mechanisms of moral disengagement. In W. Reich (Ed.), *Origins of terrorism: Psychologies, ideologies, theologies, states of mind* (pp. 161–191). Cambridge: Cambridge University Press.

Bandura, A., & Walters, R. H. (1959). *Adolescent aggression.* New York: Ronald Press.

Banks, C., Maloney, E., & Wittrock, H. (1975). Public attitudes toward crime and the penal system. *British Journal of Criminology, 15,* 228–240.

Banks, E. M., Wood-Gush, D. G., Hughes, B. O., & Mankovich, N. J. (1979). Social rank and priority of access to resources in domestic fowl. *Behavioral Processes, 4,* 197–209.

Barbaree, H. & Marshall, W. (1991). The role of male sexual arousal in rape: Six models. *Journal of Consulting and Clinical Psychology, 59,* 621–630.

Barber, N. (1998). Sex differences in disposition towards kin, security of adult attachment, and sociosexuality as a function of parental divorce. *Evolution and Human Behavior, 19,* 125–132.

Barber, R. N., & Wilson, P. R. (1968). Deterrent aspect of capital punishment and its effect on conviction rates: The Queensland experience. *Australian and New Zealand Journal of Criminology, 2,* 100–108.

Barberet, R., Rechea-Aberola, C., & Montanes-Rodriguez, J. (1994). Self-reported juvenile delinquency in Spain. In J.-T. Josine, G.-J. Terlouw, & M. W. Klein (Eds.), *Delinquent behavior among young people in the Western world: First results of the international self-report delinquency study* (pp. 238–266). Amsterdam: Kugler.

Barboriak, J. J. (1984). Alcohol, lipids and heart disease. *Alcohol, 1,* 341–345.

Barcelo, G., Sanz, M., Molina, V., & Rubia, G. J. (1997). The Wisconsin Card Sorting Test and the assessment of frontal function: A validation study with event-related potentials. *Neuropsychologia, 35,* 399–408.

Bardone, A. M., Moffitt, T. E., Caspi, A., Dickson, N., & Silva, P. A. (1996). Adult mental health and social outcomes of adolescent girls with depression and conduct disorder. *Development and Psychopathology, 8,* 811–829.

Barfield, A. (1976). Biological influences on sex differences in behavior. In M. S. Teitelbaum (Ed.), *Sex differences* (pp. 62–121). Garden City, NY: Anchor.

Barker, G., & Adams, W. (1961). Comparison of the delinquencies of boys and girls. *Journal of Criminal Law and Criminology, 53,* 470–475.

Barkley, R. A. (1987). Child behavior rating scales and checklists. In M. Rutter, A. H. Tuma, & I. S. Lann (Eds.), *Assessment and diagnosis in child psychopathology* (pp. 113–155). New York: Guilford.

Barkley, R. A. (1997). Behavioral inhibition, sustained attention, and executive functions: Constructing a unifying theory of ADHD. *Psychological Bulletin, 121,* 65–94.

Barkley, R. A., McMurray, M. B., Edelbrock, C. S., & Robbins, K. (1989). The response of aggressive and nonaggressive ADHA children to two doses of methylphenidate. *Journal of the American Academy of Child and Adolescent Psychiatry, 28,* 873–881.

Barkow, J. H. (1991). Evolved self-interest and the cross-cultural survey. *Behavioral and Brain Sciences, 14,* 261–263.

Barlow, H. D. (1993). *Introduction to criminology,* (6th ed.). New York: HarperCollins.

Barnes, D. M. (1988). Drugs: Running the numbers. *Science, 240,* 1729–1731.

Barnett, R. C., & Baruch, G. K. (1987). Social roles, gender, and psychological distress. In R. C. Barnett, L. Biener, & G. K. Baruch (Eds.), *Gender and stress* (pp. 122-143). New York: Free Press.

Barnett, S. A. (1963). *The rat: A study in behavior.* Chicago: Aldine.

Baron, R. A., & Straus, M. A. (1984). Sexual stratification, pornography, and rape in the United States. In N. M. Malamuth & E. Donnerstein (Eds.), *Pornography and sexual aggression* (pp. 185–209). New York: Academic Press.

Baron, R. A., & Straus, M. A. (1989). *Four theories of rape.* New Haven, CT: Yale University Press.

Baron, S. W., & Hartnagel, T. F. (1997). Attributions, affect, and crime: Street youths' reactions to unemployment. *Criminology, 35,* 409–434.

Barratt, E. S. (1994). Impulsiveness and aggression. In J. Monahan & H. J. Steadman (Eds.), *Violence and mental disorder* (pp. 61–79). Chicago: University of Chicago Press.

Barro, S. M., & Kolstad, A. (1987). *Who drops out of high school? Findings from high school and beyond.* Washington, DC: U.S. Government Printing Office.

Bartels, S. J., Drake, R. E., Wallach, M. A., & Freeman, D. H. (1991). Characteristic hostility in schizophrenic outpatients. *Schizophrenia Bulletin, 17,* 163–171.

Bartol, C. R. (1980). *Criminal behavior: A psychosocial approach.* Englewood Cliffs, NJ: Prentice-Hall.

Bartol, C. R. (1995). *Criminal behavior: A psychosocial approach* (3rd ed.). Englewood Cliffs, NJ: Prentice-Hall.

Bartusch, D. R. J., Lynam, D. R., Moffitt, T. E., & Silva, P. A. (1997). Is age important? Testing a general versus a developmental theory of antisocial behavior. *Criminology, 35,* 13–48.

Bass, A. H. (1996). Shaping brain sexuality: Male plainfin midshipman fish exercise alternative reproductive tactics. The developmental trade-offs involved shape two brain phenotypes. *American Scientist, 84,* 352–363.

Bastian, L. D. (1993). *Criminal victimization, 1992.* Washington, DC: Bureau of Justice Statistics, U.S. Department of Justice.

Bateman, A. J. (1948). Intra-sexual selection in drosophila. *Heredity, 2,* 349–368.

Bateson, P. P. G. (Ed.). (1983). *Mate choice.* Cambridge: Cambridge University Press.

Batta, I. D. (1975). A study of juvenile delinquency among Asians and half-Asians. *British Journal of Criminology, 15,* 32–42.

Baucus, Melissa (1994). Pressure, opportunity and predisposition: A multivariate model of corporate illegality. *Journal of Management, 20,* 699–721.

Baucus, Melissa, & Dworkin, Terry (1991). What is corporate crime? It is not illegal corporate behavior. *Law & Policy,* 13, 231–244.

Baucus, Melissa, & Near, Janet (1991). Can illegal corporate behavior be predicted? An event history analysis. *Academy of Management Journal, 34,* 9–36.

Bauer, L. O. (1997). Frontal P300 decrements, childhood conduct disorder, family history, and the prediction of relapse among abstinent cocaine abusers. *Drug and Alcohol Dependence, 44,* 1–10.

Bauer, L. O., & Hesselbrock, V. M. (1993). EEG, autonomic, and subjective correlates of risk for alcoholism. *Journal of Studies of Alcohol, 54,* 577–589.

Bauer, L., O., O'Connor, S., O., & Hesselbrock, V., M. (1994). Frontal P300 decrements in antisocial personality disorder. *Alcoholism: Clinical and Experimental Research, 18,* 1300–1305.

Baur, J. E. (1964). The trends of juvenile offenses in the Netherlands and the United States. *Journal of Criminal Law, Criminology, and Police Science, 55,* 359–69.

Beattie, J. M. (1975). The criminality of women in eighteenth-century England. *Journal of Social History, 9,* 80–116.

Beattie, J. M. (1977). Crime and the courts in Surrey—1737–1753. In S. Cockburn (Ed.), *Crime in England—1550–1800* (pp. 155–186). NJ: Princeton University Press.

Beattie, J. M. (1986). *Crime and the courts in England, 1660–1800.* New York: Oxford University Press.

Beatty, W. W. (1978). DRL behavior in gerbils and hamsters of both sexes. *Bulletin of the Psychonomic Society, 11,* 41–42.

Beatty, W. W., & Beatty, P. A. (1970). Hormonal determinants of sex differences in avoidance behavior and reactivity to electric shock in rats. *Journal of Comparative and Physiological Psychology, 73,* 446–455.

Beatty, W. W., & Fessler, R. G. (1977). Gonadectomy and sensitivity to electric shock in the rat. *Physiology & Behavior, 19,* 1–6.

Beccaria, C. (1764/1963). *On crimes and punishment* (Henry Paulucci, Trans.). Indianapolis: Bobbs-Merrill.

Beck, A., Gilliard, D., Greenfeld, L., Harlow, C., Hester, T., Jankowski, L., Snell, T., & Stephan, J. (1993). *Survey of prison inmates, 1991.* Washington, DC: U.S. Department of Justice, Office of Justice Programs, Bureau of Justice Statistics (NCJ-136949).

Becker, H. S. (1963). *Outsiders: Studies in the sociology of deviance.* New York: Free Press.

Becker, H. S., & Barnes, A. (1961). *Social thought: From lore to science,* vol. 2. New York: Dover.

Beckstrom, J. H. (1993) *Darwinism applied: Evolutionary paths to social goals.* Westport, CT: Praeger.

Begleiter, H., Porjesz, B., Bihari, B., & Kissin, B. (1984). Event-related brain potentials in boys at risk for alcoholism. *Science, 225,* 1493–1496.

Behar, D., & Stewart, M. A. (1984). Aggressive conduct disorder: The influence of social class, sex, and age on the clinical picture. *Journal of Child Psychology and Psychiatry, 25,* 119–124.

Behrman, J. R., Hrubec, Z., Taubman, P., & Wales, T. J. (1980). *Socioeconomic success: A study of the effects of genetic endowments, family environment and schooling.* Amsterdam: North-Holland.

Beirne, P. (1993). *Inventing criminology:* Albany, NY: State University of New York Press.

Bell, Daniel (1962). *The end of ideology.* New York: Collier Books.

Bell, R. Q. (1968). A reinterpretation of the direction of effects in studies of socialization. *Psychological Review, 75,* 81–95.

Bell, R. Q., & Costello, N. S. (1964). Three tests for sex differences in the tactile sensitivity in the newborn. *Biology of the Neonate, 7,* 335–337.

Bellafante, G. (1998). Feminism: It's all about me! *Time,* June 29, 54–60.

Belmaker, R. H., Ebbesen, K., Ebstein, R., & Rimon, R. (1976). Platelet monoamine oxidase in schizophrenia and manic-depressive illness. *British Journal of Psychiatry, 129,* 227–232.

Belsky, J. (1980). Child maltreatment: An ecological integration. *American Psychologist, 35,* 320–335.

Belsky, J. (1993). Etiology of child maltreatment: A developmental-ecological analysis. *Psychological Bulletin, 114,* 413–434.

Belsky, J. (1997). Attachment, mating, and parenting. *Human Nature, 8,* 361–381.

Belsky, J. (1999). Conditional and alternative reproductive strategies: Individual differences in susceptibility to rearing experience. In J. Rogers & D. Rowe (Eds.), *Genetic influences on fertility and sexuality.* Boston: Klumer.

Belsky, J., Laurence, S., & Draper, P. (1991). Childhood experience, interpersonal development, and reproductive strategy: an evolutionary theory of socialization. *Child Development, 62,* 647–670.

Benbow, C. P. (1988). Neuropsychological perspectives on mathematical talent. In L. K. Obler & D. Fein (Eds.), *The exceptional brain: Neuropsychology of talent and special abilities* (pp. 48–69). New York: Guilford.

Bennett, L. A., Sorenson, D. E., & Forshay, H. (1971). The application of self-esteem measures in a correctional setting: I. Reliability of the scale and relationship to other measures. *Research in Crime & Delinquency, 8,* 1–9.

Bennett, R. R. (1980). Constructing cross-cultural theories in criminology: Application of the generative approach. *Criminology, 18,* 252–268.

Bennett, R. R., & Lynch, J. P. (1990). Does difference make a difference? Comparing cross-national crime indicators. *Criminology, 28,* 153–182.

Benson, B. N. (1980). Dominance relationships, mating behavior and scent marking in fox squirrels (*Sciureus niger*). *Mammalia, 44,* 143–160.

Bentham, J. (1789/1948). *A fragment on government and an introduction to the principles of morals and legislation.* Oxford: Basil Blackwell.

Benton, D., Kumari, N., & Brain, P. F. (1982). Mild hypoglycemia and questionnaire measures of aggression. *Biological Psychology, 14,* 129–135.

Ben-Veniste, R. (1971). *Pornography and sex-crime: The Danish experience. Technical Reports of the Commission on Obscenity and Pornography,* vol. 8. Washington, DC: U.S. Government Printing Office.

Benward, J., & Densen-Gerber, J. (1975). Incest as a causative factor in antisocial behavior. *Contemporary Drug Problems, 4,* 323–340.

Bereczkei, T., Voros, S., Gal, A., & Bernath, L. (1997). Resources, attractiveness, family commitment; reproductive decisions in human mate choice. *Ethology, 103,* 681–699.

Berkley, K. J. (1997). Sex differences in pain. *Behavioral and Brain Sciences, 20,* 371–380.

Berkowitz, L. (1982). Aversive conditions as stimuli to aggression. In L. Berkowitz (Ed.), *Advances in Experimental Social Psychology* (Vol. 15, pp. 249–288). New York: Academic Press.

Berman, K. F., Ostrem, J. L., Randolph, C., Gold, J., Goldberg, T. E., Coppola, R., Carson, R. E., Herscovitch, P., & Weinberger, D. R. (1995). Physiological activation of a cortical network during performance of the Wisconsin card sorting test: A positron emission tomography study. *Neuropsychologia, 33,* 1027–1046.

Bernard, J., Bernard, S., & Bernard, M. (1985). Courtship violence and sex-typing. *Family Relations, 34,* 573–576.

Bernard, T. J. (1990a). Angry aggression among the truly disadvantaged. *Criminology, 28,* 73–96.

Bernard, T. J. (1990b). Twenty years of testing theories: What have we learned and why? *Journal of Research in Crime and Delinquency, 27,* 325–347.

Bernard, T. J., & Snipes, J., B. (1996). Theoretical integration in criminology. *Crime and Justice: A Review of Research, 20,* 301–348.

Bernstein, I. S., Gordon, T. P., Rose, R. M., & Peterson, M. S. (1978). Influences of sexual and social stimuli upon circulating levels of testosterone in male pigtail macaques. *Behavioral Biology, 24,* 400–404.

Bernstein, I. S., Gordon, T. P., & Rose, R. M. (1983). The interaction of hormones, behavior and social context in nonhuman primates. In B. B. Svare (Ed.), *Hormones and aggressive behavior* (pp. 535–561). New York: Plenum.

Berrueta-Clement, J. R., Schweinhart, L. J., Barnett, W. S., Epstein, A. S., & Weikart, D. P. (1984). *Changed lives: The effects of the Perry preschool program on youths through age 19.* Ypsilanti, MI: High/Scope.

Berscheid, E. (1980). An overview of the psychological effects of physical attractiveness. In G. W. Lucker, K. A. Ribbens, & J. A. McNamara (Eds.), *Psychological aspects of facial form* (pp. 1–43). Ann Arbor, MI: University of Michigan Center for Human Growth and Development.

Besharov, D. J. (1981). Toward better research on child abuse and neglect: Making definitional issues an explicit concern. *Child Abuse and Neglect, 5,* 383–390.

Beyleveld, D. (1980). *A bibliography on general deterrence research.* Farnborough: Saxon House.

Bianchi, S. M., & Spain, D. (1986). Women, work, and family in America. *Population Bulletin, 51,* 1–48.

Biderman, A. D., & Reiss, A. J. (1967). On exploring the "dark figure" of crime. *The Annals, 374,* 1–15.

Biederman, J., Faraone, S. V., Milberger, S., Garcia Jetton, J., Chen, L., Mick, E., Greene, R. W., & Russell, R. L. (1996). Is childhood oppositional defiant disorder a precursor to adolescent conduct disorder? Findings from a four-year follow-up study of children with ADHD. *Journal of American Academy of Child Adolescent Psychiatry, 35,* 1193–1204.

Biesheuvel, S. (1972). An examination of Jensen's theory concerning educability, heritability and population differences. *Psychologia Africana, 14,* 87–94.

Binder, A. (1988). Juvenile delinquency. *Annual Review in Psychology, 39,* 253–282.

Binder, A., Geis, G., & Bruce, D. (1988). *Juvenile delinquency: Historical, cultural, legal perspectives.* New York: MacMillan.

Bird, H., Canino, G., & Rubio-Stipec, M. (1988). Estimates of the prevalence of childhood maladjustment in a community survey in Puerto Rico. *Archives of General Psychiatry, 45,* 1120–1126.

Black, D. J. (1970). Production of crime rates. *American Sociological Review, 35,* 733–742.

Black, D. W., Baumgard, C. H., & Bell, S. E. (1995). A 16- to 45-year follow-up of 71 men with antisocial personality disorder. *Comprehensive Psychiatry, 36,* 130–140.

Black, D. W., Warrack, G., & Winokur, G. (1985). The Iowa record linkage study. III. Excess mortality among patients with "functional" disorders. *Archives of General Psychiatry, 42,* 58–66.

Black, S., & Casswell, S. (1991). *Recreational drug use in New Zealand.* Auckland, New Zealand: Alcohol and Public Health Research Unit, University of Auckland.

Black, W. A. M., & Hornblow, A. R. (1973). Intelligence and criminality. *Australian and New Zealand Journal of Criminology, 6,* 83–92.

Blackburn, R., & Maybury, C. (1985). Identifying the psychopath: The relation of Cleckly's criteria to the interpersonal domain. *Personality and Individual Differences, 6,* 375–386.

Blair, D. (1975). Medicolegal implications of the terms "psychopath," "psychopathic personality" and "psychopathic disorder," (part 2). *Medicine, Science, and the Law, 15,* 110–123.

Blair, R. J. R., Sellars, C., Strickland, I., Clark, F., Williams, A. O., Smith, M., & Jones, L. (1995). Emotion attributions in the psychopath. *Personality and Individual Differences, 19,* 431–437.

Blake, P., Pincus, J. H., & Buckner, C. (1995). Neurologic abnormalities in murderers. *Neurology, 45,* 1641–1647.

Blakely, C. H., & Davidson, W. S. (1984). Behavioral approaches to delinquency: A review. In P. Karoly & J. J. Steffen (Eds.), Adolescent behavior disorders: Foundations and contemporary concerns (pp. 241–271). Lexington, MA: Lexington Books.

Blakely, C. H., Kushler, M. G., Parisian, J. A., & Davidson W. S., II. (1980). Self-reported delinquency as an evaluation measure. *Criminal Justice and Behavior, 7,* 369–386.

Blanchard, D. C., & Blanchard, R. J. (1983). Hawaii: Violence, a preliminary analysis. In A. P. Goldstein & M. H. Segall (Eds.), *Aggression in global perspective* (pp. 157–191). New York: Pergamon.

Blasi, A. (1980). Bridging moral cognition and moral action: A critical review of the literature. *Psychological Bulletin, 88,* 1–45.

Blaszcyznski, A., McConaghy, N., & Frankova, A. (1989). Crime, antisocial personality and pathological gambling. *Journal of Gambling Behavior, 5,* 137–152.

Blatt, M., & Kohlberg, L. (1975). Effects of classroom moral discussion upon children's level of moral judgement. *Journal of Moral Education, 4,* 129–161.

Blau, J. R., & Blau, P. M. (1982). The cost of inequality: Metropolitan structure and violent crime. *American Sociological Review, 47,* 114–129.

Blaxter, M. (1989). A comparison of measures of inequality in morbidity. In J. Fox (Ed.), *Health inequalities in European countries* (pp. 199–230). Aldershot, England: Gower.

Blechman, E. A., Berberian, R., & Thompson, W. D. (1977). How well does the number of parents explain unique variance in self-reported drug use? *Journal of Consulting Clinical Psychology, 45,* 1182–1183.

Bloch, H., & Thompson, D. (1993). Seeking the roots of violence. *Time,* April 19, 52–53.

Block, R. (1984a). Introduction. In R. Block (Ed.), *Victimization and fear of crime: World perspectives* (pp. 1–2). Washington, DC: U.S. Government Printing Office.

Block, R. (1984b). The impact of victimization, rates, and patterns: A comparison of the Netherlands and the United States. In R. Block (Ed.), *Victimization and fear of crime: World perspectives* (pp. 23–28). Washington, DC: U.S. Government Printing Office.

Bloom, B. S. (1964). *Stability and change in human characteristics.* New York: Wiley.

Bloom, B. S., & Peters, F. (1961). *The use of academic prediction scales for counseling and selecting college entrants.* Glencoe, IL: Free Press.

Blue, H. C., & Griffith, E. E. H. (1995). Sociocultural and therapeutic perspectives on violence. *Psychiatric Clinics of North America, 18,* 571–587.

Blumberg, L., Shipley, T. E., & Shandler, I. (1973). *Skid row and its alternatives: Research and recommendations from Philadelphia.* Philadelphia: Temple University Press.

Blumer, M. (1984). *The Chicago school of sociology: Institutionalization, diversity and the rise of sociological research.* Chicago: University of Chicago Press.

Blumstein, A. (1982). On the racial disproportionality of United States's prison population. *Journal of Criminal Law and Criminology, 73,* 1259–1281.

Blumstein, A., & Cohen, J. (1987). Characterizing criminal careers. *Science, 237,* 985–991.

Blumstein, A., Cohen, J., & Rosenfeld, R. (1991). Trend and deviation in crime rates: A comparison of VCR and NCS data for burglary and robbery. *Criminology, 29,* 237–263.

Blumstein, A., Cohen, J., & Rosenfeld, R. (1992). The UCR-NCS relationship revisited: A reply to Menard. *Criminology, 30,* 115–124.

Boehm, C. (1984). *Blood revenge: The anthropology of feuding in Montenegro and other tribal societies.* Lawrence: University of Kansas Press.

Boehnke, K., Silbereisen, R. K., Eisenberg, N., Reykowski, J., & Palmonari, A. (1989). Developmental pattern of prosocial motivation: A cross-national study. *Journal of Cross-Cultural Psychology, 20,* 219–243.

Boeringer, S. B. (1992). Sexual coercion among college males: Assessing three theoretical models of coercive sexual behavior. Unpublished Ph.D. Dissertation, University of Florida, Gainesville.

Boeringer, S. B. (1994). Pornography and sexual aggression: Associations of violent and nonviolent depictions with rape and rape proclivity. *Deviant Behavior, 15,* 289–304.

Boeringer, S. B., Shehan, C., & Akers, R. (1991). Social contexts and social learning in sexual coercion and aggression: Assessing the contribution of fraternity membership. *Family Relations, 40,* 58–64.

Bohannan, P. (1973). The differing realms of law. In D. Black & M. Mileski (Eds.), *The social organization of law* (pp. 306–317). New York: Seminar Press.

Bohm, R. (1982). Radical criminology: An explication. *Criminology, 19,* 565–589.

Bohmer, C., & Parrot, A. (1993). *Sexual assault on campus.* New York: Lexington Books.

Bolton, F. G., Reich, J. W., & Gutierres, S. E. (1977). Delinquency patterns in maltreated children and siblings. *Victimology, 2,* 349–357.

Bolton, R. (1973). Aggression and hypoglycemia among the Qolla: A study in psychobiological anthropology. *Ethnology, 12,* 227–257.

Bolton, R. (1974). *Aggression in Qolla society.* Palo Alto, CA: National Press.

Bolton, R. (1976). Hostility in fantasy: A further test of the hypoglycemia–aggression hypothesis. *Aggressive Behavior, 2,* 257–274.

Bolton, R. (1984). The hypoglycemia–aggression hypothesis: Debate versus research. *Current Anthropology, 25,* 1–53.

Bolton, R., & Bolton, C. (1975). *Conflictos en la familia Andina.* Cuzco, Peru: Centro de Estudios Andina.

Bonger, W. A. (1905). *Criminalité et conditions économiques.* Amsterdam: G. P. Thierie.

Bonger, W. A. (1916). *Criminality and economic conditions.* Boston: Little, Brown.

Bonger, W. A. (1936). *An introduction to criminology.* London: Methuen.

Bonger, W. A. (1969). *Criminality and economic conditions.* Bloomington, IN: Indiana University Press.

Bonnet, P. L., & Pfeiffer, C. C. (1978). Biochemical diagnosis for delinquent behavior. In L. J. Hippchen (Ed.), *Ecologic-biochemical approaches to treatment of delinquents and criminals* (pp. 183–205). New York: van Nostrand Reinhold.

Bonnet, C. (1993). Adoption at birth: Prevention against abandonment or neonaticide. *Child Abuse & Neglect, 17,* 501–513.

Bonta, J., Pang, B., & Wallace-Capretta, S. (1995). Predictors of recidivism among incarcerated female offenders. *Prison Journal, 75,* 277–294.

Boor, M. (1981). Relationship of 1977 state suicide rates to population increases and immigration. *Psychological Reports, 49,* 856–858.

Booth, A., Mazur, A. C., & Dabbs, J. M., Jr. (1993). Endogenous testosterone and competition: The effect of "fasting." *Steroids, 58,* 348–350.

Bordua, D. J. (1986). Firearms ownership and violent crime: A comparison of Illinois counties. In J. M. Byrne & R. J. Sampson (Eds.), *The social ecology of crime* (pp. 156–188). New York: Springer-Verlag.

Borg, I. (1985). Judged seriousness of crimes and offenses: 1927, 1967, and 1984. *Archives of Psychology, 137,* 115–122.

Borg, M. J. (1998). Vicarious homicide victimization and support for capital punishment: A test of Black's theory of law. *Criminology, 36,* 537–568.

Boritch, H., & Hagen, J. (1990). A century of crime in Toronto: Gender, class, and patterns of social control, 1859 to 1955. *Criminology, 28,* 567–600.

Bornoff, N. (1991). *Pink samurai: Love, marriage, and sex in contemporary Japan.* New York: Pocket Books.

Bortner, N. A. (1988). *Delinquency and justice: An age of crisis.* New York: McGraw-Hill.

Bossert, S., Berger, M., Krieg, J. C., Schreiber, W., Junker, M., & von Zerssen, D. (1988). Cortisol response to various stressful situations: Relationship to personality variables and coping styles. *Neuropsychobiology, 20,* 36–42.

Bottomley, A. K., & Coleman, C. A. (1976). Criminal statistics: The police role in the discovery and detection of crime. *International Journal of Criminology and Penology, 4,* 33–58.

Botvin, G. J. (1986). Substance abuse prevention research: Recent developments and future directions. *Journal of School Health, 56,* 369–374.

Bouchard, T., Lykken, D., McGue, M., Segal, N., & Tellegen, A. (1990). Sources of human psychological differences: The Minnesota study of twins reared apart. *Science, 250,* 223–228.

Bourne, P. G., Rose, R. M., & Mason, J. W. (1967). Urinary 17-OHCS levels: Data on seven helicopter ambulance medics in combat. *Archives of General Psychiatry, 17,* 104–110.

Bourne, P. G., Rose, R. M., & Mason, J. W. (1968). 17-OHCS levels in combat: Special forces "A" team under threat of attack. *Archives of General Psychiatry, 19,* 135–140.

Bowker, L. H. (1977). The incidence of female crime and delinquency—a comparison of official and self-report statistics. *International Journal of Women's Studies, 1,* 178–192.

Bowker, L. H. (1978). International perspective on female crime and its correlation. In L. Bowker (Ed.), *Women, crime and the criminal justice system* (pp. 261–282). Lexington, Mass.: Heath.

Bowling, B., Graham, J., & Ross, A. (1994). Self-reported offending among young people in England and Wales. In J. Junger-Tas, G.-J. Terlouw, & M. W. Klein (Eds.), *Delinquent behavior among young people in the Western world: First results of the international self-report delinquency study* (pp. 42–59). Amsterdam: Kugler.

Bowman, L. A., Dilley, S. R., & Keverne, E. B. (1978). Suppression of oestrogen-induced LH surges by social subordination in talapoin monkeys. *Nature, 275,* 56–58.

Braaten, E. B., & Rosen, L. A. (1997). Emotional reactions in adults with symptoms of attention deficit hyperactivity disorder. *Personality and Individual Differences, 22,* 355–361.

Brabeck, M. (1983). Moral judgment: Theory and research on differences between men and women. *Developmental Review, 3,* 274–291.

Bradford, J. (1990). The antiandrogen and hormonal treatment of sex offenders. In Marshall, W., Laws, D., and Barbaree, H. (Eds.), *Handbook of sexual assault: Issues, theories, and treatment of the offender* (pp. 297–310). New York: Plenum.

Bradshaw, J. L. (1991). Animal asymmetry and human heredity: Dextrality, tool use and language in evolution—10 years after Walker (1980). *British Journal of Psychology, 82,* 39–59.

Braithwaite, J. (1981). The myth of social class and criminality reconsidered. *American Sociological Review, 46,* 36–57.

Braithwaite, J. (1989). *Crime, shame, and reintegration.* Cambridge: Cambridge University Press.

Braithwaite, J., & Biles, D. (1984). National studies of victimization. In R. Block (Ed.), *Victimization and fear of crime: World perspectives* (pp. 3–10). Washington, DC: U.S. Government Printing Office.

Braithwaite, J., & Biles, D. (1980). Overview of findings from the first Australian national crime victims survey. *Australian and New Zealand Journal of Criminology, 13,* 41–51.

Braithwaite, J., & Braithwaite, V. (1978). An exploratory study of delinquency and the nature of schooling. *Australian and New Zealand Journal of Sociology, 14,* 25–31.

Braithwaite, J. (1993). Crime and the average American. *Law & Society Review, 27,* 215–231.

Braithwaite, J., & Braithwaite, V. (1980). The effect of income inequality and social democracy on homicide. *British Journal of Criminology, 20,* 45–35.

Braithwaite, J., & Mugford, S. (1994). Conditions of successful reintegration ceremonies. *British Journal of Criminology, 34,* 139–171.

Bramblett, C. A. (1976). *Patterns of primate behavior.* Palo Alto: Mayfield.

Branchey, M. H., Buydens-Branchey, L., & Horvath, T. B. (1993). Event related potentials in substance abusing individuals after long term abstinence. *American Journal of Addiction, 2,* 141–148.

Branchey, M. H., Buydens-Branchey, L., & Lieber, C. S. (1988). P3 alcoholics with disordered regulation of aggression. *Psychiatry Research, 25,* 49–58.

Brannigan, A. (1984). *Crimes, courts and corrections: An introduction to crime and social control in Canada.* Toronto: Holt, Rinehart and Winston.

Brannigan, A. (1997). Self control, social control and evolutionary psychology: Towards an integrated perspective on crime. *Canadian Journal of Criminology, 39,* 403–431.

Brannigan, A. (1998). Criminology and the Holocaust: Xenophobia, evolution, and genocide. *Crime & Delinquency, 44,* 257–276.

Brantley, P. J., Dietz, L. S., McKnight, G. T., Jones, G. N., & Tulley, R. (1988). Convergence between the daily stress inventory and endocrine measures of stress. *Journal of Consulting and Clinical Psychology, 56,* 549–551.

Brase, D. A., & Loh, H. H. (1975). Possible role of 5-hydroxytryptamine in minimal brain dysfunction. *Life Sciences, 16,* 1005–1016.

Braukmann, C. J., & Montrose, M. W. (1987). Behaviorally based group homes for juvenile offenders. In E. K. Morris & C. J. Braukmann (Eds.), *Behavioral approaches to crime and delinquency: A handbook of application, research, and concepts* (pp. 135–159). New York: Plenum.

Braukmann, C. J. & Wolf, M. M. (1997). Behaviorally based group homes for juvenile offenders. In E. K. Morris & C. J. Braukmann (Eds.), Behavioral approaches to crime and delinquency: A handbook of application, research, and concepts (pp. 135–159). New York: Plenum.

Braungart, M., Braungart, R., & Hoyer, W. (1980). Age, gender, and social factors in fear or crime. *Sociological Focus, 13,* 55–66.

Brearley, H. C. (1932). *Homicide in the United States.* Chapel Hill, NC: University of North Carolina Press.

Brennan, T., Elliott, D. S., & Knowles, B. A. (1981). *Patterns of multiple drug use: A descriptive analysis of static types and change patterns, 1976–1978.* Boulder, CO: Behavior Research Institute.

Brenner, M. H. (1976). Effects of the economy on criminal behaviour and the administration of criminal justice in the United States, Canada, England, and Wales and Scotland. In U.N.S.D.R. Institute (Ed.), *Economic crises and crime.* Rome: United Nations Publication, No. 15.

Brewer, V. E., & Smith, M. D. (1995). Gender inequality and rates of female homicide victimization across U.S. cities. *Journal of Research in Crime and Delinquency, 32,* 175–190.

Brezina, T. (1998). Adolescent maltreatment and delinquency: The question of intervening processes. *Journal of Research in Crime and Delinquency, 35,* 71–99.

Bridges, G. S., & Crutchfield, R. D. (1988). Law, social standing and racial disparities in imprisonment. *Social Forces, 66,* 699–724.

Bridges, G. S., Crutchfield, R. D., & Simpson, E. E. (1987). Crime, social structure, and criminal punishment: White and non-White rates of imprisonment. *Social Problems, 34,* 345–360.

Briggs, M. (1972). Relationship between monoamine oxidase activity and sex hormone concentration in human blood plasma. *Journal of Reproduction and Fertility, 29,* 447–450.

Brim, J. A., & Nelson, J. M. (1981). Moral idiocy: A new look at an old concept. *Corrective and Social Psychiatry, 27,* 167–169.

Broder, P. K., Dunivant, M., Smith, E. C., & Sutton, L. P. (1981). Further observations on the link between learning disabilities and juvenile delinquency. *Journal of Educational Psychology, 73,* 838–50.

Brody, M. E. (1987). *The relationship between adolescent drug-use and parental and peer variables using the student substance use survey.* Auburn, AL: Auburn University Press.

Broida, J., & Svare, B. (1982). Strain-typical patterns of pregnancy-induced nest building in mice: Maternal and experiential influences. *Physiology & Behavior, 25,* 153–57.

Broidy, L., & Agnew, R. (1997). Gender and crime: A general strain theory perspective. *Journal of Research in Crime and Delinquency, 34,* 275–306.

Brooks, P., Devine, M., Green, T., Hart, B., & Moore, M. (1987). Serial murder: Criminal justice response. *Police Chief, 54,* 37–45.

Broom, L., & Selznick, P. (1958). *Sociology* (2nd ed.). Evanston, IL: Row, Peterson.

Broverman, D. M., Klaiber, E. L., Kobavashi, Y., & Vogel, W. (1968). Roles of activation and inhibition in sex differences in cognitive abilities. *Psychological Review, 75,* 23–50.

Brown, F., & Epps, P. (1966). Childhood bereavement and subsequent crime. *British Journal of Psychiatry, 112,* 1031–1048.

Brown, G. L., Ebert, M. H., Goyer, P. F., Jimerson, D. C., Klein, W., Bunney, W. E., & Goodwin, F. K. (1982a). Aggression, suicide, and serotonin: Relationships to CSF amine metabolites. *American Journal of Psychiatry, 139,* 741–746

Brown, G., Ebert, M., Mikkelsen, E., & Hunt, R. (1979). Clinical pharmacology of d-amphetamine in hyperactive children. In L. A. Gottschalk (Ed.), *Pharmacokinetics of psychoactive drugs* (pp. 137–153). New York: Spectrum.

Brown, G., Ebert, M., Mikkelsen, E., & Hunt, R. (1980). Behavior and motor activity response in hyperactive children and plasma amphetamine levels following a sustained release preparation. *Journal of American Academy of Child Psychiatry, 19,* 225–239.

Brown, G. L., Goodwin, F. K., & Bunney, W. E. J. (1982b). Human aggression and suicide: Their relationship to neuropsychiatric diagnoses and serotonin metabolism. In B. T. Ho, J. C. Schoolar, & E. Usdin (Eds.), *Serotonin in biological psychiatry.* (pp. 287–307). New York: Raven.

Brown, J. A. (1952). A comparative study of deviation from sexual mores. *American Sociological Review, 17,* 135–146.

Brown, M. J., McCulloch, J. W., & Hiscox, J. (1972). Criminal offences in an urban area and their associated social variables. *Journal of Criminology, 12,* 250–268.

Brown, S. E. (1985). The class-delinquency hypothesis and juvenile justice system bias. *Sociological Inquiry, 55,* 212–223.

Brownfield, D. (1986). Social class and violent behavior. *Criminology, 24,* 421–438.

Browning, Frank, & Gerassi, J. (1980). *The American way of crime.* New York: G. P. Putnam.

Brownmiller, S. (1975). *Against our will: Men, women, and rape.* New York: Simon and Schuster.

Brownmiller, S., and Mehrof, B. (1992). A feminist response to rape as an adaptation in men. *Behavioral and Brain Sciences, 15,* 380–381.

Brunner, H. G., Nelson, M., Breakefield, X. O., Ropers, H. H., & van Oost, B. A. (1993). Abnormal behavior associated with a point mutation in the structural gene for monoamine oxidase A. *Science, 262,* 578–580.

Brush, F. R., Froehlich, J. C., & Sakellaris, P. C. (1979). Genetic selection for avoidance behavior in the rat. *Behavior Genetics, 9,* 309–316.

Brush, F. R., Del Paine, S. N., Pellegrino, L. J., Rykaszewski, I. M., Dess, N. K., & Collins, P. Y. (1988). CER suppression, passive-avoidance learning, and stress-induced suppression of drinking in the Syracuse high and low avoidance strains of rats. *Journal of Comparative Psychology, 102,* 337–349.

Bryden, M. P., McManus, I. C., & Bulman-Fleming, M. B. (1994). Evaluating the empirical support for the Geschwind-Behan-Galaburda model of cerebral lateralization. *Brain and Cognition, 26,* 103–167.

Buchholz, E. R., Hartman, R., Lekshas, J., & Stiller, G. (1974). *Socialist criminology: Theory and methodology.* Westmead, England: Saxon House.

Buchsbaum, M. S., Davis, G. C., Coppola, R., & Dieter, N. (1981a). Opiate pharmacology and individual differences. I. Psychophysical pain measurement. *Pain, 10,* 357–366.

Buchsbaum, M. S., Davis, G. C., Coppola, R., & Dieter, N. (1981b). Opiate pharmacology and individual differences. II. Somatosensory evoked potentials. *Pain, 10,* 367–377.

Buck-Morss, S. (1975). Socio-economic bias in Piaget's theory and its implications for cross-cultural studies. *Human Development, 18,* 35–49.

Buffalo, M. D., & Rogers, J. W. (1971). Behavioral norms, moral norms and attachment: Problems of deviance and conformity. *Social Problems, 19,* 101–113.

Buikhuisen, W. (1987). Cerebral dysfunctions and persistent juvenile delinquency. In S. A. Mednick, T. E. Moffitt, & S. A. Stack (Eds.), *The causes of crime: New biological approaches* (pp. 168–184). Cambridge, England: Cambridge University Press.

Buikhuisen, W., & Mednick, S. A. (1988). The need for an integrative approach in criminology. In W. Buikhuisen & S. A. Mednick (Eds.), *Explaining criminal behaviour* (pp. 3–7). Leiden: E. J. Brill.

Bullock, H. A. (1955). Urban homicide in theory and fact. *Journal of Criminal Law, Criminology, and Police Science, 45,* 565–575.

Bureau of Justice Statistics (1996). *The crime of rape.* Washington, DC: U.S. Department of Justice.

Bureau of Justice Statistics (1991). America behind bars: One year later: The sentencing project. Washington, DC: U.S. Goverment Printing Office.

Burgess, A., Hartman, C., Ressler, R., Douglas, J. & McCormack, A. (1986) Sexual homicide: A motivational model. *Journal of Interpersonal Violence, 1,* 251–272.

Burgess, R. L., & Akers, R. L. (1966). A differential association-reinforcement theory of criminal behavior. *Social Problems, 14,* 128–147.

Burgess, R. L., & Draper, P. (1989). The explanation of family violence: The role of biological, behavioral, and cultural selection. In L. Ohlin & M. Tonry (Eds.), *Family violence* (Vol. 2, pp. 59–116). Chicago: University of Chicago Press.

Burkett, S. R., & Ward, D. A. (1993). A note on perceptual deterrence, religiously based on moral condemnation, and social control. *Criminology, 31,* 119–134.

Burkett, S. R., & White, W. (1974). Hellfire and delinquency: Another look. *Journal for the Scientific Study of Religion, 13,* 455–462.

Bursik, R. J., Jr. (1986). Ecological stability and the dynamics of delinquency. In A. J. Reiss, Jr. & M. Tonry (Eds.), *Communities and crime* (Vol. 8, pp. 35–66). Chicago: University of Chicago Press.

Bursik, R. J., Jr., & Grasmick, H. G. (1993a). Economic deprivation and neighborhood crime rates, 1960–1980. *Law & Society Review, 27,* 263–283.

Bursik, R. J., Jr., & Grasmick, H. (1993b). *Neighborhoods and crime: The dimensions of effective community control.* New York: Lexington Books.

Burton, V., & Cullen, F. (1992). The empirical status of strain theory. *Journal of Crime and Justice, 15,* 1–30.

Bush, D., Simmons, R., & Simmons, M. (1987). Gender and coping with entry into early adolescence. In R. C. Barnett, L. Biener, & G. K. Baruch (Eds.), *Gender and stress* (pp. 185–218). New York: Free Press.

Buss, D. M. (1989). Sex differences in human mate preference: Evolutionary hypothesis tested in 37 cultures. *Behavioral and Brain Sciences, 12,* 1–14.

Buss, D. M. (1994). *The evolution of desire.* New York: Basic Books.

Bussey, K., & Maughan, B. (1982). Gender differences in moral reasoning. *Journal of Personality and Social Psychology, 42,* 701–706.

Butler, G., Walker, R., Walker, R., Teague, P., Fiad-Fahmy, D., & Ratcliffe, S. (1989). Salivary testosterone levels and the progress of puberty in the normal boy. *Clinical Endocrinology, 30,* 587–596.

Butler, N., & Goldstein, H. (1973). Smoking in pregnancy and subsequent child development. *British Medical Journal, 4,* (573–575.

Butler, W. (1992). Crime in the Soviet Union: Early glimpses of the true story. *British Journal of Criminology, 32,* 144–159.

Buydens-Branchey, L., & Branchey, M. H. (1992). Cortisol in alcoholics with a disordered aggression control. *Psychoneuroendocrinology, 17,* 45–54.

Bynner, J. M., O'Malley, P. M., & Bachman, J. G. (1981). Self-esteem and delinquency revisited. *Journal of Youth and Adolescence, 10,* 407–441.

Bynum, Timothy (1987). Controversies in the study of organized crime. In T. Bynum (Ed.), *Organized crime in America: Concepts and controversies* (pp. 3–11). Monsey, NY: Willow Tree Press.

Byrd, R. S., Weitzman, M., Lamphear, N. E., & Auimger, P. (1996). Bed-wetting in U.S. children: Epidemiology and related behavior problems. *Pediatrics, 98,* 414–419.

Byrnes, N. (1984). The smoke at General Electric. *Financial World,* Fall, 32–34.

Cadoret, R. J. (1986). Adoption studies: Historical and methodological critique. *Psychiatric Developments, 1,* 45–64.

Cadoret, R. J., Troughton, E., Bagford, J., & Woodworth, G. (1990). Genetic and environmental factors in adoptee antisocial personality. *European Archives of Psychiatry & Neurological Science, 239,* 231–240.

Cadoret, R. J., Troughton, E., & O'Gorman, T. W. (1987). Genetic and environmental factors in alcohol abuse and antisocial personality. *Journal of Studies on Alcohol, 48,* 1–8.

Cahalan, M. (1979). Trends in incarceration in the United States since 1880. *Crime and Delinquency, 25,* 9–25.

Cairns, R. B., Cairns, B. D., & Neckerman, H. J. (1989). Early school dropout: Configurations and determinants. *Child Development, 60,* 1437–1452.

Calavita, K., & Pointell, H. (1994). "Heads I win, tails you lose": Deregulation, crime, and crisis in the savings and loan industry. In D. Curran & C. Renzetti (Eds.), *Contemporary societies: Problems and prospects* (pp. 460–480).

Calavita, K., & Pontell, H. (1994). Savings and loan fraud as organized crime: Toward a conceptual typology of corporate illegality. *Criminology, 31,* 519–548.

Caldwell, J. C., Orubuloye, I. O., & Caldwell, P. (1997). Male and female circumcision in Africa from a regional to specific Nigerian examination. *Social Science and Medicine, 44,* 1181–1193.

Calhoun, G. J., Connley, S., & Bolton, J. A. (1984). Comparison of delinquents and nondelinquents in ethnicity, ordinal position and self-perception. *Journal of Clinical Psychology, 40,* 323–328.

Callan, T. (1991). Male-female wage differentials in Ireland, *Economic and Social Review, 23,* 55–72.

Campagna, A., & Harter, S. (1975). Moral judgment in socio-pathic and normal children. *Journal of Personality and Social Psychology, 31,* 199–205.

Campbell, A., & Muncer, S. (1990). Causes of crime: Uncovering a lay model. *Criminal Justice and Behavior, 17,* 410–419.

Campbell, J. B., & Reynolds, J. H. (1984). A comparison of the Guilford and Eysenck factors of personality. *Journal of Research in Personality, 18,* 305–320.

Campbell, M., Geller, B., Small, A., Petti, T., & Ferris, S. (1978). Minor physical anomalies in young psychotic children. *American Journal of Psychiatry, 135,* 573–575.

Campbell, M., Gonzalez, N. M., & Silva, R. R. (1992). The pharmacologic treatment of conduct disorders and rage outbursts. *Psychiatric Clinics of North America, 15,* 69–85.

Campbell, R. L., & Christopher, J. C. (1996a). Beyond formalism and altruism: The prospects for moral personality. *Developmental Review, 16,* 108–123.

Campbell, R. L., & Christopher, J. C. (1996b). Moral development theory: A critique of its Kantian presuppositions. *Developmental Review, 16,* 1–47.

Canter, R. J. (1982). Family correlates of male and female delinquency. *Criminology, 20,* 149–167.

Cantor, D., & Land, K. C. (1985). Unemployment and crime rates in the post-World War II United States: A theoretical and empirical analysis. *American Sociological Review, 50,* 317–332.

Cao, L., Adam, A., & Jensen, V. J. (1997). A test of the black subculture of violence thesis: A research note. *Criminology, 35,* 367–379.

Caputi, J. (1989). The sexual politics of murder. *Gender & Society, 3,* 437–456.

Cardarelli, A. P., & Hicks, S. C. (1993). Radicalism in law and criminology: A retrospective view of critical legal studies and radical criminology. *Journal of Criminal Law & Criminology, 84,* 502–553.

Carey, A. D., & Lopreato, J. (1994). Sociobiology and the wayward critic. *Sociological Perspectives, 37,* 403–430.

Carey, G. (1994). *Genetics and violence.* Washington, DC: National Academy of Science.

Carey, G. (1992). Twin imitation for antisocial behavior: Implications for genetic and family environment research. *Journal of Abnormal Psychology, 101,* 18–25.

Carlisle, A. L. (1993). The divided self: Toward an understanding of the dark side of the serial killer. *American Journal of Criminal Justice, 17,* 23–26.

Carlo, B. (1999). Flight into sanity: Jones's allegation of Ferenczis mental deterioration reconsidered. *International Journal of Psycho Analysis, 80,* 507–542.

Carlo, G., Roesch, S. C., & Melby, J. (1998). The multiplicative relations of parenting and temperament to prosocial and antisocial behaviors in adolescence. *Journal of Early Adolescence, 18,* 266–290.

Carlson, J. M., & Williams, T. (1993). Perspectives on the seriousness of crimes. *Social Science Research, 22,* 190–207.

Carlton, P. L., & Advokat, C. (1973). Attenuated habituation due to parachlorophenylalanine. *Pharmacology, Biochemistry, and Behavior, 1,* 657–663.

Carpini, M. X. D., & Keeter, S. (1991). Stability and change in the U.S. public's knowledge of politics. *Public Opinion Quarterly, 55,* 583–612.

Carroll, L., & Jackson, P. (1983). Inequality, opportunity, and crime rates in central cities. *Criminology, 21,* 178–194.

Carroll, A., Durkin, K., Houghton, S., & Hattie, J. (1996). An adaption of Mak's self-reported delinquency scale for western Australian adolescents. *Australian Journal of Psychology, 48,* 1–7.

Carter, C. J., & Pycock, C. J. (1980). Behavioural and biochemical effects of dopamine and noradrenaline depletion within the medial prefrontal cortex of the rat. *Brain Research, 192,* 163–176.

Carter, David (1994). International organized crime: Emerging trends in entrepreneurial crime. *Journal of Contemporary Criminal Justice, 10,* 239–266.

Carter, Lief (1984). *Reason in law.* Boston: Little, Brown.

Carter, T. (1979). Juvenile court dispositions. *Criminology, 17,* 341–350.

Carter, T., & Clelland, D. (1979). A neo-Marxian critique, formulation and test of juvenile dispositions as a function of social class. *Social Problems, 27,* 96–108.

Cartwright, D. C., Howard, K. I., & Reuterman, N. A. (1970). Multivariate analysis of gang delinquency. *Multivariate Behavioral Research, 5,* 303–323.

Casanovas, L., Alvarez, A., Martin, L. H., Carvajal, A., & Martin, I. (1996). Self-medication and addictive drug consumption among university students. Is there any relationship? *Adolescence, 8,* 441–446.

Cases, O., Seif, I., Grimsby, J., Gaspar, P., Chen, K., Pourin, S., Mueller, U., Aguet, M., Babinet, C., Shih, J., & De Mayer, E. (1995). Aggressive behavior and altered amounts of brain serotonin and norepinephrine in mice lacking MAO-A. *Science, 268,* 1763–1766.

Caspi, A., Lynam, D., Moffitt, T. E. & Silva, P. A. (1993). Unraveling girls' delinquency: Biological, dispositional, and contextual contributions to adolescent misbehavior. *Developmental Psychology 29,* 19–30.

Caspi, A., Moffitt, T. E., Silva, P. A., Stouthamer-Loeber, M., Krueger, R. F., & Schmutte, P. S. (1994). Are some people crime prone? Replications of the personality–crime relationship across countries, genders, races, and methods. *Criminology, 32,* 163–195.

Castleman, M. (1984). *Crime free.* New York: Simon and Schuster.

Catalano, R. F., & Hawkins, J. D. (1996). The social development model: A theory of antisocial behavior. In J. D. Hawkins (Ed.), *Delinquency and crime: Current theories* (pp. 149–197). Cambridge, England: Cambridge University Press.

Catalano, R. F., Kosterman, R., Hawkins, J. D., Newcomb, M. D., & Abbot, R. D. (1996). Modeling the etiology of adolescent substance use: A test of the social development model. *Journal of Drug Issues, 26,* 429–455.

Caulfield, S., L. (1996). Peacemaking criminology: Introduction and implications for the intersection of race, class, and gender. In M. D. Schwartz & D. Milovanovic (Eds.), *Race, gender, and class in criminology* (pp. 91–103). New York: Garland.

Cavalli-Sforza, L. L., & Bodmer, W. R. (1971). *The genetics of human populations.* San Francisco: Freeman.

Cavior, N., & Dokecki, P. R. (1973). Physical attractiveness, perceived attitude similarity, and academic achievement as a contributor to interpersonal attraction among adolescents. *Developmental Psychology, 9,* 44–54.

Cavior, N., & Howard, L. R. (1973). Facial attractiveness and juvenile delinquency among black offenders and white offenders. *Journal of Abnormal Child Psychology, 1,* 202–213.

Centerwall, B. S. (1984). Race, socioeconomic status, and domestic homicide, Atlanta, 1971–2. *American Journal of Public Health, 74,* 813–815.

Cernkovich, S. A., & Giordano, P. C. (1979a). A comparative analysis of male and female delinquency. *Sociological Quarterly, 20,* 131–145.

Cernkovich, S., & Giordano, P. C. (1979b). Delinquency, opportunity and gender. *Journal of Criminal Law and Criminology, 70,* 145–151.

Cernkovich, S. A., & Giordano, P. C. (1987). Family relationships and delinquency. *Criminology, 25,* 295–321.

Cernkovich, S. A., Giordano, P. C., & Pugh, M. D. (1985). Chronic offenders: The missing cases in self-report delinquency research. *Journal of Criminal Law and Criminology, 76,* 705–732.

Cervenka, K., A., Dembo, R., & Brown, H. C. (1996). A family empowerment intervention for families of juvenile offenders. *Aggression and Violent Behavior, 1,* 205–216.

Chabot, R. J., & Serfontein, G. (1996). Quantitative electroencephalographic profiles of children with attention deficit disorder. *Biological Psychiatry, 40,* 951–963.

Chambliss, W. J. (1964). A sociological analysis of the law of vagrancy. *Social Problems, 12,* 67–77.

Chambliss, W. J. (1969). *Crime and the legal process.* New York: McGraw-Hill.

Chambliss, W. J. (1974). The state, the law and the definition of behavior as criminal or delinquent. In D. Glaser (Ed.), *Handbook of criminology* (pp. 24–46). Chicago: Rand McNally.

Chambliss, W. J. (1975). *Criminal law in action.* Santa Barbara, CA: Hamilton.

Chambliss, W. J. (1976). Functional and conflict theories of crime: The heritage of Emile Durkheim and Karl Marx. In W. J. Chambliss & M. Mankoff (Eds.), *Whose law, what order? A conflict approach to criminology* (pp. 1–28). New York: John Wiley.

Chamlin, M. B., & Cochran, J. K. (1997). Social altruism and crime. *Criminology, 35,* 203–227.

Chandler, M. (1973). Egocentrism and antisocial behavior: The assessment and training of social perspective-taking skills. *Developmental Psychology, 9,* 326–332.

Chandler, M., & Moran, T. (1990). Psychopathy and moral-development: A comparative study of delinquent and nondelinquent youth. *Development and Psychopathology, 2,* 227–246.

Chang, D. H. (1976). The study of criminology—A cross-cultural approach. In D. H. Chang (Ed.), *Criminology: A cross-cultural perspective, Volume 1* (pp. 3–137). Durham, NC: Carolina Academic Press.

Chapa, J., & Valencia, R. R. (1993). Latino population growth, demographic characteristics and educational stagnation: An examination of recent trends. *Hispanic Journal of Behavioral Sciences, 15,* 165–187.

Chapman, D. (1968). *Sociology and the stereotype of the criminal.* London: Tavistock.

Chapman, J. I. (1976). An economic model of crime and police. *Journal of Research on Crime and Delinquency, 13,* 48–63.

Chapman, L. J., & Chapman, J. P. (1987). The measurement of handedness. *Brain and Cognition, 6,* 175–183.

Chase, S. (1963). *The proper study of mankind.* New York: Harper and Row.

Cheney, D., Seyfarth, R., & Smuts, B. (1986). Social relationships and social cognition in nonhuman primates. *Science, 234,* 1361–1366.

Cherpitel, C. J. (1997). Alcohol and injuries resulting from violence: A comparison of emergency room samples from two regions of the U.S. *Journal of Addictive Diseases, 16,* 25–40.

Chesney-Lind, M. (1978). Chivalry re-examined: Women and the criminal justice system. In L. H. Bowker, M. Cesney-Lind, & J. Pollock (Eds.), *Women, crime and the criminal justice system* (pp. 197–223). Lexington, KY: D. C. Heath and Co.

Chesney-Lind, M. (1980). Re-discovering Lilith: Misogyny and the new female criminal. In C. T. Griffiths & M. Nance (Eds.), *The female offender: Selected papers from an international symposium* (pp. 1–37). Vancouver: Criminology Research Centre, Simon Fraser University.

Chesney-Lind, M., & Shelden, R. (1992). *Girl's delinquency and juvenile justice.* Pacific Grove, CA: Brooks/Cole.

Chess, S., & Thomas, A. (1984). *Origins and evolution of behavior disorders from infancy to early adult life.* New York: Brunner/Mazel.

Chilton, R., & deAmicis, J. (1975). Overcriminalization and the measurement of consensus. *Sociology and Social Research, 59,* 318–329.

Chiricos, T. G., & Waldo, G. P. (1975). Socioeconomic status and criminal sentencing: An empirical assessment of a conflict proposition. *American Sociological Review, 40,* 753–772.

Chisholm, J. S. (1988). Toward a developmental evolutionary ecology of humans. In K. B. MacDonald (Ed.), *Sociobiological perspectives on human development* (pp. 78–102). New York: Springer-Verlag.

Chiu, L.-H. (1990). A comparison of moral reasoning in American and Chinese school children. *International Journal of Adolescence and Youth, 2,* 185–198.

Chlopan, B. E., McCain, M. L., Carbonell, J. L., & Hagen, R. L. (1985). Empathy: Review of available measures. *Personality and Social Psychology, 48,* 635–653.

Chollar, S. (1988). Food for thought. *Psychology Today, 22* (April), 30–34.

Claridge, G. (1983). The Eysenck psychoticism scale. In J. N. Butcher & C. D. Spielberger (Eds.), *Advances in personality assessment* (Vol. 2, pp. 71–114). Hillsdale, NJ: Erlbaum.

Clark, G. R., Telfer, M. A., Baker, D., & Rosen, M. (1970). Sex chromosomes, crime, and psychosis. *American Journal of Psychiatry, 126,* 1659.

Clark, J. P., & Tifft, L. L. (1966). Polygraph and interview validation of self-reported deviant behavior. *American Sociological Review, 31,* 516–523.

Clark, L., & D. Lewis (1977). *Rape: The price of coercive sexuality.* Toronto: The Woman's Press.

Clarke, R. V., & Felson, M. (1993). *Routine activity and rational choice.* New Brunswick, NJ: Transaction.

Clary, E. G., & Miller, J. (1986). Socialization and situational influences on sustained altruism. *Child Development, 57,* 1358–1369.

Claster, D. S. (1967). Comparison of risk perception between delinquents and non-delinquents. *Journal of Criminal Law, Criminology, and Police Science, 58,* 80–86.

Clayton, R. R. (1981). The delinquency and drug use relationship among adolescents: A critical review. In D. J. Lettieri & J. P. Lodford (Eds.), *Drug abuse and the American adolescent* (pp. 82–103). Rockville, MD: National Institute on Drug Abuse.

Clayton, R. R. (1992). Transitions in drug use: Risk and protective factors. In M. Glantz & R. Pickens (Eds.), *Vulnerability to drug abuse* (pp. 15–51). Washington, DC: American Psychological Association.

Cleckley, H. (1982). *The mask of sensitivity* (rev. ed.). St. Louis: C. V. Mosby.

Clemente, F., & Kleiman, M. B. (1977). Fear of crime in the United States: A multivariate analysis. *Social Forces, 56,* 519–531.

Clifford, W. (1976). *Crime control in Japan.* Lexington, MA: D. C. Heath.

Clinard, M. B. (1959). Criminological research. In R. K. Merton, L. Broom, & L. S. Cottrell (Eds.), *Sociology today* (pp. 509–536). New York: Harper Torchbooks.

Clinard, M. B. (1978b). Comparative crime victimization surveys: Some problems and results. *International Journal of Criminology and Penology, 6,* 221–231.

Clinard, M. B. (1978a). Cities with little crime: The case of Switzerland. Cambridge: Cambridge University Press.

Clinnard, M., & Quinney, Richard (1973). *Criminal behavior system* (2nd ed.). New York: Holt, Rinehart and Winston.

Clinnard, M., & Yeager, P. (1980). *Corporate crime.* New York: Free Press.

Clive, J., Woodbury, M. A., & Siegler, I. A. (1983). Fuzzy and crisp set-theoretic-based classification of health and disease: A Qualitative and quantitative comparison. *Journal of Medical Systems, 7,* 317–332.

Cloninger, C. R. (1986). A unified biosocial theory of personality and its role in the development of anxiety states. *Psychiatric Developments, 3,* 167–226.

Cloninger, C. R., & Guze, S. B. (1970a). Female criminals: Their personal, familial, and social backgrounds, and the relation of these to the diagnosis of sociopathy and hysteria. *Archives of General Psychiatry, 23,* 554–558.

Cloninger, C. R., & Guze, S. B. (1970b). Psychiatric illness and female criminality: The role of sociopathy and hysteria in the antisocial woman. *American Journal of Psychiatry, 127,* 303–311.

Cloninger, C. R., Bohman, M. & Sigvardsson, S. (1981). Inheritance of alcohol abuse: Cross-fostering analysis of adopted men. *Archives of General Psychiatry, 38,* 861–868.

Cloward, R. A., & Ohlin, L. E. (1960). *Delinquency and opportunity.* New York: Free Press.

CNN Presents (1995). *Wild, Wild East.* CNN Television documentary, July 16.

Cobb, S., Brooks, G. W., Kasl, S. V., & Connelly, W. (1966). The health of people changing jobs. *American Journal of Public Health, 56,* 1476–1481.

Coccaro, E. F., & Kavoussi, R. J. (1997). Fluoxetine and impulsive aggressive behavior in personality disordered subjects. *Archives of General Psychiatry, 54,* 1081–1088.

Coccaro, E. F., Siever, L. J., Klar, H., Maurer, G., Cochrane, K., Cooper, T. B., Mohs, R. C., & Davis, K. L. (1989). Serotonergic studies in affective and personality disorder patients: Correlates with suicidal and impulsive aggressive behavior. *Archives of General Psychiatry, 46,* 587–599.

Cochran, J. K., Wood, P. B., & Arneklev, B. J. (1994). Is the religiosity–delinquency relationship spurious? A test of arousal and social control theories. *Journal of Research in Crime and Delinquency, 31,* 92–123.

Cochrane, D., & Manley-Casimir, M. (Eds.). (1980). *Development of moral reasoning: Practical approaches.* New York: Praeger.

Cochrane, R. (1979). Psychological and behavioral disturbance in West Indians, Indians and Pakistanis in Britain: A comparison of rates among children and adults. *British Journal of Psychiatry, 134,* 201–210.

Cockburn, J. S. (Ed.). (1977). *Crime in England—1500–1800.* Princeton, NJ: Princeton University Press.

Cockburn, J. S. (1991). Patterns of violence in English Society: Homicide in Kent, 1560–1985. *Past and Present, 130,* 93–96.

Cockerham, W. C. (1977). Patterns of alcohol and multiple drug use among rural white and American Indian adolescents. *International Journal of the Addictions, 12,* 271–285.

Cohen, A. K. (1955). *Delinquent boys.* New York: Free Press.

Cohen, A. K. (1965). The sociology of the deviant act: Anomie theory and beyond. *American Sociological Review, 30,* 5–14.

Cohen, Fred. (1995). Introduction to legal issues: How the legal framework developed. In B. Schwartz & H. Cellini (Eds.), *The sex offender: Corrections, treatment, and legal practice.* Kingston, NJ: Civic Research Institute.

Cohen, G. N., Bronson, M. B., & Casey, M. B. (1995). Planning as a factor in school achievement. *Journal of Applied Developmental Psychology, 16,* 405–428.

Cohen, L. E., & Felson, M. (1979). Social change and crime rate trends: A routine activity approach. *American Sociological Review, 44,* 588–608.

Cohen, L. E., & Land, K. C. (1984). Discrepancies between crime reports and crime surveys. *Criminology, 22,* 499–530.

Cohen, L. E., & Machalek, R. (1988). A general theory of expropriative crime: An evolutionary ecological approach. *American Journal of Sociology, 94,* 465–501.

Cohen, M. A. (1988). Some new evidence on the seriousness of crime. *Criminology, 26,* 343–352.

Cohen, W., & Boucher, R. (1972). Misunderstandings about sex criminals. *Sexual Behavior, 2,* 24–35.

Cohn, E. G., & Farrington, D. P. (1994). Who are the most influential criminologists in the English-speaking world? *British Journal of Criminology, 34,* 204–225.

Cohn, E. G., & Farrington, D. P. (1998). Changes in the most-cited scholars in major American criminology and criminal justice journals between 1986–1990 and 1991–1995. *Journal of Criminal Justice, 26,* 99–116.

Colby, A., Kohlberg, L., Gibbs, J., & Lieberman, M. (1984). Age patterns in moral reasoning. *Monographs on Social Research and Child Development, 48,* 1–96.

Coleman, C. A., & Bottomley, A. K. (1976). Police conceptions of crime and "no crime." *Criminal Law Review, 2,* 344–360.

Coleman, James (1985). *The criminal elite: The sociology of white collar crime.* New York: St. Martin's.

Coleman, J. S., & Hoffer, T. (1987). *Public and private schools: The impact of communities.* New York: Basic Books.

Coleman, L. S. (1974). Perspectives on the medical research of violence. *American Journal of Orthopsychiatry, 44,* 1–10.

Coleman, M. (1971). Serotonin concentrations in whole blood of hyperactive children. *Journal of Pediatrics, 78,* 985–990.

Collins, A., Frezal, J., Teague, J., & Morton, N. E. (1996). A metric map of humans: 23,500 loci in 850 bands. *Proceedings of National Academy of Sciences, 93,* 14771–14775.

Collins, H. M. (1981). Son of seven sexes: The social destruction of a physical phenomenon. *Social Studies of Science, 11,* 33–62.

Collins, J. J. (1981). Alcohol careers and criminal careers. In J. J. Collins (Ed.), *Drinking and crime* (pp. 152–206). New York: Guilford.

Collins, J. J., & Schlenger, W. E. (1988). Acute and chronic effects of alcohol use on violence. *Journal of Studies on Alcohol, 49,* 516–521.

Collins, R. (1981). On the microfoundations of macrosociology. *American Journal of Sociology, 86,* 984–1014.

Colman, A. M., & Wilson, J. C. (1997). Antisocial personality disorder: An evolutionary game theory analysis. *Legal and Criminological Psychology, 2,* 23–34.

Comings, D. E. (1995). The role of genetic factors in conduct disorder based on studies of Tourette syndrome and attention-deficit hyperactivity disorder probands and their relatives. *Developmental and Behaviorial Pediatrics, 16,* 142–157.

Comings, D. E., Comings, B. G., Muhleman, D., Dietz, G., Shahbahrami, M. S., Tast, D., Knell, E., Kocsis, P., Baumgarten, R., Kovacs, B. W., Levy, D. L., Smith, M., Borison, R. L., Evans, D. D., Klein, D. N., MacMurray, J., Tosk, J. M., Sverd, J., Gysin, R., & Flanagan, S. E. (1991). The dopamine D2 receptor locus as a modifying gene in neuropsychiatric disorders. *Journal of the American Medical Association, 266,* 1793–1800.

Comings, D. E., Muhleman, D., Ahn, C., Gysin, R., & Flanagan, S. D. (1994). The dopamine D2 receptor gene: A genetic risk factor in substance abuse. *Drug and Alcohol Dependence, 34,* 175–180.

Comings, D. E., Rosenthal, R. J., Lesieur, H. R., Rugle, L. J., Muhleman, D., Chiu, C., Dietz, G., & Gade, R. (1996a). A study of the dopamine D2 receptor gene in pathological gambling. *Pharmacogenetics, 6,* 223–234.

Comings, D. E., Wu, S., Chiu, C., Ring, R. H., Gade, R., Ahn, C., MacMurray, J. P., Dietz, G., & Muhleman, D. (1996b). Polygenic inheritance of Tourette syndrome, stuttering, attention deficit hyperactivity, conduct, and oppositional defiant disorder: The additive and subtractive effect of the three dopaminergic genes DRD2, DBH, and DAT1. *American Journal of Medical Genetics (Neuropsychiatric Genetics), 67,* 264–288.

Compas, B. E. (1987). Stress and life events during childhood and adolescence. *Clinical Psychology Review, 7,* 275–302.

Compas, B. E., Davis, G. E., & forsythe, C. J. (1985). Characteristics of life events during adolescence. *American Journal of Community Psychology, 13,* 677–691.

Conklin, J. E. (1986). *Criminology* (2nd ed.). New York: Macmillan.

Conley, D. J. (1994). Adding color to a Black and White picture: Using qualitative data to explain racial dispropor-

tionality in the juvenile justice system. *Journal of Research in Crime and Delinquency, 31,* 135–148.

Connell, A., & Farrington, D. P. (1997). The reliability and validity of resident, staff and peer reports of bullying in young offender institutions. *Psychology, Crime & Law, 3,* 287–300.

Conners, C. K. (1980). *Food additives and hyperactive children.* New York: Plenum Press.

Conrad, J. (1973). Corrections and simple justice. *Journal of Criminal Law and Criminology, 64,* 208–217.

Constantino, J. N., Grosz, D., Saenger, P., Chandler, D., Nandi, R., & Earls, F. J. (1993). Testosterone and aggression in children. *Journal of the American Academy of Child and Adolescent Psychiatry, 32,* 1217–1222.

Cook, P. J. (1980). Research in crime deterrence: Laying the groundwork for the second decade. In N. Morris & M. Tonry (Eds.), *Crime and justice* (Vol. 2, pp. 211–268). Chicago: University of Chicago Press.

Cooke, W. R. (1945). Presidential address: The differential psychology of the American woman. *American Journal of Obstetrics and Gynecology, 49,* 457–472.

Cooley, C. H. (1902). *Human nature and the social order.* Glencoe, IL: Free Press.

Coombs, C. H. (1967). Thurstone's measurement of social values revisited forty years later. *Journal of Personality and Social Psychology, 6,* 85–91.

Cordilia, A. (1985). Alcohol and property crime: Exploring the causal nexus. *Journal Studies on Alcohol, 46,* 161–171.

Coren, S. (1990). The arousal predisposition scale: Normative data. *Bulletin of the Psychonomic Society, 28,* 551–552.

Coren, S., & Porac, C. (1977). Fifty centuries of right-handedness: The historical record. *Science, 198,* 631–632.

Coren, S., & Porac, C. (1978). The validity and reliability of self-report items from the measurement of lateral preference. *British Journal of Psychology, 69,* 207–211.

Coren, S., Porac, C., & Duncan, P. (1979). A behaviorally validated self-report inventory to assess four types of lateral preference. *Journal of Clinical Neuropsychology, 1,* 55–64.

Cormier, B. M., & Boyer, R. (1963). *Retaliation and primitive justice, Proceedings of the 12th international course in criminology* (Vol 1, pp. 71–80). Jerusalem: Institute of Criminology.

Cornish, D., & Clarke, R. (1986). *The reasoning criminal: Rational choice perspectives on offending.* New York: Springer-Verlag.

Cornish, D., & Clarke, R. (1987). Understanding crime displacement: An application of rational choice theory. *Criminology, 25,* 933–947.

Cortes, J. B., & Gatti, F. M. (1972). *Delinquency and crime: A biopsychosocial approach.* New York: Seminar Press.

Cortese, A. J. (1984). Standard issue scoring of moral reasoning: A critique. *Merrill-Palmer Quarterly, 30,* 227–246.

Cortese, A. J. (1990). *Toward a sociology of moral judgment.* Albany: State University of New York Press.

Cosenza, R. M., & Mingoti, S. A. (1993). Career choice and handedness: A survey among university applicants. *Neuropsychologia, 31,* 487–497.

Cosmides, L., & Tooby, J. (1992). Cognitive adaptations for social exchange. In J. H. Barkow, L. Cosmides, & J. Tooby (Eds.), *The adapted mind: Evolutionary psychology and the generation of culture* (pp. 163–228). New York: Oxford University Press.

Costa, P. T., McCrae, R. R., Zonderman, A. B., Barbano, H. E., Lebowitz, B. & Larson, D. M. (1983). Cross-sectional studies of personality in a national sample: 2. Stability in neuroticism, extroversion, and openness. *Psychology and Aging, 1,* 14–149.

Costello, E. J., & Angold, A. (1993). Toward a developmental epidemiology of the disruptive behavior disorders. *Development and Psychopathology, 5,* 91–101.

Court, J. H. (1976). Pornography and sex-crimes: A reevaluation in the light of recent trends around the world. *International Journal of Criminology and Penology, 5,* 129–157.

Court, J. H. (1980). *Pornography and the harm condition: A response to the report of obscenity and film censorship.* Adelaide: Flinders University.

Court, J. H. (1984). Sex and violence: A ripple effect. In N. M. Malamuth & D. Donnerstein (Eds.), *Pornography and sexual aggression* (pp. 143–172). New York: Academic Press.

Cozad, R., & Rousey, C. (1966). Hearing and speech disorders among delinquent children. *Corrective Psychiatry and the Journal of Social Therapy, 12,* 250–255.

Craft, M. J. (1969). The natural history of psychopathic disorder. *British Journal of Psychiatry, 115,* 39–44.

Crenshaw, M. (1990). Questions to be answered, research to be done, knowledge to be applied. In W. Reich (Ed.), *Origins of terrorism: Psychologies, ideologies, theologies, states of mind* (pp. 247–260). New York: Cambridge University Press.

Crenshaw, M. (1991). How terrorism declines. In C. McCauley (Ed.), *Terrorism research and public policy* (pp. 69–87). London: Frank Cass.

Cressey, D. R. (1953). *Other people's money.* Glencoe, IL: Free Press.

Critchley, M. (1972). *The dyslexic child.* London: William Heinemann Medical Books.

Crompton, M. R. (1971). Hypothalamic lesions following closed head injury. *Brain, 94,* 165–172.

Cronin, J., Daniels, N., Hurley, A., Kroch, A., & Webber, R. (1975). Race, class, and intelligence: A critical look at the IQ controversy. *International Journal of Mental Health, 3,* 46–132.

Cronin, T., Cronon, T., & Milakolich, M. (1981). *US vs. crime in the streets.* Bloomington, IN: Indiana University Press.

Crowley, T. J., Mikulich, S. K., MacDonald, M., Young, S. E., & Zerbe, G. O. (1998). Substance-dependent, conduct-disordered adolescent males: Severity of diagnosis predicts 2-year outcome. *Drug and Alcohol Dependence, 49,* 225–237.

Cuffell, B. J., Shumway, M., Chouljian, T. L., & Macdonald, T. (1994). A longitudinal study of substance use and community violence in schizophrenia. *Nervous and Mental Disease, 182,* 704–708.

Cullen, F., Larson, M. T., & Mathers, R. A. (1985). Having money and delinquent involvement: The neglect of power in delinquency theory. *Criminal Justice and Behavior, 12,* 171–192.

Cullen, F., Link, B. G., & Polanzi, C. W. (1982). The seriousness of crime revisited: Have attitudes toward white-collar crime changed? *Criminology, 20,* 83–102.

Cullen, F., Maakestad, W., & Cavender, G. (1987). Corporate crime under attack: The Ford Pinto case and beyond. Cincinnati, OH: Anderson.

Cullen, Robert (1993). *The killer department.* New York: Pantheon.

Cummings, J. L. (1985). *Clinical neuropsychiatry.* Orlando, FL: Grune & Stratton.

Cunningham, Alison, & Griffiths, Curt (1997). *Canadian criminal justice: A primer.* Toronto: Harcourt Brace.

Cunningham, M. R. (1981). Sociobiology as a supplementary paradigm for social psychological research. In L. Wheeler (Ed.), *Review of personality and social psychology* (Vol. 2, pp. 69–106). Beverly Hills, CA: Sage.

Cunningham, M. R., & Barbee, A. P. (1991). Differential K-selection versus ecological determinants of race differences in sexual behavior. *Journal of Research in Personality, 25,* 205–217.

Cuomo, M. J., Dyment, P. G., & Gammino, V. M. (1994). Increasing use of "ecstasy" (MDMA) and other hallucinogens on a college campus. *Journal of American Health, 42,* 271–274.

Curtis, L. A. (1975). *Violence, race, and culture.* Lexington, MA: Lexington Books.

Curtis, L. A. (1977). Violent crime. In L. Radzinowicz & M. E. Wolfgang (Eds.), *Crime and justice* (Vol. 1, pp. XX). New York: Basic Books.

Czeisler, C. A., Moore, E., Regestein, Q. R., Kisch, E. S., Fang, V. S., & Ehrlich, E. N. (1976). Episodic 24-hour cortisol secretory patterns in patients awaiting elective cardiac surgery. *Journal of Clinical Endocrinology and Metabolism, 42,* 273–283.

Czudner, G., & Mueller, R. (1987). The role of guilt and its implication in the treatment of criminals. *International Journal of Offender Therapy and Comparative Criminology, 31,*.

Dabbs, J. (1990). Salivary testosterone measurements: Reliability across hours, days, and weeks. *Physiology and Behavior,* 48:83–86.

Dabbs, J. M., Frady, R. L., Carr, T. S., & Besch, N. F. (1987). Saliva testosterone and criminal violence in young adult prison inmates. *Psychosomatic Medicine, 49,* 174–182.

Dabbs, J. M., Jurkovic, G. J., & Frady, R. L. (1991). Salivary testosterone and cortisol among late adolescent male offenders. *Journal of Abnormal Child Psychology, 19,* 469–478.

Dabbs, J. M., Jr., & Morris, R. (1990). Testosterone, social class, and antisocial behavior in a sample of 4,462 men. *Psychological Science, 1,* 1–3.

Dabbs, J. M., Jr., Ruback, R. B., & Besch, N. F. (1987). Males' saliva testosterone following conversations with male and female partners: American Psychological Association Poster Session.

Daboub, A., Rasheed, A., Priem, R., & Gray, D. (1995). Top management team characteristics and corporate illegal activities. *Academy of Management Review, 20,* 138–170.

Dalecki, M. G., & Price, J. (1994). Dimensions of pornography. *Sociological Spectrum, 14,* 205–219.

Dalton, K. (1964). *The premenstrual syndrome.* Springfield, IL: Thomas.

Daly, K., & Chesney-Lind, M. (1988). Feminism and criminology. *Justice Quarterly, 5,* 97–538.

Daly, M., & Wilson, M. (1988). *Homicide.* New York: Aldine de Gruyter.

Damasio, A. R., Tranel, D., & Damasio, H. (1990). Individuals with sociopathic behavior caused by frontal damage fail to respond autonomically to social stimuli. *Behavioural Brain Research, 41,* 81–94.

Damasio, H., Grabowski, T., Frank, R., Galaburda, A. M., & Damasio, A. R. (1994). The return of Phineas Gage: Clues about the brain from the skull of a famous patient. *Science, 264,* 1102–1105. Department of Neurology and Image Analysis faculty, University of Iowa.

Dannefer, D., & Schutt, R. K. (1982). Race and juvenile justice processing in court and police agencies. *American Journal of Sociology, 87,* 113–132.

Danner, M., J. E. (1996). Gender inequality and criminalization: A socialist feminist perspective on the legal social control of women. In M. D. Schwartz & D. Milovanovic (Eds.), *Race, gender, and class in criminology* (pp. 29–48). New York: Garland.

Danziger, S., & Wheeler, D. (1975). The economics of crime: Punishment or income redistribution? *Review of Social Economy, 33,* Oct, 113–131.

Darley, J. M., Sanderson, C. A., & LaMantia, P. S. (1996). Community standards for defining attempt: Inconsistencies with the model penal code. *American Behavioral Scientist, 39,* 405–420.

Darley, J. M., & Shultz, T. R. (1990). Moral rules: Their content and acquisition. *Annual Review for Psychology, 41,* 52–56.

Darrow, C. (1922). *Crime: Its causes and treatment.* London: Thomas Crowell.

Dashkov, Gennady (1992). Quantitative and qualitative changes in crime in the USSR. *British Journal of Criminology, 32,* 160–165.

Datesman, S. K., & Scarpitti, F. R. (1977). *Unequal protection for males and females in juvenile court.* Beverly Hills, CA: Sage.

Daugherty, T. K., & Quay, H. C. (1991). Response perseveration and delayed responding in childhood behavior disorders. *Journal of Child Psychology and Psychiatry, 32,* 453–461.

Davidson, R., & Wang, Z. (1996). *The court system in the People's Republic of China with a case study of criminal trial.* Boston, MA: Butterworth-Heinemann.

Davidson, R. J., & Fox, N. A. (1989). Frontal brain asymmetry predicts infant's response to maternal separation. *Journal of Abnormal Psychology, 98,* 127–131.

Davis, B. A., Yu, P. H., Boulton, A. A., Wormith, J. S., & Addington, D. (1983). Correlative relationship between biochemical activity and aggressive behavior. *Progress in Neuropsychopharmacology and Biological Psychiatry, 7,* 29–35.

Davis, S. A. B., & Kemp, S. (1994). Judged seriousness of crime in New Zealand. *Journal of Criminology, 27,* 250–263.

Davis, T. L., Severy, L. J., Kraus, S. J., & Whitaker, J. M. (1993). Predictors of sentencing decisions: The beliefs, personality variables, and demographic factors of juvenile justice personnel. *Journal of Applied Social Psychology, 23,* 451–477.

Dawkins, R. (1976). *The selfish gene.* New York: Oxford University Press.

Dawson, G., Klinger, L. D., Panagiotides, H., Hill, D., & Spieker, S. (1992). Frontal lobe activity and behavior of infants of mothers with depressive symptoms. *Child Development, 63,* 725–737.

Dean, R. S., Schwartz, N. H., & Smith, L. S. (1981). Lateral preference patterns as a discriminator of learning difficulties. *Journal of consulting and clinical psychology, 49,* 227–235.

de Beaumont, G., & de Tocqueville, A. (1964). *On the penitentiary system in the United States and its application in France.* Carbondale, IL: Southern Illinois University Press.

de Castro, J. M. (1993). Genetic influences on daily intake and meal patterns of humans. *Physiology and Behavior, 53,* 777–782.

Deckel, W., A., Bauer, L., & Hesselbrock, V. (1995). Anterior brain dysfunctioning as a risk factor in alcoholic behaviors. *Addiction, 90,* 1323–1334.

Deckel, W. A., Hesselbrock, V., & Bauer, L. (1996). Antisocial personality disorder, childhood delinquency, and frontal brain functioning: EEG and neuropsychological findings. *Journal of Clinical Psychology, 52,* 639–650.

Decker, S. H., & Kohfield, C. W. (1986). Crimes, crime rates, arrests, and arrest ratios: Implications for deterrence theory. *Criminology, 23,* 437–450.

de Waal, F. (1982). *Chimpanzee politics: Power and sex among apes.* New York: Harper & Row.

DeFronzo, J. (1984). Climate and crime: Tests of an FBI assumption. *Environment and Behavior, 16,* 185–210.

Degl'Innocenti, A., Agren, H., Backman, L. (1998). Executive deficits in major depression. *Acta Psychiatrica Scandinavica, 97,* 182–188.

De Grazia, J. (1948). *The political community: A study of anomie.* Chicago: University of Chicago Press.

DeHart, Dana, & Mahoney, John (1994). The serial murderer's motivations: An interdisciplinary review. *Omega: Journal of Death and Dying, 29,* 29–45.

DeKeseredy, W. S. (1996). The left realist perspective on race, class, gender. In M. D. Schwartz & D. Milovanovic (Eds.), *Race, gender, and class in criminology* (pp. 49–73). New York: Garland.

Delgado-Escueta, A. V., Mattson, R. H., King, L., Goldensohn, E. S., Speigel, H., Madsen, J., Crandall, P., Dreifuss, F., & Porter, R. J. (1981). The nature of aggression during epileptic seizures. *New England Journal of Medicine, 305,* 711–176.

DeLisi, L. E., Wise, C. D., Bridge, R. P., Rosenblatt, J. E., Wagner, R., Morihisa, J., Karson, C., Potkin, S. G., & Wyatt, R. J. (1981). A probable neuroleptic effect on platelet monoamine oxidase in chronic schizophrenic patients. *Psychiatry Research 4,* 95–107.

DeLongis, A., Coyne, J. C., Dakof, G., Folkman, S., & Lazarus, R. S. (1982). Relationship of daily hassles, uplifts, and major life events to health status. *Health Psychology, 1,* 119–136.

Del Rio, M. C., Gomollon, A., & Alvarez, F. J. (1994). *Patterns of Drug Use by Valladolid University Students.* Valladolid: Secretariado de Publicaciones de la Universidad de Valladolid.

Dembo, R., Dertke, M., la Voie, L., Borders, S., Washburn, M., & Schmeidler, J. (1987). Physical abuse, sexual victimization, and illicit drug use: A structural analysis among high risk adolescents. *Adolescence, 10,* 13–34.

Dembo, R. M., Williams, L., la Voie, L., Berry, E., Getreu, A., Wish, E., Schmeidler, J., & Washburn, M. (1989). Physical abuse, sexual victimization, and illicit drug use: Replication of a structural analysis among a new sample of high-risk youths. *Violence and Victims, 4,* 121–138.

Demo, D. H., & Acock, A. C. (1988). The impact of divorce on children. *Journal of Marriage and the Family, 50,* 619–648.

Dennett, D. (1995). *Darwin's dangerous idea: Evolution and the meanings of life.* New York: Simon and Schuster.

Dentler, R. A., & Monroe, L. J. (1961). Social correlates of early adolescent theft. *American Sociological Review, 26,* 733–743.

Derrett, J. Duncan (1968). *An introduction to legal systems.* New York: Frederick A. Praeger.

Desdevises, M. C. (1980). *La délinquance des étrangers et la réaction judiciare à la delinquance étrangère, les juenes immigrés.* Vaucressin: CFRES.

Deutsch, S. J. (1978). Deterrence effectiveness measurement. *Criminology, 16,* 115–131.

Devor, E. J. (1993). Why there is no gene for alcoholism. *Behavior Genetics, 23,* 145–151.

DeWolfe, T. E., Jackson, L. A., & Winterberger, P. (1988). A comparison of moral reasoning and moral character in male and female incarcerated felons. *Sex Roles, 18,* 583–593.

Dewsbury, D. A. (1978). *Comparative animal behavior.* New York: McGraw-Hill.

Dias, R., Robbins, T. W., & Roberts, A. C. (1996). Primate analogue of the Wisconsin card sorting tests: Lesions of the prefrontal cortex in the marmoset. *Behavioral Neuroscience, 110,* 872–886.

Dickstein, E. B. (1979). Biological and cognitive bases of moral functioning. *Human Development, 22,* 37–59.

DiLalla, L. F., & Gottesman, I. I. (1989). Heterogeneity of causes for delinquency and criminality: Lifespan perspectives. *Development and Psychopathology, 1,* 339–349.

DiLalla, L., F., & Gottesman, I. I. (1991). Biological and genetic contributors to violence—Widom's untold tale. *Psychological Bulletin, 109,* 125–129.

Dinitz, S. (1987). Coping with deviant behavior through technology. *Criminal Justice Research Bulletin, 3,* 1–15.

Dinwiddie, S. H. (1996). Genetics, antisocial personality, and criminal responsibility. *Bulletin of the American Academy of Psychiatry and the Law, 24,* 95–108.

Dion, K. K., & Berscheid, E. (1974). Physical attractiveness and peer perception among children. *Sociometry, 37,* 1–12.

Dion, K. K., Berscheid, E., & Walster, E. (1972). What is beautiful is good. *Journal of Personality and Social Psychology, 24,* 285–290.

Dishion, T. J., Patterson, G. R., Stoolmiller, M., & Skinner, M. L. (1991). Family, school, and behavioral antecedents to early adolescent involvment with antisocial peers. *Developmental Psychology* 27, 172–180.

Dobash, E. R., & Dobash, R. P. (1992). *Women, violence and social change.* London: Routledge.

Dobash, R. P., Dobash, E. R., Wilson, M., & Daly, M. (1992). The myth of sexual symmetry in marital violence. *Social Problems, 39,* 71–91.

Doerner, W. G., & Speir, J. C. (1986). Stitch and sew: The impact of medical resources upon criminally induced lethality. *Criminology, 24,* 319–330.

Doherty, P., & Joyal, R. (1979). *Some selected statistics on homicide and other violent crime in Canada.* Ottawa: Ministry of the Solicitor General.

Dohrenwend, B. P., Levav, I., Shrout, P. E., Schwatrz, S., Naveh, G., Link, B. G., Skodol, A. E., & Stueve, A. (1992). Socioeconomic status and psychiatric disorders: The casuation–selection issue. *Science, 255,* 946–952.

Doleschal, E., & Klapmuts, N. (1973). Towards a new criminology. *Crime and Delinquency Literature, 5,* 607–626.

Donnelly, C. H., & Murphy, D. L. (1977). Substrate-and-inhibitor-related characteristics of human platelet monoamine oxidase. *Biochemistry and Pharmacology, 26,* 853–858.

Donnelly, P. G. (1978). Alcohol problems and sales in counties of Pennsylvania: A social area investigation. *Journal of Studies on Alcohol, 39,* 848–858.

Donnermeyer, J. F. (1992). The use of alcohol, marijuana, and hard drugs by rural adolescents: A review of recent research. In R. W. Edwards (Ed.), *Drug use in rural American communities* (pp. 31–75). New York: Harrington Park Press.

Donovan, S. j., & Nunes, E. V. (1998). Treatment of comorbid affective and substance use disorders: Therapeutic potential of anticonvulsants. *American Journal of Addiction, 7,* 210–220.

Donovan, S. J., Susser, E. S., & Nunes, E. V. (1997). Divalproex treatment of disruptive adolescents: A report of 10 cases. *Journal of Clinical Psychiatry, 58,* 12–15.

Doria, J. J. (1995). Gene variability and vulnerability to alcoholism. *Alcohol Health & Research World, 19,* 245–248.

Dornbusch, S. M., Carlsmith, M. J., Bushwall, S. J., Ritter, P. L., Leiderman, H., Hastorf, A. H., & Gross, R. T. (1985). Single parents, extended households, and the control of adolescents. *Child Development, 56,* 326–341.

Dougherty, D. M., Bjork, J. M., Huang, D., & Moeller, F. G. (1997). The relationship between self-reported menstrual symptomatology and aggression measured in the laboratory. *Personality and Individual Differences, 22,* 381–391.

Douglas, J., Ressler, R., Burgess, A., & Hartman, C. (1986). Criminal profiling from crime scene analysis. *Behavioral Sciences and the Law, 4,* 401–421.

Downes, D. (1996). The future of criminologies. *British Journal of Sociology, 47,* 360–365.

Downs, W. R., Robertson, J. F., & Harrison, L. R. (1997). Control theory, labeling theory, and the delivery of services for drug abuse to adolescents. *Adolescence, 32,* 1–23.

Dozier, J., & Miceli, M. (1985). Potential predictors of whisleblowing: A prosocial behavior perspective. *Academy of Management Review, 10,* 823–836.

Drake, R. A. (1984). Lateral asymmetry of personal optimism. *Journal of Research in Personality, 18,* 497–507.

Drake, R. A. (1985). Lateral asymmetry of risky recommendations. *Personality and Social Psychology Bulletin, 11,* 409–417.

Draper, P., & Belsky, J. (1990). Personality development in evolutionary perspective. *Journal of Personality, 58,* 141–161.

Draper, P., & Harpending, H. (1982). Father absence and reproductive strategy: An evolutionary perspective. *Journal of Anthropological Research, 38,* 255–273.

Drewe, E. A. (1974). The effect of type and area of brain lesion on Wisconsin card sorting test performance. *Cortex, 10,* 159–170.

Drukteinis, Albert (1992). Serial murder—the heart of darkness. *Psychiatric Annals, 22,* 532–538.

Duncan, J., Emslie, H., Williams, P., Johnson, R., & Freer, C. (1996). Intelligence and the frontal lobe: The organization of goal-directed behavior. *Cognitive Psychology, 30,* 257–303.

Duncan, P. D., Ritter, P. L., Dornbusch, S. M., Gross, T. R., & Carlsmith, J. M. (1985). The effects of pubertal timing on body image, school behavior, and deviance. *Journal of Youth and Adolescence, 14*, 227–235.

Duncan, R. (1995). Four-factor model of recidivism in male juvenile offenders. *Journal of Clinical Child Psychology, 24*, 250–257.

D'Unger, A. V., Land, K. C., McCall, P. L., & Nagin, D. S. (1998). How many latent classes of delinquent/criminal careers? Results from mixed Poisson regression analyses. *American Journal of Sociology, 103*, 1593–1630.

Dupre, John (1992). Blinded by "science": How not to think about social problems. *Behavioral and Brain Sciences, 15*, 382–383.

Durbin, M., DiClemente, R. J., Siegel, D., Krasovsky, F., Lazarus, N., & Camacho, T. (1993). Factors associated with multiple sex partners among junior high school students. *Journal of Adolescent Health, 14*, 202–207.

Durea, M. A. (1933). An experimental study of attitudes toward juvenile delinquency. *Journal of Applied Psychology, 17*, 522–534.

Durkheim, E. (1937). *De la division du travail social.* Paris, France: Collier.

Durkheim, E. (1933). *The division of labor* (G. Simpson, Trans.). New York: Free Press.

Durkheim, E. (1952). *Suicide: A study in sociology.* Glencoe, IL: Free Press.

Duterte-Boucher, D., Leclere, J. F., Panissaud, C., & Coustantin, J. (1988). Acute effects of direct dopamine agonists in the mouse behavioral despair test. *European Journal of Pharmacology, 154*, 185–190.

Duyme, M. (1990). Antisocial behaviour and postnatal environment: A French adoption study. *Journal of Child Psychology and Psychiatry, 31*, 699–710.

Dworkin, A. (1981). *Pornography: Men possessing women.* New York: G. P. Putnam's Sons.

Earls, C., & Proulx, J. (1987). The differentiation of Francophone rapists and non-rapists using penile circumferential measures. *Criminal Justice and Behavior, 13*, 419–429.

Eaton, G. G. (1976). The social order of Japanese macaques. *Scientific American, 235*, October, 95–106.

Eaton, J. W., & Polk, K. (1961). *Measuring delinquency: A study of probation department referrals.* Pittsburgh: University of Pittsburgh Press.

Eckberg, D. L. (1995). Estimates of early Twentieth-Century U.S. homicide rates: An eceonometric forecasting approach. *Demography, 32*, 1–16.

The Economist (1997). Executions in China: World leader. *The Economist, 344*(August 30), 27.

Edelbrock, C., Rende, R., Plomin, R., & Thompson, L. A. (1995). A twin study of competence and problem behavior in childhood and early adolescence. *Journal of Child Psychology and Psychiatry, 36*, 775–785.

Edelmann, R. J., & Vivian, S. E. (1988). Further analysis of the social psychopathy scale. *Personality and Individual Differences, 9*, 581–587.

Edwards, S. S. (1989). *Policing "domestic" violence: Women, the law and the state.* London: Sage.

Efron, Jarman, & Barker, (1997). Methylphenidate vs. Dexamphetamine in Children with ADHD: A double-blind, crossover trial. *Pediatrics, 100*, 1–7.

Egger, S. (1998). *The killers among us: An examination of serial murder and its investigation.* Upper Saddle River, NJ: Prentice Hall.

Ehrenkranz, J., Bliss, E., & Sheard, M. H. (1974). Plasma testosterone: Correlation with aggressive behaviour and social dominance in man. *Psychosomatic Medicine, 36*, 469–475.

Eichelman, B. (1983). The limbic system and aggression in humans. *Neuroscience & Biobehavioral Reviews, 7*, 391–394.

Eichelman, B. (1987). Neurochemical and psychopharmacologic aspects of aggressive behavior. In H. Y. Meltzer (Ed.), *Psychopharmacology: The third generation of progress* (pp. 697–704). New York: Raven.

Einfeld, S., Hall, W., & Levy, F. (1991). Hyperactivity and the fragile X syndrome. *Journal of Abnormal Child Psychology, 19*, 253–262.

Eisdorfer, C., Doerr, H., & Follette, W. (1980). Effects of age and sex on electrodermal reactivity. *Journal of Human Stress, 6*, 39–42.

Ekblad, S. (1984). Children's thoughts and attitudes in China and Sweden: Impacts of a restrictive versus a permissive environment. *Acta Psychiatrica Scandinavica, 70*, 578–590.

Ekblad, S. (1990). The children's behaviour questionnaire for completion by parents and teachers in a Chinese sample. *Journal of Child Psychology and Psychiatry, 31*, 775–791.

Ekehammer, B., Nilsson, I., & Sidanius, J. (1987). Education and ideology: Basic aspects of education related to adolescents' sociopolitical attitudes. *Political Psychology, 8*, 395–410.

Elifson, K. W., Peterson, D. M., & Hadaway, C. K. (1983). Religiosity and delinquency. *Criminology, 21*, 505–527.

Elliott, D. (1962). Delinquency and perceived opportunity. *Sociological Inquiry, 32*, 216–222.

Elliott, D., & Huizinga, D. (1983). Social class and delinquency in a national youth panel. *Criminology, 21*, 149–177.

Elliott, D. (1985). The assumption that theories can be combined with increased explanatory power: Theoretical integrations. In F. Meier (Ed.), *Theoretical methods in criminology* (pp. 123–150). Sage.

Elliott, D. (1994). Serious violent offenders: Onset, developmental course, and termination—The American Society of Criminology 1993 Presidential Address. *Criminology, 32*, 1–21.

Elliott, D., & Ageton, S. (1980). Reconciling race and class differences in self-reported and official estimates of delinquency. *American Sociological Review, 45*, 95–110.

Elliott, D., Ageton, S., & Cantor, R. (1979). An integrated theoretical perspective on delinquent behavior. *Journal of Research in Crime and Delinquency, 16*, 3–27.

Elliott, D., Huizinga, D., & Ageton, S. S. (1985). *Explaining delinquency and drug use.* Beverly Hills, CA: Sage.

Elliott, D., Huizinga, D., & Menard, S. (1989). *Multiple problem youth: Delinquency, substance use, and mental health problems.* New York: Springer-Verlag.

Elliott, D., Huizinga, D., & Morse, B. (1986). Self-reported violent offending: A descriptive analysis of juvenile violent offenders and their offending careers. *Journal of Interpersonal Violence, 1*, 472–514.

Elliott, F. A. (1976). The neurology of explosive rage: The dyscontrol syndrome. *Practitioner, 217*, 51–60.

Elliott, F. A. (1978). Neurological aspects of antisocial behavior. In W. H. Reid (Ed.), *The psychopath: A comprehensive study of antisocial disorders and behaviors* (pp. 146–189). New York: Brunner/Mazel.

Ellis, B. J. (1992). The evolution of sexual attraction: Evaluative mechanisms in women. In J. H. Barkow, L. Cosmides, & J. Tooby (Eds.), *The adapted mind* (pp. 267–288). New York: Oxford.

Ellis, D. P., & Austin, P. (1971). Menstruation and aggressive behavior in a correctional center for women. *Journal of Criminal Law, Criminology, and Police Science, 62,* 388–395.

Ellis, L. (1982). Genetics and criminal behavior: Evidence through the end of the 1970's. *Criminology, 20,* 43–66.

Ellis, L. (1985). Religiosity and criminality: Evidence and explanations surrounding complex relationships. *Sociological Perspective, 28,* 501–520.

Ellis, L. (1986a). Evolution and the nonlegal equivalent of criminal behavior. *Aggressive Behavior, 12,* 57–71.

Ellis, L. (1986b). Evidence of neuroandrogenic etiology of sex roles from a combined analysis of human, nonhuman primate and nonprimate mammalian studies. *Personality and Individual Differences, 7,* 519–552.

Ellis, L. (1987a). Criminal behavior and r/K selection: An extension of gene-based evolutionary theory. *Deviant Behavior, 8,* 149–176.

Ellis, L. (1987b). Neurohormonal bases of varying tendencies to learn delinquent and criminal behavior. In E. K. Morris & C. J. Braukmann (Eds.), *Behavioral approaches to crime and delinquency* (pp. 499–518). New York: Plenum.

Ellis, L. (1987c). Relationships of criminality and psychopathy with eight other apparent behavioral manifestations of sub-optimal arousal. *Personality and Individual Differences, 8,* 905–925.

Ellis, L. (1987d). Religiosity and criminality from the perspective of the arousal theory. *Journal of Research on Crime and Delinquency, 24,* 215–232.

Ellis, L. (1988). The victimful–victimless crime distinction, and seven universal demographic correlates of victimful criminal behavior. *Personality and Individual Differences, 9,* 525–548.

Ellis, L. (1989b). Evolutionary and neurochemical causes of sex differences in victimizing behavior: Toward a unified theory of criminal behavior. *Social Science Information, 28,* 605–636.

Ellis, L. (1989a). *Theories of rape: Inquiries into the causes of sexual aggression.* New York: Hemisphere.

Ellis, L. (1989/1990). Sex differences in criminality: An explanation based on the concept of r/K selection. *Mankind Quarterly, 30,* 399–417.

Ellis, L. (1990a). Conceptualizing criminal and related behavior from a biosocial perspective. In L. Ellis & H. Hoffman (Eds.), *Crime in biological, social, and moral contexts* (pp. 18–35). New York: Praeger.

Ellis, L. (1990b). The evolution of collective counterstrategies to crime: From the primate control role to the criminal justice system. In L. Ellis & H. Hoffman (Eds.), *Crime in biological, social, and moral contexts.* New York: Praeger.

Ellis, L. (1990c). The evolution of violent criminal behavior and its nonlegal equivalent. In L. Ellis & H. Hoffman (Eds.), *Crime in biological, social, and moral contexts* (pp. 81–99). New York: Praeger.

Ellis, L. (1991a). Monoamine oxidase and criminality: Identifying an apparent biological marker for antisocial behavior. *Journal of Research on Crime and Delinquency, 28,* 227–251.

Ellis, L. (1991b). A synthesized (biosocial) theory of rape. *Journal of Consulting and Clinical Psychology, 59,* 631–642.

Ellis, L. (1993a). Conceptually defining social stratification in human and nonhuman animals. In L. Ellis (Ed.), *Social stratification and socioeconomic inequality,* vol. 1: *A comparative biosocial analysis* (pp. 1–14). Westport, CT: Praeger.

Ellis, L. (1993b). Rape as a biosocial phenomenon. In G. C. N. Hall (Ed.), *Sexual aggression: Issues in etiology, assessment, and treatment* (pp. 17–41). Washington, DC: Taylor and Francis.

Ellis, L. (1994). *Research methods in the social sciences.* New York; McGraw Hill-Brown & Benchmark.

Ellis, L. (1996). The role of perinatal factors in determining sexual orientation. In R. C. Savin-Williams & K. M. Cohen (Eds.), *The lives of lesbians, gays, and bisexuals* (pp. 35–70). Fort Worth: Harcourt Brace College.

Ellis, L. (1998). NeoDarwinian theories of violent criminality and antisocial behavior: Photographic evidence from nonhuman animals and a review of the literature. *Aggression and Violent Behavior, 3,* 61–110.

Ellis, L., & Ames, M. A. (1989a). Delinquency, sidedness, and sex. *Journal of General Psychology, 116,* 57–62.

Ellis, L., & Beattie, C. (1983). The feminist explanation for rape: An empirical test. *Journal of Sex Research, 19,* 74–93.

Ellis, L., & Coontz, P. D. (1990). Androgens, brain functioning, and criminality: The neurohormonal foundations of antisociality. In L. Ellis & H. Hoffman (Eds.), *Crime in biological, social, and moral contexts* (pp. 162–193). New York: Praeger.

Ellis, L., & Hoffman, H. (1990). Views of contemporary criminologists on causes and theories of crime. In L. Ellis & H. Hoffman (Eds.), *Crime in biological, social, and moral contexts* (pp. 50–58). New York: Praeger.

Ellis, L., Miller, C., & Widmayer, A. (1988). Content analysis of biological approaches in psychology: 1894–1985. *Sociology and Social Research, 72,* 145–149.

Ellis, L., & Thompson, R. (1989). Relating religion, crime, arousal and boredom. *Sociology and Social Research, 73,* 132–139.

Ellis, L., & Walsh, A. (1997). Gene-based evolutionary theories in criminology. *Criminology, 35,* 229–276.

Ellis, L., & Walsh, A. (1999). Criminologists' opinions about causes and theories of crime and delinquency. *The Criminologist, 24* (July/August), 1–6.

Ellis, P. L. (1982). Empathy: A factor in antisocial behavior. *Journal of Abnormal Child Psychology, 10,* 123–134.

Ellwood, C. A. (1919). *Sociology and modern social problems.* New York: American Book.

Elmer, E. E. (1991). Ecology. In R. Lachmann (Ed.), *The encyclopedic dictionary of sociology* (4th Ed., pp. 97–98). Guilford, CT: Dushkin.

Elmer-DeWitt, P. (1990). Why junior won't sit still, *Time,* November 26, 59.

Eltis, D. (1993). Europeans and the rise and fall of African slavery in the Americas: An interpretation. *American Historical Review,* December, 1399–1423.

Ely, D. L., Greene, E. G. & Henry, J. P. (1977). Effect of hippocampal lesion on cardiovascular, adrenocortical and behavioral response patterns in mice. *Physiology and Behavior, 18,* 1075–1083.

Ember, C. R. (1981). A cross-cultural perspective on sex differences. In R. H. Munroe, R. L. Munroe, & B. B. Whiting (Eds.), *Handbook of cross-cultural human development* (pp. 531–580). New York: Garland.

Ember, C. R., & Ember, M. (1985). *Anthropology,* 4th ed. Englewood Cliffs, NJ: Prentice-Hall.

Ember, C. R., & Ember, M. (1988). *Anthropology,* 5th ed. Englewood Cliffs, NJ: Prentice-Hall.

Eme, R. F. (1984). Sex-related differences in the epidemiology of child psychopathology. In C. S. Widom (Ed.), *Sex roles and psychopathology* (pp. 279–308). New York: Plenum.

Eme, R. F., & Kavanaugh, L. (1995). Sex differences in conduct disorder. *Journal of Clinical Child Psychology, 24,* 406–426.

Emler, N. (1984). Differential involvement in delinquency: Toward an interpretation in terms of reputation management. *Progress in Experimental Personality Research, 13,* 173–239.

Emler, N., Heather, N., & Winton, M. (1978). Delinquency and the development of moral reasoning. *British Journal of Social and Clinical Psychology, 17,* 325–331.

Emler, N., Renwick, S., & Malone, B. (1983). The relationship between moral reasoning and political orientation. *Journal of Personality and Social Psychology, 45,* 1073–1080.

Emory, L., Cole, C., & Meyer, W. (1992). The Texas experience with DepoProvera: 1980–1990. *Journal of Offender Rehabilitation, 18,* 125–139.

Empey, L. T. (1982). *American delinquency: Its meaning and construction* (rev. ed.). Homewood, IL: Dorsey.

Ennis, P. H. (1967). *Criminal victimization in the United States: A report of a national survey.* Washington DC: U.S. Government Printing Office.

Enns, R. A., & Reddon, J. R. (1998). The factor structure of the Wechsler Adult Intelligence Scale-Revised: One or two but not three factors. *Journal of Clinical Psychology, 5,* 447–459.

Eppright, T. D., Kashani, J. H., Robinson, B. D., & Reid, J. C. (1993). Comorbidity of conduct disorder and personality disorders in an incarcerated juvenile population. *American Journal of Psychiatry, 150,* 1233–1236.

Erbas, B., Bekdik, C., & Erbengi, G. (1992). Regional cerebral blood flow changes in chronic alcoholism using Tc-99m HMPAO SPECT, comparison with CT parameters. *Clinical Nuclear Medicine, 17,* 123–127.

Erickson, M. L., & Empey, L. T. (1963). Court records, undetected delinquency and decision making. *Journal of Criminal Law, Criminology, and Police Science, 54,* 456–469.

Erlanger, H. S. (1974). Social class and corporal punishment in child rearing: A reassessment. *American Sociological Review, 39,* 68–85.

Erlanger, H. S. (1978). The empirical status of the subculture of violence thesis. In L. D. Savitz & N. Johnston (Eds.), *Crime in society* (pp. 163–173). New York: Wiley.

Eron, L. D., Guerra, N., & Huesmann, L. R. (1997). Poverty and violence. In S. Feshbach & J. Zagrodzka (Eds.), *Aggression: Biological, developmental, and social perspectives.* New York: Plenum.

Erskine, H. (1974a). Polls: Causes of crime. *Public Opinion Quarterly, 38,* 288–297.

Erskine, H. (1974b). The polls: Fear of violence and crime. *Public Opinion Quarterly, 38,* 131–145.

Esbensen, F., & Huizinga, D. (1993). Gangs, drugs, and delinquency in a survey of urban youth. *Criminology, 31,* 565–589.

Etienne, A. S., Emmanuelli, E., & Zinder, M. (1982). Ontogeny of hoarding in the golden hamster: The development of motor patterns and their sequential coordination. *Developmental Psychobiology, 15,* 33–45.

Evans, J., & Himelfarb, (1987). Counting crime. In R. Linden (Ed.), *Criminology: A Canadian perspective* (pp. 43–73). Toronto: Holt, Rinehart and Winston.

Evans, J., & Himelfarb, A. (1992). Counting crime. In R. Linden (Ed.), *Criminology: A Canadian perspective,* 2nd ed., (pp. 57–212). Toronto: Harcourt, Brace.

Evans, R. C., Levy, L., Sullenberger, T., & Vyas, A. (1991). Self concept and delinquency: The on-going debate. *Journal of Offender Rehabilitation, 16,* 59–74.

Evans, S., & Hodges, J. (1984). Reproductive status of adult daughters in family groups of common marmosets (*Callithrix jacchus jacchus*). *Folia Primatologica, 42,* 127–133.

Evans, S., & Scott, J. (1984). The seriousness of crime cross-culturally: The impact of religiosity. *Criminology, 22,* 39–59.

Evans, T. D., Cullen, F. T., Burton, V. S. J., Dunaway, R. G., & Benson, M. L. (1997). The social consequences of self-control: Testing the general theory of crime. *Criminology, 35,* 475–504.

Everitt, B. J. (1984). Monoamines and the control of sexual behaviour. In M. Sheperd (Ed.), *The spectrum of psychiatric research* (pp. 26–32). Cambridge: Cambridge University Press.

Exner, F. (1939). *Kriminalbiologie in ihren grundzugen.* Hamburg, Germany: Hanseatische Verlagsanstalt.

Eysenck, H. J. (1951). Primary social attitudes as related to social class and political party. *British Journal of Sociology, 11,* 198–209.

Eysenck, H. J. (1967). *The biological basis of personality.* Springfield, IL: C. C. Thomas.

Eysenck, H. J., (1977). *Crime and personality,* 3rd ed. London: Routledge and Kegan Paul.

Eysenck, H. J. (1979). *The structure and measurement of intelligence.* Berlin: Springer.

Eysenck, H. J., & Gudjonsson, G. H. (1989). *The causes and cures of criminality.* New York: Plenum.

Eysenck, H. J., & Nias, D. K. B. (1978). *Sex, violence and the media.* London: Maurice Temple Smith.

Eysenck, H. J., & Wilson, G. D. (1978). *The psychological basis of ideology.* Lancaster, England: MTB Press.

Eysenck, S. B. G., & Zuckerman, M. (1978). The relationship between sensation seeking and Eysenck's dimensions of personality. *British Journal of Psychology, 69,* 483–487.

Ezekiel, M. (1941). *Methods of correlational analysis* (2nd ed.). New York: Wiley.

Ezeldin, Ahmed (1989). Terrorism in the 1990's: New strategies and the nuclear threat. *International Journal of Comparative and Applied Criminal Justice, 13,* 7–16.

Faigel, H. C., Sznajderman, S., Tishby, O., Turel, M., & Pinus, U. (1995). Attention deficit disorder during adolescence: A review. *Journal of Adolescent Health, 16,* 174–184.

Fairchild, Erika (1993). *Comparative criminal justice systems.* Belmont, CA: Wadsworth.

Faller, Kathleen (1987). Women who sexually abuse children. *Violence and Victims, 2,* 263–276.

Falshaw, L., Browne, K. D., & Hollin, C. R. (1996). Victim to offender: A review. *Aggression and Violent Behavior, 1,* 389–404.

Fantino, M., & Cabanac, M. (1980). Body weight regulation with a proportional hoarding response in the rat. *Physiology and Behavior, 24,* 939–942.

Farley, F. H., & Sewell, T. (1976). Test of an arousal theory of delinquency: Stimulation-seeking in delinquent and nondelinquent Black adolescents. *Criminal Justice and Behavior, 3,* 315–320.

Farley, F. H., Steinberger, H., Cohen, A., & Barr, H. L. (1979). Test of a theory of delinquency: Delinquent behaviors among institutionalized drug addicts as a function of arousal and the sensation-seeking motive. *Criminal Justice and Behavior, 6,* 41–48.

Farley, J. E. (1998). *Sociology* (4th ed.). Upper Saddle River, NJ: Prentice-Hall.

Farley, R. (1980). Homicide trends in the United States. *Demography, 17,* 177–188.

Farley, R. (1984). *Blacks and whites: Narrowing the gap.* Cambridge, MA: Harvard University Press.

Farnworth, M., & Lieber, M. J. (1989). Strain theory revisited: Economic goals, educational means, and delinquency. *American Sociological Review, 54,* 259–270.

Farrington, D. P. (1973). Self-reports of deviant behavior: Productive and stable? *Journal of Criminal Law and Criminology, 64,* 99–110.

Farrington, D. P. (1977). The effects of public labeling. *British Journal of Criminology, 17,* 112–125.

Farrington, D. P. (1978). The family background of aggressive youths. In L. A. Hersov, M. Berger, & D. Schaffer (Eds.), *Aggression and antisocial behavior in childhood and adolescence.* Oxford: Pergamon.

Farrington, D. P. (1982). Longitudinal analyses of criminal violence. In M. E. Wolfgang & N. A. Weiner (Eds.), *Criminal Violence.* Beverly Hills, CA: Sage.

Farrington, D. P. (1986a). Age and crime. In M. Tonry & N. Morris (Eds.), *Crime and justice,* Vol. 7 (pp. 29–90). Chicago: University of Chicago Press.

Farrington, D. P. (1986b). Stepping stones to adult criminal careers. In D. Olweus, J. Block, & M. Radke-Yarrow (Eds.), *Development of Antisocial and Prosocial Behavior* (pp. 359–384). Orlando, FL: Academic.

Farrington, D. P. (1987a). Early precursors of frequent offending. In J. Q. Wilson & G. C. Loury (Eds.), *From child to citizens,* Vol. III: *Families, schools, and delinquency prevention* (pp. 27–50). London: Springer-Verlag.

Farrington, D. P. (1987b). Epidemiology. In H. C. Quay (Ed.), *Handbook of juvenile delinquency* (pp. 33–61). New York: Wiley.

Farrington, D. P. (1987c). Implications of biological findings for criminological research. In S. A. Mednick, T. E. Moffitt, & S. A. Stack (Eds.), *The causes of crime: New biological approaches* (pp. 42–64). New York: Cambridge University Press.

Farrington, D. P. (1989). Early predictors of adolescent aggression and adult violence. *Violence and Victims, 4,* 79–100.

Farrington, D. P. (1989). Self-reported and official offending from adolescence to adulthood. In M. W. Klein (Ed.), *Cross-national research in self-reported crime and delinquency* (pp. 399–423). Dordrecht: Kluwer.

Farrington, D. P. (1991). Antisocial personality from childhood to adulthood. *Psychologist, 4,* 389–394.

Farrington, D. P. (1992). Criminal career research in the United Kingdom. *British Journal of Criminology, 32,* 521–536.

Farrington, D. P. (1992). Juvenile delinquency. In J. Coleman (Ed.), *The school years: Current issues in the socialization of young people, 2nd edition.* London: Routledge.

Farrington, D. P. (1997). The relationship between low resting heart rate and violence. In A. Raine, P. A. Brennan, D. P. Farrington, & S. A. Mednick (Eds.), *Biosocial bases of violence* (pp. 89–105). New York: Plenum.

Farrington, D. P., Biron, L., & LeBlanc, M. (1982). Personality and delinquency in London and Montreal. In J. Gunn & D. P. Farrington (Eds.), *Abnormal offenders, delinquency, and the criminal justice system* (pp. 153–197). New York: John Wiley & Sons.

Farrington, D. P., Gallagher, B., Morley, L., Ledger, R., & West, D. J. (1986). Unemployment, school leaving, and crime. *British Journal of Criminology, 26,* 335–356.

Farrington, D. P., & Hawkins, J. D. (1991). Predicting participation, early onset, and later persistence in officially recorded offending. *Criminal Behavior and Mental Health, 1,* 1–33.

Farrington, D. P., Loeber, R., & Van Kammen, W. (1990). Long-term criminal outcomes of hyperactivity-impulsivity-attention deficit and conduct problems in childhood. In L. N. Robins & M. Rutter (Eds.), *Straight and devious pathways from childhood to adulthood* (pp. 62–81). New York: Cambridge University Press.

Farrington, D. P., Osborn, S. G., & West, D. J. (1978). The persistence of labelling effects. *British Journal of Criminology London, 18*(3), 277–284.

Fattah, E. A. (1993). The rational choice/opportunity perspectives as a vehicle for integrating criminological and victimological theories. In R. V. Clarke & M. Felson (Eds.), *Routine activity and rational choice* (pp. 225–258). Brunswick: Transaction.

Federal Bureau of Investigation. (1969). *Crime in the United States: Uniform Crime Reports 1968.* Washington, DC: United States Department of Justice.

Federal Bureau, of Investigation (1991). *Crime in the United States: Uniform Crime Reports 1990.* Washington, DC: United States Department of Justice.

Fedora, O., & Reddon, J. R. (1993). Psychopathic and nonpsychopathic inmates differ from normal controls in tolerance levels of electrical stimulation. *Journal of Clinical Psychology, 49,* 326–331.

Feeley, M. M., & Little, D. L. (1991). The vanishing female: The decline of women in the criminal process, 1687–1912. *Law & Society Review, 25,* 719–757.

Feinberg, J., & Gross, H. (1986). *The Philosophy of Law* (3rd ed.). CA: Wadsworth.

Feine, J. S., Bushnell, M. C., Miron, D., & Duncan, G. H. (1991). Sex differences in the perception of noxious heat stimuli. *Pain, 44,* 255–262.

Fejer, D. (1971). *Drug use among high school students in North Bay, Ontario.* Toronto, ON: Manuscript from Addiction Research Foundation.

Feldman, M. P. (1977). *Criminal behaviour: A psychological analysis.* New York: Wiley.

Feldman, R. A. (1992). The St. Louis Experiment: Effective treatment of antisocial youths in prosocial peer groups. In J. McCord & R. E. Tremblay (Eds.), *Preventing antisocial behavior: Interventions from birth through adolescence.* New York: Guilford.

Feldman, S. S., Nash, S. C., & Cutrona, C. (1977). The influence of age and sex on responsiveness to babies. *Developmental Psychology, 13,* 675–676.

Felner, R. D., & Adan, A. M. (1988). The school transitional environment project: An ecological intervention and evaluation. In R. H. Price, E. L. Cowen, R. P. Lorion, & J. Ramos-McKay (Eds.), *14 ounces of prevention: A casebook for practitioners* (pp. 111–122). Washington, DC: American Psychological Association.

Felson, M. (1987). Routine activities and crime prevention in the developing metropolis. *Criminology, 25,* 911–932.

Felson, M. (1998). *Crime and everyday life* (2nd ed.) Thousand Oaks: Pine Forge Press.

Felson, R. B., & Steadman, H. J. (1983). Situational factors in disputes leading to criminal violence. *Criminology, 21,* 59–74.

Ferdinand, T. N. (1977). Introduction. In T. N. Ferdinand (Ed.), *Juvenile delinquency: Little brother grows up* (pp. 7–16). Beverly Hills, CA: Sage.

Ferentz, E. J. (1954). Mental deficiency related to crime. *Journal of Criminal Law, Criminology, and Police Science, 45,* 299–307.

Ferguson, T. (1952). *The young delinquent in his social setting.* London: Oxford University Press.

Fergusson, D., & Horwood, L. (1994). Nocturnal enuresis and behavioral problems in adolescence: A 15-year longitudinal study. *Pediatrics, 94,* 662–668.

Fergusson, D. M., Hons, B., & Horwood, L. J. (1986). Factors related to the age of attainment of nocturnal bladder control: An 8-year longitudinal study. *Pediatrics, 78,* 884–890.

Fergusson, D. M., Horwood, L. J., & Lynskey, M. T. (1993a). Ethnicity, social background and young offending: A 14-year longitudinal study. *Australian and New Zealand Journal of Criminology, 26,* 155–170.

Fergusson, D. M., Horwood, L. J., & Lynskey, M. T. (1994a). The childhoods of multiple problem adolescents: A 15-year longitudinal study. *Journal of Child Psychology and Psychiatry, 35,* 1123–1140.

Fergusson, D. M., Horwood, L. J., & Lynskey, M. D. (1994b). The comorbidities of adolescent problem behaviors: A latent class model. *Journal of Abnormal Child Psychology, 22,* 339–354.

Fergusson, D. M., Horwood, L. J., & Lynskey, M. T. (1993b). Ethnicity and bias in police contact statistics. *Australian and New Zealand Journal of Criminology, 26,* 193–206.

Fergusson, D. M., Lynskey, M., & Horwood, L. J. (1995a). The adolescent outcomes of adoption: A 16-year longitudinal study. *Journal of Child Psychology, 36,* 597–615.

Fergusson, D. M., Lynskey, M. T., & Horwood, L., J. (1995b). Truancy in adolescence. *New Zealand Journal of Educational Studies, 30,* 25–37.

Fernquist, R. M. (1995). A research note on the association between religion and delinquency. *Deviant Behavior: An Interdisciplinary Journal, 16,* 169–175.

Ferracuti, S. (1996). Cesare Lombroso (1835–1907). *Journal of Forensic Psychiatry, 7,* 130–149.

Ferraro, K. F. (1995). *Fear of crime: Interpreting victimization risk.* Albany: State University of New York Press.

Feshbach, S., & Feshbach, N. D. (1986). Aggression and altruism: a personality perspective. In C. Zahn-Waxler, E. M. Cummings, and R. Ianotti (Eds.), *Altruism and Aggression* (pp. 189–217). Cambridge: Cambridge University Press.

Feyerherm, W. (1981). Gender differences in delinquency: Quantity and quality. In L. Bowker (Ed.), *Women and crime in America* (pp. 82–97). New York: Macmillan.

Fielding, N. G., & Fielding, J. (1991). Police attitudes to crime and punishment. *British Journal of Criminology, 31,* 39–53.

Fifield, J. K., & Donnell, A. A. (1980). *Socio-economic status, race, and offending in New Zealand.* Christs Church: New Zealand Government Printer.

Figlio, R. M. (1975). The seriousness of offenses: An evaluation by offenders and nonoffenders. *Journal of Criminal Law and Criminology, 66,* 189–200.

Finckenauer, J. O. (1979). Scared crooked. *Psychology Today, 13 August,* 6.

Finckenauer, J. O. (1982). *Scared straight! and the panacea phenomenon.* Englewood Cliffs, NJ: Prentice-Hall.

Fingerhut, L. A., & Kleinman, J. D. (1990). International and interstate comparisons of homicide among young males. *Journal of the American Medical Association, 263,* 3292–3295.

Finkelhor, D. (1984). *Child sexual abuse: New theory and research.* New York: Free Press.

Finkelhor, D., Hotaling, G., Lewis, I. A., & Smith, C. (1990). Sexual abuse in a national survey of adult men and women: Prevalence, characteristics and risk factors. *Child Abuse and Neglect, 13,* 533–542.

Finn, P., & Brown, J. (1971). Risks entailed in teenage intoxication as perceived by junior and senior high school students. *Journal of Youth and Adolescence, 10,* 61–71.

Firestone, P., & Prabhu, A. N. (1983). Minor physical anomalies and obstetrical complications: Their relationship to hyperactive, psychoneurotic, and normal children and their families. *Journal of Abnormal Child Psychology, 11,* 207–216.

Firestone, Thomas (1993). Mafia memoirs: What they tell us about organized crime. *Journal of Contemporary Criminal Justice, 9,* 197–221.

Fisch, G. S. (1993). What is associated with the fragile X syndrome? *American Journal of Medical Genetics, 48,* 112–121.

Fiselier, J. P. S. (1979). Opfer von straftaten-art und umfang der kriminalitat in den Niederlanden (Victims of crime-incidence of crime in the Netherlands). In G. F. Kirchhoff & K. Sessar (Eds.), *Das verbrechensopfer. Ein reader zur viktimologie* (pp. 111–132). The Netherlands: Bochum.

Fishbein, D. H., & Pease, S. E. (1996). *The dynamics of drug abuse.* Boston: Allyn and Bacon.

Fisher, G. A., & Erickson, M. L. (1973). On assessing the effects of official reactions to juvenile delinquency. *Journal of Research in Crime and Delinquency, 2,* 177–194.

Fishman, G. (1984). Differential victimization patterns: An analysis of crime victims in polar neighborhoods in

Haifa. In R. Block (Ed.), *Victimization and fear of crime: World perspectives* (pp. 45–49). Washington, DC: U.S. Government Printing Office.

Fitts, W., & Hammer, W. (1969). *The self-concept and delinquency.* Nashville, TN: Nashville Mental Health Center (2410 White Avenue).

Flannery, D. J., Vazsonyi, A. T., & Rowe, D. C. (1996). Caucasian and Hispanic early adolescent substance use: Parenting, personality, and school adjustment. *Early Adolescence, 16,* 71–89.

Flicek, M. (1992). Social status of boys with both academic problems and Attention-Deficit Hyperactivity Disorder. *Journal of Abnormal Child Psychology, 20,* 353–366.

Flor-Henry, P. (1973). Psychiatric syndromes considered as manifestations of lateralized temporal-limbic dysfunction. In L. V. Laitinen & K. E. Livingston (Eds.), *Surgical approaches in psychiatry* (pp. 22–26). Lancaster, England: Medical and Technical Publishing.

Flor-Henry, P. (1978). Gender, hemispheric specialization and psychopathology. *Social Science and Medicine, 12B,* 155–162.

Flor-Henry, P. (1989). Psychopathology and hemispheric specialization: Left hemisphere dysfunction in schizophrenia, psychopathy, hysteria and the obsessional syndrome. In F. Boller & J. Grafman (Eds.), *Handbook of neuropsychology* (pp. 477–494). Amsterdam: Elsevier.

Flowers, R. B. (1988). *Minorities and criminality.* New York: Greenwood.

Flynn, J. P., Vanegas, H., Foote, W., & Edwards, S. (1970). Neural mechanisms involved in a cat's attack on a rat. In R. E. Whalen, R. F. Thompson, M. Verzeano, and N. M. Weinberger (Eds.), *The neural control of behavior* (pp. 135–173). New York: Academic Press.

Fogel, C. A., Mednick, S. A., & Michelson, N. (1985). Hyperactive behavior and minor physical anomalies. *Acta Psychiatrica Scandinavica, 72,* 551–556.

Fogelman, K. P., & Manor, O. (1988). Smoking in pregnancy and development into early adulthood. *British Journal of Medicine, 297,* 1233–1236.

Fonseca, A. C., & Yule, W. (1995). Personality and antisocial behavior in children and adolescents: An enquiry into Eysenck's and Gray's theories. *Journal of Abnormal Child Psychology, 23,* 767–781.

Ford, S. F., & Campos, S. (1977). *Summary of validity data from the admissions testing program validity study service.* New York: College Entrance Examination Board.

Forehand, R., Wierson, M., Frame, C., Kempton, T., & Armistead, L. (1991). Juvenile delinquency entry and persistence: Do attention problems contribute to conduct problems? *Journal of Behavior Therapy and Experimental Psychiatry, 22,* 261–164.

Foreman, D. M., & Goodyer, I. M. (1988). Salivary cortisol hyper-secretion in juvenile depression. *Journal of Child Psychology Psychiatry, 29,* 311–320.

Fors, S. W., & Rojek, D. G. (1983). The social and demographic correlates of adolescent drug use patterns. *Journal of Drug Education, 13,* 205–222.

Forsyth, D. R., & Scott, W. L. (1984). Attributions and moral judgments: Kohlberg's stage theory as a taxonomy of moral attributes. *Bulletin of the Psychonomic Society, 22,* 321–323.

Forth, A. E., Brown, S. L., Hart, S. D., & Hare, R. D. (1996). The assessment of psychopathy in male and female non-criminals: Reliability and validity. *Personality and Individual Differences, 20,* 531–543.

Fowler, C. J., Tipton, K. F., MacKay, A. V. P., & Youdim, M. B. H. (1982). Human platelet monoamine oxidase: A useful enzyme in the study of psychiatric disorders. *Neuroscience, 7,* 1577–1594.

Fowler-Kerry, S., & Lander, J. (1991). Assessment of sex differences in children's and adolescents' self-reported pain from vein-puncture. *Journal of Pediatric Psychology, 16,* 783–793.

Fowles, D. C. (1980). The three arousal model: Implications of Gray's two-factors learning theory for heart rate electro dermal activity and psychopathy. *Psychophysiology, 17,* 87–104.

Fowles, D. C. (1988). Psychophysiology and psychopathology: A motivational approach. *Psychophysiology, 25,* 373–391.

Fowles, D. C. (1993). Electrodermal activity and antisocial behavior: Empirical findings and theoretical issues. In J. C. Roy, W. Boucsein, D. C. Fowles, & J. Gruzelier (Eds.), *Progress in electrodermal research* (pp. 223–237). London: Plenum.

Fox, N. A., Bell, M. A., & Jones, N. A. (1992). Individual differences in response to stress and cerebral asymmetry. *Developmental Neuropsychology, 8,* 161–184.

Fox, S. J. (1961). Delinquency and biology. *University of Miami Law Review, 16,* 65–91.

Francis, L., & Pearson, P. R. (1988). The development of a short form of the (JEPQ-S): Its use in measuring personality and religion. *Personality and Individual Differences, 9,* 911–916.

Francis, L., Pearson, P. R., Carter, M., & Kay, W. K. (1981). Are introverts more religious? *British Journal of Social Psychology, 20,* 101–104.

Frank, R. (1931). The hormonal causes of premenstrual tension. *Archives of Neurology and Psychiatry, 26,* 1053–1057.

Franke, P., Barbe, B., Leboyer, M., & Maier, W. (1996). Fragile X syndrome. II. Cognitive and behavioral correlates of mutations of the FMR-1 gene. *Eur Psychiatry, 11,* 233–243.

Frankenburg, F. R. (1984). Hoarding in anorexia nervosa. *British Journal of Medical Psychology, 57,* 57–60.

Franks, S., Kiddy, D., & Hamilton-Fairley, D. (1991). The role of nutrition and insulin in the regulation of sex hormone binding globulin. *Molecular Biology, 39,* 835–8.

Frazier, C. E., Bishop, D. M., & Henretta, J. C. (1992). The social context of race differentials in juvenile justice dispositions. *Sociological Quarterly, 33,* 447–458.

Free, M. D., Jr. (1994). Religiosity, religious conservatism, bonds to school, and juvenile delinquency among three categories of drug users. *Deviant Behavior: An Interdisciplinary Journal, 15,* 151–170.

Freund, Kurt (1990a). Courtship disorders: Toward a biosocial understanding of voyeurism, exhibitionism, toucheurism, and the preferential rape pattern. In L. Ellis, & H. Hoffman (Eds.), *Crime in biological, social and moral contexts* (pp. 100–114). New York: Praeger.

Freund, Kurt (1990b). Courtship disorder. In W. Marshall, D. Laws, & H. Barbaree (Eds.), *Handbook of sexual assault: Issues, theories, and treatment of the offender* (pp. 195–207). New York: Plenum.

Frey, J. H., & Eadington, W. R. (Eds.). (1984). *Gambling: Views from the social sciences.* Beverly Hills, CA: Sage.

Friday, P. C. (1977). Changing theory and research in criminology. *International Journal of Criminology and Penology, 5,* 159–170.

Friedman, R. (1988). The hungry brain. *Psychology Today, 22* (June), 9.

Friedman, R. C., & Downey, J. I. (1994). Homosexuality. *New England Journal of Medicine, 331,* 923–930.

Friedrich, D. O. (1980). Radical criminology in the United States: An interpretive understanding. In J. A. Inciardi (Ed.), *Radical criminology: The coming Crises* (pp. 35–60). London: Sage.

Fuller, T. D., Edwards, J. N., Sermsri, S., & Vorakitphokatorn, S. (1993). Gender and health: Some Asian evidence. *Journal of Health and Social Behavior, 34,* 252–271.

Furnham, A. (1984). Personality, social skills, anomie and delinquency: A self-report study of a group of normal non-delinquent adolescents. *Journal of Child Psychology and Psychiatry, 25,* 409–420.

Furnham, A., & Alison, L. (1994). Theories of crime, attitudes to punishment and juror bias amongst police, offenders and the general public. *Personality and Individual Differences, 17,* 35–48.

Furnham, A., & Henderson, M. (1983). Lay theories of delinquency. *European Journal of Social Psychology, 13,* 107–120.

Fuster, J. M. (1995). Memory and planning: Two temporal perspectives of frontal lobe function. In H. H. Jasper, S. Riggio, & P. S. Goldman-Rakic (Eds.), *Epilepsy and the functional anatomy of the frontal lobe* (pp. 9–18). New York: Raven.

Fustero, S. (1984). Home on the street. *Psychology Today, 18* (February), 56–63.

Gabel, S., & Shindledecker, R. (1991). Aggressive behavior in youth: Characteristics, outcome, and psychiatric diagnoses. *Journal of the Academy of Child Adolescent Psychiatry, 30,* 982–987.

Gabel, S., Stadler, J., Bjorn, J., Shindledecker, R., & Bowden, C. L. (1994). Monoamine oxidase and homovanillic acid in boys with predispositions to substance abuse. *Alcoholism: Clinical and Experimental Research, 18,* 1137–1142.

Gabor, T. (1994). The suppression of crime statistics on race and ethnicity: The price of political correctness. *Canadian Journal of Criminology, 36,* 153–163.

Gabrielli, W. F., Jr., & Mednick, S. A. (1983). Genetic correlates of criminal behavior. *American Behavioral Scientist, 27,* 59–74.

Gale, F., Bailey-Harris, R., & Wundersitz, J. (1990). *Aboriginal youth and the criminal justice system: The injustice of justice?* New York: Cambridge University Press.

Gallard, C. (1995). Female genital mutilation in France. *British Journal of Medicine, 310,* 1592–1593.

Gallup, G. H. (1973). *The Gallup Poll: Public opinion 1935–1971.* New York: Random House.

Gandelman, R. (1983). Gonadal hormones and sensory function. *Neuroscience & Biobehavioural Review, 7,* 1–17.

Gandossy, R. P., Williams, J. R., Cohen, J., & Harwood, H. J. (1980). *Drugs and crimes: A survey and analysis of the literature.* Washington, DC: U.S. Department of Justice.

Gans, D., Harper, A., Bachorowski, J., Newman, J., Shrago, E., & Taylor, S. (1990). Sucrose and delinquency: Oral sucrose tolerance test and nutritional assessment. *Pediatrics, 86,* 254–262.

Ganzer, F. J., & Sarason, I. G. (1973). Variables associated with recidivism among juvenile delinquents. *Journal of Consulting and Clinical Psychology, 40,* 1–5.

Garattini, S., Giacolone, E., & Valzelli, L. (1969). Biochemical changes during isolation-induced aggressiveness in mice. In S. Garattini & E. Sigg (Eds.), *Aggressive behavior* (pp. 179–187). New York: Wiley.

Garbarino, J., & Plantz, M. C. (1986). *Child abuse and juvenile delinquency: What are the links?* New York: Aldine de Gruyter.

Garcia, Jean (1987). Pedophilia: A mirror of our culture. *Corrective and Social Psychiatry and Journal of Behavior Technology Methods and Therapy, 33,* 137–144.

Garcia-Larrea, L., & Cezanne-Bert, G. (1998). P3, positive slow wave and working memory load: A study on the functional correlates of slow wave activity. *Electroencephalography and Clinical Neurophysiology, 108,* 260–273.

Gardner, L., & Shoemaker, D. J. (1989). Social bonding and delinquency: A comparative analysis. *Sociological Quarterly, 30,* 481–500.

Garfinkel, H. (1967). Inter- and intra-racial homicides. In M. E. Wolfgang (Ed.), *Studies in homicide* (pp. 45–56). New York: Harper and Row.

Garreau, B., Barthelemy, C., Jouve, J., Bruneau, N., Muh, J. P., & Lelord, G. (1988). Urinary homovanillic acid levels of autistic children. *Developmental Medicine and Child Neurology, 30,* 93–98.

Garrett, M., & Short, J. F. (1975). Social class and delinquency: Predictions and outcomes of police-juvenile encounters. *Social Problems, 22,* 368–382.

Gartner, R. (1995). Homicide in Canada. In J. I. Ross (Ed.), *Violence in Canada: Sociopolitical perspectives.* Oxford, England: Oxford University Press.

Gartner, R., Baker, K., & Pampel, F. C. (1990). Gender stratification and the gender gap in homicide victimization. *Social Problems, 37,* 593–610.

Gastil, R. D. (1971). Homicide and a regional culture of violence. *American Sociological Review, 36,* 412–427.

Gatrell, V. A. C. (1980). The decline of theft and violence in Victorian and Edwardian England. In V. A. C. Gatrell, B. Lenman, & G. Parker (Eds.), *Crime and the law: The social history of crime in Western Europe since 1500* (pp. 238–364). London, England: Staples Printers.

Gavigan, S. (1982). Women's crime and feminist critiques: A review of the literature. *Canadian Criminology Forum, 5,* 40–53.

Gayford, J. J. (1975). Wife battering: A preliminary survey of 100 cases. *British Medical Journal, 1,* 194–197.

Gazzaniga, M. (1985). *The social brain.* New York: Basic Books.

Ge, X., Cadoret, R. J., Conger, R. D., Neiderhiser, J. M., Yates, W., Troughton, E., & Stewart, M. A. (1996). The developmental interface between nature and nurture: A mutual influence model of child antisocial behavior and parent behaviors. *Developmental Psychology, 32,* 574–589.

Gebhard, P. H., Gagnon, J. H., Pomeroy, W. B., & Christenson, C. (1965). *Sex offenders: An analysis of types.* New York: Harper and Row.

Geis, Gilbert, & Meier, Robert (1986). The white collar offender. In H. Toch (Ed.), *Psychology of crime and criminal justice* (pp. 427–443). Prospect Heights, IL: Waveland.

Geis, Gilbert (1967). White collar crime: The heavy electrical equipment antitrust cases of 1961. In M. Clinard & R. Quinney (Eds.), *Criminal behavior systems: A typology* (pp. 139–151). New York: Holt, Rinehart and Winston.

Gendreau, Paul, & Ross, Robert (1987). Revivification of rehabilitation: Evidence from the 1980's. *Justice Quarterly, 4,* 349–406.

Gensheimer, L. K., Mayer, J. P., Gottschalk, R., & Davidson, W. S., II. (1986). Diverting youth from the juvenile justice system: A meta-analysis of intervention efficacy. In S. J. Apter & A. P. Goldstein (Eds.), *Youth violence: Programs and prospects* (pp. 39–57). New York: Pergamon.

George, C., & Main, M. (1979). Social interactions of young abused children: Approach, avoidance, and aggression. *Child Development, 50,* 306–318.

Gerbing, D. W., Ahadi, S. A., & Patton, J. H. (1987). Toward a conceptualization of impulsivity: Components across the behavioral and self-report domains. *Multivariate Behavioral Research, 22,* 357–379.

Gersao, E., & Lisboa, M. (1994). The self-report delinquency study in Portugal. In J. Gertz, M. G., & Gould, L. C. (1995). Fear of punishment and the willingness to engage in criminal behavior: A research note. *Journal of Criminal Justice, 23,* 377–384.

Geschwind, N. (1975). The clinical setting of aggression in temporal lobe epilepsy. In W. S. Fields & W. H. Sweet (Eds.), *Neural bases of violence and aggression.* St. Louis, MO: Warren H. Green.

Geschwind, N., & Galaburda, A. M. (1985). Cerebral lateralization. Biological mechanisms, associations and pathology: II A hypothesis and a program for research. *Archives of Neurology, 42,* 521–552.

Geschwind, N., & Galaburda, A. (1987). *Cerebral lateralization.* Cambridge, MA: MIT Press.

Giacopassi, D. J. (1992). The effects of emergency medical care. *Journal of Criminal Justice, 20,* 249–259.

Giallombardo, R. (1982). Female delinquency. In R. Giallombardo (Ed.), *Juvenile delinquency: A book of readings* (pp. 37–51). New York: Wiley.

Giambra, L. M., & Quilter, R. E. (1989). Sex differences in sustained attention across the adult life span. *Journal of Applied Psychology, 74,* 91–95.

Giancola, P. R., Moss, H. B., Martin, C. S., Kirisci, L., & Tarter, R. E. (1995). Executive cognitive functioning predicts reactive but not proactive aggression in young boys at high risk for substance abuse: A prospective study. *Alcoholism: Clinical and Experimental Psychology, 30,* 740–744.

Giancola, P. R., Peterson, J. B., & Pihl, R. O. (1993). Risk for alcoholism, antisocial behavior, and response perseveration. *Journal of Clinical Psychology, 49,* 423–428.

Giannangelo, Stephen (1996). *The psychopathology of serial murder: A theory of violence.* Westport, CT: Praeger.

Gibbens, T. C., Pond, D. A., & Stafford-Clark, D. (1955). A follow-up study of criminal psychopaths. *British Journal of Delinquency, 5,* 126–136.

Gibbons, D. C. (1987). *Sociry, crime, and criminal behaviors* (5th ed.). Englewood Cliffs, NJ: Prentice-Hall.

Gibbons, D. C., & Krohn, M. D. (1986). *Delinquent behavior* (4th ed.). Englewood Cliffs, New Jersey: Prentice-Hall.

Gibbons, D. C., & Krohn, M. D. (1991). *Delinquent behavior* (5th ed.). Englewood Cliffs, NJ: Prentice-Hall.

Gibbs, J. C., Arnold, K. C., Ahlborn, H. H., & Chessman, F. L. (1984). Facilitation of sociomoral reasoning in delinquents. *Journal of Consulting and Clinical Psychology, 52,* 37–45.

Gibbs, J. C., & Schnell, S. V. (1985). Moral development "versus" socialization. *American Psychologist, 40,* 1071–1080.

Gibbs, J. C., Potter, G. B., & Goldstein, A. P. (1995). *The EQUIP Program: Teaching young people to think and act responsibly through a peer-helping approach.* Champaign, IL: Research Press.

Gibbs, J. J., Giever, D., & Martin, J. S. (1998). Parental management and self-control: An empirical test of Gottfredson and Hirschi's general theory. *Journal of Research in Crime and Delinquency, 35,* 40–70.

Gibbs, J. P. (1974). The effects of juvenile legal procedures on juvenile offenders' self-attitudes. *Journal of Research in Crime and Delinquency, 11,* 51–55.

Gibbs, J. P. (1987). The state of criminological theory. *Criminology, 25,* 821–840.

Gibson, J. (1978). Race as a determinant of criminal sentencing: A methodological critique and case study. *Law and Society Review, 12,* 437–453.

Gibson, C. L., & Tibbetts, S. G. (1998). Interaction between maternal cigarette smoking and apgar scores in predicting offending behavior. *Psychological Reports, 83,* 579–586.

Gilbert, D., & Kahl, J. A. (1987). *The American class structure* (3rd ed.). Chicago: Dorsey.

Gillberg, C., Carlstrom, G., & Rasmussen, P. (1983). Hyperkinetic disorder in seven-year-old children with perceptual, motor, and attentional disorder deficits. *Child Psychology and Psychiatry, 24,* 377–403.

Gillespie, N. C. (1979). *Charles Darwin and the problem of creation.* Chicago: University of Chicago Press.

Gilligan, C. (1982). *In a different voice: Psychological theory and women's development.* Cambridge: Harvard University Press.

Gillin, J. L. (1946). *The Wisconsin prisoner.* Madison, WI: University of Wisconsin Press.

Gillis, A. R. (1989). Crime and state surveillance in nineteenth-century France. *American Journal of Sociology, 95,* 307–341.

Gillis, R., A., & Hagan, J. (1982). Density, delinquency, and design. *Criminology, 19,* 514–529.

Gilmartin, Pat (1994). *Rape, incest, and child sexual abuse: Consequences and recovery.* New York: Garland.

Gilsinan, J. (1990). *Criminology and public policy: An introduction.* Englewood Cliffs, NJ: Prentice-Hall.

Gin, N. E., Rucker, L., Frayne, S., Cygan, R., & Hubell, F. A. (1991). Prevalence of domestic violence among patients in three ambulatory care internal medicine clinics. *Journal of General and Internal Medicine, 6,* 317–322.

Ginsberg, M. (1965). *On justice in society.* Baltimore, MD: Penguin.

Giordano, P., Kerbel, S., & Dudley, S. (1981). The economics of female criminality: An analysis of police blotters 1890–1975. In L. H. Bowker (Ed.), *Women and crime in America.* New York: Macmillan.

Giovannoni, J. M., & Gurel, L. (1967). Socially disruptive behavior of ex-mental patients. *Archives of General Psychiatry, 17,* 146–53.

Gittelman, R., Mannuzza, S., Shenker, R., & Bonagura, N. (1985). Hyperactive boys almost grownup: 1. Psychiatric status. *Archives of General Psychiatry, 42,* 937–947.

Giulian, A., Pohorecky, A. & McEwen, B. S. (1973). Effects of gonadal steroids upon brain 5-Hydroxytryptamine levels in the neonatal rat. *Endocrinology 3,* 1329–1335.

Glaser, D. (1971). *Social deviance.* Chicago: Markham.

Glaser, D. (1978a). *Crime in our changing society.* New York: Holt, Rinehart and Winston.

Glaser, D. (1978b). Evaluation of sex offender treatment programs. In E. M. Brecher (Ed.), *Treatment programs for sex offenders* (pp. 85–92, Appendix B). Washington, DC: U.S. Government Printing Office.

Glaser, D. (1990). Book review. *Contemporary Sociology, 19,* 427–428.

Glaser, D. & Frosh, S. (1993). *Child sex abuse.* Toronto: University of Toronto Press.

Glass, J., DeVel, H. J., & Wright, C. A. (1940). Sex hormone studies in male homosexuality. *Endocrinology, 26,* 590–594.

Glendon, M., Gordon, M., and Osakwe, C. (1985). *Comparative legal traditions.* St. Paul, MN: West.

Glover, N. M., Janikowski, T. P., & Benshoff, J. J. (1996). Substance abuse and past incest contact: A national perspective. *Substance Abuse Treatment, 13,* 185–193.

Glueck, S., & Glueck, E. (1950). *Unraveling juvenile delinquency.* Cambridge, MA: Harvard University Press.

Glueck, S., & Glueck, T. (1956). *Physique and delinquency.* New York: Harper.

Goddard, G., McIntyre, D., & Leech, C. (1969). A permanent change in brain function resulting from daily electrical stimulation. *Experimental Neurology, 25,* 295–330.

Goddard, H. H. (1921). *Juvenile delinquency.* New York: Dodd, Mead.

Goff, C. H., & Kim, R. J. (1987). Seriousness of crimes: A comparison of Canadian and American chiefs of police and detachment commanders. *Canadian Police College Journal, 11,* 1–12.

Gold, M. (1970). *Delinquent behavior in an American city.* Belmont, CA: Brooks-Cole.

Gold, M., & Williams, J. R. (1969). National study of the aftermath of apprehension. *Prospectus, 3,* 3–12.

Goldberg, E. (1981). Depression and suicide ideation in the young adult. *American Journal of Psychiatry, 138,* 35–40.

Goldberg, N. (1950). Jews in the police records of Los Angeles, 1933–1947. *Yivo Annual of Jewish Social Science, 5,* 266–291.

Goldberg, S. (1993). *Why men rule: A theory of male dominance.* Chicago: Open Court.

Goldberg, W. G., & Tomlanovich, M. C. (1984). Domestic violence victims in the emergency department: New findings. *Journal of the American Medical Association, 251,* 3259–3264.

Goldsby, R. A. (1971). *Race and races.* New York: Macmillan.

Goldschmidt, W. (1976). *Culture and behavior of the Sebei.* Berkeley: University of California Press.

Goldsmith, H. H., & Gottesman, I. I. (1995). *Heritable variability and variable heritability in developmental psychopathology.* New York, NY: Oxford University.

Gonczol, Katalin. (1993). Anxiety over crime. *Hungarian Quarterly, 129,* 87–99.

Gondolf, E. W., & Foster, R. A. (1991). Wife assault among VA alcohol rehabilitation patients. *Hospital and Community Psychiatry, 42,* 74–79.

Gondolf, E. W., & Shestakov, D. (1997). Spousal homicide in Russia versus the United States: Preliminary findings and implications. *Journal of Family Violence, 12,* 63–74.

Gonzales, N. A., Cauce, A. M., Friedman, R. J., & Mason, C. A. (1996). Family, peer, and neighborhood influences on academic achievement among African-American adolescents: One-year prospective effects. *American Journal of Community Psychology, 24,* 365–387.

Goodchilds, J., & Zellman, G. (1984). Sexual signaling and sexual aggression in adolescent relationships. In N. Malamuth & E. Donnerstein (Eds.), *Pornography and sexual aggression* (pp. 233–243). New York: Academic Press.

Goode, E. (1990). Phenomenology and structure in the study of crime and deviance. *Contemporary Sociology, 19,* 5–12.

Goode, S. (1984). *Violence in America.* New York: Julian Messner.

Goodey, J. (1996). Adolescence and the socialization of gendered fear. In M. D. Schwartz & D. Milovanovic (Eds.), *Race, gender, and class in criminology* (pp. 267–289). New York: Garland.

Goodwin, D. W., & Guze, S. B. (1984). *Psychiatric diagnosis* (3rd ed.). New York. Oxford University Press.

Gordon, D. A., & Arbuthnot, J. (1987). *Individual group, and family interventions.* New York: John Wiley & Sons.

Gordon, D. M. (1971). Class and the economics of crime. *Review of Radical Political Economics, 3,* 51–75.

Gordon, M. T., Riger, S., LeBailly, R. K., & Heath, L. (1980). Crime, women, and the quality of urban life. *Signs: Journal of Women in Culture and Society, 5,* 144–160.

Gordon, R. A. (1976). Prevalence: The rare data in delinquency measurement and its implications for the theory of delinquency. In Klein (Ed.), *The juvenile justice system* (pp. 201–284). Beverly Hills, CA: Sage.

Gordon, R. A., Short, J. F., Cartwright, D. S., & Strodtbeck, F. L. (1963). Values and gang delinquency: A study of street-corner groups. *American Journal of Sociology, 69,* 109–128.

Gorenstein, E. E. (1982). Frontal lobe functions in psychopaths. *Journal of Abnormal Psychology, 91,* 368–379.

Goring, C. (1913). *The English convict: A statistical study.* London: His Majesty's Stationary Office (republished in 1972 by Patterson Smith, Montclair, NJ).

Gorsuch, R. L. (1995). Religious aspects of substance abuse and recovery. *Journal of Social Issues, 51,* 65–83.

Gorsuch, R. L., & Butler, M. C. (1976). Initial drug abuse: A review of predisposing social psychological factors. *Psychological Bulletin, 83,* 120–137.

Gottfredson, M. R. (1981). On the etiology of criminal victimization. *Journal of Criminal Law & Criminology, 72,* 714–726.

Gottfredson, M. R. (1986). Substantive contributions of victimization surveys. In M. Tonry & N. Morris (Eds.), *Crime and justice: An annual review of research* (Vol. 7, pp. 251–287). Chicago, IL: University of Chicago Press.

Gottfredson, M. R., & Gottfredson, D. M. (1980). *Decision making in criminal justice.* Cambridge, MA: Ballinger.

Gottfredson, M. R., & Hirschi, T. (1990). *A general theory of crime.* Stanford, CA: Stanford University Press.

Gottlieb, B. (1979). The way they ate was a crime. *Prevention, 31,* 64–68.

Gould, L. C. (1969). Juvenile entrepreneurs. *American Journal of Sociology, 74,* 710–19.

Gould, L. C. (1981). Discrepancies between self-reported and official measures of delinquency. *American Sociological Review, 46,* 367–368.

Gouldner, A. (1970). *The coming crisis in Western sociology.* New York: Basic Books.

Gove, W. R. (1975). *The labeling of deviance: Evaluating a perspective.* Beverly Hills, CA: Sage.

Gove, W. R. (1979). Sex differences in the epidemiology of mental disorder: Evidence and explanations. In E. S. Gomberg & V. Franks (Eds.), *Gender and disorder behavior* (pp. 23–68). New York: Brunner/Mazel.

Gove, W. R. (1985). The effect of age and gender on deviant behavior: A biopsychological perspective. In A. S. Rossi (Ed.), *Gender and the life course* (pp. 115–144). Hawthorne, NY: Aldine.

Gove, W. R., Hughes, M., & Geerken, M. (1985). Are uniform crime reports a valid indicator of the index crimes? An affirmative answer with minor qualifications. *Criminology, 23,* 451–491.

Gove, W. R., & Wilmoth, C. (1990). Risk, crime, and neurophysiologic highs: A consideration of brain processes that may reinforce delinquent and criminal behavior. In L. Ellis & H. Hoffman (Eds.), *Crime in biological, social, and moral contexts* (Vol. 17, pp. 261–293). New York: Praeger.

Graber, J., Brooks-Gunn, J., & Warren, M. (1995). The antecedents of monarchal age. *Child Development, 66,* 346–359.

Graham, J. R. (1990). *MMPI-2: Assessing personality and psychopathology.* New York: Oxford University Press.

Gramza, A. F. (1967). Responses of brooding nighthawks to a disturbance stimulus. *Auk, 84,* 72–86.

Grant, D. A., & Berg, E. A. (1948). A behavioral analysis of degree of reinforcement and ease of shifting to a new response in a Weigle-type card-sorting problem. *Journal of Experimental Psychology, 38,* 404–411.

Grasmick, H. G., Tittle, C. R., Bursik, R. J., & Arneklev, B. J. (1993). Testing the core empirical implications of Gottfredson and Hirschi's general theory of crime. *Journal of Research in Crime and Delinquency, 30,* 5–29.

Grasmick, H. G., Bursik, R. J., Jr., & Arneklev, B. J. (1993). Reduction in drunk driving as a response to increased threats of shame, embarrassment, and legal sanctions. *Criminology, 31,* 41–67.

Grauerholz, Elizabeth, & Koralewski, Mary (1991). What is known and not known about sexual coercion. In E. Grauerholz & M. Koralewski (Eds.), *Sexual coercion: A sourcebook on its nature, causes, and prevention* (pp. 187–198). Lexington, MA: Lexington Books.

Graves, T. D. (1967). Acculturation, access, and alcohol in a tri-ethnic community. *American Anthropologist, 69,* 306–321.

Gray, D., & Ashmore, R. (1976). Biasing influence of defendants' characteristics on simulated sentencing. *Psychological Reports, 38,* 727–738.

Gray, J. A. (1975). *Elements of a two-process theory of learning.* New York: Academic Press.

Gray, J. A. (1976). The neuropsychology of anxiety. In G. Sarason & C. D. Spielberger (Eds.), *Stress and anxiety* (Vol. 3, pp. 3–26). Washington, DC: Hemisphere.

Gray, J. A. (1981). A critique of Eysenck's theory of personality. In H. J. Eysenck (Ed.), *A model of personality* (pp. 246–276). New York: Springer.

Gray, J. A. (1987). Perspectives on anxiety and impulsivity: A commentary. *Journal of Research in Personality, 21,* 493–509.

Gray, J. A., Davis, N., & Tsaltas, E. (1983). Psychological and physiological relations between anxiety and impulsivity. In M. Zuckerman (Ed.), *Biological bases of sensation seeking, impulsivity, and anxiety* (pp. 181–217). Hillsdale, NY: Lawrence Erlbaum.

Green, E. (1964). Inter- and intra-racial crime relative to sentencing. *Journal of Criminal Law, Criminology and Police Science, 55,* 348–358.

Green, J. B., & Hartlage, L. C. (1971). Comparative performance of epileptic and non-epileptic children and adolescents on tests of academic, communicative and social skills. *Diseases of the Nervous System, 32,* 418–421.

Green, L., & Warshauer, D. (1981). A note on the "paradoxical" effect of stimulants on hyperactivity with reference to rate-dependency effect of drugs. *Journal of Nervous and Mental Disease, 169,* 196–198.

Greenberg, A., & Coleman, M. (1973). Use of blood serotonin levels for the classification and treatment of hyperkinetic behavior disorders. *Neurology, 23,* 428.

Greenberg, D. F. (1976). On one-dimension criminology. *Theory and Society, 3,* 610–621.

Greenberg, D. F. (1977). Delinquency and the age structure of society. *Contemporary Crisis, 1,* 189–223.

Greenberg, D. F. (1985). Age, crime, and social explanation. *American Journal of Sociology 90,* 1–21.

Greenberg, D. F., Kessler, R. C., & Loftin, C. (1983). The effect of police employment on crime. *Criminology, 21,* 375–394.

Greenberg, N. (1988). Moderating the material aspirations of criminals and delinquents. *Journal of Offender Counseling, Services & Rehabilitation, 13,* 193–209.

Greer, J., & Stuart, I. (1983). The sexual aggressor: Current perspectives and treatment. New York: Van Nostrand Reinhold.

Gregg, V., Gibbs, J. C., & Basinger, K. S. (1994). Patterns of developmental delay in moral judgment by male and female delinquents. *Merrill-Palmer Quarterly, 40,* 538–553.

Gregory, J. (1986). Sex, class and crime: Toward a non-sexist criminology. In R. Matthews & J. Young (Eds.), *Confronting crime.* Beverly Hills, CA: Sage.

Grene, M. (1982). Introduction. In M. Grene (Ed.), *Dimensions of Darwinism* (pp. 1–16). Cambridge, England: Cambridge University Press.

Gress-Wright, J. (1993). The contraception paradox. *Public Interest, 113,* 15–25.

Gresswell, David, & Clive Hollin (1994). Multiple murder: A review. *British Journal of Criminology, 34,* 1–14.

Greulich, W. W. (1957). A comparison of the physical growth and development of American-born and native Japanese children. *American Journal of Physical Anthropology, 15,* 489–515.

Grichting, W. L. (1979). The subjective probability of being labeled criminal in juvenile corrections. *Australian and New Zealand Journal of Criminology, 12,* 162–174.

Griffith, N., Engel, J., & Bandler, R. (1987). Ictal and enduring interictal disturbances in emotional behaviour in an animal model of temporal lobe epilepsy. *Brain Research, 400,* 360–364.

Griffiths, C., & Verdun-Jones, S. (1989). *Canadian criminal justice.* Toronto: Butterworths.

Grizenko, N., & Pawliuk, N. (1994). Risk and protective factors for disruptive behavior disorders in children. *American Journal of Orthopsychiatry, 64,* 534–544.

Groshong, R., Baldessarini, R. J., Gibson, A., Lipinski, J. G., Axelrod, D., & Pope, A. (1978). Activities of types A and B MAO and catechol-o-methyltransferase in blood cells and skin fibroblasts of normal and chronic schizophrenic subjects. *Archives of General Psychiatry 35,* 1198–1205.

Groth, A. (1979). *Men who rape.* New York: Plenum.

Grove, W. M., Eckert, E. D., Heston, L., Bouchard, T. J., Segal, N., & Lykken, D. T. (1990). Heritability of substance abuse and antisocial behavior: A study of monozygotic twins reared apart. *Biological Psychiatry, 27,* 1293–1304.

Groves, W. B., & Sampson, R. J. (1987). Traditional contributions to radical criminology. *Journal of Research in Crime Delinquency, 24,* 181–214.

Grunhut, M. (1951). Statistics in criminology. *Journal of the Royal Statistical Society, 114,* 10–163.

Gruter, M. (1979). The origins of legal behavior. *Journal of Social and Biological Structure, 2,* 43–51.

Grygier, T. (1966). The concept of "the State of Delinquency": An obituary. *Journal of Legal Education, 18,* 131–141.

Guilford, J. P. (1967). *The nature of intelligence.* New York: McGraw-Hill.

Guillot, E. E. (1943). *Social factors in crime as explained by American writers of the Civil War and post Civil War period.* Philadelphia: Saunders.

Gunnar, M., Fissch, R., Korscik, S., & Donhowe, J. (1981). The effect of circumcision on serum cortisol and behavior. *Psychoneuroendocrinology, 6,* 269–276.

Gunner, M., Malone, S., Vance, G., & Fisch, R. O. (1985). Coping with aversive stimulation in the neonatal period: Quiet sleep and levels of plasma cortisol during recovery from circumcision in newborns. *Child Development, 56,* 824–834.

Gurr, T. R. (1976). *Rogues, rebels, and reformers.* Beverly Hills, CA: Sage.

Gurr, T. R. (1981). Historical trends in violent crime: A critical review of the evidence. In N. Morris & M. Tonry (Eds.), *Crime and justice: An annual review of research* (pp. 295–353). Chicago: University of Chicago Press.

Gutterman, S. (1979). I. Q. tests in research on social stratification: The cross-class validity of the tests. *Sociology of Education, 52,* 163–173.

Guze, S. B. (1976). *Criminality and psychiatric disorders.* New York: Oxford University Press.

Guze, S. B., Cloninger, C. R., Martin, R. L., & Clayton, P. J. (1986). A follow-up and family study of Briquet's syndrome. *British Journal of Psychiatry, 149,* 17–23.

Haapanen, R. A., & Jesness, C. F. (1982). *Early identification of the chronic offender: Final report.* Sacramento, CA: Department of Youth Authority.

Habermas, J. (1973). *Theory and practice.* Boston: Beacon.

Hack, M., Weissman, B., Breslau, N., Klein, N., Borawskiclark, E., & Fanaroff, A. A. (1993). Health of very low birth weight children during their first eight years. *Journal of Pediatrics, 122,* 887–892.

Hacker, Frederick (1977). *Crusaders, criminals, crazies: Terror and terrorism in our time.* New York: Norton.

Hadders-Algra, M., & Touwen, B. C. L. (1990). Body measurements, neurological and behavioural development in six-year-old children born preterm and/or small-for-gestational-age. *Early Human Development, 22,* 1–13.

Hagan, Frank (1994). *Introduction to criminology.* Chicago: Nelson-Hall.

Hagan, J. (1975). The social and legal construction of criminal justice: A study of the pre-sentencing process. *Social Problems, 22,* 620–637.

Hagan, J., Gillis, A. R., & Simpson, J. (1985). The class structure of gender and delinquency: Toward a power-control theory of common delinquent behavior. *American Journal of Sociology, 90,* 1151–1178.

Hagan, J., Hefler, G., Classen, G., Boehnke, K., & Merkens, H. (1998). Subterranean sources of subcultural delinquency beyond the American dream. *Criminology, 36,* 309–341.

Hagan, J. and Leon, J. (1978). Philosophy and sociology of crime control: Canadian-American comparisons. *Sociological Inquiry, 47,* 181–208.

Hagan, J., & Palloni, A. (1986). Toward a structural criminology: Method and theory in criminological research. *Annual Review of Sociology, 12,* 431–449.

Hagan, J., & Palloni, A. (1988). Crimes as social events in the life course: Preconceiving a criminological controversy. *Criminology, 26,* 87–100.

Hagan, J., Simpson, J., & Gillis, A. R. (1987). Class in the household: A power-control theory of gender and delinquency. *American Journal of Sociology, 92,* 788–816.

Hagberg, B. (1987). Behaviour correlates to frontal lobe dysfunction. *Archives of Gerontology and Geriatrics, 6,* 311–321.

Hagerman, R. J., Jackson, C., Amiri, K., Silverman, A. C., O'Connor, R., & Sobesky, W. (1992). Girls with fragile X syndrome: Physical and neurocognitive status and outcome. *Pediatrics, 89,* 395–400.

Hagerman, R. J., Wilson, P., Staley, L. W., Lang, K. A., Fan, T., Uhlhorn, C., S., J.-S., Hull, C., Drisko, J., Flom, K., & Taylor, A. K. (1994). Evaluation of school children at high risk for fragile X syndrome utilizing bauccal cell EMR-1 testing. *American Journal of Medical Genetics, 51,* 474–481.

Haier, R. J., Buchsbaum, M. S., L., M. D., Gottesman, I. I., & Corsey, R. D. (1980). Psychiatric vulnerability, monoamine oxidase, and the average evoked potential. *Archives of General Psychiatry, 37,* 340–347.

Hall, E. (1987). Adolescents' perceptions of sexual assault. *Journal of Sex Education and Therapy, 13,* 37–42.

Hall, G., Maiuro, R., Vitaliano, P., & Proctor, W. (1986). The utility of the MMPI with men who have sexually assaulted children. *Journal of Consulting and Clinical Psychology, 54,* 493–496.

Hall, G., & Proctor, W. (1987). Criminological predictors of recidivism in a sexual offender population. *Journal of Consulting and Clinical Psychology, 55,* 111–112.

Hall, J. (1952). *Theft, law and society.* Indianapolis: Bobbs-Merrill.

Hall, K. R., & DeVore, I. (1965). Baboon social behavior. In I. DeVore (Ed.), *Primate behavior* (pp. 53–110). New York: Holt, Rinehart and Winston.

Hall, W., Hunter, E., & Spargo, R. (1994). Alcohol use and incarceration in a police lockup among Aboriginals in the Kimberely region of Western Australia. *Australian and New Zealand Journal of Criminology, 27,* 57–73.

Hallman, J. (1986). The perimenstrual syndrome—an equivalent of depression? *Acta Psychiatrica Scandinavica, 73,* 403–411.

Hallman, J., von Knorring, L., & Oreland, L. (1990). Clinical characteristics of female alcoholics with low platelet monoamine oxidase activity. *Alcoholism: Clinical and Experimental Research, 14,* 227–231.

Halstead, W. C. (1947). *Brain and intelligence: A quantitative study of the frontal lobes.* Chicago: University of Chicago Press.

Halverson, C. F., & Victor, J. B. (1976). Minor physical anomalies and problem behaviour in elementary school children. *Child Development, 47,* 281–285.

Hamilton, V. L., & Sanders, J. (1983). Universals in judging wrongdoing: Japanese and Americans compared. *American Sociological Review, 48,* 199–211.

Hamilton, V. L., & Rotkin, L. (1976). Interpreting the Eighth Amendment: Perceived seriousness of crime and severity of punishment. In H. A. Bedau & C. Pierce (Eds.), *Capital punishment in the United States* (pp. 502–504). New York: AMS Press.

Hamilton, W. D. (1963). The evolution of altruistic behavior. *American Naturalist, 97,* 354–356.

Hanson, R. A., & Mullis, R. L. (1985). Age and gender differences in empathy and moral reasoning among adolescents. *Child Study Journal, 15,* 181–187.

Haraway, D. (1989). *Primate visions: Gender, race, and nature in the world of modern science.* New York: Routledge.

Hare, R. D. (1970). *Psychopathy: Theory and research.* New York: Wiley.

Hare, R. D. (1980). A research scale for the assessment of psychopathy in criminal populations. *Personality and Individual Differences, 1,* 111–119.

Hare, R. D. (1985). Comparison of the procedures for the assessment of psychopathy. *Journal of Consulting and Clinical Psychology, 53,* 7–16.

Hare, R. D. (1986). Criminal psychopaths. In J. C. Yuille (Ed.), *Police selection and training: The role of psychology.* (pp. 187–206). Toronto, Ontario: Davis.

Hare, R. D. (1991). *The revised psychopathy checklist.* Toronto, Ontario: Multi-health Systems.

Hare, R. D., Harpur, T. J., Hakstian, A. R., Forth, A. E., Hart, S. D., & Newman, J. P. (1990). The revised psychopathy checklist: Reliability and factor structure. *Psychological Assessment: A Journal of Consulting and Clinical Psychology, 2,* 338–341.

Hare, R. D., & McPherson, L. M. (1984a). Psychopathy and perceptual asymmetry during verbal dichotic listening. *Journal of Abnormal Psychology, 93,* 141–149.

Hare, R. D., & McPherson, L. M. (1984b). Violent and aggressive behaviour by criminal psychopaths. *International Journal of Law and Psychiatry, 7,* 35–50.

Hare, R. D., McPherson, L. D., & Forth, A. (1988). Male psychopaths and their criminal careers. *Journal of Consulting and Clinical Psychology, 56,* 710–714.

Harer, M. D., & Steffensmeier, D. (1992). The differing effects of economic inequality on black and white rates of violence. *Social Forces, 70,* 1035–1054.

Harman, D. W., & Ray, W. J. (1977). Hemispheric activity during effective verbal stimuli: An EEG study. *Neuropsychologia, 15,* 457–460.

Harmon-Jones, E., Barratt, E. S., & Wigg, C. (1997). Impulsiveness, aggression, reading, and the P300 of the event-related potential. *Personality and Individual Differences, 22,* 439–445.

Harney, Patricia, & Muehlenhard, Charlene (1991). Rape. In E. Grauerholz & M. Koralewski (Eds.), *Sexual coercion: A sourcebook on its nature, causes, and prevention* (pp. 1–15). Lexington, MA: Lexington Books.

Harpending, H., & Draper, P. (1988). Antisocial behavior and the other side of cultural evolution. In T. E. Moffitt & S. A. Mednick (Eds.), *Biological contributions to crime causation* (pp. 293–307). Dordrecht: Martinus Nyhoff.

Harpending, H., & Sobus, J. (1987). Sociopathy as an adaptation. *Ethology and Sociobiology, 8,* 63S–72S.

Harper-Jaques, S., & Reimer, M. (1992). Aggressive behavior and the brain: A different perspective for the mental health nurse. *Archives of Psychiatric Nursing, 6,* 312–320.

Harrington, M. (1969). *The other America.* New York: Macmillan.

Harris, A. R. (1976). Race, commitment to deviance and spoiled identity. *American Sociological Review, 41,* 432–442.

Harris, C. D., & Ullman, E. L. (1945). The nature of cities. *Annals of the American Academy of Political and Social Science, 245,* 1–32.

Harris, G. T., Rice, M. E., & Cormier, C. A. (1991). Psychopathy and violent recidivism. *Law and Human Behavior, 15,* 625–637.

Harris, G. T., Rice, M. E., & Quinsey, V. L. (1994). Psychopathy as a taxon: Evidence that psychopaths are a discrete class. *Journal of Consulting and Clinical Psychology, 62,* 387–397.

Harris, G. T., Rice, M. E., & Quinsey, V. L. (1993). Violent recidivism of mentally disordered offenders: The development of a statistical prediction instrument. *Criminal Justice and Behavior, 20,* 315–335.

Harris, J. R. (1998). *The nurture assumption: Why children turn out the way they do.* New York: Free Press.

Harris, L. J. (1990). Cultural influences on handedness: Historical and contemporary theory and evidence. In S. Coren (Ed.), *Left-handedness: Behavioral implications and anomalies* (pp. 195–258). Amsterdam: North-Holland.

Harris, Marvin (1987). *Cultural anthropology.* New York: Harper & Row.

Harris, Marvin (1988). *Culture, people, nature.* New York: Harper & Row.

Harry, B., & Balcer, C. M. (1987). Menstruation and crime: A critical review of the literature from the clinical criminology perspective. *Behavioral Sciences & the Law, 5,* 307–321.

Hart, S. D., Kropp, P. R., & Hare, R. D. (1988). Performance of male psychopaths following conditional release from prison. *Journal of Consulting and Clinical Psychology, 56,* 227–232.

Hartmann, D. J., Wolk, J. L., Johnston, J. S., & Colyer, C. J. (1997). Recidivism and substance abuse outcomes in a prison-based therapeutic community. *Federal Probation, 61,* 18–25.

Hartmann, H. (1976). Capitalism, patriarchy and job segregation by sex. In M. Blaxall & B. Reagan (Eds.), *Women and workplace: The implications of occupational segreation* (pp. 137–169). Chicago: University of Chicago Press.

Hartnagel, T. F. (1987). Correlates of criminal behaviour. In R. Linden (Ed.), *Criminology: A Canadian perspective* (pp. 74–101). Toronto: Holt, Rinehart, Winston.

Hartshorne, H., & May, M. A. (1928). *Studies in the nature of character.* New York: Macmillan.

Hartshorne, H., May, M. A., & Maller, J. B. (1929). *Studies in the nature of character,* Vol. II: *Studies in self-control.* New York: Macmillan.

Hartshorne, H., May, M. A., & Shuttleworth, F. K. (1930). *Studies in the nature of character,* Vol. III: *Studies in the organization of character.* New York: Macmillan.

Hassett, J. (1978). *A primer of psychophysiology.* San Francisco: W. H. Freeman.

Hauge, R., & Wolf, P. (1974). Criminal violence in three Scandinavian countries. *Scandinavian Studies in Criminology, 5,* 25–33.

Haurin, J. R. (1992). Patterns of childhood residence and the relationship to young adult outcomes. *Journal of Marriage and the Family, 54,* 846–860.

Hauser, W. A., & Kurland, L. T. (1975). The epidemiology of epilepsy in Rochester, Minnesota 1935 through 1967. *Epilepsia, 16,* 1–66.

Haviland, W. A. (1990). *Anthropology* (6th ed.). Fort Worth, TX: Holt, Rinehart & Winston.

Haviland, W. A. (2000). *Anthropology, 9th ed.* Fort Worth, TX: Harcourt.

Hawkins, D. F. (1981). Causal attribution and punishment for crime. *Deviant Behavior, 2,* 207–230.

Hawkins, D. F. (1986). Black and white homicide differentials: Alternatives to an inadequate theory. In D. F. Hawkins (Ed.), *Homicide among Black Americans* (pp. 109–135). Lanham, MD: University Press of America.

Hawkins, D. F. (1987). Beyond anomalies: Rethinking the conflict perspective on race and criminal punishment. *Social Forces, 65,* 719–745.

Hawkins, D. J., Jenson, J. M., & Catalano, R. F. (1988). Delinquency and drug abuse: Implications for social services. *Social Service Review, 60,* 259–275.

Hawkins, D. J., Von Cleve, E., & Catalano, R. F. (1991a). Reducing early childhood aggression: Results of a primary prevention program. *Journal of the American Academy for Child and Adolescent Psychiatry, 30,* 208–217.

Hawkins, J. D., Arthur, W. M., & Catalano, R. F. (1995). Preventing substance abuse. In M. Tonry & D. Farrington (Eds.), *Crime and justice: A review of research* (Vol. 19, pp. 343–427). Chicago: University of Chicago Press.

Hawkins, J. D., Catalano, R. F., Jr., Gillmore, M. R., & Wells, E. A. (1989). Skill training for drug abusers: Generalization, maintenance, and effects on drug use. *Journal of Consulting and Clinical Psychology, 57,* 559–563.

Hawkins, J. D., Catalano, R. F., & Kent, L. A. (1991b). Combining broadcast media and parent education to prevent teenage drug abuse. In L. Donohew, H. E. Sypher, & W. J. Bukoski (Eds.), *Persuasive communication and drug abuse prevention* (pp. 283–294). Hillsdale, NJ: Erlbaum.

Hawkins, J. D., Catalano, R. F., & Miller, J. Y. (1992). Risk and protective factors for alcohol and other drug problems in adolescence and early adulthood: Implications for substance abuse prevention. *Psychological Bulletin, 112,* 64–105.

Hawkins, J. D., Catalano, R. F., Morrison, D. M., O'Donnell, J., Abbott, R. D., & Day, L. E. (1992). The Seattle social development project: Effects of the first four years on protective factors and problem behaviors. In J. McCord & R. E. Tremblay (Eds.), *Preventing antisocial behavior* (pp. 139–232). New York: Guilford.

Hawkins, J. D., Lishner, D., Catalano, R., & Howard, M. (1986). Childhood predictors of adolescent substance use: Toward an empirically grounded theory. *Journal of Children in Contemporary Society, 8,* 11–48.

Hawkins, J. D., & Wall, J. S. (1980). *Alternative education: Exploring the delinquency prevention potential.* Washington, DC: U.S. Government Printing Office.

Hawkins, J. D., & Weis, J. G. (1985). The social development model: An integrated approach to delinquency prevention. *Journal of Primary Prevention, 6,* 73–97.

Hay, D. A. (1990). Roubertoux and Capron are wrong—behaviour genetics is very relevant to cognitive science. *Cahiers de Psychologie Cognitive, 10,* 637–646.

Hayes, B. L. (1972). *Self-conception and delinquency: A test of labeling theory.* Kansas City: University of Kansas Press.

Hayes, S. C., & Walker, W.-L. (1986). Intellectual and moral development in offenders: A review. *Australian and New Zealand Journal of Criminology, 19,* 53–64.

Haynes, J. P., & Bensch, M. (1981). The P>V sign on the WISC-R and recidivism in delinquents. *Journal of Consulting and Clinical Psychology, 49,* 480–481.

Healy, W., & Bronner, A. (1939). *Treatment and what happened afterward.* Boston: Judge Baker Guidance Center.

Heaven, P. C. L. (1991). The Protestant work ethic and economic beliefs. *Australian Psychologist, 26,* 59–63.

Heaven, P. C. L. (1996). Personality and self-reported delinquency: A longitudinal analysis. *Child Psychology and Psychiatry, 37,* 747–751.

Hebb, D. O. (1978). Watching self get old. *Psychology Today, 12,* November, 15–17.

Hebb, D. O., & Penfield, W. (1940). Human behaviour after extensive bilateral removal from the frontal lobes. *Archives of Neurological Psychiatry, 44,* 421–438.

Hecaen, H., & Sauguet, J. (1971). Cerebral dominance in left-handed subjects. *Cortex, 7,* 19–48.

Hechter, M. (1994). The role of values in rational choice theory. *Rational Sociology, 6,* 318–333.

Hechter, M., & Kanazawa, S. (1993). Group solidarity and social order in Japan. *Journal of Theoretical Politics, 5,* 455–493.

Hechter, M., & Kanazawa, S. (1997). Sociological rational choice theory. *Annual Review of Sociology, 23,* 191–214.

Heilman, K. M., & Van Den Abell, T. (1980). Right hemisphere dominance for attention: The mechanism underlying hemispheric asymmetries of inattention (neglect). *Neurology, 30,* 327–330.

Heimburger, R. F., Whitlock, C. C., & Kalsbeck, J. E. (1966). Stereotaxic amnygdalotomy for epilepsy with aggressive behavior. *Journal of the American Medical Association, 198,* 741–745.

Heimer, K. (1997). Socioeconomic status, subcultural definitions, and violent delinquency. *Social Forces, 75,* 799–833.

Heimer, K., & Matsueda, R. L. (1994). Role-taking, role commitment, and delinquency: A theory of differential social control. *American Sociological Review, 59,* 365–390.

Heitz, D., Rousseau, F., Devys, D., Saccone, S., Abderrahim, H., Le Paslier, D., Cohen, D., Vincent, A., Toniolo, D., Valle, D. G., Johnson, S., Schlessinger, D., Oberle, I., & Mandel, J. L. (1991). Isolation of sequences that span the fragile X and identification of a fragile X related CPG island. *Science, 251,* 1236–1242.

Hellhammer, D. H., Hubert, W., & Schurmeyer, T. (1985). Changes in saliva testosterone after psychological stimulation in men. *Psychoneuroendocrinology, 10,* 77–81.

Helzer, J. E., Burnam, A., & McEvoy, L. T. (1991). Alcohol abuse and dependence. In L. N. Robins & D. A. Regier (Eds.), *Psychiatric disorders in America* (pp. 81–115). New York: Free Press.

Hendrix, J. E. (1972). A study in neglect: A report on women prisoners: Ford Foundation Travel-Study Grants.

Hendricks, J. E., & Byers, B. (Eds.). (1994). *Multicultural perspectives in criminal justice and criminology.* Springfield, IL: Charles C. Thomas

Hendrixson, L. L. (1989). Care versus justice: Two moral perspectives in the baby "M" surrogacy case. *Journal of Sex Education & Therapy, 15,* 247–256.

Henningham, J. P. (1996). A 12-item scale of social conservatism. *Personality and Individual Differences, 20,* 517–519.

Henry, A. F., & Short, J. F. (1954). *Suicide and homicide.* Glencoe, IL: Free Press.

Henry, P., & Stansky, T. F. (1982). *God on our minds.* Philadelphia: Fortress.

Henry, S., & Milovanovic, D. (1991). Constitutive criminology: The maturation of critical theory. *Criminology, 29,* 293–316.

Hepburn, J. R. (1977). Testing alternative models of delinquency causation. *Journal of Criminal Law and Criminology, 67,* 450–460.

Herman, Judith (1990). Sex offenders: A feminist perspective. In W. Marshall, D. Laws, and H. Barbaree (Eds.), *Handbook of sexual assault: Issues, theories, and treatment of the offender* (pp. 177–193). New York: Plenum.

Herman, R. (1984). The genetic relationship between identical twins. *Early Child Development and Care, 16,* 265–276.

Hernandez, L., Gonzalez, L., Murzi, E., Paez, X., Gottberg, E., & Baptista, T. (1994). Testosterone modulates mesolimbic dopaminergic activity in male rats. *Neuroscience Letters, 171,* 172–174.

Herrenkohl, R. C., & Herrenkohl, E. C. (1981). Some antecedents and developmental consequences of child maltreatment. In R. Rizley & D. Cicchetti (Eds.), *New directions for child development: Developmental perspectives on child maltreatment* (pp. 57–76). San Francisco: Jossey-Bass.

Herreros, O., Gonzalez, M. P., Perez, C. E., & Bobes, J. (1997). Tobacco, alcohol and illicit drug use by health sciences students at Oviedo University. *Adiciones, 9,* 363–373.

Herrnstein, R. J., & Murray, C. (1994). *The bell curve: Intelligence and class structure in American life.* New York: Free Press.

Herron, J. (1980). *Neuropsychology of left-handedness.* New York: Academic Press.

Hersch, L. (1936). Delinquency among Jews. *Journal of Criminal Law and Criminology, 27,* 515–516.

Hersch, L. (1937). Complementary data on Jewish delinquency in Poland. *Journal of Criminal Law and Criminology, 27,* 857–873.

Herz, F. O. (1908). *Verbrechen und verbrechertum in Oesterreich.* Tubingen: Mohr.

Herzog, E., & Sudia, C. E. (1973). Children in fatherless families. In B. M. Caldwell & Ricciuti (Eds.), *Review of child development research* (Vol. 3, pp. 141–232). Chicago: University of Chicago Press.

Heston, L. L. (1970). The genetics of schizophrenic and schizoid disease. *Science, 167,* 249–256.

Hickey, Eric (1991). *Serial murderers and their victims.* Monterey, CA: Brooks/Cole.

Hickey, Eric (1997). *Serial murderers and their victims* (2nd ed.). Belmont, CA: Wadsworth.

Hickey, J. F. (1972). The effects of guided moral discussion upon youthful offenders' level of moral judgment. *Dissertation Abstracts International, 33,* 1551A.

Hickey, J. E. (1972). The effects of guided moral discussion upon youthful offenders level of moral judgment., Boston University School of Education, Boston.

Hicks, E. K. (1986). *Infibulation: Status through mutilation.* Amsterdam: Offsetdrukkerij Kanters.

Higley, J. D., King, S. T., Hasert, M. F., Champoux, M., Suomi, S. J., & Limmoila, M. (1996a). Stability of inter-individual differences in serotonin function and its relationship to aggressive wounding and competent social behavior in rhesus macaque females. *Neuropsychopharmacology, 14,* 67–76.

Higley, J. D., Mehlman, P. T., Higley, S. B., Fernald, B., Vickers, J., Lindell, S. G., Taub, D. M., Suomi, S. J., & Linnoila, M. (1996b). Excessive mortality in young free-ranging male nonhuman primates with low cerebrospinal fluid 5-hydroxyindoleacetic acid concentrations. *Archives of General Psychiatry, 53,* 537–543.

Higley, J. D., Mehlman, P. T., Poland, R. E., Taub, D. M., Vickers, J., Suomi, S. J., & Linnoila, M. (1996c). CSF testosterone and 5-HIAA correlate with different types of aggressive behaviors. *Biological Psychiatry, 40,* 1067–1082.

Higley, J. D., Suomi, S. J., & Linnoila, M. A. (1992). A longitudinal assessment of CSF monoamine metabolite and plasma cortisol concentrations in young rhesus monkeys. *Biological Psychiatry, 32,* 127–145.

Hill, E. M., Thompson Ross, L., & Low, B. S. (1997). The role of future unpredictability in human risk-taking. *Human Nature,* 287–325.

Hill, G. D., & Crawford, E. M. (1990). Women, race, and crime. *Criminology, 28,* 601–626.

Hill, G. D., Howell, F. M., & Driver, E. T. (1985). Gender, fear and protective handgun ownership. *Criminology, 23,* 541–552.

Hill, P. C., Dill, C. A., & Davenport, E. C., Jr. (1988). A reexamination of the bogus pipeline. *Educational and Psychological Measurement, 48,* 587–601.

Hill, T. D., Reddon, J. R., & Jackson, D. N. (1985). The factor structure of the Wechsler Scales: A brief review. *Clinical Psychology Review, 5,* 287–306.

Hillbrand, M., & Foster, H. G. (1993). Serum cholesterol and severity of aggression. *Psychology Research, 72,* 270.

Hillbrand, M., Spitz, R. T., & Foster, H. G. (1995). Serum cholesterol and aggression in hospitalized male forensic patients. *Journal of Behavioral Medicine, 18,* 33–43.

Hilton, N. Z. (1989). When is assault not an assault? The Canadian public's attitudes toward wife and stranger assault. *Journal of Family Violence, 4,* 323–337.

Hinde, R. A. (1986). Some implications of evolutionary theory and comparative data for the study of human prosocial and aggressive behaviour. In D. Olweus, J. Block, & M. Radke-Yarrow (Eds.), *Development of antisocial and prosocial behavior: Research, theories, and issues* (pp. 13–32). Orlando, FL: Academic Press.

Hindelang, M. (1981). Variations in sex-race-age-specific incidence rates of offending. *American Sociological Review, 90,* 461–474.

Hindelang, M. J. (1969). Equality under the law. *Journal of criminal Law, Criminology and Police Science, 60,* 306–313.

Hindelang, M. J. (1970). The commitment of delinquents to their misdeeds: Do delinquents drift? *Social Problems, 17,* 502–509.

Hindelang, M. J. (1974). Moral evaluation of illegal behaviors. *Social Problems, 21,* 370–385.

Hindelang, M. J. (1978a). Extroversion, neuroticism, and delinquency. In L. D. Savitz & N. Johnston (Eds.), *Crime in society* (pp. 359–365). New York: Wiley.

Hindelang, M. J. (1978b). Race and involvement in common law personal crimes. *American Sociological Review, 43,* 93–109.

Hindelang, M. J., Hirschi, T., & Weis, J. (1979). Correlates of delinquency: The illusion of discrepancy between self-report and official measures. *American Sociological Review, 44,* 995–1014.

Hindelang, M. J. (1979). Race and involvement in common law personal crimes. *American Sociological Review, 43,* 93–109.

Hindelang, M. J., Hirschi, T., & Weis, J. G. (1981). *Measuring delinquency.* Beverly Hills, CA: Sage.

Hinojal, R., Fernandez, M., Riestra, S., & Bobes, J. (1983). A study of drug use among adolescents in the Gijon area. *Medical and Clinical, 80,* 108–111.

Hinshaw, S. P. (1992a). Academic underachievement, attention deficits, and aggression: Comorbidity and implications for intervention. *Journal of Consulting and Clinical Psychology, 60,* 893–903.

Hinshaw, S. P. (1992b). Externalizing behavior problems and academic underachievement in childhood and adolescence: Causal relationships and underlying mechanisms. *Psychological Bulletin, 111,* 127–155.

Hinshaw, S. P. (1994). *Attention deficits and hyperactivity in children.* Thousand Oaks, CA: Sage.

Hippchen, L. J. (1978). The need for a new approach to the delinquent-criminal problem. In L. J. Hippchen (Ed.), *Ecologic-biochemical approaches to treatment of delinquents and criminals* (pp. 3–19). New York: Van Nostrand Reinhold.

Hirschi, T. (1969). *The causes of delinquency.* Berkeley: University of California Press.

Hirschi, T. (1977). Causes and prevention of juvenile delinquency. *Sociological Inquiry, 47,* 322–341.

Hirschi, T., & Gottfredson, M. (1987). Causes of white-collar crime. *Criminology, 25,* 949–974.

Hirschi, T., & Gottfredson, M. (1990). Substantive positivism and the idea of crime. *Rationality and Society, 2,* 412–428.

Hirschi, T., & Gottfredson, M. R. (1994). Substantive positivism and the idea of crime. In T. Hirschi & M. R. Gottfredson (Eds.), *The generality of deviance* (pp. 253–271). New Brunswick, NJ: Transaction.

Hirschi, T., & Gottfredson, M. R. (1995). Control: Theory and the life-course perspective. *Studies on crime and crime prevention, 4,* 131–142.

Hirschi, T., & Hindelang, M. (1977). Intelligence and delinquency: A revisionist view. *American Sociological Review, 42,* 571–587.

Hirschi, T., Hindelang, M. J., & Weis, J. G. (1980). The status of self-report measures. In M. W. Klein & K. S. Teilman (Eds.), *Handbook of criminal justice evaluation* (pp. 473–488). Beverly Hills, CA: Sage.

Hirschi, T., & Stark, R. (1969). Hellfire and delinquency. *Social Problems, 17,* 202–213.

Hirskowitz, M., Karacan, I., Thornby, J. I., & Ware, C. (1984). Nocturnal penile tumescence and EEG asymmetry. *Research Communications in Psychology, Psychiatry and Behavior, 9,* 87–94.

Hirst, P., Q. (1972). Marx and Engels on crime, law and morality. *Economy and Society, 1,* 28–56.

Hobbes, T. (1914). *Leviathan.* London: J. M. Dent & Sons.

Hobcraft, J. N., McDonald, J. W., & Rutstein, S. O. (1984). Socio-economic factors in infant and child mortality: A cross-national comparison. *Population Studies, 38,* 193–224.

Hoberman, H., & Garfinkel, B. D. (1988). Completed suicide in children and adolescents. *Journal of the American Academy of Child Psychiatry, 27,* 689–695.

Hodgins, S., & Von Grunau, M. (1988). Biology, mental disorder, aggression and violence: What do we know? In T. E. Moffitt & S. A. Mednick (Eds.), *Biological contributions to crime causation* (pp. 161–182). Boston: Martinus Nijhoff.

Hoebel, E. A. (1954). *The law of primitive man.* Cambridge, MA: Harvard University Press.

Hoffman, B. F. (1977). Two new cases of XYY chromosome complement. *Canadian Psychiatric Association Journal, 22,* 447–455.

Hoffman, H. (1986). *Rationalization of insanity.* Ph.D. dissertation. Southern Illinois University-Carbondale.

Hoffman, J. J., Hall, R. W., & Bartsch, T. W. (1987). On the relative importance of "psychopathic" personality and alcoholism on neuropsychological measures of frontal lobe dysfunction. *Journal of Abnormal Psychology, 45,* 158–160.

Hoffman, M. (1975). Empathy, role-taking, guilt, and development of altruistic motives. In T. Lickona (Ed.), *Moral development and behavior: Theory research, and social problems.* New York: Holt, Rinehart & Winston.

Hoffman-Plotkin, D., & Twentyman, C. (1984). A multimodal assessment of behavioral and cognitive deficits in abused and neglected preschoolers. *Child Development, 55,* 794–802.

Hoffmann, J. P. (1995). The effects of family structure and family relations on adolescent marijuana use. *International Journal of the Addictions, 30,* 1207–1241.

Hofman, M. A. (1982). Encephalization in mammals in relation to the size of the cerebral cortex. *Brain, Behavior, and Evolution, 20,* 84–96.

Hofman, M. A. (1983). Encephalization in hominids: Evidence for the model of punctuationalism. *Brain, Behavior, and Evolution, 22,* 102–117.

Hogan, R. (1969). Development of an empathy scale. *Consulting and Clinical Psychology, 33,* 307–316.

Hogan, R. (1973). Moral conduct and moral character: A psychological perspective. *Psychological Bulletin, 79,* 217–232.

Hogan, R., & Jones, W. H. (1983). A role-theoretical model of criminal conduct. In W. S. Laufer & J. M. Day (Eds.), *Personality theory, moral development, and criminal behavior* (pp. 3–80). Lexington, MA: Lexington Books.

Hogenson, D. L. (1974). Reading failure and juvenile delinquency. *Bulletin of the Orton Society, 24,* 164–169.

Hogg, J. T. (1984). Mating in bighorn sheep: Multiple creative male strategies. *Science, 225,* 526–528.

Hogg, J. T., & Forbes, S. H. (1997). Mating in bighorn sheep: Frequent male reproduction via a high-risk, "unconventional" tactic. *Behavioral Ecology and Sociobiology, 41,* 33–48.

Holcomb, P. J., Ackerman, P. T. & Dykman, R. A. (1985). Cognitive event-related brain potentials in children with attention and reading deficits. *Psychophysiology, 22,* 656–667.

Holden, C. (1987a). The genetics of personality. *Science, 237,* 598–601.

Holden, C. (1987b). Why do women live longer than men? *Science, 238,* 158–160.

Holden, C. (1990). Head start enters adulthood. *Science, 247,* 1400–1402.

Holdsworth, L., & Whitmore, K. (1974). A study of children attending ordinary school I: Their seizure patterns, progress and behaviour in school. *Developmental Medicine and Child Neurology, 16,* 746–758.

Holinger, P. C. (1979). Violent deaths among the young: Recent trends in suicide, homicide and accidents. *American Journal of Psychiatry, 136,* 1144–1147.

Hollin, C. R., & Howells, K. (1987). Lay explanations of delinquency: Global or offence-specific? *British Journal of Social Psychology, 26,* 203–210.

Hollis, W. A. (1875). Lopsided generations. *Journal of Anatomy and Physiology, 9,* 263–275.

Holmes, Ronald & DeBurger, James. (1985). Profiles in terror: The serial murderer. *Federal Probation, 49,* 29–34.

Holmes, Ronald & Holmes, Stephen. (1992). Understanding mass murder: A starting point. *Federal Probation, 56,* 53–61.

Holmes, Stephen, Hickey, Eric, & Holmes, Ronald (1991). Female serial murderesses: Constructing differentiating typologies. *Journal of Contemporary Criminal Justice, 7,* 245–256.

Holms, T. H., & Masuda, M. (1974). Life change and illness susceptibility. In B. Dohrenwend & B. Dohrenwend (Eds.), *Stressful life events: Their nature and effects* (pp. 45–72). New York: Wiley.

Holzman, H. (1979). Learning disabilities and juvenile delinquency: Biological and sociological theories. In C. R. Jeffery (Ed.), *Biology and crime* (pp. 77–86). Beverly Hills, CA: Sage.

Homant, R. J., & Kennedy, D. B. (1982). Attitudes toward ex-offenders: A comparison of social stigmas. *Criminal Justice, 10,* 383–391.

Homer, A. C., & Gilleard, C. (1990). Abuse of elderly people by their caregivers. *British Medical Journal, 301,* 1359–1362.

Hood, R. (1992). *Race and sentencing.* Oxford: Clarendon Press.

Hooton, E. A. (1939). *The American criminal: An anthropological study.* Cambridge, MA: Harvard University Press.

Hopkins, A. (1975). On the sociology of criminal law. *Social Problems, 22,* 608–619.

Horgan, J. (1993). Eugenics revisited. *Scientific American, 254,* June, 122–131.

Horney, J. (1978). Menstrual cycles and criminal responsibility. *Law and Human Behavior, 2,* 25–36.

Horney, J., & Marshall, I. H. (1992). Risk perceptions among serious offenders: The role of crime and punishment. *Criminology, 30,* 575–594.

Horney, J., Osgood, D. W., & Marshall, I. (1995). Criminal careers in the short-term: Intra-individual variability in crime and its relation to local life circumstances. *American Sociological Review, 60,* 655–673.

Hoshino, K. (1988). *Organized crime and its origins in Japan.* Paper presented at the annual meeting of the American Society of Criminology, Chicago, IL (November).

Hosken, F. P. (1979). *The Hosken report: Genital and sexual mutilation of females* (2nd rev. ed.). Lexington, MA: Women's International Network News.

Howard, M. C., & Dunaif-Hattis, J. (1992). *Anthropology: Understanding human adaptation.* New York: Harper Collins.

Hoyenga, K. T., & Hoyenga, K. B. (1988). Psychobiology: The neuron and behavior. Belmont, CA: Brooks/Cole.

Huang, Frank, & Vaughn, Michael (1992). A descriptive analysis of Japanese organized crime: The boryokudan from 1945 to 1988. *International Criminal Justice Review, 2,* 19–57.

Hudgins, W., & Prentice, N. M. (1973). Moral judgment in delinquent and nondelinquent adolescents and their mothers. *Journal of Abnormal Psychology, 82,* 145–152.

Huessy, H., Metoyer, M., & Townsend, M. (1974). Eight-ten year follow-up of 84 children treated for behavioral disorder in rural Vermont. *Acta Paedopsychiatrica, 40,* 230–235.

Huff, C. L., Corzine, J., & Moore, D. C. (1986). Southern exposure: Deciphering the south's influence on homicide rates. *Social Forces, 64,* 906–924.

Huff, C. R., & Stahura, J. M. (1980). Police employment and suburban crime. *Criminology, 17,* 461–470.

Hugdahl, K., & Franzon, M. (1985). Visual half-field presentations of incongruent color-words reveal mirror-reversal of language lateralization in dextral and sinistral subjects. *Cortex, 21,* 359–374.

Hugdahl, K., Synnevag, B., & Satz, P. (1990). Immune and autoimmune diseases in dyslexic children. *Neuropsychologia, 28,* 673–679.

Hughes, M., & Carter, T. J. (1981). A declining economy and sociological theories of crime: Predictions and explications. In K. N. Wright (Ed.), *Crime and criminal justice in a declining economy.* Cambridge: Gunn & Hain.

Hui, W. M. (1993). Negative social events, stress, and health. *Journal of Epidemiology and Community Health, 47,* 181–185.

Hunter, H. (1977). XYY males. *British Journal of Psychiatry, 131,* 468–477.

Hurwitz, S., & Christiansen, K. O. (1983). *Criminology.* London: Fairleigh Dickonson University Press.

Hyde, J. S., & Sawyer, T. F. (1979). Correlated characters in selection for aggressiveness in female mice, II: Maternal aggressiveness. *Behavioral Genetics, 9,* 571–577.

Hyde, J. S., & Sawyer, T. F. (1980). Selection for agonistic behavior in wild female mice. *Behavioral Genetics, 10,* 349–359.

Iaccino, J. F., & Sowa, S. J. (1989). Asymmetrical processing of dichotic inputs in undergraduates across sex, handedness, ear-side, and experimental instructions. *Perceptual and Motor Skills, 68,* 1003–1010.

Ichniowski, T. (1985). Lotteries: Hoping the luck will last. *Business Week, September 9, 39,*

Inciardi, J. A. (Ed.). (1981a). *The drugs-crime connection.* Beverly Hills, CA: Sage.

Inciardi, J. A. (1981b). Drug use and criminal behavior. In J. A. Inciardi (Ed.), *The drugs-crime connection* (pp. 7–17). Beverly Hills, CA: Sage.

Inciardi, J. A. (1976). Criminal statistics and victim survey research for effective law enforcement planning. In E. C. Viano (Ed.), *Victims and society* (pp. 177–189). Washington DC: Visage Press.

Inciardi, J. A. (1994). *Criminal justice* (4th ed.). Fort Worth, TX: Harcourt, Brace & Jovanovich.

INTERPOL (1992). *International Crime Statistics.* Lyon, France: Author.

Israely, Y. (1985). The moral development of mentally retarded children: Review of the literature. *Journal of Moral Education, 14,* 33–42.

Itil, T. M. (1976). Rebirth of hormones in psychiatry. *Psychiatric Journal of the University of Ottawa, 1,* 105–112.

Iwai, H. (1986). Organized crime in Japan. In R. Kelly (Ed.), *Organized crime: A global perspective* (pp. 208–233). Totowa, NJ: Rowman & Littlefield.

Iwasa, N. (1992). Postconventional reasoning and moral education in Japan. *Journal of Moral Education, 21,* 3–16.

Jackman, R. (1975). *Politics and social equality.* New York: Wiley.

Jackson, L. A. (1992). *Physical appearance and gender: Sociobiological and sociocultural perspectives.* Albany, NY: State University of New York Press.

Jackson, P. I., & Carroll, L. (1981). Race and the war on crime: The sociopolitical determinants of municipal police expenditures in 90 non-southern U.S. cities. *American Sociological Review, 46,* 290–305.

Jacobs, D., & Brill, D. (1979). Inequality and police use of deadly force: An empirical assessment of the conflict hypothesis. *Social Problems, 26,* 403–411.

Jacobs, J. B. (1978). What prison guards think: A profile of the Illinois force. *Crime and Delinquency,* April, 185–196.

Jacobsen, C. (1995). Book review of *Making violence sexy, Women and Health, 22,* 96–98.

James, J. (1996). *Resisting state violence: Radicalism, gender, and race in U.S. culture.* Minneapolis: University of Minnesota Press.

James, J., & Thornton, W. (1980). Women's liberation and the female delinquent. *Journal of Research in Crime and Delinquency, 17,* 230–244.

Jaquith, S. M. (1981). Adolescent marijuana and alcohol use: An empirical test of differential association theory. *Criminology, 19,* 271–280.

Jarjoura, G. R. (1993). Does dropping out of school enhance delinquent involvement? Results from a large-scale national probability sample. *Criminology, 31,* 149–171.

Jarjoura, G. R. (1996). The conditional effect of social class on the dropout–delinquency relationship. *Journal of Research in Crime and Delinquency, 33,* 232–255.

Jarjoura, G. R., & Triplett, R. A. (1997). The effects of social area characteristics on the relationship between social class and delinquency. *Journal of Criminal Justice* 25, 125–139.

Jarmain, R., Kilgore, L., Nelson, H., & Trevathan, W. (1998). *Essentials of physical anthropology* (3rd ed.). Belmont, CA: West/Wadsworth.

Jaynes, G. D., & Williams, R. M., Jr. (1989). *A common destiny: Blacks and American society.* Washington, DC: National Academy Press.

Jeffery, C. R. (1973). The historical development of criminology. In H. Mannheim (Ed.), *Pioneers in criminology* (pp. 458–498). Montclair, NJ: Patterson Smith.

Jeffery, C. R. (1977). *Crime prevention through environmental design.* Beverly Hills, CA: Sage.

Jenkins, Philip (1994). *Using murder: The social construction of serial homicide.* New York: Aldine De Gruyter.

Jenkins, Philip (1992). A murder "wave"? Trends in American serial homicide 1940–1990. *Criminal Justice Review, 17,* 1–19.

Jenkins, Philip (1989). Serial murder in the United States 1900–1940: A historical perspective. *Journal of Criminal Justice, 17,* 377–392.

Jenkins, Philip (1988a). Myth and murder: The serial killer panic of 1983–5. *Criminal Justice Research Bulletin, 3,* 1–8.

Jenkins, Philip (1988b). Serial murder in England 1940–1985. *Journal of Criminal Justice, 16,* 1–15.

Jenkins, W. O., Witherspoon, A. D., Devine, M. D., deValera, E. K., Muller, J. B., Barton, M. C., & McKee, J. M. (1974). *The post-prison analysis of criminal behavior and longitudinal follow-up evaluation of institutional treatment.* Elmore, AL: Rehabilitation Research Foundation.

Jennings, W. S., Kilkenny, R., & Kohlberg, L. (1983). Moral development theory and practice for youthful and adult offenders. In W. S. Laufer & J. M. Day (Eds.), *Personality theory, moral development, and criminal behaviour* (pp. 281–294). Lexington, MA: Lexington Books.

Jensen, A. R., & Faulstich, E. (1988). Differences between prisoners and the general population in psychometric "g." *Personality and Individual Differences, 9,* 925–928.

Jensen, G. F. (1969). Crime doesn't pay: Correlates of a shared misunderstanding. *Social Problems, 17,* 189–201.

Jensen, G. F. (1972a). Delinquency and adolescent self-conceptions: A study of the personal relevance of infraction. *Social Problems, 20,* 84–103.

Jensen, G. F. (1972b). Parents, peers and delinquent action: A test of the differential association perspective. *American Journal of Sociology, 78,* 63–72.

Jensen, G. F. (1976). Race, achievement and delinquency: A further look at delinquency in a birth cohort. *American Journal of Sociology, 82,* 379–387.

Jensen, G. F., & Erickson, M. L. (1979). The religious factor and delinquency: Another look at the hellfire hypothesis. In R. Wuthnow (Ed.), *The religious dimension* (pp. 157–177). New York: Academic Press.

Jensen, G. F., & Eve, R. (1976). Sex differences in delinquency. *Criminology, 13,* 427–448.

Jensen, G. F., & Karpos, M. (1993). Managing rape: Exploratory research on the behavior of rape statistics. *Criminology, 31,* 363–385.

Jensen, G. F., Strauss, J. H., & Harris, V. W. (1977). Crime, delinquency and the American Indian. *Human Organization, 36,* 252–257.

Jensen, G. F., & Thompson, K. (1990). What's class got to do with it? A further examination of power–control theory. *American Journal of Sociology, 95,* 1009–1023.

Jensen, J. B., & Garfinkel, B. D. (1988). Neuroendocrine aspects of attention deficit hyperactivity disorder. *Endocrinology and Metabolism Clinics of North America, 17,* 111–129.

Jescheck, H. (1970). Principles of German criminal procedure in comparison with American law. *Virginia Law Review, 56,* 239–253.

Jessor, R. (1979). Marihuana: A review of recent psychosocial research. In R. Dupont, A. Goldstein, & J. O'Donnell (Eds.), *Handbook on drug abuse* (pp. 337–354). Washington, DC: National Institute of Drug Abuse.

Jessor, R., Close, A., & Donovan, J. E. (1980). Psychological correlates of marijuana use and problem drinking in a national sample of adolescents. *American Journal of Public Health, 70,* 604–613.

Jessor, R., Donovan, J. E., & Widmer, K. (1980). *Psychosocial factors in adolescent alcohol and drug use: The 1978 National Sample Study, and the 1974–78 panel study.* Boulder, CO: Institute of Behavioral Science, University of Colorado.

John, E. R., Ahn, H., & Prichep, L. (1980). Developmental equations for the electroencephalogram. *Science, 210,* 1255–1258.

John, E. R., Karmel, B. Z., Corning, W. C., Easton, P., Brown, H. A., Harmony, T., & Schwartz, E. (1977). Neurometrics. *Science, 196,* 1393–1410.

Johnson, D. R., & Scheuble, L., K. (1991). Gender bias in the disposition of juvenile court referrals: The effects of time and location. *Criminology, 29,* 677–699.

Johnson, E. A. (1982). The roots of crime in Imperial Germany. *Central European History, 15,* 351–376.

Johnson, E. A., & Monkkonen, E. H. (1996). Introduction. In E. A. Johnson & E. H. Monkkonen (Eds.), *The civilization of crime: Violence in town and country since the Middle Ages* (pp. 7–10). Urbana, IL: University of Illinois Press.

Johnson, E. H. (1980). Praxis and radical criminology in the United States. In J. A. Inciardi (Ed.), *Radical criminology the coming crises* (pp. 161–168). Beverly Hills, CA: Sage.

Johnson, Elmer (1990). Yakuza (criminal gangs) in Japan: Characteristics and management in prison. *Journal of Contemporary Criminal Justice, 6,* 113–126.

Johnson, E. O., Van den Bree, M. B. M., & Pickens, R. W. (1996). Indicators of genetic and environmental influence in alcohol-dependent individuals. *Alcoholism: Clinical and Experimental Research, 20,* 67–74.

Johnson, H. (1986). *Women and crime in Canada.* Ottawa: Solicitor General.

Johnson, J. (1997). Americans' views on crime and law enforcement. *National Institute of Justice Journal,* September(#233), 9–14.

Johnson, K. (1996). Homicide, rape, robbery: The numbers are falling. *USA Today,* May 6, 8A.

Johnson, K. A., & Wasielewski, P. L. (1982). A commentary on victimization research and the importance of meaning structures. *Criminology, 20,* 205–222.

Johnson, Phillip, & Feldman, Theodore (1992). Personality types and terrorism: self-psychology perspectives. *Forensic Reports, 5,* 293–303.

Johnson, R. (1986). Family structure and delinquency: General patterns and gender differences. *Criminology, 24,* 65–83.

Johnson, R. E., & Marcos, A. C. (1988). Correlates of adolescent drug use by gender and geographic location. *American Journal of Drug and Alcohol Abuse, 14,* 51–63.

Johnson, V., & Pandina, R. J. (1991). Effects of the family environment of adolescent substance use, delinquency, and coping styles. *American Journal of Drug and Alcohol Abuse, 17,* 71–88.

Johnston, F. E., & Selby, H. (1978). *Anthropology: The biocultural view.* Dubuque, Iowa: W. C. Brown.

Johnston, L. D., O'Malley, P. M., & Bachman, J. G. (1995). *National survey results on drug use from the monitoring the future study, 1975–1994: Volume I, Secondary school students.* Rockville, MD: National Institute on Drug Abuse.

Johnston, L. D., O'Malley, P. M., & Eveland, L. K. (1978). Drugs and delinquency: A search for causal connections. In D. B. Kandel (Ed.), *Longitudinal research on drug use* (pp. 137–156). New York: Wiley.

Johnston, L. D., O'Malley, P. M., & Bachman, J. G. (1993). *National survey results on drug use from monitoring the future study, 1975–1992,* Vol. 1: *Secondary school students.* Washington, DC: U.S. Department of Health and Human Services (NIH Publication No. 933597).

Johnston, P. J. (1994). Academic approaches to race-crime statistics do not justify their collection. *Canadian Journal of Criminologie, 36,* 149–185.

Jolly, A. (1985a). *The evolution of primate behavior* (2nd ed.). New York: MacMillan.

Jolly, A. (1985b). A new science that sees animals as conscious beings. *Smithsonian, 15* March, 65–75.

Jones, D. (1986). *History of criminology: A philosophical perspective.* Westport, CT: Greenwood Press.

Jones, K. L., Shainberg, L. W., & Byer, C., O. (1969). *Drugs and alcohol.* New York: Harper & Row.

Jones, Mark (1992). Islamic law in Saudi Arabia: A responsive view. *International Journal of Comparative and Applied Criminal Justice, 16,* 43–56.

Jones, O. D. (1994). Law and evolutionary biology: Obstacles and opportunities. *Journal of Contemporary Health, Law and Policy, 10,* 265–283.

Jonsson, G. (1967). Delinquent boys: Their parents and grandparents. *Acta Psychiatrica Scandinavica, Supplement 43,* 1–264.

Jonsson, G. (1975). Negative social inheritance. In L. Levi (Ed.), *Society, stress and disease* (Vol. 2, pp. 181–186). London: Oxford University Press.

Joppa, M., Rowe, R. K., & Meisel, R. L. (1997). Effects of serotonin 1A or 1B receptor agonists on social aggression in male and female Syrian hamsters. *Pharmacology, Biochemistry, and Behavior, 58,* 349–353.

Junger, M., & Wiegersma, A. (1994). *Risky behaviour and accidents* (NSCR WD94–04). Leiden, The Netherlands: Netherlands Institute for the Study of Criminality and Law Enforcement.

Junger, M., & Wiegersma, A. (1995). The relations between accidents, deviance and leisure time. *Criminal Behavior and Mental Health, 5,* 144–173.

Junger-Tas, J. (1994). The international self-report delinquency study: Some methodological and theoretical issues. In J. Junger-Tas, G.-J. Terlouw, & M. W. Klein (Eds.), *Delinquent behavior among young people in the Western world: First results of the international self-report delinquency study* (pp. 1–13). Amsterdam: Kugler.

Junger-Tas, J., Terlouw, G.-J., & Klein, M. W. (Eds.). (1994). *Delinquent behavior among young people in the Western world: First results of the international self-report delinquency study* (pp. 212–237). Amsterdam: Kugler.

Jurich, A. P., & Polson, C. J. (1984). Reasons for drug use: Comparison of drug users and abusers. *Psychological Reports, 55,* 371–378.

Jurik, N. C., & Winn, R. (1990). Gender and homicide: A comparison of men and women who kill. *Violence and Victims, 5,* 227–242.

Jurkovic, G. J. (1980). The juvenile delinquent as a moral philosopher: A structural–developmental perspective. *Psychological Bulletin, 88,* 709–727.

Jurkovic, G. K., & Prentice, N. M. (1977). Relation of moral and cognitive development to dimensions of juvenile delinquency. *Journal of Abnormal Psychology, 86,* 414–420.

Jutai, J. W., Hare, R. D., & Connolly, J. F. (1987). Psychopathy and event related potentials (ERPs) associated with attention to speech stimuli. *Personality and Individual Differences, 8,* 175–184.

Kaariainen, J. (1997). The production of "criminals" in Finland in the 1980's. *Scandinavia Journal of Social Welfare, 6,* 61–67.

Kachur, S. P., Stennies, G. M., Powell, K. E., Modzeleski, W., Stephens, R., Murphy, R., Kagan, J., & Freeman, M. (1970). Relation of childhood intelligence, maternal behavior and social class to behavior during adolescence. In H. E. Fitzgerald & J. F. McKinney (Eds.), *Developmental psychology* (pp. 508–516). Homewood, IL: Dorsey.

Kachur, S. P., Stennies, G. M., Powell, K. E., Modzeleski, W., Stephens, R., Murphy, R., Kresnow, M.-J., Sleet, D., & Lowry, R. (1996). School-associated violent deaths in the United States, 1992 to 1994. *Journal of the American Medical Association, 275,* 1729–1733.

Kadish, Carol (1988). International crime rates. Bureau of Justice Statistics, U.S. Department of Justice.

Kagan, J., Reznick, S., & Snidman, N. (1987). The physiology and psychology of behavioral inhibition in children. *Child Development, 58,* 1459–1473.

Kagan, J., Reznick, J. S., & Snidman, N. (1988). Biological bases of childhood shyness. *Science, 240,* 167–171.

Kahn, J. R., Kalsbeek, W. D., & Hofferth, S. L. (1988). National estimates of teenage sexual activity: Evaluating the comparability of three national surveys. *Demography, 25,* 189–204.

Kaironen, K. A. (1966). *A study of the criminality of Finnish immigrants in Sweden.* Strasbourg: Council of Europe.

Kaiser, G. (1985). *Kriminologie: Eine Einfuhrung in die Grundlagen.* Heidelberg, Germany: Muchen.

Kalat, J. W. (1992). *Biological psychology.* Belmont, CA: Wadsworth.

Kalish, C. B. (1988). International crime rates. *Bureau of Justice Statistics Special Report,* May, 1–11.

Kalus, O., Asnis, G. M., & Van Praag, H. M. (1989). The role of serotonin in depression. *Psychiatric Annals, 19,* 348–353.

Kandel, D. B. (1980a). Development stages in adolescent drug involvement. In D. Letirei (Ed.), *Theories of drug abuse.* Washington, DC: U.S. Government Printing Office.

Kandel, D. B. (1980b). Drug and drinking behavior among youth. *Annual Review of Sociology, 6,* 235–285.

Kandel, D. B. (1982). Epidemiological and psychosocial perspectives on adolescent drug use. *Journal of Child Psychiatry, 21,* 328–347.

Kandel, D. B. (1992). The social demography of drug abuse. *Milbank Quarterly, 69,* 365–414.

Kandel, D. B., & Faust, R. (1975). Sequence and stages in patterns of adolescent drug use. *Archives of General Psychiatry, 32,* 923–932.

Kandel, D. B., Simcha-Fafan, O., & Davies, M. (1986). Risk factors for delinquency and illicit drug use from adolescence to young adulthood. *Journal of Drug Issues, 16,* 67–70.

Kandel, D. B., Kessler, R. C., & Margulies, R. S. (1978). Antecedents of adolescent initiation into stages of drug use: A developmental analysis. *Journal of Youth and Adolescence, 7,* 13–40.

Kandel, D. B., Tremiman, D., Faust, R., & Single, E. (1976). Adolescent involvement in legal and illegal drug use: A multiple classification analysis. *Social Forces, 55,* 438–458.

Kandel, E., & Freed, D. (1989). Frontal-lobe dysfunction and antisocial behavior: A review. *Journal of Clinical Psychology, 45,* 404–413.

Kantrowitz, B., Quade, V., & Fisher, B. (1991). The pregnancy police. *Newsweek,* April 29, 52–53.

Kaplan, H. B. (1975b). *Self-attitudes and deviant behavior.* Pacific Palisades, CA: Goodyear.

Kaplan, H. B. (1975a). Increases in self-rejection as an antecedent of deviant response. *Journal of Youth and Adolescence, 4,* 281–292.

Kaplan, J. R., Manuck, S. B., & Shivley, C. (1991). The effects of fat and cholesterol on social behavior in monkeys. *Psychosomatic Medicine, 53,* 634–642.

Kappeler, Victor, Blumberg, Mark, & Potter, Gary (1993). *The mythology of crime and criminal justice.* Prospect Heights, IL: Waveland.

Karlen, A. (1980). Homosexual behavior. In J. Marmor (Ed.), *Homosexuality in history* (pp. 75–99). New York: Basic Books.

Karmen, A. A. (1991). Victims of crime. In J. F. Sheley (Ed.), *Criminology: A contemporary handbook* (pp. 121–138). Belmont, CA: Wadsworth.

Katzenelson, S. (1975). *The female offender in Washington, D.C.* Washington, DC: Institute of Law and Social Research.

Kavaliers, M., & Innes, D. G. L. (1990). Developmental changes in opiate-induced analgesia in deer mice: Sex and population differences. *Brain Research, 516,* 326–331.

Kawi, A. A., & Pasamanick, B. (1959). Prenatal and parental factors in the development of childhood reading disorders. *Monographs of the Society for Research in Child Development, 24,* 1–108.

Kay, S. R. (1990). Significance of the positive–negative distinction in schizophrenia. *Schizophrenia Bulletin, 16,* 635–652.

Kazdin, A. E. (1987). Treatment of antisocial behavior in children: Current status and future directions. *Psychological Bulletin, 102,* 187–203.

Kazdin, A. E., & Esveldt-Dawson, K. (1986). The interview for antisocial behavior: Psychometric characteristics and concurrent validity with child psychiatric inpatients. *Journal of Psychopathology and Behavioral Assessment, 8,* 289–303.

Kazdin, A. K. (1987). *Conduct disorders in childhood and adolescence.* Newbury Park, CA: Sage.

Keane, C. (1993). The impact of financial performance on frequency of corporate crime: A latent variable test of strain theory. *Canadian Journal of Criminology, 35,* 293–308.

Keane, C., Maxim, P. S., & Teevan, J. J. (1993). Drinking and driving, self-control, and gender: Testing a general theory of crime. *Journal of Research in Crime and Delinquency, 30,* 30–46.

Keeney, Belea & Heide, Kathleen (1994). Gender differences in serial murderers: A preliminary analysis. *Journal of Interpersonal Violence, 9,* 383–398.

Keeney, Belea & Heide, Kathleen (1995). Serial murder: A more accurate and inclusive definition. *International Journal of Offender Therapy and Comparative Criminology, 39,* 299–306.

Keil, T. J., & Vito, G. F. (1989). Race, homicide severity, and application of the death penalty: A consideration of the Barnett scale. *Criminology, 27,* 511–531.

Kelley, B. T., Huizinga, D., Thornberry, T. P., & Loeber, R. (1997). Epidemiology of serious violence. *Juvenile Justice Bulletin,* June, 1–11.

Kelley, B. T., Thornberry, T. P., & Smith, C. A. (1997). In the wake of childhood maltreatment. *Juvenile Justice Bulletin,* August, 1–15.

Kelley, C. (1981). Reliability of the behavior problem checklist with institutionalized male delinquents. *Journal of Abnormal Child Psychology, 9,* 243–250.

Kelley, T. M. (1996). A critique of social bonding and control theory of delinquency using the principles of psychology of mind. *Adolescence, 31,* 321–337.

Kelly, D. H., & Pink, W. T. (1973). School commitment, youth rebellion and delinquency. *Criminology, 10,* 473–85.

Kelly, F. J., & Baer, D. J. (1969). Jesness inventory and self-concept for delinquents before and after participation in Outward Bound. *Psychological Reports, 25,* 719–724.

Kelly, K. H., & Balch, R. W. (1971). Social origins and school failure: A reexamination of Cohen's theory of working-class delinquency. *Pacific Sociological Review, 14,* 413–430.

Kemper, T. D. (1990). *Social structure and testosterone: Essays on the socio-bio-social chain.* New Brunswick, NJ: Rutgers University Press.

Kempf, K. L. (1989). The empirical status of Hirschi's control theory. In W. F. Laufer & F. R. Adler (Eds.), *Advances in criminological theory* (pp. 143–185). New Brunswick, NJ: Transaction.

Kendall, P. C., Chansky, T. E., Freidman, M., Kim, R., Kortlander, E., Sessa, F. M., & Sizueland, L. (1991). Child and adolescent therapy: Cognitive-behavioral procedures (pp. 131–164). New York: Guilford.

Kendall, P., Deardorff, P., & Finch, A. (1977). Empathy and socialization in first and repeat offenders and normals. *Journal of Abnormal Psychology, 5,* 93–97.

Kendler, K. S., & Gardner, C. O. J. (1998). Twin studies of adult psychiatric and substance dependence disorders: Are they biased by differences in the environmental experiences of monozygotic and dizygotic twins in childhood and adolescence? *Psychological Medicine, 28,* 625–633.

Kennedy, D. B., & Homant, R. J. (1986). Security managers' attitudes toward locus of responsibility for crime. *Psychological Reports, 59,* 199–205.

Kenrick, D. Gutierres, S., & Goldberg, L. (1989). Influences of popular erotica on judgments of strangers and mates. *Journal of Experimental Psychology, 25,* 159–167.

Kercher, K. (1988). Criminology. In E. F. Borgatta & K. S. Cook (Eds.), *The future of sociology* (pp. 294–316). Beverly Hills, CA: Sage.

Kerstetter, Wayne (1983). Terrorism. In Kadish, S. (Ed.), *Encyclopedia of crime and justice* (Vol. 4, pp. 1529–1537). New York: Free Press

Keys, C. B. (1987). Synergy, prevention and the Chicago School of Sociology. *Prevention in the Human Services, 5,* 11–34.

Khan, A., & Cataio, A. (1984). *Men and women in biological perspective: A review of the literature.* New York: Praeger.

Kidd, R. F., & Chayet, E. F. (1984). Why do victims fail to report? The psychology of criminal victimization. *Journal of Social Issues, 40,* 39–50.

Killias, M., Villettaz, P., & Rabasa, J. (1994). Self-reported juvenile delinquency in Switzerland. In J. Junger-Tas, G.-J. Terlouw, & M. W. Klein (Eds.), *Delinquent behavior among young people in the western world: First results of the international self-report delinquency study* (pp. 186–211). Amsterdam: Kugler.

Kim, K., Smith, P. K., & Palermiti, A. (1997). Conflict in childhood and reproductive development. *Evolution and Human Behavior, 18,* 109–142.

Kimura, D. (1967). Functional asymmetry of the brain in dichotic listening. *Cortex, 3,* 163–178.

Kimura, D., & Folb, S. (1968). Neural processing of backwards speech sounds. *Science, 161,* 395–396.

Kindlon, D., J.,, Tremblay, R. E., Mezzacappa, E., Earls, F., Laurent, D., & Schaal, B. (1995). Longitudinal patterns of heart rate and fighting behavior in 9- through 12-year-old boys. *Journal of the American Academy of Child and Adolescent Psychiatry, 34,* 371–377.

King, R. J., Jones, J., Scheuer, J. W., Curtis, D., & Zarcone, V. P. (1990). Plasma cortisol correlates of impulsivity and substance abuse. *Personality and Individual Differences, 11,* 287–291.

Kingery, P. M., Pruitt, B. E., & Hurley, R. S. (1992). Violence and illegal drug use among adolescents: Evidence from the U.S. national adolescent health survey. *International Journal of the Addictions, 27,* 1445–1464.

Kinnunen, J. (1996). Gabriel Tarde as a founding father of innovation diffusion research. *Acta Sociologica, 39,* 431–442.

Kirchhoff, G. F., & Kirchhoff, C. (1984). Victimological research in Germany: Victim surveys and research on sexual victimization. In R. Block (Ed.), *Victimization and fear of crime: World perspectives* (pp. 57–64). Washington, DC: U.S. Department of Justice.

Kirigin, K. A., Braukmann, C. J., Atwater, J. D., & Wolf, M. M. (1982). An evaluation of teaching-family (Achievement Place) group homes for juvenile offenders. *Journal of Applied Behavior Analysis, 15,* 1–16.

Kirschbaum, C., Bartussek, D., & Strasburger, C. J. (1992). Cortisol responses to psychological stress and correlations with personality traits. *Personality and Individual Differences, 13,* 1353–1357.

Kirschbaum, C., & Hellhammer, D. H. (1994). Salivary cortisol in psychoneuroendocrine research: Recent developments and applications. *Psychoneuroendocrinology, 19,* 313–333.

Kitsuse, J., & Cicourel, A. (1963). A note on the use of official statisitics. *Social Problems, 12,* 131–139.

Klaiber, E. L., Broverman, D. M., Vogel, W., & Kobayashi, Y. (1976). The use of steroid hormones in depression. In T. M. Itil, G. Laudahn, & W. H. Hermann (Eds.) *Psychotrophic action of hormones.* New York, NY: Spectrum

Kleck, G. (1981). Racial discrimination in criminal sentencing: A critical evaluation of the evidence with additional data on the death penalty. *American Sociological Review, 46,* 783–805.

Kleck, G. (1985). Life support for ailing hypothesis: Modes of summarizing the evidence for racial discrimination in sentencing. *Law and Human Behavior, 9,* 271–285.

Klein, D. (1986). Labeling theory and delinquency policy: An experimental test. *Criminal Justice and Behavior, 13,* 47–79.

Klein, D., & Kress, J. (1976). Any woman's blues: A critical overview of women, crime and the criminal justice system. *Crime and Social Justice, 5* (Spring-Summer), 34–49.

Klein, M. W. (1974). Labeling, deterrence, and recidivism: A study of police disposition of juvenile offenders. *Social Problems, 22,* 292–303.

Klein, R. G., & Mannuzza, S. (1991). Long-term outcome of hyperactive children: A review. *Journal of American Academy of Child Adolescent Psychiatry, 30,* 383–7.

Kleinman, P. H., & Lukoff, I. F. (1978). Ethnic differences in factors related to drug abuse. *Health and Social Behaviors, 19,* 190–99.

Kligman, D., & Goldberg, D. A. (1975). Temporal lobe epilepsy and aggression. *Journal of Nervous and Mental Disorders, 160,* 324–341.

Klinteberg, A., Humble, K., & Schalling, D. (1992). Personality and psychopathy of males with a history of early criminal behaviour. *European Journal of Personality, 6,* 245–266.

Klockars, C. B. (1980). The contemporary crises of Marxist criminology. In J. Inciardi, (Ed.), *Radical criminology: The coming crises* (pp. 92–123). Beverly Hills, CA: Sage.

Klonoff, E. A., & Landrine, H. (1992). Sex roles, occupational roles, and symptom-reporting: A test of competing hypotheses on sex differences. *Journal of Behavioral Medicine, 15,* 335–364.

Klorman, R., Coons, H. W., Brumaghim, J. T., Borgstedt, A. D., & Fitzpatrick, P. (1988). Stimulant treatment for adolescents with attention deficit disorder. *Psychopharmacological Bulletin, 24,* 88–92.

Klotter, J. C. (1994). *Criminal law* (4th ed.) Cincinatti, OH: Anderson.

Kluger, G., Bohm, I., Laub, M. C., & Waldenmaier, C. (1996). Epilepsy and fragile X gene mutations. *Pediatric Neurology, 15,* 358–360.

Knottnerus, J. D., & Maguire, B. (1995). The status of sociology departments: An assessment of their current and future prospects. *Sociological Spectrum, 15,* 17–38.

Knudsen, Dean (1991). Child sexual coercion. In E. Grauerholz and M. Koralewski (Eds.), *Sexual coercion: A sourcebook on its nature, causes, and prevention* (pp. 17–28). Lexington, MA: D. C. Heath.

Knussman, R. K., Christiansen, & Couwenbergs, C. (1986). Relations between sex hormones levels and sexual behavior in men. *Archives of Sexual Behavior, 15,* 429–445.

Kobrin, S. (1959). *The Chicago Area Project: A 25-year assessment. Annals of the American Academy of Political Science, 322,* 19–29.

Koch, Larry (1995). Interracial rape: Examining the increasing frequency argument. *American Sociologist, 26,* 76–86.

Kofoed, L. (1988). Selective dimensions of personality: Psychiatry and sociobiology in collision. *Perspective in Biology and Medicine, 31,* 228–242.

Kohlberg, L. A. (1958). *The development of modes of moral thinking and choice in the years 10 to 16.* Unpublished Ph.D. dissertation, University of Chicago.

Kohlberg, L. A. (1979). The cognitive-developmental approach to moral development. In C. Borg (Ed.), *Psychology 79/80* (pp. 158–165). Guilford, CT: Dushkin.

Kohlberg, L. A. (1981). *Essays on moral development,* Vol. 1: *The philosophy of moral development.* New York: Harper & Row.

Kohlberg, L. A. (1984a). *Essays on moral development, Vol. 2: The psychology of moral development.* New York: Harper & Row.

Kohlberg, L. A. (1984b). *The psychology of moral development: The nature and validity of moral stages.* New York: Harper & Row.

Kohlberg, L. A., & Candee, D. (1984). The relationship of moral judgement to moral action. In L. Kohlberg (Ed.), *The psychology of moral development.* San Francisco: Harper & Row.

Kohlberg, L. A., & Kramer, R. (1969). Continuities and discontinuities in childhood moral development. *Human Development, 12,* 93–120.

Kolb, B., & Nonneman, A. J. (1974). Frontolimbic lesions and social behavior in the rat. *Physiology and Behavior, 13,* 637–643.

Kolb, B., & Whishaw, I. Q. (1980). *Fundamentals of human neuropsychology.* San Francisco: Freeman.

Konner, M. (1982). *The tangled wing.* New York: Holt, Rinehart & Winston.

Kooi, K. A., Tucker, R. R., & Marshall, R. E. (1978). *Fundamentals of electroencephalography.* Hagerstown, MD: Harper & Row.

Kormos, K. C., White, D. C., & Brooks, C. I. (1992). Sex differences in rated seriousness of crimes. *Psychological reports, 70,* 867–870.

Kornhauser, R. (1978). Social sources of delinquency: A critique of subcultural theorization. In R. Giallombardo (Ed.), *Juvenile delinquency* (4th ed., pp. 143–158). New York: Wiley.

Koss, M., & Leonard, K. 1984. Sexually aggressive men: Empirical findings and theoretical implications. In N. Malamuth & E. Donnerstein (Eds.), *Pornography and sexual aggression.* New York: Academic Press.

Kosson, D. S. (1998). Divided visual attention in psychopathic and nonpsychopathic offenders. *Personality and Individual Differences, 24,* 373–391.

Kosten, T. R. (1998). The pharmacotherapy of relapse prevention using anticonvulsants. *American Journal of Addiction, 7,* 205–209.

Kovach, J. K., & Wilson, G. (1981). Behaviour and pleilotrophy: Generalization of gene effects in the colour preferences of Japanese quail chicks (*C. coturnix japonica*). *Animal Behaviour, 29,* 746–759.

Kovandzic, T. V., Vieraitis, L. M., & Yeisley, M. R. (1998). The structural covariates of urban homicide: Reassessing the impact of income inequality and poverty in the post-Reagan era. *Criminology, 36,* 569–600.

Kozeki, B., & Berghammer, R. (1992). The role of empathy in the motivational structure of school children. *Personality and Individual Differences, 13,* 191–203.

Koziey, P. W., & Davies, L. (1982). Broken homes: Impact on adolescents. *Alberta Journal of Educational Research, 28,* 95–99.

Kposowa, A. J., Breault, K. D., & Harrison, B. M. (1995). Reassessing the structural covariates of violent and property crimes in the USA: A county level analysis. *British Journal of Sociology, 46,* 79–105.

Kraemer, G. W., Ebert, M. H., Schmidt, D. E., & McKinney, W. T. (1989). A longitudinal study of the effect of different social rearing conditions on cerebrospinalfluid norepinephrine and biogenic amine metabolites in rhesus monkeys. *Neuropsychopharmacology, 2,* 175–189.

Krahn, H., Hartnagel, T. F., & Gartrell, J. W. (1986). Income inequality and homicide rates: Cross-national data and criminological theories. *Criminology, 24,* 269–295.

Kramer, J., & Steffensmeir, D. (1993). Race and imprisonment decisions. *Sociological Quarterly, 34,* 357–376.

Kramer, Martin (1990). The moral logic of Hizballah. In W. Reich (Ed.), *Origins of terrorism: Psychologies, ideologies, theologies, states of mind* (pp. 131–157). New York: Cambridge University Press.

Kramer, R. C. (1980). Book review. *Contemporary Sociology, 9,* 533–534.

Kratcoski, P. C., & Kratcoski, L. D. (1982). The relationship of victimization through child abuse to aggressive delinquent behavior. *Victimology, 7,* 199–203.

Kraus, N., McGee, T. J., Carrell, T. D., Zecker, S. G., Nicol, T. G., & Koch, D. B. (1996). Auditory neurophysiologic responses and discrimination deficits in children with learning problems. *Science, 273,* 971–974.

Krebs, D. L. (1975). Empathy and altruism. *Journal of Personality and Social Psychology, 32,* 1134–1146.

Krebs, D. L., & Gilmore, J. (1982). The relationship among the first stages of cognitive development, role-taking abilities, and moral development. *Child Development, 53,* 877–886.

Kress, J. (1982). Book review. *Contemporary Sociology, 11,* 39–40.

Kreuz, L., Rose, R., & Jennings, J. (1972). Suppression of plasma testosterone levels and psychological stress. *Archives of General Psychiatry, 26,* 479–482.

Krisberg, B. (1975). *Crime and privilege: Toward a new criminology.* Englewood Cliffs, NJ: Prentice-Hall.

Krohn, M. D. (1978). A Durkheimian analysis of international crime rates. *Social Forces, 57,* 654–670.

Krohn, M. D. (1986). Review essay. *Criminology, 24,* 593–602.

Krohn, M. D., Curry, J. P., & Nelson-Kilger, S. (1983). Is chivalry dead? *Criminology, 21,* 417–435.

Krohn, M. D., Massey, J. L., & Skinner, W. F. (1987). A sociological theory of crime and delinquency: Social learning theory. In E. K. Morris & C. J. Braukmann (Eds.), *Behavioral approaches to crime and delinquency* (pp. 455–456). New York: Plenum.

Krueger, R. F., Caspi, A., Moffitt, T. E., White, J., & Stouthamer-Loeber, M. (1996). Delay of gratification, psychopathology, and personality: Is low self-control specific to externalizing problems? *Journal of Personality, 64,* 107–129.

Krueger, R. F., Schmutte, P. S., Caspi, A., Moffitt, T. E., Campbell, K., & Silva, P. A. (1994). Personality traits are linked to crime among men and women: Evidence from a birth cohort. *Journal of Abnormal Psychology, 103,* 328–338.

Kruesi, M. J. P., Rapoport, J. L., Cummings, E. M., Berg, C. J., Ismond, D. R., Flament, M., Yarrow, M., & Zahn-Waxler, C. (1987). Effects of sugar and aspartame on aggression and activity in children. *American Journal of Psychiatry, 144,* 1487–1490.

Kruesi, M. J., Rapoport, J. L., Hamburger, S., Hibbs, E., Potter, W. Z., Lenane, M., & Brown, G. L. (1990). Cerebrospinal fluid monoamine metabolites, aggression, and impulsivity in disruptive behavior disorders of children and adolescents. *Archives of General Psychiatry, 47,* 419–426.

Krus, D. J., Nelsen, E. A., & Webb, J. M. (1997). Changes in crime rates and family related values in selected east European countries. *Psychological Reports, 81,* 747–751.

Krus, D. J., Sherman, J. L., & Krus, P. H. (1977). Changing values over the last half-century: The story of Thurstone's crime scales. *Psychological Reports, 40,* 207–211.

Kruttschnitt, C., & Dornfeld, M. (1991). Childhood victimization, race, and violent crime. *Criminal Justice and Behavior, 18,* 448–463.

Krynicki, V. E. L. (1978). Cerebral dysfunction in repetitively assaultive adolescents. *Journal of Nervous and Mental Disease, 166,* 59–67.

Kubicka, L., Matejcek, Z., David, H. P., Dytrych, Z., Miller, W. B., & Roth, Z. (1995). Children from unwanted pregnancies in Prague, Czech Republic revisited at age thirty. *Acta Psychiatrica Scandinavica, 91,* 361–369.

Kuhmerker, L. (1975). Learning to care—the development of empathy. *Moral Education, 5,* 24–33.

Kulik, J. A., Stein, K. B., & Sarbin, T. R. (1968). Disclosure of delinquent behavior under conditions of anonymity and nonanonymity. *Journal of Consulting and Clinical Psychology, 32,* 506–509.

Kurdek, L. A. (1978). Perspective taking as the cognitive basis of children's moral development. *Genetic Psychology Monographs, 95,* 97–188.

Kurland, L. A. (1959). Incidence of epilepsy in a small urban community. *Epilepsia, 1,* 143.

Kuruoglu, A. C., Arikan, Z., Vural, G., Karatas, M., Arac, M., & Isik, E. (1996). Single photon emission computerized tomography in chronic alcoholism: Antisocial personality disorder may be associated with decreased frontal perfusion. *British Journal of Psychiatry, 169,* 348–354.

Kutchinski, B. (1971). *Towards an exploration of the decrease in registered sex crimes in Copenhagen, Technical report of the commission on obscenity and pornography* Vol. 7. Washington, DC: U.S. Government Printing Office.

Kutchinski, B. (1973). The effect of easy availability of pornography on the incidence of sex crimes: The Danish empire. *Journal of Social Issues, 29,* 163–181.

Kutnick, P. (1986). The relationship of moral judgement and moral action: Kohlberg's theory, criticism and revision. In S. Modgil & C. Modgil (Eds.), *Lawrence Kohlberg: Consensus and controversy* (pp. 125–148). Philadelphia: Falmer.

Kvaraceus, W. C. (1944). Delinquent behavior and church attendance. *Sociology and Social Research, 28,* 284–289.

Kvaraceus, W. C. (1945). *Juvenile delinquency and the school.* New York: World Books.

Lachiewicz, A. M., & Dawson, D. V. (1994). Behavior problems of young girls with fragile X syndrome: Factor scores on the Conners' parents questionnaire. *American Journal of Medical Genetics, 51,* 364–369.

Lachiewicz, A. M., Spiridigliozzi, G. A., Gullion, C. M., Ransford, S. N., & Rao, K. (1994). Aberrant behaviors of young boys with fragile X syndrome. *American Journal of Mental Retardation, 98,* 567–579.

Lachmann, R. (Ed.). (1991). *The encyclopedic dictionary of sociology* (4th ed.). Guilford, CT: Dushkin.

Ladosky, W., & Gaziri, L. C. J. (1970). Brain serotonin and sexual differentiation of the nervous system. *Neuroendocrinology 6,* 168–174.

LaFree, G. (1982). Male power and female victimization: Toward a theory of interracial rape. *American Journal of Sociology, 88,* 311–328.

LaFree, G. (1995). *Race and crime trends in the United States 1946–1990.* Albany, NY: State University of New York Press.

LaFree, G., & Drass, K. A. (1996). The effect of changes in intraracial income inequality and educational attainment on changes in arrest rates for African Americans and Whites, 1957 to 1990. *American Sociological Review, 61,* 614–634.

Lagerspetz, K. M. (1964). *Studies on the aggressive behavior of mice.* Helsinki: Sulmalainen Tredeakatemia.

Lagerspetz, K. M., & Westman, M. (1980). Moral approval of aggressive acts: A preliminary investigation. *Aggressive Behavior, 6,* 119–130.

Lagerstrom, M., Bremme, K., Eneroth, P., & Magnusson, D. (1989). *Intelligence level and school achievement at age 10 as related to birth weight and gestational age,* No. 687: Stockholm University, Psychology Department.

LaGrange, R. (1993). *Policing American society.* Chicago: Nelson-Hall.

LaGrange, R. L., & Ferraro, K. (1989). Assessing age and gender differences in perceived risk and fear of crime. *Criminology, 27,* 697–719.

LaGrange, R. L., & White, H. R. (1985). Age differences in delinquency: A test of theory. *Criminology, 23,* 19–45.

Lahey, B. B., Appelgate, B., Barkley, R. A., Garfinkel, B., McBurnett, K., Kerdyk, L., Greenhill, L., Hynd, G. W., Frick, P. J., Newcorn, J., Biederman, J., Ollendick, P., Hart, E. L., Perez, D., Waldman, I., & Shaffer, D. (1994). DSM-IV field trials for oppositional defiant disorder and conduct disorder in children and adolescents. *American Journal of Psychiatry, 151,* 1163–1171.

Land, K. C., McCall, P. L., & Cohen, L. E. (1990). Structural covariates of homicide rates: Are there any invariances across time and social space? *American Journal of Sociology, 95,* 922–963.

Landau, S. F., & Fridman, D. (1993). The seasonality of violent crime: The case of robbery and homicide in Israel. *Journal of Research in Crime and Delinquency, 30,* 163–191.

Lander, E. S. (1996). The new genomics: Global views of biology. *Science, 274,* 536–539.

Landsheer, J. A., Hart, H., & Kox, W. (1994). Delinquent values and victim damage: Exploring the limits of neutralization theory. *British Journal of Criminology, 34,* 44–53.

Lane, R. (1980). *Urban homicide in the nineteenth century: Some lessons for the twentieth century.* Beverly Hills, CA: Sage.

Langan, P. A., & Farrington, D. P. (1998). *Crime and justice in the United States and in England and Wales, 1981–96.* Washington, DC: U.S. Department of Justice (NCJ 169284).

Langevin, Ron (1990). Sexual anomalies and the brain. In W. Marshall, D. Laws, and H. Barbaree (Eds.), *Handbook of sexual assault: Issues, theories, and treatment of the offender* (pp. 103–113). New York: Plenum.

Langlois, J. H., Roggman, L. A., Casey, R. J., Ritter, J. M., Rieser-Danner, L. A., & Jenkins, V. Y. (1987). Infant preferences for attractive faces: Rudiments of a stereotype. *Developmental Psychology, 23,* 363–369.

Langone, J. (1984). Heart attack and cholesterol. *Discover, 5,* March, 21–23.

Lanza-Kaduce, L., Radosevich, M., & Krohn, M. D. (1983). Cognitive moral development, neutralizing definitions, and delinquency. In W. S. Laufer & J. M. Day (Eds.), *Personality theory, moral development, and criminal behavior* (pp. 441–465). Lexington, MA: Lexington Books.

Larner, C. (1984). *Witchcraft and religion.* New York: Blockwell.

Laron, Z. (1998). Hypoglycemia due to hormone deficiencies. *Journal of Pediatric Endocrinology & Metabolism, 11,* 117–120.

Larragoite, V. (1994). Rape. In T. Hirschi & M. R. Gottfredson (Eds.), *The generality of deviance* (pp. 159–172). New Brunswick, NJ: Transaction.

Larzelere, R. E., & Patterson, G. R. (1990). Parental management: Mediator of the effect of socioeconomic status of early delinquency. *Criminology, 28,* 301–324.

Lasker, G. W., & Tyzzer, R. N. (1982). *Physical anthropology* (3rd ed.). New York: Holt, Rinehart and Winston.

Laub, J. H. (1983). Urbanism, race, and crime. *Journal of Research in Crime and Delinquency, 20,* 183–198.

Laub, J., & Sampson, R. (1991). The Sutherland-Gleuck debate: On the sociology of criminological knowledge. *American Journal of Sociology, 96,* 1402–1440.

Laub, J., & Sampson, R. (1993). Turning points in the life course: Why change matters in the study of crime. *Criminology, 31,* 301–325.

Launay, G. (1985). Bringing victims and offenders together: A comparison of two models. *Howard Journal, 24,* 200–212.

Law, J. G., Jr. (Faison, L.). (1996). WISC-III and kait results in adolescent delinquent males. *Journal of Clinical Psychology, 52,* 699–703.

Lawrence, J. A. (1979). *The component procedure of moral judgment making. Dissertation Abstracts International, 40,* 896B.

Laws, D., & Marshall, W. (1990). A conditioning theory of the etiology and maintenance of deviant sexual preference and behavior. In W. Marshall, D. Laws, & H. Barbaree (Eds.), *Handbook of sexual assault: Issues, theories, and treatment of the offender* (pp. 209–229). New York: Plenum.

Laye, J. D. (1981). Effects of demand for performance, self-monitoring of arousal, and increased SNS activity on male erectile tissue. *Archives of Sexual Behavior, 10,* 443–464.

Lea, J., & Young, J. (1984). *What is to be done about law and order?* Harmondsworth, England: Penguin.

Leavitt, M. L., Yudofsky, S. C., Maroon, J. C., Riley, E. J., & Bavitz, M. B. (1989). Effect of intraventricular nadolol infusion on shock-induced aggression in 6-hydroxydopamine-treated rats. *Journal of Neuropsychiatry and Clinical Neuroscience, 1,* 167–172.

Lebergott, S. (1976). *Wealth and want.* Princeton, NJ: Princeton University Press.

Le Blanc, M. (1992). Family dynamics, adolescent delinquency, and adult criminality. *Psychiatry, 55,* 336–353.

Leckliter, I. N., Matarazzo, J. D., & Silverstein, A. B. (1986). A literature review of the factor analytic studies of the WAIS-R. *Journal of Clinical Psychology, 42,* 332–342.

Lee, L. C. S. (1976). Malaysia. In D. H. Chang (Ed.), *Criminology: A cross-cultural perspective* (Vol. 2, pp. 657–761). Durham, NC: Carolina Academic Press.

Lee, M. (1983). *The relationship of empathy, role-taking and moral reasoning to dimensions of juvenile delinquency. Dissertation Abstracts International, 37,* 1032B.

Lee, M., & Prentice, N. M. (1988). Interrelations of empathy, cognition, and moral reasoning with dimensions of juvenile delinquency. *Journal of Abnormal Child Psychology, 16,* 127–139.

Lee, Richard (1979). *The !Kung San: Men, women and work in a foraging society.* New York: Cambridge University Press.

Leitner, M., Shapland, J., & Wiles, P. (1993). *Drug usage and drugs prevention: The views and habits of the general public.* London: HMSO (Report prepared for the Home Office Drugs Prevention Initiative).

Lemert, E. M. (1951). *Social pathology.* New York: McGraw-Hill.

Lemert, E. M. (1953). An isolation and closure theory of naive check forgery. *Journal of Criminal Law, Criminology, and Police Science, 44,* 296–307.

Lemert, E. M. (1974). Beyond mead: the societal reaction to deviance. *Social Problems, 21,* 457–468.

Lengermann, P. M. (1974). *Definitions of Sociology.* Columbus, OH: Merrill.

Lenzer, G. E. (Editor). (1997). *Auguste Comte and positivism.* Newark, NJ: Transection.

Leonard, E. (1995). Theoretical criminology and gender. In B. Price & N. Sokoloff (Eds.), *The criminal justice system and women: Offenders, victims, and workers* (pp. 54–70). New York: McGraw-Hill.

Lerner, R. M., & Lerner, J. V. (1977). Effects of age, sex, and physical attractiveness on child-peer relations, academic performance, and elementary school adjustment. *Developmental Psychology, 13,* 585–590.

Lester, D. (1973). *Comparative psychology.* New York: Alfred.

Lester, D. (1995). *Serial killers: The insatiable passion.* Philadelphia: Charles Press.

Lester, D. (1996). Religion and suicide. *Psychological Reports, 78,* 1090.

Lester, D., & Shephard, R. (1998). Variation of suicide and homicide rates by longitude and latitude. *Perceptual and Motor Skills, 87,* 186.

Levenson, M. R., Kiehl, K. A., & Fitzpatrick, C. M. (1995). Assessing psychopathic attributes in a noninstitutionalized population. *Journal of Personality and Social Psychology, 68,* 151–158.

Levi, M., & Jones, S. (1985). Public and police perception of crime seriousness in England and Wales. *British Journal of Criminology, 25,* 234–50.

Levin, Jack & Fox, James (1985). *Mass murder: America's growing menace.* New York: Plenum.

Levinger, L. J. (1940). A note on Jewish prisoners in Ohio. *Jewish Social Studies, 2,* 209–212.

Levy, F., Hay, D. A., McStephen, M., & Wood, C. (1997). Attention-deficit hyperactivity disorder: A category or a continuum? Genetic analysis of a large-scale twin study. *Journal of the American Academy of Child and Adolescent Psychiatry, 36,* 737–744.

Lewin, R. (1988). Linguists search for the mother tongue. *Science, 242,* 1128–1129.

Lewis, C. E., Cloninger, C. R., & Pais, J. (1983). Alcoholism, antisocial personality and drug use in a criminal population. *Alcohol & Alcoholism, 18,* 53–60.

Lewis, D. E. (1986). The general deterrent effect of longer sentences. *British Journal of Criminology, 26,* 47–62.

Lewis, D. O., Pincus, J. H., Lovely, R., Spitzer, E., & Moy, E. (1987). Biopsychosocial characteristics of matched samples of delinquents and nondelinquents. *Journal of the American Academy for Child and Adolescent Psychiatry, 26,* 744–752.

Lewis, R. S., Orsini, D. L., & Satz, P. (1988). Individual differences in the cerebral organization of language using input and output interference measures of lateralization. *Archives of Clinical Neuropsychology, 3,* 111–119.

Leyton, Elliot (1986). *Hunting humans: Inside the minds of mass murderers.* New York: Pocket.

Lezak, M. D. (1988). IQ: R. I. P. *Journal of Clinical and Experimental Neuropsychology, 10,* 351–361.

Lickona, T. (1976). Research on Piaget's theory of moral development. In T. Lickona (Ed.), *Moral development and behavior* (pp. 219–265). New York: Holt, Rinehart and Winston.

Lidz, C. W., Mulvey, E. P., & Gardner, W. (1993). The accuracy of predictions of violence to others. *Journal of the American Medical Association, 269,* 1007–1011.

Lie, N. (1992). Follow-ups of children with attention deficit. *Acta Psychiatrica Scandinavia, 85,* 5–40.

Lieberman, L., & Jackson, F. L. C. (1995). Race and three models of human origin. *American Anthropologist, 97,* 231–242.

Lilly, R., Cullen, F., & Ball, R. (1995). *Criminological theories: Contexts and consequences.* Thousand Oaks, CA: Sage.

Lind, G. (1986). Cultural differences in moral judgment competence? A study of West and East European university students. *Behavior Science Research, 20,* 208–225.

Lindesmith, A., & Levin, Y. (1937). The Lombrosian myth in criminology. *American Journal of Sociology, 42,* 653–571.

Lindholm, B. W., & Touliatos, J. (1981). Mothers' and fathers' perception of their children's psychological adjustment. *Journal of Genetic Psychology, 139,* 245–255.

Lindhout, D., & Omtzigt, J. D. (1992). Pregnancy and the risk of teratogenicity. *Epilepsia, 33 Suppl 4,* 41–48.

Linfield, H. S. (1940). Jewish inmates of the state prisons of the United States. *American Jewish Yearbook, 33,* 203–211.

Link, B. G., Andrews, H., & Cullen, F. T. (1992). The violent and illegal behavior of mental patients reconsidered. *American Sociological Review, 57,* 275–292.

Link, B. G., Andrews, H., Cullen, F. T., & Stueve, A. (1994). Psychiatric symptoms and the violent/illegal behaviour of mental patients compared to community controls. In J. Monahan & H. Steadman (Eds.), *Violence and mental disorder: Developments in risk assessment* (pp. 137–159). Chicago: University of Chicago Press.

Linnoila, M., Virkunnen, M., Scheinin, M., Nuutila, A., Rimon, R., & Goodwin, F. K. (1983). Low cerebrospinal fluid 5-hydroxy-indoleacetic acid concentration differentiates impulsive from nonimpulsive violent behavior. *Life Sciences, 33,* 2609–2614.

Lira, L. R., & Andrade-Palos, P. (1993). Fear of victimization in Mexico. *Journal of Community & Applied Social Psychology, 3,* 41–51.

Littler, D. S. (1996). A discussion of findings on a study of multicultural education. *The criminologist, 21*(5), 1–4.

Liu, X., & Kaplan, H. B. (1996). Gender-related differences in circumstances surrounding initiation and escalation of alcohol and other substance use/abuse. *Deviant Behavior, 17,* 71.

Liune, V. N., Khylchevskaya, R. I., & McEwan, B. S. (1975). Effect of gonadal steroids on activities of monoamine oxidase and choline acetylase in rat brains. *Brain Research 293,* 306.

Livingston, E. (1822/1968). *The complete works of Edward Livingston on criminal jurisprudence.* Montclair, NJ: Patterson Smith.

Lizotte, A. J. (1978). Extra-legal factors in Chicago's criminal courts: Testing the conflict model of criminal justice. *Social Problems, 25,* 564–580.

Loeber, R. (1982). The stability of antisocial and delinquent child behavior: A review. *Child Development, 53,* 1431–1446.

Loeber, R. (1987). The prevalence, correlates and continuity of serious conduct problems in elementary school children. *Criminology, 25,* 615–542.

Loeber, R. (1988). Natural histories of conduct problems, delinquency, and associated substance use: Evidence for developmental progressions. In B. B. Lahey & A. E. Kazdin (Eds.), *Advances in clinical child psychology* (pp. 73–124). New York: Plenum.

Loeber, R. (1990). Development and risk factors of juvenile antisocial behavior and delinquency. *Clinical Psychology Review, 10,* 1–41.

Loeber, R., & Dishion, T. J. (1983). Early predictors of male delinquency: A review. *Psychological Bulletin, 94,* 68–99.

Loeber, R., & Stouthamer-Loeber, M. (1987). Prediction. In H. C. Quay (Ed.), *Handbook of juvenile delinquency* (pp. 325–382). New York: Wiley.

Lofland, J. (1969). *Deviance and identity.* Englewood Cliffs, NJ: Prentice-Hall.

Loftin, C., & Hill, R. H. (1974). Regional subculture and homicide: An examination of the Gastil-Hackney thesis. *American Sociological Review, 39,* 714–724.

Logli, P. A. (1990). Drugs in the womb: The newest battlefield in the war on drugs. *Criminal Justice Ethics, 9,* 23–29.

Lohdi, A. Q., & Tilly, C. (1973). Urbanization, crime and collective violence in 19th-century France. *American Journal of Sociology, 70,* 396–418.

Lombroso, C. (1911). *Crime: Its causes and remedies.* London: Heinemann.

Lombroso-Ferreo, G. (1972). The criminal man according to the classification of Cesare Lombroso. Montclair, NJ: Patterson Smith.

Long, D. (1990). *The anatomy of terrorism.* New York, NY: Free Press.

Longshore, D. (1998). Self-control and criminal opportunity: A prospective test of the general theory of crime. *Social Problems, 45,* 102–113.

Longshore, D., Turner, S., & Stein, J. A. (1996). Self-control in a criminal sample: An examination of construct validity. *Criminology, 34,* 209–228.

Lonsway, K. A., & Fitzgerald, L. F. (1994). Rape myths. *Psychology of Woman Quarterly, 18,* 133–164.

Lopez Alvarez, M. J., Gutierrez Rendedo, T., Hernandez Mejia, R., & Bobes Garcia, J. (1989). Extent and patterns of drug use by students at a Spanish university. *Bulletin of Narcotics, 41,* 117–119.

Loria, A. (1902). *Economic foundations of society.* New York: Scribner's & Sons.

Lotke, E. (1996). Sex offenders: Can treatment work? *Corrections Compendium, 21,* 1–3.

Lott, J. R. J. (1998). *More guns, less crime.* Chicago: University of Chicago Press.

Lubelcova, G. (1996). Social conditions of regional difference in crime in Slovakia. *Sociologia, 28,* 575–586.

Lueger, R. J., & Gill, K. J. (1990). Frontal-lobe cognitive dysfunction in conduct disorder adolescents. *Journal of Clinical Psychology, 46,* 696–706.

Luengo, M. A., Carrillo-de-la-Pena, M. T., Otero, J. M., & Romero, E. (1994). A short-term longitudinal study of impulsivity and antisocial behavior. *Journal of Personality and Social Psychology, 66,* 542–548.

Luke, G., & Cunneen, C. (1995). *Aboriginal over-representation and discretionary decisions in the NSW juvenile justice system.* Sydney: Juvenile Justice Advisory Council of New South Wales.

Lunden, W. A. (1942). *Statistics on crime and criminals.* New York: Stevenson Foster.

Lunden, W. A. (1964). *Statistics on delinquents and delinquency.* Springfield, IL: Charles C. Thomas.

Lundman, R. J. (1984). *Prevention and control of juvenile delinquency.* New York: Oxford University Press.

Lupsha, Peter (1986). Organized crime in the United States. In Robert Kelly (Ed.), *Organized crime: A global perspective* (pp. 34–57). Totawa, NJ: Rowman & Littlefield.

Lupsha, Peter (1987). La Cosa Nostra in drug trafficking. In T. Bynum (Ed.), *Organized crime in America: Concepts and controversies* (pp. 31–41). Monsey, NY: Willow Tree Press.

Luria, A. R. (1966). *Higher cortical functions in man.* New York: Basic Books.

Lyerly, R. R., & Skipper, J. K., Jr. (1981). Differential rates of rural-urban delinquency. *Criminology, 19,* 385–399.

Lykken, D. T. (1957). A study of anxiety in the sociopathic personality. *Journal of Abnormal Social Psychology, 55,* 6–10.

Lykken, D. T. (1982). Fearlessness. *Psychology Today, 16,* September, 20–28.

Lykken, D. T., Tellegen, A., & Iacono, W. G. (1982). EEG spectra in twins: Evidence for a neglected mechanism of genetic determination. *Physiological Psychology, 10,* 60–65.

Lykken, D. T. (1995). *The antisocial personalities.* Hillsdale, NJ: Lawrence Erlbaum.

Lykken, D. T. (1998). *The case for parental licensure.* In T. Millin, E. Simonsen, M. Birket-Smith, & R. D. Davis (Eds.), *Psychopathy: Antisocial, criminal, and violent behavior* (pp. 122–143). New York: Guilford.

Lynam, D., Moffitt, T. E., & Stouthamer-Loeber, M. (1993). Explaining the relation between IQ and delinquency: Class, race, test motivation, school failure, or self control? *Journal of Abnormal Psychology, 102,* 187–196.

Lynch, C. B. (1981). Genetic correlation between two types of nesting in *Mus musculas:* Direct and indirect selection. *Behavior Genetics, 11,* 267–272.

Lynch, James (1987a). A comparison of prison use in England, Canada, West Germany, and the United States: A limited test of the punitiveness hypothesis. *Journal of Criminal Law and Criminology, 79,* 180–217.

Lynch, James (1987b). *A comparison of prison use in four countries.* Washington, DC: Bureau of Justice Statistics.

Lynch, James (1993). A cross-national comparison of the length of custodial sentences for serious crimes. *Justice Quarterly, 10,* 630–660.

Lynch, M. J., & Groves, W. B. (1986). *A primer in radical criminology.* Albany, NY: Harrow & Heston.

Lynch, M. J., Groves, W. B., & Lizotte, A. (1994). The rate of surplus value and crime: A theoretical and empirical examination of Marxian economic theory and criminology. *Crime, Law & Social Change, 21,* 15–48.

Lyons, M. J., True, W. R., Eisen, S. A., Goldberg, J., Meyer, J. M., Faraone, S. V., Eaves, L. J., & Tsuang, M. T. (1995). Differential heritability of adult and juvenile antisocial traits. *Archives of General Psychiatry, 52,* 906–915.

Ma, H. K. (1988). Objective moral judgment in Hong Kong, Mainland China, and England. *Journal of Cross-Cultural Psychology, 19,* 78–95.

Ma, H. K., & Leung, M. C. (1991). Altruistic orientation in children: Construction and validation of the child altruism inventory. *International Journal of Psychology, 26,* 745–759.

MacArthur, R. H., & Wilson, E. O. (1967). *The theory of island biogeography.* Princeton, NJ: Princeton University Press.

Maccoby, E. E., Johnson, J. P., & Church, R. M. (1958). Community integration and the social control of juvenile delinquency. *Journal of Social Issues, 14,* 38–51.

MacDonald, K. (1997). Life history theory and human reproductive behavior: Environmental/contextual influences and heritable variation. *Human Nature, 8,* 327–359.

MacDonald, L. (1976). *The sociology of law and order.* Boulder, CO: Westview.

MacDonnell, M. F., & Ehmer, M. (1969). Some effects of ethanol on aggressive behavior in cats. *Quarterly Journal of Studies on Alcohol, 30,* 312–319.

MacKinnon, C. (1984). Not a moral issue. *Yale Law Policy Review, 2,* 321–345.

MacKinnon, D. F., Jamison, K. R., & DePaulo, J. R. (1997). Genetics of manic depressive illness. *Annual Review of Neuroscience, 20,* 355–373.

MacLean, P. D. (1982). On the origin and progressive evolution of the triune brain. In E. Armstrong & D. Falk (Eds.), *Primate brain evolution* (291–316). New York: Plenum.

MacLean, P. D. (1985a). Brain evolution relating to family, play, and the separation call. *Archives of General Psychiatry, 42,* 405–417.

MacLean, P. D. (1985b). Evolutionary psychiatry and the triune brain. *Psychological Medicine, 15,* 219–221.

MacMillian, J., & Kofoed, L. (1984). Sociobiology and antisocial personality: An alternative perspective. *Journal of Nervous Mental Disease, 172,* 701–706.

Maden, T. (1993). Crime, culture and ethnicity. *International Review of Psychiatry, 5,* 281–289.

Maeching, Charles (1993). The adversarial system should be replaced. In M. Biskup (Ed.), *Criminal justice, opposing viewpoints* (pp. 35–42). San Diego, CA: Greenhaven.

Magnusson, D. (1988). Antisocial behavior of boys and autonomic activity/reactivity. In T. E. Moffitt & S. A. Mednick (Eds.), *Biological contributions to crime causation* (pp. 137–146). Dordrecht, The Netherlands: Martious Nijhoff.

Magnusson, D., Statin, H., & Allen, V. L. (1985). Biological maturation and social development: A longitudinal study of some adjustment processes from mid-adolescence to adulthood. *Journal of Youth and Adolescence, 14,* 267–283.

Magnusson, D., Stattin, H., & Allen, V. (1986). Differential maturation among girls and its relations to social adjustment: A longitudinal perspective. In P. B. Baltes, D. L. Featherman, & R. M. Lerner (Eds.), *Life-span development and behavior* (Vol. 7). Hillsdale, NJ: Lawrence Erlbaum.

Maguin, E., & Loeber, R. (1996). Academic performance and delinquency. *Crime and Justice: A Review, 20,* 145–264.

Maguire, M. (1994). Crime statistics, patterns, and trends: Changing perceptions and their implications. In M.

Maguire, R. Morgan, & R. Reiner (Eds.), *The Oxford handbook of criminology* (pp. 233–291). Oxford, England: Clarendon Press.

Mahoney, A. R. (1974). The effect of labeling upon youths in the juvenile justice system: A review of the evidence. *Law and Society Review, 8,* 582–614.

Mak, A. S. (1993). A self-report delinquency scale for Australian adolescents. *Australian Journal of Psychology, 45,* 75–79.

Mak, A. S. (1994). Parental neglect and overprotection as risk factors in delinquency. *Australian Journal of Psychology, 46,* 107–111.

Malasanos, L., Barkauskas, V., Moss, M., & Stoltenberg-Allen, K. (1986). *Health assessment* (3rd ed.). St. Louis, MO: C. V. Mosby.

Maletzky, B. M. (1973). The episodic dyscontrol syndrome. *Diseases of the Nervous System, 34,* 178–185.

Maletzky, B. M. (1987). *Data generated by an outpatient sexual abuse clinic.* Paper presented at the 3rd Annual Conference of the Association for the Behavioral Treatment of Sexual Abusers, Portland, Oregon.

Maletzky, B. M., & Klotter, J. (1974). Episodic dyscontrol: A controlled replication. *Diseases of the Nervous System, 35,* 175–179.

Malinowski, C. I., & Smith, C. P. (1985). Moral reasoning and moral conduct: An investigation prompted by Kohlberg's theory. *Journal of Personality and Social Psychology, 49,* 1016–1027.

Maller, J. B. (1932). Juvenile delinquency among the Jews in New York. *Social Forces, 10,* 542–549.

Mangweth, B., Pope, H. G., Jr., Ionescu-Pioggia, M., Kinzl, J., & Biebl, W. (1997). Drug use and lifestyle among college students in Austria and the United states. *Substance Use & Misuse, 32,* 461–473.

Mann, C. C. (1994). War of words continues in violence research. *Science, 263,* 1375.

Mann, C. R. (1979). Differential treatment between runaway boys and girls in juvenile court. *Juvenile and Family Court Journal, 30,* 37–48.

Mannuzza, S., Gittelman-Klein, R., Horowitz-Konig, P., & Giampino, T. L. (1989). Hyperactive boys almost grown up, IV: Criminality and its relationship to psychiatric status. *Archives of General Psychiatry, 46,* 1073–1079.

Mannuzza, S., Klein, R. G., & Addalli, K. A. (1991). Young adult mental status of hyperactive boys and their brothers: A prospective follow-up study. *Journal of American Academy of Child & Adolescent Psychiatry, 30,* 743–751.

Mannuzza, S., Klein, R. G., Bessler, A., & Malloy, P. (1993). Adult outcome of hyperactive boys: Educational achievement, occupational rank, and psychiatric status. *Archives of General Psychiatry, 50,* 565–576.

Manolakes, L. A. (1997). Cognitive ability, environmental factors, and crime: Prediction of frequent criminal activity. In B. Devlin, D. P. Resnick, S. E. Fienberg, & K. Roeder (Eds.), *Intelligence, genes and success* (pp. 235–255). New York: Springer-Verlag.

Manzanera, L. R. (1984). Victimization in a Mexican city. In R. Block (Ed.), *Victimization and fear of crime: World perspectives* (pp. 51–56). Washington, DC: U.S. Government Printing Office.

Marcos, A. C., Bahr, S. J., & Johnson, R. E. (1986). Test of a bonding association theory of adolescent drug use. *Social Forces, 65,* 135–161.

Margerison, J. H., St. John-Loe, P., & Binnie, C. D. (1967). Electroencephalography. In P. H. Venables & I. Martin (Eds.), *A manual of psychophysiological methods.* New York: Wiley.

Margolin, G., Gordis, E. B., Oliver, P. H., & Raine, A. (1995). A physiologically based typology of batterers promising but preliminary: Comment on Gottman et al. (1995). *Journal of Family Psychology, 9,* 253–263.

Mariani, M. A., & Barkley, R. A. (1997). Neuropsychological and academic functioning in preschool boys with attention deficit hyperactivity disorder. *Developmental Neuropsychology, 13,* 111–129.

Mark, V. H., & Ervin, F. R. (1970). *Violence and the brain.* New York: Harper & Row.

Mark, V. H., Sweet, W., & Ervin, F. (1975). Deep temporal lobe stimulation and destructive lesions in episodically violent temporal epileptics. In W. S. Fields, & W. H. Sweet (Eds.), *Neutral bases of violence and aggression* (pp. 379–393). St. Louis: Warren H. Green.

Marlow, N., Roberts, L., & Cooke, R. (1993). Outcome at 8 years for children with birthweights of 1250 g or less. *Archives of Disease in Childhood, 68,* 286–290.

Marmot, M. G., Kogevinas, M., & Elston, M. A. (1991). Socioeconomic status and disease. *Health Promotion Research, 37,* 113–146.

Marsh, R. M. (1998). Gender and pay in Taiwan: Men's attitudes in 1963 and 1991. *International Journal of Comparative Sociology, 39,* 115–137.

Marsh, Robert & Walsh, Anthony (1995). Physiological and psychosocial assessment and treatment of sex offenders: A comprehensive victim-oriented program. *Journal of Offender Rehabilitation, 22,* 77–96.

Marshall, G. A. (1968). Racial classifications: Popular and scientific. In M. Mead, T. Dobzhansky, E. Tobach, & A. E. Light (Eds.), *Science and the concept of race* (pp. 149–164). New York: Columbia University Press.

Marshall, I. H., & Webb, V. J. (1994). Self-reported delinquency in a midwestern American city. In J. Junger-Tas, G.-J. Terlouw & M. W. Klein (Eds.), *Delinquent behavior among young people in the Western world: First results of the international self-report delinquency study* (pp. 319–342). Amsterdam: Kugler.

Marshall, W. (1988). The use of sexually explicit stimuli by rapists, child molesters and nonoffenders. *Journal of Sex Research, 25,* 267–288.

Marshall, W., & Barbaree, H. (1990). An integrated theory of the etiology of sexual offending. In Marshall, W., Laws, D., and Barbaree, H. (Eds.), *Handbook of sexual assault: Issues, theories, and treatment of the offender* (pp. 257–275). New York: Plenum.

Marshall, W., Laws, D., and Barbaree, H. (Eds.). (1990) *Handbook of sexual assault: Issues, theories, and treatment of the offender.* New York: Plenum.

Martin, R., Jr., & Conger, R. D. (1980). A comparison of delinquency trends: Japan and the United States. *Criminology, 18,* 53–61.

Martindale, D. (1960). *Nature and types of sociological theory.* Boston: Houghton Mifflin.

Martinez, R., Jr. (1996). Latinos and lethal violence: The impact of poverty and inequality. *Social Problems, 43,* 131–146.

Martinez-Selva, J. M., Gomez-Amor, J., Olmos, E., Navarro, N., & Roman, F. (1987). Sex and menstrual cycle differences in the habituation and spontaneous recovery ot the electrodermal orienting reaction. *Personality and Individual Differences, 8,* 211–217.

Maslow, A. H. (1936). The role of dominance in the social and sexual behavior of infra-human primates: IV. The determination of hierarchy in pairs and in a group. *Journal of Genetic Psychology, 49,* 161–198.

Maslow, A. H. (1940). Dominance-quality and social behavior in infra-human primates. *Journal of Social Psychology, 11,* 313–324.

Mason, D. A., & Frick, P. J. (1994). The heritability of antisocial behavior: A meta-analysis of twin and adoption studies. *Journal of Psychopathology and Behavioral Assessment, 16,* 310–321.

Mason, E. J., & Bramble, W. J. (1989). *Understanding and conducting research, 2nd ed.* New York: McGraw-Hill.

Mason, J. W., Giller, E. L., & Kosten, T. R. (1986). Urinary free cortisol levels in posttraumatic stress disorder patients. *Journal of Nervous and Mental Disorder, 174,* 145–149.

Mason, W. J., Kripke, D. F., Messin, S., & Ancoli-Israll, S. (1986). The application and utilization of an ambulaton record in system for the screening of sleep disorders. *26,* 145–156.

Masters, R. D. (1990). *Law, biology, and the sense of justice: An inquiry. Gruter Institute for Law and Behavioral Research, 3* (Spring), 1–7.

Masters, R. D., & Roberson, C. (1990). *Inside criminology.* Englewood Cliffs, NJ: Prentice-Hall.

Mathias, R. (1999). NIDA. *NIDA (National Institute of Drug Abuse) Notes, 14,* s1–s8.

Matsueda, R. (1982). Testing control theory and differential association: A causal modeling approach. *American Sociological Review, 47,* 489–504.

Matsueda, R. (1988). The current state of differential association theory. *Crime and Delinquency, 34,* 277–306.

Matsueda, R., & Heimer, K. (1987). Race, family structure, and delinquency: A test of differential association and social control theories. *American Sociological Review, 52,* 826–840.

Matthys, W., van Goozen, S. H. M., de Vries, H., Cohen-Kettenis, P. T., & van Engeland, H. (1998). The dominance of behavioural activation over behavioural inhibition in conduct disordered boys with or without attention deficit hyperactivity disorder. *Journal of Psychology and Psychiatry, 39,* 643–651.

Mattson, A. J., & Leuin, H. S. (1990). Frontal lobe dysfunction following closed head injury. *Journal of Nervous and Mental Disease, 178,* 282–291.

Matykiewicz, L., LaGrange, L., Vance, P., Wang, M., & Reyes, E. (1997). Adjudicated adolescent males: Measures of urinary 5-hydroxyindoleacetic acid and reactive hypoglycemia. *Personality and Individual Differences, 22,* 327–332.

Matza, D. (1964). *Delinquency and drift.* New York: Wiley.

Matza, D., & Sykes, F. (1961). Juvenile delinquency and subterranean values. *American Sociological Review, 26,* 712–719.

Mawby, R. I., McCullcoh, J. W., & Batta, I. D. (1979). Crime amongst Asian juveniles in Bradford. *International Journal of the Sociology of Law, 7,* 297–306.

Mayer, J. P., Gensheimer, L. K., Davidson, W. S., II, & Gottschalk, R. (1986). Social learning treatment within juvenile justice: A meta-analysis of impact in the natural environment. In S. J. Apter & A. P. Goldstein (Eds.), *Youth violence: Programs and prospects* (pp. 24–38). New York: Pergamon.

Mayer, S. E., and Jencks, C. (1989). Growing up in poor neighborhoods: How much does it matter? *Science, 243,* 1441–1445.

Mayfield, D. (1976). Alcoholism, alcohol, intoxication and assaultive behavior. *Diseases of the Nervous System, 37,* 288–291.

Mayhew, P., & Elliot, D. (1990). Self-reported offending, victimization, and the British crime survey. *Violence and Victims, 5,* 83–96.

Mazur, A. (1994). A neurohormonal model of social stratification among humans: A microsocial perspective. In L. Ellis (Ed.), *Social stratification and socioeconomic inequality* (Vol. 2): *Reproductive and interpersonal aspects of dominance and status* (pp. 37–46). Westport, CT.: Praeger.

Mazur, A. (1995). Biosocial models of deviant behavior among male army veterans. *Biological Psychology, 41,* 271–293.

Mazur, A., & Michalek, J. (1998). Marriage, divorce, and male testosterone. *Social Forces, 77,* 315–330.

McAlister, A. L., Perry, C., & MacCoby, N. (1979). Adolescent smoking: Quest and prevention. *Pediatrics, 63,* 650–658.

McCabe, B., O'Reilly, C., & Pfeffer, J. (1991). Context, values and moral dilemmas: Comparing the choices of business and law school students. *Journal of Business Ethics, 10,* 951–960.

McCabe, D. (1992). The influence of situational ethics on cheating among college students. *Sociological Inquiry, 62,* 365–374.

McCabe, E. (1989). *Structural elements of contemporary criminal justice in the People's Republic of China.* New York: Praeger.

McCaghy, Charles & Capron, Timothy (1994). *Deviant behavior: Crime, conflict, and interest groups* (3rd. ed.). New York: Macmillan.

McCall, P. L., Land, K. C., & Cohen, L. E. (1992). Violent criminal behavior: Is there a general and continuing influence of the South? *Social Science Research, 21,* 286–310.

McCall, R. B., & Kagan, J. (1970). Individual differences in the infant's distribution of attention to stimulus discrepancy. *Developmental Psychology, 2,* 90–98.

McCarthy, B., & Hagan, J. (1987). Gender delinquency and the great depression: A test of power-control theory. *Canadian Review of Sociology and Anthropology, 224*(2), 153–177.

McCarthy, B. R., & Smith, B. L. (1986). The conceptualization of discrimination in the juvenile justice process: The impact of administrative factors and screening decisions on juvenile court dispositions. *Criminology, 24,* 41–64.

McCarthy, J. D., & Hoge, D. R. (1984). The dynamics of self-esteem and delinquency. *American Journal of Sociology, 90,* 396–410.

McCleary, R., Nienstedt, C., & Erven, J. M. (1982). Uniform crime reports as organizational outcomes: Three-time series experiments. *Social Problems, 29,* 361–372.

McClintock, F. H. (1970). The dark figure. *Collected Studies in Criminological Research* (Council of Europe), *4,* 7–34.

McCord, J. (1978). A thirty-year follow-up of treatment effects. *American Psychologist, 33,* 284–289.

McCord, J. (1981a). Alcoholism and criminality: Confounding and differentiating factors. *Journal of Studies on Alcohol, 42,* 739–748.

McCord, J. (1981b). A longitudinal perspective on patterns of crime. *Criminology, 19,* 211–218.

McCord, J. (1990). Long-term perspectives on parental absence. In L. N. Robins & M. Rutter (Eds.), *Straight and devious pathways from childhood to adulthood* (pp. 116–133). Cambridge, England: Cambridge University Press.

McCord, W., McCord, J., & Zola, I. K. (1959). *Origins of crime.* New York: Columbia University Press.

McCormick, M. C. (1989). Long-term follow up of infants discharged from neonatal intensive care units. *Journal of the American Medical Association, 261,* 1767–1772.

McCormick, M. C., Gortmaker, S. L., & Sobol, A. M. (1990). Very low birth weight children: Behavior problems and school difficulty in a national sample. *Journal of Pediatrics, 117,* 687–693.

McCormick, R. A., & Smith, M. (1995). Aggression and hostility in substance abusers: The relationship to abuse patterns, coping style, and relapse triggers. *Addictive Behaviors, 20,* 555–562.

McDermott, D. (1984). The relationship of parental drug use and parent's attitude concerning adolescent drug use to adolescent drug use. *Adolescence, 19,* 89–97.

McDowall, D., & Loftin, C. (1992). Comparing the UCR and NCS over time. *Criminology, 30,* 125–132.

McEwen, B. S., & Stellar, E. (1993). Stress and the individual: Mechanisms leading to disease. *Archives of Internal Medicine, 153,* 2093–2101.

McFarelane, A. H., Norman, G. R., Streiner, D. L., Roy, R., & Scott, D. J. (1980). A longitudinal study of the influence of the psychological environment on health status: A preliminary report. *Journal of Health and Social Behavior, 21,* 124–133.

McFarland, D. (Ed.). (1981). *The Oxford companion to animal behaviour.* Oxford, England: Oxford University Press.

McGarell, E. F., & Castellano, T. C. (1991). An integrative conflict model of the criminal law process. *Journal of Research in crime and delinquency, 28*(2), 174–196.

McGarrell, E. F., & Flanagan, T. J. (Eds.). (1985). *Sourcebook of criminal justice statistics, 1984.* Washington, DC: U.S. Department of Justice.

McGarvey, B., Gabrielli, W. F., Bentler, P. M., & Mednick, S. A. (1981). Rearing social class, education, and criminality: A multiple indicator model. *Journal of Abnormal Psychology, 90,* 354–364.

McGee, R., Feehan, M., Williams, S., Partridge, F., Silva, P. A., & Kelly, J. (1990). DMS-III disorders in a large sample of adolescents. *Journal of the American Academy of Child Adolescence Psychiatry, 29,* 611–619.

McGrew, W. C. (1979). Evolutionary implications of sex differences in chimpanzees' predation and tool use. In D. A. Hamburg & E. R. McCowen (Eds.), *The great apes* (pp. 440–462). Menlo Park, CA: Benjamin/Cummings.

McGuffin, P., Owen, M. J., O'Donovan, M. C., Thapar, A., & Gottesman, I. I. (1994). *Seminars in Psychiatric Genetics.* London: Gaskell.

McIntosh, M. (1977). Review symposium: Women, crime and criminology. *British Journal of Criminology, 17,* 395.

McIntosh, M. (1978). The state and oppression of women. In A. Kuhn & A. Wolpe (Eds.), *Feminism and materialism: Women and modes of production* (pp. 254–289). London: Routledge & Kegan Paul.

McIntosh, T. K., Davis, P. G., & Barfield, R. J. (1979). Urine marking and sexual behavior in the rat. *Rattos norvegicos, 26,* 161–168.

McKelvey, B. (1977). *American prisons: A history of good intentions.* Montclair, NJ: Patterson Smith.

McKenna, C., Kelleher, M. J., & Corcoran, P. (1997). Suicide, homicide, and crime in Ireland: What are the relationships? *Archives of Suicide Research, 3,* 53–64.

McKissack, I. J. (1975). Early socialization: the baseline in delinquency research. *International Journal of Criminology & Penology, 3,* 43–51.

McLead, J. D., & Shanahan, M. J. (1996). Trajectories of poverty and children's mental health. *Journal of Health and Social Behavior, 37,* 207–220.

McLeer, S. V., & Anwar, R. A. (1989). A study of battered women presenting in an emergency department. *American Journal of Public Health, 79,* 65–66.

McLeod, J., D., Kruttschnitt, C., & Dornfeld, M. (1994). Does parenting explain the effects of structural conditions on children's antisocial behavior? A comparison of blacks and whites. *Social Force, 73,* 575–604.

McMahon, R. C. (1980). Genetic etiology in the hyperactive child syndrome: A critical review. *American Journal Orthopsychiatry, 50,* 145–150.

McMichael, P. (1979). The hen or the egg? Which comes first—antisocial emotional disorders or reading disability? *British Journal of Educational Psychology, 49,* 226–238.

McNeill, P. (1990). Female trouble. *New Statesman & Society, 3* (Jan. 26), 28.

Mealey, L. (1995). The sociobiology of sociopathy: An integrated evolutionary model. *Behavioral and Brain Sciences, 18,* 523–599.

Mechanic, D. (1975). Response factors in illness: The study of illness behavior. In T. Millon (Ed.), *Medical behavioral science* (pp. 354–367). Philadelphia, PA: Sanders.

Mednick, B. R., Baker, R. L., & Carothers, L. E. (1990). Patterns of family instability and crime: The association of timing of the family's disruption with subsequent adolescent and young adult criminality. *Youth and Adolescence, 19,* 201–219.

Mednick, S. A., Gabrielli, W. F., Jr., & Hutchings, B. (1987a). Genetic factors in the etiology of criminal behavior. In S. A. Mednick, T. E. Moffitt, & S. A. Stack (Eds.), *The causes of crime: New biological approaches* (pp. 74–109). New York: Cambridge University Press.

Mednick, S. A., & Hutchings, B. (1978). Genetic and psychophysiological factors in asocial behavior. In R. D. Hare & D. Schalling (Eds.), *Psychopathic behavior: Approaches to research* (pp. 239–253). New York: Wiley.

Mednick, S. A., & Kandel, E. S. (1988). Congenital determinants of violence. *Bulletin of American Academy of Psychiatry & Law, 16,* 101–109.

Mednick, S. A., Parnas, J., & Schulsinger, F. (1987b). The Copenhagen high-risk project 1962–1986. *Schizophrenia Bulletin, 13,* 485–496.

Mednick, S. A., Pollock, V., Volavka, J., & Gabrielli, W. F. J. (1982). Biology and violence. In M. E. Wolfgang & N. A.

Weiner (Eds.), *Criminal violence* (pp. 21–80). Beverly Hills, CA: Sage.

Mednick, B., Reznick, C., Hocevar, D., & Baker, R. (1987c). Long-term effects of parental divorce on young adult male crime. *Youth and Adolescence, 16,* 31–45.

Mednick, S. A., & Volavka, J. (1980). Biology and crime. In N. Morris & M. Tonry (Eds.), *Criminal justice: An annual review of research* (Vol. 2, pp. 85–158). Chicago: University of Chicago Press.

Mehlman, P. T., Higley, J. D., Fernald, B. J., Sallee, F. R., Suomi, S. J., & Linnoila, M. (1997). CSF 5-HIAA, testosterone, and sociosexual behaviors in free-ranging male rhesus macaques in the mating season. *Psychiatry Research, 72,* 89–102.

Meier, R. F., & Short, J. F. (1985). Crime as hazard: Perceptions of risk and seriousness. *Criminology, 23,* 389–399.

Melossi, D., & Pavarini, M. (1981). *The prison and the factory: Origins of the penitentiary system.* Totowa, NJ: Barnes & Noble.

Menard, S. (1988). UCR and NCS: Comparisons over space and time. *Journal of Criminal Justice, 16,* 371–384.

Menard, S. (1992a). Demographic and theoretical variables in the age-period-cohort analysis of illegal behavior. *Journal of Research in Crime and Delinquency, 29,* 178–199.

Menard, S. (1992b). Residual gains, reliability, and the UCR-NCS relationship: A comment on Blumstein, Cohen, and Rosenfeld (1991). *Criminology, 30,* 105–113.

Menard, S. (1995). A developmental test of Mertonian anomie theory. *Journal of Research in Crime and Delinquency, 32,* 136–174.

Menard, S., & Huizinga, D. (1994). Changes in conventional attitudes and delinquent behavior in adolescence. *Youth & Society, 26,* 23–53.

Mendez, M. F., Doss, R. C., & L., T. J. (1993). Interictal violence in epilepsy: Relationship to behavior and seizure variables. *Journal of Nervous and Mental Disease, 181,* 566–569.

Merritt, H. (1973). *A textbook of neurology.* Philadelphia: Lea and Febiger.

Merryman, J. (1985). *The civil law tradition.* Stanford, CA: Stanford University Press.

Merton, R. K. (1938). Social structure and anomie. *American Sociological Review, 3,* 672–82.

Merton, R. K. (1957). *Social theory and social structure.* New York: Free Press.

Merton, R. K. (1968). *Social theory and social structure* (enlarged ed.). New York: Free Press.

Messerschmidt, J. W. (1986). *Capitalism, patriarchy and crime: Toward a socialist feminist criminology.* Lanham, MD: Rowman and Littlefield.

Messerschmidt, J. W. (1988). From Marx to Bonger: Socialist writings on women, gender, and crime. *Sociological Inquiry, 58,* 379–412.

Messner, S. F. (1983). Regional and racial effects on the urban homicide rate: The subculture of violence revisited. *American Journal of Sociology, 88,* 997–1007.

Messner, S. F. (1984). The "dark figure" and composite indexes of crime: Some empirical explorations of alternative data sources. *Journal of Criminal Justice, 12,* 435–444.

Messner, S. F., & Sampson, R. J. (1991). The sex ratio, family disruption, and rates of violent crime: The paradox of demographic structure. *Social Forces, 69,* 696–707.

Metfessel, M., & Lovell, C. (1942). Recent literature on individual correlates of crime. *Psychological Bulletin, 39,* 133–164.

Mezzacappa, E., Tremblay, R. E., Kindlon, D., Saul, J. P., Arseneault, L., Seguin, J., Pihl, R. O., & Earls, F. (1997). Anxiety, antisocial behavior, and heart rate regulation in adolescent males. *Journal of Psychiatry, 38,* 457–469.

Michaels, J. J. (1961). Enuresis in murderous aggressive children and adolescents. *Archives General Psychiatry, 5,* 94–97.

Michalowski, R. J. (1977). Perspective and paradigm. In R. F. Meier (Ed.), *Theory in criminology* (pp. 17–39). Beverly Hills, CA: Sage.

Miczek, K. A., Brykczynski, T., & Grossman, S. P. (1974). Differential effects of lesions in the amygdala, periamygdaloid cortex, and stria terminalis on aggressive behaviors in rats. *Journal of Comparative and Physiological Psychology, 87,* 760–771.

Midanik, L. T. (1988). Validity of self-reported alcohol use: A literature review and assessment. *British Journal of Addiction, 83,* 1019–1029.

Middleton, R., & Putney, S. (1962). Religion, normative standards, and behavior. *Sociometry, 25,* 141–152.

Mieczkowski, T. M. (1990). The accuracy of self-reported drug use: An evaluation and analysis of new data. In R. Weisheit (Ed.), *Drugs, crime, and the criminal justice system* (pp. 275–302). Cincinnati: Anderson.

Mieczkowski, T. M. (1996). The prevalence of drug use in the United States. *Crime and Justice: A Review, 20,* 349–414.

Mieczkowski, T. M., Barzelay, D., Gropper, B., & Wish, E. (1991). Concordance of three measures of cocaine use in an arrestee population: Hair, urine, and self-report. *Journal of Psychoactive Drugs, 23,* 241–249.

Mieczkowski, T. M., Launderss, H. J., Neeewel, R., & Coletti, S. D. (1993, January). Testing hair for illicit drug use. National Institute of Justice—Research in Brief, NCJ 138539.

Miethe, T. D. (1982). Public consensus on crime seriousness. *Criminology, 20,* 515–526.

Milan, M. A. (1987). Token economy programs in closed institutions. In E. K. Morris & C. J. Braukmann (Eds.), *Behavioral approaches to crime and delinquency* (pp. 195–222). New York: Plenum.

Milavsky, J. R., Kessler, R., Stipp, H., & Rubens, W. S. (1982). Television and aggression: Results of a panel study. In D. Pearl, L. Bouthilet, & J. Lazar (Eds.), *Television and behavior: Ten years of scientific progress and implications for the eighties* (Vol. 2, pp. 138–157). Rockville, MD: U.S. Department of Health and Human Services.

Milberger, S., Biederman, J., Faraone, S. V., Chen, L., & Jones, J. (1996). Is maternal smoking during pregnancy a risk factor for attention deficit hyperactivity disorder in children? *American Journal of Psychiatry, 153,* 1138–1142.

Milberger, S., Biederman, J., Faraone, S. V. & Jones, J. (1998). Further evidence of an association between maternal smoking during pregnancy and Attention Deficit Hyperactivity Disorder: Findings from a high-risk sample of siblings. *Journal of Clinical Psychology, 27,* 352–358.

Millar, J. (1991). Changes in income distribution during the Thatcher years. In S. Becker (Ed.), *Windows of opportunity* (pp. 23–38). London, England: CPAG.

Miller, B. A. (1990). The interrelationships between alcohol and drugs and family violence. *National Institute of Drug Abuse Research Monograph Series, 103,* 177–207.

Miller, B. L., Darby, A., Benson, D. F., Cummings, J. L., & Miller, M. H. (1997). Aggressive, socially disruptive and antisocial behaviour associated with fronto-temporal dementia. *British Journal of Psychiatry, 170,* 150–155.

Miller, E. M. (1994a). Paternal provisioning versus mate seeking in human populations. *Personality and Individual Differences, 17,* 227–255.

Miller, E. M. (1994b). Prenatal sex hormone transfer: A reason to study opposite-sex twins. *Personality and Individual Differences, 17,* 511–529.

Miller, K. S., & Knutson, J. F. (1997). Reports of severe physical punishment and exposure to animal cruelty by inmates convicted of felonies and by university students. *Child Abuse and Neglect, 21,* 59–82.

Miller, L. S. (1994a). Preventive interventions for conduct disorders: A review. *Child and Adolescent Psychiatric Clinics of North America, 3,* 405–420.

Miller, L. S. (1994b). Primary prevention of conduct disorder. *Psychiatric Quarterly, 65,* 273–285.

Miller, S. L., & Burack, C. (1993). A critique of Gottfredson and Hirschi's general theory of crime: Selective (in)attention to gender and power positions. *Women and Criminal Justice, 4,* 115–134.

Miller, T. Q. (1994). A test of alternative explanations for the stage-like progression of adolescent substance use in four national samples. *Addictive Behaviors, 19,* 287–293.

Miller, T. Q., & Volk, R. J. (1996). Weekly marijuana use as a risk factor for initial cocaine use: Results from a six-wave national survey. *Journal of Child & Adolescent Substance Abuse, 5,* 55–78.

Millon, T. (1981). *Antisocial personality: The aggressive pattern, in disorders of personality,* DSM III. New York: John Wiley & Sons.

Mills, D. K. (1991). Alcohol and crime on the reservation: A 10-year perspective. *Federal Probation, 55,* 12–15.

Milman, D. H., & Su, W. (1973). Patterns of illicit drug and alcohol use among secondary school students. *Journal of Pediatrics, 83,* 314–320.

Milner, B. (1963). Effects of different brain lesions on card sorting. *Archives of Neurology, 9,* 90–100.

Milner, B. (1964). Some effects of frontal lobectomy in man. In J. M. Warren & K. Akert (Eds.), *The frontal granular cortex and behavior* (pp. 313–334). New York: McGraw-Hill.

Milner, B., & Petrides, M. (1984). Behavioural effects of frontal-lobe lesions in man. *Trends in Neurosciences, 7,* 403–407.

Milovanovic, D. (1989). Critical criminology and the challenge of postmodernism. *Critical Criminology, 1,* 9–10, 17.

Milstein, V. (1988). EEG topography in patients with aggressive violent behavior. In T. E. Moffitt & S. A. Mednick (Eds.), *Biological contributions to crime causation* (pp. 40–54). Dordrecht, North Holland: Martinus Nijhoff.

Minor, W. W. (1981). Techniques of neutralization: A reconceptualization and empirical examination. *Journal of Research in Crime and Delinquency, 18,* 295–318.

Mirkin, A. M., & Coppen, A. (1980). Electrodermal activity in depression: Clinical and biochemical correlates. *British Journal of Psychiatry, 137,* 93–97.

Mischel, W., Shoda, Y., & Roduguez, M. L. (1989). Delay of gratification in children. *Science, 244,* 933–938.

Misra, V. D. (1981). Direction of aggression and reaction to frustration in juvenile delinquents. *Indian Journal of Criminology, 9,* 110–113.

Mitchell, J., Dodder, R. A., & Norris, T. D. (1990). Neutralization and delinquency: A comparison by sex and ethnicity. *Adolescence, 25,* 487–492.

Mitchell, John (1987). Reasonable doubts are where you find them: A response to Professor Subin's position on the criminal lawyer's "different mission." *Georgetown Journal of Legal Ethics, 1,* 339–361.

Mitchell, R. W., & Thompson, N. S. (Eds.). (1986). *Deception: Perspectives on human and nonhuman deceit.* Albany: State University of New York Press.

Mockhiber, Russell (1988). *Corporate crime and violence: Big business power and the abuse of the public trust.* San Francisco: Sierra Club Books.

Modestin, J., Berger, A., & Ammann, R. (1996a). Mental disorder and criminality: Male alcoholism. *Journal of Nervous and Mental Disease, 184,* 393–402.

Modestin, J., Hug, A., & Ammann, R. (1996b). Criminal behavior in males with affective disorders. *Journal of Affective Disorders, 42,* 29–38.

Moffitt, T. E. (1990a). Juvenile delinquency and attention deficit disorder: Boys' developmental trajectories from age 3 to age 15. *Child Development, 61,* 893–910.

Moffitt, T. E. (1990b). The neuropsychology of juvenile delinquency: A critical review. In M. Tonry & N. Morris (Eds.), *In Crime and justice: A review of research* (Vol. 12, p#s). Chicago: University of Chicago Press.

Moffitt, T. E. (1993). Adolescent-limited and life-course-persistent antisocial behavior: A developmental taxonomy. *Psychological Review, 100,* 674–701.

Moffitt, T. E., (1994). Natural histories of delinquency. *Human Development and Criminal Behavior,* 3–61.

Moffitt, T. E. (1996a). Measuring children's antisocial behaviors. *Journal of the American Medical Association, 275,* 403–404.

Moffitt, T. E. (1996b). The neuropsychology of conduct disorder. In P. Cordella & L. Siegel (Eds.), *Readings in contemporary criminological theory* (pp. 85–106). Boston, MA: Northeastern University Press.

Moffitt, T. E. (1997). Adolescence-limited and life-course-persistent offending: A complementary pair of developmental theories. In T. P. Thornberry (Ed.), *Developmental theories of crime and delinquency* (pp. 11–54). New Brunswick, NJ: Transaction.

Moffitt, T. E., Caspi, A., Dickson, N., Silva, P., & Stanton, W. (1996). Childhood-onset versus adolescent-onset antisocial conduct problems in males: Natural history from ages 3 to 18 years. *Development and Psychopathology, 8,* 399–424.

Moffitt, T. E., Caspi, A., Silva, P., & Belsky, J. (1992). Childhood experiences and the onset of menarche: A test of a sociobiological model. *Child Development, 63,* 47–58.

Moffitt, T., & Silva, P. (1988). IQ and delinquency: A test of the differential detection hypothesis. *Journal of Abnormal Psychology, 97,* 330–333.

Moffitt, T. E., & Silva, P. A. (1988). Self-reported delinquency, neuropsychological deficit, and history of attention deficit disorder. *Journal of Abnormal Child Psychology, 16,* 553–569.

Moffitt, T. E., & Silva, P. A. (1988). Self-reported delinquency: Results from an instrument for New Zealand. *Australian and New Zealand Journal of Criminology, 21,* 227–240.

Moffitt, T. E., Silva, P. A., Lynam, D. R., & Henry, B. (1994). Self-reported delinquency at age 18: New Zealand's Dunedin multidisciplinary health and development study. In J. Junger-Tas, G.-J. Terlouw, & M. W. Klein (Eds.), *Delinquent behavior among young people in the Western world: First results of the international self-report delinquency study* (pp. 354–369). Amsterdam: Kugler.

Mogek, Judy (1996). Former Soviet Union-based organized crime: A historical perspective. *Gazette: A Canadian Police Service, 58,* 4–10.

Mogil, J. S., Sternberg, W. F., Kest, B., Marek, M., & Liebeskind, J. C. (1993). Sex differences in the antagonism of swim stress-induced analgesia: Effects of gonadectomy and estrogen replacement. *Pain, 53,* 17–25.

Molotch, H. (1986). Moral alarms. *Science, 233,* 175–176.

Monahan, J. (1981a). *The clinical prediction of violent behavior.* Washington DC: Government Printing Office.

Monahan, J. (1981b). *Predicting violent behavior: An assessment of clinical techniques.* Beverly Hills, CA: Sage.

Monahan, J. (1992). Mental disorder and violent behavior: Perceptions and evidence. *American Psychologist, 47,* 511–521.

Monroe, R. R. (1970). *Episodic behavioral disorder: A psychodynamic and neurological analysis.* Cambridge, MA: Harvard University Press.

Monroe, R. R., Hulfish, B., Balis, G., Lion, J., Rubin, J., McDonald, M., & Barcik, J. D. (1977). Neurologic findings in recidivist aggressors. In C. Shagass, S. Gershon, & A. J. Friedhoff (Eds.), *Psychopathology and Brain Dysfunction* (pp. 241–253). New York: Raven.

Montgomery, Reid (1987). Costly prison riots: United States and Canada. *Journal of Justice Issues, 2,* 53–64.

Moore, D., Richardson, B., & Wuillemin, D. (1984). A comparison of rural and legal ranking of seriousness of crimes in Papua, New Guinea. *Melanesian Law Journal, 12,* 149–158.

Moore, J. W. (1978). *Homeboys: Gangs, drugs, and prison in the barrios of Los Angeles.* Philadelphia: Temple University Press.

Moore, M. H., & Trojanowicz, R. C. (1988). Policing and the fear of crime. *Perspectives on Policing, 3,* June, 1–7.

Moore, S., Laflin, M. T., & Weis, D. L. (1996). The role of cultural norms in the self-esteem and drug use relationship. *Adolescence, 31,* 523–542.

Morell, V. (1993). Evidence found for a possible "aggression gene." *Science, 260,* 1722–1723.

Morgan, R. (1980). Theory and practice: Pornography and rape. In L. Lwederer (Ed.), *Take back the night: Women on pornography* (pp. 134–140). New York: William Morrow.

MORI. (1994). Crime and the police. *British Public Opinion,* April, 7–8.

Morris, A (1987). *Women, crime and criminal justice.* Oxford, England: Basil Blackwell.

Morrison, J. R. (1979). Diagnosis of adult psychiatric patients with childhood hyperactivity. *American Journal of Psychiatry, 136,* 955–958.

Morrison, W. D. (1897). The interpretation of criminal statistics. *Journal of the Royal Statistical Society, 60,* 1–24.

Moyer, K. E. (1974). Sex differences in aggression. In R. C. Friedman, R. M. Richart, & R. L. Van de Wiele (Eds.), *Sex differences in behavior* (pp. 335–372). New York: Wiley.

Moyer, S. (1992). Race, gender, and homicide: Comparisons between Aboriginals and other Canadians. *Canadian Journal of Criminology, 34,* 387–402.

Mucha, R. F., & Pinel, J. P. J. (1979). Increased susceptibility to kindled seizures in rats following a single injection of alcohol. *Journal of Studies on Alcohol, 40,* 258–271.

Mueller, C. W. (1983). Environmental stressors and aggressive behavior. In R. G. Green & E. I. Donnerstein (Eds.), *Aggression: Theoretical and empirical reviews* (Vol. 2). New York: Academic Press.

Mueller, D. P., Edwards, D. W., & Yarvis, R. M. (1977). Stressful life events and psychiatric symptomology: Change or undesirability? *Journal of Health and Social Behavior, 18,* 307–317.

Mukherjee, S. K. (1981). *Crime trends in twentieth-century Australia.* Winchester, MA: Allen and Unwin.

Mulder, R. T., Wells, J. E., Joyce, P. R., & Bushnell, J. A. (1994). Antisocial women. *Journal of Personality Disorders, 8,* 279–287.

Muldoon, M. F., Kaplan, J. R., Manuck, S. B., & Mann, J. J. (1992). Effects of a low-fat diet on brain serotonergic responsivity in cynomolgus monkeys. *Biological Psychiatry, 31,* 739–742.

Mullis, R. L., & Hanson, R. A. (1983). Perspective taking among offender and nonoffender youth. *Adolescence, 18,* 72.

Mulvey, E. P., Arthur, M. W., & Reppucci, N. D. (1993). The prevention and treatment of juvenile delinquency: A review of the research. *Clinical Psychology Review, 13,* 133–167.

Mungas, D. (1983). An empirical analysis of specific syndromes of violent behavior. *Journal of Nervous and Mental Disease, 171,* 354–361.

Murchison, C. (1926). *Criminal intelligence.* Worcester, MA: Clark University.

Murdoch, B. D. (1972). Electroencephalograms, aggression and emotional maturity in psychopathic and non-psychopathic prisoners. *Psychologia Africana, 144,* 59–68.

Murdoch, D., Pihl, R. O., & Ross, D. (1990). Alcohol and crimes of violence: Present issues. *International Journal of Addiction, 25,* 1065–1081.

Murphy, D. L., Wright, C., Buchsbaum, M., Nichols, A., Costa, J. L. & Wyatt, R. J. (1976). Platelet and plasma amine oxidase activity in 680 normals: Sex and age differences and stablility over time. *Biochemistry and Medicine 16,* 254–265.

Murrell, M. E., & Lester, D. (1981). *Introduction to juvenile delinquency.* New York: Macmillan.

Murrin, Mary & D. R. Laws (1990). The influence of pornography on sexual crimes. In Marshall, W., Laws, D., and Barbaree, H. (eds.), *Handbook of Sexual Assault: Issues, Theories, and Treatment of the Offender* (pp. 73–91). New York: Plenum.

Mutzell, S. (1993). Alcoholic parents and their children. *Child: Care, Health and Development, 19,* 327–340.

Myerhoff, H. L., & Myerhoff, B. G. (1964). Field observations of middle class gangs. *Social Forces, 42,* 328–336.

Myers, Margaret (1979). Offended parties and official reactions: Victims and the sentencing of criminal defendants. *Sociological Quarterly, 20,* 529–540.

Myers, T. (1982). Alcohol and violent crime re-examined. *British Journal of Addiction, 77,* 399–413.

Myren, Richard (1986). The developing legal system of China. *Criminal Justice International, 2,* March-April, 9–20.

Nadler, R. D., Wallis, L. C., R.-M., Cooper, R., & Baulieu, E. E. (1987). Hormones and behavior of prepubertal and peripubertal chimpanzees. *Hormones and Behavior, 21,* 118–131.

Naeye, R. L., & Peters, E. C. (1984). Mental development of children whose mothers smoked during pregnancy. *Obstetrics and Gynecology, 64,* 601–607.

Naffine, N., & Gale, F. (1989). Testing the nexus: Crime, gender, and unemployment. *British Journal of Criminology, 29,* 144–156.

Nagel, S., & Weitzman, L. (1971). Women as litigants. *Hastings Law Review,* November, 171–198.

Nagin, D. S., & Land, K. C. (1993). Age, criminal careers, and population heterogeneity: Specification and estimation of a nonparametric, mixed Poisson model. *Criminology, 31,* 327–362.

Nagin, D., & Paternoster, R. (1991). The preventative effects of perceived risk of arrest: Testing an expanded conception of deterrence. *Criminology, 29,* 561–588.

Nagin, D. S., & Paternoster, R. (1994). Personal capital and social control: The deterrence implications of a theory of individual differences in criminal offending. *Criminology, 32,* 581–606.

Najam, N., Tarter, R. E., & Kirisci, L. (1997). Language deficits in children at high risk for drug abuse. *Journal of Child and Adolescent Substance Abuse, 6,* 69–80.

Nakazato, K., & Shimonaka, Y. (1989). The Japanese state-trait anxiety inventory: Age and sex differences. *Perceptual and Motor Skills, 69,* 611–617.

Nathanson, C. A. (1975). Illness and the feminine role. *Social Science Medicine, 9,* 57–62.

Nathanson, C. A. (1978). Sex roles as variables in the interpretation of morbidity data. *International Journal of Epidemiology, 7,* 253.

National Council of Crime and Delinquency. (1975). Jurisdiction over status offenses should be removed from the juvenile court: A policy statement. *Crime and Delinquency, 21,* 97–99.

National Institute on Drug Abuse. (1994). Drug abuse warning network (DAWN): Annual medical examiner data—1992. Ser. 1, no. 12-B. Rockville, MD: U.S. Department of Health and Human Services.

Nauta, W. J. H. (1971). The problem of the frontal lobes: A reinterpretation. *Journal of Psychiatric Research, 8,* 167–187.

Nazroo, J. (1995). Uncovering gender differences in the use of marital violence: The effect of methodology. *Sociology, 29,* 475–494.

Nelson, J. F. (1979). Implications for the ecological study of crime: A research note. In W. H. Parsonage (Ed.), *Perspectives on victimology* (pp. 21–28). Beverly Hills, CA: Sage.

Nelson, J. R., Smith, D. J., & Dodd, J. (1990). The moral reasoning of juvenile delinquents: A meta-analysis. *Journal of Abnormal Child Psychology, 18,* 231–239.

Nelson, N. (1987). "Selling her kiosk": Kikuyu notions of sexuality and sex for sale in Mathare Valley, Kenya. In Caplan, P. (Ed.), *The cultural construction of sexuality* (pp. 217–239). London: Routledge.

Netter, P., & Rammsayer, T. (1991). Reactivity to dopaminergic drugs and aggression related personality traits. *Personality and Individual Differences, 12,* 1009–1017.

Nettler, G. (1978a). *Explaining crime* (2nd ed.). New York: McGraw-Hill.

Nettler, G. (1978b). Social status and self-reported criminality. *Social Forces, 57,* 304–305.

Nettler, G. (1984). *Explaining crime* (3rd ed.). New York: McGraw-Hill.

Newcomb, M. D., & Bentler, P. M. (1986). Drug use, educational aspirations, and work force involvement: The transition from adolescence to young adulthood. *American Journal of Community Psychology, 14,* 303–321.

Newman, G. (1976). *Comparative deviance: Perception and law in sex cultures.* New York: Elsevier.

Newman, J. P., & Kossen, D. S. (1986). Passive avoidance learning in psychopathic and nonpsychopathic offenders. *Journal of Abnormal Psychology, 96,* 252–256.

Newman, J. P., Kosson, D. S., & Patterson, C. M. (1992). Delay of gratification in psychopathic and nonpsychopathic offenders. *Journal of Abnormal Psychology, 101,* 630–636.

Newman, J. P., Patterson, C. M., Howland, E. W., & Nichols, S. L. (1990). Passive avoidance in psychopaths: The effects of reward. *Personality and Individual Differences, 11,* 1101–1114.

Newman, J. P., Patterson, C. M., & Kossen, D. S. (1987). Response perseveration in psychopaths. *Journal of Abnormal Psychology, 96,* 145–148.

Newton, Michael (1992). *Serial slaughter.* Port Washington, WA: Loompanics.

Nicholas, J., Catafau, M. A., & Esturch, R. (1993). Regional cerebral blood flow-SPECT in chronic alcoholism: Relationship to neuropsychological testing. *Journal of Nuclear Medicine, 37,* 1452–1459.

Nield, J. B. (1976). A study of birth order and family constellation among high school and delinquent students. *Dissertation Abstracts International, 37,* 3527-A.

Nielsen, J., & Tsuboi, T. (1970). Correlation between stature, character disorder and criminality. *British Journal of Psychiatry, 116,* 145–150.

Noble, E. P. (1993). The D2 dopamine receptor gene: A review of association studies in alcoholism. *Behavioral Genetics, 23,* 119–129.

Noble, E. P. (1996). Alcoholism and the dopaminergic system: A review. *Addiction Biology, 1,* 333–348.

Nolen-Hoeksema, S. (1987). Sex differences in unipolar depression: Evidence and theory. *Psychology Bulletin, 101,* 259–282.

Norris, Joel (1988). *Serial killers.* New York: Doubleday.

Nowicki, S., & Strickland, B. L. (1973). A locus of control scale for children. *Journal of Consulting and Clinical Psychology, 401,* 148–154.

Nurnberger, J. I., Gerhson, E. S., Jimerson, D. C., Buchsbaum, M. S., Gold, P., Brown, G., & Ebert, M. (1981). Pharmacogenetics of d-amphetamine response in man. In E. S. Gershon, S. Matthysse, X. O. Breakefield, & R. D. Ciaranello (Eds.), *Genetic research strategies for psychobiology and psychiatry* (pp. 257–268). Pacific Grove, CA: Boxwood.

Nutter, D. E., & Kearns, M. E. (1993). Patterns of exposure to sexually explicit material among sex offenders, child molesters, and controls. *Journal of Sex & Marital Therapy, 19*, 77–85.

Nye, I. F. (1958). *Family relationships and delinquent behavior.* New York: Wiley.

Nye, I. F., Short, J., & Olson, V. J. (1958). Socioeconomic status and delinquent behavior. *American Journal of Sociology, 63*, 381–389.

Oakley-Browne, M. A., Joyce, P. R., Wells, J. E., Bushnell, J. A., & Hornblow, A. R. (1989). Christchurch psychiatric epidemiology study, Part II: Six month and other period prevalences of specific psychiatric disorders. *Australian and New Zealand Journal of Psychiatry, 23*, 327–340.

Oaxaca, R. (1973). Male-female wage differentials in urban labor markets. *International Economic Review, 14*, 693–709.

O'Brien, B. S., & Frick, P. J. (1996). Reward dominance: Associations with anxiety, conduct problems, and psychopathy in children. *Journal of Abnormal Child Psychology, 24*, 223–240.

O'Brien, B. S., Frick, P. J., & Lyman, R. D. (1994). Reward dominance among children with disruptive behavior disorders. *Journal of Psychopathology and Behavioral Assessment, 16*, 131–145.

O'Brien, R. M. (1996). Police productivity and crime rates: 1973–1992. *Criminology, 34*, 183–207.

O'Brien, Robert (1987). The interracial nature of violent crimes: A reexamination. *American Journal of Sociology, 92*, 817–835.

Ockenfels, M. C., Porter, L., Smyth, J., Kirschbaum, C., Hellhammer, D. H., & Stone, A. A. (1995). Effects of chronic stress associated with unemployment on salivary cortisol: Overall cortisol levels, diurnal rhythm, and acute stress reactivity. *Psychosomatic Medicine, 57*, 460–467.

O'Connor, A. (1987). Female sex offenders. *British Journal of Psychiatry, 150*, 615–620.

O'Connor, S., Hesselbrock, V., Tasman, A., & DePalma, N. (1987). P3 amplitudes in two distinct tasks are decreased in young men with a history of paternal alcoholism. *Alcohol, 4*, 323–330.

O'Connor, T. G., Neiderhiser, J. M., Reiss, D., Hetherington, E. M., & Plomin, R. (1998). Genetic contributions to continuity, change, and co-occurrence of antisocial and depressive symptoms in adolescence. *Journal of Child Psychology & Psychiatry, 39*, 323–336.

O'Dea, J. P., Wieland, R. G., & Hallberg, M. C. (1979). Effect of dietary weight loss on sex steroid binding sex steroids, and gonadotropins in obese post-menopausal women. *Journal of Laboratory and Clinical Medicine, 93*, 1004–1008.

O'Donnell, J. P., Hawkins, J. D., Catalano, R. F., Abbott, R. D., & Day, L. E. (1995). Preventing school failure, drug use, and delinquency among low-income children: Long-term intervention in elementary schools. *American Journal of Orthopsychiatry, 65*, 87–123.

O'Donnell, J. P., & Van Tuinan, M. (1979a). Behaviour problems of preschool children: Dimensions and congenital correlations. *Journal of Abnormal Child Psychology, 7*, 61–75.

Odum, H. W. (1927). *Man's quest for social guidance.* New York: Henry Holt.

Offord, D. R., Alder, R. J., & Boyle, M. H. (1986). Prevalence and sociodemographic correlates of conduct disorder. *American Journal of Social Psychiatry, 6*, 272–278.

Offord, D. R., Boyle, M. H., Szatmari, P., Rae-Grant, N. I., Links, P. S., Cadman, D. T., Byles, J. A., Crawford, J. W., Blum, H. M., Byrne, C., Thomas, H., & Woodward, C. A. (1987). Ontario child health study: Six-month prevalence of disorder and rates of service utilization. *Archives of General Psychiatry, 44*, 832–836.

Ogburn, W. F., & Nimkoff, M. F. (1958). *Sociology* (3rd ed.). Boston: Houghton Mifflin.

Oi, T. (1990). Patterns of dominance and affiliation in wild pig-tailed macaques (*Macaca nemestrina nemestrina*) in West Sumatra. *International Journal of Primatology, 11*, 339–356.

O'Leary, V. (1982). Editor's comments. *Journal of Research in Crime and Delinquency, 18*, 1–3.

Olds, M. E. (1982). Reinforcing effects of morphine in the nucleus accumbens. *Brain Research, 237*, 429–440.

Olds, D. L., Eckenrode, J., Henderson, C. R., Jr., Kitzman, H., Powers, J., Cole, R., Sidora, K., Morris, P., Pettitt, L. M., & Luckey, D. (1997). Long-term effects of home visitation on maternal life course and child abuse and neglect: Fifteen-year follow-up of a randomized trial. *Journal of the American Medical Association, 278*, 637–643.

Olds, D. L., Henderson, C. R., Cole, R., Eckenrode, J., Kitzman, H., Luckey, D., Pettitt, L., Sidora, K., Morris, P., & Powers, J. (1998). Long-term effects of nurse home visitation on children's criminal and antisocial behavior: 15-year follow-up of a randomized trial. *Journal of the American Medical Association, 280*, 1238–1244.

Olds, D. L., Henderson, C., Tatalbaum, R., & Chamberlin, R. (1988). Improving the life-course development of socially disadvantaged mothers: A randomized trial of nurse home visitation. *American Journal of Public Health, 78*, 1436–1445.

Olds, D. L., Kitzman, H., Cole, R., & Robinson, J. (1987). Theoretical foundations of a program of home visitation for pregnant women and parents of young children. *Journal of Community Psychology, 25*, 9–25.

Olds, J., & Olds, M. E. (1965). Drives, rewards, and the brain. In T. M. Newcombe (Ed.), *New directions in psychology* (pp. 327–410). New York: Holt, Rinehart and Winston.

Olweus, D. (1973). Personality and aggression. In J. K. Cole & D. D. Jensen (Eds.), *1972 Nebraska symposium on motivation.* Lincoln, NE: University of Nebraska Press.

Olweus, D. (1979). Stability of aggressive reaction patterns in males: A review. *Psychological Bulletin, 86*, 852–875.

Olweus, D. (1980). Familial and temperamental determinants of aggressive behavior in adolescent boys: A causal analysis. *Developmental Psychology, 16*, 644–660.

Olweus, D. (1986). Aggression and hormones: Behavioral relationship with testosterone and adrenaline. In D. Olweus, J. Block, & M. Radke-Yarrow (Eds.), *Development of antisocial and prosocial behavior* (pp. 51–72). New York: Academic Press.

Olweus, D. (1987). Testosterone and adrenaline: Aggressive antisocial behavior in normal adolescent males. In S. A. Mednick, T. E. Moffitt, & S. A. Stack (Eds.), *The causes of crime: New biological approaches* (pp. 239–262). Cambridge, England: Cambridge University Press.

Olweus, D., Mattsson, A., Schalling, D., & Low, H. (1980). Testosterone, aggression, physical, and personality dimensions in normal adolescent males. *Psychosomatic Medicine, 42,* 253–269.

Ononye, F., & Morakinyo, O. (1994). Drug abuse, psychopathology and juvenile delinquency in south-western Nigeria. *Journal of Forensic Psychiatry, 5,* 527–537.

Onstad, S., Skre, I., Torgensen, S., & Kringlen, E. (1991). Twin concordance for DSM-III-R schizophrenia. *Acta Psychiatica Scandinavica, 1991,* 395–401.

Oosterlaan, J., & Sergeant, J. A. (1996). Inhibition in ADHD, aggressive, and anxious children: A biologically based model of child psychopathology. *Journal of Abnormal Child Psychology, 24,* 19–36.

Oostra, B. A., & Halley, D. J. J. (1995). Complex behavior of simple repeats: The fragile X syndrome. *Pediatric Research, 38,* 629–637.

Opitz, A., Marschall, M., Degan, R., Koch, D. (1983). General anesthesia in patients with epilepsy and status epilepticus. In A. V. Delgado-Esqueta, C. G. Waserlain, D. M. Treiman, and R. J. Porter (Eds.) *Advances in neurology* (Vol. 34), *Status epilepticus: Mechanisms of brain damage and treatment* (pp. 531–535). New York: Raven.

Opolot, James (1981). *World legal traditions and institutions.* Jonesboro, TN: Pilgrimage.

Opstad, P. K., & Aakvaag, A. (1983). The effect of sleep deprivation on the plasma levels of hormones during prolonged physical strain and calorie deficiency. *European Journal of Applied Physiology, 51,* 97–107.

Oreland, L., Fowler, C. J., & Schalling, D. (1981a). Low platelet monoamine oxidase activity in cigarette smokers. *Life Sciences, 29,* 2511–2513.

Oreland, L., Wiberg, A., & Asberg, M. (1981b). Platelet MAO activity and monoamine metabolites in CSF in depressed and suicidal patients and in healthy controls. *Psychiatric Research, 4,* 21–29.

Oreland, L., Wiberg, A., & Fowler, C. J. (1981c). Monamine oxidase activity in platelets as related to monamine oxidase activity and monaminergic function in the brain. In A. Angrist, M. Burrows, M. Lader, O. Ligjaerde, G. Sedvall, & J. Wheatley (Eds.), *Recent advances in neuropsychopharmacology* (pp. 195–201). New York: Pergamon.

Ortega, S. T., & Myles, J. L. (1987). Race and gender effects on fear of crime: An interactive model with age. *Criminology, 25,* 133–152.

Ortet-Fabregat, G., & Perez, J. (1992). An assessment of the attitudes towards crime among professionals in the criminal justice system. *British Journal of Criminology, 32,* 193–207.

Osborn, S. G., & West, B. J. (1978). The effectiveness of various predictors of criminal careers. *Journal of Adolescence, 1,* 101–117.

Osgood, W. D. (1998). Interdisciplinary integration: Building criminology by stealing from our friends. *Criminologist, 23,* 1–4, 41.

Osgood, D. W., Wilson, J. K., O'Malley, P. M., Bachman, J. G., & Johnston, L. D. (1996). Routine activities and individual deviant behavior. *American Sociological Review, 61,* 635–655.

Osterberg, E. (1992). Criminality, social control, and the early modern state: Evidence and interpretation in Scandinavian historiography. *Social Science History, 16,* 67–98.

Osterberg, E. (1996). Criminality, social control, and the early modern state: Evidence and interpretations in Scandinavian historiography. In E. A. Johnson & E. H. Monkkonen (Eds.), *The civilization of crime: Violence in town and country since the Middle Ages* (pp. 41–62). Urbana, IL: University of Illinois Press.

Ota, T., Toyoshima, R., & Yamauchi, T. (1996). Measurements by biphasic changes of the alpha band amplitude as indicators of arousal level. *International Journal of Psychophysiology, 24,* 25–37.

Oxenstierna, G., Edman, G., Iselius, L., Oreland, L., Ross, S., & Sedvall, G. (1986). Concentrations of monoamine metabloites in the CSF of twins and unrelated subjects. A genetic study. *Journal of Psychiatric Research, 20,* 19–29.

Paetsch, J. J., & Bertrand, L. D. (1997). The relationship between peer, social, and school factors and delinquency among youth. *Journal of School Health, 67,* 27–32.

Pagani, L., Tremblay, R. E., Vitaro, F., Kerr, M., & McDuff, P. (1998a). The impact of family transition on the development of delinquency in adolescent boys: A 9-year longitudinal study. *Journal of Child Psychology and Psychiatry, 39,* 489–499.

Pagani, L., Tremblay, R. E., Vitaro, F., & Parent, S. (1998b). Does preschool help prevent delinquency in boys with a history of perinatal complications? *Criminology, 36,* 245–267.

Pain, R. H. (1995). Elderly women and fear of violent crime: The least likely victims? *British Journal of Criminology, 35,* 584–598.

Palamara, F., Cullen, F., & Gersten, J. (1986). The effects of police and mental health intervention on juvenile deviance: Specifying contingencies in the impact of formal reaction. *Journal of Health and Social Behavior, 27,* 90–105.

Palermo, George (1997). The berserk syndrome: A review of mass murder. *Aggression and Violent Behavior, 2,* 1–8.

Palermo, G. B., Gumz, E. J., & Liska, F. J. (1992a). Mental illness and criminal behavior revisited. *International Journal of Offender Therapy and Comparative Criminology, 36,* 53–61.

Palermo, G. B., Smith, M. B., DiMotto, J., & Christopher, T. P. (1992b). Soaring crime in a midwestern American city: A statistical analysis. *International Journal of Offender Therapy and Comparative Criminology, 36,* 291–305.

Pallone, Nathaniel (1990). *Rehabilitating criminal sexual psychopaths: Legislative mandates, clinical quandries.* New Brunswick, NJ: Transaction.

Palmer, Craig (1994). Twelve reasons why rape is not sexually motivated: A skeptical examination. In R. Francoeur (Ed.), *Taking sides: Clashing views on controversial issues in human sexuality* (pp. 32–59). Guilford, CT: Dushkin.

Palmer, E. J., & Hollon, C. R. (1996). Sociomoral reasoning, perceptions of own parenting and self-reported delinquency. *Personality and Individual Differences, 21,* 175–182.

Palmer, S. (1968). Murder and suicide in forty non-literate societies. In J. P. Gibbs (Ed.), *Suicide* (pp. 246–254). New York: Harper and Row.

Pargament, K. I., & Hahn, J. (1986). God and the just world: Causal and coping attributions to God in health situations. *Journal for the Scientific Study of Religion, 25,* 193–207.

Park, R. E., & Burgess, E. W. (1921). *Introduction to the science of sociology.* Chicago: University of Chicago Press.

Park, R. E., Burgess, E., & McKenzie, R. (1925). *The city.* Chicago: University of Chicago Press.

Parker, K. D., McMorris, B., Smith, E., & Murty, K. S. (1993). Fear of crime and the likelihood of victimization: A bi-ethnic comparison. *Journal of Social Psychology, 133,* 723–732.

Parker, K. D., & Ray, M. C. (1990). Fear of crime: An assessment of related factors. *Sociological Spectrum, 10,* 29–40.

Parmelee, M. (1921). *Criminology.* New York: MacMillan.

Passler, M. A., Isaac, W., & Hynd, G. W. (1985). Neuropsychological development of behavior attributed to frontal lobe functioning in children. *Developmental Neuropsychology, 1,* 349–370.

Paternoster, R., & Brame, R. (1998). The structural similarity of processes generating criminal and analogous behaviors. *Criminology, 36,* 633–670.

Paternoster, R., & Iovanni, L. (1989). The labeling perspective and delinquency: An elaboration of the theory and an assessment of the evidence. *Justice Quarterly, 6,* 359–394.

Paternoster, R., & Mazerolle, P. (1994). General strain theory and delinquency: A replication and extension. *Journal of Research in Crime and Delinquency, 31,* 235–263.

Patterson, E. B. (1991). Poverty, income inequality, and community crime rates. *Criminology, 29,* 755–776.

Patterson, G. R. (1982). *A social learning approach: Vol. 3. coercive family process.* Eugene, OR: Costalia.

Patterson, G. R. (1996). *Some characteristics of a developmental theory for early onset delinquency.* New York, NY: Oxford University Press.

Patterson, G. R. (1997). *Performance models for parenting: A social interactional perspective.* New York, NY: John Wiley & Sons.

Patterson, G. R., & Bank, L. (1989). Some amplifying mechanisms for pathologic processes in family. In M. G. Gunner & E. Thelen (Eds.), *The Minnesota symposium on child psychology* (Vol. 22, pp. 167–209). Hillsdale, NJ: Erlbaum.

Patterson, G. R., DeBaryshe, B. D., & Ramsey, E. (1989). A developmental perspective on antisocial behavior. *American Psychologist, 44,* 329–355.

Patterson, G. R., Forgatch, M. S., Yoerger, K. L., & Stoolmiller, M. (1998). Variables that initiate and maintain an early-onset trajectory for juvenile offending. *Development and Psychopathology, 10,* 531–547.

Patterson, G. R., & Moore, D. R. (1979). Interactive patterns as units of behavior. In M. E. Lamb, S. J. Suomi, & G. R. Stephenson (Eds.), *Social interaction analysis: Methodological issues* (pp. 77–96). Madison, WI: University of Wisconsin Press.

Patterson, G. R., & Reid, J. B. (1970). Reciprocity and coercion: Two facets of social systems. In C. Neuringer & J. L. Michael (Eds.), *Behavior modification in clinical psychology.* New York: Appleton-Century-Crofts.

Patterson, G. R., & Reid, J. B. (1984). Social interactional processes within the family: The study of moment-by-moment family transactions in which human social development is embedded. *Journal of Applied Developmental Psychology, 5,* 237–262.

Patterson, G. R., Reid, J. B., & Dishion, T. J. (1992). *Antisocial boys: A social interactional approach.* Eugene, OR: Castalia.

Patterson, G. R., & Yoerger, K. (1993). Developmental models for delinquent behavior. In S. Hodgins (Ed.), *Crime and mental disorder* (pp. 140–172). Newbury Park, CA: Sage.

Patterson, G. R., & Yoerger, K. (1997). A developmental model for late-onset delinquency. In D. W. Osgood (Ed.), *Motivation and delinquency* (pp. 119–177). Lincoln, NE: University of Nebraska Press.

Paulsen, K., & Johnson, M. (1980). Impulsivity: A multidimensional concept with developmental aspects. *Journal of Abnormal Child Psychology, 8,* 269–277.

Pazzaglia, P., & Frank-Pazzaglia, L. (1976). Record in grade school of pupils with epilepsy: An epidemiological study. *Epilepsia, 17,* 361–366.

Pearson, J. L., Lalongo, N. S., Hunter, A. G., & Kellam, S. G. (1994). Family structure and aggressive behavior in a population of urban elementary school children. *Journal of the American Academy of Child and Adolescent Psychiatry, 33,* 540–548.

Peck, H. B., Harrower, M., Hariri, C., Beck, M. B., Maryjohn, J. B., & Roman, M. (1955). A new pattern for mental health services in a children's court: Round table 1954. *American Journal of Orthopsychiatry, 25,* 1–50.

Pedersen, N. L., Oreland, L., Reynolds, C. H., & McCleam, G. E. (1993). Importance of genetic effects for monoamine oxidase activity in thrombocytes in twins reared apart and twins reared together. *Psychiatry Research, 46,* 239–251.

Peeples, F., & Loeber, R. (1994). Do individual factors and neighborhood context explain ethnic differences in juvenile delinquency? *Journal of Quantitative Criminology, 10,* 141–157.

Pelfrey, W. V. (1979). Mainstream criminology: More new than old. *Criminology, 17,* 323–329.

Pelfrey, W. V. (1980). The new criminology: Acceptance within academe. In J. A. Inciardi (Ed.), *Radical criminology: The coming crises* (pp. 233–244). Beverly Hills, CA: Sage.

Penner, L. A., & Spielberger, C. D. (1988). Assessment of sociopathic tendencies. In C. D. Spielberger & J. N. Butcher (Eds.), *Advances in personality assessment* (pp. 1–22). Hillsdale, NJ: Erlbaum.

Pennington, B. F., Groisser, D., & Welsh, M. (1993). Contrasting cognitive deficits in attention deficit hyperactivity disorder versus reading disability. *Developmental Psychology, 29,* 511–523.

Pennington, B. F., & Ozonoff, S. (1996). Executive functions and developmental psychopathology. *Journal of Child Psychology and Psychiatry, 37,* 51–87.

Pentz, M. A., Dwyer, J. H., MacKinnon, D. P., Flay, B. R., Hansen, W. B., Wang, E. Y. I., & Johnson, C. A. (1989). A multi-community trial for primary prevention of adolescent drug abuse: Effects on drug use prevalence. *Journal of the American Medical Association, 261,* 3259–3266.

Pepinsky, H. E. (1983). Book review. *Contemporary Sociology, 12,* 56–57.

Perelle, I. B., & Ehrman, L. (1994). An international study of human handedness: The data. *Behavior Genetics, 24,* 217–227.

Perry, S. E., Summar, M. L., Phillips, J. A., & Roberson, D. (1991). Linkage analysis of the human dopamine B-hydroxylase gene. *Genomics, 10,* 493–495.

Petee, Thomas, Padgett, Kathy, & York, Thomas (1997). Debunking the stereotypes: An examination of mass murder in public places. *Homicide Studies,* Vol. 317–337.

Petersilia, J. (1980). Criminal career research: A review of recent evidence. In N. Morris & M. Tonry (Eds.), *Crime and research* (Vol. 2, pp. 321–379). Chicago: University of Chicago Press.

Petersilia, J. (1985). Racial disparities in the criminal justice system: A summary. *Crime and Delinquency, 31,* 15–34.

Peterson, J. B., Finn, P. R., & Pihl, R. O. (1992). Cognitive dysfunction and the inherited predisposition to alcoholism. *Journal of Studies on Alcohol, 53,* 154–160.

Peterson, R. D., & Hagan, J. (1984). Changing conceptions of race: Toward an account of anomalous findings of sentencing research. *American Sociological Review, 49,* 56–70.

Peterson, V. (1983). *The mob: 2000 years of organized crime in New York City.* Ottawa, IL: Green Hills.

Pettiway, L. E. (1985). The internal structure of the ghetto and the criminal commute. *Journal of Black Studies, 16,* 189–210.

Pfeffer, K., Cole, B., & Dada, K. (1996). British and Nigerian adolescents' lay theories of youth crime. *Psychology, Crime & Law, 3,* 21–35.

Pfeiffer, J. E. (1977). *The emergence of society: A prehistory of the establishment.* New York: McGraw-Hill.

Pharoah, P. O. D., Stevenson, C. J., Cooke, R. W. I., & Stevenson, R. C. (1994). Clinical and subclinical deficits at 8 years in a geographically defined cohort of low birthweight infants. *Archives of Disease in Childhood, 70,* 264–270.

Phillips, D. (1985). Defensive attributions of responsibility in juridic decisions. *Applied Social Psychology, 15,* 483–501.

Phillips, J. A. (1997). Variation in African-American homicide rates: An assessment of potential explanations. *Criminology, 35,* 527–559.

Piaget, J. (1932/1965). *The moral judgment of the child.* New York: Free Press. (republished in 1965).

Piaget, J. (1978). Development and learning. In J. K. Gardner (Ed.), *Readings in developmental psychology* (pp. 228–237). Boston: Little, Brown.

Piaget, J., & Inhelder, B. (1969). *The psychology of the child.* New York: Harper & Row.

Piaka, E. R. (1970). On r- and K-selection. *American Naturalist, 104,* 592–597.

Pihl, R. O., & Bruce, K. R. (1995). Cognitive impairment in children of alcoholics. *Alcohol, Health & Research World, 19,* 142–147.

Pihl, R. O., Peterson, J. B., & Finn, P. R. (1990). Inherited predisposition to alcoholism: Characteristics of sons of male alcoholics. *Journal of Abnormal Psychology, 99,* 291–301.

Piletz, J. E., Segraves, K. B., Feng, Y. Z., Maguire, E., Dunger, B., & Halaris, A. (1998). Plasma MHPG response to yohimbine treatment in women with hypoactive sexual desire. *24, 1,* 43–54.

Piliavin, I., Thornton, C., Gartner, R., & Matsueda, R. L. (1986). Crime, deterrence, and rational choice. *American Sociological Review, 51,* 101–119.

Pilke, A., Partinen, M., & Kovanen, J. (1984). Status epilepticus and alcohol abuse: An analysis of 82 status epilepticus admissions. *Acta Neurologica Scandinavica, 70,* 443–450.

Pine, D. S., Shaffer, D., Schonfeld, I. S., & Davies, M. (1997). Minor physical anomalies: Modifiers of environmental risks for psychiatric impairment? *American Academy of Child and Adolescent Psychiatry, 36,* 395–403.

Pine, D. S., Wasserman, G., Coplan, J., Staghezza-Jaramillo, B., Davies, M., Fried, J. E., Greenhill, L., & Shaffer, D. (1996). Cardiac profile and disruptive behavior in boys at risk for delinquency. *Psychosomatic Medicine, 58,* 342–353.

Pine, M. (1983). The human difference. *Psychology Today, 17,* September, 62–68.

Pinel, J. P., Treit, D., & Rovner, L. I. (1977). Temporal lobe aggression in rats. *Science, 197,* 1088–1089.

Piness, G., Miller, H., & Sullivan, E. B. (1937). The intelligence rating of the allergic child. *Journal of Allergy, 8,* 168–174.

Pirozzolo, F. J., Dunn, K., Zetusky, W. (1983). Physiological approaches to subtypes of developmental reading disability. *Topics in Learning & Learning Disabilities,* April, 40–41.

Plant, J. T. (1937). *Personality and the cultural pattern.* New York: Commonwealth Fund.

Plaznik, A., Kostowski, W., & Archer, T. (1989). Serotonin and depression: Old problems and new data. *Progress in Neuro-Psychopharmacology and Biochemical Psychiatry, 13,* 623–633.

Pliszka, S. R., Maas, J. W., Javors, M. A., Rogness, G. A., & Baker, J. (1994). Urinary catecholamines in attention-deficit hyperactivity disorder with and without comorbid anxiety. *Journal of the American Academy of Child and Adolescent Psychiatry, 33,* 1165–1173.

Pliszka, S. R., McCracken, J. T., & Maas, J. W. (1996). Catecholamines in attention-deficit hyperactivity disorder: Current perspectives. *Journal of the American Academy for Child and Adolescent Psychiatry, 35,* 264–272.

Pliszka, S. R., Rogeness, G. A., Renner, P., Sherman, J., & Broussard, T. (1988). Plasma neurochemistry in juvenile offenders. *Journal of the American Academy of Child and Adolescent Psychiatry, 27,* 588–594.

Ploeger, M. (1997). Youth employment and delinquency: Reconsidering a problematic relationship. *Criminology, 35,* 659–675.

Plomin, R., & Neiderhiser, J. M. (1992). Quantitative genetics, molecular genetics, and intelligence. *Intelligence, 15,* 369–387.

Plomin, R., Willerman, L., & Loehlin, J. C. (1976). Resemblance in appearance and the equal environments assumption in twin studies of personality traits. *Behavior Genetics, 6,* 43–52.

Pokorny, A. D. (1965). A comparison of homicides in two cities. *Journal of Criminal Law, Criminology, and Police Science. 56,* 479–487.

Polakowski, M. (1994). Linking self and social control with deviance: Illuminating the structure underlying a general theory of crime and its relation to deviant activity. *Journal of Quantitative Criminology, 10,* 41–78.

Poland, J. M. (1978). Subculture of violence: Youth offender value systems. *Criminal Justice and Behavior, 5,* 159–164.

Polednak, A. P. (1989). *Racial and ethnic differences in diseases.* New York: Oxford University Press.

Polk, K. (1969). Class, strain and rebellion among adolescents. *Social Problems, 17,* 214–224.

Pollack, O. (1950). *The criminality of women.* Philadelphia: University of Pennsylvania Press.

Pontius, A. A. (1974). Bais for a neurological test of frontal lobe system functioning up to adolescence-A form analysis of action expression in narratives. *Adolescence, 9,* 221–232.

Pope, C. E. (1979). Race and crime revisited. *Crime and Delinquency, 25,* 347–357.

Pope, C. E., & Feyerherm, W. (1992). *Minorities in the juvenile justice system.* Rockville, MD: U.S. Department of Justice, Office of Juvenile Justice and Delinquency Prevention, Juvenile Justice Clearing House.

Pope, C. E., & McNeely, R. L. (1981). An overview. In R. L. McNeely & C. E. Pope (Eds.), *Race, crime, and criminal justice* (pp. 9–27). Beverly Hills, CA: Sage.

Popenoe, David (1993). American family decline, 1960–1990: A review and appraisal. *Journal of Marriage and the Family, 55,* 527–542.

Porterfield, A. (1946). *Youth in trouble.* Fort Worth, TX: Leo Potishman Foundation.

Potegal, M., Blau, A. D., Black, M., & Glusman, M. (1980). Effects of castration of male Golden Hamsters on their aggression toward a restrained target. *Behavioral and Neural Biology, 29,* 315–330.

Potvin, R. H., & Lee, C. (1980). Multistage path models of adolescent alcohol and drug use. *Journal of Studies on Alcohol, 41,* 531–542.

Powell, Paul (1996). Man who admits killing 9 women baffles experts. *Idaho Statesman,* December 18, p. 15a.

Power, K. G., Dyson, G. P., & Wozniak, E. (1997). Bullying among Scottish young offenders: Inmates' self-reported attitudes and behaviour. *Community & Applied Social Psychology, 7,* 209–218.

Poznaniak, W. (1980). Attitudes of criminals and non-criminals toward moral norms and moral rigorism. *Polish Psychological Bulletin, 11,* 87–97.

Pratt, M. W., Golding, G., Hunter, W., & Sampson, R. (1988). Sex differences in adult moral orientations. *Journal of Personality, 56,* 373–391.

Prendergast, M. L. (1994). Substance use and abuse among college students: A review of recent literature. *Journal of American College Health, 43,* 99–113.

Prentice, N. M., & Kelly, F. J. (1973). Intelligence and delinquency: A reconsideration. *Journal of Social Psychology, 60,* 327–337.

Prentky, R. A., & Knight, R. A. (1986). Impulsivity in the lifestyle and criminal behavior of sexual offenders. *Criminal Justice and Behavior, 13,* 141–164.

President's Commission on Organized Crime (PCOC) (1986). *The impact: Organized crime today.* Washington, DC: U.S. Government Printing Office.

Press, O. (1981). The plague of violent crime. *Newsweek,* March 23, 46–54.

Previc, F. H. (1996). Nonright-handedness, central nervous system and related pathology, and its lateralization: A reformulation and synthesis. *Developmental Neuropsychology, 12,* 443–515.

Price, B. J. (1984). Competition, productive intensification, and ranked society: Speculations from evolutionary theory. In R. B. Ferguson (Ed.), *Warfare, culture, and environment* (pp. 209–240). Orlando, FL: Academic Press.

Price, W. H., & Whatmore, P. B. (1967). Behavior disorders and patterns of crime among XYY males identified at a maximum security hospital. *British Medical Journal, 1,* 533–537.

Prince, M., Thompsen, V., McLaughlin, T. F. (1988). Hyperkinesis and Feingold's K-P Diet. *Corrective and Social Psychiatry and Journal of Behavior Technology Methods and Therapy, 34,* 13–17.

Prinz, R. J., Roberts, W. A., & Hantman, E. (1980). Dietary correlates of hyperactive behavior in children. *Journal of Consulting and Clinical Psychology, 48,* 760–769.

Pronovost, L., & LeBlanc, M. (1980). Transition statutaire et delinquance. *Canadian Journal of Criminology, 22,* 288–297.

Pucilowski, O., & Kostowski, W. (1983). Aggressive behaviour and the central serotonergic systems. *Behavioural Brain Research, 9,* 33–48.

Puffer, J. A. (1912). *The boy and his gang.* Boston: Houghton Mifflin.

Putins, A. L. (1997). Victim awareness programs for delinquent youths: Effects on moral reasoning maturity. *Adolescence, 32,* 709–714.

Quay, H. C. (1965). Psychopathic personality as pathological sensation-seeking. *American Journal of Psychiatry, 122,* 180–183.

Quay, H. C. (1979). *Classification* (2nd Ed.). New York: Wiley.

Quay, H. C. (1986). Conduct disorders. In H. C. Quay & J. S. Werry (Eds.), *Psychopathological disorders of childhood* (pp. 35–46). New York: Wiley.

Quay, H. C. (1987a). Intelligence. In H. C. Quay (Ed.), *Handbook of juvenile delinquency* (pp. 106–117). New York: Wiley.

Quay, H. C. (1987b). Patterns of delinquent behavior. In H. C. Quay (Ed.), *Handbook of juvenile delinquency* (pp. 118–138). New York: Wiley.

Quay, H. C. (1988). The behavioral reward and inhibition system in childhood behavior disorders. In L. M. Bloomingdale (Ed.), *Attention deficit disorder* (Vol. 3, pp. 176–186). Oxford, England: Pergamon.

Quay, H. C. (1993). The psychobiology of undersocialized aggressive conduct disorder: A theoretical perspective. *Development and Psychopathology, 5,* 165–180.

Queipo, D., Alvarez, F. J., & Velasco, A. (1988). Drug consumption among university students in Spain. *British Journal of Addiction, 83,* 91–98.

Quetelet, A. (1831). *Research on the propensity for crime at different ages.* Cincinnati, OH: Anderson.

Quetelet, A. (1842/1972) Treatise on man. In S. Sylvester (Ed.), *The heritage of modern criminology* (pp. 27–46). Cambridge, MA: Schenkman.

Quicker, J. C. (1974). The effect of goal discrepance on delinquency. *Social Problems, 22,* 76–86.

Quinney, R. (1970). *The social reality of crime.* Boston: Little, Brown.

Quinney, R. (1974). *Critique of legal order: Crime control in capitalist society.* Boston: Little, Brown.

Quinney, R. (1975). Crime control in capitalist society: A critical philosophy of legal order. In I. Taylor, P. Walton, & J. Young (Eds.), *Critical criminology* (pp. 181–202). Boston: Routledge & Kegan Paul.

Quinney, R. (1977). *Class, state, and crime.* New York: David Mckay.

Quinney, R. (1989). The theory and practice of peacemaking in the development of radical criminology. *Critical Criminologist, 1.*

Quinney, R. (1991). *The way of peace: On crime, suffering and service.* Bloomington, IN: Indiana University Press.

Quinton, D., Pickles, A., Maughan, B., & Rutter, M. (1993). Partners, peers and pathways: Assortative pairing and continuities in conduct disorder. *Development and Psychopathology, 5,* 763–783.

Rada, R. I. (1975). Alcoholism and forcible rape. *American Journal of Psychiatry, 132,* 444–446.

Rafter, N. H., & Natalizia, E. M. (1981). Marxist feminism: Implications for criminal justice. *Crime and Delinquency, 27,* 81.

Rahe, R. H., Meyer, M., Smith, M., Kiaser, G., & Holms, T. H. (1967). Social stress and illness onset. *Journal of Psychosomatic Research, 8,* 35–44.

Rahkonen, O., & Lahelma, E. (1992). Gender, social class and illness among young people. *Social Science and Medicine, 34,* 649–656.

Raine, A. (1988). Antisocial behavior and social psychophysiology. In H. L. Wagner (Ed.), *Social psychophysiology and emotion: Theory and clinical applications* (pp. 231–250). New York: Wiley.

Raine, A. (1989). Evoked potentials and psychopathy. *International Journal of Psychophysiology, 8,* 1–16.

Raine, A. (1993). *The psychopathology of crime: Criminal behavior as a clinical disorder.* San Diego, CA: Academic Press.

Raine, A. (1996). Autonomic nervous system activity and violence. In D. M. Stoff & R. B. Cairns (Eds.), *Neurobiological approaches to clinical aggression research.* Mahwah, NJ:

Raine, A., Brennan, P., & Mednick, S. A. (1994). Birth complications combined with early maternal rejection at age 1 year predispose to violent crime at age 18 years. *Archives of General Psychiatry, 51,* 984–988.

Raine, A., & Jones, F. (1987). Attention, autonomic arousal, and personality in behaviorally disordered children. *Journal of Abnormal Child Psychology, 15,* 583–599.

Raine, A., O'Brien, M., Smiley, N., Scerbo, A. S., & Chan, C. J. (1990). Reduced lateralization in verbal dichotic listening in adolescent psychopaths. *Journal of Abnormal Psychology, 99,* 272–277.

Raine, A., Venables, P. H., & Williams, M. (1990a). Autonomic orienting responses in 15-year-old male subjects and criminal behavior at age 24. *American Journal of Psychiatry, 147,* 933–937.

Raine, A., Venables, P. H., & Williams, M. (1990b). Relationships between central and autonomic measures of arousal at age 15 years and criminality at age 25 years. *Archives of General Psychiatry, 47,* 1003–1007.

Ramsey, S. E., & Finn, P. R. (1997). P300 from men with a family history of alcoholism under different incentive conditions. *Journal of Studies on Alcohol, 58,* 606–616.

Rankin, J. H., & Kern, R. (1994). Parental attachments and delinquency. *Criminology, 32,* 495–513.

Rantakallio, P. (1983). A follow-up study up to the age of 14 of children whose mothers smoked during pregnancy. *Acta Paediatrica Scandinavica, 72,* 747–753.

Rantakallio, P., Laara, E., Isohanni, M., & Moilanen, I. (1992). Maternal smoking during pregnancy and delinquency of the offspring: An association without causation? *International Journal of Epidemiology, 21,* 1106–1113.

Rantakallio, P., Myhrman, A., & Koiranen, M. (1995). Juvenile offenders, with special reference to sex differences. *Social Psychiatry Psychiatric Epidemiology, 30,* 113–120.

Ratcliffe, S. G., Masera, N., Pan, H., & McKie, M. (1994). Head circumference and IQ of children with sex chromosome abnormalities. *Developmental Medicine and Child Neurology, 36,* 533–544.

Ray, A., Alkondon, M., & Sen, P. (1987). Involvement of brain transmitters in the modulation of shock-induced aggression in rats by propranolol and related drugs. *Pharmacological and Biochemical Behavior, 26,* 229–234.

Ray, M. C., & Downs, W. R. (1986). An empirical test of labeling theory using longitudinal data. *Journal of Research in Crime and Delinquency, 23,* 169–194.

Redmond, D. E., Baulu, J., Murphy, D. L., Loriaux, D. L., Zeigler, M., & Lake, C. R. (1976). The effects of testosterone on plasma and platelet monoamine oxidase (MAO) and plasma dopamine-beta-hydroxylase (DBH) activities in the male rhesus monkey. *Psychosomatic Medicine, 38,* 315–326.

Redner, R., Snellman, L., & Davidson, W. S. (1983). A review of behavioral methods in the treatment of delinquency. In R. J. Morris & T. Kratochwill (Eds.), *Practice of therapy with children: A textbook of methods.* New York: Pergamon.

Reed, D., & Weinberg, M. S. (1984). Premarital coitus: Developing and established sexual scripts. *Social Psychology Quarterly, 47,* 129–138.

Reed, J. (1996). Psychopathy—A clinical and legal dilemma. *British Journal of Psychiatry, 168,* 4–9.

Reed, J. S. (1972). *The enduring South: Subcultural persistence in mass society.* Lexington, MA: Lexington Books.

Reed, M. D., & Rountree, P. W. (1997). Peer pressure and adolescent substance use. *Journal of Quantitative Criminology, 13,* 143–180.

Reed, R. (1988). Education and achievement of young black males. In J. T. Gibbs (Ed.), *Young, black, and male in America: An endangered species* (pp. 37–96). Dover, MA: Auburn House.

Regan, D. O., Ehrlich, S. M., & Finnegan, L. P. (1987). Infants of drug addicts: At risk for child abuse, neglect, and placement in foster care. *Neurotoxicology and Teratology, 9,* 315–319.

Reich, Walter (1990). Understanding terrorist behavior: The limits and opportunities of psychological inquiry. In W. Reich (Ed.), *Origins of terrorism: Psychologies, ideologies, theologies, states of mind* (pp. 261–279). New York: Cambridge University Press.

Reichel, P. (1994). *Comparative criminal justice systems: A topical approach.* Upper Saddle River, NY: Prentice Hall.

Reicher, S., & Emler, N. (1985). Delinquent behavior and attitudes to formal authority. *British Journal of Social Psychology, 24,* 199–203.

Reiman, J. (1995). *The rich get richer and the poor get prison.* Boston, MA: Allyn & Bacon.

Reiman, J. (1998). *The rich get richer and the poor get prison* (5th ed.). Boston: Allyn and Bacon.

Reiss, A. J. (1951). Delinquency and the failure of personal and social controls. *American Sociological Review, 16,* 196–207.

Reiss, A. J., Jr. (1986). Why are communities important in understanding crime? In A. J. Reiss, Jr. & M. Tonry (Eds.), *Communities and crime* (pp. 15–33). Chicago: University of Chicago Press.

Reiss, A. J., Jr., & Roth, J. A. (1993). *Understanding and preventing violence.* Washington, DC: National Academy Press.

Reiss, A. L., Abrams, M. T., Singer, H. S., Ross, J. L., & Benckla, M. B. (1996). Brain development, gender and IQ in children: A volumetric imaging study. *Brain, 119,* 1763–1774.

Relethford, J. (1990). *The human species: An introduction to biological anthropology.* Mountain View, CA: Mayfield.

Remes, K., Kuoppasalmi, K., & Adlercreutz, H. (1985). Effect of physical exercise and sleep deprivation on plasma androgen levels. *International Journal of Sports Medicine, 6,* 131–135.

Ressler, Robert, Burgess, Ann, & Douglas, John (1988). *Sexual homicide: Patterns and motives.* New York: Lexington.

Rest, J. R. (1979). *Development in judging moral issues.* Minneapolis: University of Minnesota Press.

Rest, J. R. (1986). *Moral development: Advances in research and theory.* New York: Praeger.

Rest, J. R., Thoma, S. J., Moon, Y. L., & Getz, I. (1986). Different cultures, sexes, and religions. In J. R. Rest (Ed.), *Moral development* (pp. 133–175). NY: Praeger.

Reuterman, N. A. (1978). The public's view of delinquency causation: A consideration in comprehensive juvenile justice planning. *Juvenile and Family Court Journal, 29,* 39–47.

Reuterman, N. A., & Durbin, M. J. (1988). Inter-generational views of delinquency causation: A consideration in program effectiveness. *Psychology, 25,* 32–40.

Revely, M. A., Revely, A. M., Clifford, C. A., & Murray, R. M. (1983). Genetics of platelet MAO activity in discordant schizophrenic and normal twins. *British Journal of Psychiatry, 42,* 560–565.

Reznick, J. S., Kagan, J., Snidman, N., Gersten, M., Baak, K., & Rosenberg, A. (1986). Inhibited and uninhibited children: A follow-up study. *Journal of Child Development, 57,* 660–680.

Rhodes, A., & Reiss Jr., A. (1970). The religious factor and delinquent behavior. *Journal of Research in Crime and Delinquency, 7,* 83–98.

Ribak, C. E., Harris, A. B., Vaughn, J. E., & Roberts, E. (1979). Inhibitory, GABAergic nerve terminals decrease at sites of focal epilepsy. *Science, 205,* 211–214.

Rice, B. (1980). The erratic life of "scared straight." *Psychology Today,* October, 28.

Rice, D. (1980). Homicide from the perspective of NCHS statistics on blacks-meeting. *Public Health Reports, 95,* 550–552.

Rice, M. E., & Harris, G. T. (1995). Psychopathy, schizophrenia, alcohol abuse, and violent recidivism. *International Journal of Law and Psychiatry, 18,* 333–342.

Rice, M. E., Harris, G. T., & Quinsey, V. L. (1990). A follow-up of rapists assessed in a maximum-security psychiatric facility. *Journal of Interpersonal Violence, 5,* 435–448.

Rice, T. W., & Goldman, C. R. (1994). Another look at the subculture of violence thesis: Who murders whom and under what circumstances. *Sociological Spectrum, 14,* 371–384.

Richter, P., Scheurer, H., Barnett, W., & Krober, H. L. (1996). Forecasting recidivism in delinquency by intelligence and related constructs. *Medicine, Science, and the Law, 36,* 337–342.

Richters, J. E. (1993). Community violence and children's development: Toward a research agenda for the 1990s. *Psychiatry, 56,* 3–6.

Rigby, K., Schofield, P., & Slee, P. T. (1987). The similarity of attitudes towards personal and impersonal types of authority among adolescent schoolchildren. *Journal of Adolescence, 10,* 241–253.

Riley, J. (1986). *Empathy and criminal behavior: A look at man's inhumanity to man.* Unpublished Ph.D. Dissertation, Florida State University, Tallahassee, FL.

Riley, J. L., III, Robinson, M. E., Wise, E. A., Myers, C. D., & Fillingim, R. B. (1998). Sex differences in the perception of noxious experimental stimuli: A meta-analysis. *Pain, 74,* 181–187.

Rimmer, J., Reich, T., & Winokur, G. (1972). Alcoholism: V. Diagnosis and clinical variation among alcoholics. *Quarterly Journal of the Studies of Alcoholism, 33,* 658–666.

Ritchie, J., & Ritchie, J. (1983). New Zealand: Developmental and social antecedents and concomitants of aggression. In J. Ritchie (Ed.), *Aggression in global perspective* (pp. 325–365). New York: Pergamon.

Robbins, M. C., DeWalt, B. R., & Pelto, P. J. (1972). Climate and behavior: A biocultural study. *Journal of Cross-Cultural Psychology, 3,* 331–344.

Roberts, J., & Doob, A. N. (1997). Race, ethnicity, and criminal justice in Canada. *Crime and Justice: A Review of Research, 21,* 469–522.

Roberts, J. V., & Gabor, T. (1990). Lombrosian wine in a new bottle: Research on crime and race. *Canadian Journal of Criminology, 32,* 291–313.

Roberts, Simon (1979). *Order and dispute, An introduction to legal anthropology.* New York: St. Martin's Press.

Robertson, I. (1987). *Sociology.* New York: Worth.

Robin, Gerald & Anson, Richard (1990). *Introduction to the criminal justice system.* New York: Harper & Row.

Robins, L. N. (1966). *Deviant children grown up: A sociological and psychiatric study of sociopathic personality.* Baltimore, MD: Williams and Wilkes.

Robins, L. N. (1978). Aetiological implications in studies of childhood histories relating to antisocial personality. In R. D. Hare & D. Schalling (Eds.), *Psychopathic behaviour: Approaches to research* (pp. 255–271). New York: Wiley.

Robins, L. N. (1985). Epidemiology of antisocial personality. In G. L. Klerman, M. M. Weissman, P. S. Appelbaum, & L. H. Roth (Eds.), *Psychiatry,* Vol. 5: *Social, epidemiologic, and legal psychiatry* (pp. 231–244). New York: Basic Books.

Robins, L. N. (1991). Conduct disorder: Annual research review. *Child Psychology and Psychiatry, 32,* 193–213.

Robins, L. N., & McEvoy, L. (1990). Conduct problems as predictors of substance abuse. In L. N. Robins & M. Rutter

(Eds.), *Straight and devious pathways from childhood to adulthood* (pp. 182–204). Cambridge, England: Cambridge University Press.

Robins, L. N., & Price, R. K. (1991). Adult disorders predicted by childhood conduct problems: Results from the NIMH Epidemiologic Catchment Area Project. *Psychiatry, 54,* 116–132.

Robins, L. N., Tipp, J., & Przybeck, T. (1991). Antisocial personality. In L. N. Robins & D. Regier (Eds.), *Psychiatric disorders in America* (pp. 258–290). New York: Free Press.

Robins, L. N., West, P. A., & Herjanic, B. L. (1975). Arrests and delinquency in two generations: A study of black urban families and their children. *Journal of Child Psychology and Psychiatry, 16,* 125–140.

Robinson, D. S., Davis, J. M., Nies, A., Ravans, C. L., & Sylvester, D. (1971). Relation of sex and aging to monoamine oxidase activity of human brain, plasma, and platelets. *Archives of General Psychiatry, 24,* 536–539.

Robinson, R. G., & Stitt, G. (1981). Intracortical 6-hydroxydopamine induces an asymmetrical behavioral response in the rat. *Brain Research, 213,* 387–395.

Robinson, S. M. (1958). A study of delinquency among Jewish children in New York City. In M. Sklare (Ed.), *The Jews: Social patterns of an American group* (pp. 535–542). Glencoe, IL: Free Press.

Robinson, W. S. (1950). Ecological correlations and the behavior of individuals. *American Sociological Review, 15,* 351–357.

Rock, P. (1979). Another common-sense conception of deviancy. *Sociology, 13,* 75–88.

Rocklin, T., & Revelle, W. (1981). The measurement of extroversion: A comparison of the Eysenck Personality Inventory and the Eysenck Personality Questionnaire. *British Journal of Social Psychology, 20,* 279–284.

Rodgers, J. L., Billy, J. O. G., & Undry, J. R. (1982). The rescission of behaviors: Inconsistent responses in adolescent sexuality data. *Social Science Research, 11,* 280–296.

Rogeness, G. A., Cepeda, C., Macedo, C. A., Fischer, C., & Harris, W. R. (1990b). Differences in heart rate and blood pressure in children with conduct disorder, major depression, and separation anxiety. *Psychiatry Research, 33,* 199–206.

Rogeness, G. A., Javors, M. A., Maas, J. W., & Macedo, C. A. (1990a). Catecholamines and diagnoses in children. *Journal of American Academy of Child Adolescent Psychiatry, 29,* 234–241.

Rogers, J. D. (1989). Theories of crime and development: An historical perspective. *Journal of Development Studies, 25,* 315–328.

Rokeach, M. (1979). The two-value model of political ideology and British politics. In M. Rokeach (Ed.), *Understanding human values: Individual and social* (pp. 179–191). New York: Free Press.

Roland, J. G. (1998). *The Jewish community in India: Identity in a colonial era* (2nd ed.). New Brunswick, NJ: Transaction.

Roncek, D. W., & Maier, P. A. (1991). Bars, blocks, and crimes revisited: Linking the theory of routine activities to the empricism of "hot spots." *Criminology, 29,* 725–753.

Roschke, J., & Fell, J. (1997). Spectral analysis of P300 generation in depression and schizophrenia. *Neuropsychobiology, 35,* 108–114.

Rose, D. R., & Clear, T. R. (1998). Incarceration, social capital, and crime: Implications for social disorganization theory. *Criminology, 36,* 441–480.

Rose, D. F., Smith, P. D., & Sato, S. (1987). Magnetoencephalography and epilepsy research. *Science, 238,* 329–335.

Rosen, L. (1985). Family and delinquency: Structure or function? *Criminology, 23,* 553–573.

Rosenberg, F. R. (1978). Self-esteem and delinquency. *Journal of Youth and Adolescence, 7,* 279–291.

Rosenberg, J. B., & Weller, G. M. (1973). Minor physical anomalies and academic performance in young school children. *Developmental Medicine and Child Neurology, 15,* 131–135.

Rosenberg, M. (1965). *Society and the adolescent self-image.* Princeton, NJ: Princeton University Press.

Rosenfeld, R., & Decker, S. (1993). Discrepant values, correlates measures: Cross-city and longitudinal comparisons of self-reports and urine tests of cocaine use among arrestees. *Journal of Criminal Justice, 21,* 223–31.

Rosoff, Stephen, Pontell, Henry, & Tillman, Robert (1998). *Profit without honor: White-collar crime and the looting of America.* Upper Saddle River, NJ: Prentice-Hall.

Ross, L. E. (1996). The relationship between religion, self-esteem, and delinquency. *Journal of Crime and Justice, 19,* 195–214.

Ross, Shelly (1988). *Fall from grace: Sex, scandal, and corruption in American politics from 1702 to the present.* New York: Ballantine.

Rossi, A., & Rossi, P. (1980). Body time and social time: Mood patterns by menstrual cycle phase and day of week. In J. Parsons (Ed.), *The psychobiology of sex differences in sex roles* (pp. 269–304). New York: McGraw-Hill.

Rossi, P. H., Bose, C. E., & Berk, R. E. (1974). The seriousness of crimes: Normative structure and the individual differences. *American Sociological Review, 39,* 224–237.

Roth, L. R., & Erwin, F. R. (1971). Psychiatric care of federal prisoners. *American Journal of Psychiatry, 127,* 424–430.

Rothenberger, A. (1995). Electrical brain activity in children with hyperkinetic syndrome: Evidence of a frontal cortical dysfunction. In J. Sergeant (Ed.), *European approaches to hyperkinetic disorders* (pp. 255–270). Zurich: Trumpi.

Rothman, R. A. (1993). *Inequality and Stratification: Class, color, and gender.* Englewood Cliffs, NJ: Prentice Hall.

Rotten, J. (1986). Determinism reduces climate and cultural correlates of violence. *Environment and Behavior, 18,* 346–368.

Rotter, J. B. (1966). Generalized expectancies for internal vs. external control of reinforcement. *Psychological Monograms, 80,* Whole No. 609.

Rountree, P. W., & Land, K. C. (1996). Perceived risk versus fear of crime: Empirical evidence of conceptually distinct reactions in survey data. *Social Forces, 74,* 1353–1376.

Rouse, B. A., Carter, J. H., & Rodriguez-Andrew, S. (1995). *Race/ethnicity and other sociocultural influences on alcoholism treatment for women* (vol. 12). New York: Plenum.

Roush, W. (1995). Conflict marks crime conference. *Science, 269,* 1808–1809.

Roussounis, S. H., Hubley, P. A., & Dear, P. R. F. (1993). Five-year follow-up of very low birthweight infants: Neurological and psychological outcome. *Child: Care, Health and Development, 19,* 45–59.

Rowe, D. C. (1983). Biometrical genetic models of self-reported delinquent behavior: A twin study. *Behavior Genetics, 13,* 473–489.

Rowe, D. C. (1986). Genetic and environmental components of antisocial behavior: A study of 265 twin pairs. *Criminology, 24,* 513–532.

Rowe, D. C. (1994). *The limits of family influence: Genes, experience and behavior.* New York: Guilford.

Rowe, D. C. (1996). An adaptive strategy theory of crime and delinquency. In J. D. Hawkins (Ed.), *Delinquency and crime: Current theories* (pp. 268–314). Cambridge: Cambridge University Press.

Rowe, D. C., Linver, M. R., & Rodgers, J. L. (1996). Delinquency and IQ: Using siblings to find sources of variation. In G. H. Brody (Ed.), *Sibling relationships: Their causes and consequences* (pp. 147–171). Norwood, NJ: Ablex.

Rowe, D. C., & Osgood, D. W. (1984). Heredity and sociological theories of delinquency: A reconsideration. *American Sociological Review, 49,* 526–540.

Rowe, D. C., Vazsonyi, A. T., & Figueredo, A. J. (1997). Mating-effort in adolescence: A conditional or alternative strategy. *Personality and Individual Differences, 23,* 105–115.

Rowe, D. C., Vazsonyi, A. T., & Flannery, D. J. (1995). Sex differences in crime: Do means and within-sex variation have similar causes? *Journal of Research in Crime and Delinquency, 32,* 84–100.

Rowen, Edward, Langelier, Pamela, & Rowan, Judith. (1988). Female pedophiles. *Corrective and Social Psychiatry, 34,* 17–20.

Roy, A., Virkkunen, M., Guthrie, S., & Linnoila, M. (1986). Indices of serotonin and glucose metabolism in violent offenders, arsonists and alcoholics. In J. J. Mann & M. Stanley (Eds.), *Psychobiology of suicidal behavior* (pp. 202–220). New York: New York Academy of Science.

Rubin, H. T. (1985). *Juvenile Justice: Policy, practice, and law.* New York: Random House.

Rubin, K. H., & Schneider, F. W. (1973). The relationship between moral judgment, egocentrism, and altruistic behavior. *Child Development, 44,* 661–665.

Rubin, S. (1949). The legal character of juvenile delinquency. *Annals of the American Academy of Political and Social Sciences, 261,* 1–8.

Rubinow, D. R., Post, R. M., Gold, P. W., Ballenger, J. C., & Wolff, E. A. (1984). The relationship between cortisol and clinical phenomenology. In R. M. Post & J. C. Ballenger (Eds.), *Neurobiology of mood disorders* (pp. 619–628). Baltimore, MD: Williams & Wilkins.

Rubio, A. M., Garcia, J. L., Duenas, A., Gonzalez, J. L., Casal, M., & Velasco, A. (1984). A comparative study of drug use among university students in Cordoba and Valladoid. *Psicopatologia, 4,* 373–384.

Rudel, L. L., Leathers, C. W., Bond, M. G., & Bullock, B. C. (1981). Dietary ethanol induced modifications in hyperlipoproteinemia and atherosclerosis in nonhuman primates (*Macaca nemestrina*). *Arteriosclerosis, 1,* 144–155.

Rudolf, M. C. J., Tomanovich, O., Greenberg, J., Friend, L., & Alario, A. J. (1992). Gender differences in infirmary use at a residential summer camp. *Developmental and Behavioral Pediatrics, 13,* 261–265.

Rueckert, L., & Grafman, J. (1996). Sustained attention deficits in patients with right frontal lesions. *Neuropsychologia, 34,* 953–963.

Rufford, Nick (1996). The misfit behind the massacre. *The Sunday Times* (London), May 5, 3C.

Rummel, R. (1992). Megamurderers. *Society, 29,* 47–52.

Ruse, M. (1982). *Darwinism defended: A guide to the evolution controversy.* Reading, MA: Addison-Wesley.

Rush, George (1991). *The dictionary of criminal justice.* Guilford, CT: Dushkin.

Rushton, J. P. (1980). *Altruism, socialization, and society.* Englewood Cliffs, NJ: Prentice-Hall.

Rushton, J. P. (1990). Race and crime: A reply to Roberts and Gabor. *Canadian Journal of Criminology, 32,* 315–334.

Rushton, J. P. (1995). Race and crime: International data for 1989–1990. *Psychological Reports, 76,* 307–312.

Rushton, J. P. (1996). Self-report delinquency and violence in adult twins. *Psychiatric Genetics, 6,* 87–89.

Rushton, J. P., & Chrisjohn, R. (1981). Extraversion, neuroticism, psychoticism and self-reported delinquency. *Personality and Individual Differences, 2,* 11–20.

Rushton, J. P., Chrisjohn, R. D., & Fekken, G. C. (1981). The altruistic personality and the self-report altruism scale. *Personality and Individual Differences, 2,* 293–302.

Russell, G. W., & Baenninger, R. (1996). Murder most foul: Predictors of an affirmative response to an outrageous question. *Aggressive Behavior, 22,* 175–181.

Rutter, M. (1971). Parent-child separation: Psychological effects on the children. *Journal of Child Psychology and Psychiatry, 12,* 233–260.

Rutter, M. (1994). Family discord and conduct disorder: Cause, consequence, or correlate? *Family Psychology, 8,* 170–186.

Rutter, M. (1996). Testing causal hypotheses about mechanisms in comorbidity. *Addiction, 91,* 495–510.

Rutter, M., & Gillis, H. (1984). *Juvenile delinquency: Trends and perspectives.* New York: Guilford.

Rutter, M., Tizard, J., & Whitmore, K. (1970). *Education, health, and behavior.* New York: Wiley.

Rutter, M., Yule, W., Berger, M., Yule, B., Morton, J., & Bagley, C. (1974). Children of West Indian immigrants, I. Rates of behavioural deviance and of psychiatric disorder. *Journal of Child Psychology and Psychiatry, 15,* 241–262.

Rwiza, H. T., Kilonzo, G. P., & Haule, J. (1992). Prevalence and incidence of epilepsy in Ulanga, a rural Tanzanian district: A community based study. *Epilepsia, 33,* 1051–1056.

Safer, D. J., & Krager, J. M. (1988). A survey of medication treatment for hyperactive/inattentive students. *Journal of the American Medical Association, 260,* 2256–2258.

Saffron, Inga (1997). Chance leads to capture in serial killer–cannibal case. *Idaho Statesman,* February 2, 19a.

Saigal, S., Sxatmari, P., Rosenbaum, P., Campbell, D., & King, S. (1991). Cognitive abilities and school performance of extremely low birthweight children and matched term control children at age 8 years: A regional study. *Journal of Pediatrics, 118,* 751–760.

Salama, A. A. (1988). The antisocial personality (The sociopathic personality). *Psychiatric Journal of the University of Ottawa, 13,* 149–153.

Salzman, C., Wolfson, A. N., Schatzberg, A., Looper, J., Henke, R., & Albanese, M. (1995). Effect of fluoxetine on anger in symptomatic volunteers with borderline personality disorder. *Journal of Clinical Psychopharmacology, 15,* 23–29.

Sampson, R. J. (1985a). Race and criminal violence: A demographically disaggregated analysis of urban homicide. *Crime and Delinquency, 31,* 147–81.

Sampson, R. J. (1985b). Structural sources of variation in race-age-specific rates of offending across major U.S. cities. *Criminology, 23,* 647–673.

Sampson, R. J., & Laub, J. H. (1993). *Crime in the making: Pathways and turning points through life.* Cambridge, MA: Harvard University Press.

Sampson, R. J., & Laub, J. H. (1994). Urban poverty and the family context of delinquency: A new look at structure and process in a classic study. *Child Development, 65,* 523–540.

Sampson, R. J., & Lauritsen, J. L. (1994). Violent victimization and offending: Individual-, situational-, and community-level risk factors. In A. Reiss & J. Roth (Eds.), *Understanding and preventing violence,* Vol. 3: *Social influences* (pp. 1–114). Washington, DC: National Academy Press.

Samuel, W., Soto, D., Parks, M., Ngissah, P., & Jones, B. (1976). Motivation, race, social-class and IQ. *Journal of Educational Psychology, 68,* 273–285.

Sandberg, S. T., Wieselberg, M., & Shaffer, D. (1980). Hyperkenetic and conduct problem children in a primary school population: Some epidemiological considerations. *Journal of Child Psychology and Psychiatry, 21,* 293–311.

Sander, J. W., & Sharvon, S. D. (1996). Epidemiology of the epilepsies. *Journal of Neurology, Neurosurgery, and Psychiatry, 61,* 433–443.

Sarich, V. M. (1995). In defense of the Bell Curve. *Skeptic, 3,* 84–93.

Sarnecki, J. (1986). *Delinquent networks.* Stockholm: National Council for Crime Prevention.

Sarrel, P., & Masters, W. (1982). Sexual molestation of men by women. *Archives of Sexual Behavior, 11,* 117–131.

Sarri, R. (1983). Gender issues in juvenile justice. *Crime and Delinquency, 29,* 381–397.

Sarvela, P. D., & McClendon, E. J. (1988). Indicators of rural youth drug use. *Journal of Youth and Adolescence, 17,* 335–347.

Satinder, K. P. (1980). Interaction among scopolamine, conditioned stimulus modality, genotype, and either-way avoidance behavior of rats. *Psychopharmacology, 67,* 97–99.

Satterfield, J. H. (1987). Childhood diagnostic and neurophysiological predictors of teenage arrest rates: An eight year prospective study. In S. A. Mendick, T. E. Moffitt, & S. A. Stack (Eds.), *The causes of crime* (pp. 199–207). Cambridge, England: Cambridge University Press.

Satterfield, J. H., Swanson, J., Schell, A., & Lee, F. (1994). Prediction of antisocial behavior in attention-deficit hyperactivity disorder boys from aggression/defiance scores. *Journal of the American Child Adolescence Psychiatry, 33,* 185–190.

Saver, J. L., & Damasio, A. R. (1991). Preserved access and processing of social knowledge in a patient with acquired sociopathy due to ventromedial frontal damage. *Neuropsychologica, 29,* 1241–1249.

Savitz, L. D. (1978). Offical police statistics and their limitations. In L. D. Savitz & N. Johnston (Eds.), *Crime in society* (pp. 69–81). New York: John Wiley & Sons.

Savona, E. U. (1993). Experiences, fear, and attitudes of victims of crime in Italy. In A. A. del Frate, U. Zuekic, & J. J. van Dijk (Eds.), *Understanding crime* (pp. 93–125). Rome: United Nations Interregional Crime and Justice Research Institute.

Sawhill, I. (1973). The economics of discrimination against women: Some new findings. *Journal of Human Resources, 8,* 386–387.

Sawyer, J. (1965). The altruism scale: A measure of co-operative, individualistic, and competitive orientation. *American Journal of Sociology, 71,* 407–416.

Scaramella, T. J., & Brown, W. A. (1978). Serum testosterone and aggressiveness in hockey players. *Psychosomatic Medicine,* Vol. # 262–265.

Scarr, S. (1981). *Race, social class and individual differences in IQ.* Hillsdale, NJ: Erlbaum.

Scarr, S., & Carter-Saltzman, L. (1982). Genetics and Intelligence. In R. J. Sternberg (Ed.), *Handbook of human intelligence* (pp. 820). Cambridge, England: Cambridge University Press.

Scarr, S., Webber, P. L., Weinberg, R. A., & Wittig, M. A. (1981). Personality resemblance among adolescents and their parents in biologically related and adoptive families. *Journal of Personality and Social Psychology, 40,* 885–898.

Scerbo, A. S., & Kolko, D. J. (1994). Salivary testosterone and cortisol in disruptive children: Relationship to aggressive, hyperactive, and internalizing behaviors. *Journal of American Academy of Child and Adolescent Psychiatry, 33,* 1174–1184.

Scerbo, A. S., Raine, A., O'Brien, M., Chan, C.-J., Rhee, C., & Smiley, N. (1990). Reward dominance and passive avoidance learning in adolescent psychopaths. *Journal of Abnormal Child Psychology, 18,* 451–463.

Schaffer, C. E., Davidson, R. J., & Saron, C. (1983). Frontal and parietal ectroencephalogram asymmetrics in depressed and non-depressed subjects. *Biological Psychiatry, 18,* 753–762.

Schaffer, D., & Fisher, P. (1981). The epidemiology of suicide in children and young adolescents. *Journal of the American Academy of Child Psychiatry, 20,* 545–565.

Schalling, D. (1987). Personality correlates of plasma testosterone levels in young delinquents: An example of person–situation interaction? In S. A. Mednick, E. E. Moffitt, & S. A. Stack (Eds.), *The causes of crime: New biological approaches* (pp. 283–291). Cambridge, England: Cambridge University Press.

Schauss, A. (1981). *Diet, crime and delinquency.* Berkeley, CA: Parker House.

Scheff, T. J. (1988). Shame and conformity: The deference-emotion system. *American Sociological Review, 53,* 395–406.

Schichor, D. (1980). Some problems of credibility in radical criminology. In J. A. Inciardi (Ed.), *Radical criminology: The coming crises* (pp. 191–212). Beverly Hills, CA: Sage.

Schilmoeller, G. L., Schilmoeller, K. J., Etzel, B. C., & Leblanc, J. M. (1979). Conditional discrimination after errorless and trial-and-error training. *Journal of the experimental analysis of behavior, 31,* 405–420.

Schinke, S. P., Schilling, R. F., Gilchrist, L. D., Barth, R. P., Bobo, J. K., Trimble, J. E., & Cvetkovich, G. T. (1985).

Preventing substance abuse with American Indian youth. *Journal of Contemporary Social Work,* Vol # 213–218.

Schloss, B., & Giesbrecht, N. A. (1972). *Murder in Canada: A report on capital and non-capital murder statistics 1961–1970.* Toronto: Centre of Criminology, University of Toronto.

Schmalleger, F. (1993). *Criminal justice today.* Englewood Cliffs, NJ: Prentice-Hall.

Schmalleger, F. (1995). *Criminal justice today.* Englewood Cliffs, NJ: Prentice-Hall.

Schmalleger, F. (1996). *Criminology today.* Englewoods Cliffs, NJ: Prentice-Hall.

Schneider, A. L., Burcart, J. M., & Wilson, L. A. (1976). The role of attitudes in the decision to report crimes to the police. In W. F. McDonald (Ed.), *Criminal justice and the victim* (Vol. pp. 89–113). Beverly Hills, CA: Sage.

Schoenthaler, S. J. (1982). The effect of sugar on the treatment and control of antisocial behavior: A double-blind study of an incarcerated juvenile population. *International Journal for Biosocial Research, 3,* 1–9.

Schonfeld, I. S., Shaffer, D., O'Connor, P., & Portnoy, S. (1988). Conduct disorder and cognitive functioning: Testing three causal hypotheses. *Child Development, 59,* 993–1007.

Schroeder, P. L. (1936). Criminal behavior in the later period of life. *American Journal of Psychiatry, 92,* 915–924.

Schuckit, M. A., & Morrissey, E. R. (1979). Psychiatric problems in women admitted to an alcohol detoxification center. *American Journal of Psychiatry, 136,* 611–617.

Schulman, K., Rubenstein, E., Chesley, F. D., & Eisenberg, J. M. (1995). The roles of race and socioeconomic factors in health services research. *Health Science Journal, 30,* 179–195.

Schur, E. M. (1965). *Crimes without victims.* Englewood Cliffs, NJ: Prentice-Hall.

Schur, E. M. (1969). *Our criminal society.* Englewood Cliffs, NJ: Prentice-Hall.

Schur, E. M. (1973). *Radical non-intervention: Rethinking the delinquency problem.* Englewood Cliffs, NJ: Prentice-Hall.

Schuster, R. L. (1981). Black and white violent delinquents: A longitudinal study. In M. R. L. Pope & C. E. Pope (Eds.), *Race, crime, and criminal justice* (pp. 109–123). Beverly Hills, CA: Sage.

Schwartz, Barbara (1995). Characteristics and typologies of sex offenders. In B. Schwartz & H. Cellini (Eds.), *The sex offender: Corrections, treatment, and legal practice,* pp. 22-1–21-12. Kingston, NJ: Civic Research Institute.

Schwartz, Barbara & Cellini, Henry (1995). Female sex offenders. In B. Schwartz & H. Cellini (Eds.), *The sex offender: Corrections, treatment, and legal practice* pp. 5-1–5-22. Kingston, NJ: Civic Research Institute.

Schwartz, M., & DeKeseredy, W. (1991). Left realist criminology: Strengths, weaknesses, and the feminist critique. *Crime Law and Social Change, 15,* 51–72.

Schwartz, M. D., & Friedrichs, D. O. (1994). Postmodern thought and criminological discontent: New metaphors for understanding violence. *Criminology, 32,* 221–246.

Schwartz, Martin & Pitts, Victoria (1995). Exploring a feminist routine activities approach to explaining sexual assault. *Justice Quarterly, 12,* 9–31.

Schwartz, R. D., & Orleans, S. (1967). On legal sanctions. *University of Chicago Law Review, 34,* 274–300.

Schwartz, R. M., Burkhart, B. B., & Green, B. (1978). Turning on or turning off: Sensation seeking or tension reduction as motivational determinants of alcohol use. *Journal of Consulting of Clinical Psychology, 46,* 1144–1145.

Schweinhart, L. J., Baarnes, H. V., & Weikart, D. P. (1993). *Significant benefits: The High/Scope Perry preschool study through age 27.* Ypsilanti, MI: High/Scope.

Schwendinger, H., & Schwendinger, J. S. (1985). *Adolescent subcultures and delinquency.* New York: Praeger.

Schwind, H.-D. (1984). Investigations of nonreported offenses. In R. Block (Ed.), *Victimization and fear of crime: World perspectives* (pp. 65–74). Washington, DC: U.S. Department of Justice.

Scott, E. C. (1997). Antievolution and creationism in the United States. *Annual Review of Anthropology, 26,* 263–289.

Scott, J. E., & Schwalm, L. A. (1988a). Rape rates and the circulation rates of adult magazines. *Journal of Sex Research, 24,* 241–250.

Scott, J. E., & Schwalm, L. A. (1988b). Pornography and rape: An examination of adult theater rates and rape rates by state. In J. E. Scott & T. Hirschi (Eds.), *Controversial issues in crime and justice.* Beverly Hills, CA: Sage.

Scott, P. (1972). The spatial analysis of crime and delinquency. *Australian Geographical Studies, 10,* 1–15.

Scully, Diana & Marolla, Joseph (1995). Riding the bull at Gilley's: Convicted rapists describe the rewards of rape. *Social Problems, 32,* 251–263.

Scupin, R., & DeCourse, C. R. (1998). *Anthropology: A global perspective* (3rd ed.). Upper Saddle River, NJ: Prentice-Hall.

Scutt, J. A. (1979). The myth of the chivalry factor in female crime. *Australian Journal of Social Issues, 14,* 3–20.

Searcy, W. A. (1982). The evolutionary effects of mate selection. *Annual Review of Ecological Systems, 13,* 57–85.

Sears, Donald (1991). *To kill again: The motivation and development of serial murder.* Wilmington, DE: Scholarly Resources.

Sederberg, P. (1989). *Terrorist myths: Illusions, rhetoric, and reality.* Englewood Cliffs, NJ: Prentice Hall.

Segal, B., Huba, G. J., & Singer, J. L. (1980). *Drugs, daydreaming, and personality: A study of college youth.* Hillsdale, NJ: Erlbaum.

Segall, M. H. (1983). Aggression in global perspective: A research strategy. In A. P. Goldstein & M. H. Segall (Eds.), *Aggression in global perspective* (pp. 1–19). New York: Pergamon.

Segrave, Kerry (1992). *Women serial and mass murderers: A worldwide reference, 1580 through 1990.* Jefferson, NC: McFarland.

Seguin, J., R., Pihl, R. O., Boulerice, B., Tremblay, R. E., & Harden, P. W. (1996). Pain sensitivity and stability of physical aggression in boys. *Journal of Child Psychology and Psychiatry, 37,* 823–834.

Seguin, J. R., Pihl, R. O., & Harden, P. W. (1995). Cognitive and neuropsychological characteristics of physically aggressive boys. *Journal of Abnormal Psychology, 104,* 614–624.

Sellin, T. (1931). Crime. In E. R. A. Seligman (Ed.), *Encyclopedia of the Social Sciences* (Vol. 4, pp. 563–569). New York: Macmillan.

Sellin, T. (1938). *Culture conflict and crime.* New York: Social Science Research Council.

Sellin, T. (1968). Enrico Ferri: Pioneer in criminology, 1856–1929. In S. E. Grupp (Ed.), *The positive school of criminology: Three lectures by Enrico Ferri* (pp. 5–21). Pittsburgh, PA: University of Pittsburgh Press.

Sellin, T., & Wolfgang, M. E. (1964). *The measurement of delinquency.* New York: Wiley.

Sellin, T., & Wolfgang, M. E. (1982). The legal basis of juvenile delinquency. In R. Giallombardo (Ed.), *Juvenile delinquency* (pp. 22–31). New York: Wiley.

Selman, R. L. (1976). Social-cognitive understanding: A guide to educational and clinical practice. In T. Lickona (Ed.), *Moral development and behavior* (pp. 299–314). New York: Holt, Rinehart and Winston.

Selman, R. L. (1980). *The growth of interpersonal understanding: Developmental and clinical analyses.* New York: Academic Press.

Seltzer, A., & Langford, A. (1984). Forensic psychiatric assessments in the Northwest Territories. *Canadian Journal of Psychiatry, 29,* 665–668.

Selye, H. (1936). A syndrome produced by diverse noxious agents. *Nature, 138,* 32–39.

Selye, H. (1950). *Stress: The physiology and pathology of exposure to stress.* Montreal: Acta Medical.

Serin, R. C. (1993). Diagnosis of psychopathology with and without an interview. *Journal of Clinical Psychology, 49,* 367–372.

Serin, R. C. (1996). Violent recidivism in criminal psychopaths. *Law and Human Behavior, 20,* 207–217.

Serin, R. C., & Amos, N. L. (1995). The role of psychopathy in the assessment of dangerousness. *International Journal of Law and Psychiatry, 18,* 231–238.

Serin, R. C., Peters, R. D., & Barbaree, H. E. (1990). Predictors of psychopathy and release outcome in a criminal population. Psychological Assessment: *A Journal of Consulting and Clinical Psychology, 2,* 419–422.

Serio, Joseph (1992a). Shunning tradition; ethnic organized crime in the former Soviet Union. *Criminal Justice International, 8,* 5–6.

Serio, J. T. (1992b). *USSR crime statistics and summaries: 1989 and 1990.* Chicago: University of Illinois Office of International Criminal Justice.

Serio, Joseph (1993a). Organized crime in the former Soviet Union: New Directions, new locations. *Criminal Justice International, 9:*15–21.

Serio, Joseph (1993b). Organized crime in the former Soviet Union: Only the name is new. *Criminal Justice International, 9,* 11–17.

Seto, M. C., Khattar, N. A., Lalumiere, M. L., & Quinsey, V. L. (1997). Deception and sexual strategy in psychopathy. *Personality and Individual Differences, 22,* 301–307.

Seydlitz, R. (1993). Complexity in the relationships among direct and indirect parental controls and delinquency. *Youth & Society, 24,* 243–275.

Shallice, T. (1982). Specific impairments in planning. In D. E. Broadbent & L. Weiskrantz (Eds.), *The neuropsychology of cognitive function* (pp. 199–209). London: Royal Society.

Shamsie, S. J. (1982). Antisocial adolescents: Out treatments do not work—Where do we go from here? *Annual Progress in Child Psychology and Child Development, 12,* 631–647.

Shannon, I. L., Prigmore, J. R., Hester, W. R., McCall, C. M., & Isbell, C. M. (1961). Stress patterns in dental patients: I. Serum free 17-hydroxycorticosteroids, sodium and potassium in subjects undergoing local anesthesia and simple exodontic procedures. *Journal of Oral Surgery Anesthesiology Hospital Dental Services, 19,* 486–491.

Shapiro, Martin (1981). *Courts: A comparative and political analysis.* Chicago: University of Chicago Press.

Shapiro, S. K., Quay, H. C., Hogan, A. E., & Schwartz, K. P. (1988). Response preservation and delayed responding in under-socialized aggressive conduct disorder. *Journal of Abnormal Psychology, 97,* 371–373.

Sharma, V., & Kaur, K. (1992). Moral judgement as a function of intelligence, birth-order and age of the children. *Psychologia, 35,* 121–124.

Sharpe, K. J. (1992). Biology intersects religion and morality. *Biology and Philosophy, 7,* 77–88.

Shaughnessy, M. F. (1994). An interview with Arthur R. Jensen. *School Field, 4,* 129–154.

Shaw, C. R. (1929). *Delinquency areas.* Chicago: University of Chicago Press.

Shaw, C. R., & McKay, H. D. (1942). *Juvenile delinquency in urban areas.* Chicago: University of Chicago Press.

Shaw, C. R., & McKay, H. D. (1969). *Juvenile delinquency and urban areas.* Chicago: University of Chicago Press.

Shaw, C. R., & McKay, H. D. (1972). *Juvenile delinquency and the urban areas* (rev. ed.). Chicago: University of Chicago Press.

Shaw, D. S., & Bell, R. Q. (1993). Developmental theories of parental contributions to antisocial behavior. *Journal of Abnormal Child Psychology, 21,* 493–518.

Shaw, D. S., & Vondra, J. I. (1995). Infant attachment security and maternal predictors of early behavior problems: A longitudinal study of low-income families. *Journal of Abnormal Child Psychology, 23,* 335–357.

Shaw, J. M., & Scott, W. A. (1991). Influence of parent discipline style on delinquent behaviour: The mediating role of control orientation. *Australian Journal of Psychology, 13,* 61–67.

Sheard, M. H. (1979). The role of drugs affecting catecholamines on shock-elicited fighting in rats. In E. Usdin, I. J. Kopin, & J. Barchas (Eds.), *Catecholamines: Basic and clinical frontiers* (Vol. 2, pp. 1690–1692). New York: Pergamon.

Sheard, M. H., Marini, J. L., Bridges, C. I. (1976). The effect of lithium on impulsive aggressive behavior in man. *American Journal of Psychiatry 133,* 1409–1413.

Shelden, R. G., & Chesney-Lind, M. (1993). Gender and race differences in delinquent careers. *Juvenile & Family Court Journal,* 73–90.

Sheldon, W. H., Hartl, E. M., & McDermott, E. (1949). *Varieties of delinquent youth: An introduction to constitutional psychology.* New York: Harper & Row.

Sheley, J. F. (1985). *America's crime problem: An introduction to criminology.* Belmont, CA: Wadsworth.

Shelley, L. I. (1981). *Crime and modernization: The impact of industrialization and urbanization on crime.* Carbondale: Southern Illinois University Press.

Sher, K. J., & Trull, T. J. (1994). Personality and disinhibitory psychopathology: Alcoholism and antisocial personality disorder. *Journal of Abnormal Psychology, 103,* 92–102.

Sherman, D. K., Iacono, W. G., & McGue, M. K. (1997a). Attention-deficit hyperactivity disorder dimensions: A twin study of inattention and impulsivity-hyperactivity. *Journal of the American Academy of Child and Adolescent Psychiatry, 36,* 745–753.

Sherman, D., McGue, M. K., & Iacono, W. (1997b). Twin concordance for attention deficit hyperactivity disorder: A comparison of teachers' and mothers' reports. *American Journal of Psychiatry, 154,* 532–535.

Sherman, L. W., Smith, D. A., Schmidt, J. D., & Rogan, D. P. (1992). Crime, punishment, and stake in conformity: Legal and informal control of domestic violence. *American Sociological Review, 57,* 680–690.

Sherwin, B. B., Gelfand, M. M., & Brender, W. (1985). Androgen enhances sexual motivation in females: A prospective crossover study of sex steroid administration in the surgical menopause. *Psychosomatic Medicine, 47,* 339–351.

Shichor, D. (1990). Crime patterns and socioeconomic development: A cross-national analysis. *Criminal Justice Review, 15,* 64–78.

Shikita, M., & Tsuchiya, S. (1992). *Crime and criminal policy in Japan.* New York: Springer.

Shimizu, A., & Endo, M. (1983). Handedness and familial sinistrality in a Japanese student population. *Cortex, 19,* 265–272.

Shin, Y., Jedlicka, D., & Lee, E. S. (1977). Homicide among blacks. *Phylon,* vol # 398–407.

Shoemaker, D. J. (1994). Male-female delinquency in the Philippines: A comparative analysis. *Youth and Society, 25,* 299–329.

Short, G. (1991). Perceptions of inequality: Primary school children's discourse on social class. *Educational Studies, 17,* 89–105.

Short, J. F. (1957). Differential association and delinquency. *Social Problems, 4,* 233–239.

Short, J. F., & Nye, F. I. (1957). Reported behavior as a criterion of deviant behavior. *Social Problems, 5,* 207–213.

Short, J. F., & Strodtbeck, F. L. (1965). *Group process and gang delinquency.* Chicago: University of Chicago Press.

Short, J. F., Jr. (1985). Book review. *Criminology, 23,* 181–191.

Short, J. F., Jr. (1998). The level of explanation problem revisited: The American Society of Criminology 1997 presidential address. *Criminology, 36,* 3–36.

Shrenker, P., & Maxson, S. C. (1982). The Y chromosomes of DBA/1Bg and DBA/2Bg compare for effects on intermale aggression. *Behavior Genetics, 12,* 429–434.

Shrier, L. A., Emans, S. J., Woods, E. R., & DuRant, R. H. (1996). The association of sexual risk behaviors and problem drug behaviors in high school students. *Adolescent Health, 20,* 377–383.

Shriver, J. (1989). Frustrated by criminal justice system, public demands harsher penalties. *Gallup Reports, 285,* June, 23–25.

Shue, K. L., & Douglas, V. I. (1992). Attention deficit hyperactivity disorder and the frontal lobe syndrome. *Brain and Cognition, 20,* 104–124.

Shulman, H. M. (1961). *Juvenile delinquency in American society.* New York: Harper.

Shweder, R. (1991). *Thinking through cultures: Expeditions in cultural psychology.* Cambridge, MA: Harvard University Press.

Siassi, I. (1982). Lithium treatment of impulsive behavior in children. *Journal of Clinical Psychiatry, 43,* 482–484.

Siconolfi, Michael & Johnson, Robert (1991). Broker grandmother accused of losing clients' cash at baccarat. *Wall Street Journal,* August 29, pp. C1–C11.

Sidanius, J., Ekehammer, B., & Lukowsky, J. (1983). Social status and sociopolitical ideology among Swedish youth. *Youth Society, 14,* 395–415.

Siegel, L. J. (1989). *Criminology* (3rd ed.). St. Paul, MN: West.

Siegel, L. J., Rathus, S. A., & Ruppert, C. A. (1973). Values and delinquent youth: An empirical re-examination of theories of delinquency. *British Journal of Criminology, 13,* 237–244.

Siegel, L. J., & Senna, J. J. (1988). *Juvenile delinquency: Theory, practice, and law* (3rd ed.). St. Paul, MN: West.

Sigvardsson, S., Bohman, M., & Cloninger, R. C. (1996). Replication of the Stockholm adoption study of alcoholism: Confirmatory cross-fostering analysis. *Archives of General Psychiatry, 53,* 681–687.

Sigvardsson, S., Cloninger, C. R., Bohman, M., & Von Knorring, A. (1982). Predisposition to petty criminality in Swedish adoptees: III. Sex differences and validation of male typology. *Archives of General Psychiatry, 39,* 1248–1253.

Silberberg, N. E., & Silberberg, M. C. (1971). School achievement and delinquency. *Review of Educational Research, 41,* 17–33.

Silberman, C. (1978). *Criminal violence–criminal justice: Criminals, police, courts, and prisons in America.* New York: Random House.

Silberman, E. K., & Weingartner, H. (1986). Hemispheric lateralization of functions related to emotion. *Brain and Cognition, 5,* 322–353.

Silberman, M. (1994). Book review. *Contemporary Sociology, 23,* 108–109.

Silva, P. A., & Stanton, W. (1996). *From child to adult: The Dunedin Multidisciplinary Health and Development Study.* New York: Oxford University Press.

Silver, A. (1966). The demand for order in civil society: A review of some themes in the history of urban crime, police and riot. In D. Bordua (Ed.), *The police: Six sociological essays* (pp. 1–24). New York: Wiley.

Simmons, J. L. (1969). *Deviants.* Berkeley, CA: Glendessary.

Simon, R. J. (1975a). Arrest statistics. In F. Alder & R. J. Simon (Eds.), *The criminology of deviant women* (pp. 34–48). Washington, DC: National Institute of Mental Health.

Simon, R. J. (1975b). *Women and crime.* Lexington, MA: Lexington Books.

Simon, R. J., & Landis, J. (1991). *The crimes women commit, the punishments they receive.* Lexington, MA: Lexington Books.

Simon, R. J., & Sharma, N. (1979). Women and crime: Does the American experience generalize? In F. Alder & R. J. Simon (Eds.), *Criminology of deviant women.* Boston: Houghton Mifflin.

Simons, R. L., Conger, R. D., & Whitbeck, L. B. (1988). A multistage social learning model of the influences of family and peers upon adolescent substance abuse. *Journal of Drug Issues, 18,* 293–315.

Simons, R. L., Johnsson, C., & Conger, R. D. (1994). Harsh corporal punishment versus quality of parental involvement as an explanation of adolescent maladjustment. *Journal of Marriage and the Family, 56,* 591–607.

Simons, R. L., Miller, M. G., & Aigner, S. M. (1980). Contemporary theories of deviance and female delinquency: An empirical test. *Journal of Research in Crime and Delinquency, 17,* 42–53.

Simons, R. L., Wu, C. I., Conger, R. D., & Lorenz, F. O. (1994). Two routes to delinquency: Differences between early and late starters in the impact of parenting and deviant peers. *Criminology, 32,* 247–276.

Simpson, E. L. (1974). Moral development research. A case of scientific cultural bias. *Human Development, 17,* 81–106.

Simpson, S. S., & Elis, L. (1994). Is gender subordinate to class? An empirical assessment of Colvin and Pauly's structural Marxist theory of delinquency. *Journal of Criminal Law and Criminology, 85,* 453–463.

Simpson, S. S. (1989). Feminist theory, crime and justice. *Criminology, 27,* 605–631.

Simpson, S. S. (1991). Caste, class, and violent crime: Explaining differences in female offending. *Criminology, 29,* 115–135.

Singer, F., & Zumoff, B. (1992). Subnormal serum testosterone levels in male internal medicine residents. *Steroids, 57,* 86–89.

Singer, S. I. (1981). Homogeneous victim-offender populations: A review and some research implications. *Journal of Criminal Law and Criminology, 72,* 779–788.

Singer, S. I., & Levine, M. (1988). Power–control theory, gender, and delinquency: A partial replication with additional evidence on the effects of peers. *Criminology, 26,* 627–647.

Single, E., Kandel, D., & Faust, R. (1974). Patterns of multiple drug use in high school. *Journal of Health and Social Behaviors, 15,* 344–57.

Skinner, Linda, Carrol, Kelly, & Berry, Kenneth (1995). A typology for sexually aggressive males in dating relationships. *Journal of Offender Rehabilitation, 22,* 29–45.

Skinner, B. F. (1953). *Science and human behavior.* New York: Free Press.

Skogan, W. G. (1976). *Sample surveys of the victims of crime.* Cambridge, MA: Ballinger.

Skogan, W. G. (1977a). The changing distance of big-city crime. *Urban Affairs Quarterly, 13,* 33–48.

Skogan, W. G. (1977b). The "dark figure" of unreported crime. *Crime and Delinquency, 23,* 41–50.

Skogan, W. G., & Maxfield, M. G. (1981). *Coping with crime: Individual and neighborhood reactions.* Beverly Hills, CA: Sage.

Skolnick, J. H. (1966). *Justice without trial.* New York: Wiley.

Slade, P. (1984). Premenstrual emotional changes in normal women: Fact or fiction? *Journal of Psychosomatic Research, 28,* 1–7.

Slawson, J. (1926). *The delinquent boy.* Boston: Badger.

Sletto, R. F. (1934). Sibling position and juvenile delinquency. *American Journal of Sociology, 39,* 657–669.

Small, J. G. (1966). The organic dimension of crime. *Archives of General Psychiatry, 15,* 82–89.

Smart, R. G., Fejer, D., & White, W. J. (1970). *The extent of drug use in metropolitan Toronto Schools: A study of changes from 1968–1970.* Toronto: Addiction Research Foundation.

Smith, Adam (1776/1953). *The wealth of nations.* Cambridge: Harvard University Press.

Smith, A. H., Pool, D. I., Pearce, N. E., Lyon, J. L., Lilley, B. M., Davis, P. B., & Prior, I. A. M. (1985). Mortality among New Zealand Maori and non-Maori Mormons. *International Journal of Epidemiology, 14,* 265–271.

Smith, B. (1994). *Terrorism: An introduction.* Belmont, CA: West/Wadsworth. Soler, P., Carretero, M. D., Martin, C., Soler, M., Gazquez, J. A., Perez, E., Delgado, A., & Mavarro, R. (1992). Alcohol and drug use by medical university students. *Folia Neuropsiquiatrica 27,* 99–108.

Smith, B. H., & Tompkins, R. L. (1995). Toward a life history of the hominidae. *Annual Review of Anthropology, 24,* 257–279.

Smith, Brent (1994). *Terrorism in America: Pipe bombs and pipe dreams.* Albany: State University of New York Press.

Smith, C. A., & Stern, S. B. (1997). Delinquency and antisocial behavior: A review of family process and intervention research. *Social Service Review, 71,* 382–420.

Smith, D. A., & Brame, R. (1994). Of the initiation and continuation of delinquency. *Criminology, 32,* 607–629.

Smith, D. A., & Paternoster, R. (1987). The gender gap in theories of deviance: Issues and evidence. *Journal of Research in Crime and Delinquency, 24,* 140–172.

Smith, D. A., & Visher, C. A. (1980). Sex and involvement in deviance/crime: A quantitative review of the empirical literature. *American Sociological Review, 45,* 691–701.

Smith, D. J. (1995). Youth crime and conduct disorders: Trends, patterns, and casual explanations. In M. Rutter & D. J. Smith (Eds.), *Psychological disorders in young people* (pp. 389–489). New York: Wiley.

Smith, D. J. (1997). Ethnic origins, crime, and criminal justice in England and Wales. *Crime and Justice: A Review of Research, 21,* 101–178.

Smith, E., Udry, J., & Morris, N. (1985). Pubertal development and friends: A biosocial explanation of adolescent sexual behavior. *Health and Social Behavior, 26,* 183–192.

Smith, E. O. (1973). A further description of the control role in pigtail macaques, *Macaca nemestrina. Primates, 14,* 413–419.

Smith, J. C., Mercy, J. A., & Rosenberg, M. L. (1986). Suicide and homicide among Hispanics in the Southwest. *Public Health Reports, 101,* 265–270.

Smith, J. S. (1980). Episodic rage. In M. Girgus & L. G. Kiloh (Eds.), *Limbic epilepsy and the dyscontrol syndrome* (pp. 255–265). Amsterdam: Elsevier/North Holland Biomedical Press.

Smith, R. J. (1985). The concept and measurement of social psychopathy. *Journal of Research in Personality, 19,* 219–231.

Smith, S. S., O'Hara, B. F., & Persico, A. M. (1992). Genetic vulnerability to drug abuse: The D2 dopamine receptor TaqI B restriction fragment length polymorphism appears more frequently in polysubstance abusers. *Archives of General Psychiatry, 49,* 723–727.

Smith, W., & Monastersky, C. (1986). Assessing juvenile sexual offenders' risk for reoffending. *Criminal Justice and Behavior, 13,* 115–140.

Smithson, M., & Amato, P. (1982). An unstudied region of helping: An extension of the Pearce-Amato cognitive taxonomy. *Social Psychology Quarterly, 45,* 67–76.

Smuts, Barbara (1992). Male aggression against women: An evolutionary perspective. *Human Nature, 3,* 1–44.

Snarey, J. R. (1985). Cross-cultural universality of social-moral development: A critical review of Kohlbergian research. *Psychological Bulletin, 97,* 202–232.

Snider, Laureen (1990). Cooperative models and corporate crime: Panacea or cop-out? *Crime and Delinquency, 36,* 373–390.

Snyder, J., & Patterson, G. (1987). Family interaction and delinquent behavior. In H. C. Quay (Ed.), *Handbook of juvenile delinquency* (pp. 216–243). New York: Wiley.

Snyder, S. H., Banerjee, S. P., Yamamura, H. I., & Greenberg, D. (1974). Drugs, neurotransmitters, and schizophrenia. *Science, 184,* 1243–1253.

Sobell, L. C. (1979). Reliability of alcohol abusers' self-reports of drinking behavior. *Behavioral Research and Therapy, 17,* 157–160.

Sobotka, S., & Grodzicka, J. (1989). Hemispheric differences in evoked potentials to faces and words. *Acta Neurobiologica Experimenta,*

Sokoloff, L., Fitzgerald, G. G., & Kaufman, E. E. (1977). Cerebral nutrition and energy metabolism. In R. J. Wurtman & J. J. Wurtman (Eds.), *Nutrition and the brain,* vol. 1: *Determinants of the availability of nutrients to the brain* (pp. 87–139). New York: Raven.

Solomon, P., Draine, J., & Meyerson, A. (1994). Jail recidivism and receipt of community mental health services. *Hospital and Community Psychiatry, 45,* 793–797.

Sonis, W., Comite, F., Blue, J., Pescovitz, O. H., Rahn, C. W., Hench, K. D., Cutler, G., Loriaux, D., & Klein, R. P. (1985). Behavior problems and social competence in girls with true precocious puberty. *Journal of Pediatrics, 106,* 156–160.

Soubrie, P. (1986). Reconciling the role of central serotonin neurons in human and animal behavior. *Behavioral and Brain Sciences, 9,* 316–364.

Soudek, D., & Laraya, P. (1974). Longer Y chromosome in criminals. *Clinical Genetics, 6,* 225–229.

Souryal, Sam, Potts, Dennis, & Alobied, Abdullah (1994). The penalty of hand amputation for theft in Islamic justice. *Journal of Criminal Justice, 22,* 249–265.

Sparks, R. F. (1976). Crime and victims in London. In W. G. Skogan (Ed.), *Sample surveys of the victims of crime* (pp. 43–71). Cambridge, MA: Ballinger.

Sparks, R. F. (1980). A critique of Marxist criminology. In N. Morris & M. Tonry (Eds.), *Crime and justice* (Vol. 2, pp. 159–210). Chicago: University of Chicago Press.

Speer, P. W., Gorman, D. M., Labouvie, E. W., & Ontkush, M. J. (1998). Violent crime and alcohol availability: Relationships in an urban community. *Journal of Public Health Policy, 19,* 303–317.

Spennemann, D. R. (1984). Handedness data on the European neolithic. *Neuropsychologia, 22,* 613–615.

Sperry, R. (1982). Some effects of disconnecting the cerebral hemispheres. *Science, 217,* 1223–1226.

Spierenburg, P. (1994). Faces of violence: Homicide trends and cultural meanings, Amsterdam, 1431–1816. *Journal of Social History, 27,* 701–716.

Spierenburg, P. (1996). Long-term trends in homicide: Theoretical reflections and Dutch evidence, fifteenth to twentieth centuries. In E. A. Johnson & E. H. Monkkonen (Eds.), *The civilization of crime: Violence in town and country since the Middle Ages* (pp. 63–105). Urbana and Chicago, IL: Univ of Illinois Press.

Sprague, R. L., Barnes, K. R., & Werry, J. S. (1970). Methyphenidate and thioridazine: Learning, activity, and behavior in emotionally disturbed boys. *American Journal of Orthopsychiatry, 40,* 615–628.

Springer, A., & Deutsch, G. (1981). *Left brain, right brain.* San Francisco: Freeman.

Sprinzak, Ehud (1991). The process of delegitimation: Towards a linkage theory of political terrorism. In C. McCauley (Ed.), *Terrorism research and public policy* (pp. 50–68). London: Frank Cass.

Stabenau, J. R., & Pollin, W. (1993). Heredity and environment in schizophrenia, revisited: The contribution of twin and high-risk studies. *Journal of Nervous and Mental Disease, 181,* 290–297.

Stack, S. (1984). Income inequality and property crime. *Criminology, 22,* 229–257.

Stack, S. (1992). The effect of divorce on suicide in Japan: A time series analysis, 1950–1980. *Journal of Marriage and the Family, 54,* 327–334.

Stacy, A. W., Widaman, K. F., & Hays, R. (1985). Validity of self-reports of alcohol and other drug use: A multitrait–multimethod assessment. *Journal of Personal Social Psychology, 49,* 219–232.

Staffieri, J. R. (1967). A study of social stereotype of body image in children. *Journal of Personality and Social Psychology, 1,* 101–104.

Stalans, L. J., & Lurigio, A. J. (1990). Lay and professionals' beliefs about crime and criminal sentencing: A need for theory, perhaps schema theory. *Criminal Justice and Behavior, 17,* 333–349.

Stang, D., Snare, T., & Snare, A. (1978). The coercion of privacy: A feminist perspective. In C. Smart & B. Smart (Eds.), *Women, sexuality and social control* (pp. 8–26). London: Routledge and Kegan Paul.

Stang, H., Gunnar, M., Snellman, L., Condon, L., & Kestenbaum, R. (1988). Local anesthesia for neonatal circumcision: Effects on distress and cortisol response. *Journal of the American Medical Association, 259,* 1507–1511.

Stanton, B., Baldwin, R. M., & Rachuba, L. (1997). A quarter century of violence in the United States: An epidemiologic assessment. *Psychiatric Clinics of North America, 20,* 269–282.

Stanton, M. E., Wallstrom, J., & Kevine, S. (1987). Maternal contact inhibits pituitary-adrenal stress responses in preweanling rats. *Developmental Psychobiology, 20,* 131–145.

Staples, R. (1986). The masculine way of violence. In D. F. Hawkins (Ed.), *Homicide among Black Americans* (pp. 137–152). Lanham, MD: University Press of America.

Stark, E., Flitcraft, A., & Frazier, W. (1981). *Wife abuse in the medical setting: An introduction for health personnel.* Washington, DC: Office of Domestic Violence.

Stark, R., Kent, L., & Doyle, S. P. (1982). Religion and delinquency: The ecology of a "lost" relationship. *Journal of Research in Crime and Delinquency, 19,* 4–24.

Stattin, H., & Magnusson, D. (1991). Stability and change in criminal behavior up to age 30. *British Journal of Criminology, 31,* 327–346.

Stattin, H., & Magnusson, D. (1996). Antisocial development: A holistic approach. *Developmental Psychopathology, 8,* 617–645.

Staub, S. (1965). *Ursachen und erscheinungs-formen bei der bildung jugendlicher banden (Causes of the formation of juvenile gangs and their typology*). Zurich, Switzerland: Herausgegeben von Mitgliedern der Rechts, University of Zurich [see *Crime and Delinquency Abstracts, 1966, 4,* 266].

Steenhuis, R. E., Bryden, M. P., Schwartz, M., & Lawson, S. (1990). Reliability of hand preference items and factors. *Journal of Clinical and Experimental Neuropsychology, 12,* 921–930.

Steffensmeier, D. J. (1980a). Assessing the impact of the women's movement on sex-based differences in the handling of adult criminal defendants. *Crime and Delinquency, 26,* 344–357.

Steffensmeier, D. J. (1980b). Sex differences in patterns of adult crime, 1967–1977: A review and assessment. *Social Forces, 58,* 1080–1108.

Steffensmeier, D. J. (1989). On the causes of "white collar" crime: An assessment of Hirschi and Gottfredson's claims. *Criminology, 27,* 345–358.

Steffensmeier, D. J., & Allan, E. A. (1988). Sex disparities in arrests by residence, race and age: An assessment of the gender convergence/crime hypothesis. *Justice Quarterly, 5,* 53–80.

Steffensmeier, D. J., Allan, E., & Streifel, C. (1989). Development and female crime: A cross-national test of alternative explanations. *Social Forces, 68,* 262–283.

Steffensmeier, D. J., Kramer, J., & Streifer, C. (1993). Gender and imprisonment decisions. *Criminology, 31,* 411–446.

Steffensmeier, D. J., & Steffensmeier, R. H. (1980). Trends in female delinquency: An examination of arrest, juvenile court, self-report and field data. *Criminology, 18,* 62–85.

Steg, J. P., & Rapaport, J. L. (1975). Minor physical anomalies in normal, neurotic, learning-disabled and severely disturbed children. *Journal of Autism and Childhood Schizophrenia, 5,* 299–307.

Steinberg, L. (1986). Latchkey children and susceptibility to peer pressure: An ecological analysis. *Developmental Psychology, 22,* 433–439.

Steinberg, L. (1988). Reciprocal relation between parent–child distance and pubertal maturation. *Developmental Psychology, 24,* 122–128.

Stelmack, R. M., Rourke, B. P., & Van der Vlugt, H. (1995). Intelligence, learning disabilities, and event-related potentials. *Developmental Neuropsychology, 11,* 445–465.

Stermac, Lana, Segal, Zindel, & Gillis, Roy (1990). Social and cultural factors in sexual assault. In W. Marshall, D. Laws, and H. Barbaree (Eds.), *Handbook of sexual assault: Issues, theories, and treatment of the offender* (pp. 143–159). New York: Plenum.

Stets, J. E., & Straus, M. A. (1990). Gender differences in reporting marital violence and its medical and psychological consequences. In M. A. Straus & R. Gelles (Eds.), *Physical violence in American families: Risk factors and adaptation to violence in 8,145 families* (pp. 151–165). New Brunswick, NJ: Transaction.

Stevens, J. R. (1983). Epilepsy, personality, behavior and psychopathology: The state of the evidence and directions for future research and treatment. *Folia Psychiatrica et Neurologica Japonica, 37,* 203–212.

Stevens, J. R., & Hermann, B. P. (1981). Temporal lobe epilepsy, psychopathology, and violence: The state of the evidence. *Neurology, 31,* 1127–1132.

Stevenson, J., & Graham, P. (1988). Behavioral deviance in 13-year-old twins: kAn item analysis. *Journal of American Academy of Child and Adolescent Psychiatry, 27,* 791–797.

Stewart, M. A. (1985). Aggressive conduct disorder: A brief review. *Aggressive Behavior, 11,* 323–331.

Stewart, M. A., & de Blois, S. (1985). Diagnostic criteria for aggressive conduct disorder. *Psychopathology, 18,* 11–17.

Stewart, M. A., & Leone, L. (1978). A family study of unsocialized aggressive boys. *Biological Psychiatry, 13,* 107–117.

Stinson, James (1987). Domestic terrorism in the United States. *Police Chief, 54,* 62–69.

Stitt, B. G. (1988). Victimless crime: A definitional issue. *Journal of Crime and Justice, 11,* 87–102.

Stitt, B. G., & Giacopassi, D. J. (1992). Trends in the connectivity of theory and research in criminology. *Criminologist, 17,* 1–6.

Stock, Wendy (1991). Feminist explanations: Male power, hostility, and sexual coercion. In E. Grauerholz & M. Koralewski (Eds.), *Sexual coercion: A sourcebook on its nature, causes, and prevention* (pp. 61–73). Lexington, MA: Lexington Books.

Stoff, D. M., & Vitiello, B. (1996). Role of serotonin in aggression of children and adolescents: Biochemical and pharmacological studies. In D. M. Stoff & R. B. Cairns (Eds.), *Neurobiological approaches to clinical aggression research.* Mahwah, NJ: Erlbaum.

Stone, L. (1983). Interpersonal violence in English society 1300–1980. *Past and Present, 102,* 23–33.

Stott, D. (1982). *Delinquency: The problem and its prevention.* New York: SP Medical and Scientific Books.

Strayer, J., & Roberts, W. (1989). Children's empathy and role taking: Child and parental factors and relations to prosocial behaviour. *Journal of Applied Developmental Psychology, 10,* 227–239.

Streit, F. (1981). Differences among youthful criminal offenders based on their perceptions of parental behavior. *Adolescence, 16,* 409–415.

Stricker, E. M., & Zigmond, M. J. (1986). Brain monoamines, homeostasis, and adaptive behavior. In South American Physiological (Ed.), *Handbook of physiology,* Section 1: *The nervous system,* vol. 4. *Intrinsic regulatory systems of the brain* (pp. 677–700). Bethesda, MD: American Physiological Society.

Stromberg, A. H., & Harkess, (Eds.). (1978). *Women working.* Palo Alto: Mayfield.

Stuart, R. B. (1971). Behavioral contracting within the families of delinquents. *Journal of Behavior Therapy and Experimental Psychiatry, 2,* 1–11.

Sturge, C. (1982). Reading retardation and antisocial behaviour. *Journal of Child Psychology and Psychiatry, 23,* 21–31.

Stuss, D. T., Benson, D. F., Kaplan, E. F., Weir, W. S., Naeser, M. A., Lieberman, L., and Ferrill, D. (1983). The involvement of orbitofrontal cerebrum in cognitive tasks. *Neuropsychologia, 21,* 235–248.

Suchy, Y., Blint, A., & Osman, D. C. (1997). Behavioral dyscontrol scale: Criterion and predictive validity in an inpatient rehabilitation unit population. *Clinical Neuropsychologist, 11,* 258–265.

Suedfeld, P., & Landon, P. B. (1978). Approaches to treatment. In R. D. Hare & D. Schalling (Eds.), *Psychopathic Behavior* (pp. 347–376). New York: Wiley.

Sullivan, E. (1977). A study of Kohlberg's structural theory of moral development. A critique of liberal social science ideology. *Human Development, 20,* 325–376.

Sumner, W. G. (1940). *Folkways.* Boston: Ginn.

Sundberg, N. D., Latkin, C. A., Farmer, R. F., & Saoud, J. (1991). Boredom in young adults. *Journal of Cross-Cultural Psychology, 22,* 209–223.

Surbey, M. (1990). Family composition, stress, and human menarche. In F. Bercovitch & T. Zeigler (Eds.), *The socioendocrinology of primate reproduction* (pp. 71–97). New York: Liss.

Susman, E. J., Innoff-Germain, G., Nottelmann, E. D., Loriaux, D. L., Cutler, G. B., Jr., & Chrousos, G. P. (1987). Hormones, emotional dispositions, and aggressive attributes in young adolescents. *Child Development, 58,* 1114–1134.

Sutherland, E. H. (1931). Mental deficiency and crime. In K. Young (Ed.), *Social attitudes.* New York: Holt.

Sutherland, E. H. (1934). *Principles of criminology.* Philadelphia, PA: Lippincott.

Sutherland, E. H. (1939). *Principles of criminology* (2nd ed.). Philadelphia, PA: Lippincott.

Sutherland, E. H. (1940). White collar criminality. *American Sociological Review, 5,* 1–20.

Sutherland, E. H., & Cressey, D. (1966). *Principles of criminology* (7th ed.). Philadelphia: Lippincott.

Sutherland, E. H., & Cressey, D. (1974). *Principles of criminology* (8th ed.). Philadelphia: Lippincott.

Swanson, J. W., Holzer, C. E., Ganju, V. K., & Jono, R. T. (1990). Violence and psychiatric disorder in the community: Evidence from the epidemiologic catchment area surveys. *Hospital Community of Psychiatry, 41,* 761–770.

Sweeney, L. T., & Haney, C. (1992). The influence of race on sentencing: A meta-analytic review of experimental studies. *Behavioral Sciences and the Law, 10,* 179–195.

Sweet, W. H., Ervin, F., & Mark, V. H. (1969). The relationship of violent behavior to focal cerebral disease. In S. Garrattini & E. B. Sigg (Eds.), *Aggressive behavior* (pp. 336–352). New York: Wiley.

Swigert, V. L. (1975). *Criminal homicide: A socio-legal analysis.* State University of New York, Albany, Ph.D. dissertation.

Sykes, G. M., & Matza, D. (1957). Techniques of naturalization: A theory of delinquency. *American Sociological Review, 22,* 664–670.

Sykes, G. M. (1980). *Future of crime.* Washington, DC: U.S. Government Printing Office.

Syndulko, K. (1978). Electrocortical investigations of sociopathy. In R. D. Hare & D. Schalling (Eds.), *Psychopathic behavior* (pp. 145–156). New York: Wiley.

Taft, D. R., & England, R. W. (1964). *Criminology* (4th ed.). New York: Macmillan.

Tancredi, L. R., & Volkow, N. (1988). Neural substrates of violent behavior: Implications for law and public policy. *International Journal of Law and Psychiatry, 11,* 13–49.

Tannenbaum, F. (1938). *Crime and community.* New York: Columbia University Press.

Tarde, G. (1890). *La philosophie pénale.* Paris: Lyon.

Tardif, S. (1984). Social influences on sexual maturation of female Saguinus oedipus oedipus. *Ethology and Sociobiology, 10,* 131–144.

Tardiff, K. (1985). Patterns and major determinants of homicide in the United States. *Hospital and Community Psychiatry, 36,* 632–639.

Tausig, M. (1982). Measuring life events. *Journal of Health and Social Behavior, 23,* 52–64.

Taylor, E., Chadwick, O., Heptinstall, E., & Danckaerts, M. (1996). Hyperactivity and conduct problems as risk factors for adolescent development. *Journal of American Academy of Child Adolescent Psychiatry, 35,* 1213–1226.

Taylor, I., Walton, P., & Young, J. (1973). *The new criminology.* New York: Harper & Row.

Taylor, I., Walton, P., & Young, J. (1975). Critical criminology in Britain: Review and prospects. In I. Taylor, P. Walton, & J. Young (Eds.), *Critical criminology* (pp. 6–62). London: Routledge and Kegan Paul.

Taylor, J. H., & Walker, L. J. (1997). Moral climate and the development of moral reasoning: The effects of dyadic discussions between young offenders. *Journal of Moral Education, 26,* 21–43.

Teasdale, T. W., & Owen, D. R. (1984). Heredity and familial environment in intelligence and educational level—a sibling study. *Nature, 309,* 620–622.

Teicher, M. H., Ito, Y. M. D., Glod, C. A., & Barber, N. I. (1996). Objective measurement of hyperactivity and attentional problems in ADHD. *Journal of the American Academy of Child and Adolescent Psychiatry, 35,* 334–342.

Teplin, L. (1983). The criminalization of the mentally ill: Speculation in search of data. *Psychology Bulletin, 94,* 54–67.

Terlouw, G.-J., & Bruinsma, G. J. N. (1994). Self-reported delinquency in the Netherlands. In J. Junger-Tas, G.-J. Terlouw, & M. W. Klein (Eds.), *Delinquent behavior among young people in the Western world: First results of the international self-report delinquency study* (pp. 102–130). Amsterdam: Kugler.

Terrill, Richard (1984). *World criminal justice systems* (1st ed.). Cincinnati, OH: Anderson.

Terrill, Richard (1997). *World criminal justice systems,* (3rd ed.). Cincinnati, OH: Anderson.

Teuber, H. L. (1964). The riddle of frontal lobe function in man. In J. M. Warren & K. Akert (Eds.), *The frontal granular cortex and behavior* (pp. 333, 410–458). New York: McGraw-Hill.

Thapar, A., Hervas, A., & McGuffin, P. (1995). Childhood hyperactivity scores are highly heritable and show sibling competition effects: Twin study evidence. *Behavior Genetics, 25,* 537–544.

Thapar, A., & McGuffin, P. (1996). A twin study of antisocial and neurotic symptoms in childhood. *Psychological Medicine, 26,* 1111–1118.

The European (1996). Forester admits 52 murders. April 25–May 1, 7A.

Thio, A. (1986). *Sociology: An introduction.* New York: Harper & Row.

Thoma, S. (1986). Estimating gender differences in the comprehension and preferences of moral issues. *Developmental Review, 6,* 165–180.

Thomas, A., & Chess, S. (1980). *The dynamics of psychological development.* New York: Brunner/Mazel.

Thompson, I. A. A. (1968). A map of crime in sixteenth-century Spain. *Economic History Review, 21,* 244–251.

Thompson, L. A. (1993). Genetic contributions to intellectual development in infancy and childhood. In P. A. Vernon (Ed.), *Biological approaches to the study of human intelligence* (pp. 95–138). Norwood, NJ: Ablex.

Thompson, Wayne (1985). *Canada 1985*. Washington, DC: Stryker-Post Publications.

Thornberry, T. P., & Christenson, R. L. (1984). Unemployment and criminal involvement: An investigation of reciprocal casual structures. *American Sociological Review, 49,* 398–411.

Thornberry, T. P., Moore, M., & Christenson, R. L. (1985). The effect of dropping out of high school on subsequent criminal behavior. *Criminology, 23,* 3–18.

Thornhill, Randy, & Thornhill, Nancy (1987). Human rape: The strength of the evolutionary perspective. In C. Crawford, M. Smith, & D. Krebs (Eds.), *Sociobiology and psychology.*

Thornhill, Randy, & Thornhill, Nancy (1992). The evolutionary psychology of men's coercive sexuality. *Behavioral and Brain Sciences, 15,* 363–421.

Thornquist, M. H., & Zuckerman, M. (1995). Psychopathy, passive-avoidance learning and basic dimensions of personality. *Personality and Individual Differences, 19,* 525–533.

Thurman, Q. C. (1984). Deviance and the neutralization of moral commitment: An empirical analysis. *Deviant Behavior, 5,* 291–304.

Thurow, L. C. (1987). A surge in inequality. *Scientific American,* vol # 30–37.

Tibbetts, S. G., & Herz, D. C. (1996). Gender differences in factors of social control and rational choice. *Deviant Behavior, 17,* 183–208.

Tierney, J. (1987). Stress, success, and Samoa. *Hippocrates, 1,* (May/June), 74–85.

Tiihonen, J., Hakola, P., & Eronen, M. (1995). Homicidal behaviour and mental disorders. *British Journal of Psychiatry, 167,* 821.

Tinklenbert, J. R. (1973). Alcohol and violence. In P. Bourne & R. Fox (Eds.), *Alcoholism: Progress in research and treatment* (Chapter 8). New York: Academic Press.

Tittle, C. R. (1975). Deterrents or labelling. *Social Forces, 53,* 399–410.

Tittle, C. R. (1991). Book review. *American Journal of Sociology, 96,* 1609–1611.

Tittle, C. R., Villemez, W. J., & Smith, D. A. (1978). The myth of social class and criminality: An empirical assessment of the empirical evidence. *American Sociological Review, 43,* 623–656.

Tobias, J. J. (1967). *Crime and industrial society in the 19th century.* New York: Schocken Books.

Tobin, M. B., Schmidt, P. J., & Rubinow, D. R. (1994). Reported alcohol use in women with premenstrual syndrome. *American Journal of Psychiatry, 151,* 1503–1504.

Toby, J. (1980). The new criminology is the old baloney. In J. Inciardi, A. (Ed.), *Radical criminology: The coming crises* (pp. 124–132). Beverly Hills, CA: Sage.

Tocker, D. M., & Dawson, S. L. (1984). Asymmetric EEG changes as method actors generated emotions. *Biological Psychology, 19,* 63–75.

Tonry, M. (1995). *Malign neglect.* New York: Oxford University Press.

Tooke, W., & Camire, L. (1991). Patterns of deception in intersexual and intrasexual mating strategies. *Ethology and Sociobiology, 12,* 345–364.

Torrey, E. Fuller (1997). The release of the mentally ill from institutions: A well-intentioned disaster. *Chronical of Higher Education, 153,* B4–B5.

Toubia, N. (1994). Female circumcision as a public health issue. *New England Journal of Medicine, 331,* 712–740.

Touliatos, J., & Lindholm, B. W. (1980). Behavioral disturbance in children of native-born and immigrant parents. *Journal of Community Psychology, 8,* 28–33.

Townsend, J. M. (1989). Mate selection criteria: A pilot study. *Ethology and Sociobiology, 10,* 241–253.

Tracy, P., Wolfgang, M., & Figlio, R. (1990). *Delinquency careers in two birth cohorts.* New York: Plenum.

Trandaburu, T., Mincu, I., Petrescu-Rainanu, A., & Popescu, V. (1979). The effects of short-term exposure to crowding stress on the pancreatic islets morphology and glycemia in mice. *Experimental Pathology, 17,* 280–292.

Traskman, L., Tybring, G., Asberg, M., Bertlisson, L., Lanlto, O., & Schalling, D. (1980). Cortisol in the CSF of depressed and suicidal patients. *Archives of General Psychiatry, 27,* 761–767.

Treiman, D. M. (1991). Psychobiology of ictal aggression. In D. B. Smith, D. M. Treiman, & M. R. Trimble (Eds.), *Neurobehavioral problems in epilepsy* (pp. 341–356). New York: Raven.

Tremblay, R. E., & Craig, W. M. (1995). *Developmental crime prevention.* In M. Tonry & D. P. Farrington (Eds.), *Building a safer society: Strategic approaches to crime prevention* (pp. 151–236). Chicago: University of Chicago Press.

Tremblay, R. E., Masse, B., Perron, D., Leblanc, M., Schwartzman, A. E., & Ledingham, J. E. (1992a). Early disruptive behavior, poor school achievement, delinquent behavior, and delinquent personality: Longitudinal analyses. *Journal of Consulting and Clinical Psychology, 60,* 64–72.

Tremblay, R. E., Pihl, R. O., Vitaro, F., & Dobkin, P. L. (1994). Predicting early onset of male antisocial behavior from preschool behavior. *Archives of General Psychiatry, 51,* 732–739.

Tremblay, R. E., Vitaro, F., Bertrand, L., LeBlanc, M., Beauchesne, H., Boileau, H., & David, L. (1992b). Parent and child training to prevent early onset of delinquency: The Montreal Longitudinal-Experimental Study. In J. McCord & R. E. Tremblay (Eds.), *Preventing antisocial behavior* (pp. 117–138). New York: Guilford.

Trevino, L., & Youngblood, S. (1990). Bad apples in bad barrels: A causal analysis of ethical decision-making behavior. *Journal of Applied Psychology, 78,* 378–385.

Trickett, A., Ellingworth, D., Hope, T., & Pease, K. (1995). Crime victimization in the eighties: Changes in area and regional inequality. *British Journal of Criminology, 35,* 343–359.

Triplett, R., & Jarjoura, G. R. (1997). Specifying the gender-class-delinquency relationship: Exploring the effects of educational expectations. *Sociological Perspectives, 40,* 287–316.

Trivers, R. (1985). *Social evolution.* Menlo Park, CA: Benjamin/Cummings.

Troup, G. A., Bradshaw, J. L., & Nettleton, N. C. (1983). The lateralization of arithmetic and number processing: A review. *International Journal of Neuroscience, 19,* 231–242.

Truett, K. R. (1993). Age differences in conservatism. *Personality and Individual Differences, 14,* 405–411.

Tuddenham, R. D., Brooks, J., & Milkovich, L. (1974). Mother's reports of behavior of ten-year-olds: Relationship with sex, ethnicity, and mother's education. *Developmental Psychology, 10,* 959–995.

Turk, A. T. (1969). *Criminality and the legal order.* Chicago: Rand McNally.

Turk, A. T. (1980). Analyzing official deviance: Four nonpartisan conflict analyses in criminology. In J. Inciardi, A. (Ed.), Radical criminology: The coming crises (pp. 78–91). Beverly Hills, CA: Sage.

Turner, W. D. (1948). Altruism and its measurement in children. *Journal of Abnormal and Social Psychology, 43,* 502–516.

Turner, W. J., & Merlis, S. (1962). Clinical correlations between EEGs and antisocial behavior. *Medical Times, 90,* 505–511.

Udry, J. R., & Talbert, L. M. (1988). Sex hormones effects on personality at puberty. *Journal of Personality and Social Psychology, 54,* 291–295.

Uhlman, T., & Walker, N. (1980). "He takes some of my time; I take some of his": An analysis of judicial sentencing patterns in jury cases. *Law and Society Review, 14,* 323–339.

Underwood, B., & Moore, B. (1982). Perspective-taking and altruism. *Psychological Bulletin, 91,* 143–173.

United Nations Asia and Far East Institute for the Prevention of Crime & Treatment of Offenders and the Australian Institute of Criminology (1990). *Crime and justice in Asia and the Pacific.* Tokyo: UNAFEI/AIC.

United Nations, General Assembly (1977). *Crime prevention and control* (Report of the Secretary-General). New York: UN Publications.

United States Indian Health Service (1978). *Indian health trends and services.* Washington, DC: U.S. Government Printing Office.

United States, Department of Justice. (1983). *Report to the nation on crime and justice, the data.* Washington, DC: U.S. Bureau of Justice Statistics.

United States, Department of Justice. (1988). *Report to the nation on crime and justice.* Washington, DC: U.S. Bureau of Justice Statistics.

United States, Department of Justice (1993). Highlights from 20 years of surveying crime victimization. Washington, DC: U.S. Bureau of Crime Statistics (NCJ–144525).

United States Department of Justice. (1991). *Criminal victimization in the United States: 1973–1988 trends.* Washington, DC: U.S. Department of Justice (NJC–129392).

United States, Department of Justice (1997). *1996 Uniform Crime Reports.* Washington, DC: U.S. Department of Justice.

United States, Department of State (1995). *Patterns of global terrorism: 1994.* Washington, DC:

United States, Department of State (1996). *Patterns of global terrorism: 1995.* Washington, DC:

United States Federal Bureau of Investigation (1993). *Uniform crime reports.* Washington, DC: U.S. Department of Justice.

Unnever, J. D., & Hembroff, L. A. (1988). The prediction of racial/ethnic sentencing disparities: An expectation states approach. *Journal of Research in Crime and Delinquency, 25,* 53–82.

Useem, Michael (1989). *Liberal education and the corporation.* Hawthorn, NY: Aldine de Gruyter.

Vaernet, K., & Madison, A. (1970). Sterotaxic amygdalotomy and baso-frontal tractotomy in psychotics with aggressve behavior. *Journal of Neurology, Neurosurgery, and Psychiatry, 33,* 858–863.

Vago, Steven (1991). *Law and society.* Englewood Cliffs, NJ: Prentice-Hall.

Valez-Diaz, A., & Megargee, E. (1970). An investigation of differences in value judgements between youthful offenders and non-offenders in Puerto-Rico. *Journal of Criminal Law, Criminology, and Police Science, 61,* 549–553.

Valzelli, L. (1974). 5-Hydroxytryptamine in aggressiveness. In E. Costa, G. Gessa, & M. Sandler (Eds.), *Advances in biochemical psychopharmacology.* New York: Raven.

Vanagunas, S. (1979). Police diversion of juvenile offenders: An ambiguous state of the act. *Federal Probation,* September, 48–52.

van den Broek, M. D., Bradshaw C. M., & Szabadi E. (1992). The relationship between "impulsiveness" and hemispheric functional asymmetry: Investigated with a divided visual field word recognition task. In (eds), (Title), etc. (pp. 355–360). Great Britain: Pergamon.

van den Oord, E. J., Verhulst, F. C., & Boomsma, D. I. (1996). A genetic study of maternal and paternal ratings of problem behaviors in 3-year-old twins. *Journal of Abnormal Psychology, 105,* 349–357.

van Dijk, J. J. M. (1979). The extent of public information and the nature of public attitudes towards crime. In O.C.P. European Committee (Ed.), *Public opinion on crime and criminal justice* (pp. 7–42). Strasbourg: European Committee on Crime Problems.

van Dijk, J. J. M., & Mayhew, P. (1993). Criminal victimization in the industrialized world: Key findings of the 1989 and 1992 international crime surveys. In A. A. del Frate, U. Zuekic, & J. J. van Dijk (Eds.), *Understanding crime* (pp. 1–29). Rome, Italy: United Nations Interregional Crime and Justice Research Institute.

van Dijk, J. J. M., Mayhew, P., & Killias, M. (1991). *Experiences of crime across the world* (2nd ed.). Boston: Kluwer Law and Taxation Publishers.

Van Dusen, K. T., Mednick, S. A., Gabrielli, W. F., & Hutchings, B. (1983). Social class and crime in a adoption cohort. *Journal of Criminal Law and Criminology, 74,* 249–254.

Van Kammen, W. B., Loeber, R., & Southamer-Loeber, M. (1991). Substance use and its relationship to conduct problems and delinquency in young boys. *Journal of Youth and Adolescence, 20,* 399–413.

van Pragg, H. M. (1986). Affective disorders and aggression disorders: Evidence for a common biological mechanism. *Suicide and Life-Threatening Behavior, 16,* 103–132.

van Swaaningen, R., & Taylor, I. (1994). Rethinking critical criminology. *Crime, Law & Social Change, 21,* 183–190.

Van Voorhis, P., Cullen, F. T., Mathers, R. A., & Garner, C. C. (1988). The impact of family structure and quality on delinquency: A comparative assessment of structural and functional factors. *Criminology, 26,* 235–261.

Vasudev, J., & Hummel, R. C. (1987). Moral stage sequence and principled reasoning in an Indian sample. *Human Development, 30,* 105–118.

Vazsonyi, A. T. (1995). Etiological risk factors in juvenile delinquency: A comparison of Swiss and American adolescents. *Dissertation Abstracts International, 56,* 6A, 2424.

Vazsonyi, A. T., & Flannery, D. J. (1997). Early adolescent delinquent behaviors: Associations with family and school domains. *Journal of Early Adolescence, 17,* 271–293.

Venables, P. H. (1988). Psychophysiology and crime: Theory and data. In T. E. Moffitt & S. A. Mednick (Eds.), *Biological contributions to crime causation.* Dordrecht, Holland: Martinus Nijhoff.

Venables, P. H. (1987). Autonomic and central nervous system factors in criminal behavior. In S. A. Mednick, T. Moffitt, & S. Stack (Eds.), *The causes of crime: New biological approaches* (pp. 110–136). New York: Cambridge University Press.

Verdugo, N. (1998). Crimes and punishment: Blacks in the Army's criminal justice system. *Military Psychology, 10,* 107–125.

Vetter, H. J., & Silverman, I. J. (1986). *Crime and criminology: An introduction.* New York: Harper & Row.

Vetter, Harold & Perlstein, Gary (1991). *Perspectives on terrorism.* Pacific Grove, CA: Brooks/Cole.

Viemero, V. (1996). Factors in childhood that predict later criminal behavior. *Aggressive Behavior, 22,* 87–97.

Vigil, J. D. (1988). *Barrio gangs: Street life and identity in Southern California.* Austin: University of Texas Press.

Vila, B. J. (1994). A general paradigm for understanding criminal behavior: Extending evolutionary ecological theory. *Criminology, 32,* 311–359.

Vila, B. J.(1997). Human nature and crime control: Improving the feasibility of nurturant strategies. *Politics and the Life Sciences, 16,* 3–21.

Vila, B. J., & Cohen, L. E. (1993). Crime as strategy: Testing an evolutionary ecological theory of expropriative crime. *American Journal of Sociology, 98,* 873–912.

Vinokur, A., & Kaplan, R. D. (1986). Cognitive and affective components of life events: Their relations and effects on well-being. *American Journal of Community Psychology, 14,* 351–370.

Virkkunen, M. (1976). Parental deprivation and recidivism in juvenile delinquents. *British Journal of Criminology, 16,* 378–384.

Virkkunen, M. (1982). Reactive hypoglycemic tendency among habitually violent offenders: A further study by means of the glucose tolerance test. *Neuropsychobiology, 5,* 35–40.

Virkkunen, M. (1987). Metabolic dysfunctions among habitually violent offenders: Reactive hypoglycemia and cholesterol levels. In S. A. Mednick, T. Moffitt, E., & S. A. Stack, (Eds.), *The cause of crime* (pp. 292–311). Cambridge, England: Cambridge University Press.

Virkkunen, M. (1988). Cerebrospinal fluid: Monoamine metabolites among habitually violent and impulsive offenders. In T. E. Moffitt & S. A. Mednick (Eds.), *Biological contributions to crime causation* (pp. 147–157). Boston: Martinus Nijhoff.

Visher, C. A. (1983). Gender, police arrest decisions, and notions of chivalry. *Criminology, 18,* 26–34.

Vitella, R. (1996). Prevalence of childhood conduct and attention-deficit hyperactivity disorders in adult maximum-security inmates. *International Journal of Offender Therapy and Comparative Criminology, 40,* 263–271.

Vitiello, B., Stoff, D., Atkins, M., & Mahoney, A. (1990). Soft neurological signs and impulsivity in children. *Developmental and Behavioral Pediatrics, 11,* 112–115.

Vodanovich, S. J., & Kass, S. J. (1990). Age and gender differences in boredom proneness. *Journal of Social Behavior and Personality, 5,* 297–307.

Vogel, F., & Motulsky, A. G. (1979). *Human genetics: Problems and approaches.* New York: Springer-Verlag.

Volberg, R. A. (1994). The prevalence and demographics of pathological gamblers: Implications for public health. *Journal of Public Health, 84,* 237–241.

Vold, G. B., & Bernard, T. J. (1987). *Theoretical criminology* (3rd ed.). New York: Oxford, University Press.

Vold, G. B., Bernard, T. J., & Snipes, J. B. (1998). *Theoretical criminology* (4th ed.). New York: Oxford University Press.

Volkwein, J. F., Szelest, B. P., & Lizotte, A. J. (1995). The relationship of campus crime to campus and student characteristics. *Research in Higher Education, 36,* 647–670.

Volobueve, Anatoli (1990). Combating organized crime in the U.S. S. R.: Problems and Perspectives. In J. Buckwalter (Ed.), *International perspectives on organized crime* (pp. 75–82). Chicago: Offfice of International Criminal Justice.

von Hentig, H. (1948). *The criminal and his victim.* New Haven, CT: Yale University Press.

von Hofer, H., & Tham, H. (1989). General deterrence in a longitudinal perspective: A Swedish case: Theft, 1841–1985. *European Sociological Review, 5,* 25–45.

von Knorring, A. L., Bohman, M., von Knorring, L., & Oreland, L. (1985a). Platelet MAO activity as a biological marker in subgroups of alcoholism. *Acta Psychiatrica Scandinavica, 72,* 51–58.

von Knorring, L., Oreland, L., & von Knorring, A. L. (1987). Personality traits and platelet MAO activity in alcohol and drug abusing teenage boys. *Acta Psychiatrica Scandinavica, 75,* 307–314.

von Knorring, L., Oreland, L., & Winblad, B. (1984). Personality traits related to monoamine oxidase activity in platelets. *Psychiatry Research, 12,* 11–26.

von Knorring, L., Palm, U., & Andersson, H.-E. (1985b). Relationship between treatment outcome and subtype of alcoholism in men. *Journal of Studies on Alcohol, 46,* 388–391.

Von Mayr, G. (1917). *Statiiisik und Gesellschaftslehre.* Tubingen: Mohr.

Voss, H. (1963). Ethnic differentials in delinquency in Honolulu. *Journal of Criminal Law, Criminality, and Police Science, 54,* 322–327.

Voss, H. L., & Hepburn, J. R. (1968). Patterns in criminal homicide in Chicago. *Journal of Criminal Law, Criminology, and Police Science. 59,* 499–508.

Wadsworth, J., Bornell, I., Taylor, B., & Butler, N. (1985). The influence of family type on children's behaviour and development at five years. *Journal of Child Psychology and Psychiatry and Allied Disciplines, 26,* 245–254.

Wadsworth, M. E. J. (1976). Delinquency, pulse rate and early emotional deprivation. *British Journal of Criminology, 16,* 245–256.

Wadsworth, M. E. J. (1979). *Roots of delinquency: Infancy, adolescence and crime.* New York: Barnes and Noble.

Wakschlag, L. S., Lahey, B. B., Loeber, R., Green, S. M., Gordon, R. A., & Leventhal, B. L. (1997). Maternal smoking during pregnancy and the risk of conduct disorder in boys. *Archives of General Psychiatry, 54,* 670–676.

Waldrop, M. F., Bell, R. Q., McLaughlin, B., & Halverson, C. F. (1978). Newborn minor physical anomalies predict short attention span, peer aggression, and impulsivity at age 3. *Science, 199,* 563–564.

Waldrop, M. F., & Halverson, C. (1971). Minor physical anomalies and hyperactive behavior in young children. *Exceptional Infant, 2,* 343–380.

Waldrop, M. M. (1984). The necessity of knowledge. *Science, 223,* 1279–1282.

Walker, A., & Walker, C. (1987). *The growing divide: A social audit 1979–1987.* London, England: CPAG.

Walker, L. J. (1984). Sex differences in the development of moral reasoning: A critical review. *Child Development, 55,* 677–691.

Walker, M. A. (1994). Measuring concern about crime: Some inter-racial comparisons. *British Journal of Criminology, 34,* 366–378.

Walker, N. (1971). *Crimes, courts, and figures: An introduction to criminal statistics.* England: Penguin.

Walker, N. (1988). Crime and penal measures. In A. H. Halsey (Ed.), *British social trends since 1900* (pp. 616–644). London: Macmillan.

Walker, R. F. (1984). Salivary cortisol determinations in the assessment of adrena activity. In D. B. Ferguson (Ed.), *Steroid hormones in saliva* (pp. 33–50). New York: Karger.

Wallace, D. C., Garrison, K., & Knowels, W. C. (1985). Dramatic founder effects in Amerindian mitochondria DNA. *American Journal of Physical Anthropology, 68,* 149–155.

Wallace, J. M., & Bachman, J. G. (1991). Explaining racial/ethnic differences in adolescent drug use: The impact of background and lifestyle. *Social Problems, 38,* 333–357.

Wallerstein, J. S., & Wyle, C. (1947). Our law-abiding law-breakers. *Probation, 25,* 107–112.

Walsh, A. (1985). The role of the probation officer in the sentencing process: Independent professional or judicial hack? *Criminal Justice and Behavior, 12,* 289–303.

Walsh, A. (1988). Lessons and concerns from a case study of a "scientific" molester. *Corrective and Social Psychiatry, 34,* 18–23.

Walsh, A. (1990). Standing trial versus copping a plea: Is there a penalty? *Journal of Contemporary Criminal Justice, 6,* 226–236.

Walsh, A. (1991). *Intellectual imbalance, love deprivation and violent delinquency: A biosocial perspective.* Springfield, IL: Charles C. Thomas.

Walsh, A. (1992). Genetic and environmental explanations of juvenile violence in advantaged and disadvantaged environments. *Aggressive Behavior, 18,* 187–199.

Walsh, A. (1994). Homosexual and heterosexual child molestation: Case characteristics and sentencing differentials. *International Journal of Offender Therapy and Comparative Criminology, 38,* 339–353.

Walsh, A. (1997). *Correctional assessment, casework & counseling* (2nd ed.). Lanham, MD: American Correctional Association.

Walsh, R. A. (1994). Effects of maternal smoking on adverse pregnancy outcomes: Examination of the criteria of causation. *Human Biology, 66,* 1059–1092.

Walters, G. D. (1992). A meta-analysis of the gene–crime relationship. *Criminology, 30,* 595–613.

Wang, C., Chan, V., Tse, T. F., & Yeung, R. T. (1978). Effect of acute myocardial infarction on pituitary–testicular function. *Clinical Endocrinology, 9,* 249–253.

Wang, Zheng (1994). An exploratory analysis of the "China trail": Causations, methods, and policy implications. *Criminal Justice International, 10,* May-June, 11–14.

Wapner, W., Hamby, S., & Garner, H. (1981). The role of the right hemisphere in the apprehension of complex linguistic materials. *Brain and Language, 14,* 15–32.

Ward, Dick (1992). Crime and violence in the "new" Europe. *Criminal Justice Europe, 2,* 1–4.

Warm, J. S., & Dember, W. (1986). Awake at the switch. *Psychology Today, 20,* 46–53.

Warr, M. (1982). The accuracy of public beliefs about crime. *Criminology, 20,* 185–204.

Warr, M. (1984). Fear of victimization: Why are women and the elderly more afraid? *Social Science Quarterly, 65,* 681–702.

Warr, M. (1989). What is the perceived seriousness of crimes? *Criminology, 27,* 795–814.

Warr, M., & Stafford, M. (1991). The influence of delinquent peers: What they think or what they do. *Criminology, 29,* 851–866.

Warren, M. (1979). The female offender in psychology of crime and criminal justice. In H. Toch (Ed.), *The psychology of crime and criminal justice* (pp. 444–469). New York: Holt, Rinehart and Winston.

Wasserman, E. (1980). An alternative high school based on Kohlberg's just community approach to education. In R. Mosher (Ed.), *Moral education: A first generation of research and development* (pp. 265–278). New York: Praeger.

Waters, H. F., & Wilson, C. H. (1979). Telling it like it is. *Newsweek,* April 23, 101.

Waters, M. C., & Eschbach, K. (1995). Immigration and ethnic and racial inequality in the United States. *Annual Review of Sociology, 21,* 419–446.

Watts, W. D., & Wright, L. S. (1990). The relationship of alcohol, tobacco, marijuana, and other illegal drug use to delinquency among Mexican-American, Black, and White adolescent males. *Adolescence, 25,* 171–181.

Weber, J. (1990). Managers' moral reasoning: Assessing their responses to three moral dilemmas. *Human Relations, 43,* 687–702.

Weigend, Thomas (1983). Criminal procedure: Comparative aspects. In S. Kadish, (Ed.), *Encyclopedia of crime and justice* (pp. 537–546). New York: Free Press.

Weiger, W. A., & Bear, D. M. (1988). An approach to the neurology of aggression. *Journal of Psychiatric Research, 22,* 85–98.

Weiner, C. (1975). Sex roles and crime in late Elizabethan Herefordshire. *Journal of Social History, 8,* 38–60.

Weinstein, S., & Teuber, H. L. (1957). Effects of penetrating brain injury on intelligence test scores. *Science, 125,* 1036–103

Weis, J. G. (1976). Liberation and crime: The invention if the new-female criminal. *Crime and Social Justice, 6,* (Fall–Winter), 17–27.

Weis, J. G., & Hawkins, J. D. (1981). *Preventing delinquency: The social development approach.* Washington, DC: U.S. Government Printing Office.

Weisburd, David, Wheeler, Stanton, Waring, Elin, & Bode, Nancy, (1991). *Crimes of the middle classes: White-collar offenders in the federal courts.* New Haven, CT: Yale University Press.

Weisheit, R. A. (1984). Women and crime: Issues and perspectives. *Sex Roles, 11,* 567–581.

Weisheit, R. A., & Culbertson, R. G. (1985). *Juvenile delinquency: A justice perspective.* Prospect Heights, IL: Waveland.

Weiss, B. (1982). Food additives and environmental chemicals as sources of childhood behavior disorders. *Journal of the American Academy of Child Psychiatry, 21,* 144–152.

Weiss, G., Hechtman, L., Milroy, T., & Perlman, T. (1985). Psychiatric status of hyperactives as adults: A controlled prospective 15-year follow-up of 63 hyperactive children. *Journal of American Academy of Child Psychiatry, 24,* 211–220.

Weiss, G., Minde, K., Werry, J. S., Douglas, V. I., & Nemeth, E. (1971). Studies on the hyperactive child, VIII. *Archives of General Psychiatry, 24,* 409–414.

Weiss, H. R., & Sampliner, R. (1944). A study of adolescent felony violators. *Journal of Criminal Law, 34,* 377–391.

Weitekamp, E. (Ed.). (1994). *Cross-national longitudinal research on human development and criminal behavior.* Boston: Kluwer.

Weller, G. M., & Bell, R. Q. (1965). Basal skin conductance and neonatal state. *Child Development, 36,* 647–657.

Wellford, C. (1975). Labelling theory and criminology: An assessment. *Social Problems, 22,* 332–345.

Wellford, C. (1982). Labelling theory and criminology: An assessment. In R. Giallombardo (Ed.), *Juvenile delinquency: A book of readings* (4th ed., pp. 189–200). New York: Wiley.

Wellford, C. F., & Triplett, R. A. (1993). The future of labeling theory: Foundations and promises. In F. Adler & W. S. Laufer (Eds.), *New directions in criminological theory: Advances in criminological theory* (Vol. 4, pp. 1–22). New Brunswick: Transaction.

Wells, B. (1980). *Personality and heredity.* London: Longman.

Wells, E. A., Morrison, D. M., Gillmore, M. R., Catalano, R. F., Iritani, B., & Hawkins, J. D. (1992). Race differences in antisocial behaviors and attitudes and early initiation of substance use. *Journal of Drug Education, 22,* 115–130.

Wells, E. L., & Rankin, J. H. (1995). Juvenile victimization: Convergent validation of alternative measurements. *Journal of Research in Crime and Delinquency, 32,* 287–307.

Wells, L. E., & Rankin, J. H. (1983). Self-concept as mediating factor in delinquency. *Social Psychology Quarterly, 46,* 11–22.

Wells, Rob (1995). Study finds fines don't deter Wall Street cheating. *Idaho Statesman,* June 16, 1e–2e.

Welte, J. W., & Barnes, G. (1987). Alcohol use among adolescent minority groups. *Journal of Studies on Alcohol, 48,* 329–336.

Wender, P. H. (1969). Platelet-serotonin level in children with "minimal brain dysfunction." *Lancet, 2,* 1012.

Weng, L. J., Newcomb, M. D., & Bentler, P. M. (1988). Factors influencing noncompletion of high school: A compari-son of methodologies. *Educational Research Quarterly, 12,* 8–22.

Werner, E. E., & Smith, R. S. (1992). *Overcoming the odds.* Ithica, NY: Cornell University Press.

Werry, J. S. (1988). Differential diagnosis of attention deficits and conduct disorders. In L. Bloomingdale & J. Sergeant (Eds.), *Attention deficit disorder: Criteria, cognition and intervention* (pp. 83–96). New York: Pergamon.

West, D. J. (1967). *The young offender.* Harmondsworth, England: Penguin.

West, D. J. (1982). *Delinquency: Its roots, careers and prospects.* Cambridge, MA: Harvard University Press.

West, D. J., & Farrington, D. P. (1973). *Who becomes delinquent? Second report of the Cambridge study in delinquent development.* London: Heinemann Educational Books.

West, D. J., & Farrington, D. P. (1977). *The delinquent way of life.* New York: Crane Russak.

West-Eberhard, M. J. (1986). Alternative adaptations, speciation, and phylogeny, a review. *Proceedings of the National Academy of Science, 83,* 1388–1392.

Westermann, T. D., & Burfeind, J. W. (1991). *Crime and justice in two societies: Japan and the United States.* Grove, CA: Brooks/Cole.

Westlund, K. N., Denney, R. M., Kochersperger, L. M., Rose, R. M., & Abell, C. W. (1985). Distinct monoamine oxidase A and B populations in primate brain. *Science, 230,* 181–182.

Wexler, H. K. (1994). Progress in prison substance abuse treatment: A five year report. *Journal of Drug Issues, 24,* 349–360.

Wexler, H. K., Falkin, G. P., & Lipton, D. S. (1988). A model prison rehabilitation program: An evaluation of the Stay'n Out therapeutic community. A final report to the National Institute on Drug Abuse. Washington, DC.

Wexler, H. K., Falkin, G. P., & Lipton, D. S. (1990). Outcome evaluation of a prison therapeutic community for substance abuse treatment. *Criminal Justice and Behavior, 17,* 71–92.

Whalen, C. (1989). Attention deficit and hyperactivity disorders. In T. Ollendich & M. Hersen (Eds.), *Handbook of child psychopathology* (2nd ed., pp. 151–200). New York: Plenum.

Wheeler, Everett (1991). Terrorism and military theory: An historical perspective. In C. McCauley (Ed.), *Terrorism research and public policy* (pp. 6–33). London: Frank Cass.

Wheeler, J., & Carlson, C. L. (1994). The social functioning of children with ADD with hyperactivity and ADD without hyperactivity: A comparison of their peer relations and social deficits. *Journal of Emotional and Behavioral Disorders, 2,* 2–12.

Wheeler, Stanton (1983). White-collar crime: History of a concept. In S. Kadish (Ed.), *Encyclopedia of crime and justice* (pp. 1652–1656).

White, C. B. (1988). Age, education, and sex effects on adult moral reasoning. *International Journal of Aging and Human Development, 27,* 271–281.

White, H., Pandina, R., & LaGrange, R. L. (1987). Longitudinal predictors of serious substance use and delinquency. *Criminology, 25,* 715–740.

White, H. R. (1990). The drug use-delinquency connection in adolescence. In R. Weisheit (Ed.), *Drugs, crime, and the criminal justice system.* Cincinnati: Anderson.

White, J. L., Moffitt, T. E., & Silva, P. A. (1989). A prospective replication of the protective effects of IQ in subjects at high risk for juvenile delinquency. *Journal of Consulting and Clinical Psychology, 57,* 719–724.

Whitehead, J. T., & Lab, S. P. (1989). A meta-analysis of juvenile correctional treatment. *Journal of Research in Crime and Delinquency, 26,* 276–295.

Whitehouse, R., & Wilkins, J. (1986). *The making of a civilization: History discovered through archaeology.* New York: Alfred A. Knopf.

Widmayer, A., & Marquart, J. (1992). Capital punishment and structured discretion: Arbitrariness and discrimination after Furman. In C. Hartjen & E. E. Rhine (Eds.), *Correctional theory and practice* (pp. 178–196). Chicago: Nelson-Hall.

Widom, C. S. (1988). Sampling biases and implications for child abuse research. *American Journal of Orthopsychiatry, 58,* 260–270.

Widom, C. (1989a). Child abuse, neglect, and violent criminal behavior. *Criminology, 27,* 251–271.

Widom, C. S. (1989b). The cycle of violence. *Science, 244,* 160–166.

Widom, C. S. (1994). *Childhood victimization and risk for adolescent problem behavior.* New York: Lawrence Erlbaum.

Wiederman, Michael and Allgeier, Elizabeth (1994). Male economic status and gender differences in mate selection preferences: Evolutionary versus sociocultural explanations. In Lee Ellis (Ed.), *Social stratification and socioeconomic inequality* (Vol. 2). Westport, CT: Praeger.

Wilbanks, W. (1985). Is violent crime intraracial? *Crime and Delinquency, 31,* 117–128.

Wilbanks, W. (1986). Criminal homicide offenders in the U.S.: Black vs. white. In D. F. Hawkins (Ed.), *Homicide among Black Americans* (pp. 43–55). Lanham, MD: University Press of America.

Wilbanks, W. (1987). *The myth of a racist criminal justice system.* Monterey, CA: Brooks/Cole.

Wilcox, R. G., Hughes, J., & Roland, J. (1979). Verification of smoking history in patients after infarction using urinary nicotine and cotinine measurements. *British Medical Journal, 6197,* 1026–1028.

Wilder, J. (1947). Sugar metabolism in its relation to criminology. In S. Linduer (Ed.), *Handbook of correctional psychology.* New York: Philosophical Library.

Wilkins, A. J., Shallice, T., & McCarthy, R. (1987). Frontal lesions and sustained attention. *Neuropsychologia, 25,* 359–365.

Wilkins, L. T. (1964). *Social deviance: Social policy, action, and research.* London: Tavistock.

Wilkinson, K. R. (1980). The broken home and delinquent behavior: An alternative interpretation of contradictory findings. In T. Hirschi & M. Gottfreson (Eds.), *Understanding crime* (pp. 21–42). Beverly Hills, CA: Sage.

Wilkinson, K. R., Stitt, G., & Erickson, M. (1982). Siblings and delinquent behavior: An exploratory study of a neglected variable. *Criminology, 20,* 223–239.

Willhoite, F. H., Jr. (1977). Evolution and collective intolerance. *Journal of Politics, 39,* 667–686.

Williams. D. T., Mehl, R., Yudofsky, S., Adams, D., & Roseman, B. (1982). The effect of Propranolol on uncontrolled rage outbursts in children and adolescents with organic brain dysfunction. *Journal of the American Academy of Child Psychiatry, 21,* 129–135.

Williams, J. R., & Gold, M. (1972). From delinquent behavior to official delinquency. *Social Problems, 29,* 209–229.

Williams, K. (1984). Economic sources of homicide: Re-estimating the effect of poverty and inequality. *American Sociological Review, 49,* 283–289.

Williams, S., & McGee, R. (1994). Reading attainment and juvenile delinquency. *Journal of Child Psychology and Psychiatry, 35,* 441–459.

Williams, S. M. (1991). Handedness inventories: Edinburgh versus Annett. *Neuropsychology, 5,* 43–48.

Williamson, S., Hare, R. D., & Wong, S. (1987). Violence: Criminal psychopaths and their victims. *Canadian Journal of Behavioral Science, 19,* 454–462.

Wilson, Colin (1984). *A criminal history of mankind.* London: Panther Books.

Wilson, Colin (1988). *The mammoth book of true crime.* New York: Carroll & Graff.

Wilson, D. M. (1986). Growth and intellectual development. *Pediatrics, 78,* 646–650.

Wilson, G. D. (1990). Personality, time of day and arousal. *Personality and Individual Differences, 11,* 153–168.

Wilson, G. D., & Patterson, J. R. (1968). A new measure of conservatism. *British Journal of Social and Clinical Psychology, 8,* 264–269.

Wilson, J. Q. (1975). *Thinking about crime.* New York: Basic.

Wilson, J. Q. (1976). Crime and punishment, 1776–1976. *Time,* April 26, 82–84.

Wilson, J. Q., & Herrnstein, R. J. (1985). *Crime and human nature.* New York: Simon and Schuster.

Wilson, J. R., Erwin, G., DeFries, J. C., Peterson, D. R., & Cole-Harding, S. (1984). Ethanol dependence in mice: Direct and correlated responses to ten generations of selective breeding. *Behavior Genetics, 14,* 235–256.

Wilson, M. S. (1954). Pioneers in criminology—Gabriel Tarde (1843–1904). *Journal of Criminal Law, Criminology, and Police Science, 45,* 3–11.

Wilson, P. R., Braithwaite, J. B., Guthrie, A., & Smith, G. (1975). *Truancy: Report to the Poverty Commission,* Education section.

Wimer, R. E., & Wimer, C. C. (1985). Animal behavior genetics: A search for the biological foundations of behavior. *Annual Review of Psychology, 36,* 171–218.

Winfree, L. T., Jr., Backstrom, T., & Mays, G. L. (1994). Social learning theory, self-reported delinquency, and youth gangs: A new twist on a general theory of crime and delinquency. *Youth & Society, 26,* 117–177.

Winfree, T. C., Jr., Bernat, F. P. (1998). Social learning, self control, & substance abuse by eight grade students: A Tale of two cities. *Journal of Drug Issues, 28,* 539–558.

Winters, C. A. (1997). Learning disabilities, crime, delinquency, and special education placement. *Adolescence, 32,* 451–462.

Wirth, L. (1938). Urbanism as a way of life. *American Journal of Sociology, 44,* 1–24.

Wise, R. A. (1996). Addictive drugs and brain stimulation reward. *Annual Review of Neuroscience, 19,* 319–340.

Witkin, Gordon, Friedman, Dorian, & Guttman, Monika (1992). Health care fraud. *U.S. News and World Report,* February 24, 34–43.

Witkin, H. A., Mednick, S. A., Schulsinger, F., Bakkestrom, E., Christiansen, K. O., Goodenough, D. R., Hirschhorn, K., Lundsteen, C., Owen, D. R., Phillip, J., Rubin, D. B., & Stocking, M. (1976). XYY and XXY men: Criminality and aggression. *Science, 193,* 547–555.

Wittling, W., & Pfluger, M. (1990). Neuroendocrine hemisphere asymmetries: Salivary cortisol secretion during lateralized viewing of emotion-related and neutral films. *Brain and Cognition, 14,* 243–265.

Wolff, S. (1987). Antisocial conduct: Whose concern? *Adolescence, 10,* 105–118.

Wolfgang, M. E. (1967). *A sociological analysis of criminal homicide.* New York: Harper & Row.

Wolfgang, M. E. (1968). Urban crime. In J. Q. Wilson (Ed.), *The metropolitan enigma.* Cambridge, MA: Harvard University Press.

Wolfgang, M. E. (1973). Cesare Lombroso, 1835–1909. In H. Mannheim (Ed.), Pioneers in criminology (pp. 232–291). Montclair, NJ: Patterson Smith.

Wolfgang, M. E. (1975a). Delinquency and violence from the viewpoint of criminology. In W. S. Fields & W. H. Sweet (Eds.), *Neural bases of violence and aggression* (pp. 456–489). St. Louis, MO: Warren H. Green.

Wolfgang, M. E. (1975b). *Patterns in criminal homicide.* Monclair, NJ: Patterson Smith.

Wolfgang, M. E., & Ferracutti, F. (1967). *The subculture of violence: Towards an integrated theory in criminology.* London: Tavistock.

Wolfgang, P., Figlio, R., & Sellin, T. (1972). *Delinquency in a birth cohort.* Chicago: University of Chicago Press.

Wolfner, G. D., & Gelles, R. J. (1993). A profile of violence toward children: A national study. *Child Abuse & Neglect, 17,* 197–212.

Wong, D. F., Wagner, H. N., Dannals, R. F., Links, J. M., Frost, J., Ravert, H. T., Wilson, A. A., Rosenbaum, A. E., Gjedde, A., Douglass, K. H., Petronis, J. D., Folstein, M. F., Toung, J. K. T., Burns, H. D., & Kuhar, M. J. (1984). Effects of age on dopamine and serotonin receptors measured by positron tomography in the living human brain. *Science, 226,* 1393–1396.

Wong, S. (1984). *The criminal and institutional behaviors of psychopaths.* Ottawa: Program Branch User Report, Ministry of the Solicitor General of Canada.

Wong, S. (1988). Is Hare's psychopathy checklist reliable without the interview? *Psychological Reports, 62,* 931–934.

Wood, P. B., Cochran, J. K., Pfefferbaum, B., & Arneklev, B. J. (1995). Sensation-seeking and delinquent substance use: An extension of learning theory. *Journal of Drug Issues, 25,* 173–193.

Wood, P. B., Gove, W. R., & Cochran, J. K. (1994). Motivations for violent crime among incarcerated adults: A consideration of reinforcement processes. *Journal of the Oklahoma Criminal Justice Research Consortium, 1,* 75–93.

Wood, P., Pfefferbaum, B., & Arneklev, B. (1993). Risk-taking and self-control: Social psychological correlates of delinquency. *Journal of Crime and Justice, 16,* 11–130.

Woodruff, R. A., Clayton, P. J., & Guze, S. B. (1972). Suicide attempts and psychiatric diagnosis. *Diseases of the Nervous System, 33,* 617–621.

Woods, N. F., Most, A., & Dery, G. K. (1982). Prevalence of perimenstrual symptoms. *American Journal of Public Health, 72,* 1257–1264.

Woodward, M. (1963). Low intelligence and delinquency. London: Institute for the Study and Treatment of Delinquency.

Wright, Burton & Fox, Vernon, (1978). *Criminal justice and the social sciences.* Philadelphia: W. B. Saunders.

Wright, K. N., & Wright, K. E. (1995). *Family life, delinquency, and crime: A policymaker's guide, research summary.* Washington DC: Department of Justice.

Wright, L. S., & Moore, R. (1982). Correlates of reported drug abuse problems among college undergraduates. *Journal of Drug Education, 12,* 65–73.

Wright, Marcus (1974). *Understanding human behavior.* New York: Columbia House.

Wright, R. A., & Miller, J. M. (1998). Taboo until today? The coverage of biological arguments in criminology textbooks, 1961 to 1970 and 1987 to 1996. *Journal of Criminal Justice, 26,* 1–19.

Wrong, D. H. (1958). Trends in class fertility in Western nations. *Canadian Journal of Economics and Political Science, 24,* 216–229.

Wuillemin, D., Richardson, B., & Moore, D. (1986). Ranking of crime seriousness in Papua New Guinea. *Journal of Cross-Cultural Psychology, 17,* 29–44.

Yahroes, H. (1979). Why young people become antisocial, Publication number ADM 79–642. Washington DC: Department of Health, Education, and Welfare.

Yamazaki, K., Yamaguchi, M., Andrews, P. W., Peake, B., & Boyse, E. A. (1978). Mating preferences of F2 segregants of crosses between MHC-congenic mouse strains. *Immunogenetics, 6,* 253–59.

Yehuda, R., Resnick, H., & Kahana, B. (1993). Long-lasting hormonal alterations to extreme stress in humans: Normative or mal-adaptive? *Psychosomatic Medicine, 55,* 287–297.

Yehuda, R., Southwick, S. M., & Nussbaum, G. (1990). Low urinary cortisol excretion in patients with posttraumatic stress disorder. *Journal of Nervous and Mental Disorder, 178,* 366–369.

Yeudall, L. T. (1977). Neuropsychological assessment of forensic disorders. *Canadian Mental Health, 25,* 7–15.

Yeudall, L. T. (1978). *The neuropsychology of aggression.* Paper for Clarence M. Hincks Memorial Lectures, Psychobiological Approaches to Aggression in Mental Illness and Mental Retardation.

Yeudall, L. T., Fedora, O., & Fromm, D. (1985). A neuropsychosocial theory of persistant criminality: Implications for assessment and treatment. *Advances in Forensic Psychology, 2.*

Yochelson, S., & Samenow, S. (1976). *The criminal personality (Vol. 1). A profile for change.* New York: Jason Aronson.

Yoder, J., & Khan, A. (1992). Toward a feminist understanding of women and power. *Psychology of Women Quarterly, 16,* 381–388.

Yosef, R., & Pinshow, B. (1989). Cache size in shrikes influences female mate choice and reproductive success. *Auk, 106,* 418–421.

Yoshikawa, H. (1994). Prevention as cumulative protection: Effects of early family support and education on chronic delinquency and its risks. *Psychological Bulletin, 115,* 28–54.

Young, V. D. (1980). Woman, race, and crime. *Criminology, 18,* 26–34.

Yu, P. H., Davis, B. A., Bowen, R. C., Wormith, R. C., Addington, D., & Boulton, A. A. (1984). Platelet monamine oxidase activity and plasma trace acid levels in agrophobic patients and violent offenders. In K. F. Tipton, P. Dosert, & M. Strolin-Benedeti (Eds.), *Monamine oxidase and disease* (pp. 643–675). London: Academic Press.

Zahn, M. A. (1987). *Homicide in nine American cities: The Hispanic case.* Paper presented at the Conference on Violence and Homicide in Hispanic Communities, Office of Minority Health, U.S. Department of Health and Human Services, Washington, DC.

Zahn, M. (1989). Homicide in the twentieth century: Trends, types and causes. In T. R. Gurr (Ed.), *Violence in America* (Vol. 1, pp. 217–234). Newbury Park, CA: Sage.

Zahn-Waxler, C. (1993). Warriors and worriers: Gender and psychopathology. *Development and Psychopathology, 5,* 79–89.

Zahn-Waxler, C., Cole, P. M., Welsh, J. D., & Fox, N. A. (1995). Psychophysiological correlates of empathy and prosocial behaviors in preschool children with behavior problems. *Development and Psycholpathology, 7,* 27–48.

Zahn-Waxler, C., Cummings, E. M., & Ianotti, R. (1986). Altruism and aggression: Problems and progress in research. In C. Zahn-Waxler, E. M. Cummings, & R. Ianotti (Eds.), *Altruism and aggression* (pp. 1–15). London, England: Cambridge University Press.

Zahn-Waxler, C., & Radke-Yarrow, M. (1990). The origins of empathic concern. *Motivation and Emotion, 14,* 107–130.

Zametkin, A. J., Liebemauer, I. L., Fitzgerald, G. A., King, A. C., Minkumas, D. V., Herscovitch, P., Yamada, E. M., & Cohen, R. M. (1993). Brain metabolism in teenagers with attention-deficit hyperactivity disorder. *Archives of General Psychiatry, 50,* 333–340.

Zarski, J. J. (1984). Hassoes and health. A replication. *Health Psychology, 3,* 243–251.

Zatorre, R. J. (1989). Perceptual asymmetry on the dichotic fused words test and cerebral speech lateralization determined by the carotid sodium amytal test. *Neurophychologia, 27,* 1207–1219.

Zatz, M. S. (1987). The changing forms of racial/ethnic biases in sentencing. *Journal of Research in Crime and Delinquency, 24,* 69–92.

Zawitz, Marianne, Klaus, Patsy, Bachman, Ronet, Bastian, Lisa, Debarry, Marshal, Rand, Michael, & Taylor, Bruce (1993). Highlights from 20 years of surveying crime victims: The National Crime Victimization Survey, 1973–1992. Washington, DC: Bureau of Justice Statistics.

Zehr, H. (1975). The modernization of crime in Germany and France, 1830–1913. *Journal of Social History, 8,* 117–141.

Zehr, H. (1976). *Crime and the development of modern society.* Totowa, NJ: Rowman and Littlefield.

Zeichner, A., & Pihl, R. O. (1980). Effects of alcohol and instigator intent on human aggression. *Journal of Studies on Alcohol, 41,* 265–276.

Zeleny, L. D. (1933). Feeble-mindedness and criminal conduct. *American Journal of Sociology, 38,* 564–576.

Zeller, E. A., & Davis, J. M. (1980). Protein content and monoamine oxidase activity platelets. *Schizophrenia Bulletin, 6,* 267–274.

Zhang, L., & Messner, S., F. (1995). Family deviance and delinquency in China. *Criminology, 33,* 359–387.

Zhang, L., & Messner, S. E. (1996). School attachment and official delinquency status in the People's Republic of China. *Sociological Forum, 11,* 285–303.

Zigmond, M. J., Heffner, T. G., & Stricker, E. M. (1980). The effect of altered dopaminergic activity on food intake in the rat: Evidence for an optimal level of dopaminergic activity for behavior. *Progress in Neuro-Psychopharmacology, 4,* 351–362.

Zimmerman, H. G. (1966). Die Kriminalitat der ausiandischern Arbeiter. *Kriminalistik, 2,* 623–625.

Zingraff, M. T., Leiter, J., Johnson, M. C., & Myers, K. A. (1994). The mediating effect of good school performance on the maltreatment delinquency relationship. *Journal of Research in Crime and Delinquency, 31,* 62–91.

Zingraff, M. T., Leiter, J., Myers, K. A., & Johnsen, M. C. (1993). Child maltreatment and youthful problem behavior. *Criminology, 31,* 173–202.

Zinkhan, G., Bisei, M., & Saxton, M. (1989). MBAs' changing attitudes toward marketing dilemmas: 1981–1987. *Journal of Business Ethics, 8,* 963–9742.

Zuckerman, K., Ambuel, J. P., & Bandman, R. (1972). Child neglect and abuse: A study of cases evaluated at Columbus Children's Hospital in 1968–69. *Ohio State Medical Journal, 68,* 629–632.

Zuckerman, M. (1971). Dimensions of sensation seeking. *Journal of Consulting and Clinical Psychology, 36,* 45–52.

Zuckerman, M. (1979). *Sensation seeking: Beyond the optimal level of arousal.* Hillsdale, NJ: Lawrence Erlbaum.

Zuckerman, M. (1984). Sensation seeking: A comparative approach to a human trait. *Behavioral and Brain Sciences, 7,* 413–471.

Zuckerman, M. (1994). *Behavioral expressions and biosocial bases of sensation seeking.* Cambridge, England: Cambridge University Press.

Zuckerman, M., Bone, R. N., Neary, R., Mangelsdorff, D., & Brustman, B. (1972). What is the sensation seeker?: Personality trait and experience correlates of the sensation seeking scales. *Journal of Consulting and Clinical Psychology, 39,* 308–321.

Zuckerman, M., Buchsbaum, M. S., Monte, S., & Murphy, D. L. (1980). Sensation seeking and its biological correlates. *Psychological Bulletin, 88,* 187–214.

Zuckerman, M., Eyesenck, S., & Eyesenck, H. J. (1978). Sensation seeking in England and America: Cross-cultural, age, and sex comparisons. *Journal of Consulting and Clinical Psychology, 26,* 139–149.

Zuckerman, M., & Neeb, M. (1980). Demographic influences in sensation-seeking and expression of sensation-seeking in religion, smoking, and driving habits. *Personality and Individual Differences, 1,* 197–206.

NAME INDEX

SUBJECT INDEX